Guide to Gale Literary Criticism Series

For criticism on	Consult these Gale series
Authors now living or who died after December 31, 1999	***CONTEMPORARY LITERARY CRITICISM (CLC)***
Authors who died between 1900 and 1999	***TWENTIETH-CENTURY LITERARY CRITICISM (TCLC)***
Authors who died between 1800 and 1899	***NINETEENTH-CENTURY LITERATURE CRITICISM (NCLC)***
Authors who died between 1400 and 1799	***LITERATURE CRITICISM FROM 1400 TO 1800 (LC)*** ***SHAKESPEAREAN CRITICISM (SC)***
Authors who died before 1400	***CLASSICAL AND MEDIEVAL LITERATURE CRITICISM (CMLC)***
Authors of books for children and young adults	***CHILDREN'S LITERATURE REVIEW (CLR)***
Dramatists	***DRAMA CRITICISM (DC)***
Poets	***POETRY CRITICISM (PC)***
Short story writers	***SHORT STORY CRITICISM (SSC)***
Literary topics and movements	***HARLEM RENAISSANCE: A GALE CRITICAL COMPANION (HR)*** ***THE BEAT GENERATION: A GALE CRITICAL COMPANION (BG)***
Asian American writers of the last two hundred years	***ASIAN AMERICAN LITERATURE (AAL)***
Black writers of the past two hundred years	***BLACK LITERATURE CRITICISM (BLC)*** ***BLACK LITERATURE CRITICISM SUPPLEMENT (BLCS)***
Hispanic writers of the late nineteenth and twentieth centuries	***HISPANIC LITERATURE CRITICISM (HLC)*** ***HISPANIC LITERATURE CRITICISM SUPPLEMENT (HLCS)***
Native North American writers and orators of the eighteenth, nineteenth, and twentieth centuries	***NATIVE NORTH AMERICAN LITERATURE (NNAL)***
Major authors from the Renaissance to the present	***WORLD LITERATURE CRITICISM, 1500 TO THE PRESENT (WLC)*** ***WORLD LITERATURE CRITICISM SUPPLEMENT (WLCS)***

Twentieth-Century
Literary Criticism

Volume 164

Twentieth-Century Literary Criticism

Criticism of the
Works of Novelists, Poets, Playwrights,
Short Story Writers, and Other Creative Writers
Who Lived between 1900 and 1999,
from the First Published Critical
Appraisals to Current Evaluations

Thomas J. Schoenberg
Lawrence J. Trudeau
Project Editors

Detroit • New York • San Francisco • San Diego • New Haven, Conn. • Waterville, Maine • London • Munich

Twentieth-Century Literary Criticism, Vol. 164

Project Editors
Thomas J. Schoenberg and Lawrence J. Trudeau

Editorial
Jessica Bomarito, Kathy D. Darrow, Jeffrey W. Hunter, Jelena O. Krstović, Michelle Lee, Russel Whitaker

Data Capture
Francis Monroe, Gwen Tucker

Indexing Services
Laurie Andriot

Rights and Acquisitions
Margaret Abendroth, Edna Hedblad, Ron Montgomery

Imaging and Multimedia
Dean Dauphinais, Robert Duncan, Leitha Etheridge-Sims, Mary Grimes, Lezlie Light, Michael Logusz, Dan Newell, Kelly A. Quin, Denay Wilding

Composition and Electronic Capture
Kathy Sauer

Manufacturing
Rhonda Dover

Associate Product Manager
Marc Cormier

© 2005 Thomson Gale, a part of The Thomson Corporation. Thomson and Star Logo are trademarks and Gale is a registered trademark used herein under license.

For more information, contact
Thomson Gale
27500 Drake Rd.
Farmington Hills, MI 48331-3535
Or you can visit our internet site at
http://www.gale.com

ALL RIGHTS RESERVED
No part of this work covered by the copyright herein may be reproduced or used in any form or by any means—graphic, electronic, or mechanical, including photocopying, recording, taping, Web distribution, or information storage retrieval systems—without the written permission of the publisher.

This publication is a creative work fully protected by all applicable copyright laws, as well as by misappropriation, trade secret, unfair competition, and other applicable laws. The authors and editors of this work have added value to the underlying factual material herein through one or more of the following: unique and original selection, coordination, expression, arrangement, and classification of the information.

For permission to use material from the product, submit your request via the Web at http://www.gale-edit.com/permissions, or you may download our Permissions Request form and submit your request by fax or mail to:

Permisssions Department
Thomson Gale
27500 Drake Rd.
Farmington Hills, MI 48331-3535
Permissions Hotline:
248-699-8006 or 800-877-4253, ext. 8006
Fax 248-699-8074 or 800-762-4058

Since this page cannot legibly accommodate all copyright notices, the acknowledgments constitute an extension of the copyright notice.

While every effort has been made to secure permission to reprint material and to ensure the reliability of the information presented in this publication, Thomson Gale neither guarantees the accuracy of the data contained herein nor assumes any responsibility for errors, omissions or discrepancies. Thomson Gale accepts no payment for listing; and inclusion in the publication of any organization, agency, institution, publication, service, or individual does not imply endorsement of the editors or publisher. Errors brought to the attention of the publisher and verified to the satisfaction of the publisher will be corrected in future editions.

LIBRARY OF CONGRESS CATALOG CARD NUMBER 76-46132

ISBN 0-7876-8918-1
ISSN 0276-8178

Printed in the United States of America
10 9 8 7 6 5 4 3 2 1

Contents

Preface vii

Acknowledgments xi

Literary Criticism Series Advisory Board xiii

J. M. Barrie 1860-1937 1
    Scottish playwright, novelist, short story writer, journalist, and biographer

Truman Capote 1924-1984 97
    American novelist, short story writer, nonfiction writer, essayist, playwright, scriptwriter,
    and memoirist

Katherine Mansfield 1888-1923 222
    New Zealander short story writer, critic, and poet

Literary Criticism Series Cumulative Author Index 349

Literary Criticism Series Cumulative Topic Index 449

TCLC Cumulative Nationality Index 461

TCLC-164 Title Index 467

Preface

Since its inception more than fifteen years ago, *Twentieth-Century Literary Criticism* (*TCLC*) has been purchased and used by nearly 10,000 school, public, and college or university libraries. *TCLC* has covered more than 500 authors, representing 58 nationalities and over 25,000 titles. No other reference source has surveyed the critical response to twentieth-century authors and literature as thoroughly as *TCLC*. In the words of one reviewer, "there is nothing comparable available." *TCLC* "is a gold mine of information—dates, pseudonyms, biographical information, and criticism from books and periodicals—which many librarians would have difficulty assembling on their own."

Scope of the Series

TCLC is designed to serve as an introduction to authors who died between 1900 and 1999 and to the most significant interpretations of these author's works. Volumes published from 1978 through 1999 included authors who died between 1900 and 1960. The great poets, novelists, short story writers, playwrights, and philosophers of the period are frequently studied in high school and college literature courses. In organizing and reprinting the vast amount of critical material written on these authors, *TCLC* helps students develop valuable insight into literary history, promotes a better understanding of the texts, and sparks ideas for papers and assignments. Each entry in *TCLC* presents a comprehensive survey on an author's career or an individual work of literature and provides the user with a multiplicity of interpretations and assessments. Such variety allows students to pursue their own interests; furthermore, it fosters an awareness that literature is dynamic and responsive to many different opinions.

Every fourth volume of *TCLC* is devoted to literary topics. These topics widen the focus of the series from the individual authors to such broader subjects as literary movements, prominent themes in twentieth-century literature, literary reaction to political and historical events, significant eras in literary history, prominent literary anniversaries, and the literatures of cultures that are often overlooked by English-speaking readers.

TCLC is designed as a companion series to Thomson Gale's *Contemporary Literary Criticism*, (*CLC*) which reprints commentary on authors who died after 1999. Because of the different time periods under consideration, there is no duplication of material between *CLC* and *TCLC*.

Organization of the Book

A *TCLC* entry consists of the following elements:

- The **Author Heading** cites the name under which the author most commonly wrote, followed by birth and death dates. Also located here are any name variations under which an author wrote, including transliterated forms for authors whose native languages use nonroman alphabets. If the author wrote consistently under a pseudonym, the pseudonym will be listed in the author heading and the author's actual name given in parenthesis on the first line of the biographical and critical information. Uncertain birth or death dates are indicated by question marks. Single-work entries are preceded by a heading that consists of the most common form of the title in English translation (if applicable) and the original date of composition.

- A **Portrait of the Author** is included when available.

- The **Introduction** contains background information that introduces the reader to the author, work, or topic that is the subject of the entry.

- The list of **Principal Works** is ordered chronologically by date of first publication and lists the most important works by the author. The genre and publication date of each work is given. In the case of foreign authors whose works have been translated into English, the English-language version of the title follows in brackets. Unless otherwise indicated, dramas are dated by first performance, not first publication.

- Reprinted **Criticism** is arranged chronologically in each entry to provide a useful perspective on changes in critical evaluation over time. The critic's name and the date of composition or publication of the critical work are given at the beginning of each piece of criticism. Unsigned criticism is preceded by the title of the source in which it appeared. All titles by the author featured in the text are printed in boldface type. Footnotes are reprinted at the end of each essay or excerpt. In the case of excerpted criticism, only those footnotes that pertain to the excerpted texts are included.

- A complete **Bibliographical Citation** of the original essay or book precedes each piece of criticism. Source citations in the Literary Criticism Series follow University of Chicago Press style, as outlined in *The Chicago Manual of Style,* 14th ed. (Chicago: The University of Chicago Press, 1993).

- Critical essays are prefaced by brief **Annotations** explicating each piece.

- An annotated bibliography of **Further Reading** appears at the end of each entry and suggests resources for additional study. In some cases, significant essays for which the editors could not obtain reprint rights are included here. Boxed material following the further reading list provides references to other biographical and critical sources on the author in series published by Thomson Gale.

Indexes

A **Cumulative Author Index** lists all of the authors that appear in a wide variety of reference sources published by Thomson Gale, including *TCLC*. A complete list of these sources is found facing the first page of the Author Index. The index also includes birth and death dates and cross references between pseudonyms and actual names.

A **Cumulative Nationality Index** lists all authors featured in *TCLC* by nationality, followed by the number of the *TCLC* volume in which their entry appears.

A **Cumulative Topic Index** lists the literary themes and topics treated in the series as well as in *Classical and Medieval Literature Criticism, Literature Criticism from 1400 to 1800, Nineteenth-Century Literature Criticism,* and the *Contemporary Literary Criticism* Yearbook, which was discontinued in 1998.

An alphabetical **Title Index** accompanies each volume of *TCLC*. Listings of titles by authors covered in the given volume are followed by the author's name and the corresponding page numbers where the titles are discussed. English translations of foreign titles and variations of titles are cross-referenced to the title under which a work was originally published. Titles of novels, dramas, nonfiction books, and poetry, short story, or essay collections are printed in italics, while individual poems, short stories, and essays are printed in roman type within quotation marks.

In response to numerous suggestions from librarians, Thomson Gale also produces a paperbound edition of the *TCLC* cumulative title index. This annual cumulation, which alphabetically lists all titles reviewed in the series, is available to all customers. Additional copies of this index are available upon request. Librarians and patrons will welcome this separate index; it saves shelf space, is easy to use, and is recyclable upon receipt of the next edition.

Citing *Twentieth-Century Literary Criticism*

When citing criticism reprinted in the Literary Criticism Series, students should provide complete bibliographic information so that the cited essay can be located in the original print or electronic source. Students who quote directly from reprinted criticism may use any accepted bibliographic format, such as University of Chicago Press style or Modern Language Association (MLA) style. Both the MLA and the University of Chicago formats are acceptable and recognized as being the current standards for citations. It is important, however, to choose one format for all citations; do not mix the two formats within a list of citations.

The examples below follow recommendations for preparing a bibliography set forth in *The Chicago Manual of Style,* 14th ed. (Chicago: The University of Chicago Press, (1993); the first example pertains to material drawn from periodicals, the second to material reprinted from books:

Morrison, Jago. "Narration and Unease in Ian McEwan's Later Fiction." *Critique* 42, no. 3 (spring 2001): 253-68. Reprinted in *Twentieth-Century Literary Criticism.* Vol. 127, edited by Janet Witalec, 212-20. Detroit: Gale, 2003.

Brossard, Nicole. "Poetic Politics." In *The Politics of Poetic Form: Poetry and Public Policy,* edited by Charles Bernstein, 73-82. New York: Roof Books, 1990. Reprinted in *Twentieth-Century Literary Criticism.* Vol. 127, edited by Janet Witalec, 3-8. Detroit: Gale, 2003.

The examples below follow recommendations for preparing a works cited list set forth in the *MLA Handbook for Writers of Research Papers,* 5th ed. (New York: The Modern Language Association of America, 1999); the first example pertains to material drawn from periodicals, the second to material reprinted from books:

Morrison, Jago. "Narration and Unease in Ian McEwan's Later Fiction." *Critique* 42.3 (spring 2001): 253-68. Reprinted in *Twentieth-Century Literary Criticism.* Ed. Janet Witalec. Vol. 127. Detroit: Gale, 2003. 212-20.

Brossard, Nicole. "Poetic Politics." *The Politics of Poetic Form: Poetry and Public Policy.* Ed. Charles Bernstein. New York: Roof Books, 1990. 73-82. Reprinted in *Twentieth-Century Literary Criticism.* Ed. Janet Witalec. Vol. 127. Detroit: Gale, 2003. 3-8.

Suggestions are Welcome

Readers who wish to suggest new features, topics, or authors to appear in future volumes, or who have other suggestions or comments are cordially invited to call, write, or fax the Associate Product Manager:

Associate Product Manager, Literary Criticism Series
Thomson Gale
27500 Drake Road
Farmington Hills, MI 48331-3535
1-800-347-4253 (GALE)
Fax: 248-699-8054

Acknowledgments

The editors wish to thank the copyright holders of the criticism included in this volume and the permissions managers of many book and magazine publishing companies for assisting us in securing reproduction rights. We are also grateful to the staffs of the Detroit Public Library, the Library of Congress, the University of Detroit Mercy Library, Wayne State University Purdy/Kresge Library Complex, and the University of Michigan Libraries for making their resources available to us. Following is a list of the copyright holders who have granted us permission to reproduce material in this volume of *TCLC*. Every effort has been made to trace copyright, but if omissions have been made, please let us know.

COPYRIGHTED MATERIAL IN *TCLC*, VOLUME 164, WAS REPRODUCED FROM THE FOLLOWING PERIODICALS:

Arizona Quarterly: A Journal of American Literature Culture and Theory, v. 53, autumn, 1997 for "Capote's *In Cold Blood*: The Search for Meaningful Design" by John Hollowell. Copyright © 1997 by the Regents of the University of Arizona. Reproduced by permission of the publisher and author.—*Children's Literature: Annual of The Modern Language Association Division on Children's Literature and The Children's Literature Association*, v. 9, 1981; v. 18, 1990. Copyright © 1981, 1990 by Children's Literature, An International Journal, Inc. All rights reserved. Both reproduced by permission.—*Contemporary Literature*, v. 25, winter, 1984. Copyright © 1984 The Board of Regents of the University of Wisconsin System. All rights reserved. Reproduced by permission.—*The Explicator*, v. 61, fall, 2002. Copyright © 2002 by Helen Dwight Reid Educational Foundation. Reproduced with permission of the Helen Dwight Reid Educational Foundation, published by Heldref Publications, 1319 18th Street, NW, Washington, DC 20036-1802.—*Forum for Modern Language Studies*, v. 35, April, 1999 for "Trying to Be a Man: J. M. Barrie and Sentimental Masculinity" by Andrew Nash. Copyright © 1999 Forum for Modern Language Studies. Reproduced by permission of the publisher and author.—*Journal of Homosexuality*, v. 39, 2000. Copyright © 2000 by The Haworth Press, Inc. All rights reserved. Reproduced by permission.—*LIT: Literature Interpretation Theory*, v. 8, 1998. Copyright © 1998 by OPA (Amsterdam) B.V. All rights reserved. Reproduced by permission of Taylor & Francis, Inc., http://www.taylorandfrancis.com.—*Literature and Theology: An Interdisciplinary Journal of Theory and Criticism*, v. 8, June, 1994 for "*Peter Pan* as Darwinian Creation Myth" by R. D. S. Jack. Copyright © 1994 Oxford University Press. Reproduced by permission of the publisher and author.—*The Midwest Quarterly: A Journal of Contemporary Thought*, v. 35, autumn, 1993. Copyright © 1993 by *The Midwest Quarterly*, Pittsburgh State University. Reproduced by permission.—*The Mississippi Quarterly: The Journal of Southern Culture*, v. 51, fall, 1998. Copyright © 1998 Mississippi State University. Reproduced by permission.—*Modern Drama*, v. 23, March, 1980; v. 43, winter, 2000. Copyright © 1980, 2000 by the University of Toronto, Graduate Centre for Study of Drama. Both reproduced by permission.—*PMLA: Publications of the Modern Language Association of America*, v. 106, March, 1991. Copyright © 1991 by the Modern Language Association of America. Reprinted by permission of the Modern Language Association of America.—*Studies in Short Fiction*, v. 26, fall, 1989. Copyright © 1989 by *Studies in Short Fiction*. Reproduced by permission.—*Twentieth Century Literature*, v. 28, winter, 1982; v. 32, summer, 1986. Copyright © 1982, 1986 Hofstra University Press. Both reproduced by permission.—*The Virginia Quarterly Review*, v. 72, summer, 1996. Copyright © 1996, by *The Virginia Quarterly Review*, The University of Virginia. Reproduced by permission.

COPYRIGHTED MATERIAL IN *TCLC*, VOLUME 164, WAS REPRODUCED FROM THE FOLLOWING BOOKS:

Anderson, Chris. From *Style as Argument: Contemporary American Nonfiction*. Southern Illinois University Press, 1987. Copyright © 1987 by the Board of Trustees, Southern Illinois University. All rights reserved. Reproduced by permission of the publisher.—Bennett, Andrew. From *Katherine Mansfield*. Northcote House Publishers Ltd., 2004. Copyright © 2004 by Andrew Bennett. All rights reserved. Reproduced by permission.—Cochrane, Kirsty. From "Katherine Mansfield's Images of Art," in *Critical Essays on Katherine Mansfield*. Edited by Rhoda B. Nathan. G. K. Hall & Co., 1993. Copyright © 1993 by Rhoda B. Nathan. All rights reserved. Reproduced by permission of The Gale Group.—Dickson, Katherine Murphy. From *Katherine Mansfield's New Zealand Stories*. University Press of America Inc., 1998. Copyright © 1998 by University Press of America, Inc. All rights reserved. Reproduced by permission.—Donaldson, Laura E. From *Decolonizing Feminisms: Race, Gender, and Empire-Building*. The University of North Carolina Press, 1992. Copyright © 1992 The University of North Carolina Press. All rights reserved. Used by permission of the publisher.—Dunbar, Pamela. From *Radical Mansfield: Double Discourse in Katherine Mansfield's Short Stories*. St. Martin's Press Inc., 1997. Copyright © 1997 by Pamela Dunbar. All rights reserved. Reprinted by permission of St. Martin's Press, LLC.—Ferguson, Suzanne. From "Genre and the Work of Reading in Mansfield's 'Prelude' and 'At the Bay,'" in **Postmodern Approaches to the Short Story**. Edited by Farhat Iftekharrudin, Joseph Boyden, Joseph Longo and Mary Rohrberger. Praeger Publishers, 2003. Copyright © 2003 by the Society for the Study of the Short Story. All rights reserved. Reproduced by permission of Greenwood Publishing Group, Inc., Westport, CT.—Galloway, David. From "Real Toads in Real Gardens: Reflections on the Art of Non-Fiction Fiction and the Legacy of Truman Capote," in **Gattungsprobleme in der Anglo-Amerikanischen Literature**. Edited by Raimund Borgmeier. Niemeyer, 1986. Copyright © 1995 by David Galloway. Reprinted by permission of the author.—Garson, Helen S. From **Truman Capote: A Study of the Short Fiction**. Twayne Publishers, 1992. Copyright © 1992 by Twayne Publishers. All rights reserved. Reproduced by permission of The Gale Group.—Grobel, Lawrence. From **Conversations with Capote**. New American Library, 1982-1984. Copyright © 1985 by Lawrence Grobel. All rights reserved. Reprinted by permission of SLL/Sterling Lord Literistic, Inc.—Guest, David. From **Sentenced to Death: The American Novel and Capital Punishment**. University Press of Mississippi, 1997. Copyright © 1977 by University Press of Mississippi. All rights reserved. Reproduced by permission.—Hicks, Jack. From "'Fire, Fire, Fire Flowing Like a River, River, River': History and Postmodernism in Truman Capote's *Handcarved Coffins*," in **History and Post-War Writing**. Edited by Theo D'haen and Hans Bertens. Rodopi B.V., 1990. Copyright © Editions Rodopi B. V. Reproduced by permission.—Holbrook, David. From **Images of Woman in Literature**. New York University Press, 1989. Copyright © 1989 by New York University. All rights reserved. Reproduced by permission.—Kaplan, Sydney Janet. From **Katherine Mansfield and the Origins of Modernist Fiction**. Cornell University Press, 1991. Copyright © 1991 by Cornell University. All rights reserved. Used by permission of the publisher, Cornell University Press.—Markgraf, Carl. From **J. M. Barrie: An Annotated Secondary Bibliography**. ELT Press, 1989. Copyright © 1989 ELT Press. All rights reserved. Reproduced by permission.—McFall, Gardner. From "Poetry and Performance in Katherine Mansfield's 'Bliss,'" in **Critical Essays on Katherine Mansfield**. Edited by Rhoda B. Nathan. G. K. Hall & Co., 1993. Copyright © 1993 by Rhoda B. Nathan. Reproduced by permission of The Gale Group.—McGee, Diane. From **Writing the Meal: Dinner in the Fiction of Early Twentieth-Century Women Writers**. University of Toronto Press Inc., 2001. Copyright © 2001 University of Toronto Press, Inc. Reprinted with permission of the publisher.—Moran, Patricia. From **Word of Mouth: Body Language in Katherine Mansfield and Virginia Woolf**. University Press of Virginia, 1996. Copyright © 1996 The University Press of Virginia by the Rector and Visitors of the University of Virginia. Reprinted with permission of the University of Virginia Press.—Nathan, Rhoda B. From **Katherine Mansfield**. Continuum Publishing Co., 1988. Copyright © 1988 by Rhoda B. Nathan. All rights reserved. Reproduced by permission of The Continuum International Publishing Group.—New, W. H. From **Reading Mansfield and Metaphors of Form**. McGill-Queens University Press, 1999. Copyright © 1999 McGill-Queen's University Press. Reproduced by permission.—Ormond, Leonee. From **J. M. Barrie**. Scottish Academic Press Ltd., 1987. Copyright © 1987 by Leonee Ormond. All right reserved. Reproduced by permission.—Reed, Kenneth T. From **Truman Capote**. Twayne Publishers, 1981. Copyright © 1981 by Twayne Publishers. All rights reserved. Reproduced by permission of The Gale Group.—Tolron, Francine. From "Fauna and Flora in Katherine Mansfield's Short Stories," in **The Fine Instrument: Essays on Katherine Mansfield**. Edited by Paulette Michel and Michel Dupuis. Dangaroo Press, 1989. Copyright © Paulette Michel and Michel Dupuis. Reproduced by permission.—Waldmeir, John C. From "Religion and Style in *The Dogs Bark* and *Music for Chameleons*," in **The Critical Response to Truman Capote**. Edited by Joseph J. Waldmeir and John C. Waldmeir. Greenwood Press, 1999. Copyright © 1999 by Joseph J. Waldmeir and John C. Waldmeir. All rights reserved. Reproduced by permission of Greenwood Publishing Group, Inc., Westport, CT.—Yeoman, Ann. From **Now or Neverland: Peter Pan and the Myth of Eternal Youth. A Psychological Perspective on a Cultural Icon**. Inner City Books, 1998. Copyright © 1998 by Ann Yeoman. All rights reserved. Reproduced by permission.—York, R. A. From **The Rules of Time: Time and Rhythm in the Twentieth-Century Novel**. Fairleigh Dickinson University Press, 1999. Copyright © 1999 by Associated University Presses, Inc. Reproduced by permission.

PHOTOGRAPHS AND ILLUSTRATIONS APPEARING IN TCLC, VOLUME 164, WERE RECEIVED FROM THE FOLLOWING SOURCES:

Barrie, Sir James M., photograph. The Library of Congress.—Capote, Truman, photograph. Hulton Archive/Getty Images.—Mansfield, Katherine, photograph. Reprinted with permission of the Alexander Turnbull Library, Wellington, New Zealand.

Thomson Gale Literature Product Advisory Board

The members of the Thomson Gale Literature Product Advisory Board—reference librarians from public and academic library systems—represent a cross-section of our customer base and offer a variety of informed perspectives on both the presentation and content of our literature products. Advisory board members assess and define such quality issues as the relevance, currency, and usefulness of the author coverage, critical content, and literary topics included in our series; evaluate the layout, presentation, and general quality of our printed volumes; provide feedback on the criteria used for selecting authors and topics covered in our series; provide suggestions for potential enhancements to our series; identify any gaps in our coverage of authors or literary topics, recommending authors or topics for inclusion; analyze the appropriateness of our content and presentation for various user audiences, such as high school students, undergraduates, graduate students, librarians, and educators; and offer feedback on any proposed changes/enhancements to our series. We wish to thank the following advisors for their advice throughout the year.

Barbara M. Bibel
Librarian
Oakland Public Library
Oakland, California

Dr. Toby Burrows
Principal Librarian
The Scholars' Centre
University of Western Australia Library
Nedlands, Western Australia

Celia C. Daniel
Associate Reference Librarian
Howard University Libraries
Washington, D.C.

David M. Durant
Reference Librarian
Joyner Library
East Carolina University
Greenville, North Carolina

Nancy T. Guidry
Librarian
Bakersfield Community College
Bakersfield, California

Heather Martin
Arts & Humanities Librarian
University of Alabama at Birmingham, Sterne Library
Birmingham, Alabama

Susan Mikula
Librarian
Indiana Free Library
Indiana, Pennsylvania

Thomas Nixon
Humanities Reference Librarian
University of North Carolina at Chapel Hill, Davis Library
Chapel Hill, North Carolina

Mark Schumacher
Jackson Library
University of North Carolina at Greensboro
Greensboro, North Carolina

Gwen Scott-Miller
Assistant Director
Sno-Isle Regional Library System
Marysville, Washington

J. M. Barrie
1860-1937

(Full name James Matthew Barrie) Scottish playwright, novelist, short story writer, journalist, and biographer.

The following entry provides an overview of Barrie's life and works. For additional information on his career, see *TCLC,* Volume 2.

INTRODUCTION

Although he wrote more than forty plays and dozens of short stories, novels, and magazine articles, Barrie is best known today for a single creation: the tale of Peter Pan, which he told in various forms in stories, novels, and most notably the play *Peter Pan* (1904). The play has been staged throughout the Western world, particularly in Britain and America, where it has been nearly continuously performed since its first production. Part fantasy, fairy tale, adventure story, and pantomime, *Peter Pan* has been described as a modern myth in its archetypal treatment of childhood innocence, separation, and death, and Barrie has been compared to Lewis Carroll and Hans Christian Andersen for his creation of one of the most popular children's works ever written.

BIOGRAPHICAL INFORMATION

James Matthew Barrie was born May 9, 1860, in Kirriemuir, Scotland, the third son and seventh surviving child of Margaret Ogilvy and David Barrie, a weaver. Barrie's mother was a delicate woman who had an immense influence on her children's lives, especially James's. Though the Barrie family lived in modest circumstances, they were not impoverished, as was later suggested by Barrie in his autobiographical writings. In fact, the family managed to make enough money to send their sons to private schools and to college. Barrie's earliest years were uneventful. However, when he was six years old his elder brother David died in an ice skating accident. David's death had a debilitating effect on Barrie's mother, who thereafter became a near-invalid. As recounted in his biography of his mother, *Margaret Ogilvy* (1896), Barrie assumed the persona of his dead brother in order to comfort her and become the center of her affections. Critics have repeatedly linked the theme of "youth frozen in time" in Barrie's works, especially in *Peter Pan,* to David's untimely death and Barrie's attempt to become the lost son in his mother's eyes.

At the age of thirteen Barrie attended Dumfries Academy to receive a formal education. By his own account, he enjoyed the five years he spent at the academy, making friends quickly and easily, and finding at the school a welcome outlet for his love of adventure and play-acting. While at Dumfries, Barrie became interested in the theater, attending local productions as often as possible. When he left the school in 1878, he returned home determined to become a writer. His parents, however, had plans for their son to become a minister, the occupation his brother David was to have pursued. With help from his elder siblings, Barrie reached a compromise with his parents: he would attend Edinburgh University and study literature. Unlike his time at Dumfries, Barrie's years at Edinburgh were uncomfortable. He became painfully shy and intensely self-conscious over his height (he was five feet tall). Despite having difficulties with his studies, Barrie graduated from Edinburgh University with an M.A. in 1882, at the age of twenty-one.

After leaving Edinburgh, Barrie took a job as a writer for the *Nottingham Journal,* in January 1883. The position was short-lived, however, as the paper's owners decided it was less expensive to buy syndicated articles than to pay for its own writers. Back home in Kirriemuir, Barrie began to write and submit dozens of articles to a number of London periodicals. One piece, based on his mother's tales of her childhood in Kirriemuir, was published in the *St. James Gazette* in 1884. The publisher urged Barrie to submit more articles on "that Scotch thing," and the stylized, humorous sketches were popular with readers. A collection of the pieces, *Auld Licht Idylls,* was issued in 1888. (The title refers to the Auld Lichts, or "old lights," a strict religious sect in Kirriemuir to which Barrie's grandfather belonged.) The success of *Auld Licht Idylls* led to the publication of two sequels, the collection of sketches *A Window in Thrums* (1889) and the novel *The Little Minister* (1891), all three of which came to be called the Thrums books, so named after the fictional Scottish town in which all are set. With the success of the Thrums books, Barrie moved permanently to London to pursue his career as a writer.

During the next fifteen years, Barrie wrote more than twenty stories, novels, and plays, including *When a Man's Single* (1888), *Walker, London* (1892), *Sentimental Tommy* (1896), *Tommy and Grizel* (1900), and *The Little White Bird* (1902). Although not all of his works were successes, either critically or financially, Barrie's literary reputation was established by the time he wrote *Peter Pan* in 1904. As Barrie's literary fame was rising, three events occurred that had a significant impact on his life and work. The first was his marriage to a young actress named Mary Ansell in 1894. The marriage was a failure; the couple remained childless, and Barrie spent less and less time with his wife after his career as a writer was established. Even so, Mary served as the model for a number of Barrie's heroines, and for many years he gave her name to characters in his books and plays. The two were eventually divorced in 1909. The second event was the death of Barrie's mother in 1895. Within a year of her passing, Barrie wrote and published his biography and tribute, *Margaret Ogilvy,* which became an instant success, though some reviewers found the emotionally charged and overly sentimental memoir distasteful. Even after writing the memoir, Barrie continued to demonstrate the powerful influence of his mother's life and death in many of his later works. The final event was Barrie's chance meeting and eventual friendship with the young sons of Arthur and Sylvia Llewelyn Davies. There were three boys—George, Jack, and Peter—at the time of their first meeting; two others—Michael and Nicholas—were born after. During his frequent walks in Kensington Gardens, Barrie would keep company with the boys despite the disapproval of their nursemaid, and would entertain them with stories of adventure and fantasy. During the summers the boys would join Barrie and his wife at Black Lake Cottage, their vacation home. Their games together and storytelling provided Barrie with the spark that led to *Peter Pan.*

The last three decades of Barrie's life were filled with continued literary success and even greater public recognition, as well as personal setbacks. In 1911 he published the novel *Peter and Wendy,* an adaptation of *Peter Pan,* to positive reviews and a receptive audience. In fact, the novel version of the Peter Pan story for a time supplanted the play in terms of popularity. Barrie received a number of public honors during this period in his life: he was elected rector of Saint Andrews in 1919 and chancellor of Edinburgh in 1930; he received honorary doctorate degrees from Oxford University in 1926 and Cambridge University in 1930; he was bestowed with a baronetcy by King George V in 1913; and he was presented with the Order of Merit in 1922. But these years were also filled with emotional hardships. Barrie saw his popularity decline after World War I; two of the Davies children—to whom he served as legal guardian after the deaths of their parents—died; several of his literary friends also passed on; after 1920, he could write only sporadically; and he spent his last years in poor health and deeply depressed. Barrie died on June 19, 1937, in London.

MAJOR WORKS

Peter Pan and its adaptation as a novel, *Peter and Wendy,* stand apart in the Barrie cannon in their successful treatment of themes found throughout his works, such as childhood innocence, the island as a retreat from society, separation, the fantastic, and the need for social order. Barrie first told the story of children who can fly and who leave their parents for a magical world in the privately printed *The Boy Castaways of Black Lake Island* (1901), a photographic record of the fantasy games Barrie and the Davies boys played at their summer vacation cottage. He initially developed the central Peter Pan story in *The Little White Bird.* In this novel, Captain W, a lonely bachelor, acts the role of an anonymous benefactor to an impoverished young couple and ultimately befriends their young son, David, with whom he goes for walks in Kensington Gardens. In the course of their friendship, Captain W tells David a story about a baby—named Peter Pan—who flies out of his nursery to return to the island of the birds. Eventually, Peter learns that he isn't a bird but a baby and immediately loses his ability to fly. The novel also includes an image that would recur in *Peter Pan,* in which Peter returns to his nursery to be reunited with his mother and family, only to find that the nursery window is barred and a new baby has taken his place.

Barrie continued to think about the Peter Pan story after he finished *The Little White Bird* and began to add further adventures, characters, and scenes to the original tale. By the time he finished *Peter Pan*, Barrie had combined his childhood love of adventure, his memories of the Davies boys, his ambivalence about Edwardian domestic life, and his desire to create a modern myth of childhood into something new and original. As many critics have noted, nothing like *Peter Pan* had ever been seen on the British stage. Audiences of Barrie's plays were accustomed to his humorous realism and sentimentality, but they were entirely unprepared for such extensive fantasy: a nursery supervised by a Newfoundland dog, an enchanted lagoon, pirates and Indians, the magic of flight, and a glowing fairy named Tinker Bell. The play was an immediate success.

The fantasy world and childhood themes in *Peter Pan* often hide Barrie's serious concerns. Although many of his works repeatedly affirm the need for social conventions, especially marriage, Wendy's role as mother to the Lost Boys is rife with ambiguities over the domestic place of women in British society. The adult male figures in Barrie's story are depicted as childish and vindictive, while maintaining the veneer of gentlemen. The themes of death and separation are omnipresent in the story. And Peter Pan himself is anything but childlike and charming: he lives completely in the present, is cruel and selfish, and often leads the children into dangerous situations without concern for their well-being. Many critics note the nightmarish qualities of the story. *Peter Pan* and *Peter and Wendy* are in many ways works for adults, which makes it even more remarkable that the Peter Pan story would become a children's classic, a paradox noted by many commentators.

While *Peter Pan* is by far the most widely read, most frequently performed, and most discussed of all Barrie's works, there are several others that critics argue demonstrate the best qualities of Barrie's craft as a writer. These include the Thrums books, the play *The Admirable Crichton* (1902), and the novel *Farewell, Miss Julie Logan* (1932). The stories collected in the first two Thrums books—*Auld Licht Idylls* and *A Window in Thrums*—and the novel *The Little Minister* all deal with the pathos and daily lives of the ministers, weavers, farmers, and wives who inhabit the idealized Scottish village of Thrums. The stories in the first two works share common characteristics and themes: the narrators are typically unobtrusive yet observant schoolmasters or ministers; the village and its inhabitants are presented as a microcosm of Scottish rural life; and the various complications of the characters are all resolved by the ideals of love, devotion, and lasting support for one another. The stories also reaffirm the importance of social conventions, especially marriage, in controlling unhealthy behavior and maintaining happiness and order. This is particularly true in *The Little Minister*, which portrays the excessive and destructive behavior of Lady Barbara, who disguises herself as the captivating gypsy Babbie. Social order, disrupted by Babbie's actions, is restored through marriage, as the heroine ultimately marries the minister Gavin Dishart. The theme of marriage as the proper corrective to wayward or destructive energies is one found often in Barrie's work.

The Admirable Crichton deals with the need for, and inevitability of, class distinction, which is defended by the play's title character. Crichton, the epitome of the gentleman's gentleman, disagrees with his employer's attempt to eliminate class distinctions. Crichton considers these ideas as violations of nature, which in his view governs the establishment of class structure. Crichton's vision is put to the test when both he and his employer, Lord Loam, are among a group shipwrecked on a remote island. Without the support of society, the butler becomes the "governor" on the island, since he has the survival skills that the other, aristocratic, characters lack. In the end, Crichton leads the survivors off the island and willingly returns to his former rank as Lord Loam's butler. The play demonstrates that the superior man is not necessarily the one typically held up by society; it is, as Harry M. Geduld has observed, the person who "knows his place in society and respects the limitations imposed on him by class barriers."

Written late in his life, at a time when Barrie himself believed that his career as a writer had ended, *Farewell, Miss Julie Logan* is frequently praised by critics as Barrie's best work of fiction. It is considered one of his few fictional pieces that displays a thematic treatment of adult romantic love and successfully weaves a supernatural element and fantasy into the story's plot. The story, told through the diary of a young minister named Adam Yestreen, depicts the minister's battle with a beautiful spirit, Julie Logan, whom he meets while snowbound on a winter's night. The two picnic in a small ruin and ultimately kiss, at which point Julie abruptly and rather comically declares, "I am a Papist." Yestreen is thereupon released from his lover's spell. The story concludes when, twenty-five years later, the minister revisits the place of his former encounter and, to his surprise, finds the picnic basket he and Julie Logan shared, though he long ago convinced himself that the events that night were the product of his imagination.

CRITICAL RECEPTION

More than sixty years after his death, modern critics often marvel at how far the reputation of Barrie, once the most popular, acclaimed, and financially successful writer of his time, has declined. During most of his lifetime, Barrie was esteemed by both the British public and literary critics. He was friends with many of the leading authors of the age and praised by Robert Louis Stevenson, Thomas Hardy, and other noted writers. His plays attracted the best actors and actresses, engaged the most respected directors and production staff, and were staged in the top theaters of London. Although Barrie's display of personal emotions and his reliance on sentimentality disturbed some British theater-goers and critics, he was more often lauded for his deft characterizations, his clever dialogue, his ironic sense of humor, and his craft as a dramatist.

After the horrors of World War I, Barrie's popularity fell considerably. The mawkishness, predictability, and childlike innocence of his works were out of fashion in an age contemplating the violence of war and the alienation of the artist. Many saw Barrie solely as the author of *Peter Pan* and dismissed him as a children's writer unworthy of serious consideration. The popularity of Freudian theory and psychoanalytic criticism led commentators to find disturbing qualities in Barrie's works. Freudian analysts found unresolved Oedipal longings in his fixation on his mother and in the depictions of mother figures in his stories and plays. He was often disparaged for his inability to deal with adult emotions and themes, a fact that was always linked to his dependence on his mother and his need to remain a child in her eyes in order to experience her love. Barrie was also labeled a pedophile because of the dominance of boys in both his writing and his life. Much of this criticism was based on the uncomfortably close relationship of Captain W and the boy David in the novel *The Little White Bird*. One scene in particular, in which the Captain helps undress David for bed, was identified as proof of Barrie's obsessive love of children.

Since the 1980s critics have generally tried to move away from interpretations based on Barrie's personal life and have instead focused on his skill as a writer, the role of fantasy in his stories and plays, and the overt or subtextual commentary in his works on the social conventions of his age. In 1987 Leonee Ormond signaled this change with the publication of her reassessment of Barrie's life and writings. What has since emerged is a more balanced view of Barrie's art. Whereas previous critics saw in the author's dependence on sentimentality a repetitive pandering to the taste of his public at best, or an inability to confront serious themes at worst, recent scholars have maintained that Barrie was actually "interrogating the concept of sentimentalism itself," as stated by Andrew Nash in his analysis of the two "Tommy" novels. A similar view of Barrie's use of fantasy and the fantastic in his works has been put forth, especially by such critics as Lynette Hunter, Sarah Gilead, and Ann Yeoman. Rather than being dismissed as an artless proponent of the social conventions of late Victorian and Edwardian society, such as the domestic role of women, the cult of childhood innocence, and the separation of the classes, Barrie is now more often seen as questioning or showing ambivalence toward these conventions. This is especially the case with *Peter Pan*, which critics now interpret as Barrie's condemnation—rather than celebration—of perpetual childhood. Many find a central tension in the story in Wendy's role as "mother" to the Lost Boys and her precarious stature as both child and sexually aware adolescent. At the same time, scholars continue to recognize shortcomings in Barrie's handling of serious themes such as death, childhood separation, class, and marriage, noting, like earlier critics, his inability to express emotions directly and fully explore the human ramifications of his themes.

Despite such limitations, *Peter Pan* continues to fascinate both adults and children. Carl Markgraf has located the enduring appeal of Barrie's works in his ability to make us "not only think, but feel." In Markgraf's view, Barrie's best works "take us out of our world into a world of his creation. We return having been moved, as well as moved to thought, by his experience. I can think of no greater praise for any playwright."

PRINCIPAL WORKS

Auld Licht Idylls (short stories) 1888
Better Dead (novel) 1888
*When a Man's Single: A Tale of Literary Life (novel) 1888
A Window in Thrums (short stories) 1889
The Little Minister (novel) 1891
Richard Savage [with H. B. Marriott Watson] (play) 1891
Walker, London (play) 1892
Margaret Ogilvy. By Her Son (biography) 1896
†Sentimental Tommy: The Story of His Boyhood (novel) 1896
‡The Little Minister (play) 1897
§Tommy and Grizel (novel) 1900
Quality Street (play) 1901
The Admirable Crichton (play) 1902
The Little White Bird; or, Adventures in Kensington Garden (novel) 1902
Peter Pan; or, The Boy Who Wouldn't Grow Up (play) 1904
Alice Sit-by-the-Fire: A Page from a Daughter's Diary (play) 1905
Pantaloon; or, A Plea for an Ancient Family (play) 1905
What Every Woman Knows (play) 1908
The Twelve-Pound Look (play) 1910
‖Peter and Wendy (novel) 1911
Der Tag; or, The Tragic Man (play) 1914
A Kiss for Cinderella (play) 1916
Dear Brutus (play) 1917
The Old Lady Shows Her Medals (play) 1917

Mary Rose (play) 1920

The Plays of J. M. Barrie (plays) 1928; revised edition, 1942

The Works of J. M. Barrie. 16 vols. (novels, sketches, biography, and plays) 1929-40

Farewell, Miss Julie Logan: A Wintry Tale (novel) 1932

The Boy David (play) 1936

The Letters of J. M. Barrie [edited by Viola Meynell] (letters) 1942

*This novel first appeared serially in *The British Weekly,* 1887-88.

†This novel first appeared serially in *Scribner's Magazine,* 1896.

‡This play is an adaptation of the novel by the same name.

§This novel first appeared serially in *Scribner's Magazine,* 1900.

‖This novel is an adaptation of the play *Peter Pan.*

CRITICISM

Lynette Hunter (essay date March 1980)

SOURCE: Hunter, Lynette. "J. M. Barrie's Islands of Fantasy." *Modern Drama* 23, no. 1 (March 1980): 65-74.

[*In the following essay, Hunter examines why Barrie shifted from writing novels to composing plays after 1902, claiming that the author became disillusioned with fiction as a form of artistic communication and came to regard drama as the best medium for expressing his growing condemnation of fantasy literature.*]

I

James Barrie's plays offer a consistency of approach to ideas about artistic communication that has been seriously neglected. The neglect partly results from a separation between the criticism of his novels and that of his plays, which obscures the development of theme, structure and imagery from the one medium to the other. The criticism of the drama itself has suffered from an avoidance of the published scripts. There has been little if any attention paid to the commentary of the plays which provides a function similar to that of the narrator in the novels, and is invaluable in understanding the author's ironic perspective. The product of the dramatic criticism has been an enormously diversified assessment of Barrie, leaving an impression of a man of dilettante interests rather than complexity.[1] But if we examine the plays as generated from the novels, we find in their author not only a more thoughtful and mature literary figure, but also one who is placed firmly among early twentieth century concerns about communication and art.

On examination, the similarity between the later novels and early plays of the period 1890 to 1902 is so close[2] that it poses the interesting question: why did Barrie change his medium to drama alone after 1902? It could not have been solely for financial reasons, because his novels were selling well;[3] and while he had written four very mediocre plays by 1902, only the first, **Walker, London,** a light farce, had more than a respectable run. I would suggest that the change in medium was due to a change in the author's understanding of art and what he saw as the artist's responsibilities. Barrie's early critical work of the late 1880's indicates that he had a strong belief in the possibility of absolute communication through words.[4] But by the time he was writing **Tommy and Grizel** in 1900, he had personally discarded this belief, or developed it into a discussion of the fantasist who is a specific kind of artist defined by his belief in absolute personal communication. He is a man who thinks that he can create perfect alternative worlds, and that by initiating them from actual experience he can generate trust in them from his audience. Once created, the worlds are controlled absolutely by the fantasist who builds defenses against the intrusion of reality by providing detailed accounts of language, customs, and a way of life that needs no reference to an external standard. Both the creation and control of these worlds demand a passive audience accepting and believing rather than involved and experiencing.

In **Tommy and Grizel** Barrie follows up the implications of these totally self-sufficient worlds. It is interesting that the one chapter explicitly demonstrating the process of Tommy's fantasizing corresponds exactly to Walter Pater's description of image-making in the last chapter of *The Renaissance,*[5] and significantly, in **Sentimental Tommy** Barrie connects the fantasy process with what he saw as the "art for art's sake" movement led by Pater. His point is that if art is totally self-sufficient, its responsibility is to itself, and its morality becomes relative. Barrie points out on many occasions that while this kind of irresponsibility to others is acceptable in a child who is mainly unconscious of the process, it is not so in a man consciously producing a piece of art.[6] Both novels by Barrie also contain many instances of the ambivalent and dangerous nature of fantasy. The ambivalence stems from the fact that fantasy is something to escape to, and escape can be effective only if one becomes unconscious of the limits of the story. Yet if one is to control the story, one cannot become entirely unconscious of its existence. Tommy himself is killed when he follows his fantasy into an extreme situation which he cannot control. The danger of fantasy is that its final realization ends in madness or death.

The "Tommy" stories provide an obvious study of Barrie's early beliefs about the powers of a writer through the central character. Yet he also examines his own motives for writing about Tommy through the narrator of each work, and the tone becomes increasingly cynical and bitter as he approaches the year 1900. In *Tommy and Grizel* the narrator interrupts a sarcastic comment on Tommy's obituaries to ask himself why he even wrote about such a despicable character. He concludes that although Tommy failed to conquer his selfishness and egoism, at least he tried. Barrie wishes not just to condemn fantasy, but also to demonstrate the essential battle with it if man is to avoid self-delusion.

To achieve the fantasy worlds in his novels Barrie uses a four-part structure intrinsically connected to the tone of the narrator. The first section creates trust in the narrator, who in the second presents a situation that arises from actual events. This leads to the third part, which produces the central fantasy, usually the main character's personal interpretation of the situation, presented as the only reality. The final part of each book places in a perspective the interpretation of the central fantasy. In earlier work such as *The Little Minister*, Barrie allows the fantasy to be reinforced, but in the later work, the narrator ironically removes all the bases for belief in the interpretation built up by the central character.

The Little White Bird is an exception to this structural pattern and anticipates the later three-part structure of Barrie's plays. Here the author also fuses the roles of narrator and fantasist. The narrator is the ironic voice conscious of reality, yet the character side of him is the fantasist trying to escape responsibilities. The first part of the book becomes a series of episodes with the narrator constantly exposing his delusions and then creating new desires. There is a central fantasy, but it is here isolated, recognized as fantasy, not brought into real life. The fantasy itself reflects this condition, for it presents Peter Pan as the very young child, an unconscious fantasist. The conditions for his survival are complete separation from human beings, and isolation beyond his control not only in a park but on a real island in a river. It should be noted that the increasing isolation in which Barrie places the physical and mental islands of his work indicates his growing awareness of the dangers of fantasy. The final part of the book shows the narrator slowly and painfully trying to get rid of the lady Romance, who makes a sentimental fool of him in the first part, and to accept the reality of a real woman, Mary.

II

Before moving on to the plays which succeed *The Little White Bird,* it is important to note the relationship of Barrie's ideas to the comments on fantasy made by other major contemporary authors. Barrie's attitude to fantasy distinguished the pure fantasy of the child and an equation of adult fantasy with sentimentalism in both "sentimental" Tommy and the sentimental narrator of *The Little White Bird.* Behind this definition we can see the immensely influential figure of Meredith. In Meredith's *The Egoist,* the central character, like Tommy, is a supreme fantasist creating a fantasy of self-limited perfection in his home and life. The related essay, *An Essay on Comedy . . .*, explicitly examines the egoist as sentimentalist.[7] The influence of Meredith can also be found in the work of most of Barrie's contemporaries.[8] But the closest to Barrie is D. H. Lawrence. He speaks of fantasy as a circle of self-consciousness evading the "real *being* of men. . . ."[9] He too notes that when fantasy becomes conscious, it becomes egoistical and sentimental,[10] and sentimentalism is linked with an adult wish to regain the fantasy of childhood, which Lawrence condemns as "disgusting."[11]

For all these critics, the big point is the questionable use of personal authority over reality through fantasy, and the demand of fantasists for a passive audience to evade reality. All also perceive a need for some external authority, social, political or religious. Significantly, the most comprehensive modern study of fantasy, Colin Manlove's *Modern Fantasy*, concludes by saying that "the only basis in our reality . . . became the creator and not his audience." Further, the fantasist's self-involvement leads to sentimentality and escapism for himself and a "benign determinism" towards his audience.[12] It is the concept of human authority and control taken to its extreme that makes possible the isolated fantasies of potential perfection. It is interesting that the dominant image of an island in Barrie's works, which he himself notes in the dedication of *Peter Pan* (1928), is present in many other works of fantasy.[13] Islands are important because it is insularity that removes the invented world from actuality. But fantasy's potential perfection is only potential, for it is an unavoidable situation that "No man is an *Iland*, intire of it selfe. . . ."[14] It is the assumption of perfection that the fantasist makes when he creates his worlds; and it is the danger in this assumption about which Barrie and other critics were worried.

Between 1892 and 1902 there is a marked decline in Barrie's satisfaction with the novel as a mode. The amount of dialogue increases enormously until *The Little White Bird* with its narrator/character, which has some later chapters virtually entirely spoken.[15] Here also the chapter structures and thematically consistent units of the previous novels break up to produce an episodic, scene-like progression. It is important that this growing disenchantment with the novel is coincident with Barrie's condemnation of fantasy writing. The structure of drama is the practical solution to his technical need for more dialogue and scenic development of plot. But the questions remain: why does he develop more towards a dramatic technique, and how does the mode provide a medium more suitable for his change in attitude towards the artist's responsibilities in communication?

One obvious difference between novelistic and dramatic modes is the relationship of the audience to the work of art. The novel is intensely individual, usually functioning on a one-to-one, reader-to-book, response. The control that the author can exercise over that response is therefore immense. Theatre, as George Steiner comments, provides immediate social implications not found in the novel.[16] The very fact that one sits in an audience not only creates a greater mental distance between the art and the spectator, but also partially conditions one's response to the surrounding public response. Further, theatre is based on illusion. The spectator actively chooses at some point to accept this convention, and at any given moment the suspension of disbelief may be stopped. T. S. Eliot makes an interesting distinction between the actively involved audience in the theatre as opposed to the more passive audience of film. In a broad generalization he notes that the intent of film is to create "the illusion that we are observing the actual event. . . ."[17] Many novels have a similar intent, and certainly those which are based on fantasy, yet the manifest illusion of the theatre is far less conducive to the realizing of fantasy.

Barrie tried to stabilize the presence of fantasy in his novels either by isolating it or by treating it ironically. In drama he found that the implicit separation between the spectator and the play controlled and pointed out the inescapable limits of the story more successfully than novelistic convention. Technically, the increased use of dialogue and episodic development in *The Little White Bird* cuts down on descriptive interpretation that can be used to control response. In the drama he still can and does exercise an editorial role through his extensive commentary; yet this does not intrude upon the play as the audience sees it. But fundamentally, Barrie recognizes the positive role of illusion in the theatre. As he comments in the bitter, autobiographical allegory *Pantaloon*: "It is well known . . . that actors in general are not the same off the stage as on; . . . they dress for their parts, speak words written for them which they do not necessarily believe. . . ."[18] It is the public and conscious knowledge of the illusory nature of theatre that Barrie needs in coming to terms with his new sense of artistic responsibility.

III

The role of the narrator is instrumental in understanding Barrie's perspective on fantasy and his attitude to his art. One can only, like the narrator/character of *The Little White Bird*, face the delusion, expose it and experience reality, and then fall into another. Just so the role of the commentator is necessary to an understanding of the plays. Yet here the invisibility of the commentator in the work as theatre is the safeguard Barrie seeks, for his personal control is one step away, transformed and interpreted.

Quality Street, the first of Barrie's really successful plays, has many aspects of the earlier work, but points to his later style and thematic content. The play has a four-act structure, and a central fantasy: Brown's desire for Phoebe to become a girl again. But when he is faced with this possibility in the third act, he is dissatisfied. In the final act the commentator hints that Brown's new vision of Phoebe may yet become fantasy again, for he refuses to accept that she will grow older. But this potential delusion is not emphasized. The audience is allowed to entertain its possible reality.

Just as *The Little White Bird* indicates a shift to a three-part structure and a clearer isolation of the island of fantasy, so *The Admirable Crichton*, although in four acts, shifts to three main parts: London society, the island, and London society. After this play only one of Barrie's full-length dramas is in four acts; the others clearly reserve the central act for fantasy. *The Admirable Crichton* also anticipates another development. Both London society and the island society exist only as personal interpretations of social rules; they appear arbitrary and fantastic. What is interesting is that the transitional periods between societies provide the characters with opportunities to find out about themselves, just as the narrator in *The Little White Bird* did between fantasies. But in *The Admirable Crichton*, only Crichton and Mary even realize other aspects of themselves, and they have not the strength to act upon them.

The movement from fantasy to fantasy, with the possibility of discovering one's self in between and even changing, becomes a central theme of all Barrie's plays. The dedication to *Peter Pan* speaks of people usually passing without change from room to room, but concedes that one may change "through effort of will, which is a brave affair . . ." (492). Yet as Barrie continues to become more aware of the potential influence of words in art, his attitude to the role of the man who makes this movement possible, the fantasist, gradually shifts its perspective.

Peter Pan, as the boy "who would not grow up," not the boy who did not grow up, is the conscious fantasist, no longer a child yet determined to stay within his invented world. The commentator explicitly notes that Never Land is Peter's island; he has made it.[19] The creation of a complete personal world is the first of Barrie's conditions of fantasy. The second, absolute control over the actions and events, is also fulfilled. Peter controls not only the events but also their interpretations. At the end of each day when Wendy asks him what he has been doing, Peter tells her his version; but she is "*never quite sure . . . ; indeed the only one who is sure about anything on the island is* PETER" (549). She becomes a passive audience "*too guarded by this time to ask . . .*" (538) for any truth.

The price Peter pays for this fantasy is his humanity. He is given a second chance to return to reality, but he refuses to accept the responsibility. In a key passage the commentator describes Peter saying to himself, "*with a drum beating in his breast as if he were a real boy at last,*" "To die will be an awfully big adventure" (545). He echoes the observation in the final note to the play, saying: "*If he could get the hang of the thing his cry might become 'To live would be an awfully big adventure!' but he can never quite get the hang of it, and so no one is as gay as he*" (576). Peter wants to become a real boy, and to maintain his fantasy world. But the two are mutually exclusive, so Peter forfeits his humanity to preserve his fantasy. Wendy, on the other hand, acknowledges the desirability of fantasy but also the need to reject it. She provides a constant standard of reality within Never Land which allows her to learn about herself.

While Peter himself is the pure fantasist, Barrie creates the man with the *Thesaurus* who is similar to the narrator of the novels. The character is at times Barrie himself,[20] the commentator (503), Mr. Darling (513), and Captain Hook (557). He is the adult who wishes to return to fantasy and cannot. He is the sentimentalist, aware of an external standard of reality negating the value of personal desire. Barrie himself observes in the dedication the "fragments of immortality . . ." (502) left him if he attempts fantasy, for reality always intrudes. The fantasy is always shattered. Rather than an escapist play, **Peter Pan** is a comment on the stasis and delusion of fantasy. The strength of the play is the tension between the desirability of Peter's fantasy-making power and the knowledge of the impossibility of using it without losing one's humanity.

Dear Brutus and **Mary Rose** are the best of the later plays. In the former Barrie extends his attitude to the nature of an artist's responsibility. He takes the ironic occurrence of self-knowledge reached between fantasies and makes it a positive goal. The artist is not just clearly distinguishing between reality and fantasy, but making it possible for people to move between the two. The idea of moving from reality to fantasy to reality, or from island to island, yet needing to question the fantastic nature of reality itself, is the predominant theme of **Dear Brutus.** The central character, Lob, like Peter Pan, creates a fantasy; but his guests choose to participate in and experience the fantasy without his control over their responses. Yet he too is inhuman; along with Peter, "*he is so light that the subject must not be mentioned in his presence . . .*" (1004). Like, yet unlike, the conscious fantasist, Lob lives an intermediate existence, always conscious of fantasy and providing it for others, but never indulging in it himself. We understand from the commentator that all Lob's guests but one suffer a delusion about the reality in which they live. Lob provides them with a "second chance" to change their lives in the fantasy world of the wood beyond his garden.

It is impossible not to correlate the function of Lob with the role Barrie sees for himself. Barrie has moved away from the duality of Peter as the complete fantasist and the man with the *Thesaurus* as the sentimentalist, to a perspective through which he tries to use the deluding nature of his art positively in exposing the deluding nature of life. He comes to see this role as a further responsibility to his audience, yet without the convention of theatrical illusion it would be difficult to maintain the necessary balance.

Barrie's last successful full-length play is **Mary Rose,** written in 1920. Here he squarely faces the question occupying all the theorists on fantasy: that of control by personal authority and its dangerous potential. In **Peter Pan** the fantasist exercises totalitarian control over the invented world; Lob controls the presence of the fantasy but not the response to it. In **Mary Rose** Harry, like the narrator of **The Little White Bird,** has to control the fantasy of his mother, Mary Rose, not for others but for himself. The complex situation that results produces an atmosphere of elusive reality: layers of delusion and desire interpenetrating, shifting, fading, obscuring the actual events and revealing the difficulty of true self-knowledge.

Again from the commentator we learn that Mary Rose is similar to all the previous fantasists, especially in her femininity.[21] They also share an "oddness" with her; like her, they are all frozen into eternal age or eternal youth. She too has her island with only an evergreen for eternal youth and a rowan tree for witchcraft on it; for Barrie increasingly equates fantasy with witchcraft and superstition, not only in **Farewell, Miss Julie Logan** but also in **The Boy David.** And just as Peter forsook his second chance and condemned himself to fantasy, when Mary Rose tries to return a second time she can do so only as a ghost.

What Harry sees in the central act of the play is the memory of what he has been told of his mother. He learns to perceive the reality between what he wants Mary Rose to be to him and what she herself expects to find in him; and he realizes that his desire for a mother can never be fulfilled. Once Mary Rose as a mother figure has been exposed as a fantasy, she can finally die, and release is achieved at the end of the play for her and for Harry. This is one of the first discardings of fantasy that Barrie writes about; and significantly the commentator tells us that it happens through prayer. The exposure of fantasy is not an act of human authority but an act of will requiring more than human strength. Barrie's brief but clear answer to the need for some external authority to relieve man's dilemma of delusion and desire is found in a God to whom one can pray for strength of will. In this conclusion he also clearly connects artistic responsibility with a moral responsibility to indicate an external power that will lessen what he sees as the dangers of human authority in fantasy.

The Boy David, which was written fifteen years after *Mary Rose* and the year before Barrie's death, provides a summary of his mature ideas about communication. It indicates that the gradual internalizing of the role of the fantasist has progressed to the stage where the writer feels that an artist should communicate absolutely, or not at all. In other words the fantasist has no moral right to re-create his fantasies for an audience without indicating the extent of personal authority within them. The purest communication in this play is Samuel's; one understands exactly what he means even when he does not speak. The most abased is Saul's, and his downfall is caused by a misunderstanding of his words. David enacts the supremely human conflict as he fluctuates between both. Barrie also tries hard to make his meaning totally understandable; but in doing so he produces a creaky play. The attention to biblical detail provides only a superficial reality; and the schematic development of characters, although clear, leaves them cold.

Samuel is presented as completely free from self-delusion. He communicates with God through prayer and vision, and speaks to man through allegorical action, prophecy and poetry. Saul, the corrupted king, insists on personal authority and must therefore depend upon Samuel to communicate with God for him. As a man-made authority, he must do things by himself, as Jonathan points out.[22] Kings, just like fantasists, are entirely dependent on themselves for everything in their world. Like fantasists they insist on their personal points of view and impose their authority on others. In the end Saul begins to believe in his own fantasies, here portrayed as witchcraft, and he kills himself.

David's career throughout the play is a conflict between the two poles of fantasy and reality that the two men represent. Here it is important that David is still a boy; his fantasies are not yet dangerous. He is still the child fantasist, but in contrast to Peter, he is never allowed to indulge in an isolated fantasy. To accommodate this change in action, Barrie changes the structure of his play: there is no longer a "central fantasy," but a series of incidents in which David fluctuates between self-knowledge and desire. Initially it is Samuel's vision of God that helps David to know himself, but gradually he is given visions himself and can realize his true potential. When at the end of the play he loses a fight with Jonathan and finally has to accept his limitations, the commentator notes that he is changing from boy to man. In accepting reality he reaches *"the most tragic moment of his boyhood's story"* (1268).

The commentator carefully contrasts Saul's fantasies with David's visions which make up most of the final act of the play. The visions are real "as if they lived" (1249); and David is not "in" them, as with a fantasy, but "at" them Significantly, in his visions the boy David sees himself grown up to be a king, and hurls a stone at himself; for man must always try to destroy in himself the delusion of personal power so dangerous in an adult. But he also sees the dead Saul made innocent again, and using David's own words to express himself. David will always remain in danger of becoming a Saul and only the constant recognition of God can prevent it.

In his straightforward writing, Barrie is specifically emulating Samuel's responsibility to communicate God's presence so that David can release himself from fantasy. Samuel's responsibility is identified with the artist's responsibility to point to an external standard of reality and lessen the dangers of fantasy. In this we find another hint of Barrie's preference for the theatre. Samuel's main mode of communication is through the allegory of his prophecies and actions. Action on a stage made it possible for Barrie to stop talking about his personal interpretations of ideas and concepts except in the commentary, and to realize them instead. At least in the theatre Barrie's view of the insidious intangibility of fiction is made physical in three dimensions with real people. There is less room for authorial manipulation. However, the control over manipulation is taken too far in *The Boy David.* It is the tension between fantasy and reality not only in the characters, but also in the structures of the plays that strengthens Barrie's best work. Here the tension is hardly present at all. We are told that the characters have changed or will change, but the "brave affair" is not realized for us.

It is ironic that while Barrie's concern about the dangers of fantasy leads him to create some brilliant pieces of theatre, it also leads him to reject his particular artistic skill. The positive side of the later style is its experiment with action and attempt at allegory. Although the experiment fails, it indicates great courage on Barrie's own part; he himself has tried to change. The final form of his ideas about communication reveals a thoughtful and mature design. It is also surprisingly consistent in its assessment of action and prophecy as the purest communication, with contemporary developments in the philosophy of language, and with a growing interest in the use of allegory. That Barrie transformed his original, rather facile, acceptance of the absolute ability of words to communicate meaning into a consistent analysis of fantasy, poetry, and action or prophecy, deserves recognition. And that he was willing to put the ideas into practice, at the eventual cost of his own particular style, deserves admiration. Barrie's epilogue is exactly Prospero's, when he too has to leave his island:

> But release me from my bands
> With the help of your good hands:

Gentle breath of yours my sails
Must fill, or else my project fails,
Which was to please. Now I want
Spirits to enforce, art to enchant;
And my ending is despair,
Unless I be relieved by prayer,
Which pierces so, that it assaults
Mercy itself, and frees all faults.[23]

Notes

1. See David Daiches, "The Sexless Sentimentalist," *The Listener,* 63, No. 1624 (12 May 1960), pp. 841-843; Sheila Kaye-Smith, "J. M. Barrie, The Tragedian," *The Bookman,* 59 (Dec. 1920), 107-108; Patrick Braybrooke, *J. M. Barrie: A Study in Fairies and Mortals* (London, [1924]); and Janet Dunbar, *J. M. Barrie: The Man Behind the Image* (London, 1970), for opinions on Barrie as a writer of tragedy, comedy, and farce.

2. Lynette Hunter, "J. M. Barrie: The Rejection of Fantasy," *Scottish Literary Studies* (May 1978).

3. Denis MacKail, *The Story of J. M. B.* (London, 1941), pp. 302 and 337.

4. *The British Weekly,* 25 Oct. 1888, pp. 415-416.

5. Walter Pater, *The Renaissance: Studies in Art and Poetry* (1910; rpt. London, 1967), pp. 234-6.

6. See *Sentimental Tommy* (London, 1896), p. 385; and *The Letters of J. M. Barrie,* ed. Viola Meynell (London, 1942), p. 10.

7. George Meredith, "Prelude to *The Egoist*," in *An Essay on Comedy, and The Uses of the Comic Spirit,* ed. Lane Cooper (London, 1972), p. 91.

8. For example, see G. K. Chesterton, "Sentimental Literature," *The Speaker,* July 1901, p. 464.

9. D. H. Lawrence, "Pornography and Obscenity," in *A Selection from Phoenix,* ed. A. A. M. Inglis (Harmondsworth, 1971), p. 318.

10. "The Crown," p. 435.

11. *Ibid.,* pp. 440-441.

12. C. N. Manlove, *Modern Fantasy: Five Studies* (Cambridge, 1975), pp. 259-260.

13. Among many examples are such diverse works as William Golding's *Lord of the Flies,* or *Perelandra* by C. S. Lewis; it should also be noted that Meredith refers to the egoist's home as an "island of perfection," "Prelude to *The Egoist*," p. 40.

14. John Donne, "Devotion 17," in *Selected Prose,* chosen by Evelyn Simpson, ed. Helen Gardner and Timothy Healy (Oxford, 1967), p. 101.

15. For example, see the chapter on Pilkington's, or the final chapter.

16. George Steiner, *Tolstoy or Dostoievsky* (London, 1959).

17. T. S. Eliot, and George Hoellering, *The Film of Murder in the Cathedral* (London, 1952), p. 8.

18. *The Plays of J. M. Barrie,* ed. A. E. Wilson (London, 1928), p. 581; all quotations from Barrie's plays are from this edition and page numbers follow in brackets.

19. *Peter Pan,* p. 523.

20. For example, there is Barrie's reference to himself coming to London armed with only his *Thesaurus* in *The Greenwood Hat* (London, 1937), here alluded to on p. 503.

21. Barrie's attitude to women is ambivalent: they are not only more resistant to fantasy but also at its base. The ambivalence is clarified partly by an early article on actors as both supreme fantasists and sexless, *The Edinburgh Evening Dispatch,* March 1887. From Tommy in "sexless garments," to Peter Pan, always acted by a woman, and Captain Hook, great because of "a touch of the feminine" (546), to Lob with his "little feminine touches. . . ." (996), the fantasists are not so much female as bisexual or nonsexual.

22. It is interesting to note that Walter J. Ong connects Pater with the man-made and personalized art with which Barrie's concept of fantasy began, *The Barbarian Within* (New York, 1962), p. 21.

23. William Shakespeare, *The Tempest,* ed. Morton Luce, 4th ed., rev. (London, 1938), pp. 147-8.

Martin Green (essay date 1981)

SOURCE: Green, Martin. "The Charm of *Peter Pan*." *Children's Literature* 9 (1981): 19-27.

[*In the following essay, Green compares Barrie and Walt Disney in their respective treatments of the Peter Pan story. He maintains that Barrie is likely "more responsible than anyone else for the English disease of charm."*]

Family circumstances led me to visit both Disneyland and Disneyworld last summer, experiences I found less rewarding than I'd been promised. I took the Peter Pan Ride in both places, and since the same circumstances had led me to see the Disney movie *Peter Pan* during the spring, I naturally began to think about the conjunction of Disney and Barrie.

One's first thought must be how very badly Disney handles such stories, how crudely and clumsily he draws such figures and renders their charms. Of course, Disney *is* crude and clumsy in his handling of so many subjects; what can one say but "obscene" even to his drawing of animals and his photographing of flowers—those speeded-up blossomings which turn all of nature into a florist's shop stocked with prize blooms, fresh every morning from the cosmetician? But there is a peculiar wrongness in his choosing Barrie to work on.

Disney's humor is naturalist and primitive and seems to derive from the Southwest humorists of nineteenth-century America. He has their love of exaggeration, particularly of size and speed, and their obsession with aggression and violence—everything gets smashed into a pulp, everyone skids at top speed into a wall or over a cliff, or gets scalped or flayed or dropped into wet concrete. Like them, he also takes a sadistic interest in domestic animals, delighting to reverse the movement, the personality, even the physique of a vigorous animal like a cat or a bulldog with that of a feeble one, like a canary or a mouse. (His treatment of cats is especially unpleasant.) Allied to these traits is a Gothic strain I think of as more German—an interest in dwarfs and witches and castled crags and (as their correlative) dewy damsels.

Barrie is not interested in any of those. He treats animals with exaggerated respect—for instance, Nana in **Peter Pan.** Moreover, the fantasy of the children is far from naturalist or primitive. In **Peter Pan** it is firmly limited and located within a highly civilized social setting and is motivated by the parents' life, full of stresses and strains, and Wendy's incipient adolescence. This is *conscious* fantasy, designed by an adult who has a truly remarkable sympathy with children, quite exquisitely shot through with the ironies of a game both sides consciously are playing, though from different points of view. The island is made up out of a dozen books which the children know about, and is treated ironically—not, of course, satirically—by all concerned. The children are treated with great regard for their dignity, and there is a clear distinction between their reality and the fantasy of the island and its inhabitants—though of course we and they play at obliterating that distinction. But in his **Peter Pan,** Disney caricatures—and then sentimentalizes—everything equally. Nana, the dog-nurserymaid, is made to skid and smash just like every Disney animal, though it is essential to Barrie's scheme of ideas that she should be allowed her dignity. The point of Barrie's conception—in its way a brilliant conceit about the situation of employing servants—is that beneath the fond playfulness of a-dog-just-like-a-person lies the forbidden wickedness of a-person-just-like-a-dog. And Tinker Bell, that Cockney Ariel, a drop of waspish venom in the sweetness of faery, is dressed by Disney like a sex symbol and is given a Marilyn Monroe bosom and bottom and Marilyn Monroe problems in squeezing through keyholes.

Not that I feel any indignation on Barrie's behalf against Disney. What I feel is glee. Let me not to the marriage of true minds admit impediment; let the two great seducers of English-speaking childhood hold hands and simper at each other. Barrie is in his way an artist, but he is none the less disgusting for that. Probably he is more responsible than anyone else for the English disease of charm.

About 1900, it seems, the English began to cultivate charm—above all, the charm of childhood—with sinister intensity. Before then, as far as I know, it was not a quality anyone had attributed to John Bull. But suddenly we had Lewis Carroll and Edward Lear and Puck of Pook's Hill, and Christopher Robin was Saying his Prayers. We had whimsy and fantasy and well-bred infantilism. Stories of adventure and action were replaced by stories of fairies and flowers. Men were replaced—in children's minds—by women. Culture became playful.

The deleterious effects of this on the arts have been pointed out by W. H. Auden; the writers of England have preferred playing family games with their audiences to creating works of art.[1] And that is what *Brideshead Revisited* is about, the ruin of a gifted painter by his preference for English charm over artistic seriousness. Auden's and Waugh's whole generation was blighted by charm.

One sees that charm incarnate in Mrs. Darling. "She is the loveliest lady in Bloomsbury, with a sweet mocking mouth," Barrie tells us in the stage directions. "Her evening gown is a delicious confection made by herself out of nothing and other people's mistakes." But however seductive, she is purely and untouchably a mother, a priestess of childhood. She made her nursery into the hub of the universe, Barrie says, by her certainty that such it was. While her children slept, she sat beside their beds, "tidying up their minds. . . . When they wake . . . on the top, beautifully aired, are their prettier thoughts, ready for the new day."[2]

What makes one feel that Disney and Barrie are made for each other is that the single effective scene in the movie (effective in making one's hair stand on end) portrays Wendy in a role just like this. (Wendy is Mrs. Darling in an earlier phase.) Her brothers have been getting out of hand, playing at Indians, and not wanting to go back home, not wanting to be children. They have forgotten what a mother is. So Wendy sings them a celebration of that idea. And as they listen, the boys begin to droop and to snivel, to rub off their war-paint, to break their arrows, and to cuddle up to the virgin mother. And we are asked to do the same. A strongly ambivalent scene is packaged for us with a single name-tag.

And that is very true to Barrie. Of course, he would never have written anything so blatant, but he does mean us to see Wendy as poised nervously on the edge of motherhood, or on the edge of the abyss of sexuality, beyond which is motherhood. She has to learn to fly. She is already a woman in every other way. She is a perfectly formed adult (that is her charm and her odiousness), but she has somehow to get through the unpleasant business of sex in order to get her license to operate as a woman—to exercise her talents as a mother. By falling in love with a boy who has refused to grow up, by dealing in fancy with the emotions of competition, possession, jealousy, alliance in responsibility, Wendy prepares herself for that difficult rite of passage.

But what makes Barrie's Mrs. Darling so powerful a figure is the sisterhood of her motherhood. The loveliest lady in Bloomsbury—doesn't that title suggest other women of that time and place, for instance, Mrs. Ramsay of *To the Lighthouse*? And aren't they both essentially the same figure, sweetly mocking virgin mothers, managing the exigent husbands? Mr. Darling, Barrie tells us, is "really a good man, as breadwinners go" (exit the male principle, to universal laughter); and it is "hard luck" for him that Barrie has to introduce him "as a tornado . . . brandishing a recalcitrant white tie" (p. 21). Like Mr. Ramsay, Mr. Darling is full of bluster—"Am I the master in this house or is she [Nana]?"—and always disrupting the sweet playfulness of his wife and children (p. 28). But Mrs. Darling uncomplainingly manages him. Besides Virginia Woolf's Mrs. Ramsay, there were Shaw's Candida, Waugh's Lady Marchmain, and many others. The imagination of England was in the charm business—nursery charm—and Barrie was ahead of the industry. I really wonder how Virginia Woolf could for shame repeat the formula seriously when he had worked it out playfully beforehand.

All these fictional ladies had their real-life originals; in Barrie's case it was Sylvia Llewellyn Davies. She was the daughter of George du Maurier (author of the bestselling *Trilby*) but the wife of a rather unsuccessful barrister. Barrie "adopted" first her five children and then Sylvia herself, to the dismay of Arthur Llewellyn Davies, who found himself excluded from the inner circle of his own family. Barrie told the Davies boys the stories which he later published, to great applause, and which he adapted in **Peter Pan**. The play's intimation that this is a small-group fantasy, a shared joke, cunningly adapted to a large-group participation, is no illusion; that complexity of intent is one source of its vitality—one which Disney of course misses.

Sylvia Llewellyn Davies was adored by other men and other writers besides Barrie, for instance, A. E. W. Mason, the bestselling author of *The Four Feathers*. She can be recognized in some of *his* heroines, the lovely women of London to whom the men of empire humbly return from their various frontiers—the ladies for whom the empire was built. Mason and Barrie and Sylvia went to Paris for a holiday together, but there was no question of sexual misconduct. Mason "put all beautiful women on a pedestal," we are told, while Barrie saw Sylvia's seductions as the graces of maternity.

The Davieses were at the center of a good deal of semi-artistic and semiliterary activity of the type that spread the cult of charm. They were friendly with the Mackails, whose daughter Angela became a popular novelist—very popular after World War II—writing under the name of Angela Thirkell. Sylvia's brother, Gerald, was an actor (he played Captain Hook in *Peter Pan*) and a matinée idol. Her niece, Daphne du Maurier, became the bestselling author of *Rebecca* and other such books. Her son, Peter, after whom **Peter Pan** was named, founded the publishing firm of Peter Davies, Ltd. So the story Barrie told, and the cult of boy-charm to which it belongs, was deeply interwoven with the imaginative life of England for the next couple of generations.

Barrie became literal godfather to a lot of English boys and metaphorical patron saint to the cult. A certain range of upper-class males began to hit their peaks—the phase when they were proudest to be themselves, because that was when other people were fondest of them—at age eight. After the early deaths of both Arthur and Sylvia Llewellyn Davies, Barrie formally adopted their five boys and incidentally steered them away from poetry, ballet, and opera, towards healthy outdoor sports and competitive games. (He didn't want any little Oscar Wildes around the house; in fact, he wanted little Kiplings.) He became godfather to the sons of heroes. He was asked by Captain Scott (Scott of the Antarctic) to look after *his* wife and son when Scott departed for his explorations in 1913. And many gifted mothers brought him their sons for a consecration in charm. One such case was the actress Carmel Haden Guest, whose little boy David told Barrie at this first meeting that he too did not want to grow up.

David was indeed a Peter Pan in real life, and as a child wrote a Barrie-esque poem about himself.

> My poetical self
>   Is just like an elf,
>   Capricious and shy;
>   He is certain to fly,
>   If placed on a shelf.[3]

Many such whimsies were written by gifted and privileged children in the 1920s. But David, who had brains, pulled himself out of the charm-marsh. His only publication is entitled *A Textbook of Dialectical Materialism*. Politicized by a visit to Germany in 1930-31, he helped to found the Cambridge University Communist Party and went to fight in Spain. He had made the transition, as Harry Pollitt said when he died, from elf to comrade. Pollitt was the boss of the Communist Party of Great Britain, whose ranks included quite a few ex-Peter Pans in the 1930s.

Why was this? Well, Barrie represented the end of a line—the line of adventure-tale tellers, selling values designed for administrative class trainees but disguised as humanist to please the mothers and uncles, the playful and poetical cohorts of that class. He was at the end of the line in infantilism: we have come a long way from *Robinson Crusoe,* via *Coral Island,* to end up with **Peter Pan.** He was at the end of the line in indirection: the allusiveness, the whimsy, the paradox, the sprightliness almost completely obscure the basic message, of loyalty to throne and flag, to school and church and regiment. He was at the end of the line in sweetness: the high good humor of Defoe, Scott, Borrow, Kingsley has crystallized in the preserve into lumps of sugar.

Once one had seen **Peter Pan,** or once all London had seen it, from the pit to the gallery, there was nothing to do but change one's life, start from scratch on another principle. Boys like David Guest had to wash that sugar out of their mouths. They could either become perverse parodists like Ronald Firbank, archly self-conscious Peter Pans sporting the gilded horns of diabolism, or else Communist comrades, making clear and simple affirmations, re-entering manhood and adventure without irony or whimsy, made new. (Or, of course, like Auden and Isherwood, become both at the same time.)

The reaction against Disney is likely to be different, because the concentration of allegiance to him is not to be found among the most privileged in wealth and power, taste and education. Rather the reverse is true. But Disney surely represents the end of the line in American pop taste. The reaction against him is likely to take the form of pop diabolism; surely Disneyworld and Disneyland offer themselves to the imagination as a setting for Hell's Angels' exploits. *They* are the reality that seems ever about to burst through those sugar-candy façades; *they* are the denial that echoes behind the Voice's cheerfulness. The Merry Pranksters of Ken Kesey (as related by Tom Wolfe in *The Electric Kool-Aid Acid Test*) stand to Disney as Firbank and the Twenties' dandies stood to Barrie. And the American equivalents of David Guest are no doubt to be found in ecological communes, baking their own bread and refusing to go to the movies.

The question really is—the question I pondered as I took the Peter Pan Ride—why should the sick fancies of London in 1900 return to corrupt the imagination of America in the 1970s? Dreams that were natural in a world of nannies and nurseries and those very *literary* storybooks are not natural here and now. Two shaping drives of Barrie's imagination derive from sexual repression—not just his own but the cultural convention of the time—and a plethora of servants, neither of which can be there for the world of Disney's audience. And yet it is Barrie and *Mary Poppins* and *Winnie the Pooh* and *Alice in Wonderland* and so on that he keeps serving up. (The merchandising rights to *Winnie the Pooh,* now in the hands of Sears Roebuck, are worth from two to five million dollars a year.) Can it be that Disney's audience *demands* this fare? It is true that a lot of girls at Disneyland wore badges saying "I am Wendy," and I have heard children coming out of that appalling movie, which portrays Wendy as a monster of priggishness, enthusiastically identifying with her.

But I think that is consequence, not cause, of Disney's use of this material. What draws him to Barrie is an instinct for the debasing and demoralizing. He knows another great liar when he sees one. And they are both lying in the same cause. The cult of nationalist complacency which is blatant and brash in Disney is indirect and oblique in Barrie—full of qualms and queasiness, implicitly—but it adds up to the same thing.

When it grew dark in Disneyland, after the parades of plastic "characters" and barely distinguishable starlets singing "Freedom! America! Freedom!" passed by, the Voice of the place played patriotic songs; thousands of people more or less stood to attention, and the man in front of me took off his hat, while the blurry music and blurrier words bounced off the plaster turrets and the papier mâché gargoyles. It seemed only fitting that the senile whimsy of English Imperial culture at the end of its tether should blend in with the rest.

Notes

1. W. H. Auden, "One of the Family," *Forewords and Afterwords* (New York: Random House, 1973), pp. 367-83.
2. J. M. Barrie, *The Plays of J. M. Barrie* (New York: Charles Scribner's Sons, 1929), pp. 19-20. Subsequent references will appear in the text.
3. Carmel H. Guest, *David Guest: A Scientist Fights* (London: Lawrence and Wishart, 1939).

Leonee Ormond (essay date 1987)

SOURCE: Ormond, Leonee. "*Farewell, Miss Julie Logan*" and "*The Boy David.*" In *J. M. Barrie,* pp. 137-44; 145-48, Edinburgh: Scottish Academic Press Ltd., 1987.

[*In the following chapters from her book-length study of Barrie, Ormond describes* Farewell, Miss Julie Logan *as a "traditional winter's tale" dealing with the central theme of isolation and repression, and discusses the Biblical origins of* The Boy David, *locating the play's dramatic failings in Barrie's inability to portray the tragic relationship of David and Saul.*]

In March 1927, the editor of *The Times,* Geoffrey Dawson, asked Barrie for a piece about Adelphi Terrace. Refusing, Barrie said: 'Just leave it at this, that if I do see anything promising, I'll have a shot at it—as perhaps at something else. It isn't that I'm busy. The fact is I think that I am dead. I only seem to be able to do tom fool things'.[1] By 1930, Barrie had recovered sufficiently to begin work on his memoirs. He reprinted a number of early articles, revised for the occasion, and interspersed them with passages of reminiscence. The volume was published privately under the title *The Greenwood Hat,* and distributed to fifty of Barrie's friends for Christmas.

Work on the book seems to have stimulated an unexpected response to Dawson's suggestion. Early in 1931, Barrie started a new story, completed by 30 June. On 6 July, he told Cynthia Asquith: 'It is terribly "elusive" I fear and perhaps mad, but was I not dogged to go through with it!' (*L* [*Letters*], 224) Barrie offered the story to *The Times,* and asked that it should appear as a free six page supplement to the Christmas Eve number. He himself accepted no payment.

Coming at a time when Barrie's writing career seemed at an end, *Farewell, Miss Julie Logan* is his one undoubted masterpiece in prose. For this late work, Barrie returned to the Scots setting of his early writing. In 1890 and 1891, he had published a series of sketches about a country manse, where the minister's life is dominated by an inquisitive and intrusive servant girl. The background of the new story is much the same, but this 'wintry tale' is very different from the discursive and amusing sketches of forty years before.

Farewell, Miss Julie Logan takes the form of a diary, written by a minister of twenty-six, Adam Yestreen, when he is snowed-in during the winter of 186-. Yestreen meets Julie Logan, a beautiful young girl. In reality she is a 'stranger', the ghost of a Jacobite heroine reputed to have succoured the Young Pretender. Her name refers to a 'rocking' or 'logan' stone, popularly associated with the supernatural. According to local legend, the Jacobite girl was said to have leapt onto a logan stone while searching for game to feed Prince Charlie.

By telling the story through the words of Adam Yestreen, Barrie is able, as in his plays, to project an individual character without the intervention of a narrating voice. The development of the later plays, through a series of evolving texts, had taught him economy. *Julie Logan* is not a compressed work, but, in dealing with a single theme, it has real virtues of control and organisation. The diary form gives a sense of immediacy, and limits the operation of hind-sight to Yestreen's summing-up in the Epilogue, supposedly written twenty-five years later.

Yestreen's diary reveals how the young minister's struggles after spiritual perfection are constantly undermined from within. Like Gavin Dishart in *The Little Minister,* Yestreen is an innately sensual man whose emotion is unnaturally blocked by the outward demands of his calling. Where the improbable Babbie is conjured up to resolve these tensions in the early novel, here we remain within the mind of Yestreen himself. The story never becomes tortured, or depressing, but it does probe deeply into the fantasies of isolation and repression.

When *Julie Logan* was published in book form in 1932, Barrie took the opportunity to make certain emendations. Early in the story, he added a passage where Yestreen speaks of his response to the trees and shrubs of the manse garden:

> My predecessor, Mr. Carluke, tore down the jargonelle tree, which used to cling to my gable-end, because he considered that, when in flourish (or as the English say, in blossom, a word with no gallantry intilt), it gave the manse the appearance of a light woman.

(*MJL* [*Farewell, Miss Julie Logan*], 4)

This not only illustrates Yestreen's love of beauty, but also his use of dialect. There are few dialect words in the *Times* version, but, for the book, many English terms were replaced by Scots ones, 'speel' for 'climb'; 'hallan' for 'passage'; 'half nine on the clock' for 'nine o'clock'; 'stramash' for 'distress' (*MJL,* 23, 35, 37, 47). The changes in Yestreen's vocabulary suggest greater humanity and individuality, and set him further apart from the English visitors, who play with Scots terms in much the same spirit as they wear the tartan. As Yestreen says, they 'have a happy knack of skimming life that has a sort of attraction for deeper but undoubtedly slower natures' (*MJL,* 12).

Yestreen's private comments on the English reveal the unflattering awareness of the perceptive outsider. When he is asked to take an attractive lady to dinner, the most popular man is placed on 'the other side of her to make up for me' (*MJL,* 14). When the 'popular man' asks Yestreen to agree that the lady is very pretty, 'all I could reply was that I had not given the subject sufficient consideration to be able to make a definite statement about it' (*MJL,* 15).

The sharp satire on the English in Scotland introduces Yestreen's diary. It is they who have challenged him to describe his experiences during the winter months, and he accepts with an ill-founded confidence, believing that local stories of 'strangers' are 'superstitious havers, bred of folk who are used to the travail of out of doors, and take ill with having to squat by the saut-bucket' (*MJL,* 2).

Yestreen's account of the locked glen is in some ways a rewriting of the fine opening section of *Auld Licht Idylls,* 'The School House'. There too, Barrie describes the freezing hens brought into the house, the black burn cutting through the white snow, but a close reading shows a marked difference in emphasis. The ridge 'struggling ineffectually to cast off his shroud' (*ALI* [*Auld Licht Idylls*], 2) of *Auld Licht Idylls*, becomes, in a stronger and more threatening image, 'White hillocks of the shape of eggs' which 'have arisen here and there, and are dangerous too, for they wobble as though some great beast beneath were trying to turn round' (*MJL*, 32-3).

The early 'School House' passage is largely descriptive and consoling. The narrator manages to rescue a freezing bird, and drags a water-hen from a weasel. In *Julie Logan,* the imprisoning snow has a more profound significance. Snow becomes the outward symbol of Yestreen's isolation from warmth and affection. We are constantly reminded, through the deceptive simplicity of his narrative, that the outer and inner man are at odds, as are the outer and inner statements of the diary entries. Yestreen is not without insight into his own state of mind. He knows, for example, that on his arrival in the glen he walked 'with affected humility' (*MJL*, 3), conscious of being stared at from every window along the route. With touching dignity, he acknowledges his own immaturity. He looks 'maybe younger than is seemly in my sacred calling, being clean-shaven without any need to use an implement' (*MJL*, 3).

Yestreen continually reveals his suppressed response to beauty. He loves his garden and his study. He alone likes the ancient yellow-tinted glass in the window at the Grand House. Most telling of all are his references to his violin, which distracted him as an undergraduate and which he fears he should not have brought to the glen: 'I have never once performed on the instrument here, though I may have taken it out of its case nows and nans to fondle the strings' (*MJL*, 3).

Almost in solitary confinement, cut off from his neighbours by snow, Yestreen begins to hear his fiddle playing to itself. His reproving commentary on his apparent hallucination is expressed in sensible statements which gradually dissolve away as his emotion metamorphoses the violin into a sensuous human being:

> Of course there was nobody. I had come back with the tune in my ears, or it was caused by some vibration in the air. I found my fiddle in the locked press just as I had left it, except that it must have been leaning against the door, for it fell into my arms as I opened the press, and I had the queer notion that it clung to me. I could not compose myself till I had gone through my manse with the candle, and even after that I let the instrument sleep with me.
>
> (*MJL*, 35-6)

Yestreen's response is to decide that 'it might be hard on a fiddle never to be let do the one thing it can do' (*MJL*, 36), an indirect reflection on what is happening to himself. So he lends the violin to the local postman, with the proviso, often disobeyed, that it shall not be used to play Jacobite lilts. The postman yields himself to the wayward, feminine, qualities of the violin: '"She likes that kind best, and she is ill to control once she's off"' (*MJL*, 36). Even Yestreen cannot resist the forbidden tunes: 'It is pretty to hear him in the gloaming, letting the songs loose like pigeons' (*MJL*, 36-7).

As the snow locks him in, Yestreen's only contact with the outside world is waiting for the old lady at the Grand House to let up her blind twice every evening, and then responding three times with his own.[2] The snow-bound glen is like the night 'waiting, as it must have done once, for the first day. It is the stillness that is so terrible. If only something would crack the stillness' (*MJL*, 38).

Yestreen's hold on reality gradually evaporates. He thinks that he has written up his diary, but finds only a few broken lines, with 'God help me' written 'as if I were a bird caught in a trap' (*MJL*, 37). The violin can release songs like pigeons, but, in a reversal of the image, Yestreen is the caged bird.

Local gossip has it that one of Yestreen's distant predecessors, Mr. H., who also kept a diary during the snowy weather, was locked in a desperate struggle against a 'spectrum' with a 'wicked desire to drive the lawful possessor out of the house and take his place' (*MJL*, 29). Mr. H., like Mr. Lapraik in Barrie's one-act play, was driven out of the house, while the incubus took possession. Doctor John, talking to Yestreen of Julie Logan, hazards a guess that the enchanting young girl is a manifestation of Mr. H's 'spectrum', and that she has appeared in other forms at other times. One of her appearances is in a remote cottage where a woman is about to give birth. Here the 'stranger' brings warmth and close physical contact. After relighting the fire, and helping to deliver the baby, she strips naked and lies next to the mother to act as a hot-water bottle.

In revision, Barrie played down Julie Logan's 'spectrum' side, and put more stress on her romantic, Jacobite, appeal. As a low-church minister, Yestreen officially frowns upon Catholic legends. Half a highlander himself, however, he has to admit privately the attraction of the forbidden.

In the chapter called 'The End of a Song', Yestreen, searching for Julie Logan on New Year's Eve, sits down on the bank of the loch by the Grand House. In the distance, he hears what he calls 'the most reprehensible but the loveliest of all the Jacobite cries, "Will you no come back again?"' (*MJL*, 76). When the music fades there is complete silence, and, as he looks into the water, Yestreen sees reflected there a scene taking place in the ballroom. His statements are positive, 'I saw', 'I could see', he repeats several times. The indefinite statements, so characteristic of Barrie's prose, relate here, not to doubts about what Yestreen 'sees', but to his uncertainty about the meaning of the vision: 'I could see the trews and an occasional flashing silver button or a gleam of steel; but near all colour had been washed out of them, as if they had been ower long among the caves and the eagles' (*MJL,* 77).

Encouraged by the silence, Yestreen tries to see directly into the hall, but when he moves, the figures in the reflection become aware of his presence. They are distracted from him by the arrival of Julie Logan, her clothes in tatters, searching for food for the hidden Pretender. Moving out of the mirrored world of the hall, she comes down the steps to the minister, and they eat together in a sheltered corner. The end of the love scene comes when Yestreen, responding to a playful challenge, carries the girl into the middle of the burn. There she tells him that she is a Catholic, and, overcome by the shock, he drops her into the water. Yestreen falls into a nervous collapse, and is ill for weeks, but, when he recovers, the enchantment is over.

By setting his story in the 1860s, the decade of his own birth, Barrie again chose a period when rigid and restricted religious beliefs provided a foil for the aesthetic and the passionate. The choice of the minister's names is significant. Adam Yestreen dislikes his Christian name, 'with its unfortunate associations' (*MJL,* 2); and his surname, meaning 'yesterday evening', points back to the more immediate past. Another level of time is introduced by the references to the Jacobite rising. In Stevenson's *Kidnapped,* a book which Barrie knew intimately, the lowland whig, David Balfour, finds himself both attracted and repelled by the highlander, Alan Breck Stewart. Here the half-highlander Yestreen is unable to resist the attractions of the Jacobite and Catholic Julie Logan.

The Epilogue, set twenty-five years later, allows Yestreen to reconsider events. He has moved away from danger, settled in an industrial town and married there. But for all his reiterations that she never existed, he has never forgotten Julie Logan, and the concluding paragraph speculates that, after his death, his younger self will escape into the glen.

Published on Christmas Eve, ***Julie Logan*** is a traditional winter's tale and ghost story. 1931 is the year in which M. R. James's ghost stories were first published in one volume, and the comparison is instructive. Barrie's supernatural tale offers us a seductive rather than a terrifying visitation. Yestreen has gained rather than lost through his brief release from repression. Because the protagonist is essentially good, the effect of the haunting has been benign.

. . . . .

Sixteen years separated the first production of the ***The Boy David*** from that of ***Mary Rose.*** Now in his seventies, Barrie resisted the temptation to relive old glories, and struck off across new territories. A career in the theatre which opened with a disastrous historical play, ***Richard Savage,*** closed with a Biblical drama. Between the two, Barrie had ventured no further than the Napoleonic era for his subject-matter. Neither the Jacobite rebellion nor the story of Mary Queen of Scots ever inspired the Scottish drama of which he intermittently dreamed. Instead, at the request of the actress, Elizabeth Bergner, he turned to the Old Testament story of King David.

A new tradition of historical drama emerged in the 1920s and 1930s. The pioneering work was Shaw's *Saint Joan* of 1924, a play which Barrie greatly admired, and in which Elizabeth Bergner had starred. Through a powerful historical figure, Shaw presents a commentary on contemporary and historical issues. In their very different ways, Bertolt Brecht and T. S. Eliot were among the dramatists who followed his example.

Barrie's research work on Jewish tradition did not lead him to proclaim political or religious truths in his play, although, given its date, he might have done. An assertion of nationality was clearly in the exiled actress's mind when she chose the subject. Barrie's interest lies in the clash of the generations. David, like Shaw's Joan, is a representative figure of youth and power, part of a force destined to sweep away darkness and corruption. Both authors use a well-known story which leads towards an inevitable end. Both decided to quote certain passages from original sources. Barrie's David speaks the opening verses of the twenty-third psalm, and the lamentation over Saul and Jonathan. Unlike Shaw, Barrie makes no startling use of anachronistic dialogue. His characters speak in a heightened style, marked by the prose rhythms and cadences of the Authorized Version.

The writing of ***The Boy David*** followed a familiar Barrie pattern. He began enthusiastically on the first act, set in the home of Jesse in Bethlehem. David, the youngest son, is despised by his brothers, but loved by his mother. When he says that he has killed a lion, and a bear, no-one believes him. The coming of Samuel, searching for the chosen king among the sons of Jesse, proceeds in the manner of a fairy-tale. David, like a tentative Cinderella, is the chosen one. Barrie departs from the First Book of Samuel in insisting upon Jesse's absence during this scene. When he returns, the father finds that David has eaten his supper. His wrath is deflected, however, by his belief that the boy is in some way possessed. The act ends with David's announcement that he is called to kill Goliath.

Barrie wrote the first act swiftly enough, but then became anxious and uncertain about how to continue. The killing of Goliath was a major obstacle, and scenes were written, rewritten and rearranged as he tried to find a way round. The confidence and completeness of the first act gives way to the more uncertain and uncomfortable second act, laid out in three scenes. Barrie's intention was to run the relationship of Saul and David on parallel lines, and the dramatic tension comes from this relationship, which mingles love, hate and fear. Saul is to some extent the father; loving David, but fearing usurpation by him. Like David's actual father, he falls under the spell of the boy's personality. Barrie originally intended to call the play 'The Two Farmers' or 'The Two Shepherds', and the scene where David and Saul, meeting for the first time, talk of their flocks of sheep, is the finest piece of writing in the play.

By comparison, the crowd scenes seem disastrously stilted. Augustus John's sets for the first production proved theatrically hopeless, but, even without them, it is easy to see why Barrie found the Goliath episode such a problem. At first, he hoped to bring Goliath onto the stage. Then a dummy was tried, but in the end the Philistine giant was reduced to off-stage voice.

Barrie's play is a prologue to the story of King David. Having killed Goliath, David returns to his home and family. Saul continues to reign. The author, however, decided that this was not enough, and incorporated a series of dream visions of the future into the final act. These represent some of the major episodes of David's relationship with Saul, leading up to the death of Saul and Jonathan. David wakes, and the play closes with him as a boy once more, talking with Jonathan.

The visions were a serious problem on stage. The director, Komisarjevsky, failed to unify the third act effectively. There were long pauses while the scenes were changed, often involving the fall of the curtain, and Barrie protested that the status of the visions as dreams was undermined by the lighting, which failed to pick out the sleeping family clearly. Elizabeth Bergner herself, with good reason, felt that an adult man should have played the fully-grown David of the future.

Barrie's venture into the timeless world of dream again suggests the influence of expressionism, or perhaps of the epilogue to *Saint Joan*. *Macbeth* is, however, a more potent source for Barrie's doomed Saul. Like Macbeth with the weird sisters, Saul summons the Witch of Endor only to receive a grim announcement of death and disaster.

Looking back on the play's comparative failure, Barrie said that he had not found the means to express himself. Illness limited his attendance at rehearsals, and, when he finally saw the production, it was too late to make his usual alterations and amendments. Elizabeth Bergner failed to carry off the part of David, a role which surely needs a boy actor. If the play were to be revived, it would be for the tormented and divided figure of Saul. The stage directions tell us that Barrie had Browning's poem and Rembrandt's painting in his mind as he wrote the play. Both works bring out the inherent tragedy in the relationship of David and Saul. Barrie too was acutely aware of this, but seems to have made David too charming to bear the weight of his role. In the end *The Boy David* fell between two stools.

Notes

1. Bodleian Library, Dawson Papers, f. 98.
2. Barrie seems to have borrowed this idea from Hardy's *Two on a Tower*, and the same author's 'The Distracted Preacher' may have suggested the character of the young clergyman.

Select Bibliography

COLLECTIONS

The Thistle Edition. New York, 1896-1902.

The Kirriemuir Edition. 1913-22.

The Uniform Edition of the Works. 1913-22.

The Uniform Edition of the Plays. 1918-38.

Plays, ed. A. E. Wilson. 1942. (Definitive Edition).

BIBLIOGRAPHY

H. Garland. *A Bibliography of the Writings Of Barrie.* 1928

B. D. Cutler. *Barrie: A Bibliography.* 1931.

W. M. Jones. *Writings on Sir J. M. Barrie,* unpublished dissertation for the London University Diploma in Librarianship. 1964.

BIOGRAPHY

D. Mackail. *The Story of JMB.* 1941.

C. Asquith. *Portrait of Barrie.* 1954.

J. Dunbar. *J. M. Barrie.* 1970.

A. Birkin. *J. M. Barrie and the Lost Boys.* 1979.

STAGE HISTORY

I. F. Marcosson and D. Frohman. *Charles Frohman.* 1916. With an appreciation by J. M. Barrie.

I. Vanbrugh. *To Tell My Story.* 1948.

J. C. Trewin. *The Theatre Since 1900.* 1951.

A. Nicol. *A History of English Drama,* Vol. V: 1850-1900. 1959.

A. Nicol *English Drama: 1900-1930.* 1973.

David Holbrook (essay date 1989)

SOURCE: Holbrook, David. "Woman, Death, and Meaning in *Peter Pan* and *Mary Rose*." In *Images of Woman in Literature*, pp. 71-114. New York: New York University Press, 1989.

[*In the following essay, Holbrook focuses on the interrelated themes of death and the role of mothers in* Peter Pan *and* Mary Rose. *He argues that the latter play reflects Barrie's attempt to "re-create the mother who can give him (psychic) birth as his real mother never did."*]

It may seem odd for a literary critic to turn from psychoanalysis to *Peter Pan*. To most serious critics, this play might seem to be a trivial popular fantasy. To Edgell Rickword, writing on Barrie in *Scrutinies* by various writers (1928), the sentimentality was disastrous. He quotes from the film version:

PETER PAN:

When was I born?

MRS. DARLING:

At midnight, dear.

PETER PAN:

I hope I didn't wake you, Mummy.

However, as a social phenomenon alone, the work of Sir James Barrie poses a problem. The plays seem really quite mad; yet, they are enormously popular. *Peter Pan* continues to be performed. It is a remarkable success, even though—or perhaps because—it lies totally outside of rationality and is sheer fantasy. Barrie's *Mary Rose* was revived in Edinburgh in 1988 and the National Theatre in London experimented recently by having a man play Peter Pan.

I was surprised to find myself discussing Barrie's *Mary Rose,* that mysterious play, in my study of Mahler. I alluded to the play in relation to the Holy Mary syndrome—that is, the impulse to impose a certain kind of idealization upon woman. Here, I pursue the matter further. Clearly, from all the biographical accounts, Barrie had a serious problem with woman. And, I believe, it is his cultural engagement with the problem of woman that makes his plays everlastingly and universally fascinating, despite their madness. They are about woman as the focus of 'being-in-existence,' 'going-out-of-existence,' and of life and death.

As is so often true, where we encounter the image of woman at the heart of a literary work (as in D. H. Lawrence, C. S. Lewis, and George MacDonald and in Coleridges's *The Rime of the Ancient Mariner* and the poetry of Sylvia Plath and the music of Mahler), what we encounter is a problem of death.

The problem of woman is often linked in some way with the problem of mourning. How do we explain this? I intend to show that the exploration of the problem of woman in literature continually returns to the association of woman with death. In this, I believe, *Peter Pan* and other works of Sir James Barrie are illuminating.

One important clue is to be found in D. W. Winnicott's insight that the mother has a mirror role—that is, she creates us by her creative reflection. If she dies or turns a blank face upon us, then we are faced with extinction. In desperation, we seek another source of confirmation of our 'being'; if we cannot find it, our life is forfeit. It is her face and eyes that connect woman with death. Of course, I am talking phenomenologically about the symbols and meaning of the unconscious mind and of the phenomena of consciousness.

Peter Pan is thought of as a play for children. But from my phenomenological perspective, it is a play about 'being-unto-death' in relation to woman and the mother. We only have to open *Peter Pan* to see the problem of 'being-unto-death' evoked in symbolism that focuses on the mother in ways related to existential meanings. The first tension in the play involves a face at the window:

(*As . . . [Mrs. Darling] enters the room she is startled to see a strange little face outside the window and a hand groping as if it wanted to come in.*)

MRS. DARLING:

Who are you? (*The unknown disappears; she hurries to the window.*) No one there. And yet I feel sure I saw a face. My children!

It is a moment of yearning for creative reflection and a yearning to make substantial the ghost of someone who isn't there.[1] Here we have too the presence of the dead sibling in Barrie's life. His brother David was killed suddenly in a skating accident at the age of fourteen. His mother withdrew completely and lived shut in her room, refusing food. James took it upon himself to try to bring her back to life by engaging in childish antics like standing on his head—by play. In desperation, he would count the number of times she smiled, in an attempt to relieve her deathlike depressions. His mother kept the lost child's christening robe, and it seems to have been the most important memento in her life. She would talk to the dead David as if he were there. We have in this phenomenon a terrible threat to the meaning of existence, which generated the strange phenomenology of Barrie's work. For Barrie, as a child, was deeply involved in his mother's failure to mourn, while at the same time as an adult he wrote all his books for her, in a way parallel to his attempts as a boy to lift her depressions by amusing her. The ghost of his brother, too, wanted to "come in," for his mother yearned for David to come back from the world of death to this world.

There was another problem that I shall examine further. Marietta Karpe and Richard Karpe (1957) suggest that Barrie was traumatized earlier by the birth of a sister when he was an infant. We may say, I believe, that he needed more creative reflection *to be born*. Mrs. Darling in **Peter Pan** responds immediately and wants to see the face, exclaiming "My children!" We have a similar moment in Mahler's *Kindertotenlieder* (Songs on the death of children) when the poet Friedrich Rückert seems to see his dead child come into the room with the mother ("*Dort wo würde dein lieb Gesichtchen sein*"). The reference to mothering is even more plain in **Peter Pan**:

WENDY:

Now let us pretend we have a baby.

JOHN:

(*Good-naturedly.*) I am happy to inform you, Mrs. Darling, that you are now a mother. (*Wendy gives way to ecstasy.*) You have missed the chief thing; you haven't asked, "boy or girl?"

At once it seems of primary importance as to whether reflection establishes that the new creature is a boy or a girl—that is, there is an underlying craving for one's gender identity and authenticity. On this theme Barrie develops the following playful exchange, where Michael pretends to want to be born:

MICHAEL:

(*Expanding.*) Now, John, have me.

JOHN:

We don't want any more.

MICHAEL:

(*Contracting.*) Am I not to be born at all?

JOHN:

Two is enough.

MICHAEL:

(*Wheedling.*) Come, John; boy, John. (*Appalled.*) Nobody wants me!

MRS. DARLING:

I do.

MICHAEL:

(*With a glimmer of hope.*) Boy or girl?

MRS. DARLING:

(*With one of those happy thoughts of hers.*) Boy.

In his essay on Barrie, Rickword (1928) points out the ineptitude of Barrie's art in dealing with adult emotions, love, and death. Rickword exposes the "infantile" element in Barrie's works. Yet; what we still have to explain is the astonishing appeal of Barrie's plays and the way people attend them and love them. His plays are popular despite their embarrassing and even rather mad episodes—those that one really cannot give a rational account of. The plays appeal to the unconscious level and to the primitive *Dasein* need (as evidence in the previously quoted dialogue)—that is, the urgent need to come into being and to be someone *for* the 'other'.

Peter has lost his shadow. Whatever strictures the literary critic may make on Barrie's art, the achievement is in one sense remarkable. He managed to present quite surrealistic material in a normal domestic setting and to open up in the nursery setting strange aspects of the *Dasin* problem—that is, the fundamental problems of existence as the child dreads them. If one is real, one has a shadow. Peter has had his cut off by the window falling:

> (*She produces it from a drawer. They unroll and examine the flimsy thing, which is not more material than a puff of smoke, and if let go would probably float into the ceiling without discolouring it. Yet it has human shape. As they nod their heads over it they present the most satisfying picture on earth, two happy parents conspiring cosily by the fire for the good of their children.*)[2]

The literary problem is that the playfulness of the language is at odds with the dreadfulness of the essential theme, which is the fear of going out of existence. Just as Coleridge, in close relationship with his sleeping baby, fears the extinction of consciousness if the flame on his fire goes out (in "Frost at Midnight") so Barrie evokes the fear of one's substance going out like "smoke." At the same time, there is the reassurance that parental love *is* a guarantee of one's identity; but this, again by the weakness of the language (which is an emotional weakness), is sentimentalized. The shadow is that of the dead sibling, and the stage direction evokes the strange evanescence of the human personality that, after death, when one becomes shadowless, *is* less substantial than a puff of smoke and "might float to the ceiling without discolouring it." The ineptitude of Barrie's capacity to deal with such an existential theme is revealed if one compares with this playful passage Mahler's funeral march on a childhood theme in the second movement of his First Symphony in which the depths of the heart are touched in relation to the death of a child.

But there is also a grim undercurrent to **Peter Pan**. Although Peter Pan is the fairy protagonist of the play, he is menacing because he is going to take the children out of this world into the world of shadowless death in which he exists (or nonexists). The mother leaves a symbol of her eyes to watch over her children because she suspects some ghostly presence is after them:

MICHAEL:

> Can anything harm us, Mother, after the night-lights are lit?

MRS. DARLING:

> Nothing, precious. They are the eyes a mother leaves behind to guard her children. . . . Dear night-lights that protect my sleeping babes, burn clear and steadfast tonight.

These "eyes" are a guarantee that the children will not be left to go out of existence by a failure of reflection or because of the ghost that comes from the world of death. This scene fascinates audiences because it evokes the fears we all suffered in infancy of going out of existence when mummy put out the light. Len Chaloner writes in *Feeling and Perception in Young Children* (1963) of our fears about what would happen (as in the *Kindertotenlieder*) if the mother's eyes stopped reflecting us. They go out like children:

> *(They blink three times one after the other and go out, precisely as children (whom familiarity has made them resemble) fall asleep.)*

Again, we hear almost an echo of the *Kindertotenlieder* ("*Ein Lämplein verlosch in meinem Zelt!*" and "*O Augen!*"). Their light is taken over by the light of Tinker Bell.

The children are taught to fly. (The theatrical device by which they are fixed up to fly is stressed, as Barrie keeps our minds fixed on the need for a willingness to suspend disbelief.) In one sense, flying represents the growth of sexuality and adulthood (after latency), by which children, in fact, fly away from the nest. But flying is also an adventure into the world of nonexistence, into the Never Land:

> *(The broken-hearted Father and Mother arrive just in time to get a nip from Tink as she too sets out for the Never Land.)*

While Barrie never allows us to feel deep adult feelings, as does Mahler in the *Kindertotenlieder,* he does offer play with the real problems. However, the disturbing quality about this play is its manic quality: it derives from antics intended to overcome the depression derived from the fear of death. Mahler tried to distract his dying brother Ernst, and this is manifest in his music. The difference in quality has to do with the capacity to find the 'other". Barrie's fairy tale has limits because it is too much in a mode that denies death. It is this denial of death that we see in Barrie that we simply do not in Mahler. In the background of Barrie's work lurks a fear of the mother: Can the mother, or the female element, be trusted to reflect and confirm us? Is she good or bad? If she is bad (hate rather than love), then we may be annihilated; if she responds to us and helps create us, she is love and goodness. Thus, these symbols may be related to the *Dasein* problem—that is, what can be set against the nothingness that death thrusts at us?

In the end, Peter Pan cannot stay (any more than the dead ghost of the dead brother could stay). Wendy cannot fly as she once did as a child, and she has to use a broomstick. (She is growing up to adult sexuality, and the broomstick represents a penis. This growth to adult sensuality divides her forever from Peter, who died as a child and must remain a child.) Mrs. Darling does what she can; but there remains for Peter "the riddle of his being," which she cannot solve because he is a ghost. ("*If he could get the hang of the thing his cry might become 'To live would be an awfully big adventure!'*") What is so fascinating about **Peter Pan** is that such unusual explorations of schizoid existence anxiety, of death, and of 'nonbeing,' should be dealt with in such a way that adults and children in the theater take it all in their stride and allow themselves (in a sense) to go mad and to perceive the play's surrealistic fantasy as quite acceptable. In trying to solve the existentialist problems in the play, the mother does what she can ("I mean to keep you"); but Peter is beyond her power. By the end, we almost feel that Mrs. Darling is a foe, as she closes and bars the windows, which surely are acts of manic denial.

The word *manic* is important in connection with the play. It is all play, and it is significant that Peter chooses never to grow up and will play on forever ("He plays on until we wake up"). In the introduction, Barrie writes: "*all the characters, whether grown-ups or babies, must wear a child's outlook on life as their only important adornment.*" To put on one's shadow is to come back from the dead and become real. But when Wendy sews on Peter's shadow, he does not become real. Barrie's mother obviously wanted her son to return from the world of death, but her hopes could not be fulfilled. He, like Peter, could remain in the world of the house only as some kind of dreadful untouchable: As a stage direction tells us, "*He [Peter] is never touched by anyone in the play.*"

Although the play is remembered for its dealings with fairies and pirates and seems a bit of fey nonsense for the children being walked round Kensington Gardens, it is persistently about death. Its play about death is child's play—about death in the home. Appropriately, the term

Wendy House has entered the educational establishments and its vocabulary, in recognition that children, in playing mothers and fathers, are engaged in serious play with notions of sexuality, existence, and death. In **Peter Pan** we return to the earliest fears of the child, so beautifully discussed by Chaloner (1963). The boys encountered in Never Land are those children who fall out their prams: *"not that they are really worrying about their mothers, who are now as important to them as a piece of string."*

The pirates are embodiments of the threat of death in the world. The crocodile with a clock inside it is death itself. The crocodile has "killed" Captain Hook's arm and yearns for him. When he dies, he enters "the yawning cavity . . . like one greeting a friend." (Melville's *Moby-Dick* is in the background here.) Tootles, believing Wendy to be a bird, shoots her. The woman who the lost boys hope will be a mother to them is shot. In the background, of course, is the *The Rime of the Ancient Mariner*. The reference is highly significant because in Coleridge the symbolism belongs to that of "the stage of concern." The mariner's act is a thoughtless one, like an infant directing a fantasy of hate at the source of life. He has, painfully, to dwell on the possibility of having blighted his world by his assault on life. Through the benign light of the moon shining on the stark sea, in which swim the water snakes, he is able to find a spring of love rising in his heart: "I blessed them unawares." The moon is the mother, and her light enables him to find the power of reparation.[3]

The level of the action had to be kept at the level of child's play, for Barrie could not aspire to deal with realism through the dreadfulness of the tragic. But Wendy is the child's ideal object:

TOOTLES:

When ladies used to come to me in dreams I said 'Pretty mother,' but when she really came I shot her!

A kiss has saved Wendy; and Omnes cries, "Wendy lady, be our mother!" Later, even the pirates want a mother:

SMEE:

(*Not usually a man of ideas.*) Captain, could we not kidnap these boys' mother and make her our mother?

But then the female is dangerous, and even the fairy Tinker Bell gets up to some vengeful tricks. The mermaids try to pull you under the water to drown you. And behind this fear of the dangerous woman lurks the problem of sex. Tiger Lily wants to be "something else" to Peter Pan, not his mother. Peter Pan wants Wendy so much that he shuts the window at the end so she cannot return to her mother. Mrs. Darling is heard moaning, "Wendy, Wendy, Wendy." Peter says.

She wants me to unbar the window. I won't. She is awfully fond of Wendy. I am fond of her too. We can't both have her, lady! (*A funny feeling comes over him.*) Come on, Tink; we don't want any silly mothers.

The "funny feeling" is a recognition that begins to dawn on him, of feeling a need that belongs to "something else." Peter, however, does not want to grow up: "I just want always to be a little boy and to have fun." When the water is rising, he says, "To die will be an awfully big adventure." And reality is again dissolved in play. At the end, Barrie writes:

(*If he could get the hand of the thing his cry might become "To live would be an awfully big adventure!" but he can never quite get the hang of it, and no one is as gay as he.*)

Peter Pan tells us why Barrie could "never get the hang of it"—woman is too dangerous. We may interpret the phrase "get the hang of it" in a sexual sense. While most of the play is play with death, there is also play with sexuality, as there is when children play mothers and fathers. The danger in Barrie's life was that his mother yearned to bring her dead son back into the world, as Mrs. Darling yearns to bring her lost children back: "When they call I stretch out my arms to them, but they never come, they never come!" The lost boys come with them. The maid Liza immediately becomes the mother of Slightly; they are born at this very moment, so to speak.

But how could one bear to approach woman if (like Barrie's mother) she is capable of exercising with such poignant intensity evocative powers over life and death? How could one bear sexuality with her, to enter her body, and to create from there new life? Such a mother was terribly dangerous; thus as one can see from Peter, any suggestion of love intimacy with woman in the sexual sense must be playfully avoided because for him it is impossible.

Toward the end of the play, Wendy is inclined, like a teenage girl, to want to fly away to Peter, while Peter wants to keep her for himself, like any young suitor, rejecting the mother's claims. Wendy's inclination to fly into Peter's world horrifies Mrs. Darling. But Peter cannot accept the challenge of sexual commitment:

WENDY:

(*Making a last attempt.*) You don't feel you would like to say anything to my parents, Peter, about a very sweet subject?

PETER:

No, Wendy

Mrs. Darling offers to adopt Peter as well as the lost boys. Would she send him to school and to an office? "I suppose so" So, Peter would be threatened with becoming like Mr. Darling, who is a nonentity and at last retires into the dog kennel. Peter, who larks with the fairies, still needs a mother. But Wendy will be released to him, for "spring cleaning."

"Spring cleaning" may be read as a euphemism for the kind of duties a wife performs for her husband. We see Never Land a year hence. The little Wendy House appears; Wendy looks a year older but Peter looks the same. As I have pointed out earlier, Wendy "flies so badly now that she has to use a broomstick." Instead of the magical, playful love of the latency period, Wendy now has libidinal urges for a phallus. It is the instrument with which you do the "spring cleaning."

WENDY:

> When you come for me next year, Peter—you will come, won't you?

And then she becomes worried:

> If another little girl—if one younger than I am—(*She can't go on.*) Oh, Peter, how I wish I could take you up and squdge you! (*He draws back.*) Yes, I know. (*She gets astride her broomstick.*) Home! (*It carries her from him over the treetops.*)

Wendy's maturing sexuality carries her away from Peter Pan, who is impotent.

> (*In a sort of way he understands what she means by "Yes, I know," but in most sorts of ways he doesn't. It has something to do with the riddle of his being.*)

The appeal of **Peter Pan** lies in the way it plays upon this "riddle of being." For what the play says is that Barrie himself had become mystified by the strange psychic state of his mother, in her unrelievable grief of bereavement and that he was possessed by such a fear of woman that he could never advance beyond the state of childishness in relation to woman. If a woman wanted to "squdge" him, he could only draw back; and then her broomstick would carry her away from him over the treetops.[4]

There are two remarkable essays from the psychoanalytical point of view that have been of considerable use to me in developing a phenomenological approach to the work of Sir James Barrie and, indeed, to the works of other fantasists. One is an essay by P. Lionel Goitein, entitled "A New Approach to Analysis of 'Mary Rose,'" published in 1926. This is an oddly old-fashioned account that finds Barrie's play to be a religious analogy, yet also brings to it some remarkable intuitive insights. The other is by Marietta Karpe and Richard Karpe, entitled "The Meaning of Barrie's 'Mary Rose,'" published in 1957. The latter provides many insights into the connections between motherhood and the problem of death. The implied connections among mothering, death, and images of woman in these essays have helped me in my studies of C. S. Lewis, Sylvia Plath, George MacDonald, Gustav Mahler, and D. H. Lawrence.

Before I discuss the play **Mary Rose,** I should like to pursue further certain clues from these essays and elsewhere to Barrie's uncanny preoccupation with woman as a focus of the problem of life and death, and the mystery that surrounds her. I hope to show how some of D. W. Winnicott's concepts illuminate the problems outlined in these essays. One of these is primary maternal preoccupation and the mysterious state into which a woman goes when she is giving psychic parturition to her infant—especially the concept of the mother's reflecting role as creative mirror. In these processes, the mother draws out the potentialities of the infant—his 'soul', his 'being'. What happens if this process is disastrously disturbed, either by death or by the effects of death, as when a sibling dies? I believe that with Barrie, as with Dylan Thomas, Mahler, MacDonald, Lewis, and Lawrence, the death of a sibling so disturbed the psychic processes between mother and infant that the result was catastrophic in one sense but was the mainspring of a creative drive in another.

One of the chapters in Barrie's book about his mother, *Margaret Ogilvie, by Her Son* (1896), is called "How My Mother Got Her Soft Face." Among other things, his book deals with the crisis provoked in Barrie when his mother became severely traumatized by the sudden death of his brother at the age of fourteen, in a skating accident. As we shall see, Barrie's mother withdrew completely; and the boy Barrie took it upon himself to try to draw her back into the world, into reality. In a similar spirit he wrote all his books for her, and so we can see that his creative effort has to do with the problem of life and death in the woman and in consequence in himself, insofar as he was totally dependent upon the woman. Yet, at the same time, in complex with this urge was a drive to deny reality altogether. In Barrie's shadow plays there is, of course, a massive dynamic of denial of reality, of the need to grow up and find one's adult reality—that is, one's mortality. To accept one's mortality also means, incidentally, finding and accepting one's sexuality. The mother's sexuality, which produced the offspring to which she should have conveyed reflection, is seen, in the background, as being part of the problem.

Out of these problems, a troubled mind can devise an ideal woman, a woman who has none of the difficulties and dangers of being mortal or sexual. Barrie evidently picked up from his mother the impulse to deny reality, in favor of manic denial. As we shall see, although Barrie wrote all of his books for her and they were a deeply significant element in her life, there was one story to which she needed always to be blind. The story is "Dead These Twenty Years," in which Barrie wrote of a death similar to his brother's. Such a denial of the reality of death and such a failure of the processes of mourning can only be achieved by a kind of magic—by the invention of a mother-woman who is perfect, beautiful, gentle, eternal, never suffers from depression, never hates or rejects, is magically nonmortal, is never weak, and never threatens rejection. We may, I believe, relate Peter Pan's failure to grow up and Mary Rose's uncannily nonhuman presence to this fantasy of a magical woman of the *Geist* (spirit).

Margaret Ogilvie, for whom Barrie wrote his books, is such an immortal magical woman. She is eternally manic:

> Her face beamed and ripped with mirth as before, and her laugh that I had tried so hard to force came running home again. I have heard no such laugh as hers save from merry children; the laughter of most of us ages, and wears out with the body, but hers remained gleeful to the last, as if it were born afresh every morning. There was always something of the child in her, and her laugh was its voice, as eloquent of the past to me as was the christening robe to her.
>
> (Barrie 1896, 18)

As a child Barrie strove to transform the actual mortal, ailing, threatening, depressed mother into this idolized woman.

Of course, there were other lesser psychic conditions that affected Barrie. Family life must have been difficult enough, as was the problem of adjusting to new siblings. The Karpes write:

> Barrie was born at Kirriemuir, a small Scottish town, the ninth of the children and the third son in the family of a poor weaver. When he was three and two months old, the last child, his youngest sister was born. In his autobiographical book *Margaret Ogilvie* Barrie tells us that he has a complete amnesia for the first six years of his life. . . . We thus have no direct description of little James's reaction to his sister's birth, but we can guess from the unusually intensive relationship which later developed with his mother that he must have felt very deeply her preoccupation with her new baby.
>
> (Karpe and Karpe 1957, 409)

But then the normal difficulties were exacerbated by his brother's death:

> At the age of six a tragic event occurred which had a deep and lasting influence on Barrie's whole life. He then had two older brothers, the oldest Alexander, already grown up, and an adolescent brother David . . . much loved by the mother. When David was killed in an accident on the eve of his fourteenth birthday . . . the mother went into a deep depression. For many days she stayed in bed in a darkened room, her face to the wall, refusing food and paying no attention to her children, until little six-year-old James *succeeded in arousing her interest in him again* [italics mine]. From then on James took it upon himself to cheer his bereaved mother, and these attempts provide his first childhood memories.
>
> (408)

Perhaps in such a large family, Barrie had experienced already a deficiency of creative reflection. There was perhaps a deficiency in his earliest infant life, of that telepathic experience of total identification in which the child's emerging identity has its basis. Thus, he may have known the sense of being totally threatened in his existence by a lack of confirmation, which we find in his plays. Perhaps even before his mother's withdrawal he had experienced that the mother could disappear into "another world" and thus virtually go out of existence, leaving him in existlessness, while yet obviously physically still alive and growing. Certainly, what we find in Barrie's work is an intense need to try to find the mother who can give him more reflection. He cannot grow up psychically unless he finds her; and finding her seems to involve an immense effort to get into another world, back in time, and back into the primal relationship. Yet, there is a poignant sense that the time is gone.

As we have seen, there is a good deal of childish magic in this; and this may be seen in connection with the mother's magic, of trying to bring the dead sibling back to life:

> But I had not made her forget the bit of her that was dead; in those nine-and twenty years he was not removed one day farther from her. Many a time she fell asleep speaking to him, and even while she slept her lips moved and she smiled as if he had come back to her, and when she woke he might vanish so suddenly that she started up bewildered and looked about her, and then said slowly "My David's dead!" or perhaps he remained long enough to whisper why he must leave her now, and then she lay silent with filmy eyes. When I became a man and he was still a boy of thirteen, I wrote a little paper called "Dead this Twenty Years," which was about a similar tragedy in another woman's life, and it is the only thing I have written that she never spoke about, not even to that daughter she loved the best. No one ever spoke of it to her, or asked her if she had read it: one does not ask a mother if she knows that there is a little coffin in the house. She read many times the book in which it is printed, but when she came to that chapter she would put her hands to her heart or even over her ears.
>
> (Barrie 1896, 18)

The conflict in Barrie's work is thus between the ghost that persists in existence, like Mary Rose in his play of that name, and those who seek to put it to rest. The conflict is between those who cannot become real or perhaps do not want to become real, like Peter Pan, and those who mourn the loss of their shadows, who have fallen out of their prams and have never been convinced by the mother that they were real. As Peter Coveney writes in *Poor Monkey* (1957), there is one central image in Barrie's works. It is not the "central image of Barrie's neurosis"; it is an image of an existence problem:

> But the window was closed, and there were iron bars on it, and peering inside he saw his mother sleeping peacefully with her arm round another little boy. Peter called "Mother! Mother!" but she heard him not; in vain he beat his little limbs against the iron bars. He had to fly back, sobbing, to the Gardens, and he never saw his dear again.
>
> (Barrie, 1902, 186)

Peter cannot be confirmed in his existence because the mother is given over to another. This seems like a final catastrophe. There is no second chance:

> Ah Peter! we who have made the great mistake, how differently we should all act at the second chance. But Solomon was right—there is no second chance, not for most of us. When we reach the window it is Lock-out Time. The iron bars are up for life.
>
> (187)

For Barrie, "the iron bars were up" because his mother remained forever in a state of primary maternal preoccupation for the ghost of his sibling and not for him. For Barrie, because the time of psychic parturition is over forever, it is too late; and in both plays we have a poignant sense that the time that could have brought fulfillment is gone forever. Even at the end:

> All this time there seemed to be something that she wanted, but the one was dead who always knew what she wanted, and they produced many things at which she shook her head. They did not know then that she was dying, but they followed her through the house in some apprehension, and after she returned to bed they say that she was becoming very weak. Once she said eagerly, "Is that you, David?" and again she thought she heard her father knocking the snow off his boots. Her desire for that which she could not name came back to her, and at last they saw that what she wanted was the old christening robe. It was brought to her, and she unfolded it with trembling exultant hands, and when she had made sure that it was still of virgin fairness her old arms went round it adoringly, and upon her face there was the ineffable mysterious glow of motherhood.
>
> (Barrie 1896, 200)

This mysterious state of the mother belongs to the same *participation mystique* by which Tolstoy's Kitty in *Anna Karenina* feels that her baby needs her:

> It was not a mere guess—the bond between herself and the baby had not yet been severed—and she knew surely by the flow of milk within herself that he was wanting food. She knew he was screaming before she reached the nursery. And so he was. She heard his voice and increased her speed.
>
> (Tolstoy 1878; part 8, sec. 6)

But for Margaret Ogilvie, this mysterious state was for a dead child; and its magic power was terrible because it spelled everlasting immaturity for Barrie. Over him she exerted an obliterating possessiveness. Since all he wrote was for her, it was necessarily manic and in it was always the denial of death. Just as Barrie's mother had scotomized the death of her son forever and had kept him as a baby, she kept herself in a state of permanent 'being for' that baby. Caught in such psychic toils, Barrie could achieve nothing of the *Dasein*—nothing that is, to set in terms of 'being there' against death and 'being-unto-death'. He could never find the true path toward separateness, out of union, so that he could exist alone and become a man with his shadow attached but also with life and freedom. Thus, as Coveney writes, Barrie's fixation on his mother meant his exclusion from creative fulfillment. We may add to this the possibility that because of her state of mind, this meant exclusion for Barrie from an adequate relationship with reality—in truth, "disillusionment." By "dissolutionment" Winnicott means the process by which the mother gradually enables her child to find the real world as painful as this may be for him (and for her). Barrie, like Peter Pan, withdraws from reality; his woman fades into evanescence like Mary Rose, who periodically slips out of this world.

In view of the problems I am discussing of the mother and her role in the formation of identity as they are explored in psychoanalysis, it should be no surprise to find chapters in Sir James Barrie's **Margaret Ogilvie** headed "What I Should Be" and "How My Mother Got Her Soft Face." Coveney quotes Barrie as saying, "the love of mother and son has written everything of mine that is of any worth" (Coveney 1957, 204).

Barrie's books, he said, were written to "please one woman who is now dead." But there is an element in his urgent activity that make his reparation incapable of really restoring his object and the world, thus establishing a "living principle" between him and the world. His is a manic reparation, directed at trying to keep alive what cannot be kept alive and to make the woman perfect in a magical way, so that she has no ambivalence and no unreliability—no human qualities, indeed. Barrie thus made his mother his heroine and put himself entirely in her hands, becoming whatever she wanted him to be. It is this sacrifice of authenticity that both fascinates and appalls his readers. It is also what makes a critic like Rickword so scathing, since such a denial of adult freedom seems to involve us in an emotional "mess"—that is, a forfeiture of appropriate responses. In chapter 8 of **Margaret Ogilvie,** Barrie reports with affection his mother's dominance of his work:

> We had read somewhere that a novelist is better equipped than most of his trade if he knows himself and one woman, my mother said, "You know yourself,

for everybody must know himself" (there never was a woman who knew less about herself than she), and she would add dolefully, "but I doubt I'm the only woman you know well."

"Then I must make you my heroine," I said lightly.

"A gey auld-farrant-like heroine!" she said, and we both laughed at the notion—so little did we read the future.

(Barrie 1896, 60)

And in the following chapter he writes:

My Heroine

When it was known that I had begun another story my mother might ask what it was to be about this time.

"Fine we can guess who it is about," my sister would say pointedly.

"Maybe you can guess, but it is beyond me," says my mother, with the meekness of one who knows that she is a dull person.

My sister scorned her at such time. "What woman is in all books?" she would demand.

"I'm sure I canna say," replies my mother determinedly. "I thought the women were different every time."

"Mother, I wonder you can be so audacious! Fine you know what woman I mean."

(163)

On her part, Barrie's mother identified closely with Barrie's struggle to become a writer:

After her death I found that she had preserved in a little box, with a photograph of me as a child, the envelopes which had contained my first cheques. There was a little ribbon round them. (82)

On the last day, my mother insisted on rising from bed and going through the house. The arms that had so often helped her on that journey were now cold in death, but there were others only less loving, and she went slowly from room to room like one bidding goodbye, and in mine she said, "The beautiful rows upon rows of books, and he said every one of them was mine, all mine!"

If creative work is to be judged by the degree to which it is successful in establishing existential authenticity and freedom, Barrie seems to have made few gains in the way of genuine creativity. He never found his freedom because his view of self, world, and others never escaped from the confines of his mother's need to preserve her denial of time, death, and growth (rather like Miss Havisham in Dickens's *Great Expectations*).

As Coveney points out, Barrie himself came to see in the end that he had been unable to escape from this "flight from life." Later in his life he wrote, "It is as if long after writing **Peter Pan,** its true meaning came to me. Desperate attempts to grow up but can't" (Coveney 1957, 209).

However, the phrase "unable to grow up" masks the deeper problem. Coveney concludes his discussion of Barrie with a moralizing tone of discrimination, by which he conveys that it is somehow reprehensible and "uncreative" to "fail to grow up," despite heroic efforts to solve the problem of one's existential self.

Coveney recounts how Elizabeth Bergner[5] was able to coax Barrie's talents into life with the suggestion that he write a drama based upon the legend of David and Goliath, in which "the main and eccentric dramatic point of the whole play should reside in David's obsession with acquiring Goliath's spear" (209).

After the battle the boy trails the stage disconsolately, because he cannot raise the treasured possession onto his shoulder. In the final scene he confides to Jonathan that he can at last raise it, and the final curtain finds the boy on the highest rock on the stage with the spear shaft as wide as a "weaver's beam" mounted on his shoulder. From anyone who would deny the phallic character of the symbol (it is to be remembered that Barrie's father was in fact a weaver) it would be interesting to have an explanation of the dramatic point of **The Boy David.**

(209-10)

Barrie's work often is based on fantasies of stealing the father's penis and using it to possess the mother: "For the rest of the night he lay on me and across me. . . . He always retained possession of my finger" (Barrie 1902, 232). But this approach seems both too Freudian and deterministic, as if the work can be explained in terms of such oedipal material. This leads to "oedipal morbidities," says Coveney.

An approach based on phenomenology, however, acknowledges that the symbolism has a deeper meaning. The struggle of David against Goliath can be interpreted as the struggle to discover and assert against impossible odds (the weight of the mother's sickness and dread) a certain male-element strength of identity. The symbolism of phallic sexual desire for the mother can rather be interpreted as a yearning to find sustenance, to receive more reflection from her, and even to receive "disillusionment" from her in order to discover one's own independent strength of identity—so that, in adulthood, one could, in turn, support the mother against nothingness and loss of meaning. When the Boy David holds the mother's finger, it is possible that what he wants of her is something from her male element (*her* penis) that will enable him as an adult to deal with a "difficult and sometimes dangerous" world. But because of her need to depend so manically on Barrie, Margaret Ogilvie disarmed her son for such creative dealings with reality. What Coveney calls "oedipal morbidities" may thus be interpreted as a quest for genuine creative potentialities in an impossible situation—and so are not so blameworthy as they appear from Coveney's somewhat moralizing approach. If we hold back for the moment from moralizing discrimination, we may understand better and see that what we are dealing with is magic. (Of course, the trouble is that magic doesn't work in the real world.)

But the recognition of the element of magic will help us to understand such things as the mysterious way in which Mary Rose, in the play of that name, disappears periodically into another world while her son grows up.[6] At the end of the play, Mary Rose's son takes her on his lap like a child. What the author himself seeks is to be released from his problem of identity. This Barrie achieves in *Mary Rose* by inverting the problem, so that Harry's aim is to release Mary Rose:

HARRY:

> All I know about them for certain is that they are unhappy because they can't find something, and then once they've got the thing they want, they go away happy and never come back.

MARY ROSE:

> Oh, nice.

HARRY:

> The one thing clear to me is that you have got that thing at last, but you are too dog-tired to know or care. What you need now is to get back to the place you say is lovely, lovely.

MARY ROSE:

> Yes, yes.

From the Freudian way of looking at the problem, it might seem, as it does to Goitein, as if the creator of Mary Rose is "keeping her for his sexual pleasure":

> This means the author of her being, the father creator, has kept her for himself and his pleasure, has drawn her back into his mind and ultimately suppressed her from consciousness, even as he did years before, when she became the object of sexual desire in the fullness of his youth—lost her in the mists of the unconscious.[7]

(Goitein 1926, 196)

But if we look at the problem in light of Winnicott's exploration of the origins of existence in the experience of total identification with the mother, as a problem of existence, we can penetrate beneath the sexual pattern (which is undeniably there) and see a schizoid pattern. That is, what Barrie is seeking is existential rebirth of the regressed ego—the rebirth of 'being' in the experience of the female element. Goitein sees that there is a theme of rebirth:

> What is the problem Mary Rose really endeavours to settle when she comes to earth? It is stated in the play as the question of eternity which is of course, "How can man live forever, how reclaim his lost youth, and be born again, how come to be a little child once more to enter the Kingdom of Heaven?" Or, expressed in the "projected" form, "What is it Mary is ever searching for and longing for, and returned for?—a baby." Indeed she goes through a *"nightly travail that can never be completed"* till this Harry is here *"to provide the end."*

(187)

But the "baby" is Barrie's own regressed libidinal ego—that is, the unborn infant self in himself.

Barrie wants to re-create the mother who can give him (psychic) birth as his real mother never did. Thus, he creates a dream mother who is forever anguished by her need to complete her baby, so that he can "enter the kingdom of heaven" of integration. Goitein continues:

> Now the latest content of this question is the personal heart-searching: "How can a man tear himself away from the mother, and yet be at one with her . . . ?" Mary herself is eternal, always virgin, ever young.

(187)

Mary is the "ideal object" who is not prone to the threats to her survival inherent in becoming an adult. An adult is capable of libidinal sexual creativity and in this is at one with his mortality. Mary may not have this. She must be kept in pseudoinnocence. (Goitein says that Mary Rose is a virgin throughout the play and that the marriage is never consummated.) A mother kept magically in this state is not susceptible, of course, to one's own dangerous envy. Therefore, she cannot then—as castrating mother—turn jealously against one's oedipal involvement in parental sex. She will always be there to reflect one in a totally controllable manner and will never threaten withdrawal or rejection, as a mother does when she mourns, attends to a new sibling, belongs to her husband, or recovers her self-interest. This mother is kept in a state of perpetual primary maternal preoccupation; and she lives, therefore, is a magical world:

> She has solved the problem, but she is from another world, for which "the loch" and the "vale of the shadow" separate us. ("There was a door for which I had no key. There was a veil past which I could not see.")

(187)

This other world is the world where the dead mother is. There, if one can find her, she will prove to be the creatively reflecting mother who was not adequately experienced. The new world—the spirit world—is a world in which one may experience psychic birth as one never could before (as in George MacDonald's other world or the world at the end of Charles Kingsley's *The Water-Babies*). It is the inheritance of love and encounter that one has never had as a neonate. The problem for, us, of course, is to estimate the value the re-creation of the world may have for us: How much rebirth do we need? "How is it with us?" asks Goitein.

> We cannot be Peter Pans, that is certain: reverie and dream are not enough, if as men we would live again we must recreate ourselves: go back to the womb from whence we came—and this must mean reunion with the mother. Or man may create himself by 'being one with' his own grandchild—by union with his daughter. Of course, this is but deep, unconscious reasoning; in life it is but metaphor, it satisfied the mind's censor in the guise of religious drama; and on the stage it is but the enacting of a dream: and so again may pass the world's censorship.
>
> (187)

Goitein discusses the play in Freudian terms of sexual impulses expressed in Christian symbolism:

> His [Harry's] answer to the immortality problem is "Through the creation of a daughter" . . . the union of the Father with the daughter and the rise of the immortal Son and Lord. . . . He makes love to her: the sparks of the fire he has made "leap up as often as they are trampled down," but as he approaches her, "an unholy organ" of another "increasing in volume" rakes the bushes for her. . . . The Father has drawn her in unto Himself; she is no more.
>
> (188)

Goitein also discusses problems of identity:

> He [Harry] returns to the "old home," the fabric of the mother, and dandles on his knee a little girl spirit; whose childish patter and babyish ways show best what age Mary Rose has reached.
>
> (188)

As Goitein sees, Mary Rose is *"the beautiful youthful maiden form the mother is unconsciously ever thought to be."* (188) Perhaps Mary Rose is the mother who is remembered as having allowed her baby to make her the subjective object. She is re-created now as still being able to allow him to make use of her in primary maternal preoccupation, yet she is made into a controllable little toy girl. Thus, at the end of the play we have the disturbing image of a man holding on his lap the mother—who has become so identified with her baby that she now is the baby, while the adult writer is a man.

According to Goitein, the implication is that "the problem of the ages can only be settled on earth as it is in heaven," and "in reality the solution is a poor one as far as the human race is concerned":

> It is an ideal of a kind, harboured by many desperate minds who would fly in the face of conventions of racial evolution, and eventually be their own unwitting slayers. It may hold for the phantasy [sic] of the family in heaven; it must fail for the families on earth.
>
> (189)

Isn't the point, instead, that what we have here is a symbolism of schizoid suicide—that is, a weariness with life, in the absence of an inward confirming possession of the female element of the mother, that tends to lead to withdrawal into death, into a ghostly world. There may be in this a hope of rebirth, but could it prove to be a negative path of ultimate regression? An underlying feeling of the lure of death permeates the play. It is the malevolent call to which Mary Rose herself gives such ecstatic assent.[8]

But at the same time, a real need is being expressed—the intense need for reexperiencing that confirmation of identity that the mother reflection should originally have provided. The problem with **Mary Rose** is that the solution to the problem of the need to have one's existence confirmed *is* simply magical; it belongs not to heaven but to the preservation of an attitude of magical infantile omnipotence. Harry retains an ability such as a child believes in, even to defy God, to manipulate the universe, and to restore the object to heavenly perfection by sheer manic necromancy:

HARRY:

. . . If there was any way of getting you to that glory place!

MARY ROSE:

Tell me.

HARRY:

(*Desperate.*) He would surely send for you if he wanted you.

MARY ROSE:

(*Crushed.*) Yes.

HARRY:

It's like as if He had forgotten you.

MARY ROSE:

Yes.

HARRY:

It's as if nobody wanted you, either there or here.

MARY ROSE:

Yes. (*She rises.*) Bad man.

HARRY:

It's easy to call me names, but the thing fair beats me. There is nothing I wouldn't do for you, but a mere man is so helpless.

From Barrie's childhood experience we can recognize the origins of this combination of feelings of hopelessness and the urge to restore the object:

From then on (from the moment when he managed to "arouse her interest in him again") James took it upon himself to cheer his bereaved mother, and these attempts provide his first childhood memories. He recalls in his autobiography how he sat in his mother's room, trying to entertain her by standing on his head or by similar childish tricks and counting how often she laughed. He devoted a great deal of his boyish efforts and energies to cheering his mother by letting her talk about herself, and, almost like a psychotherapist, encouraged her to talk of her own childhood, her father whom she had adored, and her early hopes and experiences. This intensive relationship continued for the next *twenty-eight years* until her death, even though James never completely succeeded in making her forget David, *to whom she was always talking in whispers as if he were constantly with her* [italics mine]. Barrie's mother also remained on intimate terms with other dead persons, a fact which must have been of great importance to him. When one of his sisters, after the death of her fiancé, decided to marry the dead man's brother, her mother begged the dead man's forgiveness, asking him to understand how sad and lonely is the life of a friendless girl.

(Karpe and Karpe 1957, 409)

As Marietta Karpe and Richard Karpe write, "the tragic loss of a love object seems able to become a stimulating factor for an artist's or a child's creativity, and the revival in fantasy of a lost object is one way of mastering that loss" (408). The problem, I believe, is deeper than one of loss and mastering loss. Loss presents the problem of existential despair, which in turn presents the question "What is the point of life?" This question then requires engagement with the *Dasein* problem.

It is interesting at this point to note that, as the Karpes point out, the basic idea of **Mary Rose** first occurs in a story book, **The Little White Bird** (1902). Among the episodes are fantastic answers to the question "Where do I come from?" One chapter, "A Nightpiece," deals with the birth of David.

> The author tells David, a little boy of five, what happened on the night of his birth. He tells how he, the author, walked the streets all night with David's father waiting for David's mother to have her baby, and surprisingly enough their thoughts turn to death and to ghosts. "The only ghosts, I believe," he writes, "who creep into this world, are dead young mothers: returned to see how their children fare. There is no other inducement great enough to bring the departed back.... But what is saddest about these ghosts is that they may not know their child. They expect him to be just as he was when they left him, and they are easily bewildered, and search for him from room to room, and hate the *unknown boy he has become.*"

(Karpe and Karpe 1957, 409)

It is true, as the Karpes say, that in this we have the synopsis of **Mary Rose**; but within in it, we also can see several important themes that address existence anxiety. In talking to David, who is five years old, the author is talking to the boy who died in 1867 at the age of fourteen, when Barrie was six. The Karpes suggest that the fantasy of death associated with birth may have had its origin in Barrie's experience of the birth of his younger sister. But isn't it better explained in terms of a failure in early babyhood to be confirmed as alive and real? Barrie may well have sensed that the birth of David (as well as his sister) meant even a greater lessening of his mother's capacity to confirm him, while David's birth becomes merged with his death, by the consequences of which all confirmation and hope of confirmation seemed lost. Barrie's young mother was to him a "dead young mother" because she did not make him feel alive, while the ghosts' bewilderment ("they may not know their child") springs from the terrible experience of being unconfirmed by a dissociated mother and then being confused by her with the ghosts of a dead sibling by being put on the same existential plane.

Surely, the relationship of Barrie's mother to dead persons manifests a form of dissociation from reality that gives the reader a clue to Barrie's own existence problem. A mother who confused real persons and ghosts in this way would obviously prove less than dependable in the formation of the child's identity, since the child could never be sure whether he was being treated as a real person or as a ghost.

Barrie's attachment to his mother can thus be seen as an attempt to help her become real and alive because she had not enabled *him* to feel real and alive. However, the attachment involved him in accepting her dissociation, so that the problem of integration comes into conflict with the magic by which he sought to preserve her. When these manic processes broke down he would be subject to one of his own "periods of deep depression in which he refused to see anyone and cut himself off from all contacts" (409).

Thus, even Harry seeks to persuade Mary Rose that in being indifferent to her God is being cruel—a paranoid attitude that often accompanies an inability to tolerate and accept one's mortal reality.[9] In Barrie's writings, we often find such resentment expressed in terms that surely derive from his own puzzlement over his brother's death—a death that the mother herself seems to have been unable to accept. At the end of **Mary Rose,** Harry says:

> I wonder if what it means is that you broke some law.
>
> If it was that, it's surely time He overlooked it.

Here surely is the attitude of a bemused child who feels that the woman's suffering must be a consequence of some guilt and that what is needed to overcome this is a mollifying and propitiation of some persecutor. Lifting his mother's depression was also sharing her paranoia and so trying to propitiate her persecutors.

Mary Rose, Harry supposes, may have broken some law, "just to come back for the sake of—of that Harry?" The recognition that the mother is dead and inaccessible as a source of rebirth is impossible; therefore, the law that has been broken is the law of the need to accept reality. For breaking this law, Mary Rose has alienated herself from God. She is stuck unhappily in existence, although really out of existence, just as David, although really out of existence, became stuck in existence because Barrie's mother continually recognized the presence of his ghost and refused to recognize his death.

Thus, we can see the infantile logic of those twenty-eight years: My brother is dead, but my mother continues to confirm his (non-existent) existence as a person. What does my core of feeling of nonexistence mean, since I am living? Why do I not feel confirmed even so? The answer was to change the *malevolent call* that called the mother out of confirming existence, which is what caused the damage in the first place, into a *benign call*. Yet, this transformation happens only by magic. At first, the stars of the actual universe seem indifferent. Harry says, "You are too small a thing to get a helping hand from them"

But then, as God's hard heart is softened by Harry's remonstrances, comes the celestial music that is "the only sound in the world." The stage direction is intensely sentimental and is imbued with a force of tremendous magical desire that things should not be as they are and never have been:

> (*The call is heard again, but there is in it now no unholy sound. It is a celestial music that is calling for Mary Rose, Mary Rose. . . . As it wraps her round, the wearly little ghost knows that her long day is done. Her face is shining. The smallest star shoots down as if it were her star sent for her, and with her arms stretched forth to it trustingly she walks though the window into the empyrean. The music passes with her.* HARRY *hears nothing, but he knows that somehow a prayer has been answered.*)
>
> THE END

This is the epitome of manic reparation. The problems of existence anxiety and identity are solved by the capacity of the infant to move a star out of heaven, to make his object good enough for him to "begin." This is cosmic infant monism indeed—to make the stars into the mother's eyes! Strangely enough, after *Mary Rose* Barrie was able to produce nothing more that was creative. He had somehow re-created and magically assuaged his anguish for the female element of 'being'. Significantly, perhaps, his next attempts at plays were called **Shall We Join the Ladies?**, **Farewell Miss Julie Logan**, and, his last, **Boy David**. As the Karpes write, "The free flow of his creativity seemed cut off after the writing of *Mary Rose*" (Karpe and Karpe 1957, 408).

These writers argue that *Mary Rose* fulfilled an important "dynamic function" in Barrie's life. However, "dynamic function" seems a positive term for a strangely negative process. For example, it seems likely that one of the motives for writing the play was an attempt at reconciliation with his former wife, Mary. In fact, she was later hospitalized with a paranoid condition; and *Mary Rose*, as the Karpes say, "helped him to reject the idea of marriage." They go on to say that writing the play "liberated him temporarily from his lifelong struggle with his mother's youthful image" (411). The word "liberated" seems strange here, when, in fact, Barrie seems to have solved the problem of his turmoil over Mary's reappearance on the scene at the time by making Lady Cynthia Asquith his "private secretary" and forming a close relationship both with her mother Lady Wemyss and Lady Cynthia's two little boys. (Barrie "always loved little boys and needed their proximity"—presumably because they fulfilled the intense need in his own relationship with his mother to resurrect David). Lady Cynthia simply provided the mother relationship:

> Lady Cynthia describes the days of depression and gloom when nothing could cheer him, with one exception; if she presented him with some trouble of her own, he immediately became interested in her problem and forgot his own sadness, obviously a repetition of his old tendency to cheer his grieving mother.
>
> (410)

Barrie's sense of identity depended upon having a mother object whose confirming regard he gained by seeking to lift her grief, but this was no solution. Nor did it lead him to mature engagement with existential problems (as he would have had to had he rejoined his former wife). Barrie merely became a child again who was faced with an impossible task. Therefore, like a child, he asks existential questions but; he cannot answer them except in childish terms:

> His attempt to free himself from the ghosts of his childhood proved unsuccessful. Should the dead come back from their graves? Where are the children before they are born?—the eternal questions of life and death. Barrie's gallant attempt at solving them in his magical, illogical and philosophical way did not succeed, and he died discouraged, a lonely old man, in spite of many friendships.
>
> (411)

Barrie's play may have begun as a "parable of life," but even the terms in which he phrases his philosophical questions are not philosophically mature or "disillusioned" enough. He is too content with the terms and concepts of a Victorian nursery and a Sunday-school Christian cosmology—little stars, heavenly voices, the dear dead, and the innocent souls of children. One existential question is "Where do they go when they die?"—

for the essential question is "How do I know I exist, especially when others (who should confirm my existence) go out of existence?" It is rather like Alice and the Red King. However, instead of waking up and ceasing to dream of her, so that Alice ceases to exist, the Red King dies—and where would Alice be then?[10]

Barrie speaks of the "narrow loch" that separates us from nonexistence, but his nonexistence remains a dream. He cannot accept utter loss. He stays in the metaphysical state of childhood, in which the child cannot accept nonexistence but must believe in another world of easily available ghosts. Thus, Barrie's method of expressing loss is merely childish:

MARY ROSE:

> The last time of anything is sad, don't you think, Simon?

MARY ROSE:

> Simon, if one of us had to—to go—and we could choose which one . . .

Barrie's world is disturbing because we are never allowed, and the characters are never allowed, to develop an adult's self-interest. The characters and the readers always must go over into the state of confirming the existence of another or letting another confirm their identity in terms of total identification. In other words, all are subjective objects. We are involved in striving to bring Mary Rose out of the world beyond existence, and we yearn for others to do this for us—from Mary Rose herself, to the voices of the spheres at the end, to Harry. In responding to the play, we hear a shriek in our ears that means "let me never be confounded!"

To avoid going out of existence in truth, a mystic and magical power *is* needed. In reality, that power is the uncanny state of the mother—that is, primary maternal preoccupation, her schizoid extension of identity in creative reflection that establishes our sanity, a kind of telepathy. When this power cannot be found, we have a desperate quest for all kind of magic to take its place. Goitein says of Barrie in relation to *Mary Rose*:

> He is not only anxious, but troubled, for the essential incident seems to worry him; and he, therefore, seeks as many outlets of expression as possible. For no discovery in science is left untried that can be enlisted to throw light on his theme and support his inmost contention. "Haunting", Hallucinations, Sublimation, Brain Waves, "telepathy," and Wireless Waves, are in turn offered as explanations to justify the pet delusion.
>
> (Goitein 1926, 181)

As Goitein writes, all these preoccupations enabled Barrie to combine nearness to truth and "probability of genuine occurrence" with a "quasi-scientific attitude" and phenomena of "abnormal psychology." In truth,

Mary Rose is a mad play, with all the madness of primal existence anxiety, when the uncanny state of primary maternal preoccupation has gone "wrong":

> . . . its power of skipping over time, and leaving some of its images uninfluenced by time; its logic, its confusion of the characters, its sudden appearance, and its fading away.
>
> (181)

There are images of *as-if*: "As if . . . as if a cold finger has touched my Mary Rose." There are also hallucinations: "the old woman on the stairs" seen by Mary and the baby waving his bib seen from the island ("you needn't pretend you can see him"). Mary Rose has been seen "talking to some person who wasn't there and listening as it were for some sound that never came." She herself is like a "collective hallucination," says Goitein, "we cannot see her quite so clearly." The whole play is a "beautiful illusion." Goitein writes "that in going back to the "Home" and its "little room" we are going back to the Mother" (183).

Thus, the play is an act of symbolic magical regression. As Goitein points out, the imagery of the anatomy of the "Home" is full of imagery of being "inside" the mother. This is an expanded metaphor for the reconstructed memory of intrauterine life. (From my point of view, this is symbolism of being inside the *psychic* uterus):

> For the house and its rooms, more especially the Mother's Room, . . . is the mother of the family. It wears "her disturbing smile,", "the smiles that she has left about";[11] and its aspect "takes on a semblance of herself"; even as every room is "full of herself, hanging on nails and folded away in drawers." We are privileged to see a Vision of life "in the old manner" (old manor) in the confines of the old-time mother. Small wonder they "whimper and thrill at his coming." Our attention is focused first on the garden external to her, with a blossoming tree as the open window, whose foliage scrapes the glass. This leads to a big room and (with-) drawingroom, where the baby first learnt to swim; and by a "fearsome narrow dark passage" into a single room—the baby's room "where he used to sleep"—the oldest part of the mother. It has two windows of stone and spanned above with wooden rafters: the door is never locked, it is often held, but the key is lost (only the grim blade—"the visiting card"—is to be thrust against its door). It is here that the ghost-mother pauses, hunting still for her child. Down below is the kitchen with its well-known smells (and rat holes) and the front door. Over our head and "so near us" is the Apple-room so called (?) from the large apples pressing against its walls. It is gloomy within—a chamber from which the *thumping* cry now and then to be answered by a thump quicker and happier from the big room below "when things are getting on, and going well." As we trace our way outward we observe a picture of a "waterfall" on the wall of the (with-) drawingroom; its "window opens outward" and it was

down the parent trunk of the foliaged tree that her baby "slipped away" into the garden.

(184)

(Incidentally, this is a superb piece of phenomenological analysis.) Harry unwittingly hurls his knife (= penis) at the door of her chamber, "the oldest room" in the fabric of the mother. As Goitein points out, Mr. Morland, on "calling" Mary to himself, is thinking of Mary Rose rather as "the old lady with wrinkles" and of the name on the island trunk which forever stops at MAR. (Barrie's mother's name was Margaret.) The knife breaks in the middle of her. The knife, Goitein believes, is a symbol of the dangers of incestuous desire for the mother. Perhaps the knife symbolizes instead the unconscious hatred that is directed against the mother's failure in psychic parturition. Here, the existence problems meet the oedipal problems. The consequence of both is the need for splitting to preserve existence because hate must be kept apart from love and goodness; hence, the "Holy Mary syndrome". Goitein's analysis of the religious elements in the play (with Freudian interpretations he does not quite make explicit) is fascinating:

> As a woman she is certainly not of this world, "she is different from other girls," "a little odd" with that peculiar "attribute of her that never plays with them." Like the Madonna, she is likened to a flower, "*a rare and lovely flower,*" and her parents were never anxious "*to take the bloom off her.*" Like the Virgin [likened to a blood red rose] Mary-the-Rose is her name. Her little calyx (bassinette) holds the Babe; but that flower has inherited eternal youth by the cold finger of fate—a "cold finger had once touched my Mary Rose," as "frost may stop the *growth* of a plant and yet leave it *blooming.*" . . . her saintlike purity is hinted at in many places. "*What you are worrying about is just her innocence—which seems a holy thing to me.*" . . . "Marriage . . . it is so fearfully solemn." "We'll try to be good, won't we?" says Mary Rose: and while Simon is craving for her hand, Mary is sitting in the cold room above "*thinking holy things*" about love; and in her simple way, says Barrie, is worlds above the average "secret women" so much less innocent than she. Her island, which embodies herself (her soul) is a bird *sanctuary*: silent and "still as an empty *church*": and when in the shadow of a church she is buried, that site is a "holy spot." That is the dust, but her spirit rises "to the stars" of "the empyrean," when the "celestial music" calls her to her Father.
>
> . . . Mary is a virgin throughout the play (virgin-mother), but we may spare references to what the reader will detect for himself (e.g. How her child is adopted . . . "some baby you had borrowed . . ." "I sometimes think so still . . ." It was a phantom pregnancy and an imaginary delivery when Simon was sent away to Plymouth—an artifice suggested to the author's mind by the recently prominent case of Mrs. Slingsby and almost identical; the *ear* rather than a tuft of hair that being stressed in the imagined likeness to the father. The "holding of her tongue," her being told "to dry up" at the end of the scene of making love, both of these metaphorically and in fact, she does. For her, the reflection that she is an island, a garden enclosed, whose whins [whims] have first to be torn down to get through to her and win her—even at the risk of bleeding limbs. And finally, when the "call" does come, is the "attempt to beat them back and put a girdle of *safety* round her"—all these point to her successful guarding of her virginity).
>
> Finally, she is Maria Stellarum when the "smallest star shoots down from heaven for her." ("My star" as Simon calls her;) and the little thing ascends at the divine call (the music of the spheres) into a "night of stars." Then surely she "*hid her head amid a crown of stars,*" and the moment was the Ascension of the Virgin.

(189-90)

Such a split-off, pure, ideal object (deprived of all bodily sensibility) can exist ultimately only in "the land where the dead dreams go," since Mary Rose is so much divided from any real libidinal and ambivalent woman. Such a splitting must also accompany a division within the subject. Since to keep the subject's goodness unspoiled by hate requires an equal feat of internal splitting and projection, there is necessarily paranoia; hence, the "unseen devils" and Harry's remark:

> As if in a way there were two kinds of dogs out hunting you, the good and the bad.

—while the call is malevolent:

> A storm and whistling winds, increasing in volume till the mere loudness is horrible.

There are two observations to be made here: One is that the splitting prevents the acceptance of ambivalence in experience—our mixture of love and hate. The other is that the call which removes Mary is the libidinal power of "the Father," which is felt to be bad, even malevolent. Again, both symbolize a failure to embrace humanness in a whole way. This may be associated with the barrenness of Barrie's play, about which Goitein notes:

> One fact must surely emerge from the study of **Mary Rose,** and one of which the author is consciously unaware, and that is the hopeless barrenness of every character in the play.

(207)

Simon never married again; Cameron will remain a bachelor "until . . ." and does so; Harry is unattached; and so on. As Goitein suggests, they are all waiting

> for the hand of Mary Rose—a creature who is the perfection ideal of their dreams—*an unreal phantasy* [sic] *that cannot be*—a woman that cannot be.

(207)

Thus, the infant gravely unconfirmed in his identity, in the aspect that should have been confirmed by the female element of 'being', needs to invent a hallucinatory split-off female element that will confirm him, although he has no capacity in himself to realize feminineness. Desperately the infant tries, but the image remains too good to be true, too heavenly, too pure, too ideal to be anything but barren and sterile. It remains (as Goitein says) the "image of a child," and its only place is among the cold, dead stars. The implicit impossibility is paralleled in Barrie's own relationships with women.

Mary Rose, too, is about woman and death, about 'being-in-existence' and 'going-out-of-existence'. As the Karpes and Goitein point out, at the time of the play's first appearance there was much discussion of the meaning of *Mary Rose*. The play was puzzling not only to audiences but to the author himself. It was also virtually the last creative work Barrie wrote. "According to the Karpes, the free flow of his creativity seemed cut off after *Mary Rose*" (Karpe and Karpe 1957, 408). It ended a period of twenty-nine years of intensive productivity, during which Barrie wrote twenty-seven plays. His secretary, Lady Cynthia Asquith, reports that he asked her, "I wish you could tell me what it means and settle the matter for once and for all" (Asquith 1954, quoted in Karpe and Karpe 1957, 408) But she could not tell, and she says in her book, *Portrait of Barrie,* that she preferred to leave the play unexplained.

The Karpes see that the play is about "the loss by death of a loved one we were not ready to give up" (408). Goitein points to the symbolism in the play: The apple tree that grows up toward the dining room, from whose branches we first hear the voice of Mary Rose, is the tree of life. The Island is "life," divided by a narrow channel from eternity. We arrive on it, have experiences there, as Mary does with her lover-husband, and then disappear. Goitein also examines in detail the complex time sequence of the play.

As will be seen, the play relates to the very question of woman as the *mysterium tremendum*; and I have tried to show how the play is illuminated by Winnicott's concepts. In the response of the mother—the *participation mystique*—the new human being finds his own sense of 'being'. There are various ways in which this process can be broken, and one is death—the death of the mother or the death of a sibling (which can leave the mother in a schizoid state). As the Karpes say, a loss by death is often the mainspring for that existential anguish by which a creative writer is driven to try to find a sense of meaning in existence. In Barrie's plays, while their meaning is not evident at the explicit level, it is clear from their very mysteriousness and ghostliness that they have to do with 'being-unto-death'. As Mary Rose, "the last of anything is always sad." In *Peter Pan,* the clock ticks away inside the voracious crocodile, while in *Mary Rose* there is the "wheezy smith in the corner" who hammers out the time.

There does seem to be a problem of time, in relation to the mother's capacity to reflect the infant. Perhaps this is so because there is a certain period during which the formative psychic processes take place. If these are not completed in this period, then serious consequences follow. George MacDonald, the Victorian fantasist, kept in his drawer a lock of his mother's hair and a letter she wrote about his sudden weaning. (In a poem in *Phantastes* (1858), he wrote:

> Alas, how easily things go wrong!
> A sigh too much, or a kiss too long,
> And there follows a mist and a weeping rain,
> And life is never the same again.
>
> (MacDonald, "Sir Aglovaile")

The chance of 'reflection' can be missed, and then the individual may spend his life looking for the opportunity to make it up. But then profound problems arise: the child, by degrees, becomes another person; and the child is lost forever. In *Mary Rose,* Mary as a ghost at the end is looking for her baby; but the person in the house, Harry, is now a man, come back from Australia. Harry ran away at the age of twelve, and Mary disappeared when he was two and a bit. Now, twenty-five years later, he is twenty-seven years old. The solution to her problem seems to involve her sitting on his lap like a baby. In this, we can see the intense bafflement that is felt about experience and time. Where is the mother? She exists only in the child's memory. Can she be put together again, so that the process of mothering can be reexperienced? If she is in the world of death, might she not, when she comes back, be malevolent—a mother capable of such rejection again as she was once culpable of? These perplexities are worked out in fantasy again and again by George MacDonald and by Barrie in *Mary Rose.*

As well as time, there is the puzzle of place. A central theme is that of "talking to some person who wasn't there and listening as it were for some sound that never came." David is "there": "To whom she [the mother] was always talking in whispers as if he were constantly with her." Barrie's mother, the Karpes point out, also remained on intimate terms with other dead persons. She must be suspected, therefore, of mystifying the young Barrie (who worked so hard to relieve her grief), so that he became doubtful as to whether people were really there or not. His house must have been full of ghosts. And he himself was powerfully involved in her quest. His mother, like Mary Rose, was one of those who "are unhappy because they can't find something, and then once they've got the thing they want, they go away happy and never come back." Such a statement sounds as if it emerged from a fear that the mother was so preoccupied with the (dead) rival sibling that her withdrawal in this respect threatened Barrie's very existence.

> The only ghosts . . . who creep into this world are dead young mothers, returned to see how their children fare. . . . What is saddest about these ghosts is that they may not know their child. They expect him to be just as he was when they left him, and they are easily bewildered, and search for him from room to room, and hate the unknown boy he has become.
>
> (Barrie 1902, 40-41)

Behind this theme we can sense the child's most terrible dread that his own existence is threatened by the mother's failure, when he needed more maternal reflection, to respond to him and to confirm his identity. She threatens him with eternal nonexistence. As Goitein says, Barrie has identified himself with his characters and silhouetted himself in his shadow plays; and his more mysterious plays are clearly about the problem of woman being the key to staying in existence. Yet Mary Rose, of course, spends much of her time in the play in a trance and becomes increasingly evasive ("*perhaps a little indistinct*"; "*we cannot see her quite so clearly*"), as if she were a mother the child is trying to hold together in his memory but cannot hold in focus as the mirror to his emerging identity.

It is perhaps worth adding that, even though I have been thinking about **Mary Rose** for years, there are still many aspects of it I cannot fathom. This is worth admitting of any work of literature. In my experience, it cheers undergraduates to find that one is still in perplexity about a work such as *Antony and Cleopatra*—so they are quite in order if they continue to be baffled. And, indeed, how much less interesting art would be if we could understand or explain its meaning. It is satisfying because it is ineffable.

My perplexities remain concerning the symbolism of sexuality in **Mary Rose** and also concerning the uncanny theme of "the last time." I am also puzzled by the religious element—what Barrie meant exactly about the good and bad days, about "the Father," and about the end, when Mary goes to heaven. When I say "exactly meant," I am of course asking too much. It seems clear that Barrie had an explicit meaning for himself, as did MacDonald about his fantasies. It is also clear, however, that much of the unconscious meaning was not clear to Barrie himself.

I cannot agree with Goitein that Mary remains a virgin throughout. How could she give birth to a baby if she were? I suppose the Christian answer would be that the Spirit of the Lord came upon her, but that doesn't seem to fit the play. What is extraordinary is that Barrie writes like one who does not have experience of sexual play and sexual love. He seems to be childishly ignorant, as if he were in the latency period.

The way Mary and Simon talk about "making love" seems to belong to such ignorance. We have seen how in **Peter Pan** there are dark hints about love, but now there seems to be a shrinking from it. Here the absence of sexuality seems to be cold and deathly: "a cold finger had once touched my Mary Rose." Simon replies, "her innocence which seems a holy thing to me." But her "holiness" seems to go with her uncanniness, as if she were bewitched or a changeling. If we take the "finger" in the spirit of the symbolism of the passage discussed above and see it by the displacement of imagery as a penis, it seems a dead penis, while Mary is swept away on the Island by an "unholy organ" that is "raking every bush." Behind these images is a sense that sexuality is dangerous and liable to bring annihilation.

Mary discusses making love with her lover, and there seems to lie behind her questioning a deep dread of sexuality. There is some discussion of play. We have seen how play is an aspect of **Peter Pan**. In light of Winnicott's insights, play is part of that imaginative exchange between mother and infant that brings out in the child a sense of his own reality and that of the world. It is also the beginning of symbolism and culture and so of the quest for meaning. Sexual play has qualities that develop out of infant play; and it, too, has to do with meaning. When the quest for meaning through sexual play becomes desperate, we have perversions. These are often found to be related to the problems of 'being' and 'nonbeing'—sometimes even linking sex and death.

Simon and Mary talk about being "us":

SIMON:

. . . Do you like it?

MARY ROSE:

It is so fearfully solemn.

SIMON:

You are not frightened are you? (*She nods.*)

Then Mary suddenly says, "Simon, after we are married you will sometimes let me play, won't you?" He replies, "Lots of married people play games."

A little later she says, "I may be wrong, but I think I'll sometimes love you to kiss me, and sometimes it will be better not." I am puzzled by these uncertainties, but I link them with her special characteristics. Peter Pan is not touched by anyone in the play; in **Mary Rose,** it would seem, there will be times when Mary Rose is not real enough to be kissed, or there is some special danger in close contact with her. Just after the above exchanges, Simon and Mary Rose discuss their wedding day and honeymoon, and she proposes they go for their honeymoon to the Island, thus connecting the dangers of disappearing with sexual intimacy.

As one often finds in fairy stories and fantasies for children, there is play on the infant belief that sex is a form of eating. There is, therefore, an inherent danger of going out of existence as a result of close sexual contact, because when things are eaten they disappear. Mary Rose is a creature who is more than usually liable to disappear. For example, when her father rows her back from the Island (after she has reappeared), he sits facing her so he can see her all the time. There is also much play throughout on keeping an eye on Mary to make sure she stays in existence. Being looked at should be a way of being confirmed in one's reality ("Thou God seest me"), but Mary Rose is terrifyingly likely to slip away under one's eyes all the same and becomes increasingly difficult to see.

I have suggested that this is like a child trying to hold his mother together in his memory, so she can reflect him. In light of the autobiographical details of Barrie's life, I think we can put the matter in a different way. There could have been times in Barrie's life when it seemed as if the mother had stopped seeing him—seeing him, that is, in the way he needed. Barrie's mother talked to a ghost as if it were real, while ostracizing the real child who needed her, turning to him a blank, depressed face. It would seem, then, that there was a terrible possibility—that there might be a last chance, a last time for confirming exchanges. If one needed love, there was always the problem of this last time, it therefore, would perhaps be better never to allow oneself this mortal reality at all.

Thus, Mary says, "Some day, Simon, you will kiss me for the last time":

SIMON:

> That wasn't the last time, at any rate. (*To prove it he kisses her again, sportively, little thinking that this may be the last time. She quivers.*) What is it?

MARY ROSE:

> I don't know; something seemed to pass over me.

This moment seems to indicate quite clearly that Barrie felt that sexuality was dangerous and that any physical contact could prove to be the "last time": the Island is jealous; or, God the Father is jealous; or, the good or bad dogs are jealous.

And there is a last time of seeing a baby. Immediately, Simon says:

> You and your last time. Let me tell you, Mistress Blake, there will be a last time of seeing your baby.

and he refers to the fact that children disappear and become adults. Mary Rose then declares, that it will be lovely when her baby can take her on his lap, as she now puts him on hers. It is this that happens at the end of the play, but the truly terrifying thing is that Mary Rose disappears out of the life of her baby for twenty-five years.

If there can be a last kiss, there can also be a last act of sexual intercourse. I interpret the tuft of hair on Simon's head to be a displacement image of a penis. Mary says the "loveliest thing on Lieutenant Simon Sobersides is the little tuft of hair which will keep standing up at the back of his head," and she immediately talks about how "I—have—got—a baby!" In the conversation about "last times," Mary says:

> There must be a last time I shall see you, Simon (*playing with his hair*). Some day I shall flatten this tuft for the thousandth time, and then never do it again.

SIMON:

> Sometime I shall look for it and it won't be there. That day I shall say, "good riddance."

MARY:

> I shall cry.

In other words, she will be sad that he has become impotent.

If the tuft is a penis, then the butter dish is the woman's genital. It is as close to the reality of woman's sexuality as we get. When Mary Rose becomes pregnant, she throws the butter dish at Simon.

SIMON:

> I had always understood that when a young wife—that when she took her husband aside and went red, or white, and her head on his bosom, and whispered the rest, I admit I was hoping for that; but all I got was the butter dish.

But Barrie cannot give us the reality of birth. Mary plays a "dastard trick" on Simon; she doesn't tell him she has had a baby. She asks him what that funny thing was in the bassinette, and he thinks, "it was some baby you had borrowed." Although Barrie shrinks in his Peter Pan way from the reality of months of pregnancy and the pain of birth, he can allow his lovers to discuss which of them will die first. And he makes Simon speak of how the mother's polarity must be for her child—the one who must be reflected.

SIMON:

> If I did go, I know your first thought would be "The happiness of Harry must not be interfered with for a moment." *You would blot me out for ever, Mary Rose,* rather than he should lose one of his hundred laughs a day [italics mine].

Behind this we surely see the child Barrie who felt "blotted out" by his mother's devotion to her dead son. We also see his attempt to give her a "hundred laughs," so that he could be reflected. This discussion occurs only moments before Mary disappears for twenty-five years.

The strangest aspect of the final relationship between Harry and his mother (he never calls her mother) is that the love play with the tuft of hair is transferred to him:

HARRY:

    I like your hair.

MARY ROSE:

    Pretty hair.

HARRY:

    Do you mind the tuft that used to stand up at the back of—of Simon's head?

MARY ROSE:

    (*Merrily.*) Naughty tuft.

HARRY:

    I have one like that.

MARY ROSE:

    (*Smoothing it down.*) Oh dear, oh dear, what a naughty tuft.

It is at this moment he tells her his name is Harry. He has taken the father's place. He adds, "But you don't know what Harry I am." He goes on trying to instruct his mother on how she can be freed as a ghost. He wants to get her to that "Glory place." Mary can go to heaven because she has found her baby at last, even though she never recognizes him as such. She even suspects him at one point of having stolen her baby, which, in a sense, he has since the child Harry has been absorbed into the adult.

However, the end, or the solution, is magical and manic. But what is the religious significance of Mary's departure? When she is carried away on the Island, it seems to be by a horrible force: "in a fury as of storm and whistling winds that might seem an unholy organ." It seems like a hostile male force, "raking the bushes". Perhaps it is a spirit like Heathcliff. The loudness of the sounds is "horrible."

But there is opposition: "They are not without an opponent. Struggling through them, and also calling her name, is to be heard music of an unearthly sweetness that is seeking perhaps to beat them back and put a girdle of safety round her." Later, there are references to the good and bad days. But the call at the end has "now no unholy sound." Indeed, "a prayer has been answered."

I find myself baffled by these good and bad forces, and I cannot accept Goitein's explanation that the father wants her for himself. I believe the play is a gesture at the completion of mourning, so that the burden of the ghost of the dead mother can be released. The development can be seen as analogous to the resolution of a destructive dynamic (hate) by the power of love, as in Mahler's later works.

Is it the powers of evil (like Macbeth's witches which are bubbles of the earth) that have taken Mary away? And what has happened at the end, to release her only to the powers of love?

Harry has penetrated to the womblike room in the house and has used his knife to find the ghost of his mother. She sits on his lap, like a child, to be instructed in the secret of her haunted and everquesting state. Can he tell her what only the dead know? Actually, she exits having seemingly learned nothing of the reality of her predicament—that is, she seeks what time has changed out of all recognition and what can never be refound. All that can be accepted is the reality of her son as an adult; but she doesn't come to terms with that either, and so the end is a magical piece of manic denial.

Yet, the ending still leaves me baffled as to what its meaning might be, except that it seems no solution to turn the mother, who is the focus of perplexity about 'being', into a little girl child who needs playful elucidation as to the nature of existence—which is what one never got from her.

The strangest thing of all is that the end is virtually an act of sexual intimacy with the mother. This seems to lead in a totally false direction, if one supposes the goal to be a grasp of adult reality and meaningful existence. But men with an intense fixation on their mothers do seem to seek a relationship with woman as a mother, even though this is ultimately sterile and deadly. Behind *Mary Rose* is a cold air of loss, sterility, and death—which the ending does not alleviate.

The strange case of J. M. Barrie and his plays shows that the public can enjoy literary works, recognizing intuitively that, though they make no explicit sense at all, they relate to the deepest problems of 'being-in-existence' and 'going-out-of-existence'. Upon examination, Barrie's works also show that they are bound up with problems of woman and that we cannot explain or understand these works at all unless we draw on the insights of dynamic psychoanalysis. Even so, when we apply these insights, we encounter immense difficulties, as demonstrated by this brief study of Barrie. When we turn to a major writer such as Shakespeare, these difficulties become even more acute.

Notes

1. Another example can be found in Gustav Mahler's *Kindertotenlieder*, especially in "Wen der Mutterlein."
2. The "flimsy thing" has evident analogies with the brother's christening robe. As a child, Barrie lived with the problem that his mother talked to a dead sibling who was not really there.
3. There are, actually, many literary references in *Peter Pan*. Behind the playfulness, we can recognize certain important moments in Shakespeare. At one moment, for example, Wendy is Cordelia, as when she seems to be dead; but she then gives signs of being alive: Peter cries, "She lives!" See also "the way to dusty death" from Macbeth's famous speech about the futility of life and references to *The Tempest* and the sounds and voices on the island.
4. It is a mark of the period that often in plays and novels young lovers show their love by baby talk. See, for example, how the lovers talk in George Bernard Shaw's *Mrs. Warren's Profession*. It is a very English form of emotional ineptitude.
5. The only reference Coveney gives is to Denis MacKeil, *The Story of J. M. B.* (London: Peter Davies, 1941), from which, presumably, he takes the account of Elizabeth Bergner's influence.
6. There is also, of course, the "other world" of *Peter Pan* that is sometimes so threatening.
7. Goitein draws attention also to the phrase used about Mary Rose, "a finger has . . . stopped her growth"; he believes "the Father" has kept her for himself.
8. An analysis of Sylvia Plath's kind of predicament exposes the dangers here of the regression becoming total and final.
9. See also Ted Hughes's "Song for Phallus," in *Crow* (London: Faber and Faber, 1970), 77. In this poem Hughes writes, "What a cruel bastard God is."
10. Goitein writes, "It is not pleasant being a dream-child. Whatever her parents think must perforce be the thoughts of Mary Rose. . . . All the while attention is being focussed on her image; she lives, indeed she shines forth with the hallucinatory vividness; without it she must die" (Goitein 1926, 192-93).
11. See Bachelard, *Poetics of Space*, passim, on the room as a symbol of the mother's body and other such symbolism.

Bibliography

Bachelard, Gaston. *The Poetics of Space*. Boston: Beacon Press, 1969.

Coveney, Peter. *Poor Monkey*. London: Rockliff, 1957.

Goitein, P. Lionel. "A New Approach to Analysis of 'Mary Rose'" *British Journal of Medical Psychology* 6 (1926): 178.

Carl Markgraf (essay date 1989)

SOURCE: Markgraf, Carl. "The Elusive Barrie." In *J. M. Barrie: An Annotated Secondary Bibliography*, pp. vii-xiii. Greensboro: ELT Press, 1989.

[*In the following introduction to his book-length bibliography of Barrie criticism, Markgraf discusses the "elusiveness" of Barrie's success as a writer, stating that his plays continue to attract audiences because they make people "not only think, but feel."*]

The thousands of references in this bibliography to books and articles on Barrie are sufficient evidence of continuing interest in the man and his works. Having surveyed all of them, I suppose that I am the last person who would wish to add more words to those already written about "JMB." However, I would like to offer some thoughts to which my work has led.

First is the surprising fact that in our time Barrie is so little known, despite all his honors: his Baronetcy, his Order of Merit, his four honorary doctorates—St. Andrews, Edinburgh, Oxford, and Cambridge—despite the fact that he was the first British playwright since Shakespeare to be presented by the Comédie Française and the first living British author to be printed in the London *Times*; and despite the enormous financial success and worldwide popularity that Barrie and his works enjoyed during his lifetime. I found to my amazement during work on this project that few of my literary colleagues recognized his name. Of those who did, only a couple could connect him with anything beyond **Peter Pan**.

Naturally enough, **Peter Pan** was my own introduction to Barrie, as is the case with most English-speaking children of this century. But my serious acquaintance with his work came through the theatre. In college after World War II, I performed in Barrie's one-act, *A Well-Remembered Voice*. It was, I felt then, a rather touching story about a young Englishman's ghost who returns, after being killed in the First World War, for a brief chat with his father. Knowing now that it first played in London while the blood-bath in France was still decimating British manhood, I realize that, like most of JMB's work, it was more than it seemed. In those grim days it must have been taken as anything but "touching"; rather, it must have given its first audiences a terrible emotional wrench. My next work with a Barrie play occurred ten or so years later, when I directed his comedy, *Alice Sit-by-the-Fire,* in which he created a charming, but ironic, love-triangle satire on the love-triangle pot-boilers then in vogue. As with *A Well-Remembered Voice,* this play also worked its audience on more than one level. Since then, I have not had any personal theatrical experience with Barrie's work, although over the years, besides reading and teaching some of his work, I have enjoyed seeing a number of JMB's plays performed. My latest contact with the Barrie theatre magic occurred recently, when I watched the television re-broadcast, after twenty-nine years, of the 1960 Mary Martin television musical production of *Peter Pan.* To my surprise, I found it as charming and as affecting as at first view, when I had watched it with my young children. Knowing from my work that the television audience for its first broadcast was the largest in history, I continue to puzzle over JMB's relative obscurity.

Though I have not seen all his plays performed, from what I know of them, a Barrie play—as they say in the theatre—is far from being "actor-proof," or, by extension, "reader-proof." After all, Barrie generally had in mind specific actors for the parts he wrote, and those actors were the best people performing on the stages of London's West End. His reputation for producing "winners" assured him his choice of players. Furthermore, for the same reason, during most of his playwriting career he could count on the kind of financial backing that would support the finest in what we today call "production values": very large casts, specially written musical scores performed by good orchestras, numerous and elaborate—hence expensive—settings, extraordinary lighting, and special scenic effects. The production requirements of his best-known work, *Peter Pan,* give sufficient evidence of the above: the "stars" Nina Boucicault and Gerald Du Maurier in the lead roles of Peter Pan and Captain Hook/Mr. Darling, multiple sets that included The House in the Treetops and The Mermaids' Lagoon, the Tinkerbell lighting effects, and the specially developed "flying" apparatus. Beyond the acting, settings, and technical elements, there was the production factor of Barrie himself. Unlike other playwrights, some of whom went so far as to iron-clad their texts, printing them before the play even went into rehearsal, Barrie was noted for being ever-present during rehearsals—revising, cutting, and supplying new material where needed—and open-mindedly collaborating with his players: he was not above changing his text when experienced actors demonstrated the need for revision. This creative Barrie touch continued to shape his plays all the way up to—and even after—opening night. In the latter regard, he is known to have called together the actors of long-running productions so as to delete the added "gags" and bits of "business" which had, weedlike, sprouted up in his original play.

But setting aside the expensive paraphernalia of star actors, grand sets, and the like which were available to him, in my experience, a Barrie play, given half a chance, "works" on stage, though it does not always appear to work quite so well on the page. Why? Because in his best work JMB did not settle for theatrical clichés, and because he knew his audience and how his stagecraft would affect them right down to the ground.

Many theatrical reviewers cited in these pages have found this somehow very annoying; much of their criticism of his plays as staged sounds rather shrill. Other critics who write about his printed plays—which JMB painstakingly revised into a new form something between a play and a novel—frequently demonstrate that they lack the "theatre of the mind" which Barrie's plays—as plays—demand of the reader. Sometimes drama critics have written that the audiences, and even they, were moved to tears, or laughter, and occasionally even to thought. Even so, these same critics often turned on Barrie to blame him for their own failures to explain How Barrie had managed it. Other critics, in order to praise what was obviously inexplicable success, ascribed it to those undefinable Barrie qualities that became almost mandatory language in their reviews: the plays succeeded because of the Barrie "charm," or the Barrie "whimsy," or "that Barrie magic." The affectionate term "Barrieism" grew up to cover this. Even the French began to use it, and one British playwright was downright chided for his employing "Barrieisms," since he had rudely stepped foot in JMB's private preserve.

Most discussion of Barrie's work struggles with what I have suggested above: his elusiveness. He formed no school, nor did he adhere to one. He was at home in many camps. Some of his plays, such as ***The Will,*** are grimly realistic—for the writing of which he was chided by those who loved his "whimsy." On the other hand, we find William Archer, the eminent drama critic, speaking for the Realists who were riding the rising Ibsen tide; he would not concede that Barrie was a playwright at all, until Barrie produced ***The Admirable Crichton,*** a play which finally met an Ibsenite criterion, being demonstrably critical of the existing social structure.

Similarly, Barrie's work in fiction ranged widely, from the carefully drawn, realistic, local color work of his "Thrums" creations to the fantastic, such as his ghost story, ***Farewell, Miss Julie Logan.*** But being an adherent of no particular school draws the fire of all schools, and Barrie could count on only the reading and playgoing public. Their judgment, as the following pages of comment and partial lists of performances show, has sustained his reputation.

In the course of his enormously successful career as novelist and his later even more successful career as playwright, Barrie amassed a fortune which was described at the time of his death in 1937 as the largest sum, up to that date, that a writer had ever acquired through his work. The enormous, and unexpected, success of **Peter Pan** gave Western civilization a wholly new and powerful myth—an original fairy tale that places Barrie among that group of truly creative geniuses such as Hans Christian Andersen and Lewis Carroll. But it is indicative of Barrie the man that little of his great personal wealth came from **Peter Pan**'s success.

In fact, **Peter Pan,** for most of Barrie's lifetime, did not contribute a penny to his income. Early on he assigned its proceeds, later bequeathing them to continue after his death, to the support of London's Hospital for Sick Children, Great Ormond Street. That expiring copyright has recently been extended into perpetuity, at least within the United Kingdom, by a Special Act of Parliament. Thus Barrie's aid, which helped to provide the Peter Pan Ward and the Peter Pan Canteen, will continue to live on like their namesake.

Barrie's philanthropy is evident not only from such monetary support of worthy causes, but also from the lavish outlay of his talent as a writer. He allowed numerous productions of his "commercial" plays to be performed gratis for charity, it is true. However he also devoted considerable time and effort to writing plays and sketches specifically intended for charitable fundraising. Skimming through a list of his plays, one is struck by the fact that a large number of them have never been heard of since their initial productions—and rightly so. They were written for specific charitable occasions, many of them benefit productions for servicemen's hospitals during the Great War and for similar war-connected charities. Surprising to me in this respect was the fact that some critics cited herein, instead of praising him for his altruism, chided him for squandering his talent in pieces of so little merit. But few, if any, writers of his stature can make claim to the generosity Barrie displayed.

Some of Barrie's many other charitable gifts, most of which he provided anonymously, are described by Cynthia Asquith, his secretary during his last twenty years. One benefice is strikingly similar to his gift to the Sick Children's Hospital—in France he outfitted and maintained a hospital and shelter for French children during the Great War. It is perhaps a signal of this century's cynicism that the childless Barrie's kindnesses have resulted in an ambivalent modern attitude toward his affection for children.

Paedophilia, say some. Once Freud's ideas had become commonplace, the chorus of that notion, if not use of the word itself, began to swell. Numerous articles cited in these pages sing that tune. Predictably, in nearly all writings by psychiatrists or psychologists about Barrie or his works, we find it the burden of their arguments, circularly finding evidence of aberration in his works and thereby explicating his works in terms of abnormality. However, this din seems to be subsiding. A fairly recent psychological essay on Barrie and **Peter Pan** goes so far as to point out that before Freud's ideas were common knowledge, people weren't finding sexual significance in anything and everything. This essay's historical approach notes the realities of Victorian and Edwardian home life, in which Father—often called "the Governor," rather as if he were a prison official—was a distant and awesome figure. In this milieu, an uncle or family friend, for instance, was a welcome father-substitute in children's games.

Such a one was Barrie in the lives of the five Llewelyn Davies children. After the death of their father, Barrie provided financial assistance. On the death of their mother, and at her request, Barrie legally adopted them and offered them all the luxuries of an upper class upbringing, including Eton and Oxford. As the companion of their childhood—and *with* them, Barrie said—he composed his classic about The Boy Who Wouldn't Grow Up, which Andrew Birkin describes so marvelously well in his *J. M. Barrie and the Lost Boys.* The blood-soaked fifty years that followed Barrie's death seem to have disillusioned us into a cynicism that makes it nearly impossible for us to accept genuine kindness such as his at face value.

Given Barrie's personal oddities, the biographical approach, of which the psychoanalytical is one manifestation, is to be expected. As a Scot, he was by nature an oddity to the English public. And in his earliest work he exploited his Scottishness, many would say. Though he did not initiate the "Kailyard School" of Scottish local-color writing, his early work was its most successful example, thereby drawing upon himself the fire of those critics who disliked the "mawkishness" of its sentimentality. But not only was he not English, he also was extremely short and exceedingly reserved—a curious little man who never seemed to smile. Socially retiring, with an impenetrable reticence, his idea of a sociable time was to sit quietly with someone, puffing away at his pipe, while the silence between them lengthened interminably.

Another strand of Barrie's oddity, as comment on him reveals, connects with what is often called an excessive affection for his mother, as shown in the book he devoted to her: **Margaret Ogilvy.**

Had Barrie not written **Margaret Ogilvy,** one wonders how much less ink might have been spilled over his presumed mother-fixation. Surely, mother-figures appear in most of his work, and critics would certainly have discussed all this "mothering" as a recurring subject. But in **Margaret Ogilvy** Barrie unabashedly poured out his devotion to her. Some, mainly Americans, spoke of it as a marvelous filial tribute. But Barrie offended British sensibilities by this book—it was not the sort of thing done in public; it was an act some critics described as coining money from his mother's coffin. The impact of *Margaret Ogilvy* seems not only to have increased the critics' barely-suppressed tone of virtual outrage about mother-figures in his works, but also to have encouraged his biographers to see his mother's influence as another of his oddities. As a playwright, he was certainly odd—once established, he maintained his singularity.

After his earliest playwriting ventures, he followed neither the dramatic mainstream, rapidly turning its course toward the intellectual vogue of realism—as represented by his friends and theatrical co-workers, Shaw and Barker—nor did he stay with the standard pot-boiler techniques of writers who had learned only too well the crafts of the well-made play.

A few of the writers cited in these pages recognized that Barrie was not to be pigeonholed. Some even recognized the novelty he afforded: at long last, here was a playwright who could provide the hoped-for relief from Realism, and in his own, truly unique, way. No slave to Ibsen, nor bound to the grinding out of formula "triangle" plays, Barrie produced burlesques of such playwriting vogues, not only in his popularly successful one-act, *Ibsen's Ghost; or, Toole Up-to-Date,* but also in *A Slice of Life, Alice Sit-by-the-Fire,* and elsewhere. The "elsewhere" included taking on his friend and producing colleague, the great GBS, whom he put on stage in *Punch* as the character, "Superpunch," replete with red beard and Jaeger suit.

Shaw, Barrie, and Harley Granville Barker were collaborators in the theatrical revolution sometimes called the "theatre of the playwright," a movement most clearly exemplified in Granville Barker's famous Court Theatre productions, 1904-1907. These banished the time-honored but pernicious "star" system, substituting for its emphasis on the star performer—which often led to cutting the script to focus on the star—their emphasis on the play as a whole, often relegating erstwhile stars to minor parts. To accomplish this, they maintained directorial control over all production elements. In Britain, therefore, they were primarily responsible for bringing about the present-day means of managing theatrical creativity. Although Barker's energetic activities rightly deserve the major credit for this breakthrough in the British theatre, some have said that Barrie made it all possible.

Barrie continues to live on in his plays. As in his lifetime, however, he cannot be categorized as one sort of playwright or another. His best work—the work that continues to be performed—is neither one thing nor the other. He is not merely a fantasist, as *Peter Pan* would suggest. Nor is he a local-color realist, as *What Every Woman Knows* might indicate. He is not only a "women's libber"; though *The Twelve-Pound Look* would support that notion, *The Adored One* contradicts it. Nor is he just a "problem-play" writer, however much *The Admirable Crichton* is a demonstration of the "Two Englands" idea. He is all of these, hence none of these alone.

Barrie resists all attempts to classify him. His plays make his audiences not only think, but feel. One is tempted, when reading some of the critics who are made uncomfortable by their own emotions at one of his plays—therefore calling the plays sentimental—to remind them of Aristotle's maxim: rational evidence is insufficient to move humankind to action—their emotions must be stirred as well. Barrie's best plays, as do those of all great playwrights, take us out of our world into a world of his creation. We return having been moved, as well as moved to thought, by this experience. I can think of no greater praise for any playwright.

Richard Rotert (essay date 1990)

SOURCE: Rotert, Richard. "The Kiss in a Box." *Children's Literature* 18 (1990): 114-23.

[*In the following essay, Rotert examines the novel version of* Peter Pan, *maintaining that Peter's character is completely defined by "his acknowledged lack of and desire for the mother imago."*]

> Long ago I thought like you that my mother would always keep the window open for me; so I stayed away for moons and moons and moons, and then flew back; but the window was barred, for mother had forgotten all about me, and there was another little boy sleeping in my bed.
>
> —*Peter Pan* (106)

In spite of Peter Pan's history of recurrent amnesia—he says of pirates, "I forget them after I kill them," (161)—the distressing memory of being barred from returning to his mother persists. Considering the preponderance of material purged or repressed in the adolescent mind, it is crucial for an analysis of subsequent behavior to identify which details of a child's life escape general oblivion. What remains in conscious memory is likely the most significant element in that whole period of life, regardless of whether it possessed such importance at the time or gained importance from the influence of later events (Freud, *Character* 193). In the traumatic memory cited above, Peter acknowledges his estrangement from the mother imago, an estrangement that persists without hope of redress. The barred window excludes Peter as participant in the previously abandoned familial context of mother and child in a nursery. Peter's personal story, mirroring that of the text, begins and ends with a flight from and return to the nursery window, the locus of his unresolved dilemma. Peter Pan was—and is—on the outside looking in.

By returning to this locus Peter acknowledges his deprivation and reveals the purpose of his original flight. "'Wendy, I ran away the day I was born. . . . It was because I heard father and mother,' he explained in a low voice, 'talking about what I was to be when I became a man.' He was extraordinarily agitated now. 'I don't ever want to be a man,' he said with passion" (26). Peter's repudiation of "manhood" may also be affirmed in the conspicuous absence of the father from the iterative nursery scene, an absence indicative of the fulfilled wish by a son who sees the father as denying access to the mother. The normal wish to eliminate the father imago is revealed in a wistful encounter with a dead father in a wood, later to be identified as the Island of Neverland. "Children have the strangest adventures without being troubled by them. For instance, they may remember to mention, a week after the event happened, that when they were in the wood they met their dead father and had a game with him" (8). Here the apparent merriment of the children suggests the ultimate resurrection or replacement of the father, or adult, in their own eventual maturity. But Peter Pan permanently rejects fatherliness, including his own, by refusing to enter the prerequisite order of manhood. By denying his manhood, Peter also denies the possibility of a mature, loving relationship with any of the female characters, considering them only surrogates for the desired but inaccessible mother.

Peter's necessary conflict with a specular image of the father is displaced onto Neverland battles with pirates whose captain, James Hook, is associated by parallel episodes to the one identifiable father in the text, Mr. Darling. In a nursery scene with Michael, Mr. Darling invokes parental authority by demanding the consumption of medicine by his son. "Strong man though [Mr. Darling] was, there is no doubt that he had behaved rather foolishly over the medicine. . . . When Michael dodged the spoon in Nana's mouth, he had said reprovingly, 'Be a man, Michael . . . when I was your age I took medicine without a murmur' (16). Later, in Neverland, Captain Hook adds a poisonous concoction to Peter's medicine in an effort to murder the boy: "But what was that? The red in his eye had caught sight of Peter's medicine standing on a ledge within easy reach. Lest he should be taken alive, Hook always carried about his person a dreadful drug . . . which was probably the most virulent poison in existence. Five drops of this he now added to Peter's cup" (122-23). The father-pirate analogy exposes the tyranny of authority, and the pirates become fathers against whom the children, urged on by Peter, avenge prior transgressions.

When Peter returns to the nursery window, he discovers that the affection he seeks from his mother has been directed toward another. The mother as object of desire is inaccessible to him within the sealed enclosure of the nursery which she shares with other children. This quandary is elaborated metaphorically in a *mise-en-abyme* image of Mrs. Darling as a puzzle box of desirable contents.

> Her romantic mind was like the tiny boxes, one within the other, that come from the puzzling East, however many you discover there is always one more; and her sweet mocking mouth had one kiss on it that Wendy could never get, though there it was, perfectly conspicuous in the righthand corner.
>
> He [Mr. Darling] got all of her, except the innermost box and the kiss. He never knew about the box, and in time he gave up trying for the kiss.
>
> [1-2]

Peter, as subject, is constituted by his acknowledged lack of and desire for the mother imago. His enigmatic relation with the feminine, represented by the missing kiss, is underscored by his incomprehension of the word "kiss," as revealed in a dialogue with Wendy.

> She also said she would give him a kiss if he liked, but Peter did not know what she meant, and he held out his hand expectantly.
>
> "Surely you know what a kiss is?" she asked aghast.
>
> "I shall know when you give it to me," he replied stiffly; and not wanting to hurt his feelings she gave him a thimble.
>
> "Now," said he, "shall I give you a kiss?" and she replied with a slight primness, "If you please." She made herself rather cheap by inclining her face toward him, but he dropped an acorn button into her hand.
>
> [25]

Even when Peter and Wendy "play house" on Neverland, the island retreat emblematic of his emotionally remote, isolated identity, he fails to develop a fuller relationship with her. Because of his prior displacement from the nursery, Peter's instinctual desire for the feminine, which would normally shift from the mother to a lover, was arrested at an infantile stage. His fixation[1] on the mother-son dyad allows Peter to imagine Wendy only as a potential mother imago, as he does all the female characters.[2] When Wendy suggests to him that he is indeed father to the island boys, to whom she is surrogate mother, Peter rejects the assertion of his fatherhood not only because to accept it would mean foreclosure upon the desired mother-son relationship, but also because he equates fatherliness with the adult world he repudiates.

Peter Pan's inability to imagine an object-love relationship with the feminine is elaborated during his interrogation by Wendy regarding the island family.

"Peter, what is it?"

"I was just thinking," he said, a little scared. "It is only make-believe, isn't it, that I am their father?"

"Oh yes," Wendy said primly.

"You see," he continued apologetically, "it would make me seem so old to be their real father."

"But they are ours, Peter, yours and mine."

"But not really, Wendy?" he asked anxiously.

"Not if you don't wish it," she replied; and she distinctly heard his sigh of relief. "Peter," she asked, trying to speak firmly, "what are your exact feelings for me?"

"Those of a devoted son, Wendy."

"I thought so," she said, and went and sat by herself at the extreme end of the room.

"You are so queer," he said, frankly puzzled, "and Tiger Lily is just the same. There is something she wants to be to me, but she says it is not my mother."

"No, indeed, it is not," Wendy replied with frightful emphasis. . . .

"Then what is it?"

"It isn't for a lady to tell."

"Oh, very well," Peter said, a little nettled. "Perhaps Tinker Bell will tell me."

. . . . .

He had a sudden idea. "Perhaps Tink wants to be my mother?"

"You silly ass!" cried Tinker Bell in a passion.

[100-01]

Peter's demeanor bespeaks intact narcissism. Even on the island his self-sufficiency differentiates him from the other boys. Though part of the group, he remains aloof from it, to the extent of forbidding anyone even to look like him. As the narrator insists, Peter is a self-contained unit of conceit; and Wendy agrees, noting that the only stories he enjoys are those about himself.

At the center of each of the many family units is a female who draws it together. Mrs. Darling, Wendy, Tinker Bell, and Tiger Lily, the lovely Indian maiden, all exert a centripetal force on their constituent groups; even the pirates have a "feminine" character in Smee. As the adhesive, bonding agent, each is associated with the act of sewing or mending. Tinker Bell, the sarcastic anima figure darting about the text and literally hovering over the stage as a beam of light in the theatrical version of *Peter Pan*, is so named "because she mends pots and kettles" (28), a reference to the traditional occupation of gypsies or tinkers. After putting her children to bed, Mrs. Darling "sat down by the fire to sew" (9). Unity or wholeness is precisely what Peter lacks; he entices Wendy, whose kiss was represented by a thimble, to the Neverland Island family by promising, "you could darn our clothes, and make pockets for us. None of us have any pockets" (31). It would seem that the feminine task is to suture the jagged edges of a youthful world in disarray.

An inclination toward orderliness, as another form of unity, is stated explicitly in a passage that compares Mrs. Darling's arranging of her children's minds to the tidying of a room. This citation also implicates motherhood in the dynamic of the superego (Egan 42).

> Mrs. Darling first heard of Peter when she was tidying up her children's minds. It is the nightly custom of every good mother after her children are asleep to rummage in their minds and put things straight for the next morning, repacking into their proper places the many articles that have wandered during the day. If you could keep awake (but of course you can't) you would see your own mother doing this, and you would find it very interesting to watch her. It is quite like tidying up drawers. You would see her on her knees, I expect, lingering humorously over some of your contents, wondering where on earth you had picked this thing up, making discoveries sweet and not so sweet, pressing this to her cheek as if it were nice as a kitten, and hurriedly stowing that out of sight. When you wake in the morning, the naughtiness and evil passions with which you went to bed have been folded up small and placed at the bottom of your mind; and on the top, beautifully aired, are spread out your prettier thoughts, ready for you to put on.
>
> [5]

The text bequeaths Peter Pan's shadow to feminine ordering and mending when the boy loses it in the Darling nursery. On discovering it, Mrs. Darling "decided to roll the shadow up and put it away carefully in a drawer, until a fitting opportunity came along for telling her husband" (12). But the adult Mrs. Darling forgets Peter; it is her young daughter who must enter his world to cure him. The feminine as unifying agent reunites Peter with his shadow, returning him to wholeness. For Wendy awakens at Peter's sobbing over his lack (the missing shadow, the fragmented self), and she sews his shadow back on for him.

Clearly Mr. Darling would not have been as receptive as his wife to the little boy's intrusion. The text resonates not only with the oedipal conflict, but also with the *puer-senex* conflict, itself integral to the oedipal.[3] The *puer*, representative of the imaginativeness and spontaneity of youth, contends with the *senex*, which exemplifies the rigidity of tradition and adulthood. These mutually exclusive configurations strive to displace rather than incorporate each other. Peter Pan would kill Captain Hook, who would kill Peter Pan.

Adulthood kills children figuratively, since each individual who attains maturity abandons his own youth. Captain Hook plots to kill youth by having children in

Neverland walk the plank of death. The maturation process kills fairies as well, those figures of the imagination and the hallmark of Neverland who succumb to the rational. As Peter explains to Wendy, "when the first baby laughed for the first time, its laugh broke into a thousand pieces, and they all went skipping about, and that was the beginning of fairies. . . . [But] you see children know such a lot now they soon don't believe in fairies, and every time a child says, 'I don't believe in fairies,' there is a fairy somewhere that falls down dead" (26-27). But Peter, the standard-bearer of youth, counters this process with a somatic response to his neurotic compulsion against the adult enemy: "He was so full of wrath against grown-ups, who, as usual, were spoiling everything, that as soon as he got inside his tree he breathed intentionally quick short breaths at the rate of about five to a second. He did this because there is a saying in the Neverland that, every time you breathe, a grown-up dies; and Peter was killing them off vindictively as fast as possible" (107). And Peter himself culls his troops on the basis of advancing age, the fatal flaw. "The boys on the island vary, of course, in numbers, according as they get killed and so on; and when they seem to be growing up, which is against the rules, Peter thins them out" (48).

This conflict culminates in the battle between Peter Pan, captain of the children, and James Hook, captain of the grown-up pirates. Peter comes face to face with him and with his own "grown-up" potential on Marooners' Rock: "Hook rose to the rock to breathe, and at the same moment Peter scaled it on the opposite side. The rock was slippery as a ball, and they had to crawl rather than climb. Neither knew that the other was coming. Each feeling for a grip met the other's arm: in surprise they raised their heads; their faces were almost touching; so they met" (87). In this specular projection Peter sees his despised manhood, which he feels he must eliminate. But also juxtaposed are a physically mutilated Captain Hook (Peter having previously severed his hand) and a psychically fragmented Peter. To complete an oedipal scenario of castration in this scene of recognition, Captain Hook actually bites Peter Pan. Some time later Peter vicariously experiences adulthood by figuratively becoming Hook as captain of the captured pirate ship, with the island boys as crew.

> Some of them wanted it to be an honest ship and others were in favour of keeping it a pirate; but the captain treated them as dogs, and they dared not express their wishes to him even in a round robin. Instant obedience was the only safe thing. . . . The general feeling was that Peter was honest just now to lull Wendy's suspicions, but that there might be a change when the new suit was ready, which, against her will, she was making for him out of some of Hook's wickedest garments. It was afterward whispered among them that on the first night he wore this suit he sat long in the cabin with Hook's cigar-holder in his mouth and one hand clenched, all but the forefinger, which he bent and held threateningly aloft like a hook.
>
> [148]

Ultimately the boys return to the Darling household, where they abandon their youthful Neverland identities to become adults, although Peter will again refuse the invitation. The children's displacement of Hook's entire group on the pirate ship marks their ascension to the order of adulthood. The feminine remains integral to each group: Wendy to the boys and Smee, whom Hook observed "hemming placidly" on a sewing machine before the battle, to the pirates.

The mutually exclusive concepts of youth and adulthood are isolated and defined in the Pan-Hook conflict and elaborated by the leitmotiv of the exclusionary circle. Peter challenges the lions "when he drew a circle round him on the ground with an arrow and defied them to cross it" (75); later Hook with "his iron claw made a circle of dead water round him, from which they [the boys] fled like affrighted fishes" (87). The interchangeable "arrow" and "claw" designate the perimeters of identity within which none may intrude without forfeiture of self. The climactic combat joins the enemies in a ring where only one can survive. "Proud and insolent youth" challenges the "dark and sinister man."

> I think all [pirates] were gone when a group of savage boys surrounded Hook, who seemed to have a charmed life, as he kept them at bay in that circle of fire. They had done with his dogs, but this man alone seemed a match for them all. . . .
>
> "Put up your swords, boys," cried the newcomer, "this man is mine."
>
> Thus suddenly Hook found himself face to face with Peter. The others drew back and formed a ring round them.
>
> For long the two enemies looked at one another; Hook shuddering slightly, and Peter with the strange smile upon his face.
>
> "So, Pan," said Hook at last, "this is all your doing."
>
> "Ay, James Hook," came the stern answer, "it is all my doing."
>
> [143]

The man-image was indeed Peter's, and its "murder" was Peter's doing when, on the day of his birth, his flight denied the eventuality of his own manhood. The threat of Hook is eliminated, lost for all time to the belly of a crocodile whose belly ticks. And Peter, the eternal *puer*, survives in timeless youth.

As the rest of the children approach the nursery window, the father once more assumes an exclusionary role: Mr. Darling instructs his wife to shut the window of the nursery (152). But the children are now liberated from the tyranny of adulthood, for they have resigned themselves to their own maturation and incorporated the very confidence which previously had intimidated them. Michael says, "'Let me see father, . . .' and he took a good look. 'He is not so big as the pirate I killed.'" (154).

Peter Pan retains his youth and continues to haunt the imagination of the young, who have intuitive knowledge of him. But in their rational advance to adulthood, the Darling children will forget him, just as their parents have: "At first Mrs. Darling did not know, but after thinking back into her childhood she just remembered a Peter Pan who was said to live with the fairies. . . . She had believed in him at the time, but now that she was married and full of sense she quite doubted whether there was any such person" (7). Bowing to the dictates of generational cycles the characters successively replace one another. Only Peter's youthful nature remains constant, surfacing repeatedly from the unconscious as the return of the repressed. Eventually the mature Wendy, like Mrs. Darling before her, acknowledges the repressed youthfulness her adulthood would conceal. "'Hullo, Peter,' she replied faintly, squeezing herself as small as possible. Something inside her was crying 'Woman, woman, let go of me'" (166). Peter Pan's return reminds Wendy of her childhood and of the repressed, figuratively dead child within her.

Because of his unfulfilled wish for reciprocity with the mother, Peter is bound to sterile and iterative behavior. During one more of his many returns to the Darling nursery, a little girl there wakens to the sounds of someone sobbing. It is Peter. She asks, "Boy, why are you crying?" (167). This is the question asked verbatim years ago by her mother, of a little boy who had lost his shadow. This time it is Jane, Wendy's daughter, who speaks; for Wendy, with husband and family, has realized her "favorite story" of "Cinderella."

"Hullo," he said.

"Hullo," said Jane.

"My name is Peter Pan," he told her.

"Yes, I know."

"I came back for my mother," he explained, "to take her to Neverland."

"Yes, I know," Jane said, "I been [sic] waiting for you."

[167]

The "*mise-en-abyme,*" box-within-a-box enigma of inaccessibility is replicated by female progeny. Jane's place is taken by her daughter Margaret, and "when Margaret grows up she will have a daughter, who is to be Peter's mother in turn; and thus it will go on" (168). Peter's yearning for the mother imago will never end. When Mrs. Darling finds the returned children—

"George, George," she cried when she could speak; and Mr. Darling woke to share her bliss, and Nana came rushing in. There could not have been a lovelier sight; but there was none to see it except a strange boy who was staring in at the window. He had ecstasies innumerable that other children can never know; but he was looking through the window at the one joy from which he must be for ever barred.

[156]

Notes

1. In volume 3 of his *Collected Papers,* Sigmund Freud writes: "Fixation can be described in this way. One instinctual component fails to accompany the rest along the anticipated normal paths of development, and, in consequence . . . it is left behind at a more infantile state."

2. The following dialogue between Tiger Lily, the Indian maiden who speaks in overtly sexual terms, and Peter Pan appears in the 1903-04 manuscript, in scene 3:

TIGER LILY:

If Peter paleface chase Tiger Lily, she no run very fast. She tumble in a heap, what then?

. . . . .

PETER PAN:

Are you wanting to be my mother, Tiger Lily?

3. See Jacqueline Rose for additional applications of Freudian principles to *Peter Pan.*

Works Cited

Barrie, J. M. *Peter Pan.* New York: Bantam, 1985.

———. Manuscript dated 1903-04 of Peter Pan, cited with permission of the Manuscript Department of the Lilly Library, Indiana University, at Bloomington, Indiana.

Egan, Michael. "The Neverland of Id: Barrie, *Peter Pan,* and Freud." *Children's Literature,* 10 (1982), 37-55.

Freud, Sigmund. *Character and Culture.* New York: Macmillan, 1963.

———. *Collected Papers.* London: Hogarth, 1925. Vol. 3, 453.

Rose, Jacqueline. *The Case of Peter Pan or the Impossibility of Children's Fiction.* London: Macmillan, 1984.

Sarah Gilead (essay date March 1991)

SOURCE: Gilead, Sarah. "Magic Abjured: Closure in Children's Fantasy Fiction." *PMLA* 106, no. 2 (March 1991): 277-93.

[*In the following excerpt, Gilead analyzes the flight to fantasy and "return-to-reality" structure inherent in a number of popular children's works, including* Peter Pan.]

Children's literature, like any literature, bears examining from the viewpoint of adult readers. Even its child-directed projects reflect the adult writer's intentions and satisfy adult readers' notions about children's tastes and needs, as well as fulfilling the needs of the adult societies to which the children belong. In addition, the works are shaped by conscious or unconscious goals that diverge from the conventional (one might say official) child-directed ones. Unless otherwise specified, therefore, the term *reader* in this essay refers to the adult reader.

As U. C. Knoepflmacher has observed, the socializing tendency in children's literature consorts with its appeal to adults' "regressive yearnings." Works of fantasy in particular

> can be said to hover between the states of perception that William Blake had labeled innocence and experience. From the vantage point of experience, an adult imagination re-creates an earlier childhood self in order to steer it towards the reality principle. From the vantage point of innocence . . . that childhood agent may resist the imposition of adult values. . . .
>
> ("Balancing" 497)

In a particular work, the differing perspectives may be manifest in a dramatic clash between characters, in the protagonist's internal conflict, in patterns of imagery or symbol, or in narrative structure. A return-to-reality closure tends to concentrate these dramatic, psychological, or figurative expressions of the work's opposing purposes and themes.[1]

Such a device recurs in many classic works of children's fantasy fiction: the adventurers return home, the dreamer awakens, or the magical beings depart. Often the ending completes a frame around the fantasy, reestablishing the fictional reality of the opening. Despite its commonness, indeed its seeming naturalness, the pattern is surprisingly varied in dramatic mode and in meaning. So familiar is the return-to-reality closing, embedded as it is in literary tradition and convention, that the reader's interpretive query is disarmed by the satisfaction of formal expectations.[2] Though apparently paralleling the initial frame segment, the return may in fact undo the narrative work of the opening: the first segment justifies as well as generates the ensuing fantasy or dream; the conclusion may question that justification. The simple aesthetics of parallel or circular narrative framing may function for obvious interpretations but falter on closer scrutiny. The familiarity and self-evident validity of both process (return) and ontological locus (reality) reassure the reader. At the same time, the return almost inevitably requires a reinterpretation (even a radical one) of the fantasy and may embody a metaliterary comment on the work's cogency or purpose.[3]

While officially resolving and fixing meanings (offering, in particular, the "correct" interpretation of what precedes), the return seems in fact to pose many more questions than it settles. It may legitimize the fantasy narrative as a necessary lapse from structured reality, a lapse that paradoxically supports reality. But often such a reading noticeably simplifies the fantasy's rich and multiple meanings (the misprision tending to give itself away by a patronizing or sentimental tone). From the vantage point of the return, is the fantasy a socializing, ego-forming expression of anxieties, fears, or grievances? or is it a stimulus to subversive desires or cognitions and hence a threat to socialization? Does the fantasy plot yield knowledge, consolation, or moral significance and thus fit the concept of children's literature as comforting and educative? or does the return assert such purposes only to imply more dubious ones? Does the return neutralize the social criticism implicit in the fantasy? Does the frame, as a "safe" container, enable the fantasy to challenge the norms of reality? or does it, in swerving from such criticism, paradoxically reveal an even more profound disaffection with reality? Does the return imply faith that a coherent and mature self can abjure the crutch of escapist fantasy? Indeed, the return may be viewed as resolving a narrative rivalry between realism and fantasy and thus as analogous to a self that has worked out internal conflicts. But what if the return instigates this rivalry even as it appears to offer resolution? Does the framed narrative imply a self that is fragmented into dream self and waking self? or into child and adult? Perhaps the overall narrative, like the self, acquiesces to the ideologies that fix its patterns and meanings but, at the very point of acquiescence, registers discomfort with such constraints. Indeed, the strange blending of acquiescence and resistance may account for the dramatic power of the return, at once a positivist assertion of fantasy's usefulness, of fantasy as reality's tool, and a demonstration of narrative's dependence on nonreality, since storytelling energy lapses when reality returns.

The works of children's fantasy literature that feature the return-to-reality closural frame can be classified into three basic types. In the first, the return completes a history of psychic growth and interprets the fantasy narrative as a salutary exposure of forbidden wishes and emotions. The exposure neutralizes antisocial impulses. Obsessive inquiry, resentment, anger, or anxiety is symbolically enacted in the fantasy and thus reduced to an acceptable level, so that the formerly fragile or threatened ego returns as a more fully formed social entity. Examples of this type include *The Wizard of Oz*, by L. Frank Baum, and two picture books by Maurice Sendak.[4]

The second type features a return that rejects or denies the fantasy by misreading it sentimentally and ignoring its subversive force. This return simulates the closural effects of the first type but disrupts rather than smoothly concludes a linear socialization plot. Implied is a conflicted and unsuccessful straining toward such a plot. Examples are Lewis Carroll's *Alice* books and Edith Nesbit's *Enchanted Castle*.

In the third type, the return neither normalizes fantasy as socializing therapy for the protagonist (and implicitly for the child reader) nor rejects fantasy as fostering a neurotic avoidance of social and psychic realities. The return turns against fantasy but, unlike the second type, acts in a tragic mode that reveals, without an assuring sense of mediation, both the seductive force and the dangerous potentiality of fantasy. Examples of the third type are J. M. Barrie's **Peter Pan** (the prose-narrative version) and P. L. Travers's *Mary Poppins*.[5] . . .

The Return as Tragic Ambiguity

The third type of children's fantasy narrative is perhaps the most problematic. In the first type of closural return we considered, fantasy's energies are appropriated for socializing purposes and are thus defined as controllable and usable. In the second type, fantasy is misread through the interpretive screen of sentimental comedy. But the tragic mode of return is dominated by a sense of loss unmitigated by a playful or softened tone. Indeed, the meaning of the return remains indeterminate. Ironically, such indeterminacy leaves the value of fantasy intrinsic, independent of other frames of reference. Missing is the closural translation of fantasy or magic into some readable, culturally encoded set of religious, moral, or psychological meanings.

Throughout J. M. Barrie's prose version of **Peter Pan**, the titular hero is an emissary from the fantasy world (Neverland) and thus the children's and reader's guide in a symbolic flight from reality. Yet Peter is magnetized by that reality, to which he constantly returns. Forever young, he embodies the adult obsession with time and death. Peter is at once the idealized child and the regressive, impotent adult who is compelled to kidnap the very concept of childhood to alleviate the intolerable burden of adult existence. Free of mortality, sexuality, and social responsibility, Peter is imprisoned by his inability to grow up. Condemned to repeat the same story of denial with each generation and insatiably hungry for new stories, Peter exemplifies the unacknowledged power of children's literature over adults.[6]

In the initial framing segment, the narrator locates the Island of Neverland in a child's mind. Like the derivative figure Mary Poppins, discussed below, Peter represents the child's escapist imagination—more properly, the adult's romantic view of childhood as the liberated imagination itself. Peter also reveals the adult's fearful or even guilt-laden desire for the idealized imagination of the child. Mrs. Darling dreams "that the Neverland had come too near and that a strange boy had broken through from it. . . . [S]he thought she had seen him before in the faces of many women who have no children" (9). What escapes repression here is the adult desire not only for children but for childhood. Peter, then, embodies both repressed adult wishes and the absence or loss of childhood, the lack that breeds regressive desire. That desire, while exposed and partly satisfied in fantasy writing, requires the assuring frame structure of children's literature, with the genre's nominal but official child audience and purposes. But here the initial frame invokes only to repudiate the dream of eternal childhood and thus educates the adult reader in the elusive ways of desire that perpetuate lack even as they promise to assuage it. In keeping with the familiar Romantic model, only death—literal or metaphoric—makes Barrie's child eternal; only after childhood ends can the adult reconstitute it as the object of desire, so that the concept originates in loss. The return to childhood through fantasy narrative inevitably traces the route toward childhood's end: the way back turns into the way forward once again. With inevitable logic, then, the close must mirror the beginning. Escape into an idealized past cannot, as in the works examined above, fuel even an illusory progress toward adult consciousness but must, rather, collapse into cyclicality.[7]

Thus, Peter is death itself as well as the desire for eternal childhood. Death is the strategy of refusal in the self's war against biological, generational processes. Through a familiar slippage of psychic signifiers, the fear of death becomes a death wish. Peter is the product of a guilt-ridden, self-consciously sentimental swerve from adult fears of sexuality and death. We remember that in Mr. Darling's economy children are threats: they cost too much. In fact, they cost one's own life. The existence of the next generation guarantees the expendability of the present. In Mr. Darling the adult's fear of mortality is expressed as thinly concealed hostility toward and envy of the child. For the child, adults are threatening examples of aging and mortality. Peter's strategy is to short-circuit those species-serving systems that collaborate with nature's indifference toward the individual: socialization, marriage, the family (at one point, Peter rejects three importunate females: Tinker Bell, Tiger Lily, and Wendy [100]). But that means taking the shorter route to the same end and enduring constant hauntings by the returned repressed, nicely imaged in Peter's haunting of the nurseries he has escaped. His very presence turns Wendy into a little mother, linking her to the adult future he abhors and fears (24, 31, 67).[8]

Not surprisingly, **Peter Pan** is a morbid book, rich in themes of guilt, revenge, obsession, and murder. The adult's regressive desires produce the idealized fantasy figure of the child, but the fantasy reveals itself to be a self-defeating and paradox-ridden strategy against the fear of death. Peter's charm, his immortality, his flight, his realm—all are death-ridden. The true paradox of the "never" in Neverland is in its double meaning of stark denial—on the one hand, the refusal of the self to conceive of its own end and, on the other, the absolute reality of death. When Peter first appears, he is described as "lovely" but "clad in skeleton leaves and the juices that ooze out of trees" (10). Both boy eternal and rotting corpse, he arrives like a dream of immortality come true but also like a plague deadly to children—like aging and death, he empties the nursery. As he kidnaps the Darling children in retaliation for their father's childish bullying, he fulfills both the child's revengeful wishes to punish powerful parents (like the other "lost boys," he is a victim of and an escapee from adult reality in general and from parental neglect in particular) and the parents' unconscious wishes to rid themselves of children, evidence of their own aging and mortality. As in the Romantic paradox discussed above, the real child must give way to the symbolic substitute. Like the author of children's literature, Peter kidnaps the child to escape the nursery, gravity, and other limitations and burdens of ordinary reality; but he takes us to a world infused with morbid reminders of that reality.[9]

Neverland is a realm of death under the cover story of boyish fun and adventure. The boys live underground, each in a house whose entrance fits him exactly, like a coffin. Peter, like death, changes the boys to fit the entrances. When they shoot Wendy, they build a tiny house around her, like a tomb. The ticking crocodile is death itself (when the clock runs down, the prey is caught) or it is ourselves, doomed to the brief lifespans measured by our ticking hearts. Neverland is a stew of murderous rivalry or revenge (Tink against Wendy, Hook against Peter). Hook is a comic-melancholy and murderously resentful adult obsessed with Peter, the pristine image of childhood and the past: envied, desired, and hated. An obvious analogue for Mr. Darling (in productions of the play, the roles were often performed by the same actor), Hook is the time-burdened adult living with the painful consciousness of mortality and with a romantic sense of adulthood as the loss of perceptual and emotional force. For Hook, Peter and the ticking crocodile are doubles, each a living symbol of relentless temporality (135). In a metatextual sense, Peter exemplifies a vitiated or defunct psychocultural strategy against the fear of death. Hook is bemused by the image of the innocent and inviolable child, but his anxiety and anger are thereby deepened, not assuaged. In symmetrical fashion Peter hates Hook, the adult who seems to the child to embody the facts of generation, time, and mortality. Not surprisingly, Pan slays Hook only to become him (148).

Though the Darling children and the Lost Boys are "found" again by the powerful social realities and narrative conventions that appear to triumph at the end, the return does not bring stability but, rather, generates further losses and returns. The children lose their powers of flight, their belief in the possibility of escape through fantasy, and also, perhaps, their belief in the inviolability of childhood itself. Peter, forgetting the past, is entrapped in an eternal present without emotional or cognitive meaning. Those who have returned to reality are "grown up and done for." Mrs. Darling is "now dead and forgotten," and Nana, we are told bluntly, "died of old age" (162). We glimpse the generations come and go (Wendy's, Jane's, Margaret's); and while Peter, as the resistant impulse, accompanies them, his unchanging presence only emphasizes and seems somehow to hasten the speed of generational process. And, of course, he himself only exists by means of—indeed, has come to epitomize—the narrative genre whose putative agenda he dismantles.[10]

Like Peter, Mary Poppins is associated with flight and nature (the wind, animals, heavenly bodies). Her "pop-ins" appear spontaneous, like the wind that blows her into and out of the narrative. Mary is a semidivine "Cousin" of the zoo animals; for the children who accompany her to the transformed, moonlit, "upside-down" zoo, she is a teacher of truths transcending adult conceptual narrowness and selfishness (134). Defying gravity, she seems also to defy adult "gravity" (see especially chapter 3, "Laughing Gas," where comic fantasy temporarily defeats anxieties concerning loss and death). But Mary is also a governess, a socializing agent and at times even a repressor who denies magic or uses it for punishment of moral lapses. For example, at the end of chapter 3, the scene of the hilarious, floating tea, she sniffily denies that the incident took place. In chapter 6 she whisks the children off to hobnob with animals, only later to use this fantasy journey, in the form of a nightmare, to punish one of her charges (80-81). Thus, Mary embodies the ambivalence of fantasy writing for children, now escapist and frankly unsocial (or even antisocial), now framed by the justifying context of moral didacticism.

In the overall narrative's closural frame, the fictional world is restored to its original, prefantasy condition. When Mary departs, magic, fantasy, and nature myths depart too. But the child protagonists experience this departure as loss, not as restoration. Further, the meaning of the departed fantasy is not established: no particular lessons have been learned, self-concepts are not strengthened, religious truths vaguely hinted at remain unrevealed. The closure points to an absolute barrier between fantasy and reality, between childhood and adulthood; Mary's presence obscures that barrier, but her absence makes it manifest. Oddly, though, when her magic disappears, the very sense of its loss suggests that magic is an intrinsic, though ambiguous, good—not justified by, and apparently not needing to be justified by, any other frame of reference.

Like Peter Pan, Mary and her magic come into the initial reality frame to fill a parental gap and, more broadly, to compensate for the multiple inadequacies of adult reality. In the initial frame, adult activities are presented as trivial, the adults as obtuse and selfish, remote from the children and indifferent to their needs; and these qualities are exacerbated in the closing frame (see especially pages 156-57, where Michael now fully comprehends his mother's selfishness). The closural loss of magic and of its consolations thus sharpens the critique of adults and of their version of reality and makes the loss of the fantasy world tragic. Reality is not rectified; fantasy and reality are not aligned.

The series of episodes and interpolated tales that make up the narrative mostly follow the reality-fantasy-reality pattern of the whole. Fantasy never becomes fully present; it is temporary, risky, and unstable in duration and meaning (ironically, adult reality is even more unstable and much less satisfying and comprehensible). For example, chapter 2, "The Day Out," repeats the general frame narrative in structure but opposes it in meaning. Mary's day off is indeed "off" the plane of reality. Initially described in realistic terms, it soon enters the "framed" world of fantasy—here, almost literally: she and her sidewalk-artist friend, Bert, "enter" a picture he has painted, a pastoral landscape where they enjoy an idyllic tea. Returning to reality, Mary tells the children that she has been in a fairyland all her own, that is, one derived from her wishes. In the demarcated spaces of art, fantasy offers temporary gratifications for reality's omissions (the "real" tea was foiled by Mary's and Bert's lack of money). In confusing contrast, chapter 9, "John and Barbara's Story," shows infants outgrowing their ability to understand the speech of natural objects and creatures. In chapter 2 Mary seems to offer fantasy as a compensatory resource. In chapter 9 she presides over the "natural" loss of the "magical" delights of perceptual and cognitive unity with nature. Does her leaving reflect childhood's inevitable end? If so, why have her equivocal lessons in fantasy reinforced the children's sense of reality's inadequacy? As reality even more clearly resumes its initial shape of barren and joyless necessity, the children are left with a framed portrait of Mary and her hint of return ("au revoir"). That is, they hope that once again ordinary reality may be reduced to a mere frame around a more exciting and variable realm. Almost cruelly, Mary has forced them back to reality without reconciling them to it; she has, if anything, spoiled them for it by her tantalizing range of modes of escape and by her refusal or inability to define the uses of enchantment.[11]

In one sense, the return-to-reality closure asserts the conventional, ideologically mandated meanings and indeed relations between the concept pairs "child" and "adult," "fantasy" (or "dream") and "reality." But to do so, it must counter a potential obscuring of such meanings and relations: the initial narrative movement from fictional reality to fantasy raises the possibility of regressive slippage from adulthood to an idealized realm of childhood. But if the ending abjures such childhood, relegating it to a mere stage in the progress toward adult selfhood, the ending also confesses the attraction of childhood for adults. The return seems to relegate to the child (as subject and reader) the desire for fantasy, but at the same time it expropriates these desires, as well as the child as subject, for possibly conflicting adult projects, such as socialization and escape. Well or thinly concealed is the fact of fantasy as object of adult desires and as response to adult anxieties and wishes. The closural narrator may be an idealized adult purveyor of controlled fantasy—that is, fantasy as therapeutic or monitory for the nominal child audience or as merely playful entertainment. The same closural narrator may also be an image of the adult consumer of fantasy, with the child as a projection of the regressive adult.

M. M. Bakhtin's observation about novelistic closure may be applicable here. In postmythic literature, the "absence of internal conclusiveness and exhaustiveness creates a sharp increase in demands for an external and formal completedness and exhaustiveness, especially in regard to the plot-line" (31). The official discursive thrust of children's literature in particular is toward linear plotting leading to a conventionally closed ending. Socialization plots tend to present life-process transitions as manageable; the traditional role of adults and of adult institutions vis-à-vis the child is virtually defined as the regulation of the transitional state of childhood. Writing for children thus permits the adult to recuperate the familiar—the authorized quality of folk, mythic, and ritualistic discourse—and to link slippery modern culture to the lost wholeness and stability of an imagined (and largely imaginary) past. The self-doubt and anxiety behind such recuperative desire are particularly evident in the most problematic of the narrative transitions, the ending: the point at which we are invited to relax our attentiveness and interpretive energy and at which, for that very reason, the greatest demands are placed on our understanding.

The return seems to offer the reassuring concept of reality as that which is familiar and ordinary, that which loyally awaits our return even though we turn from it. But such a cozy view points to reality's idealized, simplified, fictional status. There is of course a never eliminable gap between extra-literary reality and the fictional reality of the realistic frame segments. The separate fictional realms of the frame and the central narrative may suggest a fixed hierarchy of realities, with extra-literary reality supreme, the fantasy narrative at the lowest level of reality, and the fictional reality of the frame segments in the middle and possibly mediating between the other two. But this hierarchy is unstable: the fantasy may satirize the reality claims of ordinary modes of perception and experience, and the frame reality may be more consoling and escapist than the preceding fantasy narrative. The return frame may establish the hierarchy of realities by classifying the foregoing fantasy as dangerously—or safely—remote from extraliterary reality; or it may, ironically, reveal the equal or even deeper fictionality of both literary and extraliterary versions of reality. Thus, instead of restoring or inverting conventional orders of significance, the return may function as the point at which the text most dramatically turns on itself to reveal its duplicities and discords.

Notes

1. Recognizing the double appeal that children's literature has for the adult reader, U. C. Knoepflmacher suggests that the superimposition of outward frames or bridges may reflect the author's conflicts of intention and selfhood ("Balancing" 500).

   Humphrey Carpenter (11, 13) and Peter Coveney (31) characterize children's literature as an escapist exercise for adult authors. Christopher Clausen offers as a taxonomic criterion for the genre the thematics of home, often in the form of a closural return, and sees the homecoming as the fulfillment of an escapist impulse, a retreat to safe domesticity. So considered, is the return an escape from fantasy rather than from reality? I take up this question in discussing the *Alice* books later in this essay. Eric S. Rabkin defines literary fantasy as "the continuing diametric reversal of the ground rules within a narrative world" (73). Fantastic reversal is both escape from and constant reminder of the world diametrically escaped (48), presumably the extratextual world as well as the narrative locus. He does not discuss the frame-narrative structure but does consider the use of a nominal child audience for adult fantasy projects (96, 97).

   Tzvetan Todorov derives the literary fantastic from characters' and readers' "uncertainty" regarding the laws that govern reality (25). Presumably, a closural return to reality would eliminate the fantasy element by resolving the uncertainty. Todorov is in fact unclear in discussing closure as a generic determinant. At one point he seems to define the fantastic as an "evanescent genre" whose attributes may well dissipate at closure—for example, at an awakening that dispels the fantasy (42). But, he also argues, by restoring the hero or the reader to reality's rule, the ending retroactively defines the foregoing narrative as the uncanny, not the fantastic (41). Even more problematic is Todorov's narrowly cognitive approach, which leads him to characterize the fantastic as evidence of, and thus somehow party to, premodern repressive discourse; the fantastic becomes anachronistic when replaced by a more liberal discourse, that is, by psychoanalysis (160). Clearly, his limited view of the usefulness of the fantastic seems to stem from the positivist notion that defines symbolic discourse as primitive and sees analytical-rationalist discourse as progressive and superior. Further, Todorov dismisses the capacity of the literary fantastic to question the normatively real and even insists, against massive evidence to the contrary, that the fantastic died with the nineteenth century. For him, the very positing of a dichotomy like language/reality or real/unreal is naive, so that fantasy writing cannot avoid postulating the very reality it attacks (166-68). In contrast, I believe that fantasy writing in general and children's fantasy writing in particular continue to flourish and to generate critical and theoretical responses such as Todorov's precisely because fantasy both collaborates in the ongoing invention of reality and teases us with the possibility of refusal.

2. Most critics of fantasy literature have minimized or misread the significance of the frame device. T. E. Apter believes that works set in a realm separate from "our world" do not qualify as fantasy literature. He does not consider the possibility that the separation of the fantasy narrative from the realistic frame may heighten, not diminish, the effect of the fantasy. Rosemary Jackson is interested in fantasy's subversive thrust and in the dream of fantasy as a doomed escape from sociocultural reality. Jackson observes that fantasy texts often express desire first by manifesting it and then by expelling it (4). Does the return to reality mark such a shift? Following Todorov, she excludes literary works that provoke no true ambiguity of response (144) or that legalize fantasy by a framing device that neutralizes its force. She does not examine how the frame, by providing a safe "cover story," enables fantasy to function transgressively. J. R. R. Tolkien also excludes dream tales from true fantasy literature, because they "cheat" the reader of "imagined wonder" (19).

3. For Jacqueline Rose, the meaning of language in children's literature and the reality of cultural categories such as child and adult are open to question (1). Her study centers on the adult's desire revealed "in the very act of construing the child as object of its speech" (2). She considers the "cover-up" aspect in children's literature, as I do, and emphasizes the way children's literature conceals its instrumentality in repressing adult desire.

   In an essay especially pertinent to the present study, Knoepflmacher discusses the endings in children's books centering on a journey and in adult books featuring child travelers ("Roads Half-Taken"). The closures of such works are inevitably problematic: while the journey provides a gratifying delay in socialization, the closural return "necessarily reactivates questions about goals and directions, about the very teleology of growth" (48). "Endings . . . inevitably compel us to reassess the journey we undertook with our child or childlike agents" (49).

4. In a much cited study of fairy tales, Bruno Bettelheim eloquently asserts the therapeutic power of the genre. Although he dismisses the bulk of children's literature (4), his descriptive-prescriptive view of fairy tales clearly derives in part from a long tradition of writing for children that aims at helping them grow up in the way adults think they should. For Bettelheim, literary fantasy is a legitimate cultural-collective extension of a child's actual fantasizing; but since personal fantasy may be inadequate, the fairy tale may assist in carrying out the psychosocial work of fantasy. He points out that the fairy-tale hero typically returns to reality at the story's end ("a happy reality, but one devoid of magic"); thus the tale teaches the child that "permitting one's fantasy to take hold of oneself for a while is not detrimental, provided one does not remain permanently caught up in it. . . . As we awake refreshed from our dreams, better able to meet the tasks of reality, so the fairy story ends with the hero returning, or being returned, to the real world, much better able to master life" (63).

D. W. Winnicott's concept of transitional objects and phenomena should be mentioned here. An intermediate state between an infant's inability to recognize reality and the child's growing ability to do so is at once illusion and creative play. Eventually, this transitional state is diffused into large cultural fields that are similarly between inner and outer reality: play, dreaming, the arts, drug addiction, fetishism, and criminality (2-6). Equally necessary for the infant's development is first the illusion of an external reality that corresponds to the infant's own capacity to create and then the disillusion of such an idea. Winnicott distinguishes between creative play, which carries on the never completed task of accepting reality, and escapist fantasy, which is regressive and dysfunctional (37). Literary and other forms of creative play are for Winnicott, as for Bettelheim, essentially therapeutic, necessary for discovering the self and for adjusting to reality. In this respect, the closural return of literary fantasy could replay the necessary illusion-disillusion process of the infant's education in the ways of reality. For the adult as reader, the literary fantasy could fuel the ongoing process of reality acceptance; for the adult as teacher, literary fantasy may proffer the reassuring notion that reality can be sufficiently mastered to be passed down, as a cultural endowment, to the next generation, to the child reader. The adult writer-reader could enjoy the transitional phenomenon while disavowing a need for it, defining the need as exclusively the child's.

John H. Timmerman's view of literary fantasy, its assumptions and effects (on adults and children), accords with Bettelheim's view of the fairy tale. Offering a relief from structured reality, fantasy in fact enables the reader to engage the ordinary world with clearer insight and sharper perspective, even with renewed faith.

5. Since this essay is intended to be preliminary and suggestive rather than comprehensive or final and since space is limited, it evades the ticklish difficulties of classifying the frame effects of other major children's fantasy works. Some of these works use frame devices not discussed here and not included in the proposed tripartite taxonomy: for example, the absence of the expected return (as in E. B. White's *Charlotte's Web* or C. S. Lewis's final book of the Narnia series, *The Last Battle*).

6. Carpenter notes that "*Peter Pan* . . . manages . . . both to celebrate imagination, and to give a rather chilling warning of its limitations" (179). Elliott Simon also points out that Never-Never Land (the name of the fantasy locale in the play version) is finally not an antithesis of the adult world but an extension of it (227, 229), implying that the problem of how to link fantasy to reality is in fact not solved.

7. Carpenter, discussing the play *Peter Pan,* notes that there "can be no ending, only a return to the beginning" (180).

8. On the notion of flight from death as producing an obsession with death, see Norman O. Brown, especially 88, 95, 249.

9. Simon discusses the sinister and violent quality of the magic of Never-Never Land and comments on Peter's fascination with death (228). Andrew Birkin's and Janet Dunbar's biographical studies reveal how Barrie's many versions of *Peter Pan* strangely reflect and even more bizarrely anticipate the deaths of children Barrie knew (the deaths, appropriately, are both literal and figurative, with Barrie himself providing the chief example of figurative death). For a traditional psychoanalytical view of Barrie's fantasy locales and figures, see Geduld, especially 53-67.

10. Jacqueline Rose argues that the adventures in *Peter Pan* are contained "by the nursery which is the start and the finishing point of the whole story," so that here, as elsewhere in children's literature, the reality frame contains and neutralizes fantasy

(33). We have seen that the frame may point to other, less reassuring interpretive possibilities, even while seeming to exclude them.

11. A topic for further consideration would be the ways that a particular author experiments with the frame device, either in a series of fantasy works or in separate works. The foregoing discussion of two Sendak picture books offers an abbreviated example of such a study (which, if expanded, should include *Outside, Over There,* the third part of what Sendak himself considered a loose trilogy). The fantasies of Nesbit (noted above) and Travers seem amenable to such a comparative approach, as do Baum's thirteen Oz sequels. Other fantasy serialists might include Mary Norton (the *Borrowers* series) and C. S. Lewis (*The Chronicles of Narnia*). There are of course many individual fantasy works with the frame structure; notable examples include Andersen's "Snow Queen" and George MacDonald's *At the Back of the North Wind,* as well as the contemporary *A Wrinkle in Time* (Madeleine l'Engle) and Chris Van Allsberg's picture books (especially *Jumanji, Ben's Dream,* and *The Wreck of the Zephyr*).

The closural frame of the second Mary Poppins book, *Mary Poppins Comes Back* (1935), is far more consoling than that of the original *Mary Poppins* (1934); similarly, the third book, *Mary Poppins Opens the Door* (1943), where Mary's "gifts" to the children (including the gift of renewed parental warmth) compensate for her departure. *Mary Poppins in the Park* (1952) and *Mary Poppins in Cherry Tree Lane* (1982) dispense with the frame device entirely and generate dramatic interest by intensifying the liminal quality of their incidents.

Works Cited

Apter, T. E. *Fantasy Literature: An Approach to Reality.* Bloomington: Indiana UP, 1982.

Auerbach, Nina. "Alice in Wonderland: A Curious Child." Bloom 31-44.

Bakhtin, M. M. *The Dialogic Imagination: Four Essays by M. M. Bakhtin.* Ed. Michael Holquist. Austin: U of Texas P, 1981.

Barrie, J. M. *Peter Pan.* 1911 [*Peter Pan and Wendy*]. New York: Bantam, 1985.

Baum, L. Frank. *The Wizard of Oz.* 1900. New York: Scholastic, 1958.

Bettelheim, Bruno. *The Uses of Enchantment: The Meaning and Importance of Fairy Tales.* Harmondsworth, Eng.: Penguin, 1978.

Birkin, Andrew. *J. M. Barrie and the Lost Boys: The Love Story That Gave Birth to* Peter Pan. New York: Potter, 1979.

Bloom, Harold, ed. *Lewis Carroll.* New York: Chelsea, 1987.

Briggs, Julia. *A Woman of Passion: The Life of E. Nesbit, 1858-1924.* New York: New Amsterdam, 1987.

Brown, Norman O. *Life against Death: The Psychoanalytic Meaning of History.* London: Sphere, 1959.

Carpenter, Humphrey. *Secret Gardens: A Study of the Golden Age of Children's Literature.* Boston: Houghton, 1985.

Carroll, Lewis. *Alice's Adventures in Wonderland* and *Through the Looking-Glass. The Annotated Alice.* Ed. Martin Gardner. Harmondsworth, Eng.: Penguin, 1960.

———. "The Wasp in the Wig." A "Suppressed" Episode of Through the Looking-Glass and What Alice Found There. Ed. and introd. Martin Gardner. New York: Potter, 1977.

Clausen, Christopher. "Home and Away in Children's Fiction." *Children's Literature* 10 (1982): 141-52.

Cott, Jonathan. *Pipers at the Gates of Dawn: The Wisdom of Children's Literature.* New York: Random, 1981.

Coveney, Peter. *The Image of Childhood. The Individual and Society: A Study of the Theme in English Literature.* Baltimore: Penguin, 1967.

Dunbar, Janet. *J. M. Barrie: The Man and the Image.* Boston: Houghton, 1970.

Empson, William. "*Alice in Wonderland*: The Child as Swain." *Some Versions of Pastoral.* 1935. London: Chatto, 1950. 251-94.

Geduld, Harry M. *Sir James Barrie.* New York: Twayne, 1971.

Gordon, Jan B. "The *Alice* Books and the Metaphors of Victorian Childhood." Bloom 17-30.

Jackson, Rosemary. *Fantasy: The Literature of Subversion.* London: Methuen, 1981.

Knoepflmacher, U. C. "Avenging Alice: Christina Rossetti and Lewis Carroll." *Nineteenth-Century Literature* 41 (1986): 299-328.

———. "The Balancing of Child and Adult: An Approach to Victorian Fantasies for Children." *Nineteenth-Century Fiction* 37 (1983): 497-530.

———. "Of Babylands and Babylons: E. Nesbit and the Reclamation of the Fairy Tale." *Tulsa Studies in Women's Literature* 6 (1987): 299-325.

———. "Roads Half-Taken: Travel, Fantasy, and Growing Up." *Proceedings of the Thirteenth Annual Conference of the Children's Literature Association.* N.p.: ChLA, 1988. 48-59.

Lanes, Selma G. *Down the Rabbit Hole: Adventures and Misadventures in the Realms of Children's Literature.* New York: Atheneum, 1971.

Madden, William A. "Framing the *Alices*." *PMLA* 101 (1986): 362-73.

Nesbit, E. *The Enchanted Castle*. Harmondsworth, Eng.: Puffin, 1956.

Rabkin, Eric S. *The Fantastic in Literature*. Princeton: Princeton UP, 1976.

Rackin, Donald. "Blessed Rage: Lewis Carroll and the Modern Quest for Order." *Lewis Carroll: A Celebration*. Ed. Edward Guiliano. New York: Potter, 1982. 15-25.

———. "Love and Death in Carroll's *Alices*." Bloom 111-27.

Rose, Jacqueline. *The Case of Peter Pan: Or, The Impossibility of Children's Fiction*. London: Macmillan, 1984.

Sendak, Maurice. *In the Night Kitchen*. Harmondsworth, Eng.: Puffin, 1973.

———. *Where the Wild Things Are*. New York: Scholastic, 1963.

Simon, Elliott M. *The Problem Play in British Drama, 1890-1914*. Ed. James Hogg. Salzburg Studies in English Literature: Poetic Drama and Poetic Theory. Salzburg: U of Salzburg P, 1978.

Streatfeild, Noel. *Magic and the Magician: E. Nesbit and Her Children's Books*. London: Schuman, 1958.

Timmerman, John H. *The Fantasy Genre*. Bowling Green: Bowling Green U Popular P, 1983.

Todorov, Tzvetan. *The Fantastic: A Structural Approach to a Literary Genre*. Trans. Richard Howard. Cleveland: P of Case Western Reserve U, 1973.

Tolkien, J. R. R. "On Fairy Stories." *Tree and Leaf*. London: Unum, 1964. 11-70.

Travers, P. L. *Mary Poppins*. 1934. Harmondsworth, Eng.: Puffin, 1961.

Winnicott, D. W. *Playing and Reality*. Harmondsworth, Eng.: Penguin, 1971.

Laura E. Donaldson (essay date 1992)

SOURCE: Donaldson, Laura E. "Of 'Piccaninnies' and Peter Pan: The Problem of Discourse in a Marxist Never-Never Land." In *Decolonizing Feminisms: Race, Gender, and Empire-Building*, pp. 66-87. Chapel Hill: University of North Carolina Press, 1992.

[*In the following essay, Donaldson investigates the role of Tiger Lily in* Peter Pan, *demonstrating how Barrie—by means of conflating Tiger Lily's image with that of the "piccaninnies"—undercuts the feminist challenge to the traditional role of women in the Edwardian world of the story.*]

ON FALSE DICHOTOMIES

Is there no way out except submission to the heart of the colonial community or departure? Yes, still one. . . . Why not knock at the door of the colonized whom he defends and who would surely open their arms to him in gratitude? He has discovered that one of the camps is that of injustice, the other, then, is that of righteousness. Let him take one more step, let him complete his revolt to the full. The colony is not made up only of Europeans! Refusing the colonizers, damned by them: let him adopt the colonized people and be adopted by them; let him become a turncoat.

Albert Memmi, *The Colonizer and the Colonized*

If it wishes to survive as a revolutionary movement, Euro-American feminism must ask the question posed by Albert Memmi: Are there no alternatives to colonialism except presence or absence? According to Memmi, one could intervene in this false dichotomy with a third position: that of "adoption" by the colonized. However, a colonizer who merely sympathizes with the plight of the colonized falls short of this position; the colonizer must also be loved by the colonized.[1] Memmi's insistence on the colonizer's existential, and not just intellectual, participation in the life of the oppressed also captures Gayatri Spivak's meaning when she describes how Anglo-European feminists usually "wander out of our own academic and First-World enclosure": "When we speak for ourselves, we urge with conviction: the personal is also the political. For the rest of the world's women, the sense of whose personal micrology is difficult (though not impossible) for us to acquire, we fall back on a colonialist theory of most efficient information retrieval."[2] Information retrieval can never liberate one from the position of the colonizer because the "Third World" woman still remains the "object" of information and the "First World" feminist the distanced and superior interpreter of that information.

If we look for female members of colonizing groups who have renounced their positions and become adopted by the colonized, the unforgettable image of Daisy Bates (1861-1951), "the Great White Queen of the Never-Never," comes vividly to mind. Bates, who left a journalistic career in England to live in the northern Australian desert wilderness with the Ngalli-a, the Arunta, the Wong-gai-i-Waddi, and the Koogurda, began her life's vocation with an offer in 1899 to investigate exploitation of Aboriginal cultures by white settlers. Douglas Glass's famous photograph of her frames a formidable woman seated on a porch, with an umbrella firmly clasped in one white-gloved hand and a large leather purse clutched in the other, her high-top boots neatly laced, and a crisply starched high-necked collar highlighting the stubborn jut of her jaw. In his foreword to Bates's memoirs, Alan Moorehead muses upon this remarkable photograph: "A glance at the photograph and one feels one knows her pretty well—the eccentric, voyaging, Victorian spinster, pert and indestructible, the missionary figure: Florence Nightingale or perhaps the lady who went off to the court of the King of Siam. She is one's well-loved maiden aunt."[3] If the journeys of Bates's life share some particulars with those of her historical sister, Mrs. Anna Leonowens, then they also share some of the contradictions.

On one level, Daisy Bates seems to exemplify Memmi's portrait of the colonizer who "refuses," for she quickly passed beyond the task of retrieving information about the Aborigines and became an adopted member of their tribe: "They accepted me as a kindred spirit. . . . They even allowed me free access to the sacred places and the sacred ceremonies of the initiations of the men, which their own women must never see under penalty of death."[4] Further, according to Bates, "at the men's hidden corroborees, far from my own people in the heart of the bush, because I showed no quiver of timidity, or of revulsion of feeling, or of levity, because I was thinking with my 'black man's mind,' I have never been a stranger" (*PA* 25). "Thinking black" was Daisy Bates's articulation of identification with the oppressed, and no one could deny that they greatly loved her. After all, what other white person voluntarily lived for years in a fourteen-foot circular tent in extremes of heat, wind, and cold for the sole purpose of ameliorating the disruptions of colonization by tending and comforting its aboriginal victims?

While Bates remained highly skeptical of women's emancipation and the appearance of the New Woman in Britain (once denouncing such women as "Public Nuisances"), she nevertheless became an ardent advocate for Aboriginal women. Kabbarli, or "grandmother," as Bates was called, particularly resisted their exchange as commodified objects and mounted a vigorous campaign to rectify the situation: "There were four Manilamen at Beagle Bay married to native women. By tribal custom the women had all been betrothed in infancy to their rightful tribal husbands. They were therefore merely on hire by their own men to the Asiatics, and, in spite of the church marriage, remained, not only their husband's property, but that of all his brothers, and all of the Manila husband's brothers who paid for the accommodation. It was hard to convince the Bishop and the little abbot of this fact and of the terrible cruelty to the women and girls of such a system" (*PA* 12). Her outrage at the exploitation of these women knew no racial bounds, and she criticized both Anglo and Aboriginal men for perpetuating this oppressive and brutal misogynist network.

However, despite an adoption by the colonized that transgressed virtually every British social more, Bates simultaneously embodied the difficulties of refusal. Memmi persuasively argues in *The Colonizer and the Colonized* that privilege lies at the heart of the colonial relationship. Indeed, he asks, what is colonialism "if not a regime of oppression for the benefit of a few? The entire administrative and political machinery of a colony has no other goal. The human relationships have arisen from the severest exploitation, founded on inequality and contempt, guaranteed by police authoritarianism" (*CC* 62). In her own relationships with Aboriginal peoples, Daisy Bates seemed to jettison the flotsam of colonialism, for her severely nomadic life exhibited few of the qualities that one might describe as "privileged." However, colonial privilege is not solely economic (*CC* xii)—or, for Daisy Bates, related to the refusal of middle-class living arrangements.

As the analysis of Mrs. Anna Leonowens has shown, empires exist through complex relationships of control, and we can disregard no strategy or micrology of power that disseminates them. Paternalism is one such strategy. This "astonishing mental attitude" stretches racism and inequality to its tautest logical extremes: "It is, if you like, a charitable racism—which is not thereby less skillful nor less profitable. . . . Having found this new moral order where he is by definition master and innocent, the colonialist would at last have given himself absolution" (*CC* 760). In spite of her profound concern for the "dying" Aborigines and her protestation of the paternalistic "kindness that killed as surely and as swiftly as cruelty would have done," Daisy Bates acts as what one might call a colonial maternalist because she ensnares the very groups she protects with discourses of control.

Like a mother tending her children, Bates found it impossible "to leave these people, to be deaf to their appeal for human kindliness, and of the hopelessness of any movement except one of help and personal example. So savage and so simple, so much astray and so utterly helpless were they, that somehow they became my responsibility" (*PA* 207). This perception of Aboriginal society as infantile functioned as the basis for the colonialist discourse of the "piccaninny"—one of the most powerful justifications of Anglo-European imperialism and the subject of this chapter. However, it is the memoirs of Mrs. Aeneas Gunn, another great white queen of the Never-Never, that most tellingly expose the disparity between action and speech in the crucible of colonialism. Precisely *because* of their contradictory social positioning, the differences within themselves, the women of colonial Australia illuminate some of the most complex historical and theoretical issues of the imperialist project.

WILL MARXISM EVER GROW UP?; OR, HOW NEVER-NEVER LAND RE-VISIONS REVOLUTION

Marxism is a revolutionary world outlook which must always strive for new discoveries, which completely despises rigidity in once-valid theses, and whose living

> force is best preserved in the intellectual clash of self-criticism and the rough and tumble of history.
>
> Rosa Luxemburg, *The Anti-Critique*

"1701: Sao Salvador de Bahia, *Voice of America*: Father António Vieira died at the turn of the century, but not so his voice. . . . The words of this missionary to the poor and persecuted still echo with the same lively ring throughout the lands of Brazil."[5] Father António Vieira—or more precisely, Father Vieira's voice—articulates a question from beyond the grave that continues to haunt Marxist analysis: How can such an intimate effect of the body survive the body itself? Of course, the passage implies that what survives is not his physiological voice but rather a mode of communication, a discourse, that resonates independently of its actual speaker. Following Emile Benveniste, we could label "discourse" any enunciation "distinguished . . . by its integration of both the locutor and the listener with the desire of the former to influence the latter."[6] This definition does not quite account for Father Vieira's spectral echo, however, since in this instance the desire to influence listeners survives his mortal ability to converse.

In *The History of Sexuality,* Michel Foucault extends the problem of Father Vieira's "voice," or discourse, beyond the sphere of the individual in his assertion that discourses constitute tactical blocks which operate in the field of force relations and which "we must question on the two levels of their productivity (what reciprocal effects of power and knowledge they ensure) and their strategical integration (what conjunction and what force relationship make their utilization necessary in a given episode of the various confrontations that occur)."[7] It is precisely this involvement in the production and transmission of power that makes the interpretation of discourse so indispensable for Marxist analysis—particularly for its analysis of colonialism.

An example that illustrates the importance of discursive processes to the success of the colonialist project emerges in the link that the discourse of the Catholic church forged between the economic exploitation of indigenous South American groups and the subordination of women. In her research on the historical role of the church in the colonization of the Americas, anthropologist Eleanor Leacock documents the efforts of orders such as the Jesuits to impose a model of the patriarchal nuclear family, complete with Europeanized norms of sexual and conjugal behavior, upon such tribes as the Montagnais-Maskape:

> The Jesuit attack on the autonomy of women was compounded by a systematic attack on individual autonomy specifically and egalitarian relations in general. Control of a husband and father over a wife and offspring, along with control of men over other men, were seen by the Jesuits as the key to restructuring productive relations and attitudes toward colonial domination, bringing the Indians from "savagery" to "civilization." The Jesuit program of conversion had devastating effects on zealots and their victims, fomenting internal conflict and creating the divide-and-rule situation that is the ever present tool of colonization.[8]

The theological discourses of Catholicism exacerbated inequalities and effectively undermined those social, political, and economic institutions that guaranteed women's rights and, by extension, the rights of indigenous peoples.[9]

Marx himself suggests the centrality of such discourses to any analysis of colonialism in his sweeping reference to the "Christian colonial system" and his directive that "this stuff ought to be studied in detail, to see what the bourgeois makes of himself and of the worker when he can model the world according to his own image without any interference."[10] A bourgeois remodeling of the world with no interference from resisting forces could easily describe the ideological core of the discursive process and, at the very least, implies an intersection of language and power that demands further investigation. In spite of these provocative allusions, however, discourse's life on the margins of historical materialism—literally, confined to a footnote of *Capital*—has limited Marxism's ability to explain the semiotic means by which groups maintain their power. Perhaps the most important message of Father Vieira's voice, then, is the inadequacy of Marxism's traditional base-superstructure paradigm for considering these cultural phenomena, since it elucidates neither how discourses are formed nor the roles they play within social formations.[11]

I will attempt to explore the relationship of discourse and its social grounding by reading it through the lens of two turn-of-the-century texts: James M. Barrie's classic children's tale ***Peter Pan*** (originally *Peter and Wendy,* 1911) and *We of the Never-Never* (1905), Mrs. Aeneas Gunn's autobiographical account of the year that she spent on a cattle station in the northern outback of Australia. At this point, one might legitimately ask about the appropriateness of using literary works as vehicles for reformulating Marxist analysis. I would answer such questions by appealing to Antonio Gramsci's insight that narrative provides "a means of ideological diffusion which has a rapidity, a field of action, and an emotional simultaneity" which makes it an extremely potent yet contradictory instrument:[12] it exists not only as a weapon in disseminating ideology but also as a tool for unraveling the very disseminations it weaves.

Both ***Peter Pan*** and *We of the Never-Never* are deeply embedded in the historical context of British imperialism, and both possess fields of narrative action that reveal how discourses not only empower but also perpetuate this colonialist project. For example, through its reliance upon the enthymeme, or the rhetorical construction of an incomplete syllogism, **Peter Pan** dramatizes the importance of "articulating practices" to a hegemonic group, while *We of the Never-Never* indicates that discourses assume an "anaclitic" (literally, a "leaning-up-against") relationship with their material bases. I hope to demonstrate that discourses occupy a position which resists not only those "vulgar" Marxist interpretations that regard them merely as reflections of an economic base but also those which believe that discourses, like Never-Never Land, are only "make-believe" constructs of the bourgeois imagination.

"Second to the right, and straight on 'til morning." Everyone—that is, every Anglo-European child whose parents lulled him or her to sleep with bedtime stories—knows that these are the directions to Never-Never Land in **Peter Pan**, James M. Barrie's delightfully wicked tale of juvenile mayhem and adventure.[13] I myself dreamed longingly of waking like Wendy in the middle of the night and discovering Peter crying softly for his lost shadow. In gratitude for sewing his shadow back on, he would sprinkle me with fairy dust and I would fly to his magic island, fight Captain Hook, and become a mother to the Lost Boys. But much to my childish dismay, I learned that, like Santa Claus, Peter Pan's Never-Never Land was only "make-believe"; or, in more adult terms, it "relinquished any ostensive function, i.e., any connection with the 'here' and 'now' of reality, and therefore, any claim to 'truth value.'"[14] (Perhaps this insight conjures in different terms Peter's passionate desire always to be a boy and have fun.)

In *Marxism and Philosophy,* Alex Callinicos notes the limitations of this view for a Marxist, and indeed any other kind of politically committed, analysis:

> A Truth-conditional theory of meaning gives a formal and structural account of language.... Such an account may be valid as an explanation of how expressions are assigned their sense and reference and can probably be extended to deal with the force with which utterances are taken (as commands, assertions, etc.). It is, however, only an imperfect guide to the study of linguistic usage, and of its imbrication in social practice.... The reason is that formal semanticists, like analytical philosophers generally, are concerned with the *logical form* of expressions.... Now logic is concerned with valid inference; it appraises arguments in terms of their structure, sentences related in a particular inference. Entirely justifiably, it is not concerned with the question of whether or not there are relations between sentences other than those which transmit truth or falsity.[15]

By displaying a propensity toward "make-believe so real . . . that during a meal of it you could see him getting rounder" (**PP** [*Peter Pan*] 66), Peter Pan himself exists as a more reliable guide to these "other" relations that imbricate language within social practice. Peter's expanding girth whimsically emphasizes not only the text as discourse, or a communicative interaction of implied speakers, consciousness, and communities,[16] but also its materialist character. For Barrie's text, worldliness is not like some thief in the night who breaks into and out of textuality (or windows of the Darlings' house) at will, for the discursive effect of the meal (that we see him getting rounder) replaces the meal itself as the consuming—and consumed—interpretive matter.

However, the Lost Boys complain loudly about the coerciveness of Peter's particular propensity, since "if they broke down in their make-believe he [Peter] rapped them on the knuckles" (**PP** 59). The painful experience of the Lost Boys in Never-Never Land highlights the more somber fact that discourses and their various effects do not exist solely in the realm of consciousness, or, in Marxist terminology, in the superstructure. Indeed, the Lost Boys beg the question of articulating practices for a Marxist analysis, a question that emerges most urgently in the search for **Peter Pan**'s lost girl—the "belle of the Piccaninnies," Tiger Lily.

I conceived my own passion for **Peter Pan** during its revival as a Leonard Bernstein musical in the 1950s. One of my most vivid memories from this play was the duet sung by Peter and Tiger Lily celebrating Peter's heroic rescue of the Indian princess from the evil machinations of Captain Hook. Its chorus repeatedly professed undying mutuality and regard; however, if we examine the sociopolitical actualities of Barrie's text, a much different dynamic emerges:

> On the trail of the pirates, stealing noiselessly down the warpath, which is not visible to inexperienced eyes, come the redskins, every one of them with his eyes peeled. They carry tomahawks and knives, and their naked bodies gleam with paint and oil. Strung around them are scalps, of boys as well as of pirates, for these are the Piccaninny tribe. . . . Bringing up the rear, the place of greatest danger, comes Tiger Lily, proudly erect, a princess in her own right. She is the most beautiful of dusky Dianas and the belle of the Piccaninnies, coquettish, cold and amorous by turns; there is not a brave who would not have the wayward thing to wife, but she staves off the altar with a hatchet.
>
> (**PP** [*Peter Pan*], 46)

At first glance, Tiger Lily seems literally to embody her name: "Tiger" evoking fierceness and amazonian stature, and "Lily," beauty and whiteness. Since Never-Never Land had never never allowed women to immigrate there as "real" citizens, Tiger Lily also appears as a welcome antidote to the staunchly conservative maternalism of Wendy (Peter: "What we need is just a nice motherly person." "Oh dear!" Wendy said, "You see I feel that is exactly what I am"). Although Peter explains that the absence of female inhabitants is merely because girls are too clever to fall out of their prams, one could just as easily conjecture that it is because women and women's traditional domestic labors are not highly thought of on Peter's island—an attitude (melo)dramatized by the fate of Starkey the pirate. During the final rout of Captain Hook and his crew by Peter and the Lost Boys, Starkey flees by swimming ashore. He is captured by the redskins, who, by way of punishment, "made him nurse for all their papooses, a melancholy come-down for a pirate" (*PP* 135). Against this misogyny, Tiger Lily inscribes a subversive female presence by refusing either to become the surrogate mother or to surrender her independence to Edwardian wifehood.

Yet something peculiar happens when we examine Barrie's portrayal of Tiger Lily as the belle of the Piccaninnies, for "piccaninny"—the West Indian derivative of *pequeño*—connotes "tiny," or "very little," and was commonly applied to black indigenous populations by their Anglo-European colonizers. Marlon Riggs's important documentary *Ethnic Notions* highlights the influence of the "piccaninny" as one of the most important images shaping Western attitudes about race.[17] For example, it shows a relief carved for the 1915 entrance gate of the San Francisco Exposition that metamorphoses a small black child into a "piccaninny" by making its braids stick out with a preternatural energy, emphasizing its wide toothless grin and imbuing its face with a decidedly demonic expression. Even more revealing are early cartoons included in the documentary that often portrayed "piccaninnies" as partially naked, dirty, and unkempt victims of nonhuman predators such as alligators or wolves—a scenario whose subhuman savagery betrays a deep racial ambivalence about the participation of African Americans in Anglo-European society. Indeed, this image of the "piccaninny" implies that only white law and morality can contain black lawlessness and amorality, and one could argue that its message not only reflects but also creates the rationale for maintaining white racial hegemony. As the narrator observes, "these caricatures did as much harm as any lynch mob" to African Americans, and the fact that they inflicted their wounds indirectly only meant that they were far more difficult to heal.

The question then becomes how **Peter Pan** yokes the apparent oxymoron of the full-sized white adult and the small black "piccaninny" in the character of Tiger Lily with such seeming ease and noncontradiction. To understand this phenomenon, we need to delve into the discipline of classical rhetoric and its practice of the incomplete syllogism or "enthymeme." Although Aristotle identified the enthymeme as a form of public reasoning used only by ignorant men, later Roman and medieval rhetoric defined it somewhat more kindly in terms of its elliptical argument, or the suppression of one or more relevant propositions.[18] Aristotle's *Rhetoric* captures this ellipticism when it states that "the Enthymeme must consist of a few propositions, fewer often than those which make up the normal syllogism. For if any of these propositions is a familiar fact, there is no need even to mention it; the hearer adds it himself" (1.2). The way an enthymeme both depends upon and solicits the suppressed premise surfaces in a contemporary version of it: the often heard accusation "since you are not pro-life [on the question of abortion], you are not a Christian":

(Suppressed) Premise I: All Christians must be pro-life.

Premise II: You are not pro-life.

Conclusion: You are not a Christian.

This succinct constellation of statements is an enthymeme because its major premise—that all Christians must be pro-life—is suppressed. To those "pro-lifers" articulating the syllogism, the hidden proposition seems an incontestable one that they simply keep in mind, or *en thumo*, as classical rhetoricians would say.[19] However, this suppression *en thumo* illustrates perhaps the primary ideological manipulation performed by enthymemes: based on a previous bias (here, a certain politics of Christianity), it chooses a given circumstantial selection that attributes a certain property to a sememe ("pro-life") and thereby conceals other contradictory properties that are equally predicable.[20] Of course, the equally predicable conclusion that our pro-life enthymeme suppresses is that one can be a Christian and favor a pro-choice position on abortion. By an enthymemic sleight of hand, however, one can superimpose the marker "pro-life" with its conservative political code onto the marker "Christian" with its diverse religious codes and reach a "foregone," albeit unsound, conclusion. In the case of abortion, the pro-life motivation for suppressing the crucial premise seems overwhelmingly clear: if God is on your side, you possess a potent argument indeed.

Although the text of **Peter Pan** imbues Tiger Lily with the possibility of challenging dominant interpretations of gender in fin-de-siècle imperial England, it also takes away this possibility by recuperating her within an implied enthymeme of the "Piccaninny"—that colonialist and paternalistic marker of a childish and less developed, therefore unequal, person. As Michèle Barrett remarks in *Women's Oppression Today: Problems in Marxist Feminist Analysis,* "'Recuperation' . . . [is] the ideological effort that goes into negating and defusing challenges to the historically dominant meaning of gender in particular periods"—it takes away with one hand what you have given with the other.[21] **Peter Pan** accomplishes this process by constructing the following enthymeme:

Premise I: Tiger Lily is a woman.

(Suppressed) Premise II: Women and Piccaninnies are coextensive.

Conclusion: Tiger Lily is belle of the Piccaninnies.

Like the above pro-life syllogism, this one also suppresses its critical premise that women have become coextensive with the "piccaninny" or "native" Other. This suppression successfully recuperates Tiger Lily's implicitly feminist challenge to traditional roles for women by subsuming her under the racist discourses of Anglo-European colonialism.

Peter Pan's use of the enthymeme clearly demonstrates the function and importance of a dominant group's "articulatory practices" to a radical political analysis. In *Hegemony and Socialist Strategy: Towards a Radical Democratic Politics*, Ernesto Laclau and Chantal Mouffe's provocative re-visioning of Marxism, articulatory practices establish "a relation among elements such that their identity is modified as a result."[22] In other words, just as a "practice" transforms material through time, a written practice (such as the enthymeme) exerts a continuously transformative effect upon the signifying material of language.[23] Articulatory practices work by constructing "nodal points," or privileged points that partially fix the meaning of a discursive chain; rather than expressing a previously self-defined totality (a deterministic base-superstructure argument), however, they create new positions of difference and invest any stable system of differences such as class, race, or sex with an incomplete "floating" character.[24] For Laclau and Mouffe, framing hegemony in the terms of articulatory practice redresses the spectacular failure of Marxism's base-superstructure model to detect how dominant groups such as the church or ruling classes constantly reinscribe their interests within society and successfully reorganize the result of this struggle.[25]

In *Peter Pan,* Tiger Lily's enthymeme becomes an articulatory practice when it creates new positions of difference by establishing a relation (syllogistic) among elements (woman and "piccaninny") that consequently modifies their identities (each becomes assimilated to the other). Since biographical testimony reveals that James M. Barrie "never talked politics himself,"[26] one cannot assume that this ideological transformation is intentional on the part of the author; yet, this particular inscription of difference becomes politically crucial to the continued success of English colonial ambitions. It also greatly enlarges the field of categories that a Marxist analysis can use to account for imperialist social relations.[27] As Laclau and Mouffe note, such articulatory practices as synonymy, metonymy, metaphor—and I would add, the enthymeme—"are not forms of thought that add a second sense to a primary, constitutive literality of social relations; instead, they are part of the primary terrain itself in which the social is constituted."[28]

If articulatory practices "pierce the entire material density" of the multiplicitous institutions and rituals through which a discursive formation becomes structured,[29] then *Peter Pan*'s practice of the enthymeme constitutes a part of the primary social terrain that structures colonialist discourses. For example, the recuperation of Tiger Lily to the status of colonized object uncovers one of the most important sociocultural processes that enabled England to become the empire upon which the sun never set—a process that unfolds most revealingly in *Peter Pan*'s description of Peter and Tiger Lily's ultimate fate:

> Peter had saved Tiger Lily from a dreadful fate, and now there was nothing she and her braves would not do for him. . . . They called Peter the Great White Father, prostrating themselves before him; and he liked this tremendously, so that it was not really good for him. "The Great White Father," he would say to them in a very lordly manner, as they grovelled at his feet, "is glad to see the Piccaninny warriors protecting his wigwam from the pirates." "Me Tiger Lily," that lovely creature would reply, "Peter Pan save me, me his velly nice friend. Me no let pirates hurt him." She was far too pretty to cringe in this way, but Peter thought it his due, and he would answer condescendingly, "It is good. Peter Pan has spoken."
>
> (*PP* 91)

In Michael Doyle's extensive study of imperialism, he defines empires as relationships of political control over a people that assume two basic forms: formal, which controls through annexation and rule by a colonial governor with the collaboration of local elites, and informal, which controls through the collaboration of legally independent but politically dependent indigenous rulers.[30] England relied mainly upon the latter form of imperialism, buttressed by an occasional but strategic use of force (for example, the Opium Wars, suppression of the Indian Mutiny, and its blockade of the River Plate),[31] and it is precisely this political paradigm that Barrie's text helps empower. If control is evidenced by the behavioral effects it exerts on those who are controlled, then Peter's control of Tiger Lily textually reproduces the paternalistic ideology at the heart of England's colonialist project and the imperialist ideology at the heart of its paternalism. Like the "piccaninny," Peter's signifier of "Great White Father" tightly imbricates the dominating hierarchies of both colonizer and patriarch into an overdetermined articulation of nationalist interests and, in so doing, pierces the density of the institutions, rituals, and practices that disseminate colonialist discourses.

Geopolitics in the "Real" Never-Never Land

The *we*, which articulates natural philosophical consciousness with each other . . . is the unity of absolute knowledge and anthropology, of God and man, of onto-theo-teleology and humanism. "Being" and language—the group of languages—that the *we* governs or opens: such is the name of that which assures the transition between metaphysics and humanism via the *we*.

Jacques Derrida, "The Ends of Man"

We of the Never-Never, Mrs. Aeneas Gunn's diary of a year in the Australian outback, continues to map the discursive terrain that we began exploring in chapter 3 by uncovering the asymmetries of power and subject positions mediated and produced within articulatory practices. At first glance, the "we" of Mrs. Gunn's title and her declaration in the Prelude that "All of Us . . . shared each other's lives for one bright, sunny year" suggest a mutuality which contravenes the coerciveness of the discourses explored in **Peter Pan.** Since the territory of the cattle station Elsey included not only its Anglo-European settlers but also a once independent Aboriginal group who now labored as indentured servants, one begins to grasp the enormous claim implied by Mrs. Gunn's first-person plural pronoun. Without necessarily supporting a "universal pragmatics," or reconstructing the universally valid bases of speech, the "we" of *We of the Never-Never* constructs a localized version of what Jürgen Habermas identifies as "an ideal speech situation." Such a situation creates mutual understanding between participants because it allows its participants equal chances to employ speech acts, recognizes the legitimacy of each to engage in dialogue as an autonomous and equal partner, and reaches consensus simply through the better argument.[32] According to Habermas, "Agreement arrived at through communication, which is measured by the intersubjective recognition of validity claims, makes possible a networking of social interactions and lifeworld contexts. Of course, these validity claims have a Janus face: As claims, they transcend any local context; at the same time, they have to be raised here and now and be de facto recognized if they are going to bear the agreement of interaction participants that is needed for effective cooperation."[33]

The signifying practice of *We of the Never-Never* bequeaths us the first clue about what this claim might be. If a title not only figures a beginning but also binds its own utterance to the contingency of that which follows,[34] then "The Unknown Woman"—Mrs. Gunn's first chapter heading—implodes the inclusiveness of the text's primary title. Instead of a We, where the collective knows every person, the presence of an unknown divides We into Us and Them: "us" inside the Never-Never and "them" outside of it. The "Unknown Woman" refers in this case to the newlywed Mrs. Gunn, who has followed her husband to his position as manager of the Elsey, and who ascribes her status to the obvious fact that "everyone . . . was blissfully unconscious of even the existence of the Maluka's [Mr. Gunn's] missus."[35] Her "unknown" status also exists as a prerequisite for the claim of the bushmen that the Never-Never should remain the privileged territory of the Anglo-European male. As one of the men so baldly pronounces: the cattle station is "not a fit place for a woman, and besides, nobody wants her!" (WNN [*We of the Never-Never*] 9).

The whitemale crew of the Elsey work feverishly to make sure that Mrs. Gunn never enters their world by attempting to "block" her arrival at the Elsey: "The Sanguine Scot had been thinking rapidly, and, with characteristic hopefulness, felt he had the bull by the horns. 'We'll just have to block her, chaps; that's all,' he said. 'A wire or two should do it'; [he] led the way to the telegraph office; and presently there quivered into Darwin the first hint that a missus was not wanted at the Elsey" (WNN 2). The men of the Elsey tax their imaginations to the limit in their attempts to "block" the "missus." First, they "would advise leaving wife behind till homestead can be repaired" (WNN 2). When his wife stands firm in her decision and the Maluka requests a buggy, they reply that no buggy is available, not to mention no sidesaddle and no suitable stock horses. Further, no woman in her right mind would want to travel in the rainy season, and even if she did, "she'll be bored to death if she does reach the homestead alive" (WNN 3).

This resistance is particularly interesting from the standpoint of discourse because the attempted exclusion takes place over the Darwin-Pine Creek telegraph lines. In this passage, the telegraph functions as an extremely appropriate trope of discourse: just as the telegraph transmits messages between a sender and a receiver, discourse stresses meaning as communication; just as the Darwin-Pine Creek telegraph facilitates a particular historical and political goal—in this case, the "civilization" of Australia's last frontier and the colonization of Aboriginal lands—discourse operates for particular ideological ends; and just as the Elsey's crew transforms the telegraph into the site of a sexual struggle for power, discourse often becomes a site of ideological domination. As a metadiscourse—that is, a discourse about discourse—this not so innocent act of communication rips apart the consensual fabric from which *We of the Never-Never* weaves its textuality.

In fact, the strenuous endeavors of the bushmen to "unknow" Mrs. Gunn systematically distort the ideal speech situation that *We of the Never-Never* initially presents to the reader. From the earlier thought of Habermas, the concept of systematically distorted communication draws on the methodology of psychoanalysis and illuminates the significance of behavior that has been deformed by repression or censorship: "The psychically most effective way to render undesired need dispositions harmless is to *exclude from public communication* the interpretations to which they are attached—in other words, *repression.*"[36] This exclusion of undesired voices from public communication has historically functioned as one of the most potent weapons in the maintenance of power—men over women, colonizer over colonized, white over black. Indeed, the interpretive gloss that the Maluka places on the behavior of his crew vividly dramatizes how pervasive such repression can be: "The

Unknown Woman is brimful of possibilities to a bushman . . . for although she may be all womanly strength and tenderness, she may also be anything, from a weak timid fool to a self-righteous shrew, bristling with virtue and indignation. Still . . . when a woman does come into our lives, whatever type she may be, she lacks nothing in the way of chivalry, and it rests with her whether she remains an outsider or becomes just One of Us" (*WNN* 5). While the Maluka characterizes the situation as one that offers a genuine choice, it actually presents Mrs. Gunn with only one desirable course of action: to identify with the bush's dominant masculine community or else be exiled to its social and communicative margins. In this respect, Mrs. Gunn's position exhibits a common female dis-ease whose pathology includes expulsion from conversational communities solely on the basis of gender. Like most women under Western patriarchy, Mrs. Gunn is known but not knowing; seen but not seeing; repressed and Signified but unable herself to participate in these operations.[37]

It is precisely this power-induced asymmetry that systematically distorts *We of the Never-Never*'s initial ideal speech situation, and as in **Peter Pan,** the discourse of the "piccaninny" intervenes to uncover the contradictions of Mrs. Gunn's oppression. In her memoirs, Mrs. Gunn adopts the articulating practice of the Never-Never's white community by substituting the generic "piccaninny" for the individual identities of the Aboriginal children living on the Elsey: "He [the Maluka] reduced the house staff to two, allowing a shadow or two extra in the persons of a few old blackfellows and a piccaninny or two, sending the rejected to camp" (*WNN* 47). As we have seen, the rhetoric of difference that spawns the "piccaninny" functions as an integral part of the Anglo-European imperialist project, and its discursive usage implies participation not only in the discourse itself but also in the sociopolitical privilege it bestows upon its users.

Such participation is paradoxical in Mrs. Gunn's case, however, for although she benefits from the discourse of white privilege, its racist figures turn back on her and literally keep the "missus" in a lower social position. Soon after her own use of "piccaninny," for example, the Maluka describes his wife as "a poor homeless little mite," and she thereafter becomes known to all as "the little Missus." One could loosely write the enthymeme this way:

> Premise I: The Missus is a woman.
>
> (Suppressed) Premise II: Women and piccaninnies are little.
>
> Conclusion: The Missus is a piccaninny.

While it is true that standing on her tiptoes, Mrs. Gunn could not have measured much over five feet, her characterization as "little"—the etymological root of "piccaninny"—goes far beyond any spatial definition. Instead, it marks one who is dominated and colonized, whose lower/higher relationship to discourse infers nothing less than that of inferior to superior, oppressed to oppressor.

The "piccaninny" conjures this system of distorted communication because it attempts to conceal the logic of whitemale supremacy in which it is embedded. As David Silverman and Brian Torode explain in *The Material Word: Some Theories of Language and Its Limits*, "Where the sociality of linguistic practice is concealed or fixed in some apparently fixed natural order, we have distorted communication."[38] Mrs. Gunn thus deceives herself about the mutuality, equality, and reciprocity of the linguistic and social "we" that the unknown woman and the known men of the bush create. However, her growing powers of self-reflection ultimately enable her to penetrate the "piccaninny's" ideological veil. Indeed, she laments, "the mistress had long ceased to be anything but the little Missus—something to rule or educate or take care of, according to the nature of her subordinates" (*WNN* 94).

Mrs. Gunn's liberatory self-reflection not only ruptures the bush's systematically distorted communication but also exposed the weakness of one of the most influential contemporary analytics of power—Michel Foucault's elaboration of "fellowships of discourse." According to Foucault, fellowships of discourse preserve or reproduce discourses so that they will circulate within a closed community without those in possession of them becoming dispossessed.[39] Although these fellowships assume myriad forms, they all share schemas of exclusivity and disclosure and a "secret-appropriation and non-interchangeability." Further, they all require a speaking subject (the position from which power/knowledge is exercised) and a spoken subject (the position brought into existence through the exercise of power/knowledge).

However, the positions generated by *We of the Never-Never*'s discursive grid belie these sharp distinctions: although the Maluka and his fellow bushmen appropriate the stance of speaking subjects, the long-suffering Mrs. Gunn simultaneously inhabits the position of both speaking and spoken subject. Foucault's schema fails to account for the contradictory worlds and selves set into play by colonialist discourse itself.[40] According to Habermas, Foucault's "speaking subjects are either masters or shepherds of their linguistic systems. Either they make use of language in a way that is creative of meaning, to disclose their world innovatively, or they are always already moving around within a horizon of world-disclosure taken care of by language itself."[41] The overdetermined status of one who both participates in and is excluded from colonizing discourse eludes his sharply dichotomized positions. Further, in spite of the bushmen's attempts to "block" her from their territory and fellowship of discourse, Mrs. Gunn resists their arguments and, like Wendy, transgresses the boundaries of the Never-Never's rugged and forbidding No (wo)Man's Land. Mrs. Gunn's historical experience requires us to look beyond binary opposition and grasp the multiplicity of positions and contradiction of responses generated by the communicative interaction of the bush.

By arguing for the importance of discourses to Marxist analysis, I do not mean to imply that the material bases for these discourses are at best unimportant or at worst unnecessary. This is an idealist abyss into which too many theorists have fallen—although doubting the reality of the base means that their superstructural fall never comes to a concrete and finite end. The two interpretive poles for any discussion of the relationship between discourse and its material base are two versions of cause and effect: either an unmediated base causes the effects of discourse (vulgar Marxism), or discourse causes the effects of the base (conservative versions of deconstruction). Neither of these positions accurately characterizes the very complex and overdetermined symbiosis between discourse and reality.

In her essay "Histoire d'O: The Construction of a Female Subject," Kaja Silverman suggests that the concept which most accurately characterizes the relationship between real and discursive bodies is that of *anaclisis*.[42] From the Greek verb εφκλινω ("to lean on or upon"), the concept of anaclisis was first articulated by Sigmund Freud as a process in which the sexual instincts satisfy themselves through a propping upon or "leaning up against" the self-preservative instincts.[43] Silverman argues that in an analogous way, discursive bodies lean upon real ones: "lean both in the sense of finding their physical support in, and of exerting their own pressure upon, real bodies. Thus real bodies are tied to, and in the process shaped by, discursive formations."[44] In this ideological symbiosis, discourse territorializes and then maps meaning onto bodies[45]—a description more than faintly reminiscent of nineteenth-century imperialism.

The discourse of the "piccaninny" found its original material support in the European conquest of the West Indies, and it helped to enable this territorialization by mapping the binary oppositions high/low, adult/child, culture/nature, light/dark, and superior/inferior onto European/"native" bodies, respectively. In the colonialist version of anaclisis, then, the interpretation of the "native" Other as childish, dark, and inferior in turn supported Europe's occupation of foreign lands and its paternalistic deracination of their indigenous peoples. Further, as the "piccaninny" became more widely disseminated within the Anglo-European grammar of power, its discourse of difference bound racial and sexual inferiority together through articulating practices such as those we have explored in **Peter Pan** and *We of the Never-Never*. Such are the lessons that Never-Never Land teaches its inhabitants at a very early age.

"Second to the right, and straight on 'til morning." Both the "make-believe" Never-Never Land of Peter Pan and the "true" one of Mrs. Gunn dramatize some of the most insidious discursive means by which women and people of color are marginalized on the boundaries of society. Indeed, I would hope that our imaginary journey to this fabled country has illuminated the necessity for Marxism to profess the analysis of discourse as an inextricable part of its still powerful materialist analysis of colonialism. Short of developing this more adequate model both for reading differently and for reading difference, it might discover second to the right; it will, however, never go straight on 'til morning and complete the journey to a revolutionary, postcolonial methodology.

Notes

1. Memmi, *The Colonizer and the Colonized*, 37 (hereafter cited in text as *CC*).

2. Spivak, *In Other Worlds*, 179.

3. Moorehead, Foreword, ix.

4. Bates, *The Passing of the Aborigines*, 24 (hereafter cited in text as *PA*).

5. Galeano, *Memory of Fire*, 4.

6. Kristeva, *Language, the Unknown*, 11.

7. Foucault, *History of Sexuality*, 102.

8. Etienne and Leacock, *Women and Colonization*, 18.

9. Ibid.

10. Marx, *Capital*, 1:916.

11. Callinicos, *Marxism and Philosophy*, 151.

12. Gramsci, *Cultural Writings*, 382.

13. Barrie, *Peter Pan* (hereafter cited in text as *PP*). While the novel *Peter Pan* was not published until 1911, the character of Peter first appeared in Barrie's 1902 tale, *The Little White Band*, followed by the play *Peter Pan* two years later.

14. Ricoeur, "Hermeneutical Function," 140.

15. Callinicos, *Marxism and Philosophy*, 147.

16. Fowler, *Literature as Social Discourse*, 94. For an excellent discussion of discourse and the meanings it has accrued within contemporary critical debates, see *A Dictionary of Modern Critical Terms*, rev. ed., edited by Roger Fowler (London: Routledge and Kegan Paul, 1987), 62-66.

17. *Ethnic Notions,* documentary.
18. Barthes, *The Semiotic Challenge,* 58.
19. Ibid., 59.
20. Eco, *A Theory of Semiotics,* 293. The general semiotic analysis is Eco's, but the constructed enthymeme and particular interpretation of the abortion question are my own.
21. Barrett, *Women's Oppression Today* (1980), 111.
22. Laclau and Mouffe, *Hegemony and Socialist Strategy,* 113.
23. MacCabe, "On Discourse," 91.
24. Laclau and Mouffe, *Hegemony and Socialist Strategy,* 113-14.
25. Callinicos, *Marxism and Philosophy,* 153.
26. Dunbar, *J. M. Barrie,* 307.
27. Laclau and Mouffe, *Hegemony and Socialist Strategy,* 110.
28. Ibid.
29. Ibid., 109.
30. Doyle, *Empires,* 130.
31. Ibid., 236.
32. Held, *Introduction to Critical Theory,* 343.
33. Habermas, *Philosophical Discourse,* 322.
34. Barthes, *The Semiotic Challenge,* 267.
35. Gunn, *We of the Never-Never,* 1 (hereafter cited in text as *WNN*).
36. Habermas, *Knowledge and Human Interests,* 223-24.
37. Silverman, "Histoire d'O," 326-27.
38. Silverman and Torode, *The Material Word,* 343.
39. Foucault, "Discourse on Language," 225.
40. Silverman and Torode, *The Material Word,* 342.
41. Habermas, *Philosophical Discourse,* 317.
42. Silverman, "Histoire d'O," 324.
43. Freud, "On Narcissism," 69.
44. Silverman, "Histoire d'O," 325.
45. Ibid., 324.

Bibliography

Barrett, Michèle. *Women's Oppression Today: Problems in Marxist Feminist Analysis.* 1980. Rev. ed. London: Verso Press, 1988.

Barrie, J. M. *Peter Pan.* Illustrated by Michael Hague. New York: Henry Holt and Company, 1987.

Barthes, Roland. *The Semiotic Challenge.* Translated by Richard Howard. New York: Hill and Wang, 1988.

Bates, Daisy. *The Passing of the Aborigines: A Lifetime Spent among the Natives of Australia.* Foreword by Alan Moorehead; Introduction by Arthur Mee. 1938. Reprint. New York: Frederick A. Praeger, 1967.

Callinicos, Alex. *Marxism and Philosophy.* New York: Oxford University Press, 1985.

Doyle, Michael W. *Empires.* Ithaca, N.Y.: Cornell University Press, 1986.

Dunbar, Janet. *J. M. Barrie: The Man behind the Image.* Boston: Houghton Mifflin, 1970.

Eco, Umberto. *A Theory of Semiotics.* Bloomington: Indiana University Press, 1976.

Etienne, Mona, and Eleanor Leacock, eds. *Women and Colonization: Anthropological Perspectives.* New York: Praeger, 1980.

Foucault, Michel. "Discourse on Language." In *The Archaeology of Knowledge,* translated by A. M. Sheridan Smith, 215-37. New York: Harper and Row, 1972.

———. *The History of Sexuality.* Vol. 1, *An Introduction,* translated by Robert Hurley. New York: Vintage Books, 1980.

Fowler, Roger. *Literature as Social Discourse: The Practice of Linguistic Criticism.* Bloomington: Indiana University Press, 1981.

Freud, Sigmund. "On Narcissism: An Introduction." In *General Psychological Theory: Papers on Metapsychology,* Introduction by Philip Rieff, 56-82. New York: Collier Books, 1963.

Galeano, Eduardo. *Memory of Fire.* Vol. 2, *Faces and Masks,* translated by Cedric Befrage. New York: Pantheon Books, 1987.

Gramsci, Antonio. *Selections from the Critical Writings.* Edited by David Forgacs and Geoffrey Nowell-Smith; translated by William Boelhower. Boston: Harvard University Press, 1985.

Gunn, Mrs. Aeneas. *We of the Never-Never.* 1905. Reprint. New York: Avon Books, 1982.

Habermas, Jürgen. *Knowledge and Human Interests.* Translated by Jeremy J. Shapiro. Boston: Beacon Press, 1971.

———. *The Philosophical Discourse of Modernity: Twelve Lectures.* Translated by Frederick Lawrence. Cambridge: MIT Press, 1987.

Held, David. *Introduction to Critical Theory: Horkheimer to Habermas.* Berkeley and Los Angeles: University of California Press, 1980.

Kristeva, Julia. *Language, the Unknown: An Initiation into Linguistics.* Translated by Anne M. Menke. New York: Columbia University Press, 1989.

Laclau, Ernesto, and Chantal Mouffe. *Hegemony and Socialist Strategy: Towards a Radical Democratic Politics.* Translated by Winston Moore and Paul Cammack. London: Verso Press, 1985.

MacCabe, Colin. "On Discourse." In *Tracking the Signifier: Theoretical Essays—Film, Linguistics, Literature,* 82-112. Minneapolis: University of Minnesota Press, 1985.

Marx, Karl. *Capital: A Critique of Political Economy.* Introduction by Ernest Mandel; translated by Ben Fowkes. 3 vols. 1867. Reprint. New York: Vintage Books, 1977.

Memmi, Albert. *The Colonizer and the Colonized.* Introduction by Jean-Paul Sartre. Boston: Beacon Press, 1965.

Moorehead, Alan. Foreword to *The Passing of the Aborigines: A Lifetime Spent among the Natives of Australia,* by Daisy Bates. 1938. Reprint. New York: Frederick A. Praeger, 1967.

Ricoeur, Paul. "The Hermeneutical Function of Distanciation." in *Hermeneutics and the Human Sciences: Essays on Language, Action, and Interpretation,* edited and translated by John. B. Thompson, 131-44. London: Cambridge University Press; Paris: Edition de la Maison des Sciences de l'Homme, 1981.

Silverman, David, and Brian Torode. *The Material Word: Some Theories of Language and Its Limits.* London: Routledge and Kegan Paul, 1980.

Silverman, Kaja. "Histoire d'O: The Construction of a Female Subject." In *Pleasure and Danger: Exploring Female Sexuality,* edited by Carole S. Vance, 320-49. Boston: Routledge and Kegan Paul, 1984.

Spivak, Gayatri Chakravorty. *In Other Worlds: Essays in Cultural Politics.* New York: Methuen, 1987.

R. D. S. Jack (essay date June 1994)

SOURCE: Jack, R. D. S. "*Peter Pan* as Darwinian Creation Myth." *Literature and Theology* 8 no. 2 (June 1994): 157-73.

[*In the following essay, Jack maintains that* Peter Pan *dramatizes Barrie's Darwinian belief in life as a conflict of opposing forces.*]

That **Peter Pan** abounds in battles is self-evident; that it is a creation myth is universally accepted; that the two are linked by Darwin's theories of life as conflict is not discussed. The reason for this lies in another myth—that of James Barrie's Christian escapism. George Blake represents the voice of critical orthodoxy when he laments the playwright's refusal to move with the times. Was not his village of Thrums as represented in **Auld Licht Idylls** (1888) or **A Window in Thrums** (1889) set in a safe pre-industrial past? Was he not deaf to revolutions in thought and practice because his was a Christianity unwilling to accept Milton's challenge in *Areopagitica* to "sallie out and see her adversary"? After all, Barrie admits in **An Edinburgh Eleven** (1888) that, during his five years at Edinburgh University, he "never entered any but Free churches."[1] Blake concludes:

> There were probably too many old books and ideas about those Free Kirk manses, too few new ones—and a wonderful faith that, in spite of all the signs, the Kirk's hegemony was really not about to collapse.[2]

This is to discount strong contrary evidence from the very books cited and from Barrie's early journalism. In *The Nottingham Journal* of 15th September 1884 he reviews two articles on agnostic metaphysics. He agrees with Frederic Harrison that Darwin's discoveries must at the very least force Christians to redefine their position and shares G. J. Romanes' view that Nature draws evolution onwards via power struggles. Earlier, in leader-articles for the same newspaper, he had revealed his acceptance of the Darwinian world view unequivocally. Relating it to ambition, the self-styled 'Scotsman on the make' notes that "The fight for life is now far sterner . . . and the ladder of fame can only, except in rare instances, be climbed by inches." In looking forward socially rather than personally, he also follows "the Darwinian method of reasoning" adopting it for "determining the man of the future as well as the man of the past".[3]

In **An Edinburgh Eleven** the young Christian's traditional theology meets the advanced views of the University teachers whose pen portraits form the core of that book. As Barrie followed the broad curriculum set for the Scottish Ordinary degree, the worlds of Mathematics, Natural Philosophy and Metaphysics were opened to him as well as those of language and literature. Campbell Fraser in the class of Metaphysics introduced the young writer to perspectivism. In so doing he gave academic respectability to Barrie's own difficulties in defining the real through a personality which changed constantly.[4] Science drew him towards anthropology and the books of explorers, bringing the youthful traveller Joseph Thomson into the team.[5] In short, Edinburgh University brought an enquiring mind into contact with new philosophical and scientific ideas. Educated in one of the major centres of Scottish Darwinism and committed to Berkeley's view that there are as many truths as persons perceiving them, Barrie visited his old church in a new spirit.

Blake fails to account for all this evidence in texts he does not cite. More perniciously, he fails to cope with evidence against his thesis in the very texts he does cite. True, **Auld Licht Idylls** is, historically, set in the past and narrated by a Free Church precentor. But the Nature he observes is far from idealised. The opening chapter of **Auld Licht Idylls** describes a world of battle. Before the precentor's troubled eyes, animals and birds devour each other with the strong destroying the weak. That scenario is translated into human terms via the 'roup' where villagers squabble over the possessions of a ruined neighbour. Later, the problem is given a literary dimension when he enters a bothy to find the farm labourers reading "one of Darwin's books" (p. 49). He remarks to himself that they scarcely needed academic confirmation of a fact they knew at first hand.

If Blake fails to understand the fictive perspective of the Narrator, he also fails to understand the literary perspective of that Narrator's creator. Bringing realistic, sociological criteria to the text, he condemns it as historical escapism. Barrie had made it quite clear that he was not presenting history in this way. If you wish to live in his Thrums, the very person you must *not* rely upon is a historian—("ask not a dull historian" p. 10). The first change of *your* perspective must be away from empirical criteria ("nor even go to Thrums" p. 10) into shared imaginary identification with the plight of individuals ("but to those rather who have been as boys and girls there and now are exiles" p. 10). The second is to understand historical change not through facts and events but through artifice and individuality. For there *is* no Thrums, only a village of words ("Thrums is the name I give here to the handful of houses" p. 9). At the same time, there are as many Thrums as there are Scots villagers thrown out of their secure village world, needing to "use" images of home as a means of proclaiming dignity and identity in the face of unemployment and the uniformity of city life ("Everyone dreams of it, though not all call it Thrums" p. 26). Barrie does not attempt to imitate the actual world of the Industrial Revolution but to inhabit the minds and emotions of those who convert their rustic homelands into a mythic protection against unbearable reality.

The Nature proposed by Darwin was, essentially, one of advance through conflict:

> Consequently, each new variety or species, during the progress of its formation, will generally press hardest on its nearest kindred and tend to exterminate them.[6]

Peter Pan is, throughout, a tale of battles—pirates against redskins against lost boys; Tiger Lily against Wendy against Tinker Bell. Structurally, it is based on the circular form of Shakespearean Romance with its variations and contrasts, all suggestive of the seasonal cycle. That it is meant to represent the mystery of an apparently cruel nature is underlined by the various rituals demanded by its author. At the first rehearsal, the actors were given scripts carrying only their words and the name of the next character cued. They were as blind to the play's development as to their future fortune in life; made to experience the dramatist's godhead in the theatre as we from day to day experience unforeseeability in creaturehood. A second ritual confirmed the intention of likening the play to Nature—its run must be regarded as continuous, with each particular production differing from the last; merely a chance, concrete viewing of the mysteries of origin played out by us all—audience, actors, authors. A third underlined Nature's cruelty in excluding those who did not fit its patterns. "Every December a terrifying ceremony takes place before **Peter Pan** is produced, and this is the measuring of the children who play in it. They are measured to see whether they have grown too tall."[7]

When Barrie wrote the Dedication to **Peter Pan** he expressed this belief in a more explicit manner. He began by suggesting that he had "no recollection of having written it" himself. He then, in turn, granted hypothetical authorship or part-authorship to the Llewelyn Davies children, whose adventure games had been its source material; to members of the audience, including "a depressed man in overalls" who thinks it is bound to be a failure; and to Wendy whose feminine nature provided the "disturbing element" necessary to turn picture book into drama. Returning to the question of his own role, he concluded that he probably did have some part in the "inky" production of the text but only after calling attention to the original programme in which Ela Q. May, the youngest actress is designated "Author of the Play".[8]

Any question of Barrie actually forgetting his authorship of the play may be put aside. All his work issues first from notes compiled over a long planning stage. **Peter Pan** (1904) not only has 466 'Fairy Notes' specifically relating to it,[9] its hero and theme have earlier appeared in the photograph collection, **The Boy Castaways** (1901) and in a novel, **The Little White Bird** (1902).[10] By positing multi-authorship, Barrie is calling attention to his own limitations as creature-creator of an inky text, which originates from events shared with others, introduces characters with a life of their own interpreted by actors with views of their own for audiences whose reactions will kill it or grant it continuing life until the breath of their applause fails.

The problem of authorship is of especial importance for an age of Darwinian doubt. Once the certainty of a benevolent creator is withdrawn, the comfort of syntheses in mystery is replaced by the very dialectic of oppositions-unreconciled enacted in **Peter Pan**. One can either remain free, young and anarchic with Peter or responsible, mature and beloved with Wendy. One cannot choose both. And if that is the pessimism of doubt enacted, Peter's name embodies the new challenge of Darwinism for man contemplating a creation revealed in conflict yet still veiled by mystery.

No author toiled more over names than did James Barrie. Almost always they are significant. Pan is the god whose own origins had been described by Sir Francis Bacon. Barrie had read Bacon with some enthusiasm in Masson's literature classes at University at a time when the Elizabethan's status as a precursor of Darwinism, guaranteed him newfound popularity. *The Wisdom of the Ancients and New Atlantis* had been re-published in 1886. In it the conflicting accounts of Pan were drawn together:

> PAN: Pan, as his name imports, represents and lays open the ALL of things, or Nature. Concerning his origin, there are only two opinions that go for current: either he came of Mercury, that is the Word of God . . . or else from the confused seed of things . . . But as touching the third conceit of Pan's origins, it points to the state of the world not considered of Adam, exposed and made subject to death and corruption.[11]

Pan economically represents 'all' by possibly meaning God, world or devil. Peter Pan can affirm Peter as type of the Church and gatekeeper of heaven, whose symbol of the cock the eternal boy constantly arrogates to himself. Or Peter can conflict with Pan as Satan, the goat-god, an idea followed through in the 'Fairy Notes'—as demon (n. 106), type of pride (n. 347) and usurper (n. 268). Or Peter can join with Pan as child of the world, of pantheism and the fall, unable to face up to the cruel facts of death and decay. In name he is all meaning and no meaning and so any meaning; in conception he is, therefore, the perfect character-tool to re-frame, in a new intellectual context, the age-old questions of origins and ontology.

My argument is that Darwinian conflict and its upsetting of the traditional Christian world view constitute, for Barrie, that new dramatic frame. He had already addressed similar issues in **Quality Street** (1902) and **Little Mary** (1903).[12] But in **Peter Pan** he specifically deals with Creation. The play's rituals and Dedication have turned creation as authorship into a contest for godlike power. I shall now demonstrate the thoroughness with which Barrie pursues his chosen theme. Using the Manuscript and earlier drafts as well as the Collected Edition text I shall in turn look at the battles over creation—original, sexual, artistic and linguistic.[13]

The opening scene in the drama appropriately turns the idea of birth into a children's game with John and Wendy playing fathers and mothers. At the most immediate level, this is effective light comedy. Barrie knew that one did not fill popular London theatres with overtly philosophical drama. His favourite dramatic models—Shakespeare and Skelton—had taught him however that different audiences can be addressed at different levels and by different poetic means.[14] And if we listen with more care to John and Wendy, we notice that they literally 'call' their game-children into being.

JOHN:

> (*Good-naturedly*) I am happy to inform you, Mrs Darling, that you are now a mother.

(p. 20)

Twice Wendy will "acquaint" John in his turn of fatherhood. It was the God of *Genesis* who spoke things into being in this manner ("And God SAID, Let there be Light" *Genesis* I, verse 3). If Barrie suggests rivalry with the deity, he also stresses that this claim is being made *in game* by children. (JOHN: (histrionically) We are doing an act; we are playing at being you and father.) As with authorship, the battle begins by relinquishing the highest ground. As with authorship, the manipulative, negative potential of such power is also explored. If one creature can 'call' another into being, so it can destroy potential existence by silence.

MICHAEL:

> (*expanding*) Now, John, have me.

JOHN:

> We don't want any more.

MICHAEL:

> (*contracting*) Am I not to be born at all?

JOHN:

> Two is enough.

(p. 20)

The stage directions are important. Michael acts his growth and destruction before being spoken into being by his real mother. As the Idea of the shadow play ("we are playing at being you"), she has the right so to do. To Michael's despairing cry that nobody wants him, she not only gives the positive word "I do" but confirms his gender—"Boy."

If the opening of Act One dramatises Creation as birth in primarily metaphysical terms, so Act Two deals with Creation in its natural and sexual context. The 'Fairy Notes' clearly reveal that, at first, Barrie had intended Cupids to have character status as well as Pan.

> 2) Cupids teaching girl to fly away.
> 51) Cupids shooting arrows into Prince.

The same range of positive (generative) and worldly/fallen (pantheistic/pagan) associations were being explored for sexual love as for origins; for Cupids as well as Pan. In addition, the malevolent, anti-Christian side of the personification was being followed through. Note 134, for example, links the blindness of the deity to the games played by the torturers at the foot of the cross: "134) Cupids playing Blind Man's Buff". Later, Barrie decided to translate these ideas without recall to the pagan deities. The sexual battle was, first of all, mythically translated and diminished through the Lost Boys shooting Wendy. Then it was dramatised in the battle for Peter's favours conducted among Wendy, Tiger Lily and Tinker Bell.

In Act Two Scene One, Wendy flies over the Never Never Land. Mistaking her for a bird, Tootles shoots her with an arrow. She falls to earth apparently dead; Peter orders a house to be constructed around her and from that house she emerges to claim motherhood. The sexual overtones are clear. The arrow penetrates the woman and is followed by a brief 'death'. As an avid student of Renaissance drama, Barrie knew what he was doing in suggesting the 'little death' of the sexual act followed by the womb house. It is this aspect of the motif which is stressed by those critics who wish to demonstrate the playwright's Oedipal complex.[15] If so, it is certainly a self-conscious artistic presentation of the condition for the Notes show that all the sexual details of the Cupid myth had to be translated as part of the play's intellectual plan.

The blindness of the new Cupids is overlooked in the desire to turn the play into a mirror of its author's psyche. It is essential that the shooting is done by creatures unaware of their own nature—representatives of *our* fallen state as well as Wendy's. That is why the shooting is preceded by evidence that they all are Pan's creations in his fantasy land, unaware of the laws of the real world, unaware even of their own names.

SLIGHTLY:

> My mother had wrote my name on the pinafore I was lost in. 'Slightly Soiled'; that's my name.
>
> (p. 39)

In facing the new questions raised by Darwin's view of Nature as battle, Barrie honestly re-translates both the images of warfare *and* of lost spiritual comfort. If our new origin is an ape or a tadpole, that does not eradicate our unwilled existence; it only gives it a less exalted mythological framework. And if science has given us one new and necessary insight, it serves only to highlight the darkness of the minds with which we fail to understand our own existence and essence. Wendy is shot down by a lost boy who understands nothing and serves, in Peter, a master of protective mythologies. Denying the real world, Pan builds a comforting fantasy around him. Denying death, he teaches the lost boys that only flowers decay and die. Denying sex, he claims that Wendy was not pierced by the arrow but protected by an acorn. His calling the acorn a kiss reflects a different, verbal type of shield. Seeing that his childishness prevented him from understanding the nature of the concept 'kiss', she had diverted its word-sign to an object and so provided him with a protection in linguistic reference:

WENDY:

> (*aghast*) Don't you know what a kiss is?

PETER:

> I shall know when you give it me. (*Not to hurt his feelings she gives him her thimble.*)
>
> (p. 31)

He in his turn matches the thimble with an object of the same shape drawn from his own life, so fusing the sound of kiss and the shape of the nut in his mind. Every one of these primitive myths are enacted before Wendy becomes a mother. Here, Barrie translates birth as warfare; a warfare in which man's arrow cruelly brings life down from the skies. But he dramatises this descent through the blind eyes of wilful escapism, denying the facts of life (literally) to remain happy in error.

From this point of view, it is Peter and his non-existent ("Never Never") land which represents the temptation to deny new evidence. So long as one sees Peter as Barrie's alter-ego, it is possible to view the author as another escapist. To do so, however, is to deny the evidence of the 'Fairy Notes' in which Peter's diabolic aspect is more fully explored than any other;[16] to deny the evidence of his earlier journalism and to deny the way in which the sexual battle, in particular, is presented. In this instance, it is helpful to look at the earlier manuscript evidence. The original plan for **Peter Pan** proved too ambitious and too lengthy for actual stage production. But often, as in this case, it provides evidence of the pattern of Barrie's thought before it faced the compromise of theatrical pragmatics.[17]

The conflict among the female characters in the manuscript is more developed and more adult. Tiger Lily represents the coquette with references to her appearing in her neglig'ee and her ostentatious flirting. Wendy is at once the mother figure and possessor of all the trickery of the 'very woman' in *Seven Women*.[18] These 'humours' are much more clearly defined but it is the directly sexual approach of Tiger Lily which obviously distinguishes the early texts from later versions. In Scene Three of the manuscript, for example, she forces the eternal boy to face his sexuality:

TIGER LILY:

> Suppose Tiger Lily runs into wood—Peter Paleface catch her—what then?

PETER:

> (*bewildered*) Paleface can never catch Indian Girl, they run so fast.

TIGER LILY:

> If Peter Paleface chase Tiger Lily—she no run very fast—she tumble in a heap what then? (*Peter puzzled. She addresses Indians.*) What then?

ALL INDIANS:

> She him's squaw.

In Scene Four, when she finally comes to accept the impregnability of his innocence, her reaction is that of the rejected, passionate lover. Furiously, she abandons him to his fate. "Then Tiger Lily leave you here—you starve, or else wild beasts come to eat you little bit here, little bit there." The sexual competitiveness essential to Darwinian theory becomes less obvious as the play is abbreviated in subsequent drafts. But it remains as does the superiority of the sexually aware female characters over the asexual boy.

The major flaw in most psychological readings of the play lies in their more or less exact equation between Pan and his creator; between Barrie's desire to escape and Peter's. All the planning evidence suggests exactly the opposite—that Barrie admired and gave the victory to Wendy.[19] I shall test this thesis again as I move from the sexual battle per se to the sexual battle in Art.

As a perspectivist, Barrie had to translate battling Nature via medium as well as message; via the origins and conventions of Art as well as the origins and perceptions of mankind. That is why the Pan theme is, itself, re-examined by Sir James in nine different art forms—photograph collection, novel, full length play, one act play, ballet, children's novel, film scenario, short story and speech.[20] If every individual recreates the tale anew when seeing it or reading it, then its author must also view it through the maximal range of artistic convention available to him.

The most obvious support for the validity of this view within **Peter Pan** lies in the preference shown by the major characters for different types of artistic expression. Hook is at once the *rhetorician* and the *literary critic*. His soliloquies with their many Shakespearean echoes are usually pessimistically virtuosic. But they express an awareness of entire impotence in Darwinian battle terms:

HOOK:

> (*communing with his ego*) How still the night is; nothing sounds alive. Now is the hour when children in their homes are a-bed; . . . Split my infinitives, but 'tis my hour of triumph! (*Clinging to this fair prospect he dances a few jubilant steps but they fall below his usual form.*) And yet some disky spirit compels me now to make my dying speech, lest when dying there may be no time for it. All mortals envy me, yet better perhaps for Hook to have had less ambition!
>
> (p. 74)

Of course Hook shares many of Barrie's characteristics—his love for accurate language is revealed by viewing a split infinitive as the worst of swearwords and by his having a *Thesaurus* in his cabin. But in the battle for power within the text, he is the creation of another creation (Pan) and as such is sacrificed by a writer who loves him.

Peter is the *actor-director*. The Never Never Land is his play and within it he orders the around; revises the rules whenever he wishes and usually does so in order to highlight his own acting role. In Peter, the spirit of Bottom the Weaver lives on with the wish to direct, re-write and play all parts. It is easy to assume that he, therefore, is the victor in any struggle conducted within a play (*his* chosen mode) bearing *his* name. But Barrie seems anxious to stop us making this assumption. In pitting Peter against Wendy the *storyteller,* he even explicitly warns us against leaping to this easy conclusion against the precise meaning conveyed by the text.

In the Dedication, he notes that many people seem to take away the idea that Peter leads Wendy and the others into the Never Never Land. Look again, he suggests for "It may be that even Peter did not really bring her to the Never Land of his free will, but merely pretended to do so because she would not stay away." (p. 13) The relevant part of the text reveals Peter's desire to learn the end of *Cinderella* from Mrs Darling. In her absence, Wendy adopts the position of narrator successfully for the first time. Knowing the conclusion, Peter is about to set off and it is Wendy who uses the promise of further tales to restrain him—"Don't go, Peter. I know lots of stories." It is Wendy who makes him take her brothers by appealing to his male ego: "Of course it's awfully fas-cin-a-ting! Would you teach John and Michael to fly too?" And it is Wendy, who 'tells' the boys out of the Never Never Land after having 'told' them into it. Once she is quite sure that Peter is a sexual lost cause, incapable of making her a real mother—and only then—she begins her sagas of the homeland:

WENDY:

> Who are the two noble portly figures accompanying her? Can they be John and Michael? They are. (*Pride of Michael*) "See, dear brothers," says Wendy, pointing upward, "there is the window standing open." So up they flew to their loving parents and pen cannot inscribe the happy scene over which we draw a veil.
>
> (p. 66)

Her psychological technique is identical. She relies on male pride. But she also invades Peter's mode and *dramatises* herself as storyteller. Peter is not the victor for he rules only within the fantasy kernel of the play's structure. Wendy defeats him by telling herself into that land and out of it. The Dedication reminds us also that she is the male principle, who has "bored her way" into the safe land of Black Lake Island with its all-male games.[21] She is, therefore, the dramatic impetus as well as the victor revealed by the dramatic form.

The thoroughly planned victory for Wendy can be demonstrated by looking at the sexual/artistic battle from two other angles. First, if the image of Wendy-triumphant is of a moving, adaptable force drawing characters from fantasy towards fact, where is the balancing image of Peter? The answer is to be found in the tableau which concludes Act Five Scene One. The Curtain falls on Pan's most complete victory in battle and then rises again "to show PETER a very Napoleon on his ship." This scene was one which Barrie retained despite strenuous opposition. It posed a major directing problem for Peter had to be given time to change and that involved having a gymnast cover his part from his last speech ("I'm youth I'm joy! . . .") until the fall of the curtain. In its turn the curtain had to remain down until the exact scene depicted by Orchardson in his painting of Napoleon on the Bellerophon had been reproduced.[22] Barrie never moved from the position spelt out in the 'Fairy Notes':

> 362) P. in black a stern figure of Fate—after success is drunk in himself a la Tommy—struts deck along with others staring at him—like Napoleon on Bellerophon.

That is—at the moment of apparent victory, Peter mimics a defeated male hero as represented in Fine Art for the benefit of self-created images on a fantasy island within the artifice of drama.

The contrast with Wendy could not be more extreme; nor could it work more obviously in her favour. In Bergsonean terms, she is the fluid, adaptable, real figure at one with the demands of evolutionary development; he is frozen in the tableau form at four removes from actuality. Barrie also refers to the novel in which Peter's own birth is first mooted. "A la Tommy" reminds us that the flawed artist-hero of *Tommy and Grizel,* had declared his intention of writing a novel about a boy who would not grow up.[23] Barrie needs to sign Peter's inadequacy in both the sexual and artistic dimensions of Origin. He does so by referring to a literary *source* in which man's inadequacy as artist (Tommy) is highlighted through contrast with a more mature woman (Grizel).

A similar technique had been used at the end of Act Three. There, Peter had celebrated another victory within the limitations of dramatic fantasy. On the lagoon, Peter 'saves' Wendy by letting her fly off on the kite, while he remains behind, proclaiming, "To die will be an awfully big adventure." But the stage directions remind us, first of all, that he has no weight and so has chosen to remain in this quasi-heroic position only in order to steal the scene from her. He cannot die in his own deathless land. In a manner which again reminds us of Nature teaching the strong to usurp the weak, he simply removes two eggs from the bird's nest which obligingly swims towards him. Barrie then makes Peter literally life the eggs from a nest while himself 'lifting' the symbolism for the scene from the major source of the play, *The Little White Bird.*

In that novel, Peter had first come to life in Kensington Gardens as part of the male narrator's failed attempt to defeat through tale-telling the greater powers of a rival heroine. That heroine would have a real child *and* write a better novel than his, so winning both battles of creation in Nature and in Art. In this context, Peter is "born" when he takes a thrush's nest and crosses in it to an island where the God-Bird Solomon Caw distributes babies. He is created by the male author-narrator, therefore, in one of a series of failed attempts to precede the act of copulation from which he is, by his own nature, barred. Another attempt to claim pre-natal creation takes the form of his having written a letter which caused the real mother to be reconciled with the father and so 'caused' their child to be born—his word preceding the Word. The sophistry of such arguments and man's inadequacy in the face of woman's superior Nature as birthgiver are, therefore, the dramatic context for Pan's own birth in Art.

The coding is complex but very thorough and available to anyone who reads the 'Fairy Notes' and earlier drafts. As originally planned, the play made these links much clearer as it contained additional scenes which gave Peter's failure in the face of Nature and Art a more explicit dramatic context. One of these involved twenty mothers claiming the lost boys; the other (set in Kensington Gardens) translated all the characters into their original dramatic equivalents within the harlequinade.[24] It is easy to see why both were dropped. The play as originally conceived and performed was far too long. The twenty women appeared for only one scene and, unfortunately, reminded the audience on the first night of prostitutes on parade. Commercial and theatrical considerations doomed them at once to oblivion.

The harlequinade did not, in one sense, disappear. Barrie converted its message into the one act play, *Pantaloon* (1905). In so doing he faced the sad fact that the metadramatic line in his play had evaded the understanding of even his most perceptive critics. They failed to see that a work on origins had, in his terms, to embrace origins in art. First night criticism had also focussed on the metadrama of Hook recalling past actors:

> We have unfortunately to endure a 'front-scene', as meaningless and as exasperating as it is paltry. The only excuse for its introduction, if excuse it can be

considered, is that it affords Mr Gerald du Maurier an opportunity of imitating the bearing and style of Sir Henry Irving, Mr Tree and Mr Martin Harvey.[25]

In bowing to incomprehension, Barrie confessed not to meaninglessness but to an attempt at being too meaning-*full* within the immediacy of the dramatic mode. The pattern of the first production, however, had made clear the full range of origin battles comprehended in the playwright's thought—nature (mothers), fiction (Kensington Gardens), drama (harlequinade), acting (Irving, Harvey) and Fine Art (Orchardson).[26] Abbreviation and pragmatic accommodations did not narrow the range of imaginative reference; they only obscured the clarity of formal signing and so made future audiences' continued sense of having felt and understood more than the apparent triviality of the piece warranted less amenable to easy critical demonstration.

Darwin's battling Nature was, therefore, recreated in **Peter Pan** through character conflicts. These centred on claims for power—*authorial*, *sexual* and *artistic*. Sometimes, Barrie's own claim is stressed but within the drama it would appear that Peter's victories over Hook are shadowed by his failures to control or even match Wendy. Students of Barrie's earlier writings will know that a final battle remains to be evaluated—the *linguistic* battle of words and names. In **Sentimental Tommy** the artist-hero learned that words did not embody facts; that the word 'tree', for example, only signified a type of plant life to those initiated into the code of the English language. This gave potential power to those who could use language most subtly. Tommy then proved his suppositions by writing letters on behalf of his less literate acquaintances, so manipulating their lives.[27]

The presence of Roget as, literally, the household god of **Peter Pan** relates to Barrie's awareness of this fact. He enjoyed practising verbal power, which he saw as his own claim to genius. But he also, like Tommy, knew the other side of the equation—that there was no perfect word to 'speak' things, only grades of greater or lesser referential accuracy. Tommy discovers this when he enters an essay competition and sits throughout searching for that impossible word (pp. 423-40). Barrie reflected the need to be as precise as possible by always composing with the *Thesaurus* at his side. It is more than 'whimsy', therefore, when the opening stage direction to **Peter Pan** credits the setting of the Darlings' home to Roget:

> The night nursery of the Darling family, which is the scene of our opening act is at the top of a rather depressed street in Bloomsbury. We have a right to place it where we will, and the reason that Bloomsbury is chosen is that Mr Roget once lived there.
>
> (p. 17)

In claiming his own "inky" power, Barrie admits the major source of its subtlety.

What may not be so clear is the link between Roget and Darwin. The former was not first and foremost a linguist but a physiologist, who later held the Fullerian Chair of Physiology at the Royal Institution. He had met Darwin as a fellow student in the Medical Faculty at Edinburgh University and subsequently structured his *Thesaurus* around the zoological phyla. That is, if Nature could not be exactly and necessarily expressed by language, at least language could be arranged to mirror the perceived organisation of and distinctions within Nature. Both Roget and Darwin saw stronger languages ousting weaker ones and more effective words ousting less effective ones in this verbal reflection of evolutionary progress:

> A struggle for life is constantly going on amongst the words and grammatical forms in each language. . . . The survival or preservation of certain favoured words in the struggle for existence is natural selection.[28]

Darwin made these claims without losing faith in the Word (the Speaker of things); Barrie's own faith may or may not have remained firm but as mirroring and questioning playwright he saw it as his duty to present the personal, social and metaphysical problems of starting anthropologically with Babel.

Clearly, **Peter Pan** does explore less refined communication battles. Tom-toms, smoke signals, the crocodile's clock, the fairy language, the birds' language are all used and treacherously misused in the Never Never Land. The crucial question remains—*in language*, which characters have the greatest power? I shall look at the opening dialogues between Peter and Hook then between Peter and Wendy to discover whether Barrie is consciously thinking of conversation as a battle for power in Darwinian terms. If so, who is revealed as the hero or heroine in power?

Peter confronts the pirate captain for the first time verbally in Act Three. By mimicking the latter's voice, he has tricked the pirate's crew into releasing Tiger Lily. Hook learns of this and sees the boy first as a claimant for his own identity:

HOOK:

> (*gripping the stave for support*) Who are you, stranger, speak.

PETER:

> (*who is only too happy to speak*) I am Jas Hook, Captain of the *Jolly Roger*.

HOOK:

> (*now white to the gills*) No, no, you are not.

PETER:

> Brimstone and gall, say that again and I'll cast anchor in you.

HOOK:

   If you are Hook, come tell me, who am I?

PETER:

   A codfish, only a codfish.

HOOK:

   (*aghast*). A codfish?

SMEE:

   (*drawing back from him*) Have we been captained all this time by a codfish?

STARKEY:

   It's lowering to our pride.

HOOK:

   (*feeling his ego is slipping from him*) Don't desert me, bullies.

(p. 55)

If this dialogue is not intended to reflect the power of Peter, through language, to rob Hook of his essence, then why does he imitate the very language patterns of his victim ("Brimstone and gall"); why does Hook take the matter so seriously ("aghast") and why does he construe it in Freudian terms ("feeling his ego is slipping from him")? More specifically, why does he see himself being drawn backwards in the evolutionary process? The theory that we may have derived from fish was popular at this time as reflected in the music hall ditty—"When you were a tadpole, I was a fish / In the Palaeozoic age." The codfish references surely have this force.

But there is even more to it than that. Peter has actually created Hook, as he has created all the creatures on *his* fantasy island. The hook (iconographically associated with the devil) is at once a sign of this difference in ontological status and a nickname given as a sign of former victory. Here theology and anthropology merge. As the Devil cannot defeat Christ, only rhetorically defy him, so Hook cannot defeat his creator. His knowledge of that stems from a past defeat, just as Hook's name reflects the past defeat which Pan had signed on his body.[29] If the Bible revealed that to Barrie, it was the work of those explorers whom he idolised and those anthropologists whose writings he had reviewed in the *Nottingham Journal,* which explained to him the magical power of 'naming' in primitive societies. Smee, whose name proclaims the very security in identity ('It's me!') which his history denies[30] is, unsurprisingly, the first of the crew to accept the theft of Hook's name as identical with lost essence. In so doing Barrie dramatises one of the scenes recently described in Frazer's *Golden Bough*:

> Unable to discriminate clearly between words and things, the savage commonly fancies that the link between a name and the person or thing denominated by it is not merely an arbitrary and ideal association, but a real and substantial bond which unites the two.[31]

In particular, nicknames and names referring to *parts* of a person's appearance were held to give the namer magical power over the individual named. 'Hook', therefore, gives Peter dual power as it fulfils both criteria. No wonder, at the height of later apparent victory, that "some disky spirit" dictates he prophesy death. That spirit is Pan (the diminished and selfish Christ figure) who only creates him for the greater glorification of self.

In **Sentimental Tommy,** the 'naming' victory had also been anticipated through the character of Tommy's earthbound friend, Corp (i.e. body). He is defeated in the fantasy games devised by the hero because he has been given so many different role-names that "which he was at any particular moment he never knew, till Stroke (i.e. Tommy) told him, and even then he forgot and had to be put in irons." (p. 251) The distinction between naming and other types of conversation battle and their potential for mastery had been noted well before **Peter Pan** but are most powerfully presented in that text.

The first discussion between Peter and Wendy leads into the 'kiss'/'thimble'/'nut' situation earlier noted, where Peter's more limited understanding makes him "unable to distinguish clearly between words and things" and so puts him in the vulnerable position of the savage identified by Frazer. Although Wendy first of all meets his expectation of a kiss-object by benevolent perversion of her richer vocabulary range, soon she will attempt to manipulate action through the new coding. Her demonstration of what a "thimble" *really* means led (in the earlier drafts) to their only actual kiss.

But all this follows from what amounts to a nominal knock-out in Wendy's favour in Round One:

PETER:

   What is your name?

WENDY:

   (*well-satisfied*) Wendy Moira Angela Darling. What is yours?

PETER:

   (*finding it lamentably brief*) Peter Pan.

WENDY:

   Is that all?

PETER:

   (*biting his lip*) Yes.

WENDY:

   (*politely*) I am so sorry.

(p. 29)

Every stage direction demands enactment of the felt victory. If Hook constantly looks back to the first deciding 'nominal' battle as the sign of his tragic definition, only Peter's inability to live outside the present shields him from a similar fate.[32] A more adult consciousness might have used the Biblical and Baconian potentials of 'Peter Pan' to contest Wendy's confidence but it is precisely that consciousness which the child, frozen in childhood, cannot have. For Peter, Wendy simply has a longer and, therefore, better name. For Barrie, that name had undergone a lengthy period of revision and thought. In the manuscript she was called 'Wendy Maria Elizabeth' with Wendy a coinage drawn from the actual attempt by W. E. Henley's daughter to call Barrie her "friend." (Friend—*fwendy.*)[33] If that represents the particular, empirical side of guidance in love, so 'Moira's echoing of the loving guide figure, Moira Loney, in *Little Mary* (1903) and 'Angela's' association with the role of the angels as our guides within the theological hierarchy lead naturally into 'Darling' as sign of family love. From all these identity-contexts, as the barred window symbolises, Peter is locked out.

My argument is not intended to draw attention away from the simpler comic effectiveness of **Peter Pan**. As a writer for the popular theatre, Barrie sought to enchant the many through his comic skills. Like Boccaccio, however, he held that a work might be structured vertically. A direct and light narrative line might carry darker and more complex meanings poetically conveyed to those whose intellects could face their message while remaining veiled from those who could not. Much of the imagery of **Peter Pan**, most of its stage directions and all of its precise dramatic argument re-present the unanswerable problems of origin diminished and softened through the perspective of children at play but darkened by Darwin's view of internecine Nature evolving from primitive animalism rather than Eden. The questions are posed starkly and considered thoroughly in their ontological, sexual, artistic and linguistic dimensions. The clear storyline may end happily enough but its implications will trouble the minds and emotions of those who think deeply about it or allow its imagery and visions to take them over. As one of Barrie's most perceptive critics noted, "He has been inspired to see that the greatest tragedy of human life to-day is that its tragedy cannot be faced, that it can only be shown us by a trick—the trick of Laughter."[34]

Notes

1. J. M. Barrie, *An Edinburgh Eleven*, Uniform Edition (London, 1888), p. 125.
2. George Blake, *Barrie and the Kailyard School* (London, 1961), p. 52.
3. *Nottingham Journal,* 15th September, 1884; 16th April and 8th May, 1883.
4. *An Edinburgh Eleven,* Uniform Edition (London, 1888), p. 68. "Phenomenal or sense dependent existence can be substantiated and caused only by a self-conscious spirit . . ." et seq.
5. *Ibid.,* Chapter 9. The comic lead in Barrie's first major play, *Walker, London* tries to pass himself off as an African explorer, based on Thomson as model.
6. Charles Darwin, *The Origin of Species* (London, 1950), p. 97.
7. Pauline Chase, *Peter Pan's Postbag* (London, 1909), Introduction, p. v.
8. The Dedication was composed for the Collected Edition of the *Plays of J. M. Barrie* (London, 1928) from which all dramatic quotations in this article are taken. Placing Ela Q. May's name as author on the programme did not prevent Barrie "having the large letters and standing at the top". *Times,* December 28th 1904.
9. Beinecke Library, University of Yale, Barrie MSS: P45/1903. A fellowship at this library during Spring 1993 allowed me to complete the research for this article.
10. The photographs were of the actual games played by Barrie with the Llewelyn Davies boys. Only two copies were printed, the full title being *The Boy Castaways of Black Lake Island*. Chapters XIV ('Peter Pan') and XV ('The Thrush's Nest').
11. Francis Bacon, *The Wisdom of the Ancients and New Atlantis* (London, 1886), Section 6, p. 36.
12. See R. D. S. Jack, *The Road to the Never Land* (Aberdeen, 1990), pp. 79-104; 131-154.
13. The Manuscript is held in the Lilly Library, University of Indiana.
14. Barrie's early critical essay on Skelton, 'The Satirical Rector of Diss', is held in Beinecke: Barrie MSS S354.
15. The most thorough Oedipal reading is by Harry M. Geduld, *James Barrie* (New York, 1971).
16. Especially through references to his egoism in pride and desire to steal the souls of children. Later, Pan is sometimes deleted and "pirate" interpolated.
17. See R. D. S. Jack, 'The Manuscript of *Peter Pan,*' *Children's Literature* 18 (1990) pp. 101-13.
18. *Seven Women* (1917) constituted the first Act of the unsuccessful *Legend of Leonora* (1913). It was retained in One Act form and subsequently printed in the Uniform and Collected Editions.
19. This case is also argued by Frederic L. Meisel in 'The Myth of *Peter Pan*,' *The Psychoanalytic*

Study of the Child, Vol. 32 (New Haven, 1977), pp. 545-64; and by Jacqueline Rose, *The Case of Peter Pan* (London, 1984).

20. See Jack, *Road to Never Land,* pp. 164-65.

21. See Note 10. Barrie played the role of the pirate leader, Captain Swarthy.

22. Roger Lancelyn Green, *Fifty Years of Peter Pan* (London, 1954) re-traces Barrie's battles to retain the tableau in its exact form, imitating the painting.

23. Published in 1900.

24. The one act drama re-translated the cruel battles of the commedia dell'arte one year after the material was withdrawn from *Peter Pan.*

25. *Daily Telegraph,* 28th December, 1904.

26. In modern productions, all of these clear analytic signs of authorial intention have disappeared. In Barrie's own time, all but the last had been sacrificed. He retained his major ideas by a variety of subtler devices including the growth of Hook's part at the expense of Mr Darling's. See Jack, 'Manuscript of Pan'.

27. E.g. p. 419, where the schoolmaster exposes Tommy's practice. "'If these letters had been addressed to me they would have taken me in.' Tommy tried to look modest, but his chest would have its way."

28. Charles Darwin, *The Descent of Man* (London, 1885), p. 91. He is citing Max Muller in *Nature.* (1870) p. 257, with approval.

29. "HOOK: Most of all I want their captain, Peter Pan. 'Twas he cut off my arm." (Act 2, p. 41).

30. "HOOK: Pathetic Smee, the Nonconformist pirate, a happy smile upon his face because he thinks they fear him! How can I break it to him that they think him lovable?" (Act 5, p. 74).

31. J. G. Frazer, *The Golden Bough* (London, 1900) 3 vols. I, 403.

32. 'Fairy Notes' No. 296. "P's worst agony of all that he will forget girl in month."

33. Denis Mackail, *J. M. B.* (London, 1941), p. 148.

34. Sheila Kaye-Smith, *The Bookman* (Christmas Supplement). (1920), p. 108.

Ann Yeoman (essay date 1998)

SOURCE: Yeoman, Ann. "*Peter Pan,* the Novel: J. M. Barrie's Twentieth-Century Image of the Eternal Boy." In *Now or Neverland: Peter Pan and the Myth of Eternal Youth,: A Psychological Perspective on a Cultural Icon,* pp. 81-156. Toronto: Inner City Books, 1998.

[*In the following excerpt, Yeoman contends that in the novel* Peter Pan, *"Barrie aligns his narrative with the Romance genre, and modern literary fantasy may be seen as the successor to Medieval Romance, thematically as well as structurally."*]

SOME PLACE ELSE: STRUCTURES OF FANTASY AND FAIRY TALE

In the sparse page and a quarter John Rowe Townsend devotes to *Peter Pan* in his outline of literature for children, he makes three points which, despite their decidedly critical and dismissive tone, are instructive in our study of Peter Pan: 1) "Peter Pan, as everyone knows, is the boy who wouldn't grow up"; 2) "It is doubtful whether the idea of a boy who never grows up is as appealing to children as it is to parents"; and 3) "All in all, *Peter and Wendy* is not a very good book; I am sure it benefits unduly from the fame of the play."[1]

Townsend's comments return us to our earlier remarks about the artistic faults of Barrie's work and introduce the question of literary genre. How are we to classify *Peter Pan*? Why bother? How might an attempt at classification further our hermeneutic quest for possibilities of meaning in the text? Seamless, faultless and genre-specific Barrie's tale is not. Yet the more seamless and reassuringly coherent the narrative, the less provocative or rich it may prove to the searcher for new meaning. The sudden, disquieting, cryptic images of tale and dream narrative are those that open our perception to the previously unknown as they disturb our complacency and explode our preconceptions.

His elusive character makes Peter Pan impossible to fix. His tale remains equally elusive to literary definition, as Barrie draws from myth, and from the forms of fairy tale, Romance, adventure tale and fantasy, for the structure of his novel. As a result, the novel presents a collage of styles and genres, as it introduces a confusion of voices and points of view. Barrie now sides with his characters ("Some like Peter best and some like Wendy best, but I like [Mrs Darling] best"), now observes from the distance of a cynical adult ("You see, the woman [Mrs Darling] had no proper spirit"); he is now inside, now outside, of the action; he contradicts later what he, or the narrative, affirms earlier, changes his authorial mind in mid-paragraph, and then writes as though he, with the reader, is discovering the narrative as he proceeds:

> Now I understand what had hitherto puzzled me, why when Peter had exterminated the pirates he did not return to the island and leave Tink to escort the children back to the mainland. This trick [of closing the nursery window so the children would not be able to return home] had been in his head all the time.[2]

This veritable Babel of authorial voice and point of view introduces the possibility of Barrie's uncertain relationship with his material and is indicative of his profound ambivalence toward children and childhood as much as toward mothers, fathers and adulthood.

Townsend is right when he states that everyone knows Peter Pan and that the 1911 novel benefits from the 1904 play. In writing the novel, Barrie was not creating a character but writing about a figure already six and a half years old with a vibrant life of its own in the imagination of the theater-going public. Barrie was faced with the extraordinary task of capturing the ever-deepening popular "myth" of Peter Pan *as fiction,* as well as the essence of the immortal and eternal boy of classical myth embodied by Peter Pan *as figure.*

No wonder he resisted requests to write the novel for so many years and finally published the play only in 1928. No wonder Barrie's repeated changes to the script, particularly the ending, from production to production, and the mystery about the outcome of the plot during the first 1904 production, when cast members were not given copies of the entire script or informed of the fates of the characters they were playing. After all, the theater seems far more Peter Pan's element than the printed word. In the theater, he makes his sudden appearances and disappearances, and may never be exactly the same from year to year. It is, perhaps, the Peter Pan in Barrie, as much as the irreducible quality of Peter Pan's own mythic resonance, that refuses easy containment in print and genre.

Drawing from fairy tale as well as from myth, Barrie does not, however, locate the action of his novel in mythic time, the "Once upon a time" of traditional fairy tale. We are introduced to a specific time, place and family (the Darlings), and to a sense of normalcy ("All children grow up . . .") in what might appear the beginning of a domestic "nursery" story. The disturbing anomaly is the exception of the first line: All children, except one, grow up. It raises the question of whose tale is to be told: the opening pages indicate this to be Wendy's story but it is Peter Pan who is the one who does not grow up, and he soon commands center stage. An extension of this question of the relative centrality of Peter or Wendy to the tale is seen in the problematic relation of Edwardian London to Neverland, "this" or Wendy's world to that "other" world of Peter Pan. Barrie seems to struggle throughout the novel to decide whether his story has a hero or a heroine, or both, and on which side of the dividing line between London and Neverland, the real and the imaginal, he wants to position himself.

Although it lacks the flatness of characterization and description, and the objective starkness of the fairy story, in many ways the structure of Barrie's novel is similar to that of the traditional tale. Neverland and Edwardian London present two different realities; the plot involves the relation of one to the other and an exploration of the values implicit in each. In traditional tales also, two worlds are usually presented: the conscious, familiar, mundane world, in which a problem or missing value is evident, and the magical world indicative of the unfamiliar and unconscious, which nonetheless harbors the means to resolve the initial problem and restore the lost value. Movement from the mundane to the magical realm is often abrupt at the opening of the tale, for the hero or heroine is generally unaware of the existence and certainly of the potency of the unconscious, and so falls unwittingly into its power. We see this in the sudden appearance of the Beast's castle to Beauty's father in "Beauty and the Beast," and in how Hansel and Gretel stumble unexpectedly on the witch's gingerbread house in the forest. Typically, the protagonist from *this* world falls into the realm of the *other* world. In the case of Peter Pan, however, it happens the other way around, with Peter's sudden appearance in the nursery.

In the course of the traditional tale, the unfamiliar becomes increasingly familiar as the hero/heroine learns to cope, aided by magical animals and helpers, with the strangeness of the other world, until a bridge, or connection, is established between the disparate realms. The fairy tale, in its customary flatness, offers no interpretive clues to its possible meaning through the insights of characters or the intrusion of the narrator's opinion: there is no self-conscious narration and the narrative is not self-reflexive. The tale serves as a blank canvas, inviting the audience's projections and interpretations alike, and speaking to each listener insofar as it reflects his or her psychological truth.

Analytical psychology usually understands the bridge which develops between conscious and unconscious, as each is portrayed in the tale, to signify the development of a dialogue or flow of energy between the two levels (consciousness and the unconscious) of the psyche. This dialogue results from the ego's increased awareness of the reality of the unconscious or objective psyche, an awareness represented in the developing consciousness and strength of the hero/heroine. On the one hand, the boundary separating the two worlds becomes more clearly defined as an enhancement of ego-consciousness develops, and, on the other, the hero/heroine learns more readily to differentiate the two realms. With every expansion of consciousness, symbolized by such things as a royal wedding or success in finding the lost treasure, the ego is strengthened and so becomes less liable to fall into a strange world or psychic state of which it has no prior inkling and against which it is consequently unprotected.

The metaphorical bridge or psychological awareness of which we are talking is represented symbolically in "Hansel and Gretel" by the white duck who ferries the children back across the lake to their father's cottage. In "Beauty and the Beast" the link between the two worlds is effected through the mirror; in "Cinderella" through the slipper. In Barrie's children's fantasy the two worlds are linked through Peter Pan, his fairy dust and magical power of flight, although the inclusion of fairies and fairy dust in the tale arguably has more to do with Barrie's debt to Celtic mythology, as we shall see in our later discussion of Neverland, than with the fairy tale genre.

Modern literary fantasy's concern with alternate realities links it structurally to the fairy story. Often the alternate reality is explicitly represented in the creation of a secondary world (as in utopian- and science-fiction). In many cases the alternate realm is implicit, appearing as the other, inner world of a dissociated psyche (for example, in the figure of Golyadkin in Dostoyevsky's narrative of a descent into madness in *The Double*), or in the form of an inner prerogative or state of mind (as in the case of Kafka's protagonist K. in *The Trial* and *The Castle*). So J. R. R. Tolkien, author of the popular fantasies *The Hobbit* and *Lord of the Rings,* argues that the fantasist becomes the sub-creator of a world which stands in opposition to the primary world of consensus reality. This secondary creation of self-contained fantasy realms serves as a means to awaken desire in the reader for a different reality, for what is missing from the primary but promised in the secondary world. The implication is that ultimate value lies elsewhere, in the spiritual fantasy world of which this world is a poor reflection. If the work is successful, in Tolkien's view, desire for this other world must remain unsatisfied, for according to Tolkien fantasy should continually direct the reader toward the type of spiritual consolation and joy afforded by, in the Christian context, the greatest fairy story of all time, the Gospels.[3]

The type of fantasy tale of which Tolkien speaks is far removed from the noncommittal flatness of the traditional tale. On the one hand, it is overtly moralistic and, on the other, serves as a Christian allegory, offering a fictional Great Escape from the primary world, and consequently, for the duration of the story, from our fear of death. Tolkien's successful tale securely locates the longed-for grace intimated by the happy-ever-after resolution of the typical fairy story in a transcendent realm "beyond the walls of the world."

At first glance, Barrie's secondary world of Neverland may seem to belong in the tradition of Christian fantasists such as George MacDonald, Tolkien and C. S. Lewis, and we are tempted to draw comparisons between Neverland, Middle Earth and Narnia. Neverland presents a childhood paradise filled with adventure, joy and youth, promising the Great Escape from a primary world of grown-up consensus reality. It does not, however, afford a satisfactory allegory of the Christian message. As well as Barrie's more or less overt pagan references, we discover in Neverland a continuous round of violence and intrigue, the only moral ingredient of which is the somewhat ambiguous "good form" or "fair play" insisted upon by Hook and Pan. When the cycle of action is seemingly broken in Pan's defeat of Hook at the end, there is no symbolic resolution or expectation of redemption through the final victory of a Christian ethic: Hook is devoured by the crocodile; the pirates are dead or have fled the scene; the Indians have been brutally massacred; the lost boys return with Wendy to the grown-up world; and Peter Pan is left alone, trapped in an endless web of makebelieve, which confirms Wendy's sense when she first encounters him that she is "in the presence of a tragedy."[4]

Perhaps, then, more than may be immediately apparent, Barrie uses his children's fantasy as a vehicle to challenge collective mores and traditional concepts of what is real by proposing Neverland as an imaginative alternative to the consensus reality of Edwardian England. Certainly, the opposition of two worlds in fantasy provides a structure which may be exploited by the author to social, political or moral ends. This mode of fantasy enjoys a long tradition and we know that Barrie acknowledged the influence of many such fantasists and satirists.[5]

However, while we may read Barrie's tale for his commentary on Empire, and on contemporary political, military and social matters, the satirical strain in the narrative is faint indeed compared to the author's questioning of the nature of the actual and the imaginal, imagination and dream, conscious experience and the reality of the unconscious psyche. Hence the story's ambiguities and equivocations: If Peter is part of Wendy's dream, how may Mrs Darling explain the leaves left behind on the nursery floor, leaves which do not come "from any tree that grew in England"? The children are missing from their beds, yet the Neverland to which they fly is something that "you play at . . . by day with the chairs and table-cloth . . . but [which] in the two minutes before you go to sleep . . . becomes very nearly real."[6]

By questioning the boundary between the real and the imaginal in this way, Barrie aligns his narrative with the Romance genre, and modern literary fantasy may be seen as the successor to Medieval Romance, thematically as well as structurally. We have only to recall those most familiar Romances which focus on the quest of King Arthur's knights for the Holy Grail, the tragedy of Tristan and Isolde, and Sir Gawain's encounter with the Green Knight, to realize that Medieval Romance exemplifies the pattern of the hero's journey, in which the protagonist is challenged, among other things, to differentiate worldly from spiritual values.

The Romance genre addresses the hero's search for identity and meaning, both on an outer and an inner level. Two worlds are usually posited, representing the known and the unknown, in which opposition we discover Romance's structural similarity to myth and fairy tale. The quester must journey into the night world in search of knowledge or a value missing from the daytime world. Above all, Romance concerns "man's vision of his own life as quest,"[7] the outer journey standing as a metaphor for the inner. Consequently Romance, and fantasy as its modern equivalent, have as much to do with individual identity and the protagonist's achieving a secure sense of being in the world as with the desire, more explicit in science-fiction and allegorical or didactic fantasy, to change givens and alter reality, whether out of boredom, play, moral or political vision, or the longing for something lacking.

We can, then, make an argument for two principal modes of fantasy: The focus of one involves the conscious creation of imaginative alternatives to the everyday world (science-fiction, moral and Christian allegory, fantasy with a didactic or satirical intent) and brings to mind Jung's commentary on "psychological" literature as writing ostensibly directed and controlled by the intent of the author. The other addresses the eruption of the unfamiliar within the context of familiar, apparently logical, rational experience (magic realism, fantastic, grotesque and horror fiction), and is closer to Jung's description of "visionary" writing, where the author becomes the vehicle of an autonomous complex.

The fairy tale would seem to demand a category of its own: In the "pure" folk tale there is usually little or no evidence of allegorical intent, and in analytical psychology's approach to the tale, the primary world is understood as already serving as a metaphor for the dynamics of psyche represented in and through the characters and objects, while the appearance of a secondary world in the images of forest, magical castle, ocean, cave, etc., symbolizes psychic activity at a deeper archetypal substratum of the unconscious. Consequently, Marie-Louise von Franz and others attribute the origin of folk and fairy tales to their being a symbolic expression of a direct, and otherwise irrepresentable and unintelligible, experience of the autonomous psyche.[8]

The first mode of fantasy described above may be seen as subversive in that it questions, challenges and inverts the real. The chief characteristic of the second is disjuncture: it focuses on the uncanny and our struggle to understand and relate to the unreal; it explores the anomalous and fantastic event as it erupts into everyday life, and in this way is a "form of writing which is about opening up subversive spaces within the mainstream rather than ghettoizing fantasy by encasing it within genres."[9] There is, of course, no literary law that precludes the coexistence of both strains of fantasy in a single work, and this is what I believe we find in *Peter Pan*. On the one hand, Barrie's depiction of life in Neverland enables a critique of Edwardian institutions—childhood, the family, motherhood, fatherhood, social and sexual mores: it is subversive.[10] However, the very title of Barrie's first chapter, "Peter Breaks Through," suggests something of the nonrational has indeed broken through the veil of rational experience in the figure of Peter Pan: it is disjunctive and concerns the fantastic.

Certainly Barrie did not manage, and probably did not even try, to make a "good" piece of children's literature, as that was conceived in his day. This is evident in the number of abridgments and versions of *Peter and Wendy* written by others to make the tale more "suitable for children" than Barrie's original. All the usual distinctions between fairy story, fantasy, domestic story and boys' adventure tale are violated: Neverland and Peter Pan are as inappropriate to the domestic tale as is Wendy's domesticating presence in Neverland to the boys' adventure story. So in the novel it seems that Barrie was less concerned with elaborating the tale and profile of his 1904 dramatic hero than with finding a way to describe his experience of an autonomous force, with a life of its own, that cannot be contained within the boundaries of genre or the collective norms of Edwardian culture.

To return to a remark of Townsend's we have not yet addressed, namely, that the idea of a boy who never grows up is more appealing to parents than to children, we may certainly agree that Peter Pan presents an enigma of considerable concern to parents, but also argue that such an enigma must surely *engage* adults in general and one in particular: J. M. Barrie.

The Darlings: Stocks, Shares and Tidy Drawers

In order better to appreciate Barrie's eternal boy from a psychological and symbolical perspective, we will engage the novel through an interpretative lens similar to that applied by analytical psychology to the study of fairy tales. We will read *Peter Pan* for what its symbology and symbolic action may reveal about the dynamics of puer psychology in general, and about the psychodynamics represented in Barrie's compelling hero in particular. This approach is not the stretch it might at first appear to be. As Jung reminds us:

> Since it is a characteristic of the psyche not only to be the source of all productivity but, more especially, to express itself in all the activities and achievements of the human mind, we can nowhere grasp the nature of the psyche *per se* but can meet it only in its various manifestations.[11]

We find an artistic recognition of this truth in the literary term *psychomachia* ("battle for the soul"), and in the many pieces of literature where authors explicitly refer to their works as dramas of the psyche, for example Christopher Marlowe's *Dr. Faustus*, Lord Byron's "Manfred," Shelley's *Prometheus Unbound* and "Alastor," to name but a few.

Barrie tells us, "Of course [the Darling family] lived at 14." No. 14 therefore represents the primary world of consensus reality (Tolkien), and certainly the conscious, everyday world of middle-class Edwardian family and social life. The somewhat off-hand expression, "Of course," asks the reader to assume the portrait of the family which follows to be a portrait of the social norm. We know that Barrie looked on the Llewelyn Davies as the embodiment of a family ideal of which he could never fully be a part, and that this family formed the basis of his characterization of the Darlings. However, we can assume, from Barrie's ambivalence toward Mrs Darling and his sometimes gentle, sometimes more cruelly satirical portrayal of Mr Darling, that he only loosely based his characterization of the Darling parents on Arthur and Sylvia Llewelyn Davies, the parents of his "boys." Sylvia had, on the one hand, an "innate and underlying tendency towards melancholy," as described by her son, Peter Llewelyn Davies, and on the other an "appetite for luxury that [her husband] neither shared nor could hope to satisfy," while Arthur was "in no sense the typical Edwardian father of the Mr Darling variety . . . [being] so tender and gentle with children . . . [and with] a more parental instinct than Sylvia."[12]

Nevertheless, the predominant values of the Darlings' world, as summarized and satirized by Barrie, present us with a family dynamic that promotes the early development of mother's son psychology, as well as its perpetuation in adult life. Mr and Mrs Darling provide a parental background and environment which encourages that quality of psyche represented in the puer as carrier of spirit to be "split off" and relegated to a Neverland of the unconscious. As we shall see, Mr and Mrs Darling seem to represent everything the puer most fears: routine, groundedness, the dull round of adult responsibility. Theirs is the "buttoned up" conscious attitude that produces in the Neverland of the unconscious a Peter Pan and a Captain Hook, fairies, pirates and redskins, mermaids, sirens, wild beasts and a devouring crocodile, all of which add up to the inventory of a child's odyssey that has been domesticated, neither recognized nor valued, but discarded in a dusty corner of the nursery.

What ego-consciousness rejects falls into shadow in the unconscious. We must bear this in mind in our discussion of the Darlings which follows: collective values, in the guise of perceptions of gender roles and the norms of social interaction, change, and often quite rapidly. What was considered acceptable behavior in Victorian and Edwardian England may appear as neurotic or perhaps even pathological to an observer from a different era or culture. In comparison, psychological dynamics remain constant. While the psychology of the typical Edwardian family may today be far more subtly differentiated than at the time Barrie's novel, we regularly encounter Mr Darling's intransigence and need for control, Mrs Darling's tendency to smother her children, and Peter Pan's challenge to adventure, in various forms of generalized anxiety, "over-parenting," and the current popular phenomenon of the business executive who rides his Harley-Davidson to a bikers' convention.

We will first consider Mr Darling. He is depicted as a businessman who knows "about stocks and shares" but has "no real mastery of his tie." Barrie's picture of Mr Darling is of one whose main psychological function and values are identified with persona, with the opinion of neighbors and colleagues, to the point where his excessive attention to the rational and to social and professional propriety leads him to absurd, inappropriate behavior. He says:

> I warn you of this, mother, that unless this tie is around my neck we don't go out to dinner tonight, and if I don't go out to dinner tonight, I never go to the office again, and if I don't go to the office again, you and I starve, and our children will be flung into the streets.[13]

The image of Mr Darling's having difficulty with his tie and his feeling that his world will collapse unless it is securely around his neck introduces a marked tendency to paranoid thinking that points to an overdefended because weak ego, a tendency that increasingly dominates Mr Darling's personality in the course of the novel. It points also to his obsession with appearances and to his psychology and world-view as a whole. The tie identifies Mr Darling as a prestigious member of the business community; however, it also suggests that he is confined—as later he confines Nana to her kennel by placing a leash around her neck—by an allegiance to the status quo and an attitude to the world that over-values success and materialism at the expense of spirit and intuition.

Mr Darling's adherence to the rational is so exaggerated that it pushes him to the inhuman extreme of looking upon his children primarily in terms of economics: his being "very honourable" entails a hardening of the heart that allows him coldly and carefully to calculate the cost of raising a child in order to decide whether or not to keep Wendy "as she was another mouth to feed." This presents a picture of frozen feeling that is often the consequence of a fragile ego's tendency to overadaptation in a characteristic attempt to compensate a deep fear of falling apart. So Mr Darling exhibits many of the behavior traits of a person suffering profound emotional abandonment and which include, according to Kathrin Asper, overadaptation, an almost robotic conformity and identification with collective values, a reliance on intellect, a tendency to withdraw and an effort "to lead a shadowless existence," among others.[14]

In many ways Barrie's portrait of Mr Darling suggests such a case of arrested development and deep emotional abandonment or narcissistic wounding. A "simple man" able to pass "for a boy again if he had been able to take his baldness off," Mr Darling does everything in excess, and we deduce from the opening chapters that he has a labile, infantile personality ungrounded in any secure sense of self. He takes to Nana's kennel when the children disappear, blaming himself for the disaster and assuming a disproportionate sense of guilt, which may be understood as his falling into a negative inflation and becoming fixated with the notion that no one is at fault, or suffers, as much as he. His mood fluctuates uncontrollably from joy to rage to petulance to arrogance to tears; he refers to his wife as "mother," and to the nursery as "my nursery." In his puerility, Mr Darling seems to identify most closely with his youngest son but in the histrionic charade he plays with Michael about taking medicine it is the child who proves to be father to the man.

Mr Darling's infantile behavior indicates that he has little or no mature connection either to feeling or instinct (for which psychic situation, again, the tie around the neck is an appropriate image marking, as it does, the separation of head from body). Accordingly, he acts now as the petulant child, now as the cynical, severe paternal figure serving a rigid ideal of the father as lawgiver. What he is *not* is a figure for mature masculinity. He denies creative masculine spirit, in the figure of Peter Pan, which is rendered inaccessible and unconscious as a result (i.e., relegated to Neverland and attributed to Wendy's childish fantasy). Laughing even at the idea of Peter Pan and seeing himself as strong (a claim he makes when sitting half in and half out of the kennel), Mr Darling shows himself to be, as we earlier saw in Pentheus, the unconscious victim of the same impulses he denies. In this way he serves as an embodiment of the Victorian shadow, as in evident in his temper tantrums, his spontaneous tears, his effeminacy, his alternating rigidity and emotionality.

The vehemence of Mr Darling's denial of Peter Pan suggests that Peter represents a part of the personality that has been split off from consciousness. Such a split-off part, though inactivated, is only apparently so. As Jung writes:

> In actual fact it brings about a possession of the personality, with the result that the individual's aims are falsified in the interests of the split-off part. If, then, the childhood state of the collective psyche is repressed to the point of total exclusion [as in Mr Darling's denial of Peter Pan], the unconscious content overwhelms the conscious aim and inhibits, falsifies, even destroys its realization. Viable progress only comes from the co-operation of both.[15]

The way in which we have so far described Mr Darling points to his manifesting a number of the negative qualities attributed to puer psychology (or pathology), but Mr Darling also shares several characteristics with the "old king" of alchemy. This old king is the "chief-dictator-father spirit" or senex into which extreme position the puer may swing unwittingly in his refusal to become grounded in time and adulthood, but in distinct opposition to which he must define himself if puer and senex values are not to remain unconsciously contaminated, the one by the other. Von Franz writes:

> The figure of the old king is usually portrayed . . . as defective, unredeemed, rigidified, sick, or even evil. The defective quality corresponds to an intensified egotism and hardening of the heart that must be broken down in the alchemical bath. Power hunger and concupiscence often also ingloriously characterize the old king . . . [who may] . . . embody a pure attitude of power and [be] characterized by a total lack of eros. The spirit, which in itself is no "adversary of the soul," degenerates in such personifications to the level of intellect, and in this contracted and rigidified form stands in the way of all the psyche's fertile and creative impulses. It is an enemy of emotionality and instinct, but precisely for this reason it secretly lets itself be negatively influenced by primitive impulses.[16]

To attribute to Mr Darling characteristics of the old king, or the wounded Fisher-King of Grail mythology, might seem harsh. However, there is much in his behavior to indicate a contamination, or lack of differentiation, of puer and senex qualities: his weak, labile ego causes him to act out traits of both puer and senex in an unconscious, irrational manner, and so we see in him similarities to Captain Hook as well as to Peter Pan. Although Mr Darling is described as "grander" than his wife, we are led to believe that this is solely by virtue of his being a male. (We are told, when the children are playing at mothers and fathers, of "the extra pomp . . . [occasioned by] . . . the birth of a male"). The psychological portrait Barrie gives us, then, is of a man who is not in the least bit grand but who remains unconsciously trapped in the realm of the Mother because he is caught at an instinctual level of identification in the role of son. So we see him behaving like his children, with Mrs Darling treating him accordingly.

Although there are in Mr Darling several positive qualities of the puer—like Peter Pan he is playful, spontaneous and loves to dance—the "fun" he has with his family may equally be understood as part of a protective shield which masks the viciousness we see him act out with Michael and with Nana. Mr Darling's victimization by the primitive impulses he either energetically denies or believes he controls is further captured in the image of him being brushed like a dog by his wife, in his having taken "a dog for a nurse" in the first place, in his banishment of Nana to the yard, and finally in his self-imposed punishment of going "down on all fours and . . . [crawling] into the kennel" until the children return.

Barrie dubs Mr Darling "quixotic," which brings to mind the delusional quality of Don Quixote's quest to right the wrongs of his world. Not unlike Cervantes' Knight of the Mournful Countenance—and arguably also to the point of delusion—Mr Darling is unconsciously impelled by forces which his fragile ego identifies as his own conscious choices and desires, as, for example, the determination to live in Nana's kennel. He does not appear to enjoy the stable sense of identity which Jeffrey Satinover associates with the development of a "proper narcissism" in early development. We know nothing of Mr Darling's childhood, but see that he exhibits many of the characteristics we later find in Peter Pan and the narcissistic personality: extreme highs followed by extreme lows; rapid shifts from positive to negative inflation, pointing to a damaged ego-Self axis or, in other words, to a basic mistrust of the world and an inability to embrace the ineluctable quality of life and of one's own destiny.

We see grandiosity and "lion courage," succeeded by feelings of failure and remorse; a stubborn need for control in an attempt to suppress a rising fear of the unknown and chaotic. ("Mr Darling was frightfully ashamed of himself, but he would not give in.") We see an egocentric need for attention and admiration; an inflexibility which results in black and white and often mistaken or paranoid thinking; a lack of either eros or insight, and so a tendency to act out emotions and impulses in an unrelated and often destructive manner; and, finally, a tendency to depression which often serves to mask the pain of the emotionally wounded. ("When he tied [Nana] up in the backyard, the wretched father went and sat in the passage, with his knuckles to his eyes.")

Overall, Mr Darling's quixotic, unstable and essentially narcissistic personality points to his alleged success in the social and business world being the result of a rigid persona supported by a somewhat paranoid system of defenses. In this regard, Erich Neumann writes of the juxtaposition of rigidity and chaos as a protection against what Kohut later calls "disintegration anxiety," the threat of falling apart or being flooded by the unconscious;[17] and James Hillman observes that "the dissolution of any paranoid system will release panic."[18]

We witness this process activated in Mr Darling: when his carefully constructed safeguards against all eventualities are rendered ineffectual by the arrival of Peter Pan in the nursery, he behaves in an erratic, irrational manner. Just as Pentheus's refusal of Dionysus spells his own destruction by the very Bacchanalian forces he despises, the more vehemently Mr Darling denies the reality of Peter Pan, or an incursion from the unconscious, the greater his panic and the less effective his precautions to protect his children.

Hillman points out that "where panic is, there too is Pan,"[19] and whether we understand in Peter Pan a dim vestige of the instinctual goat-god, a figment of the childish imagination, a figure for the unconscious, a symbol of autonomous creativity or spirit of renewal, the effect of his intrusion into the rational order of life at No. 14 returns Mr Darling to the level of instinct. So what Barrie gives us in the character of Mr Darling is, perhaps, under the softening guise of fantasy, an otherwise quite brutal portrayal of what may happen when puer and senex qualities of psychic energy have remained unconscious, and consequently undifferentiated, unrealized and unintegrated: they manifest autonomously in their negative aspects as puerility and irrational rigidity, with little evidence of creative reciprocity between the two.

In many ways Mr Darling's neurotic behavior provides a picture of how a distortion of the archetypal configuration of *puer-et-senex* often appears in conscious life: in extreme narcissism, and in the effeminacy and decadence associated with Victorian life at the turn of the century. Missing is a realization of the chthonic masculine as well as a differentiated relationship to the mature feminine which would enable Mr Darling to acknowledge both his personal shadow and that of the collective.

Barrie gives several indications in his opening paragraph that in visiting No. 14 we are entering a world dominated by feminine, specifically maternal, values: there is an implicit resistance to growth, differentiation and conflict—so long considered aspects of masculine energy—in statements such as, "All children, except one, grow up," and "Two is the beginning of the end." More importantly, the first image we have of Mrs Darling is of her delight at the gift of a flower from the two-year-old Wendy who is "playing in a garden." Barrie's image is of Paradise, and of Demeter and Persephone—mother and daughter—before Persephone's abduction by Pluto/Hades to the Underworld. Mrs Darling's cry, "Oh, why can't you remain like this for ever!" expresses a lament for the passing of springtime and for the inevitability of process and change, and at the same time nostalgia for a world that is static, perfect and devoid of conflict. Her cry marks her resistance to an intrusion of chthonic masculine energy into the gentle refinement of her female domain. It is the cry of Demeter who refuses to allow the masculine, in the form of Hades, to objectify the mother-daughter dyad and who begs Zeus to permit Persephone to return to her for six months of the year.

In an ironic reversal at the end of the novel, when she again assumes the role of Demeter, Mrs Darling makes Peter Pan a "handsome offer: to let Wendy go to him for a week every year to do his spring cleaning." We understand the strength of the mother-daughter bond in Barrie's novel when we realize the extent of Wendy's identification with and idealization of her mother and when, in the final chapter, we learn how the powerfully introverted maternal instinct embodied in Mrs Darling is passed unchanged and unchallenged from mother to daughter for successive generations:

> As you look at Wendy you may see her hair becoming white, and her figure little again, for all this happened long ago. Jane is now a common grown-up, with a daughter called Margaret; and every spring-cleaning time, except when he forgets, Peter comes for Margaret and takes her to Neverland, where she tells him stories about himself, to which he listens eagerly. When Margaret grows up she will have a daughter, who is to be Peter's mother in turn; and thus it will go on . . .[20]

As much as Mr Darling has a passion for exactitude, Mrs Darling also loves "to have everything just so," and she conforms in many ways to a collective idea of woman- and mother-hood that is narrowly traditional and suggestive of her own unconscious tendency to be murderously exacting. Husband and wife are presented as nothing-but-father and nothing-but-mother, respectively, their individual personalities subsumed by their collective parental personae. Mrs Darling fulfills the role of the conventional wife, supporting her husband, taking care of the household, the children, and all personal and social matters; she can keep the books perfectly, remain placid when her husband is irrational, and dances "gayest of all" as occasion demands. Jung suggests that such an exaggeration of the maternal element results in the type of mother who comes to regard her husband

> as an object to be looked after, along with children, poor relations, cats, dogs, and household furniture. Even her own personality is of secondary importance; she often remains entirely unconscious of it, for her life is lived in and through others, in more or less complete identification with all the objects of her care. First she gives birth to the children, and from then on she clings to them, for without them she has no existence whatsoever.[21]

Although this description may seem overly condemning when applied to Mrs Darling, it does bring the singular quality of her maternal instinct into relief: she keeps her husband's books perfectly, it is true, but "as if it were a game," and quickly substitutes "pictures of babies without faces" for the figures "she should have been totting up"; she treats her husband like a child, as mentioned above, on a mythological level playing Cybele to his Attis by "coddling" him and so figuratively rendering him impotent, his masculine spirit reduced to nothing more than a laughable childish charade as he hides in Nana's kennel; and she spends a great deal of time "tidying up her children's minds"—an activity, or attitude to life, that indicates a need for power, control and absolute right of possession that traditionally belongs to the father.

This type of fanatical insistence on "maternal rights" may arise when the instinct to bear children dominates the personality to the point of becoming an impersonal drive. (Mrs Darling draws "babies without faces" in her husband's books.) Jung writes: "Eros [then] develops exclusively as a maternal relationship while remaining unconscious as a personal one . . . [and such] an unconscious Eros always expresses itself as will to power"[22] which manifests as the devouring aspect of the archetypal Mother, a quality we see on the personal level in Mrs Darling's self-effacing but suffocating love for her children, and in her psychological emasculation of her husband.

We may speculate that as a nothing-but-mother, Mrs Darling grew up as the nothing-but-daughter of a woman much like herself, identifying with her mother's maternal values to the detriment of her own feminine initiative. A strong overidentification with the mother in this way may result in the type of woman whom Jung describes, with little apparent sympathy, as a "pallid maiden . . . often visibly sucked dry by the mother." This "empty vessel" attracts all of a man's unconscious projections and she readily forms herself according to his image of the feminine:

> Such women may become devoted and self-sacrificing wives of husbands whose whole existence turns on their identification with a profession or a great talent, but who, for the rest, are unconscious and remain so. Since they are nothing but masks themselves, the wife, too, must be able to play the accompanying part with a semblance of naturalness.[23]

Mrs Darling seems to have been just such a type of woman, whose feminine indeterminateness "sucks up all masculine projections and this pleases men enormously."[24] Barrie describes Mr Darling's courtship of her in the following way: "The many gentlemen who had been boys when she was a girl discovered simultaneously that they loved her, and they all ran to her house to propose to her except Mr Darling, who took a cab and nipped in first."[25]

Mrs Darling accepts the first suitor to arrive on her doorstep and Mr Darling, it would seem, marries his wife more because he is impelled by unconscious impulse (projection) and accident than by conscious relatedness and love, because Mrs Darling appears to embody something of the mystery and fascination of the archetypal feminine. She is, after all, "the chief one" at No. 14 until the birth of Wendy, and she has an elusive, enigmatic quality which is that of the woman whose innocence (or emptiness) suggests the "great feminine secret . . . absolutely alien to man":

> Her romantic mind was like the tiny boxes, one within the other, that come from the puzzling East, however many you discover there is always one more; and her sweet mocking mouth had one kiss on it that Wendy could never get, though there it was, perfectly conspicuous in the righthand corner.[26]

Barrie's depiction, however sentimental, is also subtly ambivalent. On the one hand, in the kiss that may never be taken and the "tiny box" about which Mr Darling never even knew, it affords Mrs Darling a certain sense of selfhood and inner integrity. It paints the feminine as essentially *other,* mysterious and exotic ("from the puzzling East"). The "tiny box," however, also serves as a negative image of control; it is equally the locked inner chamber of Mrs Darling's affections (and, we may surmise, of the affections of Barrie's own mother), as inaccessible and taboo as the elusive kiss.

Throughout the novel, there is a marked ambivalence in Barrie's picture of Mrs Darling in particular and of mothers in general, an ambivalence echoed by Peter pan who takes Wendy to Neverland because the lost boys need a mother, yet remembers little or nothing of his own mother, and considers he and Tinker Bell "don't want any silly mothers" anyway. When the children are on their way home from Neverland, Barrie's authorial voice intrudes to denounce Mrs Darling as a woman who has "no proper spirit." By this Barrie means the type of mother who declares "What do I matter?" and sacrifices everything—including her own personality— for her children and her role. (Recall the selfless devotion of Sylvia Llewelyn Davies to her five boys.) "So long as mothers are like this their children will take advantage of them," Barrie tells us, yet this self-sacrificing love may mask the seductive quality of the negative mother—the witch in the gingerbread house—promising her children ease and security in a potentially devouring embrace which nevertheless shields them from consciousness of moral conflict and so from life.

However, as soon as he has conjured again a sentimental image of her as "a very sad-eyed woman . . . because she has lost her babes," Barrie decides he does indeed like Mrs Darling best. Barrie's ambivalence is more clearly embodied in Peter Pan who projects onto Mrs Darling what must be an inner archetypal image of the mother as he has no experience of a personal mother himself; at the same time he energetically rejects her outstretched arms. On the one hand Peter whispers to Tinker Bell, "She is a pretty lady, but not so pretty as my mother"; on the other he warns Mrs Darling, "Keep back, lady, no one is going to catch me and make me a man."

Peter Pan is convinced that if he does not repulse Mrs Darling's offer of mothering he will become a solemn man with a beard—that is, only-senex. In the context of Barrie's tale he is right. We see what happens to John, Michael and the lost boys who come under Mrs Darling's care: the ambivalence they once felt about "grown-ups," and the "No!" with which they resisted growing up themselves, is forgotten (or becomes unconscious). Whereas Peter Pan defines himself, and so creates and recreates himself continually, by saying "No!" to the adult world, the Darling children and the lost boys are soon adult and "done for":

So it is scarcely worth while saying anything more about them. You may see the Twins and Nibs and Curly any day going to an office, each carrying a little bag and an umbrella. Michael is an engine-driver. Slightly married a lady of title, and so he became a lord. You see that judge in a wig coming out at the iron door? That used to be Tootles. The bearded man who doesn't know any story to tell his children was once John.[27]

In John's inability to remember any stories we see Barrie's association of the only-senex quality of the adult world with the death of imagination. We recall how Mr Darling either denies the reality of Peter Pan or denounces him as a "fiend," and we wonder if Barrie ever felt himself a fiend in Arthur Llewelyn Davies' eyes for stealing away the affection of his children. Although it would seem that storytelling is kept alive and passes from generation to generation through the mother-line (as was true of Barrie's own experience), stories—and the indulgence of fancy—are clearly confined to the nursery and to childhood: Mrs Darling is confident that Wendy will outgrow her fascination for Peter Pan, and to Wendy, who from the beginning emulates the quality of mothering she experiences in her own mother and who consequently "grew up of her own free will a day quicker than other girls," Peter Pan is soon "no more to her than a little dust in the box in which she had kept her toys."

Nothing changes at No. 14 because of the rigidity and fixity of the conscious structures. Wendy is little different from her mother, despite her experience of Neverland. Although initially she resists the tyranny of Mrs Darling by following Peter Pan, she is so identified with her nothing-but mother that even in Neverland— that is, unconsciously—she both acts out the "mother" and initiates the return to her real mother on the mainland, all earlier ambivalence overcome.

Jung writes that when there is a disturbance of instincts in the relation of parent to child (particularly in the relation of mother to child), archetypal fantasies are produced which "come between the child and its mother as an alien and often frightening element."[28] There is sufficient evidence in Barrie's tale to pin the origin of any disturbance of instinct in the Darling family on the conscious attitudes of the parents, especially those of the mother. Figures that might stand for natural wisdom (Liza the maid) and instinct (the dog) are either immature and consequently ignored (Liza is little more than ten years old) or banished (Nana, who provides an image of distorted, over-domesticated instinct at best, is chained in her kennel).

We may argue that Peter Pan and the lure of Neverland appear as intervening fantasies arising out of the children's need to resist and separate from their parents, a need symbolized in their flight. In the experience of ambivalence which the children naturally and necessarily feel toward the parents (are mothers good or bad? are parents necessary?), Peter Pan represents one compelling alternative or pole while the other is kept alive by Wendy's stories of Mr and Mrs Darling. Eventually fear of separation and abandonment wins out and the children return to No. 14. Negative emotions toward mother, father and adulthood are again repressed. A final image is of the closed family circle from which "ecstasy" Peter Pan is barred, as Barrie, that entertaining but idiosyncratic genius from Scotland, was himself relegated to the position of outsider, always "listening in" on the Llewelyn Davies, unable to identify with many of the values embodied in the decidedly English parents of "his boys."

However, we know that Peter Pan is not entirely forgotten. He survives in the imaginations of generations of daughters, although Mrs Darling's dim sense of foreboding on the night he abducts Wendy and her brothers from the nursery is insufficiently strong to keep her from leaving her children alone. Barrie also tells us that there was a commotion in the firmament that night. There is much to suggest, then, that the perpetuation of Peter Pan and the inevitability (if unreliability) of his springtime return are symbolic of orchestrations of the archetypal psyche against which imperative the conscious ego has little recourse.

Such a reading would make Pan a figure for a quality of the Self, which appears now and again as fate to shape destiny and further the process of individuation; such a figure manifests a potentiality for positive, creative development, unless thwarted and perverted by an inflexible ego's will to power or unconscious enthrallment to a petrifying complex.

Notes

1. *Written for Children*, pp. 106f.
2. *Peter Pan*, p. 207. [Quoted passages, sentences and phrases from Barrie's novel are ubiquitous in this chapter. In order not to overburden the reader, footnote references to these are hereafter given only for lengthy or significant extracts.—Ed.]
3. "On Fairy-Stories," in Tolkien, *Tree and Leaf,* pp. 64ff.
4. *Peter Pan*, p. 53.
5. Michael Hearn notes in his Introduction to *Peter Pan* that "The names of other writers [besides Defoe, Ballantyne and Cooper] whom Barrie aligned himself to through his play, if in spirit only, were included on the curtain the author himself designed for the 1908 revival, supposedly a sampler stitched by Wendy, nine years old: Hans Christian Andersen, Charles Lamb, Robert Louis Stevenson and Lewis Carroll." (p. 13)
6. *Peter Pan*, pp. 35, 33.
7. Northrop Frye, *The Secular Scripture: A Study of the Structure of Romance*, p. 15.
8. *An Introduction to the Psychology of Fairy Tales*, chap. 1.
9. Lucie Armitt, *Theorising the Fantastic*, p. 3.
10. Jonathan Rutherford argues that Peter Pan was "the culminating adventure story of the Victorian era and revealed what had been repressed and denied in the imperial fantasy of manly racial supremacy—the domestic world of mothers, sexuality and emotional need. It was an act of acute, if unconscious, reflexivity." (*Forever England: Reflections on Masculinity and Empire*, p. 25)
11. "Psychology and Literature," *The Spirit in Man, Art and Literature*, CW 15, p. 85.
12. Birkin, *J. M. Barrie and the Lost Boys*, chap. 9.
13. *Peter Pan*, p. 43.
14. *The Abandoned Child Within*, pp. 162ff.
15. The Psychology of the Child Archetype," *The Archetypes and the Collective Unconscious*, CW 9i par. 277.
16. "The Religious Background of the Puer Aeternus Problem," in von Franz, *Psychotherapy*, p. 312.
17. Cited in Kathrin Asper, *The Abandoned Child Within*, p. 157.
18. *Pan and the Nightmare*, p. xxxi.
19. Ibid.
20. *Peter Pan*, p. 225.
21. "Psychological Aspects of the Mother Complex," *The Archetypes of the Collective Unconscious*, CW 9i, par. 167.
22. Ibid.
23. Ibid., par. 182.
24. Ibid., par. 169.
25. *Peter Pan*, p. 28.
26. "Psychological Aspects of the Mother Complex," *The Archetypes of the Collective Unconscious*, CW 9i, par. 183.
27. Ibid., p. 219.
28. "Psychological Aspects of the Mother Complex," *The Archetypes of the Collective Unconscious*, CW 9i, par. 161.

Bibliography

Armitt, Lucie. *Theorizing the Fantastic*. London: Arnold, 1996.

Asper, Kathrin. *The Abandoned Child Within: On Losing and Regaining Self-Worth.* Trans. Sharon E. Rooks. New York: Fromm International, 1993.

Barrie, J. M. *Peter Pan.* Intro. Michael P. Hearn. Illus. Susan Hudson. Montreal: Tundra Books, 1988. (Originally *Peter and Wendy.* London: Hodder and Stoughton, 1911.)

———.*Peter Pan and Other Plays.* New York: Oxford University Press, 1995.

———.*Peter Pan and Wendy.* Adapted for children by Jane Carruth. Illus. Anne Grahame Johnstone. London: Award Publications Limited, 1988.

Birkin, Andrew. *J. M. Barrie & the Lost Boys.* London: Constable, 1979.

Frye, Northrop. *The Secular Scripture: A Study of the Structure of Romance.* Cambridge, MA: Harvard University Press, 1976.

Hillman, James. *Pan and the Nightmare.* Zurich: Spring Publications, 1972.

Jung, C. G. *The Collected Works of C. G. Jung* (Bollingen Series XX). 20 vols. Trans. R. F. C. Hull. Ed. Herbert Read, Michael Fordham, Gerhard Adler, William McGuire. Princeton: Princeton University Press, 1953-1979.

Rutherford, Jonathan. *Forever England: Reflections on Masculinity and Empire.* London: Lawrence and Wishart, 1997.

Tolkien, J. R. R. *Tree and Leaf.* London: Allen and Unwin, 1975.

Townsend, John Rowe. *Written for Children: An Outline of English-Language Children's Literature.* Middlesex, England: Pelican Books, 1980.

von Franz, Marie-Louise. *An Introduction to the Psychology of Fairy Tales.* Zurich: Spring Publications, 1970.

———. *Psychotherapy.* Boston: Shambhala Publications, 1993.

Andrew Nash (essay date April 1999)

SOURCE: Nash, Andrew. "'Trying to Be a Man': J. M. Barrie and Sentimental Masculinity." *Forum for Modern Language Studies* 35, no. 2 (April 1999): 113-25.

[*In the following essay, Nash contends that in* Sentimental Tommy *and* Tommy and Grizel *Barrie was not simply trying to create sentimental works of art, but was "concerned with interrogating the concept of sentimentalism itself."*]

Writing to Conrad Aiken in 1914, T. S. Eliot asked: "Do you think it possible, if I brought out the 'Inventions of a March Hare', and gave a few lectures, at 5 p.m. with wax candles, that I could become a sentimental Tommy."[1] The reference is to the eponymous hero of two novels by J. M. Barrie and it is suggestive that Eliot, when wanting to indicate in his letter the issue of sentimentalism, should use a literary allusion that obviously did not require any elucidation. By 1914, J. M. Barrie was an established playwright with important successes such as **The Admirable Crichton** (1902), **Peter Pan** (1904) and **What Every Woman Knows** (1908) behind him. His most recent novel, **The Little White Bird,** was already twelve years distant, and **Sentimental Tommy** itself had been published as far back as 1896. Eliot's remark thus indicates the longevity of impact not only of Barrie's novel but of the resonance of its subject matter: for Eliot, the best way of imagining himself as a sentimentalist was to refer to Barrie's hero, and as the remarks of a reviewer of **Tommy and Grizel** (1900) suggest, Barrie was seen by his contemporaries as a writer primarily concerned with the issue of sentimentalism: "Just as Thackeray became haunted by a suspicion of snobbery, so with Mr Barrie the fear of sentiment becomes an obsession."[2]

Posterity has dealt harshly with Barrie for principally this association; he is often swept from critical view on account of being a sentimental writer. But with the possible exception of **A Window in Thrums,** an early work published in 1889, Barrie was not a writer who set out to create a sentimental work of art which aimed to arouse its readers into a specific emotional response. He was more concerned with interrogating the concept of sentimentalism itself.

Sentimentalism and sentimentality are words which have come to be used in generalised ways: to label something "sentimental" is to dismiss it curtly as beneath intellectual concern. Worse still, sentimentality is widely accepted as unethical. As Robert C. Solomon has summarised, "it seems to be all but agreed that sentimentality is no virtue even if it is not, like cruelty and hypocrisy, intrinsically vicious. Something is wrong with sentimentality."[3] The pejorativeness of the term is often built into the way in which the word is defined. The *OED* defines sentimentality as "the *affectation* of sensibility", and sentimentalism as "the disposition to attribute *undue* importance to sentimental considerations" and "the tendency to *excessive* indulgence or *insincere* display of sentiment" [my italics]. The pejorativeness thus resides not in sentiment itself but in the uses to which it is put. Under this definition, the raw material of emotion which an individual might be said to possess is seen as redundant in meaning; it is only when the situation at hand is deemed appropriate enough to warrant it that a show of emotion is endorsed as being sincere. A sentimentalist, therefore, is one who overlooks the question of sincerity and appropriateness and expresses emotion regardless of the significance of the situation in hand. This is what Oscar Wilde means when he says in *De Profundis* that "a sentimentalist is simply one who desires to have the luxury of an emotion without paying for it."[4]

At the time when Barrie was writing, sentimentalism was a more visibly pertinent issue than it is now, and in a sketch which he contributed early in his career to the *Young Man*, he illustrates very clearly what is at stake. Describing an imaginary character called "The Sentimentalist", Barrie wrote:

> sentiment was a horse ever standing ready for him. He jumped on, and away they went. Then he dismounted with a proud chest, and at once did a mean thing, if convenient. All he remembered next day was his galop.[5]

The sentimentalist only remembers the galop—the luxury of the emotion—not what the purpose of it was. But whereas in the 18th century the ability to respond with sympathetic emotion to any situation encountered was a sign of ethical strength, the utilitarian strain in Victorian morals viewed sentimentalism negatively.

Like most things in the Victorian period, attitudes toward sentimentalism were influenced by Thomas Carlyle, whose importance in shaping opinion is evident in the way in which the present *OED* definition is clearly visible in his writings. Carlyle was concerned about the separation of sentiment from moral considerations; for him sentiment only became meaningful when it was applied to an external referent and seen within a moral paradigm. In his essay "Characteristics", he wrote:

> The barrenest of all mortals is the Sentimentalist. Granting even that he were sincere, and did not wilfully deceive us, or without first deceiving himself, what good is in him? Does he not lie there as a perpetual lesson of despair, and type of bedrid valetudinarian impotence?[6]

The word impotence points to the concomitant relationship in Carlyle's thought between industry and sexuality, and I want in this essay to show how sentimentalism came to be clearly defined in the late Victorian period along lines of gender, because it is in this context that J. M. Barrie's fictional voice attains a dissident note: throughout his fiction—and indeed in most of his plays—Barrie was intent on writing about men who seemed to embody an extreme level of sentimentality at a time when it was becoming identified as incompatible with successful manliness.

Herbert Sussman's recent book on *Victorian Masculinities* has shown how many of the ideas about successful manliness in the Victorian era emanate from Carlyle, who imagined the male self as a fluid, seminal energy which needed to be controlled and channelled towards industrial productivity.[7] Masculinity was only acquired when things were seen objectively and energy turned outward, and so by inevitable contrast the inward viewing sentimentalist came to be seen in Carlyle's thought as solipsistic and fundamentally unmanly. Recent work on Victorian masculinity has shown how such Carlylean ideas permeated all areas of life and became so deeply ingrained in institutions—particularly schools and youth organisations—that their persistence as part of an accepted moral code remains clearly visible to the present day.[8] Partly through the assistance of biological studies and the inevitable strength of authority they carried, manliness became encased in tropes of athleticism and the healthy body, and such ideas received a powerful cultural authority through the phenomenon of muscular Christianity. A recent book on this influential movement is so confident of its subject's cultural significance that it is subtitled "Embodying the Victorian Age", and it could be said that because of its influence in schools and print media, and the utilisation of its ideals in political and imperial arguments, muscular Christianity represents the coming together of science, religion, education, literature, politics and nationalism into one gigantic theory of manliness.[9] The outward-looking, physically active, stoical Victorian male was a testament to scientific fact, but he was also Godly and affirmatively British.

The cult of manliness had an important effect on the direction of fiction because the novel was not exempt from the mass gender theorising taking place elsewhere in society. The second half of the century witnessed an attempt at transforming the gendered identity of the novel which by many writers (both male and female) was seen to be restricted by its identification with women and its subsequent association with the social taboo of sentimentalism. In one of the many manifestos for Romance which were written in the 1880s and 1890s, Henry Rider Haggard asked a pertinent question:

> Why do *men* hardly ever read a novel? Because in ninety-nine cases out of a hundred, it is utterly false as a picture of life [. . .]. The ordinary popular English novel represents life as it is considered desirable that schoolgirls should suppose it to be.[10]

The question of whether a novel provided suitable reading matter for young women was firmly entrenched in the Victorian age and "unsuitable for girls" became a general maxim of the tacit controls of censorship keeping the idea of novels and novel-reading within the realms of femininity. George Eliot's infamous destruction of "Silly Novels by Lady Novelists" typified the growing ridicule associated with this branch of the fiction market, and J. M. Barrie's critical writing shows a clear awareness of the gendered identity of novel-reading. In a critical article on Thomas Hardy he wrote:

> Novels have been divided according as they are popular with men or with women, though, indeed, only the

favourites of the latter go into many editions. The lady who is at Mudie's counter daily may not skip everything except the love passages, but she prefers novels that are "sentimental" and has an aversion to complex characters.[11]

As Sally Mitchell has argued, fiction written by and for women was identified in the second half of the century largely as a recreational activity that aimed to elicit an emotional rather than an intellectual response.[12] Writing in 1859, W. R. Greg argued that "novels constitute a principal part of the reading of women, who are always impressionable, in whom at all times the emotional element is more awake and more powerful than the critical [and] whose feelings are more easily influenced than ours."[13] What really made the difference in the attempt to demarcate novel-reading along lines of gender was the impact of biological studies which claimed to legitimise scientifically the idea that women's mode of reading differed from that of men because of a greater biological capacity for sensitivity and sensibility. The voracious female taste for reading was put down, however inaccurately, to a biological weakness which needed to be disciplined, and so for young men, to whom this sentimental capacity was already attributed in a smaller biological measure, the paths of discipline inevitably led even further away from the legitimisation of conveying and trusting emotion.[14] As a result, the second half of the century witnessed a growing increase in the availability of books and newspapers designed specifically for boys.[15] Adventure romances like those of Stevenson and Rider Haggard, coupled with the emergence of the school-story as a distinctive genre, helped to draw a clear line around what was identified as acceptable reading matter for boys and young men. Moreover, there was a marked difference between fiction for boys at the end of the century and that at mid-century.[16] Whilst Thomas Hughes's hugely influential *Tom Brown's Schooldays* (1856) had allowed for a certain level of emotional expression in young men—Tom is moved and enriched by sympathising with George Arthur during his illness—as the century wore on boys' stories became less and less able to tolerate any hint of the sentimental. Writing in a preface to Talbot Baines Reed's highly successful *The Fifth Form at St. Dominic's* (1881), G. A. Hutchinson wrote that the boys in the book "stand at the very antipodes alike of an effeminate sentimentality".[17] With regard to fiction in particular, sentimentalism was explicitly a gendered term.

By focusing on a male who seems to embody such an effeminate sentimentality, Barrie's *Tommy* novels are disruptive not only of prevailing ideas of successful masculinity, but also of the newly masculinised idea of the novel. As the anonymous reviewer in *Blackwood's* noted of **Sentimental Tommy,** the "excursion into boyhood in pursuit of its sentimental qualities [. . .] is something new in fiction".[18] Barrie had earlier argued in favour of men expressing emotion in the *Young Man* sketch, and it is important to remember that he is writing this inside the covers of a boys' newspaper—a publication whose pages elsewhere would ideologically endorse the rejection of sentimentality in favour of muscular Christianity:

> Young men who can talk readily with each other about their books and their pipes are still shy about their feelings, which they consider too sacred to mention in ordinary conversation. Often when they would like to blurt out little bits of sentiment they are tongue-tied less [sic] derision be the result—which is a pity, for their friends (if worth their salt) would like to unlock their bosoms too, and the exchange would be mutually beneficial.[19]

The life of Tommy Sandys is told in two novels: **Sentimental Tommy** (1896), subtitled "The Story of his Boyhood", and **Tommy and Grizel** (1900), which takes up the story of Tommy when he is in his twenties. Tommy is sentimental for the reasons outlined above: he values emotion for its own sake rather than for its appropriateness for the reality of the situation in hand. On one occasion in his boyhood, Tommy acts as a letter-writer for those members of his home community who are unable to write themselves. Forced to take on the emotional conditions of others, Tommy revels in the opportunity to express powerful sentiments which do not really belong to him and which he does not have the right to hold. In one instance he has to write as a woman who wishes to tell her mother about the death of a friend, and not only do his words induce tears in the eyes of both the person he is writing for and writing to, but they move *him* to tears also. Tommy displays emotion not because he genuinely feels that way about the situation at hand—he has no stake in it. His emotion is, rather, purely love of emotion itself, and it is specifically this which has come to be considered as the ethical weakness of sentimentality.

But of course what Tommy is in effect doing here is writing fiction; a fiction which enables other people to experience something more profound and more powerfully moving than the reality which it is supposed to be serving. His sentimentalism is close to an accepted idea of the artist's sympathetic engagement, and in the sequel, **Tommy and Grizel,** the links between sentimentalism and Art are strengthened as it follows Tommy's growth into a successful author. At the beginning of this book he is employed as an amanuensis and ends up writing some of the monthly instalments of his employer's ludicrously formulaic "Penny Numbers". His particular love is in altering Pym's portrayal of ladies, and whenever he rewrites the love passages he becomes so engrossed in the products of his own creation that he himself is aroused into an emotional response to them: "with a pen in his hand and a woman in his head he had such noble thoughts that his tears of exaltation damped the pages as he wrote."[20] This image of a man crying over his own fantasies is at the furthest remove from the representation of manliness in boys' stories and Adventure fiction of the same period, and it is this very deviation from normative constructions of gender which becomes the central theme of the novel. Tommy's sentimentalism and artistic ability are identified as taking him far away from contemporary ideals of manliness; they literally unsex him.

The writer who is able to write love stories but unable to love in real life was a frequent theme in Barrie's extensive journalistic output and Tommy's artistic abilities and real-life experiences are explicitly counterpointed. In real life he appears indifferent to female society but in art he is able to write about women's desires with such insight that his book, *Letters to a young Man about to be Married*, proves to be an outrageous best seller, becoming known simply as "Sandys on Women" (***TG***, [***Tommy and Grizel***], 29). He becomes so famous that his book is even quoted in the House of Commons and when he is invited to move about fashionable society everybody assumes that because of his book he must have had extensive experience with women. A number of rumours circulate about his sexual history including one that his wife is dead which, although entirely false, Tommy is quite happy to go along with because it gives him an outlet to express his sentiment. In a scene with a lady at dinner we see him playing the part of the mourning husband still coming to terms with his imaginary wife's imaginary death:

> "I suppose," she said gently, to bring him out of the reverie into which he had sunk, "I suppose it happened some time ago?"
>
> "Long, long ago," he answered. Having written as an aged person, he often found it difficult to remember suddenly that he was two-and-twenty.
>
> (***TG***, 32)

The emotions Tommy expresses which so convince Mrs Jerry of his sincerity are entirely imaginary and completely without referent to any real-life situation. Tommy is constantly out to test the powers of his sentiment by finding out whether he can move or disturb the emotions of others, and this leads him to exercise sentiment even when it involves social implications he would rather avoid. After impressing Mrs Jerry with his imaginary mourning for his imaginary wife, he actually ends up proposing to her. She becomes so impressed by his depth of insight into matters of love that she immediately seeks his advice when she receives an unexpected proposal of marriage by letter. Tommy, however, cannot let an opportunity of playing a part go by. He is so stirred by the sentiments of Mrs Jerry's unknown admirer that he pretends to have written the letter himself and proceeds to declare his imaginary love for her and to propose in a passionate display of emotion whilst all the time saying to himself "'What am I doing? [. . .]. Oh Heavens, if she should accept him!'" (***TG***, 38). Tommy's is a virtuoso performance and he actually convinces Mrs Jerry that he really does love her—"'I know you love me now,' she said softly"—which is simply not true. Fortunately, she rejects him after some deliberation.

In this instance, and in contrast to the letter-writing, Tommy's sentimentality appears dangerous because it manipulates Mrs Jerry's own feelings. But this early episode sets the scene for the overall theme of this book which is the contribution sentimentalism makes towards the failure of male sexual desire. ***Tommy and Grizel*** is an extended study of Tommy's failure to desire Grizel, and Eve Kosofsky Sedgwick has briefly discussed the text as representative of the many novels at the end of the century which focus on the complications placed on male desire by the new proliferation of discourses on sexuality.[21] The work of Foucault has highlighted how the last third of the 19th century was a crucial moment in the history of sexuality: studies in science and sexology contributed to an enormously influential paradigm shift where sexuality was no longer seen predominantly in terms of sexual acts but in terms of personality traits. From this period on, not only was one male or female in identity but homosexual or heterosexual as well. Foucault argues that this resulted in "a new specification of individuals" which inevitably resulted in sexuality becoming the controlling force in the construction of human subjectivity.[22] Taking up this approach, Kosofsky Sedgwick argues that from this point on, anxiety over sexual identity has structured much of the organisation of western culture. She shows how in contrast to the fiction of Thackeray, for example, the bachelor figure in late Victorian fiction sees his absence of sexual desire as an issue of acute anxiety and often desperately tries to convince himself that he does desire women in order to escape the inevitable consequences of the newly forged, unyielding homosexual/heterosexual binary. As she remarks with regard to ***Tommy and Grizel***, "Grizel's tragedy is not that the man she desires fails to desire her—which would be sad, but, the book makes clear, endurable—but that he *pretends* to desire her."[23] Tommy pretends because of the anxiety of identity which is brought about by the pressure exerted upon him to fulfil the ascribed conditions of normative masculinity: "want of interest is almost immoral" roars Tommy's employer Pym, "At your age the blood would have been coursing through my veins. Love! You are incapable of it" (***TG***, 21). Sedgwick's discussion has introduced an important new context with which to analyse Barrie's work, but her brief discussion cannot do the book full justice and she does not mention the crucial issue of sentimentalism which is identified as the explanation for Tommy's failure to desire.

Tommy's sentimentalism sends him inward and prevents him from achieving socially ascribed normative relations with women because he is always liable to fall in love with the products of his own imagination:

> While he sat there with eyes riveted he had her to dinner at a restaurant, and took her up the river, and called her "little woman," and when she held up her mouth he said, tantalisingly, that she must wait until he had finished his cigar. This queer delight enjoyed, back he popped her into the story.
>
> (*TG*, 16-17)

The only women Tommy can fall in love with are those of his own fantasy, and this situation is exposed in a key episode where Tommy and a group of friends are taking lunch on a riverbank. Tommy, who is lost in his own creative mind, has noticed a glove in his pocket and is not at all concerned to explain to himself why it is there but instead begins to live out in his mind the role of a young man whose love for a faithless woman has been unrequited. Suddenly, reality offers to intrude on Tommy's fantasy when a little boy is spotted drowning in the river. Tommy duly jumps in to save him but before doing so he thrusts the glove into the hand of his friend, Corp, saying "Give her that, and tell her it never left my heart" (*TG*, 115). But as the narrator points out, reality has not intruded on Tommy's dream at all, "it was his dream intruding on reality", because Tommy is not responding to the drowning boy in terms of reality—he is still inside his fantasy. The man who jumps into the river and risks his life is not Tommy but the imaginary rejected young man. The owner of the glove is not Grizel, as Corp assumes, but the imaginary faithless woman. Tommy has, quite literally, fallen in love with his own creation.

Tommy's love of his own fantasies, his constant embrace of self and his inability to regulate his own emotion by transferring it outward, place him at the very antithesis of the idea of successful manliness outlined by Carlyle and fixed in place by forces like muscular Christianity. Tommy emerges instead as more in line with the figure of the masturbator—the Victorians' most feared sexual type. Masturbation was easily the most written-about sexual subject in a period which wrote about sex a lot. In the words of Peter Gay, "throughout the nineteenth century, the vice of 'self-abuse' or 'self-pollution' propelled learned men, and some learned women, into postures of perspiring alarm; they flooded the literatures of medical advice and moral uplift with macabre case-histories and desperate, repetitive pleas for action before it was too late."[24] Ed Cohen has argued that it was the medicalisation of theories on masturbation which, more than anything else, legitimated familial ideologies of masculinity, because the masturbator, placed outside reproductive sex, was defined in medical texts as the "negation of 'manliness'" and became increasingly identified according to a personality type rather than a simple matter of acts.[25] A new medical condition was created—masturbatory insanity—whose ubiquitousness as a diagnosis for any young man who showed symptoms of timidity, solitude, physical weakness, ill-discipline or, significantly for *Tommy and Grizel,* sexual impotence, was really quite remarkable. Victorian society lived in absolute fear of masturbatory insanity, and a sentimentalist would have been seen as dangerously close to this new medical type. If he was to be capable of desiring women, a sentimentalist like Tommy had to learn to reject the masturbatory tendency by overcoming the preoccupation with his own mind, and it is made clear at the end of the book that Tommy could give Grizel affection but not passion—"his passion, like an outlaw, had ever to hunt alone" (*TG*, 411). Tommy's sexual impotence derives from his masturbatory sentimentalism which throughout the book is seen as incompatible with the acquisition of manhood: at one stage the narrator describes Tommy as "a sentimentalist trying to be a man" (*TG*, 158), and Grizel tells him that "I am trying only to help you to be what a man should be" (*TG*, 291).

Haunted by his inability to satisfy the woman who loves him, Tommy pretends to fall in love with Grizel in a desperate response to conform to the social strictures of successful masculinity. His sentimentalism is so acute, however, that he is unable to recognise when he is only pretending, and his attempt to love Grizel emerges as just another attempt to love the products of his own fantasy, because "he so loved the thing he had created that in his exultation he mistook it for her" (*TG*, 158). He relates to Grizel not according to how he feels but how he thinks he should relate to her:

> He looked at her long and adoringly, not, as he thought because he adored her, but because it was thus that look should answer look; he pressed her wet eyes reverently because thus it was written in his delicious part, his heart throbbed with hers that they might beat in time, he did not love, but he was the perfect lover, he was the artist trying in a mad moment to be as well as to do.
>
> (*TG*, 158-9)

It is acceptance of this new role—the perfect lover—which leads Tommy into believing that he really must desire Grizel. When they become engaged it is made absolutely clear that Tommy is not consciously deceiving Grizel: the narrator says that "during those weeks he had *honestly thought* that he was in a passion to be married" (*TG*, 276; [my italics]). His capacity to believe completely in any fantastical situation he creates leads him into not knowing the lines of demarcation between acting and being: "he passed between dreams and reality as through tissue-paper" (*TG*, 180).

Tommy's problem, then, brought on by his sentimentality, is chiefly one of ambiguity: he cannot know for certain what his passion is, or indeed whether he has one at all, and it is this secret of not knowing that he keeps locked up in his closet. In a section where the language mirrors that used by any individual across time who is forced to embody a socially-dissident sexuality, he imagines telling Grizel his secret:

> in a flood of feeling he had a fierce desire to tell her the truth about himself. But he did not know what it was [. . .]. "Grizel, I seem to be different from all other men; there seems to be some curse upon me [. . .] I want to love you [. . .] but apparently I can't."
>
> (*TG*, 178-9)

"It would have been an honest speech," says the narrator, "and it was in a passion to be *out*" [my italics]. What prevents Tommy from coming out is his sentimentality, the very same condition which prevents him from loving Grizel in the first place; because as he gets further involved in this "honest speech" he sees the opportunity to play out another part. As his imaginary revelation to Grizel continues, he becomes more and more preoccupied with self:

> He forgot that she was there, except as a figure needed to complete the picture of the man who could not love; he saw himself a splendidly haggard creature with burning eyes standing aside while all the world rolled by in pursuit of the one thing needful; it was a river and he must stand parched on the bank for ever and ever.
>
> (*TG*, 179-80)

This condition of the sentimentalist is brought out strongly in the scenes which cover his relations with Alice Pippinworth, a fashionable lady in whom Tommy becomes interested not because he desires her—"he had not even the excuse of being passionately drawn to this woman (*TG*, 339)"—but because of her "reputation as a duellist whose defence none of his sex could pass" (*TG*, 340). She is a test case for his sentimental powers. Can he, like Prince Calaf in Puccini's *Turandot*, move this "icy woman" (*TG*, 338) to love where no other had so far managed? He pretends to desire her, but because of his sentimentalism he loses the boundary between reality and pretence; he plays the part so well that without realising it he becomes unsure whether he does not in fact really desire her and literally loses himself in his fantasy: "he was in a frenzy of passion now", observes the narrator, "he meant every word of it".

The sentimentalist thus cannot know whether he really means something or not because the sentimentalist's "real" self is located in his capacity for sentiment and not in any rational faculty which governs the deployment of it. As was implied by the *OED*'s definition which I analysed at the beginning of this essay, the sentimentalist is thus essentially solipsistic and amoral. In ***Tommy and Grizel***, Tommy attempts to repress this "real" self and to assimilate himself to the society he lives in. He is said to be "afraid" of his sentimentality (*TG*, 402) and the narrator says that "he craved mastery over self" (*TG*, 117). Society demands that he sacrifice his sentimentality, transfer his emotion outward onto women and conform to the pre-ordained social and sexual roles of a man. When he pretends to love Grizel we are told that "never in his life had he tried so hard to deceive at the sacrifice of himself." He is aware that "he had made believe in order that she might remain happy" (*TG*, 179), but the unanswered question remains "Was it even make-believe? Assuredly he did love her in his own way [. . .]. I think I love you in my own way," he tells Grizel, "but I thought I loved you in their way, and it is the only way that counts in this world of theirs. It does not seem to be my world" (*TG*, 278).

The final sections of the book deal with Tommy's desperate attempt to accommodate himself to "this world of theirs"; to reject his sentimentality and try and love in "their" way. He finally marries Grizel after she has gone mad, and in an attempt to negate the artist in him resorts to writing for magazine papers only, because if Tommy is to negate his self he must deny his creative artistry. As Leonee Ormond has suggested, the clash between Tommy and Grizel is "on one level, the archetypal one between creative man and domestic woman".[26] Grizel distrusts Tommy's writing because she sees the solipsistic dangers into which it can lead him: "if writing makes you live in such an unreal world it must do you harm" (*TG*, 101). There is a suggestion that Grizel comes to admire him for trying to love her but it becomes clear that Tommy values his art more than he does Grizel and that his true potency always exists there. In marrying her he sacrifices himself, but he proves unable to repress the creative intensity and when he finds out that the missing manuscript of his new novel is not lost but has been stolen by Alice Pippinworth he leaves Grizel and renews his pursuit of Alice, again unsure over whether he really desires her or not. Finding that she has already burned the manuscript he is eventually hanged accidentally when the collar of his coat gets hooked on an iron spike on the top of a wall when he is trying to reach her.

Viewed one way Tommy is the sentimental masturbator who cannot prevent himself veering towards solipsism; viewed another way, however, he is the creative artist whose inability or refusal to desire becomes the very touchstone of artistic greatness. It is significant that on each occasion that Tommy's (imaginary) love has been rejected—by Mrs Jerry, Alice Pippinworth and Grizel—he is described as "in fine fettle for writing" (*TG*, 39). His sentimentalism makes him a more capable artist but it must be at the cost of sexual potency; as Alice Pippinworth tells him, he loves his manuscripts too much to love her. Tommy emerges here as the decadent aesthete who feels more at home in the inner life of art and the very profundity of his own emotions than in the external social issues to which he might at any stage deploy those emotions. In this context, Barrie's presentation of the sentimental male contributes to a newly emerging attitude towards male sexuality and creativity. The Victorian model of masculinity was transformed towards the end of the century by writers like Walter Pater who legitimised inwardness and viewed the retreat from heterosexual compulsion as a sign of intense mental consciousness.[27] The inner life became valorised as a more complex but more authoritative subjectivity and throughout *Tommy and Grizel* we witness Tommy living his life according to his own fantasies rather than the mundane facts of the real world around him. As such he emerges as the artist whose creative powers are stifled by a world which subordinates creative intensity (and thus sentimentality) to the direction of moral purposefulness. Tommy is always trying to make the events of his life more profound then they really are; for him the "truth" about a situation is not how it is but how he *imagines* it:

> He had told the truth, and if what he imagined was twenty times more real to him than what was really there, how could Tommy help it?
>
> (*TG*, 77)

In his presentation of Tommy, Barrie seems to be striking out, at least to some extent, in favour of sentimentality. After all, it is not really Tommy's sentimentality which proves so disruptive but the pressure exerted upon him to reject it and to embrace socially prescribed norms. Society demands that he love Grizel, and in so trying he destroys both her and himself. By contrast, Tommy's sentimentalism leads him to do great things. When Grizel says to Tommy "I think you could do the most courageous things [. . .] so long as there was no real reason why you should do them" (*TG*, 102), she strikes at the heart of the issue. Tommy *is* courageous—we see that when he jumps in the water to save the drowning boy—but his courage is an aesthetic not a moral courage. He jumps not because he feels it is morally right but because he is in a state of intense mental emotion. Without that intensity of emotion, however, the boy would have drowned.

In its representation of a creative artist who oscillates between externally imposed moral paradigms and solipsism, Barrie's work can be identified as an important contribution to one of the most forward-looking literary idioms of his age. Anxiety over male sexuality and its relationship with creativity was to become a commonplace of modernism and it is perhaps not surprising that the young D. H. Lawrence responded to the *Tommy* novels with great enthusiasm, suggesting, in a letter to Jessie Chambers, that they helped define the way he felt about himself.[28] Barrie's novel is an important book in the literary representation of masculinity; that it remains out of print is absolutely scandalous.

Notes

1. *The Letters of T. S. Eliot,* ed. Valerie Eliot, 2 Vols (London, 1988), Vol. 1, p. 59.

2. Stephen Gwynn, "The Autumn's Books", *Fortnightly Review* 74 (1900), 1028-38 (p. 1037).

3. Robert C. Solomon, "In Defense of Sentimentality", *Philosophy and Literature* 14, 2 (October, 1990), 304-23, (p. 305).

4. Oscar Wilde, *De Profundis and other Writings* (Harmondsworth, 1954), p. 196.

5. J. M. Barrie, "Young Men I have Met. I—The Sentimentalist", *Young Man,* IV (1890), p. 6.

6. Thomas Carlyle, "Characteristics", *Edinburgh Review* (1831), reprinted in *The Works of Thomas Carlyle,* 30 vols (London, 1895) Vol. 28, p. 9.

7. Herbert Sussman, *Victorian Masculinities: Manhood and Masculine Poetics in Early Victorian Literature and Art* (Cambridge, 1995).

8. See J. A. Mangan & James Walvin (eds), *Manliness and Morality: Middle-class masculinity in Britain and America 1800-1940* (Manchester, 1987).

9. Donald E. Hall (ed.), *Muscular Christianity: Embodying the Victorian Age* (Cambridge, 1994).

10. Henry Rider Haggard, "About Fiction", *Contemporary Review* LI (1887), 172-80 (p. 177).

11. J. M. Barrie, "Thomas Hardy: The Historian of Wessex", *Contemporary Review* LVI (1889), 57-66 (p. 63).

12. Sally Mitchell, "Sentiment and suffering: women's recreational reading in the 1860s", *Victorian Studies* 21, 1 (1977), 29-45.

13. Quoted by Kate Flint, *The Woman Reader: 1837-1914* (Oxford, 1993), p. 4.

14. See ibid., chapter 4.

15. See Joseph Bristow, *Empire Boys: Adventures in a Man's World* (London, 1991).

16. See Kimberley Reynolds, *Girls Only? Gender and popular children's fiction in Britain, 1880-1910* (New York, London etc., 1990), p. 50.

17. Quoted in ibid., p. 36.

18. "A New Boy in Fiction", *Blackwood's Magazine* 160 (December, 1896), 800-13 (p. 805).

19. "Young Men I have Met", p. 6.

20. J. M. Barrie, *Tommy and Grizel* (Uniform edition, London, n/d), p. 16. Further references are given in the text.

21. Eve Kosofsky Sedgwick, *Epistemology of the Closet* (New York & London, 1991 [1990]).

22. Michel Foucault, *The History of Sexuality: An Introduction,* 1976, trans. Robert Hurley (Harmondsworth, 1981), pp. 42-3.

23. *Epistemology of the Closet,* p. 198.

24. Peter Gay, *The Bourgeois Experience: Victoria to Freud* (New York, 1984), p. 295.

25. Ed Cohen, *Talk on the Wilde Side: Towards a Genealogy of Male Sexualities* (New York, 1993).

26. Leonee Ormond, *J. M. Barrie* (Edinburgh, 1987), p. 78.

27. See Sussman, *Victorian Masculinities,* chapter 4.

28. See *The Letters of D. H. Lawrence,* Volume I, ed. James T. Boulton (Cambridge, 1979), p. 175.

Ann Wilson (essay date winter 2000)

SOURCE: Wilson, Ann. "Hauntings: Anxiety, Technology, and Gender in *Peter Pan.*" *Modern Drama* 43, no. 4 (winter 2000): 595-610.

[*In the following essay, Wilson emphasizes the undercurrent of anxiety in* Peter Pan, *which she attributes to the changes in masculine identity in modern life that Barrie explores in the play.*]

J. M. Barrie's ***Peter Pan*** (1904) circulates in the popular imagination as a happy tale for children that, through the adventures of Peter and the other children in Never Land, celebrates playfulness. As Mark Twain commented, "It is my belief that ***Peter Pan*** is a great and refining and uplifting benefaction to this sordid and money-mad age; and the next best play is a long way behind" (qtd. in Jack 158). Tellingly, Twain's comment that ***Peter Pan*** is uplifting seems to depend on ignoring the fact that each of the "lost" boys is a baby who has fallen out of his pram "when the nurse is looking the other way" and who, if not claimed within seven days, is "sent far away to the Never Land" (Barrie 101). The boys of Never Land are dead, and so Peter Pan, arriving at the window of the Darling family, is a ghost. As the stage direction before Peter's arrival indicates, "*the nursery darkens [. . .]. Something uncanny is going to happen, we expect, for a quiver has passed through the room, just sufficient to touch the night-lights*" (97). As Freud suggests in his 1919 essay, the "uncanny" arouses an experience of "dread and horror," partially because the familiar (*heimlich*) evokes the unfamiliar (*unheimlich*), rendering the comfortable and "homey" uncomfortable and alien (224). The familiar, now both familiar and unfamiliar, generates anxiety.

Peter Pan, as a ghost whose first appearance is announced as "uncanny," is the sign of anxiety within the play. Beneath the familiarity of middle-class life, in the opening and closing scenes, and the culture of children's play evident in the adventures in Never Land is the anxiety aroused by the shifts in masculine identity in relation to modern life, including the new technologies of the workplace and the demise of Empire. Barrie's response is anxious and nostalgic, the desire to return to an imagined past of stability that, if it ever existed, is impossible to recuperate, a point marked by the setting of the play in "Never Land."

The "modern," as the experience of recent times, involves the memory of the past and anticipates a future. Thus, the experience of the "modern" is change. In the flux, the familiar may be lost or altered. If change is a characteristic of the modern, then *heimlich* and *unheimlich*—the familiar and the unfamiliar—with the resulting dread and anxiety produced by change are important features. One of the implications of this understanding of "modern" is that as capitalism emerges as the economic ethos of Western countries, the changing technologies of industry that buttress capitalism become key to understanding the "modern." Industrial technologies are not simply tools within the workplace; because they change the terms of work, they inevitably have an impact on the relation of workers to their labour and, hence, on the identities of workers, particularly in terms of redefining class and gender. As industrial technologies evolve, they effect radical change, which generates anxiety, particularly for the middle class, which, located between the upper and working classes, is in a site of negotiation and inherent instability.

Industry and its technologies opened a set of social relations that gave rise to the middle class. It is relatively easy to define the upper class as those who enjoy social privilege by virtue of aristocratic birth and those with established fortunes—either made or inherited—that allow access to social institutions of power. In contrast, as Ed Cohen notes in *Talk on the Wilde Side,* "agricultural labourers and the industrial working classes [. . .] were largely determined by the material constraints circumscribing their lives" (19), which is to say that the work in which they engaged was mainly physical, intellectually disengaged, and under-waged, so that there was little possibility of accruing excess capital. Members of the working class did not have the luxury of imagining that their financial circumstances would improve significantly.

The middle class seems more difficult to define. Cohen, synthesizing a wide range of commentary on class formation, suggests that understanding the middle class depends partially on the empirical and partially on understanding the epistemological underpinnings of the concept (19). As its name implies the middle class falls between the upper and working classes as an unstable site of mediation between the two. The instability of the middle class means that arriving at a definition is difficult, but a point of departure might be the consideration of the broad terms of work for the middle class, which requires a degree of intellectual engagement and is remunerated at a level above subsistence; in these two ways it differs from the work performed by the working class. The accumulation of savings, frequently resulting in members of the middle class buying property, results in a horizon of expectation and imagined possibilities: affluence brings the promise of a better life, which seemed a consequence of the economics of Empire. As Cohen comments,

> Without too much quibbling [. . .] we might say that the denizens of the Victorian middle class were those who had been able to advance themselves financially and socially in the accelerating, expanding, and industrializing British economy. Hence it included a wide array of individuals from merchant princes and entrepreneurial wizards, to an ever-growing number of professionals, bankers, bureaucrats, and civil servants, to local shopkeepers, artisans, teachers, clergy, and clerks, along with their families.
>
> (19, 20)

The broad range of individuals who make up the middle class means that; given the differing social locations of these individuals, it is relatively difficult for this class to coalesce around common interests: the aspirations of a curate serving in a rural parish are not those of a shopkeeper in an urban setting, although both are "middle class." The lack of commonality contributes to the instability of the middle class. Further, its instability is an effect of the cycles of capitalism, which means that being middle class is not secure. In times of affluence, some members of the middle class acquire savings. But the margin of comfort afforded by such savings tends to be limited, and so an economic depression can lead to financial demise for those in the middle class. Hence, as Cohen notes, the spectre of failure haunts the middle class even as it anticipates a better life (19-21). Put another way, to be middle class is to be located within a social sphere of inherent instability marked by the lack of homogenous interests amongst members of the class and by the reality that the defining economic location is precariously uninsulated from vacilations in the economy. The optimistic investment—psychological and fiscal—that the future brings possibilities of affluence and a better life is the underlying anxiety that the conditions of capital generate in the middle class. A valence of the "uncanny" that renders the comfort of the "homey" uncomfortable may well stem from the fundamental instability of the middle class, which, given its investments, cannot acknowledge that "instability" is its condition. It is a class that, as Cohen suggests, is haunted by the possibility of failure.

The strain of having limited and insecure affluence is the context of *Peter Pan*, which opens in the nursery of a house "at the top of a rather depressed street in Bloomsbury" (87). The house is so nondescript that Barrie advises, "you may dump it down anywhere you like, and if you think it was your house you are very probably right" (87). While this is a particular house, belonging to the Darling family, Barrie assumes that members of his audience recognize and identify with it because they, like the Darlings, are middle class: if they don't live in a house like the Darlings', they know of people who do.

The opening scene of *Peter Pan* continues to offer a glimpse of the middle class, particularly in terms of the negotiation of gender. The action of the play begins with the Darling children pretending to be their parents. Says John to his mother, "We are doing an act; we are playing at being you and father" (89), as if gender roles are performed. John and Wendy's rehearsal of their parents seems like a recurring part of the dynamic of the family, so that Mr Darling's entrance and his petulant demand that his wife fix his tie read like an extension of the role playing: as the children play their parents, so the father plays his child. Says Mr Darling to his wife, "I warn you, Mary, that unless this tie is round my neck we don't go out to dinner to-night, and if I don't go out to dinner to-night I never go to the office again, and if I don't go to the office again you and I starve, and our children will be thrown into the streets" (91). Given that the audience does not have access to the stage directions while they watch the play, and given that Mr Darling does later self-consciously play his son, the audience might be forgiven for seeing Mr Darling as entering the spirit of the domestic scene by "playing along." The stage directions suggest that it would be a misreading to see Mr Darling as naturally given to the sulks and resentful of others being the centre of attention:

> *Mr Darling arrives, in no mood unfortunately to gloat over this domestic scene. He is really a good man as breadwinners go, and it is hard luck for him to be propelled into the room now, when if we had brought him in a few minutes earlier or later he might have made a fairer impression. In the city where he sits on a stool all day, as fixed as a postage stamp, he is so like all the others on stools that you recognise him not by his face but by his stool, but at home the way to gratify him is to say that he has a distinct personality. He is very conscientious, and in the days when Mrs Darling gave up keeping the house books correctly and drew pictures instead (which he called her guesses), he did all the totting up for her, holding her hand while he calculated whether they could have Wendy or not, and coming down on the right side.*
>
> (90)

This stage direction is extraordinary in a number of ways, not the least of which is that Barrie includes important information in a stage direction that an actor would have difficulty conveying in performance. The information amounts to a curious recognition and, given that the information is unplayable, suppression by Barrie of the effect of the economic on the lives of individuals. In a moment that one might expect to find in a play by Ibsen in which characters are anxious about their finances (such as *A Doll's House*), Barrie tells us that the Darlings are not flush and had to calculate whether they could afford to have a child (with the interesting implication that they must have been practising contraception). As well, the stage direction establishes a tension between Mr Darling's identity at work, where he is anonymous, and his demeanour at home, where he is the protective husband who, as the master of his house, takes responsibility for reconciling the household finances. Barrie establishes the beginnings of a critique of masculinity in which there is a separation between the identity of a man in the workplace and his identity at home. Work alienates and dehumanizes the labourer, whereas within the sphere of home, his humanity is restored within the codes of manhood that make him the first element of the dyad man/woman. At home, he is ostensibly the breadwinner, provider, and protector of his family.

This scene seems to suggest two types of instability: the instability of masculine identity as a man moves between work and home; and financial instability or insecurity. Given the Mr Darling to whom the audience is introduced in the opening act, the strain seems too much. "George, not so loud, the servants will hear you," instructs Mrs Darling after Mr Darling has petulantly compared his situation to that of Nana, the governess of his children, who, because the family is in economic straits, is a Newfoundland dog.[2] When, in this moment, his daughter, Wendy, tells her father that he has made Nana cry, he responds, "Coddle her; nobody coddles me. Oh dear no. I am only the breadwinner, why should I be coddled? Why, why, why?" (95). It is then that Mrs Darling tries to regulate her husband, to insist that he lower his voice, presumably in order to maintain the illusion of middle-class decorum, and financial solvency, before the servants. Mr Darling responds, "Let them hear me; bring in the whole world," because he is *"The desperate man, who has not been in fresh air for days, [and] has now lost all self-control"* (96). Mr Darling's desperation, it is implied, is a consequence of his being cooped up at work, where he is denied a sense of individuality and autonomy, a cipher in the workings of the office.

Mr Darling is faceless, known by his stool, and is likened to a postage stamp, which dehumanizes him in a particular way. By being made into a piece of furniture in the workplace and a postage stamp, which marks that the cost of sending a piece of mail has been paid, he is rendered a part of the technology of industrial capital. Given that postage stamps were introduced in England in 1839, Mr Darling seems not even to be a part of current technologies. What is at stake here is more than a rhetorical figure of synecdoche in which a stool or a stamp stands for Mr Darling. Barrie suggests that under capitalism, human identity becomes a technology. The social codes of masculinity are thrown into crisis because notions of "mastery" that were key to middle-class masculinity are impossible for men like Mr Darling in the context of their work, which shapes a significant aspect of their identity. Rendered less than fully human in the workplace, Mr Darling is not even the "master" within his own home, where the terms of his livelihood as a clerk mean that his ability to provide for his family is uncertain; and, given the shabbiness of the house and the fact that the family has a dog as its governess, Mr Darling's inadequacies as a provider seem to announce his "failed" manhood.

Part of this sense of "failure" is a consequence of the shifting demographics of the workforce. The expansion of industrial capital involved the expansion of the business end of the operations. With this expansion, women entered the labour force as clerks, which, in the early part of the nineteenth century, had been a male occupation. As the offices of industry enlarged, the nature of clerical work shifted, creating a "dual labour market": "highly trained, trusted and well rewarded employees [undertook] the demanding and responsible work, while the routine work was performed by a shifting group of low-paid, easily replaced workers who could be hired and fired as pressure of work demanded" (Jordan 12). As Elizabeth Roberts notes in her study *Women's Work, 1840-1940,* "In 1914 about 20 per cent of clerical workers were women. Between 1861 and 1911 the number of male clerks had increased fivefold while the number of women clerks had risen by 400 per cent" (28). From the description of Mr Darling on his stool, it is clear that he does not hold a senior position of responsibility but performs "routine" work that offers little job security and is increasingly becoming the domain of women. As routine clerical work became feminized and devalued, the sense of failure for men like Mr Darling became pronounced. The workplace is a site of emasculation that denies men performing clerical work the sense that they can provide assuredly for their families. As a result, failure is the condition of masculinity for Mr Darling and men like him, who, under the changing terms of work in industrial capital, can never be "masterful" men.

The emasculation of Mr Darling is emphasized in the final scene of the play, in which Mr Darling is, literally, in the doghouse. As he emerges from the kennel, the stage direction indicates that *"It ought to melt us when we see how humbly grateful he is for a kiss from his wife, so much more than he feels he deserves"* (148). The play suggests that Mr Darling is being punished for losing his temper. As I have argued, however, his outbursts are not symptomatic of his limitations as an individual but, rather, are socially produced through the irreconcilable codes of masculinity that he has to negotiate. The anger and the feeling of impotence, which lead to childish outbursts, become modes of social regulation that ensure that middle-class men will not enjoy consistent identities within the public and domestic spheres. Put another way, the full title of the play is ***Peter Pan or the Boy Who Would Not Grow Up.*** "Would" suggests agency and choice. In Mr Darling's case, the contradictions of masculinity may amount to the man who could not grow up. Faced with the impossibility of coming to terms with the eroding sense of masculinity as the demographics of the workplace shift and women perform clerical tasks but the imperative remains for middle-class men to be the "bread winners" of the family, Mr Darling "plays" the child at home. The play rehearses this regression when it moves to Never Land, the world of childish adventure that is an escape from the pressures of adult life.

In Never Land, the parental figures—Mr and Mrs Darling—are left behind, and so Barrie abandons the critique of the middle class that he seemed to offer in the first act. Never Land, as its name implies, doesn't exist, save in its imaginative rendering within the constraints of the proscenium arch. It is a place of play within a play. The terms of Never Land are nostalgic and gendered. Never Land is a boy's world, "very compact, not large and sprawly with tedious distances between one adventure and another, but nicely crammed" (105).

Act Two introduces Never Land and begins while Peter Pan is still off in London, where he is trying to recover his shadow, which he lost in the Darlings' house, which Mrs Darling found and Mr Darling is keen to sell: "There is money in this, my love. I shall take it to the British Museum to-morrow and have it priced" (93). Without Peter Pan, their leader, the other boys in Never Land are "lost," trying to imagine the mothers from whom they were separated as small children (107). Enter the pirates, led by Captain Hook, who, in the context of the adventure, are the enemy. Barrie provides a long and detailed description of Hook, who, among his other features, is described as having his hair "*dressed in long curls which look like black candles about to melt, his eyes blue as the forget-me-not*" (108). Further, he is described as having elegant diction, which, along with "*the distinction of his demeanour, show him one of a different class from his crew, a solitary among uncultured companions. [. . .] At his public school they said of him that he 'bled yellow.' In dress he apes the dandiacal associated with Charles II*" (108).

The identification of Captain Hook as a "dandy," in the wake of the trials of Oscar Wilde in 1895, is significant inasmuch as it opens the complex issue of Hook's sexuality. As Ed Cohen (in *Talk on the Wilde Side*) and Alan Sinfield (in *The Wilde Century*) argue, the trials (which were widely reported in the popular press in England and, indeed, throughout Europe and the United States) were crucial in the construction of the homosexual as a recognizable social identity. As Sinfield notes, "The dominant twentieth-century queer identity [. . .] has been constructed [. . .] mainly out of elements that came together at the Wilde trials: effeminacy, leisure, idleness, immorality, luxury, insouciance, decadence and aestheticism" (*Wilde Century* 12). Sinfield's point is that while these characteristics have since become associated with homosexuality, Wilde's public personae of aesthete and, later, dandy were not read by his contemporaries as obvious signs of his homosexuality. While Wilde's dandyism was recognized, celebrated, and reviled, his self-staging did not lead "either his friends or strangers to regard him as obviously, even probably, queer" (2).

With the case of Wilde serving as the cautionary note, a reading of Captain Hook as "queer" is problematic. Certainly, that he is the only adult in Never Land, engaged in "play" with the boys, does suggest a latent anxiety about the homosexual as arrested in his development, invested in the culture of youth, inclined to pederasty. Given that the "lost boys" are dead, a sexuality that eroticizes death could be added to the list of anxieties about the homosexual. Captain Hook, rather than being obviously homosexual, is a dandy. As Sinfield suggests in "'Effeminacy' and 'Femininity': Sexual Politics in Wilde's Comedies,"

> Dandy effeminacy signalled class, far more than sexuality. The newly dominant middle class justified itself by claiming manly purity, purpose, and responsibility, and identified the leisure class, correspondingly, with effeminate idleness and immorality. In the face of this manoeuvre, there were two alternatives for the wealthy and those who sought to seem wealthy. One was to attempt to appear useful and good; the other was to repudiate middle-class authority by displaying conspicuous idleness, immorality, and effeminacy; in other words, by being a dandy.
>
> (38)

Given that a theatrical convention is to have the role of Captain Hook played by the actor performing the role of Mr Darling, and given that middle-class masculinity has failed Mr Darling, Captain Hook can been seen as Barrie's inscription of what amounts to a fantasy, for Mr Darling, of his having access to the privilege of leisure and luxury associated with the upper classes. This is not to discount the idea that there is a homoerotic undercurrent in ***Peter Pan***; this is another mode of haunting in the play because at issue is masculinity, related to issues of class, rather than simply sexuality. The interrelation between sexuality and class is complex, and, as Sinfield's comments imply, adopting the guise of a dandy may signal more than homosexual inclinations.

In some sense, Mr Darling might be read as a figure in Never Land who escapes the pressures of being an adult by donning the guise of Captain Hook, a dandy—leisured and effeminate—who has the time (which is to say, financial security) to indulge in play and is free of the necessity to work. Further, playing an effeminate male figure offers Mr Darling the fantasy of recuperating a sense of masculinity that is eroded in his working life, in which the role of clerk increasingly is becoming the domain of women. If a cause of Mr. Darling's anxiety about his masculinity is the feminization of clerical work, playing the dandy—the feminized man of wealth—is a way of managing that anxiety because the dandy is a figure of financial means; Mr Darling is anxious about his ability to provide for his family. Never Land is a haunted world, not just because the boys are "dead" but because it is not free of the spectre of social and economic pressures on the middle class.

It seems impossible for Barrie to imagine a place without class, perhaps because Never Land is the nostalgic response to the conditions of the middle class that Barrie established in Act One. The fantasy circulating around the ethos of Never Land rehearses that of the public schools, which were, as Jonathan Rutherford has suggested, implicated in establishing codes of manliness associated with a virtuous Englishness that justified imperialism. He suggests that "public schools sought to inculcate four qualities in their boys": "sport," "readiness," "character," and "religion" (15). While the last, "religion," is not particularly evident in **Peter Pan,** the others are. In Never Land, the culture of the public school is rehearsed in the separation of the boys from family and, particularly, the influence of mother. In the face of the loss of family, the boys become a "family" and forge close, intense bonds that are homosocial and, inasmuch as these affective relations are "between boys" (to borrow and adapt Eve Kosofsky Sedgwick's phrase), open an emotional terrain that allows the intimacy to become homosexual. Through their "games" or adventures, they learn not only about readiness in responding to the surprise attacks by Hook but about submitting to enforced regimes, and so they become obedient. As the opening of Act Two suggests, without Peter Pan as their leader, the other boys flounder, remembering mother but, as the stage direction reminds us, *"not that they are really worrying about their mothers"* (107).

Codes of manliness involve physicality through the games/adventures but a pronounced avoidance of the body as sexual. When Wendy reaches out to touch Peter in their initial encounter, he recoils and says, "You mustn't touch me" (98). As the stage directions note, *"He is never touched by any one in the play"* (98). Indeed, the play establishes a curious economy of desire in which Wendy, Tinker Bell (the fairy) and Tiger Lily (the Indian maid) are all attracted to Peter Pan, who doesn't reciprocate their interest. Wendy, in Act One, offers herself to receive a kiss from Peter Pan, who "*offers her the thimble*" (101). "Thimble" becomes a means for negotiating the awkwardness of the moment as Wendy leans forward to kiss Peter, who seems perplexed and doesn't recognize her attraction to him. Their faces don't meet; Wendy screams, saying that she felt as if someone were pulling her hair (101). "That must have been Tink," explains Peter. By Act Four, when Wendy has established a household where she plays mother and Peter plays father to the boys, Wendy asks, "What are your exact feelings for me, Peter?" (130). "Those of a devoted son, Wendy," he replies. Apparently disappointed, Wendy turns away, causing Peter to comment, "You are so puzzling. Tiger Lily is just the same; there is something or other she wants to be to me, but she says it is not my mother" (130). "No, indeed it isn't," retorts Wendy (130).

Each of the three female figures attracted to Peter Pan recognizes the other's desire for him, even if he is oblivious. Tinker Bell reacts with obvious jealousy, pulling at Wendy's hair and, when Wendy is arriving in Never Land, telling the boys that Peter has ordered them to shoot her. Given that they have been trained to obediently follow the orders of their Captain, they shoot arrows at her until she falls to earth, which Tootles believes will make Peter proud of him (112). Wendy recognizes Tiger Lily's desire for Peter because it parallels her own. The terms under which Barrie represents female desire are worth considering because they suggests how class and ethnicity are elements in producing codes of middle-class femininity.

When Wendy offers to give Peter a kiss, and he reveals that he doesn't know what a kiss is, she gives him a thimble. Peter then asks if he should give her a kiss, and then offers her an acorn (99). The scene, played between a young boy and girl, seems innocuous enough but, even so, provides cues about middle-class perceptions of female sexuality. Wendy has the opportunity to take the lead and give Peter a kiss, but instead offers him a thimble. His reciprocating by offering her an acorn creates an economy in which the exchange of tokens of affection substitutes for the expression of affection itself. A few moments later, Wendy seems to feel that the opportunity might be right for a kiss, but this time, rather than offering to kiss Peter, she offers herself: "Peter, you may give me a kiss" (101). It is as if the codes of middle-class femininity prevent Wendy from expressing sexual agency; her role is to make herself passively available, despite her own desires.

The play hints at a logic behind the suppression of sexuality. Never Land, rehearsing the culture of public school, is homosocial, a site for establishing relations between men in which women, if they figure at all, do so as currency in the exchange.[3] While the homosocial is not homoerotic, the spectre of the homoerotic, lurking as the unspoken possibility, haunts the scene. The negative connotations of "lurking" are deliberate, because by the time Barrie wrote **Peter Pan** the dissident figure of the homosexual as pathological and criminal was established in the cultural imaginary of England through press accounts of the trials of Oscar Wilde. The castigation of Wilde in the popular press speaks to an already established anxiety about homosexuality and, indeed, about sexuality in general. To gesture to this anxiety, it is worth remembering that in 1864 Britain implemented the Contagious Diseases Acts, which allowed the police to apprehend any woman who *appeared* to be infected with venereal disease and subject her to medical examinations in hospital, where she was held for three (and later nine) months. The women who appeared to be infected were prostitutes, and the cultural context of prostitution is important. Prostitution was a mode of casual employment for working-class women employed in the three major occupations which were available to them (laundry, needlework, and domestic service), none of which paid adequate wages (Clark 642). Occasional stints as prostitutes supplemented the income of these women. Prostitution came to be seen as a threat to the nation in the aftermath of Crimean Wars, in which men in the military had high rates of infection from sexually transmitted diseases.

There is little evidence to suggest that the castigation of working-class women who supplemented their incomes through prostitution had any effect on rates of venereal disease infection amongst the military. My reference to this moment of history is intended to serve as a reminder of the terms of the Acts: sexually engaged women were cited as contaminating men. Because the women were from the working class, the measures against them were severe. Women were apprehended on the basis of appearing to be infected, held for months in hospitals, segregated from their families and communities, and subjected to the regulation of being put on a register. Further, the police, having identified the women, patrolled the areas where they lived, and so all women within those communities became suspect (Clark 644). This hyper-vigilance gave rise to suspicion about female desire. Wrote Henry Mayhew in *London Labour and the London Poor* in 1862, "'Literally, every woman who yields to her passions and loses her virtue is a prostitute'" (qtd. in Clark 642). The mid-nineteenth-century concern over sexuality transmitted disease was understandable, but it became a panicked response that made manifest fears of female sexuality as dangerous and needing regulation. While men were the agents of the Empire that fuelled the economy and the commensurate sense of nation, they somehow were not responsible for their own sexual conduct or for availing themselves of prostitutes, apparently rendered powerless by the allure of female sexuality. Socially engaged women responded to the Contagious Diseases Acts with an evangelical fervour, but part of the movement involved notions of purity and eschewing sex outside marriage because it was dangerous and sinful. Further, the purity movement, with its distrust of the body as sexual, included the regulation of homosexuality, which, like prostitution, was seen as undermining a "manliness" that was crucial to the project of Empire, even if the ethos of Empire seems to have depended on the homosocial. The result of the anxiety around homosexuality was the 1885 Labouchère amendment, which made homosexual acts, whether in public or in private, criminal. As Sinfield notes, the title of the amendment is "Outrages on public decency" (*Wilde Century* 9). These references to the regulation of sexuality in Victorian England speak not only to the public anxiety about sexuality but to the recognition of the body as sexual, even if that body is reviled. This history of sexual regulation is another mode of haunting in **Peter Pan** in which Peter, forever the boy, panics and avoids the advances of the three female figures in Never Land.

Although Wendy desires Peter, she is reticent about acting; not Tinker Bell, who tries to cut Wendy from Peter's affections so she can have him to herself. Tinker Bell is brazen and, as Peter remarks, "not very polite. [. . .] She is quite a common girl, you know. She is called Tinker Bell because she mends the fairy pots and kettles" (100). It would seem that even the fairy world is marked by class and that Tinker Bell, who is working-class, is impure and suspect in ways that are consistent with the middle class's imagining of the working class. Later on in the play, at the opening of Act Four (titled "The Home Under the Ground"), Barrie establishes a contrast between Tinker Bell, who has retreated to her unseen bedchamber, where she "is probably wasting valuable time just now wondering whether to put on the smoky blue or the apple blossom" (126), and Wendy. While Tinker Bell indulges in attiring herself, presumably for the pleasure of Peter, who isn't home, Wendy presides over the dinner as if she were mother of the boys (126). It would seem that the role envisioned for middle-class women is that of mother, evacuated of any sexuality—which, because it contaminates, is displaced onto the working class, becoming another reason to sanction the regulation and containment of that class.

There are other implications to rendering the figure of mother as pure and asexual: as I mentioned earlier in commenting on Mr Darling, middle-class masculinity, produced within industrial capital, may militate against men growing up. As well, the fear of female sexuality as diseased and the resulting celebration of the middle-class woman as "pure" and "chaste," occurring within the context of a homosocial ethos haunted by fear of homosexuality, which is seen also as diseased, leads to suspicion of the sexualized body. This point is made by Barrie's depiction of the sexualized female as Tinker Bell, the fairy who is a coloured light and so without a body.

In mapping the construction of middle-class sexuality through *Peter Pan,* I want to draw attention to another aspect of the contrast between Tinker Bell and Wendy. Tinker Bell is a light, but one that is coloured, while Wendy—in keeping with tropes of purity—is associated with white. As Wendy and her brothers approach Never Land, Tinker Bell offers a feigned alert and tells the boys in fairy language that Peter wants Wendy shot (111). The boys shoot at Wendy, who has been *"fluttering among the tree-tops in her white nightgown,"* almost like a ghost. As if to emphasize the visual cue of the fluttering figure, one of the boys comments, "How white it is!" (111). Wendy is "it" and not "she," the feminine denied gender, looking ghostly but representing such a threat to the boyish culture of Never Land that she has to be shot down on the instruction of Tinker Bell, who pretends that the instruction comes from Peter. Women (or, at least, female figures—Tinker Bell is hardly a woman) are key to the regulation of sexuality, as evinced historically by the involvement of middle-class women in social purity movements; Tinker Bell's wanting Wendy shot is a mode of regulation, but one motivated by her selfish desire to have Peter to herself, and so she makes no pretence about serving the social good.

Multiple anxieties are at work in this scene, beginning with the implications of "whiteness." "Whiteness" is a crucial critical category in the production of discourse around race because, as Henry Louis Gates, Jr., reminds his readers in the introduction to *"Race," Writing, and Difference,* "Race, as a meaningful criterion within the biological sciences, has long been recognized to be a fiction. When we speak of 'the white race' or 'the black race,' 'the Jewish race' or 'the Aryan race,' we speak in biological misnomers and, more generally, in metaphors" (4). Wendy's "whiteness" marks her purity and effectively announces visually that she is sexually pure. As we have noted, the legacy of the Contagious Diseases Acts was to mark working-class women as licentious and dangerous, carriers of disease that threatened to exceed the working class and infect the middle class. Taking my cue from Gates's comments, the force of the metaphoric deployment of whiteness in *Peter Pan* is a referent to the set of social understandings around the relation of feminine sexuality to class. Perhaps the latent anxiety around female sexuality resonates most strongly in Tinker Bell being a fairy, and so having desire but no body that might unleash that dangerous working-class desire.

The purity of whiteness figures strongly on another valence in *Peter Pan.* Through the figure of Tiger Lily, the stereotype of the over-sexed aboriginal figure is introduced. Like Tinker Bell, Tiger Lily desires Peter Pan. In an early manuscript, that desire is articulated through a rape fantasy:

TIGER LILY:

Suppose Tiger Lily runs into the wood—Peter Paleface attack her—what then?

PETER:

(*bewildered*) Paleface can never catch Indian girl, they run so fast.

TIGER LILY:

If Peter Paleface chase Tiger Lily—she no run very fast—she tumble into a heap what then? (*Peter puzzled. She addresses Indians.*) What then?

ALL INDIANS:

She him's squaw.

(qtd. in Jack 169)

In a play marked by the negotiation of anxiety and filled with the playwright's self-censoring (including the displacement to the stage directions of concerns about how industrial technologies impact on Mr Darling), *Peter Pan* starts to seem to be a play with an unconscious. Lurking in that unconscious is an anxiety about female sexuality as dangerous and, in the case of aboriginal populations subjugated in the colonizing enterprise of imperialism, wanting to be raped. To the contemporary reader, Barrie's depiction of the aboriginal is embarrassing, for, while the play depends on stereotypes of femininity—of the middle-class Wendy as the figure of mother, of the working-class Tinker Bell as self-absorbed in her desire for Peter—the early manuscripts, which feature a stronger presence of Tiger Lily, are horrific in their suggestion that aboriginal women so strongly desire white men that they want to be violently conquered through rape. While the rape fantasy does not figure in the version of *Peter Pan* that was finally staged, Barrie depicts the aboriginals as stereotypes of the primal and pre-social, so that the braves can say little beyond "Ugh, ugh, wah!" and Tiger Lily's command of language is only slightly better: "The Great White Father save me from pirates. Me his velly nice friend now; no let pirates hurt him" (129). Indeed, the use of "velly" sounds like a racist stage depiction of a Chinese person, suggesting that all who are not white meld into an undifferentiated "other." The deployment of the phrase "The Great White Father," mimicking the nineteenth-century appellations of Queen Victoria as the Great White Mother, signals that Never Land is not just a recreation of the public school ethic—although it is that—but an invocation of Empire that ties the public school ethic to imperialism.

Jacqueline Rose, in *The Case of Peter Pan or The Impossibility of Children's Fiction,* devotes a chapter to issues of language. The chapter titled "Peter Pan, Language and the State," with the subtitle "Captain Hook Goes to Eton," offers a useful reminder that in Barrie's short story "Jas Hook at Eton," Hook's final words before jumping overboard are "Floreat Etona" (115). Given that the story was written in 1925, the contrast with the "plain" language of the play, written just over twenty years earlier, serves as another useful index of Barrie's anxiety about the changing world brought about by the industrial technologies of capitalism. The specifics of Rose's argument about the tension of various levels of language in Barrie's iterations of the Peter Pan story, at a time when there were state initiatives around literacy and more accessible education based on the deployment of a standardized vernacular, have limited applicability to the concerns of this paper. But her comments do draw attention to the use of language and its implications for maintaining class distinctions. Barrie has Tinker Bell's utterances unheard by the audience but clearly marked as being in a foreign tongue—that of the fairies—that needs translation and is ungrammatical (136). The figure of Tinker Bell, so innocuously presented as a disembodied fairy, is Barrie's management not just of the working class but of the working-class immigrant for whom English was not a first language. Similarly, Tiger Lily and her braves seem to have limited abilities in English, marking the xenophobia of the English middle class to the "other." It is Wendy, that figure of purity and the virtues of English womanhood, who has full command of English. To return to the earlier scene in which a "kiss" was interpreted by Peter Pan as a "thimble," R. D. S. Jack reminds readers that the issue is one of understanding referentiality: Wendy knows the referent to "kiss" and Peter Pan doesn't (232). The middle-class English woman is figured as the sign of purity, a repository of Englishness marked by her command of language.

To state what at this juncture must be patently obvious, **Peter Pan** is a fable of modernity, anxiously negotiating industrial technologies that produced a middle class predicated on instability and which encoded impossible roles for men and women. Given the circulating ideologies of manliness that involved notions of their agency, of being patriarchal masters in their immediate households and in that enterprise of nation predicated on a lexis of "family," middle-class men at the turn of the twentieth century seem to have been denied any actual way of becoming "real" men. The evolution of industrial capital inscribed their failure. But no less did it regulate middle-class women by locating them as asexual, pure figures whose "natural" inclinations to maternity became the sign of the inherent virtue of whiteness. Mr Darling may be *"really a good man as breadwinners go,"* but the implication is that "goodness" is accessible only to a middle-class woman like Mrs Darling.

The experience of the modern is that of the present or the very recent past, which is marked as different from the more distant past. This difference is, in effect, change, which, since the Enlightenment, Western culture has understood as cumulatively amounting to "progress" and, ultimately, to social betterment. Given that the various aspects of society do not function as discrete entities but are interrelated, change in one aspect has some degree of impact on others, including gender and sexual identities. Barrie's strategy for managing the anxiety is a nostalgic retreat to Never Land, the fantasy of boyish adventure, which rehearses the ethos of the public school and Empire. Never Land, as its very name suggests, is an impossibility, an idealization of what never was, because part of the strategy of managing anxiety about the changes that the modern brings is nostalgia for a (mis)remembered past now gone.

Selective remembering is not restricted to **Peter Pan**; it also characterizes the response to the play, as Twain's comment about it being an "uplifting benefaction" suggests. Twain forgets that Never Land is inhabited by dead boys who are ghosts. For the most part, the play's reception has been marked by its being read as a play for children, a jolly fantasy of fun-filled adventure. As a consequence, it is not included in the canon of modern drama, as if a work for children cannot tackle issues with the gravity of a writer like Ibsen. So, for example, Elaine Showalter writes,

> New Women and male aesthetes redefined the meanings of femininity and masculinity. There were fears that emancipated women would bear children outside of marriage in the free union, or worse, that they would not have children at all. In the wake of Ibsen, women's oppression became the theme of successful plays by Arthur Pinero, Oscar Wilde, Harley Granville-Barker, and George Bernard Shaw. . . .
>
> (3)

Showalter's comment is instructive inasmuch as her list of playwrights who address issues relating to the shifts in gender and sexual identities celebrates those whose works anticipate, and are compatible with, changing roles for women and a greater social acceptance of homosexuality in the late twentieth century. In the move to inscribe a genealogy for the social movements of the present, Showalter and others ignore plays that do not seem politically "progressive." The remarkable longevity of **Peter Pan,** which receives more productions today than do the works of Pinero or Granville-Barker, suggests that it appeals to audiences. While much of the appeal is, no doubt, the highly theatrical fantasy of the play, this fantasy is a means of managing the anxiety of loss. It may well be that Barrie's anxieties resonate with audiences who are haunted by the loss that change brings and seek escape in fantasy.

Notes

1. My thanks to Alan Filewod for his careful reading of an early draft of this paper. I owe a tremendous debt of thanks to the students in a senior seminar

on dramatic literature that I taught at the University of Guelph in winter 2000. The course focused on ideologies of gender and sexuality in relation to nation in the late nineteenth and early twentieth centuries. The students' enthusiastic, thoughtful engagement did much to shape my thinking.

2. Bendure notes, "In addition to being something of a status symbol, Newfoundlands were also employed as canine nannies and personal companions, and saw great popularity as gun dogs. There is even a story from the last century of a husband trading his wife for a Newfoundland dog" (70).

3. Sedgwick notes in her introduction to *Between Men* that "'Homosocial' is a word occasionally used in history and the social sciences, where it describes social bonds between persons of the same sex; it is a neologism, obviously formed by analogy with 'homosexual,' and just as obviously meant to be distinguished from 'homosexual'" (1).

Works Cited

Barrie, J. M. *Peter Pan. Peter Pan and Other Plays.* Ed. Peter Hollindale. Oxford: Oxford UP, 1995. 73-154.

Bendure, Joan C. *The Newfoundland Dog: Companion Dog-Water Dog.* New York: Macmillan, 1994.

Clark, Anna. "Prostitution." *Victorian Britain: An Encyclopedia.* Ed. Sally Mitchell. New York and London: Garland, 1988. 642-45.

Cohen, Ed. *Talk on the Wilde Side: Toward a Genealogy of a Discourse on Male Sexualities.* New York and London: Routledge, 1993.

Freud, Sigmund. "The 'Uncanny.'" *The Standard Edition of the Complete Psychological Works of Sigmund Freud.* Vol. 17. Trans. and Ed. James Strachey. London: Hogarth P and Inst. of Psycho-Analysis, 1955. 217-56.

Gates, Henry Louis, Jr. "Editor's Introduction: Writing 'Race' and the Difference It Makes." *"Race," Writing, and Difference.* Ed. Henry Louis Gates, Jr. Chicago and London: U of Chicago P, 1985. 1-20.

Jack, R. D. S. *The Road to the Never Land: A Reassessment of J. M. Barrie's Dramatic Art.* Aberdeen: Aberdeen UP, 1991.

Jordan, Ellen. *The Women's Movement and Women's Employment in Nineteenth Century Britain.* London and New York: Routledge, 1999.

Roberts, Elizabeth. *Women's Work, 1840-1940.* 1988. Cambridge: Cambridge UP, 1995.

Rose, Jacqueline. *The Case of Peter Pan or The Impossibility of Children's Fiction.* London: Macmillan, 1984.

Rutherford, Jonathan. *Forever England: Reflections on Race, Masculinity and Empire.* London: Lawrence, 1997.

Sedgwick, Eve Kosofsky. *Between Men: English Literature and Male Homosocial Desire.* New York: Columbia UP, 1985.

Sinfield, Alan. "'Effeminacy' and 'Femininity': Sexual Politics in Wilde's Comedies." *Modern Drama* 37 (1994): 34-52.

———. *The Wilde Century: Effeminacy, Oscar Wilde and the Queer Moment.* London: Cassell, 1994.

FURTHER READING

Bibliography

Garland, Herbert. *A Bibliography of the Writings of Sir James Matthew Barrie.* London: The Bookman's Journal, 1928, 146 p.

The first comprehensive bibliography of Barrie's writings, written while the author was still alive.

Biographies

Asquith, Cynthia. *Portrait of Barrie.* London: James Barrie Ltd., 1954, 230 p.

A favorable and apologetic biography of Barrie, written by the author's personal secretary, who assisted Barrie during the last twenty years of his life.

Darton, F. J. Harvey. *J. M. Barrie.* St. Clair Shores, Mich.: Scholarly Press, 1970, 127 p.

Biography of Barrie by an admirer of his works. Originally published in 1929.

Mackail, Denis. *The Story of J. M. B.: A Biography.* London: Peter Davies Ltd., 1941, 736 p.

Considered the most authoritative and comprehensive biography of Barrie.

Roy, James A. *James Matthew Barrie: An Appreciation.* London: Jarrolds, 1937, 256 p.

An admiring biography of Barrie that includes critical assessments of a number of his works.

Criticism

Billone, Amy. "The Boy Who Lived: From Carroll's Alice and Barrie's Peter Pan to Rowling's Harry Potter." *Children's Literature* 32 (2004): 178-202.

Compares J. K. Rowling's character Harry Potter to Lewis Carroll's Alice and Barrie's Peter Pan, in order to determine if today's readers have expanded their idea of childhood "so that girls participate as comfortably in fantasylands as boys do."

Blake, George. *Barrie and the Kailyard School.* London: Arthur Barker Ltd., 1951, 103 p.
> Study of Barrie that discusses his relation to the Scottish Kailyard School of regional literature.

Geduld, Harry M. *Sir James Barrie.* New York: Twayne Publishers, Inc., 1971, 187 p.
> Attempts to provide a "new and deeper understanding" of Barrie by focusing on the author's often-criticized sentimentality and his inability to overcome his own fantasies.

Green, Roger Lancelyn. *J. M. Barrie.* London: The Bodley Head, 1960, 64 p.
> Short study of Barrie's most popular works. Also provides a comprehensive bibliography of Barrie's writings, including his unpublished and uncollected plays.

Hammer, Stephanie Barbé. "Nasty Boys, Feminine Longing, and Mourning the Mother in J. M. Barrie's *Peter Pan* and Anne Rice's *The Witching Hour.*" In *Nursery Realms: Children in the Worlds of Science Fiction, Fantasy, and Horror,* edited by Gary Westfahl and George Slusser, pp. 171-84. Athens: University of Georgia Press, 1999.
> Offers a re-reading of *Peter Pan,* focusing on Wendy's role as mother in the fantasy world of Neverland.

Hammerton, J. A. *J. M. Barrie and His Books.* London: Horace Marshall & Son, 1900, 264 p.
> Study of Barrie's writings and the author's early days in journalism.

Jack, R. D. S. "The Manuscript of *Peter Pan.*" *Children's Literature* 18 (1990): 101-13.
> Analyzes the earliest-known manuscript of *Peter Pan,* discovered in 1964, and discusses how its differences from the published play shed light on Barrie's original intent.

——. "J. M. Barrie's Jekyll and Hyde Drama: Lifting the curtain on *The House of Fear.*" *Studies in Scottish Literature* 27 (1992): 28-46.
> Discusses the legitimacy and historic value of the unpublished drama *The House of Fear,* which the author attributes to Barrie.

Lundquist, Lynne. "Living Dolls: Images of Immortality in Children's Literature." In *Immortal Engines: Life Extension and Immortality in Science Fiction and Fantasy,* edited by George Slusser, Gary Westfahl, and Eric S. Rabkin, pp. 201-10. Athens: University of Georgia Press, 1996.
> Analyzes the theme of immortality in Barrie's *Peter Pan* and Rachel Field's *Hitty, Her First Hundred Years.*

Nash, Andrew. "The Compilation of J. M. Barrie's *Auld Licht Idylls.*" *Bibliotheck* 23 (1998): 85-96.
> Traces the origins of the tales and sketches included in *Auld Licht Idylls* to various journalistic pieces Barrie wrote during the 1880s.

Nelson, Claudia. "The Reforming Impulse and the Fantasy." In *Boys Will Be Girls: The Feminine Ethic and British Children's Fiction, 1857-1917,* pp. 147-74. New Brunswick, N.J.: Rutgers University Press, 1991.
> Discusses the central organizing theme of opposing tensions, such as that between adult and child or male and female, in *Peter Pan.*

Waterston, Elizabeth. "Barrie, Montgomery, and the Mists of Sentiment." In *Rapt in Plaid: Canadian Literature and Scottish Tradition,* pp. 175-91. Toronto: University of Toronto Press, 2001.
> Offers a bio-critical assessment of Barrie's work, claiming that the author's own complex psychological problems pressured him to sublimate his distress and the ugly aspects of Victorian life in fairy tales and "misty evasions."

Additional coverage of Barrie's life and career is contained in the following sources published by Thomson Gale: *Beacham's Guide to Literature for Young Adults,* Vols. 4, 5; *British Writers Supplement,* Vol. 3; *Children's Literature Review,* Vol. 16; *Concise Dictionary of British Literary Biography, 1890-1914; Contemporary Authors,* Vols. 104; 136; *Contemporary Authors New Revision Series,* Vol. 77; *Dictionary of Literary Biography,* Vols. 10, 141, 156; *DISCovering Authors: British Edition; DISCovering Authors: Canadian Edition; DISCovering Authors Modules: Dramatists; DISCovering Authors 3.0; Drama for Students,* Vol. 7; *Encyclopedia of World Literature in the 20th Century,* Ed. 3; *Literature Resource Center; Major Authors and Illustrators for Children and Young Adults,* Eds. 1, 2; *Major 20th-Century Writers,* Ed. 1; *St. James Guide to Children's Writers,* Vol. 5; *St. James Guide to Fantasy Writers; Something About the Author,* Vol. 100; *Supernatural Fiction Writers; Twentieth-Century Literary Criticism,* Vol. 2; *World Literature and Its Times,* Vol. 4; *Writers for Children;* and *Yesterday's Authors of Books for Children,* Vol. 1.

Truman Capote
1924-1984

(Born Truman Streckfus Persons) American novelist, short story writer, nonfiction writer, essayist, playwright, scriptwriter, and memoirist.

The following entry provides an overview of Capote's life and works. For additional information on his career, see *CLC,* Volumes 1, 3, 8, 13, 19, 34, and 38; for discussion of the journalistic novel, see *CLC,* Volume 58.

INTRODUCTION

Capote was a prolific prose stylist and celebrity, as well-known for his flamboyant public persona as he was for his numerous essays, short stories and novels. His greatest contribution to the body of world literature, however, was his 1965 journalistic novel *In Cold Blood,* which established Capote as one of the leading innovators of the New Journalism movement that flourished during the 1960s and influenced Tom Wolfe and Norman Mailer, among others. *In Cold Blood* was both immensely popular and controversial from the moment it was published. The work, which retells the gruesome murder of the Clutter family in Holcomb, Kansas, in 1959, is neither pure journalism nor pure fiction but a synthesis of both into a hybrid genre variously referred to as the "nonfiction novel," "journalistic novel," or "novel of fact." The result was a true story that riveted readers in a way conventional reporting could not. Though many commentators question the proper place and literary value of his experiments in blending journalism and fiction, most praise Capote for his willingness to experiment with his craft and test the boundaries of the established genres as well as his gifted prose.

BIOGRAPHICAL INFORMATION

Capote was born Truman Streckfus Persons on September 30, 1924, in New Orleans, the only child of Archuylus (Archie) and Lillie May Persons. When Capote was four years old, his parents divorced, and he spent his youth traveling between relatives. To compensate for his loneliness and sense of displacement, he developed a flamboyant personality, which he would exaggerate as an adult. Often left to himself, Capote began writing stories as a youth—at the age of ten, his short story "Old Mr. Busybody" was run in a local newspaper as part of a fiction contest, and garnered praise until

locals discovered that the tale was based on real people. In 1939, at the age of 15, Capote went to live with his mother and her second husband, Joseph Capote, in New York. Capote was sent to several boarding schools in New York and then to high school in Connecticut; he dropped out at the age of seventeen. He then took a job as a copyboy for *The New Yorker* magazine. In the early 1940s, Capote began publishing his short stories. In 1948 he published his first novel, *Other Voices, Other Rooms,* which received considerable attention from literary critics and established Capote's career as an author. The work was controversial due both to the theme of male homosexuality and the suggestive photograph of Capote on the back of the book's dust jacket. This incident established a pattern in which Capote's public persona would overshadow his work as an author, a situation he sustained through his eccentric behavior, biting wit, and love of publicity.

Capote continued to write and publish numerous short stories and novels, and became interested in creating a nonfiction novel, combining the research and reporting found in journalism with the techniques and atmosphere of fiction. In 1959, he read a brief story in the *New York Times* regarding the murder of Herbert W. Clutter and his family in Kansas, which Capote immediately recognized as an ideal topic for his literary experiment. Capote moved to Kansas and devoted the next six years of his life to researching and writing his novel. The resulting work, *In Cold Blood,* was an immediate success with the reading public, topping the *New York Times* bestseller list and generating a highly publicized, lucrative film contract. Already well known in New York and in literary circles, Capote became a national media celebrity after the publication of *In Cold Blood.* He was a regular guest on television talk shows, and was the focus of numerous articles in newspapers and popular magazines. This publicity seriously curtailed Capote's work, however, and he published little significant work after its completion. Capote devoted most of his later years to a work meant to elevate gossip and portraits of high society to a new art form, a work he alluded to frequently as his masterpiece. During the 1960s and '70s, Capote's use of drugs and alcohol steadily increased, and his health deteriorated significantly. On August 25, 1984, Capote died of complications from liver disease.

MAJOR WORKS

Critics often place Capote's early fiction, leading up to his nonfiction phase and the publication of *In Cold Blood,* into two categories: one comprising dark and sinister works, the other light and humorous stories. *Other Voices, Other Rooms* centers on a young man's search for his father and his loss of innocence as he becomes an adult. The work displays many elements of the grotesque and for this reason has often been placed in the tradition of Southern Gothicism depicted by such writers as William Faulkner, Carson McCullers, and Flannery O'Connor. The sinister scenes which populate the novel result in a surreal, nightmarish quality. Most of the stories in *A Tree of Night and Other Stories* (1949) continue to portray grotesque incidents and characters who suffer from mental and physical abnormalities. Several of the stories in *A Tree of Night,* however—including "My Side of the Matter" and "Children on Their Birthdays"—are humorous, light, and ironic, foreshadowing Capote's subsequent work. Capote's later works are often ironic comedies. *The Grass Harp* is a lyrical, humorous novel focusing on the conflict between the idealized and unconventional, and authority, wealth, and conformity. In the novel, Capote clearly sides with eccentrics and innocents who pursue their dreams in the face of the suppression of individuality. Capote's next major publication, *Breakfast at Tiffany's,* is regarded as his most urbane, ironic, and character-centered work. The story's protagonist, Holly Golightly, is another of the author's innocent social outcasts. *Breakfast at Tiffany's* celebrates innocence and romance in an evil world. The story shares with most of Capote's fiction a sympathy for people who are liberated from the conventions of social and cultural life, and who deliberately contradict middle-class values of respectability and conformity.

During the 1950s, Capote turned away from fiction and began experimenting with other genres. He began to develop his own brand of narrative or "creative reporting." Capote's experiments in creative reporting resulted in *In Cold Blood.* Originally serialized in *The New Yorker,* the novel chronicles the murder of Kansas farmer Herbert W. Clutter and his family, who were bound, gagged, robbed, and shot by two ex-convicts in November, 1959. Capote's narrative derives its interest not from the crime itself, but from the psychology of the killers, the social and psychological forces that shaped their lives, and the impact of senseless, random violence on the safe, secure, and innocent Midwestern town of Holcomb. Capote's use of fictional techniques provide the narrative with a power and immediacy that mere reporting of facts could not achieve.

CRITICAL RECEPTION

Critical assessment of Capote's career is highly divided, both in terms of individual works and his overall contribution to literature. As critics like Kenneth T. Reed and Helen S. Garson note, Capote's place in literary history has been undermined as much by his controversial personality as by the quality of his writings. After he achieved notoriety early in his career, and especially after the immense success of *In Cold Blood,* Capote seemed more concerned about his celebrity status and role as social gadfly than his literature. His bold and unabashed promoting of his work, such as his claim that he invented a new literary genre with *In Cold Blood,* alienated many critics. Since the 1980s, commentators have been less concerned over weighing the significance of Capote's brand of journalistic fiction and, instead, have focused more closely on the techniques he employs to create powerful literature. This can be seen in the essays by such critics as Robert Siegle, David Galloway, Brian Conniff, John Hollowell, and David Guest. Others have offered structural analyses of Capote's art, especially the story *Handcarved Coffins* and *In Cold Blood,* to demonstrate how the author uses narrative techniques—such as the lack of narrative explication, self-reflexive language, disordering of events, and psychological development of character—to underscore broader themes in his work. The theme of homosexuality, overtly or latently present in much of Capote's writing, has received considerable critical attention as well. Capote's relation to Southern Gothic fiction is also often adressed by critics, some claiming that the author ironically employs the "tropes" of Gothicism to achieve a greater sympathy for his gay and outcast characters.

Ultimately, most critics agree that Capote's literary reputation rests on *In Cold Blood*. In retrospect, whether he created a new art form, the novel's legacy can be found in its blurring of the dividing line between fact and fiction. The continuing popularity of nonfiction novels testifies that the "novel of fact" continues to intrigue and challenge readers.

PRINCIPAL WORKS

Other Voices, Other Rooms (novel) 1948
A Tree of Night and Other Stories (short stories) 1949
Local Color (nonfiction) 1950
The Grass Harp (novel) 1951
The Grass Harp: A Play (play) 1952
The Muses Are Heard, an Account (journalism) 1956
Breakfast at Tiffany's: A Short Novel and Three Stories (novella and short stories) 1958
The Selected Writings of Truman Capote (novella, short stories, nonfiction, and journalism) 1963
A Christmas Memory (nonfiction novella) 1966
In Cold Blood: A True Account of a Multiple Murder and Its Consequences (journalistic novel) 1966
The Thanksgiving Visitor (nonfiction novella) 1967
House of Flowers [with Harold Arlen; adaptor; from a short story by O. Henry] (drama) 1968
The Dogs Bark: Public People and Private Places (nonfiction and journalism) 1973
Music for Chameleons (novella, short stories, and nonfiction) 1980
Answered Prayers: The Unfinished Novel (unfinished novel) 1986

CRITICISM

Kenneth T. Reed (essay date 1981)

SOURCE: Reed, Kenneth T. "Short Fiction: The Ten Dollar Dream." In *Truman Capote,* pp. 34-70. Boston: Twayne Publishers, 1981.

[*In the following essay, Reed surveys Capote's short fiction, categorizing the works into those set in New York and those set in the south.*]

Capote remarked once to an interviewer that his "more unswerving ambitions still revolve around" the complex art of the short story. "When seriously explored," he continued, "the short story seems to me the most difficult and disciplining form of prose writing extant. Whatever control and technique I have," he said, "I owe entirely to my training in this medium."[1] The expression "my training" should be borne in mind especially, for in a general way, Capote began as a writer of short fiction before turning his attention to the novel-romance. Finally, except for a foray or two into the theater, he developed the craft of reportage which became the artistic mainstay of his more recent years. Still, the great bulk of his short fiction was written in the 1940s, beginning most notably with **"A Tree of Night"** which was published originally in 1943. The more recent of his shorter fiction, however, is the chronologically isolated **"Mojave"** which appeared in 1975.

An examination of the tales in order of chronology, however, does not altogether illuminate the intriguing diversity of the shorter pieces. Much depends on Capote's keen sense of place, and the diversity of his short stories is compounded by his tendency to select either the rural South or metropolitan New York as the locality-setting for most of his work. Undoubtedly, the kinds of characters that appear, as well as the particular kinds of dilemmas in which they find themselves, are closely related either to the urbanized impersonality of city life, or to the hidebound agrarian personality of the southern mode of life as it is lived mostly in Louisiana and Alabama. It is impossible that the southern tales could have been rewritten with New York as the setting, nor could his citified stories been adapted to the isolated back-lands of rural Alabama.

I TALES OF NEW YORK

Eight of the stories, namely **"The Walls Are Cold"** (1943), **"A Mink of One's Own"** (1944), **"Miriam"** (1945), **"The Headless Hawk"** (1946), **"Shut a Final Door"** (1947), **"Master Misery"** (1949), **"Among the Paths to Eden"** (1960), and (to a limited extent) **"Mojave"** (1975), are tales of New York. In general, the care and the subsequent artistic quality with which the pieces were written, tended to improve, predictably enough, with Capote's growth as a writer. The stories gradually become richer both in linguistic skill as well as in dark thematic implications—so much so, in fact, that the earlier tales show surprisingly little stylistic resemblance to the later ones.

For example, **"The Walls Are Cold"** is perhaps closer to a vignette than to one of Capote's later and far more finished short stories. The scene is set in one of the upper floors of a relatively plush city apartment building where a drinking party, presided over by a fickle sixteen-year-old girl named Louise, is well in progress. The hour is two o'clock in the morning, and among the guests is a group of sailors, all of them strangers to Louise. She singles out one of them, a Mississippian known only as Jake, and proceeds to tease him with a succession of sexual overtures, eventually inviting him into the confines of her bedroom where the walls are done in a "cold green." When, after some hesitation, he accepts her invitation to kiss, he also moves his hand against her breasts. She reacts by giving him a "violent shove" that sends him "sprawling across the cold, green rug," and he in turn reacts by vacating the premises. Louise then resolves to sleep that night in the security of her mother's bedroom where "the walls were pale rose and warm."

There are contrasting elements in this brief narrative that give it some slight significance. The first of these is Louise herself, a spoiled and indulged citified adolescent girl living in the midst of fairly opulent circumstances, and Jake, a hapless and far less privileged young person, eight months into a wartime interlude with the Navy. Another of the contrasts is the more pastoral life Jake had known back in Mississippi versus the life he sees at the party: "I never saw anything like it," he exclaims as she users him around her apartment. Still another contrast is the change that the girl's adolescent temperament undergoes, a jolting shift from being coyly seductive to outrightly belligerent within the space of a few minutes.

But the story, such as it is, belongs to Louise, whose lack of empathy toward others such as Jake, who are actively involved in the waging of a war, prefigures the otherwise nameless "white pompadoured woman" in **"The Shape of Things"** which was published a year later. Otherwise, Louise is like the walls of her bedroom: both cold and green. Jake, on the other hand, is at least partially initiated into some of life's more unpleasant realities, and perhaps as a result of this he lives a less self-absorbed, narcissistic way of life. He is forced to accept, after all, the regimentation of military existence in spite of his aversion to it: "I don't take to this kind of life, I don't like others bossin' me around."

"The Walls Are Cold" shares with **"A Mink of One's Own"** a certain vague consciousness that somewhere in the distance there is indeed a war being waged, except that in **"A Mink of One's Own"** Capote chose to intensify the elements of irony and deception. Set in New York, it is a wartime story centering upon Mrs. Bertha Munson, a vaguely discontented middle-aged woman who, as the story opens, nervously anticipates brightening one of her otherwise dreary afternoons with a visit from a younger woman named Vini Rondo who has supposedly lived a far more colorful, and altogether more privileged, existence than Mrs. Munson ever had. Vini, an American living in Paris until the German occupation, has (according to newspaper gossip columns) been married to "some Count or Baron or something."

The story's irony becomes evident when Vini Rondo arrives at Mrs. Munson's apartment door on this January afternoon with her hair uncombed, her teeth unbrushed, her nails revealing chipped enamel, her fingers "jewelless," and her body clothed only in a summer print dress. She carries a large pink box containing a mink coat and says that she wants Mrs. Munson to have it, meaning that she expects Mrs. Munson to offer her money for it. ("I feel I should get something back on my investment," she says.) Distinctly ill at ease, Mrs. Munson tenders an offer of $400.00 which she evidently cannot afford, judging from her standard of living. She writes Vini Rondo a check, primarily, no doubt, to terminate the strained and difficult conversation between them. But once Vini has accepted the check and departed, Mrs. Munson gives the coat "a little yank" and is "terrified to hear the sound of ripping." The coat has disintegrated.

The chief deception in the story is evident at this moment when Mrs. Munson realizes that the coat is literally rotten and therefore worthless. Too late to rectify the situation, she realizes also that "Vini wouldn't phone tomorrow or ever again," and that she must somehow justify the expenditure to her husband, admitting that she has "been taken and taken good." And yet it is not Vini who provides all of the story's deceptions, for when she alleges that for the past year she has been living in California, Mrs. Munson replies, "Oh California, I love California!" even though "she had never been farther west than Chicago."

"A Mink of One's Own" is not a memorable piece of fiction from any point of view, although there are signs to be found in it that point the direction that Capote's writing was about to take. Vini Rondo herself is the forerunner of certain other emotionally disturbed, urbanized young women characters, especially Miriam (in the story of the same name), D. J. in **"The Headless Hawk,"** Sylvia in **"Master Misery,"** and Holly Golightly in *Breakfast at Tiffany's*. As an easily intimidated New York apartment dweller, Mrs. Munson bears an obvious similarity to the neurotic Mrs. Miller in **"Miriam."** Furthermore, the deceptions used against these women are fairly typical of Capote's use of deceptions in his 1943 story **"A Tree of Night"** as well as in a good deal of the fiction he had yet to write, especially **"Preacher's Legend," "The Headless Hawk," "Shut a Final Door," "Children on Their Birthdays," "Master Misery," "Jug of Silver,"** *House of Flowers*, **"Among the Paths to Eden,"** *The Thanksgiving Visitor*, and the more ambitious *Other Voices, Other Rooms*, *The Grass Harp*, and *Breakfast at Tiffany's*.

"Miriam" is a far better story than either **"The Walls Are Cold"** or **"A Mink of One's Own"** primarily because of its growing and sustained dramatic intensity and because of its improved handling of psychological crisis. Capote himself evidently cared little for it. "I like . . . several of my short stories," he revealed once during an interview with *The Paris Review*, "though not

'Miriam,' which was a good stunt but nothing more."[2] **"Miriam"** is, in fact, a kind of tour-de-force, but perhaps no more so than several of the other stories published by that time, especially **"A Tree of Night."** His lack of enthusiasm for it was apparently a question of personal taste.

"Miriam" has to do with the progressive emotional disintegration of a sixty-one-year-old woman named Mrs. H. T. (Miriam) Miller, a widow who, until the story opens, had led a comfortably conservative private existence in a remodeled brownstone close to New York's East River. Her sedate life and habits are interrupted, however, by the appearance of a child, also named Miriam, whom the woman encounters for the first time on a cold and snowy night while they both queue up for tickets to a movie house. From this point on the child subtly torments Mrs. Miller by making personal visits at unlikely hours of the night, and by moving, bag and baggage, into Mrs. Miller's two rooms with kitchenette. Mrs. Miller's response to this outlandish series of events is first puzzlement, then outrage, and finally desperation to escape the veiled threat to her sanity that Miriam has come to represent. Mrs. Miller gradually loses her composure, as indicated by her inability to keep track of the days as they pass, and then by her inhaling from the wrong end of a cork-tipped cigarette. Driven to desperation, Mrs. Miller eventually runs down the hallway outside of her apartment and down one landing, where she attempts to seek help from another tenant in dealing with her child-intruder, who by this time has provoked her into genuine fear. When the tenant returns with Mrs. Miller, however, there is no sign of the child. Only when Mrs. Miller comes back by herself to her apartment is the girl once again in evidence. "In times of terror or immense distress," Capote writes, "there are moments when the mind waits, as though for a revelation, while a skein of calm is woven over thought; it is like a sleep, or a supernatural trance." When last seen, the woman "stiffens" to Miriam's "dull, direct stare."

"Miriam" contains the not unusual pattern in Capote's writing of the victim and the victimizer, wherein the victim's will is besieged until it finally weakens and collapses into submission. Mrs. Miller is a likely victim, however, since she obviously has not far to travel before she is forced over the line that divides rationality from despondency. She is also easily threatened and intimidated, as in the scene where the child takes possession of the cameo Mrs. Miller's late husband had given her. Like Mrs. Bertha Munson in **"A Mink of One's Own,"** Mrs. Miller is an inconspicuous, plain woman living in a state of isolation in the midst of a huge, densely populated, and largely indifferent city where she is an ideal target for petty tyranny. In both of these stories the main characters are threatened by females different in both age and temperament. Moreover, and this is quite significant in the development of Capote's fiction, Mrs. Miller chances at one point to come upon a version of the "wizard man," a threatening and recurring male figure in Capote's consciousness; for on the corner of Third Avenue she becomes aware of "an old man, bowlegged and stooped under an arm-load of bulging packages" who gives her a sinister smile. And although she walks some five blocks, she continues to be aware of "the steady crunch of his footfalls" in the city snow. There is the vague suggestion that he is the same man with whom the child Miriam had last lived, for she has said that "he was terribly poor and we never had good things to eat."

Capote was rather clearly concerned with the question of identity when he wrote **"Miriam,"** for at the end of the story Mrs. Miller is not altogether certain whether she ever did, indeed, "really [know] a girl named Miriam," or whether the encounter she supposedly had with the child was some kind of trick of her own imagination. "For the only thing she had lost to Miriam was her identity," and until the story's final two lines, she believes that she has recovered that illusive identity once more. The question therefore arises whether the child is the alter-ego of the woman, and as in Nathaniel Hawthorne's celebrated short story "Young Goodman Brown," the reader can scarcely distinguish between the dream and the reality of what he has witnessed. Besides the name that the two protagonists share, there is the remark, made on the story's second page, that the child is "lacking [in] any childlike quality whatsoever." But whether literally or figuratively, the child is an expression of the emotional dislocation that lurks just beneath the neat and orderly surface of the upper middle class world of Mrs. Miller.

Perhaps the least interesting of the New York group of stories is **"The Headless Hawk"** which, because of its structural diffuseness and consequent lack of artistic unity, makes it less compelling than a number of Capote's other pieces. The center of the narrative belongs not, as it would first appear, to a thoroughly perverse runaway from a mental asylum, a girl known only as "D. J.," but to the New York picture gallery manager, Vincent Waters; for it is he, and not the seventeen-year-old girl, who is alluded to in the story's preface from *Job* as one of "those that rebel against the light."

The story is as enigmatic as its two protagonists. Vincent meets the girl when she enters the gallery in the despondent hope of selling her painting which was apparently done in the secure confines of a mental hospital. Too preoccupied to pay her much attention, Waters asks the girl to leave her address, and agrees to send her a check amounting to thirty dollars for the painting. The address, however, turns out to be only "D. J.—Y. M. C. A." which is far too cryptic a guide to tracking down a young woman in New York. He takes the painting back to his basement apartment and eventually begins to form a certain identification between himself and the picture's provocative content, consisting of "a headless figure in a monk-like robe reclining complacently on top a tacky vaudeville trunk; in one hand she held a flaming blue candle, in another a miniature gold cage, and her severed head lay bleeding at her feet: it was the girl's head, but here her hair was long, very long, and a snowball kitten with crystal spitfire eyes playfully pawed, as it would a spool of yarn, the sprawling ends. The wings of a hawk, headless, scarlet-breasted, copper clawed, curtained the background like a nightfall sky."

There can be little question but that the headless girl reclining on the vaudeville trunk represents the mentally ill D. J., whose aimless peregrinations have extended from New Orleans to New York. Nor can there be much doubt that the headless hawk is a representation of Vincent Waters himself, for the reader is told that Waters also is not emotionally fit; he has, like D. J., absorbed a succession of painfully thwarted quests. He finds himself at the age of thirty-six "a man of the sea, fifty miles from shore; a victim, born to be murdered, either by himself or another; an actor unemployed." He is furthermore, and by his own admission, "a poet who had never written poetry, a painter who had never painted, a lover who had never loved . . . someone, in short, without direction, and quite headless." As one of those who, again in the words from *Job,* "Know not the light," Vincent is depicted early in the story "tap-tap-tapping" with his umbrella-cane down the sidewalk in the manner of a blind man. Later, in an act of self-destruction, Vincent impulsively stabs the hawk's heart with a pair of scissors, causing the canvas to flake dried paint on the floor.

Like **"The Walls Are Cold," "A Mink of One's Own,"** and **"Miriam," "The Headless Hawk"** centers upon mental and emotional disintegration, although D. J. proceeds further and more permanently over the line of irrationality than Capote's earlier characters had. **"The Headless Hawk"** also illustrates Capote's growing interest in characters with no particular concrete identity, for, like the child Miriam, D. J. seemingly has no origins, and is on the loose in New York. She does as Miriam does, moves in on a person she does not know and who does not know her. Waters never discovers D. J.'s true name or her background, but regards her with the same "feeling he's had as a child toward carnival freaks."

D. J.'s shadowy references to a certain Mr. Destronelli suggest that this person, somehow connected with her mental hospital experiences, is another of Capote's wizard men whose foreboding presence is felt in the story even though he never appears. If **"The Headless Hawk"** were not so consistently dark and pathetic, it would, in its outward characteristics, be not so far removed from the setting and tone of *Breakfast at Tiffany's* where the character of Holly Golightly can be recognized as a cheerful, delightfully self-possessed D. J.

Instead, the story has certain technical and structural flaws that prevent its being the finished piece of fiction that it might have been. It is, for one thing, full of details that appear to have no function in the story as a whole. The reader may wonder, for example, why he finds Vincent Waters absorbed in a story by James Thurber in an old issue of *The New Yorker,* and why he observes the same character taking such an unusually narcissistic pleasure in his own nakedness. Why does Waters pay twenty-five cents to view the moon and stars? What is the function of Ruby the popcorn man? Such apparently nonessential tag ends detract from the story's real center: Vincent's lonely and vacant urban existence, his "talents unexploited, voyages never taken, promises unfulfilled," as well as his many abortive love affairs with men and women alike. Neither is there the slightest ray of illumination leading to self-understanding in the hopelessly confused mind of D. J., who, like her friend Waters, becomes more pitiable (if not tending to invite sympathy) as the story reaches its conclusion.

Capote once revealed that **"Shut a Final Door"** was one of his favorites among the short stories,[3] and the reasons for his preference are not difficult to ascertain. Unlike **"The Headless Hawk,"** it has both thematic and tonal control, as well as a keener sense of purpose and direction. Nevertheless, there is an element in **"Shut a Final Door"** that evades rational explanation, for the story centers around a character named Walter Ranney, an unsuccessful businessman who receives two unnerving and sinister long-distance telephone calls. His anonymous caller possesses an uncanny ability to reach him in unlikely and far removed places. The caller reaches him once in New York ("Oh, you know me, Walter. You've known me a long time"), and locates him again in the hotel room belonging to a club-footed woman under scrutiny at a medical convention in Saratoga. This aura of mystery, as unexplained as the child in **"Miriam"** or the character of D. J. in **"The Headless Hawk,"** is by no means untypical of the perplexing enigmas present in most of Capote's writing.

The most imposing theme of the story is failure, and, although such earlier characters as Mrs. Miller and Vincent Waters were also in one sense or another portraits in failure, Walter Ranney's propensity for losing life's battles is drawn into sharper focus than had been the case with these and other earlier characters. At the beginning of **"Shut a Final Door"** Ranney has managed to alienate his friend Anna by gossiping about her. After that, he spoils his relationship with another woman (Margaret) when he becomes an assistant in an advertising house and fawns too much on the boss (who subsequently fires him). The reader learns that as a child Ranney had been caught plagiarizing a poem that he had published in the school magazine under his own name. On another occasion he had blatantly provoked a homosexual liaison, only to jump into a waiting taxi, slam the door, lean out a window, and laugh contemptuously at the man he had allowed to follow him for several blocks: "the look on his face, it was awful, it was like Christ." About his friend Rosa Cooper, he had apparently leaked the erroneous information to Walter Winchell's newspaper column that "big shot ad exec Walter Ranney and dairy heiress Rosa Cooper are telling intimates to start buying rice." To all appearances, he thrives on failure: "It was like the time he'd failed algebra and felt so relieved, so free: failure was definite, a certainty, and there is always peace in certainties."

Beyond the emphasis on failure is the almost unendurable isolation that Walter Ranney, as well as a number of his fictional predecessors, has been forced to withstand. At the outset of the story he is at his nadir, installed in a hot and seamy little New Orleans hotel room, eating peanut butter crackers, washing them down with a finger of Four Roses, and finally vomiting in a wastebasket. Like Saul Bellow's Tommy Wilhelm in *Seize the Day,* Ranney is the pitiably isolated and unloved loser who is forced eventually to own up to the reality of his condition, for he sees that "no matter what you did or how hard you tried, it all came finally to zero."

A substantial number of Capote's stories have what, for want of a better term, can be called grotesques. It was Vincent Waters in **"The Headless Hawk"** who found that he could love only those who had "a little something wrong [or] broken" about them, and **"Shut a Final Door"** has its share of such people. Margaret, for example, with her bulging eyes and her teeth reddened by lipstick, dresses like a ten-year-old child. Her friend Irving looks "like a little boy playing grownup," his legs too short to reach the footrest on a barstool. Others are still more within the category of the comic-grotesque. Rosa's companion Anna Stimson is "almost six feet tall, wore black suits, affected a monocle, a walking cane, and pounds of jingling Mexican silver." Stimson's son by a former husband ("Buck Strong, the horse-opera idol") is currently incarcerated in a "corrective academy" for having stolen from Woolworths, throwing things, and taking "potshots out the window with a .22." At a bar in Saratoga, Ranney encounters such "summer-season grotesques" as "sagging silver-foxed ladies, and little stunted jockeys." Chief among the grotesques, however, is the unnamed woman afflicted with a club foot who explains that "my doctor's . . . going to talk about me and my foot on account of I'm pretty special." Because all of the other hotel rooms are occupied, Ranney accepts an invitation to share hers. It is here that the anonymous telephone call reaches him, after which he clutches her in dismay. Her comment is to the point: "we're awfully alone in this world, aren't we?" Thus in each of Capote's stories discussed to this point (1947), the chance encounters that happen lead to emotionally debilitating results. For when last seen, Walter Ranney is, like Louise in **"The Walls Are Cold,"** pushing his face into a pillow in a final gesture of anguish. Indications are that, just as the demonic child in **"Miriam"** is a projection of Mrs. Miller herself, the sinister long-distance telephone caller is in reality an expression of Ranney's conscience and his fear.

"Master Misery" is another of the New York group of stories dealing in failure and broken dreams. Its protagonist, a young woman named Sylvia, lives for a time with her friends Henry and Estelle (a Columbia law student and his wife), whose "trouble" in Sylvia's estimation, "was that they were excruciatingly married." But Sylvia has other problems. She loses her dreary job as a typist for an underwear manufacturing company known as Snug Fare, sells her watch, her beaver coat, her gold mesh evening bag, and finally, her dreams. Having moved into a depressingly furnished room in the East Sixties, she has fallen into the company of an ex-clown, the hopeless alcoholic Mr. Oreilly, whose spiritual bankruptcy parallels her own. Walking the crowded streets of Manhattan, she sees on different occasions the symbol of herself and Oreilly; in the window of a Madison Avenue shop she encounters "a life-sized, mechanical Santa Claus" who slaps his stomach and rocks "back and forth in a frenzy of electrical mirth." In the same window at a later time Sylvia and Oreilly find another exhibit that is no less suggestive; this time it is "a plastic girl with intense glass eyes [sitting] astride a bicycle pedaling at the maddest pace" and although "its wheel spokes [spin] hypnotically, the bicycle never [moves]."

In need both of money and spiritual "meaning" in her life, Sylvia overhears a conversation between two men at an Automat, to the effect that a certain Mr. A. F. Revercomb on East Seventy-eight Street is a broker in dreams ("regular night-time dreams"), and will pay, according to their intrinsic merit, cash for the disclosure of anybody's dream experiences. Revercomb, whose name denotes his occupation, has no dreams of his own, as suggested by his very appearance: His "flat gray eyes planted like seed in the anonymity of his face and sealed within steel-dull lenses." Revercomb, however, is no fraud; he knows the real dream-article from mere imaginary fabrications of dreams.

Oreilly, however, recognizes Revercomb for what he really is, another version of the wizard man (although not referred to as such); the dream broker is "the same fellow," says Oreilly, that Sylvia must have been aware of as a child. "All mothers tell their kids about him," Oreilly says. "He lives in hollows of trees, he comes down chimneys late at night, he lurks in graveyards, and you can hear his step in the attic. The sonofabitch, he is a thief and a threat: he will take everything you have and end by leaving you nothing, not even a dream." Sylvia *is* aware of Revercomb's identity: "My family called him something else. But I can't remember what." Oreilly knows him as Master Misery.

Sylvia and Oreilly share the same world of loneliness, stress, and unproductivity that is captured in the fragments of the newspaper headline before her: "*Lana Denies, Russia Rejects, Miners Conciliate.*" The external New York scene, with its frigid temperatures, snow and ice, contribute to the sense of desolation that they both feel. Sylvia's childhood friend, Estelle, feels that her predicament would be solved if she were to get married. ("I'm here to tell you, honey, that there is nothing like lying in bed at night with a man's arms around you and. . . .") But the man that Sylvia was to marry, whoever that might be, "must've fallen down a manhole," for every ostensible candidate for marriage that she has identified in New York "who seemed the slightest bit attractive was either married, too poor to get married, or queer." Her desperation causes her to lose track of reality for short periods, and her signs of emotional instability are not dissimilar to Capote's other women characters introduced earlier.

Oreilly, too, is reminiscent of certain other emotionally depleted characters in Capote's earlier fiction, not the least of whom are Vincent Waters and Walter Ranney. He has sought a number of solutions to his spiritual dilemma, as hinted at in the song he jauntily sings: "*cherryberry, moneyberry, happyberry pie, but the best old pie is a loveberry pie. . . .*" Later in the story he changes the ending of his song to "the best old pie is a whiskeyberry pie!" Irretrievably alcoholic, Oreilly has sold all his dreams to Master Misery and used the money to satisfy his habit and also, he hopes, to create a few more marketable dreams. When "you get a couple of bucks," he tells Sylvia, "you rush to the nearest liquor store—or the nearest sleepingpill machine." When he runs out of cash, he either borrows more money or steals the whiskey he is seeking. Realizing that alcoholism is Oreilly's last hold on life, Sylvia is last seen slipping a five dollar bill into his pocket as she kisses him. And when, in the story's final paragraph, two boys emerge from a bar and stare menacingly in her direction, she knows she is no longer afraid because "there was nothing left to steal."

Still, there is nothing particularly pathological about Sylvia's morbid depression and loneliness. Her former job at the underwear company (where in a single day she has typed some ninety-seven letters) is no more pointless than the plastic girl in the storefront who monotonously spins the wheels of her bicycle, but goes nowhere. Equally devoid of meaning, to her mind, is the delusion of marital harmony and bliss as represented by her struggling married friends. Only in her dreams, the essentials of which are kept hidden in a music box, can she arrive at any possibility of meaning. Eventually, however, her dreams are extracted from her by Revercomb for money, and she is left with nothing. The difficulty of Sylvia's facing another day is emphasized by the "disorganized version of 'Oh How I Hate To Get Up in the Morning'" that emanates from within her music box.

There is nothing amusing in **"Master Misery,"** but the same cannot be said with respect to **"Among the Paths to Eden"** which is a dark tale with oddly humorous overtones. It is also one of the simpler, more anecdotal of the Capote stories. The scene is a huge cemetery in Queens which, besides being a haven for the deceased, offers "an unhindered view of Manhattan's skyline" for the living. On a chilly and windy day in March, a fifty-one-year-old Jew named Ivor Belli arrives at the cemetery bearing "a fine mass of jonquils" to place at the grave of his wife who had once been "a woman of many natures, most of them trying." His motive for coming out this day is less to pay tribute to his wife's memory than it is an opportunity to breathe the fresh air. He wishes also to be able to assure his two married daughters that he has paid his respects to their mother.

As he stoops "to jam the jonquils into a rock urn," he takes a certain secret comfort in the knowledge that "the woman's tongue was finally stilled." Turning to leave the gravesite, Belli encounters a husband-stalker who introduces herself as Mary O'Meaghan who detains him by feeding him peanuts while she leads him to believe that she has come to the cemetery to visit the grave of her father. Her late father, however, has "absolutely refused" burial, and has been cremated and left "at home." After some preliminary ploys, Mary O'Meaghan emphasizes her prowess as a cook and then launches into an imitation of Helen Morgan while perched on the late Sarah Belli's gravestone. This much accomplished, she comes to her point by asking Belli "a very personal question," to wit, if he had "considered marrying again." With twenty-seven years of matrimony behind him, Belli replies in all candor that that much marriage is "enough for any lifetime." But by this time, her inattention to his words is revealed by "her eyes [that] played hookey, [roaming] as though she were hunting at a party for a different, more promising face." Finally, "a new pilgrim, just entering through the gates of the cemetery" attracts her interest, while Belli takes the opportunity to make as graceful an exit as the occasion allows. He thanks Mary O'Meaghan for the peanuts and wishes her good luck.

Mary, as eccentric and as uninhibited as she is, evinces the desperate, underlying loneliness of certain other of

Capote's earlier women characters. Capote, however, does not allow the pathos of Mary O'Meaghan to preclude a slight comic effect, for while Mary is not altogether unattractive, she wears "shoes which were of the sturdy, so-called sensible type," and "her chunky cheeks" assert themselves "under a drab felt hat." Although Belli does not view her as obese, neither can he "imagine that she mounted scales too cheerfully."

Consistent with a number of Capote's short stories, **"Among the Paths to Eden"** develops from the moment when complete strangers meet and interact. The idea of matrimonial disharmony, a not unusual element in his fiction, is present here, as well. The apparent significance of the title is in itself matrimonial in implication inasmuch as the story concerns itself primarily with Mary's effort to locate a husband who, for as much time as remains, will suffice as her Adam. For the time being, however, she has taken the wrong path toward her dreams of Edenic bliss.

Nor is there anything blissful about the digressive **"Mojave,"** which did not appear until the June, 1975 issue of *Esquire*. **"Mojave"** is a different kind of a story which examines with still greater intensity (and far less whimsy) the ironic complications of mature love relationships. The story has a point to make, and that point is reinforced a number of times. It is articulated, however, only toward the conclusion: "We all, sometimes, leave each other out there under the skies. And we never understand why." **"Mojave"** does not suggest "why," but it does explore the theme of love and its betrayal to a considerable extent.

The protagonist is Sarah Whitelaw, thirty-six, wife of the wealthy New Yorker George Whitelaw, fifteen years older than she, and a man who "had graduated third in his class at Yale Law School, never practiced law but had gone on to top his class at Harvard Business School, [and who] had been offered a Presidential Cabinet post, and an ambassadorship to England or France, or wherever he wanted." Married at the age of twenty-four, two months after the death of her father, Sarah had once seen in George the approximation of "her great lost love"—her father. Nevertheless, the opening scene of **"Mojave"** finds Sarah Whitelaw in the midst of one of her regular acts of infidelity with the oafish Dr. Ezra Bentsen, "formerly her psychoanalyst and presently her lover." But after George Whitelaw, Ezra Bentsen is an unlikely sexual partner ("two hundred and twenty pounds of shortish, fiftyish, frizzly-haired, hip-heavy, myopic Manhattan Intellectual") whom Sarah actively loathes.

It is her husband she loves, and betrays, for the company of Bentsen, whose greed demands that she present him with expensive gifts at each of their trysts, until she breaks their liaison. Meanwhile, Bentsen has told Sarah of the breach that erupted the previous evening between himself and his child-psychiatrist wife: "I slapped Thelma. But good. And I punched her in the stomach, too." Sarah's mind had earlier ranged over a not-unrelated incident that had happened to her the day before: Jaime Sanchez, her hairdresser, has told her that he intends to murder his homosexual companion Carlos, a dentist, because Carlos has fallen in love with Sanchez's cousin Angelita. But Carlos does not fully comprehend Sanchez's admonition to him: "You love or you do not. You destroy or you do not."

When George Whitelaw enters the story, he tells Sarah about the summer after he left Yale when he had hitchhiked to New Mexico and California. He goes on to say that he had met an abandoned, seventy-year-old blind man named George Schmidt on the highway in the Mojave desert. Schmidt had told him a story of his betrayal by two women, one of whom (the ex-stripper Ivory Hunter, his wife) was responsible for his abandonment "helpless, in the middle of nowhere." But whereas Schmidt is wary of women ("women are like flies: they settle on sugar or shit"), he is also understanding ("a woman can do you like that, and still you love her").

George Whitelaw, it develops, has betrayed his wife Sarah, but not without her aid, "for when they had stopped sleeping together, they had been discussing together—indeed, collaborating on—each of his affairs." Neither is his involvement with other women without its consequences, for it has triggered still other betrayals:

> Alice Kent: five months; ended because she demanded he divorce and marry her. Sister Jones: terminated after one year when her husband found out about it. Pat Simpson: a *Vogue* model who had gone to Hollywood, promised to return and never had. Adele O'Hara: beautiful, and alcoholic, a rambunctious scene-maker; he had broken that one off himself. Mary Campbell. Mary Chester. Jane Vere-Jones. Others. And now, Christine.

If the truth be known, however, George Whitelaw feels secretly "emasculated by women."

The relation between **"Mojave"** and some of Capote's earlier work is apparent enough. Although **"Mojave"** is basically a story of New York, it contains scenes of the Southwest that echo some of his earlier excursions into local color fiction. In that part of the country, he writes, "there wasn't any shade. Nothing but sand and mesquite and this boiling blue sky." The character Freddy Feo, who takes up with Ivory Hunter, is a carry-over from another Capote character, Tico Feo, the prisoner in **"A Diamond Guitar"** (1950). Both Tico and Freddy are closely identified with guitars decorated in rhinestone. Capote's attention to problems related to homosexuality (such as exists in *Other Voices, Other Rooms* and *In Cold Blood*) is evidenced once again in the strained relations between Jaime and Carlos, as well as in Freddy Feo, recently hired by a trailer park manager who "had picked him up in one of those fag bars in Cat City and put him to work as a handyman."

Capote's fascination with snow, a symbol of isolation and estrangement in such works as **Other Voices, Other Rooms** and in the short story **"Master Misery,"** is again present in **"Mojave."** When, for example, Sarah and George embrace, "the flesh against her lips felt as cold as the snowflakes at the window." In the next-to-last paragraph in the story the heavy silk window draperies in the Whitelaws' apartment conceal "the night river and the lighted riverboats, so snow-misted that they were as muted as the design in a Japanese scroll of winter night."

The New York stories are those in which a cold, impersonal, and uncongenial environment seems to foster characters who are, in the main, the victims of loneliness, alienation, and despair. As a consequence, their behavior not infrequently hovers somewhere between the engagingly eccentric and the certifiably deranged. Generally humorless, the New York fiction lacks some of the occasional warmth and familiarity that is often (but certainly not always) present in Capote's southern stories.

II Stories of the South

The earliest (1944) of these is **"The Shape of Things"** which, like **"A Mink of One's Own,"** is a wartime narrative. It brings four characters together on a moving train somewhere between the Carolinas and Virginia. Three of them are related directly in one sense or another to the war itself, and they are brought in touch with one another on a railway diner for a brief interlude that is perhaps more felt than articulated. The three consist of "a ruddy-cheeked marine and a heart-faced girl" (his wife), as well as a severely battle-fatigued corporal from the Army. The fourth character, and the central one, is "a wispish-sized, white pompadoured woman" who, at least ostensibly, has no relation to the war and its attendant human dilemmas. She regards the girl (who comes from Alabama) merely as a "war bride." When the corporal suddenly makes his appearance in the dining car and lurches "awkwardly toward them and [collapses] in the table's empty seat like a rag," she regards him as a drunk. The marine, by contrast to the woman, understands the corporal's condition and evinces some degree of sympathetic understanding: "Listen, fella, you better get a doctor." The corporal, in spite of his erratic, nervous behavior, is aware of his own condition and attempts to reveal this understanding to the other three by saying "D'ya think I want to sit down at a table with . . . someone like you and make 'em sick? D'ya think I want to scare a kid like this one over here and put ideas in her head about her own guy! I've been waiting months, and they tell me I'm well, but the first time . . ." With this somewhat stilted outburst he bolts out of the diner, leaving the three alone again. The white-pompadoured woman's response to this is merely to pay for the coffee that the corporal has left behind.

Capote also used the unifying device of characters brought together on a train in his next story, **"A Tree of Night,"** although the implications of **"The Shape of Things"** are quite different. In the latter story the central idea is one that is anything but unusual in war-related literature—William Faulkner had used it in *Soldiers' Pay* in 1926, for example—that persons like the white-pompadoured woman who are well insulated from the unspeakable realities of war seem unable or unwilling to comprehend the effects of war upon those who have been touched directly by it. **"The Shape of Things"** is therefore partly an exercise in point of view wherein the woman is somewhat ironically unable to imagine the grave predicaments faced by others in her midst, and reacts mostly by silence and indignation.

As a short story, **"A Tree of Night"** succeeds much more than **"The Shape of Things"** for a number of reasons. It is, first of all, well sustained in its tone. The icicles that are suspended from the remote southern railway depot at night, are "like some crystal monster's vicious teeth," and they establish the prevailing mood for the rest of the narration. On the lonely railway platform it is windy, cold, and dark, except for "a string of naked light bulbs." As the story's protagonist, a college sophomore named Kay, climbs aboard the last remaining dingy railway coach, the gloom of the deserted depot extends to the tawdriness of the coach's interior, with its disarray of partly eaten sandwiches, remnants of apples and oranges, discarded paper cups, newspapers, and soft drink bottles—all of which combine with the staleness of tobacco smoke, the prospect of dozing travellers, and a leaking water-cooler to produce a singularly depressing scene.

The story traces the gradual undoing of Kay, who is finally coerced into surrendering the contents of her purse to a hypnotically grotesque pair of travelling con-artists. The man and woman who with ironic subtlety break her will as she falls into a macabre trance, accomplish their ends not only by their relentless insistence, but also by the lighting on the train and by the cadence of the moving locomotive. Kay, a nineteen-year-old, is on her way back to college after having attended the funeral of an uncle who has willed her a green Western guitar. Her decidedly funereal point of view is heightened by other elements in the story, such as the ghoulish monster teeth suspended from the station house and the gloom of entering the coffin-like interior of the last coach on this dreary, nocturnal passenger train. Kay settles in the car's only vacant seat where across from her are situated the two con-artists, she in her lavender hat with its cluster of celluloid cherries drooping from it, he deaf and dumb. Their game, as it turns out, is the reenactment of live burial for the entertainment of the curious in "every tank town in the South." The woman's advertising handbill comes, no doubt, as an unpleasant reminder of the funeral from which Kay has just returned:

> LAZARUS
> The Man Who Is Buried Alive
> A Miracle
> See For Yourself
> Adults, 25¢———Children, 10¢

With a description that invites comparison with Eudora Welty's story "Petrified Man," the eccentric woman explains to Kay their routine reenactment of his mock funeral: "*He* wears a gorgeous made-to-order bridegroom suit and a turban and lotsa talcum on his face," she states matter-of-factly. "After the hymn, after the sermon, we bury him." The deaf-mute, she says, has the ability to lie motionless for hours in a coffin by putting himself into a hypnotic trance. Then people come to view him in a storefront window. "Stays there all night stiff as a poker and people come and look: scares the livin' hell out of 'em. . . ." The details of their act are ludicrous, even funny, except that both the present moment and certain of Kay's sinister childhood memories each conspire against her, breaking her will. The coldness of the car's platform makes her head ache, and outside the coach window the tall trees seem "misty, painted pale by a malicious moonshine." The stars overhead remind the reader of the stars painted on the lid of the mute's casket, and the mute himself recalls for Kay the white image of her dead uncle's head resting on its casket pillow.

She is reminded too, and this is central to the story's "meaning," of her childhood memories "of terrors that once, long ago, had hovered above her like haunted limbs on a tree of night," and of "the unfailing threat of the wizard man." For her, the mute quite obviously becomes the living embodiment of the dreaded wizard man of her girlhood imagination. His desire is to sell her a love charm in the form of a shellacked peach seed. Too terrified either to ask the railway conductor to find her another seat, or to cry out and thus awaken the deathlike slumber of those around her, she submits, pulling her raincoat up "like a shroud" as the woman takes possession of Kay's purse.

"A Tree of Night" contains certain ironic elements, not the least of which is the complete surrender of an apparently rational and intelligent young college woman to the purely emotional forces of the moment and to the wiles of an exceedingly crude (and yet not unskilled), partially drunken, self-proclaimed fraud and her afflicted partner who utters not a single word. In spite of Kay's protestations, she is emotionally seduced into co-operating with the couple when the woman tries to force her to drink some cheap gin, although Kay finally manages to pour the paper cup of gin into the sound hole of her green guitar.

Other ironic details are also present; at one point the woman admonishes Kay for not telling the truth when Kay has tried to break away, allegedly to meet a friend on the same train; it is the woman and her accomplice, of course, who trade professionally in lies. The woman then suggests that for Kay to leave her seat would hurt the mute's feelings. Only a page later, however, the woman notes that her companion is immune to having his feelings trampled on by incredulous "smart alecks" because "he's afflicted." A short time later the woman hoists her skirt and blows her nose enthusiastically on the ragged hem of her petticoat, only to rearrange her skirt "with considerable primness." As for the rest of the passengers seated in this veritable mobile garbage dump rolling through a siege of foul weather in a dimly lit and offensive-smelling antiquated railway car, they seem "not . . . at all conscious of any discomfort" because they are asleep.

The story is made coherent by a series of leitmotifs and images. The most imposing of these is the awareness of death as suggested by entombment, morbid fear of supernatural forces, bodies, shrouds, and caskets. Another recurring image in the tale is that of devoured fruit. On the floor of the coach are apple cores and orange hulls. The lacquered peach seed that the mute desires to palm off on Kay is another such image, as is the cluster of faintly comic artificial cherries that are sewn to the woman's hat. Such images are but a reminder of the otherwise spent and artificial atmosphere that engulfs the whole narrative, particularly the funeral that Kay has just witnessed, and later the gloomy interior of the coach. The result of these unpleasant experiences for her is but another step in the loss of her youthful innocence.

Capote's early fiction is characterized in part by an unevenness in artistic quality. There is probably no better illustration of this than the differences that exist between **"A Tree of Night"** and **"Preacher's Legend,"** both of which appeared in 1945. The deficiencies of **"Preacher's Legend"** lie in both its narrative style and its dubious thematic import. The story centers around "an old colored man" of advanced age ("ninety or a hundred, maybe") who lives alone in the rural South and who is preoccupied by the passing of his wife Evelina long ago, as well as by certain fundamentalist religious persuasions. At one juncture in the story he retires alone into the woods to pray at a location known to him simply as The Place. But when he opens his Bible, clasps his hands, and lifts his head, he is interrupted by two sinister white hunters bearing a slain wildcat. The hunters are identified only as Curly Head and Yellow Hair. Owing to his generally confused state and to his preoccupation with the Bible (despite the Preacher's illiteracy), "he knew who the strangers were—knew it from the Good Book." Accordingly, he addresses one of the hunters as "Mistuh Jesus," and the other as "Mistuh Saint," evidently believing that the two have come to deliver him to his heavenly reward.

But Preacher is not ready to go. To Mistuh Jesus he says, "I'se been turnin' de whole mattah ovah an' I'se come to conclude I don't wants to go wid y'all." Curly Head and Yellow Hair do not take the old black man seriously, and are of the opinion that "he's just been sitting in the sun too long, that's all." As the two make their departure, however, Preacher asks Mistuh Jesus to do him one favor: "If you can see yo' way clear to do me one mo' favuh, I'd 'preciate it if you evah gits de time iffen you'd find my ol' woman . . . names Evelina . . . an' say hello from Preacher an' tells her what a good happy man I is." Curly Head promises to fulfill Preacher's request "first thing in the morning," but as the two hunters make their way down the road they burst into derisive laughter.

The story has relatively little to say. Capote reveals something of Preacher's private world, a world of myth and memory that is contrasted in the story with some harsher realities of the intrusive "outside" world of violence and cynicism represented by the two hunters. Preacher's remarks to himself, and to them, make the narrative partly a dialect story, and the Preacher himself is sketched in the tradition of the childlike, subservient, equivocal black man of the Uncle Remus stories.

Some of Capote's early interest in the gothic mode that found its flowering in *Other Voices, Other Rooms* is to be found in **"Preacher's Legend,"** just as in **"A Tree of Night."** Evelina had been "dead and buried two springs ago," and Preacher is mindful that some of his own children have gone "to their graves" and that "on the eve of his puppy's death, it was said, a great red-winged bird with a fearsome beak had sailed into the room from nowhere." Other images and suggestions reinforce the morose tone of the narration. From his wall stares "a wonderful poster-picture of a golden-haired girl holding a bottle of NE-HI [that is] torn at the mouth, so that her smile was wicked and leering." Outside, meanwhile, a rooster crows and the dogwood blossoms. Preacher recalls Evelina's admonition to him against believing in spirits: ("I ain't gonna listen to no mo' of dat spook talk."). And yet, when he first hears the approach of the hunters in the woods, he regards them as apparitions. Such details as these point to the story's affinity with local color tradition as evidenced by its whole cultural milieu, its rural southern setting, its re-use of black colloquialisms, and its somewhat paternalistic view of the black man.

After **"Preacher's Legend,"** comedy prevailed in Capote's southern stories, and one of the better comic tales is **"My Side of the Matter"** which is written (uncharacteristically for Capote) in the first person. The narrator is a seriocomic sixteen-year-old bridegroom and expectant father who, to his infinite regret, has been persuaded to relinquish his "swell position clerking at the Cash'n'Carry to accompany his bride to her aunts' house in Admiral's Mill" which, he says, "is nothing but a damn gap in the road any way you care to consider it."

Domestic differences of opinion have culminated in his being attacked by his wife Marge's two aunts. One of them, Eunice, has threatened him with a Civil War sword, and the other (Olivia-Ann) has brandished a "fourteen-inch hog knife" against him. The result of these disputes is the young man's barricading himself in the family parlor by pushing heavy furniture against the doors, locking the windows, and lowering the shades. Last seen, he is "munching a juicy, creamy, chocolate cherry" from out of a "five pound box of Sweet Love candy." As his would-be attackers plead for him to surrender, his reply is to give them "a tune on the piano every now and then just to let them know" that he is still "cheerful."

The story is as light and comic as most of the others were dark and serious, and yet throughout his career Capote persists in concentrating upon the grotesque characters he had used before, except that in **"My Side of the Matter"** they are devoted to comic ends. Here the narrator himself admits to being "slightly stocky," but he attributes that to his not having "got [his] full growth yet." Eunice, seeing him in a less understanding light, regards him merely as "the runt of the litter." But Marge protests: "you seem to forget, Aunt Olivia-Ann, that this is my husband, the father of my unborn child." Eunice then makes a nasty sound. "Well, all I can say is I most certainly wouldn't be bragging about it."

The other characters are scarcely more appealing. Marge, the child bride, according to her husband, "has no looks, no body, and no brains whatever," and on top of those shortcomings, "ups and gets pregnant" after the couple are betrothed less than three months. Eunice, on the other hand, has "a behind that must weight [sic] a tenth of a ton," and tries vainly to chew her tobacco with ladylike decorum. Olivia-Ann, according to the sixteen-year-old, is worse still, "for she is a natural-born half-wit and ought really to be kept in somebody's attic." To make matters worse, he says, "she's real pale and skinny and has a mustache. She squats around most of the time whittling on a stick with her fourteen-inch hog knife."

The women make no pretense about their disapproval of the young man, compelling him as they do to sleep apart from his wife on a cot erected on the screenless back porch, which is besieged both by mosquitoes "that could murder a buffalo" and by "dangerous flying roaches and a posse of local rats big enough to haul a wagon train." With continued vehemence, the women accuse him of ineptitude and outright laziness. Says Eunice, "if you think I'd let that runt drive my just-as-good-as-brand-new 1934 Chevrolet as far as the privy and back you must've gone clear out of your head." Alluding to his laziness, she continues, "if he's ever so much as driven a plow I'll eat a dozen gophers fried in turpentine."

The humor of the tale is at once sophisticated and slapstick, for while the narrator retains an astutely ironic point of view throughout, he also speaks with an ingenious crudity. In the end, the story turns into a free-for-all. Marge hands Eunice a Civil War sword with which to restrain the narrator, while Olivia-Ann rushes into the yard bellowing "The Battle Hymn of the Republic." The effect of all this is hilarious Faulknerian fun, as pointless, perhaps, as it is funny.

Like a number of stories before and after it, **"My Side of the Matter"** concerns a less-than-welcome guest in an alien household, a circumstance that Capote uses in such stories as **"Miriam," "The Headless Hawk," "Shut a Final Door," "Master Misery,"** as well as in *Other Voices, Other Rooms*. And although the young man's involuntary exile in **"My Side of the Matter"** is comic, he is still another of Capote's isolated and unloved outcasts.

"Jug of Silver" is another comic story, and the chief difference between it and **"My Side of the Matter"** is that the former is a much more charming narrative, though no less enigmatic in its message. It is the story of a waifish boy known only as Appleseed who is credited with guessing the amount of money ($77.35, in all) contained in a gallon jug that had once contained "store-bought" Italian wine.

The scene is a small town in the deep South where the narrator, looking fondly back to his boyhood, recalls Mr. Ed Marshall, his uncle, "a squat, square-faced, pink-fleshed man with looping, manly white mustaches" who owns and manages the Valhalla drugstore. Early in the story Marshall appears as "a renowned teetotaler" drinking red wine with his companion, a somewhat mysterious, supposedly Egyptian, dentist named Hamurabi who unaccountably possesses no foreign accent, and who, in the opinion of the narrator, "wasn't any more Egyptian than the man in the moon." Marshall, a little tipsy from the wine, and a great deal concerned about the sudden appearance of an old man named Rufus McPherson who has opened a rival drugstore across the town square, decides to fill the jug with nickels and dimes. His idea is to promote business by allowing his customers to estimate the value of the jug's contents, and to award the same contents on Christmas eve to the nearest estimator. To Hamurabi, the jug represents "the pot at the end of the rainbow," but to Marshall, it is a sensational piece of business promotion. He tells his customers that "the more you buy, the more chances you get. And I'll keep all guesses in a ledger till Christmas Eve, at which time whoever comes closest to the right amount will get the whole shebang."

The plan succeeds enormously. "Why," the narrator says, "the Valhalla hadn't done so much business since Station Master Tully, poor soul, went stark raving mad and claimed to have discovered oil back of the depot, causing the town to be overrun with wildcat prospectors." But moral and sentimental problems confront Marshall and Hamurabi when Appleseed arrives on the scene and claims to live on a farm outside the town limits. Appleseed also claims to be twelve years old, but his sister Middy ("a said looking kid" who resembles "a regular bean pole" and who has something wrong with her teeth) says that her brother is only eight. Obviously down on his luck, Appleseed never changes his outfit which consists of "a red sweater, blue denim britches, and a pair of man-sized boots that went clop clop with every step." His mother, he says, weighs but seventy-four pounds, his brother plays the fiddle at weddings for a fee of fifty cents, and his father is apparently one short step ahead of the sheriff.

Appleseed resolves to ascertain the correct amount contained in the jug, but instead of taking a mere educated guess, he intends somehow to count the money: "Now, the way I got it figured, there ain't but one sure-fire thing and that's to count every nickel and dime." Hamurabi is incredulous: "Count! You better have X-ray eyes, son, that's all I can say." Moved by the sight of the pathetic boy and his even more pathetic sister, Hamurabi has not the heart to see the child's face on Christmas Eve when he, in all probability, will be grievously disappointed: "I don't want to see that kid's face. This is Christmas and I mean to have a rip-roaring time."

At the climax of the story at the Valhalla on Christmas Eve, the store fills with an anxious assemblage in only twenty minute's time. Capote's handling of the suspense element is perfectly timed. Appleseed is accorded the honor of opening an envelope containing a slip with the prize-winning figure on it, and it becomes clear that Marshall, in the spirit of yuletide charity and holiday good will, has altered the figure to coincide precisely with Appleseed's estimate. Only the town drunk who masquerades as Santa Claus and "who had a snootful by this time" causes a rumpus, although it develops that he has been paid to do so by Rufus McPherson.

The story is related with an engaging oral quality in the tradition of the American tall tale. Appleseed wins the contents of the jug, so Capote's explanation goes, because he had been fortuitously born with a caul over his head. But all this happened long ago. In the ensuing years Appleseed moved with his family to Florida and was never again heard from. In the remaining time before his death, Marshall "was invited each Christmas day to tell the story of Appleseed to the Baptist Bible class." Later, Hamurabi had recorded the "legend" of Appleseed and had attempted to interest an editor in publishing it, but was unsuccessful. Capote's story ends on still another ironic note, for the editor who had turned down Hamurabi's version of the story had done so because Hamurabi had not stressed the fact that Middy supposedly "turned out to be a movie star" after she acquired enough money to pay for false teeth. "But that's not what happened," says the narrator, "so why should you lie?" The real center of the story is, of course, predicated on Marshall's charitable distortion of the truth.

As in so many of Capote's short stories, **"Jug of Silver"** offers the reader an array of colorful and eccentric characters, especially in the form of precocious, determined children. The children in the story are much like those in **"Children on Their Birthdays"** which appeared next, and which is similar in situation, setting, and atmosphere. **"Jug of Silver"** also shares with a number of other stories, such as **"A Tree of Night," "Miriam,"** and **"The Headless Hawk,"** a certain counter-realistic quality which, if it makes the story no less believable, is still considerably removed from stark, photographic reality. It makes effective use of some genuinely warm and comic southern local color elements; but comic or not, it contains a touch of sadness growing out of the use of deprived characters that makes the texture of the narrative decidedly bittersweet.

That same bittersweetness prevails in another of Capote's favorite stories, the hilarious **"Children on Their Birthdays."** The tale begins and ends on a poignant note, however, for the protagonist (an enigmatic ten-year-old named Miss Lily Jane Bobbit) is eventually run over and killed by the same six o'clock bus that had originally brought her and her mother to the tiny southern town which is the scene of the narrative. The story, withal, is a remarkable piece of local color narration told by an anonymous first-person observer. Much like **"My Side of the Matter," "Children on Their Birthdays"** has no imposing thematic point to make, although it is rich in a variety of kinds of suggestiveness.

Structurally, the story is framed by Miss Bobbit's arrival and would-be departure, for as she runs toward "those moons of roses" prepared by her childhood friends as a going-away tribute, she runs into the path of the bus and is killed. The story itself ends on this note, and the immensely comic aspects of the story are therefore tempered.

Still, "enigmatic" is the word that applies best to Miss Bobbit's character and behavior. From the moment she makes her appearance in town, there is a certain disruption of the usual patterns of social and psychological behavior among a whole colony of provincial southern children in whom change is ultimately brought about. The "wiry little girl in a starched, lemon-colored party dress [carrying a] spinsterish umbrella" proceeds to evoke a wide range of responses (jealousy, awe, admiration, outrage, and finally love) among those children who are attentive to her. Miss Bobbit is another of Capote's somewhat disarmingly precocious child characters. The narrator's Aunt El, for one, is bothered by this ten-year-old child's wearing makeup, but aside from that, Miss Bobbit possesses an adult dignity, for "she was a lady, and, what is more, she looked you in the eye with a manlike directness."

The story consists of a series of loosely related anecdotes involving the child, each of which is progressively more comic and revealing of character. At the outset, the eccentric child moves into an eccentric-looking house, "an old dark place with about two dozen lightning rods scattered on the roof." The gossipy Mrs. Sawyer who owns the place and who is terrified by storms, spreads the rumor that the child's father, "the sweetest singing man in the whole of Tennessee," is serving time in a state penitentiary, and that Miss Bobbit and her suspiciously silent mother subsist on a raw vegetarian diet. When the child befriends a young black girl named Sister Rosalba ("baby-fat and sugar-plum shaped"), Mrs. Sawyer tells Aunt El "that it went against her grain to have a nigger lolling smack there in plain sight on her front porch." And when Miss Bobbit announces that Rosalba is to be considered as her sister, the initial racial slurs from the white population are finally discontinued. On the occasion when Miss Bobbit becomes incensed over the dogs that station themselves under her window at night and keep her awake, she and Sister Rosalba take the matter into their own hands after the sheriff refuses to do anything, and after Sister Rosalba reveals that she does not regard them as dogs at all, but as "some kind of devil." The two are "seen stalking through town carrying a flower basket filled with rocks." When they come upon a dog, Miss Bobbit scrutinizes it, and if it is one of the condemned, Sister Rosalba, "with ferocious aim, would take a rock from her basket and crack the dog between the eyes."

Later, when Miss Bobbit becomes the county subscription representative for a list of magazines that include "*Reader's Digest, Popular Mechanics, Dime Detective* and *Child's Life*," she enlists the help of the unruly Billy Bob and his exceedingly ornery companion who is ironically misnamed Preacher Star. Sister Rosalba, meanwhile, begins to market an assortment of cosmetics called Dewdrop, and also hires the boys to make deliveries. The work is surprisingly difficult, for "Billy

Bob used to be so tired in the evening that he would hardly chew his supper." But the most comic part of the story involves the appearance of the town con-man (Manny Fox) who, in the manner of Mark Twain, promotes a show featuring a "Fan Dancer Without the Fan" as well as an array of local talent elicited from among the townspeople who will compete for "A Genuine Hollywood Screen Test." The fanless dancer (clad in a bathing suit, much to the disappointment of the local hangers-on) turns out to be none other than Mrs. Manny Fox ("A deadpan pimento-tongued redhead with wet lips and moist eyelids"), currently residing at the Chucklewood Tourist Camp.

The main attraction for the narrator and his companions is Miss Bobbit, the ladylike Miss Bobbit, who has been practicing her "act" behind drawn window shades at Mrs. Sawyer's. When another local performer (Buster Riley) has finished "Waltzing Matilda" on a saw, Miss Bobbit proceeds to shock the townfolk by singing in "a rowdy sandpaper voice": "I was born in China, and raised in Jay-pan . . . if you don't like my peaches, stay away from my can oho o-ho!" Aunt El gasps as, "with a bump [Miss Bobbit] up-ended her skirt to display her blue-lace underwear." Her act terminates in a grand flourish when "in the midst of a full split" a Roman candle bursts "into firey balls of red, white and blue," as the audience rises for her to bellow out "The Star Spangled Banner."

In the meantime, Manny Fox skips town, and after two weeks of non-action on the promised Hollywood screen test, Miss Bobbit organizes the "Manny Fox Hangman's Club" which leads eventually to his arrest in Uphill, Arkansas. For her efforts, she receives the "Good Deed Merit Award" from the Sunbeam Girls of America, of which she takes a dim view because of "all that rowdy bugle blowing." By the time the Hangman's Club proposes to send her to Hollywood for a screen test (in return for ten percent of her lifetime earnings) Billy Bob has fallen in love with Miss Bobbit. But after the farewell festivities which involve "boys in flower masked faces," she runs into the path of the bus.

Miss Bobbit, remotely the same kind of self-determined, totally independent, and enterprising child that Capote's Miriam had been, can be viewed as the forerunner of certain other characters yet to be created, not the least of which are Idabel Tomkins in **Other Voices, Other Rooms** and Holly Golightly in **Breakfast at Tiffany's.** Similarly, Billy Bob's habit of escaping up the nearest tree in moments of stress prefigures **The Grass Harp** where a whole colony of characters select the same arboreal refuge. Capote's attention to the elements of hoax and childhood problems, also evident in **"Jug of Silver,"** foreshadows *The Thanksgiving Visitor*.

But Capote's next story in the southern group was **"A Diamond Guitar"** which appeared in 1950 and which belongs among the darker of his short stories. The scene is a prison farm set in the midst of a pine forest in the South, where the prisoners pass their days tapping the trees for turpentine. The protagonist is a certain Mr. Schaeffer who is serving a sentence of ninety-nine years and a day for having killed a man who, according to the omniscient narrator, "deserved to die." Schaeffer enjoys a limited measure of prestige among the prison guards and inmates, in whose eyes he has "a mask of special respect." He is literate, for one thing, and prisoners not infrequently bring letters from outside for him to read aloud, although he has the habit of improvising "more cheerful messages and does not read what is written on the page."

One Sunday a truck arrives bearing a young Cuban named Tico Feo, "a knifer" who has allegedly "cut up a sailor in Mobile" and who brings with him, among other cherished items, "a guitar studded with glass diamonds." Given to telling outlandish lies, the young Cuban causes most of the men in the green wooden sleep house to feel a kind of love for him, inspired, perhaps, by his songs sung to the accompaniment of his guitar. "Except that they did not combine their bodies or think to do so," the narrator says, "they were as lovers."

Tico reveals to Schaeffer that he has a friend named Frederico in Mobile who will put them on his boat and carry them to freedom if they can first manage to escape from the prison camp. And as Schaeffer fantasizes about his prospects for making an escape, he hears the sound of a coffin being assembled in the yard for one of the prisoners who has died. Thinks Schaeffer, "This is for me, it is mine." But it is Tico's plan to hide in a tree until dark, and then make an escape by running through a creek and thereby leave no scent for search dogs to follow. The last act that Tico performs before attempting his escape is to put his guitar in tune. When the moment of their prison break comes, the two men run through the creek as "icy geysers [spray] around them." While Tico makes his successful escape, Schaeffer breaks an ankle when he runs into a fallen tree. The captain of the guards ironically interprets the whole episode to mean that Schaeffer has been injured in an attempt to capture Tico, for which he is honored by having his picture in the local newspaper. Tico, meanwhile, makes good on his bid for freedom, and, in his typically romantic fashion, is said to have entered the home of a spinster woman, kissed her twice, and fled.

Three winters go by, and Schaeffer's hair has become progressively whiter. He still keeps the "diamond guitar with its glass gems turning yellow with age. A new prisoner is assigned to the sleep house, and although he is said to be an accomplished guitar player, his songs come out sour, "for it was as though Tico Feo, tuning his guitar that last morning, had put a curse on it." When last seen, the guitar is beneath Schaeffer's cot, where in the night the old man "sometimes reaches it out, and his fingers drift across the strings: then, the world."

Like so many other Capote tales (such as **"A Tree of Night," "Miriam," "My Side of the Matter," "The Headless Hawk," "Shut a Final Door," "Jug of Silver,"** and **"Master Misery"**) **"A Diamond Guitar"** is set in motion when complete strangers begin to interact. Tico Feo's rather brief influence over the dreary, hopeless life of Schaeffer has provided the old man with not only a ray of hope for an eventual escape, but also some colorful memories to fuel his romantic imagination. Tico himself shares with Billy Bob (of **"Children on Their Birthdays"**) the notion that one can find solace and safety if he will but climb a tree. But in general, Tico is another of Capote's array of fiercely independent characters who, like Miss Bobbit and Holly Golightly, are far more motivated from within than from without.

In **"A Diamond Guitar,"** Schaeffer functions as the protagonist because he is the person to whom development occurs. And although Tico himself undergoes no significant change, the monotony of Schaeffer's life is alleviated by Tico's brief presence. Tico, with his "bottle of Evening in Paris cologne" and his "Rand McNally map of the world," enjoys a kind of life far removed from Schaeffer's; for to Tico, being alive "was to remember brown rivers where the fish run, and sunlight on a lady's hair." He leaves behind him only the diamond guitar, an emblematic reminder of himself.

The most warmly engaging of all Capote's ventures into short fiction is *A Christmas Memory* (1956), a blend of fiction and autobiography concentrating once more on the author's remembered life in the South. His powers of description in *A Christmas Memory* are quite possibly unparalleled anywhere else in his work. When the book begins, it is "a morning in late November. A coming of winter morning more than twenty years ago." Capote remembers himself at the age of seven. His guardian, "a woman with snow white hair," is at the window "wearing tennis shoes and a shapeless gray sweater over a summer calico dress," and looking like "a bantam hen." Because "it's fruitcake weather," the boy and the old woman set out in a buggy, the wheels of which "wobble like a drunkard's legs" to find the ingredients necessary to bake thirty cakes: "cherries and citron, ginger and vanilla and canned Hawaiian pineapple, rinds and raisins and walnuts and whiskey and oh, so much flour, butter, so many eggs, spices, flavorings. . . ."

Like much of his earlier fiction (such as *Other Voices, Other Rooms* and *The Grass Harp*), *A Christmas Memory* can be read as a moving expression of lost childhood innocence and idyllic simplicity. The texture of the prose is also similar to those earlier pieces, for it is both subtle and impressionistic. There is probably no better instance of this kind of writing in *A Christmas Memory* than Capote's description of a late fall southern dawn:

> Morning. Frozen rime lusters the grass; the sun, round as an orange and orange as hot-weather moons, balances on the horizon, burnishes the silvered winter weeks. A wild turkey calls. A renegade hog grunts in the undergrowth. Soon, by the edge of knee-deep, rapid-running water, we have to abandon the buggy. Queenie [a dog] wades the stream first, paddles across barking complaints at the swiftness of the current, the pneumonia-making coldness of it. We follow, holding our shoes and equipment (a hatchet, a burlap sack) above our heads. A mile more: of chastising thorns, burs and briers that catch at our clothes; of rusty pine needles brilliant with gaudy fungus and melted feathers. Here, there, a flash, a flutter, an ecstasy of shrillings remind us that not all the birds have flown south. Always, the path unwinds through lemony sun pools and pitch vine tunnels. Another creek to cross: a disturbed armada of speckled trout froths the water round us, frogs the size of plates practice belly flops; beaver workmen are building a dam. On the farther shore, Queenie shakes herself and trembles. My friend [Miss Sook Faulk] shivers too: not with cold but enthusiasm. One of her hat's ragged roses sheds a petal as she lifts her head and inhales the pine-heavy hair. "We're almost there; can you smell it, Buddy?" she says, as though we were approaching an ocean.

Curiously enough, Capote once said that *A Christmas Memory* was the only piece he ever wrote "that *depended* on its southern setting. The moment I wrote that story I knew that I would never write another word about the South. I'm not going to be haunted by it anymore."[4] Haunted or not, Capote succeeded in creating in *A Christmas Memory* a high watermark of personal feeling and dramatic intensity; he recalls at one point that for Christmas he had wanted a bicycle, but that because of his guardian Miss Faulk's impoverished state, he anticipated receiving a kite (made by her), along with "socks, a Sunday school shirt, some handkerchiefs, a hand-me-down sweater and a year's subscription to a religious magazine for children." This will be the last Christmas with Miss Faulk. Her mind begins to fail, and the boy is to be sent to a series of military schools, "a miserable succession of bugle-blowing prisons, grim, reveille-ridden summer camps." Back in the present, some twenty years after these childhood experiences, he learns of her death, which he regards as a "severing [of an] irreplaceable part of [himself]." He concludes, "that is why, walking across a school campus on this particular December morning, I keep searching the sky. As if I expected to see, rather like hearts, a lost pair of kites hurrying toward heaven."

Capote's *The Thanksgiving Visitor* shares with **"A Diamond Guitar"** and *A Christmas Memory* not only a remote southern locality, but also a tone of wistfulness born out of the narrator's sense of profound loneliness. The narrator in *The Thanksgiving Visitor,* however, is a child, and the story itself can be read in more than one light. Perhaps the most obvious way of seeing the narrative is as a documentary of life in rural Alabama in one of the worst of the Depression years, 1932. At the climactic Thanksgiving dinner, Uncle B (one of the narrator's four guardians) offers a prayer appropriate to the occasion: "Bless You, O Lord, for the bounty of our table, the varied fruits we can be thankful for on this Thanksgiving Day of a troubled year." Buddy, a Capote self-portrait, recalls having been fed magnificently on "cockcrow repasts of ham and fried chicken, fried pork chops, fried catfish, fried squirrel (in season), fried eggs, hominy grits with gravy, blackeyed peas, collards with collard liquor and cornbread to mush it in, biscuits, pound cake, pancakes and molasses, honey in the comb, homemade jams and jellies, sweetmilk, buttermilk, coffee chickory-flavored and hot as Hades." But he is understandably troubled by the thought of those who have to make do with less. "Throughout the Depression Years," he says, "our school distributed free milk and sandwiches to all children whose families were too poor to provide them with a lunch box." But a few children were still harder hit by the bad times: "some boys, girls too, were forced to go barefoot right through the bitterest weather—that's how hard the Depression had hit Alabama."

For Buddy, the times were also difficult, but for reasons somewhat independent of the country's depressed economy. An autobiographic story, *The Thanksgiving Visitor* is a bittersweet, retrospective, illumination of his early life with three aunts and an uncle. The protagonist is Buddy's only "friend," Miss Sook Faulk, for "as she was a child herself . . . she understood children, and understood me absolutely." Even so, Buddy's life is not an easy one, inasmuch as they "had taken me under their roof because of a disturbance among my more immediate family, a custody battle that, for involved reasons, had left me stranded in this somewhat eccentric Alabama household. Not that I was unhappy there: indeed, moments of those few years turned out to be the happiest part of an otherwise difficult childhood. . . ."

The conflict in the story centers around Buddy's unhappy relations with a twelve-year-old contemporary named Odd Henderson. "Talk about mean!" says Buddy, "Odd Henderson was the meanest human creature in my experience." Odd, who has failed the first grade twice, vents his hostilities on the more passive Buddy by knocking him to the ground and rubbing prickly cockleburs into his scalp as "a circle of kids ganged around to titter, or pretend to." Malicious acts of this nature cause Buddy to find excuses not to attend school, and when Miss Sook comprehends the problem, she develops a stratagem to solve Buddy's dilemma, while she finds a way to advance the cause of Christian charity at the same time. Convinced that Buddy must somehow "come to terms with people like Odd Henderson," Miss Sook pays a call on Molly Henderson, Odd's destitute, toothless mother who is faced with a house full of children and an absentee, jailbird husband. Miss Sook extends an invitation to Odd for Thanksgiving dinner.

The dinner itself ends in a debacle when Odd steals Miss Sook's prize cameo. At the dinner table, Buddy does what he can to expose the crime, but with continued holiday charity, Miss Sook covers up for Odd's act of petty theft. Because, in Buddy's judgment, "she'd lied to save his skin, [and] betrayed our friendship," Buddy is all the more disconsolate. Even so, the Thanksgiving invitation solved the original problem of Odd's harassment of Buddy, for "afterward, Odd Henderson let me alone," Buddy recalls.

But the object of the story lies much deeper than the alleviation of Buddy's problems with Odd Henderson. "The whole family (there were ten of them, not counting Dad Henderson, who was a bootlegger and usually in jail, all scrunched together in a four-room house next door to a Negro church) was a shiftless, surly bunch, every one of them ready to do you a bad turn; Odd wasn't the worst of the lot, and brother, that is *saying* something." The story makes use of the somewhat outmoded philosophy of determinism to some extent, for Odd himself is depicted as "a skinny, freckled scarecrow in sweaty cast-off overalls that would have been a humiliation to a chain-gang convict," and the conditions of his environment shape his behavior. As Miss Sook puts it, "this boy can't help acting ugly; he doesn't know any different. All those Henderson children have had it hard."

There is much more to her understanding of the Hendersons: at the end of the story, Miss Sook puts her arm around Buddy's shoulder. "There's just this I want to say, Buddy. Two wrongs never made a right. It was wrong of him to take the cameo. But we don't know why he took it. Maybe he never meant to keep it. Whatever his reason, it can't be calculated. Which is why what you did was much worse: you *planned* to humiliate him. It was deliberate. Now listen to me, Buddy: there is only one unpardonable sin—*deliberate cruelty.* All else can be forgiven. That, never. Do you understand me, Buddy?" Miss Sook's words are central to an understanding of *The Thanksgiving Visitor.* Furthermore, they have far-reaching implications in Capote's system of values because they clarify some of the perplexities of evil and its origins that occur in the pages of *In Cold Blood.* In that book, the murderers Richard Hickock and Perry Smith are, in a very real sense, prisoners of their pathological childhood. As a consequence, their crimes are rendered understandable, but not forgivable.

In its narrative style, ***The Thanksgiving Visitor*** is one of the more quotable of Truman Capote's stories because of his occasional flashes of linguistic brilliance. As Miss Armstrong (a strong-armed schoolteacher) beats Buddy's hands for having called Odd a "sonafabitch," Odd looks on with "a small citric smile." Somewhat later, Buddy comments that "my mind wandered through a maze as melancholy as the wet twilight." Observing Odd's ears, Buddy regards them as "a pair of eye-catchers, like Alfalfa's in the *Our Gang* comedy pictures," and as he watches Odd urinate, he sees him "unbuttoning his trousers and letting go with a forceful splash [as] he whistled along, jaunty as a jaybird in a field of sunflowers."

Capote's stories are frequently invested with certain gothic elements. In a fight with a tomboy named Ann "Jumbo" Finchburg, Odd suffers "a broken thumb, plus scratch scars that will stay with him to the day they shut his coffin." And of the "Henderson breed," he writes that they might well "gouge the gold out of a dead man's teeth." While Odd's act of thievery is being exposed at the Thanksgiving dinner, he "seemed calm as a corpse," and as Buddy fantasizes about his own funeral, he says it would be "worth it to hear the human wails and Queenie's howls as my coffin was lowered into cemetery depths."

III *House of Flowers*

House of Flowers (1950) must be considered among the lighter tales, although like those it is not altogether made up of sweetness and light. The central character is a comely prostitute named Ottilie who in the early part of the narrative is in the employ of a "spinsterish, smooth-looking invalid" woman who operates the Champs Elysées bordello in Port-au-Prince from an upstairs room. Ottilie, notwithstanding her pleasant and engaging manner, has not passed an easy life. Her mother has died, her father has returned to France, and Ottilie herself has been left in the custody of "a rough peasant family, the sons of whom had each at a young age lain with her in some green and shadowy place." At fourteen, she had walked two days and a night to Port-au-Prince carrying what was originally a ten-pound sack of grain. To ease the strain, she has allowed the grain to run out gradually until there was little of it remaining at her arrival. "A jolly nice man" has dried the girl's tears and has taken her "to see his cousin," the proprietress of the Champs Elysées, where she has become the only employee under thirty, and easily "the most talked about girl on the road."

At a cockfight she meets Royal Bonaparte who spirits her away as his wife to his house of flowers. Convinced by a Houngan in the hills above town that love has come to her at last, she has also been led to believe that if she clutches a wild bee in her bare hand, and if the bee does not sting, then love is real. Although this test has disproven her love for a bordello customer named Mr. Jamison, it indicates the genuineness of her attachment to Royal. Her main problem after five months of marriage to Royal is not so much that he has been spending great amounts of time at cafes and cockfights, but that she has been tormented by her mother-in-law, a more than petulant woman known as Old Bonaparte. The old woman not only spies on Ottilie's love-making, but also harasses her by placing the severed head of a yellow cat on Ottilie's sewing basket. Later, Old Bonaparte places other things in the basket, such as a green snake, spiders, a lizard, and a buzzard's breast. Ottilie retaliates by incorporating such morsels as these in her cooking for the old woman. She drops the cat head into a boiling pot and serves Old Bonaparte a soup that turns out to be "surprisingly tasty." But when Ottilie reveals her culinary practices to her mother-in-law, the shock is so extreme that the woman dies by nightfall. Ottilie, however, imagines at night that "Old Bonaparte was dead but not gone," and she confesses to her husband that she has served the old woman such things as snake stew. Royal concludes that she must be punished by being tied to a tree for an entire day without food or water as "the goat Juno and the chickens [gather] to stare at her humiliation."

Still tied to the tree, Ottilie thinks she is dreaming when Baby and Rosita, two of her former associates from the Champs Elysée, arrive in an automobile hired by Jamison, and attempt to bring Ottilie back to Port-au-Prince where her absence has caused trade at the bordello to fall sharply. They untie the girl and drain a bottle of rum in "a toast to old times, and those to be." Finally, Ottilie insists on being retied so that, as she explains, "no bee is ever going to sting me." Thus, rather than being "dead," as the invalid proprietress has said of Ottilie, Ottilie is not only alive, but in love. "Chewing eucalyptus leaves to sweeten her breath," Ottilie throws "her arms akimbo, [lets] her neck go limp, [and lolls] her eyes far back into their sockets [so that] seen from a distance it would look as though she had come to some violent, pitiful end." This, she concludes, will give Royal "a good scare."

In spite of the story's sometimes unsavory and unfunny elements, the narrative is not only witty, but curiously innocent and romantic, inasmuch as Ottilie possesses a childlike mentality and lives a life (in spite of her shady past) that seems idyllic. Ottilie's story is fundamentally consistent with the pattern established by other Capote protagonists, for she is a virtual stranger whose influence is strongly felt by those with whom she comes into contact. At seventeen, her precocity at handling people and situations invites a comparison with (for example) Lily Jane Bobbit of **"Children on Their Birthdays."** Both characters prove to be virtually irresistible to those around them, and it is precisely this irresistibility that distinguishes some of Capote's other key short-story protagonists such as Appleseed ("**Jug of Silver**") and Tico Feo ("**A Diamond Guitar**"). Moreover, Capote's three longer narratives (*Other Voices, Other Rooms*; *Breakfast at Tiffany's*; and *The Grass Harp*) have as central characters individuals with considerable personal appeal. Gone are such unattractive and audibly introspective personalities as Mrs. Miller ("**Miriam**"), Walter Ranny ("**Shut a Final Door**"), and Sylvia ("**Master Misery**").

Notes

1. Malcolm Cowley (ed.), *Writers at Work: The Paris Review Interviews,* (New York, 1960), p. 287.
2. Ibid., p. 290.
3. Ibid.
4. Roy Newquist, *Counterpoint* (Chicago, 1964), p. 80.

Selected Bibliography

Primary Sources

This bibliography is based on Robert J. Stanton's *Truman Capote: A Reference Guide* (Boston: G. K. Hall, 1980). For further details about reprints and foreign editions, consult the Stanton Guide. Detailed information about publications and reprints through 1967 is also contained in Jackson R. Bryer's "Truman Capote: A Bibliography," which is included in Irving Malin's *Truman Capote's "In Cold Blood": A Critical Handbook* (Belmont, Cal.: Wadsworth, 1969), pp. 239-69.

1. Novels and Short Story Collections

Breakfast at Tiffany's: A Short Novel and Three Stories. New York: Random House, 1958. [Contains "A Diamond Guitar," "The House of Flowers," and "A Christmas Memory."]

A Christmas Memory. New York: Random House, 1966.

The Grass Harp. New York: Random House, 1951.

Other Voices, Other Rooms. New York: Random House, 1948.

The Thanksgiving Visitor. New York: Random House, 1968.

A Tree of Night and Other Stories. New York: Random House, 1949. [Contains, besides the title story, "Children on Their Birthdays," "The Headless Hawk," "Master Misery," "Miriam," "My Side of the Matter," "Shut a Final Door."]

3. Nonfiction

In Cold Blood: A True Account of a Multiple Murder and Its Consequences. New York: Random House, 1965.

5. Short Stories (original periodical publications arranged chronologically).

"The Walls Are Cold," *Decade of Short Stories,* 4 (Fourth Quarter, 1943), 27-30.

"A Mink of One's Own," *Decade of Short Stories,* 6 (Third Quarter, 1944), 1-4.

"The Shape of Things," *Decade of Short Stories,* 6 (Fourth Quarter, 1944), 21-23.

[All three of the above are uncollected.]

"My Side of the Matter," *Story,* 26 (May-June, 1945), 34-40.

"Miriam," *Mademoiselle,* June, 1945, 114-15, 184, 186-90.

"A Tree of Night," *Harper's Bazaar,* October, 1945, pp. 110, 176-88.

"Jug of Silver," *Mademoiselle,* December, 1945, pp. 142-43, 238-47.

"Preacher's Legend," *Prairie Schooner,* 19 (December, 1945), 265-74 [uncollected].

"The Headless Hawk," *Harper's Bazaar,* November, 1946, pp. 254-55, 330-58.

"Shut a Final Door," *Atlantic Monthly,* August, 1947, pp. 49-55.

"Children on Their Birthdays," *Mademoiselle,* January, 1949, pp. 88-90, 146-51.

"Master Misery," *Horizon,* 19 (January, 1949), 19-37; *Harper's Magazine,* February, 1949, pp. 38-48.

"A Diamond Guitar," *Harper's Bazaar,* November, 1950, pp. 164, 170-78, 188.

"House of Flowers," *Botthege Oscure,* 6 (1950), 414-29.

"A Christmas Memory," *Mademoiselle,* December, 1956, pp. 70-71, 125-31.

"Breakfast at Tiffany's," *Esquire,* November, 1958, pp. 134-62.

"Among the Paths to Eden," *Esquire,* July, 1960, pp. 53-57.

"The Thanksgiving Visitor," *McCalls,* November, 1967, pp. 75, 155-62.

Truman Capote with Lawrence Grobel (interview date 1982-84)

SOURCE: Grobel, Lawrence. "In Cold Blood." In *Conversations with Capote,* pp. 109-27. New York: New American Library, 1985.

[*In the following interview, based on meetings between Grobel and Capote from 1982 to 1984, Capote discusses the facts surrounding and impetus to writing* In

Cold Blood. *It is in the interview below that Capote made his controversial disparaging comment on Norman Mailer's* The Executioner's Song.]

"Everybody has their field. My field is the multiple murderer."

Capote never claimed—as many critics thought he did—that he invented narrative journalism or, as *In Cold Blood* came to be labeled, the nonfiction novel. He *did* consider it to be a serious new literary form and he did feel he had made a major contribution toward its establishment. And he also staked the claim to have undertaken the most comprehensive and far-reaching experiment in the medium of reportage.

When he began his investigation into the murder of the Clutter family in Holcomb, Kansas, Perry Smith and Richard Hickock had not yet been apprehended. Once they were, Capote needed their cooperation before he could write his book. He got more than he bargained for. "Short of actually living in a death cell myself," he said, "I couldn't have come closer to their experience."

He spent long hours with them as they waited to be hanged; he shared their emotions. It was a life totally alien to anything he had ever undergone, and he told *Playboy*, "I came to understand that death is the central factor of life. And the simple comprehension of this fact alters your entire perspective. . . .

"The experience served to heighten my feeling of the tragic view of life, which I've always held and which accounts for the side of me that appears extremely frivolous; that part of me is always standing in a darkened hallway, mocking tragedy and death. That's why I love champagne and stay at the Ritz."

[*Grobel*]: *In* **Music for Chameleons** *you quoted a line from Henry James: "We live in the dark, we do what we can, the rest is the madness of art." The line impressed you and you later describe yourself sitting alone in your dark madness. How dark and how mad is it?*

[Capote]: What I meant by that was, for instance, in a book like **In Cold Blood**, which took me six years to write, I know a writer has to be alone a good deal of the time and, as I've told you, at one point I spent seven months on a mountain in Switzerland virtually isolated, not seeing anyone, writing or working on that book—and the subject matter and the loneliness led to a definite darkness and terrific apprehension. I've never been so nervous and so agitated. I never slept more than three hours a night for the seven months there.

What was it that led to such agitation? Was it the solving of the problems of the book or was it the reliving of what had happened to Hickock and Smith and the Clutter family?

It's just very difficult to write. It's difficult for anyone to write, but I find it *extremely* difficult. I'd just as soon have not been a writer if I'd had a choice.

But you've never had a choice?

No, not really.

What about your choice of subject matter? Was it the idea of writing about a gruesome murder which attracted you to writing **In Cold Blood**?

I didn't choose that subject because of any great interest in it. It was because I wanted to write what I called a nonfiction novel—a book that would read exactly like a novel except that every word of it would be absolutely true. I had written a book that was like that called **The Muses Are Heard.** It was a short book about Russia and every word of it was true and it reads like a short novel, but I wanted to do it on a grand scale. I had two sort of dry runs with subjects that just turned out not to have enough material in them to do what I wanted to do and finally I settled on this obscure crime in this remote part of Kansas because, I felt, if I followed this from beginning to end it would provide me with the material to really accomplish what was a technical feat. It was a literary experiment where I was choosing a subject not because of a great attraction to the subject, because that was not true, but because it suited my purposes literarily speaking.

Yet, you weren't able to remain detached once you got involved in the story of the murders; did you find yourself being sucked into the story almost against your will?

Yes, because I became so totally involved in it personally that it just took over and consumed my life. All the trials, the appeals, the endless research I had to do—something like eight thousand pages of pure research—and my involvement with the two boys who had committed the crime. Everything. It was a matter of living with something day in and day out. That's why I have no respect for Norman Mailer's book *The Executioner's Song,* which, as far as I'm concerned, is a nonbook. He didn't live through it day by day, he didn't know Utah, he didn't know Gary Gilmore, he never even *met* Gary Gilmore, he didn't do an ounce of research on the book—two other people did all of the research. He was just a rewrite man like you have over at the *Daily News*. I spent six *years* on **In Cold Blood** and not only knew the people I was writing about, I've known them better than I've known *anybody*. So Mailer's book just really *annoyed* me. Can you see why it annoyed me?

Sure, but when you read his book, couldn't you appreciate the fact that he was even able to do it?

No! I was so annoyed by the whole thing about the book. I didn't like the book, I didn't like his attitude about the characters, I didn't like his point of view, I didn't like the writing . . . but most of all, I didn't like the fact he hadn't done it!

Well, it's true he had help with the research, but he did actually write the book. Do you feel that without your book he wouldn't have been able to do his?

No, he never would have. Norman and I were quite good friends until the last year or two. And now I don't feel friendly toward Norman *at all.* He said something to me on a television program to the effect that I had criticized him on his book *The Executioner's Song* as being a copycat. Well, Norman *has* been copying me for years, but it started back with **The Muses Are Heard.** Norman didn't understand my whole feeling about nonfiction narrative writing, he never understood what I was talking about. I remember an extremely violent conversation with him when I was in the middle of writing **In Cold Blood** because he told me it was a failure of the imagination which caused me to have this extreme drive in this direction. I said, "It's exactly the opposite. It's imagination that's causing me to *have* the drive!" But this television thing brought it up. Well, in the introduction in **Music for Chameleons** I said, but very lightly and very jokingly, that I was so glad to be of such help to Norman Mailer. It really was meant as a joke but he brought it up and said that I had said things in interviews about him. I actually never had, up to that point. As a matter of fact, up to *this* point.

Mailer says he feels guilty about saying certain things about you, especially when he was quoted as saying your life was wrecked, not very long ago. He said it was a journalist who led him down that garden path to get a provocative quote.

How do you know that Norman feels guilty about saying those things about me?

He told me. I did an interview with him for cable television. He said that the reason he didn't publicly acknowledge **In Cold Blood** *when he published his book was because he felt that your book was so famous that everyone would know it.*

That's what he said to me on television. That's ridiculous. I mean, I acknowledged the fact that why I wrote **The Muses Are Heard** was because of Lillian Ross's *Picture.* I wanted to see if I did it using all the techniques of a fiction writer, but I certainly mentioned Lillian Ross over and over. Without her, I don't think it really would have occurred to me at that point. It would have occurred to me later because I was doing it all the time, but not on a very large scale. Lillian did a wonderful job. She's a very good reporter, but she's not a very good writer in the sense that we're talking about. She just doesn't have the *lift*—that final, dreadful thing that it takes. There's a moment in writing when it's either going to really lift or it's not.

Is it usually within the first seventy-five pages?

Not necessarily. I read Norman's book *Ancient Evenings* and it never lifted once.

Did you read the whole thing?

Most of it. It never even got off the page anywhere.

He says it's the best writing he's ever done.

I can understand *why* he said that. He feels on the defensive. But he's written far better things than that.

What of his work do you like?

Norman's book that I liked best was *Advertisements for Myself.* There was good writing in it and it was more truthful and honest and more like what's best about him. I never liked his fiction, but I've liked his nonfiction. I thought *Armies of the Night* was quite a good book.

What about his book on Marilyn Monroe?

Oh, that was so ridiculous it isn't worth discussing. I, at least, have the courtesy to ignore what is so obviously insane. Norman sits down to ostensibly write a reasonably short book and he ends up writing *Gone With the Wind* about somebody he never even knew. Marilyn was a great friend of mine and I wrote a piece about her that was really a wonderful piece—**"A Beautiful Child"**—but he never even met Marilyn. It was that same guy [Lawrence Schiller] who put him up to that as put him up to *The Executioner's Song.* Well, I can understand that Norman needs the money, but . . .

(*What Norman Mailer actually said when I told him that Capote said—long before* Ancient Evenings *was published—that* Ancient Evenings *couldn't possibly be a good book because Mailer was only good at writing about what he knew and he didn't know anything about ancient Egypt, any more than he knew about Gary Gilmore or Marilyn Monroe, was: "Well, Truman's very upset about* The Executioner's Song. *He feels that I should have made a pilgrimage and gotten down on my knees and said, 'Oh, great Cardinal Capote, do I have your blessing? May I proceed to write a book about a killer?' And I didn't. He went around saying, 'He never gave any credit to* **In Cold Blood.**' *Well, I just thought that book was so famous that you didn't have to give credit to it. Anyone assumed that I did* The Executioner's Song *having* **In Cold Blood** *in mind. But I reread* **In Cold Blood** *after I finished* The Executioner's Song *and it's a very good novel. It's probably as much of a novel as* The Executioner's Song. *Maybe more. And it's very nicely written. And it may end up being a classic because it is something that is remarkable. But I don't* know what he's talking about, it just sort of struck me as kind of a dumb remark. Truman is canny as hell, but he's not the brightest guy in the world.")

If you ever tackled a long investigative piece like **In Cold Blood** *again, would you follow Mailer's route and hire researchers?*

Never. I think that is so unbelievable.

Malcolm Cowley, among others, took exception to your claim that you had invented the nonfiction novel—pointing out that Henry Adams did this in 1907 when he wrote The Education of Henry Adams *and Hemingway did it with* Green Hills of Africa *in 1935.*

That's not true. I don't know about Henry Adams but I know *Green Hills of Africa,* which is nothing but a kind of autobiographical travel piece. And, in any event, he has himself in it all the time. The great accomplishment of **In Cold Blood** is that I never appear once. There's never an *I* in it at all.

So there's no doubt in your mind that you achieved literary history with that book?

Yes, I did. Just look at the multitude of copycats.

Have any of them surpassed what you've done?

No.

Do any of them get close?

Not that I've read.

You've spoken of the experience of writing **In Cold Blood** *as being too painful, saying nothing was worth it. In retrospect, do you still feel that way?*

Well, I certainly wouldn't do it again. If I knew or had known when I started it what was going to be involved, I never would have started it, regardless of what the end result would have been.

How close did you get to the death-row experiences of Dick Hickock and Perry Smith?

What do you mean, get to it?

To what it was actually like. You were there. You saw the hangings. It affected you. I believe you've said that you vomited from it.

It was the most emotional experience of my creative life, yes.

And of your personal life?

No.

You've talked about their stark and brutal conversations with you—

I don't remember *talking* about it.

Mentioning that they were stark and brutal, anyway. Were you the last person to speak with them?

Yes, I was the *very* last person to speak to them.

Have you ever talked about what they said to you?

Well, they just wished me good-bye. (*Pauses.*) Perry said to me, "Good-bye. I love you and I always have." Perry Smith.

And how did you react to that?

Well, I was standing there at the foot of the gallows. There were about fifty people surrounding me. They couldn't hear what he said to me because he was whispering. I was very upset. . . . But I was upset terrifically about the whole thing. That was just the straw that was a little too heavy.

Did you reciprocate that love in any way? Did you feel you loved either of them, after being so close and intimate with them?

I didn't love either one of them, but I had a great understanding for both of them, and for Perry I had a tremendous amount of sympathy. Dick, I thought, was just a small-time crook who got into water way over his head and was really responsible for this whole murder, which Perry actually committed. But Perry would not have committed it if he hadn't been led on in what the French call a *folie à deux.*

Although they so cold-bloodedly murdered a family of four, you didn't think they should have been killed, did you?

No. I'm very much against capital punishment. But I've seen a number of people executed.

Is it something that you are attracted to see, as a writer?

No, I did it as research. I saw two people executed after Perry and Dick. I was going to write a thing about executions and about my feelings against capital punishment, which I actually never wrote. I've written it in my journal, but I've never done a piece about it.

You've spent a considerable amount of time interviewing killers, haven't you?

Most of the interviews I did during the ten years I went into and out of **In Cold Blood.** Since then I've only done about a hundred and seven interviews. Maybe more. I could kill that Whizzer White for what he did with that man who was being executed in Texas. They put the needle in his arm and darling little Whizzer White was waiting until they were shooting the juice into his arm to bother to telephone and say, "Well, let's just hold this off." I mean, that's just such a terrible level of tragedy. The man has to go through it over again, he should have been left alone. That's one person I really despise, Byron White. I follow the Supreme Court very closely. I began to twenty years ago when I first became so involved in crimes and I began to follow the Supreme Court and their decisions and I have an opinion about every one.

Is there any Justice on the Supreme Court you respect?

The only person at the moment on the Supreme Court whose grave I wouldn't spit on is Brennan. The rest of them, I would spit on their graves. Except the lady. She hasn't been on there long enough—although I have followed her decisions and I don't think she's been too bright.

Sandra O'Connor seems to be a very conservative woman.

Yes. She hasn't done anything that you can make any particular judgment about her. But the person who is a real hypocrite and who is not only *conservative* but is a cruel person is Byron White.

Do you know any of the Supreme Court justices personally?

I guess I've met them all, except I haven't seen any of them in the last five years.

Who would you like to see on the Supreme Court?

I don't know. I'd like to see the whole Supreme Court change.

In what ways?

I think they should have something like the Soviet Politburo.

Isn't that just a bit radical?

I don't believe in the Supreme Court as it is. I don't believe the setup is right. I don't believe that the Supreme Court is large enough.

Should it have twice as many justices?

Yes. At least. It's too small a group handling too much, trying to do more than it's possible for any group of people to do. I know they don't have the time and they have too many cases. If they double the Supreme Court, it doesn't mean that the whole court has to decide each issue. They can be divided. Some cases are obviously so much more important than others. The whole court should decide once and for all on the death penalty, which they keep avoiding and avoiding and avoiding. That whole thing with the death sentence is one of the most serious issues in American life, although it may seem minor, in a way. But it isn't. And the fact that there are twelve hundred and seventy people on death row waiting day and night to know whether they're going to be executed is absolutely outrageous beyond words. Just because the Supreme Court can't make up its mind one way or the other.

If they made up their mind and voted for the death penalty . . .

Then I think they should carry out the executions and stop this torture.

One of the more infamous prisoners you know is Charles Manson. How well do you know him?

I know him, but I don't know him all that well. But I don't want to know him, I hate him.

Didn't you know four of the five people who were killed in the Sharon Tate house?

Yes. Isn't it fabulous?

You don't think, though, that Manson was the mastermind behind that little band of crazies, do you?

No, Bobby Beausoleil was.

You met him in San Quentin prison and he was apparently impressed that you walked freely in the yard. Is it dangerous for you to walk around in prison yards?

I don't feel it is. Prisoners think that it is. Bobby Beausoleil said, "Somebody will kill you just to get their name in the papers."

What about Sirhan Sirhan. You've known him . . .

. . . A long time.

And do you think he should be released?

Oh . . . yes.

Why?

Because he certainly would never kill anybody again. I don't think he should have been in prison in the first place. He should have been in a hospital for treatment for a few years. He's a harmless little toad. I don't have any sympathy for him at all, but I don't think there's any point keeping him in prison. It's just a gesture to do so.

Do you think that Robert Kennedy would have been President if he hadn't been killed?

No. I despised Kennedy.

Besides Sirhan Sirhan, you also knew Lee Harvey Oswald and both Jack and Bobby Kennedy, didn't you?

Yeah, isn't that fabulous?

Are you the only person in the world who can make that connection?

I only know one other person who knew both Jack Kennedy and Lee Harvey Oswald, a girl called Priscilla Johnson, who worked for U.P. in Moscow. That's the only other person in the world that knew both of them.

What is your opinion of Oswald?

Highly neurotic. Certainly crazy. I only saw him twice. I'd say my total encounter with him altogether would add up to about five hours.

Where were your encounters?

In Moscow, just when he defected. I was living in Moscow.

Do you think he acted alone?

Oh, yes.

So, there's no conspiracy in your mind. What about Martin Luther King, Jr.? Again, single killer?

Mm-hmmm. I think it's very strange they're making this legal holiday, because I don't think they know the truth (*laughs*) about Martin Luther King.

And you do?

Well, Martin Luther King had many sides. (*Laughs.*)

There's a devilish twinkle in your eye—what sides do you know about?

Nothing that nobody doesn't know. I think everybody knows.

Do you think he was a great man at all?

Oh, yes, mm-hmmm. I think he's just fine. (*Laughs.*)

Getting back to the men on death row—is a lot of your mail letters from these condemned men?

I guess I get more mail from death-penalty prisoners than anybody. I certainly get an awful lot. There's scarcely a literate person on death row who hasn't written me at one time or another.

Is it always the same? Some kind of plea for help?

They want me to write something about their case.

Are they all innocent, in their minds?

Ah-hah. Or, at least they don't feel that their case has been presented by the media in a true light. Like this John Gacy. Did I tell you about him?

No.

He isn't saying, "I didn't murder the thirty-three people," but that his whole case has been misrepresented to the public, which turns out to be absolutely true. To give you a simple example: the way his case was presented to the public was that he was a sort of child molester who got fourteen-year-old boys and raped and murdered them. Not one word of that is true, not at all. All of his victims were between ages seventeen and twenty-eight and all of them were whores. They were boys who would walk a particular stretch of park in Chicago where cars just circulate around and around picking them out as they choose. And almost every single one of the victims came from that particular thing. He'd just drive his car around until he finally would pick out a boy and take him home and have sex with him and then murder him. Now, the thing that was wrong in the way the media addressed it was you would think he was taking innocent little high-school kids and doing this instead of really tough ones who were being paid twenty-five dollars for whatever it was that they did. But the thing that was strange to me about the case is why—having, in a sense, not committed any kind of crime at all in his sexual relationship—why did he murder them? I mean, it wasn't as though they were what the papers made it sound like.

Did you talk to him? Did you ask him?

I asked him that question and it was the last I heard from him. He didn't want to answer that question.

Wasn't he a man who was struggling with his homosexuality? He would have sex with them but then kill them because he was depressed by it?

I don't think that that was it. I don't know what the answer is.

Couldn't there have been a part of himself that hated what he was doing sexually and so he felt he had to kill that part? Isn't that one reason a killer kills?

Maybe you've got the answer . . . but I think the killing was part of the pleasure. I don't think it came about because of any sense of guilt or retribution. I've talked to many a strangler. They get a curious pleasure out of it, like the awful thing with children who strangle a cat. You know, they get some terrible, awful sensations from it.

Is that the case with all stranglers, you think?

I think definitely with stranglers. Stranglers get a pleasure out of killing.

Isn't that supposedly true with killers who use a knife as well? That they get a great deal of pleasure sticking the knife in?

That's what they say.

It isn't easy sticking a knife in deep enough to kill, is it? You have to really push to get it in.

They say it's very easy, the few people who will talk about it. So few of them are ever willing to talk to you about what they actually do and how they feel. The few that have actually been willing to talk to me about what they feel about knifing, they get a real pleasure from the actual feel of the knife going into the body. For instance, that Jack Abbott, in his book, described this thing of how it felt pushing the knife into somebody, knowing just where to put it under the ribs, seeing the expression on the person's face . . .

Why do murderers almost always laugh when discussing their crimes?

I think they feel a sudden rush of embarrassment. You know, what's called an embarrassed laugh? That's how I would describe it. It comes over them despite whatever their mentality is. They feel suddenly a sense of shame.

You feel that murderers do *feel a sense of shame about their crimes?*

Oh, yes. That's why they find it so difficult to talk about it.

Have you ever wondered why you are able to relate so well to murderers?

Because right away they realized that I wasn't passing any judgment on them. I had no opinion about them as a person regarding the fact that they'd killed or no matter what their crime had been, because I don't.

I know magazines have asked you to write about the multiple murderer. Why haven't you?

I started one particular piece. It was called "Darker Corridors: Opinions on the Mind of the Multiple Murderer." But I'm not sure I'm going to finish it. I certainly have my opinions on the mind of the multiple murderer. I knew over four hundred of them. Everybody has their field. My field is the multiple murderer.

Is there anything they all have in common?

I'm not going to go into that now. There is one thing that eighty percent of them have in common, and it's the only thing I'll tell you. Eighty percent of multiple murderers have tattoos. Interview after interview after interview, the person always turned out to be tattooed, either a little bit or a lot.

So when you see someone with a tattoo, stay away?

You should do that for a lot of reasons. There's something really the matter with most people who wear tattoos. There's at least some terrible story. I know from experience that there's always something terribly flawed about people who are tattooed, above some little something that Johnny had done in the Navy, even though that's a bad sign.

What about the Japanese who are tattooed from head to foot? Is that a whole other thing?

It's terrible. Psychologically it's crazy. Most people who are tattooed, it's the sign of some feeling of inferiority, they're trying to establish some macho identification for themselves.

Have you known many Jewish multiple murderers with tattoos?

They're rarer than most. Not as gangsters, Jewish gangsters are just as prevalent as Italian gangsters.

Did you know that a Jew with a tattoo cannot be buried in a Jewish cemetery?

I didn't know that. (*Pauses, thinking.*) That's fascinating. I'm glad you told me that. I wish I had known that a long time ago.

Do most multiple murderers believe in God, or are they atheists?

They all believe in God.

Do they have a sense of shame or remorse about what they've done?

That's where it's very hard, very difficult, because it's so hard to get them to talk about what they did and what they feel about it. There's the real turning point. I can know a person for years, talk to them any number of times, know every single thing in their lives, about the first time they ever masturbated, and they're not able to rise to the occasion to acknowledge that they really did kill their mother, father, brother, and two sisters.

How long does it take a murderer to feel comfortable enough around you for him to open up to you?

It depends on the person. After I get to know them, usually they like to talk, because they don't have anybody to talk to.

Do they always know who you are?

Oh yes.

Most of them have read **In Cold Blood***?*

Yes, that's how I get the interviews.

How many of them may have read your work before *they killed?*

I don't know. (*Pauses.*) I haven't thought about that.

Robert Siegle (essay date winter 1984)

SOURCE: Siegle, Robert. "Capote's *Handcarved Coffins* and the Nonfiction Novel." *Contemporary Literature* 25, no. 4 (winter 1984): 437-51.

[*In the following essay, Siegle argues that the nonfiction novel is not an oxymoron but a "tautology," and that works of this type take the reader into a "vortex" where both "nonfiction reality and fictional narrative" merge together.*]

The nonfiction novel makes us uneasy by its apparently oxymoronic nature—its mixing of reality and fiction, of journalist and novelist, of factuality and imagination. Uncomfortable with so indiscrete a mixture, many writers on the subject resolve specific works back into either the novel or nonfiction. William L. Nance, for example, speaks of the "flaws" and "limitations . . . inherent in the very concept of a non-fiction novel" and concludes that *In Cold Blood* "falls back into a category which may as well be labeled 'documentary novel.'"[1] In the most extended reflection on the type, Mas'ud Zavarzadeh shifts it in the opposite direction by calling it the "fiction" of the metaphysical void. In the absence of shared, preestablished norms, it maps the surrounding objectal world, without imposing a projected pattern of meaning on the neutral massiveness and amorphous identity of actual people and events. Its response to the confused and contradictory interpretations of reality, which are all the product of an Aristotelian compulsion to explain and label experience at all levels, is to return to noninterpretive, direct contact with actuality.[2]

Zavarzadeh's ideal of objectivity—"direct contact with reality"—may be stated so extremely in order to contrast the type with the two principal alternatives he sees in contemporary fiction, the "liberal-humanist novel" (Bellow, Malamud, Updike), and "transfiction" (Barth, Pynchon, Barthelme), but he nonetheless argues that the "fictual" realm of the nonfiction novel has both the factual authority of reality and the "aesthetic control" of the fictional.[3] One side of the debate approaches the work in terms of its novelistic artistry, the other side in terms of its ability "to circumvent the intervening imposed interpretations and to return to the elementals."[4]

This curious split response can be explained by thinking of the "nonfiction novel" not as an oxymoron, but as a tautology. That is, works of this type bring us not up to a barrier between two distinct regions, nonfictional reality and fictional narrative, but into a vortex in which both kinds of accounts, together with the presumably meta-linguistic commentary upon them, are drawn into the same discursive swirl. Each grounds itself by means of a figurative space, a literary triangle delegating specific zones to each, and allowing each to "cover" its limitations as discourse, as a way of knowing, by deferring elements of the "full picture" to the others—the way science defers matters of the heart to fiction, and fiction defers precise explanations of quantum mechanics to physics. Such a strategy of differentiation seeks to stabilize each kind of discourse by suiting its method to its material. But part of the problem critics seem to have with the nonfiction novel is that nothing new or unique emerges from the "synthesis" of these supposedly distinct zones—not because it "falls back" into one or the other familiar kind, but because these kinds turn out to have been the same. Different methods all turn out to be varying conventions for framing, proportioning, and selecting from the same basic cultural myth of reality.[5] If such material is as much fiction as "reality," and if "method" is mainly convention—that is, fiction—then even the distinction of method and material turns out to be a version of the basic cultural logic from which all these illusory oppositions derive. They are, in other words, diacritical rather than independent variables.[6]

This redundancy in the nonfiction novel is the key to sorting out the anomalies readers find in it, and to look at Truman Capote's **Handcarved Coffins**—a brief and thus convenient piece for illustration—is to see how immediately useful this approach can be. In the preface to **Music for Chameleons,** the volume in which the story appears, Capote calls the book a "nonfiction short novel," and thus launches from outside the discourse of the narrative a presumably authoritative commentary upon it.[7] The rest of the document explains Capote's period of disorder after enraging critics with the publication of chapters from **Answered Prayers** in *Esquire.* Feeling himself "in a helluva lot of trouble," "suffering a creative crisis and a personal one at the same time," moving through a period of "creative chaos" that was "torment," Capote tells us he came to a new understanding "of the difference between what is true and what is *really* true" (p. xvi). The nonfiction novel, then, is the means of answering on both the personal and professional levels what amounts to the fundamental hermeneutical question, and **Handcarved Coffins** accordingly reproduces the hermeneutic investigator in the form of the sleuth and his scribe endeavoring to discover the truth and put it in writing.

This effort to establish the *"really* true" is the root of all cultural fictions. But as truth is a difficult goal at best, we had best return to Capote's preface to discover why and how he feels able to achieve it. There are curious aspects to the two basic ideas he advances at this point. Capote apparently considers the crisis in his writing as an unsatisfactory ratio between "the powers at my command" and "the total potential" of "all the energy and esthetic excitements that material contained" (p. xvii). If Nietzsche is right that "powers" are versions of a will to mastery over the materials of one's experience, then this passage presents the dramatic confrontation of order with the "energy" and "excitements" of its counterpart, the chaos of the material before the writer brings out of it the "total potential" of its truth. The dream of "total potential" or plenitude is not reached, however; for some reason the resources of writing cannot triumph totally over the recalcitrance of its material. We may at this point at least speculate as to why: if fiction and nonfiction, or perhaps even method and material, are no different, then such a triumph is impossible. It is like the dream of sign and referent merging, text and world, desire and fulfillment.

Capote remains buoyant, however. He exudes the ecstasy of desire for such a crossing, and bubbles with metaphors that command our attention. The "apparently unsolvable problem" he poses is this:

> how can a writer successfully combine within a single form—say the short story—all he knows about every other form of writing? For this was why my work was often insufficiently illuminated; the voltage was there, but by restricting myself to the techniques of whatever form I was working in, I was not using everything I knew about writing—all I'd learned from film scripts, reportage, poetry, the short story, novellas, the novel. A writer ought to have all his colors, all his abilities available on the same palette for mingling (and, in suitable instances, simultaneous application).
>
> (p. xvii)

It is no wonder that the work he returns to is **Answered Prayers,** for this wish amounts to the theological conception of fulfilling the inner truth of the spirit. Capote seeks to make his practice of writing as comprehensive as possible, absorbing into this application all the forms he has known, as if sheer range of generic conventions and techniques would achieve his dream of plenitude. The "voltage was there," it seems, although one cannot tell whether the voltage derives from the material as an inner truth to be brought out, or from Capote's earnestness despite his self-restrictions in technique. Perhaps it is enough to see, however, that the voltage raging through the material left the work "insufficiently illuminated," darkened in its partial order. If, somehow, an additional intensity of the light of order could be brought to bear upon the material, it would shine brightly with its "total potential." The truth is there; it needs illumination.

But strangely enough, as the paragraph moves towards Capote's own enlightenment, the metaphoric configuration shifts, and what the writer needs is not more light, but all his "colors" on "the same palette." His techniques now are an impasto smeared upon the canvas, covering what is there in order to portray on one surface the illusion of what exists elsewhere. Here the truth is no longer within, an actual order to be illuminated, but a virtual order to be created, fictionalized, in a medium unmistakably alien to the material it pictures. The first of these images suggests a metaphysical ontology of truth, the second a rhetoric of figuration which obviously can at best only approximate, only disfigure, the subject. It clearly marks its difference from that subject, and indeed is what it is because of that difference. We are back, in other words, to the two views of writing with which we began—as a direct rendering of the actual entities whose inner truths we must reveal, or as virtual points in a fictional matrix. The novel itself suggests ways of thinking through the relation between the two as diacritical conventions of the basic interpretive activity of culture.

The extent to which narrative practice in the novel shows interpretive interests at work on the "nonfiction" material can be seen in a number of ways that echo the previously cited work of Nance, De Bellis, and Tompkins on **In Cold Blood.** Jake, a detective and a friend of Capote's, is one narrator worth comment. He selects the case for the character "TC" as "something that he thought might interest" a novelist (p. 68), and he draws on his own literary tastes (Dickens, Trollope, Melville, and Twain are mentioned) to present matters to TC. One sees a number of instances of this literary framing of the event. Jake literally reads from fiction to explain Quinn, he paces the timing of information for maximum effect, and he allows metaphor to introduce figurative displacement into a supposedly denotative case history in criminology (as when his chief is "jittery as a killer on Death Row," an interesting mixing of contraries). Perhaps he has no choice but to perceive events in terms of Dickens's search for hidden connections, people in terms of characters in nineteenth-century novels, referential "facts" in terms of metaphorical figures—nonfiction in terms of fiction.

As for the larger topic of TC's narrative practice, one's first observation is that he plays well the role of "narratee" for Jake. For example, when Jake tells him of the rattlesnake murders, TC plays the role of ideal reader, co-creating in his imagination the scene Jake outlines:

> But the sound of the wind was only a murmur in my head underneath the racket of rattling rattlesnakes, hissing tongues. I saw the car dark under a hot sun, the swirling serpents, the human heads growing green, expanding with poison. I listened to the wind, letting it wipe the scene away.
>
> (p. 70)

Besides being a prime example of Capote's skill at description, the passage shows TC's willingness to go beyond the factual to imagine how it has come to be. A fictional narrative line is projected back of the "facts" of corpses to explain them, a quite mythic origin posited that in its fictiveness reiterates the book's qualification of any naïve understanding of its method, or that of detection, interpretation, or nonfiction. It also, of course, shapes the responses of TC's own readers—of us, that is—as he does later when he marvels at the "mathematical element" in Clem Anderson's decapitation (p. 76), or when he underlines the suspense in Jake's tale of Addie ("You mean you're going to leave me hanging out here?" [p. 83]).

Lest we neglect our hermeneutic responsibilities, TC prods us from time to time by rendering facts as clues: "There were nine snakes. And nine members of the Blue River Committee. Nice quaint coincidence" (p. 97). By playing narratee so well, TC plots out within his novel the "real" readers' responses. In other words, those supposedly external to the narrative find themselves already anticipated there inside the text. One hears in the distance Roland Barthes collapsing the distinction between reader and text, but more conservatively, for the moment, we may note that TC exploits fully, as Capote's preface promises, the resources of fictional narratees in his nonfiction work.

TC exploits fictional narrators too, as it turns out. He paces his story as much like the omniscient novelist as Jake does; he finally remembers at one point of whom Quinn reminds him, but won't tell us until the time is ripe (p. 110). And he makes good use of Dickensian dreams; he speaks of "Addie: her hair, tangled in watery undergrowths, drifted, in my dream, across her wavering drowned face like a bridal veil" (p. 127), anything but an innocent metaphor. An even more intense example of the classic dream device occurs earlier in the narrative:

> Oddly, sleep struck me as though I'd been hit by a thief's blackjack . . . I entered some sphere between sleep and wakefulness, my mind like a crystal lozenge, a suspended instrument that caught the reflections of spiraling images: a man's head among leaves, the windows of a car streaked with venom, the eyes of serpents sliding through heat-mist, fire flowing from the earth, scorched fists pounding at a cellar door, taut wire gleaming in the twilight, a torso on a roadway, a head among leaves, fire, fire, fire flowing like a river, river, river. Then a telephone rings.
>
> (p. 84)

At first glance this seems only a marvelously evocative passage that collects for the reader the various murders that have taken place. But the least bit of attention to its figures finds more of interest as well. The puzzle of reality, represented in the novel as crime, seems to have become pervasive, as TC cannot even nap without theft and assault giving shape to his sleep. Moreover, the "spheres" that normally exhaust the alternatives are here split by another, nameless sphere in which he finds himself.

Perhaps more interesting than the cosmology is what takes place there. His mind becomes "a crystal lozenge" that "caught the reflections" of the images he lists. The very materiality of his mental theater is an interesting anachronism for our age, but its epistemological implications may be even more so. That is, the lozenge is "crystal" or clear, and the images are "reflections" of something external to that mind, since crystals reflect particularly those images "spiraling" around the crystal. But if Jake has indeed not described, but TC imagined, the details, as we saw a moment ago, then these cannot be external images at all. And if they are made by TC, then he is hardly the neutral, objective, crystal clear window upon them, but rather the opaque colorist or producer of them. The super-realist, the nonfiction journalist reporting on "the way it was," might indeed aspire to the method of the crystal lozenge, but it seems oddly out of place here. Ah—one remembers, this is a dream, Capote only dreams of himself as the objective, nonfiction reporter. If nonfiction is thus the dream element of the narrative, that is to say of the fictional element, does that make the fictional element *more* real, deriving as it does from the flow of actual fictional narratives in culture? The interchange of contraries remains confusing, as in this passage when fire and water are equivalent. Fortunately for the analyst, "the telephone rings," giving us a line out of a literary device that absorbs pretensions to the non-literary, nonverbal, and nonfictional into its own dream structure.

What he finds "outside" the dream-set is not necessarily reassuring, however. Apparently casual allusions turn out to be not at all innocent. Early in the narrative, for example, while TC is watching Addie and Jake together, the allusions are to mannerists like Edith Wharton (p. 87) and Jane Austen (p. 94). By the time the mystery heats up, the allusions are to the likes of Eric Ambler (p. 105). After TC has left the scene for a while, another phone call takes him back—and, appropriately enough, it is Proust he reads (p. 120), the prime retrospective interpretive narrative that, as TC notes, is "rather like plunging into a tidal wave, destination unknown" (p. 120). The catastrophic imagery is justified, since Addie's life is swept away and, consistent with the imagery, by drowning. In other words, apparently inert allusions, always "justified" by the "realistic" context that cues them, are in fact a narrative line of literary frames that provide the appropriate sort of context within which to see these events taking place. To see them take place in such a context is not only to see them already interpreted in accordance with those frames, but to have one's responses plotted within the narrative by an all-but-omniscient narrator who exploits his knowledge of the materials, placing our responses in the sequence best suited to increasing their narrative impact upon us.

The imagery of the novel is no more crystalline in its treatment of fiction and nonfiction. In playing up the romance developing between Jake and Addie, a sort of sentimental subplot in this multi-plotted novel, TC deploys some curious images. He says, for example, that "the style of the woman implied an erotic history complete with footnotes," a remarkably textual metaphor implying that either TC's perceptual framework or Addie's self-creation—or both—complies with specific narrative conventions. In the next sentence TC says that "the tension between them was as taut as the steel wire that had severed Clem Anderson's head" (pp. 86-87), a grotesque image conflating the desires of murder and sex, and prophetic of the consequences of the relationship fatal to both, though to Jake only metaphorically. Both metaphors invade reportage of objective facts with the interpretive figures of fiction.

The extent to which a mode of understanding preconstructs observation shows in passages like that in which TC notices Jake blowing smoke rings and decides that "the empty oval, floating through the air, seemed to carry with it an erotic message" (p. 89). Perhaps as another type of crystal lozenge this "empty oval" may be filled with whatever plot the narrator constructs, but it is clearly less a transparent window or neutral reflection than a flamboyant splash of rhetorical color upon the page. It is as heavy-handed as TC's parenthetical break away from Jake's vow to protect Addie to a scene he dreams up of wintry clumps of grass and "two spotted calves huddled side by side, lending each other comfort, protection: like Jake, like Addie" (pp. 107-8). Knowing when winter calves are sent to slaughter strengthens the reader's expectations that, come summer, Addie must die: after all, we have learned as well as Jake from Dickens and Trollope that plot resolutions conform to the miniature narrative epitomized in foregrounded imagery. It appears that when Capote combines the denotative language of journalism with the figurative language of fiction, he (inadvertently?) ends up clarifying how figures work in any discourse to betray the interpretive plots that writers-as-narrators impose upon whatever type of experience they set out to inscribe within their respective discursive orders. Baldly put, language as figure points to discourse as fiction.

To turn to the substance of TC's relation to the mystery late in the novel is to see how such confusions come to fruition. Good novel reader that he is, TC keeps looking for the univocal "key" to Quinn-as-character, finding it finally—or perhaps constructing it finally—by identifying him with a character in his own private psychodrama, the traumatically austere Reverend Snow. Perhaps it is worth pointing out that snow is another crystal lozenge allowing the narrative projectionist full freedom. On the basis of this identification, TC finds Quinn guilty, seeing him as a sufficiently self-righteous monomaniac to perpetrate the crimes. He even constructs the scenario for us; he is again not quite sleeping, and tells us that "Images formed, faded; it was as though I were mentally editing a motion picture" (p. 129). We might take him to be simply an earnest editor of images that form themselves or are otherwise external if we had not already been disabused of such a naïve sense of the narrative act. What we are in fact doing is watching TC fit the images *he* has imagined to the criteria for causal coherence, character consistency, and the like that he inherits from the genre of film and, by extension, from the history of philosophical assumptions presupposed by that genre.

For a full page, TC elaborates his feature-length dream of the way it was, but then after daybreak had "lessened my enthusiasm for fevered fantasizing," concludes that "unless Jake had evolved a theory more convincing than my own imagination had managed, then I preferred to forget it; I was satisfied to fall asleep remembering the coroner's common-sense verdict: *Accidental death by drowning*" (p. 130). Having followed through the dream version Jake cues him to, TC finds it wavering in the illumination of daybreak, the light of common sense—that journalistic look at just the facts that presumably dispenses with imaginative reconstruction. A few pages later, however, he is angry to discover that his "fevered fantasizing" "*is* Jake's story," according to a colleague of Jake's, "give or take a lotta little details" (p. 132). TC is "angry at him [Jake] for not having produced a solid solution, crestfallen that his conjectures were no better than mine." Strangely enough, the narratives constructed by detective and novelist coincide, the plot lines of nonfiction and fiction cross. Movie editor, novelist, reporter, sleuth, metalinguistic hermeneutic theorist—they are all the same, it would seem.

The novel presses even further, however, in the way in which it subtly allies and even confounds the discourse of interpretive narrative with those of madness and religion. The figure of madness appears in a number of forms, some of them quite bizarre. Mrs. Parsons, for example, is a morphine addict whom Jake describes as "a woman who has already left life. She's looking back through a door—without regret" (p. 78). But she is nonetheless important to Jake because on first seeing the little coffin her husband receives, and without knowing of its presence in the other cases, she feels "a shadow" fall across their lives, and knows he has been murdered despite the lack of any evidence to that effect. That is, although a morphine-crazed recluse, she duplicates Jake's reasoning and conclusion.

This connection might seem far-fetched were there not other and closer ties established between the writer/detective and the madman. Juanita Quinn is another strange case with hair "too black to be true," a "narrow skull" with a face "like a fist" featuring "bored onyx eyes" (p. 112). More strange than her appearance is her drugged behavior; she sits regally in a chair that "may well have once decorated the throne room of an Iberian castle" (p. 111), with a shivering Chihuahua and a guitar on her lap, watching a TV game show with the volume turned down: she is difficult to distract. But her case gets more curious when she explains herself to TC:

> You asked why I have the sound off. The only time I have the sound on is to hear the weather report. Otherwise, I just watch and imagine what's being said. If I actually listen, it puts me right to sleep. But just imagining keeps me awake. And I have to stay awake—at least till midnight. Otherwise, I'd never get any sleep at all. Where do you live?
>
> (p. 113)

She, like TC, struggles in a confusing zone between sleeping and waking, she too has her trials with the night, and she too busies herself "imagining" plots in order to keep the demons at bay.

If we look at TC himself, we find not only these general parallels to Juanita's patterns, but passages like this one that more specifically ally him to the figure of madness:

> Anxiety, as any expensive psychiatrist will tell you, is caused by depression; but depression, as the same psychiatrist will inform you on a second visit and for an additional fee, is caused by anxiety. I rotated around in that humdrum circle all afternoon. By nightfall the two demons had combined; while anxiety copulated with depression, I sat staring at Mr. Bell's controversial invention, fearing the moment when I would have to dial the Prairie Motel and hear Jake admit that the Bureau was taking him off the case.
>
> (p. 133)

As it turns out, his plot no more fits the silent technology he stares at than Juanita's—Jake is not off the case, at least not yet. But in following the pattern he shares with Juanita of giving voice to the silent machine, a pattern peculiarly appropriate to the writer, he enacts the epistemological model in which one "explains" a silent truth supposedly within the material, voicing the presence of what had been only partly apparent before. But he also enacts the recurrent confusion of that model when its verbal account turns out to differ from the merely visible, nonverbal order we call "facts." He attempts, in other words, to reflect like a crystal lozenge though in fact he is painting like an ardent colorist. Moreover, he is doing all this within the context of neurosis, the low level rage of anxiety and its quiet intransigence as depression, each of which are to be "explained" by the other in a typically circular hermeneutic. It is only in these strange fringe states that he can give form to the material, it would seem, but the form derives not from within the material or even necessarily within him, but from the cultural imagination, which transpires in a mental space outlawed by the categorizing order of reason.

Perhaps Capote is simply being inconsistent in repeatedly conflating such contraries, but perhaps also the text demonstrates that the difference between them is illusory, a rhetorical strategy to make way for creativity. In keeping with this recurrent theme, the novel also places religion within the same philosophical template. Jake seems almost serious in attributing his continuation on the case to an answered prayer (p. 82), suggesting that a hermeneutic of prayer (the "help me?" answered by Addie) is at times an essential detail within the detective's picture. TC adds another analogical element to the religious and the detective hermeneutics when he, as writer, makes use of the connection between Quinn and the Reverend Snow to decide upon his characterization of Quinn. Dragged as a boy into the river during a revival, TC tells us that

> I shut my eyes; I smelled the Jesus hair, felt the Reverend's arms carrying me downward into drowning blackness, then hours later lifting me into sunlight. My eyes, opening, looked into his grey, manic eyes. His face, broad but gaunt, moved closer, and he kissed my lips. I heard a loud laugh, an eruption like gunfire: "Checkmate!"
>
> (p. 118)

The passage is like a Church Homecoming for our critical themes: blackness and sunlight as the two extremes, the strange grey zone where stable qualities like time become distorted, the fusion of the religious order and the "manic" rage, the identification of preacher and (presumed) murderer, the seepage of raging metaphoric gunfire into a "friendly" game of chess. The transubstantiation of Jesus, Reverend Snow, and Quinn is an example of a basic movement of logocentric logic, the however temporary effacement of difference in order to produce identity out of mere similarity, just as TC here effaces the distinctions among the three and transfers from Snow to Quinn the messianic ego. The point is not whether the process achieves a working insight, but that figurative displacement is its basis.

This would seem, however, to produce a problem for us. Up to this point we have been undoing the false dichotomy of fiction and nonfiction, created as a space-making strategy by which they can take place, and can take the place of the unnamable, dreamlike, inconsistently imaged state wherein they seem to originate. Now, it seems, there is a simultaneous countermovement in which the culture is accused of assimilating different entities into (deceptive) identities. How does one explain this? Perhaps by first seeing that it is not an isolated occurrence, that Capote apparently felt it an important enough gesture to repeat it, and in fact to let it stand as the end of his multiple hermeneutic venture—as sleuth, as novelist, as nonfiction chronicler, and as personally involved inquirer.

In a last, powerful scene, TC goes back to the Blue River after Addie's death and Jake's departure from the case. Drawn to Quinn as the center of the question—the party he must imagine guilty without knowing for sure—TC comes to him, appropriately enough, while Quinn is wading in the river itself. Quinn laments that Jake had too many suspicions for them to have become friends, and that

> "he even thought I drowned poor Addie Mason!" He laughed; then scowled. "The way I look at it is: it was the hand of God." He raised his own hand, and the river, viewed between his spread fingers, seemed to weave between them like a dark ribbon. "God's work. His will."
>
> (p. 147)

He invokes the novel's version of the hermeneutic issue (whodunit?), and then in a manner more straightforward than that of other figures of the novel, makes explicit that what follows is *not* the way it is, but the "way I look at it." A narrator who affirms that his product is a fictive framework, a commentator upon nonfictional "realities," a monomaniac assuming cosmic knowledge, a possible murderer who may have chosen to appear before TC in the rubber suit that would provide the missing "how?" to TC's account of a death in those same waters, a religious believer who assigns causality to providence, Quinn here subsumes all the roles distributed throughout the novel to others. He becomes, were this one of Propp's folktales, all roles and functions. He even embodies in one sense the voice of TC, the actual narrator, for the river is a "dark ribbon," dark with the sinister themes of mass murder and hyperrational madness, and is figuratively woven as an implement in *his* fingers. It is a type of the writer's pen leaking its black flow of ink, and the final words of TC's narrative are the Answer Quinn proposes. It is an appropriately theological answer: God's work, the Word embodied in fact.

A madman utters the culture's central, commanding image for order: all cases, all differences, resolve themselves in the Word. Does it then require madness of a kind to affirm and maintain such an order, the order assumed by the kind of hermeneutic search that is reflected in this novel from the central cultural tradition? One notes the steady increase in TC's depressive anxieties and Jake's mania for evidence, ever more intense the longer circumstances resist reduction to the univocal question their inquiry poses; one begins as a result to doubt their binary logic of madness and order, guilt and innocence, fiction and nonfiction, figure and fact. Quinn thus becomes a figure that threatens the very ground rules of the project's nonfiction dimension, for he handles the ancillary discourses as all the same kind of (fictional) ordering, and collapses them into a self-mystifying narrative delusion.

Hence one must turn back to the text itself, to the preface to the text, and recognize the implications for our thinking about literary genres. What Capote set out to do was to discover the "*really* true," and he set out with the classic logocentric dichotomies of fiction and nonfiction—that is to say, figurative and literal or referential language—with its attendant tools of inside-outside divisions and the hierarchical rankings of the two. Capote seems to have sought to bring the reality outside fiction into its inside, and thus make it more real; or, alternatively, he wanted to bring the fiction outside reality into the nonfiction, to increase its "energy and esthetic excitements," as he put it in the preface. As these dichotomies fold in on one another, we discover not the naïve realist's belief that fiction is adequate to reality, but the contrary, that nonfiction is never adequate to reality, that its distinction from fiction is one of the primary deceptive maneuvers of logocentric logic by which it hypothesizes the space in which it transpires. The "nonfiction novel" is thus a tautology, not an oxymoron.

Moreover, by talking of the "*really* true," Capote seems to have raised again the notion that truth is the indwelling meaning of events or entities themselves, and that the nonfictional discourses to which he resorts will give him privileged access: logical deduction solves the hermeneutic crisis. What we find, in fact, is a great deal of disorientation on TC's part as he tries to carry out this program. We see him deploying all manner of interpretive frames—both the fictional devices of allusion, figurative language, generic conventions, and the nonfictional devices of the assumptions implicit in these ancillary discourses. The "really true" inheres in the discursive order of intelligibility. It is outside the events, in the narrative covering them with the writer's colors, not in them; or, alternatively, it is not inside the "faithful" narrative version of events, but outside that order in the assumptions implicit in the language and the discursive conventions from which and by which and in which that narrative is cast. Either way, Capote's "invention" of the nonfiction novel is both hoax and ingenious gathering of the full cultural resources into the act of narration, even if those resources have always been in fiction, if in slightly different guises, just as the fictional has always been there in alternative cultural discourses.

When Capote tells us that, after his conceptual breakthrough, "I set myself center stage, and reconstructed" experiences in his writing (p. xviii), he goes back to the necessarily egoistic positing of the frameworks within which those experiences are seen to take place. It doesn't matter whether such fictions are generated by creating binary myths to divide—and conquer—reality, or by assimilating that multifarious reality into an all but monomaniacal logocentric ego. The point in either case, as a tactician might put it, is to deploy your forces so that things begin happening.

Notes

1. *The Worlds of Truman Capote* (New York: Stein and Day, 1970), pp. 184, 178. Most commentaries on the novel follow Nance's lead, perhaps most explicitly John Hollowell in his *Fact & Fiction: The New Journalism and the Nonfiction Novel* (Chapel Hill: Univ. of North Carolina Press, 1977). Hollowell quotes Nance and Meyer Levin's definition of the "documentary novel" with approval. Jack De Bellis surveys some five thousand revisions Capote worked into the novel between its serialized and book forms, concluding that its factual accuracy is questionable and apparently subordinated to the subliminal goal of working out, novelistically, Capote's complex relationship to the South and to "the dual vision of his fiction" it gave him (p. 535), and he alludes to an earlier criticism of the novel's factual reliability by Phillip K. Tompkins in an article in *Esquire*. The De Bellis essay is "Visions and Revisions: Truman Capote's *In Cold Blood*", *Journal of Modern Literature*, 7 (1979), 519-36. Helen S. Garson talks of the way the novel is "mingling realism with novelistic imagination" (p. 143), an opposition that shows how completely within the fictional field she considers the type (in *Truman Capote* [New York: Frederick Ungar, 1980]). Kenneth T. Reed shows anxiety closer to the surface in emphasizing the "reordering and proportioning" of the orchestration but in seeing also no "distortion of fact" (in *Truman Capote* [Boston: Twayne Publishers, 1981], p. 112). See too Ronald Weber's *The Literature of Fact: Literary Nonfiction in American Writing* (Athens: Ohio Univ. Press, 1980); Weber admires the extent to which Capote draws us "into a world of meaning and inner coherence" (p. 73), "while remaining strictly within the historical record" (p. 80), a judgment perhaps too indulgent.

2. Mas'ud Zavarzadeh, *The Mythopoeic Reality: The Postwar American Nonfiction Novel* (Urbana: Univ. of Illinois Press, 1976), p. 68.

3. Alfred Kazin, in *Bright Book of Life: American Novelists and Storytellers from Hemingway to Mailer* (Notre Dame: Univ. of Notre Dame Press, 1980 [1973]), makes the same shift from quite a different perspective, summing up *In Cold Blood* as "a 'novel' in the form of fact" (p. 210). Both writers, in other words, feel the need for quotation marks around the same half of the nonfiction novel. Kazin, however, is more what Zavarzadeh would call a "liberal-humanist," with his concern for the tension between "our participation in the story [being] more narrow and helpless than [in] a real novel" (p. 218) and the book's aim "to give us this mental control over the frightening example of what is most uncontrolled in human nature" (p. 216). The trouble with the genre for Kazin is that the preoccupation with senseless crime "relieves the liberal imagination of responsibility and keeps it a spectator" (p. 219) of reality, rather than achieving what Zavarzadeh disparages as the "totalizing" goals of "liberal-humanist" fiction.

4. Zavarzadeh, p. 68.

5. Perhaps a work like Derrida's *Writing and Difference* (trans. Alan Bass [Chicago: Univ. of Chicago Press, 1978]) is the most notorious demonstration of a basic cultural myth he calls "logocentrism" in a whole galaxy of discourses including mysticism, sociology, psychology, linguistics, anthropology, and so forth. But see also Wilson Snipes, "The Biographer as a Center of Reference," *biography* 5, No. 3 (1982), 215-25, for a study of that nonfictional genre as a version of the way relativity figures in history as well as in physics. One may think also of Thomas Kuhn's *The Structure of Scientific Revolutions* (2nd ed. [Chicago: Univ. of Chicago Press, 1970]) as a study of a kind of cul-

tural fiction he calls "paradigms," imaginative orderings of the universe which shape even science, that bastion of supposedly objective nonfiction.

6. John Hellmann comes closer to this position than any commentator I know, in *Fables of Fact: The New Journalism as New Fiction* (Urbana: Univ. of Illinois Press, 1981). He argues the distinction between new journalism (and the nonfiction novel) and other forms of fiction as that between the contracts they establish with the reader: the latter "points outward toward the actual world without ever deviating from observations of that world except in forms—such as authorial speculation or fantasy—which are immediately obvious as such to the reader" (p. 27). As in all fiction, the focus is upon "a microcosmic selection, shaping, and interpretation of events of the macrocosm into a text, a construct representing not events, but an individual consciousness's experience of them" (pp. 25-26). Hellmann is acutely alert to the illusoriness of any direct, unmediated perception of actual events, pointing out that even an historical character like Hubert Humphrey "that the reader knows outside his experience of a text is an interpretively selected and ordered construct of impressions, as is the author's, whether arrived at through first-hand knowledge or (more typically) already interpreted as received from the mass media" (p. 31). But Hellmann is probably more inclined than I to accept that there is something called "external facts" with which a writer can begin. In actual practice, such "facts" are inevitably textual episodes from the moment they form in one's consciousness.

7. The quotations from the preface and the novel come from the paperback edition (New York: New American Library, 1981) and are noted parenthetically.

David Galloway (essay date 1986)

SOURCE: Galloway, David. "Real Toads in Real Gardens: Reflections on the Art of Non-Fiction Fiction and the Legacy of Truman Capote." In *The Critical Response to Truman Capote*, edited by Joseph J. Waldmeir and John C. Waldmeir, pp. 143-54. Westport, Conn.: Greenwood Press, 1999.

[*In the following essay, originally published in 1986, Galloway discusses Capote's contribution to the nonfiction novel, praising the author's use of techniques from fiction to create a more immediate reality than straight narrative reporting could accomplish in* In Cold Blood.]

Two decades have passed since Truman Capote electrified *New Yorker* readers in the fall of 1965 with his account of the brutal and senseless murder of a Kansas farm family. Even before its official release the following spring, the hardcover version of *In Cold Blood* had soared to the top of bestseller lists, and translation rights were being auctioned off to the highest bidder. The writer himself, never shy of the media, became a familiar face on late-night talk-shows, together with his contentious contemporaries Norman Mailer and Gore Vidal. The author as pop-culture commodity was a new phenomenon for Americans; even Scott and Zelda Fitzgerald, at the peak of their photogenic zaniness, could not have dreamed of such celebrity. The much-publicized loss of Capote's private address book sent a seismic tremor through the upper social registers on both sides of the Atlantic. The self-proclaimed "nonfiction novelist," furthermore, was as likely to provide headlines for literary quarterlies and high-brow newspapers as for gossip-columns and decorating magazines.

For many critics schooled in the Great Tradition, stardom and seriousness were an incompatible combination. In a pragmatic, materialistic society, the true artist's fate was callous rejection (as in Hawthorne's "The Artist of the Beautiful"), posthumous acclaim (Melville and Poe), the dissipation of creative energies (Fitzgerald, Hemingway, Miller), self-destruction (Poe, Fitzgerald, Wolfe, Hemingway, Kerouac). In time, of course, Capote would richly fulfill the latter two criteria, but in 1966 he rode the crest of an improbable wave. Unlike the narrative junk-food of Grace Metalious or Jacqueline Susann, his writings had been praised as "minor classics." Recognition came early, with the publication of *Other Voices, Other Rooms* in 1948, though the image it projected of a Wilde-Huysmans decadent owed as much to the Cecil Beaton portrait on the cover as it did to the novel's sultry and sensuous tone. Another short novel, a play, a short-story collection and the novella *Breakfast at Tiffany's* (1958) consolidated the image, and critics waited impatiently for the major work that would confirm the promise of a decade's graceful achievements.

When that work appeared, many academic critics expressed outrage over the author's presumptuousness in describing *In Cold Blood* as a "Nonfiction Novel" and subtitling it "A True Account of a Multiple Murder." The blatant contradictions of the title-page provoked Kenneth Tynan to vent his rage week after week and across page after page of the London *Observer*. He disputed the "truth" of Capote's account, the hybrid genre in which it was composed, and the author's own moral cowardice in not fighting for the reprieve of the convicted murderers. By implication, the novelist required their execution for a dramatic climax to his story of crime and punishment. Capote was not, in principle, opposed to capital punishment, and he had no doubt of the guilt of Perry Smith and Eugene Hickock. The only hope for commuting their sentence from the death penalty to life in prison rested entirely on psychiatric testimony which the novelist—however great his insights into the troubled minds of the killers—was not qualified to give. He might, of course, have used his influence to organize an additional defense fund, to press for retrial, to raise the larger question of whether a society has the right to destroy "monsters" of its own creation or an obligation to rehabilitate them. (Fellow nonfiction novelist Norman Mailer would later initiate such a campaign, with tragic results.)

Capote chose, instead, to adapt the classic novelistic stance of observing consciousness; unlike Norman Mailer in *The Armies of the Night* or *Of a Fire on the Moon* he does not even appear as a narrative persona in his own work. However we read the moral implications of the author's detachment, **In Cold Blood** plainly contributed to a shift in public opinion that led to the temporary abolishment of the death penalty in the United States. Kenneth Tynan's charge that Capote exploited the anti-heroes of his book is best settled by the novelist's future biographers. The assertion that he consciously tampered with truth to add color and suspense to the story has already been verified,[1] though the discrepancies might be described as peripheral rather than substantive. Fine-combing the text for "falsehoods" is a variation on Tynan's more general (and more serious) question of artistic ethics. The formal controversy, which stirred tempests in so many fragile academic teacups, is another matter entirely, for it presupposed that fiction and fact were congenitally antagonistic. How, traditional readers asked, could a work be simultaneously "true" (as the author claimed) and novelistic? Yet those same readers had accepted without so much as an intellectual gulp the traditional disclaimer that libel-wary publishers once automatically included behind the title page of a novel. The familiar formula appears, even, in James Jones's *Go to the Widowmaker*, published like **In Cold Blood** in 1966: "This novel is a work of fiction, and any resemblance to real people, living or dead, is completely coincidental, and totally outside the author's intention."[2]

Regardless of the writer's avowals or disavowals, one of the greatest and most frequent compliments that the average reader of fiction pays to a work is that its characters "seem so real"—i.e., so much like living, breathing, flesh-and-bone mortals. Negatively formulated, the response becomes "I couldn't identify with X or Y" or "I didn't believe in the character." Whatever else it attempts, the sense of a felt reality remains one of the novel's greatest strengths—whether the reality of a desert island, a whaling ship, a battlefield, a dinner-party, or a voyage to the heart of darkness. Even the later works of Samuel Beckett cannot entirely banish the note of "resemblance." One can, of course, tamper with it—ghoulishly, fantastically, absurdly and metafictionally, but without the sense of a "real" counterpart, the variation itself—whether hissing Hydra or glaring Cyclops—is meaningless. For James Jones himself, verisimilitude was always a novelistic prerequisite, and his professed "intention" thus seems far more preposterous than Capote's insistence on dubbing his own work a "nonfiction novel." The latter term, however, had to contend with a Puritan inheritance that equated fiction with lying, together with genre classifications firmly ratified by George Orwell's "Geneva conventions of the mind."

For five years Capote researched the apparently motiveless murders of four members of the Clutter family on a farm near Holcomb, Kansas. Observing that a tape-recorder often inhibited interview subjects, he trained himself to recall lengthy passages from books read aloud to him by a friend. As the facts emerged, they assumed metaphorical patterns of their own: the scene of the crime, near a suburb of Garden City, was situated at the geographical center of the United States; the Clutters seemed, at first glance, an apple-pie embodiment of the American Dream; the killers were the classic victims of a success-oriented society. Underprivileged, dispossessed, resentful of those who had achieved their dreams, Perry Smith and Eugene Hickock struck out at a world from which they felt unjustly excluded—like the sensation-hungry mob in Nathaniel West's *The Day of the Locust*, originally entitled *The Cheated*. The details and implications and insinuations that gathered about this frame-story were often of the sort popularly described as "beggaring the imagination." Capote saw no necessity to invent or to disguise—no necessity, that is, to "fictionalize" his findings.[3]

The author had long toyed with the idea of a nonfiction novel, and first practiced its techniques in **The Muses Are Heard** (1956), an account of his journey through Russia with the all-Negro cast of *Porgy and Bess*. A violent crime, however, seemed to him the ideal subject of such a work,[4] and he gave detailed advice to his friend and childhood neighbor Harper Lee, whose Pulitzer Prize-winning novel *To Kill a Mockingbird* (1960) focused on the sensational trial of a Negro charged with raping a white woman. (Harper Lee, in turn, accompanied Capote on his first visit to Holcomb, only three days after the murders were committed, and when there seemed little hope of apprehending the culprits.) For his own purposes, a sensational murder case seemed most likely to deliver the basic ingredients of a "found" narration, and he would have been aware of his literary antecedents—Poe's "The Mystery of Marie Rogêt," Dostojevsky's *The Possessed,* Dreiser's *An American Tragedy.* All were based on actual murder cases, which the authors had transformed not merely with the banal intention of "protecting the innocent," but in the interest of art. As Alfred Kazin has observed, Capote wanted to go a step further: while remaining literally true to the record, he was "not content to make a work of record. He wanted, wholly and exclusively, to make a work of art. . . . He wanted, ultimately, not the specificity of fiction, which must be content to be itself alone, but to make an emblematic human situation for our time that would relieve it of mere factuality."[5]

Why, then, should he stir the critical hornets' nest by evoking the word fiction? If a subtitle was necessary at all to establish the authenticity of persons, places, and events, "A Documentary Novel" would surely have sufficed. The term works admirably well for a book like John Hersey's *The Algiers Motel Incident*, which offers a chronological reconstruction of the killing of three Negroes during the bloody Detroit riots of 1967. It is written in a functional, reportorial style complete with maps, coroners' reports, confessions, lengthy swatches of official transcripts, and interviews conducted by the author himself. Hersey's work is passionately committed to what he sees as one of the most shocking episodes in American race relations, but the very rigor of its documentary method—its zeal to record the specific facts of a specific incident, together with all possible variants—precludes its achieving the larger metaphoric dimension of *In Cold Blood*.

In one of the rare passages in which he gives rein to a modest poetic license, Hersey describes the setting of Detroit's sniper battle:

> The Algiers Motel was one of many transients' hostelries on Woodward Avenue, a rod-straight street, the city's spine, that divides eastern Detroit from western Detroit. A couple of miles north of the cluster of massive buildings called "downtown," and only a few blocks from the section of Twelfth Street where the black uprising of those July days and nights had started, the Algiers stood at the corner of Woodward and Virginia Park, an elm-lined street elegantly brick-paved in the old days but pot-holed now and patched with asphalt, a street of once prosperous wooden and brick houses with boastful porches and backyard carriage houses recently declined into rooming houses and fraternity houses and blind pigs, as Detroit calls its illegal after-hours drinking spots.[6]

Beyond a "rod-straight street" and "boastful porches," Hersey is even here, where he might have sought to generalize or elaborate the theme of urban decay, making a conscious effort to restrict himself to photographically verifiable details: "elm-lined," "brick-paved," "pot-holed," "patched." Even the faint evocation of "the old days," when this was a peaceful, elegant neighborhood, is substantiated by visible remnants of that earlier time—trees, brick paving, porches, carriages, houses.

It is instructive to compare this restrained and calculatedly objective style with Capote's own *mise-en-scène*:

> The village of Holcomb stands on the high wheat plains of western Kansas, a lonesome area that other Kansans call "out there." Some seventy miles east of the Colorado border, the countryside, with its hard blue skies and desert-clear air, has an atmosphere that is rather more Far West than Middle West. The local accent is barbed with a prairie twang, a ranch-hand nasalness, and the men, many of them, wear narrow frontier trousers, Stetsons, and high-heeled boots with pointed toes. The land is flat, and the views are awesomely extensive; horses, herds of cattle, a white cluster of grain elevators rising as gracefully as Greek temples are visible long before a traveler reaches them.[7]

A comparison of Hersey's "cluster of massive buildings called 'downtown'" with Capote's "cluster of grain elevators rising as gracefully as Greek temples" offers a compact demonstration of the authors' divergent methods. It is not simply that the latter indulges in poetic simile. Nor is it a question of his being a more gifted and original writer (though the argument would not be difficult to substantiate), but of being a different kind of writer composing a very different kind of book that required the application of techniques more commonly associated with fiction.

Throughout the opening paragraph of *In Cold Blood* the author is systematically and artfully shaping our initial vision of the scene; observations are made—narrow trousers and high-heeled boots, for example—that go beyond documentary necessity to create an explicit sense of place. The reader becomes a "traveler," approaching across the wide plains; unlike the objective camera-eye, however, his also registers emotions and insinuations: "lonesome," "awesomely," "gracefully." Every physical detail contributes to the overall realism of the passage, yet each slots into a larger scheme of inference if not, literally, of symbolism. From this point individual images begin to cluster into leitmotifs—birds wedged into the grills of pick-up trucks, dead animals beside the highway, a beaten dog, a slaughtered pig, the corpses of the Clutters. Perry Smith's technicolor fantasy-world finds unexpected parallel in Mrs. Clutter's retreat into a realm of glittering baubles; the cabin-building adventure of his childhood is an ironic echo of the myth of the self-made farmer which Mr. Clutter embodies.

Structurally, too, *In Cold Blood* departs from the linear mode of documentary reporting; Capote has rearranged chronology and introduced flash-backs to lend narrative drama and thematic richness to the story. He has, furthermore, reconstructed long, vividly detailed conversations that he could not possibly have overheard. Such intrusions and overt manipulations of point-of-view are hostile to the documentary. In describing his own method, John Hersey piously insisted "that the events could not be described as if witnessed from above by an all-seeing eye opening on an all-knowing novelistic mind; the merest suspicion that anything had been altered, or made up, for art's sake, or for the sake of effect, would be absolutely disastrous. There could be no 'creative reconstruction.'"[8] There can be no doubt that

Hersey wrote this passage with the Capote controversy in mind, and consciously sought to distance himself from the two-headed beast known as "the nonfiction novel." Others, including new-journalist Tom Wolfe, saw Capote's novel as confirmation of their own efforts to break down the barriers between so-called fiction and so-called fact, high-brow and low-brow, art and journalism, and ultimately between art and life.

With twenty years of hindsight to focus the critical faculties, one can now see that Capote's experiment was neither unique nor unprecedented. Far more, it was symptomatic of a richly fertile period in the cultural life of the United States—the most creative eruption of talent since that early nineteenth-century flowering which F. O. Matthiessen dubbed "The New England Renaissance." The once-impervious Geneva conventions of the mind were assailed from all sides. While novelists like Truman Capote and Norman Mailer coopted the techniques of journalism, journalists like Tom Wolfe and Gay Talese raided the camp of the novelist. Andy Warhol took soup cans from the supermarket and displayed them in galleries and museums; he proclaimed the Coca-Cola bottle to be as worthy of aesthetic contemplation as the wine-bottle; and he transformed the jerky, out-of-focus home-movie into an underground art form. Choreographer Merce Cunningham, composer John Cage, and painter Robert Rauschenberg collaborated on improvised "happenings"—multimedia events that mingled conventional disciplines with an indiscriminate zest and contagious irreverence for traditions.

In the new, anything-goes aesthetic, nothing was quite where one expected it to be. Accustomed to films based on novels (and generally convinced of the "superiority" of the book both in time and in quality), moviegoers were confronted with bestsellers based on films: *Love Story, Last Tango in Paris, Deep Throat, 2001.* Where music fans had once awaited recordings of popular performances, they now attended performances based, like *Jesus Christ Superstar* or *Tommy,* on recordings. Such apparent displacements of the technological or "synthetic" event offer an important key to the revolutionary spirit of the times. Roy Lichtenstein, James Rosenquist, and Andy Warhol did not merely take commercial icons as their subjects; they also put aside traditional painterly tools in favor of commercial mass-reproduction techniques—stencils, spray-guns, photo-offset screens. Warhol referred to his studio as "The Factory," and developed assembly-line methods for producing and signing his canvases. In *The Philosophy of Andy Warhol from A to B and Back Again,* the prince of pop (who had illustrated a volume of Capote short stories in 1952) recalled his youthful affair with a television set, "which has continued to the present, when I play around in my bedroom with as many as four at a time. But I didn't get married," he confesses, "until 1964 when I got my first tape recorder."[9]

By the mid-1960's, an estimated 95 percent of American households had at least one television set; before the end of the decade, a third of those were two-TV households.[10] Establishment guardians direly predicted that the resulting image-bombardment would deprive the arts (both literary and visual) of one of their most time-honored components, for the image itself was rapidly becoming a throw-away commodity, no more precious or cherished than the beer-can or disposable diaper. (The introduction of a mass-produced photocopier in 1960 further aggravated the problem; and since the first Xerox machines were too heavy for salesmen to carry about, they were marketed primarily through television.) Narrative also seemed bankrupted by the new fad—not just through serials, televised plays, and movie reruns, but by the medium's overall preference for organizing information into instantly digestible mini-narratives with recognizable beginnings, middles, and ends. Even the ubiquitous commercial followed suit: from the disgrace of dingy laundry to the wind-flapping pennants of cleanliness, godliness, motherhood; from bad-breath ostracism to Pepsodent romance; from a tyrannizing Excedrin-headache to the serene control of hearth and home, office and classroom—from Mr. Hyde to Dr. Jekyll within minutes. Many writers, to be sure, reacted to this overkill by retreating into fabulism or intellectual riddles; others consciously stripped the novel and short story of contaminating traces of plot, scene, and character. Non-objective painting had already become the fine-arts dogma, and serious composers strove for increasing "abstraction." Such artists demanded aesthetic results that were not accessible to the hyperliteral modes of film and television or the banalities of popular culture. Others, however, began to experiment with such media, producing results through the underground cinema or video art that have, in turn, exercised a measurable influence on their commercial counterparts. It was, after all, a time-honored American principle: "If you can't beat 'em, join 'em."

Though he assailed the documentary as "the bleeding heart of television land," Mailer adapted several of its devices to his own ends in *The Armies of the Night*. That idiosyncratic venture into the realms of nonfiction marked the beginning of a vital stage of experimentation in Mailer's art. Whereas Capote intentionally excluded himself from the structure of **In Cold Blood,** Mailer placed himself at the vital center of his work—a metaphysical and political commitment too often dismissed by hostile readers as simple narcissism. But if fiction, like history, is always the distinct and biased hypothesis of an individual intelligence, then the intelligencer must be prepared to submit to such scrutiny. In the oft-quoted metaphor that introduces Part II of *The Armies of the Night,* the author compares both historian and novelist to an astronomer working with faulty tools. "Of course," he argues, the tower is crooked, and the telescopes warped, but the instruments of all sciences—history so much as physics—are always constructed in small or large error; what supports the use of them now is that our intimacy with the master builder of the tower, and the lens grinder of the telescopes (yes, even the machinist of the barrels) has given some advantage for correcting the error of the instruments and the imbalance of his tower.[11]

Capote systemically denies us this advantage. What we can never know about his view of Holcomb, Kansas, and its citizens is the degree to which their responses to him as a lisping Easterner/intellectual/homosexual colored their response to his tireless questionings. We see too little of him to make such corrections. In *The Armies of the Night* as in *Of a Fire on the Moon* Mailer stands before us with his psyche bared, loudly proclaiming his faults and fears, his broken marriages, his drinking habits, his political prejudices. The book opens with a brief article from *Time* magazine describing the author's drunken misbehavior at the Ambassador Theater rally preceding the march on the Pentagon in October 1967; it is followed by Mailer's own confessional account of that episode and the events surrounding it. Then, in the book's concluding section, he adopts the sober and objective voice of the historian to comment on the Pentagon march. Which of these versions of reality can one trust? On the basis of its tone, the historical treatment would seem more reliable than the subjective one, but the author of "History as a Novel" presumably shares the same flaws revealed by the author of "The Novel as History." It is, after all, the same man; he has merely donned a different hat.

Mailer's projection of himself as imperfect spokesman for his time continues in *Miami and the Siege of Chicago* (1968), but finds its richest expression in *Of a Fire on the Moon* (1970). In the narrative persona of Aquarius, the author reflects on the Apollo launch as a human undertaking deeply resonant with meaning, and therefore despairs that it has been reduced for much of the world to a second-rate television spectacular. The horror of our time, he suggests, is "the size of each new event, and the paucity of its reverberation."[12] In an inversion of Nick Carraway's romantic contemplation of the moon hanging over Gatsby's house, he refers to America as an "empty country filled with wonders."[13] Yet through the sheer generative power of his own language, he restores the wonder, guides us into unplumbed, metaphysical depths, launches us on a fantastic voyage into the unknown, transforms NASA's nuts-and-bolts technologies into soaring poetry. The immense satellite is a grain elevator, a chalice, a cathedral, a white whale, Icarus and Madonna, ghost, angel, and devil. Mailer has done his journalistic homework, but it is the allusive, self-doubting, probing mind of the novelist that produces the following description of lift-off:

> Flames flew in cataract against the cusp of the flame shield, and then sluiced along the paved ground down two opposite channels in the concrete, two underground rivers of flame which poured into the air on either side a hundred feet away, then flew a hundred feet further. Two mighty torches of flame like the wings of a yellow bird of fire flew over a field, covered a field with brilliant yellow bloomings of flame, and in the midst of it, white as a ghost, white as the white of Melville's Moby Dick, white as the shrine of the Madonna in half the churches of the world, this slim angelic mysterious ship of stages rose without sound out of its incarnation of flame and began to ascend slowly into the sky, slow as Melville's Leviathan might swim, slowly as we might swim upward in a dream looking for the air.[14]

The Apollo-Saturn moon launch also plays a central role in Tom Wolfe's *The Right Stuff* (1979), but the later book never achieves the demonic energy that animates Mailer's account. (Furthermore, having so brilliantly recapitulated a "media event" that his readers have all witnessed for themselves, Mailer has the audacity to relate it a second time within the same volume.) Though his more recent anatomies of the art and architecture establishments are at best extended essay-harangues, Tom Wolfe remains a central figure in the emergence of the nonfiction novel. Like Gay Talese and Hunter Thompson he began his career as a journalist, but was uncomfortable with the formal hegemonies of his craft. He entered the arena of nonfiction fiction in 1963 with an article in *Esquire* magazine entitled "There Goes (Varoom! Varoom!) That Kandy-Kolored (thphhhhhh!) Tangerine-Flake Streamline Baby (Raghhh!) Around the Bend (Brummmmmmmmmm-mmmmmmmm) . . ." The first of a series of remarkable pieces on pop-culture fads and personalities, it was allegedly composed as a memorandum, which the *Esquire* editors chose to publish in the "unfinished" form.

The discovery that Wolfe and a number of his colleagues were making was that "it just might be possible to write journalism that would . . . read like a novel."[15] With his first, serendipitous venture into "parajournalism," the young reporter discovered a heady sense of liberation. As he later recalled,

> What interested me was not simply the discovery that it was possible to write accurate nonfiction with techniques usually associated with novels and short stories. It was that—plus. It was the discovery that it was possible in nonfiction, in journalism, to use any literary device, from the traditional dialogisms of the essay to stream-of-consciousness, and to use many different kinds simultaneously, or within a relatively short space . . . to excite the reader both intellectually and emotionally. I am not laying all those gladiolas on that rather curious first article of mine, you understand. I'm only talking about what it suggested to me.[16]

The suggestions were to flower into *The Electric Kool-Aid Acid Test* (1968)—a psychedelic picaresque, a wistful reminder of the paradoxical need for heroes in a faceless society, and a comment on technological clutter. Wolfe's protagonist, the novelist Ken Kesey, is a charismatic leader of tremendous energy and frenetic drive who acts as the compelling center for a new family of man. On the darker side, his career suggests parallels to that of Charles Manson: both "families" travel across the country in busses; both experiment heavily in drugs; both are so intimately linked to technology that individuals themselves often seem no more than cyborgs. The American Dream in its spatial, spiritual, and economic dimensions is once more turned to nightmare—as in *The Great Gatsby* or **In Cold Blood**. And the long sought earthly paradise that inspired countless pioneers has now been wired for sound.

Stylistically, Wolfe's work helps focus some of the most tantalizing questions concerning the nature and responsibilities of art in a technological society. He himself creates a style directly dependent on the technical variables of the printed page. "I found," he says, "a great many pieces of punctuation and typography lying around dormant when I came along—and I must say I had a good time using them [. . .]. I found that things like exclamation points, italics, and abrupt shifts (dashes) and syncopations (dots) helped to give the illusion not only of a person talking but of a person thinking."[17] Together with the use of the historical present, such devices lend *The Electric Kool-Aid Acid Test* an electrifying feeling of immediacy. The language of the book spits and curls and drips and turns in upon itself; it races ahead, slows to a near stand-still, or chirps and whines and drones like the machines compulsively manipulated by Kesey's Merry Pranksters. Ken Kesey himself emerges here as a seminal figure for his generation—not merely as the creator of two distinguished novels, but more significantly as the champion of a lifestyle intensely dependent on technology and the drugs of technology; as initiator, too, of such technological phenomena as the multimedia show and acid rock.

Kesey is, in short, not merely an individual but a commodity, a phenomenon, an event—for the culture of the West what Warhol was for the East; and Wolfe's style provided uniquely suited to explore such a personality, suggesting the various forces, fads, compulsions, illusions, and needs that spiral round him. The figure is a compelling one, to both author and reader, but only a frail line separates the ego of a Kesey from the psychopathology of a Manson, and Wolfe clearly sees the threat, reflecting it in the very disintegration that attacks his prose in the concluding chapter. Plugged into their instruments, Kesey and one of his lieutenants sit alone in The Barn, communicating through variable-lag microphones, and the very images of their dissociative dialogue are significant—soldiers, fleas, latrines, suicide, Hitler, psychedelics, heroin, trading stamps. Like the book itself, this final duet is a study of creative frenzy as it verges on madness; the grandfather of this particular acid test is Edgar Allan Poe. Such are the themes that Mailer reiterates two years later in *Of a Fire on the Moon*—the aching need for heroes, the journey as a search for human definition, the obsession with technology, the fear of technology. Phrased in more traditional terms, Capote and Wolfe and Mailer are all obsessed by the loss of innocence; their protagonists, whether bound for a farm, a barn, or the caverns of the moon, are all picaresque voyagers. But unlike the resourceful Huckleberry Finn, who makes a charade of murder, Capote's vagabonds are ruthless killers. Mailer, too, would focus his own most compelling nonfiction novel on a vicious murderer—Gary Gilmore of the *Executioner's Song* (1979).

Mailer referred to his gargantuan book on Gilmore as "a true life story,"[18] perhaps consciously echoing a popular-fiction formula that has recurred since Defoe's *Moll Flanders*. Indeed, the nonfiction novel, however directly it responded to contemporary realities, was also a return to an older narrative idiom that freely mixed observed fact with imaginative elaboration—as in Defoe's *Journal of the Plague Year* or Sterne's *Sentimental Journey*. Audiences were once blissfully untroubled by such liberties, as the early Norse sagas, Greek epics, or Shakespeare's history plays richly confirm. Tom Wolfe cites, as more immediate antecedents, DeQuincey's *Confessions of an English Opium Eater*, Dickens's *Sketches of Boz*, Twain's *Innocents Abroad*, and Orwell's *Down and Out in Paris and London*. But he repeatedly suggests that, for his generation—for novelizing journalists and journalizing novelists alike—**In Cold Blood** was the catalyzing experience.

Its author never again found the "true life" materials from which he could mold a major work of fiction. Significantly, the rambling and self-indulgent *magnum opus* with which he wrestled in the final years of his life was hopefully entitled **Answered Prayers**. The few chapters to appear in print reveal a progressive blurring of critical faculties—a fundamental confusion between social history and tittering gossip that would suffice to set the ghost of Samuel Pepys on chain-rattling midnight rambles. Sporadically, Capote published shorter works—essays, interviews, and short stories—that recalled the virtuoso performances of the 1950's; in addition to composing television and film scripts, the aging *Wunderkind* of American letters made his own shrill film debut. The best of his later writings were collected in 1980 as **Music for Chameleons**. The lyric title story is a bravura performance, but the book's real strength lies in the gothically grim novella **Handcarved Coffins**, subtitled "A Nonfiction Account of an American Crime." That the author found an entirely new voice for this second exploration of the theme is a final tribute to the genius pathetically dissipated in drugs and alcohol.

And it was a reminder that *In Cold Blood,* more than any other single work of the postwar period, had helped to redraw the map of American fiction.

Notes

1. See, for example, William L. Nance, *The Worlds of Truman Capote* (New York, 1970), 179-180.

2. James Jones, *Go to the Widowmaker* (New York, 1966), unnumbered page with a "Special Note" by the author.

3. The "instant metaphors" of the case are discussed in detail in my own article, "Why the Chickens Came Home to Roost in Holcomb, Kansas." See Truman Capote's *In Cold Blood: A Critical Handbook,* ed. Irving Malin (Belmont/Cal., 1968), 154-163.

4. In an interview with George Plimpton, Capote recalled reading the first, brief article on the Kansas murders: "[. . . .] it suddenly struck me that a crime, the study of one such, might provide the broad scope I needed to write the kind of book I wanted to write. Moreover, the human heart being what it is, murder was a theme not likely to darken and yellow with time." See George Plimpton, "The Story Behind a Nonfiction Novel," *New York Times Book Review* (January 16, 1966), 3.

5. Alfred Kazin, "The World as a Novel: From Capote to Mailer," *The New York Review of Books* (April 8, 1971), 26.

6. John Hersey, *The Algiers Motel Incident,* Bantam (New York, 1968), 10.

7. Truman Capote, *In Cold Blood* (New York, 1966), 3.

8. Hersey, 27.

9. Andy Warhol, *The Philosophy of Andy Warhol (From A to B & Back Again)* (New York, 1975), 26.

10. The statistics are taken from Daniel J. Boorstin, *The Americans: The Democratic Experience* (New York, 1973), 393-394.

11. Norman Mailer, *The Armies of the Night,* Signet (New York, 1968), 245.

12. Norman Mailer, *Of a Fire on the Moon* (Boston, 1970), 40.

13. *Ibid.,* 98.

14. *Ibid.,* 95-96.

15. Tom Wolfe, *The New Journalism, With an Anthology* Edited by Tom Wolfe and E. W. Johnson (New York, 1973), 9.

16. *Ibid.,* 15.

17. Tom Wolfe, "The Birth of 'The New Journalism,'" New York, 5 (February 14, 1972), 37.

18. Norman Mailer, *The Executioner's Song* (Boston, 1979), 1053. The context in which the phrase appears, with Mailer's own italics, is the following: "Let it be said then that without the cooperation of Nicole Baker, there would not have been a way to do this factual account—this, dare I say it, *true life story,* with its real names and real lives—as if it were a novel."

Chris Anderson (essay date 1987)

SOURCE: Anderson, Chris. "Truman Capote: A Ceremony of Style." In *Style as Argument: Contemporary American Nonfiction,* pp. 48-81. Carbondale, Ill.: Southern Illinois University Press, 1987.

[*In the following essay, Anderson examines the manner in which Capote uses silence, or the lack of narrative explication, as both a technique and theme in his fiction and nonfiction work.*]

I

Much has been said in recent criticism about what makes the nonfiction novel novelistic, what makes nonfiction fictive, and in most of these discussions Capote's *In Cold Blood* is a prominent example. Its textures and subtle symbolisms give it the feel of a novel. But in all the debate about the epistemological status of subject matter and the truth or falsity of characterization in the nonfiction novel, no one has recognized that one of the key similarities between fiction and nonfiction in Capote is the use of authorial silence. Capote's nonfiction is like his fiction in what it does not say, and this is true not only in *In Cold Blood* but in all the other major nonfiction as well.

By "silence" I mean that throughout his narratives Capote remains silent about important details, avoiding explicit interpretation and commentary. He repeatedly puts himself in the position of an outside observer forced to make inferences and read meanings on the basis of external detail. Silence in this sense is the underlying metaphor throughout Booth's *Rhetoric of Fiction.* Unlike eighteenth and nineteenth century narrators who comment directly on their stories, the silent author of modern fiction, according to Booth, has "effaced himself, renounced the privilege of direct intervention." The modern narrator "leaves his characters to work out their own destinies and tell their own stories"—he gives "the illusion that he is sitting silently behind scenes" of the story itself (7, 273, 50).

Silence in this sense is also related to Wolfgang Iser's notion that the reading experience depends on "gaps" or "blanks," the gaps arising from dialogue, for example, or from unexplained events, delayed revelations, and uninterpreted concrete images. At these junctures, "what *is* said only appears to take on significance as a reference to what is not said; it is the implications and not the statements themselves that give shape and weight to the meaning" (168). In the space left by the withdrawal of the narrator, meaning takes place. Information withheld, intepretation withdrawn, the reader is left to draw inferences and make connections.

In ***Other Voices, Other Rooms,*** for example, Capote's first and perhaps most representative novel, the narrator is silent for most of the story about Joel's father. Joel has come to Skully's Landing to live with a father he has never known, but from the beginning of his stay no one will tell him anything about the man—where he is, what he is like, when he can see him:

> "Miss Amy," he said, as they started down the stairs, "where is my dad? I mean, couldn't I see him, please, ma'am?"
>
> She did not answer.
>
> (50)

As narrator Capote doesn't answer this question either. He deliberately withholds information and interpretation throughout the first half of the novel. We know no more than Joel. With him we must explore the strange, silent house and deal with its enigmatic inhabitants—Randolph, Miss Amy—drawing what conclusions we can. At one point Joel hears a strange thumping on the stairs. It stops, there is "an instant of quiet," "then an ordinary red tennis ball roll[s] silently through the archway" (87). Later we find that this is a signal from Joel's invalid father for Randolph or Amy to come upstairs, but at this point it is a strange, mysterious sign, silent and uninterpreted. Like many other events and details in the novel, it puzzles Joel and it puzzles us. Capote leaves us with Joel to work out its significance.

Just as importantly, silence has to do with the way Capote dramatizes rather than explicates his central themes, relying on symbolism and the implications of concreteness to convey meaning. He shows rather than tells. In the conclusion of ***Other Voices*** Joel stands in the garden at Skully's Landing and looks up at the clouds: "The clouds traveled slower than a clock's hands, and, as he waited, became thunder-dark, became John Brown and horrid boys in panama hats and the Cloud Hotel and Isabel's old hound, and when they were gone, Mr. Sansom was the sun." There is a sense of anticipation now. Something, some revelation, is about to take place:

> His mind was absolutely clear. He was like a camera waiting for its subject to enter focus. The wall yellowed in the meticulous setting of the October sun, and the windows were rippling mirrors of cold, seasonal color. Beyond one, someone was watching him. All of him was dumb except his eyes. They knew. And it was Randolph's window. Gradually the blinding sunset drained from the glass, darkened, and it was as if snow were falling there, flakes shaping snow-eyes, hair: a face trembled like a white beautiful moth, smiled. She beckoned to him, shining and silver, and he knew he must go: unhurried, not hesitating, he paused only at the garden's edge where, as though he'd forgotten something, he stopped and looked back at the bloomless, descending blue, at the boy he had left behind.
>
> (230-31)

Many threads of symbolism and implication developed from the beginning of the novel come together here, too complicated to explicate now. For our purposes it is enough to note that Capote does not explicitly comment on Joel's rite of passage. The moment is fundamentally symbolic, rendered concretely rather than openly interpreted. We must *read* the detail. On one level Joel is leaving the garden of his youthful innocence. On another he has learned the importance of passively accepting the darkness around him as the only way of escaping that darkness. He has come to see his father, Mr. Sansom, free of the clouds that have always surrounded him. He has come to accept Randolph, his sexually ambiguous cousin, who apparently is the mysterious woman he has repeatedly glimpsed in the upstairs window. In the moment in the garden, a moment where nothing essentially "happens" in any external sense—where everything, in fact, is literally silent—Joel moves from boyhood to manhood, although in Capote's rich silence it is unclear how full or healthy this manhood will be.

As in all literary expression, it is the concrete details of the dramatized situation that carry the weight of meaning. Capote does not "say" what he means here. What he says is the scene itself; what he means is what the scene implies, points to, causes us to think about for ourselves. This is the strategy in all of Capote's fiction, from the early stories to the later novels. He grounds his narratives in uninterpreted concrete images and leaves his characters ambiguous and enigmatic. It's not that we don't have any sense of the symbolic value of these images or characters. Capote provides us with clues throughout the stories to their philosophical and psychological importance, establishing their meaning through pattern and implication. The point is that as narrator Capote does not establish these correspondences directly. He is Booth's modern narrator, sitting silently behind the scenes as his characters deal with mysterious and troubling circumstance. He is Weaver's new rhetorician, relying on pictorial realism and photographic detail to convey meaning rather than engaging in panoramic commentary.

In this large sense, Wolfe, too, employs authorial silence, for the most part remaining detached from his narratives, allowing his characters to work out their own fates and speak for themselves, implying rather than stating his own interpretation of events. Though we would not associate Wolfe, in his intensity and verbosity, with silence in any narrow meaning of the word, he is remarkably similar to Capote in his decision to remain behind the scenes or within character.

The rhetorical effect of these silences is twofold. First, they draw us as readers into the action. In the absence of explicit commentary, we are made to "assemble" the text ourselves, generate meaning from the "instructions" implicit in the narrative. As Iser puts it, "the unwritten aspects of apparently trivial scenes and the unspoken dialogue within the twists and turns not only draw the reader into the action but also lead him to shade in the many outlines suggested by a given situation, so that they take on a reality of their own" (168). Gaps are the places of reconstitution in the act of reading, creating moments of what Iser would call "indeterminacy" in which we must discover or anticipate the meaning ourselves.

Second, and perhaps somewhat at odds with the first, silences demand reading. A silence does not readily disclose its meaning. It exists by definition in the absence of speech, in the absence, therefore, of explicit explanation. It requires interpretation. Although silences present us with puzzles which we are drawn toward assembling—although they invite us, or entice us, to fill in the gaps—they also require us to work harder as readers. The narrator is not doing all the work for us. We must participate. We must see past the words on the page, make connections between the dramatization before us and the larger themes it implies.

In fact, Iser differentiates between fiction and nonfiction, or what he calls "expository" prose, in precisely these terms. In a fictional text "connectability" is broken up by blanks and meaning becomes "multifarious." But in an expository text, he says, a text which "unfolds an argument or conveys information," the goal is to narrow down the "multiplicity of possible meanings" "by observing the connectability of textual segments." That is, exposition depends on explicitness. The expositor is to make his connections as clear as possible, his conclusions obvious and readily understandable. The reader should not have to fill any gaps or participate in the work of meaning. The utterance should be continuously "individualized," the meaning made as "precise" as possible (184).

In this light it is all the more interesting that Capote's non-fiction, like his fiction, depends on the rhetoric of silence. At the end of **"A Duke in His Domain,"** Capote sums up his impressions of Brando, not with explicit commentary and interpretation, a direct analysis of character, but with a description of Brando's image—"sixty feet tall," his head "as huge as the greatest Buddha's"—projected on a billboard above a Tokyo theatre. It is an ironic portrait, and the irony depends on understatement: "Rather Buddha-like, too, was his pose, for he was depicted in a squatting position, a serene smile on a face that glistened in the rain and the light of a street lamp. A deity, yes; but, more than that, really, just a young man sitting on a pile of candy" (*Dogs Bark* 353). The last sentence here, the last sentence of the piece, is the only place where Capote does more than record, select, synthesize his impression of surfaces, and this is spare, restrained. The piece resolves itself in an image, a concrete detail from Capote's actual experience with obvious symbolic implications. In an earlier essay, **"A Ride through Spain,"** Capote concludes a description of the Spanish landscape with a similarly evocative image, a one sentence paragraph that emphasizes the blank space at the end of the page: "The train moved away so slowly butterflies blew in and out of the windows" (*Dogs Bark* 104). There are no apostrophes here to the beauty of Europe or the end of an era. There is just the recreation of the scene itself, concrete and compact.

Capote claims a degree of omniscience in **In Cold Blood,** entering the minds of his characters and occasionally describing their feelings and attitudes—feelings and attitudes he has carefully reconstructed from extensive interviews. But it is significant that for the most part he renounces omniscience and maintains authorial silence in the narrative, withdrawing to the point of view of an outside observer restricted to making deductions from available evidence and testimony.

In the beginning Capote is careful to foreshadow the impending murder. Mr. Clutter heads for home and the day's work, "unaware that it would be his last"; Nancy lays out her prettiest red dress, "the dress in which she was to be buried" (13, 56). As narrator, these phrases suggest, Capote is in possession of the facts but is withholding what he knows as he prepares for the climax. When the climax finally comes and Dick and Perry drive their car up the Clutter driveway, Capote immediately cuts away, turning to a description of how the bodies were discovered rather than detailing the events of the murder itself. In fact, it is not until Perry's confession in the last half of the book that we know what exactly happened that night. Between this first section of preliminaries, "The Last To See Them Alive," and the third, "The Answer," he inserts a second, "Persons Unknown," establishing the character of Dick and Perry and detailing the reaction of the townspeople to the murder. Throughout this long intervening section he remains silent about the central event of the narrative.

As a result, we must join Alvin Dewey, the detective in charge of the case, as he struggles to decipher clues. With him we must try to account for the position of the bodies, the nature of the wounds, the state of the house. In the absence of answers, we must form hypotheses. It's "like those puzzles," Dewey himself puts it, "the ones that ask, 'How many animals can you find in this picture?'" (83). The animals are hidden for us precisely because of Capote's authorial silence. He doesn't tell us what he knows.

Capote continually puts us in the position of reading externals, even in the most apparently trivial scenes. Mrs. Clutter's room is austere, without personal ornament, "as though by keeping this room impersonal, by not importing her intimate belongings but leaving them mingled with those of her husband, she lessened the offense of not sharing his quarters" (29). The handwriting in Nancy's diary varies from entry to entry, sometimes slanted to the right, sometimes to the left, sometimes round, sometimes steep, "as though she were asking, 'Is this Nancy? Or that? Or that? Which is me?'" (57). "As though" conjectures are a necessary response to silence. Without the certainty of fact we can only deduce internals from the character of externals. Even near the end, when Perry is captured and brought in for questioning, Capote chooses to present him to us from a distance. With the detectives we view him through the one-way observation window of the interrogation room, deducing what we can from his "stiff Indian hair," his "pert, impish features," his flickering, lizard-like tongue (224).

It is from this perspective that we can understand the symbolic resonances characteristic of *In Cold Blood.* The cats who fish through the gutters for dead birds outside the courthouse are meant to be symbolic of people within the story—Dick and Perry, the journalists coming to cover the murder (258). Capote notes that over a Las Vegas motel where the police are searching for the killers the "R" and the "S" are missing from "rooms." The truncated word "OOM" seems to resonate in the rest of the story, a symbol of the disintegration of language and meaning in the face of violence (174). Earlier in this section Capote records part of a radio broadcast that awakens a prisoner in the Kansas State Penitentiary ("Chancellor Konrad Adenauer arrived in London today for talks with Prime Minister Harold Macmillan. . . . President Eisenhower put in seventy minutes going over space problems and the budget for space exploration with Dr. T. Keith Glennan" [159]), subtly linking the events that took place in Holcomb, Kansas, with world events on the eve of a new decade. These details are all presumably "true," yet selected from their context they assume a symbolic, evocative value beyond their literal meaning. As in Capote's fiction, concreteness does not mean what it says; it points beyond itself, evokes via association or metaphor something not stated.

In his later nonfiction Capote continues to assume an objective point of view, only this time eschewing omniscience entirely and acknowledging the perceiving "I."

In **"Hello Stranger"** (*Chameleons*), he presents without commentary a conversation with a friend who confesses a strange sexual indiscretion. The sketch is constructed around the interview form itself—"TC's" question followed by "George's" answer—with a minimum of connecting description. The surface of the story and of the man who tells it are presented, without explicit interpretation, for us to judge. In **Handcarved Coffins** (*Chameleons*), a longer nonfiction piece reminiscent of *In Cold Blood,* Capote again features the bare skeleton of the interview, the give-and-take of question and answer without the narrator's all-seeing interventions. Occasionally he adds, in tight, almost minimalist parentheses, some description of the surrounding scene or landscape. There is never commentary. Here in these later pieces there are just the lineaments of the act of experiencing itself, the "I" in its immediate transactions with the world. By making himself nominally present in the story, Capote emphasizes silence even more than in *In Cold Blood.* Acknowledging the "I" in its act of observation calls our attention to the opaqueness of surfaces we must interpret for ourselves.

In an important statement in a *Paris Review* interview, Capote identifies this kind of rhetorical silence as the common strategy of both his fiction and his nonfiction:

> In reporting one is occupied with literalness and surfaces, with implication without comment—one can't achieve immediate depths the way one may in fiction. However, one of the reasons I've wanted to do reportage was to prove that I could apply my style to the realities of journalism. But I believe my fictional method is equally detached—emotionality makes me lose writing control: I have to exhaust the emotion before I feel clinical enough to analyze and project it, and as far as I'm concerned that's one of the laws of achieving true technique.
>
> (Cowley 291)

In a sense the rhetoric of silence is more appropriate to nonfiction than to fiction. After all, in nonfiction the author cannot finally claim total omniscience. Capote can't say with absolute certainty why Nancy Clutter varies her handwriting, because she is a real person, not a fictional creation of his own. He can't say why Mrs. Clutter would keep her separate bedroom so austere, because he cannot read her mind. The rhetoric of silence acknowledges the limits of factual reporting. But at the same time Capote recognizes that the rhetoric of silence is the central strategy of his fiction (and, we would add, of most modern fiction). The technique of reading "surfaces" and making inferences from those surfaces is a choice for the novelist in a way it cannot be for the nonfiction writer, but its purposes and effects are the same in both modes. There is still the same insistence on the reader participating in the making of deductions, still the narrator's refusal to speak in his own voice and comment on the meaning of the action he has dramatized, the character he has described. The key to technique in both modes is "detachment"—control, distance, concreteness, the dramatization rather than explication of events. Both fiction and nonfiction depend, in this view, on "implication without comment."

Thus Capote's nonfiction has the same two contradictory rhetorical effects as his fiction. It elicits and at the same time demands a reading. It draws us into the narrative and at the same time makes it harder for us to understand the meaning of the words before us. Unlike more conventional narrative exposition, where everything is spelled out as completely as possible in its turn, Capote's nonfiction develops from implicitness, restraint, withholding. It is riddled with at least temporary moments of indeterminacy.

In a series of prefaces to his various collections of nonfiction, Capote has discussed his effort over a career to fashion a prose style of understatement and conciseness. He has striven, he says, for a "technical virtuosity as strong and flexible as a fisherman's net," a sentence structure "simple, clear as a country creek" (*Chameleons* xviii). This involves cutting and condensing, a radical revising away of what he perceives as the former "density" of his prose so that he can achieve the same effects in a single paragraph that he achieved before in three pages (vii). Or as he puts it in the preface to *The Dogs Bark*, he is struggling to control his "static" writing, "to reveal character and sustain mood unaided by a narrative line" (xviii), an interesting parallel to Wolfe's stated intention of developing narrative through "scene-by-scene reconstruction" with as little "historical narration" as possible. In the terms I have been developing, it seems clear that what Capote is really describing here is the rhetoric of silence, an attempt to create language which means more than it says, which shows rather than tells, which depends in the end on the author's strategic decision to stay out of what is ultimately pure narration and description.

Capote says it best, perhaps, in a tribute to the style of Japanese art. In his view all Japanese art depends on the "dread of the explicit." Thus, "the single blade of grass describing a whole universe of summer, the slightly lowered eyes left to suggest the deepest passion." The withholding of interpretation, the restraining of comment, is "all a ceremony of Style, a phenomenon that seems to rotate, in a manner quite separate from emotional content, on absolute style alone" (*Dogs Bark* 356). This is a spare and understated piece in itself, no more than 500 words long, richer in implication than in analysis. It is a fitting critical analysis of the rhetoric of silence, even though the word "silence" is never mentioned. In Capote, too, a blade of grass is "left" to describe the whole universe of summer, lowered eyes left to suggest deeper realities of character.

II

There is another dimension of silence in Capote, not just technical but thematic. Capote's fiction and nonfiction are saturated with explicit references to silence—the silence of landscape, of character, of scene and event. In *In Cold Blood* in particular silence becomes the central figure for the inexplicability of contemporary American experience: it defines Capote's effort to communicate experiences which are fundamentally nonverbal or antiverbal.

Mr. Clutter is a speech-maker, a man used to standing up and talking to hundreds of people at the Rotary or the 4-H. He can "convince anybody about whatever," according to a friend (36). "No matter what the situation was, he could talk his way out of it" (117). Language is community. It provides the structures and continuities and contacts that govern everyday experience.

But as Perry explains in his confession, language fails on the night of the murders. Mr. Clutter can't convince Dick and Perry that he doesn't have a safe, then can't talk them out of the violence to follow. "You couldn't argue with him," Perry says of Dick, "he was so excited" (239). When Mr. Clutter tries to calm Dick down, Dick shouts: "Shut up! When we want you to talk, we'll tell you" (238). Violence takes place after the failure of language. It is fundamentally nonverbal, a rejection of the compromises and accommodations that language can make possible.

The act of murder is oddly noiseless in Perry's account. "The only sound was the wind," he remembers (236). Despite the noise of the shotgun blasts, no one hears anything unusual. As Capote subtly emphasizes, violence is a silencing: the plan of the murder, he says, was flawlessly devised, "from first footfall to final silence" (37). When Nancy's friend Susan comes to pick her up for church the next morning, she is struck by the similarly unnatural quiet of the aftermath. "Everything looked too bright and quiet," she says in a later statement (59). The other friends who discover the bodies also experience that unnerving soundlessness. The normal chatter and flow of phatic conversation has ceased in this family.

As the investigation into the murders proceeds, the silence of the Clutter house comes to figure the inexplicability of the event. In an essay on the filming of the movie *In Cold Blood,* Capote remarks that it is "a curious experience to find myself once more in this house where I have so often been, and heretofore under such silent circumstances: the silent house, the plain rooms, the hardwood floors that echo every footstep, the windows that look out on solemn prairies and fields tawny with wheat stubble" (*Dogs Bark* 398). In *In Cold Blood* itself he uses similar imagery to describe Dewey's perceptions of the house:

> The detective moved from room to room. He had toured the house many times; indeed, he went out there almost every day, and, in one sense, could be said to find these visits pleasurable, for the place, unlike his own home, or the sheriff's office, with its hullabaloo, was peaceful. The telephones, their wires still severed, were silent. The great quiet of the prairies surrounded him. He could sit in Herb's parlor rocking chair, and rock and think.
>
> (152-53)

Later, too, Capote describes Nancy's boyfriend returning to the house, only to find it "shadowed, and hushed, and motionless" (207).

Despite the apparent peacefulness of these scenes, the silence surrounding the murder is maddening for Dewey and the other detectives involved in the case, maddening as well for the townspeople. The facts of the case, and the reasons for them, will not declare themselves. They constitute a kind of text to be read. "Writing has this strange quality," Socrates explains to Phaedrus, a quality it shares with painting. If one asks the creatures in a painting any questions, "they preserve a solemn silence." If one questions written words in the hope of better understanding their meaning, "they always say only one and the same thing" (69). So, too, with the silent texts in *In Cold Blood*. They simply reiterate themselves rather than refining, extending, explicating their mysteries: Why wasn't Nancy bound and gagged like the rest of the family? Were there two murderers? Is it just coincidence that Mr. Clutter took out a forty-thousand dollar life insurance policy the day of the murder? More importantly, why were the murders committed? Revenge? Robbery? For Dewey the silent details of the house—the physical evidence left at the scene, silently declaring itself over and over—don't "add up." "It doesn't make sense. But then, come right down to it, nothing does" (83).

Even though the details of the case are eventually resolved, over the course of the narrative the murder assumes a symbolic importance greater than its superficial mysteries of fact. Ultimately it is linked to a pervading sense of meaninglessness in the community and the nation as a whole. After all, Garden City is "just another fair-sized town in the middle—almost the exact middle—of the continental United States" (33). It is central, representative of the heartland. And the Clutters are representative of the city. A resident says of them, "I never heard a word against them; they were about as popular as a family can be, and if something like this could happen to *them,* then who's safe, I ask you?" (70). When the Clutters are murdered the community is threatened; their pain and horror are not just personal but an enactment of universal horrors. The Clutter murder is just one of many multiple murders beginning to take place throughout the country (271). The order of society seems to be threatened by bursts of arbitrary violence symptomatic of some intrinsic unrest or instability in the structure of things. It is the eve of a new decade. In the background are radios announcing the progress of the space program and new attempts to accommodate the Russians. The Bible admonition on Mrs. Clutter's bookmark evokes the mood of the times: "Take ye heed, watch and pray: for ye know not when the time is" (30).

In perhaps the most telling statement of all, a schoolteacher links the Clutter murders with a kind of existential dread:

> Feeling wouldn't run half so high if this had happened to anyone *except* the Clutters. Anyone *less* admired. Prosperous. Secure. But that family represented everything people hereabouts really value and respect, and that such a thing could happen to them—well, it's like being told there is no God. It makes life seem pointless. I don't think people are so much frightened as they are deeply depressed
>
> (88)

If God exists and is just, how could the Clutters be murdered? If God can be silent when people are suffering, can he be just? Can he exist? The murders in Holcomb raise the possibility that the world is not governed by a benevolent deity. Because they are apparently random and senseless—because no reason for them is discernible—they threaten to undermine the faith and values of the community. In this sense they come to represent the general malaise of the decade to come. The murder of the Clutters becomes for Capote a representative anecdote for dramatizing the fearfulness and uncertainty of contemporary American society.

In the face of such mystery and meaninglessness, language repeatedly fails. Ironically, the silent text of the event in *In Cold Blood* generates many other texts. Wordlessness engenders pages of ultimately futile testimony and interpretation. The detectives, of course, generate their "theories" and "hypotheses": that there were two murderers, that the motive was robbery, that the murderers were not known to the Clutter family, and so on—hypotheses which are then written up and recorded in volumes of police reports. Dewey goes on to formulate theories about the character of the murderers to account for some of the anomalies at the scene, for example, the fact that Bonnie and Nancy were tied up and then tucked into bed before they were shot or that a pillow was put under Kenyon's head. "At first I thought maybe the pillow was put there to make his head a simpler target." But "now I think, No, it was done . . . to make the victim more comfortable." One of the murderers at least exhibits a certain "twisted tenderness" (103). The townspeople also try to interpret and understand. Was it someone from town or one of the surrounding farms? Had Mr. Clutter made enemies? Was it Nancy's boyfriend? And there are conjectures about the motives.

All are duly recorded—Mother Truitt's, Mrs. Clare's, the schoolteacher's, the friends'. Similarly, the newspapers write their blurbs and headlines trying to account for the murders: "a tragedy, unbelievable and shocking beyond words" (69). Eventually, convinced that the case will never be solved, the newsmen leave Garden City (113).

Perry's father and sister both write long letters which try to account for Perry's personality and motives. His father's manuscript, entitled "A History of My Boy's Life," details Perry's birth, childhood, education, jobs, even "recreation" and "interests." He was a "normal" boy, Mr. Perry insists, raised with the golden rule, sensitive and artistic. There are possible explanations here for Perry's behavior, hints that Capote later develops himself: an accident that left Perry crippled, perhaps damaged his brain; more importantly, and this Mr. Perry suggests only inadvertently, fatherly neglect and abuse. Yet as text the letter says more about the father than the son. Mr. Perry cannot express himself well enough to persuade us that his son should be paroled—the purpose of the letter—or give us insight into the murders he later commits (125-30).

Perry's sister, Barbara, also writes to persuade, this time to persuade her brother to reform his ways. The letter is full of attempts to explain why he has turned out the way he has. "I truthfully feel none of us have *anyone* to blame for *whatever* we have done with our own personal lives," she says, yet "of course, environment plays an awfully important part in our lives"—an allusion to the influence of their father. More important than the content of the letter, however, is the fact that it is another text which tries to interpret and which must in turn be interpreted. In fact, a prison counselor and confidant responds to the letter with a intricately reasoned piece of rhetorical criticism. "It is a foolish letter, but born of human failing," Willie-Jay writes. It fails in its objectives. "What could be *more* conventional than a housewife with three children, who is 'dedicated' to her family???? What could be more natural than that she would resent an unconventional person." Her letter "failed because she couldn't conceive of the profundity of your problem—she couldn't fathom the pressures brought to bear upon you because of environment, intellectual frustration and a growing tendency toward isolationism" (143-145). Willie-Jay is right in his analysis that ultimately communication is impossible between two people from two such different worlds. In the end language can only beget more language, text lead to text.

Perry himself provides texts in the form of notebooks, lyrics, and poems piled up in two heavy boxes, although there doesn't seem to be any order in the language. The notebooks consist of a nonalphabetical dictionary of useful words and an anthology consisting of obscure facts, poems, and literary quotations. He quotes from a Blackfoot Indian chief, "What is life? It is the flash of a firefly in the night. It is a breath of a buffalo in the wintertime" (147). His confession is also a text, recorded and then transcribed on paper. It is his own effort to explain in language the silence of his act. "It was like I was outside myself," he tells the detectives. "Watching myself in some nutty movie." Mr. Clutter strikes him as a gentleman, "soft-spoken." "I thought so right up to the moment I cut his throat." Later: "I aimed the gun. The room just exploded. Went blue. Just blazed up. Jesus, I'll never understand why they didn't hear the noise twenty miles around" (240-44).

Still more texts develop in the trial. There is the academic language of the forensic psychiatrist, later published in an article in *The American Journal of Psychiatry*: Dick and Perry are "predisposed to severe lapses in ego-control which make possible the open expression of primitive violence, born out of previous, and now unconscious, traumatic experiences" (299). There is the language of the prosecution, oratorical rather than clinical, ascribing motives in its own way: "These were strange, ferocious murders. Four of your fellow citizens were slaughtered like hogs in a pen. And for what reason? Not out of vengeance or hatred. But for money. *Money*" (304).

For that matter, Capote's omniscient narration itself is a matter of textuality, since it is based on extensive interviews and exhaustive review of all the available transcripts from the police and the trial. Everything Capote is able to say about Perry's inner state or Clutter's frame of mind is grounded in the language of others, first spoken and then transcribed. It is all documented, in the literal sense, based on documents.

But in the end, even after the details of the murder are sorted out, the mystery persists: "The confessions, though they answered questions of how and why, failed to satisfy his [Dewey's] sense of meaningful design. The crime was a psychological accident, virtually an impersonal act; the victims might as well have been killed by lightning. Except for one thing: they had experienced prolonged terror, they had suffered" (246). It is not just the reason for the murders that remains inexplicable. The imagination fails to comprehend the quality and degree of the suffering the Clutters endured. Even Perry himself cannot explain what happened. Despite all the psychological and forensic and journalistic jargon, the event is beyond language: "and yet—How can I explain this? It was like I wasn't part of it. More as though I was reading a story. And I had to know what was going to happen. The end" (240). Perhaps Perry was driven by hatred of his father; perhaps he had lost his ability to reason and feel because of brain damage suffered in the earlier accident; perhaps he was victimized by society in some way. But in the end things just happened; at the key moment there is a blank: "I didn't realize what I'd done till I heard the sound. Like somebody drowning" (244). As Perry puts it in a prophetic statement early on, "The ineffable happens, things *do* take a turn" (37). The emphasis on textuality ironically heightens our sense of the original silence. All these texts are attempts through language to find meaning, yet all fail in the end.

Silences dominate all of Capote's work. He is obsessed with the implications of silence for character and mood, landscape and scene. The history of the household in **Other Voices** is too various and intricate for the child's mind of the narrator to understand. It is no accident that when Joel does finally meet his father, the old man is unable to speak more than a few monosyllables. It is no accident either that Capote describes the interiors and the landscapes of the novel as silent (27, 151, 187, 198, 216, 217). In **"Miriam"** a young girl suddenly appears in the life of an older widow, ghostlike, haunting. She doesn't explain herself, doesn't answer Mrs. Miller's questions. She is a silent apparition, appearing and disappearing without a trace. In the end, standing in her bedroom "in the hushed snow-city," Mrs. Miller "strives to shape a sentence" to save herself but fails, falling silent (*Tree of Night* 123). What's striking about the old man sitting across from Kay in **"A Tree of Night"** is his absolute silence. He is deaf and dumb, sitting with "mute detachment," unmoving, unresponsive. There is about the man's face a "shocking, embalmed stillness," a "mysterious silence" which finally overpowers the protagonist in the story's ambiguous conclusion (*Tree of Night* 203-04).

Brando is Buddha-like in **"The Duke in His Domain,"** his answers contradictory and jumbled, significant silences punctuating his digressions and mumblings. Bob Quinn is enigmatic and self-contradictory in **Handcarved Coffins,** a sophisticated and intelligent murderer who never betrays himself. There are unsolved mysteries in the nonfiction landscapes as well. New Orleans is a "secret place," a place of "silent, suffocated gardens" (***Dogs Bark*** 22-23). Of Ischai Capote remembers the "silent, shadowless afternoons" when the "whispering people wander back and forth and through the piazza and into some secret dark" (***Dogs Bark*** 86). He is compelled, he says in **"Hidden Gardens,"** by the "concealed" and "secret delights" of certain cities like New Orleans, cities which will "always remain wrapped boxes, containers of riddles never to be solved" (***Chameleons*** 193).

Indeed, there is a crucial sense in which silence is fundamental to the very enterprise of the New Journalism for Capote. **The Muses Are Heard,** Capote's first long work of nonfiction, describes the experiences of an American acting company traveling by train to Leningrad to perform *Porgy and Bess*. It is really a short parable about the impenetrability of appearances. For pages and pages Capote records every random detail in his immediate experience, much like the camera in cinéma vérité: snatches of scenery, little vignettes involving the actors and their entourage, glimpses of strangers, and, especially, bits of conversation. In the objective, documentary style characteristic of *The New Yorker,* where ***Muses*** was first published, every surface is duly recorded.

Near the end, in his only direct authorial comment on the experience, Capote attests to the impossibility of ever getting beyond mere surface, ever understanding the truth silently underneath the phenomena we sense every second in our daily lives. What really happened? Capote is asked about the actual performance of the opera: "There is no absolute truth in these matters, only opinion, and as I attempted to formulate my own, tried to decide what I was going to tell Shapiro, I stretched on the bed and switched out the light" (164). In acknowledging his own subjectivity, Capote puts the entire cataloguing of the previous pages in a new light. These random details take on significance precisely as random details: this is all we can know, he is saying, all that we can determine with any certainty—what we actually experience, not what these experiences might mean. There is no absolute truth. From this perspective the language problems of the travelers assume new importance as well. The difficulty of the Americans in trying to understand the Russians, and of the Russians trying to understand the Americans—particularly the subtly nuanced slang of the play itself—comes to figure the inability of all people finally to understand each other. We are locked inside ourselves; the interiors of others are finally inaccessible—silent.

In **"A Day's Work,"** Capote follows a housekeeper through her daily routine, carefully observing details from the interiors she cleans—a "leather-framed photograph" of a "swarthy macho man," for example, a copy of *True Detective* magazine, lipstick on the sheets—all clues to the identity of the man who lives in the apartment. Capote's technique is to read character as it is manifested in physical things. But all the evidence in the apartments is evidence of isolation and despair, from girly magazines left out in a bachelor's studio to a plastic dildo in the bathroom of a single woman. The tenants live alone, unable to communicate with each other, their letters unanswered, their notes indecipherable. Neither Capote nor Mary, the housekeeper, can hope to understand or reach them. The inhabitants are literally and figuratively absent. The meaning behind their surfaces remains a thing-in-itself, unknowable. In the telling epitaph to **Other Voices,** quoted from Jeremiah, "the heart is deceitful above all things, and desperately wicked. Who can know it?" In the end of **"A Day's Work"** Capote tells Mary, "I'm praying for you," and she replies: "Don't pray for me. I'm already saved.

(She takes my hand and holds it). Pray for your mother. Pray for all those souls lost out there in the dark" (*Chameleons* 166).

The mysteriousness of everyday existence is implicit in the controversy surrounding Capote's omniscience in *In Cold Blood*. How can he know that Dick swerved to hit a dog on the way back from the murders? How can he know Perry's dreams, or what Mr. Clutter was thinking as he stood on the morning of the murder and faced the house? These questions suggest our instinctive sense of the mysteriousness of character. Our conclusions about motives and feelings in the real world are always in the nature of conjecture. Critics have attacked Capote because he misrepresented the basketball skill of Nancy's boyfriend or got the facts wrong on the sale of Nancy's horse. Even fact is finally beyond certainty when the author is not inventing the story. Experience is too various and complex, too fine, to be represented completely in words.

In the acknowledgments to *In Cold Blood* Capote concedes this problem, carefully bracketing all of his subsequent omniscient observations. "All the material in this book not derived from my own observation," he says, "is either taken from official records or is the result of interviews with the persons directly concerned." Underneath the apparent omniscience is still a reliance on external indicators of internal states or second hand reports of past events. Capote must rely on written testimony which is by definition removed from the event itself, an interpretation of an individual. He cannot get at the truth. He can only make his interpretations on the basis of evidence. Perhaps this, in the end, is the attraction of nonfiction for Capote. He has given many accounts of why he moved from fiction to nonfiction at the turning point in his career, but perhaps after all it is his attraction to mystery which draws him to the nonfiction novel.

III

Authorial detachment can be a technique in any narrative, whatever the themes. It is not necessarily linked to the problems of wordlessness that concern us in this study. But the nuances and patterns of silence we have seen operating within Capote's texts give a new dimension to the silences *of* the text, establishing a thematic link between the narrative and the point of view of the narrative. The richness of silence as a theme in Capote creates an atmosphere, a set of symbolic resonances, in which narrative detachment and withholding become symbolically important in themselves.

When Capote focuses on the "great quiet of the prairies" which surrounds Dewey as he sits in Herb's rocking chair, and then falls silent himself; when he allows the chilling remarks of the towns-people to resonate without qualification or consolation or commentary ("if it can happen to them, who's safe I ask you?" or "well, it's like being told there is no God"); when he describes for a moment a hawk circling over the wheat-fields, isolating the image, leaving it stark, enigmatic—whenever Capote records a significant detail or bit of conversation or glimpse of the landscape without comment in these climactic scenes, he forces us as readers to experience the wordlessness at the heart of the events in Holcomb. Because he remains silent as narrator, withholding interpretation, we find ourselves as readers in the same position as Dewey, the townspeople, Capote himself: we must read details, generate theories and hypotheses, speculate about meaning behind phenomena, all without knowing whether our speculations are valid.

When he refuses to arbitrate among the competing readings his characters offer, refuses to intrude as narrator to declare truth or even to offer a theory of his own, Capote traps *us* in language. For us, too, as for Dewey and the townspeople, the truth remains a thing-in-itself, unknowable. "I didn't realize what I'd done till I heard the sound"—Perry's statement is fundamentally opaque, meaningless. It reveals nothing. As language, as text, it only highlights a more fundamental silence. Capote's authorial detachment at this point—he does not comment on this statement, does not qualify it, interpret it in his own voice—forces us into the position of limited observers faced with the opaqueness of phenomena, statements.

When Capote does not tell us what the clues of the murder might mean, when he does not give us direct insight into the motives for the murders, when he does not betray his own presence in the situation, he is reinforcing on the level of the narrative frame the thematic implications of the story: "In the parlor, a sheet of music, 'Comin Thro' the Rye,' stood open on the piano rack. In the hall, a sweat-stained Stetson hat—Herb's—hung on a hat peg. Upstairs in Kenyon's room, on a shelf above his bed, the lenses of the dead boy's spectacles gleamed with reflected light" (152). The language is spare and constrained and resolutely superficial, restricted to what can be observed. Details are made present—the dead boy's spectacles—but nothing more. They are random, part of no pattern. Narrative detachment can heighten suspense and involvement in any context, but in the context of *In Cold Blood* the rhetorical effect is greater. Capote's authorial silence here enables us to experience the implication of *In Cold Blood* that the final meaning of the event is inexplicable: the sheet music and the glittering glasses are merely poignant details, not symbols or clues, reminders of the pointlessness and randomness of the murders. In what Capote doesn't say, we experience what can't be said. When we join Dewey in the struggle to interpret the evidence—accounting for the position of the bodies and the nature of the wounds—when we participate with him in discovering the "animals in the picture," we experience more than the narrative suspense of a murder mystery. Because point of view is implicated in the symbolic resonances of the text, all the dilemmas of language and expression in the story are played out in the very act of reading.

In the process, ironically, Capote succeeds in magnifying the presence of the wordless reality he cannot finally describe. Absence creates presence. It is a psychological fact that the dimly seen and far away appear larger and more imposing in the mind. Obscurity arouses curiosity and activates imagination. "As nothing that is wholly seen through has other than a trivial character," Thomas Carlyle says, "so anything professing to be great, and yet wholly to see through it, is already known to be false, and a failure" (17). Unmarred by partial and inadequate description, the unseen object of expression—what happened to the Clutters, why it happened, what it means—becomes interesting and compelling. As Perelman puts it, "one of the benefits resulting from the obscurity of certain texts" is that such obscurity "quickens the attention." The "very lack of precision" gives the object of expression "a mysterious, magical character" (145, 157). Kenneth Burke agrees that we must concede "the great persuasive power of mystery" (*Rhetoric of Motives* 278). In fact, this is the rhetorical principle at work in Iser's notion that gaps elicit participation. Because the rhetoric of gaps depends on the mystique of withholding, it is ideally suited for magnifying the presence of an experience that can't be reproduced in language.

Here, then, is the central problem of contemporary American nonfiction. Silences represent for Capote both the danger of apocalypse and the attraction of mystery, the disintegration of culture and the intensely personal revelations of the self. Wolfe defines the American experience as sublime and in some ways mystical, and he embraces that sublimity. In Capote there is a greater sense of impending catastrophe, of threat and fear—the violence at Holcomb represents the beginning of some dimly understood but powerful incursion of evil and anarchy. Yet there is also in Capote a greater preoccupation with the seductions and fascinations of secrecy and concealment. Capote is drawn to silence as he is drawn to the poetic, the imaginative, the nuanced and layered. Silence seems to represent for him the claims of a certain kind of transcendence.

The rhetoric of silence, furthermore, is Capote's response to this problem. Wolfe pushes the outside of the envelope of language through rhetorical intensification and figures of sublimity in an effort to reach an experience beyond the limits of conventional journalism. Narrative detachment, in a sense, is Capote's way of pushing the outside of the envelope in an effort to attain mystery, wordlessness. If explicit commentary is impossible, the writer must seek some indirect means of suggesting, pointing to, hinting at his subject. Silence is a means of indirection, of pointing. It gives the readers instructions for an operation of meaning they must perform themselves. It implicitly asks readers to assemble, infer, deduce for themselves what as text it cannot explicitly say. As rhetoric, it circumvents the problem of representation: it seeks to entice us to imagine what cannot be represented.

But Capote, unlike Wolfe, does not approach the problem of apocalypse head on. He does not make a direct assault. He does not strain and struggle like Wolfe in the effort at direct evocation. Rather, he adopts narrative detachment as a strategy from the beginning of the story, carefully positioning himself from the outset.

In the starkness and tension of Capote's spare sentences there is some sense of strain or failure. The absence of reconciling commentary in Capote can be regarded on a basic level as symptomatic of his inability to interpret the event, a kind of zero-degree interpretive stance. From this perspective we would say that Capote does not arbitrate among these competing readings of the central silence because as narrator the experience literally overwhelms him. He is not working for effect but, in the face of such extreme and shocking brutality, resigning all efforts to create effects. This is the implication of Zavarzadeh's general thesis in *The Mythopoeic Reality*. Capote eschews interpretation, Zavarzadeh would say, because the event he is trying to describe is "inherently ambiguous and so bizarre that it cannot be categorized as either factual or fictional by our current epistemological standards" (126). Or in Tony Tanner's more elegant phrasing, Capote gives the "illusion of art laying down its tools as helpless and irrelevant in front of the horrors and mysteries of life itself" ("Death in Kansas" 98).

The text itself gives cues for reading narrative detachment as a kind of shock. When the bodies are first discovered, Capote says, "nobody said anything"; they were "too stunned" (63). When the jurors are shown pictures of the bodies later at the trial, the courtroom grows "exceedingly silent" (281). "It just shut you up," a friend of Mr. Clutter remarks, "the strangeness of it" (78).

Even in the shorter pieces, in ***Muses*** or **"A Day's Work,"** Capote's decision to remain outside events emphasizes in part the limits of language and the presence of something beyond it. More than acknowledging the boundaries of journalism, Capote's careful maintaining of objectivity and his refusal to advance more than minimal hypotheses implies on the level of the narrative itself that human understanding is inherently finite. "We live in the dark," he quotes from Henry James, "we do what we can, the rest is the madness of art" (***Chameleons*** xv).

But even if this were true, as we have seen in Wolfe, the very breakdown of imagination can have the effect of signifying the grandeur and magnitude of the object in view. Zavarzadeh's notion that Capote is relinquishing all control in his narrative stance simply overlooks the figurative possibilities of failure. Yet in the end I don't think that the logic of the sublime operates in quite this way in Capote. Our impression as readers of Capote is that he is in complete control of his language in **In Cold Blood,** that he has adopted a certain strategy from the beginning and carefully maintained it throughout the text. As Capote explains in a preface, nonfiction presents him with a stylistic challenge, an opportunity to create new aesthetic effects and develop a tighter, more effective prose style:

> For several years I had been increasingly drawn toward journalism as an art form in itself. I had two reasons. First, it didn't seem to me that anything truly innovative had occurred in prose writing, or in writing generally, since the 1920's; second, journalism as art was almost virgin terrain, for the simple reason that very few literary artists ever wrote narrative journalism.
>
> (**Chameleons** xiv)

This is not literature giving up on itself, the artist renouncing art before the chaos of the age. This is the statement of a craftsman exploring the possibilities of his medium. The rhetoric of silence is a device of language for creating certain effects. As Mailer puts it—in an important analysis we will return to later—Capote's style is a kind of "jewel," "superb" in its craftsmanship and precision. Capote is one of those contemporary authors who in Mailer's view follows the prescription for style laid down by "the great physician Dr. James Joyce—'silence, exile, and cunning'" (*Cannibals* 99, 5).

"Cunning" is not exactly the right word to describe Capote; it underestimates the intensity of his commitment to language, implies a kind of insincerity. But at the same time it does express the quality of control and precision I have tried to identify in his prose, and with "silence" on the one hand and "exile" on the other it comes close to capturing the true character of his style. Indeed, the context of Mailer's discussion of Capote is a larger discussion of how contemporary American writers develop forms in direct response to the "apocalyptic" nature of the great "Beast" that is America. Capote's response to the wordless is "the ceremony of style," the strong and flexible "fishermen's net" of words. He comes to Holcomb equipped with a stylistic credo ideal for coping with the experience he eventually finds—which is perhaps no accident after all, since Capote's style in his previous works of fiction is intimately linked with a concern for human mysteries and silences. The style and subject in Capote call forth one another. This is not to diminish the tension between words and wordlessness in Capote, nor to exclude the rhetoric of the sublime from a consideration of his style. In Capote that negative logic is worked out in subtler ways. The relationship between words and wordlessness in his prose, because restrained, is tauter, more finely tuned. But the issue at stake for him is the same as for Wolfe and, we will see, for Mailer: the effort to communicate the incommunicable.

IV

In an interview after Capote's death, the Kansas lawyer who prosecuted Perry and Hickock questioned the moral and rhetorical purpose of **In Cold Blood**:

> I don't think there was one bit of redeeming social value in Capote's whole book. It was a successful idea that made him and a lot of other people a lot of money. It's a shame that our city has to be on the map for that thing. In the courthouse square, we have a statue of C. J. Buffalo Jones, our first mayor (in 1883). He should get the recognition. It's just unfortunate that we didn't have media hype back then.
>
> (Polman)

Behind the frustrated boosterism in this remark lie legitimate questions about the value and intended effect of **In Cold Blood,** questions shared by more sophisticated readers and critics.

Booth maintains that "in fiction the concept of writing well must include the successful ordering of your reader's view of a fictional world." The author "has an obligation to be as clear about his moral position as he possibly can be," whatever that moral position is (*Rhetoric* 388-89). In some modern fiction, where narrative detachment is too scrupulously maintained, the intelligent reader cannot be sure what the author is trying to imply. In his silence, we are subject to "misreadings."

If fiction has the obligation to interpret rather than simply present surfaces, nonfiction would seem to have an even greater obligation to order. Though fiction may have didactic purposes and specific rhetorical ends, its primary purpose is to create an aesthetically satisfying and credible fictive world. Rhetorical literature, in contrast, while it may have aesthetic and literary purposes, is by definition intended to serve rhetorical ends: it must inform, deliberate, reflect on experience.

It is possible to argue that Capote's stance in **In Cold Blood,** like Wolfe's in *Acid Test,* is morally ambiguous in precisely Booth's sense. Because he maintains a strict authorial silence in his non-fiction narratives, it is difficult to determine on a first or superficial reading whose side Capote is on or what he wants us to learn from the story. Because he does not argue or reflect in explicit ways, it is not immediately apparent how **In Cold Blood** is meant to inform us or guide us.

To put this another way, Capote can be seen as guilty of aestheticism. Weber rightly says of *In Cold Blood* that "no other work of literary nonfiction is so resolutely literary in its intentions" (74). As we have noted, Capote's own statements about the composition of the book are largely technical, his motives aesthetic. His sacrifices, he says, have been at "the altar of technique" (*Chameleons* xii). From this perspective the argument is that Capote is simply interested in creating aesthetic effects, not in responding to social problems. We know that Capote made the decision to experiment with nonfiction prior to discovering the subject of the Holcomb murders. The tragedy in Kansas seemed to be ideal material for creating a new, hybrid literary form.

At the same time it can be argued that in his silences Capote allows himself to identify—and allows us to identify—with Perry, just as Wolfe seems to allow us in his silences to identify with Kesey. In remaining strategically detached from the narrative, Capote engages our sympathy with a morally despicable criminal mind. In failing to correct or qualify the actions and thoughts of the mind he inhabits, Capote implicates himself in a kind of evil. More than that, it can be argued that Capote actively sympathizes with Perry's character and situation, identifying himself with Perry's appearance, his status as freak and victim, his artistic tendencies. In this light Perry becomes a prime example of what Booth calls the "seductive rogues who narrate much modern fiction." Inside views "can build sympathy even for the most vicious character," Booth points out, and while such strategies of identification can force us "to see the human worth of a character whose actions, objectively considered, we would deplore," they also run the risk of "moral confusion" (379).

But it seems to me that in my claims for the rhetorical effectiveness of silence in Capote are two important answers to these charges.

First, Capote's preoccupation in both his fiction and nonfiction is with demonstrating that the world contains silence and mystery. His underlying "moral" or "message" is that beyond the narrow and petty concerns of our day to day life are mysteries both terrible and compelling. Holcomb, like La Honda, is a metaphor for complacent Eisenhower Republicanism exploded by the energies of the age. Capote's quick sketch of the Clutters' living room suggests his subtle satire of the middle-class:

> As for the interior, there were spongy displays of liver-colored carpet intermittently abolishing the glare of varnished, resounding floors; an immense modernistic living-room couch covered in nubby fabric interwoven with glittery strands of silver metal; a breakfast alcove featuring a banquette upholstered in blue-and-white plastic. This sort of furnishing was what Mr. and Mrs. Clutter liked, as did the majority of their acquaintances, whose homes, by and large, were similarly furnished.
>
> (9)

The banal bad taste of this interior reflects the stolidity of the town as a whole. It is unimaginative. In an opening scene that recalls Wallace Stevens' "Disillusionment at 10 O'Clock" ("The houses are haunted / by white night gowns"), Capote describes Holcomb as a ghost-town, faded, empty, isolated. Its people are asleep, both literally and figuratively; they are "sufficiently unfearful of each other to seldom trouble to lock their doors" (5).

Into this landscape—figured by the silence of the deserted streets and the sleeping townspeople—come "explosions" and "foreign sounds" which foreshadow the murder. Until the murders, no "exceptional happening" had ever occurred in Holcomb. Capote's purpose from the beginning of the book, if read carefully, is to wake up the townspeople—and by implication, the reader. His silences are meant to stimulate our involvement and arouse us from complacency. They constitute both a warning and an invitation.

All the main characters in Capote's fiction are characters of imagination, enigmatic and beyond formula. As the Egyptian remarks in **"A Jug of Silver,"** "It's the mystery that's enchanting" (*Tree of Night* 152). It's not the possibility of winning a great deal of money that inspires the townspeople to gamble on how many silver coins the druggist has stored up in a clear glass jug; the people are inspired by the sense of not knowing. A feeling of uncertainty and anticipation raises the characters in this story above their ordinary life. ***The Grass Harp*** is a parable about the power of Dolly's magic versus the deadening mechanicalness of her sister's insistence on formula. Dolly is a free spirit, close to the earth, a maker of magic potions, someone suspect from the standpoint of conventional standards of conduct. Verena, her sister, is authoritarian, no-nonsense, businesslike, contemptuous of her sister's excesses and irresponsibility. At the crisis point, when after an argument Dolly runs away to live in a treehouse, Capote clearly means us to see, through the eyes of his young narrator, the desirability of the imaginative life over and against the life of convention. His sympathies, and ours, are with Dolly in the treehouse.

This is the whole tenor of Capote's work, from the early stories through the later nonfiction. He is compelled by mystery, and his argument, reinforced by the rhetoric of silence, is that mysteries have an intrinsic power and desirability. I'm not suggesting that in *In Cold Blood* Capote in some way prefers violence over peacefulness, murder over middle-class life. Yet there is in Capote's scrupulous avoidance of explanation, his insistence on the inexplicability of the event, a sense that for him there is value in some happening which challenges and raises us above the mundane inevitability of bourgeois life. "Things unspoken" are always "the center of interest," he remarks of Dick's interrogation (229).

If this is true, the rhetoric of silence, as style, performs its argument. Style is a kind of magic. It transcends simple communication, the transaction of information and fact. It exists as a kind of aura between the lines, in the blank space surrounding the text. Style develops from what is not said and what cannot be said. Perhaps from this perspective, what seems a mere "ceremony of style," a set of strategies open to the charge of aestheticism, really develops a philosophical and thematic force of its own. Style becomes an argument for style, for that which cannot be measured, explained, reduced to the explicit.

Indeed, in my view Capote's style is his most powerful argument. He is not morally ambiguous. He is not on Perry's side. He is on the side of language. The fact of his style, the fact even of his aestheticism, signals his allegiance to the controlling and conserving power of language over and against the chaos and violence and meaninglessness threatening language from the outside.

It is true that Capote identifies with Perry in certain very subtle ways. By means of the rhetoric of silence—selection, presence, connotation and imagery—he orchestrates our deepening engagement with Perry from the beginning of the book. After Perry is arrested and jailed Capote chooses to describe his situation through the eyes of Josie Meier, the sheriff's wife and Perry's cook during his imprisonment in Holcomb. Mrs. Meier is a kindly older woman, and her portrait of Perry emphasizes his vulnerability and even his gentleness: she worries about the large crowds that gather around the jail; she worries that Perry might catch pneumonia on the first "bitter cold" night; she frets because he doesn't eat any of his supper. Through her we later learn that Perry befriends a squirrel who appears on his window sill, that he cried on the night of his conviction, and that, after being sentenced to hang, he declared, "I'm embraced by shame" (308). He speaks softly, "almost a whisper," spends his time brooding quietly in his cell, standing at the window. Through Mrs. Meier's maternal eyes we see Perry as a lonely and suffering child in a thin cotton prison shirt. "He wasn't the worst young man I ever saw," she says (285). He becomes associated in her account with the homey pleasantries of apple pie and baked bread. The jail is adjacent to the Meiers' kitchen, the criminal subsumed for the moment in the domestic.

Capote has not made any explicit bids for our sympathy and compassion. He has remained detached. But just by his selection of Mrs. Meier's narrative as the organizing point of view at this juncture, and his suppression of other points of view, he has encouraged us as readers to identify with Perry. Throughout the book he selects detail and testimony that present Perry in a favorable light: Perry writes and paints, he is abused and abandoned by his father, he is deformed. According to Willie-Jay, a friend from prison, he is a frustrated poet, something "rare and savable" (45). The mere selection of such details, even without directing commentary, projects Perry's character in positive ways.

By withholding his description of the actual murders until late in the third section of the book, Capote further encourages us to sympathize with Perry. Unaware of the horrible and senseless details of Perry's behavior on the night of the killings, we are more likely to pity him for his tough luck and difficult childhood. When Capote does finally describe the murders themselves, he chooses to relay the details first through Perry's own confession. The killings are first presented through the consciousness of a character for whom we've developed some measure of sympathy. As Capote himself explained in an interview with George Plimpton:

> I believe Perry did what he did for the reasons he himself states—that his life was a constant accumulation of disillusionments and reverses and he suddenly found himself (in the Clutter house that night) in a psychological cul-de-sac. The Clutters were such a perfect set of symbols for every frustration in his life. As Perry himself said, "I didn't have anything against them, and they never did anything wrong to me—the way other people have all my life. Maybe they're just the ones who had to pay for it." Now in the particular section where Perry talks about the reason for the murders, I could have included other views. But Perry's happens to be the one I believe is the right one.
>
> (Plimpton 38)

What Capote describes here is what Perelman calls the rhetorical power of "choice" in creating "presence" (116). Because as readers we have only one interpretation to consider—because competing interpretations are set aside—we are more likely to give this version of events credence. It is more present in our minds, "overestimated" in our consciousness.

What Burke would call the "question-begging tonalities" of Capote's descriptive language also encourage identifications with Perry (*Rhetoric of Motives* 91). In the first pages of the book Capote describes Mr. Clutter with documentary style briskness. The sentences are direct and unadorned, the detail largely factual and statistical. We are told about his insurance policies, his membership in the Rotary, the value of his house and land. Clutter in fact comes off as something of a prig: "He did not smoke, and of course he did not drink; indeed, he had never tasted spirits, and was inclined to avoid people who had" (20).

But in the second chapter, simply spliced or juxtaposed after the first, the language becomes denser and richer, the character more imaginative and compelling. This is our first description of Perry:

> His own face enthralled him. Each angle of it induced a different impression. It was a changeling's face, and mirror-guided experiments had taught him how to ring

the changes, how to look now ominous, now impish, now soulful; a tilt of the head, a twist of the lips, and the corrupt gypsy became the gentle romantic. His mother had been a full-blooded Cherokee; it was from her that he inherited his coloring—the iodine skin, the dark, moist eyes, the black hair which he kept brilliantined and was plentiful enough to provide him with sideburns and a slippery spray of bangs.

(15-16)

Perry is not an entirely sympathetic character. He is vain, and as we learn later in the scene, he is also shiftless, out of work, and recently released from prison. But Capote's descriptions make him out to be a romantic, gypsy-like figure strikingly more interesting than the stick figure of Mr. Clutter. Perhaps more importantly, Capote's sentences become more heavily modified and sophisticated, not just base clauses followed by an appositive or two—the stock sentence of his prose—but long, accumulating descriptions, dense with metaphor, assonance, consonance, concrete detail ("the slippery spray of bangs," "the iodine skin"). Perry dreams of travelling to exotic places, of "drifting downward through strange waters, of plunging toward a green sea-dusk, sliding past the scaly, savage-eyed protectors of a ship's hulk that loomed ahead, a Spanish galleon—a drowned cargo of diamonds and pearls, heaping caskets of gold" (17). The poetic texture of the language both engages us and signals Capote's greater interest in Perry's character. Like Kesey for Wolfe, he is a figure of imagination, and the sentences that describe him are not transparent but translucent. The appositives lengthen and become more interesting, more metaphorical.

But ultimately Capote cannot be on Perry's side in this book because Perry represents the nonverbal and the antiverbal. It is clear that in some ways Capote saw himself in Perry; he shared with Perry the experience of deformity and isolation. It is also true that in *In Cold Blood* there are several indications that Capote views the hanging of the murderers as "pretty goddam cold-blooded, too" (306). But these are not the real issues. What Perry represents is the danger of the antiverbal and nonverbal forces which threaten American society on the eve of a new decade. He represents the rejection of language which precedes the act of violence, whatever his pretenses to poetry. Ultimately, after all the efforts to engage our sympathies, Capote reveals the facts of that night in Holcomb for what they are: a horrible silencing of the discourse that enables us to live together. Perry's silence is in some ways compelling: as a figure of imagination he embodies the possibility of transcending the mundane. But on a higher level he threatens to undermine the possibility of making sense out of the world through words.

It is from this perspective that Capote's style itself becomes the most important rhetorical act. The language presenting Perry's character and engaging our sympathies with him is at odds with the violence and wordlessness that Perry finally represents. The language that describes him controls, conserves, directs, maintains nuances and shades of meaning. Perry himself is not capable of writing the kinds of sentences that Capote uses to portray him or using the kinds of metaphor Capote discovers for suggesting his importance. His language is mumbled and fragmentary, incapable of managing his affairs in the world.

In Capote's silence and reticence we are called to read each word carefully, ponder its meaning. Capote's detachment requires us to linger on the surface of the language, drawing us into that contractual relationship that Iser describes as the filling of gaps. Ironically, the text invites our participation because it demands our interpretation. And as a result, in the experience of reading Capote, we are located in the text, we are inside it, recreating it ourselves, participating in the making of meaning. We are not implicated finally in Perry's evil but in Capote's aestheticism, his demand for and peformance of style. Because gaps create puzzles to solve, we are finally engaged with Dewey and the other detectives in the effort to establish order.

The priority of style over substance is what makes Capote's work socially valuable. It represents the battle of words against wordlessness. There is no real contradiction here. On the one hand Capote wants to create and celebrate silence, awakening his readers to experiences beyond words and in some way energizing language with the possibilities of silence. But on the other hand he wants to claim silence for language. He wants to identify with Perry's violence and mystery yet contain it for style. Silence for him does not represent the failure of rhetoric; rather, silence is the key to the dynamic possibilities of rhetoric.

Works Cited

PRIMARY

TRUMAN CAPOTE

Other Voices, Other Rooms. New York: Random House, 1948.

A Tree of Night and Other Stories. New York: Random House, 1949.

The Grass Harp. New York: Random House, 1951.

The Muses Are Heard. New York: Random House, 1956.

In Cold Blood. New York: Random House, 1965.

The Dogs Bark. New York: Random House, 1973.

Music for Chameleons. New York: Random House, 1980.

NORMAN MAILER

Cannibals and Christians. New York: Dial Press, 1966.

TOM WOLFE

The Electric Kool-Aid Acid Test. New York: Farrar, Straus, and Giroux, 1968.

SECONDARY

Booth, Wayne C. *The Rhetoric of Fiction*. Chicago: U of Chicago P, 1961.

Burke, Kenneth. *A Rhetoric of Motives*. Berkeley: U of California P, 1969.

Cowley, Malcom, ed. *Writers at Work*: The Paris Review *Interviews*. New York: Viking, 1960.

Iser, Wolfgang. *The Act of Reading: A Theory of Aesthetic Response*. Baltimore: Johns Hopkins UP, 1978.

Plimpton, George. "The Story behind a Nonfiction Novel." *New York Times Book Review* 16 Jan. 1966: 2-3, 38-42.

Polman, Dick. "'Squirrely little' Capote remembered in Kansas." Knight-Ridder Newspapers. Week of 10 Sept. 1984.

Tanner, Tony. "Death in Kansas." *Truman Capote's* In Cold Blood: *A Critical Handbook*. Ed. Irving Malin. Belmont, Calif.: Wadsworth, 1968.

Weber, Ronald. *The Literature of Fact: Literary Nonfiction in American Writing*. Athens: Ohio UP, 1980.

Zavarzadeh, Mas'ud. *The Mythopoeic Reality: The Postwar American Nonfiction Novel*. Urbana: U of Illinois P, 1976.

Jack Hicks (essay date 1990)

SOURCE: Hicks, Jack. "'Fire, Fire, Fire Flowing Like a River, River, River': History and Postmodernism in Truman Capote's *Handcarved Coffins*." In *History and Post-War Writing*, edited by Theo D'haen and Hans Bertens, pp. 171-84. Amsterdam: Rodopi B.V., 1990.

[*In the following essay, Hicks investigates the postmodern influences apparent in Capote's* Handcarved Coffins, *claiming that the text of the story reflects Capote's ultimate rejection of history and myth as organizing forces.*]

The waters of history have long made a nurturing mother for us, as they play down to us traditionally through prose in tides of genre, rivers of continuous narrative, deep mimetic lakes of character. But for many postmodern American writers of fiction and non-fiction, this mother has become a diabolical matriarch—comic, deceptive, murderous. As an informing matrix for human life, she ceases to exist.

Turn first to fiction. For prose postmoderns disparate as John Barth, Kurt Vonnegut, Jr., Jerzy Kosinski and Thomas Pynchon, history is a deceiving agent, and the fictive tropes and texts giving her voice must be self-consciously exposed and undone. Barth burlesques the founding nostalgias of the New World, limning, instead, a bawdy new *ur*-myth, at the heart of which is an America opened as a fresh market for the international opium trade. His "historical" Captain John Smith is a mythic counteragent, and the tools of his founding trade are not beads and trinkets, blunderbusses, or the healing modern sciences, but texts: a trunkful of pornography to woo the New World "salvages," and a secret diary, in which lurks an eggplant recipe guaranteeing the eternal, conquering priapus.

For Vonnegut in *Slaughterhouse-5,* the urge to history, encased in martial fiction, is a vicious comic ruse, and even the anti-war novel, which rejects warfare, valorizes the individual warrior of conscience, and is thus complicit in extending a history of senseless brutality. The form and its inevitable awakening protagonist, from Henry Fleming to Yossarian, make warfare morally palatable. Earth people are *easy*, the Tralfamadoreans tell us—they already know our accidental and absurd end—and they posit a planet and literature in which everything happens at once and leads finally nowhere. In Vonnegut's hand, they expose the petty human urge to cloak self-destruction in self-deluding myth.

In his postmodern fable *The Painted Bird,* Jerzy Kosinski also takes the historic World War II as his canvas. The will to yoke such grand terror in continuous narrative, and the need to create a young warrior who awakens in battle are both shown as annihilating impulses. The child protagonist blunders from village to village and realizes finally that the social cord itself is diseased. To be fully free, he must reject society and all its institutions, from language to history to the life narratives of others, all of which promise his extermination.

Similarly, for Thomas Pynchon in *V,* the urge to historicize is rooted in psychological paranoia, and it leads to omnivorous narratives of conspiracy that devour all of existence in quest of pattern and accounting. What once suckled us is an infernal machine here, ratcheting through phenomenal life as surely as the letter V yawns up and open, yearning forever at the acme of its own shape.

I cite Barth, Vonnegut, Kosinski and Pynchon because they are internationally known, and show in the mainstream radical doubts and revolutionary techniques deemed threatening and destructive two decades ago. In brief, while some of their postmodern peers are far more innovative and/or *avant garde,* this quartet illustrates the power of *influence,* the extent to which postmodernism has pervaded. And influence, I suggest, is one true test of any *avant garde.* The truly revolutionary can never content itself with remaining marginal or peripheral, and however violently it resists assimilation, it is most prominent—at least in literature—in how it refigures the core.

American literary postmodernism, then, brings strong counter-pressures into the mainstream, seen nowhere more vividly than in the reexamination of the will to historicize, and of the philosophical validity and implications of history herself. Note that I write of both fiction and non-fiction, and nowhere to this point have spoken of the term "novel" or of companion genres. Radical doubt now denies us the comfort of using such categories with ease. Indeed, writing free of history and thus beyond genre is a literary dream of some postmodern artists, and with the rise of serious literary non-fiction (the non-fiction novel to the new journalism, including work by Joan Didion, Norman Mailer, Tom Wolfe, Truman Capote, Edward Abbey, Hunter S. Thompson, Frederick Exley, and others), the full blurring of the lines between fiction and fact is real.

-2-

Recent research takes me into the realm of American literary non-fiction since 1960, a profound and abundant surge of work calling for serious scrutiny. Many of our finest writers—including Didion, Mailer, Wolfe, Capote and Peter Matthiessen—have turned away from fiction, either because they sense elsewhere dramatic new, uncharted potential (Mailer's *Armies of the Night* and *The Executioner's Song* are results), or feel that conventional narrative forms (fed by myth and history) cannot perceive or contain recent strangenesses in the United States. Didion's *The White Album,* Wolfe's *The Electric Kool-Aid Acid Test* and Capote's **In Cold Blood** are varying issues of such convictions. And some writers work with a special passion to amplify/diagnose symptoms of the national heart, seeking new instruments for deep work. In Matthiessen's case, *The Snow Leopard* constitutes the former, *In the Spirit of Crazy Horse* the latter urge.

Hidden in this tide has been the assumption, as well, that the familiar categories within this genre (auto/biography, confession and memoir, long nature or wilderness meditation, the narrative of national achievement or catastrophe, the diary, the character study, the travel narrative, and the occasional essay)—ill-defined as they are—now impede our vision and are no longer reflexive literary modes. Thus unfamiliar, perplexing hybrids appear, many of which question the assumption that non-fiction funtions to record history and the real and the forms it takes: Is Joan Didion's "The White Album" simply an intimate account of the profound social crises of the Manson Era? Or can it be more than the psychic historical diary it pretends to offer, a "confession" that draws power from fiction to create the certainty of intimate fact that it mimics? Is the "I" of the narrative, certified by her doctor's psychiatric evaluation, truly congruent with the "real" Joan Didion?

Against this backdrop, I will examine Truman Capote's **Handcarved Coffins,** for several purposes. First, recent American literary non-fiction is now a field of serious art requiring close attention, and Capote's *corpus* is a major mark. Second, the "fire, fire, fire flowing like a river, river, river" of **Handcarved Coffins** enacts, in the process of the text, the intrusion of the postmodern sensibility, in both a very unlikely author and in markedly atypical narrative and stylistic aspects.[1]

-3-

In contrast to that of Mailer and Didion, Capote's work is an unlikely candidate for the irruption of the postmodern, for as a literary heir to William Faulkner, he draws in fiction and non-fiction upon his Southernness. He writes with a poet's eye for exotic landscape and eccentric character in both his early fiction (***Other Voices, Other Rooms*** [1948] and ***A Tree of Night*** [1949]) and non-fiction (***Local Color*** [1950]).[2] But however misty or gothic the surfaces, he writes from a received assumption that history and myth—often tragic—are reliable informants, restless and alive. Even in the environment itself, be it New Orleans, New York, Haiti or the wild rocks of Greece. As Faulkner's, his work is implicitly traditional, even conservative, in its acceptance of home and hearth and nurturing place, all held in a dense mythic/historic matrix.

Capote is far more conventional in technique, for there are few Faulknerian soundings of point of view, chronology, plotting or interiority. Conventional, as well, in his acceptance of genre: elegant as the prose and mystic the places of ***Local Color*** may be, it is a collection of travel pieces, each written on commission from magazines catering to mass audiences.

Similarly, ***The Muses Are Heard*** (1956) is a direct non-fiction novella of a rare 1955 tour of the USSR by a wide-eyed *Porgy and Bess* troupe. **"The Duke in His Domain,"** his celebrated bitchy profile of actor Marlon Brando, brings artistry to a hitherto journalistic form—much as Lillian Ross did earlier in her *New Yorker* portraits—but it remains a character study, a genre piece.[3]

Even **In Cold Blood,** which Capote proclaimed wholecloth a new genre—"the nonfiction novel"—is decidedly realistic in philosophy and form.[4] The work remains riveting, a contemporary masterpiece, and while it is structurally informed by montage, the double narrative is continuous and unfaltering, driving the reader through with cinematic immediacy. The rich store of Midwestern detail, the lives of the Clutters, Smith, Hickock blended in a history of the newer West, offers Capote a metaphoric bank, and both victims and murderers are rendered with alarming mimetic credibility.

The arc of the plot—from random mass murder as wound to the body politic, to the purgation of evil and the restoration of communal harmony in a graveyard close—employs history and myth as organizing and nourishing modes. Indeed, the protagonist is Detective Alvin Dewey, an embodiment of the need for moral right, and his quest traces ancient mythic forms. Like many recent fictional quests (both popular and serious), his pattern has sources in an ancient literary river, with antecedents in classic Greek and Shakespearean tragedies of violation and redemption.

The power of the work issues also in auctorial repression. The point of view is omniscient, author and/or narrator rigorously excluded from narrative episodes. We know Capote was no mere after the fact recorder in *In Cold Blood*, and found himself painfully involved with his subjects, especially Smith and Hickock, but he permits himself no appearance as character, save a ghostly reference or two as "a journalist."[5] There is, as well, no hint of postmodern narrative self-consciousness or textual self-reference.

"I wanted to produce a journalistic novel," he writes of *In Cold Blood*, in the Preface to *Music for Chameleons*, his last collection of non-fiction, "something on a large scale that would have the credibility of fact, the immediacy of film, the depth and freedom of prose, and the precision of poetry."[6] He achieved that height, but almost immediately questioned its value, finding himself in deep depression. By 1975, he was central in the rise of literary non-fiction to art, but he doubted the validity of the pattern of both his life and craft. When he undertook *Handcarved Coffins* on a tip from Alvin Dewey, he quickly realized that the impulse to twin *In Cold Blood* was a decade too late and a lifetime away: a nostalgic wish, doomed.

Capote, who found himself "suffering a creative crisis and a personal one at the same time," claimed to have reread every line he ever wrote. He sensed his work had come to a dead end:

> I felt my writing was becoming too dense . . . by restricting myself to the techniques of whatever form I was working in, I was not using everything I knew about writing—all I'd learned from film scripts, plays, reportage, poetry, the short story, novellas, the novel. A writer ought to have all his colors available on the same palette for mingling (and, in suitable instances, simultaneous application). But how?[7]

The writer's crisis was personal—he was, by 1975, sorely impaired by drugs, drink, failing physical/mental health—but profoundly philosophic and artistic as well. The answer to his quandary lived in tapping the deepest sources of his dis-ease, his doubts of personal power, the social fabric, the continuing reliability of the historical impulse. And all fourteen of the pieces collected in *Music for Chameleons* reflect this decision.

Handcarved Coffins was undertaken in the sanguine hope that it would revive the time and achievement of *In Cold Blood*, that the mythic Blue River flowing through an even grislier plain than the earlier Kansas, would power another model of narrative continuity and social balance. But the dream dies, the source slows down and dries up, revealing a loss of faith in history and myth as viable patterns for life and art and in the narrative techniques that create such patterns. But this drying of old sources yields a variety of postmodern traits, at once destructive and creative: the deflection of the tide of single form into generic conflation; the disruption of mimesis once held in rushing narrative, pools of credible character. What emerges are techniques such as Capote's pastiche of diary extracts and dramatic scaffoldings, and an insistent, interrupting parenthetical style. Such devices jar the plates of social realism, bare the artifice of the narrative scape, insist on the textuality and intertextuality of setting, character, and plot.

Prior to working (c. 1970-1980) on the posthumously published *Answered Prayers* and *Music for Chameleons*, he admits, "I had tried to keep myself as invisible as possible." It is wise to be chary of writerly attribution of purpose and design well after the art has emerged; creation rarely stops at the border of the typed page. But Capote is accurate, continuing, "Now, however, I set myself at center stage . . . ," and correctly describes his new style as "a severe, minimal manner."[8]

Thus we find a highly self-conscious and self-referential narrator, with an urgent swerve from the masterly omniscience that served *In Cold Blood* so well, toward text as free assertion of personality, as a projection of the inner life: of hope, frustration, and most, fear.

-4-

The force of *In Cold Blood* flows from the dense social and psychological vision of victims and murderers, two mingled versions of the American myth of success. The Clutters make a doomed Eden in River Valley Farm, "a patch of paradise," and their prize apple orchard is not far from the county seat, Garden City. (23) Patriarch Herb Clutter embodies our dream of success by sweaty work and ingenuity, his spread won from the Kansas Depression dustbowl of the 1930s. Psychopathic killers Perry Smith and Dick Hickock are rootless, wandering, compelled by perverse democratic fantasies of utter mobility and windfall fortune. Every man a king at any moment, they tell themselves; life is a gamble each instant, as they realize ironically on their capture in Las Vegas.

The surface of *In Cold Blood* is sectioned into four books, eighty-five episodes, and it moves back and forth in time by flashback and flashforward. But it plays seamlessly as an accurately (as far as we can tell) imagined history of murder and social retribution. Under the orderly historical surface run multiple patterns that first bind us uncomfortably, then set us uncertainly free, healed for a time. Victims and murderers—two versions of our founding myths—, there are elements of each in the Other, they will not remain comfortably apart. This is a source of anxiety for the careful reader, right from the opening excerpt of François Villon's "*Ballade des Pendus,*" in which the condemned and the watching crowd are linked at the gallows.

The four Clutter killings, for example, are committed during the Thanksgiving season, an occasion with pagan, Christian and national mythic dimensions. The restoring protagonist, Detective Alvin Dewey, is an Anyman, and it is his lot to imagine the crime from clues, pursue the guilty, and set the trial in motion. On his course, he is ordained to take on the suffering (and wrath) of the community—in body and spirit—and heal himself and society in the final ritual purgation of Smith and Hickock.

Against this narrative of rich metaphor, informed by mythic and historical patterns, runs the deracinated text of *Handcarved Coffins*. The non-fiction novella is an account of multiple murder "in a small Western state" Capote fearfully elects not to name (67), and the apparent murderer a wealthy rancher he calls Bob Quinn. When a citizens' committee votes to change the course of the local Blue River, spreading water rights among his neighbours, Quinn plots and undertakes the murders of all eight members. Shortly before a grotesque death, each receives an intricately hardcarved tiny balsamwood coffin, on the pillow of which rests a candid photograph, a portent.

What originates as sequel is very quickly truncated. Bob Quinn is the murderer to Detective Jake Pepper and author Capote, but while the burden of proof is weighty, it is all circumstantial. Thus what the author hoped to find a second ritual of social violation and restoration refuses to assume that shape. The detective quest that structures *In Cold Blood* is denied certainty here. Nine victims fall, and the suspected killer's fortunes go unchanged, actually improve. The text reflects first Capote's increasing frustration with, then rejection of, history and myth as organizing and just forces, and this is most evident in the disruption of the narrative itself.

The Blue River is a metaphor for the author's desire for historical/mythic continuity, his hope for a revivified narrative flow. It is first a source of life, gathering from the snow of distant mountains, nourishing the many ranches and lives in the valley. But it is soon treacherous (an accomplice in the drowning of Pepper's fiancée, Addie Mason), and finally demonic and death-dealing, a mirror in which to see his own forced, infernal baptism forty years earlier. To be born ritually into this world, Capote implies, is to be dragged in unwillingly, to be ceremonially drowned, inundated first beneath the waters of a hell-on-earth.

The waters no longer nourishing, the narrative churns itself into broken forms, subsumes other genres, seeks power in a conflation of screenplay, confession, diary. By the end of the second page, Capote has rigorously restricted his setting to that of a stage, with dialogue set off as lines for his actors, stage directions appended in parenthetical glosses. But this artifice flags, and as the Blue River surges and people continue to die, Capote moves almost chess-like through reduced narrative modes, inscribing his growing rage at Jake Pepper's impotence (and his own), and a rising awareness that his anger is funded by fear of social collapse and a very private demonology.

First screenplay, then the text is conflated to appropriate the apparent confession, as Capote mimes the structure of admission, seeks forgiveness for his own failings and those of the world in which he now finds himself. Errant lover to questioning mate: penitent to priest: patient to therapist: political criminal to torturer: murderer to interrogator: putative autobiographer to engrossed reader: These are all confessional structures by which truth may be revealed, redemption begun in apparent admission and purgation. But as in Joan Didion's "The White Album," they may also be powerful artistic ploys by which the illusion of self-scouring candour yields a highly effective mode of deceiving narration. And this, I suggest, is what Capote is up to.

Jake Pepper is powerless, doubted even by his superiors in the State Bureau. Denied effective solution to the horror continuing around him, Capote plumbs the cause for his own terror of Quinn and the Blue River. He finds it in the flow of nightmare images the two release, as they force repressed memory to the surface in dream and flashback. Beyond personal empathy for the victims and social indignation, the narrator reimagines his own forced, hellish river baptism by Reverend Bobby Joe Snow forty years earlier. Thus the narrative is further conflated, to absorb the stream of nightmare, and in the process, deflects our attention from social outrage to personal violation.

In remembering and confessing the trauma worked on him at age eight—first to Pepper and then to the willing reader—he confirms that the waters of history, myth, narrative are now deadly, and nourish an evil world. The ritual of baptism, for example, is not a cleansing ceremony, but one of forced induction into a satanic world. Thus the Blue River is transmuted, first into a haven for poisonous snakes, then into a means of extending hell on earth, harbouring "fire, fire, fire flowing like a river, river, river" (84).

The textuality and intertextuality of *Handcarved Coffins* grows as the narrative accumulates. Capote implicitly yearns for the fixity and shelter of *In Cold Blood,* and more explicitly, seeks to undo the powers of death and evil by incorporating wholesale letters, telegrams, written telephone memoranda into the narrative. The waters are turbid, not unlike the muddy Alabama river into which he was dragged, and generic conflation soon appropriates the diary. The author includes twenty-three entries from 1975-1979, as if this disruption of the narrative, this insistence on displaying unmediated materials, can stop a mounting historical horror by violating the smooth surfaces of the text. If the desire for continuous narrative is to drink from a poisoned source, then perhaps health can be summoned by the sympathetic magic of conflation, deflection, indirection.

The river of narrative must somehow be turned aside, and this simultaneous movement of destruction and creation also takes place at the micro-level of prose style. From youth, Truman Capote was a master of literary style, writing with a true sense of the sound, rhythm and texture of language, with a feel for trenchant detail and metaphor. But convinced that his prose had grown opaque and weighed him down, he soon turned to an absolutely reduced manner in *Music for Chameleons,* pruning and simplifying the rich descriptive language so powerfully turned loose in *In Cold Blood.* Diction, sound, rhythm, syntax—all are attenuated here, for language itself is a poisoned spring.

This reduction of style is evident in every aspect of *Handcarved Coffins,* but especially in Capote's use of dialogue. Despite the gruesome deaths of the Roberts (by drugged rattlesnakes), the Baxters and their guests (fire), Clem Anderson (beheading), Dr. Parsons (poison) and Addie Mason (drowning), the pulse of the town remains quotidian. Their speech is slack, mildly slangy, colourless, bordering on direct recording. Seven **"Conversational Portraits"** (Part III) close *Music for Chameleons,* most of which continue the author's use of "commonplace conversation with everyday people" (xviii). Dialogue throughout is sunken in the text—quotation marks are not used—and the effect is that of a mechanism with a spent spring, one running on the lees of old energy.

Stylistic reduction is also evident in Capote's insistent parenthetical style. The frequent use of interrupting commas, ellipses, and dashes illustrates his diversionary technique: these all highlight disjointed thought rhythms undercutting plain language. Most explicitly, we see it in the regular stage directions for his cast—notations of their tones of voice, gestures, bodily movements—which are set off in parentheses. Parenthetical asides provide emphasis, nuance, elaboration or extension of (or from) a central notion, but in *Handcarved Coffins* the major action or mental state is held increasingly by parentheses, as if protected within lacunae of the marks themselves. On more than thirty occasions, the narrator isolates his perceptions or responses, as if to suggest that the tale of unavenged death by the Blue River is growing peripheral. The eye of the text moves to the psychic life of the narrator, and he hides these tender moments within convex walls, like pearls held in a bony shell.

Genre is conflated in *Handcarved Coffins,* and style reduced, but the role of the narrator expands considerably. Capote was no stranger to first-person narrative—almost all the early non-fiction collected in *The Dogs Bark* issues from an "I"—but he felt most comfortable and effective hidden, buried in the scapes of his narrative.

Capote's emblem is the chameleon, a creature surviving by assuming anonymity, save those rare, dangerous moments that it emerges from its backdrop, like the dozen "scarlet, green, lavender" chameleons seduced by Madame's piano, lured out on her terra cotta floor to create a living art, "a written arrangement of musical notes. A Mozartean mosaic" (12). They live in a deep lack of self-definition, an expression of the protean self. Similarly, the author finds ease in the protections of omniscient coloration.

He writes often with a keen nostalgia for a place on earth, a lost time of social and historical continuity. Many of his characters (human and beast) are driven to re-create that lost state of wholeness, and the efforts prove misguided, self-destructive. A pet raven in "Lola" is so tamed she forgets how to fly, "thought she was something else," and menaced by a cat, falls from a sixth floor balcony. A crippled boy in "Greek Paragraphs" falls in love with the Greek Isles through his reading of classical literature and convinces his doting mother to debark on an isolated speck. He wants "to see the temple by moonlight and sleep on the shores."[9] He is torn to pieces by starving rats; his mother flees into the sea, from which she watches all night. She survives in Nice, trapped mute in memory.

Even Detective Jake Pepper is an outsider, marked early as an alien—in part, the reason for his impotence—and lives six years in a motel while he stalks Bob Quinn. Pepper has no place here, can neither arrest Quinn nor save his own fiancée. Defeated, he retires to Oregon, deferring his role to the narrator.

But chameleons, confidence men, magicians, conjurers, artists survive and flourish in Capote's work. They live in their abilities to transform themselves, dwell in the illusions they create or embody.

As Jake Pepper fails, Capote succeeds him. "Just let me come there and look around," Capote implores him early on, and from that point on the narrative narrows down, the focus tightening from social threat and historical loss to the impact of each on the first-person narrator. Familiar with the point of view, Capote had usually limited it to the role of narrator-observer, almost never permitting it to swell to postmodern textual self-consciousness or self-reference.

Thus when he writes of a black mirror early in **Music for Chameleons** he signals a sudden, unexpected shift toward postmodern vision and technique: "I shall overly describe it—in the manner of those 'avant-garde' French novelists who, having chosen to discard narrative, character, and structure, restrict themselves to page-length paragraphs dealing with the contours of a single object . . . a white wall with a fly meandering across it. So: the object in Madame's drawing room is a black mirror" (7).

The narrator of **Handcarved Coffins** is fully self-revealed, but merely a midpoint between the announced self-conscious and self-reflexive intentions in the passage above and the Siamese twin narrators of **"Nocturnal Turnings,"** who talk themselves to sleep and close the collection. This is a postmodern *jeu d'esprit* comparable to that of John Barth in *Lost in the Funhouse*. Capote goes about as far as he can at this mid-point: his narrator intrudes to stage centre, and the narrative records his frustration and anger with the failure of history and myth—and with the agents (Pepper) who should continue these forces as modes of health. He projects himself further, asserting both his fear of what this drying up implies for him, as man and artist, and his resolve to take up Pepper's role as protagonist. Increasingly, he limns his inner life, puncturing the text frequently in a kind of self-flagellation caused by philosophic and literary frustration. Postmodern in impulse, yearning for what is lost and angry at failure, the narrative subsumes the fact of the death of history and older modes. Out of the failed quest grows a new power, though, and near the end of **Handcarved Coffins** he draws a strength from the flux of water run to fire.

Capote leaves Pepper behind at the Prairie Motel, and sets off to confront Bob Quinn, and, in doing so, his own trauma and fear. Quinn fishes waist-deep in the Blue River, and beckons the narrator to join him. He will not go. Capote now knows that Quinn will never be brought to trial. But his own sense of power grows, out of his knowledge that historical, literary and literal rivers are all poisoned, and out of the decision not to be submerged. If water has turned to fire in nightmare, if history is a killing mother, and if the satanic has usurped the offices of divinity, Capote finds in embracing the irruption of the postmodern in his life and art a means of standing strong in narrative and character. It is enough, the end of his non-fiction novella suggests, to record the flux that runs without and within. As Quinn finally says, "'The way I look at it is: It was the hand of God.' He raised his own hand, and the river viewed between his spread fingers, seemed to weave between them like a dark ribbon. 'God's work. His will.'" (147).

Notes

1. Truman Capote, *Handcarved Coffins*, in *Music for Chameleons* (New York: Random House, 1980). All subsequent references are to this edition and will appear in the text in parentheses.

2. Truman Capote, *Other Voices, Other Rooms* (New York: Random House, 1948); *A Tree of Night and Other Stories* (New York: Random House, 1949); *Local Color* (New York: Random House, 1950).

3. Truman Capote, *The Muses Are Heard* and "The Duke in His Domain," collected in *The Dogs Bark* (New York: Random House, 1973), 159-307; 308-353.

4. See Capote's comments to George Plimpton, "The Story Behind A Nonfiction Novel," in *Truman Capote: Conversations*, ed. M. Thomas Inge (Jackson, Miss.: University Press of Mississippi, 1987), 47-68.

5. Truman Capote, *In Cold Blood* (New York: Random House, 1966), 316; 371; 375. All subsequent references are to this edition, and appear in the text in parentheses.

6. Capote, "Preface," *Music for Chameleons*, xiv.

7. Ibid., xvi-xvii.

8. Ibid., xviii.

9. Capote, "Lola" and "Greek Paragraphs," in *The Dogs Bark*, 129; 154.

Helen S. Garson (essay date 1992)

SOURCE: Garson, Helen S. "Those Were the Lovely Years." In *Truman Capote: A Study of the Short Fiction*, pp. 28-41. New York: Twayne Publishers, 1992.

[*In the following study, Garson examines three of Capote's stories—"Children on Their Birthdays," The Grass Harp, and Breakfast at Tiffany's—arguing that these works display common themes and techniques and follow the same narrative pattern.*]

Capote's early work reveals a writer with two diametrically opposed styles. Although most of the early stories are about children or young adults, the different techniques reflect the polarity of his vision. One pattern, baring the dark and frightening shadows of existence, characterizes his gothic stories; the other reveals the joyful Capote who created stories of bright, brief, happy days that seem to hold promise and hope for the future. In three of the best-known and most successful examples of this lighthearted fiction—**"Children on Their Birthdays,"** *The Grass Harp,* and *Breakfast at Tiffany's,*—the themes are clear, the young protagonists captivating, the imagistic style haunting, the comedy both physical and verbal, the contrapuntal sounds of gaiety and melancholy always present. Lesser stories of this same period lack this totality; sometimes their humor is forced, the story derivative, or the protagonist uninteresting.

The primary force in most of the "daylight" stories is memory. Paradoxically, memory unites delight and sadness. The narrator's pleasure in recalling days—even years—of joyous youth is heightened by his and the reader's nostalgia for lost innocence and the recognition of unfulfilled desires. Out of his memory Capote selects moments in time that catch the shimmer of sunlit childhood, in its brief happiness, its expectations and longings. He reminds us that all children dream a fairytale world, but all are destined to awaken to painful reality. Although the stories differ in their plot particulars, their general outline is much the same: an event or an image triggers remembrance for the narrator, who then looks back to a childhood when everything seemed possible, and describes people from that period, friends, relatives, acquaintances. Eventually the person on whom the narrator focuses dies or goes away, and life thereafter is never the same.

"Children on Their Birthdays"

"Children on Their Birthdays," one of the earliest of Capote's published works, is a story both the author and the public favored. Miss Lily Jane Bobbit, the protagonist of the piece and a forerunner of the young woman in *Breakfast at Tiffany's,* is a 10-year-old girl who arrives in a small Alabama town with her mother one late summer afternoon. Although she lives in the community only a year, she has a powerful effect on everyone who knows her; Mr. C., the narrator of the story, declares that she will never be forgotten. Like a summer's day, Miss Bobbit's time is brief. The fact that she dies at the height of her hopes and desires, unspoiled by disappointments and failures, seems to make her ageless, untouched by process. Roses are in bloom the day of her death, and no leaves fall.

Though realistic enough in multiple ways, Lily Jane Bobbit is a fantasy child, the mirror of the longings of all children. The fantasy quality is suggested immediately upon her arrival. Although she gets off the six o'clock bus, it is as if she simply materializes from another world. We learn almost nothing about her past life. Like many a creature from other worlds, she is not destined to remain long in the world of ordinary mortals. She has no intentions of lingering to grow old in this sleepy Southern town, for she has plans to move on to Hollywood as soon as possible. She intends to be a star.

In the real world of children mothers (and fathers) exert control over their activities, but Lily Jane's mother does not interfere with anything Lily Jane does. Mrs. Bobbit has a speech defect and appears to be mute. In a role reversal that many a child might desire, Lily Jane seems to be in charge of her mother: "My mother has a disorder of the tongue, so it is necessary that I speak for her," the girl announces.[1] Further, the secret longing to be parentless and free to do whatever they want that children sometimes have is reinforced thematically by the absence of the father figure.[2] Although townspeople, church leaders, and school authorities try to control Lily Jane, nobody is able to direct her. She is what all children wish to be: free of parental restraint; free from attending school or church; free to criticize anything; free to make the friends she wants; free to earn money as she chooses and spend it as she prefers; free to do whatever she wants when she wants to do it. And, unlike a real child, who dreams impossible dreams but does nothing to achieve them, Miss Bobbit employs all her considerable energy to make her dreams reality.

She will not be diverted from her objectives in any way. From the moment of her arrival, when she interrupts Billy Bob's birthday party, everything she does is directed toward the fulfillment of her dream. However, this extraordinary child also has a practical side, the polar opposite of her romantic, dreamer side. She refuses to eat ice cream and cake because they are not good for the figure. The very night of her arrival, though she has good reason to rest after her long bus trip, she carries on with her dance practice. Although the adolescent boys fall in love with her, and the girls in their jealousy mock her, Miss Bobbit is indifferent to such behavior. Ordinary girls are silly and unkind, and ordinary boys are foolish and immature, but Lily Jane is practical, efficient, logical, and businesslike. She concentrates on her goal of achieving stardom. She will not go to school because it would be a waste of her time; school will not teach her what she needs to learn. Church too would be a waste of time, for God would be no use to her career plans. She needs the help of the devil, who is on her side, the side of dancing.

All the boys are happy to work on her behalf in any scheme she devises, but her one true friend is Rosealba, a black girl she rescued from the sexual bullying of these same white boys. Child-woman that Miss Bobbit is, a combination of innocence and worldliness, untouched by sexual stirrings and yet strangely knowing, she is totally different from all other girls. Undeterred by Billy Bob's mother, she gives Billy Bob a "refreshing" massage when he is ill; she rejects the boys' declaration of affection, but finds them entertaining; she shocks the local audience the night she wins the prize in a talent show when she sings a wicked little ditty and displays her blue-lace-covered bottom.

Most of the humor in the story is associated with Miss Bobbit's personality and character, but Capote enlivens his tale with other kinds of humor that in time became Capote trademarks. There are funny scenes associated with animals: when Miss Bobbit is disturbed at night by the howling of dogs, she and Rosealba stalk the offenders. They carry "a flower basket filled with rocks; whenever they saw a dog they paused while Miss Bobbit scrutinized him. Sometimes she would shake her head, but more often she said, 'Yes, that's one of them, Sister Rosealba,' and Sister Rosealba, with ferocious aim, would take a rock from her basket and crack the dog between the eyes" (**"Children,"** 98). The narrator notes that Miss Bobbit's landlady has a memorial sundial dedicated to a dog who met his end by lapping up paint. There is the comedy of exaggeration in the actions of the boys, particularly those of Preacher Star, who in spite of his name is the antithesis of a churchly child. There is the comedy of bizarrely inappropriate names. Rosealba Cat, for example, is neither a white rose nor a child of catlike grace—she is more like the "baby elephant" Mr. C. calls her. While Rosealba's name comically contradicts her appearance, Manny Fox's name emblemizes his personality. Fox is a sly con man so persuasive that a local woman gives him the money she had intended to use to buy an angel tombstone. Capote plays with language, as in the expression "Merci you kindly." Even food becomes a vehicle for fun; ordinary mortals eat boiled ham and deviled eggs, but Miss Bobbit will eat no meat, and only raw foods, including raw eggs. The humor of the tall tale, so popular with southern and western writers, and a device Capote employed frequently, appears here through such depictions as the old drunken boarder who has a toilet-paper phobia and the vengeance Miss Bobbit and Rosealba take on him for his behavior. Many of the girls' actions fall under the tall-tale category.

Capote gains maximum effect from humor, but the comedy, while very important to the story, is not the author's major concern. He always brings us back to the primary motif, the sweet and sad lost moments of childhood, days that can only be recaptured in idealized memory.

The imaginary and the nostalgic are brought together through the title, which comes from a statement made by Miss Bobbit, who is searching for a world where everything and everyone dances and is pretty, a special, lovely world "like children on their birthdays." Adults know that such a world does not exist, but Lily Jane is one of the creatures who lives in the sky, different from all others. She is the child who will never grow up. We have seen such a character in Oreilly, the clown who also lives in the sky, in **"Master Misery,"** and that same metaphor is used later with Holly Golightly in *Breakfast at Tiffany's*. The child or childlike creature never remains with us for long. Oreilly disappears, Holly leaves forever, and Miss Bobbit dies.

Early or late, childhood and childhood's dreams fade. The images of William Blake's *Songs of Innocence* come to mind as we look at Capote's ephemeral characters: the children who want to continue playing are watched by adults who know how short the time is, who see the darkening green all around them. Experience must come, changing, shattering, completely destroying innocence and illusions. But this will not happen to Lily Jane Bobbit, who dies in her white communion-like dress, in summer, while the air is heavy with the fragrance of wisteria and roses, the rain soft against a rainbowed sky.

Also like Blake, Capote is a colorist, and throughout **"Children on Their Birthdays"** he makes yellow the major hue. Miss Bobbit is first seen in a lemon-colored dress; her eyes are the yellow of sunflowers; yellow roses are given to her in tribute, twice. The faces of the boys who bring her flowers look like "yellow moons." But the boys with their roses bring about Miss Bobbit's death as she runs toward them: "That is when the six o'clock bus ran over her" (**"Children,"** 106). The yellow of flowers, of moons, of summer thus becomes associated with death in a gentle, melancholy, and nostalgic tone much like the one describing the yellow leaves of autumn Capote was to use in *The Grass Harp* and *Breakfast at Tiffany's*.[3]

The reader knows from the first that Miss Bobbit must die, for her death is announced by an opening line that has the same quiet finality as the conclusion: "Yesterday afternoon the six o'clock bus ran over Miss Bobbit." Death in general, and the death of Miss Bobbit in particular, is an inescapable fact for Capote and his readers. Even while spinning out the story with all its humor, the author uses delicate and transient images of summer, of mutable nature, to underscore the unalterable reality that the little girl will soon be gone, like the music heard from afar, the fireflies that swoop through the early evening, the brief blooming irises. Dressed in white and glitter soon after her arrival, the child is shown dancing just before the fall of darkness, illuminating the evening before night sets in. Fantasies, hopes, and dreams must end for those left behind, for those who must grow up. But the memory of summer and a magical child is caught and preserved forever.

THE GRASS HARP

The Grass Harp, a novella published in 1951, has many of the characteristics Capote favored in the forties, techniques seen in **"Children on Their Birthdays,"** as well as in the 1958 novella *Breakfast at Tiffany's,* and as late as 1966, in *A Christmas Memory.* Although almost 20 years separate the earliest from the last of these four works, the stories not only seem part of a whole in multiple ways, but also fall into pairs: **"Children on Their Birthdays"** with *Breakfast at Tiffany's,* **The Grass Harp** with *A Christmas Memory.* All four have a young male narrator, easily identified with Capote; each has one or more major symbols that appear and reappear to bind the work together; the four feature recurring character types; each has a circular plot structure; all employ various forms of humor, from the very gentle to the physically vaudevillian; all create a sense of nostalgia for the past; in each, the most lasting impression is the combined sense of sadness and sweetness for the irretrievably lost world of childhood.

Capote turned **The Grass Harp** into a play a year after publication of the novella, but it was a failure with both the critics and the public. Although the novella is more effective than the play, the seeds of the play's failure are already present in the novella's overt message and its sentimentality; sentimentality exists in other Capote works, but he controls it more. He conveys the delicate, magical quality of memory quite successfully in the written words of the novella, but this key feature of the novella was lost when he embodied his story with characters and actions on stage.

The major symbol in **The Grass Harp** is the Indian grass found in the meadow just below the town cemetery. The grass harp, the narrator is informed by his cousin Dolly, is a teller of tales, and this is precisely the function the narrator takes on when he reaches manhood. He becomes the bard, like the harpist of ancient times. Introduced in the very first part of the story, the special grass is mentioned several times throughout the years that pass. The final revelation comes at the end when the narrator, still a boy and about to leave his home forever, goes with an elderly friend to visit the cemetery and the meadow below it, where the September grass glows in all its fall colors. As the two stand in the field, the narrator tells the old man of the ability of the grass to sing the stories of the lives of those who are now gone. At that moment we recognize the relationship of the grass and the human storyteller, as well as the circularity of the story. The story we read is the one the narrator himself tells, the one we have just heard, of a past he has relived through the retelling.

At the beginning of **The Grass Harp** the narrator suggests that everything that follows is filtered through memory. A segment of the past is revisited, but now, because it can never be relived and experienced as it actually was, it takes on new coloration and tone because the insignificant details of daily life are forgotten and meaningful episodes are highlighted. In language similar to that of several other Capote stories, the narrator reminds us that memory is selective. The narrator, Collin Fenwick, asks, "When was it . . . ?"[4] and a little later uses words like "long before." Soon he begins to tell us a story of "the lovely years" from the time of his arrival, an orphan, at age 11, to the day of his leave-taking, several years later.

After the death of his parents, Collin is taken in by his father's cousins, two spinsters, Verena and Dolly Talbo. Also living in the household is Dolly's dearest friend and constant companion, Catherine. Catherine is a dark-skinned woman who calls herself an Indian, but the rest of the community call her a Negro and treat her as inferior. Dolly becomes Collin's closest ally and mentor, and he grows up in her and Catherine's constant company. Verena is the money-maker, the businesswoman of the family, whose greed and selfishness lead to the death of her sister, Dolly, and to the end of Collin's innocence.

Before Dolly's death, however, life follows a quiet, predictable pattern. Dolly is as much a child as Collin. She likes children's play and games, has the pink room of a little girl, and prefers sweets to any other food. She does not have to pretend to enter into the childhood stage Collin is in, for she seems to have been always caught there. Only in the last few months of her life does she become an independent, self-assured woman.

Dolly makes, and sells a tonic to alleviate dropsy. Similar to the format of the later story, *A Christmas Memory,* with its seasonal trips into the woods to collect the ingredients for fruitcake, **The Grass Harp** presents making the dropsy medicine as the focal point of the week for Dolly, Catherine, and Collin. On Saturdays they take to the woods to search out the herbs, the roots, the bark, and the leaves that go into the secret remedy. Because of the sales of her medicine, Dolly has contact through the mail with customers outside her immediate circle. These letters are her only connection with other people because she is shy and timid. The money she earns from the sales provides the three companions with games, puzzles, lessons, and whatever advertised items catch their fancy.

This happy time ends when Collin is 16. Verena decides that real money can be made from the production and sale of the medicine. Verena, unable to allow her sister anything of her own, brings in an adviser from Chicago, which, in the xenophobic South of those years, represents sin city.[5] The townspeople tag Dr. Morris Ritz as a foreigner and a troublemaker, and they are right. With Ritz's advice, Verena prepares to go into large-scale production of the dropsy cure. But the plan never comes to fruition because Dolly refuses to yield to Verena.

Ritz is a con man drawn in the mold of the earlier Manny Fox, from **"Children on Their Birthdays."**[6] Both are sly and manipulative. Fox is "greasy and leering" as he tells off-color jokes; Ritz winks suggestively as he speaks to Collin of sexual opportunities in Chicago. Fox, the vaudeville showmaster, claps his hands; Dr. Ritz, of unknown profession, snaps his fingers as if he were in a vaudeville show. The townspeople's suspicions, Dolly's fears, and Catherine's hostility to Ritz prove well-founded, for Ritz eventually takes off with Verena's money and leaves her a broken, disappointed woman.

The turning point in the story occurs on the night Verena forces a showdown with Dolly about the dropsy cure. Not only does Verena berate her; she also blames her for the lonely life she has been forced to live because she has been ashamed of Dolly and the "gurgling fool," Catherine. Now Dolly feels she can no longer live with her sister. Although Verena tells her she has no other place to go, Dolly leaves home. Dolly, joined by Catherine and Collin, walks through the sleeping town; together they pass through the Indian grass, the grass that is the harp. As the sun rises they reach the China tree where they will live until the beginning of October.

Although the first part of the novella has a childlike, magical quality, the second segment, which describes life in the treehouse, is even closer to a fairy tale, but one with strong didactic elements. Here, Dolly and Collin grow up, with Dolly discovering her strength of character as well as her womanhood. They find friendships, and they and some of the people who become their friends learn about love. Typical of a fairy tale, they must undergo a test and be physically and emotionally challenged by various forces.

When Dolly, Catherine, and Collin take up life in the treehouse—surely the dream of many a child—they find happiness for a short time. Many people seek them out. A young man, Riley Henderson, and an old man, Judge Cool, join them as allies in the ensuing battles between the forces of conservatism and the forces of change. The handsome daredevil Riley becomes Collin's much admired friend; Judge Cool and Dolly fall in love. Each fulfills the needs of the other. For Dolly, the Judge becomes the admirer she has never had, one who approves of all she is and accepts her totally. For the Judge, Dolly becomes the beloved to whom all may be told.

The people in the treehouse learn lessons, about the world, about other people, and about the self. Uncertain men change to lovers and heroes. In old age, Dolly comes of age, becomes a woman who stands tall and assured because of love. But the treedwellers also learn that there is no escape from responsibilities. Eventually each must return to face the issues and problems he or she left behind. Dolly chooses to go back to her sister, who needs her. The Judge must also resolve his family problems. Riley will no longer behave like an irresponsible, uncontrollable boy, and Collin will move toward self-sufficient manhood.

The story's underlying didacticism is mitigated by the liveliness of Capote's humor. The humor in the first part is more gentle, more verbal than that in the second: Catherine abandons French lessons after she learns how to say she is tired in French, for example, and she invents a version of history that suits her theories of race. The comedy of the second segment involves mock battle scenes and numerous farcical characters, some of whose names identify their personalities. Most of the interlopers suggest Gilbert and Sullivan figures. Capote mocks traditional religious figures and their attitudes, not only through their behavior, but also by creating a highly comic and sympathetic evangelist named Sister Ida Honey, who has an enormous brood of children, most of them illegitimate, but all loved. The tall-tale element is prevalent throughout this part of the story, as when Sister Ida recounts her various romances and ensuing pregnancies, or a meal intended for 5 is expanded to serve 16, or in the manner by which the good defeat the wicked invaders.

Comedic episodes dominate the middle section of the story, but the reader is never allowed to forget that nothing good lasts. With the departure of most of the people at the end of the battle, decisions about the future must be made. Dolly cannot resist Verena's pleas to return home. Just as Verena's claim seems to stand between Dolly and a new life, so too does the season, with its melancholy turn in the weather. As Dolly hesitates, attempting to choose, the rain seems to separate her from the Judge. The rain here, like the rain described as a curtain of glass in **"The Headless Hawk,"** suggests a barrier that cannot be breached. With the rain also comes the dissolution of cozy living in the treehouse. Everything falls, spills, or is washed away. The group leaves and takes nothing with them. What remains will be covered over by winter.

The warning of the winter to come has been present from the moment Dolly decided to leave home. From that point on in the story, the reader has a growing awareness of the swift passage of time. Before Dolly even tells Collin of her plans to go live in the treehouse with Catherine, Collin is lying in bed thinking of dead fathers—Dolly's and his own—and of the Indian grass and its stories of the dead. As Dolly agrees to permit Collin to join her in flight, a clock tolls the hour. Even in the idyllic setting of the treehouse, the Judge's gold watch is often mentioned, ticking away; although Dolly, in a magnanimous gesture, gives the watch to Sister Ida to help her and her children on their journey, time cannot be stopped. The clock is running down for Dolly, who becomes ill soon after returning home. The night of her death, just before she goes up to the attic with Collin in search of some decorations, he becomes aware of the striking of the town clock. Later, as she shows him her childhood treasures, Collin describes her face as looking like a moth's next to a lamp, so delicate is she, so brief her remaining time. Before the clock strikes again, Dolly tells Collin of the important knowledge she has gained from the Judge: "love is a chain of love. . . . Because when you can love one thing . . . you can love another, and that is owning, that is something to live with" (*Grass Harp,* 223).

Soon the sound of the clock is heard again. Moments afterward, as Dolly is dancing around the attic, she collapses. Her death at sunrise is known to Collin even before he is told, for a breeze flutters through the veil of Dolly's traveling hat, the hat she wore when they left for the treehouse, in River Woods, near the cemetery and the meadow of Indian grass. Although Dolly's death is really the end of the story, the aftermath of the lives of her friends and family are briefly summarized. Everything and everyone changes when she is gone. For Collin, childhood and the lovely years are over; he leaves home with no expectation of ever returning again.

BREAKFAST AT TIFFANY'S

From the day of its publication in 1958 **Breakfast at Tiffany's** has been a much-loved book. More than 30 years after its appearance, book reviewers continue to compare female characters to Holly Golightly, Capote's unforgettable heroine.

Numerous conflicting stories have been told about the model for Capote's portrait. An actual person sparked the fictional creation, but who that person was remains a topic of debate. Typically, Capote embroidered and embellished the truth, telling different versions of the origin of Holly Golightly to interviewers over the years, and also to his biographer. All of these statements are at odds with novelist James Michener's recollections of the original "starlet-singer-actress-raconteur" he knew to be Holly.[7]

Although an actual person may have provided the mold for the heroine, Holly is yet another fantasy creature, a beautiful, captivating, elusive, lovable, and haunting young woman, a mixture of the romantic and the tragic. Generally regarded by critics as an expanded, older version of the adolescent Lily Jane Bobbit of **"Children on Their Birthdays,"** Holly has many of the same personality traits: wisdom beyond her chronological age, brashness, courage, a longing for something that proves unattainable, and a separateness which makes her different from earthbound human beings. We respond affectionately to both Lily Jane and Holly, laughing at and with them, and mourning their loss. However, because **Breakfast at Tiffany's** is the longer, more complex fiction in which the major character is more fully drawn, the minor characters funnier, and the setting more completely realized, it is the more memorable work.

Mr. C., the narrator of **"Children,"** has an expanded role in the novella. Though he has no name except the one Holly gives him briefly, he is obviously meant to be the young Capote, starting out as a writer in New York; even the birthdays are the same, September 30.[8] In **Breakfast at Tiffany's,** however, the Capote figure is more than an observer. He is an involved participant who falls in love with Holly and helps her whenever she has problems. He is friend, listener, defender, brother, and ultimately biographer of this captivating creature.

This story, resembling other Capote pieces in its mixture of tenderness, melancholy, and humor, is enclosed and protected in a frame of memory, inviolable, like figures carved on an urn, caught in a moment of time past. As in many of Capote's stories, time is the silent yet relentless figure in the background. In reality, autumn and winter must eventually succeed spring and summer; the church clock must toll the hours, signifying the passage of time and time-bound life. But memory, misted over with all its happy and unhappy moments, remains. The narrator's recollections are stirred by a phone call and a visit to a barman named Joe Bell. Returning to a neighborhood he knew well 15 years earlier, he learns that Joe has obtained a recent photo of a sculpted African head and that this head bears an uncanny resemblance to a much-loved person out of the past, Holly Golightly. After the bartender relates what little information he has concerning the background of the photo, the narrator walks through the neighborhood streets, back to the brownstone where he first met Holly.

It was wartime when the hopeful young writer met Holly, who lived in the same building as he. Holly, not quite 19, was a young woman who lived on "powder room money," a girl who looked like a breakfast cereal ad, but lived solely for fun and excitement. The larky atmosphere, the casual encounters, the easy money, the nightclubs, the dancing in the streets and partying with service officers—all speak of a wartime philosophy. The whole world seems young. Champagne bubbles up in glasses, in spite of or because of the war, but the war is very far away, even for Holly, whose beloved brother is at the front. When he is killed, however, her one tie with the past and normal life is destroyed.

Holly's card vaguely identifies her occupation as "traveling." The word is apt for the way she lives. Holly never stays anywhere for very long. She is a person searching for love, for a home, for a happy and safe life—all symbolized in her mind by Tiffany's. Orphaned early, the then Lulamae Barnes married Doc Golightly when she was only a child. Although she loves him—he was like a kind old father to her—she ran away. From that moment she has had a series of fantasy lives. In Hollywood, where for a time she concentrated on improving herself, Lulamae became Holly; she lost her hillbilly accent, learned a little French, became a starlet, and gained enough sophistication to realize she could not become a star. She then headed for New York to try for another kind of fame and fortune as a New York socialite. The elusive Holly is depicted as someone balanced between childhood and womanhood. In spite of her numerous lovers, she appears untouched by sordidness, and is surprisingly naive in many ways. Having had no childhood, she creates a child's world where she makes up the rules. Her girlish enthusiasm is contagious, so that all men feel more alive in her company.

In New York, although fortune eludes her, she does find fame, that is, notoriety, when she unwittingly becomes a courier for a mobster named Sally Tomato. This experience ends her only "non-rat" romance, when her skittish lover abandons her. The publicity also causes her to flee the country to avoid the courts and keep from betraying Sally, for she is an advocate of the honest heart in all circumstances. The streetwise side of Holly recognizes that her "career" in New York has been blemished and part of her life is over. Because of this mishap, once again Holly becomes a traveler. After sending a single postcard to the narrator, she fades into the soft haze of the past, a past revisited briefly when Joe Bell sends for the narrator.

All of Holly's fantasizing has a melancholy side, however, for it is really only a dream. Beneath the surface of gaiety lies the knowledge that nothing lasts. There is loneliness at the core of the dreamer. Though always surrounded by people, Holly gives the impression of being alone, still the little girl, Lulamae Barnes, still running, still searching for a home never to be hers. She knows she is one of those wild creatures who live in the sky, always an empty place; her favorite song tells plaintively of traveling "through the pastures of the sky." At times Holly confesses to the narrator her awareness of transiency, and in a sorrowful moment of revelation tells him we do not even recognize the wonder of lovely days until they are gone. Then it is too late to bring them back. For the narrator, however, they can be recalled, though only in memory.

Holly may seem like Miss Bobbit in her unchanging hope for something better, something more, but there is a far greater strain of melancholy in Holly. Holly, unlike Miss Bobbit, seems to know, at least at a subliminal level, that life will never give what it seems to promise children. Miss Bobbit dies before knowledge dims her radiance. Holly, however, even as a child, never had the kind of innocence Lily Jane has. There is a depth of sadness in her unknown to the younger girl. In spite of Holly's determination to be happy and have everything possible, she has been battered by existence and has endured poverty, hunger, loss, and abandonment.

An authority on abandonment, Holly has learned to face the world with style, even if it is veneer. When the narrator tries to tell her gently about the defection of her lover, Jose, Holly first puts on her makeup, her perfume, her earrings, and her dark glasses before she reads Jose's letter, in which he informs her that he will not marry her. A young woman who has built her personality partly on dissemblance and make-believe, partly playful, partly defensive, Holly has her own kind of armor to protect her from the harsh world. This is what leads her former Hollywood agent, O. J. Berman, to call her "a phony," but also to note that "She isn't a phony because she is a *real* phony. She believes all this crap she believes."[9]

Berman also predicts that Holly one day will finish "at the bottom of a bottle of Seconals." Although Holly battles frequently with fear and depression, in the tenderness of the narrator's memory, however, she is always young and unchanged. Still, the images associated with Holly lend themselves to both visions, Berman's and the narrator's: a birdcage she presents to the young writer, given with the admonition that he must never put anything in it; the cast-off cat she takes in, refuses to name, and then abandons when she flees New York; the yellow roses she loves (reminding the reader of the death of Miss Bobbit in **"Children on Their Birthdays"**); the flowers Joe Bell attempts to give her when she is leaving, flowers that fall to the floor (again reminiscent of the flowers Miss Bobbit never gets in the last scene in the short story). The downpour of rain as Holly flees New York carries with it the wind of desolation, an ache not obviated when the narrator discovers the cat at a later time ensconced in a lace-curtained window in Harlem. He hopes then that Holly too will find a place where she belongs, but that hope, the reader recognizes, may be as ephemeral as her promise to keep in touch.

Although both the short story and the novella end with a sense of loss in their images of mist and rain, a much more powerful minor key runs through the conclusion of the later work, for summer is still in the air in **"Children on Their Birthdays."** The rainbow that crosses the sky preserves the feeling of childlike hope, but in *Breakfast at Tiffany's* the autumnal season of heavy rain and yellowed leaves suggests only the winter to come.

However, *Breakfast at Tiffany's*, like **"Children on Their Birthdays,"** is also lighthearted in many ways. Once again, Capote's humor is found in characters, dialogue, and events. He plays with names: Joe Bell takes phone messages; Rusty Trawler is a much-married man who has been involved in sex scandals.[10] Runyonesque characters from New York and Hollywood fill the novella. There is a chase scene with horses. And the star of the story herself provides slapstick and bawdy humor. *Breakfast at Tiffany's* shows Capote at his best, in total control as humorist, stylist, symbolist, imagist, and tone painter, characteristics that marked his fiction and nonfiction prose of the fifties and sixties.

Notes

1. "Children on Their Birthdays," in [Capote, Truman.] *A Capote Reader*, [New York: Random House, 1987] 93; hereafter cited in text as "Children."

2. There is an autobiographical element here, in that the author's family life was somewhat like Miss Bobbit's: her mother is mute, and her father is absent, and Capote grew up without mother or father.

3. Capote associates the color green with death, and usually combines green with gothic images of horror, terror, or violence. Capote also associates the color yellow with death, but links this color with nostalgia or sadness.

4. *The Grass Harp* in *A Capote Reader*, 155; hereafter cited in text.

5. The southern parallel, at least as described in Faulkner's novels, is Memphis.

6. Although Manny Fox, in "Children on Their Birthdays," is not called a Jew, this identity is suggested. Dr. Ritz is often referred to as the "little Jew," usually by Catherine, who is an outspoken woman. She says things others are too polite or kind to voice.

7. See Michener's "Foreword" in Lawrence Grobel's *Conversations with Capote* (New York: New American Library, 1985).

8. Capote also makes an oblique reference to another autobiographical detail, when he speaks of being fired for "an amusing misdemeanor." He is probably referring to the Robert Frost episode at *the New Yorker*. See Helen S. Garson's *Truman Capote* and Gerald Clarke's *Capote: A Biography*.

9. *Breakfast at Tiffany's*, in *A Capote Reader*, 241-242; hereafter cited in text as *Breakfast*.

10. The names Lily Jane in "Children on Their Birthdays" and Lulamae in *Breakfast at Tiffany's* appear to have a relationship to the author's mother, whose name was Lillie Mae before she changed it to Nina.

Brian Conniff (essay date autumn 1993)

SOURCE: Conniff, Brian. "'Psychological Accidents': *In Cold Blood* and Ritual Sacrifice." *The Midwest Quarterly: A Journal of Contemporary Thought* 35, no. 1 (autumn 1993): 77-94.

[*In the following essay, Conniff regards* In Cold Blood *as a work of "prison literature" and focuses, specifically, on the way in which psychological accidents, rather than "meaningful design," shape the direction of the novel.*]

American prison literature of the past twenty-five years has been preoccupied with a contradiction that is central to the national consciousness. Throughout this period, imprisonment and execution have often risen to the level of obsession; yet such authorized violence has been so normalized that any understanding of it, even in the relatively "safe" realm of literature, has rarely occurred, except through personal tragedy or accident. It is hard to imagine that even Malcolm X, whose *Autobiography* H. Bruce Franklin considers the starting point of "Contemporary American prison literature" (236), would ever have considered the institutionalized racism of the justice system if he had remained a petty hustler in Detroit. As Malcolm himself explains, it took a ten-year sentence for a first-time burglary conviction—a sentence lengthened by the involvement of two "well-to-do" white women—to begin his transformation from an ordinary con into the leading disciple of Elijah Muhammad, and then into a symbol of the "aspirations" held by those convicts of the late 1960s and early 1970s who wanted, as Eldridge Cleaver puts it, to "inject" the problems of imprisonment "into national and state politics" (59, 61). It is equally hard to imagine that Cleaver himself could ever have been transformed from a harmless "lover of marijuana" into an "insurrectionary" rapist, and then into a leading Black Panther, if he had not had the bad luck to serve a term in San Quentin on a petty charge of possession. It might very well have taken the chance correspondence with Jack Henry Abbott to allow Norman Mailer, in the course of writing *The Executioner's Song*, to see through his usual glamorizations of violence, from the 1950s hipster to Mike Tyson, into the reality of the institutionalized man, and beyond that into what he would call, in his introduction to Abbott's *In the Belly of the Beast*, "the progressive institutionalization of all society" (xv). Again and again, this literature of the prison suggests that the most fortified barriers are not the physical walls and fences between the prison, and the outside world; the most fortified barriers are the psychological walls between the preoccupations of everyday life, even the everyday life of a petty hustler or a famous novelist, and the conscious realization that punishment is the most self-destructive kind of national addiction.

Ironically, these psychological walls are confronted most forcefully, and their implications are seen most clearly, in a work that is not usually considered hardcore enough, or subversive enough, to be a part of any renegade tradition of "prison literature": Truman Capote's *In Cold Blood*. In the novel's most characteristic moment, Kansas Bureau of Investigation Agent Alvin Dewey—one of Capote's favorite "characters"—finally hears the confession of Perry Smith, one of the two former Kansas State Penitentiary cellmates who murdered Herb Clutter, a prosperous farmer, and his family. For seven months, Dewey has worked continuously, staring at grisly photos and following useless leads, in his quest "to learn 'exactly what happened in that house that night.'" But when he finally hears the entire story—told by one of the killers, step by step, shotgun blast by shotgun blast—he is strangely disappointed. The truth, he discovers, is even more disturbing than anything he had imagined. Even though he suddenly knows more about the crime than he, or Capote, would ever have hoped, the "true story" somehow "fails to satisfy his sense of meaningful design" (277). The truth, Dewey discovers, is at once more ordinary and more disturbing than anything he has been able to imagine. Contrary to his expectations, Smith and Richard Hickock did not kill the Clutters out of some aberrant sense of revenge; in fact, until the night of the crime, they had never even met their chosen victims. They certainly were not, in any sense, "criminal masterminds." In fact, they were not even very competent. Among other things, they had never even bothered to find out what everyone else in town seemed to know, that Herb Clutter never kept more than a few dollars on hand. Perhaps most disturbing of all, they acted as though they were simply putting in a rather ordinary night's work for which they believed they deserved a good night's pay—though, as it turned out, they would come away with nothing more than about forty dollars and a radio. To Agent Dewey, hearing the full story for the first time, none of this seems possible. He does not want to consider the obvious truth, that "The crime was a psychological accident, virtually an impersonal act; the victims might as well have been struck by lightning" (277).

Like the works more often recognized as "prison literature," *In Cold Blood* is primarily concerned with moments like these, in which "meaningful designs" about crime and punishment—the kind of "common sense" virtually no one sees fit to question—are disrupted by actual events. But no matter how accidental or incongruous the Clutter murders might have seemed, Capote went to Kansas with a "meaningful design" of his own, one far more serious than the literary establishment, the popular imagination, or he himself would later admit. As Gerald Clarke has written in his recent biography, Capote would tell just about anyone who happened to listen that he planned to examine "the reaction of a small town to a hideous crime" (324). For such a study, he did not believe that the solution of the crime was particularly relevant—a belief that angered Alvin Dewey, and would undoubtedly have angered most local residents, if they had been willing, at that early stage, to take him seriously. Capote was not the least bit concerned with the killers, at first, but only with the immediate victims—a category in which he included both the Clutter family and their neighbors, all those people who suddenly found their lives altered by the mere proximity of the slain bodies.

But Capote's understanding of this "reaction" was, at first, severely limited: to suppose that the effects of violence do not include the capture and punishment of the criminals is to underestimate the community's need for retribution, its need to reaffirm its "stability," its "normalcy," by authorizing and enacting a violence of its own. Capote also underestimated the extent to which he, too, was subject to the irresistible force of this need. He seems to have never been able to admit—or perhaps even understand—just how much the "appearance" of Hickock and Smith, in both senses of the word, caused him to alter, and eventually fictionalize, his "nonfiction novel."

When the good citizens of Holcomb and Garden City finally decided to talk to Capote, he found, or at least he imagined he found, the reaction he had anticipated: locked doors and sleepless nights, suspicious neighbors and frightened children, malicious gossip and charitable prayers. Accordingly, the first half of *In Cold Blood* is filled with this superficial fear, which Capote typically describes as a nostalgia for an "ordinary" life—as though he is not yet aware, or will not yet allow his narrative voice to sound aware, of the forces that lie behind this "normalcy." After all, as Capote writes, these people had always been "quite content to exist inside ordinary life." They had been reasonably happy, it seems, "to work, to hunt, to watch television, to attend school socials, choir practice, meetings of the 4-H Club." In fact, as the most banal cliché would have it, they had been "sufficiently unfearful of each other to seldom trouble to lock their doors" (15).

Once this "unfearful" life was corrupted by the Clutter murders, it could not be restored until after the killers had been found and punished. Finally compelled to lock their doors, many of them with newly purchased locks, the local residents seemed at first to be trying to keep out some kind of invader from "outside" the community, some kind of creature as alien as it was frightening. They seemed to be playing the kind of game that Agent Dewey, searching one more time through the photographs of the crime scene in the hope that "some meaningful detail would declare itself," described as "find the hidden animals" (100). As George Creeger has noted, Dewey's search for "animals" in the "puzzle" is part of an elaborate system of imagery that Capote uses "to suggest a complex relationship between the criminal and the community" (6). The "grim logic" by which Hickock and Smith are categorized as "animals" allows the community to "deprive the killers of their humanity," "exile them" and "return to the feeling it cherishes so much—that of security" (2, 6). But Capote also suggests that Dewey's search through the "puzzle" is also a little naive, almost even pathetic: it is a child's game, in relation to the events that have preceded it, and the events that will follow. "Meaning" will never declare itself. Rather, "meaning" will have to be superimposed, over and over, by all the residents of Garden City, and eventually by Capote himself, as one delusion after another is undermined by ordinary, sordid events.

Because a common "normalcy" ultimately depends upon the complete exclusion of "outsiders," the exorcism of these mysterious "animals" is just as important as their discovery and capture. In this sense, most of Holcomb's citizens are very much like Perry Smith's sister, who believes that men like Perry and his father—the Irish rodeo cowboy turned wilderness man, John "Tex" Smith—"should" always live "alone," perhaps in the "Alaskan wilderness," far away from her own kind of "timid life" (153, 209). Like all the rest of the "normals," as Perry calls them—"respectable people, safe and smug people"—she needs to convince herself that Perry's life is "an ugly and lonely progress toward one mirage and then another" (277). In other words, she needs to believe that Perry's life is completely different from her own, and completely different from the lives of those other "respectable" people with whom she tries to surround herself. Only Perry and his kind, beasts from some imagined "wilderness," could so disrupt and endanger a community in which lives are assumed to have direction—a world of progress that is always becoming, as Herb Clutter confidently remarked in an interview with C. B. Palmer not long before his death, "increasingly organized" (6). Like the residents of Holcomb, Perry's sister must convince herself that it is only people like Perry, "isolated" and "animal," who are driven by a lonely search for distant "mirages."

As the local "professional," Agent Dewey assumes the responsibility of superimposing on the evidence an official interpretation that can somehow support these delusions. Accordingly, in his efforts to explain the crime, he constructs two "concepts." Dewey realizes that both have glaring limitations, and he has difficulty deciding between them; nonetheless, these "concepts," and Dewey's inclinations in trying to decide, allow Capote to provide a commentary on the kind of respectability to which Perry's sister, like so many others, has always aspired. According to the first possible explanation, the "single killer concept," the killer would have been "a friend of the family, or, at any rate, a man with more than casual knowledge of the house and its inhabitants." This person would have known the structure of the house, the placing of the telephones, the dog's fear of guns and, of course, "that the doors were seldom locked" (98). Dewey is reluctant to accept this explanation, because it would lead him to assume elaborate and careful planning on the part of this "single killer." The killer would have had to possess the kind of rationality that, Dewey would rather believe, distinguishes people like those of his community from animals and madmen. The second "concept" follows the first "in many essentials," but suggests that the killer had an "accomplice, who helped subdue the family, tape, and time them" (99). Dewey is even more reluctant to accept this second explanation—though of course it turns out to be closer to the truth. He finds it "difficult to understand 'how two individuals could reach the same degree of rage, the kind of psychopathic rage it took to commit such a crime'" (99). "Psychopathic rage" is the one idea he could not have derived from the "facts" in which he claims to place so much faith. For that matter, this idea even allows him to deny an impressive body of evidence—the mattress box placed beneath Herb Clutter's body, the pillow beneath his son's head, the blankets tucked around the two women—all the traces of "considerate impulses . . . a certain twisted tenderness" on the part of at least one killer (122). Nonetheless, Dewey clings to this second "concept" as long as he can, because in the common scheme of things, which he wants so badly to reaffirm, the very definition of the "psychopathic" would be the murder of people like the Clutters, the embodiments of local respectability, the "least likely people in the world" to be killed (102).

Dewey's two "concepts" are revealing not only because of the extent to which they exclude the reality of the crime, but also because of the extent to which they exclude each other: he does not want to admit the possibility of either a calculated, multiple murder or the possibility of mutual psychopathology. Most of all, he does not want to admit the possibility of *both,* that two killers, together, could have performed such a crime, deliberately and without "abnormal" rage—as, in fact, they did. As a professional defender of the community—and as a defender of the very idea of a "community" by which rational "normalcy" is defined—he must always view "psychopathology" as individual. He must always believe that rational deliberation necessarily excludes excessive violence, except as they might come together within a narrowly defined category of individual psychopathology. At the same time, as a custodian of the law, he must neatly divide all offenders "into two groups, the 'sane' and the 'insane'" (335). Most basically, like Perry Smith's sister, and like most everyone else in Holcomb, Dewey wants desperately to believe that the Clutter murders were the act of someone completely isolated, mentally *and* socially.

Dewey's theories might have remained impressive, like Capote's original plan for his book, and almost convincing, if it were not for the intervention of certain "accidents." By a stroke of luck far more striking than Capote's "discovery" of the story, the crime is "solved." In the Kansas State Penitentiary, Floyd Wells, a former cellmate of Richard Hickock, happens to hear a radio account of the murder. Wanting, more than anything else, to improve his own chances of parole, Wells decides to inform the prison officials. In the meantime, by returning to their favorite motels and continuing to pass bad checks, Smith and Hickock have just about guaranteed their own arrest outside a Las Vegas post office. Capote's narrative arrangement—more or less alternating scenes involving the Clutters and their community with scenes involving Smith and Hickock—provides the kind of juxtapositions that make the murderers' simple incompetence all the more glaring, in contrast to the elaborate suspicions and theories fostered by the "normal" community.

By virtue of such unimpressive events, Capote found himself in a situation that would turn out to be far more resistant to his investigations and his art than the reticence of Kansas farmers. Perhaps it was only such events, combined with the trial and execution that would follow—in which "good" would stubbornly refuse to triumph over "evil," in which "sanity" would strangely refuse to explain and cure "insanity"—that could ever have forced him to question his initial design. Perhaps it was only such events that could have allowed him to travel—by such an unexpected route and, in the end, deeper than he had ever anticipated—into the center of the American psyche. In any case, when word got around that the killers were being brought back for trial, Capote made sure that he was at the center of the crowd forming outside the Finney County Court House to await their arrival. There, journalists anticipated "shouted abuse." Just about everyone, anxious for the display of the "hidden animals," anticipated some kind of worthwhile spectacle. But the moment the killers appeared, this design, too, was shattered. At the sight of Smith and Hickock, everyone simply fell silent, "as though amazed to find them humanly shaped" (280).

This amazement at the sight of the killers is a clue to the "effect of fear" that is, of all the effects the novel tries to document, the most resistant to conscious awareness. The capture of Smith and Hickock is not enough, in itself, to make the residents of Holcomb feel completely secure. And the public display of the two killers—"white-faced and blinking blindly" as they "glistened in the glare of flashbulbs and floodlights" (280)—only serves to undermine whatever small degree of security has been restored. In fact, Capote suggests, the combination of these two events only exposes a deeper hostility—a hostility within the community for which the two murderers cannot be completely responsible. The demonization of these "Persons Unknown" turns out to have been, all along, a defense against the very nightmare that does come true the moment they are put on show in the courthouse square: the killers, as it turns out, are not so reassuringly "alien." With the arrest of Smith and Hickock, the residents of Holcomb have been spared what might have seemed, at first, to be a worse "solution" of the crime, the possibility that the killers might be found "among themselves." So, now, one might expect them to be relieved that they no longer have "to endure the unique experience of distrusting each other" (105), at least not in exactly the same way.

But even though it has turned out that Smith and Hickock are not "locals," for some reason their appearance can not extinguish "the fires of mistrust in the glare of which many old neighbors viewed each other strangely, and as strangers" (15). Even when Hickock's detailed confession is announced—as though any further evidence is needed—the people of Holcomb still want to believe that someone else, someone more familiar, must have been involved: "the majority of Holcomb's population, having lived for seven weeks amid unwholesome rumors, general mistrust, and suspicion, appeared to feel disappointed at being told that the murderer was not someone among themselves" (262). They cannot escape the kind of internal distrust that was first expressed by Myrtle Clare, postmistress and local Jeremiah, immediately after the murders. As Mrs. Clare told her mother, it could have been anyone: "All the neighbors are rattlesnakes. Varmints looking for a chance to slam the door in your face. It's the same the world over" (85). Ironically, it is only after the killers have been caught and returned to Kansas that Mrs. Clare's vast denunciation begins to acquire a degree of general acceptance. No matter how vigorously the citizens have taken to buying new locks and to constructing psychological theories, they are still compelled to confront a beast that is within. Just as "Institutional dourness and cheerful domesticity coexist on the fourth floor of the Finney County Courthouse," where Smith and Hickock wait for their trial, institutionalized fear and domestic ritual remain inseparable in the minds of all the people who wait to see them tried (283). The arrest and display of the killers is not enough, at least not so long as they refuse to appear obviously inhuman. The community still cannot return to "normal," not until the fear and the ritual are completely fused in another act of violence.

That is why the good citizens of Finney County finally seem to be seeking—at once and, ultimately, in defiance of all evidence—a criminal without *and* a criminal within, a guilty alien *and* a guilty neighbor. Though Capote is never quite willing to pursue all of its implications, he does suggest that such a paradox is inevitably involved in the dynamics of ritual sacrifice. As René Girard explains, in *Violence and the Sacred*, the victim "must bear a sharp resemblance to the *human* categories excluded from the ranks of the sacrificable, while still maintaining a degree of difference that forbids all possible confusion" (12). To mitigate internal distrust—or even better, to pretend that it has never existed—the community must seize upon a "sacrificable" victim, or, in the case of *In Cold Blood,* victims. Otherwise, the community fears, further violence might "be vented on its own members, the people it most desires to protect" (4). Accordingly, everyone in town has demonized Hickock and Smith, turned them into "animals," in order to insist, as Girard puts it, on a "degree of difference that avoids all confusion"; and, more by chance than anything else, it has discovered the killers to be all too human—more or less ordinary looking young men, without elaborate criminal records. The killers turn out to be too a little close to "the *human* categories excluded from the ranks of the sacrificable."

Capote's depiction of the murder trial is, in effect, an attempt to demonstrate that this contradiction can only be overcome—and Hickock and Smith properly executed—if their actual mental states are treated as irrelevant. No legal consideration can be given to the car collision that left Dick Hickock, in his father's words, no longer "the same boy" (191), nor to the first seventeen months he did in the state prison at Lansing for taking a hunting knife from a neighbor's house. As Hickock's father puts it, this first imprisonment seems, more than anything else, to have been the young man's "ruination": "When he came out of Lansing, he was a total stranger to me" (191). Nor can any legal consideration be given to Smith's "personality structure," described by one psychiatrist as "very nearly that of a paranoid schizophrenic reaction" (43, 333-34). Certainly, it is necessary to exclude from the trial Smith's recurrent dream of an avenging yellow parrot, a "towering" figure that first visited him when he was a child in a California orphanage run by nuns who beat and humiliated him for wetting the bed, the "warrior-angel" that came to his rescue and "blinded the nuns with its beak, fed upon their eyes, slaughtered them as they 'pleaded for mercy,' then so gently lifted him, enfolded him, winged him away to paradise"—a magic friend that reappeared violently throughout his "several confinements in institutions and children's detention centers" (109, 111).

In this way, Capote suggests, the community reassures itself that justice is being carried out, while establishing the adequacy of the sacrificable victims. To this end, the prosecution of Smith and Hickock is aided by the M'Naghten rule, "the ancient British importation which contends that if the accused knew the nature of his act, and knew it was wrong, then he is mentally competent and responsible for his actions" (301). "Furthermore," as special assistant prosecuting attorney Logan Green reminds the Judge, there is "nothing in the Kansas statutes indicating that the physicians chosen to determine a defendant's mental condition must be of any particular qualification." They can be "just plain doctors. Medical doctors in general practice. That's all the law requires" (301). Like the two "concepts" superimposed on the case by Agent Dewey before the killers were captured, the Kansas statutes serve the community's purpose, in this case by reducing psychiatric testimony, literally, to a "yes" or "no" answer, preferably given by an "expert" who would not even be disposed, in any case, to much further elaboration. Despite the public and the media's earlier fascination with the capture and confessions of the killers, no attempt is made, once they are caught, to understand the crime in any way. Rather, as the execution of Hickock and Smith draws closer, the most troubling questions are systematically preempted. Neither the community nor the law that defends it—and, in the end, not even Capote himself, the aspiring expert on "multiple murderers"—really wants to risk any challenge to the accepted distinctions between the "sacrificable victims," Hickock and Smith, and all those local residents who must be "excluded from the ranks of the sacrificable." As one of the forensic psychiatrists asked to consult on the evaluations of the two killers admits, in the kind of testimony excluded from the trial, "murderers who seem rational, coherent, and controlled, and yet whose homicidal acts have a bizarre, apparently senseless quality, pose a difficult problem" (335).

Capote is admirably determined to confront this kind of difficult problem, mostly by including in the novel the kind of testimony that is excluded with such vigilance from the courtroom. Throughout, he dwells on the dual nature of the sacrificial victim. Early on, he describes Hickock's face, transformed by a car collision into a jumble of "mismatched parts," part "American-style 'good kid,'" part thug. Smith's body is similarly "mismatched," the result of a motorcycle accident that left his weight-lifter's upper-body balanced tenuously on two "dwarfish" legs, which "still pained him so severely that he had become an aspirin addict" (42-43). Hickock repeatedly swears, "I'm a normal" and, when Perry, reflecting on the murders, suggests that there just might be "something wrong" with them after all, Hickock denies it with all the self-righteousness of a teetotaling old aunt. Yet Hickock runs over dogs on the highway and "promises" Smith, when planning the robbery, that there will be "lots of hair on them-those walls" (50). Hickock is the one with the "sexual interest in female children" who wants to stop, in the middle of the burglary, to rape Nancy Clutter (229). For his part, Smith rather typically, if pathetically, fantasizes about "theatrical" fame, envisioning himself as Perry O'Parsons, "The One-Man Symphony," with a white top hat and a white tuxedo, with songs and instruments and tap dance steps attuned to every nuance of popular taste (62, 357). Yet he also continues to dream of the yellow parrot, his projection of isolated vengeance—and his two fantasies eventually flow together in front of an audience of "phantoms, the ghosts of the legally annihilated, the hanged, the gassed, the electrocuted" (357).

Most importantly, Capote includes the detailed psychological profiles that the defense attorney's expert witnesses would have provided, if the law had not prevented them from doing so. Most tellingly, so far as the community is concerned, Capote even includes passages from an article, "Murder Without Apparent Motive—A Study in Personality Disorganization," written by Joseph Satten in collaboration with three of his colleagues. After criticizing the ordinary legal distinctions between the "sane" and the "insane," this article describes a "specific syndrome" that would apply, Satten thinks, to Smith and Hickock. Not surprisingly, by this point in the novel, this "syndrome" seems to apply almost equally to the local community. The psychologists write of a "lapse in ego control which makes possible the open expression of primitive violence" (335), and an "unconscious traumatic configuration" that "unwittingly sets into motion . . . homicidal potential" (338). The murder of the ultra-respectable Clutters, followed by the capture of two young men who fit so well into the role of sacrificial victim, was just such a "configuration"—just such a psychological accident.

As Capote should have known, judging by his attention to such accidents throughout the book, the implications of this "testimony" are much more disturbing than either alien invaders or distrustful neighbors. Capote is not particularly determined to demonstrate that, in this particular case, justice has been denied in the courtroom. He never tries to prove that the unfortunate backgrounds of Smith and Hickock can really be used to explain why they became murderers, or even to give guidance on what sort of punishment would be appropriate for them. Instead, by including such a wide range of excluded, more or less psychiatric "testimony," he portrays the trial as little more than an official sanction to ensure that the execution will take place. In doing so, Capote demonstrates that violence is not just a foreign threat, something from "outside normal life." Sacrificial violence is the culmination of the sense of normalcy that holds the town together.

But in the end, no one, not even Capote, really wants to face this reality. At the execution of Smith and Hickock, Agent Dewey—who has become, in the course of the novel, increasingly difficult to separate from Capote's conscience—is once again mysteriously disappointed. He "had anticipated a setting of suitable dignity" (378). More importantly, he "had imagined that with the deaths of Smith and Hickock, he would experience a sense of climax, release, of a design justly completed" (382). By this point in the novel, it is no longer surprising that this imagined design is shattered by real events.

It is surprising, however, that Capote himself, after all his efforts to confront the psychological barriers between the world of the murderers and the world of victims, is compelled to falsify the ending of his "nonfiction novel" by attaching a completely fictional final scene. At the end, Dewey and Susan Kidwell, the best friend of the Clutter's murdered daughter, meet on a sunny May afternoon at the cemetery where the Clutter family is buried. Dewey recalls this meeting as he stands in the prison warehouse, having been "invited" as one of the "twenty-odd witnesses" to "the ceremony" of Smith and Hickock's hanging (378). When Dewey opens his eyes to see Smith's "childish feet, tilted, dangling"—at the moment, that is, when he realizes just how wrought with fiction his hope for "a design justly completed" really is—his thoughts jump back to a pristine moment in the past, the imagined, "casual encounter" in Garden City's "formal cemetery" (382). There, in that "good refuge from a hot day," where "fields blaze with the gold-green fire of half-grown wheat," Dewey thinks proudly of his new home and his two sons, now "deep-voiced" and "as tall as their father" (382). Susan Kidwell, only a child at the trial, is now "a willowy girl with white-gloved hands, smooth cap of dark-honeyed hair, and long, elegant legs" (383). Sexual maturity, it seems, makes up for a lot. "Normalcy" is made to reassert itself, as though it were a force of nature. It is in this setting that the book closes. Transported from the prison warehouse by an act of "novelistic" magic, Dewey strolls through that warm field, "starting home . . . toward the trees, and under them, leaving behind him the big sky, the whisper of wind voices in the wind-bent wheat" (384). Time, at least this suddenly fictional time, has finally brought all things to fullness, and has brought Dewey, like Capote, to some comforting sense of closure. All is pretty much well. The murders—and, more importantly, all the subsequent "whispers" of fear, suspicion, and vengeance—have been displaced into a distant past. Smith's dangling feet have disappeared.

So, in one act of relatively "pure fiction," Capote provides the kind of satisfaction that, he would always argue, an execution should not provide in reality. Even Capote, the eternal "outsider" who spent nearly six years interviewing and corresponding with Smith and Hickock, is finally controlled by the irresistible dynamics of community bonding. He, too, needs to impose the apparent meaning of a completed "design," needs to construct a sort of myth, to normalize and dissipate his awareness of the events surrounding the execution, perhaps even to ease his conscience for not having tried to stop it. Like the critics who praised him so early in his career, and like the citizens of Holcomb who contributed so much to his greatest work, Capote does not really want to consider the disturbing truth that *this* center of the American psyche, this vision of justice as a vengeful God who must be propitiated so that the "natural" and social order can be restored, is only reached by luck—or, to put it in his own terms, by "a psychological accident." And he does not want to admit that, even then, any consideration of this center is always resisted, if not entirely avoided, by our desire to distance ourselves from the need for violence that holds together our communities.

Bibliography

Capote, Truman. *In Cold Blood.* New York: Signet, 1965.

Clarke, Gerald. *Capote: A Biography.* New York: Simon and Schuster, 1988.

Cleaver, Eldridge. *Soul On Ice.* New York: Delta, 1968.

Creeger, George R. *Animals in Exile: Imagery and Theme in Capote's In Cold Blood.* Center for Advanced Studies, Wesleyan University, 1967.

Franklin, H. Bruce. *The Victim as Criminal and Artist: Literature from the American Prison.* New York: Oxford University Press, 1978.

Girard, René. *Violence and the Sacred.* Trans. Patrick Gregory. Baltimore: The Johns Hopkins University Press, 1977.

Mailer, Norman. "Introduction" to Jack Henry Abbott's *In The Belly of The Beast.* New York: Random House, 1981.

———. *The Executioner's Song.* New York: Warner, 1979.

Malcolm X and Alex Haley. *The Autobiography of Malcolm X.* New York: Ballantine, 1964.

Palmer, C. B. "A Farmer Looks at Farming." *Truman Capote's In Cold Blood: A Critical Handbook.* Ed. by Irving Malin. Belmont, California: Wadsworth, 1968. 2-6.

George Garrett (essay date summer 1996)

SOURCE: Garrett, George. "Then and Now: *In Cold Blood* Revisited." *The Virginia Quarterly Review* 72, no. 3 (summer 1996): 467-74.

[*In the following essay, Garrett considers* In Cold Blood, *calling it "an historical landmark" in the way in which it anticipated the violence present in modern American culture.*]

Now it is a matter of memory, but then it was an experience. Not simply a memorable event, but an experience lived in and through and worth remembering, one of those rare occurrences which, even after all is said and done, modified and revised by time, can be said to have changed things.

In my house, which is, among other things, a hopeless clutter and chaos of books, placed in no known or discernible order, I can go directly to it, no groping and searching, and lift Truman Capote's **In Cold Blood,** hardcover, first printing, off the shelf. Partly this is because of the unusual book jacket (slightly torn and frayed since 1965) consisting of nothing but words: title and author on front and spine; on the back, "Books by Truman Capote," a list of his nine published titles at that time, including this one. No blurbs, no photograph, fore or aft. On the end flap, "About the Author," we learn Capote's date of birth—September 30, 1924; that his first novel, **Other Voices, Other Rooms,** "was an international literary success and established the author in the first rank of contemporary writers—a position he has since sustained with additional novels and short stories, as well as his widely praised experiments in the field of reportage." The copy goes on to claim that this new book "represents the culmination of his long-standing desire to make a contribution toward the establishment of a serious new literary form: the Non-fiction Novel."

In an essay review written at the time, I quibbled with that claim, reminding other readers and myself of e. e. cummings' *The Enormous Room,* of Hemingway's *Green Hills of Africa, Death in the Afternoon,* and *A Moveable Feast,* of the whole line of books descending from Walter Lord's *A Night to Remember.* And at that moment I had ignored, and will not again, the major contribution to the form, Shelby Foote's magnificent achievement, *The Civil War: A Narrative,* which, by 1963, was two-thirds done, with the first two volumes in print. All of which only suggests that other writers had thought and were thinking at the same time in the same way—that, somehow, the traditional novel, as it came to them and was practiced, did not have the ways and means to deal honestly and artistically with large events of the past or with the mad reality of our own times, with what Capote described in an interview as "desperate, savage, violent America in collision with sane, safe, insular even smug America—people who have every chance against people who have none." The real world was, they thought, too wild for fiction, but the hard facts of it could be tamed and arranged in a narrative form, what Tom Wolfe would later call "the New Journalism."

The front flap of the jacket is equally spare and unusual, then or now. Title and subtitle, "A True Account of a Multiple Murder and Its Consequences." The text, a little over 100 words, deserves to be quoted in full:

> On November 15, 1959, in the small town of Holcomb, Kansas, four members of the Clutter family were sav-

agely murdered by blasts from a shotgun held a few inches from their faces. There was no apparent motive for the crime and there were almost no clues.

Five years, four months and twenty-nine days later, on April 14, 1965, Richard Eugene Hitchcock, aged thirty-three, and Perry Edward Smith, aged thirty-six, were hanged on a gallows in a warehouse in the Kansas State Penitentiary in Lansing, Kansas.

In Cold Blood is the story of the lives and deaths of these six people. It has already been hailed as a masterpiece.

All but the final sentence is made up of bare facts and numbers, might as well be a newspaper account, surprising in its flat tone (only the word "savagely" is an adverbial judgment call) and perhaps surprising in that it might seem to eliminate some of the suspense of the story. We are told what happened to the six principals before opening the book or reading a page.

But we knew that anyway. The last statement on the jacket is factual also. This book had been serialized in *The New Yorker* with great success. In his "Acknowledgements" Capote thanks "Mr. William Shawn of *The New Yorker*, who encouraged me to undertake this project, and whose judgment stood me in good stead from first to last."

I remember that, remember, after the first chunk of it appeared, waiting eagerly for the next issue of *The New Yorker*. People talked about it with excitement in the way that people only talk about good new movies nowadays. I couldn't wait to get my hands on the book. Didn't wait too long, either, to have acquired an expensive ($5.95) hardcover of the first printing. Waiting around for it we read all about Capote and the new book in all the magazines. I'll never forget the big spread in *Life* magazine where Capote, calm and matter-of-fact, allowed: "The book will be a classic." And in any case it was a huge and instantaneous success, a bestseller, a Book-of-the-Month Club selection (more important then than now); paperback rights were sold for an enormous sum; movie rights were promptly purchased.

It's true, Capote had enjoyed a good measure of literary fame and success ever since the appearance of **Other Voices, Other Rooms**; but this was a great leap, a *grande jete* into popular success. Fame became celebrity. Then that celebrity was at once confirmed and flaunted in 1967 by a party at the Plaza Hotel—"The Party," Gloria Steinem named it in *Vogue* magazine, "a great masked ball that would bring guests from Europe and Asia, not to mention Kansas, California, and Harlem"—to which Capote invited 540 people, enough of them celebrities to be called (again by Gloria Steinem) "a new Four Hundred of the World."

What else about the book itself? It is a very handsomely made and designed book, beautifully printed on the best paper and with a rare and elegant full-cloth binding. Made to last. Made to be kept and appreciated. Made to tell the world: *This is real class.* Open it up and you are soon greeted on the title page by a chilling illustration, the only one in the book or jacket—two pairs of eyes, an extreme close shot in black and white, the eyes of the killers, here brooding over the story to follow. To say the eyes of these two dead young men are haunting would be an understatement. That it is, finally, their book, their story, is underscored by the epigraph, four lines asking for pity and God's mercy, from Francois Villon's "*Ballade des pendus.*"

One thing more. We soon discover that one of the people to whom the book is dedicated is Capote's old childhood friend Harper Lee, author of *To Kill a Mockingbird,* one of the best-loved stories of our time. From all the advance publicity about the making of the book, we already knew that Harper Lee had helped him in various ways in the research and socially in winning over reticent people in Kansas.

The advance publicity, unusual for the time, and the carefully designed jacket copy for the book served a powerful technical purpose as well. Since we knew, more or less, what was coming to pass before reading the first words on the first page, knew that what was coming was horrific—"blasts from a shotgun held a few inches from their faces," to be followed in due course by a double hanging, Capote was free to do what he did, building his story quietly and inexorably. Building it around a classical four-part structure, he could, paradoxically, keep suspense at a high level throughout. The first three sections move along quickly and easily, intercutting back and forth between the murderers and their unsuspecting victims, then the hunters and the hunted. In the final section, **"The Corner,"** dealing with the trial and punishment, Capote demonstrated a virtuoso magician's sleight of hand. By now all the original suspense has been dissipated, and the announced conclusion, the hanging of the killers, was obligatory. Yet he managed to get there without any diminishment of intensity or interest. The hanging scene is one of the finest of its kind, right up there with Melville's *Billy Budd* and the hanging of Popeye in William Faulkner's *Sanctuary*. With one great difference. Melville and Faulkner scrupulously avoided the dramatic cliches, working against the grain of the material. Capote pulled out all the stops: "The hangman coughed—impatiently lifted his cowboy hat and settled it again, a gesture somehow reminiscent of a turkey buzzard huffing, then smoothing its neck feathers—and Hickcock, nudged by an attendant, mounted the scaffold steps." That others present at the scene recalled the details, including the condemned men's last words, differently is not strictly relevant. It's a hell of a hanging.

Before **In Cold Blood** Capote had written—in **Other Voices, Other Rooms, The Grass Harp,** even in the lighthearted **Breakfast at Tiffany's**—romantic fables, well-removed from the world of "realistic" fiction. Even though each of these works is different from the others, all have a clear and consistent moral frame, an inversion of conventional, middle-class values. Even the lovable Holly Golightly of **Breakfast at Tiffany's** has a hard and independent core: "Good? Honest is more what I mean. Not low-type honest—I'd rob a grave, I'd steal two-bits off a dead man's eyes if I thought it would contribute to the day's enjoyment—but unto-thyself-type honest. Be anything but a coward, a pretender, an emotional crook, a whore: I'd rather have cancer than a dishonest heart." In each of these books, and most of the short stories, it is the outsiders and the outcasts who reject conventional morality and are examples of another kind of virtue. Those who manage to prosper or get along in the duplicitous world of practical matters are usually exposed as being at heart deceitful and/or self-deceived, hypocrites at best. It is these, too, who make real mischief and cause real trouble. In the end, thanks to a kind of whimsical Providence or poetic justice they get what is coming to them.

In *In Cold Blood* it is the all-American Clutter family—Herbert William Clutter, 48, the father; Bonnie, his wife; Kenyon, 15, the only son; and Nancy, 16, "the town darling"—whom destiny has selected to represent, in Capote's telling, "sane, safe, insular, even smug America—people who have every chance against people who have none." Anyone at all familiar with the world of Capote's earlier fiction knew two things, why he had chosen this subject and not another and what doom was coming to the Clutters, from the moment he first introduced Herbert Clutter. "Always certain of what he wanted in the world, Mr. Clutter had in large measure obtained it." Poor Clutter is even physically emblematic of the doom-deserving, vulnerable losers (outward and visible winners) of Capote's universe: "Though he wore rimless glasses and was of but average height, standing just under five feet ten, Mr. Clutter cut a man's-man figure. His shoulders were broad, his hair had held its dark color, his square-jawed confident face retained a healthy-hued youthfulness, and his teeth, unstained and strong enough to shatter walnuts, were still intact." People who happened to have read Capote would read that passage and others with an awareness of his irony. People who had never read a word until the arrival of *In Cold Blood,* the huge majority of the audience that made the book a bestseller, were at once invited and allowed to take things straight, at face value. The subtext, however, is slightly camouflaged and complicated because there are some good "straights" in the story, the most important of whom, "a lean and handsome fourth-generation Kansan of forty-seven," is Alvin Adams Dewey, an agent of the Kansas Bureau of Investigation and the closest facsimile of a conventional "hero" in the book. Alvin Dewey and his family became friends of Capote in real life and was noted by Gloria Steinem in her account of "The Party" in 1967. "Alvin Dewey answered questions about problems of the Clutter case, just as dignified and direct in the Paley dining room as he had been in Kansas during the murder investigation in *In Cold Blood.*" Subtext: *There are some real people out there beyond the Hudson, Dorothy. Even in a place like Kansas.* But Dewey, as a figure in the book, is treated with a respect and consideration that, otherwise, only the killers receive.

Capote is adroitly clever here, too. He inverts the old good-cop-bad-cop convention and uses it on the murderers. One, Dick Hickcock, is from the outset the most blameworthy and the least attractive, basically a bad influence on the other, Perry Smith, who is presented with deeply dimensional sympathy. Hickcock is the heavy. There is an archetypal malevolence about him with his head "halved like an apple, then put together a fraction off center," with his "left eye being truly serpentine, with a venomous, sickly-blue squint that, although it was involuntarily acquired, seemed nevertheless to warn of bitter sediment at the bottom of his nature." That's our first impression. Not too pretty, huh? You bring a serpent and an apple together in the same paragraph and you're talking Original Sin and suchlike.

Perry Smith, though he suffers from a physical deformity as the result of an accident, has an interesting look about him: "It was a changeling's face, and mirror-guided experiments had taught him how to ring the changes, how to look now ominous, now impish, now soulful; a tilt of the head, a twist of the lips, and the corrupt gypsy became the gentle romantic." Perry Smith becomes in almost every detail we are given a spooky embodiment of Capote's early fiction. What could be more perfect for a Capote protagonist than to be the child of "a lean Cherokee girl (who) rode a wild horse, a 'bucking bronco,' and her loosened hair whipped back and forth, flew about like a flamenco dancer's"? Capote gives us an empathetic and fascinating look at a murderer's psyche through his portrait of Perry Smith.

There are a number of problems, more evident in hindsight than at the time. For one thing there is the complex matter of fact and judgment. When pictures of the people involved appeared in the magazines, it was clear how much of Capote's descriptions and judgments was subjective, *literary.* The people did not look much like the people he described. Later it turned out that they did not do or say all the things he attributed to them; and some things neither he nor anyone else could have known. Still, it was wonderful reporting and charged writing. And we have become used to the other flaws in our post-Capote non-fiction narratives.

There is also the slightly more disturbing fact that neither the Clutters nor the killers were fictional constructs. They were real people. The brains and blood and hair that splatter walls of the house at River Valley Farm were real. There remains the often asked and always unanswered question, then: were the lives and deaths of these people exploited for the sake of our titillation and the author's profit? Maybe so, but by now both titillation and profit from the real sufferings of others have become so commonplace as to leave us unfit to ask that question about a book from 31 years ago. Maybe Capote lent to the "true crime" story a patina of literary respectability; but now it seems that this was coming anyway, part of the spirit of the 1960's, as was our gradual change over from concern for victims to fascination with perpetrators. Capote's book had something to do with that change of heart and values and certainly spawned a multitude of literary imitations in both fiction and non-fiction. For that reason alone *In Cold Blood* is an important book, an historical landmark. And, finally, there is another, maybe stronger claim the book makes. The "real" world of America as revealed in this story, of which Capote said at the time "It's what I really think about America," has come to pass, is far more a matter of public fact than private vision. Who today would deny that we live in a "desperate, savage, violent America (that is) in collision with sane, safe, insular, even smug America"? In that sense *In Cold Blood* can qualify as prophecy.

What was beyond prophecy, even predictability, was that this book would be the last "big" book by Truman Capote. There would be five more books in his lifetime, none without style and merit, but none of them more than minor exercises. When he died in 1984, he had been working for many years on the novel *Answered Prayers,* dealing with his rich and powerful acquaintances, the folks who came to The Party. When something was cobbled together by Random House from published excerpts and leftover bits and pieces, it was described on the jacket as "perhaps the most famous unpublished novel in contemporary American letters." The publication of *Answered Prayers* in 1987 did little or nothing to change that judgment call. Meantime, no question about it, Truman Capote's continuing claim on our attention derives from and rests in a single extraordinary volume—*In Cold Blood.*

John Hollowell (essay date autumn 1997)

SOURCE: Hollowell, John. "Capote's *In Cold Blood*: The Search for Meaningful Design." *Arizona Quarterly: A Journal of American Literature, Culture, and Theory* 53, no. 3 (autumn 1997): 97-116.

[*In the following essay, Hollowell examines the confession, trial, and execution scenes in* In Cold Blood, *arguing that Capote's treatment of these scenes in the context of Agent Dewey's quest for a "rational framework" explaining the murder of the Clutter family is key to any interpretation of the novel.*]

However long it takes, it may be the rest of my life, I'm going to know what happened in that house: the why and the who.

Alvin Dewey, Chief Detective

I have finished the book, but in a sense I *haven't* finished it: it keeps churning around in my head. It particularizes itself now and then, but not in the sense that it brings about a total conclusion.

Capote, *New York Times Book Review,* 16 January 1966

In early studies of the new journalism and the nonfiction novel, critics have sought to identify the fictional techniques that make the nonfiction novel "read" like a novel. In *The New Journalism,* Tom Wolfe speaks of the realistic novel's "emotional involvement," or its "gripping" and "absorbing" quality (31). Perhaps the most often cited of these devices of realism, according to Wolfe, is "scene by scene reconstruction and resorting as little as possible to sheer historical narration" (31). The supposed effect on the reader is a reconstruction of events with full dialogue and psychological depth without the anonymous summary or narration of traditional journalism.

More recent readers of Capote's *In Cold Blood* have discussed the degree of closure and resolution such scenes achieve with respect to reading the overall meaning of the Clutter murders. Brian Conniff, for example, examines the crucial role of what he calls psychological accidents in the recreation of the crimes and Capote's overall narrative plan (74-94), while Phyllis Frus adopts the opposing view that Capote's method allows for the murders to be explained and rationalized within a framework of middle-class ideology and psychological analysis (120-56). I want to explore the category of "meaningful design," apparently drawn from Detective Dewey's verbal world, since it strategically offers an explanatory framework for understanding murder. In fact, the careful construction of the confession, trial, and execution scenes refers to this standard, one that promises to resolve vexing questions for readers of *In Cold Blood.* Capote's strategy, however, is to raise the possibility of rational order without ever fully endorsing it, often revealing that random and accidental events shape the history of the crime. Capote's narrative method also emphasizes two language systems—the first based on punishment, the second on psychological analysis of personality—that demonstrate opposing ways of judging human behavior. This conflict undermines any straightforward rational design for comprehending murder or its punishment. To evaluate these issues of closure and meaning in *In Cold Blood,* I examine three critical scenes in detail—the confessions of the killers, the courtroom verdicts, and the executions—to provide the best opportunity to identify a totalized, clear sense of an ending.

Until Part 3 of the book, **"Answer,"** Capote's method emphasizes the mysterious, evasive nature of the crimes and their effects on the townsfolk of Holcomb, Kansas. The three scenes I have selected are presented through the eyes of Alvin Dewey, the law-and-order hero of the book. Since Capote's narrative method does not allow the author to speak in his own, first-person voice, Dewey acts as the central intelligence guiding our integration of plot elements. The reader is likely to identify with Dewey's viewpoint as she identifies with Dewey's search for design, since it will presumably create an explanatory framework that will allow her to understand the bizarre murders. These three scenes provide a basis for reading the murders, for placing them within a coherent design for *In Cold Blood* as a whole. The narrative promises to create an understanding of the crimes and get to the bottom of the killers' motives—if not through the legal system, then perhaps through the process of psychological analysis. Dewey's role is critical since his motives and desires allow readers to identify with the eventual capture and punishment of the suspects.

The confession scene develops in **"Answer"** when Dick Hickock and Perry Smith are arrested in Las Vegas as their cross-country ride comes to an end; Capote signals the arrival of a dramatic climax in which we may find out "what really happened." It is useful to study the staging *words* and interviews in some depth, both for the portrait of Dewey's actions and for our understanding of the motivation and possible logic behind the crimes. First, recall that Capote's narrative strategy left the black Chevrolet frozen in moonlight in the Clutter driveway on the night of the murders, but the murders have never been described "in real time." Second, the confession scene promises to release pent-up curiosity about the crimes, which up to this point have been presented as motiveless and inexplicable. Our anticipation takes its cue from Dewey's solemn vow when first encountering the murder scene: "However long it takes, it may be the rest of my life, I'm going to know what happened in that house: the why and the who" (*In Cold Blood* 80).

Dewey's thoughts about the case suggest a rational framework for understanding murder—a meaningful design. The possibility of this design comes from the general human need for meaning and the specific need for closure, to put an ending to a series of plausible yet always puzzling explanations. Second, Capote's strategy raises the possibility of design and meaning by strengthening the reader's identification with Detective Dewey, who dominates every phase of the case. What I propose is to examine the confession, the trial, and the execution scenes against the standard of meaning Dewey envisions. Capote's treatment of this complex standard of resolution is linked to any interpretation of *In Cold Blood* and its overall aesthetic effects.

One test to apply to the confession and the trial scenes is the extent to which rational explanation—the why and the who—appears in the final revelation of the crimes in **"Answer."** On December 30, 1959, after more than six weeks of cluelessness and frustration, Dewey learns of Hickock and Smith's arrest in Las Vegas. While this should be an occasion for joy in the Dewey family, Alvin remains pessimistic that the case will finally be solved since the physical evidence is slim: "Yes, a big lot of good they [photographs of bloody footprints] are . . . unless those boys still happen to be wearing those boots that made them" (213). Reflecting on the flimsy evidence as he dresses for a quick departure for Las Vegas with his three Kansas Bureau of Investigation partners, Dewey tells his wife the only interviewing strategy he can think of: "the name Clutter has to hit them like a hammer, a blow they never knew was coming" (213). Such a statement anticipates a fierce struggle between law enforcement and criminals who had hoped to leave no clues behind.

Capote allows the *why* of the crimes to play itself out slowly, since at first the two suspects are allowed to believe they have been arrested for minor violations of parole and hot check writing. In Capote's chosen order, Hickock is the first to be interrogated by agents Church and Nye. After pursuing the check-writing incidents in Kansas City, Church mentions the weekend of November 14-15, while Hickock rambles on with a prepared false alibi about traveling to Fort Scott to see Smith's sister and picking up two prostitutes. By allowing Hickock to exhibit "his one true gift" of recollection, the detectives let him go on to name all the roads, hotels, and highways from Kansas to Florida, and back through Texas to Nevada. Nye then zeroes in on him: "I guess you realize we wouldn't have come all the way to Nevada to chat with a couple of two-bit check chiselers" (222). Capote cites the detectives' contemporaneous notes of the moment when Nye mentions the name "Clutter": "Suspect underwent an intense visible reaction. He turned gray" (223). The two detectives then deliver a blow intended to shatter Hickock's alibi:

> "But you made two mistakes, Dick. One was, you left a witness. A living witness. Who'll testify in court. Who'll stand in the witness box and tell a jury how Richard Hickock and Perry Smith bound and gagged and slaughtered four helpless people."
>
> (223)

While he is visibly rattled, Hickock still denies any knowledge of the murders. Detectives Nye and Church decide to cut off the interview, allowing him to brood over his guilt and a possible death sentence. Capote's interest lies in the methods of trapping suspects and forcing a confession. His goal is to dramatize the pressure applied by the detectives and Dick's wavering motives for confessing or withholding information.

When first confronted with the idea of a witness, Hickock thinks of an *eyewitness*—someone who actually saw the crime—and he soon remembers his old cellmate, Floyd Wells, but dismisses any danger figuring that "the sonofabitch was probably expecting some fancy reward" (227). Detectives finally break down Dick's protestations of innocence, however, by showing him large "one to one" blowup photographs of the bloody footprints from the murder scene, and he quickly realizes that Smith is the one witness who could damage him the most: "It was *Perry* he ought to have silenced. On a mountain road in Mexico. Or while walking across the Mojave" (228). When Hickock contemplates the photographs of the crime scene and considers their use in court, he blurts out: "'Perry Smith killed the Clutters. . . . It was Perry. I couldn't stop him. He killed them all'" (230). The interrogation of Hickock reflects his desire to hold out in the face of his fear of Smith and the physical evidence. He attempts to exculpate himself by declaring that he did not actually kill any member of the family. Capote shows Hickock's thinking as he falls back on the claim that he did not actually pull the trigger and therefore should not be charged with first-degree murder.

Capote soon switches the interrogation to Smith, since his version of events promises to answer Dewey's questions about motive. Following a similar reconstructive method throughout, Capote develops Smith's testimony more completely than Hickock's, reporting in the present tense to intensify the immediacy. After more than three hours of questioning, Agent Duntz tells Smith that on November 14, "'You were killing the Clutter family'" (225), but Smith stubbornly sticks to the cover story about Fort Scott and the prostitutes. Finally, Dewey decides to cut the interview off, leaving Smith with the guilt-inducing knowledge that the next day would have been Nancy Clutter's birthday: "'She would have been seventeen'" (226).

In portraying Smith in this section, Capote uses the most controversial technique of the nonfiction novel. Instead of quoting directly or using typical journalistic attribution, he adopts a point of view coming from inside the suspect's mind. While it seems as if an omniscient author has access to his private thoughts, everything Smith "thinks" came from extensive interviews Capote conducted much later on Death Row. Here Smith worries about Hickock's ability to hold out against sharp interrogation.

> . . . well, he damn near died, that's all. He must have lost ten pounds in two seconds. Thank God he hadn't let them see it. Or hoped he hadn't. And Dick? Presumably they'd pulled the same stunt on him. Dick was smart, a convincing performer, but his "guts" were unreliable, he panicked too easily. Even so, and however much they pressured him, Perry was sure that Dick would hold out.
>
> (227)

While Smith avoids confessing in Las Vegas, he finally breaks down and tells the "whole story" during his transport back to Kansas. Dewey inadvertently tells Smith that Hickock has spoken of "King," a black man whom Smith supposedly whipped to death in a false story he made up to impress Hickock. At first, Smith cannot believe Hickock has confessed to any involvement in the Clutter case: "'I thought it was a stunt. I didn't believe you. That Dick let fly. The tough boy!'" (232). But the revelation about the King story becomes a critical signal because if Hickock ever confessed, "'dropped his guts all over the goddamn floor—I knew he'd tell about the nigger'" (232).

This revelation launches Smith's narration into the events on the night of the murders. Dewey is attentive, having sworn to himself long ago to learn every detail of the murders, hoping for a coherent story to resolve his doubts and earlier confusion. Since the outset of the long investigation of the senseless murders, the reader follows Dewey's reactions with hope that the dramatic highlights of the book will occur in this scene. As Dewey performs the repellent act of lighting cigarettes for the handcuffed Smith, the two factors that dominate the story of the night of the murders are the bickering and macho posturing of the two men, and the obvious fact that Mr. Clutter kept no safe at his house.

Far from being a portrayal of two homicidal maniacs on a rampage, what is striking about Smith's narrative are odd moments of quiet, moments of hesitation when the whole scheme might have been ended without anyone dying. In the driveway, both men swig from a bottle of whiskey; Hickock says, "'I'll show you who's got guts,'" as the two muster courage for tying and gagging each member of the family, the women upstairs and Kenyon and Mr. Clutter in the basement (235). When it becomes apparent that there is no office safe, and Smith understands that the "big score" is a bust, he reports wanting just to leave the house: "'Why don't I walk off? Walk to the highway, hitch a ride. I sure Jesus did not want to go back in that house'" (240). But there is an odd magnet, according to Smith, almost as if he is watching someone other than himself: "'It was like I wasn't part of it. More as though I was reading a story. And I had to know what was going to happen. The end'" (240). Seeing himself in the role of spectator is a bizarre feature of Smith's narration, implying that he is watching some other person commit the crimes.

This curious dissociation of thoughts and emotions from actions permeates much of Smith's account of the night of November 14. Later, in the psychiatric analysis, it will be presented as a case of Smith's "magical thinking," his uncanny ability to separate and distance himself from events and action, as if he were watching a movie in which he was a character. Early on, Perry talks of shaking down Nancy Clutter's room and the shame of searching for her souvenir silver dollar: "'. . . it rolled across the floor. Rolled under a chair. I had to get down on my knees. And just then it was like I was outside myself. Watching myself in some nutty movie. It made me sick. . . . Dick, and all his talk about a rich man's safe, and here I am crawling on my belly to steal a child's silver dollar'" (240). Again, Capote's report of Smith's confession emphasizes the feeling of being "outside himself," as if he were watching some "movie." Capote dwells on the silver dollar incident because Smith himself understands it as a symbol of the absurdity of the theft, a shameful reminder of pointless torture and murder.

Despite the high points of action in Smith's story—the killing of Mr. Clutter, the rapid shotgun blasts—the length of time in the house with strange moments of quiet lead us to a discomfiting series of *what ifs*. Readers are cued to wait for a design that will explain the motive for the murders. For example, Smith tells of ordering Hickock to leave Nancy's room for "'that's something I despise. Anybody that can't control themselves sexually'" (243). Yet when Dick leaves the room, Perry has a surreal yet quite "normal" conversation with a girl who fears for her life:

> "She was trying hard to act casual and friendly. I really liked her. She was really nice. A very pretty girl, and not spoiled or anything. She told me quite a lot about herself. About school, and how she was going to go to a university and study music and art. Horses. Said next to dancing what she liked best was to gallop a horse, so I mentioned my mother had been a champion rodeo rider."
>
> (242)

This is an odd conversation, for here is a nice girl that Perry's criminal life has never allowed him to meet and, ironically, he is able to have a friendly chat about horses in the moments just before killing her at point-blank range. Readers may have difficulty resolving such a moment with the rapid series of shotgun blasts, and the sudden flash of anger that remains uncanny.

After telling of several such moments of pause and quiet, Smith mentions the final strategy session between the two men just before the killing of Mr. Clutter, the first in the chain reaction of killing. With the lights out and the family taped and bound, Smith presents this huddle as a prelude to the actual murders:

> "Dick and I went off in a corner. To talk it over. Remember, now, there were hard feelings between us. Just then it made my stomach turn to think I had ever admired him. . . . I said, 'Well Dick. Any qualms?' He didn't answer me. I said, 'Leave them alive, and this won't be any small rap. Ten years the very least.' . . . I asked him for [the knife], and he gave it to me, and I said, 'All right, Dick. Here goes.' But I didn't mean it. I meant to call his bluff."
>
> (244)

Shortly after this point, Smith tells of Mr. Clutter struggling "half out of his ropes" and making a gurgling sound "like somebody drowning," while Smith dares Hickock to finish killing him. In Smith's version, he takes the knife from Hickock and then uses the shotgun to kill Mr. Clutter to end his suffering:

> "Dick wanted to get the hell out of there. But I wouldn't let him go. The man would have died anyway, I know that, but I couldn't leave him like he was. I told Dick to hold the flashlight, focus it. Then I aimed the gun. The room just exploded. Went blue. Just blazed up."
>
> (244)

As Smith finishes his story, Agent Dewey's ears "ring with it," and he knows that he has wanted these details all along since this case had begun to dominate his life. Every event of the confessions—all the terrors of the victims, every shotgun blast—has been presented. Yet has the story actually fulfilled the design Dewey so desires? Does the scene as reported reveal the *true answer* of "the why and the who" that Dewey sought? Recall that from the early scattering of disconnected clues, Dewey formulated two "concepts," one involving a single killer and another involving two or more men. These two scenarios demonstrate how even Dewey's crime-solving skills could not anticipate or comprehend what these particular killers were capable of. Because of the amount of taping and tying the family suffered, Dewey favored the "double-killer concept," but earlier he found it unbelievable that "'two individuals could reach the same degree of rage, the kind of psychopathic rage it took to commit such a crime'" (82-83). Even if someone had an insane rage against Herb Clutter, "'where did he find a partner, someone crazy enough to help him? It doesn't add up. It doesn't make sense'" (83). And yet, as he learns from Smith, this scenario is close to what happened.

Does Smith's confession add up to a story that makes sense now? Within this matrix of common sense and reason, Dewey does not feel satisfied with the answers. Even though all the details have been revealed, the murders remain outside an explanatory or rational viewpoint based on the human need for order that dominates Capote's approach. Capote shapes **In Cold Blood** to present the possibility of a rational view of murder and yet systematically denies or withdraws it. The narrative dwells on Dewey's sense of dissatisfaction, even after hearing every detail: "But the confessions, though they answered the questions of how and why, failed to satisfy [Dewey's] sense of meaningful design. The crime was a psychological accident, virtually an impersonal act; the victims might as well have been killed by lightning" (245).

Reviewing these moments of terror in the account Smith gives Dewey, we find a consistent failure to arrive at the "sense of meaningful design" Dewey is seeking.

Each of the constituent elements leading to the moment of the crime is present: the failure to find a safe, the two men's anger toward each other, Smith's sense of shame, Hickock's embarrassment at not bring off "the perfect score," the final thought that more prison time will surely await them if they leave witnesses and get caught. Each of these factors plays a role in the murders, yet no single motive in itself makes the killing necessary or inevitable. If any one of these elements had been missing, the murders might have been avoided; therefore, even by the end of the story things do not "add up" or "make sense."

As Brian Conniff has persuasively argued, the case would be too simple and indeed Capote's narrative would be too determined and obvious, like Dewey's two concepts, "if it were not for the intervention of certain 'accidents'" (77-94). Conniff goes on to show how Capote blurs the usual distinctions between good and evil. It is not excellent police work that solves the case but a "stroke of luck" when the convict Floyd Wells names Hickock. Dewey is lucky, too, that the killers are so foolish:

> . . . by returning to their favorite hotels and continuing to pass bad checks, Smith and Hickock have just about guaranteed their own arrest outside a Las Vegas post office. . . . [Capote's method] provides the kind of juxtapositions that make the murderers' simple incompetence all the more glaring, in contrast to the elaborate suspicions and theories fostered by the "normal" community. . . . Perhaps it was only such events, combined with the trial and execution that would follow—in which "good" would stubbornly refuse to triumph over "evil," in which "sanity" would strangely refuse to explain and cure "insanity"—that could have forced [Capote] to question his initial design [for the book].
>
> (Conniff 84-85)

Such commentary sheds light on what happens in the confession scene, because all the details make clear that the mystery does not follow the classic means of solving a murder—looking for motive and opportunity, nor does it adhere to the logic of Dewey's two prior concepts. In fact, rejecting the formula resolution of most crime stories, Capote endorses no clear-cut motive or reason for the murders. Crimes of premeditation can be understood, and even crimes of passion may be comprehensible in psychological terms. As in the classic literature of American crime—in Dreiser's *An American Tragedy*, for example, when Clyde Griffiths' pregnant fiancée drowns when the two of them are out rowing—events seem to *happen* without premeditation and beyond the conscious control of human agents.

Capote's narrator apparently offers us a false certainty when he says, "the confessions . . . answered questions of how and why" (245), since a careful reader will seriously wonder if they do. A radical feature of Capote's book, one that has troubled many critics, is that the narrator never offers easy answers or a ready-made ethical framework for "understanding" the murders (Macdonald 44-48; Trilling 107-13). Hence, readers must confront the acts of terror and violence outside the framework of rational organization, while appreciating Garden City's long-awaited return to stability now that the perpetrators of the murders have been duly captured and jailed. As Capote sets up the equation, the dramatic work of the confessions helps establish the ground for another important scene, the trial in Garden City that once again promises to get to the bottom of the Clutter murders.

The Law vs. Psychology

If the confession scene does not fully satisfy the desire for "meaningful design," perhaps the trial of Hickock and Smith will provide the fuller explanation of the events that resist Dewey's sense of reason. Recent perspectives on language indicate that humans construct "reality" and "truth" from the vantage point of metaphorical and language systems that control our view of the world.[1] In the courtroom drama, for example, Capote manages to promote conflict by establishing two interpretations of the events—the first legal and restrictive, the second psychological—drawing arguments first from acts and then from a careful study of the killers' possible motivations. Both systems of language—the legal and the psychological—offer competing ways of reconstructing the past from different perspectives. The legal language focuses on action, responsibility, and laws of evidence—to determine whether the acts of murder were committed by these men. The psychological language provides psychiatric "testimony" to explore the unconscious motives for such "motiveless" crimes; the psychological testimony concerns personality structure and the formative events of childhood. Embedded in the psychiatric language is a definition of sanity that implicitly challenges the legal definition at the trial, by which Kansas law reduces matters to a simple yes-or-no answer.

At first glance, the outcome of the trial appears foregone: the physical evidence, the bloody photographs, the testimony of Floyd Wells, the careful reconstruction of the crime by Alvin Dewey, and the signed confessions all point to the guilt that will allow the community to restore its sense of order and quiet its fear by exacting guilty verdicts and the death penalty. The legal system, with its established rules of evidence, restricts what information can be presented to a jury. Crucial in this case is the M'Naghten rule, a British legal precedent stating that "if the accused knew the nature of his act, and knew it was wrong, then he is mentally competent" (267). Further, as prosecutor Logan Green makes clear, specialized psychiatric testimony is not required since the determination of any family doctor will suffice: "'Medical doctors in general practice. That's all the law requires. We have sanity hearings in this county every year'" (267). This ruling restricts the ground for arguments and limits the jury's view of all potential evidence.

A more distant underpinning of the legal system is the biblical view of crime and punishment, placing the prosecutors in the role of vengeful Old Testament prophets, invoking the *lex talonis*. Prosecutor Green effectively uses a "reading" of biblical passages in his summation to call for the deaths of Hickock and Smith:

> "But I anticipated that defense counsel would use the Holy Bible as an argument against the death penalty. You heard the Bible quoted. But *I* can read too . . . and here are a few things that the Good Book has to say on the subject. In Exodus Twenty, Verse Thirteen, we have one of the Ten Commandments: 'Thou shalt not kill' . . . [and] in the *next* chapter, Verse Twelve, the penalty for disobedience [is] . . . 'He that smiteth a man, so that he die, shall be surely put to death.'"
>
> (304)

While the courtroom presentation of evidence focuses on the simple knowledge of right and wrong, Capote undermines the reading of the verdicts by presenting viewpoints of those unsympathetic to the court proceedings. For example, Dick Hickock's father remarks: "'That judge up there! I never seen a man so prejudiced. Just no sense having a trial'" (281). The author also quotes two journalists, who comment on the "cold-blooded" nature of the death penalty. As Capote often stated in interviews, the context and position of quotations help to organize the reader's sense of a scene more effectively than would authorial intrusion. Capote's quotations from the journalists show that "in cold blood" applies first to the killers and then to the state.

While the trial scene is limited by restrictions of the M'Naghten rule to assess sanity, Capote's approach stresses the psychiatric examinations that were inadmissible in court. Since Capote's narrator is unfettered by any legal rulings, he relates the complex theory of Dr. W. Mitchell Jones by stating, "had Dr. Jones been allowed to speak further, here is what he would have said" (294). Jones' assessment of Dick Hickock focuses on his athletic ability and previous good health before a severe auto accident produced "'blackout spells, periods of amnesia and headaches'" (294). He concludes that Hickock's personality has "'typical characteristics of what psychiatrically would be called a severe character disorder,'" and he would have urged the court to order physical examinations to rule out the possibility of "'organic brain damage'" (295). As usual, Capote's lengthier and more penetrating presentation is devoted to psychological evidence concerning Perry Smith's early traumas and his violently explosive behavior.

Dr. Jones finds "'two features in [Smith's] personality make-up stand out as particularly pathological.'" The first is a paranoid orientation toward social interactions: "'He is suspicious and distrustful of others, tends to feel others . . . are unfair to him and do not understand him'" (297). Related to this trait, he is "'sensitive to criticism'" and "'cannot tolerate being made fun of'" (297). The second trait, related directly to the Clutter murders, concerns

> "rages, which he says 'mount up' in him, and . . . the poor control he has over them. When turned toward himself the anger has precipitated ideas of suicide . . . [and, at times] . . . his thinking [is] . . . lost in detail, and some of his thinking reflects a 'magical' quality, a disregard of reality."
>
> (297)

In addition to Dr. Jones' conclusions, Capote quotes extensively from a 1960 paper by Dr. Joseph Satten and his three colleagues, "Murder without Apparent Motive—A Study in Personality Disorganization." Studying the Clutter case, Dr. Satten finds that Smith's behavior conforms to a pattern of murders he had studied where the murderers suffered from "'severe lapses in ego control,'" leading to "'the open expression of primitive violence, born out of previous, and now unconscious, traumatic experiences'" (298-99). For more than ten pages, Capote presents the behavior pattern of such murderers who, on the surface, "'seem rational, coherent, and controlled'" but whose crimes "'have a bizarre, apparently senseless quality'" (298).

At the heart of Dr. Satten's theory is the idea of unconscious motivation, that a present action is determined by the repetition of some earlier, unresolved state of mental imbalance. The murderer in effect finds in the current situation a configuration that provokes a reenactment of old wrongs:

> "Such individuals can be considered murder-prone in the sense of carrying a surcharge of aggressive energy or having an unstable ego defense system that periodically allows the naked and archaic expression of such energy. The murderous potential can become activated, especially if some disequilibrium is already present, when the victim-to-be is unconsciously perceived as a key figure in some past traumatic configuration."
>
> (301)

Such parallels reinforce the viewpoint that Dr. Satten "feels secure in assigning [Smith] to 'their ranks'" (301). The proposed theory suggests that Mr. Clutter "was not entirely a flesh-and-blood man [that Smith] 'suddenly discovered' himself destroying" (302) but the cumulative ghost of his father, his despised Army sergeant, the nuns who beat him, and thus all the hated authority figures from his past.

After an extended presentation of these theories, Capote examines Smith's own words, heard earlier both in the confession scene and during a meeting with Don Cullivan, his old Army buddy. In that meeting Smith describes the killing of Mr. Clutter in almost exactly the same words as in the confession scene:

> "I was sore at Dick. . . . But it wasn't Dick. Or the fear of being identified. . . . And it wasn't because of anything that the Clutters did. They never hurt me. Like other people. Like people have all my life. Maybe it's just that the Clutters were the ones who had to pay for it."
>
> (290)

Capote's narrative voice concludes neutrally by showing the apparent harmony of two viewpoints, reporting that, "It would appear that by independent paths, both the professional and the amateur analyst reached conclusions not dissimilar" (302). Capote's narrator does not interpret these conclusions, but the length of time devoted to them clearly undercuts the straightforward clarity of courtroom justice.

Yet how does the psychiatric testimony work? Although it does not change anything about the laws operating in Kansas in 1960, it questions the fairness of death-penalty verdicts endorsed by the community. Readers must wonder: if Smith underwent a "brain explosion" at the time of murdering Mr. Clutter, how could he be held responsible? It may seem to be a clear case of temporary insanity. Capote's inherent plea for mercy, however, must later be subjected to cold-blooded facts of the murders of Herbert, Kenyon, Nancy, and Mrs. Clutter. It is clear that they are just as dead whether they were killed by Smith in an agitated state, or because he was intent on leaving *no witnesses* to the crime—a motive for the murders reinforced throughout "The Last to See Them Alive." The weight of the psychiatric testimony does not suggest that Smith and Hickock are *not* guilty, but it hints that leniency or perhaps life imprisonment without parole would be a more suitable punishment, although Capote never overtly makes this argument.

EXECUTION AND FINAL MEANING

The last of the trio of scenes examining the framework of a meaningful design is the execution of Hickock and Smith, depicting events at the Kansas State Penitentiary on April 14, 1965, after five years of legal appeals. As preparation for the events to come, Capote depicts the execution of Lowell Lee Andrews, a Death-Row friend of Hickock and Smith. According to Capote's narrative voice, Smith is allowed to speak a condemned man's customary last words: "'I don't believe in capital punishment, morally or legally. Maybe I had something to contribute, something—'" (340). While journalist Philip Tompkins quotes others close to the scene who stated that these words were not spoken (170), Capote depicts Smith as both penitent and critical of the state. In interviews after the publication of *In Cold Blood,* Capote echoed Smith's own sense of his potential for some future contribution:

> He wanted very deeply to paint and write and he also had genuine talent as a musician. He had a natural ear and could play five or six instruments; the guitar, in particular, he played extremely well. But one of the things he used to tell me over and over again was what a tragedy that . . . [no one] encouraged him in any single creative thing he wanted to do.
>
> (Norden 125-26)

Yet when Hickock finally dies at 12:41 A.M. and Smith follows at 1:19 A.M., Capote's narrator again turns to Alvin Dewey, the same moral barometer consulted in each phase of the case. Based on comments Dewey no doubt made to Capote, Hickock remains as always "'a small-time chiseler who got out of his depth'" (340), and yet in death Smith possesses the "aura of an exiled animal, a creature walking wounded" (341). This last description echoes the book's earlier references to Smith's childhood and his wounded adulthood, seen through sympathetic observers like Don Cullivan, Mrs. Josie Meier in Garden City, and his prison friend Willie-Jay.

The closing scene of this nonfiction novel is not the executions proper, since they, once again, fail to provide Alvin Dewey with "a sense of climax, release, of a design justly completed" (341). Capote's language suggests Aristotle's analysis of catharsis in tragedy, in which terror and pity are released in the audience by the appropriate completion of an action at the play's end (*Poetics,* ch. 13-14). In the Clutter case, however, the accidents of a "brain explosion" and the Clutters' accidental presence as victims, as well as Capote's emphasis on the long legal delays, all block the proper purging of the expected emotions at the completion of a well-made plot. Instead, Capote singles out Dewey's memory of a graveside meeting at River Valley Cemetery "a year earlier," a chance encounter with Susan Kidwell, Nancy Clutter's girlhood friend who had gone on to the university to study:

> "Everything. Art, mostly. I love it. . . . Nancy and I planned to go to college together. We were going to be roommates. I think about it sometimes. Suddenly, when I'm very happy, I think of all the plans we made."
>
> (342)

After a brief discussion of Nancy's former boyfriend's marriage, and of her own plans, Dewey acknowledges "a pretty girl in a hurry" and he privately thinks she is "just such a young woman as Nancy might have been" (343). The scene nostalgically closes with a sense of place that recalls Capote's ***The Grass Harp,*** when Collin Fenwick is reunited with Judge Cool. Here Dewey is walking home "leaving behind him the big sky, the whisper of wind voices in the wind-bent wheat" (343). At first this scene seems a fitting way to end, something out of the world of fiction. Yet it also presents a cliché in response to death, asserting the old truism that "life goes on" while survivors must resolve their own searches for meaning.

This ending's strong sense of closure has seemed to certain critics to be tacked on artificially (Tanner 101-2; Macdonald 48). Apparently, Capote did not want to end on the downbeat note of the executions, which were very troubling to him after five years of close contact with the killers. Gerald Clarke's biography asserts that Capote *invented* this graveside scene. ***In Cold Blood***'s "one act of pure fiction," was revealed as such a decade after the book's publication in a letter from Sue Kidwell's mother and Alvin Dewey (Clarke 358-59; n. 585). This is a serious blemish on the otherwise factually accurate narrative; as Clarke notes, "since events had not provided him with a happy scene, he was forced to make one up" (358-59). Despite this problem of accuracy, does Capote's concluding fiction really imply that the world is restored to order, that a rational structure has been superimposed on the baffling events? Or does the scene function as a kind of musical coda that extends or modifies the formal ending as in a symphonic movement?

In closing this discussion, I want to return once again to the standard of meaningful design to assess its influence on our final interpretation of ***In Cold Blood***. Despite the sense of closure Capote's invented ending implies, the book does not really resolve the conflicted meanings of the crimes or bring them within a larger framework that is rationalized, totalized, and complete. A strong reading of this sort is proposed by Phyllis Frus in her recent comparison of ***In Cold Blood*** with Norman Mailer's *The Executioner's Song*. She argues that Capote's novel reinforces standard class ideology by achieving a defined sense of resolution:

> The narrative of ***In Cold Blood*** implies that truth is, if not simple, at least ascertainable, if we are willing to take the trouble; and that sociologists and psychiatrists have the answers to the riddle of criminal behavior. Furthermore, the reader implied by the structure of the novel learns that violent, senseless crime can be made sensible and poignant through artistic representation; and that these repulsive, illiterate, antisocial criminals are rendered as literate, talented, redeemable. . . . ***In Cold Blood*** . . . assumes a world of cause and effect, of certitude, reason—in short, of common sense, and it expresses this world view via a realism characterized by verisimilitude, a historical narrator who assures the intelligibility of the text by "placing" the other narrations, and through its strong sense of closure.
>
> (184)

While this reading of closure and certainty of ***In Cold Blood*** raises many interesting problems, it is ultimately reductive and mistaken in terms of Capote's complex narrative strategies. Although Dewey's category of "meaningful design" is three times raised by the narrator as a possible standard for resolution, nowhere is it accepted or fully endorsed. Furthermore, while the psychiatric testimony is "placed" in an important position in **"The Corner,"** it is never accepted as the final answer to the "riddle of criminal behavior"; in fact, it is only one part of the explanatory apparatus of the narration, since the law and legal proceedings have their due, along with the desire for retribution of the people of Holcomb. I would argue that Capote's structure places the reader in a complex intersection of the law, the impulse for compassion, and the knowledge of psychiatry without fully endorsing a single, stable viewpoint naturalized by "common sense" or reason.

Chris Anderson explains that the mystery of murder in ***In Cold Blood*** is presented through what he calls a "rhetoric of silence." In effect, Capote's reluctance to impose meaning produces an uncertain ending, one that reproduces our uncertainty when "the imagination fails to comprehend the quality and degree of suffering the Clutters endured" (Anderson 84). In fact, the moment of cutting Mr. Clutter's throat is portrayed as silent and inexplicable because "in the end things just happened; at the key moment there is a blank" (Anderson 64). It is this blank—a moment that resists reduction to language—which the whole trial scene and Smith's confessional account do not domesticate or tame by reason. The events at the center of the murders, despite the full psychological backgrounds and the lengthy confessional statements, produce a reverberation of many texts resounding, while the narrator of ***In Cold Blood*** declines to single out any explanatory framework as superior or definitive.

With respect to the psychiatric testimony, despite its strong placement, the reader realizes in a way that Frus seems not to accept that psychiatric knowledge will not clear away the mystery of the case. Such thinking is a kind of trap, for, as Alan Dershowitz has recently pointed out in *The Abuse Excuse,* what murderer could not claim an abused childhood or environmental preconditions for murder? At the closing of ***In Cold Blood,*** Capote positions the reader within a competition of explanatory and rational texts without endorsing any of them and without reducing the mysteries of the case to common wisdom.

What Anderson calls "the rhetoric of silence" implies a narrator who places us in the midst of these explanatory systems, leaving a troubling series of thoughts but never leading to any easy resolution. Are these men guilty? Certainly, on the basis of the evidence at trial, most would say "yes." Are they insane? According to the M'Naghten rule they are sane, yet the psychiatric testimony makes childhood abuse and possible brain damage from motor accidents challenge this ruling. Should Smith's painting and studying of philosophy on Death Row be taken into account? Does journal-keeping indicate that Hickock and Smith are redeemable? "Yes," some might say again. Yet Capote leaves readers with an unwieldy series of accidents, as Conniff points out, brought about by real events: the pairing of these two partners, the particular set of American values the Clutters seem to represent, the feelings that Smith experiences at the precise moment of being poised with a knife above Mr. Clutter's throat. What remains is an irreducible blank and a mystery at the center not unlike Kurtz's cry, "the horror, the horror" in *Heart of Darkness*. None of this can easily be paraphrased.

Finally, do readers accept the town's need for revenge, supported by a biblical call for justice, or the chief detective's need to feel an appropriate set of emotions to achieve a personal closure? Even if they do, there are the dangers of accepting the potentially exculpatory evidence of psychiatry that might eventually lead to selfless agents lost in a world of post-Freudian determinism. *In Cold Blood,* despite its authorial omniscience and its apparent sense of closure, requires acceptance of no particular viewpoint without the simultaneous consideration of other powerful and contradictory explanations. At the end of an interview—published in the *New York Times Book Review*—Capote was asked if he personally had achieved a sense of closure with the case and he replied: "It's like the echo of E. M. Forster's Malabar Caves, the echo that's meaningless and yet it's there: one keeps hearing it all the time" (Plimpton 68). It is perhaps this memory of the vertigo beyond language that he hoped to reproduce for readers of *In Cold Blood.*

Note

1. Numerous post-structuralist theorists have explored the relationship between social reality and language. Foremost among these is Michel Foucault who, in such works as "The Discourse on Language," *Discipline and Punish,* [New York: Pantheon Books, 1977] and *The History of Sexuality, Volume 1: An Introduction,* [New York: Pantheon Books, 1978] examines the relationship between knowledge and power in social institutions such as the clinic, the prison system, and the social control of sexuality. A key tenet in this analysis is that reality does not exist independently of the language and discursive practices of social institutions that are shaped by them. In Capote's work, the narrative method heightens the sense of the tension between punishing and vengeful language (exhibited by prosecutors) and the therapeutic language of psychology (exhibited by the defense). Capote thereby positions the implied reader of *In Cold Blood* between these competing ways of conceiving of crime and criminality leading to ambiguous results.

Works Cited

Anderson, Chris. *Style as Argument*. Carbondale: Southern Illinois University Press, 1987. 48-81.

Aristotle. *The Rhetoric and Poetics*. Trans. Ingram Bywater. New York: Modern Library, 1954.

Capote, Truman. *In Cold Blood*. New York: Random House, 1965.

Clarke, Gerald. *Truman Capote: A Biography*. New York: Simon and Schuster, 1988.

Conniff, Brian. "Psychological Accidents: 'In Cold Blood' and Ritual Sacrifice." *Midwest Quarterly* 35 (Autumn 1993): 77-94.

Foucault, Michel. *Discipline and Punish: The Birth of the Prison*. Trans. A. M. Sheridan Smith. New York: Harper, 1972.

———. "The Discourse on Language." *The Archaeology of Knowledge*. Trans. A. M. Sheridan Smith. New York: Harper, 1976. 215-37.

———. *The History of Sexuality, Volume 1: An Introduction*. Trans. Robert Hurley. New York: Pantheon, 1978.

Frus, Phyllis. *The Politics and Poetics of Journalistic Narrative*. Cambridge: Cambridge University Press, 1994. 120-56.

Inge, Thomas M., ed. *Truman Capote: Conversations*. Jackson and London: University of Mississippi Press, 1987.

Macdonald, Dwight. "Cosa Nostra." *Esquire* (April 1966): 44+.

Norden, Eric. "Playboy Interview: Truman Capote." *Playboy* (March 1968); rpt. Inge: 110-63.

Plimpton, George. "The Story Behind a Nonfiction Novel." *New York Times Book Review,* 16 January 1966, 2+; rpt in Inge: 47-68.

Tanner, Tony. "Death in Kansas." *Spectator* (18 March 1966): 331-32.

Tompkins, Philip K. "In Cold Fact." *Esquire* (June 1966): 125+.

Trilling, Diana. "Capote's Crime and Punishment." *Partisan Review* (Spring 1966): 252-59. Rpt. *Truman Capote's 'In Cold Blood': A Critical Handbook*. Ed. Irving Malin. Belmont, Calif.: Wadsworth, 1968. 107-13.

Wolfe, Tom, and E. W. Johnson, eds. *The New Journalism, with an Anthology Edited by Tom Wolfe and E. W. Johnson*. New York: Harper & Row, 1973.

David Guest (essay date 1997)

SOURCE: Guest, David. "Truman Capote's *In Cold Blood*: The Novel as Prison." In *Sentenced to Death: The American Novel and Capital Punishment*, pp. 104-30. Jackson, Miss.: University Press of Mississippi, 1997.

[*In the following essay, Guest demonstrates how* In Cold Blood *"presents a sort of narrative analogue" of the modern criminal justice system in the way in which it focuses on the criminal "biographies" of the killers rather than on the crime itself.*]

> I have certainly heard it said that, on occasion he chased with a scythe a child who happened to be in his yard; but people also said that it was only in jest. Certainly no one would have thought anything more of it had it not been for the murders he has committed.
>
> —Testimony of Pierre Riviere's Priest in Foucault's *I, Pierre Riviere*

> The power in the hierarchized surveillance of the disciplines is not possessed as a thing, or transferred as a property; it functions like a piece of machinery. . . . This enables the disciplinary power to be both absolutely indiscreet, since it is everywhere and always alert, since by its very principle it leaves no zone of shade . . . and absolutely "discreet," for it functions permanently and largely in silence.
>
> —Foucault, *Discipline*

In the forty years between *An American Tragedy* and *In Cold Blood,* many of the arguments advanced in Dreiser's novel and in Wright's *Native Son* eventually brought a temporary halt to capital punishment. *An American Tragedy* showed that discretionary sentencing allows class bias and wealth to shape a judge's or jury's perceptions of dangerousness, degree of responsibility and self-control, and punishability. Around the country, and especially in the Deep South, discretionary sentencing permitted all-white juries to sentence African-Americans and the very poor to death while sparing well-to-do whites convicted of the same offenses. This demonstrably inconsistent sentencing and racist bias prompted the U.S. Supreme Court to rule in 1972, in *Furman v. Georgia,* that death sentences were being awarded in a manner so "arbitrary" and "freakish" as to be unconstitutional. There ensued an unofficial moratorium on executions. Capote's novel was published almost exactly at the beginning of a decade in which no death sentences were carried out.

Capote's novel also marks a shift in the kind of capital offender under scrutiny. *McTeague* and *An American Tragedy* depict the sudden and startling eruption of murder in previously law-abiding working-class men. Bigger Thomas is a small-time hood who finds the role of murderer forced upon him. *In Cold Blood* and *The Executioner's Song* depict state-raised convicts, willful delinquents who seem to opt for a criminal, subversive lifestyle. In one sense, the difference reflects a change in the practice of execution. Norris and Dreiser wrote about relatively anonymous offenders at a time when executions were fairly frequent. Patrick Collins and Chester Gillette were unremarkable members of a large crowd, two representative cases chosen from hundreds. Capote and Mailer wrote at a time when executions occurred rarely, if at all. Today the executed few tend to be the most violent hard-core delinquents and convicts, criminals of the sort least suited to the defense mounted by Dreiser and Darrow.

The two murderers at the center of *In Cold Blood* are Perry Smith and Richard Hickock. In mid-November of 1959, Smith, thirty-one, and Hickock, twenty-eight, murdered four members of the Clutter family in the small town of Holcomb, Kansas. The family had operated one of the most prosperous and prominent farms in the area. Herb and Bonnie Clutter had four children, but only the two youngest, sixteen-year-old Nancy and fifteen-year-old Kenyon, still lived at home. Smith and Hickock had recently been released from prison, and Hickock had learned, from an inmate who worked on the Clutter farm years earlier, that the Clutter home contained a hidden safe filled with money.

The two men entered the house in the middle of the night through an unlocked door, roused the four sleepers at gunpoint, bound and gagged them, and left them in four different rooms. After discovering that the house held no safe, and no more than fifty dollars in cash, Smith and Hickock stabbed Herb Clutter, used a shotgun to kill all four, and fled. They remained at large for more than six weeks, even spending time in Mexico, before being captured in Las Vegas. In 1965, Smith and Hickock were hanged, two of seven men executed nation-wide that year.

The Clutter murders attracted a good deal of media attention in the region and even received brief notice in the *New York Times*. When Truman Capote read the notice, he found the subject for his next book. After years of research and writing, including lengthy interviews with the principal players, Capote published his "nonfiction novel" *In Cold Blood*. The book was a startling success. It sold millions of copies and became the basis for a highly acclaimed feature film. Like *McTeague* and *An American Tragedy, In Cold Blood* was inspired by a particular real-life murder case. Capote claimed, however, that his book was not only realistic but scrupulously true. In the book, Capote referred to places and to most people by their true names, and in interviews he claimed to have neither invented nor altered any incident. Capote promoted the book as the first of a new genre, the "nonfiction novel."

In Cold Blood is a retelling of the Clutter murders using the novelistic conventions of realism. It is told by a third-person, omniscient narrator, in a style that might be termed documentary. The novel appears to recreate all of the most important scenes in the story—from the murders to the breaks in the investigation to the hangings—and scenes are typically presented with few interruptions and lots of dialogue. During one courtroom scene depicting testimony by psychiatrist Dr. W. Mitchell Jones, however, there are two curious interruptions. The first occurs when Jones is asked if he "has an opinion as to whether or not Richard Eugene Hickock knew right from wrong at the time of the commission of the crime." After replying that "within the usual definitions Mr. Hickock did know right from wrong," he is asked if he can qualify or elaborate that answer (330). The prosecuting attorney objects, the objection is sustained, and Dr. Jones is dismissed from the stand.

Dr. Jones's qualification of his answer is disallowed because, under the M'Naghten Rule, anything beyond a "yes" is irrelevant. At this moment in the narrative, however, something odd occurs. Capote's narrator interrupts the account of the trial to tell us what Dr. Jones would have said, "had [he] been allowed to speak further." In the page or so that follows we read that Hickock is "above average in intelligence," although he "seems incapable of learning from experience." He "professes usual moral standards [but] seems obviously uninfluenced by them in his actions." Finally, Dr. Jones concludes that Hickock should be tested for "organic brain damage" that "might have substantially influenced his behavior during the past several years and at the time of his crime" (330-31).

Dr. Jones is recalled to the stand to testify about Perry Smith, and this time he states that he has no opinion "as to whether or not [Smith] knew right from wrong at the time of the offense involved in this action" (333). Once again any qualification of the answer is disallowed, and once again the narrator interrupts to insert what Jones would have said, "had [he] been permitted to discourse on the cause of his indecision" (333). This time readers hear not only from Dr. Jones but also from Dr. Joseph Satten, who sees Smith as fitting the profile described in an article Satten coauthored, "Murder Without Apparent Motive—A Study in Personality Disorganization."[1]

What prompts the narrative to fill in these "gaps" in the trial? Why not simply recreate the exchange of dialogue? It should be noted that, in interpolating this testimony about psychological motive, the novel may depart somewhat from its own format. Still, it does not depart radically from the format of the trial: Dr. Jones's testimony may be strictly limited, but the court does not restrict its attention to the question of guilt or innocence. Smith and Hickock confess to the crimes before the trial, and they never withdraw these confessions. Their attorneys do not even attempt to argue for acquittal but instead mount a defense based on character witnesses in an attempt to dissuade the jury from the death penalty. By including what Dr. Jones would have said, *In Cold Blood* merely elaborates on and professionalizes this testimony about character.

It would seem, at least in the case of capital crimes, that simple proof of guilt is not enough; execution also requires particular forms of motive. If the motive seems wildly irrational, a product of insanity, the killer will be institutionalized but not executed. If the motive, on the other hand, is found to be relatively rational, the killer is also likely to be spared. It becomes most difficult to evaluate motive in the case of monstrous, apparently motiveless crimes committed by someone not clearly insane. The apparent sanity of the accused, in conjunction with the ghastly, incomprehensible nature of his crimes, seems to demand maximal punishment, but the lack of understandable motive suggests mental illness and thus diminished responsibility. Often, the criminal psychologist must unravel the knot. When the only indication of insanity is the "motiveless" crime itself, criminal psychology can provide a motive by decoding the killer's deranged logic and translating the killer's actions into a sensible form. The identification and classification of the criminal behind the crime are generally described as the end results of disinterested observation: the offender, scrutinized by a trained eye, is discovered to be a certain type of individual. But it is hard to sustain this objective stance, as we have seen, particularly in cases involving capital crimes. How can anyone be objective while evaluating the biography of a known killer? Criminal biography, as I have argued, is less a means of determining who the offender is than of constructing the offender as juridical subject. What appears to be mere observation and diagnosis is actually the exercise of power, an act that establishes the complete authority of the criminal justice system over the offender.

In the case of the delinquent or the psychopath, the criminal act is depicted as a manifestation of a criminal personality that lurked beneath the surface all along. No detail about the offender's past, even in an ostensibly journalistic work like *In Cold Blood*, can be "merely" documentary, because even minutiae prefigure moments of apocalyptic violence. The details become clues to the subject's psychopathy, and we see that the offender is no ordinary human but instead a dangerous kind of automaton or monster. This shift from specific crime to individual criminal removes the criminal act from its particular time frame in a way that effectively disguises the exercise of power. The criminal act is extended into the past, and the criminal justice system thus appears to have no part in the production of crime and delinquency: the subject was a criminal personality long before being discovered as one. The criminal act is also extended into a potential future. Incarceration becomes necessary in the interest of public safety.

In Cold Blood reproduces the strategies of power associated with modern carceral discourse, "imprisoning" Smith and Hickock within deterministic narratives while simultaneously working to disavow any connection to power. The basis of this disavowal is the term "nonfiction novel," which, as I will show, posits a complete disjunction between the realms of art and power. The novel's omniscient point of view recreates the privileged, diagnostic vision of surveillance. Like the supervising gaze, the novel moves toward classification by specific criminal type. The novel also follows official carceral discourse in its strategies for renouncing power; like the clinical diagnostician, Capote's narrator is both omniscient and impotent.

In Cold Blood bears the misleading subtitle "A True Account of a Multiple Murder and Its Consequences." The novel may probe the consequences of murder, but it is far more concerned with exploring the "souls" of Dick Hickock and Perry Smith perhaps chiefly by means of the flatly narrated but somehow evocative biographical anecdote. Consider the following passage, which concludes a chapter and immediately follows a discussion in which Smith and Hickock, driving through Mexico, marvel at the prospect of actually getting away with the murders they have committed: "The car was moving. A hundred feet ahead, a dog trotted along the side of the road. Dick swerved toward it. It was an old half-dead mongrel, brittle-boned and mangy, and the impact, as it met the car, was little more than what a bird might make. But Dick was satisfied. 'Boy!' he said—and it was what he always said after running down a dog, which was something he did whenever the opportunity arose. 'Boy! We sure splattered him!'" (133). This scene has little to do with the murders or their consequences, and in fact the narrator makes no direct connection, but the scene is included nonetheless, apparently as an illustration of Hickock's character. *In Cold Blood* links the murder of the Clutter family to makeshift, anecdotal biographies of the killers. In doing so the novel suggests that the meaning of the murders cannot be understood without a thorough, clinical knowledge of the people who committed them. Such knowledge permits killers who are intrinsically murderous to be separated from killers who are not.

The distinction between offender and delinquent is, as we have seen, a hallmark of the modern criminal justice system. In this sense, *In Cold Blood* presents a sort of narrative analogue of that system. Like the novel, the prison is designed "for the formation of clinical knowledge about the convicts" (*Discipline*, 249). Descriptions of the criminal justice system offered by social historians and criminologists often echo the language Capote uses to describe *In Cold Blood*. Both are "given over to the chores of the classification of individuals and their placement and documentation" (Cousins and Hussein, 173). In both cases, "the juridical subject becomes the focal point of a classifying and objectifying mode of perception, which recruits the individual into a complex framework of justiciable characteristics and evidentiary fact" (Breuer, 236). Capote's narrative reproduces, in effect, the assessment of the criminal that takes place within the modern criminal justice system.

The concern with criminal personality type rather than criminal act is evident not only within *In Cold Blood* but also in Capote's discussions of crime in other contexts. For example, in a 1968 interview with Eric Norden, Capote explains that he is against capital punishment in the United States only because our system is so slow and arbitrary in applying it:

> If the system were clear-cut and a person was sentenced and executed within a six-month period on an even, regularized basis, then it might become a singularly effective deterrent; I think professional murderers would really think twice. By professional murderer, of course, I mean not the killer for hire or the Syndicate assassin, but the man who commits a crime with the intention of killing the man he is robbing, often in the belief that he will thus not be identified to the police by his victim. He considers murder a necessary *by-product* of his crime.
>
> [Capote, *Conversations*, 124-25]

In the present context, the most striking feature of this passage is Capote's easy assertion that there are several particular categories of killer—the assassin and the "professional" (and the unprofessional?)—which bear little resemblance to the statutory categories of homicide.

Later in the same interview, Capote elaborates on this idea as he describes his concept of the ideal way to treat killers. He advocates a system in which all homicides are treated as federal crimes, and all convicted killers are sent to a special federal prison.

> The key to this system would be that whenever a man is convicted of first-degree homicide, he would receive no precise sentence but an indeterminate sentence of from one day to life, and the actual length of the sentence would be determined not by a parole board but by an expert psychiatric staff attached to the Federal prison. The prison itself would be as much a hospital as a jail and, unlike most of our prisons, whose so-called psychiatric staffs are merely a joke, a true effort would be made to cure the inmates. Under this system, the board might determine that the man who killed his wife in a spasm of passion would be incarcerated for only three months, since his was not a repeatable crime, while a man like Perry Smith would probably have to stay there the rest of his life.
>
> [125-26]

Under the system that Capote describes, hospitals and prisons are conflated, as are psychiatrists and prison guards, and murderers come in a variety of recognizable types.

Capote's lengthy examinations of Smith and Hickock, like his proposed psychiatric review for all first-degree murderers, result in their classification as particular criminal types. As is evident in the following excerpt from a 1966 interview with George Plimpton, Capote places himself in the position of examining psychiatrist, able to explain past crimes and predict future behavior:

> [Plimpton]: What do you think would have happened if Perry had faltered and not begun the killings? Do you think Dick would have done it?
>
> [Capote]: No. There is such a thing as the ability to kill. Perry's particular psychosis had produced this ability. Dick was mostly ambitious—he could *plan* murder but not commit it.
>
> [Capote, *Conversations*, 59]

Capote's confidence in his own typing of Smith and Hickock prompts him to make this assertion even though it contradicts the findings of the official investigation. Smith's initial confession depicts Hickock as participating in the murder of Mr. Clutter and as killing the mother and daughter. According to Phillip Tompkins, who interviewed many of the participants in the case after the publication of *In Cold Blood,* most of the investigators, including county attorney Duane West and KBI agent Alvin Dewey, continued to believe that the confession was accurate.

Capote's proposed prison/hospital posits a world with various types of killer, but *In Cold Blood* focuses on one extreme end of the spectrum. The novel depicts killers so dangerous that they must never be released. The psychological profile that Capote constructs bears a striking resemblance to homicidal monomania, although the term is never used. The novel relies instead on the term "psychopath." Like the homicidal monomaniac, the murderous psychopath may appear normal and sane to the untrained eye. In both cases the derangement may go undetected until it explodes into murderous violence. A diagnosis of psychopathy requires a trained eye. Capote speaks with the confidence of a clinician when he states, in an interview, that "Perry never meant to kill the Clutters at all. He had a brain explosion" (Capote, *Conversations,* 60). Dr. Satten's report on Perry Smith, included in the novel, is likewise rooted in the paradigm of the monomaniac or psychopath:

> Such individuals can be considered to be murder-prone in the sense of either carrying a surcharge of aggressive energy or having an unstable ego defense system that periodically allows the naked and archaic expression of such energy. The murderous potential can become activated . . . when the victim-to-be is unconsciously perceived as a key figure in some past traumatic configuration. The behavior, or even the mere presence, of this figure adds a stress to the unstable balance of forces that results in a sudden extreme discharge of violence, similar to the explosion that takes place when a percussion cap ignites a charge of dynamite.
>
> [337-38]

Capote's narrator endorses Satten's diagnosis by claiming that when Smith attacked Mr. Clutter, "he was under a mental eclipse, deep inside a schizophrenic darkness" (338).

Further evidence that Capote's novel is shaped by the myth of the psychopath or monomaniac is provided by Phillip Tompkins in his article "In Cold Fact." Tompkins claims to have uncovered a number of factual errors in the book, the most serious of these being the conclusion that Perry suffered from a "brain explosion" at the time of the murders. The transcribed confessions mention nothing resembling a trancelike state or episode of altered consciousness. They seem even to rule out the possibility of a such a state. According to Smith's confession, he and Hickock discuss who will do the killing, and then Smith approaches Mr. Clutter on the pretext of tightening the ropes that bind him. Once behind Clutter, Smith produces a knife that he has been concealing and cuts Clutter's throat. Smith then hands the knife to Hickock, who repeats the act. When Clutter continues to struggle, Smith and Hickock decide to put him out of his misery by shooting him. There is evidence of planning, discussion, and a disturbingly calm demeanor, but Smith never claims that he was out of control or that he suffered from any form of seizure during the murders.

The narrative often turns directly to psychopathy in matters of diagnosis. Drawing on psychiatric testimony, particularly Satten's article about apparently unmotivated murder, Capote produces the evidence required to fit the clinical profile of the psychopath. The psychopath paradigm in the novel, however, can also be seen at work in the very structure of the narrative. The novel's diagnosis of psychopathy is confirmed by a heightened narrative vision that sees all details as potentially meaningful, all incidents as potentially anecdotal. When we read that, in preparation for their return from Mexico to the United States, Smith and Hickock ship back a carton of clothes including "two pairs of boots, one pair with soles that left a Cat's Paw print, the other pair with diamond-pattern soles" (146), we know that these details are more than documentary. That the boots are important has already been revealed by the lens of the police photographer's camera:

> As a matter of fact, one of the photographs, a close up of Mr. Clutter and the mattress box upon which he lay, had already provided a valuable surprise: footprints, the dusty trackings of shoes with diamond-patterned soles. The prints, not noticeable to the naked eye, registered on film; indeed, the delineating glare of the flashbulb had revealed their presence with superb exactness. These prints, together with another footmark found on the same cardboard cover—the bold and bloody impression of a Cat's Paw half sole—were the only "serious clues" the investigators could claim.
>
> [100]

Like the police photographer's camera, and like the trained gaze of the expert, Capote's narrator sees more than the "naked eye."

The introduction of the all-seeing narrator recreates the heightened panoptic vision used to scrutinize the prison inmate. The penitentiary posits a kind of supervision, a privileged gaze, that allows for the classification and control of each inmate. *In Cold Blood* recreates this privileged gaze by adopting a particular form of the third-person, omniscient point of view. Smith and Hickock are placed in a sort of panopticon, while the all-seeing narrator sits, himself unseen, in the observation tower.

Nowhere is the panoptic quality of the narration more evident than in the brief section following the first interviews in which Smith and Hickock are accused of the murders. Later that evening the two sit nervously in separate cells, unable to see each other or communicate. Although we know that Capote was nowhere near this scene, he has reconstructed it in such a way that the narrator is written into the observation tower, able to see not only the men but also their thoughts and feelings. Smith worries that the witness mentioned by his interrogators is an eyewitness. Hickock knows that it is Floyd Wells, the cellmate who told Hickock that the Clutter home contained a safe full of money.

In this brief chapter the narrator seems to disappear, allowing the reader direct access to the thoughts of the two prisoners. When Hickock worries about things he should have done differently, we seem to hear him speak: "Hell, if all those cowboys had to go on was some story Floyd Wells had told, then there wasn't a lot to worry about. Come right down to it, Floyd wasn't half as dangerous as Perry. Perry, if he lost his nerve and let fly, could put them both in The Corner [Kansas's Death Row]. And suddenly he saw the truth; It was *Perry* he should have silenced. On a mountain road in Mexico. Or while walking across the Mojave. Why had it never occurred to him until now? For now, now was much too late" (258). The disappearance of the narrator assures the reader that the narrative point of view is both unlimited and objective. In this particular example the narrator's disappearance demonstrates at the same time that homicide has become a way of life for Smith and Hickock.

The no-holds-barred scrutiny to which Smith and Hickock are subjected extends to all facets of their lives. A close examination of Hickock's face, for example, reveals hints about his character:

> But neither Dick's physique nor the inky gallery adorning it made as remarkable an impression as his face, which seemed composed of mismatching parts. It was as though his head had been halved like an apple, then put together a fraction off-center. Something of the kind had happened; the imperfectly aligned features were the outcome of a car collision in 1950—an accident that left his long-jawed and narrow face tilted, the left side rather lower than the right, with the results that the lips were slightly aslant, the nose askew, and his eyes not only situated at uneven levels but of uneven size, the left eye being truly serpentine, with a venomous sickly-blue squint that although it was involuntarily acquired, seemed nevertheless to warn of bitter sediment at the bottom of his nature.
>
> [43]

Through just this sort of optic phrenology, *In Cold Blood* reproduces the methods by which the criminal justice system examines and classifies its subjects. In both cases an offender is rewritten as a delinquent by means of an anecdotal biography. In both cases, too, the transformation is enabled by the construction of a heightened form of vision, one that sees things "not noticeable to the naked eye."

In order to unmask the strategies that underlie this illusion of supervision, it is necessary first to recall that psychopathy—like other variations on the homicidal monomania theme—is inseparable from narrative. Psychopaths are always defined in terms of biographical narrative. The life histories are, by definition, revisionist histories. The "trained eye" that is able to see hints of the criminal in the precriminal always reaches the scene after the fact. We view the criminal's life through his crime and thus come, almost inescapably, to see certain incidents as prophetic. In the diagnostic biography of the capital offender, the power of the murder scene is so great that it can lend a prophetic resonance to a wide variety of past events. Childhood temper tantrums foreshadow murderous rage; the absence of childhood temper tantrums reveals a psychopathic lack of affect. When the incident happened, it lacked significance. Later, when it was seen "properly," in the light of eventual violence, it became anecdote.

In Cold Blood promotes such resonance through suggestive epigrams, titles, and subtitles and by juxtaposing scenes of people we know are about to be killed with scenes of people we know are their killers. The style of the narrative may be flat and objective, but no scene can be "merely" documentary when it is preceded by a subtitle like "The Last to See Them Alive." By the time readers catch their first glimpse of Perry Smith, they may find that they too are acquiring a trained eye: "Like Mr. Clutter, the young man breakfasting in a cafe called the 'Little Jewel' never drank coffee. He preferred root beer. Three aspirin, cold root beer, and a chain of Pall Mall cigarettes—that was his notion of a proper 'chow down.' Sipping and smoking, he studied a map spread on the counter before him—a Phillips 66 map of Mexico—but it was difficult to concentrate, for he was expecting a friend, and the friend was late" (24). This scene reverberates with prophetic meaning because of the subtitle and other textual indications that tranquillity is about to erupt into violence. The immediately preceding sentence, for example, depicts Herb Clutter with awful prescience: "Touching the brim of his cap, he headed for home and the day's work, unaware that it would be his last" (24). Mr. Clutter may be unaware, but the all-seeing narrator is not. The same privileged gaze that scrutinizes Smith and Hickock in their cells can look into the past, in effect bringing history under surveillance.

The narrative also relies on another strategy for reproducing the sort of supervision posited by the criminal justice system and by diagnostic biography: the inclusion of testimony from witnesses and experts. Just as a trial transcript assembles testimony from a wide range of witnesses and experts, the novel incorporates various documents relating to the case. Capote quotes at length from the statements of various criminologists, criminal psychiatrists, and law enforcement officials. He also reproduces autobiographical confessions by Smith and Hickock as well as biographical testimony about the two from their surviving parents. The narrative establishes and validates through expert testimony and documentation a profile of a specific criminal type and then proceeds to wed the facts of the Clutter "case" to that profile.

Among the external documents included are brief autobiographies written by each of the defendants. Dr. Jones requests these written statements and uses them, along with interviews lasting about two hours, as the basis for the psychological evaluations that are excluded from the trial but included in the novel. Near the beginning of Smith's statement, he recalls a fight with his brother:

> The next thing I can recall is living in Fort Bragg, Calif. My brother had been presented a B.B. gun. He had shot a hummingbird, and after he had shot it he was sorry. I asked him to let me shoot the B.B. gun. He pushed me away, telling me I was too small. It made me so mad I started to cry. After I finished crying, my anger mounted again, and during the evening when the B.B. gun was behind the chair my brother was sitting in, I grabbed it & held it to my brother's ear & hollered BANG! My father (or mother) beat me and made me apologize.
>
> [308]

It is difficult not to read this incident as prefiguring the later murders. The dispute with his brother recalls Smith's later altercation with brother-figure Hickock, which ended when Smith took a shotgun from Hickock and pointed it at four (or was it two?) other heads. Our sense of the line between the episodes is heightened by the fact that Smith chose to include the otherwise unremarkable memory from childhood early in his statement. It is the second story recounted in a brief autobiography that begins with the story of Smith's birth.

There are, however, some problems with reading the incident as particularly prophetic. For example, we cannot be sure what went on between Smith and Hickock in the Clutter house or even who did the killing. Even more of a problem is that the presence of ellipses in the statement indicates that it has been edited: what has been omitted? Furthermore, we have no way of knowing what sort of primacy Smith assigned to the incident. How many stories were omitted before one could be found with such sinister resonance? Who made the decision? Also, is it possible that Smith's experience with prison psychiatrists "trained" him to produce evocative anecdotes like these?

A statement that, after all, Capote did not even write thus emerges as an instrument of manipulation carefully honed for effect. Like the "trained eye" of the diagnostician, Capote's narrator is able to look into the past and identify precriminal behavior. In the sense that the narrator both exercises and renounces power by including this fragment, the BB gun story is typical of the way that both the novel and the criminal justice system make useful anecdotes from "useless" incidents.

A shadowy figure haunts the final pages of *In Cold Blood*: a journalist who is mentioned twice as he interviews Dick Hickock on Death Row. It is revealed that this journalist, who corresponds with Hickock and visits him regularly, is "equally well acquainted with [Perry] Smith" (371, 375). The journalist is not mentioned again, and we are left to wonder about his identity and role in the story. This mysterious figure is probably Capote, but why would he choose to disguise himself in this manner?

There are no direct references to Capote in the narrative. Capote claimed that this anonymity was a central element of his experiment in the "nonfiction novel": "The real demarcation between my book and anything that has gone before is that it contains a technical innovation that gives it both the reality and the atmosphere of a novel; and that device is that I never once appear in the book. Never" (Capote, *Conversations,* 120). Although Capote claims that the erasure of the "I" from the text is largely a "technical innovation" to avoid the intrusiveness of the first person, I suggest that this decision should be seen as part of a larger renunciation of power that is—paradoxically—best understood as a strategy for masking the exercise of power.

The simultaneous exercise and denial of power characterize diagnostic biography as it functions within the criminal justice system. The rewriting of an offender as a delinquent or psychopath, for example, is an act of power in which a criminal act is determined to be evidence of a criminal personality type in one offender but not another. This distinction may justify the maximum punishment in the former case and the minimum in the latter, but it is disguised as discovery or diagnosis. Once an offender is discovered to be a delinquent or a psychopath, the criminal justice system must respond, but even then disciplinary power appears to be exercised reluctantly and after the fact. Because delinquency is dangerous, the criminal justice system must step in and protect the public interest by imprisoning, and possibly executing, anyone discovered to be a delinquent. Also, because the models for delinquency and psychopathy identify visible symptoms that begin to appear during childhood (at least to properly trained eyes), diagnostic biography establishes that the criminal justice system plays no role in the production of criminality.

If we are to trace the workings of power in carceral narratives, then, we must come to terms with power's dissembling strategies. Disciplinary power manifests itself in discourse not as admonition or command but as diagnosis. For every exercise of power there is an accompanying disavowal. *In Cold Blood* reproduces strategies for the simultaneous exercise and denial of power that can also be seen at work in much carceral discourse. The novel characterizes itself as merely observing and recording what is, after all, a true story and thus works to deny that it has transformed or distorted this story in any way. This renunciation of power appears on several different levels of the narrative.

One way for a writer to renounce power is to lay a claim to realism. Capote goes further. His narrative, he declares, is not only realistic but also completely and utterly true, a nonfiction novel. Given the nature of the project, any departure from fact is unacceptable. Capote once stated that "one doesn't spend almost six years on a book, the point of which is factual accuracy, and then give way to minor distortions" (Capote, *Conversations,* 62). He goes so far as to describe himself as a "literary photographer" and also states that he spent two hours a day, for eighteen months, training himself to be a human tape-recorder (Capote, *Conversations,* 48, 54).

The narrative supports the illusion of complete objectivity by recording numerous details that later prove to have no connection to the crime. Like the camera and the tape-recorder, the narrative thus seems to record without interpreting or editing. We are told, for example, that in the days before the murders, Nancy Clutter smells cigarette smoke in the house, an oddity in a home where smoking was forbidden. On the last day of his life, Mr. Clutter encounters a group of strangers armed with shotguns and gives them permission to hunt on his land. Hours before his death, Mr. Clutter signed a new life insurance policy. These incidents will prove unrelated to the murders. Their inclusion establishes that the narrator sees with a undiscriminating eye and leads us to believe that we are not being manipulated.

The novel's reliance on external documentation and expert testimony, as previously noted, reinforces the illusion of documentary realism. Long passages are quoted verbatim from confessions, letters, psychiatric evaluations, and transcriptions of court proceedings, thus providing further evidence that the novel is reporting rather than interpreting or creating. Capote also labors to support these claims of documentary realism in interviews, as when he tells George Plimpton that his "files would almost fill a whole small room, right up to the ceiling. All my research. Hundreds of letters. Newspaper clippings. Court Records" (Capote, *Conversations,* 66).

Perhaps the primary strategy for renouncing power can be discovered through an exploration of Capote's theory of the nonfiction novel, which posits an absolute separation of art and power. Capote even denies that the nonfiction novel has anything to do with crime: "In a way, I guess it was unfortunate that I selected a crime for my first big experiment in the genre [nonfiction novel], because that made it easier for them to . . . think of it as a true crime story. But a nonfiction novel can be about *anything*—from crime to butterfly collecting" (Capote, *Conversations,* 122). Capote also claims that his work on the Clutter case grew not out of an interest in crime but out of a desire to wed the techniques of journalism to those of fiction: "the motivating factor in my choice of material—that is, choosing to write a true account of an actual murder case—was altogether literary" (Capote, *Conversations,* 47). Even in this choice of subject matter Capote seems at pains to deny any hint of exercising power, claiming that he "*didn't* select this Kansas farmer and his family; in a very real sense, they selected me" (Capote, *Conversations,* 122).

By emphasizing that his motives were "altogether literary," Capote posits a disjunction between style and subject matter, between the workings of the criminal justice system and the workings of the artist. The nonfiction novelist, like the diagnostician, is a slave to fact and makes decisions only concerning the manner of presentation. According to Capote, too, the nonfiction novelist must remain completely removed from political or ideological motivations. Capote claims to have told Perry Smith that the book "didn't have anything to do with changing the reader's opinion about anything, nor did I have any moral reasons worthy of calling them such—it was just that I had a strictly aesthetic theory about creating a book which could result in a work of art" (Nichols, 39).

All of these strategies for renouncing power—asserting factual accuracy, providing supporting documents, claiming aesthetic disinterest and egoless objectivity—are evident in carceral discourse in general and especially in diagnostic biography. They work to mask the physical mechanism of power, which, both in Capote's novel and the criminal justice system, is largely embodied in the prison and in diagnostic biography. Diagnostic biography renders the prison invisible. For example, by locating evidence of delinquency in the subject's childhood, the narrative indicates that the criminal justice system plays no role in the production of delinquency. When Capote makes the curious decision virtually to ignore the years his subjects have spent behind bars, to ignore the institution in which the murder plan was hatched, in which all of Capote's interviews with the killers took place, and which played such a profound role in the lives of his subjects, he does the same thing.

The decision to erase the author, to adopt a third-person, omniscient point of view, allows us to read the novel without thinking about the fact that Capote never saw his subjects outside police custody and that he never spoke to them outside prison. The physical fact of their incarceration seems to have been significant only as an inconvenience to Capote's project. Incarceration was fundamental to the project, however, and offered Capote certain advantages with respect to his subjects. "I could always tell when Dick or Perry wasn't telling the truth. During the first few months or so of interviewing them, they weren't allowed to speak to each other. They were in separate cells. So I would keep crossing their stories, and what correlated, what checked out identically, was the truth" (Capote, *Conversations*, 57-58).

In Cold Blood reveals little trace of the "I" of this statement or of the process by which Smith and Hickock's stories were collected and cross-checked. All that survives in the final text is the sense of absolute certitude, of complete knowledge of a subject. Erasing the "I" from the text may appear to diminish the influence of the author, but instead it allows the substitution of an objective, infallible, panoptic eye for the subjective, fallible, normally-sighted "I" of the writer. The prison disappears, and a sort of leveling effect is achieved as each incident recounted in the narrative becomes equally true. The different layers of distortion, fabrication, coercion, folklore, and twenty-twenty hindsight are hidden beneath the surface. Every episode of the narrative takes on a uniform, visual verisimilitude.

This dark area of the narrative, which allows the mechanisms of power to remain hidden, apparently distinguishes mainstream nonfiction from Capote's "nonfiction novel." Capote's paradigm is meant for a hybrid form that uses novelistic techniques in writing nonfiction narrative. The awkward term "nonfiction novel" highlights a contradiction: if the narrative is factually accurate, and thus nonfiction, why is the word "novel" necessary? The inadequacy of the term "nonfiction" as a description suggests that the story does something other than recount fact. Capote addresses this issue by introducing an intriguing metaphor:

> But what I wanted to do was bring to journalism the technique of fiction, which moves both horizontally and vertically at the same time: horizontally on the narrative side and vertically by entering inside its characters. . . . Now, in my effort to give journalism this vertical interior movement—and that was the whole purpose of my experiment—I had to remove the narrator entirely. I had to make the book flow uninterruptedly from beginning to end, just like a novel, and thus the narrator never enters the picture and there is no interpretation of people and events. . . . except for the selection of detail, I am totally absent from the development of the book, and the people are re-created as they are in life.
>
> [120]

The introduction of this vertical, novelistic axis, which moves "inside" characters and events while avoiding interpretation, creates some obvious problems; to represent the "inside" of character or plot *is* to interpret. Capote's method masks the agency of power while retaining the effects of that power. An illusion of objectivity is maintained because the author avoids stating his interpretation outright, but the narrative is structured in such a way that the reader's interpretation is managed, shaped, and controlled.

The problems inherent in an uncritical acceptance of the narrative's objectivity become apparent in passages like the following, from Kenneth T. Reed:

> It is significant that Capote at no time renders a judgment about the criminals. His determined disinterest is maintained for at least two reasons: it is important for the reader to draw his own conclusions about the philosophical-sociological-psychological circumstances of the mass murder, and Capote was determined not to interfere with the reader's judgmental process. . . . Capote is primarily concerned with motivations and circumstances that form an engrossing but inscrutable web of factors that rendered Smith and Hickock moral invalids, psychopathic criminals. It becomes evident that questions of condemnation and sympathy toward the criminals have no real bearing from an objective standpoint.
>
> [107]

Reed is confident that his assessment of Smith and Hickock as "psychopathic criminals" and "moral invalids" is his own, that it does not originate in the novel. The novel presents only raw fact, he seems to be saying, and a discerning reader like Reed knows a psychopath when he sees one.

By adopting these dissembling strategies, then, the novel, like much penal discourse, masks the exercise of power. But what does this power accomplish, and what forms does it take? In a broad sense, disciplinary power can be said to work toward exclusion and normalization. A particular segment of the population is excluded from society—through incarceration or execution—and carceral discourse produces the diagnostic biographies that justify this exclusion. These narratives explain the treatment of criminals for the benefit of the remaining, law-abiding segment of the population, but also reinforce a vision of society in which the idealized domestic hearth serves as norm. By producing, classifying, and managing various forms of criminality, the criminal justice system defines the normal and the abnormal while creating an atmosphere of danger that demands a careful distinction between the two.

Foucault argues that two of the main "instruments" of disciplinary power are hierarchical observation and normalizing judgment (*Discipline*, 170). These categories provide a useful way of approaching the subject of power in **In Cold Blood**. The narrator's vision, like the privileged gaze of surveillance, sees its subjects while remaining unseen. In a sense, the narrator subsumes the investigating detective, the examining psychiatrist, the sentencing judge, and the guard in the observation tower. From this lofty position, the narrator may even see more than these intermediary agents could, as when Agent Dewey doggedly pursues leads that we know are false.

The hierarchical nature of the relationship between narrator and subject in the novel is further illustrated by the narrator's role as confessor to Smith and Hickock. Capote takes on this position of authority, extracting confessions from Smith and Hickock and embedding those confessions in a narrative that judges, qualifies, and evaluates them. Like the police interrogators when they take official confessions, Capote verifies the accuracy of confessions by cross-checking them against one another and against other external sources. He judges Smith's official confession, in which Smith claims that Hickock killed the two women, to be false, even though it was accepted by the court and many of the chief investigators on the case. Capote rejects this confession in favor of one that credits Smith with all four murders. In doing so once again he affirms the narrator's position atop the hierarchy of observation.

Capote may also have departed from the facts in his depiction of Smith as repentant and apologetic. Capote reports that Smith cried in his cell after the trial, that he held the hand of Mrs. Meier (the wife of the undersheriff) and sobbed, "I'm embraced by shame" (Tompkins, 345). Capote also writes that Smith apologized for his crimes just before mounting the scaffold. Tompkins interviewed Mrs. Meier and several people who witnessed the executions. He claims that all disputed Capote's version. Mrs. Meier denied that she ever heard Smith cry or claim to be ashamed and, vehemently, that she ever held his hand. Tompkins also spoke with witnesses at the execution who were confident that Smith did not apologize.

The portrait of a repentant Smith may not fit the facts, but it does seem curiously consistent with the model for confession in a disciplinary hierarchy. In such a system, confession has a twofold purpose: it serves both to reveal the truth and to transform the confessor. The confession is a "ritual in which the expression alone, independently of its external consequences, produces intrinsic modification in the person who articulates it: it exonerates, redeems, and purifies" (Foucault, *History,* 62). Such a model may help explain why Capote sees remorse in Smith when others do not. Capote's role as confessor would be incomplete without Smith's repentance.

In Cold Blood exercises normalizing judgment largely in its manipulation of images of the domestic hearth. The idealized domesticity of the Clutter family contrasts especially starkly in the novel with the nomadic criminality of Smith and Hickock. Capote seems at pains to present Herb Clutter as the ideal head of a perfect family. He is "the master of River Valley Farm" (15). Although he is short and wears glasses, he is a "man's man" (16). Not the town's richest citizen, he is nonetheless its most prominent. He married "the person he had wished to marry" (16), and his daughter is the "town darling" (17). He is kind but firm with his children: "his laws were laws" (18). Through good sense and years of hard work, Clutter has come to embody the American dream of the self-made man running a successful family farm. Against this portrait of productivity and ingenuity the novel places Perry Smith, an aimless ex-convict without money or prospects, a drifter capable of killing without remorse and without a second thought.

In an interview with Eric Norden, Capote claims that Clutter and Smith embody the extremes of American life:

> The Clutter family and Smith and Hickock do represent the opposite poles in American society; if you ask me who best represents the *real* America, I have to say a very modified and much more soiled and complicated version of the Clutter family. But Perry Smith . . . does represent a very real side of American life; he is typical of the conscienceless yet perversely sensitive violence that runs through such phenomena as the motorcycle gangs and the drifting herds of brutalized children wandering across the country.
>
> [Capote, *Conversations,* 133-34]

One of the interesting things about this passage is that it posits at least a potential disjunction between criminality and domesticity; were it not for the predatory nature of these nomadic psychopaths, the idealized domestic hearth would remain intact and would never be soiled by the criminal.

The disjunction between criminality and domesticity proves, however, to be quite problematic. In the novel, the two are inseparable opposing poles of American society. The initial appearance of disjunction dissolves under scrutiny to reveal interdependence and entanglement. As *In Cold Blood* locates the source of criminality outside the criminal justice system, it tends to locate it within the family. More specifically, criminality reflects a family's failure to measure up to the domestic ideal. The murders are the manifestation of the abuse Smith suffered at the hands of a drunken mother and the final resolution of his love-hate relationship with his shiftless father. When the narrative includes its edited version of Smith's autobiography, the only story that precedes the BB gun anecdote is one in which a young Smith watches in horror as his father beats his mother because she was drinking and "entertaining" a group of sailors (308). This is Smith's "primal" scene, and it leads directly to the first sign of his murderous nature.

Criminality and the family are also linked in the future. The novel envisions the idealized domestic hearth as a site ripe for violence. Capote in his description of the relationship between Clutter and Smith insists that the murders were fated: "All this had to happen; there was a quality of inevitability about it. Given what Perry was, and what the Clutters represented, the only possible outcome of their convergence was death" (Capote, *Conversations,* 134).

It is not surprising that the novel depicts the destruction of the Clutter family as foreordained; what is surprising is that domesticity linked with violence can be seen whenever an idealized family setting is depicted. The novel describes the home of Smith's only surviving sister, for example, in terms that emphasize cheerful, all-American domesticity. The Johnson family (Capote protects the family with this appropriate pseudonym) lives in "a middle-class, middle-income real estate development" near San Francisco, in a "conventional suburban ranch house, pleasant and commonplace." Mrs. Johnson is "in love with" the house and especially its backyard: "And she was proud of the small back garden; her husband—by profession an insurance salesman, by inclination a carpenter—had built around it a white picket fence, and inside it a house for the family dog, and a sandbox and swings for the children. At the moment, all four—dog, two little boys, and a girl—were playing there under a mild sky" (205-6). Despite this idyllic setting, Mrs. Johnson is haunted by fears of violence, both at the hands of her brother Perry and in more impersonal forms. She is tormented by thoughts that she will "go mad, or contract an incurable illness, or in a fire lose all she valued—home, husband, children." At the end of the brief chapter describing Mrs. Johnson, she is troubled by her fears, hiding behind doors locked against "the dead as well as the living" (213-14).

The novel's tendency to locate the source of violent criminality in failed family units may also explain why Capote rejects the theory that Smith and Hickock were both murderers. Smith's family life was sordid enough to produce a psychopathic killer, but Hickock's childhood offers no such colorful images of squalor or abuse. Capote may have rejected the idea that Hickock could also be a murderer on the ground that his parents seemed relatively normal.

Such links between criminal violence and domestic bliss are perhaps best understood in terms of what Foucault dismisses as the "repressive hypothesis" of power. Repressive theories envision disciplinary power and criminality as adversaries, with power struggling to eliminate the criminals, namely those who resist power. Crime may persist, even flourish, but only because of failures in the execution of the penal plan, not because of flaws in the plan itself. As an alternative to repressive theories of power, Foucault argues that we see power instead as producing and using delinquency. In terms of handling offenders, delinquency allows for exclusion, for the separation of a certain segment of the population. The criminal justice system "is not intended to eliminate offences, but rather to distinguish them, to distribute them, to use them . . . to assimilate the transgression of the laws in a general tactics of subjection" (*Discipline,* 272).

The presence of delinquency can also be used, however, to exert a normalizing influence on the remaining segment of society. As has been illustrated, biographical portraits of delinquents tend to link horrific crimes to a wide array of minor illegalities and legal nonconformity. This linkage tends to make all nonconformity seem dangerous. By locating the source of criminality in domestic failures, these biographies increase the pressure on parents to "discipline" their children. Carceral narratives promote an image of normalcy under siege, depicting idealized domestic settings as the favored targets of murderous young psychopaths. Delinquents come to represent an eminent public danger that necessitates, even requires, a police presence.

Disciplinary power works, then, largely by creating a sense of danger. ***In Cold Blood*** participates in and reproduces that manufacturing of danger. Perry Smith must be presented not as a small-time hood who, one night, under extraordinary circumstances, participates in a brutal mass murder but instead as a compulsive killer, a man particularly inflamed by the sight of a happy family and eager to murder again. Capote often described Smith using such terms:

> Perry Smith was a serious psychopath and to some degree paranoid, with the kind of mind that is able to kill without passion and without remorse, just as you or I would swat a fly. I've known several Perry types, and human life means nothing to them; it's as if they have a talent for destruction, the kind of death-dealing ability hired killers have. . . . They can cut a man's throat from ear to ear and walk away and go to a movie and never think about what they've just done, because they place no value whatever on human life.
>
> [Capote, *Conversations,* 128-29]

This assessment of Smith is inconsistent not only with other accounts of the case but also with the novel itself. More than once we are told that Smith worries about his role in the murders, thinking that "there's got to be something wrong with somebody who'd do a thing like that." Smith worries this point so incessantly that Hickock, who would rather forget the incident, is irritated almost to the point of violence: "Christ Jesus, what damn good did it do, always dragging the goddamn thing up" (128-29).

In addition to this evidence of Smith's anguish and self-doubt, the novel also establishes that Smith and Hickock were never involved in any other killings. Perry may have been able to cut a man's throat as easily and thoughtlessly as he would swat a fly, but he never did so. Even so, Capote is able to assert that a "pattern of homicide had become so ingrained in them that it was inevitable they would have killed again had they remained free" (Capote, *Conversations*, 130). To support this statement, Capote can only cite plans of murder that never materialize, and Smith's admittedly fabricated story about killing a man years before the Clutter murders. Capote's assertions may not represent the facts of the case, but they do foster an aura of danger around Smith and Hickock, an aura that works both to exclude the pair from the human race and to justify the "work" of penal power.

Capote's depictions of cold-blooded killers often owe more to popular images of the psychopath than to the details of a particular case, perhaps because Capote wanted to stress the danger they represented. In describing one of the other inmates housed with Smith and Hickock on Death Row, for example, Capote seems to draw on the words of Flannery O'Connor's Misfit, from the story "A Good Man Is Hard to Find." James Douglas Latham is quoted as saying, "It's a rotten world. . . . There's no answer to it but meanness. That's all anybody understands—meanness. Burn down the man's barn—he'll understand that. Poison his dog. Kill him" (362). O'Connor's Misfit makes another appearance as Hickock tells his story to the mysterious journalist:

> When that boy read a book it stayed read. Course he didn't know a dumb-darn thing about life. Me, I'm an ignoramus except when it comes to what I know about life. I've walked along a lot of mean streets. I've seen a white man flogged. I've watched babies born. I've seen a girl, and her no more than fourteen, take on three guys at the same time and give them all their money's worth. Fell off a ship once five miles out to sea. Swam five miles with my life passing before me every stroke. Once I shook hands with President Truman in the lobby of the Hotel Muehlebach. Harry S. Truman.
>
> [373]

Capote's choice of the Misfit as model psychopath is especially noteworthy, because O'Connor's story also depicts a man, recently out of prison, who murders an entire family in cold blood.[2]

By forging these links between criminality and domesticity, and by creating the image of a family home that is besieged by inhuman monsters, the novel can be said to do for the reader what the Clutter murders do for the town of Holcomb. The once innocent, peaceful town is transformed. People begin locking their doors and eyeing one another suspiciously. Even after Smith and Hickock are arrested and have made their confessions, many residents of the town remain on guard: "a sizable faction refused to accept the fact that two unknown men, two thieving strangers, were solely responsible" (262). For these citizens, Smith and Hickock must have been hired killers working for someone who knew the Clutters, probably someone from Holcomb. The atmosphere of eminent danger creates the need for increased police surveillance and heightened security measures. Even Detective Alvin Dewey and his wife put aside their long-held dream of owning a farmhouse outside of town, too fearful to live in such isolation (382).

In Cold Blood, like many narratives of delinquency and incarceration, is generally considered sympathetic to its subjects. Capote freely admitted that he came to think of Smith and Hickock as his close friends, and many critics have noted that Capote especially identified with Smith. It has also been pointed out that the title seems to describe the executions that end the novel more aptly than the murders that begin it. Capote's inclusion of psychological profiles of the subjects that the court chose to exclude adds to our sense that the novel is deliberately critical of the judicial system and particularly of the system's stance on questions of mental illness.

These images of sympathy and criticism, however, fail under careful scrutiny. Although Capote may regard Smith and Hickock as friends, he considers them too dangerous ever to be released from prison. His novel may include the excluded psychological testimony, but this testimony makes the pair seem more dangerous by portraying them as murderous time bombs virtually guaranteed to explode and kill again. Capote's sympathy resembles the pastoral "care" that characterizes disciplinary power. His criticism of the judicial system, if acted upon, would only extend and strengthen that system. Because carceral power manages and even produces the forces that would resist it, *In Cold Blood* can only reproduce the incarceration of its subjects.

Notes

1. Published in the *American Journal of Psychiatry* 117 (July 1960): 48-53.

2. For the apparent sources of the two quoted passages, see *Three by Flannery O'Connor* (140, 142).

Bibliography

Breuer, Stephan. "Foucault and Beyond: Towards a Theory of the Disciplinary Society." *International Social Science Journal* 120 (May 1989): 235-47.

Capote, Truman. *Conversations with Truman Capote.* Edited by M. Thomas Inge. Jackson: University Press of Mississippi, 1987.

———. *In Cold Blood: A True Account of a Multiple Murder and Its Consequences.* New York: Random House, 1966.

Cousins, Mark, and Athar Hussain. *Michel Foucault. Theoretical Traditions in the Social Sciences,* ed. Anthony Giddens. New York: St. Martin's Press, 1984.

Foucault, Michel. *Discipline and Punish: The Birth of the Prison.* Translated by Alan Sheridan. New York: Vintage Books, 1979.

———. *The History of Sexuality: An Introduction.* Translated by Robert Hurley. New York: Vintage Books, 1990.

Nichols, L. "Mr. Capote." *New York Times Book Review,* 22 August 1965, p. 39.

O'Connor, Flannery. *Three by Flannery O'Connor.* New York: Signet, 1962.

Tompkins, Phillip K. "In Cold Fact." *Esquire* 65.6 (June 1966): 126-27, 166-71.

William White Tison Pugh (essay date fall 1998)

SOURCE: Pugh, William White Tison. "Boundless Hearts in a Nightmare World: Queer Sentimentalism and Southern Gothicism in Truman Capote's *Other Voices, Other Rooms.*" *The Mississippi Quarterly: The Journal of Southern Culture* 51, no. 4 (fall 1998): 663-82.

[*In the following essay, Pugh argues that labeling* Other Voices, Other Rooms *as a work of Southern Gothicism is reductive and incomplete, claiming instead that the novel merges the tropes of Gothicism and sentimentalism.*]

In the 1941 article, "The Gothic South," Louise Bogan declares, "The definite Gothic quality which characterizes so much of the work of writers from the American South has puzzled critics."[1] In addition to puzzling the critics, however, the ascription of the Southern gothic label to their writings has often puzzled, if not insulted, the Southern writers themselves. In response to Alice Walker's question whether she had ever been called a gothic writer, Eudora Welty replied, "They better not call me that! Yes, I have been, though. Inevitably, because I'm a Southerner. I've never had anybody call me that to my face."[2] Though perhaps not taking such offense at the ascription of a gothic style, Flannery O'Connor likewise believed that some critics both too quickly link the Southern with the gothic and apply the term grotesque to Southern literature when it is not appropriate: she humorously commented that "I have found that anything that comes out of the South is going to be called grotesque by the Northern reader, unless it is grotesque, in which case it is going to be called realistic."[3] Paradoxically, a review of the critical literature about these authors and other Southern writers confirms Bogan's characterization of the literature rather than Welty's and O'Connor's. The assumption of a Southern gothic style is virtually the *sine qua non* of a critical analysis of Southern literature.[4]

Another author who has often been dubbed a Southern gothicist is Truman Capote. Reading his ***Other Voices, Other Rooms*** in opposition to this background of grotesque critical interpretation,[5] I believe, offers an alternate reading of the novel in which certain characters are not interpreted merely as freakish aberrations and grotesque incarnations but as poignant and sympathetic representations of humanity. My goal is to liberate the text from a reductive critical past in order to begin a process of reinterpretation both of Capote's novel and of other Southern writings which have been too casually labeled "gothic" without sufficient analysis of how the gothic tropes interplay with other literary traditions. Specifically, I argue that Capote employs gothicism in tandem with sentimentalism. Though the gothic and the sentimental may appear to be radically discrete literary traditions, Capote merges them to great effect in ***Other Voices, Other Rooms*** both to create a hybrid style of gothic sentimentalism in which gothic terror and sentimental pathos combine to solicit the reader's sympathy for the characters, and to bring out the theme that love in any form must be cherished.[6] More specifically, one can see that Capote has created a sentimental novel designed to bring his readers into a sympathetic relationship with the protagonist as this character moves through the nightmare world in which he lives and learns, by so doing, to accept his homosexuality. Rather than merely offering a parade of grotesques and freaks to shock the reader, the didactically sentimental thematics of ***Other Voices, Other Rooms*** urge the novel's audience to a better understanding and deeper acceptance of homosexuality through a groundbreaking treatment of adolescent gay identity.

The Gothic Elements

Certainly, I do not want to minimize the gothic elements of the text in my argument that Capote is writing within the sentimental tradition. For example, the landscape of ***Other Voices, Other Rooms*** is indeed fully gothic in its terror. Capote isolates his characters in the principal setting of the novel, a secluded Southern mansion, and the name of this ancestral manor, Skully's Landing, is itself evocative of death, bones, and decay. The novel begins with the adolescent protagonist, Joel Harrison Knox, traveling from New Orleans to the Landing in order to live with his father after his mother's death, and the descriptions of the landscape through which he travels foreshadow the deterioration which he finds upon his arrival: Capote describes the swamp lands which Joel passes through as "filled with luminous green logs that shine under the dark marsh water like drowned corpses."[7] The boy is then stranded in Sydney

Katz's "gloomy café" (p. 12) until Sam Radclif drives him farther; the toy skull on Radclif's gear shift foreshadows Joel's destination, Skully's Landing, which the local townspeople refer to as "The Skulls" (p. 30). In numerous other passages of the book, Capote establishes the foreboding setting of the novel with key elements of the gothic tradition, such as ghostly presences (the mysterious woman in the window), supernatural tales (the local folklore surrounding the Cloud Hotel), and surreal dreams (Joel's delusions during his sickness).

Capote further connects the moldering landscape of Skully's Landing to gothic tropes through the piercing loneliness which plagues the characters who inhabit it; the descriptions of Joel's journey emphasize that he is traveling through "lonesome country" (p. 9). The end of his journey offers no respite to the piercing isolation Joel feels as Zoo, the housekeeper of the Landing, declares that "you ain't got no notion what lonesome is till you stayed a spell at the Landin'" (p. 61). Isolation is a key trope of the gothic novel because the characters must be removed from the safety and comfort offered by other people; as Irving Malin notes, the "Gothic employs a microcosm . . . [such as] Skully's Landing . . . [in which] there is enough room for irrational (and universal) forces to explode."[8] Certainly, the gothic setting of *Other Voices, Other Rooms* fits this description in its closed atmosphere in which gloom, skulls, and loneliness are Joel's only companions.

READING CHARACTERS SENTIMENTALLY

Though the setting and the atmosphere of the novel are indeed gothic, critics have been too quick to assume that a gothic setting necessitates that *all* of the characters be grotesques. For example, John W. Aldridge describes four of the primary personalities of the novel—Joel, Idabel Thompkins, Cousin Randolph, and Mr. Sansom—as "superbly and grotesquely effective in themselves [though they] illuminate nothing beyond themselves" (p. 202). Bruce Bawer mentions the "Southern Gothic touches" of the novel which include "grotesque characters [and] haunting scenes" (p. 39), but he does not elaborate upon why he views the characters in this way or detail specifically which of the characters are grotesques. William Nance, in a description of Zoo, writes that "she is also, *like everyone at the Landing . . . a grotesque*."[9] I agree with Nance that Zoo is a grotesque figure, for Capote describes her as "almost a freak, a human giraffe (p. 59)[10]; however, Nance does not elucidate why Joel, Cousin Randolph, Amy, and Ed Sansom should be considered grotesques. These critics see *all* of the novel's characters as equally grotesque inhabitants of a darkly gothic world; nevertheless, though they decry the "grotesque" characters of the novel over and over, they do not specify why these characters should be read as grotesques. The question then arises whether all of the characters should be interpreted as grotesques or if an alternate interpretation exists. I contend that we must look both to the gothic and to the sentimental traditions to understand how Capote constructs certain characters as grotesques while others are representatives of an affective sentimentality.

In *To Kiss the Chastening Rod*, G. M. Goshgarian outlines the basic tropes and themes of the sentimental novel, and their presence in *Other Voices, Other Rooms* supports my argument that the gothic elements of the text are working in conjunction with the sentimental. Goshgarian declares that writers of sentimental literature

> focus on middle-class home life; appeal massively to their readers' tenderest emotions; deal in types rather than psychologically individuated characters; write with evangelical ends in mind; and compulsively chronicle the improbable career of a pious, nubile, aboriginally middle-class but temporarily déclassée white American girl whose exemplary fortitude under a storm of adversities is rewarded with a spouse, solvency, and salvation.
>
> (p. 9)

With only minor modifications, all five of Goshgarian's parameters of sentimental literature appear in Capote's novel: (1) The deteriorating condition of Skully's Landing indicates that Randolph's financial situation has declined from its past heights and, thus, that the novel's setting is not in the upper class but in the middle; (2) Capote makes outright demands upon the reader's emotions and models the appropriate sympathetic responses to his characters; (3) certain characters are introduced as types rather than as fully fleshed individuals in order to accentuate their sentimental appeal; (4) though Capote does not write with evangelical objectives, he does write didactically in order to lead his readers to a better acceptance of homosexuality; (5) and Joel, forced out into the world after his mother's death, is an adolescent gay male version of the typically feminine sentimental protagonist as he withstands the onslaught of adversity and emerges with a partner (though "solvency and salvation" are not addressed in the text) through his relationship with Randolph at the novel's end. Moreover, Capote's revisions of the fourth and fifth tropes—metamorphosing evangelical objectives into a didactic appeal to accept sexual-orientation difference and replacing a heterosexual female heroine with a gay adolescent hero—suggest that the sentimentalism at the heart of his project has specifically queer objectives, and I therefore refer to Capote's sentimentalism as a queer sentimentalism. A middle-class setting, claims on the reader's sympathy, stock characters, didactic appeals, and the protagonist's perseverance in the face of overwhelming odds—all of these elements of the sentimental tradition are included in *Other Voices, Other Rooms*. With so much queer sentimentalism, why, then, should all of the characters be read as grotesques? And which of the characters should be read sentimentally?

Other than the invalid Mr. Sansom, the chief mark of difference for the characters that Aldridge labels grotesques is their respective sexual ambiguities, as Joel is a "sissy," Idabel is a tomboy, and Cousin Randolph is effeminate. The many descriptions of these characters throughout the novel underscore that they do not adhere to traditional gender roles: Joel is "too pretty, too delicate and fair-skinned, each of his features was shaped with a sensitive accuracy, and a girlish tenderness softened his eyes, which were brown and very large" (p. 11); Capote's portrait of Idabel emphasizes her masculine manners and her rough-and-tumble ways, evident in her male attire ("a pair of brown shorts and a yellow polo shirt") and her rambunctious antics ("Whooping like a wild-west Indian, the redhead whipped down the road" [p. 26]); Randolph's defining characteristics are his smoothness and his femininity, as his face "was round as a coin, smooth and hairless; . . . curly, very blond, his fine hair fell in childish yellow ringlets across his forehead, and his wide-set womanly eyes were sky-blue marbles" (p. 84). These descriptions certainly set the characters apart from heterosexuality, but they do not construct them as grotesques. Thus, because Aldridge and other critics do not specify why these characters should be read as grotesques, I surmise that their indictments of the characters are based upon both the characters' location in a gothic setting and the heterosexist labeling both of sexual-orientation difference and of gender cross-over as grotesque. Certainly, a good deal of the criticism of **Other Voices, Other Rooms** is explicitly homophobic: the reviewer of the novel for *Time* magazine declared that "the distasteful trappings of its homosexual theme overhang it like Spanish moss."[11] This and other unsympathetic critical reactions mirror the responses of many homophobic characters in the novel to those who do not adhere to traditional gender mores, as when, for example, the wife of the one-armed barber declares that "it wasn't no revelation to me cause I always knew *she was a freak*, no ma'am, never saw Idabel Thompkins in a dress yet" (p. 27; emphasis added). With critics unsympathetic to the homosexuality of the story, that Joel, Idabel, and Randolph have been read as freakish aberrations rather than as sentimental tropes refashioned from a queer perspective should come as no surprise.

Indeed, Capote shows that such closed-minded opinions have been successful to a degree in convincing the gay and lesbian characters themselves that they are grotesques. In the account of his experiences with Ed Sansom, Dolores, and Pepe, Cousin Randolph refers to his friends and himself as "grotesque quadruplets" (p. 153); however, Miss Wisteria, the dwarf in the carnival with whom Idabel later falls in love, explicitly counters this view and emphasizes that the gay and lesbian characters are not grotesques, though even they themselves may think they are freaks because of society's reaction to them. In her sympathetic encounter with Idabel, Miss Wisteria brings to light the damage which the townspeople have done to the adolescent girl when she rhetorically asks, "Poor child, is it that she believes she is a freak, too?" (p. 199). Miss Wisteria's question demonstrates her understanding that Idabel may believe herself grotesque because of the constant abuse she receives from both the townspeople and her family; nevertheless, Miss Wisteria's compassionate concern also clearly demonstrates that Idabel is not a freak but a human being who has for too long been subjected to inhumane treatment by those around her. Joel, Idabel, and Randolph are viewed as grotesques only through closed-minded misperceptions; Capote ensures that their humanity and pain are always at the forefront of the novel so that the reader is forced to confront the results of such barbarity. And it is superbly appropriate that Capote allows Miss Wisteria, who in other novels would be immediately recognizable as a grotesque character because of her dwarfism, to be the voice of this concern, as this allows a traditionally grotesque figure the symbolic opportunity to reclaim herself from misreadings. Furthermore, Capote highlights the ironic hypocrisy of the townspeople who label these characters as grotesques because the townspeople themselves are directly linked to the gothic tradition through their own grotesque features: the one-armed barber suffers an obvious physical absence; the simian Miss Roberta has "long ape-like arms that were covered with dark fuzz, and there was a wart on her chin, and decorating this wart was a single antenna-like hair" (p. 28); the avian Florabel becomes an odd parody of the model of propriety she believes herself to be, as "she talked rapidly in a flighty, too birdlike manner, as if mimicking a certain type of old lady" (p. 37).

When the gay and lesbian characters of **Other Voices, Other Rooms** are viewed as tropes of the sentimental tradition, the flatness which some critics observe becomes a necessary marker of a specific literary genre. Janet Todd, in providing an overview of the elements of the sentimental, declares that "the arousal of pathos through conventional situations, *stock familial characters* and rhetorical devices is the mark of sentimental literature."[12] Todd furthermore affirms the sentimental's need for characters who are "distressed [and] natural victims, whose misery is demanded by their predicament as defenceless women, aged men, helpless infants or melancholic youths" (p. 3). Interestingly, of the four characters of the novel whom Aldridge addresses, three specifically belong to the categories of sentimental characters which Todd delineates: Joel and Idabel are both "melancholic youths" and Mr. Sansom is an "aged man" and hopeless invalid. Craig M. Goad, though not specifically recognizing the characters' debt to the sentimental tradition, points out the symbolic nature of the text's personae:

> Joel is not a normal member of any normal society, but rather a symbol of everyone who struggles against overwhelming odds to establish an identity and to find love. . . . None of these characters, despite their lovable natures, is, properly speaking, a person. They represent abstract qualities of non-conformity, charity, understanding and other virtues. They exist, not as people, but as representations of the way people ought to be if only the world would let them be so.
>
> (p. 13)

Within a queer sentimental interpretation, Joel, Idabel, and Randolph can be read not as grotesques, but as character types integrally designed to elicit a sympathetic response from the reader.

The novel's sympathetic and sentimental tropes stress the humanity of the homosexual characters, a humanity which Capote does not allow to be stripped from them. Rather, he often stresses the appropriate emotional responses to his characters, as when, for example, Idabel laments to Joel the problems of being a girl:

> "I never think like I'm a girl; you've got to remember that, or we can't never be friends." For all its bravado, she made this declaration with a special and compelling innocence; and when she knocked one fist against the other, as, frowning, she did now, and said: "I want so much to be a boy: I would be a sailor, I would . . ." *the quality of her futility was touching.*
>
> (p. 136, emphasis added)

Capote directs the reader's response, ordering the audience to be "touched" by Idabel's plight, to understand the pain which gender codes have placed upon her. Capote employs his stock characters of the little boy lost (Joel), the tomboy (Idabel), and the loveless lonelyheart (Randolph) to guide his readers into a sympathetic relationship with them.

In *Sentimental Modernism,* Suzanne Clark declares that "tropes of sympathy argue through embodiment and an appeal to experience: the sentimental locates moral values in the (feminized) heart and denies the importance of external differences. Thus the sentimental also grounds the moral appeal to respect individual differences" (p. 22). In this light, Capote's didactic aims are apparent: the depiction of these unique characters is intended to initiate a relationship between reader and character in which the former learns to respect the latter. The difference and otherness of Joel, Idabel, and Randolph is located in their refusal of a socially assigned heterosexuality; the thematic thrust of **Other Voices, Other Rooms** seeks to bring its readers to an acceptance of homosexuality through a sympathetic relationship with its characters. Moreover, I find this didacticism to be part of the novel's sentimental, rather than its gothic, tradition. Though gothic literature may also be didactic, gothic didacticism is not predicated upon the reader's sympathetic relationship with the characters. For example, Flannery O'Connor is outrightly didactic in such short stories as "A Good Man is Hard to Find" and "Good Country People," but the moral lesson does not derive from our sympathy for such characters as the Grandmother or Joy "Hulga" Hopewell; rather, we are invited to laugh at them as we learn O'Connor's moral thematics. The didacticism of **Other Voices, Other Rooms,** however, is based upon our heartfelt sympathies for the gay and lesbian characters. Gothic didacticism may function despite an affective separation between reader and character(s); sentimental didacticism depends upon the reader's emotional cathexis with the character(s).

Boundless Hearts in a Nightmare World

Within the first few pages of the text, Capote arouses the reader's sympathy for Joel both through the many hardships and losses the boy has endured and through his effeminate character, which marks him as an outsider to the heteronormative world outside Skully's Landing. His mother has recently died from pneumonia, and he feels isolated from everyone else in the world; when he imagines himself trapped in a frozen palace, he asks himself, "What living soul would then brave robber barons for his rescue?" and concludes that "there was no one, really no one" (p. 17). Joel's isolation in his past life is mirrored by his sense of abandonment in his present: upon arriving at a town close to Noon City, he cannot finish his journey because, as he says, "no one come to meet me" (p. 11). Even the conclusion of Joel's travels will not end the solitude thrust upon him since his mother's death because Joel has never met his father: "'I've never seen him,' said Joel" (p. 15). The pathos of a little boy lost immediately demands the reader's heartfelt attention to Joel, as does the effeminacy which marks him as the "Other" to patriarchal society. Capote stresses Joel's separation from a masculine ethos, as Sam Radclif dislikes Joel immediately for his feminine qualities: "Radclif eyed the boy . . . not caring much for the looks of him. He had his notions of what a 'real' boy should look like, and this kid somehow offended them" (pp. 10-11). Capote ensures the reader's sympathy for his protagonist by marking him as totally alone in the world; Joel has no one to care for him except the audience of the text. In his little prayer, "Only how, how could you say something so indefinite, so meaningless as this: God, let me be loved" (p. 79), Capote delineates the tragically simple quest of Joel's life.

Capote further emphasizes the chasm between Joel and patriarchy by the differences in Joel's and his father's last names: Joel's mother chose "Knox" for the boy's surname after her divorce from his father, Mr. Sansom. The patronymic difference between Joel and his father stresses Joel's separation from patriarchal codes and marks him as an outsider in a predominantly masculine and heterosexual society, as evidenced by the reaction of Sam Radclif to the boy's last name: "'Aw, say, son' said Radclif, 'you oughtn't to have let [your mother] done that! Remember, your Pa's your Pa no matter what'" (pp. 14-15). Though Joel's surname distances him from the heteronormative community which his father and Radclif represent, Capote also employs Joel's name to foreshadow the boy's rejection of the homophobic society which places such an emphasis on the father's name. Judith Butler concludes in her analysis of the patronym that "patronymic names endure over time, as nominal zones of phallic control. Enduring and viable identity is thus purchased through subjection to and subjectivation by the patronym."[13] Through Joel's rejection of the patronym, Capote points forward to the character's rejection of the social codes which inhibit the development of his homosexuality. Joel's surname is thus a means both to highlight his isolation in and to foreshadow his freedom from the patriarchal parameters which hamper his acceptance of a gay identity.

Having established that Joel's search for love and acceptance is the focus of the novel, Capote develops this theme in the following scene. Before arriving at Skully's Landing, Joel meets Idabel Thompkins, the local tomboy. His desire for friendship with another outsider is evident in his unspoken address to the girl, "Hi Idabel—watchasay Idabel?" The words, however, are never uttered, and Idabel promptly ignores Joel. Though Joel does not connect with Idabel at this point of the narrative, Capote uses the scene effectively to introduce the reader to Idabel's masculine attributes. He writes that "[h]er voice was boy-husky" (p. 31) and depicts Miss Roberta admonishing Idabel both to "learn a few ladylike manners" and to "put on some decent female clothes" (p. 32). Although Joel and Idabel do not meet in this passage, Capote establishes their mutual status as outsiders due to their inabilities to conform to traditional gender roles.

Joel and Idabel become friends in the unfolding of the narrative, but his subsequent relationship with her cannot wholly free him from the isolation he feels. Though Idabel is in many ways Joel's kindred spirit, neither can give the other the love they both need, and, though they attempt to escape together from the world which traps them, they fail because such an escape would not force them to face their respective true identities. Through their ability to make "everything look a lot prettier" (p. 132), Idabel's green-colored glasses symbolize her attempt to make the world more palatable. By changing the world around her with the glasses, Idabel attempts to construct a world which she wants to see. The society in which she and Joel live, however, is not a "pretty" place for the two. Thus, when Joel attempts to kiss Idabel after they have been swimming naked together and, accordingly, to take his place in the heterosexual community, Idabel fights against him and pins him down: "Idabel was astride him, and her strong hands locked his wrists to the ground" (p. 139). In this act of simulated intercourse, as Helen Garson points out, "symbolically the male-female roles are reversed . . . Idabel becomes representative of the fierce strength of the conquering male astride the subdued figure of the female" (p. 22). Also important in this scene of reversals is that the green-colored glasses break and cut Joel in his buttocks. Joel's buttocks bear the bloodiness of the loss of virginity which is typically borne on the woman's body in heterosexual intercourse; this inversion of heterosexual bleeding foreshadows his acceptance of homosexuality, in which his virginity is not only marked by his penis but by his anus as well. In the failure of heterosexuality for Joel and Idabel, Capote shows that they cannot escape from their true selves either by an enforced heterosexual union or by the green-colored glasses changing the appearance of the world around them. They must face the struggle to accept themselves, including their homosexuality, despite the society which is unsympathetic to their needs. Green-colored glasses are not sufficient to alter the harsh reality of their lives,[14] and Joel and Idabel must find their identities not by a retreat into heterosexuality but through an acceptance of their homosexuality.

Idabel is the first of the pair successful both in her repudiation of heterosexual norms and in her acceptance of her homosexuality. In a scene which begs for a Freudian interpretation, Idabel and Joel encounter a snake—an obvious metaphor for the phallus—after they have run away from home together. Though Joel is paralyzed with fear and can only see his father in the snake ("How did Mr. Sansom's eyes come to be in a moccasin's head?"), Idabel grabs yet another phallic symbol, Joel's sword, and kills the snake as she calls it a "[b]ig granddaddy bastard" (p. 184). Thus, Idabel is capable of wielding the phallic power of the sword in order to destroy the phallic power of the snake. In her ability to move freely in roles stereotypically associated with the masculine and to eradicate symbolically the constraining influence of the phallus, Idabel liberates herself from patriarchal codes which attempt to restrict her from experiencing her homosexuality. In this newfound freedom, Idabel is able to accept her homosexuality, and she falls in love with Miss Wisteria at the carnival: "[A] queer thing happened . . . as [Idabel] continued to fawn over tiny yellow-haired Miss Wisteria it came to [Joel] that Idabel was in love" (p. 197). Joel sees that queer things and queer feelings can happen through Idabel's love for Miss Wisteria, even though the dwarf does not return the young girl's affection. Because Idabel has learned to accept herself and her emotions, Joel is able to comprehend the possibility of accepting his homosexuality.

Cousin Randolph is equally important to Joel in his realization and acceptance of his homosexuality, and Capote's depiction of Randolph similarly ensures that the character be read sympathetically. Before Randolph establishes his residence at the Landing, he has a relationship with Dolores, who introduces him to the man, Pepe, with whom he falls hopelessly in love. Though Randolph has not realized his homosexuality prior to Pepe's arrival, Dolores has deduced the truth and advises Randolph to stay away from Pepe: "'Strange how long it takes us to discover ourselves; I've known since first I saw you,' she said, adding, 'I do not think, though, that he is the one for you; I've known too many Pepes; love him if you will, it will come to nothing'" (p. 151). Dolores's conjecture proves true, and Pepe leaves Randolph. Consequently, Randolph retreats to the Landing where he attempts to regain Pepe's love by writing to him in care of postmasters throughout the world:

> "Over there," said Randolph with a tired smile, "is a five-pound volume listing every town and hamlet on the globe; it is what I believe in, this almanac: day by day I've gone through it writing Pepe always in care of the postmaster; just notes, nothing but my name and what we will for convenience call address. Oh, I know that I shall never have an answer. But it gives me something to believe in. And that is peace."
>
> (p. 158)

In this hyperbolic description of the extents to which Randolph will go to find Pepe, Capote illustrates a heart hungering for the love it craves. Speaking for all of humanity, Randolph claims that "What we most want is only to be held . . . and told . . . that everything . . . is going to be all right" (p. 152); the reader cannot help but wish that everything will be all right for him after following his tragic search for love.

As the novel closes, Joel and Randolph enter into a symbiotic relationship in which Randolph helps Joel to accept his homosexuality, and Joel helps to convince Randolph that, indeed, everything will be all right. After their trip together to the Cloud Hotel, Joel enters Skully's Landing while Randolph, dressed in drag, waves to him from the window, suggesting that the two are prepared to begin their new lives together, and will be able to support each other despite the outside world's disapproving view of their sexual orientations. Many critics have expressed negative reactions to the ending of *Other Voices, Other Rooms* because they presume that it suggests a predatory and dysfunctional sexual relationship between Randolph and Joel in which the former has molded the latter into a sexual toy and that a romance ensues with complicated inversions of traditional family relationships. Goad suggests that "with Joel's rejection of both his father and male-female sexuality, Randolph is ready to assume the dual role of father and lover" (p. 30). Marvin Mengeling, in an Oedipal interpretation, declares that "Joel, therefore, must somehow be infused with the psychological strength necessary for him to assume the position of husband, not child, in relation to Randolph, the mother image."[15] Paul Levine suggests that "Joel, like Christ, is condemned and abandoned by his father and crucified by surrendering to Randolph" (p. 614). These opinions, and others like them, assume that gay relationships are predicated upon inversions of traditional family structures in which one man loves another who fulfills the role of his parent. I offer an interpretation of the novel's denouement in which Randolph does not act as Joel's mother, father, or crucifier: Because Randolph dresses in drag does not mean that Joel wants to sleep with his mother; because Randolph is older than Joel does not mean that Joel wants to sleep with his father; because two men share a sexual relationship does not necessitate that one be crucified. Importantly, too, critics have attacked the sentimentality of the novel's close: Claude Summers considers that the ending "represent[s] an escape from reality into the make-believe of Randolph's sentimental and self-indulgent fantasies."[16] How does the novel's resolution appear when we read it sentimentally, when we interpret a loving relationship rather than a predatory one?

A Sentimental Ending

Interpretations which suggest a dysfunctional relationship between Joel and Randolph may be predicated upon Joel's desire to leave Skully's Landing and, thus, to escape from his homosexuality. That Joel wants to escape from homosexuality should not be read as a condemnation of homosexuality; rather, Joel's reluctance to accept his homosexuality serves a key role in his development. Growing up in a homophobic society is intrinsically difficult, and Capote's novel would lack depth if he glossed over this central conflict of Joel's maturation. Thus, Capote describes Joel as desperate to leave the Landing and to return to his home in New Orleans with his Aunt Ellen: "[T]he good feeling came back: Ellen would make things different, she would fix it so he could go away to a school where everybody was like everybody else" (p. 114). Joel, however, can never be "like everybody else" because of his homosexuality, and the acceptance of his gay identity must therefore take place in a setting which will nurture his unique person. The world outside Skully's Landing is wholly inappropriate and hostile to this task. Joel's denial of his homosexuality involves his attempt to run from Skully's Landing; conversely, his acceptance of homosexuality is evident at the end of the novel when he enters the mansion.

The scene in which Randolph leaves with Joel for the Cloud Hotel at the time when Aunt Ellen comes to take him to New Orleans, therefore, should not be interpreted as depicting a cruel homosexual seducer kidnapping a young boy from his loving family. Significantly, Randolph and Joel travel to the Cloud Hotel after Joel's long sickness during which Randolph nurtures him back to health, and, thus, their relationship becomes firmly established. Randolph and he are free to return to their home at Skully's Landing where homosocial and/or homosexual bonds may be forged, and Randolph's presence ensures that Joel will be able to experience his rebirth as a gay man in a gay community rather than retreating into a state of perpetual pre-adolescence in a society which will never understand him. A character who acts as such an exemplar of proper behavior is another marker of the sentimental tradition: Jane Tompkins notes that sentimental novels "always involve, prominently, a mentor-figure who initiates the pupil into the mysteries of the art, and enunciates the values the narrative is attempting to enforce" (p. 176). Is Cousin Randolph serving narratively in such a mentoring fashion?

Randolph's many didactic discourses about love certainly teach Joel how to deal with the emotions he is experiencing at this time of his maturation. Capote describes Joel's benefitting from Randolph's instruction as the boy approaches a fundamental change in which his old self is dead, replaced by the vibrancy of his new identity:

> Now at thirteen Joel was nearer a knowledge of death than in any year to come: a flower was blooming inside him, and soon, when all tight leaves unfurled, when the noon of youth burned whitest, he would turn and look, as others had, for the opening of another door.
>
> (p. 131)

Randolph, of course, represents the "others" mentioned in the quotation; as Joel "opens the door" to his homosexuality, so central to the titular thematics of **Other Voices, Other Rooms,** Randolph serves as a mentor for Joel's new self who can now accept and cherish his homosexuality. Indeed, the postcard from Idabel which Randolph burns as Joel convalesces from his illness is further evidence of the distinction between the Joel of the past and the new Joel who has experienced this rebirth; Idabel now is one "whose names concerned the old Joel" (p. 214). Joel's past, including both the good and the bad memories, is sacrificed to his new identity as he thematically opens the door to another room and another life. His quest for his homosexual self has been the overriding focus of the narrative; Randolph, in his exemplary role, assists Joel in the task of finding himself through his gay identity. Though in the novel's opening Joel feels as if he has no identity ("He felt separated, without identity, a stone-boy mounted on the rotted stump" [p. 76]), by the novel's close, Joel is able to proclaim, "I am me, . . . I am Joel, we are the same people" (p. 230). In accord, the narrator relates that Joel "knew who he was, he knew that he was strong" (p. 231).[17]

In the closing lines of the text, Capote depicts Joel's acceptance of his homosexuality as the adolescent realizes both that Randolph is the mysterious woman in the window and that his own life will change irrevocably with the acceptance of his new gay identity:

> She [Randolph] beckoned to him, shining and silver, and he knew he must go: unafraid, not hesitating, he paused only at the garden's edge where, as though he'd forgotten something, he stopped and looked back at the bloomless, descending blue, at the boy he had left behind.
>
> (p. 235)

Joel moves to enter Skully's Landing at the novel's end, but he and Randolph are not portrayed together as lovers at the novel's end; consequently, we can only hypothesize that they engage in a sexual relationship. Nonetheless, if we assume if the two do engage in a sexual relationship in their seclusion at Skully's Landing, I maintain that the paradigm of this union would not be an inversion of traditional family structures in which Joel partners with Randolph acting either as his mother- or father-figure; rather, Capote asserts throughout the text that the two are equals, nearly mirror images of each other. When Joel first sees Randolph as the mysterious woman, he recognizes aspects of himself: "the hazy substance of her face, the suffused marshmallow features, brought to mind his own vaporish reflection in the wavy chamber mirror" (p. 71). Later, Joel looks into Randolph's eyes and sees himself reflected: "So he questioned the round innocent eyes, and saw his own boy-face focused as in double camera lenses" (p. 91). Capote accentuates both Randolph's youth and Joel's age so that, despite their age difference, the two appear more as equals. Joel writes to his friend Sammy Silverstein that "Out here a person old as us is a grown-up person" (p. 96)[18]; likewise, Randolph's youthfulness is often highlighted as when, for example, Capote writes "the sudden light flattered [Randolph's] face, made the pink hairless skin more impeccably young" (p. 157) or "[Randolph's] skin seemed translucently pink in the morning light, his round smooth face bizarrely youthful" (p. 172). By stressing the likenesses between the two characters, Capote paints their relationship as sharing a fundamental equality.

Furthermore, I would like to point out that Capote is playing with tropes of Narcissism in his depiction of Joel's and Randolph's relationship. Though homosexuality has often been viewed as an excessive form of self-love, Capote redeems Narcissistic tropes from their traditional allegations of egotism and posits Narcissus as a model of human honesty in amorous concerns. In a defense of self-love, Randolph declares: "I tell you, my dear, Narcissus was no egotist . . . he was merely another of us who, in our unshatterable isolation, recognized, on seeing his reflection, the one beautiful comrade, the only inseparable love . . . poor Narcissus, possibly the only human who was ever honest on this point" (p. 144). Capote then delineates the perfect Narcissistic equality between the two when Joel falls sick and discusses with Randolph their ages and their relationship:

> "Randolph," [Joel] said, "were you ever as young as me?" And Randolph said: "I was never so old." "Randolph," he said, "do you know something? I'm very happy." To which his friend made no reply. The reason for this happiness seemed to be simply that he did not feel unhappy, *rather he knew all through him a kind of balance.* There was so little to cope with. The mist which for him had overhung so much of Randolph's conversation, even that had lifted, at least it was no longer troubling, *for it seemed as though he understood him absolutely.*
>
> (p. 212, emphases added)

In their Narcissistic balance, Joel and Randolph are free from society's bigotries and ready to embrace their gay identities. That two gay men choose to live with each other in a secluded setting should not be read as an indictment of homosexuality. The society outside Skully's Landing does not care to understand homosexuality, and the two men therefore make a haven for each other in which they are free to live as the gay men they are. Georges-Michel Sarotte believes the novel's dénouement suggests that "Joel has recognized his inner personality, and the joy he shows seems to indicate that he hopes to make his life a paradise . . . Joel's refuge in homosexuality is the only solution to the anxiety plaguing anyone who adopts against his nature the sexual mores of society."[19] Joel and Randolph are safe together in their understanding of each other; they have made a world in which self-expression liberates them from the society which would never understand their feelings of love.

In their freedom from the world's homophobia at the Landing, Joel and Randolph serve for the reader as role models of individuals unwilling to forgo their need for love in order to appease the petty dictates of society. In the novel's ending, Capote's sentimentally didactic goal is explicitly to teach his readers that all human love is beautiful. As Cousin Randolph, in his role as Joel's mentor, declares,

> "The brain may take advice, but not the heart, and love, having no geography, knows no boundaries: weight and sink it deep, no matter, it will rise and find the surface: and why not? any love is natural and beautiful that lies within a person's nature; only hypocrites would hold a man responsible for what he loves, emotional illiterates and those of righteous envy, who, in their agitated concern, mistake so frequently the arrow pointing to heaven for the one that leads to hell."
>
> (p. 151)

This passage, which expressly states the theme of the novel and speaks the beauty of boundless loves, models the proper reaction of the novel's audience to the characters and their situations. In both his outright exhortation for acceptance of love in its myriad forms and his condemnation of the hypocritically judgmental, Capote urges the reader to a sympathetic relationship with his characters, a relationship universalized to include all human beings who love in ways not condoned by the greater society.

Although Southern gothicism has long been recognized as a distinct body of American fiction, the time is long past due to reassess this label and the assumptions behind it. Rather than always designating the Southern homosexual character as a fascinating yet grotesque "Other," critics must analyze these characters with the same assumptions of fundamental humanity which heterosexual characters have received since the beginnings of literary criticism. One hopes, therefore, that blanket equations of homosexuality and grotesquerie will finally be eradicated both from criticism and from society itself.[20] Certainly, Capote includes a great deal of grotesquerie in *Other Voices, Other Rooms,* but these gothic tropes serve to highlight the plight of his sentimental gay and lesbian characters, not to construct them as freaks. We must be sure to investigate how gothicism interacts with other literary traditions employed in the delineations of gay and lesbian characters: how, for example, would the works of Carson McCullers, Tennessee Williams, and other Southern writers look to us if we looked for traces of queer sentimentalism in their gothic literatures? If they were viewed as sentimental characters, how would the critical interpretations of Frankie of *The Member of the Wedding* or Brick of *Cat on a Hot Tin Roof* change? Along with both the Southern and the gay characters receiving the sympathetic readings they so strongly deserve, perhaps sentimental literature itself would at long last receive the critical approbation which it for too long has been denied.[21]

Notes

1. Louise Bogan, "The Gothic South," *Nation,* 153 (1941), 572.

2. Alice Walker, "Eudora Welty: An Interview," in Peggy Whitman Prenshaw, ed., *Conversations with Eudora Welty* (Jackson: University Press of Mississippi, 1984), p. 137.

3. Flannery O'Connor, *Mystery and Manners: Occasional Prose,* ed. Sally and Robert Fitzgerald (New York: Farrar, Straus and Giroux, 1969), p. 40.

4. Some recent criticism on this issue includes Dieter Meindl, *American Fiction and the Metaphysics of the Grotesque* (Columbia: University of Missouri

Press, 1996) and Louis Gross, *Redefining the American Gothic* (Ann Arbor: University of Michigan Press, 1989). Given Welty's displeasure with the critical association between her literature and gothic tropes, one might wonder how she would react to Ruth Weston, *Gothic Tradition and Narrative Techniques in the Fiction of Eudora Welty* (Baton Rouge: Louisiana State University Press, 1994).

5. The assumption of Capote's gothicism is apparent in much of the criticism of his works. See, for example, the books and articles by John W. Aldridge, *After the Lost Generation: A Critical Study of the Writers of Two Wars* (New York: McGraw-Hill, 1951); Bruce Bawer, "Capote's Children," *New Criterion*, 3 (1985), 39-44; Helen S. Garson, *Truman Capote* (New York: Frederick Ungar Publishing, 1980); Craig M. Goad, "Daylight and Darkness, Dream and Delusion: The Works of Truman Capote," *Emporia State Research Studies*, 16 (1967), 5-57; and Paul Levine, "Truman Capote: The Revelation of the Broken Image," *Virginia Quarterly Review*, 34 (1958), 600-617.

6. Though sentimental literature has traditionally been viewed as inferior to other forms of fiction, recent scholarship has begun to reclaim the sentimental as a significant and relevant literary tradition in its own right. For scholarship on sentimental literature, see Jane Tompkins, *Sensational Designs: The Cultural Work of American Fiction, 1790-1840* (New York: Oxford University Press, 1985); Howard Fulweiler, *"Here a Captive Heart Busted": Studies in the Sentimental Journey of Modern Literature* (New York: Fordham University Press, 1993); Suzanne Clark, *Sentimental Modernism: Women Writers and the Revolution of the Word* (Bloomington: Indiana University Press, 1991); G. M. Goshgarian, *To Kiss the Chastening Rod: Domestic Fiction and Sexual Ideology in the American Renaissance* (Ithaca, New York: Cornell University Press, 1992); and Claudia Tate, *Domestic Allegories of Political Desire: The Black Heroine's Text at the Turn of the Century* (New York: Oxford University Press, 1992).

7. Truman Capote, *Other Voices, Other Rooms* (New York: Signet, 1948), p. 9.

8. Irving Malin, *New American Gothic* (Carbondale: Southern Illinois University Press, 1962), p. 5.

9. William L. Nance, *The Worlds of Truman Capote* (New York: Stein & Day, 1970), p. 44, emphasis added.

10. Although Capote clearly labels Zoo a grotesque, she is also linked to the sentimental tradition through the scar on her neck. The scar, a visible reminder of her relationship with the villainous Keg Brown, ensures the reader's sympathy for her. Zoo, thus, is herself an example of the gothic sentimentalism which I find in the novel.

11. "Spare the Laurels," *Time,* March 14, 1949, p. 113.

12. Janet Todd, *Sensibility: An Introduction* (London: Methuen, 1986), p. 2, emphasis added. Although Todd's analysis of the sentimental addresses the tradition's British history, her argument about the stock nature of sentimental characters certainly applies to American sentimentalism as well. as the previous quotation from Goshgarian confirms.

13. Judith Butler, *Bodies That Matter: On the Discursive Limits of "Sex"* (New York: Routledge, 1993), p. 153.

14. Green-colored glasses are a recurring motif in *Other Voices, Other Rooms,* and they repeatedly fail in the characters' attempts to use them to escape into a fantasy world (as when Joel remembers his life with the Kendall family "as if he lived those months wearing a pair of spectacles with green, cracked lenses" [p. 17] or when Idabel wins another pair at the carnival "but too large for her, they kept sliding down her nose" [p. 195]). Capote does not allow his characters to escape from their harsh worlds, but depicts them as learning to face homophobic society.

15. Marvin E. Mengeling, "*Other Voices, Other Rooms*: Oedipus Between the Covers." *American Imago*, 19 (1962), 370.

16. Claude J. Summers, *Gay Fictions: Wilde to Stonewall: Studies in a Male Homosexual Literary Tradition* (New York: Frederick Ungar, 1990), p. 132

17. Randolph's role in Joel's maturation is also evident in Capote's internal parody of the thematics of emotional and psycho-sexual development when the author depicts Joel's thirst for alcohol to mark his new-found maturity. At Miss Roberta's diner, Joel asks for beer and is embarrassed by her reply that she "[c]an't serve no beer to minors, babylove, even if you are a might cute-lookin' fella" (p. 29). Randolph's mentoring role is then evident when, by giving Joel alcohol, he provides the first clue to his position as the boy's mentor, as one who will assist him in his growth to manhood.

18. After writing this letter to Sammy, Joel realizes that "almost all he'd ever written were lies, big lies poured over the paper like a thick syrup" (p. 97). The lies, however, address Joel's fantasy vision of his father; I believe that Joel's thoughts about Randolph and his perceptions of age at Skully's Landing are accurate reflections of his world.

19. George-Michel Sarotte, *Like a Brother, Like a Lover: Male Homosexuality in the American Novel and Theater from Herman Melville to James Baldwin* (New York: Anchor Press, 1978), p. 48.

20. I do not mean to suggest that gay, lesbian, or bisexual characters should never be read as grotesques. Certainly, many authors specifically demand that sexual orientation difference be interpreted as a market of grotesquerie. I do believe, however, that we must be careful not to make universal and essentializing connections between homosexual or bisexual characters and Southern gothic conventions.

21. I thank Mary Wood, Louise Westling, Margaret Johnson, and the anonymous readers of the *Mississippi Quarterly* for their helpful suggestions throughout the composition of this essay.

John C. Waldmeir (essay date 1999)

SOURCE: Waldmeir, John C. "Religion and Style in *The Dogs Bark* and *Music for Chameleons*." In *The Critical Response to Truman Capote*, edited by Joseph J. Waldmeir and John C. Waldmeir, pp. 155-66. Westport, Conn.: Greenwood Press, 1999.

[*In the following essay, Waldmeir maintains that religion is an important and often overlooked topic in Capote's* The Dogs Bark *and* Music for Chameleons. *He then distinguishes the ways in which Capote treats religion in these two works.*]

There are several reasons to compare Truman Capote's two works, *The Dogs Bark* and *Music for Chameleons.*[1] In both Capote has collected previously published prose that varies in length and subject matter. He has structured the pieces carefully that together they might convey certain themes and intentions. In the course of organizing them he also has tended to place similar works in parallel places. Both books, for example, begin with prefaces that discuss his experiences as a writer, end with creative dialogues in which Capote converses with himself, and contain, in their respective middles, long works that Capote valued for what they contributed to his development as a writer.

In addition to these similarities, both books also treat a topic that few critics have examined in Capote's writing: religion.[2] *The Dogs Bark* introduces the topic in a number of selections, including the piece that opens the volume, "A Voice from a Cloud," Capote's early travelogue, *Local Color,* and his much publicized (and somewhat controversial) interview with Marlon Brando, "The Duke and his Domain." *Music for Chameleons* refers to the topic consistently throughout the text; all fourteen works employ a terminology that is either recognized or best interpreted as "religious."

Though long neglected, religion in fact holds a prominent place in Capote's writing. His first novel, *Other Voices, Other Rooms* opens with a quote from the prophet Jeremiah. *Answered Prayers,* his final, unfinished work, takes its title from a quote by St. Theresa. In between there are Gothic tales with religious overtones, such as "A Tree of Night," "Master Misery," and "The Headless Hawk"; extended treatments of holidays with religious significance, like *The Thanksgiving Visitor* and *One Christmas*; and an array of nonfiction prose that repeatedly describes the significance of people and events in religious terms.

If religion offers readers a basis for comparing works within Capote's corpus, it also provides them with a reason for contrasting certain texts. Despite their similarities, *The Dogs Bark* and *Music for Chameleons,* for example, assume very different positions toward the topic. The first uses words associated with traditional religious vocabularies to describe a sense of sacred "otherness." From its opening pages "God" is objective, like the statue in a New Orleans courtyard with "stark glass angel eyes" that "stare upward" (*Dogs*, 21). No narrative voice in this work experiences the deity as "close." By contrast, *Music for Chameleons* speaks of the divine as a source of "help." The confession Capote utters at the close of this collection suggests his faith: "I began to believe in God again, and understood that Sook was right: that everything was His design, the old moon and the new moon, the hard rain falling, and if only I would ask Him to help me, He would." Here the "other" is not only omnipotent but also intimate, he heals the fractured voice of the "drug addict," "homosexual," "genius" who speaks (*Music*, 264).

As a direct result of such theological assumptions about the ways of God to man, Capote's collections differ in significant ways. They are organized, for instance, toward different ends. In keeping with the emphasis upon objectivity and "otherness" in *The Dogs Bark,* that work builds toward selections anthologized from a book Capote published with photographer Richard Avedon, *Observations.* From their text Capote selects an assortment of reflections on a cast of characters, including Mae West, Louis Armstrong, Humphrey Bogart, and Marilyn Monroe. All of the selections examine the public side of these figures, Mae West speaking in a "sassy drawl" or Armstrong as a "grinning Buddha" stomping and shouting "his way into the sunny side of the street" (*Dogs*, 366, 368). *Music for Chameleons,* by contrast, ends with a section that is suited to its dialogic approach to matters of ultimate meaning, "**Conversational Portraits.**" Here Capote talks and interacts with his cleaning lady, Mary Sanchez, the proprietor of a New Orleans waterfront bar, Big Junebug Johnson, convicted murderer Robert Beausoleil, and with himself. "**Conversational Portraits**" also contains a piece on Marilyn Monroe. But unlike the essay in *The Dogs*

Bark, which celebrates the ripe sensuality that was so essential to her on-screen persona, **"A Beautiful Child"** in *Music* seeks to understand this quality and to connect it with that side of Monroe that resembles "thin fleecy clouds fragile as lace" (*Music,* 243).

To support their theological assumptions, both *The Dogs Bark* and *Music for Chameleons* refer to traditional, organized forms of religion. But they use those references in different ways. In *The Dogs Bark* Capote cites religious practices from a variety of traditions, but he does so in ways that are almost incidental to the action. In **"Tangier"** he writes of the Islamic holy month of *Ramadan,* in **"The Duke and His Domain"** he refers to "Zen meditation" and "Yogi breathing," and in **"Haiti"** he offers interesting insights into Voodou. Despite possibilities raised by each reference, however, Capote rarely develops his thoughts or integrates them into the worlds he depicts. In **"Haiti,"** for example, he never connects his final claim that "in Voodou . . . there is no boundary between the countries of the living and the dead" with his earlier depiction of Hyppolite, the country's "most popular . . . primitive painter" whose eight-month old daughter has just died as the piece opens (***Dogs,*** 67, 58-59). As a result, **"Haiti"** remains disjointed and similar to the type of "film" Capote claims he would like to make of that country: ". . . soundless, nothing but a camera brilliantly framing architecture, objects" (***Dogs,*** 60).

In *Music for Chameleons* Capote uses words and images associated with traditional forms of religion in ways that seem to offer critical commentaries on its social role. Capote's visit to the magical Mrs. Ferguson in **"Dazzle"** takes place amid a "Sabbath stillness"; Pearl Bailey's arrival at Los Angeles International Airport to save him from being arrested is called a "miracle" in **"Derring-do"**; Mary Sanchez's day of cleaning New York apartments and smoking pot ends with a visit to church to pray the "rosary."

In addition to these references, though, there are others in *Music* that seem incidental but in fact are extremely important to the stories in which they appear. Both **"A Lamp in a Window"** and **"Hospitality,"** for example, use their references to establish sustained reflections on a religious theme: hospitality. Mrs. Kelly's admission in **"A Lamp in the Window"**—"I was raised a Catholic, but now, I'm almost sorry to say I have an open mind. Too much reading, perhaps"—seems at first to be a humorous aside. A better interpretation, however, recognizes that the comment describes the dynamics of the entire tale. This story begins with the narrator as a passenger in a car driven by the drunken Mr. and Mrs. Roberts, a hostile, argumentative environment that he claims resembles a scene from *Who's Afraid of Virginia Woolf.* It moves from there to the cozy fireside hearth of Mrs. Kelly, which calls to mind the worlds of "Jane Austen . . . Thoreau, and Willa Cather," to name but three. It is Mrs. Kelly who facilitates this transition, and she succeeds because she expresses a hospitality that we should recognize as not only "religious" but decidedly "Christian." "With hazel eyes like the small lamp shining on the table beside her," she embodies the Gospel charge to be "the light of the world (*Music,* 18)." She is the "lamp . . . on a stand" that "gives light to all in the house" (Matthew 5:15). That text from the Sermon on the Mount informs the entire story as it asks readers to ponder the religious meaning of hospitality. "Too much reading" may have diminished Mrs. Kelly's "Catholic" faith, but it has not dimmed her "religious" character.

Capote continues to call our attention to the religious dimension of the host/guest relationship in **"Hospitality."** Like **"A Lamp in the Window"** this story uses an incidental reference to organized religion, this time in the form of a visiting Presbyterian missionary to the depression-weary farm of Jennings and Mary Ida Carter, to emphasize religiously-motivated acts of kindness. The fact that the visitor is a Presbyterian minister seems to be of little importance until the reader realizes that Capote contrasts him and his position with two subsequent visitors, one an escaped convict named Bancroft and the other a young unmarried mother named Zilla. Through both contrasts the religious qualifications of the missionary begin to look suspect. Bancroft may be a criminal, but at least he offers to work for a meal. Of the preacher, who devours food "with both hands," the narrator says he "never saw a greedier fellow" (*Music,* 45). Zilla comes with nothing more than a "broken-down suitcase" and a little boy named Jed. But the love between mother and child is evident in a powerful fashion as Zilla bathes him naked in a nearby creek, the two of them "laughing" during this symbolic baptism. By contrast the preacher baptizes nothing and speaks not of love but of horror and hate. His element is not water but fire, and he terrifies his listeners with tales of "cannibals" who have assured him that "the best eatin' is roasted newborn baby" because it "tastes just like lamb" (*Music,* 46).

References to religion in these and other tales suggest a great deal about the value of interpreting in religious terms the pieces that comprise *Music for Chameleons.* But the value extends far beyond a commentary on organized expressions of faith. These works introduce religion as a topic or issue that informs and shapes other literary conventions such as theme and style. The theme of hospitality, for example, assumes religious characteristics in part because Capote employs a recognizable religious vocabulary. Without the dichotomy in **"A Lamp"** between Catholicism and reading literature, for instance, the reader would have a more difficult time identifying the Sermon on the Mount as the subtext that moves both the narrator and us from a scene that is as fragmented as an Edward Albee play to another that is as seamless as a novel by Jane Austen.

Capote believed that *Music for Chameleons* differed from his previous works principally through its innovative style. "I eventually developed a style," he wrote, "into which I could assimilate everything I knew about writing" (*Music,* xviii). As Jack Hicks points out, the result is an eclectic combination of literary conventions that are "parenthetical" and "reduced." "The frequent use of interrupting commas, ellipses, and dashes," writes Hicks, "illustrates [Capote's] diversionary technique: these all highlight disjointed thought rhythms undercutting plain language."[3] In *Music for Chameleons* the style reflects a polyphony of genres and texts that includes essays, diaries, stage directions, asides to the audience, and numerous other innovations. The tendency toward control that manifests itself in Capote's earlier works gives way here to unpredictability. And if one source of these changes, as Hicks maintains, is that "the role of the narrator" has been expanded "considerably," the reason that such an expanded role should lead to change is that Capote, as narrator, is far less certain of himself.[4] His authority over his text reflects nothing less than a new understanding of God's authority over creation and the ability of sacred language to undercut its "plain" counterpart. Capote illustrates the perils of that relationship as early as the second paragraph in the book. "When God hands you a gift he also hands you a whip," he writes; "and the whip is intended solely for self-flagellation" (*Music,* xi).

In a review of *The Dogs Bark* Willie Morris writes that Capote's "attention to style, to the extraordinary pull of places," is what "gives this volume . . . durability far beyond the perfunctory compendia of [its] pieces."[5] Interestingly, however, he makes this observation while reading a passage from "To Europe," are one that describes Capote's inability to feel "part of" a place. "I was not part of Europe, I never would be," he writes. "Safe, I could leave when I wanted to. . . ."[6] Because Capote uses literary style in *The Dogs Bark* to distance himself from his reader and from the drama he depicts, style in this work is treated as an element of the prose that is distinct from the experiences of writing or reading. Capote describes this model of stylistic excellence in a brief essay from the collection entitled "Style: and the Japanese." There he writes of Mr. Frederick Mariko, a Japanese florist who ran a shop in New Orleans when Capote was a boy. Mr. Mariko's creations, which extend beyond floral arrangements to a series of toys that he fashioned for Capote, provided the future writer with nothing less than "my original aesthetic experience."

Significantly, the wire fish, paper dancers and ornate flowers that Mr. Mariko fashions are experienced by Capote as creations set apart: they are "much too exquisite to be *played* with" (*Dogs,* 354-55). As such they are emblems of a style Capote prefers and tries to imitate in his prose. Like Mr. Mariko's carefully-shaped toys, Capote's essays in *The Dogs Bark* participate in a "ceremony of style, a phenomenon that seems to rotate, in a manner quite separate from emotional content" (*Dogs,* 355). These essays are in many respects dispassionate "silhouettes and souvenirs of persons and places" that constitute, according to Capote, "a prose map, a written geography of my life over the last three decades" (*Dogs,* xvi). Capote's metaphor emphasizes distance. Essays in *The Dogs Bark* form an objective map that delineates not only a specific geographical region but also a particular historical period, 1942-1972. Capote offers them to his audience as objects of study that, like their prototypes, are too exquisite to be "played with."

Capote interprets them this way as well. He announces his attitude in the initial essay when he describes the experience of re-reading his first published novel, *Other Voices, Other Rooms*: "I stood there and looked back at the boy I had left behind" (*Dogs,* 4). Compiled and presented in this format, these pieces are set apart from one another and from Capote. They seem to fit the category of "static writing" that Capote refers to in his preface. "I am not a keen reader of my own books," he writes, "what's done is done" (*Dogs,* 10). Because they do not engage him, Capote can speak only of "controlling" them, of enacting through them the "artist's principle task: to tame and shape the raw creative vision" (*Dogs,* 7). Once it is tamed and shaped, Capote understands its product as entirely "other." In these essays "*history,*" as Warner Watson says at the end of the central piece, *The Muses Are Heard,* "is fenced in" (*Dogs,* 307).

Capote dramatizes this sense of otherness through his frequent use of enclosed spaces. *The Dogs Bark* opens with references to the bedrooms in Alabama and Louisiana where he wrote *Other Voices, Other Rooms*; it closes with his efforts to answer the question: "if you had to live in just one place—without ever leaving—where would it be?" (*Dogs,* 405) In between there is the New Orleans courtyard that begins *Local Color* and the train compartment that ends that collection. There is the old house, Fontana Vecchia, Brooklyn's **"House on the Heights,"** Marlon Brando's hotel room in Kyote, Isaac Dinesen's parlor at tea-time, and the courthouse in Western Kansas that stimulates thoughts about filming *In Cold Blood.* In each case Capote crafts spaces that "contain" action, character, mood, tone. If the writing generates a sense of energy from conflict, it does so in part because of pressure from depicted environments. Like the image of Ezra Pound (in the essay that bears his name), striding back and forth on the deck of a ship bound to carry him to Italy, each one of these pieces serves as "a cage that . . . becomes life itself."

To make the "cage" seem like "life itself"—to create what he describes in his "observation" of Marilyn Monroe as a "verbal imprisonment"—requires a style that calls attention to itself by emphasizing, even celebrating, objectivity as a source of power and authority (***Dogs***, 380). One example in ***The Dogs Bark*** of such a style is the piece **"A House on the Heights,"** which Capote admired for the fact that "all the movement depends on the writing itself," on "how the sentences sound, suspend, balance, and tumble" (***Dogs***, xviii). This rather long, highly stylized reflection on Brooklyn Heights contains the following description of a group of sailors Capote sees tanning themselves on a small stretch of beach along the river.

> But the bare-footed sailors on the beach, the three I saw reclining there, profiles against the sundown, seemed mythical as mermen: more exactly, mermaids—for their hair, striped with albino streaks, was lady-length, a savage fiber falling to their shoulders; and in their ears gold rings glinted. Whether plenipotentiaries from the pearl-floored palace of Poseidon or mariners merely, Viking-tressed seamen out of the Gothic North languishing after a long and barberless voyage, they are included permanently in my memory's curio cabinet: an object to be revolved in the light that way and this, like those crystal lozenges with secretive carvings inside.
>
> (***Dogs***, 147)

The passage is typical of much writing in this and other essays from ***The Dogs Bark***, because it turns on several characteristic elements of Capote's style. For example, alliteration runs throughout the passage, most obviously in the repetition of words beginning with the letter "m" in the first sentence—mythical, mermen, more, mermaids—and the use of words that begin with "p" in sentence two: plenipotentiaries, pearl-floored palace of Poseidon, permanently. One effect of such repetition is humor, and clearly Capote intends to make light of numerous circumstances in this text. A second effect, related to the first but more basic, is that the passage calls attention to itself.

The reader notices Capote's writing here, the way his sentences sound and the way his words tumble. To notice the writing is to recognize the presence of a writer. Such a presence, however, does not imply that the author is involved in his work in ways that reflect a deep interest or passion. On the contrary, the style suggests a craftsman who shapes his prose in a very objective way. As though to reinforce that sense of stylistic objectivity, Capote deliberately describes an object here. His sailors exist in his "memory's curio cabinet," each one "an object . . . sealed inside."

In this passage Capote's style is consonant also with the way he treats religion in the book. The "distance" Capote establishes between himself and his memories invites him to depict the sailors as possessing what he calls "mythical" qualities. Androgynous figures, these sailors are both "mermen" and "mermaids." They seem to have come "Viking-tressed" from the "Gothic North," and they shall return to a sea that is described as nothing less than "the palace of Poseidon." They are portrayed humorously as gods in language that follows naturally from the highly objective style that Capote adopts. Distant from Capote, they are like the house on the Bay of Lindos that Capote writes about in "Greek Paragraphs": "all I will ever do," Capote acknowledges, "is remember it."

This particular nexus of style and religious subject matter is no accident. ***The Dogs Bark*** opens with a piece that establishes a theological paradigm for the style of all subsequent essays in the collection, and its assumptions parallel the guiding assumptions of much Biblical prose. "It is unusual," Capote writes in this opening piece, "but occasionally it happens to almost every writer that the writing of some particular story seems outer-willed and effortless; it is as though one were a secretary transcribing the words of a voice from a cloud." (***Dogs***, 7). The words provide the essay with a title and the book with perhaps its most succinct statement of Capote's tendency to treat his creation as something decidedly "other." A vehicle of God's word, he creates as if he were that word, one who spoke "another language" and embodied "a secret spiritual geography" (***Dogs***, 6).

Such a "secret" implies privileges and indicates that this text addresses questions about power in a style that enacts a very traditional theology. In it God is sovereign and necessary to human life and character, and theology serves to translate that sovereign otherness in ways that respect its essential difference from secular realms of experience. The controlling metaphor describes God as "Lord," the fundamental text is Exodus, and the subsequent theological approach is neo-orthodox, a tradition that reaches its zenith in the twentieth-century with the writings of Karl Barth.

By the time Capote publishes ***Music for Chameleons***, this religious paradigm changes in significant ways for him, and because of these changes readers encounter a very different religious style. Central to this later collection is Capote's "nonfiction account of an American crime," ***Handcarved Coffins***, and in the middle of that tale is a scene that illustrates the fundamental theological change that underwrites Capote's style. In that scene Capote and detective Jake Pepper are visiting Bob Quinn, the rancher whom Pepper suspects is responsible for a string of murders. Quinn knows that Pepper suspects him but that he has no substantial evidence; Capote is meeting Quinn for the first time and has agreed to play him in a game of chess. While Pepper and Quinn trade barbs about whether Quinn could have taken and developed photographs of his victims before their deaths, Capote ponders moves on the chessboard. "Look here, Jake," Quinn exclaims at one point. "Your friend almost has me checkmated. *Almost*. . . ." Capote then goes on to write:

> It was true; with a skill subconsciously resurrected, I had been marching my ebony army with considerable, though unwitting, competence, and had indeed managed to maneuver Quinn's king into a perilous position. In one sense I regretted my success, for Quinn was using it to divert the angle of Jake's inquiry, to revert from the suddenly sensitive topic of photography back to chess; on the other hand, I was elated—by playing flawlessly, I might now very well win. Quinn scratched his chin, his grey eyes dedicated to the religious task of rescuing his king.
>
> (*Music*, 116)

The passage compares in interesting ways with the earlier one quoted from ***The Dogs Bark***. Here too Capote uses alliteration to help the passage flow. However, with one notable exception the sounds come in pairs: "skill subconsciously," "ebony army," "managed . . . maneuver," "Quinn's king," "perilous position," "suddenly sensitive," "well win," "Quinn . . . chin," "chessboard . . . blurred." The pairings make alliteration (and therefore the passage) far less noticeable than its predecessor in ***The Dogs Bark***. Readers pay less attention to the writing as an object in and of itself and more attention to the drama, which depicts a series of divisions between Pepper and Quinn, Quinn and Capote, and, as we soon learn, between Capote and Pepper as well. The pairings therefore emphasize the importance of cohesion over sound and rhythm or melody. As Quinn, for example, seeks to reclaim his king and all it symbolizes in this struggle between innocence and guilt, alliteration heightens the drama associated with that goal.

The exception to these pairings is the alliteration between words beginning with the prefix "re" that run like a thematic string throughout the paragraph. "Resurrected," "revert," "religious," "rescuing" all appear in the paragraph and together they suggest that cohesion, which should result from some resolution to the various dramatic conflicts, involves a re-turn to another time, place, or individual. This return is "religious" because it requires that Capote "re-ligare" or "bind-back" together what he had considered dead or forgotten. This sense of the term is very different from the one that informs ***The Dogs Bark***, and Capote's two styles clarify the difference. In that earlier work Capote seemed bound to nothing, and his distance from his subjects allowed him to describe them as both mythical creatures and figures in a curio cabinet. Although the discussion of photography and the game of chess that frame the setting in ***Music*** offer Capote an ideal opportunity to once again style a very objective scene, he chooses instead to use them to begin a most personal revelation. Suddenly he is five years old and spending his summer with relatives in a small Alabama town.

> There was a river attached to this town, too; a sluggish muddy river that repelled me, for it was full of water moccasins and whiskered catfish. However, much as I disliked their ferocious snouts, I was fond of captured catfish, fried and dripping with ketchup; we had a cook who served them often. Her name was Lucy Joy, though I've seldom known a less joyous human. She was a hefty black woman, reserved, very serious; she seemed to live from Sunday to Sunday, when she sang in the choir of some pineywoods church.
>
> (*Music*, 116-17)

The flashback continues important features of the style that precedes it. There is some pairing of words through alliteration: "river . . . repelled," "water . . . whiskered," "captured . . . ketchup." The more significant pairing, however, occurs within entire sentences. Each sentence in the passage joins two separate statements; three of them denote this union with a semicolon. None of these statements seem particularly congruent when examined closely. The river he refers to in the first part of the second sentence, the Blue River that is central to ***Handcarved Coffins***, is clear and rapid (it has at least one waterfall where Addie swims); as such it is the opposite of the "sluggish muddy" and dangerous water Capote describes in the second half of the same sentence. The third sentence describes both Capote's like and dislike for catfish (as well as a basic structuralist dichotomy between the raw and the cooked). The fourth contrasts Lucy Joy's demeanor with her name while the fifth points out that she is both "reserved, very serious" and someone who is not afraid to sing out in the choir of her Pentecostal church. Only Capote's style binds these sentences together and allows readers to move easily from one to the next.

Capote describes that style in his Preface to ***Music*** in ways that help readers understand how it enacts religious ideas, themes, even language in the book. In writing ***Music***, he states that he set himself "center stage, and reconstructed, in a severe, minimal manner, commonplace conversations with everyday people. . . ." After he writes page after page of this "simpleminded" prose, he develops "a style," what he calls a "framework into which I could assimilate everything I knew about writing." According to this passage, one way to read the alliterative pairing of words that appear, for example, in ***Handcarved Coffins***, is as an expression of the pairings Capote sought as he developed his minimalist style: relationships between himself and others. Capote challenges himself to cultivate a literary style that is true to the experience of relationship. "Commonplace" and "simpleminded," the style is also, Capote goes on to say, "underwritten" and "clear as a country creek" (*Music*, xvi-xvii).

The "severity" of the pairings help to keep the style "simple," and one could equate this simplicity with naive faith in a God to whom Capote calls at the end of **"Nocturnal Turnings"** with the traditional bedtime prayer for children: "Now I lay me down to sleep . . ." (*Music*, 264). However, the pairing is deceptively simple. Stylistically, passages from *Music* tend to bring words, clauses, sentences together only to highlight the tension that threatens to force them apart. This situation applies not only to those selections from *Handcarved Coffins* discussed above, but also to other texts. Consider the following from the title story.

> Raising my eyes from the mirror's demonic shine, I notice my hostess has momentarily retreated from the terrace into her shadowy salon. A piano chord echoes, and another. Madame is toying with the same tune. Soon the music lovers assemble, chameleons scarlet, green, lavender, an audience that, lined out on the floor of the terra-cotta terrace, resembles written arrangement of musical notes. A Mozartean mosaic.
>
> (*Music*, 12)

The passage describes a group of chameleons coming together to hear piano music. Notice, however, how fragile is their bond. Not only are the creatures likely to "scatter like sparks from an exploding star" (*Music*, 4), every element of the text threatens to do the same because of the duplicity or "doubleness" that defines its references. In the first sentence, for example, Capote raises two eyes from his image or second self in the mirror, which is both demonic (dark) and shiny (light), in order to notice that his hostess, the Martinique aristocrat who entertains him during the afternoon, has moved from the light of the terrace to the shadows of the salon. From the salon she plays two chords on her piano, which gives the narrator the sense that she is "toying with" or doubling "the same tune." As a result of her music, chameleons gather ("they are very fond of music," she points out earlier) on the terra-cotta floor of the terrace. They come as an "audience" but resemble in their arrangement the music itself. They are, therefore, both a "mosaic" of listeners and the music they hear.

For a writer who has traded throughout his career in themes of doubleness—light and dark, child and adult, good and evil—the duplicity of this passage is not entirely novel. What is new in this story and this collection is precisely what Capote calls our attention to in his Preface: his attempt to embed those traditional themes, and the corresponding tensions they create, into the style of the prose. Style now provides a "framework," he writes, to contain all facets of his prose; it becomes; he says, the palette onto which he places "all his colors" (*Music*, xvii).

Conceived of in this way, style enriches content. Within this framework, the "colors" of religion—its themes, images, vocabularies—suggest certain theological premises about the relationship between God and human life, the sacred and profane. The tension between coming together and coming apart that is evident within Capote's style both reflects the pairings he dramatizes and enacts the tensions created by that drama. Through this stylistic doubling, features of the text that readers traditionally associate with religion become theologically-rich symbols.

One example of such a symbol is Blue River, which weaves throughout *Handcarved Coffins.* Jack Hicks's analysis of this river helps link that symbol to Capote's writing, thereby indicating its "double" quality. "The Blue River is a metaphor for the author's desire for historical/mythic continuity," writes Hicks, "his hope for a revivified narrative flow." Initially it is a "source of life," Hicks says, but soon it assumes qualities that are "demonic and death-dealing" as it becomes more closely associated with the demise of several characters. When it undergoes this transformation as a symbol, it helps to transform Capote's writing. Like the river, "the narrative," Hicks points out, "churns itself into broken forms, subsumes other genres, seeks power in the conflation of screenplay, confession, diary." In a simultaneous fashion, both symbol and narrative are found doubling in their textual function and meaning.[7]

Read in the light of all the religious meaning Capote invests in Blue River—the fact that it stimulates a series of flashbacks to his own forced baptism forty years earlier, performed against his will by Lucy Joy and the reverend Bobby Joe Snow, a double of Bob Quinn—the symbol begins to illuminate the theological complexity of Capote's writing in *Music.* In addition to dramatizing all that is at stake in the ritual of baptism, the complex and dangerous exchange between life and death that Saint Paul described a "dying to Christ," this central symbol in *Handcarved Coffins* suggests the doubleness of all language about God. Through narrative and symbol, and in the style he employs to join both, Capote explicates the relation of human life to "God," that word that Paul Ricouer asserts holds a "double power to gather all the significations that issue from partial discourses [uttered by humans] and to open up a horizon that escapes from the closure of discourse."[8] Moving between these two options, and therefore following a very different trajectory than the one initiated by *The Dogs Bark,* Capote seemed prepared to embrace the leper he refers to at the conclusion of **"Nocturnal Turnings,"** the one whom St. Julien kissed and discovered to be God. *Answered Prayers* is the result of that embrace, and no critical study of it has yet been written to determine if in fact Capote continued to dramatize the tension between the joy of the gift and the lash of the whip that was his—and is our—lot.

Notes

1. Truman Capote, *The Dogs Bark: Public People and Private Places,* (New York: Random House,

1973); *Music for Chameleons,* (New York: Random House, 1980). All references in the text will be to these editions.

2. Throughout this essay I use "religion" as a concept that organizes an extensive vocabulary or "lexical field." "Religion" gives us a vocabulary for describing, analyzing, and asserting the meaning of certain traditions, texts, practices, images, etc.

3. Jack Hicks, "'Fire, Fire, Fire Flowing Like a River, River, River': History and Postmodernism in Truman Capote's *Handcarved Coffins.*" In *History and Post-War Writing,* Theo D'haen and Hans Bertens, eds. (Amsterdam: Rodopi, 1990), 182.

4. Ibid., 182.

5. Willie Morris, "Capote's Muse Is Heard: *The Dogs Bark,*" *New Republic* (13 November 1973): 22.

6. Ibid.

7. Hicks, "'Fire, Fire, Fire Flowing Like a River, River, River,'" 179.

8. Paul Ricoeur, "Philosophy and Religious Language," *Journal of Religion* 54 (1974): 71-85. Reprinted in and quoted from Ricoeur, *Figuring the Sacred: Religion, Narrative and Imagination,* ed. Mark Wallace, (Minneapolis: Fortress Press), 46.

Brian Mitchell-Peters (essay date 2000)

SOURCE: Mitchell-Peters, Brian. "Camping the Gothic: Que(e)ring Sexuality in Truman Capote's *Other Voices, Other Rooms.*" *Journal of Homosexuality* 39, no. 1 (2000): 107-38.

[*In the following essay, Mitchell-Peters asserts that in* Other Voices, Other Rooms *Capote satirically undermines the gothic paradigms present in the novel while employing "aspects of Camp sensibility" to establish his queer characters and construct a hopeful ending to his story.*]

INTRODUCTION

With possible influence from the utopian "greenwood" of E. M. Forster's *Maurice,* originally written from 1913 to 1914 and first published posthumously in 1971, Truman Capote released his first novel in the late 1940s with a striking never-never land that provided an alternative to the stifling realities for homosexuality during this time. There are three settings that exist in this text: the first is a typically redneck Southern backdrop filled with the necessary types and Capote's campy satire, the second is a mysterious rundown mock-haunted castle where the adult homosexuals and/or drag queens hide, and the third is a Peter Pan-like Oz, where queer youths gather, bond, and discover their young yet very real feelings. The novel's original setting of the Southern redneck reveals the most hostile environment for homosexuality, an environment that still exists today, not only in the South but throughout the United States, as we have witnessed recently with the grotesque murder of Matthew Sheppard in the fall of 1998. The second setting the reader is introduced to has received most of the criticism to date: its gothic feel has allowed the novella to be deemed a Southern-gothic tale, although, as this article will discuss, the use of gothic themes is equally as satirical as the mock-maleness of the redneck Southern inhabitants. The setting that has received the least amount of critical investigation is Capote's unique creation of a fantasy locale. Within this fantasy location, Capote not only moves away from the types of dismal realities that are evident in Baldwin's novel and Williams's stories, but shifts the subjects of homosexuality to queer adolescents. With the real world lurking in various forms behind the carnival of life that Joel and Idabel discover, their world—the world of queer acknowledgement and arguable homosexual awakenings—marks a hope for their inherent desires. Capote's text thus marks the first modern representation of homosexuality where a character's queerness does not lead down some version of the river Styx to a contemporary Hell. Instead, Joel and Idabel flourish and reveal that their natures are definitely queer. Truman Capote's first novel illustrates influences from a number of sources to tell the revolutionary stories of its young, queer heroes. This article will explore the literary influences in this text to illustrate how Capote reconstructs a gothic setting and employs aspects of Camp sensibility to construct his unique queer characters. Unlike Capote's contemporaries—such as James Baldwin or Tennessee Williams, who portray aspects of homosexual repression, disillusionment and violence in their texts from the 1950s—Capote's early book gives a type of literary birth to two young queer and often times detectably homosexual characters. This accomplishment—which arguably fuelled the negative, often hostile criticism that surfaced after the novel was published—is a tremendous feat in pre-Stonewall American literature. Capote is rivalled by no one in the first half of the twentieth-century, and his wondrously loaded book accomplished many tasks which were not tackled in full until the 1960s and 1970s: in *Other Voices, Other Rooms* there is no Frankensteinian arrangement of master and slave, nor questionable desire and excessive abuse and related power struggle. The destructive reality of homosexual panic is not a major part of the story Capote tells. Rather, Capote's text cleverly manipulates form and characterization and creates a number of compelling queer characters.

If a Victorian murderer is queer, if cannibalism is queer, if Marilyn Manson is queer (arguably *really* queer), if

Madonna in the early 90s was queer, and if I am going to argue how two pre-teens are queer, how can one pinpoint a definition for queer? Perhaps my question is aptly responded to: queer allows for interpretative movement, and related questioning and cultural theorizing. Queer allows for a readership which isolates aspects of uncertain, odd, and sometimes gay or lesbian characters and circumstances; not always homosexual, but definitely not only heterosexual, queer challenges the binary of straight/bent to include instances of possible homosexuality, bisexuality, cross-dressing, or uncertain or bizarre, physical interactions within such a trajectory of difference. Eve Kosofsky Sedgwick argues that queer includes

> the open mesh of possibilities, gaps, overlaps, dissonances and resonances, lapses and excesses of meaning when the constituent elements of anyone's gender, of anyone's sexuality aren't made (or *can't* be made) to signify monolithically.
>
> ("Queer and Now" 8)

Aside from opening definition and representation, Sedgwick's writing is integral to a contemporary consideration of queer as it's compound object insists that gender and the idea of meaning as well as signification cannot be static. Less complicatedly, the notion of a signifier—something we can read as queer—will shift and never have precisely the same meaning in any questioned circumstance. Hence, Marilyn Manson's neo-gothic vampiress persona, Madonna in a designer suit grabbing her nonexistent yet certainly powerful phallus as she exposes a meshy black bra, as well as characters who stray away from heterosexual advances to acknowledge same-sex ones, are all examples—however different—of queer behaviour: none exhibit direct homosexual interaction, but each example is out-of-the-ordinary, and is susceptible to a queer reading and thereby a decoding of signifiers to present gay and or lesbian undertones (at least).

To explore the relationships between queer and/or homosexual representation, gothic nuances and settings, and Camp, in this article I will: (i) introduce the relationship between gothic themes and Camp as a literary technique to counter the Southern-gothic style in the text, and present the ways the reader can rethink these categories in *Other Voices, Other Rooms*; (ii) approach the criticism which followed the book's publication, questioning the focus on Southern-gothic style and homophobic discourse in such criticisms; (iii) illustrate Capote's technique of Camping gothic themes to create a queer text, and (iv) analyze the main characters in this text to solidify their queerness and emphasize their homosexual natures. The aim of this chapter is to illustrate the ways that gothic styles are undermined by Camp sensibility—Capote's specific style of reacting to the homosexual representations in literature of the late 40s and 1950s—and focus on the developments of representation and queer sexuality through the novel's important combination of these two very different yet often interlined styles of Southern-gothic and Camp to create a readably queer text.

The Gothic and Camp: Re-Thinking Genres

As discussed throughout the preceding chapters, gothic literature reacted to norms and related representations in traditional literature during the late eighteenth and early nineteenth centuries. As such, the gothic articulated the controversial issues of incest, murder, and promiscuous sexuality, and created an exciting arena for the development of the supernatural and the occult. Gothic, in short, rebelled against traditional domesticity and sentimental literature, as a writing style which embodies and develops horror and terror (Arnaud, 123). Can **Other Voices, Other Rooms** be considered as a novel which reemploys the atrocities of a nightmarish imagination? Curiously, the Signet edition's introductory page describes the book as "terrifying." It appears that the school of criticism which highlights the gothic motifs in the text is the influence which subverts Joel's sexuality through the masked label of sensitivity, and avoids Idabel's lesbianism by focusing on her as a tomboy. On the introduction feature page of the Signet edition, Skully's Landing is described as "[a] mouldering mansion[,]" as the mysterious drag queen has been interpreted as "[a] ghostly face at a curtained window." It appears that the publishers went through great pains to emphasize the gothic-like backdrop of the novel to focus on gothic motifs and similarities to overt the then-controversial issues that Capote's novel presents. As this paper shall argue, the author deliberately uses gothic themes and gay Camp style to create eccentric, queer characters who challenge the tradition of homosexual representation in contemporary American literature.

As the pre-Stonewall homosexual character has been locked in the abyss of gothic representation since Marlowe's "Edward II" and most conveniently crystallized as the pre-modern villain in Oscar Wilde's *The Picture of Dorian Gray,* Capote manipulates a neo-gothic setting to develop characters with a particularly queer consciousness, as the text moves away from the literary tradition of homosexual desire and impending death. One may wonder why Capote employs the gothic to express queer sexualities: the gothic form is habitually indulgent, imaginative, supernatural and horrific, hence in the gothic novel almost anything can happen. The gothic novel can be read with particular attention to queer sexual spaces, where unclear, or partially veiled instances of physical intimacy can be interpreted with attention to homoerotic undercurrents. Moreover, aspects of the gothic create an often suppressed homosexual character or encoded homosexual (or homosocial) relationship between a desired male character and the corruptive monster or demon. What is gothic becomes questionable and simultaneously homosexual with the theme of a double-life in Stevenson's "Dr. Jekyll and Mr. Hyde," and with the combination of Camp, the Narcissus myth, murder, and death in Wilde's *Dorian Gray*, what was questionably homosexual in the nineteenth century becomes detectably queer almost one hundred years later. Modern literary representations of homosexuality have frequently been found in texts which re-employ gothic motifs, such as Djuna Barnes's *Nightwood* or Carson McCullers's *Reflections in a Golden Eye*. In the twentieth century the gothic monster is given a more human form, in the style of Dorian Gray, as the male homosexual. Truman Capote's Southern-gothic tale of **Other Voices, Other Rooms** borrows from this intricate tradition, as he introduces a series of gothic types, themes and settings, only to dissolve Joel's spooky, late night arrival to represent the gothic into a daytime carnival of Campy aesthetics. I would like to argue that Capote was well aware of his specific mock-gothic agenda and, as this chapter shall argue, by countering gothic with Camp the author rebels against the gothic's inscription of homosexuality and death. Robert Miles suggests that part of male representation in the gothic is the value of sight and the visual, hence, "[i]n Gothic writing, desire inheres within the visual" (57-60). Capote's first novel uses the visual in a similar manner, with a distinctly different twist: in Capote's text what is excessively visual is an acute, flamboyant and flagrant series of images that bombard the reader throughout the text. As the author uses aspects of a genre which relies inherently on the visual, he manipulates gothic motifs with a style that encompasses a strong visual intensity. The Camp style of this text allows for the amusing, new type of literary representation of queer personalities. Capote distinctly reconstructs aspects of gothic style, then Camps it: he takes an already excessive and fantastic style, creates a parody of it by adding to such a style with colourful prose, and over-the-top characters. By countering and complimenting gothic nuances with Camp, Capote is able to manoeuvre a style which will enhance the intensity of his characters, further emphasizing the open boundaries of interpretation that queer theory introduces.

Capote uses a conventional late-40s genre by adopting a Southern-gothic style, and through a precise use of camp aesthetics and language he turns it queer: as the nineteenth-century gothic challenged traditional literary form with unbelievable reincarnations of the occult-supernatural, Capote rethinks his own variety of vamps, and tones down their supposedly dangerous natures through excessive camp-humour. By employing a Camp style of satire and excess, Capote unhaunts the nighttime gothic of Skully's Landing, and as day breaks the author slowly and completely creates an absolutely queer textual space that replaces the gothic nuances with a very definite gay-Camp sensibility. Over the years, many critics have argued that Camp is gay, as others have argued that it is not. Camp style is a product of a most definitely queer sensibility, where the homosexual artist adopts a genre to create a parody of another genre, thus taking away its power and strength. Capote's use of gothic motifs allows him to desensitize the focal issues of what should be gothic, and in return he focuses on his concerns: rather than murder and monsters Capote takes the fear out of the rumoured fearful inhabitants of Skully's Landing.

Through the young queer characters of Joel and Idabel the text gives birth to two adolescents who are readably homosexual. This text tells the stories of their discoveries of their own, different, and queer sexual awareness. Susan Sontag has infamously argued that Camp is not necessarily a gay style and that Camp is not political (281). As this discussion shall exhibit, Camp is a critical part of readership appreciation, and the manner in which Camp is detected, interpreted and often appropriated is definitely a gay phenomenon, although it is by no means gay male exclusive. Sontag reads Camp as "the love of the unnatural, artifice and exaggeration" (275). In **Other Voices, Other Rooms** such aspects of Camp style intersect with the gothic themes, and undermine—if not extinguish—them. Like Wilde's important literature, in Capote's text Camp expresses a political voice. As Camp is an excessive parody, and thus incorporates satire as its principal mode of humour, when one Camps something—such as a mannerism—one often ridicules a convention, especially gender typology. Hence, this chapter will have a detailed look at how Capote Camps the Gothic as a means to create a definitive satire which allows him to create the queer personalities of **Other Voices, Other Rooms**.

The Early Critics

In most pre-Stonewall criticism, Truman Capote's **Other Voices, Other Rooms** has been explored in homophobic, pop-psychoanalytic readings, which consider the text as terrifying and perverse, and the characters are more often than not examined as deviant. Many critics slander this book, as they attempt to solve the sexual mysteries of Capote's creative characters through aspects of trivial, demeaning psychology. The negative criticism which accompanied the publication of this novel is essentially a homophobic reaction, a direct result of the anti-homosexual sentiment of the late 40s and early 50s. Chester E. Eisinger clearly illustrates his own homophobic reactions to the sexual diversity in Capote's text as he argues that **Other Voices, Other Rooms** presents a "world of flight, childhood terror, estrangement and perverted love" (16). As such, Capote's intuitive and imaginative novel is not only reviewed in regard to negative approaches to the unusual characters, settings and situations, but in regard to the main characters' lack of sexual conformity. Rather than unique or revolutionary, Capote's characters are reviewed in response to theories of sexual deviance and related ideologies of perversity. I would like to counter Eisinger's argument by emphasizing that Capote's main character Joel Knox and his equally queer sidekick Idabel Tompkins are reactionary creations, marking this text's very important position in the history of gay, lesbian, and queer literature; hence the focal point for the arguments that dominate this paper. To prove Eisinger's argument is problematic, one must note that Joel journeys willingly to the text's fantastic locations of Skully's Landing and Noon City, and both Joel and Idabel do not engage in a horrified flight from either of these locales. Rather, the unprepared reader may desire flight from the issues this novel presents, as Joel and Idabel embrace these settings as the homeland of their queer adventures. Contrary to Eisinger's homophobic remarks, Joel's arrival brings an end to his possible childhood terror and presents Joel with a series of personal discoveries which take place in his new Southern setting. As well, rather than estrangement, Joel and Idabel's camaraderie demonstrates supportive friendship: with Idabel, Joel learns how to make friends with a carousel of different people, most significantly his cousin Randolph and Miss Wisteria. The relationship between these characters creates a queer camaraderie amidst the unconventional mock-gothic and Campy settings. Sadly, Eisinger is not alone, and many of Capote's early critics use the demeaning terms grotesque and perverted to describe the characters, the identities and the sexualities in this author's early writing. Although various reconstructions of the gothic genre are part of the foundation in this text (as I shall explore throughout the next section), Capote builds away from the possible reactions of trauma and horror, and presents a Southern paradise where queer sexuality, in varying forms, flourishes in abundance.

Ihab Hassan is the one exception amongst the early critics. However, his book on the contemporary American novel was released over a decade after Capote published **Other Voices, Other Rooms**. Capote was plagued with unflattering, narrow-scoped reviews and analyses for over ten years. Conservative approaches to the gothic themes, as seen in Eisinger's criticism, dominated the questioning of setting and description in Capote's early text. Moreover, his latter works **Breakfast at Tiffany's** and **In Cold Blood** remain his most famous. Capote cleverly borrowed from the mystery and suspense of classic gothic literature to create a setting which would allow for the colourful characterizations that take place throughout the text. The use of night and day, the binaries of good/evil and straight/queer are certainly themes and sub-themes crystallized in nineteenth-century English fiction. However, as the gothic and Camp themes adequately house his characters' unconventional mannerisms, both genres reveal the revolutionary sexualities in this text. Capote purposely presents aspects of unclear or partially revealed desire which can be read as queer coding: the shy-boy, the tomboy, and the drag queen all function as signifiers for sexual queerness, creating a text which depicts queer sexuality and possible homosexuality not as dismal destruction, but as a possible option. Thus, Hassan considers Capote's use of gothic themes as an "extravaganza" where the "narcissistic overestimation of the self . . . begs for allegorical interpretation" (234 & 239). Hassan explores Capote as an author who exhibits unusual characters, sexual diversity, and double-identities in a profound post-gothic genre with an excess of Campy style. Combining the gothic with a paradoxical use of humour, the author turns the scary into a carnival of the unorthodox. In line with Hassan's arguments, Capote's text is about interpretation, somewhat allegorical, perhaps metaphoric, theoretically semiotic, but most of all revolutionary: the novel's careful representation of genre, gender, identity and sexuality challenge the established representation of queer sexuality and homosexuality in literature and create a literary arena where the author can introduce and reveal a new selection of not-so-straight characters. Gothic therefore becomes a neo-gothic style, possibly even a mock-, quasi-, or partial-gothic, which moves away from the traditions of English and American gothic as it undermines the central component of fear with curiosity. Hence, the integral binary of fear/attraction that exists in nineteenth-century gothic fiction is overthrown, and what is supposed to be scary is actually rather amusing. In this new Southern-Camp-gothic, sexuality can flourish and the characters are free enough to explore some aspects of their sexual orientation.

More than Gothic

Camping the Gothic

Far too often the adaptation of gothic themes has allowed for the creation of the doomed homosexual. The night-time and the sub-cultural haunts are part of the inevitable despair and death of the queer character in pre-Stonewall fiction. Death can be read as a metaphor, a punishment and deliverance, and the process of dying or journeying towards death is part of the pre-Stonewall homosexual character's rite of passage, hence an inevitable "moral" fate. From an exploration of coded language and ambiguous sexuality in *Frankenstein* and "Dr. Jekyll and Mr. Hyde," to *Dorian Gray*, the queer character is destined to a regimented fall and an inevitable death at the end of a given text. Capote's **Other Voices, Other Rooms** portrays sometimes gay, often lesbian, and habitually queer characters without the inevitable; the author creates the birth of queer sexuality which leads his young heroes to discover their adolescent awareness. The main characters are budding teens who are different, queer, and often homosexual, and there is no attempt to explain the different personalities of Joel and Idabel, as they do not conform to typical gender representations. No matter how "unnatural" people may seem, in Capote's fiction the eccentric characters are typical. The author represents queerness as he indirectly critiques the adaptations of the gothic genre which have been used a myriad of times to express homosexuality and related destruction. Capote reconsiders particular aspects of the gothic mode through his parody of a Campy Southern-gothic style, as he frees what is queer and gives life to the homosexual discoveries of his young characters.

Over recent years a few studies have been done which move away from the condemning attitudes of the pre-Stonewall critics. Like Hassan's text, the two books by Helen S. Garson consider *Other Voices, Other Rooms* as an example of exceptional fiction. Garson's arguments focus on the novel as a piece of literary accomplishment rather than a disruptor in a conservative literary canon; *Other Voices, Other Rooms* is explored as a text which counters the conventional novel of the 1940s. Garson suggests that "Capote's novel was a piece of a new pattern in fiction, one that was described by terms such as narcissistic, grotesque, symbolic and aesthetic" (13). Like Garson, my explorations will embrace Capote's use of the grotesque and the narcissistic to highlight and de-code the text's important queer signs. Thus, my approaches are concerned with the manner in which Capote represents the grotesque, through his own combination of Gothic motifs and his use of Camp-style(s). Along with the parody of gothic themes and the advent of Camp, this paper will explore how, in his first novel, Capote's greatest accomplishment is the insubordination of gender and the expression of personal and sexual discovery for both Joel and Idabel.

Capote suggests a future of gay and lesbian identification for his protagonists through his use of gothic parody: the author builds from a tradition of representing sexuality within an unclear and partially veiled text to imply the queer natures of his heroes through their unorthodox and often eclectic behaviour. In the pages that follow, the setting of Skully's Landing will be examined with attention to gothic similarities which house the ambiguous settings for the text's queer characters. The following section will focus on how Capote recreates a gothic style of sexual representation: a little ghoulish, and basically unconventional, Capote first haunts desire, then Camps it, and creates a strange irony between what should be scary and what is humorous. The result is a type of literary birth as *Other Voices, Other Rooms* portrays the discoveries of its young and not so young queer heroes. Joel and Idabel's rites of passage are therefore both traditionally and non-traditionally American: Capote creates the search for identity within a seemingly conventional frame—the search for ancestry and the rite of passage—as the characters achieve sexual freedom through unconventional circumstances.

Since Capote playfully borrows aspects of gothic style, the contents of his first novel are often misread and the text is labelled as exclusively Southern-gothic. Of course this text is Southern-gothic historically, but with a particular flavour of its own as the author's efforts to counter his gothic style reveal a paradoxical structure, as the reader continuously shifts between gothic themes and a Camp sensibility. As the earlier critics consider this text Southern-gothic, they search for the gothic theme of good versus evil. Accordingly, the early critics associate the homosexual aspects of the text with darkness and destruction. It should be emphasized that the early critics focus on gothic oppositions of good and evil to lighten the stylistic and creative accomplishments of the Camp text, which lessen the importance of homosexual and queer representations in this late 1940s novel. Rather than approach the novel's representations of genre, gender, identity, and sexuality, the pre-Stonewall studies concentrate on (hetero)normative polar oppositions to condemn the homosexual as a psychologically unsound and deviant subject. With the combinations of gothic and Camp, the novel is bizarre, exciting and unique, especially if one considers Capote's presentation of the rite of passage, the search for identity, and the discovery of queer sexuality. The restructuring of gothic themes demonstrates Capote's rejection of trauma and destruction. Capote first introduces a gothic-type setting and possibly dark characters, then ends the ominous night with the bright sunshine of the day that follows, and the Campy journey that follows.

As one can survey in literature from Christopher Marlowe to Anne Rice, gothic themes have been used to express tragic representations of homosexuality. As Christian England deemed homosexuality a sin against God and the nation, the occult and generally nocturnal worlds of gothic fiction aided the representation of sexuality, desire and same-sex love in pre-Stonewall literature. A queer gothic, and arguably homosexual gothic, springs forth as early as Marlowe (especially if one considers themes of disillusionment, destruction and punishment) and by the end of the nineteenth century Wilde illustrates a particularly homosexual gothic in *The Picture of Dorian Gray*. By the time Capote had started to write, many writers had already established the gothic mode as a genre which plays an integral role in the representation of ambiguous physical liaisons between people of the same sex. Capote uses the gothic motifs of a midnight arrival, lurking mystery and threatening evil, however, he does not imitate or replicate in admiration. There is no Frankenstein-like doctor and his angst-ridden monster as the characters spring forth from an unconventional, night-time dream-scape to move beyond the destructive master and servant theme. Capote presents a Campy manipulation of the gothic, resulting in a particularly satirical Southern-gothic parody: rather than scary and deathly, everything and everyone is bizarre and queer. *Other Voices, Other Rooms* will not be explored as the "sadistic fantasy [or] masturbatory horror" that Leslie A. Fiedler condemned it as in the mid-nineteen-sixties, but as a revolutionary pre-Stonewall novel (135).

William Faulkner and Bram Stoker

Before exploring Capote's most important representations of queer sexuality—Joel Knox and Idabel Tompkins—I would like to clarify my interpretation of genre in *Other Voices, Other Rooms* and clearly illustrate Capote's combined use of gothic themes and Camp styles. The Southern-gothic style is the most detectable in the text; it is central to the illustrations of homosexuality. During the pre-Stonewall decades of the twentieth century, adopting a gothic style helped the homosexual writer to publish aspects of same-sex desire in more open—yet by no means out—prose texts. It is within such a study that one can read Capote's earlier writings as an "anti-realist protest," which used gothic themes to present unreal characters in an almost surreal setting or background (Fiedler 135). Hence, the backdrop to this novel, the haunted-like mansion and the night-time arrival, demonstrates a reaction to a world which would not tolerate homosexuality in contemporary fiction, especially a positive one. It is from this Southern-gothic frame that Capote easily creates unusual heroes and their equally unorthodox sexual discoveries.

As a born and raised Southerner, Capote illustrates his influence from the popular Southern-gothic mode in early twentieth-century American literature. William Faulkner should be read as an influential predecessor, particularly in response to the overwhelming power of death in *As I Lay Dying*. Specifically, Faulkner's varying narratives in this novel present the occult as a force which overrides the everyday; the voice of the dead mother initiates the journey and haunts the text. Faulkner confidently displays a series of odd characters, strange happenings and often incomprehensible dialects. In this text, Faulkner's focus is on a number of teen-aged characters, their rite of passage and their own experiences with death, disillusionment, and sexual discovery. Similar to Cash's journey and the findings that take place throughout Faulkner's story, Capote presents Joel and his search for origins, and both young characters grapple with their identities and lineage on a strange journey which reveals their true natures. Both authors write in a style of language which the reader may not completely understand, complete with dialects, accents and regional expressions. Like *As I Lay Dying*, Capote's text reveals the discovery of life and experience through an often unclear, yet creative story which only partially reveals the secret of each location and the protagonist's genealogy and personality. Moreover, in Faulkner's book, the voice of the past is the voice of the dead mother, as in *Other Voices, Other Rooms* the voice of Joel's past is the voice of a dying father: a voice the reader never hears except through the editing, slurring voice of Joel's strange cousin Randolph. The characters are brought together by the supposed death of Joel's father, Edward Sansom. In the Gothic tradition death is often a guiding force: in "Dr. Jekyll and Mr. Hyde," Jekyll's fear of death motivates the creation of his elixir—which, ironically, brings him closer to his own death and ultimately destroys him—and in *Dracula*, Lucy's death not only reveals the reality of the vampire, but unites the vampire hunters. In Capote's novel, death motivates Joel's trip to Skully's Landing, as Joel must make contact with his father and discover his past, and arguable future, before it is too late. Aside from the motif of death and the unconventional narrative, the characters demonstrate the author's influence from Faulkner as both books display a diverse collection of misfits, and a mysterious journey filled with side-stepping interludes that reveal partial (arguably symbolic) sketches of each character. Unlike Faulkner, Capote has one official narrator: an omniscient voice with direct access into the thoughts and feelings of the story's many characters. This narrative style illustrates the eccentric personalities and the queer sexualities. As such, Capote's gothic opens the rusted gate of a not so haunted Castle, and displays not the vampire or monster but, as the following sections shall argue, the queer main characters of Joel, Idabel, and cousin Randolph.

Along with the impact of Faulkner and the tradition of the Southern-gothic, the other major gothic influence of *Other Voices, Other Rooms* is Bram Stoker and *Dracula,* and the motif of the haunted castle. Like Jonathan Harker, Joel Knox is prompted to go a mysterious home, instigated by a letter, and rather than the discovery of the vampire and ominous, deadly anti-Christian blood worship, Joel finds a series of colourful vamps who help him transform his personal consciousness. In *Dracula* the reader never sees the original letter which prompts Harker to voyage to Transylvannia, and Stoker's novel is told in an epistolary format: we read a series of letters, journal entries and newspaper clippings to find out what has happened and what is happening in the life of the sinister vampire Count. In *Other Voices, Other Rooms,* Joel receives his letter from his father, which turns out to actually have been written by cousin Randolph. Joel, like Jonathan, takes a long journey into the unknown, however, no wolves howl in Joel's new landscape, as he arrives at the mock-haunted castle of Skully's Landing. As well, Joel is included in a series of secrets, surprises and realizations, and rather than sending him to recuperate in a sanitorium, Joel's exposure to the unconventional realities of the Landing allow him to embrace the odd misfits of this new world and leads him to the discovery of his sexual difference. The secrets Joel discovers are far from ominous. Joel is brought away from the clandestine mysteriousness of the night to a bizarre, queer daytime drama.

The realities of the locale and its inhabitants are revealed by a series of eccentric characters, and the reader uncovers these secrets through varying voices in the narrative, particularly when the omniscient narrative gives way to dialogue, and the characters of Randolph and Idabel speak. These characters dramatically help the telling of Joel's story, as they illustrate the Camp style of the text, disclosing the realities of the mock-Southern-gothic environments as they slowly reveal a series of unconventional sexual identities. Joel is allowed to observe the diverse behaviour of queer personalities. From this experience, Joel will soon acknowledge his own sexual orientation. Rather than the deadly gothic monster, Joel's surprise is the gender diversity and the transvestism of Randolph (and presumably Joel's ill father), and from his discoveries Joel learns about his own sexuality. As Jonathan Harker enters the world of the vampire and never is the same, Joel enters the nurturing circus freakshow of **Other Voices, Other Rooms** and discovers aspects of his identity: through his new friends, Joel becomes involved with the carnivalesque characters and learns to accept his true self.

Unlike Jonathan, who never recovers from his contact with the vampire, the changes that affect Joel are part of his evolution and mark the journey from queer to gay consciousness. Through his manipulation of the vampire Stoker demonstrates the metaphor of queer sexuality, and with the vampy characters of Randolph and Miss Wisteria Capote articulates a more open version of queer sexual liaisons. Most of all, it is the nighttime setting of Skully's Landing which allows the untraditional characters to emerge: in the gothic novel danger happens during the night, and in the spirit of midnight mystery Capote introduces the eccentricities of Skully's Landing. Rather than roaming graveyards for blood, these oddities turn out to be the drag-personas of Joel's parental figures, as well as the butch-girl personality of Joel's young counterpart, Idabel. To counter the night-time setting's relationship to *Dracula*, Capote alludes to his influence from Faulkner with the day time carnival of Southern misfits. Like Faulkner characters, Capote's creations are odd and sometimes difficult to understand. Faulkner's characters are sad victims of limited education and often intense personalities, as Joel and his friends are only partially understood because they can't articulate their true feelings. Capote only partially discloses the sexualities of his characters; readership and decoding the text is part of the consideration of queer representation in **Other Voices, Other Rooms**. Consequently, unlike Stoker or Faulkner, Capote's characters are illustrated as far less serious, although their positioning as queer, and at times homosexual, subjects is an important one in the history of the gay and lesbian novel. Hence, Capote borrows from gothic literature's creation of the unconventional setting to give birth to strange characters, and express the queer sexuality of his young heroes.

Skully's Landing

As I have indicated in the preceding paragraphs, the most pivotal Southern-gothic setting is Skully's Landing. Negative criticism denotes the name of this location as an example of death, or as John Aldridge has argued the "aborted symbolism of evil and guilt" (194). As my introduction suggests, the application of the general, vague binaries of good and evil and innocence and guilt are difficult to successfully prove since there is no presence of puritanical light in **Other Voices Other Rooms**. Skully's Landing is a setting where the "good" pole is absent, and the "evil" pole is reconstructed to portray the dark, the sinister, and the dead or the deadly, as the not-so-sinister, the eccentric and queer. Rather than absolute Southern-gothic, Capote uses parody and Camp to question his use of gothic themes. Skully's Landing can be read in a series of ways which confirm the text's ironic use of the gothic genre: (i) the Landing recreates the classic gothic locale as the haunted-type house; (ii) Capote's construction of such a space is particularly paradoxical, as he reconstructs the clandestine into a less dangerous and humorous version of the bizarre; and (iii), which is the result of one and two, Skully's Landing presents aspects of mystery without fear, and this new, arguable mock-Southern-gothic locale functions as a post-gothic closet which hides the transvestism of Joel's father and uncle, and leads the way to Joel and Idabel's queer consciousness. Accordingly, once Joel is a part of Skully's Landing, he must confront the queer sexuality and personalities of his father and uncle, as well as the queerness of the many other characters in the text. Experiencing this diversity, Joel begins his journey towards the discovery of his own queer sexuality.

Stephen Adams argues that the gothic and homosexuality share key similarities under the scornful gaze of conservative criticism, most specifically the manner in which both are part of the lurking perverse nature of Capote's narrative (56-88). I would like to suggest that although Capote wrote **Other Voices, Other Rooms** during a time when homosexuality was judged within the negative confines of Christian moralism, he creates a confident manipulation of what is gothic and who is homosexual. This text can therefore be read as rebellion against the confines of contemporary society and homosexual representation in literature. As a result, the gothic-type setting is not life threatening—but freakish—and the queer character is not abnormal or deviant, but a standard part of such an environment. The pessimism and compulsive heterosexism in the literary representation that Adams discusses is not part of Capote's first novel, since the world and the genre are parodies of other fictional worlds. However, Capote does demonstrate the entrapment of desire in sociological and cultural realities of the text's time. Much like Dracula's towering mansion—the Count's safety from the world of light—Skully's Landing provides Joel with what it provides for Randolph and Edward: an escape and a protection from the absent yet present every day, where diversity and sexuality would stimulate unjust societal treatment in the real world. This unseen world exists beyond the pages of the text. Although the Landing functions as a type of closet for the adults, it leads Joel into the freer world which the reader experiences throughout the story: in this queer pastoral where Joel and Idabel flourish.

From Queer to Gay, Lesbian, and Drag Queen

Joel

When Joel wakes up at Skully's Landing, he remembers his one and only previous visit when he felt that "the walls were alive with the tossing shadows of candleflames" (26). He remembers the Landing as strange and old, and as he looks around he recollects the supposedly ominous surroundings which welcomed him at midnight (26). As he wakes up, he thinks about how he was led through the house by Miss Amy, up the steep stairs with a "robber['s] stealth," as his guide partially revealed the pre-modern decor with the feeble light provided by her kerosene lantern (26). Capote recreates the haunted castle, although its haunts do not threaten Joel or possess any real, life endangering secret powers, like Dracula's Castle in Transylvania. The gothic style of an unknown and shadowy locale welcome Joel, not by the proprietor himself (Joel's absent father), but by a type of mock-gothic servant who shows Joel to his room at the Landing. Joel wakes up, sits in wonder, and thinks about his new home and its mysterious inhabitants: he feels no fear, although the narrator illustrates a setting which could have been perceived as haunting. What follows Joel's arrival is not a nightmare-filled sleep (like Jonathan Harker's in the early pages of *Dracula*) but a content, full sleep which he awakes from early in the afternoon (28). The supposedly menacing night almost instantaneously breaks into a warm, Southern day, and what was set up as gothic becomes carnival-like: night-time haunts give way to day time eccentricities, and lead Joel to his own self-discoveries. Capote couples aspects of gothic nuances with a Camp sensibility which simultaneously disarms the danger of the night and allows for the developments of the bright and gay day that follows. By over riding the gothic motifs of the unknown inhabitant, the haunted house, and a candle-lit midnight arrival, Capote takes the threat out of the setting of Skully's Landing and introduces the potentially frightening as both intriguing and comforting, as Joel's long, restful sleep insinuates.

Capote crosses the two different influences from the gothic and Camp by combining gothic nuances with similarities to L. Frank Baum's *The Wizard of Oz*. Baum's book is a gothic story for children, fully equipped with an evil witch, a haunted castle, and a lot of magic; moreover, Baum illustrates a battle between the forces of good over the forces of evil. Like gothic fiction, both Baum and Capote provide the reader with a new, mysterious setting, as both novels (and the Camp-cult musical that followed Baum's book) provide both the naive Dorothy and Joel with new, odd, and interesting friends, who confirm that neither Joel nor Dorothy is as odd as they think when compared to the new people they meet. The paradoxic representations of questionable danger which proceed Joel's night-time arrival are lessened with the sunny day that follows and the Campy style Capote uses to present the characters and circumstances which take place during this day. By combining gothic motifs with Camp, Capote begins to represent the sexual diversity and the queer personalities in ***Other Voices, Other Rooms***.

Like the vampires that have no need for mortal necessities of the toilet, Miss Amy informs Joel, "we haven't modern plumbing facilities. Randolph is opposed to contrivances of that sort" (28). The absence of modernity is part of Randolph's eclectic tastes, not only aligning the setting with the haunted locations of nineteenth-century fiction, but signifying Randolph's difference through his inability to conform to basic technological realities. Joel finds himself as a natural part of this strange setting, bidding Miss Amy compliment to her ghostly hair, which is striped like a skunk's: oddly, Joel informs her that he finds it to be "a *nice* colour" (29, Capote's italics). Miss Amy's skunk-like appearance signifies questionable nocturnal habits, as Joel's almost out-of-place compliment balances the gothic surrounding with an almost Campy remark. Due to the author's use of italics, the truthfulness of this compliment is to be questioned by the reader as the italics are indicators of a Campy drawl, which adds to the specifically Southern style of the Camp Capote employs. This sequence also demonstrates how Joel is not threatened by Skully's Landing and its inhabitants. Rather, Joel's ability to accept the strange world of the Landing illustrates that Joel feels at home in his new, strange surroundings, as he is also different from the conventional world.

Joel's new environment is hardly threatening, and once he awakes from his restful sleep, the Landing is illustrated as eccentric and unique. The world Capote depicts before the Landing is a type of Southern redneck environment, and Joel's interactions with the people in this setting exhibits how he is different from them—this will be explored in the following subsection. When he arrives at the Landing he feels no fear towards his stepmother or the spooky environment, and from his deep sleep he awakes. He falls into sleep, emphasized as sleep comes to him by "falling . . . falling . . . FALLING!" (25). Aside from denoting a type of dream-like unconsciousness, the emphasis on falling illustrates that Joel falls from somewhere else, a place which is presumably more conventional. Like Dorothy who falls from a Kansas farm to a colourful world of music and danger, Joel finds himself in a freer setting once he awakes in Skully's Landing. Capote brings on the light of day by sighting an imaginary, unexplained "crocodile [which] exploded in sunshine" (25). I would like to read this part of the text as deliberately symbolic, and consider the exploding crocodile the destruction of a monstrous threat, alleviated with the arrival of sunshine. The crocodile's fate in the daylight is much like the vampire, who burns up in an immediate gust of fire when faced with arrival of the sun. In *Other Voices, Other Rooms* what is threatening is put to rest with the arrival of daylight, as the Southern-gothic surroundings give way to the Campy, queer day that lies ahead. Ironically, Randolph and Edward are paralleled to the vampire, and like the crocodile who explodes in the sunshine, they are confined to Skully's Landing during the day. In return, for isolated, brief moments, they show their feminine personalities during the evening's interludes. Joel is led away from the Landing during the day, principally by Idabel, and the day reveals a collection of queer characters, as the night partially exposes the drag personas of Joel's uncle (as well as his father). Like the crocodile, the possible threat of this new landing is put to rest, as Joel's new home poses no threat as the new, sunny day brings him closer to his self-discovery.

As the novel unfolds, it is apparent that Joel is both mystified and captivated by the secrets of the Landing. Capote's mock-gothic is embraced by the main characters, and thereby emphasizes the relationship between Southern-gothic and satire. Joel does not try to flee from or battle the vampy characters in this surrounding, but he is caught in a spell by them, fascinated and entranced. Skully's Landing, cousin Randolph and Idabel teach Joel how to settle in, how to feel at ease, even in front of odd or seemingly terrifying things. As the novel progresses, it becomes clear that Randolph and Idabel teach Joel to not only embrace queerness, but to not feel estranged. By combining gothic nuances with a definite Camp style, Capote emphasizes a liaison between his characters and a queer interpretation: the queer characters are part of an unclear, only partially exposed narrative which can only become more clear as the text progresses.

When Joel wakes from his deep slumber, a magical rite of passage begins as Joel meets a variety of different people. As *The Wizard of Oz* tells the story of four people and their personal triumphs, **Other Voices, Other Rooms** tells the story of a similar search. In *Dracula*, when Jonathan recovers in the European convalescent home, Mina brings him home, and when they return to England nothing is the same. Jonathan has been touched by the sexual unconscious of the vampire sisters, as Joel has been touched by the sexual inversion of the Drag Queen "sisters," which causes him to evolve past gender restrictions to discover his queerness. Joel too will never be the same after his visit to his father's, but his haven is antithetical to the hell that Jonathan, like most gothic heroes, must go through. When Joel wakes, Miss Amy, Randolph and Idabel—who are certainly more like Dorothy's friends in Oz than the vampire sisters of subconscious desire in *Dracula*—show him a world which changes him dramatically.

With Joel, Capote presents a queer adolescent protagonist younger than Dorian Gray and a little older than Dorothy. By creating a character as an almost child and not quite adult, Capote avoids confronting the more complex issues of sexuality and identity which Randolph's sexuality and cross-dressing embodies. Instead, like Idabel, Joel's characterization is about identity and a rebellion against fixed gender norms. Throughout the text, Capote overthrows all gender restrictions as he destructs the limitations of specifically masculine or feminine character traits. The circus of outlandish characters not only represent an unconventional world but they all emphasize the difference which is at the centre of Joel's characterization: all of these characters embody traits, either physical or part of their personality, which articulate gender insubordination, gender inversion, and/or queer desire. Thus, each character's difference(s) can be read as signifiers for their queer sexuality, and, in the case of Joel, his homosexuality.

The excitement Joel feels to the many diverse personalities and queer personas—such as Miss Wisteria, Miss Roberta and cousin Randolph—lead to the awakening of his own sexual awareness. Rather than sexual interaction and possible interpretations of physical intimacy, Capote expresses sexual awakening through the development of adolescent behaviour. Consequently, through the people he meets, Joel learns to accept the sexual insubordination of his new surroundings, as he slowly begins to express his own queerness. I emphasize the idea of consciousness or personal awakening as a coming of age and a crucial part of homosexual representation in this text because Joel's realizations come about through exposure to the queer gender rebelliousness of Idabel and Randolph, rather than a homosexual love affair with another character. Consequently, Joel's discovery is a queer-sexual awakening, rather than sexual experience. Joel acknowledges his new friends' queerness as he slowly begins to discover himself. Capote's most important contribution to pre-Stonewall literature is his characters' flamboyant, colourful personas, and how Joel learns tolerance and self-acceptance through his interaction with the wide variety of eclectic and often readably queer people. The characters in this revolutionary text demonstrate that gender typology has no bearing on the queer consciousness that Capote illustrates; as the title implies, the sexual Other is very different from prescribed visions of masculine or feminine gender restrictions. As a result, Joel has the chance to re-think what society has prescribed for him as a young man, and by identifying with the queer personalities of his new friends and family, Joel has the opportunity to embrace his own sexuality in a more open environment.

IDABEL

As the previous sub-section has illustrated, two principal story lines (and their related shorter plots) are part of the portrayal of Joel's coming of age: (i) his experiences with Idabel Tompkins, and (ii) his cousin Randolph (to be discussed in the next sub-section). Idabel's place in the text serves a faux-heterosexual story line, where the traditional reader is fooled by Joel's interest in Idabel. This is not to say that Joel has no legitimate feelings for Idabel; however, his feelings need to be considered within the concerns of this reading. Idabel may fill the gap of supposed crush for Joel, but as Capote reveals and as I shall argue, Idabel functions as a signifier for queer identification, for both herself and for Joel. As tomboy she breaks free from the stereotypical limitations of the little girl, and discovers her own sexuality. This is critical for Joel; with Idabel Joel witnesses first-hand homosexual identification, love, and coupling, as portrayed through Idabel's liaison with Miss Wisteria. Joel does not trail behind Idabel with a secret romantic interest, but identifies and bonds with her as a homosexual counterpart. Capote makes this clear when Joel first sees Idabel:

> The skinny girl with the fiery, chopped-off red hair swaggered inside, and stopped dead still, her face was flat, and rather impertinent; a network of big ugly freckles spanned her nose. Her eyes, squinty and bright green, moved swiftly from face to face, but showed no sign of recognition; they paused a cool instant on Joel, then travelled elsewhere.
>
> (18)

It seems highly unlikely that the above description is meant to imply any sexual fascination with Idabel. Rather, Joel focuses on Idabel's non-conventional appearance, specifically the way her presentation is very different from a conservative description of an adolescent girl. The attention given to Idabel's gender difference and the strength of her demeanour signifies Joel's attraction to her, and represents Joel's desire to establish a friendship with someone like himself. Capote places particular emphasis on Idabel's boyishness to counter Joel's girlishness. Joel instantly recognizes this gender insubordination. Subtly, yet clearly, the author creates an association between these young characters and the common queer-kinship that links them.

Idabel is portrayed as not attractive in a traditionally girlish manner, and like Joel she shares a type of androgyny. Her description is the counterpart to Joel's appearance. Like Idabel, Joel has been perceived as a queer boy by Radclif, the redneck truck driver. This happens when Joel first arrives in Noon City and is searching for his father's mysterious abode:

> He [Radclif] eyed the boy over the rim of his beer glass, not caring much for the looks of him. He had his notions of what a "real" boy should look like, and this kid some-how offended them. He was too pretty, too delicate and fairskinned; each of his features was shaped with a sensitive accuracy, and a girlish tenderness softened his eyes, which were brown and very large.
>
> (6)

Like Idabel, Joel's description is emphasized through the impression he makes on the other people of the town, specifically the androgynous qualities of his appearance. His lack of gender conventions and the absence of specifically masculine traits are like Idabel's absence of exclusively feminine characteristics. Both Idabel and Joel embody both forms of opposite gender conventions, from Joel's girlish completion and gaze, to Idabel's boyish hair and stance. Capote specifically marks these characters' queerness through the series of visible traits, which signify their homosexual natures. Capote creates the principal characters of **Other Voices, Other Rooms** as reactions to gender norms, and Idabel and Joel's lack of traditional gender traits are important literary accomplishments. The confident gender rebelliousness of these characters and the homosexual natures which are subsequently disclosed is not done on a regular basis until the 1960's: with the exception of Capote, major American writers, such as James Baldwin, Gore Vidal and Tennessee Williams, have employed gothic motifs to represent the homosexual as a dangerous, fatally destined contemporary monster. Not until the 1960s would another major author confidently portray young homosexuals with the open, creative style that Capote does in 1948. In this text, the naturalness of Idabel and Joel's own gender differences challenge conventional gender norms. The pairing together of these two should not be read as a type of freaky romantic liaison, rather, Idabel and Joel's friendship illustrates the mutual attraction between sexual others and their ability to gather personal strength in the company of one another. As a modern, Southern American approach to gender inversion, Idabel is similar to Radclyffe Hall's Stephen Gordon from *The Well of Loneliness,* as Joel is a version of a young Dorian Gray. Capote thus borrows not only from traditional nineteenth-century gothic tales, but, his principal characters echo the very queer constructions of Hall and Wilde, characters and stories that crystallized queer representations until the 1960s. Most of all, Capote's characters live in a much freer and more colourful environment than either of their English ancestors.

Capote introduces his commentary on traditionally masculinist typology through Joel's early interactions with Radclif the truck driver. As Joel and Radclif get acquainted, "Joel imagined a queerness in the driver's tone" (11). Capote's text instantly signifies that either Joel's perception of Radclif or the driver himself is queer. Moreover, Joel's consequence for not being boyish enough and for desiring the mysterious Landing and its implications comes from the aggressive Radclif, fully equipped with sexual undertones: "Yessir, if I was your Pa I'd take down your britches and muss you up a bit" (8). To compliment Capote's use of parody, the butch behaviour of his characterization of Radclif comes across as equally strange, satirical, and queer. The author displays the excessive unnaturalness of extreme masculinity; to emphasize this critique, Radclif's comment signifies a satiric hint of pederastic, homoerotic "punishment." What is supposed to be straight is seemingly not, as this sequence introduces and foreshadows the queerness to come.

In the spirit of reversing traditional gender roles, it is not Radclif but Idabel who musses Joel up, a little later on in the story. This takes place during Joel and Idabel's outing to the bathing pond, a sequence which marks the signalling moment of their homosexual natures: Joel tries to kiss Idabel, and winds up in a fight with her. The sequence begins with Idabel washing Joel's hair, "without clothes," and to Joel "her figure was, if anything, more boyish" (133). Even though Idabel is a girl, Capote plays with undercurrents of male-male erotics through a description of Idabel which marks her form and her mannerisms as conventionally boyish. Idabel proceeds to tell a joke, one Joel has to inquire about as he can not understand the meaning, and Joel feels that Idabel "was imitating someone" (134) and asks her who. She tells him her masculine model is "Billy Bob." Along with Idabel's boyish physique, she reveals her masculine prototype, someone she attempts to manner herself after. Idabel then tells Joel about her softer side, that she does cry, but instructs Joel not to tell anyone. Joel feels close to Idabel, understands a kinship has formed and thinks, "I am your good true friend," but instead of saying it he "kissed her cheek" (134). Opposed to stating his appreciation towards Idabel, Joel conveys his feelings in a more traditionally feminine exchange of a friendship kiss, which Idabel reacts against with more of her little-boy angst. Idabel grabs Joel by the hair and they begin to fight:

> The dark glasses fell off, and Joel, falling back, felt them crush beneath and cut his buttocks.

> "Stop," he panted, "please stop, I'm bleeding."

(75,76)

As Joel assumes a submissive position to Idabel and gives up, she ends the confrontation and cleans out his cut as she states rather flatly, "You'll be alright" (76). Joel passively apologizes about breaking the glasses and Idabel replies, "It's not your fault [. . .] Maybe someday I'll win another pair" (76). Strangely, Joel's first "sexual encounter" is part of his coming of age and results with his bloody buttocks; Capote is making a crude-Campy mockery of the loss of gay male innocence. As well, the gender conventions are aptly established as Idabel states how she "won" her glasses, much like a boy would at a fair.

What Capote manoeuvres in this section is a very careful and clever manipulation of gender-role play. The traditionally fixed binary categories of masculine and feminine are overthrown with these diverse heroes, as stereotypically aggressive and passive roles alternate: what is considered as masculine behaviour is attributed to Idabel and what is deemed feminine is executed through Joel. Joel is sentimental, he thinks about his devotion to Idabel and finally summons up enough courage to compliment her with a light kiss. Rather than asking what the kiss was for, she presumes it is her cue to rough Joel up, and does. Capote highlights Joel's bloody buttocks as a mocking gesture towards virginity or purity, something Idabel taints with her aggressive physical interaction. Capote makes abrupt statements on gender boundaries through the representation of boy and girl, as he mocks heterosexual courtship and physical violation. By reversing the gender roles, Capote demonstrates the difficulties with regimented constructions of male and female, and the complexities that these limited gender norms initiate in a homosexual rite of passage. Through Idabel and Joel, Capote illustrates how gender typology just doesn't work, and how heterosexist restrictions have no place between these characters. The author ridicules gender roles through Camp, where excess, absurdity, and humour overthrow what is supposedly fixed and unchangeable.

The Campy descriptions of physical appearances and related personalities can be read as a well thought-out reaction to the limitations of conventional gender representation. Capote's carnival of characters have distinct physical attributes and mannerisms which emphasize post-gothic grotesqueness with a humorous Camp excess: introduced as lurking night-time figures, the text reveals that the sea of misfits are far from dangerous. Moreover, the Camping of the gothic and the subsequent characterizations in this text exhibit the queer personalities and allows the author to further develop certain characters—principally Joel and Idabel—as lesbian and gay. The distortion of the physical appearances and the excessive mannerisms is Capote's particular Camp sensibility. Through his Campy style, Capote emphasizes the sexual diversity of his characters, thus marking the pre-Stonewall political consciousness of the text.

Capote introduces lesbian rivalry through Miss Roberta's scornful approach to Idabel. Roberta is very masculine, introduced early in the text with mannish movements and "dark fuzz" covering her arms (16). She is always furious with Idabel. Towards the end of the novel Capote further mocks her physical appearance when she kicks Joel and Idabel out of her diner. The author describes Roberta, "toying with the long black hair extending from her chin-wart [. . .] scratching under her armpits like a baboon" (105). Capote draws particular attention to Roberta's unusual behaviour and appearance not to simply poke fun at her, but to demonstrate that Roberta has no shame in regard to her un*lady*like appearance. Moreover, the descriptive insult—her ape-like conduct—is also a signifier of primal desires: she is un-evolved, she can embrace the instinctual and as such her hostility towards Idabel can be read as her own, internalized homophobia. **Other Voices, Other Rooms** does not try to explain or excuse gender insubordination. Rather, this text embraces gender difference and exhibits its queer personalities with confidence.

What happens after the scene when Idabel and Joel have their fight is the disclosure of Idabel's sexuality. Capote demonstrates this through her attraction to Miss Wisteria. When Joel and Idabel leave the diner they go to the fairgrounds and meet Miss Wisteria. Joel asks Miss Wisteria to join him and Idabel for soda, Miss Wisteria replies with a whole lot of Southern Camp, as the author emphasizes as she lisps (rather than declares), "Well, this is surely a treat" (106). As Miss Wisteria takes out her lipstick to freshen-up her appearance, we find out that the treat isn't just for Miss Wisteria. Curiously, "a queer thing" happens to Idabel:

> borrowing the lipstick, [Idabel] painted an awkward clownish line across her mouth, and Miss Wisteria, clapping her little hands, shrieked with a kind of sassy pleasure. Idabel met this merriment with a dumb adoring smile. Joel could not understand what had taken her. Unless it was that the Midget had cast a spell. But as she continued to fawn over tiny yellow-haired Ms Wisteria it came to him that Idabel was in love.
>
> (106, 107)

For Idabel, Miss Wisteria is as a type of good lesbian witch who "had cast a spell" on Idabel (107). This spell is successful since Idabel has been queer all along; the type of spell which ignites her homosexual desire is triggered by the outlandish, overdone Camp charm of Miss Wisteria. As the mysterious spell results with Idabel's lesbian desire she crosses the threshold between little girl and adolescent: as her appearance is never girlish—even with lipstick—her desires are never heterosexual. It takes the bizarre, Campy, and strangely glamorous Miss Wisteria to inflame Idabel's passions. Once the spell has been cast, Idabel is sent into a tranquil state of delirious love (107). Unlike Joel's attempt to kiss Idabel, there is no hostile approach to Miss Wisteria, and contrary to her previous characterization, Idabel has become sheepish under Miss Wisteria's spell. Throughout this section Miss Wisteria repeats "charmed" a number of times, and indeed, Idabel is charmed. However, through this sequence something happens to Joel, and Capote makes an interesting comment on Joel's sexual identity as well. Although Joel wants Idabel to come back to him, thinking "I love you" (108), he does nothing about this urge, and, for a brief moment he finds himself the subject of Miss Wisteria's desire, something he does not react to. Consequently, Miss Wisteria not only demonstrates Idabel's lesbian desire, but through Joel's rejection of her advances the text implies Joel's sexual orientation.

Cousin Randolph

Once Joel witnesses Idabel's crush on Miss Wisteria he flees to Skully's Landing in search of his eclectic cousin Randolph and the mysterious Lady: who is, presumably, Randolph and/or Edward in drag. Through Joel's interaction with Randolph, Capote demonstrates Joel's liaison to his cousin, gesturing towards Joel's own homosexual nature. Although one can argue that Joel is queer throughout the text, his queerness and the possibilities of his latter homosexuality is confirmed by cousin Randolph, as the novel ends. The many adventure-like story lines can be read as Idabel and Joel's coming of age, and due to their young ages, each of these characters establishes their sexual identity through a queer adult. As Idabel's lesbian awakening takes place through her attraction towards Miss Wisteria, Joel's sexuality is confirmed at the end of the text with his cousin Randolph. Throughout the story his friendship with his cousin signifies his sexual orientation: in an early scene when Joel and Randolph are in the privacy of Randolph's boudoir, the narrator explains how puzzled Joel is with the mysteries of the Lady in the window. What "she" means and who she is, as the author also demonstrates, is cleverly manipulated through Randolph's ambiguous response (or lack of response) to Joel's questions. Joel asks Randolph, "I saw that Lady, and she was real, wasn't she?" Randolph replies with "his loose kimono swaying about him"; "[a] matter of viewpoint, I suppose" (52). These words are some of the most striking words in the text, for as much of the criticism has revealed, viewpoint has a lot to do with reading this novel. The early critics label this book gothic and "terrifying"; however, **Other Voices, Other Rooms** is hardly scary, as the text mocks style, language, and human behaviour to illustrate diverse sexual awakenings. Through the intensity of Capote's Camp style, readership dictates viewpoint, as well as interpretation; to the unwilling reader Joel may not be that queer, and certainly not gay, and Skully's Landing might somehow be frightening, the Lady in the window with the kimono and the yellow wig may indeed be a "ghost" (52). However, to the inquisitive reader Joel has to be queer, the Landing can't be anything but a Camp parody, and, accordingly, the "lady" in the window must be Edward Samson in drag (52).

Rather than absolutely homosexual, I would like to emphasize Joel's queerness is a signifier of his still developing homosexuality. Joel's lack of typical boyish mannerisms coupled with his fascination with Randolph and the mysterious lady of Skully's Landing allow for Joel (and the text) to be read as queer: by queer I am implying that many aspects of this book are simply not straight, and like the unknown lady, sexuality is in disguise. As such, the uncertainties of this text are subject to readings which explore homosexual themes. It seems harder to say that Joel is gay all the time, but it is a little more accommodating to focus on Joel as different, as queer, and, in my consideration, as a young homosexual. When Joel wakes up during the last morning of the text, the narrator exclaims that Joel "was in love" (2-26). However, the reader is never privileged with the subject of Joel's love. "He hugged himself," writes Capote, confirming that Joel has found happiness in the drag house of his cousin and absent father (125). Unlike Idabel who falls in love with Miss Wisteria, we do not know who Joel is in love with: maybe Randolph or perhaps Joel is in love with his own self, alive and awake, celebrating himself in a Whitman-like manner, or a type of narcissistic self-fascination.

Although Joel has finally accepted Randolph, Capote advises the reader that Randolph will have "no part of him [Joel]" (125). Randolph's affections for Joel are consistently ambiguous. Perhaps the above reference is meant to imply that Randolph will not turn Joel into a Baroque lady, that Randolph will not seduce Joel, and transform him into a drag queen. Nonetheless, and perhaps most importantly, Randolph's double identity complicates Joel's position and his sexual awakening. Randolph and Joel have different types of sexualities, although both are presumably queer. Due to the evasive and illusive language of the last pages of *Other Voices, Other Rooms,* pinpointing what exactly happens (and what will happen) to Joel is difficult. However, it appears that this mysteriousness is part of Capote's narrative technique: through the ambiguity of the mysterious Lady, the absent father, and Randolph's strange mannerisms, Capote draws a differential separation between Randolph's queer transvestism and Joel's homosexuality. In Randolph Joel does not necessarily find a homosexual big brother. As Capote demonstrates through Joel's comfort in his new home and his relationship with his cousin, it appears that in Randolph and the mysterious Lady (Randolph and/or Edward in disguise) Joel finds a subject of Diva admiration. As such, Randolph represents a moment in the contemporary homosexual's rite of passage and the subject of gay fascination is found in a thrilling, glamorous, mysterious and often pathetic woman.

More than experienced friend, Randolph can be read as Joel's Louise Brooks, his Marlene Dietrich, his Joan Crawford, his Marilyn Monroe, his Liza Minelli, or his Madonna. Therefore, Capote gives birth to the discovery of homosexual identity, rather than the tradition in pre-Stonewall fiction which almost predestines the discovery of homosexuality with despair or death. Capote implies an interesting comment on homosexuality in the twentieth century: the male homosexuality is not only played out through sexual discovery but at times through the admiration of the gendered performances of the fabulous and glamorous (wo)man.

"I am me," says Joel to Randolph, "we are the same people" (125). Randolph has no response, and instead walks in circles as though he "were in a trance of some kind" (227).

> And Joel realized then the truth; he saw how helpless Randolph was: more paralyzed than Mr. Sansom, more childlike than Miss Wisteria, what else could he do, once outside and alone, but describe a circle, the zero of his nothingness?
>
> (125)

In the text's style of partially disclosed homosexuality the narrative further demonstrates its paradoxical nature: if Joel is happy with himself, a self which is reflective of his cousin, why is Randolph in a gloomy state and why does Joel consider Randolph a zero? This point is responded to when Amy arrives, furious with Randolph, but, of course, not stating why. Arguably, Amy considers the relationship between Randolph and Joel as the development of cross-dressing identification, something she obviously scorns. Amy wants "the truth" to be known (126) and she plans to do anything to reveal the truth. Her threats are severe and hysterical, "I'll go to the sheriff, I'll travel around the country, I'll make speeches" (126). And what will such tactics resolve, wonders the puzzled reader, what would the flaky Miss Amy tell the Sheriff and how would her complaints be interpreted? Does Capote respond to any of the mysteries he introduces throughout the text? In response to Idabel, Capote reveals a lot more than with Joel and his absent father. However, with Joel, our answers must be derived from the complex, illusive language: the evasive, suggestive language hints at interpretative solutions, attracting a particular reading by a specific audience who can read between the lines and come up with a queer theory about Joel's journey.

Concluding Thoughts

The novel, rather appropriately, does not have a conventional—hence final—ending; it is up to the reader to isolate, speculate and question, and arrive at only partial responses. As well, both Joel and Idabel identify with a queer adult, but neither receive support. Miss Wisteria and cousin Randolph remain distant from their young proteges. Nonetheless, in **Other Voices, Other Rooms** the homosexual characters live and there is no dark, sinister, morally conscious death or killing. Through this text, Capote gives birth to queer representation, related homosexual themes and homosexual developments: the author thereby demonstrates his reaction to the typecasted melo-traumas of his contemporary portrayals of homosexuality in literature. Throughout this novel Capote plays with ambiguity, illustrating a lack of specificity in the queer, homosexual, and drag-like personalities. As Idabel Tompkins is most definitely a young lesbian, Joel Knox is just as different, certainly queer, and for the correct audience, a little homosexual and possibly a soon to be drag queen.

Bibliography

Adams, Stephen. *The Homosexual as Hero in Contemporary Fiction.* New York: Barnes & Noble Books/Harper & Row, Publishers, Inc., 1980.

Austin, Roger. *Playing the Game: the Homosexual Novel in America.* Indianapolis/New York: The Bobbs-Merrill Company, Inc., 1977.

Aldridge, John W. *After the Lost Generation: A Critical Study of the Writers of Two Wars.* New York: The Noonday Press, 1951, 1958.

Arnaud, Pierre. "The Gothic Novel." *A Handbook to English Romanticism.* Jean Raimond & J. R. Watson (Eds). New York: St. Martin's Press, 1992.

Baum, L. Frank. *The Wonderful Wizard of Oz.* New York: Dover Publications, 1960.

Baym, Nina, et al, eds. *The Norton Anthology of American Literature,* Second Edition, Volume 2. New York & London: W.W. Norton & Company, 1979,1985.

Capote, Truman, *Other Voices, Other Rooms.* New York: Signet Books, 1948.

Craft, Christopher. *Another Kind of Love.* Berkeley: University of California Press, 1994.

Craft, Christopher. "'Kiss me With Those Red Lips': Gender Inversion in Bram Stoker's *Dracula,*" *Representations,* Fall 8 (1984).

Dyer, Richard. "Children of the Night: Vampirism and Homosexuality, Homosexuality as Vampirism." *Sweet Dreams: Sexuality, Gender & Popular Fiction,* Susannah Radstone (ed). London: Lawrence & Withart, 1988.

Eisinger, Chester E. *Fiction of the Forties.* Chicago & London: The University of Chicago Press, 1963, 1965.

Fiedler, Leslie A. *Love and Death in the American Novel.* New York, Stein and Day, Publishers, 1966.

Faulkner, William. *As I Lay Dying.* 1930. New York: Vintage International, Random House, Inc., 1990.

Garson, Helen S. *Truman Capote.* New York: Fredrick Ungar Publishing Co., 1980.

Garson, Helen S. *Truman Capote: A Study of the Short Fiction.* New York: Twayne Publishers, 1992.

Hassan, Ihad. *Radical Innocence: Studies in the Contemporary American Novel.* New Jersey: Princeton University Press, 1961.

Miles, Robert. "The Hygenic Self: Gender in the Gothic." *Gothic Writing 1750-1820: A Geneology.* London: Routledge, 1993.

Oates, Joyce Carol. "Dracula: the Vampire's Secret." *Southwest Review,* 76.4 (1991).

Pick, Daniel. "'Terrors of the Night': *Dracula* & 'Degeneration' in the Late 19th Century." *Critical Quarterly,* Winter 30.4 (1988).

Reed, Kenneth T. *Truman Capote.* Boston: Twayne Publishers/G.K. Hall & Co., 1981.

Sontag, Susan. *Against Interpretation and Other Essays.* New York: Farrar, Straus & Giroux, 1966.

Stoker, Bram. *Dracula.* 1897. Oxford & New York: Oxford University Press, 1991.

Tracy, Robert. "Loving You All Ways: Vamps, Vampires, Necrophiles and Necrophiles in 19th Century Fiction." *Sex and Death in Victorian Literature,* Regina Barreca (ed). Bloomingon, Indiana: Indiana University Press, 1990.

Tison Pugh (essay date fall 2002)

SOURCE: Pugh, Tison. "Capote's *Breakfast at Tiffany's.*" *The Explicator* 61, no. 1 (fall 2002): 51-3.

[*In the following essay, Pugh identifies and underscores the importance of homosexuality in Capote's* Breakfast at Tiffany's.]

The predominant heterosexuality of Holly Golightly's lifestyle has eclipsed the queer thematics of Truman Capote's **Breakfast at Tiffany's,** and thus the subtle homosexual presence in the novella has gone unnoticed by many scholars. To overlook the queer aspects of Holly Golightly's world is to miss key moments of the text that provide a better understanding of the novella's sexual dynamics.

Foremost, Capote describes Holly's two closest friends—the narrator and Joe Bell—as homosexuals, though he does so with such a delicate touch that many critics have failed to recognize these characters as gay. The first clue to the narrator's homosexuality lies in Holly's formulation of how to determine if a man is gay: "If a man doesn't like baseball, then he must like horses, and if he doesn't like either of them, well, I'm in trouble anyway: he don't like girls" (38). These words resonate in the reader's mind when the narrator reports the contents of Holly's bookshelves ("of the books there, more than half were about horses, the rest baseball") and then feigns interest in horses: "Pretending an interest in *Horseflesh and How to Tell It* gave me sufficiently private opportunity for sizing Holly's friends" (35). If this passage fails to convince us that the narrator holds no interest in horses and, therefore, no interest in heterosexuality, the episode when Holly takes him horseback riding, to disastrous effect, also figures him as a homosexual under her horse/baseball rubric.

Second, when Holly tells the narrator that she will not testify against Sally Tomato, she calls the narrator a name laden with queer meaning: "Well, I may be rotten to the core, Maude, *but*: testify against a friend I will not" (102-03). In homosexual slang, "maude" signifies a male prostitute or a male homosexual (*Dictionary of Slang and Unconventional English*). Third, the narrator himself makes a veiled reference to his homosexuality when he compares his rain-soaked trip from Holly's apartment to Joe Bell's bar to another difficult journey he had made years ago: "Never mind why, but once I walked from New Orleans to Nancy's Landing, Mississippi, just under five hundred miles. It was a lighthearted lark compared to the journey to Joe Bell's bar" (105). Nancy's Landing is Capote's creation; it does not exist geographically. According to *A Dictionary of the Underworld*, "Nancy" refers either to the posterior or to "an effeminate man, especially a passive homosexual." "Nancy's Landing," then serves as Capote's code phrase for a gay resort, a make-believe, southern Fire Island or Provincetown. Thus, the narrator's coy rejoinder that the reader should "[n]ever mind why" he made the trip appears as a subtle move to direct attention away from his self-confession.

We perceive a hint of Joe Bell's homosexuality in the list of his passions; he enjoys, in addition to hockey players and Weimaraner dogs, "Our Gal Sunday (a soap serial he had listened to for fifteen years), and Gilbert and Sullivan," both of which indicate less stereotypically masculine aspects to his character. Capote develops the reference to Gilbert and Sullivan further, noting that "[Bell] claims to be related to one or the other, I can't remember which" (4). Since Sullivan is rumored to have been a homosexual because of the many coded references to sexual partners in his diaries, the passage slyly hints that the bartender is part of Sullivan's "family," a fellow gay man to his beloved composer. One could, of course, argue that, because Capote does not specifically state to which composer Joe Bell is related, he could be "related" to the heterosexual Gilbert. Such an interpretation, however, would have to ignore a final touch of Capote's characterization of Joe Bell that emphasizes the bartender's feminine qualities: he "arranges with matronly care" the flowers at the bar (5).

Descriptions of Joe Bell's bar also subtly hint that it is a gay bar: its anonymity suggests that it is hidden from general view; the narrator remarks that it has no neon sign to attract attention to itself (5). Gay bars did not advertise themselves as such in the 1950s, and patrons had to learn about their locations through word of mouth. Furthermore, the narrator mentions that the windows of the bar are mirrors (5). Mirror windows allow patrons to see outside but do not allow passersby to look in; to this day many gay bars have such mirror windows to protect the privacy of their patrons. Though we see very few customers inside the bar besides Holly and the narrator, two men enter together when the narrator prepares to leave after conversing with Joe Bell (10).

Critics have long recognized that Holly's friendships with the narrator and Joe Bell are asexual, but it is imperative to note the queer reasons for the platonic nature of these relationships. Thus, we can see that Holly's friendships with gay men are one sign of her progressive sexual politics. Indeed, Holly's words to the narrator about gay marriage remain topical today: "A person ought to be able to marry men or women or—listen, if you came to me and said you wanted to hitch up with Man o' War, I'd respect your feeling. No, I'm serious. Love should be allowed" (83). (A possible irony: under Holly's rubric of sexuality, in which love of horses indicates heterosexuality, would the narrator be straight if he loved Man o' War?)

Holly Golightly's queer world marks her as a participant in the sexual struggle against conformity and conservatism, rather than as merely a lovely young innocent who inspires protective and paternal love. And Capote makes it clear that she leaves a queer legacy behind her when Quaintance Smith, who "entertained as many gentleman callers of a noisy nature as Holly ever had" (110), moves into her old apartment. The name "Quaintance" is an allusion to George Quaintance, a painter of the 1940s and 1950s, whose art bordered on soft-core gay pornography. Holly Golightly's queer world lives on even after she flees the constraints of New York City for her own freedom.

Works Cited

Capote, Truman. *Breakfast at Tiffany's and Three Stories*. 1958, New York: Vintage, 1993.

Partridge, Eric. *A Dictionary of the Underworld.* New York: Macmillan, 1950.

———. *A Dictionary of Slang and Unconventional English.* 8th ed. New York: Macmillan, 1984.

FURTHER READING

Bibliographies

Christensen, Peter G. "Truman Capote (1924-1984)." In *Contemporary Gay American Novelists: A Bio-Bibliographical Critical Sourcebook,* edited by Emmanuel S. Nelson, pp. 46-59. Westport, Conn.: Greenwood Press, 1993.
   Provides a short biography of Capote and traces the critical reaction to his works, themes, and overall literary reputation.

Stanton, Robert J. *Truman Capote: A Primary and Secondary Bibliography.* Boston: G. K. Hall & Company, 1980, 287 p.
   Book-length bibliography on writings by and about Capote, provides a comprehensive bibliography of Capote's writings as well as nearly 1,350 secondary references.

Biographies

Brinnin, John Malcolm. *Truman Capote: Dear Heart, Old Buddy.* New York: Delacorte Press, 1986, 182 p.
   A memoir that chronicles the author's relationship with Capote during Capote's youth and after he became a famous writer.

Clarke, Gerald. *Capote: A Biography.* New York: Simon and Schuster, 1988, 632 p.
   Often considered by critics to be the seminal biography of Capote.

Dunphy, Jack. *"Dear Genius . . .": A Memoir of My Life with Truman Capote.* New York: McGraw-Hill Book Company, 1987, 275 p.
   Combination novel and memoir written by Capote's life companion.

Moates, Marianne M. *A Bridge of Childhood: Truman Capote's Southern Years.* New York: Henry Holt and Company, 1989, 240 p.
   Biography of Capote's youth based on information provided by Capote's cousin, Jennings Faulk Carter.

Plimpton, George, ed. *Truman Capote: In Which Various Friends, Enemies, Acquaintances, and Detractors Recall His Turbulent Career.* New York: Nan A. Talese/Doubleday, 1997, 498 p.
   Collection of personal reminiscences of Capote's life and career provided by a number of the author's friends and detractors.

Criticism

Allmendinger, Blake. "The Room Was Locked, with the Key on the Inside: Female Influence in Truman Capote's 'My Side of the Matter'." *Studies in Short Fiction* 24, no. 3 (summer 1987): 279-88.
   Examines the similarities between Eudora Welty's story "Why I Live at the Post Office" and Capote's "My Side of the Matter," arguing that while Capote often denied the influence of other writers, his texts contradict him.

Frus, Phyllis. "The 'Incredibility of Reality' and the Ideology of Form." In *The Politics and Poetics of Journalistic Narrative: The Timely and the Timeless,* pp. 157-95. Cambridge: Cambridge University Press, 1994.
   Compares Norman Mailer's *The Executioner's Song* and Capote's *In Cold Blood,* asserting that Mailer's work is superior as a "journalistic narrative."

Garson, Helen S. *Truman Capote.* New York: Frederick Ungar Publishing Company, 1980, 210 p.
   General study of Capote's career, including extended summaries of the plots and some critical discussion of the author's works.

———. "From Success to Failure: Capote's *The Grass Harp.*" *The Southern Quarterly: A Journal of the Arts in the South* 33, nos. 2-3 (winter-spring 1995): 35-43.
   Contrasts the successful elements of the novel *The Grass Harp* with the shortcomings of Capote's dramatic adaptation, claiming that the play fails because the "characters do not change."

Inge, M. Thomas, ed. *Truman Capote: Conversations.* Jackson, Miss.: University Press of Mississippi, 1987, 374 p.
   Collection of interviews Capote gave with various journalists and others between 1948—shortly after the publication of *Other Voices, Other Rooms*—and 1980.

Plimpton, George A. "Truman Capote, Screenwriter." *The Paris Review* 38, no. 138 (spring 1996): 125-31.
   Provides discussion of Capote's work on the script for John Huston's film *Beat the Devil.*

Poirier, Richard. "In Cold Ink: Truman Capote." In *Trying It Out in America: Literary and Other Performances,* pp. 218-25. New York: Farrar, Straus and Giroux, 1999.
   Maintains that Capote failed to explore the serious issues and "forces at work in contemporary culture."

Rafferty, Terrence. "A Final Door." *The New Yorker* (21 September 1987): 113-19.
   Review of *Answered Prayers* that disparages Ca-

pote's unfinished novel as lacking in depth and failing to live up to its author's promise.

Richards, Gary. "Writing the Fairy *Huckleberry Finn*: William Goyen's and Truman Capote's Genderings of Male Homosexuality." *Journal of Homosexuality* 34, nos. 3-4 (1998): 67-86.

Examines how Capote's *Other Voices, Other Rooms* and William Goyen's *The House of Breath* reveal contradictory representations of male homosexuality.

Ruas, Charles. "Truman Capote." In *Conversations with American Writers*, pp. 37-56. New York: Alfred A. Knopf, 1985.

Interview with Capote following the publication of *Music for Chameleons*.

Wells, Paul. "*In Cold Blood*: Yellow Birds, New Realism and Killer Culture." In *Classics in Film and Fiction*. Vol. 5, edited by Deborah Cartmell, I. Q. Hunter, Heidi Kaye, and Imelda Whelehan, pp. 194-206. London: Pluto Press, 2000.

Examines film and television adaptations of Capote's novel, to demonstrate "the shifting paradigms of the nonfiction docudrama," and to test the claim that the novel is a classic of American postwar fiction.

Additional coverage of Capote's life and career is contained in the following sources published by Thomson Gale: *American Writers Supplement*, Vol. 3; *Beacham's Encyclopedia of Popular Fiction: Biography & Resources*, Vol. 1; *Concise Dictionary of American Literary Biography, 1941-1968*; *Contemporary Authors*, Vols. 5-8R; 113; *Contemporary Authors New Revision Series*, Vols. 18, 62; *Contemporary Literary Criticism*, Vols. 1, 3, 8, 13, 19, 34, 38, 58; *Contemporary Popular Writers*; *Dictionary of Literary Biography*, Vols. 2, 185, 227; *Dictionary of Literary Biography Yearbook*, 1980, 1984; *DISCovering Authors*; *DISCovering Authors: British Edition*; *DISCovering Authors: Canadian Edition*; *DISCovering Authors Modules: Most-studied Authors, Novelists*, and *Popular Fiction and Genre Authors*; *DISCovering Authors 3.0*; *Encyclopedia of World Literature in the 20th Century*, Ed. 3; *Exploring Short Stories*; *Gay & Lesbian Literature*, Ed. 1; *Literature and Its Times*, Vol. 3; *Literature Resource Center*; *Major 20th-Century Writers*, Eds. 1, 2; *Nonfiction Classics for Students*, Vol. 2; *Reference Guide to American Literature*, Ed. 4; *Reference Guide to Short Fiction*, Ed. 2; *Short Stories for Students*, Vol. 2; *Short Story Criticism*, Vols. 2, 47; *Something About the Author*, Vol. 91; *Twayne's United States Authors*; and *World Literature Criticism*.

Katherine Mansfield
1888-1923

(Born Kathleen Mansfield Beauchamp; also wrote under the pseudonym Boris Petrovsky) New Zealander short story writer, critic, and poet.

The following entry provides an overview of Mansfield's life and works. For additional information on her career, see *TCLC*, Volumes 2, 8, and 39.

INTRODUCTION

Mansfield is widely recognized as one of the leading contributors to the development of the modern short story in English. Though she died at the early age of thirty-four and published only three volumes of stories in her brief career, and two others after her death, her work had a profound impact on the direction and aesthetics of the short story genre in the twentieth century. Mansfield's writing style was compact, clear, and precise, and her stories—even many of her early ones—were innovative and psychologically acute. She has been especially praised for her masterful use of image and symbol in her fiction, and for her ability to distill and dissect her characters' emotions and psychological states of mind through language and form. Mansfield produced no single masterpiece, and her work treats a variety of themes, such as family and sexual conflict; the vulnerability of relationships; the insensitivity and brutality of middle-class life; the social impact of war; and, most notably, the individual's need to extract beauty and vitality from the mundane experience of everyday life. As a result of her tireless attempts to perfect her art, Mansfield remains among the most widely read short story writers in world literature.

BIOGRAPHICAL INFORMATION

Mansfield was born Kathleen Mansfield Beauchamp into a prosperous family in Wellington, New Zealand, on October 14, 1888. She was the third daughter and one of six surviving children of Harold Beauchamp and Annie Burnell Dyer Beauchamp. Her father made his money in the insurance business and eventually held a prominent position at the Bank of New Zealand. Her mother, at least according to Mansfield's recollections, was a nervous and somewhat overbearing woman. As a child young Katherine was slightly overweight and was forced to wear eyeglasses at an early age; because of

her physical characteristics, and because of her place as a middle child in the family, she often felt ignored and neglected by her parents. She did, however, form a close relationship with her maternal grandmother, who lived with the Beauchamp family. Mansfield showed an interest in writing at an early age. While in elementary school, she wrote for the school newspaper, wrote about and performed in plays, and began to write poetry. In 1903 she was sent off to Queen's College in London with two of her sisters; the girls-only school specialized in the arts and languages and allowed its students a considerable amount of freedom for the time. It was here that Mansfield experienced real intellectual freedom for the first time. She began reading and admiring the works of Oscar Wilde, Arthur Symons, Henrik Ibsen, George Bernard Shaw, and others. Mansfield left Queen's and returned to New Zealand in 1906, restless, lonely, and completely at odds with her parents' plan to have her play the social maiden and find a suitable husband to marry. Back in her native country, she struggled to find an outlet for her creative energies. She did, however, write four stories that were published in late 1907 in the Melbourne periodical *Native Companion.* In July 1908, after numerous quarrels with her parents, Mansfield received their permission and an allowance to return to London to live and pursue her work as a writer.

Biographers believe that Mansfield either arrived in London pregnant as a result of a romance onboard ship, or that she became pregnant after her arrival from an affair with a man she had known in New Zealand, named Garnet Trowell. Whatever the facts, she entered into a hasty marriage with another man, a young musician named George Bowden, whom she knew for only three weeks. On the night of her wedding, Mansfield suddenly left her new husband and, according to one theory, returned to Garnet Trowell, who was then living in Glasgow, Scotland. Shortly thereafter, Mansfield's mother arrived in England and, learning of her daughter's pregnancy, took her to a Bavarian spa in Bad Wörishofen, Germany, then to a less expensive pension. While living at the pension, Mansfield apparently had a miscarriage. She stayed on in Germany to recuperate, then in 1909 returned to London. During this time Mansfield began writing the stories that would comprise her first collection, *In a German Pension,* which was published in 1911. Based on her short stay in Germany, the stories in the collection provide satiric commentary on the attitudes and behavior of the German people and focus on such themes as sexual relationships, the subordination of women, and motherhood and childbearing. *In a German Pension* received generally favorable reviews from critics, though often for the wrong reasons: published at a time when tensions with Germany were high, commentators enjoyed Mansfield's depiction of the German people as gross and thoroughly unsympathetic. Determined to pursue a literary career, between 1911 and 1915 Mansfield published short stories, critical essays, and book reviews in such literary magazines as the *Athenaeum, Blue Review, New Age, Open Window,* and *Rhythm.* Also during this period, she met editor and critic John Middleton Murry, with whom she eventually shared the editorship of the *Blue Review* and *Rhythm.* The two began living together and were married in 1918, when Mansfield's first husband, George Bowden, finally consented to a divorce.

In 1915, during the early stages of World War I, Mansfield was reunited in London with her only brother, Leslie Heron Beauchamp, who had left New Zealand to join the war effort on the continent. Shortly after reporting for service, Leslie was killed in a military training accident. His death was devastating to Mansfield, while at the same time it galvanized her commitment and focus as a writer. During his short stay with his sister in London, Leslie had urged Mansfield to write stories about her native home and their childhood together in Karori, New Zealand. After her brother's death, Mansfield transformed that resolve into a passion, attempting a complete evocation of Karori in a number of minutely detailed stories and fictional revelations. During this time she published her two most acclaimed collections—*Bliss and Other Stories* (1920) and *The Garden Party and Other Stories* (1922)—both of which contain many of her so-called Karori stories and some of her most accomplished work as a writer, including "Prelude," "At the Bay," "The Garden Party," "The Voyage," and "A Doll's House." The success of these volumes established Mansfield as a major writer of short fiction, comparable to such contemporaries as Virginia Woolf and James Joyce. Mansfield was never in vigorous health—she was diagnosed with tuberculosis in 1917—and her condition deteriorated during the early 1920s. Despite her doctor's urging to rest, she increased her efforts as a writer, working until the last few months of her life. In a desperate act, she sought out a faith cure and admitted herself to Russian George Gurdjieff's Institute for the Harmonious Development of Man in late 1922. Mansfield died three months later, in 1923, of a massive tubercular hemorrhage at the age of thirty-four.

MAJOR WORKS

Mansfield's first volume of stories, *In a German Pension,* consists primarily of sketches, many of which are based on her life and experiences in Bad Wörishofen in 1909. Generally, these stories present the point of view of a quiet, perceptive young English woman living in Germany and offer satirical portraits of the German people, whom Mansfield depicts as crude, gross, pompous, and self-satisfied. Some of the stories, like "The Baron," focus on the snobbery and arrogance of German men, while others, like "The Luft Bad" and "Germans at Meat," deal with the purported German obsession with food, digestion, and the soul. After the outbreak of World War I and later in her career, Mansfield dismissed *In a German Pension* as an "inferior" work and a "youthful extravagance of expression and youthful disgust." While the stories are not as technically accomplished as her later fiction, many reveal the narrative skills and psychological complexities of her best work. Critics have also noted in these early stories the sense of estrangement, of severe loneliness, and the intense desire for personal connection that run through all Mansfield's work.

Mansfield's best and most characteristic work is generally considered to be included in the two collections *Bliss and Other Stories* and *The Garden Party and Other Stories.* The work of her so-called mature period, written during the last seven years of her life, these two books contain many of Mansfield's highly praised New Zealand stories as well as the most discussed and anthologized of her short fiction, including "Prelude," "At the Bay," "Bliss," "Je ne parle pas français," "The Garden Party," and "Miss Brill." These stories deal with a variety of themes—from family conflict and sexual relations in "Prelude" and "At the Bay," to lesbianism and the betrayal of innocence in "Bliss," to homosexual emotion and the complex interplay of male power, attraction, narcissism, and control in "Je ne parle pas français." Stylistically and technically they share common traits: evocative descriptions of the natural world; the effective use of image and symbol to define character and theme; the use of interior monologue, flashback, shifting narrative perspectives, and daydream; and a desire to unite form and content indissolubly, where language and words serve not only as conceptual markers but as physical entities, like notes in a musical composition. The stories in *Bliss* and *The Garden Party* display Mansfield's most successful innovations in narration and are considered by critics to be among the finest examples of the short story genre in the English language.

CRITICAL RECEPTION

Early assessments of Mansfield's works were based largely on the idealized image presented by her husband and literary executor, John Middleton Murry. After Mansfield's death Murry tightly controlled the posthumous publications of her letters, notebooks, unpublished stories, and other writings, and he manipulated her critical reception and literary stature in ways many later critics found to be exploitative and self-serving. After Murry's death in 1957, the "cult of Katherine," as it has been called by critics, underwent revision and a more objective assessment of her contribution occurred. What has emerged is an even greater appreciation for Mansfield's insight and power as a writer. Critics continue to praise the clarity of her language, especially her remarkable ability to describe flowers, plants, animals, and other natural phenomena in ways that are both naturalistic and symbolic. She is also lauded for her penetrating psychological portraits; her depiction of the complexity of human relationships, particularly sexual relationships; her astringent satire; and the organic unity—the attempt to unify form and content—of her art. Since the 1980s many critics have offered close textual analyses of her fiction, noting the ways in which her prose not only describes events and contributes to her narratives, but also defines the psychology of her characters and manifests her central themes. Whereas past critics praised Mansfield for the delicacy, sensibility, and impressionistic nature of her writing, current scholars regard her as a much more accomplished and self-conscious writer, one who worked tirelessly to compress her prose and to employ every technique of the short story form toward a perfect unity of expression. In a Mansfield story, details and literary techniques operate on multiple levels and have a symbolic as well as a narrative function. In the words of W. H. New, "Mansfield's talent lay in her stylistic control: in the way she experimented with time, point of view, language choice, and duration of silence, to reveal, in the lives of her characters, the remarkable resonances of insight and regret, and to represent the moments of desire and debilitating pain that give life, as she understood it, meaning."

PRINCIPAL WORKS

In a German Pension (short stories) 1911
*"Prelude" (short story) 1918
"Je ne parle pas français" (short story) 1919
Bliss and Other Stories (short stories) 1920
The Garden Party and Other Stories (short stories) 1922
The Doves' Nest and Other Stories (short stories) 1923
Poems (poetry) 1923
The Little Girl and Other Stories (short stories) 1924; also published as *Something Childish and Other Stories* 1924
Journal of Katherine Mansfield (journal) 1927
The Letters of Katherine Mansfield. 2 vols. (letters) 1928
Novels and Novelists (criticism) 1930
The Short Stories of Katherine Mansfield (short stories) 1937
The Scrapbook of Katherine Mansfield (journal) 1939
The Collected Stories of Katherine Mansfield (short stories) 1945
Katherine Mansfield's Letters to John Middleton Murry: 1913-1922 (letters) 1951
The Urewera Notebook (journal) 1978
The Collected Letters of Katherine Mansfield. 3 vols. (letters) 1984-93
The Critical Writings of Katherine Mansfield (criticism) 1987
Letters between Katherine Mansfield and John Middleton Murry (letters) 1988
Poems of Katherine Mansfield (poetry) 1988

*"Prelude" is a revision and compression of Mansfield's first attempted novel, *The Aloe*. The novel was not published until 1930, after Mansfield's death.

CRITICISM

Walter E. Anderson (essay date winter 1982)

SOURCE: Anderson, Walter E. "The Hidden Love Triangle in Mansfield's 'Bliss.'" *Twentieth Century Literature* 28, no. 4 (winter 1982): 397-404.

[*In the following essay, Anderson discusses the homosexual undercurrents in Mansfield's story "Bliss," claiming that Bertha's final disillusionment is not the result of her husband's infidelity, but rather her discovery that she and her husband love the same woman.*]

In her study of Katherine Mansfield's art, Anne Friis draws special attention to the style, which "hints and suggests rather than asserts. It is indirect, it is elliptic."[1] Mansfield abbreviates crucial thoughts or statements with dots and dashes, and "by the use of those punctuation marks she waives a mass of description and psychology."[2] In her short story **"Bliss"** this technique is most apparent, perhaps, in a significant passage occurring just after Bertha Young has her first experience of sexual desire for her husband: "But now—ardently! ardently! The word ached in her ardent body! Was this what that feeling of bliss had been leading up to? But then then—" (*SSM* [*The Short Stories of Katherine Mansfield*], p. 348).[3] Only a proper understanding of the psychological meaning of the story's action enables us to complete correctly that final sentence. Previous critics generally seem to agree that **"Bliss"** embodies a provocative study in mood and feeling within a conventional love-triangle plot.[4] The climax has been seen as Bertha's discovery that her husband Harry and her friend Pearl Fulton are lovers, a revelation which shatters her growing sense of marital bliss. In accordance with this interpretation, Robert Heilman identifies two main ironies: "Bertha's realization that her admired Miss Fulton shares her own unique bliss, and then her discovery that the shared mood has the same origin for each—love for Harry."[5] Edward Shanks faults Mansfield for making this central subject so obvious. All her art, he argues, goes into establishing the precarious external dependency of Bertha's bliss, "and it is a disastrous descent to a lower plane when, at the end, she appears to say, 'Disillusionment, you see, might have come in some such way as this. . . .'"[6] Actually the story is more subtle than Shanks imagines and more complexly ironic than Heilman has proposed, because the point of Bertha's disillusionment is not that both she and her friend love Harry and Harry loves Pearl instead of his wife, but that Bertha also loves Miss Fulton.

It is safe to say that Pearl Fulton does not, contra Heilman, share Bertha's "unique bliss," as Bertha, in the course of the party, imagines she must. In guessing Miss Fulton's mood, Bertha admits that she actually has "less than nothing" to justify her suspicion that their inclinations coincide. The entire bearing of the action suggests that Bertha's and Pearl's desires have neither the same origin nor the same object, yet Bertha, in her dreamy self-delusion, gives free rein to her coursing desire. Almost completely unaware of the homosexual nature of her attraction to Pearl, Bertha quite logically supposes that her passion—though fanned throughout the evening by imaginary communications with Miss Fulton—is for her husband Harry. If she desires Harry, "then then—" (the sentence Bertha is unable to complete) what has Miss Fulton had to do with it all? Being together in a "warm bed" with Harry, she asks in apparent disbelief, "was this what that feeling of bliss had been leading up to?" The answer is no. But she cannot fill in the sexual gaps—hence the all-significant dash and her wondering perplexity, both in this scene and at the close, when she recalls the "lovely pear tree—pear tree—pear tree." Earlier in the evening she had ecstatically contemplated this tree in company with Miss Fulton, the touch of whose arm kindled Bertha's passion into a blaze. After dinner, over coffee and cigarettes, Bertha imagines that Miss Fulton at last "'gave the sign'" for which she had long been waiting. The indefiniteness of the sign forces the reader to mark the disparity between Miss Fulton's words and what Bertha makes of them: "'Have you a garden?' said the cool sleepy voice." In answer, all Bertha can do is "obey," ecstatically:

> And the two women stood side by side looking at the slender, flowering tree. Although it was so still it seemed, like the flame of a candle, to stretch up, to point, to quiver in the bright air, to grow taller and taller as they gazed—almost to touch the rim of the round, silver moon.
>
> How long did they stand there? Both, as it were, caught in that circle of unearthly light, understanding each other perfectly, creatures of another world, and wondering what they were to do in this one with all this blissful treasure that burned in their bosoms and dropped, in silver flowers, from their hair and hands?
>
> For ever—for a moment? And did Miss Fulton murmur: "Yes. Just *that.*" Or did Bertha dream it?
>
> (*SSM*, p. 347)

The thoughts and feelings here belong to Bertha's dream, so different from what Pearl—the silver moon, the silver flower to Bertha's yearning desire—must be thinking as she stands next to her lover's wife. Both the "as it were" and the final question undercut Bertha's hopes for a silent communion with her "new find." Before understanding the significance of this moment for Bertha, we must consider those earlier passages of thought and feeling which resonate both with it and with the startling scene of disillusionment immediately following.

Early in the story we receive an insight into Bertha's stifled sexual feelings. "How idiotic civilization is," she thinks: "Why be given a body if you have to keep it shut up in a case like a rare, rare fiddle?" (*SSM*, p. 338). The thought of her body's not being used bears implications causing her to resist her analogy: "'No, that about the fiddle is not quite what I mean,' she thought, running up the steps and feeling in her bag for the key . . . 'It's not what I mean, because—'" (*ibid.*). Beyond a certain point, Bertha would not go, and she nervously allows herself to be distracted from pursuing her thoughts. The idea would bring Harry to mind, simultaneously forcing her to acknowledge that Harry cannot be blamed for her sexual indifference. The real issue that Bertha will not pursue is the origin of this indifference. Just before the close of the story, Mansfield reveals the crucial fact that Bertha and her husband are simply good pals:

> Oh, she'd loved him—she'd been in love with him, of course, in every other way, but just not in that way. And, equally, of course, she'd understood that he was different. They'd discussed it so often. It had worried her dreadfully at first to find that she was so cold, but after a time it had not seemed to matter. They were so frank with each other—such good pals. That was the best of being modern.
>
> (*SSM*, p. 348)

Although modernity had its advantages, civilization was idiotic if one's body was shut up in a case. When Bertha compares her lack of desire with Harry's sexual appetite (his difference), she thinks of herself as "cold." Yet she obviously is, as we have seen, a woman of ardent, though repressed, passions. Although she tries to pretend that she is happy ("She had everything": baby, money, house, cook, friends, and a husband) she still feels unsatisfied (*SSM*, p. 342). This evening gives her a sense of other possibilities, vague perhaps, yet overwhelmingly powerful.

Hours before the dinner party, Bertha's excited anticipation of Pearl's imminent visit causes her bosom to glow unbearably as if a "shower of little sparks" were exploding, though the reader only learns later that Pearl has caused this excitement. Bertha "hardly dared to breathe for fear of fanning it higher" (*SSM*, p. 338). She observes in the mirror her "trembling lips" and feels that she is "waiting for something . . . divine to happen . . . that she knew must happen . . . infallibly" (Mansfield's ellipses). To appease her excitement, she rushes up to the nursery to hold her baby girl. But when the nanny deprives her of this outlet, "all the feeling of bliss came back again, and again she didn't know how to express it—what to do with it" (*SSM*, p. 340). She flies to the phone to answer Harry's call and "to get in touch for a moment" with him, but finds "nothing to say." Her thoughts return to her expected guests and the arrangement of the living room: "As she was about to throw the last [sofa cushion] she surprised herself by suddenly hugging it to her, passionately, passionately. But it did not put out the fire in her bosom. Oh, on the contrary!" (*SSM*, p. 341). Releasing the cushion, Bertha beholds the "tall, slender pear tree in fullest, richest bloom" standing "as though becalmed" at the end of the garden. Anne Friis and Chester Eisinger interpret the tree as a symbol of nature's indifference to human suffering.[7] A few other critics, however, perceive a phallic symbolism in the tree, and connect it with Harry. The tree does not stand either for Harry's sexuality or for a pure, spiritual relationship with a woman, which Helen Nebeck claims is what Bertha seeks.[8] The flowering pear tree is a composite symbol representing in its tallness Bertha's homosexual aspirations and in its full, rich blossoms, her desire to be sexually used. As Bertha flings herself down on the couch in ecstasy, "she seemed to see on her eyelids the lovely pear tree with its wide open blossoms as a symbol of her own life" (*SSM*, p. 342): the open flowers image her female sexual self, but the meaning and object of the tree's tall assertiveness, the "masculine" part of her sexual feelings, eludes her conscious recognition. To the end of the story it remains a strongly felt urge only vaguely defined.

Mansfield initially presents Bertha in a state of unfocused, semi-hysterical bliss heightened by thoughts of Miss Fulton, her most recent "find," whom she had met at the club: "And Bertha had fallen in love with her, as she always did fall in love with beautiful women who had something strange about them" (*SSM*, pp. 340-41). Mention of her falling in love elicits at first only casual attention, since the phrase characterizes Bertha's hypersensibility and exaggerated manner of expression. We note, however, that Bertha habitually finds and picks up beautiful women, afterward trying to draw them out. Toward what end, she does not specify: "Up to a certain point Miss Fulton was rarely, wonderfully frank, but the certain point was there, and beyond that she would not go" (*SSM*, p. 341). Bertha does not consciously know herself the tendency of her own solicitations.

When her guests begin to arrive, she forgets until Harry enters the house that "Pearl Fulton had not turned up" (*SSM*, p. 344). Her thoughts shuttle back and forth from Harry to Miss Fulton in a pattern of association which gains significance as the crisis builds.[9] When Pearl does arrive, Bertha smiles, "with that little air of proprietorship that she always assumed while her women finds were new and mysterious" (*SSM*, p. 344). Upon seizing Pearl's arm, Bertha feels much as she did earlier in the afternoon when sparks seemed to light up in her bosom: "What was there in the touch of that cool arm that could fan—fan—start blazing—blazing—the fire of bliss that Bertha did not know what to do with?" Although Pearl does not look directly at her hostess, Bertha is sure, "as if the longest, most intimate look had passed between them—as if they had said to each other: 'You, too?'—that Miss Fulton . . . was feeling just what she was feeling" (*SSM*, p. 345). Mansfield repeats the "as if" to heighten the contrast between the apparent facts and what Bertha would most like to believe. For her part, Pearl is simply casual, blasé; she may be thinking about Harry, but Bertha clearly does not. In believing that she and Pearl are intimately in touch, Bertha is doomed to disappointment at the close of the evening.

For the moment everything that happens seems to fill her brimming cup of bliss: "Everything was good—was right" (*SSM*, p. 346). And always, "in the back of her mind, there was the pear tree. It would be silver now, in the light of poor dear Eddie's moon,[10] silver as Miss Fulton." After connecting the silver moon and the silvery blond Pearl, Mansfield expands her primary symbolism in an event which climaxes Bertha's mood. Bertha feels that she has read Miss Fulton's mind exactly, yet she is not absolutely certain: "she never doubted for a moment that she was right, and yet what had she to go on? Less than nothing" (*SSM*, p. 346). Consequently she hopes that her friend will "'give a sign'," though "what she meant by that she did not know, and what would happen after that she could not imagine." While she waits for the sign to come, as she feels it infallibly must, she simply has to "laugh or die." She diverts herself by observing Mrs. Norman ["Face"] Knight, who, "like a very intelligent monkey," is habitually "tucking something down the front of her bodice—as if she kept a tiny, secret hoard of nuts there" (*SSM*, p. 343). The thought causes Bertha to dig her nails into her hands. Then comes the sign, so Bertha imagines, and the visit to the garden to contemplate the pear tree, as described above.

The adjectives—"tall," "slender," and "still"—for the tree specifically recall Bertha's earlier perception of it while squeezing the sofa cushion with passion (*SSM*, p. 341). The phrase "wondering what they were to do . . . with all this blissful treasure" parallels Bertha's previous feelings, which she "didn't know how to express" or "what to do with" (*SSM*, p. 340). The latter phrase also occurred in the description of Bertha's thoughts upon taking hold of Pearl's arm after her arrival (*SSM*, p. 344). "Treasure that burned in their bosoms" echoes the earlier phrase, "in her bosom there was still that bright glowing place—that shower of little sparks coming from it" (*SSM*, p. 338). Some urge inside Bertha grows taller and taller as she stretches, quiveringly, toward the silvery blond Miss Fulton, much as the pear tree seems to her to stretch up and touch the "rim" of the round, silver, feminine moon. The color silver now draws to itself, along with previous associations, the sexually symbolic silver flowers. Bertha has no more knowledge of what her own feelings mean than she would know what to do were Miss Fulton actually to go beyond a certain point, in frankness, and give the sign she secretly longs for. She is left wondering what she is to do with her unknown and unfulfilled desires.

When the lights in her house are turned on, Bertha returns to the world in which her marriage to Harry is a simple fact. Ironies multiply as Bertha imagines that she can share with him the feelings Pearl Fulton has inspired. The conflicting tendencies within her psyche emerge in thoughts at cross-purposes: "Oh, Harry, don't dislike her. You are quite wrong about her. She's wonderful, wonderful. And, besides, how can you feel so differently about someone who means so much to me. I shall try to tell you when we are in bed tonight what has been happening. What she and I have shared" (*SSM*, p. 348). Here Bertha attempts to transfer her unconscious feelings for the woman onto her relationship with the man, according to what she knows her feeling for him conventionally ought to be. For the *first* time in her life, we are told, she feels sexual desire for her husband, and it is a "strange and almost terrifying" thought. Somehow she feels perplexed that her bliss has been leading up to Harry; it was Pearl, after all, who seemed to fan the flames of her ardor. "But then then—" why Harry? or, if Harry, what has Miss Fulton had to do with her excitement? Bertha breaks off, not pursuing the implications even this far.

As the guests take their leave, a stunned Bertha beholds Harry embrace and kiss Pearl. Her eyes focus on Miss Fulton, who laid her "moonbeam fingers" on his cheeks and smiled "her sleepy smile." The sign she had so much desired has been reserved for Harry, and her pearl slips from her grasp like quicksilver. Bertha touches those slender fingers only in parting, as Miss Fulton holds her "hand a moment longer" to praise her "lovely pear tree." The unwitting irony of her praise is devastating. In another moment she is gone, leaving Bertha feeling empty and hopeless. Bertha, confused and in pain, rushes to the window to view the pear tree: "Oh, what is going to happen now?" she wonders. Her pent-up desires are still in full flower, as are the tree and its flowers that symbolize them.

Throughout **"Bliss"** Mansfield ironically plays off a conventional love triangle against an unconventional one, forcing the reader to make the necessary adjustment. She subtly controls her symbolism and other modes of suggestion and indirection to convey both the tendency of Bertha's peculiar feelings and her lack of self-knowledge, the degree of ignorance in her bliss. In her essay examining Katherine Mansfield's theory of fiction, Eileen Baldeshwiler reveals the degree to which this author cared about her craft, how much she delighted in achieving the perfect detail and the sufficient balance between form and subject.[11] **"Bliss"** adequately illustrates both the care and the craft. But even more perfectly, it exemplifies, perhaps, the kind of joy which every practitioner of the art of fiction must feel when he successfully detaches the object from himself. Mansfield carefully articulates this feeling in her letters, parts of which Baldeshwiler summarizes: "'But when I am writing of "another" I want so to lose myself in the soul of the other that I am not.' The act of faith, of surrender, requires 'pure risk,' the absolute belief in 'one's own essential freedom.' It is hard to let go, 'yet one's creative life depends on it and one desires to do nothing else.'"[12] Certainly we may suppose that Mansfield felt her own essential freedom when lost in the soul of Bertha Young and her short-lived bliss.

Notes

1. Anne Friis, *Katherine Mansfield: Life and Stories* (Copenhagen: Munksgaard, 1946), p. 132.

2. *Ibid.*, p. 136.

3. All page references in the text (cited parenthetically as *SSM*) are to *The Short Stories of Katherine Mansfield* (New York: Knopf, 1970).

4. In addition to Anne Friis, see Nariman Hormasji, *Katherine Mansfield: An Appraisal* (London: Collins, 1967), pp. 122-24; Saralyn Daly, *Katherine Mansfield* (New York: Twayne, 1965), pp. 82-88; Sylvia Berkman, *Katherine Mansfield: A Critical Study* (New Haven: Yale Univ. Press, 1951), *passim*; Robert Heilman, ed., *Modern Short Stories* (New York: Harcourt, 1950), pp. 207-09; Chester Eisinger, "Mansfield's 'Bliss,'" *Explicator*, 7 (1949), Item 48; Dorothy Brewster and Angus Burrell, *Modern Fiction* (New York: Columbia Univ. Press, 1934), pp. 374-77; Edward Shanks, "Katherine Mansfield," *London Mercury*, 17 (Jan. 1928), 291-92; Alfred C. Ward, *Aspects of the Modern Short Story: English and American* (New York: Dial, 1925), pp. 287-89.

5. Heilman, *Modern Short Stories*, p. 208; cf. Hormasji, *Katherine Mansfield: An Appraisal*, pp. 122-23.

6. Shanks, "Katherine Mansfield," pp. 291-92. Cf. Ward, who finds Mansfield's attitude in "Bliss" cruel and pitiless: her ending is "sheer cynicism and a negation of the subtle art that she was later to develop" (*Aspects of the Modern Short Story*, p. 288). For Brewster and Burrell the story ends in dissonance, "with overtones making analysis as baffling as life itself" (*Modern Fiction*, p. 277). Cf. T. S. Eliot, *After Strange Gods* (London: Faber, 1934), pp. 38-39.

7. Friis, *Katherine Mansfield*, p. 177; Eisinger, "Mansfield's 'Bliss,'" Item 48.

8. Helen E. Nebeker, "The Pear Tree: Sexual Implications in Katherine Mansfield's 'Bliss,'" *Modern Fiction Studies*, 18 (1972-73), 545-51. Nebeker and I have independently concluded that homosexuality is central to the story and to this extent corroborate each other.

9. If, as Saralyn Daly argues (*Katherine Mansfield*, p. 85), Bertha's close association of Pearl and Harry suggests her suspicion of their affair, she fears it, I suggest, not as Daly thinks, because it would mean her losing Harry to Pearl, but vice versa.

10. With "poor, dear Eddie," the dilettante poet, Mansfield gives her story a certain tone and atmosphere appropriate to her subject, as one brief fragment of his speech discloses: "I have had such a *dreadful* experience with a taxi-man; he was most sinister. I couldn't get him to *stop*. The more I knocked and called the *faster* he went. And *in* the moonlight this bizarre figure with the *flattened* head *crouching* over the *little* wheel," and so forth (*SSM*, p. 343). Bertha associates Eddie with the silver moon at the moment she imagines an identification between it and the silver Pearl. Bertha's thinking of Eddie and of the moon as his moon reflects her dim sense of relationship between Eddie's probable propensities and her own nascent feelings. Similarly, at the end of the story Bertha associates Eddie with the image of a black cat following a gray cat, as he follows Miss Fulton to the door. The image represents Bertha's sexual thoughts almost surfacing as they creep after Miss Fulton; it recalls as well the cats she saw in the garden beneath the pear tree earlier in the afternoon (*SSM*, p. 341). Mansfield offers in the cats a generalized floating symbol of sexuality and animality—as with the monkeys in the pattern of Face's dress—which expresses Bertha's ambivalence toward sexuality.

11. Eileen Baldeshwiler, "Katherine Mansfield's Theory of Fiction," *Studies in Short Fiction*, 7 (Summer 1970), 421-32.

12. *Ibid.*, p. 423.

Judith S. Neaman (essay date summer 1986)

SOURCE: Neaman, Judith S. "Allusion, Image, and Associative Pattern: The Answers in Mansfield's 'Bliss.'" *Twentieth Century Literature* 32, no. 2 (summer 1986): 242-54.

[*In the following essay, Neaman investigates allusions to the Bible and Shakespeare's* Twelfth Night *in* "Bliss."]

"Bliss," Katherine Mansfield's most ambiguous story of initiation, poses many problems, some of which have plagued critics for years.[1] What is Bertha's "bliss"? What does Pearl Fulton represent and to what does her name allude? Why a pear tree instead of an apple? Was Bertha really cold? Is she hysterical? Would *would* "happen now"? Why, at the end of such a crisis of disillusionment, is the pear tree "as lovely as ever"?[2] Yet, Mansfield has answered these questions in the story by interweaving allusions to two sources—the Bible and Shakespeare's *Twelfth Night*—whose major role in "Bliss" has been largely ignored. These allusions not only answer the crucial questions but they also illuminate the meaning of the tale, while simultaneously charting the anatomy of its creation.

Perhaps because critics have seen all too clearly the obvious tree of knowledge blooming in Bertha's garden,[3] none seems to have detected the first overt clue to the thematic importance of the Bible. It appears as a familiar echo in the words, "for the first time in her life, she desired her husband" (p. 349). In Genesis 3.16,[4] among the punishments God metes out to the disobedient Eve is: "thy desire *shall* be to thy husband and he shall rule over thee." In visiting this affliction on Bertha at the very moment that she first experiences marital lust, Mansfield appears to indicate an easy familiarity with the long tradition of biblical commentary. According to both Augustinian and Talmudic interpretation, lust entered the world as a result of the Fall. **"Bliss"** pursues the theme by chapter and verse.

In the same chapter of Genesis, directly before and after Eve is first sentenced to a life of connubial desire, there are numerous phrases so similar in image and content to those Mansfield uses in **"Bliss"** that the story seems to be almost a gloss upon the Bible. The evidence that the words of Genesis were deeply embedded in her mind appears in a diary entry of February 1916 in which she remarks that, since she came to Bandol where she wrote **"Bliss"** in 1918, she has "read the Bible for hours on end." She wrote here of wanting to know "if Lot followed close on Noah or something like that. But I feel so bitterly that they ought to be part of my breathing."[5] Furthermore, during the same brief period of feverish work in which she produced **"Bliss,"** Mansfield wrote the story **"Psychology,"** in which a character playfully remarks, "And God said; 'Let there be cake. And there was cake. And God saw that it was Good.'"

In both stories, words or phrases from Genesis appear in brief but they set up reverberations which guide the reader's responses to all subsequent events. In **"Bliss,"** Mansfield's more indirect use of the words of Genesis is overbalanced by a closer attention to the intent and material of it. In fact, the parallels between the biblical work and Mansfield's story are so close that the words of Genesis may inform the reader not only of what Bertha's life was before the day of her maturation but also of what her future will be. In this way, Genesis answers Bertha's last question: "What is going to happen now?" If, like a modern Eve,[6] Bertha has lived in a fool's paradise which is destroyed by knowledge, then she and Harry are destined to repeat, in a modern form, the fate of their first models. This is so much the case that God himself answers Bertha's question about her future. What "will happen now" is that Bertha will desire only her husband and he will dominate her life. "In sorrow [she] will bring forth children" while Harry, who has tasted another form of the forbidden fruit of knowledge, will now eat "the herb of the field" "in sorrow . . . all the days of [his] life" (Gen. 3.17). Bertha's future children will be begotten in sorrow and bitterness born of the knowledge she has gained. She will know that Harry sees her as Adam saw Eve after the Fall—as the "mother of all living" (Gen. 3.20), which, in Mansfield's punning paraphrase, is Berth A' Young.

Because Mansfield's metamorphosis of this chapter of Genesis remains so close to its source, readers will not be surprised to find still further relations between the words and events of **"Bliss"** and those of Genesis 3. The garden in which this young pair learns the consequences of sin is populated not only by a wondrous tree about which all knowledge revolves but also by animals. Following her own associative thought patterns, Mansfield has linked the denizens of the first garden and the Youngs' garden with the behavior of Adam and Eve and also with Darwinian evolutionary theory. The Norman Knights are also compared to first forebears by their name but they are now the forebears of English society. Mansfield compares them to monkeys, for "Face" Knight, so perfectly matched with her mate, "Mug," is wearing a funny little coat with monkeys all over it and looks "like a very intelligent monkey."[7]

Here the reader must wonder if Mansfield is using her Bible to deliver a post-Darwinian stab at English society. The rest of Face's outfit echoes Adam's and Eve's first attempt at clothing, which they made in Genesis 3 to hide their shame at their newly discovered nakedness. As God created for Adam and his helpmeet "coats of skins" (3.21) to help them "hide their shame," so Face wears a yellow silk dress that looks like "scraped banana skins" and she is later described as "crouched before the fire in her banana skins" (p. 343). No sooner has Bertha noticed the simian clothing and physiognomy of her guest than Mr. Norman Knight remarks on parenthood and paradise, "This is a sad, sad fall! . . . When the perambulator comes into the hall—. . . ." The final link of this particular chain which seems to stretch through Mansfield's mind from Bible to **"Bliss"** is forged when Norman Knight remarks in parting, "You know our shame" (p. 343).

Gradually, it becomes apparent that the innocent Bertha and her hairy mate, an emotional primate if there ever was one, have opened their house and garden to beasts from a number of literary fields. Eddie Warren, his last name removing all doubt of his nature and habitat, is a stuttering rabbit. Terrified by his taxi ride, dressed in white socks and an enchanting white scarf to match, Eddie speaks in conversational tones and patterns that often echo those of Alice in Wonderland's white rabbit.

Pearl has been called a moon to Bertha's sun[8] and a parallel to the pear tree, which has also been identified with Bertha and Harry.[9] However, Mansfield's descriptions of Pearl emphasize not only Pearl's lunar qualities (she is dressed "all in silver with a silver fillet binding her head" and her fingers, "like moonbeams, are so slender that a pale light seemed to come from them") but also focus the reader's attention on her "cool arm," "heavy eyelids," and "[mysterious] half smile."[10] Pearl is such an adept at enigma that everyone who encounters her assigns her another identity. Her conversation merely amplifies the mystery, for it is barely audible; she whispers and intimates. Bertha is not even certain what Pearl murmured about the pear tree or if she had guessed that Pearl said, "just that" (p. 347) when she looked out at the tree in the garden. Yet, it is Pearl who asks if there is a garden, Pearl whose "cool arm could fan—fan—start blazing—blazing the fire of bliss that Bertha did not know what to do with" (p. 344).

Enigmatic, dressed in scaly silver, full of whispers and murmurs, Pearl is infinitely tempting. Her lidded eyes conceal her passion for Harry. But she is secretive, intimating, cool-skinned and cool-souled, in other words, "the subtlest beast of the field" (Gen. 3.3). Thus, Bertha cannot see the truth until she glimpses the kiss. With that kiss, Bertha's innocence falls and her blissful illusions are destroyed. Only then does Bertha begin to see her mysterious friend in a new light. No longer the distant and enchanting moon of Bertha's hopes, Pearl now appears to her hostess to resemble the seductive gray cat who had provoked a shiver of sexual revulsion in Bertha earlier in the evening. One critic believes that Bertha's new vision of Pearl is evoked by a horror of the bestiality she perceives in her former love, since she considers that Pearl's purity has been sullied by the heterosexual behavior Bertha abhors.[11] But, if we see Pearl as a serpent, the common Talmudic and patristic interpretation of the serpent's role in tempting Eve seems far more appropriate a view.

According to this traditional understanding of the Bible, it was the serpent's seduction of Eve that first induced her to lust for Adam. Pearl's seduction of Bertha awakens Bertha's lust for her own husband. In fact, Bertha's image of Pearl followed by Eddie, as the seductive gray cat followed the black cat, is so distorted a view of Eddie that it makes little sense if Pearl is not seen as the serpent. Mansfield has, after all, painted Eddie as effeminate at least and homosexual at most, hence hardly a likely candidate for seduction by a woman. Clearly the "grey cat, dragging its belly . . . [as it] crept across the lawn, and a black one, its shadow trail[ing] after" (p. 341), reminds Bertha, and is intended to remind readers of **"Bliss,"** of the serpent of Genesis which God punished by decreeing that it should crawl on its belly.

In every possible way, Pearl fulfills the role of the serpent in the garden. She is one of those beautiful women with "something strange about them" (p. 341) with whom Bertha is always falling in love. Like the rest of these temptresses, she is strangely secretive while seeming to be *so* open and Bertha is certain that they "share" something. Until Bertha gains the carnal knowledge which will be revealed to her, she is incapable of understanding that what they share is a lust for Harry. By the time Bertha realizes that the "bliss" with which she has burned is sexual desire and then sees that desire mocked (all within moments), she has tasted the fruit of the tree and found it a bitter dessert to the banquet of sight and taste she has laid for herself and her guests. That the discoveries which cause her so much pain should take place at a dinner party celebrated in a house with a flowering fruit tree is no coincidence.

Critics who have noted the importance of the imagery of food and eating in this tale[12] have ignored standard biblical associations among lust, fruit, and knowledge so clearly introduced in Mansfield's references to the food and eating which led to the Fall and lead to this fall. Bertha's first important act in the story is associated with these elements. The reader can see this link in her conflict between the enjoyment of temptation and her fear of succumbing to it. First she luxuriates in the beauty of the fruits she has bought for the party. Then, as she begins to fear the intensity she tries to repress it, crying, "No, no. I'm getting hysterical" (p. 339). As the tale and Bertha's growth simultaneously progress, the images of fruit and eating become less abstract and aesthetic and more active and hostile, for their connection with sex, flesh, and desire is clarified. Pearl rolls a tangerine between her luminous fingers. Harry loves the "white flesh" of lobster and "pistachio ices—green and cold like the eyelids of Egyptian dancers" (p. 345). The most emotionally evocative dish is made of eggs, reminding us of the embryonic Youngs and their new infant. In the forms of the new cook's omelettes and the "admirable soufflé," eggs become the crucial bonds in the marriage, inspiring Harry's praise which makes Bertha almost weep "with childlike pleasure" (p. 345).

After Bertha sees Harry and Pearl embracing, the nature of the imagery shifts from its focus on the food to be eaten to a new emphasis on the act of eating it. With this shift, the cannibalism which has been vaguely implied now becomes glaring.[13] When Harry kisses Pearl "with his lips curled back in a hideous grin" (p. 349), the reader, like Bertha, sees him devouring this delectable woman whose serenity he had earlier attributed to a "good stomach." Hence, fruit becomes the visible apple of temptation (at one point in the story it is a tangerine turning in Pearl's fingers), and eating becomes the act of lust born of knowledge.

If fruits and flesh and the devouring of these represent desire and consummation as well as knowledge, then instruments and the music *not* played on them represent human bodies and sexual frustration and/or repression. Marilyn Zorn quotes Mansfield's letter of May 24, 1918, to Ottoline Morrell in which Mansfield cries, "What might be so divine is out of tune—or the instruments are all silent and nobody is going to play again."[14] For her purposes, Mansfield's succeeding words are irrelevant, for ours, they are central. "There *is* no concert for us. Isn't there? Is it all over? Is our desire and longing and eagerness, quite all that's left? Shall we sit here forever in this immense wretched hall—waiting for the lights to go up—which will never go up."[15] That is precisely what Bertha does at the end, of course, and it is Harry who "shut[s] up shop" or turns out the lights (p. 350). The musical refrains, though they occur only three times in the story, are central and the association between the fruits, the passion, and the music becomes increasingly specific. Music is "the food of love." Like the eating of the fruit, the playing of music, in this tale at least, is forbidden.

At the very outset of the tale, Bertha longs to dance, bowl a hoop, or "simply laugh at nothing" (p. 337) in the streets to express her bliss. "Oh, is there no way you can express it without being 'drunk and disorderly'? How idiotic civilization is! Why be given a body if you have to keep it shut up in a case like a rare rare fiddle?" (p. 337). Bertha's protest against the social requirement that she quash her ebullience becomes a louder aria when Nanny removes the baby from her embrace: "How absurd it was. Why have a baby if it has to be kept—not in a case like a rare string fiddle—but in another woman's arms?" (p. 339).

Finally, the fiddle—shaped like a pear and analogue, like the pear, to a woman's body—grows into a piano. Now fully aware and unsuccessfully trying to repress her thoughts and fears about that moment at which she will share the bed with a husband she suddenly desires, Bertha runs to the piano. "What a pity someone does not play! What a pity someone does not play!" (p. 348). Indeed, Bertha's body has not been played, nor has she played. But now the fruit of carnal knowledge is about to be transmuted into the music of desire and the passion arising from both is about to suffer "a dying fall,"[16] a hidden pun on both the original fall from grace and the musical form of a "dying fall."

Associating the tree of knowledge with the food of love, Mansfield has subtly alluded to Shakespeare's *Twelfth Night,* a play she knew almost by heart, which celebrates the Feast of Twelfth Night or Epiphany. This reference creates a musical tie which binds all the images and references of **"Bliss."** Like the primary biblical allusion, this secondary Shakespearean allusion from the opening lines of the play not only recapitulates the theme of the Fall but, in so doing, explains in part why Bertha's beloved tree is a pear tree. The lines alone explain the musical references in **"Bliss"** and show the relations between love, food, and the shattering of Bertha's innocence:

> If music be the food of love, play on;
> Give me excess of it that surfeiting,
> The appetite may sicken and so die.—
> That strain again!—it had a dying fall!
>
> (*Twelfth Night* I.1.4)

To observe Mansfield's whole train of thought, the reader must consider the entire play. *Twelfth Night* is a play of pairing and couples, of confused and confusing sexuality, of female love which leads to male-female unions. The pear tree of **"Bliss"** may be Mansfield's conscious or unconscious pun on pair, as Magalaner suggests, for the story is itself full of pairs and even possibly alter egos.[17] More important, Mansfield was interested throughout her life in "shadow selves," as she called them in a letter to Murry of 1920.[18] But the connections among the pairing and the pear tree and the structure and imagery of *Twelfth Night* run deeper still.

Large portions of the play take place in a garden which belongs to Olivia; there, to oblige Orsino, Viola courts Olivia. Viola is dressed as a man and Olivia does, indeed, conceive a passion for her, only to discover that she is not eligible. It is only after meeting Viola's twin, Sebastian, whom Viola had feared was dead, that Olivia transfers her affection to him and gives him a pearl as a love token. Viola, one cannot help noting, is closely related to the viol or fiddle to which Bertha compares her caged body, and Bertha is, at first, Pearl's wooer, sadly winning her for Harry. Thus, the theme of sexual confusion, of pairing of opposites, of "shadow selves" which Mansfield had cherished so long and embodied in her story **"Sun and Moon,"** is everywhere in **"Bliss."** Bertha and Harry, Bertha and Pearl (Bertha's gift to Harry), the black and gray cats, Pearl and Eddie, and the spiritual twins, Mug and Face, recapitulate this favorite theme, one which Magalaner has noted.[19] In *Twelfth Night,* as in **"Bliss,"** heterosexual love is the goal toward which the play strives and pairing is, after all, just another name for copulation, suggesting the lust which the fruit of the tree evoked.

But Mansfield's personal and aesthetic interests might have been far more effective than her reading in directing her choice of associations which formed **"Bliss."** Since girlhood, Mansfield had been both a cellist and a passionate lover of gardens and pear trees. Magalaner notes that, a year before she wrote **"Bliss,"** Mansfield mentioned, in a letter to Ottoline Morrell, the importance of writing about a flower garden with people in it:

> walking in the garden—several pairs of people—their conversation—their slow pacing—their glances as they pass one another.
>
> . . . . .
>
> A kind of, musically speaking, conversation set to flowers.[20]

In Murry's volume the letter immediately succeeding the letter to Ottoline Morrell was a note to Virginia Woolf about the sketch "Kew Gardens":

> Yes, your Flower Bed is very good. There's a still, quivering changing light over it all and a sense of those couples dissolving in the bright air which fascinates me—[21]

Of all the plants and trees in a garden, a pear tree was one of the most important to Mansfield and, at the time of the writing of **"Bliss,"** she must have been thinking of it. Convinced that she was dying after the major hemorrhage which preceded the writing of this story by a few days, she thought constantly of her beloved brother, Chummie, who had recently been killed in the war. How often the two of them had sat on the bench beneath the pear tree in Tinakori Road in New Zealand and exchanged confidences. The new home which she and Murry first rented in England had a garden with a pear tree.

If these two types of sources, the biographical and the literary, consistently clarify Mansfield's use of images and symbols in the story, it would be illogical to ignore their potential influence upon the meaning of the story. Might they not also, central as they seem to be to Mansfield's consciousness at the time she wrote **"Bliss,"** shed light on the relationship between Bertha and Pearl, for example? Upon this love, some critics of the story have dwelled far too emphatically. Mansfield's friend Virginia Woolf, for example, hated **"Bliss,"** which she considered a shallow, maudlin tale of lesbianism. Later critics, like Nebeker,[22] have argued that Bertha's real goal is Pearl and that the sorrow she experiences is a result of Pearl's rejection of her for Harry. But nothing in the story suggests this. In fact, Bertha considers a bedtime discussion with Harry about what she and Pearl share. She imagines that this conversation will promote the spiritual understanding that will culminate in their first passionate physical union. In both *Twelfth Night* and **"Bliss,"** youthful and innocent love is homosexual, as if both authors were chronicling the normal English schoolgirl stage of maturation. Heterosexual love is the source of the excitement, the growth, the real passion. Bertha's "crushes" on women are nothing new in her life, but her desire for her husband is both new and startling to her. Ultimately, Bertha's disillusionment over the impossibility of fulfilling her terrifying but exciting new desire matures her, for, through this loss of hope, she learns the sorrow of knowledge. Finally, it is Harry's "cool" voice which sets the seal on Bertha's fear and suffering.

Critics have cited Bertha's frigidity as the most incontrovertible proof of her lesbianism. After all, Bertha seems to have admitted to frigidity when she reflected that "it had worried her dreadfully at first to find that she was so cold" (p. 348). Despite the fact that readers conventionally accept a narrator's statements about him or herself, Bertha's self-evaluation, in this instance, cannot be taken at face value, no matter how afraid she is of her first real sexual encounter. Too much of her behavior argues against frigidity.[23] She experiences bliss, she resents the restrictions of a society that demands she "cage" her body, she enjoys her child's flesh and resents the woman who withdraws it from her, she aches to communicate her bliss to Harry though it is hopeless to do so. Bertha is highly sensual, glorying in the colors of fruit, in smells and sights, in feelings she can hardly contain. Surely these are not the responses of a frigid woman. The source of her conviction that she is frigid lies elsewhere—at the site of her "discovery" that she is so cold. It is the same source from which she learns that her desire to dance and sing, to hold her child are symptoms of "hysteria" (pp. 337, 338). That source is the society she identifies as the one which will call her "drunk and disorderly" (p. 338) if she gives vent to her passions; it is the "idiotic civilization" which demands that she imprison her feelings and her body. Harry and she have "discussed" her problem and he has explained that he is "different" (p. 348).

That Bertha's testimony about her own proclivities is not necessarily reliable is attested to by the sardonic tone, the desperate contradiction of her "Really, really—she had everything. . . ."[24] She is missing something—something that throws a pall over her marriage, and surely part of what she is missing is the understanding husband who would not hasten her off the phone, truncate her expression of feeling. Is the rest the passion she lacks or is it, as Mansfield's portrayal of Harry's callousness suggests, the passion he tells her she lacks? Throughout the story, Bertha acts the good wife and mother, observing the conventions of social respectability which pinion her whims and moods. The purveyors of these conventions appear in the forms of Nanny and Harry, yet she still emerges as a passionate woman. When she finally experiences the marital lust so "improper" in a good English matron, Bertha learns that the fruit of desire is death, for there is always a snake in the garden and the music of passion always suffers a "dying fall."

In marrying these sources to produce so carefully unified a story, Mansfield has disclosed the cast of her mind. Critics who have often pointed out how autobiographical the tale is, have neglected one major aspect of Mansfield's autobiography to which both her letters as well as her journals draw attention. Mansfield was devoted to Shakespeare and the Bible and was especially absorbed in Genesis at the time she wrote **"Bliss."** She spoke of her desire to know the Bible as well as she knew Shakespeare, whose words she recited constantly. In a letter to Murry, dated March 4, 1918, written only a week after completing **"Bliss,"**[25] Mansfield remarked to Murry: "My Shakespeare is full of notes for my children to light on." Magalaner noted a letter to Murry written just days before the completion of **"Bliss"** in which Mansfield speaks of her love for Murry in terms of food and eating.²⁶ She concludes, "'Hang there like fruit, my soul, till the tree die!' The tree *would* die."²⁷

Twelfth Night is much on her mind. She notes often at this time that she is thinking of death (because of her own severe hemorrhage and Chummie's death), and these morbid thoughts intermingle with visions of gardens and food. She is filled with what she calls either "a rage of bliss" or bliss she longs to "share unexplained." Coincidentally perhaps, both the story and the title of **"Sun and Moon"** are conceived at this same time. The intellectual and emotional recipe for **"Bliss"** is revealed in these threads of thought recorded in Mansfield's journals and letters. How she regarded the conclusion of the story is not. Yet, the mystery of the concluding lines is solved by finishing the speech from *Twelfth Night* which both opens the play and sets the musical key of the story.

The work ends on an elegiac note: innocence dies quickly, but those who see their paradise fade survive. They live out long lives in a twilight sorrow, illuminated only by a memory of an irretrievable bliss.

> O, spirit of love, how quick and fresh art thou!
> That, notwithstanding thy capacity
> Receiveth as the sea, naught enters there,
> Of what validity or pitch soe'er,
> But falls into abatement and low price
> Even in a minute!
>
> (*Twelfth Night* I.1.9-15)

Twelfth Night tells us what has happened; Genesis tells us that what happened once will happen—again and again. The pear tree remains "as lovely as ever and as still" because, like the tree of knowledge, it remains firmly rooted in perfect Eden. Only Bertha is expelled. The lasting beauty and seductiveness of the tree sound an ironic note of contrast with the imperfection of the love they provoke and disclose. In the mythic world in which the pear tree, now forever out of Bertha's reach, blooms eternally without blemish, Eddie Warren's last words about the eternal quality of the lines: "Why must it always be tomato soup?" bear the wisdom of the Shakespearean clowns; they are set against an archetypal quest for knowledge which will always end in the "too dreadfully eternal" (p. 350) discovery that sweet fruit turns bitter when bliss fades. Accompanied by the unplayed music of *Twelfth Night* Bertha Young relives the epiphany of Genesis in a London garden.

Notes

1. Saralyn R. Daly (*Katherine Mansfield* [New York, Twayne, 1965], pp. 81-83) refers to Bertha's "bliss" as the passion she and Pearl share for Harry, and agrees with Sylvia Berkman (*Katherine Mansfield, A Critical Study* [New Haven: Yale Univ. Press, 1951]) that Bertha is hysterical. Daly believes that what Bertha first "interprets . . . as 'bliss,'" but shortly calls "hysteria," has arisen because she knows her husband is having an affair . . ." (p. 83). She believes that Bertha is uncomfortable "before animal sexuality" (p. 83) and that Bertha "physically rejects Harry" (p. 86) as the cool pear-tree analogue, Pearl, does not. The pear tree remains lovely, according to Berkman, because it reveals the "immutability of natural beauty in the face of human disaster" (p. 107), whereas Daly (p. 87) points out that "such beauty offers no promise. . . ." She asserts that Bertha knows what will inevitably happen. Pointing out how Mansfield uses autobiography to reconcile parts of the self in her writing, Marvin Magalaner ("Traces of Her 'Self' in Katherine Mansfield's 'Bliss,'" *Modern Fiction Studies*, 24 [1978], 420) sees the characters as parts of the whole, so that the lead character is the moon, Pearl, and the tree is Bertha-Pearl. The woman becomes a compound of opposites, the "virginal matron and harlot" amalgamated in "Bertha-Pearl" (p. 420). In his longer study, *The Fiction of Katherine Mansfield* (Carbondale: Southern Illinois Univ. Press, 1971), p. 85, Magalaner again equates Pearl with the moon and Harry with the tree, maintaining that Bertha wants to stave off old age, hence she sees the pear tree as always in full bloom though it is "blasted in advance by Marvell's chill observations on time and eternity." Helen F. Nebeker ("The Pear Tree: Sexual Implications in Katherine Mansfield's 'Bliss,'" *Modern Fiction Studies*, 24 [1978], 545-51) sees "Bliss" as a tale of Bertha's homosexual love for Pearl and her disillusionment at the discovery of Pearl's passion for a man. Only what Nebeker calls the "bisexual pear tree" remains perfect. Marilyn Zorn ("Visionary Flowers: Another Study of Katherine Mansfield's 'Bliss,'" *Studies in Short Fiction* [Spring 1980], 173) calls the story a romantic "cry against corruption" of Shelley's "white radiance of eternity" and speaks of her inability to find someone with whom to share her vision which will remain locked in her forever unrealized passion (p. 147).

2. "Bliss," *The Short Stories of Katherine Mansfield*, ed. J. Middleton Murry (New York: Knopf, 1937), p. 350. All further quotations of the story are from this edition and will hereafter be cited in the text by page number.

3. Magalaner casually refers to Bertha as "a more mature Eve than Laura" and to Harry as a "modern Adam" whose fall causes Bertha's "expulsion from the fantasy garden" in *The Fiction of Katherine Mansfield*, p. 77. Berkman, *Katherine Mansfield, A Critical Study*, p. 252, notes that a "ruined Eden" is one of Mansfield's major symbols in numerous stories, especially "Bliss." Zorn,

"Visionary Flowers," p. 146, also utilizes the Eden imagery noted by Magalaner. She speaks of the sun images in this story and of Mansfield's consistent use of images "which link the sun and moon" as "holistic" for Mansfield. "They suggest the earthly paradise, the condition of prelapsarian innocence."

4. All biblical citations are from the King James Version.

5. *Journal of Katherine Mansfield,* ed. John Middleton Murry (New York: McGraw-Hill, 1964), p. 56. In this same entry, Mansfield writes that her Bible reading has continued "with the same desire" as that with which she has always read Shakespeare.

6. For Edenic imagery and references to innocence, see note 3, especially Zorn, who also mentions the prevalence of these images in the story "Sun and Moon," and Magalaner, *The Fiction of Katherine Mansfield.*

7. Face's coat is described on page 343 of "Bliss." Magalaner, *The Fiction of Katherine Mansfield,* pp. 82-84, writes of Mansfield's association of the couple with monkeys who mimic and imitate and are part of the gross animalistic aspect typical of the segment of society Mansfield scorns.

8. Magalaner, *The Fiction of Katherine Mansfield,* p. 78; Zorn, "Visionary Flowers," p. 146.

9. Berkman, *Katherine Mansfield, A Critical Study,* p. 195; Magalaner, "Traces of Her 'Self,'" p. 195.

10. "Bliss" (p. 345) actually refers to Pearl's expression as a "strange half smile."

11. Nebeker, "The Pear Tree," p. 546.

12. This imagery is especially noted by Magalaner, *The Fiction of Katherine Mansfield,* p. 82, and "Traces of Her 'Self,'" pp. 415-17, and by Zorn, "Visionary Flowers," pp. 146-47.

13. Zorn, "Visionary Flowers," p. 147; Magalaner, "Traces of her 'Self,'" p. 417, speaks of Mansfield's preoccupation with "consuming and being consumed."

14. Zorn, "Visionary Flowers," p. 144, is quoting from *Katherine Mansfield's Letters to John Middleton Murry: 1913-1922,* ed. John Middleton Murry (New York: Knopf, 1951), p. 211, hereafter cited as *Letters.*

15. *Letters,* pp. 144-45.

16. This phrase appears in *Twelfth Night* in the first speech about music as "the food of love," I.1.4, as quoted below in the text.

17. Magalaner, "Traces of Her 'Self,'" pp. 419, 422.

18. Magalaner, "Traces of Her 'Self,'" pp. 418, 419, quotes this letter (from *Letters,* p. 566) and cites both other letters and journal entries dealing with the same theme. He elaborates on people as parts of one another or "pairs," p. 421.

19. Magalaner, "Traces of Her 'Self,'" pp. 420, 421, and *The Fiction of Katherine Mansfield,* p. 79.

20. Magalaner, "Traces of Her 'Self,'" p. 421.

21. *The Letters of Katherine Mansfield* (New York: Knopf, 1936), pp. 70-72.

22. Nebeker, "The Pear Tree," pp. 547, 548.

23. Magalaner, *The Fiction of Katherine Mansfield,* p. 75, accepts Bertha's testimony that she is "getting hysterical" and that she is "cold." Yet, Bertha's perception of her own marital bliss is clearly one even she doubts. Why, then, should one accept what is clearly something she was told by either society or Harry (that she is hysterical in joy and cold in bed) as accurate? In fact, the extramarital joys Harry pursues may be justified, as Mansfield suggests in the story, by his belief that he is different. If Harry sees Bertha's behavior as license to pursue other women, he is fully justified and can be "cool," even claiming about Bertha "The woman gave me of the tree and I did eat." This fractured version of Genesis 3 is part of what the story is about.

24. See Magalaner, *The Fiction of Katherine Mansfield,* p. 76, and Zorn, "Visionary Flowers," p. 145, on the irony or delusion apparent in this line from page 342 of "Bliss."

25. *Letters,* p. 127.

26. Magalaner, "Traces of Her 'Self,'" p. 416.

27. Mansfield is quoting and elaborating on the line, "Hang there like a fruit, my soul, Till the tree die," from *Cymbeline* V. 5.236. Another work about confused identities, this Shakespearean play includes the character of Imogen who has just asked her husband why he rejected her. These admiring words are his reply.

Rhoda B. Nathan (essay date 1988)

SOURCE: Nathan, Rhoda B. "Neurotics, Eccentrics, and Victims: Stories of Character." In *Katherine Mansfield,* pp. 87-112. New York: Continuum Publishing Company, 1988.

[*In the following essay, Nathan compares Mansfield to Anton Chekhov in her immense skill at developing character through imagery, description, and internal monologues. The critic examines the treatment of a number of Mansfield's protagonists to support her argument.*]

Like her acknowledged master Anton Chekhov, Mansfield became an adept at the story that anatomizes character and temperament through a significant emblem, a loaded statement, a minor idiosyncrasy. The animation of an ordinary lifeless object such as the "sea of coloured blouses" and "quivering hair-bows" of the pupils in **"The Singing Lesson"** establishes the same tension that the "flickering light" in the little servant's room does in Chekhov's "Sleepy." Mansfield began writing character studies at a very early age, and ultimately developed the genre to a high art. Even so youthful a sketch as **"A Truthful Adventure,"** in which the author scarcely bothers to disguise herself but calls the protagonist Katherine, shows evidence of that attention to the easily overlooked nuance of behavior or gesture that reveals character and conflict in a flash.

Away from home for the first time on a trip to Bruges in Belgium, the young Katherine, lonely and feeling inadequate in the face of centuries of European history, happens upon an old girlfriend from New Zealand. The meeting, which should have proved a source of comfort to her, turns out to be fraught with what Chekhov would have called "poshlost," conversation that was at once vulgar, trivial, and, to the young girl, ludicrous. Everything "touristy" that the impressionable fledgling artist was seeking to avoid in her immersion in the ancient city is thrust on her by her crass compatriot. The banality of her acquaintance's gush stands in sharp contrast with her unuttered soliloquy. "You know," her former schoolmate babbles, "Bruges is simply packed with treasures and churches and pictures. There's an outdoor concert tonight in the Grand Place and a competition of bell ringers tomorrow for the whole week." Her unimaginative sight-seeing program is superimposed on the narrator's internal resolution: "At evensong I shall lie in the long grass of the Beguinage meadow and look up at the elm trees—their leaves touched with cold light and quivering in the blue air—listening the while to the voices of nuns at prayer in the little chapel." The portrait of the artist as a young woman is of course the design of the sketchy story. The narrator, with her senses alert and simultaneously recording impressions that have nothing to do with external events or occasions, is contrasted in a single paragraph with her less inspired friend. The sharp distinction between the poetic temperament and the tourist mentality is instantly effected through a scrap of conversation. The artist has a mystical union with nature that the ordinary person lacks.

Through the alternation of dialogue and monologue, Mansfield was to hone the craft of character portraiture to a fine art. Eventually she would succeed in a complex interweaving of imagery, detailed description, and lengthy passages of internalized streams of thought to achieve fully realized characters. One of her most successful achievements, albeit of a singularly unsympathetic type, was the central figure in the story **"Mr. Reginald Peacock's Day."** The very name the author assigns her hero tells the story. Reginald Peacock is one of Mansfield's favorite types, a caricature notable for vanity and selfishness. According to Alpers's biography of Mansfield, he is supposedly modeled on her first husband, George Bowden, described as a musician who has enjoyed the patronage of well-heeled ladies through the "flowery path of a choral scholarship" and a reputation as a "gentleman-artist" with a "bedside manner." The plot of the story is nearly nonexistent. It unfolds as a species of docudrama, with the author following Peacock through his day, recording its events with meticulous fidelity. His character is neatly captured without the benefit of authorial comment, merely by showing him in his private and public roles. In his domestic life he is revealed as a whining narcissistic infant, abusing his long-suffering and gentle wife. Throughout his professional day, he is charming, flirtatious, and fawning. This two-sided and fully fleshed portrait is accomplished through a single effective device: the internal stream of thought. The entire day's schedule is filtered to the reader through Peacock's mind, from his preparation for his appointments, vocalizing, preening before the mirror, and practicing his hand-kissing techniques, to the letdown he feels when he must return to his modest home to his neglected patient wife.

The story turns on an irony that encapsulates the confusion of values and insincerity in the character of the voice teacher. All through the day he has addressed his highborn female pupils with a well-worn phrase of flattery. As he ushers them out he responds to their invitations to their musicales, their small select dinners, and their soirees with the polished formula, "Dear Lady, I shall be only too charmed." After the whirl of his glamorous day, culminating in a tête-à-tête with a nymph named Aenone Fell and a splendid dinner with Lord Timbuck who addresses him as an equal, he returns to his humble apartment and finds his wife asleep, "squeezed over to her side of the bed," as self-abnegating in repose as in her waking hours. Rousing her with his noisy bedtime rituals, he determines to make an effort to treat his wife for once as an equal as he has been regarded all day. But, the author concludes, "for some fiendish reason, the only words he could get out were, 'Dear Lady, I should be so charmed—so charmed!'"

The petty incident is vile yet painful, both to the participants and to the reader. The wife's reaction is not recorded, but the reader feels indignation for her. The author's unwavering focus remains on Peacock, a sad excuse for a man but a predictably human failure unable to utter anything but a trite sentiment to the person closest to him in the world. Contemptible as he is, he is as much a victim of his fantasies as his wife is of his selfishness. All day long he has lived in a magical world of his betters, dreaming, while he was singing, of the party to be held that evening, of "their feathers and their flowers and their fans, offered to him, laid before him, like a huge bouquet." In the story's alternation of scenes of reality and illusion, the character's real inadequacy is dramatically exposed. The wife's pain is implicit but not articulated, because Mansfield's thesis rests on the deficiency in the husband's character that causes him to worship false idols and scorn his familiar and protective household gods.

Miss Ada Moss in the story **"Pictures"** is, in direct contrast to Mr. Reginald Peacock, firmly rooted in the here and now. Much more naturalistic in style, and entirely free of decorative flourishes, the story is a detailed and unsentimental portrait of an old fat chorus girl down on her luck and pressed to the wall. The ills of aging flesh, varicose veins, and chilblains brought on by her unheated rented room are meticulously recorded, as are her unsuccessful rounds of the hiring halls for a bit part in a musical comedy. The solid fleshly ambiance of this sordid story is kept sharply in focus through carefully chosen symbols: the blue serge and artificial violets in which Ada Moss sails out in search of a job; the "great knots of greeny-blue veins" on her fat white legs that tell the story of long hours on her feet waiting for a call; and the "sausage finger" of the stout gentleman who "saves" her by paying her for the sexual work in which she is still serviceable.

Although this character study is unambiguous, any attempt to draw a message or moral from it is gratuitous. It is simply a coolly rendered slice of life, near scientific in its microscopic scrutiny. Miss Ada Moss is neither good nor bad. She is redeemed from bathos by Mansfield's naturalistic technique, and exempt from unwarranted sympathy by her perfectly credible coarseness that has been shaped by a predatory environment. Throughout the sketch, like a ship in full sail, she is always in motion, buffeted by the wayward winds while she attempts to navigate the dangerous shoals with just enough courage and know-how to keep afloat. At the end, determined to survive, she follows the "gentleman" to his rooms. "Wearing a very small hat that floated on top of her head like a little yacht," her gallant steward holds out a lifesaver to the overripe siren, and Miss Moss "sail[s] after the little yacht out of the café."

"Miss Brill" is another full portrait of a "marginal" woman, told from the subjective point of view of an aging insignificant character. However, whereas Miss Ada Moss is an embattled survivor, the genteel Miss Brill is an observer of life, one who sits on the sidelines and watches the game in all its striving, contending, cruelty, and passion. She is as frozen in time as in a sepia photograph, wearing her ratty fox fur as if she were at the theater instead of seated on her usual bench in the park on Sunday, observing the scenes played out one after another. She even fancies that she, the receptive audience, might be missed by the players if she were to fail to show up for one of the performances. Her illusion is cruelly shattered when she accidentally overhears two young lovers making fun of her as she avidly eavesdrops on their lovemaking.

In the unconscious irony of Miss Brill's final behavior, the onlooker aspect of her life is reinforced. As she puts away her Sunday fur, she imagines she hears something crying in the box. So inauthentic is her life, made up of secondhand experience as well as secondhand furs, that she is incapable of recognizing the origin of her tears, which of course, is her grief and humiliation. It is more natural to her to imagine that the weeping comes from the glass eyes of the fox's head on the boa.

The four stories discussed so far share a common narrative structure. The author follows her characters through the events of their day, alternating actual events with the characters' private interpretation of their experiences. This single technique that yields up a multifaceted character derives from the author's narrative pace, which is rapid and economical, and in full control of the scenes that are juxtaposed for the purpose of contrast between the reality of their daily lives and their private yearnings and illusions. In **"Mr. Reginald Peacock's Day,"** for example, Reginald is literally followed by the author, who dogs his footsteps through the various rooms of his modest home, then on to the salons of his wealthy clients, and finally, to complete the cycle of his day, back to the bedroom where he was first met that morning. He has been revealed in these connecting yet contrasting scenes as self-indulgent, peevish, demanding, fawning, preening, and finally, inadequate. In scene after scene the real mediocre man has been counterposed alongside the performer. In each case he responds to his environment with the spontaneity of a shallow nature imbued with large visions of self-aggrandizement.

In the study of Miss Brill, the narrator follows her from the privacy of her humble rooms to the exposure of the public park, where she partakes of other people's joys and sorrows in voyeuristic pleasure, and then accompanies her to the bakeshop where she seeks to sweeten her weekly Sunday outing with a slice of cake. Again, as in the previous tale, the cycle is complete when the author sees her safely back in her room at the end of her day. But although the setting is familiar, she has been irrevocably changed by the events of the day that evolved so naturally in the connecting scenes, but contain one small insignificant moment that ruined not only this day, but would poison her Sundays henceforward.

The dramatized scenes in Miss Ada Moss's day, like the others, are logically connected, and like the others, contrast with each other for the purpose of ironic impact. The three scenes are her shoddy room in a boarding house where she is not welcome because she cannot pay her rent; the booking agent's where she is not welcome because she is too old to be employed as a show girl; and finally, the café, where she is anonymous but welcome because some man will come along and pay for her drink and dinner. The title of the story, **"Pictures,"** is evocative of the visions of nourishing meals floating over her head in her hungry morning state, to the final picture, in which the prospect of a satisfying dinner is realized through the exchange of sexual payment.

The technique of juxtaposition of scenes dramatizing the real and wishful lives of troubled people is developed to a much more ambitious extent in Mansfield's most celebrated character stories, **"The Life of Ma Parker"** and **"The Daughters of the Late Colonel."** In the first, Mansfield once again pays tribute to Chekhov, in creating a female servant based on a male cabman in Chekhov's "Misery," who tries without success to tell his fares his tragic story; he has just lost his son and continues to recount his sorrow to a succession of strangers who have hired his cab in order to relieve his feelings and extract some sympathy from his fellows. He ends up telling his story to his little mare, who munches her oats patiently through the sad narration.

"The Life of Ma Parker" is in no sense a copy of Chekhov's, as is **"The Child Who Was Tired,"** but it does use the bare bones of the Russian writer's plot. For the rest, the story is entirely original, although it strives for the profound compassion that marks the best of Chekhov's stories about ordinary people who are victimized by their lot. Mansfield's Ma Parker is such a victim, poor and uneducated, consigned to live at the very edge of the economic and social structure by an accident of birth. Hers is an uncelebrated life. If Chekhov's servant is a male sleigh driver who transports ill-mannered gentlemen for a slave wage, Mansfield's is one of the army of "ladies who do" who let themselves into the lodgings of cultivated gentlemen for a half-day's pay to clean up a week's worth of dirty dishes and other residues of the impecunious intellectuals' genteel shabby lives.

Ma Parker is one of those characters whose marginal lives are traced through connecting scenes of present circumstance and recollected scenes of the past. In this story Mansfield has hit her stride and controls her subject through the use of meticulous naturalistic detail. The full tragedy of her life unfolds as step by step the author evokes the old woman's sad plight. She releases her information bit by bit, until the reader has a fully rounded character, contending with the present while she retraces her inexorable past, all the while drudging away with stoicism. The first scene locates Ma Parker at the flat of the literary gentleman, responding to his mechanical query about her ailing grandson. To her dispirited "We buried him yesterday, sir," he says with condescension, "I hope the funeral went off all right." It is not so much her employer's callousness as his conviction that the lower classes "set such store" by conventional rites such as funerals that encourages her to hug her secrets close to her bosom. Still, her gentleman's suggestion about the "pleasure" intrinsic to the funeral actually does set off pleasurable memories in the charwoman's mind. As she sets about her menial chores she is transported to another place in her past, sitting in a deep chair with her grandson snuggled in her arms. As she daydreams, conjuring up the delicious feeling of the small breathing presence in her sheltering arms, the boiling kettle awakens her to the sordid dregs of her reality, the indescribably filthy kitchen that she must put in order for the "gentleman." The monotony of her task triggers another recollection, and the scene shifts again to the past. In paragraph after paragraph, her debased present is connected to and contrasted with the past, which admittedly was hard but compensated by the love of her grandson. Fleeting moments of the child's freely given affection are recalled with alternating scenes of her servitude. She remembers her grandson's piping "gran" when he addressed her, in marked contrast to her employer's allusion to her as a "hag," and the child's wholehearted trust in her generosity as distinct from the gentleman's accusing her of filching a teaspoon of cocoa. The irony of the "gentleman's" boorish behavior to a poor old servant and her own gallant self-control in the face of callousness is apparent in Mansfield's carefully uninflected narration.

"The Life of Ma Parker" is not a conventional story. It has no real plot. The recollected episodes of an ordinary person's life are psychological tools for understanding the character of a simple woman whose grief is poignant although her story lacks tragic dimension. The double pathos of this elemental tale lies in her loss and her total isolation. She accepts her lot, but lacks the equipment to work through her unhappy situation. She simply has nowhere to go after the child dies. Although her material circumstances have not altered, the real core of her life is gone. Leaving her gentleman's flat, where she is an unwelcome temporary necessity in his selfish life, she dreads going home where she will have to face her daughter, the dead child's mother, and relive her sorrow. She has nothing to soften the impact of her loss, and no heroic resources to enable her to rise above it. She has had a hard life, as she once explained to her gentleman, and its single consolation is gone.

Death, or rather, its consequences, is likewise the subject of **"The Daughters of the Late Colonel,"** and here too there is nothing heroic or tragic about the deceased or those he left behind. However, whereas **"The Life of Ma Parker"** is more a sociological case study than a fully developed story, **"Daughters"** is full of action. The tone is set in the first sentence: "The week after was one of the busiest weeks in their lives." The busyness is both physical and emotional, attesting to the deep agitation and displacement experienced by the two spinster daughters of a severe autocratic father, the late colonel of the title. A deficient yet dictatorial parent in his lifetime, he has left his daughters a legacy of dread and impotence in their bereavement. Although they are well into their middle years, their behavior is decidedly childlike, if not downright childish at moments. Yet they are clearly distinguishable from each other in temperament and response. Josephine, the elder, is irascible and authoritative; Constantia, her younger sister, is soft and wavering.

"**Daughters**" is a species of black comedy. All the characters are eccentrics, from the two spinsters with their respective pallid and florid complexions and their uneventful lives mired in petty detail, to the tyrannical old man who has expired after opening just one eye in his purple face. Even the hired nurse who tends the old ramrod in his last illness is a highfalutin caricature with an exasperating laugh "like a spoon tinkling against a medicine glass." What saves Josephine with her "small bead-like eyes" and Constantia with her long pale face from being equally grotesque is the genuine pathos of their situation. They bear the psychological wounds of their father's harshness, which has left them so fearful that they have not the courage even to demand the service due them from the contemptuous kitchen maid, who alludes to them as "the old tabbies."

"**Daughters**" is a fully developed story in eight parts, one of Mansfield's longest. Each sequential scene moves the story of the women's adjustment forward by retracing their past lives under their father's iron fist, while all the time they are preparing for the funeral and their ensuing orphaned existence. Thus the events move forward and backward in time in each short chapter, revealing additional aspects of the hedged-in lives of the sisters. In parts 8 and 9 their deprivation and gullibility are demonstrated through a flashback to a recent episode. The two are lamenting the failure of their nephew Cyril, the old man's only grandson, to attend his grandfather's funeral. The old maids' emotional deprivation is manifest in their sentimental indulgence of their handsome nephew, who is a thoroughgoing rotter. While his aunts are extremely generous to him, planning to give him the old man's gold watch, the young wastrel avoids paying his respects, even though they stuff him with "rich dark cake that stood for Josephine's winter gloves or the soling and heeling of Constantia's only respectable shoes."

"**Daughters**" is one of the stories that best illustrates Mansfield's comic gifts. The two sisters are a Laurel and Hardy duo—the one plump and ineffectual, the other desiccated and prim—both ludicrous in their regressed infantilism vis-à-vis their domineering parent. Even now that he is safely dead, they are sure that their "father would never forgive them for daring to bury him," let alone having the temerity to go through his personal things for bequest. The terrifying old man, recollected by his cowed daughters, is literalized through the same frivolous emblem that serves for his playboy grandson. The costly meringues that his doting aunts have bought to lure the young man to tea are recalled later in the same scene when the colonel, just before his demise, cups his hand "like a purple meringue shell over one ear," the better to hear his daughters' silly natterings and roar his disgust like the sounding sea.

Mansfield's comic art is achieved within the emotional frame of the story and finally intensifies the pathos of the sisters' lives. The humor of a given situation is realized through symbols seen in more than one perspective. Thus, the meringue representing the extravagance of the two sisters also signifies the nephew's airy carelessness of their caring. He disremembers whether his "poor dear father" had been fond of meringues also, as he must have been, given his heredity. And finally, that some meringue, which predominates in parts 8 and 9, is given its final hilarious explication in the ensuing scene, when the irascible old man, just before his expiring, cups his meringue shell hand over his deaf meringue ear, and demands to know what his two cowed daughters are yammering about. They have been endeavoring to impart to him the information—vital to them but gibberish to him—that his late son had been fond of meringues. "What an esstraordinary [sic] thing," he broods, after the dawning light of comprehension, "to come all this way here to tell me!" The meringue itself, a fluffy insubstantial cake literally composed of beaten air, is a pertinent emblem of the content of all their insignificant lives.

The resolution of the story restores the balance necessary to its credibility. The pace of the narration itself slows down, as do the lives of the sisters after the hectic activity of the prefunerary bustle. Even their speech becomes halting and sluggish as the reality of their situation takes hold. Liberated from parental control and thrust into adult roles late in life, the sisters are unable to cope with the unprecedented challenge of their new freedom, and, in effect, fade out. Their unfinished sentences trail off into silence as they contemplate their uncertain future. The mood of the final episode is set by fragments of speculation such as "I was wondering if now . . ." and "Don't you think perhaps . . . ?" After the bustle and conflict in the roaring old man's final hours and stormy death, the sisters' tentative murmurs tell the story of the remainder of their lives. Lacking in guidance, devoid of substance, their days will drift away.

Balancing the comic vision with unflinching realism is a trick Mansfield must have learned from her long painstaking study of Chekhov. Chekhov's most memorable characters are comical in their ineffectuality, nervous tics, foolish opinions, and aimless gestures, all of which render them all too human from a psychological perspective. Josephine's most irrational utterance is the very thing that humanizes her, ludicrous as it is. Guilt-ridden and panic-stricken after the funeral, she bursts into tears and blurts to her sister: "We shouldn't have done it, Con!"

> And Constantia, pale as a lemon in all that blackness, said in a frightened whisper, "Done what, Jug?" "Let them bu-bury father like that," said Josephine. . . . "But what else could we have done?" asked Constantia wonderingly. "We couldn't have kept him, Jug—we couldn't have kept him unburied. At any rate, not in a flat that size." . . . Josephine blew her nose. . . . "I don't know," she said forlornly. "It is all so dreadful. I feel we ought to have tried to, just for a time at least. To make perfectly sure. One thing's certain"—and her tears sprang out again—"father will never forgive us for this—never!"

The hilarious effect of this passage derives from the irrational childishness of a fully grown woman. Yet there is genuine pathos in her fears and quirks. The skill with which the author chips away at the adult protective shells of the spinsters Constantia and Josephine to unearth the quaking children Con and Jug lies at the very heart of her finest character studies. These are real people, predictable products of a certain kind of inadequate rearing and emotional starvation. They are guilty, frightened, immature, and entirely credible. As characters, they are a far cry from the one-dimensional characters Mansfield drew in the **Pension** sketches as her only revenge against the national character of her "captors" during her confinement.

In this period Mansfield was as psychologically sound in her portrayal of the very young as she was of the ineffectual elderly characters in an environment that freezes out the two marginal elements. **"The Young Girl"** is a minor story, but handled in great detail, about a pretty adolescent, caught between her young brother's patently childish world of ice-cream parlors and her mother's forbidden world of gambling casinos during a Riviera holiday. The girl's petulance at being barred from the glamorous pursuits of her elders and being forced into the company of her docile small sibling is caught in two illustrative scenes. The first shows her chagrin and humiliation when she is barred from the casino and obliged to accompany her brother to the despised tea shop. She is rebellious and contemptuous. She flaunts her "soft young body in the blue dress . . . like a flower that is just emerging from its dark bud." She whips out the tools of her new maturity—a compact and a lipstick—and powders her perfect nose and rouges her rosy lips in defiance of all her heartless elders. The second scene shows her other aspect, the vulnerability of the child still intact within the burgeoning woman's body. Taken to a tea shop in compensation for being ousted from the casino, she is placated by her elders with chocolate and "little melting dreams" of pastries, which she devours even as she scorns them. Nature will have its due. Although she will design to accept only the most ethereal of nourishment—tangerine ice to be eaten with tiny silver spoons and miniature pastry cornets filled with strawberries—she is nonetheless bribable, avid for pleasure, if not of one kind, then of another, and withal, a healthy young girl with a growing girl's appetite for sweets. Her "lovely nose" sniffs the perfumed air of the tea shop, and the irresistible chocolate glides down the flawless "white throat."

Mansfield's preoccupation with food in her stories has often been remarked. There is no doubt that like her master, Chekhov, she dwells on eating, menus, hunger and its appeasement, and detailed accounts of the food and drink at dinner parties. Chekhov's obsession with food in his stories "Oysters" and "The Siren's Song" is no more extreme than Mansfield's "pageant of sensible substantial dinners" that drifts across Miss Ada Moss's field of vision in **"Pictures"** or the "shameless passion for the white flesh of the lobster" Harry Young confesses to in **"Bliss."** But, as in Chekhov, the rituals of eating and drinking, the references to certain kinds of foods, such as "the green of pistachio ices" in **"Bliss"** and grapes "green and cold like the eyelids of Egyptian dancers," are intended to release larger information about the character than the literal simile suggests. Rites, landmarks, conflicts, and unaltering values are implicit within the food symbolism in Mansfield's stories. The melted miniature ice-cream house in the story **"Sun and Moon"** distresses a small boy and causes him to howl in so "unmanly" a fashion that he infuriates his father. The subject of this story is generational conflict. In **"Bliss,"** a beautiful red soup chosen to dramatize the pale gray plates in which it is served is a symbol of the aesthetic harmony in Bertha Young's life that will end in disharmony and disillusion. In **"The Dill Pickle"** a young woman imagines a condiment so sour that it causes her to "suck in her cheeks," a sign of her keen imagination and her ability to imagine unshared experience, however acid. Death is symbolized by the broken cakes and dried-out leftover sandwiches Laura Sheridan carries to the house of mourning in **"The Garden Party."** Seeking gratification of some kind, characters in the stories eat, alone and together, foods that symbolize their nature and position. Ada Moss, common and down on her luck, craves a glass of "nourishing" stout. The fuming pubescent in **"The Young Girl,"** frustrated in her inability to indulge in the forbidden glamorous rituals of the casino, finally gives in to her appetite for some kind of pleasure, and wolfs down the despised ices, creams, and éclairs as a surrogate for unattainable emotional satisfaction.

Food, furnishings, clothing, and personal adornment are some of the meticulously handled details of Mansfield's character fiction that contribute lavishly to its psychological realism. Character in perspective is accomplished through another technique; each person is shown in at least two different lights. Both Miss Moss and Miss Brill are subjected to the scrutiny of others, Miss Moss by her landlady who sees her for the old trollop she is, and Miss Brill by the two lovers who, within her hearing, make fun of her "silly old mug" and her ratty fox fur piece. These revelations shatter illusions just as surely as the young girl's false notion of her maturity is pricked by her unceremonious ousting from the casino where only real grown-ups are allowed to play.

The attitudes of the characters are often at odds with their actual environment, their aspirations and limitations carefully juxtaposed. Two such cases, both involving old men, may be found in **"The Fly"** and **"The Ideal Family."** Each of the elderly men is a "boss," a success in business and a figure of authority. But as each story unfolds, each is seen from another perspective. In personal terms they are victims of their age, their society's values, and their own children. The old man in **"The Fly"** denies his humanity, while Mr. Neave in **"The Ideal Family"** questions the humanity around him. Each man is a variation of Stanley Burnell grown old, at the end of his forces and incapable of controlling his environment. The tragedy of the aged go-getter who has outlived his own authority has its inevitable logic as well as its natural pathos. The first "boss," the central figure of **"The Fly,"** spoiled with power, is incapable of weeping for his dead son because the boy had disobeyed him and joined the army. He vents his accumulated frustration in a brutal act of drowning a struggling fly in a drop of ink as he sits alone at his desk. The second, a man of equivalent wealth and position, the head of "an ideal family," is shown at the moment of his failing strength, dressing for dinner with his family but shunted to the sidelines by his preoccupied wife and his self-indulgent children.

Each profile is accurately drawn and devoid of sentimentality. The elderly brute drowning the struggling fly even as he admires its pluck for surfacing each time but the last, is a realistic portrait of a man whose rage must be relieved because his sorrow goes unpurged. The fatigued old businessman of the second story dozes away in his room, unnoticed as the dinner party goes on below without him. He has paid for the bounty enjoyed in the splendid dining room but his presence at the board is no longer required nor welcome. All the while dreams and reality merge in his confused state as he is caught between fading life and imminent death but participating in neither.

Although these two stories are not dream stories, Mansfield makes use of the dream in both for the purpose of perspective. Psychological realism derives from examining the inner life, in these cases presented in the form of reveries. The boss in **"The Fly"** dreams of his beloved dead son just before his savage attack on the insect. Old Mr. Neave in **"The Ideal Family"** has two opposing dreams: the past, in which he feels the soft warm arms of a vanished young girl about his neck— the girl he should have married; and the future, his vision of a withered old man painfully climbing steps leading to infinity. Both dreams are truthful interpretations of his unrealized goals and his wearisome sterile achievements.

The flashback is another version of the dream. It shows the past, often halcyon in recollection, in contrast to the grim present. In **"The Fly"** the photograph of the boss's dead son on his father's desk is a recurring image that stirs up memories of the painful vanished past. The young fellow's sunny disposition is recalled as a symbol of the old man's unrealized aspirations, but the serious expression on the boy's face affronts his father, who denies his son had ever looked like that. His rage at the cruel tricks of fate, coupled with his guilt in not being able to remember his beloved son's facial expression, finds relief in his sadistic murder of the helpless fly. Still, after the corpse is disposed of, he cannot find surcease. Instead of cathartic relief, he is seized by despair. The flashback to his son's untested youth has activated but not assuaged all the dormant repressed grief and anger in the impotent old man.

To the discomforts and idiosyncrasies of the eccentrics, victims, and outcasts in her stories, Mansfield brings an amalgam of authorial tolerance, humor, and compassion. The point of view in **"The Fly"** and **"The Ideal Family"** are cases in point. But for neurotics, the author wields a rapier. There is a world of difference between the insecure Reginald coming courting in **"Mr. and Mrs. Dove"** and the selfish spoiled Monica Tyrell in **"Revelations."** The tone in the latter story is set in the first sentence: "From eight o'clock in the morning until half-past eleven Monica Tyrell suffered from her nerves." The point of view is entirely subjective, but the reader is aware of Mansfield's moral presence as surely as he is of Henry James's stern judgment of the egotistical John Marcher in "The Beast in the Jungle" or of Chekhov's contempt for selfish Olga in "The Grasshopper." Monica Tyrell is a neurotic, and as such earns her creator's unmitigated scorn. Her story is told in gestures more than in episodes, each moving the story forward with inexorable logic to its inescapable conclusion. The heroine's gestures of "suffering" at the slightest irritation to her delicate nerves—the banging of a shutter; the ringing of a telephone; the pull of a hairbrush through her pampered tresses—cause her to press trembling fingers to pained eyes. In short, she is too fragile a flower for the indignities of everyday life. Anguished apostrophes such as "Oh, if it were as simple as that!" accompanied by pained dismissing gestures, shut out illness, poverty, and similar catastrophes from her luxurious boudoir.

But life insists on intruding, in spite of a well-regulated well-staffed household. Although he knows that his wife cannot face the morning hours, Monica's heartless husband has been thoughtless enough to send a telephone message asking that she join him for lunch. This burden entails a more grievous one, a mandatory morning visit to the hairdresser on a raw windy day that frazzles her nerves beyond endurance. The crisis takes shape the moment Monica enters the perfumed precincts of the beauty shop. She senses, with the unerring instincts of the master narcissist, that the usual muted sycophancy of the elegantly appointed salon is off by a shade. A barely identifiable pall hangs over the establishment. Her hairdresser tugs at her hair and fails to remark on its beauty and sheen. When she finally discovers, not through any sensitivity or concern, that her hairdresser's small daughter has just died, she flees in panic. She experiences an unprecedented impulse to send him flowers as she passes a florist in her cab. In a pleasurable reverie she imagines a bouquet of white lilies and pansies tied with white ribbon and her sentimental accompanying note glorifying her pain at his bereavement.

The vignette ends with a swift denouement that captures the selfishness of the neurotic. Moved by her generous impulse, Monica taps against the window just as her cab passes the florist. But the driver does not hear, and "anyway, they were at Prince's already."

The neurotic's inability to act, to think things through, to progress beyond narcissism to compassion, is manifest in the story's mode of narration. The breathless highly agitated style is formed by elliptical sentence structure, incomplete phrases punctuated by dashes to dramatize Monica's inability to sustain a thought, and irritated gestures of dismissal. Mansfield does not trouble to comment on the ludicrous aspects of Monica's resentment of being put upon by an inconsiderate spouse who requests her company for lunch. Her self-absorption juxtaposed against the real but contained grief of the bereaved hairdresser speaks for itself, as does her craven flight from the scene.

"The Escape," the story that follows **"Revelations"** in the *Collected Stories,* is a continuation of the same theme—the selfish female of neurotic temperament in a merciless pursuit of shelter and comfort. The same techniques prevail. A succession of internal monologues are truncated in midsentence as the character's restless thoughts skitter from one internal complaint to another. An undercurrent of whining is carried by a deft vocabulary—words like "hideous," "idiotic," "ridiculous"—when the woman takes stock of the people who have been put on earth to cushion her person and expedite her needs. In contrast, the character of the demanding woman's husband emerges as fine, generous, and trusting through her interior monologue:

> It was his fault, wholly and solely his fault, that they had missed the train. What if the idiotic hotel had refused to produce the bill? Wasn't that simply because he hadn't impressed upon the waiter at lunch that they must have it by two o'clock? Any other man would have sat there and refused to move until they handed it over. But no! His exquisite belief in human nature had allowed him to get up and expect one of those idiots to bring it to their room.

Her veils, scented handkerchief, silver purse, and phials of pills, the ammunition of the neurotic, are contrasted with the world about her, an impoverished area in the Mediterranean where she has been convalescing. Her insularity rejects the baby held up by its proud mother for the inspection of the fine English lady. All she can see is its "awful, awful head." The flies circling the peasant houses, the sunburned carbuncled neck of the cabman, and "the disgusting, revolting dust" are affronts to her sensibility. Even the gift of flowers brought by the local urchins is rejected. She heaps contumely upon her good-natured husband who offers the children a few coins for their goodwill. In a temper, she flings the bouquet from the carriage.

The title of the story carries a double meaning, just as **"Revelations"** does in the preceding tale. Literally, the escape is the invalid woman's, told from her point of view during her exodus from the spa. But the story ends in a sudden shift in the narrative voice. As his wife flounces from the carriage to retrieve a fallen parasol, the narrative is continued by the victimized husband, who is left with the cab to await her return. The emotionally exhausted man sees in his mind's eye "an immense tree with a round, thick silver stem and a great arc of copper leaves." He is taken by surprise, because he had been envisioning himself as a bleached skeleton buried in the valley below. From the silent silvery center of the magical tree he hears the soft full voice of a woman singing mellifluously and without strain. He is experiencing an epiphany that frees him from the shrill neurotic to whom he is yoked. Even after his return to England, the vision of the tree persists, offering him continued escape from her nagging presence. The memory of the charmed tree in its animistic power is similar to the erotic flowering of the pear tree in **"Bliss"** and the mysticism of the aloe in **"At the Bay."**

As unpleasant as the neurotics are in these stories, none can equal Raoul Duquette in **"Je ne parle pas français,"** Mansfield's longest story after **"Prelude."** Briefly, its plot, told entirely through flashbacks, is a tale of moral corruption. Duquette, the narrator, exposes his despicable character through an event in which he is only an accessory. The episode itself is recalled through an accidental reminder to the young man as he sits idly in a café and picks up a pad on which someone had scrawled "*Je ne parle pas français.*" He remembers that the same phrase had been spoken by a young English girl known only as "Mouse," perhaps because of her long snug gray fur-trimmed cloak, hat, and muff. She had been brought to Paris by Dick Harmon, a young English writer with whom Duquette had struck up an ambiguous, possibly homosexual friendship. When she had first met Duquette, she took his hand and murmured, "*Je ne parle pas français.*" She plainly needed protection, but within a few weeks was abandoned first by her lover and then by Duquette, who had promised to see her through. A self-confessed cynic and a pimp by profession, he admits being haunted by poor Mouse as he sits in his usual place arranging for a female companion for some "dirty old gallant."

The first paragraph is pure Toulouse-Lautrec, a graphic depiction of a seamy working-class café. As Duquette the pimp lounges in his booth he notes the "grey, flat-footed and withered" old waiter "in his far too long apron," smearing over the table with a "three-cornered dip of dirty napkin," or "pouring a glass of familiar purplish stuff with a green wandering light playing over it." Madame, the *patronne,* "is thin and dark, too, with white cheeks and white hands. In certain lights she looks quite transparent, shining out of her black shawl with an extraordinary effect."

Passages such as these are reminiscent of Lautrec's highly charged selective portrayals of the world of dance halls, brothels, and cafés, whose denizens come close to caricature. In this story Mansfield seems to be intent, as the painter was, on telling the "truth" about urban life through dramatic portraits intensified by a shawl, a hat, or a splash of color. She is equally preoccupied with the effects of light, painting the "thin dark girls with silver rings in their ears" against a backdrop of coarse workmen "all powdered over with flour" lounging against the bar. Through the window "one could just see the shapes of horses and carts and people, soft and white, moving through the feathery air." As the dusk thickens, the images seem to disappear in the enveloping gloom, much as in Monet's Rouen cathedral, painted variously through mist or snow. In the darkening café, Duquette fancies he sees the departed Mouse as a "soft bundle moving . . . through the feathery snow." The melancholy mood is determined by the fading light and hazy atmosphere.

Although this lengthy story is unsatisfactory because it fails to tie up a number of loose ends, it is a fascinating piece of "art," notable for its attempt to do with language what the Impressionists and Postimpressionists were doing with brush and palette. This is Mansfield's most "painterly" story, its aesthetic effects calculated, not incidental. That she was familiar with the work of the painters cited, as well as Cézanne, Manet, Matisse, and the others, is beyond conjecture. She frequented the galleries in London and attended and remarked in her letters the first Postimpressionist exhibition at the Grafton Gallery in London. The exhibit made such a profound impression on her that she wrote to her friend Dorothy Brett a dozen years later that the paintings "taught [her] something about writing which was queer, a kind of freedom—or rather, a shaking free." She began writing "impressionistic" exercises in her scrapbook, translating the pictorial effects of the painters into metaphors of light, shape, and immediacy of impression:

> There was no sound in the house any more nor any light save where the moon shone on the floors and ceilings, on the dismantled supper table, gleaming on the mirrors and fading flowers. Silence hung over the garden, but the garden was awake. Its fruit and flowers filled the air with a sweet wild scent. White and grey moths flew over the silvery branches of the syringa bushes. On the dark camellia trees flowers were poised like white and red birds.

In other exercises she shows that she is searching, as Cézanne did, for arbitrary arrangements of line and form to give coherence to related shapes and colors of objects strewn on the table:

> She bent her head, gazing with half-shut eyes at the white ring of the cup and the white ring of the saucer, the round white shape of the pot and jug, and the four crossed pieces of sugar on the table, at the cigarettes spilled out of the yellow wrapper.

"I want to reach that state of condensation of sensations which produces the picture," the painter Matisse wrote in 1908. Mansfield was aiming for the same visual initiative in 1918 when she began **"Je ne parle pas français."** Duquette produces just such a picture as Matisse envisioned with his self-portrait, which is a distillate of his corrupt and exotic character in a few phrases notable for "condensation of sensation":

> "I am little and light with an olive skin, black eyes with long lashes, black silky hair cut short, tiny square teeth that show when I smile. My hands are supple and small. . . . I am like a woman in a café who has to introduce herself with a handful of photographs. 'Me in a chemise, coming out of an eggshell . . . ; me upside down in a swing, with a frilly behind like a cauliflower.'"

Later on one sees the "Japonais" influence in Whistler and van Gogh in his continuing self-portraiture: "It was early morning. I wore a blue kimono embroidered with white birds and my hair was still wet; it lay on my forehead, wet and gleaming." There are, as well, overtones of Degas, who can capture a gleam of pearl in a dancer's ear or the texture of velvet ribbon around her throat. The imagism in Ezra Pound's translations from the Chinese poet Li Po is evident here also. Mansfield was alert to all the new movements in art, particularly those abounding in visual effects. That she was self-conscious and calculating in her painterly techniques in this daringly conceived and executed story is apparent from her own analysis of her craft within the story. In the cab, Duquette insists on taking the jump seat facing his friends, because he wished to see their faces through "the occasional flashing glimpses" of the "white circles of lamplight. They revealed Dick, . . . his broad hat shading him as if it were a part of him—a sort of wing he hid under." The play of shadows on a face, the attitude of a reclining body, the figure thrown into relief by the light of the lamp against the dark, tell an impressionistic "truth" about the narrator-artist's perception of reality more revealing than the most detailed line-for-line rendition. Mouse, sitting next to Dick, is captured by the same artist, "her lovely little face more like a drawing than a real face . . . against the swimming dark."

The suggestive imagist touches instead of the "correct" drawing revered by the Academy painters succeeded in the immediacy and emotional repercussion sought, so that each time he looked at her "it was as if for the first time":

> She came upon you with the same kind of shock that you feel when you have been drinking tea out of a thin butterfly cup and suddenly, at the bottom, you see a tiny creature, half butterfly, half woman, bowing to you with her hands in her sleeves. As far as I could make out she had dark hair and blue or black eyes. Her long lashes and the two little feathers above were most important.

Duquette's sense impressions are dependent on the moment, the light, and the emotional state of the observer. Like the Impressionist painters and the Imagist poets, Mansfield was seeking spontaneity through fleeting experience, sensory impact, and the captured moment that will evanesce as the light dims or diffuses.

Duquette's self-portrait is honest but repellent. As an acknowledged pimp and prostitute, he admits he lives through his senses. In a scene right out of Gauguin, he recalls having been kissed by his African servant until he became "very languid, very caressing, and so quickened, so sharpened, [he] seemed to understand everybody and be able to do what [he] liked with everybody." All his experience is defined in terms of the shapes and colors of objects about him. In one scene, against a background of cubist sofas, the guests drink red brandy before a homosexual seduction.

The climax of the story to which all Duquette's shocking allusions are leading is a confession:

> I don't believe in the human soul. I have made it a rule of my life never to regret and never to look back. . . .
> Regret is an appalling waste of energy. . . . It's only good for wallowing in. . . . I have no family; I don't want any. I never think about my childhood. I've forgotten it.

Duquette, of course, is Mansfield's Underground Man, which should come as no shock, because her **Journals** are almost as full of Fyodor Dostoyevski as Chekhov. Although the Russian writer's famous *Notes from the Underground* begin with the words "I am a sick man. . . . I am a spiteful man. I am an unattractive man," a less shameless confession than the cynical Duquette's, its influence is apparent. Duquette's self-revelation betrays an excessive *amour propre,* which causes him to positively enjoy infecting others through his own self-degradation. Withal, he is as rootless and alienated as Dostoyevski's Man, capable only of sterile retrospection. Dostoyevski's Underground Man concludes with a backward glance: "Even now, so many years later, all this is somehow a very evil memory. . . . And why do we fuss and fume sometimes? . . . We don't know why ourselves." Mansfield's perverse hero ends on a similar note: "Even now I don't fully understand why. Of course I knew that I couldn't have kept it up." Both are studies of minds engaged in the process of ongoing self-evaluation but incapable of change.

The unsettling conclusion of **"Je ne parle pas français"** has Duquette promising to procure a "tiny little girl" for the "dirty old gallant"; it is clear that he has Mouse in mind, if he can find her. He then kisses his fingertips in a connoisseur's gesture of appreciation and lays his hand on his heart as a pledge of his honor. In that single act of unregenerate self-mockery, he abases himself, his victim, his client, and the traditions of culture and morality of the society that shaped him and which he exploits.

The fascination of this unpleasant story, whose plot is rudimentary and theme ambiguous, is its departure from anything else Mansfield ever wrote. Like Dostoyevski, she succeeds in showing a mind in a state of agitation, a complex process of thinking, voluptuous pleasure, and moral drift. Even on the occasional moment when Duquette expresses astonishment at seeing two people "really" suffer, he is distracted by Mouse's "quivering eyelids" and "the tears pearling down her cheeks" in a novelistic sensibility rather than human compassion. He actually scrutinizes his own coldheartedness and moral opportunism with the scrupulous honesty one expects from the writer in the objective detachment dictated by his craft.

Duquette is an unsettling composite portrait of a modernist hero, one part alienated man in the Russian confessional tradition, one part gigolo straight out of the French novels of Colette. His pouting mouth, "kept" aura, and general androgyny are reminiscent of the petulant Cheri in Sidonie-Gabrielle Colette's stories of sexual exploitation. The similarity between Duquette and Cheri is not surprising in light of Mansfield's voracious reading of Colette's fiction and her self-declared identification with the French writer. Mansfield's biographer Jeffrey Meyers claims she identified with Colette because the latter was so "independent, innovative and impulsive," everything Mansfield wished to be, but it is just as likely that she was taken with Colette's open treatment of sexuality and her relationship with her husband, the managing M. Willy, which she imagined bore some resemblance to her own relationship with Murry.

Owing much to so many sources of art and literature, **"Je ne parle pas français"** emerges as Mansfield's only story with a truly "modernist" sensibility. Would she have evolved into a consistently modernist writer had she lived long enough to develop in that direction? If by "modernist" it is understood that life is little more than a process of being without purpose or value, and that existence comprises sensation rather than societal standards, then **"Je ne parle pas français"** was clearly moving in that direction. If she had gone on to develop this philosophical dimension in her fiction, she might have found her own distinct modernist voice in the wake of this first derivative piece. This one story, however, must be seen as a departure. She touched on themes never before considered in her fiction: personal estrangement from accepted societal standards; sexual ambivalence in pursuit of personal gratification; and a pervasive pessimism expressed through debased human values.

Miriam B. Mandel (essay date fall 1989)

SOURCE: Mandel, Miriam B. "Reductive Imagery in 'Miss Brill.'" *Studies in Short Fiction* 26, no. 4 (fall 1989): 473-77.

[*In the following essay, Mandel examines the sense imagery in "Miss Brill," which she describes as "reductive," that is, limited to the title character's perspective: "we see not only what Miss Brill sees, but we see how she sees what she sees." Mansfield manipulates the imagery, Mandel argues, to develop the psychological portrait of the story's protagonist.*]

Katherine Mansfield's story **"Miss Brill"** has evoked a curious double response. Critics generally feel sympathy for the character,[1] but reject the story.[2] The most positive statements about the story emphasize its careful structure and its compression.[3] But even these admiring critics have failed to notice its most impressive technical achievement: a highly functional application of figurative language which enables the reader to understand and evaluate the character.

"Miss Brill" has less action and more figurative language than any of the other stories in *The Garden Party*, figurative language which marks a departure both of kind and of purpose: **"Miss Brill"** relies on sense imagery, and not on the "trees, flowers, birds, insects, mice, rats, cats and dogs, the sun and moon, and the sea"[4] with which Mansfield regularly expounds the familiar themes of helplessness and of preying. Most fully developed are the images of sight and sound. But the senses of taste ("a faint chill, like a chill from a glass of iced water before you sip")[5] and touch ("She felt a tingling in her hands and arms" [182]) are also represented in the story. And this concrete sense imagery is, rather surprisingly, transmitted to us through the perception of a woman remarkably out of touch with the world around her.[6]

Miss Brill, an aging spinster, a foreigner (in xenophobic France) without friends or relatives, is almost a parody of the isolated expatriate. Her only relationships are with her students, in whom she naturally can't confide, and with an old invalid gentleman who is practically dead. No one else figures in her life. She maintains only the most tenuous of contacts with the outside world: once a week she observes and eavesdrops on strangers. It is a story, as David Madden points out, of a woman's forced retreat from the world.[7] What is the function, then, of the vivid sense imagery? Don't the very profusion and immediacy of the imagery contradict the theme of isolation?

A careful look at Miss Brill's imagery reveals that all of it shares a singular characteristic: all of it is reductive. The images which bring the scene to life simultaneously reduce it: we see not only what Miss Brill sees, but we see how she sees what she sees, as it is reported in her own language (free indirect discourse). This is obvious, of course, in terms of characters and action: she transforms the real, human scene in the park into a set scene from a play ("It was exactly like a play. . . . They were all on the stage. . . . they were acting" [186-87]).[8] But it is operative also in the imagery, by means of which she reduces the real world (lively, bright and joyful on a spring afternoon) to fit her own limited perspectives.

Critics have noted that Miss Brill transforms the band imagery even as she reports it.[9] But critics have not noticed that the means by which she transforms it are encoded in the sense imagery. What is important to an understanding of Miss Brill is not the fact of transformation but the manner of transformation. To give an example: music produced by a brass band playing outdoors is inevitably loud; on this Sunday, the first Sunday of the new season, it was even "louder and gayer" than usual. But filtered through Miss Brill's perception, the large brassy sounds become "a little 'flutey' bit—very pretty!—a little chain of bright drops" (183).

For part of the story, Miss Brill doesn't even hear the loud band; and then "Tum-tum-tum tiddle-um! tiddle-um! tum tiddley-um tum ta!" (185)—she has reduces a brass band to a few humming, tapping sounds. The reductive and subjective quality of the sound imagery becomes even more obvious when Miss Brill projects onto the band her interpretation of another character's emotions: "the band seemed to know what she [the woman wearing the ermine toque] was feeling and played more softly, played tenderly . . ." (186). The imagery presents not the real sounds the band makes, but Miss Brill's subjective transformation and ultimate reduction of these sounds.

Miss Brill consistently reduces the world in which she lives. In Welty's terms, Miss Brill tries to make the world "cozy" and "safe" for herself.[10] To make them fit into her diminished world, Miss Brill attempts to reduce the people in the Jardins Publiques by imaging them as small animals: the band director "scraped his foot and flapped his arms like a rooster about to crow" (183); the mother is "like a young hen . . ." (184). The older woman is reduced even further by metonymy—she is the "ermine toque"—and she dabs her lips with "a tiny yellowish paw" (185) and then "pattered away" (186). And the central image of the fox is also reduced in size: Miss Brill attaches the adjective "little" to it six times in the first paragraph: the fox is a "dear little thing" and (twice) a "Little rogue"; it has "dim little eyes," "sad little eyes," and needs "a little dab of black sealing-wax" (182) on its (presumably little) nose. We hear Miss Brill's voice and diction here.[11]

As Miss Brill catalogues what she sees, she reduces and dehumanizes it: children are "little French dolls" (184); the people on the benches are "still as statues" (184). Faces are not described; Miss Brill prefers to see people in terms of single items of clothing: "a fine old man in a velvet coat . . . a big old woman . . . with a roll of knitting on her embroidered apron" (183); "An Englishman and his wife, he wearing a dreadful Panama hat and she button boots" (184). Sometimes several characters are reduced to the same single item of clothing—"little boys with big white silk bows . . . little girls . . . dressed up in velvet and lace" (184); "Two peasant women with funny straw hats" (185). Or they are seen in terms of a single color—"a gentleman in grey," "Two young girls in red . . . with two young soldiers in blue"; describing the woman who is the ermine toque, Miss Brill sees, somewhat improbably, that "everything, her hair, her face, even her eyes, was the same colour as the shabby ermine . . ." (185). Whatever Miss Brill sees, she reduces to the parameters of her own constricted world.

The text does not provide an objective reason for the emptiness of her life. The usual Mansfield problems do not restrict Miss Brill. Money, though not plentiful, doesn't seem to worry her. She is in good health; her senses are alert. No fights or angers poison her outlook; no cruel, overbearing men establish limits for her. And yet, her condition of isolation is so extreme that one thoughtless bit of cruelty is capable of wrecking everything. By giving us Miss Brill's own imagery (instead of the narrator's), and by investing it with the quality of reductivity, Katherine Mansfield has transposed the psychological aspects of cause and effect. Instead, then, of presenting the story from the outside, and showing that a chance remark seems to make Miss Brill disproportionately unhappy, Mansfield shows us the character from the inside, in order to disclose why she could be made so unhappy by such a remark. That is to say, Miss Brill's misery is caused not by the cruelty of the unfeeling external world, represented by the young couple, but by the manipulative, restrictive, and finally destructive personality of Miss Brill herself. Her reductive imagery suggests that Miss Brill has never permitted other human beings a full and independent reality. Like Emma Woodhouse, she has seen them only as raw material to be shaped and managed by herself. And as Emma is humiliated when those upon whom she attempted to impose her will turned out to have independent wills of their own, so Miss Brill is severely shocked when the romantic young couple—"the hero and heroine, of course, just arrived from his father's yacht"—turn out to be real individuals intent on their own needs and given to rather inelegant means of expression. The proper response to Miss Brill, then, involves not only pity for her current misery but also blame for having brought that misery on herself. Reading the imagery carefully reveals that the theme of the story is not destruction but self-destruction.

Katherine Mansfield does not often require us to judge her characters so severely. But in this story she encodes a negative response into the text by attaching unflattering images to her main character. Although Saralyn Daly claims that "No distancing of emotion is allowed as the reader follows her train of thought and feeling,"[12] several clear markers obviate emotional identification with the character. First, by choosing to present Miss Brill in the act of eavesdropping (instead of teaching her students or reading to the old gentleman), Mansfield emphasizes an unattractive aspect of her character. Mansfield also distances Miss Brill from us by giving her the name of a fish.[13] The fox fur, with which Miss Brill is identified both at the beginning and the end of the story,[14] is not only dead but continues to decay even after death. And on the same narrative level, the girl at the end of the story reduces the value of the fox fur (and thus of Miss Brill) even further by comparing it to "a fried whiting" (189). Although we tend to respond sympathetically to Mansfield's troubled women, I think that in this story such a response is inappropriate. A more dispassionate examination of Miss Brill is demanded.[15]

Just as Miss Brill's imagery reveals her personality to us, so does the narrative discourse reveal the distance and attitude appropriate for the reader. Disassociation works on two levels: the character practices the technique on the world around her and thus reveals the causes for her isolation, and the author practices the technique on the reader and thus manipulates our response to the character. A careful reading, then, requires both a dispassionate attitude to the character and close attention to her imagery. That imagery reveals her method of dealing with the world: Miss Brill tries to control her environment by reducing it. But her final defeat or isolation or alienation (depending on which critic's language you use) is not the main issue of the story. The imagery draws our attention not to the defeat but to the process that has made it inevitable. The reductive imagery reveals that the defeat is caused not by the world, but by Miss Brill's attempt to work her will on it. The imagery is a powerful tool by means of which Mansfield encourages and enables us to discover how her character got to where she is: in no small measure, Miss Brill herself created the smallness of her life.

Notes

1. Eudora Welty writes that "Miss Brill was from the first defenseless," ("Katherine Mansfield's 'Miss Brill,'" rpt. in *Story and Critic*, ed. Myron Matlaw and Leonard Lief [New York: Harper and Row, 1963], p. 19). Robert L. Hull finds that "Miss Mansfield gives in this story a significant look . . . a look short and startling and at once full of pity, at the world that the lonely woman inhabits. . . . She is left, as she began, in her pathetic solitude" ("Alienation in 'Miss Brill,'" *Studies in Short Fiction*, 5, No. 1 [1967], 74, 76). The most direct statement of sympathy comes from Saralyn R. Daly, who claims that "Miss Brill . . . engages the reader's affection" (*Katherine Mansfield* [New York: Twayne, 1965], p. 90).

2. Although widely anthologized, the story has not always fared well with the critics. Sylvia Berkman condemns both the character and the story: "Miss Brill, hyperconscious, semihysterical, through feverish examination herself emphasizes the meaning of each trivial happening in her afternoon, so that the very instrument of implication—the running stream of feeling—here gives rise to the obvious, or at least the mechanical" (*Katherine Mansfield: A Critical Study* [New Haven: Yale Univ. Press, 1951], p. 163). Berkman also finds that the symbolism is flawed: "the association of emotion with the external object [the fox fur] has been pushed to an identity which Miss Brill herself points out, and we are conscious of excess" (p. 175). In the special Mansfield issue of *Modern Fiction Studies* (1978-79), "Miss Brill" comes in for much neglect and some decidedly rough treatment. Richard F. Paterson, in "The Circle of Truth: The Stories of Katherine Mansfield and Mary Lavin," reports that "Mary Lavin . . . agrees with Woolf that 'Bliss' as well as 'Miss Brill,' falls far short of the truth. . . . the reader learns the truth about . . . Miss Brill through a convenient and artificial climax. . . . when the vision . . . of the loneliness of human existence . . . arrives, it is so contrived that the reader suspects that the lack of passion and loneliness belonged more to the author than the characters in her fiction" (*Modern Fiction Studies*, 24, No. 3 [1978-79], 384, 386).

3. See Peter Thorpe, "Teaching 'Miss Brill,'" *College English*, 23 (1962), 661-63; and David Madden, "Katherine Mansfield's 'Miss Brill,'" *University Review*, 31 (1964), 89-92.

4. Toby Silverman Zinman, "'The snail under the leaf': Katherine Mansfield's Imagery," *Modern Fiction Studies*, 24, No. 3 (1978-79), 458.

5. "Miss Brill," in *The Garden Party* (New York: Modern Library, 1950), p. 182. All further citations are in the text.

6. In his Note "Alienation in 'Miss Brill'" (*Studies in Short Fiction*, 5, No. 1 [1967], 74-76), Robert L. Hull uses the word the words "estrangement" and "solitude," in addition to "alienation," to identify the theme of the story.

7. "Katherine Mansfield's 'Miss Brill,'" p. 89

8. Even the "little brown dog" is diminished: he is "like a little 'theatre' dog, a little dog that had been drugged" (p. 186).

9. David Madden accurately points out that she tries "to create her own private music out of her emotions" ("Katherine Mansfield's 'Miss Brill,'" p. 90); Peter Thorpe remarks that "the band, the music and the . . . conductor are merely raw materials for the dramatizations of Miss Brill's mind" ("Teaching 'Miss Brill,'" p. 661).

10. "Katherine Mansfield's 'Miss Brill,'" p. 18.

11. Just as in "The Fly" we can clearly distinguish the opinions and diction of the boss, Mr. Woodifield, and even of the absent Mrs. Woodifield and her daughters, when these words are not encased in the conventional quotation marks (see F. W. Bateson and B. Shahevitch, "Katherine Mansfield's 'The Fly': A Critical Exercise," *Essays in Criticism*, 12 [January 1962], 39-53), so here we are aware that "little" is Miss Brill's word.

12. *Katherine Mansfield*, p. 90.

13. James W. Gargano, "Katherine Mansfield's 'Miss Brill,'" *Explicator*, 19, No. 2 (1960), Item 10. David Madden mentions "the 'shine' and 'sparkle'

meanings [in French] of Miss Brill's name" (p. 92), as does Robert L. Hull, who finds that the name works ironically, because Miss Brill is "a dull spinster without a shining personality or the warming glow of love" ("Alienation in 'Miss Brill,'" p. 75).

14. Peter Thorpe finds that "symbol [the fox fur] and referent [Miss Brill] become one in this last sentence of the story" (p. 663).

15. Once we assume the proper distance from Miss Brill, we become aware of further limitations. Like Holden Caulfield, she has a limited vocabulary and repeats the same words over and over again, the favorite quite revealingly being "little." And although she is fond of similes, her image-making capabilities are limited: she invokes only three animals (ermine, rooster, hen), all of them small.

Francine Tolron (essay date 1989)

SOURCE: Tolron, Francine. "Fauna and Flora in Katherine Mansfield's Short Stories." In *The Fine Instrument: Essays on Katherine Mansfield*, edited by Paulette Michel and Michel Dupuis, pp. 166-72. Sydney: Dangaroo Press, 1989.

[*In the following essay, Tolron traces Mansfield's use of plant and animal imagery in her stories, stating that these images are not merely decorative but are employed by the author to express her protagonists' "transient moods and states of being, their response to life or to a particularly vital moment."*]

D. M. Davin considers that some of the obvious features of Katherine Mansfield's style are:

> a sensibility almost morbidly alert to detail and to the evidence of the senses, to colour and shape, to the feel, smell and sound of things . . . an exultation in life, movement and beauty and an appalled shrinking before the crude, the ugly and the cruel.[1]

Her great sensuousness and keen sensitiveness are reflected in her treatment of the various plants and animals which appear in her stories: they are transient but recurrent images whose sum makes up a coherent pattern which exemplifies both her 'exultation in life' and her 'shrinking before the crude'.

Nature appears in her stories as both positive and negative; the plant and animal images are never mere 'decorative' elements, they are meant to express the protagonists' psyche, their transient moods or states of being, their response to life or to a particularly vital moment.

In **'Prelude'** nature is shown as simple, carnal, domestic, as a source of joy and beneficial effects, as exemplified by the tasty jams Linda's mother intends to make. More significantly, the first attitude of Katherine Mansfield's heroes—and heroines above all—is to perceive nature as an object of admiration: it is perfect in its form and colours and thus transcends the daily humdrum. It provides a short-lived ecstasy. One thinks of Bertha, in **'Bliss',** and of the rapture which takes hold of her when she gazes at the lovely fruit on the table or at the pear tree, a true miracle of perfection. Similarly, Linda Burnell goes into ecstasy over the exquisite flowers of the manuka tree. Flowers and fruit are combined to materialize the feeling of plenitude which overcomes the characters. Leila, in **'Her First Ball'**, caught in the whirling motion of the dance, feels 'like a flower that is tossed into a pool' (p. 429); meanwhile the young men are getting ready for the ritual of seduction, like birds strutting before the love dance, 'smoothing their gloves, patting their glossy hair' (p. 428). The attachment that links the young couple in **'Psychology'** calls for a blossoming into a physical intercourse, as suggested by the author's very words: 'now was the time for harvest—harvest' (p. 319). In this respect, **'Feuille d'Album'** is delightfully explicit: the nascent love of the artist for the unknown girl he is observing materializes into flowers and his heart literally becomes the daffodils she is presently watering. The egg he gives her is the naïve, preposterous manifestation of his youthful passion. Significantly, the whole scene takes place on a background made of spring rain, of fragrances of wet earth, of budding trees: it is both cosmic and humble, touching and slightly puerile—like love shared by two young people. But one must not be deceived by the seemingly gleeful, rosy-coloured atmosphere: the satirical Katherine Mansfield, whose verve can be so acid, cannot miss out the opportunity of denouncing the mawkishness of some of her characters. Nature is sometimes linked to affectation as, for instance, in **'The Garden Party'** where José is presented as a butterfly in 'silk petticoat' and 'kimono jacket', while the bushes bow down 'as though they had been visited by archangels'. The enamoured Henry, in **'Something Childish But Very Natural'**, sees his dream-cottage walk 'on tiptoe'.

Personified and animated by a cheap imagination these elements become part of the characters' simple, childish psyche and mean yearnings. The tone becomes distressing in **'Miss Brill'** when the elderly spinster marvels at seeing, through her reductive vision, that the surrounding world is a stage and that the little dog by her side 'trotted off, like a little "theatre" dog' (p. 376). This must be interpreted as a means of depicting derision in human life.

Apart from these few, almost comical examples, the prevailing trend in her stories is to glorify the animal and the vegetal world. Plenitude and bliss shine out in

'Marriage à la Mode' where the sorrow William feels for his lost conjugal happiness is emblematically and a *contrario* expressed by the image of the rose-bush:

> When he had been a little boy, it was his delight to run into the garden after a shower of rain and shake the rose-bush over him. Isabel was that rose-bush, petal-soft, sparkling and cool.
>
> (p. 433)

In a less striking way, dead love is conjured up in **'A Dill Pickle'**, by a profusion of geranium, marigold and verbena, bathed in warm sunshine. In **'Something Childish But Very Natural'** the beloved Edna with her 'marigold hair' and 'strawberry cheeks' is a flower-woman and a fruit-woman; at the beginning of the story, the eponymous poem heralds the sentimental fervour which is to take hold of Henry by referring to the flying bird heading for his beloved.

Nature is resolutely endowed with life and a momentum which, at first, remain untouched. Henry, again, who works for a London architect, dreams of building nests, not houses. When the highly perturbed Edna refuses to yield to him, he evades his vexation and grief by gazing at the trees of the square 'with their unbroken buds'. A similar reaction is to be found in **'Psychology'**; the young woman has been deserted by her friend and is a prey to the adoration of the 'elderly virgin' with the posy:

> for a moment she did not take the violets . . . Again she saw . . . the dark garden ringed with glittering ivy, the willows . . . she put her arms round her friend.
>
> (p. 323)

And she accepts her violets, shrivelled as they may be. Nature provides an answer to an unsatisfied expectation, a transitory evasion, a brief liberation. In **'At the Bay'** Beryl changes into a turtle and a rat to have a swim and escape from Mrs Harry Kember. Through such a metamorphosis, she means to protect herself and get away from the 'poisoning', pernicious influence of 'this cold woman' whom yet 'she longed to hear'. She shuts herself up in the hermetic shell of a turtle or the swift repulsive appearance of the fleeing rat, very much in the same manner as a child at play pretends to believe that a hiding-place is a real shelter. The turtle and the rat, significantly both marine elements (as stated by the text), are synonymous with transitory safeness, away from the dangers of dry land (the blemish of adulthood?). In **'Her First Ball'**, Leila eludes the hold of the old beau and of his ill-omened talk by thinking of the pleasant comfort of home:

> She wanted to be home, or sitting on the verandah listening to those baby owls.
>
> (p. 431)

Similarly, in **'Life of Ma Parker'**, the old drudge, overwhelmed with grief, puts an end to her misfortunes by flying toward oblivion and death: 'the icy wind blew out her apron into a balloon' (p. 408).

A negative aspect of nature is becoming apparent, i.e., nature as refuge, as ersatz, deprived of its joy, disquieting. It is even presented as heavy with dangers. The beginning of **'At the Bay'** suggests an engulfment by an almost diluvian tidal wave: 'it looked as though . . . one immense wave had come rippling, rippling—how far?' (p. 441); and it is made more threatening by the apparition of the huge fish at the window. This childhood phantasmagoria, taken up throughout the story, together with the animal and vegetal imagery helps generate a feeling of uneasiness, some vague anguish powerfully shared by the characters and the reader. The threat begins to take shape with the allusion to a 'sea-forest', a sort of Gordian knot made of seaweeds and of 'thread-like creatures' where submarine sheep are heard bleating: some antipodean Lorelei and Atlantis? It may be so: in any case fauna and flora are suggestive of death; some devouring, suckling—down process is hinted at against which the characters are utterly powerless. Nature holds man under its spell.

The garden, in **'At the Bay'**, that Jonathan describes as 'vast, dangerous . . . undiscovered, unexplored', speaks and entices the frustrated Beryl into consuming sexual intercourse with the not very commendable Harry: 'How had she got here? The stern garden asked her as the gate pushed open, and quick as a cat Harry Kembler came through and snatched her to him' (p. 469). Beryl's disgusted exclamation: 'You are vile, vile' condenses the horror that human baseness and nature's conniving deceitfulness fill her with. Similarly, in **'Prelude'**, another scene, bringing together in an (imaginary?) relation Beryl and a young man in a (primeval?) garden, is bathed in a similar atmosphere of shady temptation: he is described as 'sly and laughing' and she turns him away by dressing herself. Does this mean that sexual intercourse is demeaning? Not quite, but it is referred to as difficult, impossible and bringing little gratification. These scenes take place in the night, with which the moon, cold and morbid, is associated. The phallic pear tree in **'Bliss'** is bathed in the white moonlight and the lunar Miss Fulton, turns out to be a femme fatale. In **'Prelude'** Linda turns away her husband's overtures as she finds herself shivering in the midst of 'a flood of cold light' (p. 243).

A fundamental aspect of Katherine Mansfield's universe is thus revealed, namely an overwhelming sense of waste. This is a recurrent theme in her short stories. Henry, as he is waiting for Edna, mistakes for a moth the little girl who is bringing the message whose reading will fill the garden and cottage with shadows, spinning 'a web of darkness' around him. Laura leaves the garden party with the sensation of grass crushed by the guests' feet. William, the deserted husband, calls his existence 'a filthy life' and his dejection finds a powerful metaphorical expression in the landscape he is gazing at: 'One bird drifted high like a dark fleck in a jewel'. We are here poles apart from the ecstasy of **'Bliss'**.

Animals and plants are sometimes used as 'objective correlatives' to this world-weariness. The flower of the manuka-tree soon loses its petals which get caught in Linda's hair: from an 'exquisite small thing', it turns into 'a horrid little thing'. Now, 'horrid' implies an intention, somewhere, around which the mystery remains entire: 'Why, then, flower at all?' is the only appropriate answer, an interrogation about life whether human, animal or vegetal . . . There remains only to lament, along with Linda, over 'all these things that are wasted, wasted. . . . It was uncanny' (p. 452).

Man's powerlessness is also matched by the reflection it finds in nature: in **'Prelude'**, the aloe is cruel, in **'The Canary'**, the bird dies for all the devoted love of its mistress who deplores:

> I must confess that there does seem to me something sad in life . . . It is there, deep down, deep down, part of one, like one's breathing.
>
> (p. 541)

Such bitterness is echoed in the questions punctuating **'At the Bay'**: 'What was going on down there?', 'Was there no escape?' asks Linda, feeling like a leaf that is shaken by the wind; 'the shortness of life' exclaims Jonathan, insect-like, prisoner of his own life. Through the imagery Katherine Mansfield conveys what words cannot express, i.e., a pure metaphysical anguish.

Yet, she also uses animal images to express occasional healthy outbursts of hatred against social injustice, which roots her work in the concrete. In **'The Doll's House'**, the washerwoman's poor daughters are 'shooed out like chickens'. Alice, the young maid in **'Prelude'**, is compared to the hapless duck victimized by the children:

> It was hard to say which of the two, Alice or the duck, looked the better basted . . . they both had the same air of gloss and strain.
>
> (p. 251)

As shown in these two quotations, Katherine Mansfield uses animal metaphors when she ventures into the field of social criticism, but also . . . in her rendering of married life. In **'Prelude'**, Linda sees her husband as 'a frog', 'a big fat turkey' or a good cumbersome dog:

> If only he wouldn't jump at her so, and bark so loudly, and watch her with such eager, loving eyes.
>
> (p. 254)

Childhood and art are not spared either by her scathing pen: the children in **'Prelude'** desert their improvised doll's tea party, consisting in flowers and greenery which will be eaten up by ants and snails. As to the artist, in **'Feuille d'Album'**, what he sees in the market below—a source of inspiration to him, one might think—is a swarming world of crab-like costermongers—'among the flowers the old women scuttled from side to side, like crabs' (p. 268)—on whom he spits his prune-stones . . .

'Sun and Moon' is very significant in that the short span of time it covers and the thinness of the argument (a party given at some wealthy people's, seen through their two children's eyes) heighten the value and meaning of each tiny detail. The description of the scene, both before and after the meal, and of the children is interspersed with references, comparisons and allusions to animals and plants which clearly bring out the two basic functions of Katherine Mansfield's use of nature images: 'an exultation in life, movement, and beauty and an appalled shrinking before the crude, the ugly and the cruel'. On the set table, 'the salt-cellars were tiny birds drinking out of basins', 'in the middle was a lake with rose petals floating on it', the napkins are 'made into roses', in the lit-up dining-room 'all the lights were red roses'; Sun, the little boy, is dolled up in 'a white shirt with red and white daisies speckled on it', male-guests in tailcoats look funnily 'like beetles' and the children's apparition, all dressed-up, causes the company to exclaim: 'my lamb' (Nurse), 'oh, the ducks! Oh, the lambs!' (the ladies), before their mother tells them to 'fly up to [their] little nest'. But the glee will be short-lived. Among the guests, Sun singles out one man to whom he takes an instant liking. The man asks Sun if he is fond of dogs, then vanishes. Sun 'thought perhaps he'd gone outside to fetch in a puppy' . . . but nothing comes out of the brief encounter. The only episode standing out against the ambient artificiality leads nowhere: no real dog will ever materialize. When later in the night the two children wake up, the party is drawing to an end and the atmosphere is heavy with inebriated mirth: Sun is horrified to see the shattered beauty of the table (ribbons and roses pulled untied, 'bones and bits and fruit peels and shells everywhere' (p. 304), whereas Moon, undisturbed, bites into the nut, the only remnant of the ice pudding which had been made to look like a little pink house, with white snow on the roof, green windows and a brown door where the nut served as a handle. To Sun, the broken little house is a heart-breaking sight; to Moon it is immaterial. Significantly, as early as the fifth line of the story, our attention had been drawn to a difference in the two children's perception. While watching the men carrying the flower pots for the reception, Moon said 'Look. There's a man wearing a palm on his head' (p. 300) and her remark is followed by 'But she never knew the difference between real things and not real ones'. As in **'Sun and**

Moon', much of Katherine Mansfield's writings deal with growing up i.e., the difficulty of coming to terms with reality, and with the power of imagination to transcend it.

I hope I have shown that there exists in Katherine Mansfield's stories a real bestiary, a proper Mansfieldian nature which deserves to be fully explored. The meaning of her nature imagery is as complex as that of her stories: each element in it stands both for one thing and its opposite according to how the author's perception evolves from one story to another or even within a single story. Whether used as mere narrative element integrated into the plot, or used metaphorically or metonymically, the fauna and flora references weave an almost ecological pattern which reflects a social and/or psychological reality, and eventually Katherine Mansfield's fundamental questioning about life—an ecological pattern that attracts or rejects, bewitches or repels her characters and thus forcefully and pitilessly defines the human condition.

Note

1. D. M. Davin, introduction to: Katherine Mansfield, *Selected Stories* (Oxford: Oxford University Press, 1953), p. xv.

Sydney Janet Kaplan (essay date 1991)

SOURCE: Kaplan, Sydney Janet. "From *The Aloe* to 'Prelude.'" In *Katherine Mansfield and the Origins of Modernist Fiction*, pp. 103-17. Ithaca, N.Y.: Cornell University Press, 1991.

[*In the following essay, Kaplan discusses the personal events in Mansfield's life—her dissolving friendship with D. H. and Frieda Lawrence, the death of her brother, and her association with the Bloomsbury Group and, especially, Virginia Woolf—that influenced her writing of the novel* The Aloe *and her subsequent revision of that novel into the short story "Prelude." Kaplan describes "Prelude" as a new kind of narrative and a breakthrough for Mansfield into a more concise style of writing.*]

> A certain strangeness, something of the blossoming of the aloe, is indeed an element in all true works of art.
>
> Walter Pater, *The Renaissance*

The evolution of **"Prelude"** from its initial conception as a novel, ***The Aloe,*** in 1915[1] to its publication by the Woolfs in 1918 demonstrates Mansfield's intensified process of technical and conceptual experimentation, the true beginning of her *conscious* sense of a new shape for prose fiction.[2] What began as a "novel" eventually became something new: a mixed genre, a multileveled, spatially ordered narrative. Katherine Mansfield remarked in a letter in response to a question about **"Prelude"**: "What form is it? you ask. . . . As far as I know, it's more or less my own invention" (*Letters* I, p. 331). Some years later she referred to "the **'Prelude'** method—it just unfolds and opens."[3]

But what was the impetus for this new kind of narrative? The usual account of her new direction has the flavor of Murry's style of public relations about it: Leslie Beauchamp, Mansfield's brother, arrives from New Zealand on his way to the front and renews her connections with her childhood. He is killed almost immediately after leaving for the continent, and then, through her grief and final acceptance of his death, Mansfield experiences a sudden burst of creative energy. Yet even a brief study of the chronology of her writing process provides a more complicated story, and one that begins *before* the death of her brother.

The period between **"Maata"** and *The Aloe* was not very productive for Mansfield in terms of writing and publication.[4] By December 1913, she and Murry had moved to Paris, where she met the writer Francis Carco for the first time. Returning to England at the end of February 1914, she found her attention diverted by volatile relationships with friends, new and old. Her journal reveals a preoccupation with disturbing and sexual dreams,[5] memories of New Zealand, and vacillating feelings for her friend L. M. (Ida Baker), intensified by L. M.'s imminent departure for Rhodesia at the end of March. By April 2, Mansfield recorded her concern over her difficulties in writing: "If I could write with my old fluency for *one day,* the spell would be broken. It's the continual effort—the slow building-up of my idea and then, before my eyes and out of my power, its slow dissolving" (*Journal,* p. 58). On April 4, she wrote: "Nothing that isn't satirical is really true for me to write just now. If I try to find things lovely, I turn pretty-pretty. And at the same time I am so frightened of writing mockery for satire that my pen hovers and won't settle" (pp. 58-59).

But alternating with lethargy and depression were moments of recognition and expansion. Only three days later, her journal records:

> The heavens opened for the sunset to-night. When I had thought the day folded and sealed, came a burst of heavenly bright petals. . . . I sat behind the window, pricked with rain, and looked until that hard thing in my breast melted and broke into the smallest fountain, murmuring as aforetime, and I drank the sky and the whisper. Now who is to decide between 'Let it be' and 'Force it'? J. believes in the whip: he says his steed has plenty of strength, but it is idle and shies at such a journey in prospect. I feel if mine does not gallop and dance at free will, I am not riding at all, but just swinging from its tail. For example, to-day . . . To-night he's all sparks.
>
> (pp. 59-60)

The implicit commentary on the differences between male and female modes of creativity—and of sexuality—is undeniable. But Mansfield would participate later that year in an incessant and electrifying discourse on "the masculine" and "the feminine" as her relationship with D. H. Lawrence deepened.

Lawrence and Frieda von Richthofen had returned from Italy on June 24, and on July 13 their marriage took place. Only one month later the First World War began. Throughout these same months, Mansfield grew increasingly unhappy with her life with Murry. Then, on October 26, after spending ten days as guests of the Lawrences, she and Murry moved to Rose Tree Cottage, only three miles away. Devastated by his publisher's rejection of his first version of *The Rainbow*, Lawrence was in the thick of revising it. Apparently, during this time Mansfield had many conversations with the Lawrences about her problems with Murry and gained their support for her side of the conflict.

Frieda Lawrence, in particular, was sympathetic to Mansfield's longing for a lover more intense and sensual than Murry and abetted her in her romance by mail with Francis Carco. On November 16, Mansfield received a letter from Carco and implicitly contrasted him with Murry by referring to "his warm sensational life" (*Journal*, p. 62), using a typically Lawrencian phrase. It is interesting to note how her interest in Carco countered some of Lawrence's prescriptions on male authority. Carco seemed to Mansfield soft and feminine, "with his laughing face, his pretty hair, one hand with a bangle over the sheets, he looked like a girl" (*Journal*, p. 78). She thought of Carco while riding on top of a bus in London, on January 6, 1915, and remarked in her notebook: "I longed for him so, and yet I dare not push my thoughts as far as they will go" (*Journal*, p. 66). Note how her phrasing here is the same as in the quote from Wilde in her journal of 1906: "Push everything as far as it will go" (p. 3).

Undoubtedly, these days with the Lawrences must have encouraged Mansfield's own analysis of sexuality, childhood, and parental influences. Not that these were new topics of concern for her. The earlier stories **"New Dresses"** (1910) and **"The Little Girl"** (1912) already show how astute she could be about the dynamics of family life and the power struggles inherent in a patriarchal society. But what the Lawrences may have provided was an awareness of the Freudian theory behind the observations she had already made. (Of course Lawrence's versions of psychoanalysis deviated greatly from their original sources.)

Mansfield must have been influenced as well by Lawrence's theories about "true marriage" and especially by his notions about the essences of the male and the female[6]—although, as I suggest later, much of this influence has its effect in reaction and rejection, rather than in enthusiastic acceptance.[7] At about this time Lawrence was working on the long, windy disputations on sexuality in his "Study of Thomas Hardy," and it is not improbable that Mansfield would have heard him speak of ideas like these from the "Study":

> But except in infinity, everything of life is male or female, distinct. But the consciousness, that is of both: and the flower, that is of both. Every impulse that stirs in life, every single impulse, is either male or female, distinct, except the being of the complete flower, of the complete consciousness, which is two in one, fused. These are infinite and eternal. The consciousness, what we call the truth, is eternal, beyond change or motion, beyond time or limit.[8]

This work of Lawrence's reflects his interest in Otto Weininger's ideas about the essential bisexuality of human beings. Mansfield must have found such ideas intriguing if unsettling, and they might have encouraged her to reexamine her own sexual experiences. There may even be a connection (although the notion is purely conjectural) between Lawrence's analysis of the "flower," which like "the complete consciousness" is "two in one, fused," and Mansfield's later use of the aloe in **"Prelude,"** where it seems to connote both the masculine and the feminine.

Tomalin remarks that Katherine Mansfield told Frieda much about herself during those months at the end of 1914. She might have told Frieda about her youthful sexual experiences, perhaps the affair with Edith Bendall.[9] Frieda probably told Lawrence about Mansfield's experiences or he was present himself at these storytelling sessions. Tomalin makes a convincing case that these stories influenced Lawrence. She believes that Lawrence drew on them for the chapter "Shame," about Ursula's lesbian relationship with Winifred Inger, which he added to *The Rainbow* that winter.[10]

The intensity of the atmosphere around the Lawrences confirmed Mansfield's belief that she needed independence and isolation in order to write.[11] By February 1915, she was anxious for escape. Her brother had arrived in England, and although it is true that she enjoyed their reminiscences about childhood, her greater impulse at this time was to run away to France and Francis Carco, and to escape the emotional complexities of her current life with Murry and the Lawrences. Her brother gave her the money to go to Paris on February 12. Her journey was to be a brief escape of only a few days, and by mid-February she was back in England with Murry, apparently reconciled with him.

By March 18, however, Mansfield had again returned to Paris to use Carco's flat in order to do some serious writing—writing that would become the first sections of *The Aloe* and would be dominated by a preoccupation with gender differences. This preoccupation is, I believe, a direct consequence of Mansfield's interaction with the Lawrences. But there were other influences connected with the origins of *The Aloe*. Partly, there was the atmosphere of Paris itself—wartime, air raids, a tumultuous visit with her old friend Beatrice Hastings, perhaps a lesbian flirtation (she wrote to Murry about a party at Hastings's where she met "a very lovely young woman—married & *curious*—blonde—passionate—we danced together" [*Letters* I, p. 164]), the suggestiveness of the sights, colors, and scents of early spring. Finally, in a letter to Murry on March 25, 1915, she mentions the originating moment for her new work:

> I had a great day yesterday. The Muses descended in a ring like the angels on the Botticelli Nativity roof—or so it seemed . . . and I fell into the open arms of my first novel.[12] I have finished a huge chunk but I shall have to copy it on thin paper for you. I expect you will think I am a dotty when you read it—but—tell me what you think—won't you? Its queer stuff. Its the spring makes me write like this. Yesterday I had a fair wallow in it and then I shut up shop & went for a long walk along the quai—very far. It was dusk when I started—but dark when I got home. The lights came out as I walked—& the boats danced by. Leaning over the bridge I suddenly discovered that one of those boats was exactly what I want my novel to be—Not big, almost 'grotesque' in shape I mean perhaps *heavy*—with people rather dark and seen strangely as they move in the sharp light and shadow and I want bright shivering lights in it and the sound of water. (This, my lad, by way of uplift) But I *think* the novel will be alright. Of course it is not what you could call serious—but then I cant be just at this time of year & Ive always felt a spring novel would be lovely to write
>
> (*Letters* I, pp. 167-68)

She returned to London on March 31 but was back in Paris on May 5. Several days later she told Murry:

> I have been writing my book all the afternoon. How good the fatigue is that follows after! Lovers are idling along the quai. They lean over the parapet and look at the dancing water and then they turn and kiss each other—and walk a few steps further arm in arm and then stop again and again kiss. It *is* rather the night for it, I must say.
>
> (P. 180)

It is clear from these first few remarks about the novel that Mansfield saw it originally as a lighter piece than it became, and one connected with spring, her own sexual frustration, and perhaps with a re-awakened lesbian desire. By May 12, she was writing to Murry: "My book *marche bien*—I feel I could write it anywhere—it goes so easily—and I know it so well. It will be a funny book—"(*Letters* I, p. 186). Only two days later, however, she told him: "My work is finished my freedom gained. . . . Besides which I have only to polish my work now; its all really accompli" (p. 188).

According to Vincent O'Sullivan, Mansfield at this point had only written "to the end of the dance scene in Chap. II."[13] If so, certain themes in the story were already in place, but other significant ones had not yet appeared. In place were Linda's distance from her children, the emphasis on defining gender differences, an awareness of the creative potential of the matriarchal order, and the women's responses to the masculine intrusion in their domain. Mansfield had yet to include Stanley's point of view, Linda's ambivalent feelings about Stanley, Linda's delusions about inanimate objects becoming alive, and the aloe itself. In fact, it is not clear yet that the aloe will be the story's central symbol.

After returning to England on May 19, 1915, Mansfield did not work on the story for nearly ten months. Lawrence's presence was again very much a factor. In August, he and Murry founded a new magazine, *The Signature*, for which Mansfield wrote some short stories, including **"The Little Governess."** Then, on September 30, while the sexual issues in *The Aloe* were still not fully articulated and the manuscript itself had almost been abandoned, Lawrence's *The Rainbow* was published. There is no written account of Mansfield's reaction to the lesbian episode within it. Murry's explanation of her response to the book only reflects what he believed she felt—and what she was willing to tell him. (His knowledge of her past sexual experiences was very limited.) Murry writes:

> We neither of us liked *The Rainbow* and Katherine quite definitely hated parts of it—in particular the scene where Anna, pregnant, dances naked before the mirror. That, Katherine said to me, was 'female'—her most damning adjective—and an apotheosis of the 'female': a sort of glorification of the secret, intimate talk between women, the sexual understanding of the female confraternity, which Katherine could not abide. But whereas Katherine in a sense understood the book and hated it positively, I could not understand it at all. I disliked it on instinct. There was a warm, close, heavy promiscuity of flesh about it which repelled me, and I could not understand the compulsion which was upon Lawrence to write in that fashion and of those themes.[14]

Mansfield's own treatment of pregnancy in her half-abandoned manuscript was completely at odds with Lawrence's. Linda's pregnancy is never stated explicitly; her mother looks for "smelling salts" to give her during the excitement of loading the buggy at the beginning of the story. Later, when Mansfield continued working on *The Aloe*, she developed the section of the story which emphasizes Linda's abhorrence of pregnancy and childbirth.

Katherine Mansfield spent quite a bit of time with her brother during that summer, and his visits helped to focus her imagination on their shared New Zealand past. During this period she wrote a story about a brother and sister, **"The Wind Blows,"** which was published in

The Signature. It is filled with the emotional intensity of adolescent anticipation, of the urge to start a new life, of escaping from family restrictions. It is also a story about awakening sexuality.[15] This energy of anticipation was broken by tragedy when Leslie Beauchamp was killed in France on October 7, 1915. Mansfield's reaction was intense and profound. A month later she wrote in her journal: "I am just as much dead as he is" (*Journal,* p. 89). "Then why don't I commit suicide? Because I feel I have a duty to perform to the lovely time when we were both alive. I want to write about it, and he wanted me to" (p. 90).

Consequently, by January 22, 1916, after Murry had joined her in Bandol, where she had gone to recuperate, she considered how her attitude toward her writing had been transformed by her brother's death:

> Only the form that I would choose has changed utterly. I feel no longer concerned with the same appearance of things. The people who lived or whom I wished to bring into my stories don't interest me any more. The *plots* [she underlined this word in her notebook, but Murry printed it without emphasis] of my stories leave me perfectly cold.
>
> (P. 93)

She writes here about her desire to "write recollections of my own country" (p. 93), "to make our undiscovered country leap into the eyes of the Old World" (p. 94). And then she refers to "a kind of *special prose*": "No novels, no problem stories, nothing that is not simple, open" (p. 94).

On February 16, 1916, she mentions in her journal that she had "*found The Aloe* this morning" (p. 97) and that

> *The Aloe* is right. *The Aloe* is lovely. . . . And now I know what the last chapter is. It is your birth—your coming in the autumn. You in Grandmother's arms under the tree, your solemnity, your wonderful beauty. Your hands, your head—your helplessness, lying on the earth, and above all, your tremendous solemnity. That chapter will end the book. The next book will be yours and mine. And you must mean the world to Linda; and before ever you are born Kezia must play with you—her little Bogey.
>
> (P. 98)

She also comments further in her **"Notes for the Aloe"**: "They cut down the stem when Linda is ill. She has been counting on the flowering of the Aloe" (p. 99).

Although Mansfield wrote in her journal that the story was to be an elegy for her brother and that she intended it to end with his birth, her final version in **"Prelude"** did not include that birth. Her brother is the absent center, the son whose meaning to his parents is still incipient, in potential. Stanley looks at his family at the table and thinks, "That's where my boy ought to sit" (p. 244).

But the *active* center is Kezia, the young girl; it is her en-gendering that the reader experiences, her realization of male dominance. The girl-child's later displacement by her brother, the brother who will receive the mother-love denied to her from birth, would not be treated in **"Prelude."** Mansfield would not introduce it until her later story about the Burnells, **"At the Bay"** (1921).

Yet the terrible sense of loss and grief which followed her brother's death also might have included a suppressed element of relief—with its accompanying guilt.[16] For after all, the death of that masculine intruder, the longed-for male child, must have involved some of her most deeply suppressed childhood feelings. Her renewed friendship with him in adulthood must have reawakened those feelings, but she again submerged them by absorbing him into her own self-identity. Again and again she stresses their likeness, their being two halves of one whole, as in **"The Wind Blows"** with its duplication of brother and sister on shore and on board—the same two in two time zones, but composed spatially in the same picture—and in the unspoken "understanding" between the two of them, with its unfocused, diffused quality of sexual excitement.

Mansfield apparently stopped work again on **The Aloe** when she and Murry left Bandol to join the Lawrences in Cornwall in April 1916. O'Sullivan and Scott mention that "KM wrote nothing in Cornwall, nor for several months afterwards, apart from letters and occasional jottings in her notebooks" (*Letters* I, p. 259). There is a lapse of an entire year between the move to Cornwall and the moment when Virginia Woolf asked for a story for the Hogarth Press on April 26, 1917. While the story lay dormant, however, much was happening in Mansfield's life which would eventually influence its final shape. First of all, there was the disintegrating relationship with the Lawrences, including Lawrence's abortive attempt at a *blutbruderschaft* with Murry, the violent intensity of the fights between Lawrence and Frieda, and Mansfield's increasing disgust with Lawrence's incessant theorizing about sex. Next was Mansfield's first visit to Garsington in early July, which brought her into close contact with Bloomsbury, broadening her circle of friendships and associating her with the center of British modernist activity, introducing her subsequently to Lytton Strachey, Maynard Keynes, Aldous Huxley, Dorothy Brett, Dora Carrington, Mark Gertler, Bertrand Russell, and T. S. Eliot. And finally, as a consequence of her new involvement with Bloomsbury, came her significant friendship with Virginia Woolf.

After Woolf's request for a story, in April 1917, Mansfield spent the summer revising **The Aloe**. It was not until July 10, 1918, that the first copies of **"Prelude"** were published. Mansfield's process of revision between **The Aloe** and **"Prelude"** reveals her continuing attempt to eliminate the personal intrusion—the cutting away of the author's voice. Many of Mansfield's alterations serve to bring the narration closer to a specific character's consciousness and away from interpretation by an omniscient narrator. These changes result in a more complex rendering of several female points of view. Other alterations eliminate a nostalgic, personal tone. In the earlier version she retained the second-person "you" as part of several descriptions: "From the window you saw beyond the yard a deep gully filled with tree ferns" (*The Aloe*, p. 35). The narrator seems to insinuate herself into the narrative at this point. She also inserts, in parentheses, information that Kezia would not have been able to explain: "(Kezia had been born in that room. She had come forth squealing out of a reluctant mother in the teeth of a 'Southerly Buster' . . .)" (*The Aloe,* p. 35). The expression "reluctant mother" bears some resemblance to Lawrence's diction.

Some of Mansfield's thematic concerns are strengthened, made more explicit through revision. In other places the revisions tone down a reference. For example, in *The Aloe,* the Samuel Joseph family is described as the "swarm" (p. 27); the overriding impression of too many children in messy familiarity and antagonism contrasts with Linda's desire not to have any more children. The contrast works thematically, but in revising, Mansfield de-emphasized the Josephs altogether, eliminating large sections of which they were a part. To make a simple point of contrast did not warrant allowing the story to take in so much extraneous narration. Neither did overobvious humor—even if it contributed to larger themes—remain in the final version. In a scene at the Josephs' excised in **"Prelude,"** Mansfield originally wrote:

> "You've only got one w. at your place," said Miriam scornfully. "We've got two at ours. One for men and one for ladies. The one for men hasn't got a seat."
>
> "Hasn't got a seat!" cried Kezia. "I *don't* believe you."
>
> (P. 31)

This incident is actually the first of the several contrasts between male and female that Kezia encounters in the story; these contrasts contribute to a pattern of emphasis on the process of awakening to gender differences, a pattern that includes Kezia's later conversation with the storeman about the difference between sheep and rams. But in a section of description like "Sunlight, piercing the green chinks, shone once again upon the purple urns brimming over with yellow chrysanthemums that patterned the walls—" (*The Aloe,* p. 35), Mansfield makes changes in **"Prelude"** that help to situate these descriptive lines more firmly in a discourse on sexuality: "Long pencil rays of sunlight shone through and the wavy shadow of a bush outside danced on the gold lines" (*Stories,* p. 222). In this way the masculine, in the image of the sun with its "long pencil rays," intrudes into the child's perception of the abandoned house.

The Aloe becomes, through its evolution into **"Prelude,"** an awakening into female sexuality. It is also a rejection of male modes, and this strategy is apparent in its all-over structure: its multiplicity, its fluidity, its lack of a central climax, and its many moments of encoded sexual pleasure. What makes **"Prelude"** so revolutionary as a narrative is its implicit statement that the construction of gender should be the motivating center of the text. The technical innovations are devices to reveal this process of reproduction. Reproduction in several forms dominates the text: in terms of procreation—Linda's pregnancy, the blossoming of the aloe; reproduction of gender roles in the games of the children and in Kezia's questioning about sexual differences; and the re-production of bourgeois family life in the interactions of the family members as they respond to the pressures of their "roles." This reproduction assumes the continued dominance of the patriarchal society—the dominance of Stanley as businessman, rule-maker, center of authority—and it occurs in a world of upward mobility—"fleets of aloes," more children, more property. And it relies on the proficiency of the matriarchal center in Mrs. Fairfield: her managing, bringing order, situating the process of reproduction within an aesthetically satisfying and efficient home. But **"Prelude"** also reveals that a counter-process of resistance and rebellion is always at work within these dynamics. Linda's resistance counters Stanley's demands, but ineffectively. Hers is primarily a negative force: passive resistance. The imaginative powers necessary for active rebellion are not brought into force. She fantasizes escape but cannot envision what shape it should take. Yet the imaginative powers, the talents she will never develop, are also in her daughter Kezia, who shares so many of her mother's internal responses: fears of rushing animals, a sense of things coming alive through a force that Kezia calls "It" and Linda, "THEY."

Three modes of female sexual response are suggested in this story: First, Linda's initial attraction to sexuality (the baby bird in her dream), revulsion when the bird swells, and fear when it turns into a human baby; second, Beryl's fantasies of romance, centered in self-love, narcissism, and envy, a body-consciousness purely visual—specular. The third response is that of Kezia, the child not yet completely gendered, who longs for her grandmother's arms, to be stroked and to stroke, to experience the tactile pleasures. She is still polymorphous, responsive to a whole range of stimuli. But she already fears any that might overpower her. Her sexuality requires mutuality, not assault.

A fourth possible mode is one that Mansfield deleted from **"Prelude,"** and that is the implied sexuality of

Mrs. Trout, Linda's other sister. No less a participant in fantasy than her two sisters, as neurasthenic as Linda appears to be, Mrs. Trout has sexual fantasies bound up in violence and injury; her imaginary "novels" always include the death and destruction of the male.

In **"Prelude"** we are presented with multiple viewpoints, nearly all those of female characters. Only the short sections from the point of view of the father, Stanley Burnell, allow for the intrusion of the masculine. His consciousness works as counterpoint in a minor key. It strikes me that the story is structured like a female organism (which invariably contains some subordinated masculine characteristics). In working on this story, nearly a decade before Woolf's *Mrs. Dalloway*, Mansfield was already attempting a spatial rendering of a few days in the inner lives of her characters (she was even closer to Woolf's technique in revealing several minds living through *one* day in the later story about the Burnells, **"At the Bay"**).

Remarkable as it is as a piece of experimental fiction, **"Prelude"** is even more immediately accessible to us as an exploration of feminine consciousness. Within the story Mansfield grapples with her own relationships with the members of her family—mother, father, grandmother, aunt, sisters. It is her most directly autobiographical story, but she discovers a way of exploring these relationships without centering them in the mind of a fictional alter ego. Although the child, Kezia, is a re-creation of the author herself, Kezia's consciousness is but one focus of attention in the story. Mansfield establishes connections, psychic connections that link all of the female characters. The overriding theme of the story is female sexual identity. Linda Burnell, Kezia's mother, strains against her given role and does not want to be a mother. She avoids her children and dreads the sexuality that might lead to the birth of yet another one. She thinks of her husband with a mixture of affection and revulsion: "For all her love and respect and admiration she hated him. And how tender he always was after times like those, how submissive, how thoughtful. . . . There were all her feelings for him, sharp and defined, one as true as the other. And there was this other, this hatred, just as real as the rest" (p. 258).

Linda's ambivalence toward her role is one possible direction for female sexual identity which Mansfield explores in this story. Linda's unmarried sister Beryl represents another. Her outlet is fantasy; she imagines a lover while she gazes at herself in the mirror for self-gratification. And yet another direction is embodied in the grandmother, who represents the earlier, more traditional generation and totally accepts her role. She gives Kezia the affection she craves and is always generous, practical, hard-working, and sensitive to everyone's feelings. Kezia adores her grandmother, but Mansfield makes us see that Kezia shares more deeply the fearsome personal isolation and acute imagination of the mother she does not really know very well than the placid, assured rootedness of the grandmother she hugs, strokes, and calls her "Indian brave."

Early in the story Kezia asks the storeman the difference between a ram and a sheep, expressing the central question of her awakening consciousness. The storeman, embarrassed, typically avoids the truth by saying, "well, a ram has horns and runs for you." But Kezia intuitively knows what he means:

> "I don't want to see it frightfully," she said. "I hate rushing animals like dogs and parrots. I often dream that animals rush at me—even camels—and while they are rushing, their heads swell e-enormous."
>
> (P. 225)

Kezia's language here is nearly identical to her mother's later in the story when she alludes to her husband with:

> If only he wouldn't jump at her so, and bark so loudly, and watch her with such eager, loving eyes. He was too strong for her; she had always hated things that rush at her, from a child.
>
> (P. 258)

Such similar thought patterns establish a psychic connection between mother and daughter deeper than the external aloofness of their behavior with each other. **"Prelude"** is filled with points of connection like this one: images repeated in new contexts, phrases echoed or parodied by different characters, daydreams merging into waking reality.

Older Freudian readings of **"Prelude"** often consider how Kezia's response to the killing of the duck relates to castration anxiety. But in terms of feminist revisionary theory, the most noteworthy aspect is that it is the "head" that is cut off. To lose the head—mind, intellect, consciousness—is to participate in women's fate as constructed in masculine definitions of women's position in relation to civilization. Kezia responds with excitement and then with fear. She wants the head put back on. She would like genders to be as interchangeable as the earrings she suddenly notices on Pat's ears—to recognize that one can go back and forth in the costumes of gender, that the roles are as simple as impersonation, that "death" is not permanent and loss can be reversed.[17]

"Prelude" breaks the form of the *bildungsroman* but is a narrative of *bildung* nonetheless. The spatial organization suggests simultaneity, but the typical linear pattern of individual development is rather spread out among the female characters, who tend to represent the central consciousness at various stages of her life: early childhood, late adolescence, young motherhood, and old age.

The child, aunt, mother, and grandmother embody the female life cycle. But the inevitability of the continuation of conventional female roles seems implicit in this structuring. The only opening is for Kezia, the child yet unformed, but already containing within herself the inner structure to be unfolded.

Notes

1. *The Aloe* has been printed along with "Prelude" in a beautiful edition arranged by Vincent O'Sullivan with the two stories set side by side. See Katherine Mansfield, *The Aloe: With Prelude*, ed. Vincent O'Sullivan (Wellington, N.Z.: Port Nicolson, 1982). Page references to *The Aloe* cited in the text are to this edition, which supersedes the version edited by Murry and published by Knopf in 1930.

2. Virginia Woolf refers to the first printing of "Prelude" in a letter on November 13, 1917, in *The Letters of Virginia Woolf*, vol. II, p. 196. See also Quentin Bell, *Virginia Woolf: A Biography*, vol. II (New York: Harcourt Brace Jovanovich, 1972), 48.

3. *Letters of Katherine Mansfield*, p. 359.

4. Alpers (*Life*, p. 407) mentions that Mansfield wrote only one story in 1913: "Something Childish but Very Natural."

5. For example, on March 6, 1914, she has a dream about walking with her sister along cliffs with "points of teeth"; other elements of the dream include a black fur muff, a charioteer with a quiet evil smile, horses galloping backwards, and "a dark serene rider in a wide hat, gliding past them like a ship through dark water" (*Journal*, pp. 52-53).

6. See Paul Delany, *D. H. Lawrence's Nightmare* (New York: Basic Books, 1978), p. 27, on Lawrence's completion of *The Rainbow* in winter 1914. Delany remarks that "Lawrence must have seen his celebration of Ursula's exuberant femininity as a phase of consciousness that already lay behind him. From now on he would view the relations between men and women as more deeply contradictory, and place a higher value on manly self-reliance."

7. Interestingly, Murry was also uneasy with Lawrence's notions about the essential female. He writes in his autobiography: "Rightly or wrongly, it seemed to me that Lawrence did not serve Frieda as a person, or an individual, but as a sort of incarnation of the Female principle, a sort of Magna Mater in whom he deliberately engulfed and obliterated himself. And I felt a morbidly fastidious aversion to this. It produced in me a kind of nausea." *Between Two Worlds: The Autobiography of John Middleton Murry* (New York: Julian Messner, 1936), p. 312.

8. D. H. Lawrence, "Study of Thomas Hardy," in *Phoenix: The Posthumous Papers of D. H. Lawrence,* ed. Edward D. McDonald (New York: Viking, 1972), pp. 443-44.

9. Tomalin, *Katherine Mansfield: A Secret Life*, p. 38.

10. See Tomalin, pp. 37-39. Delany, p. 397, dates the composition of the chapter as December 1914.

11. Claire Tomalin describes beautifully the details and stresses of this period; see pp. 115-44.

12. Open arms had long been associated for her with female sexuality. See *Journal*, p. 12, on one lesbian relationship: "Last night I spent in her arms"; "Nothing remains except the shelter of her arms" (p. 13); and "Now, each time I see her to put her arms round me and hold me against her" (p. 14).

13. Vincent O'Sullivan, "Introduction" to *The Aloe* (London: Virago, 1985), p. ix.

14. See Murry, *Between Two Worlds*, p. 351.

15. "The Wind Blows" retains the suggestiveness of the symbolist work she did much earlier. Hanson and Gurr comment that it "is the most purely symbolist of her stories to this date" (*Katherine Mansfield*, p. 45).

16. See Hankin's discussion of Mansfield's guilt feelings after the death of her brother, which "must have seemed in some odd way the logical outcome of her years of battling with male adversaries" (*Katherine Mansfield and Her Confessional Stories*, pp. 105-15).

17. Fullbrook remarks on Kezia's reaction to the beheading of the duck: "In this very ritualistic scene she assumes the position of suppliant before the man who has demonstrated his power of imposing death in an ordinary yet godlike display of authority. The scene is of a primal fall from innocence, and it is also a scene in which a male parent-figure initiates the children into slaughter. In 'Prelude' this is the core of masculine gender. The male is the devourer of life, the killer, and Pat's act is completed as male ritual later in the story when we see Stanley—associated with knives like the butcher in Kezia's nightmare in 'The Little Girl'—carving the same duck with professional manly pleasure. . . . Kezia is only recalled from her terror through the evidence of Pat's likeness to women" (*Katherine Mansfield*, pp. 74-75).

Selected Bibliography

Alpers, Antony. *Katherine Mansfield: A Biography*. New York: Knopf, 1954.

———. *The Life of Katherine Mansfield.* New York: Viking, 1980.

Fullbrook, Kate. *Katherine Mansfield.* Bloomington: Indiana University Press, 1986.

Hankin, C. A. *Katherine Mansfield and Her Confessional Stories.* London: Macmillan, 1983.

Hanson, Clare, and Andrew Gurr. *Katherine Mansfield.* London: Macmillan, 1981.

Mansfield, Katherine. *The Aloe.* Ed. J. Middleton Murry. New York: Knopf, 1930.

———. *The Aloe: With Prelude.* Ed. Vincent O'Sullivan. Wellington, N.Z.: Port Nicolson, 1982.

———. *The Collected Letters of Katherine Mansfield.* Vols. I-II. Ed. Vincent O'Sullivan and Margaret Scott. Oxford: Clarendon, 1984, 1987.

———. *The Critical Writings of Katherine Mansfield.* Ed. Clare Hanson. New York: St. Martin's, 1987.

———. "Fifteen Letters from Katherine Mansfield to Virginia Woolf." *Adam International Review* nos. 370-75 (1972-73), 19-24.

———. "Forty-Six Letters by Katherine Mansfield." *Adam International Review* no. 300 (1965), 88-118.

———. *Journal of Katherine Mansfield.* Ed. John Middleton Murry. London: Constable, 1954.

———. "Katherine Mansfield and S. S. Koteliansky: Some Unpublished Letters." Ed. John W. Dickinson. *Revue de Litterature Comparée* 45 (January-March 1971), 79-99.

———. *Katherine Mansfield's Letters to John Middleton Murry 1913-1922.* Ed. J. Middleton Murry. New York: Knopf, 1951.

———. *The Letters of Katherine Mansfield.* Ed. John Middleton Murry. New York: Knopf, 1929.

———. *Novels and Novelists.* New York: Knopf, 1930.

———. *Poems of Katherine Mansfield.* Ed. Vincent O'Sullivan. Auckland, N.Z.: Oxford University Press, 1988.

———. *The Scrapbook of Katherine Mansfield.* Ed. John Middleton Murry. New York: Knopf, 1940.

———. *Selected Letters.* Ed. Vincent O'Sullivan. Oxford: Clarendon, 1989.

———. *The Short Stories of Katherine Mansfield.* New York: Knopf, 1937.

———. "The Unpublished Manuscripts of Katherine Mansfield." Transcribed and edited by Margaret Scott. *The Turnbull Library Record* (n.s.): 3 (March 1970), 4-28; 3 (November 1970), 128-33; 4 (May 1971), 4-20; 5 (May 1972), 19-25; 6 (October 1973), 4-8; 6 (May 1974), 4-14; 12 (May 1979), 11-28.

———. *The Urewera Notebook.* Edited with an Introduction by Ian A. Gordon. New York: Oxford University Press, 1978.

Murry, John Middleton. *Aspects of Literature.* New York: Knopf, 1920.

———. *Between Two Worlds: The Autobiography of John Middleton Murry.* New York: Julian Messner, 1936.

———. *The Letters of John Middleton Murry to Katherine Mansfield.* Ed. C. A. Hankin. London: Constable, 1983.

O'Sullivan, Vincent. "The Magnetic Chain: Notes and Approaches to K. M." *Landfall* 114 (June 1975), 95-131.

Tomalin, Claire. *Katherine Mansfield: A Secret Life.* New York: Knopf, 1988.

Woolf, Virginia. *The Common Reader, First Series.* New York: Harcourt, Brace & World, 1925.

———. *Contemporary Writers.* New York: Harcourt Brace Jovanovich, 1965.

———. *The Diary of Virginia Woolf, Vols. I-III.* Ed. Anne Olivier Bell. New York: Harcourt Brace Jovanovich, 1977, 1978, 1980.

———. *The Letters of Virginia Woolf. Vol. II.* Ed. Nigel Nicolson and Joanne Trautmann. New York: Harcourt Brace Jovanovich, 1976.

———. *Mrs. Dalloway.* New York: Harcourt, Brace & World, 1925.

Gardner McFall (essay date 1993)

SOURCE: McFall, Gardner. "Poetry and Performance in Katherine Mansfield's 'Bliss.'" In *Critical Essays on Katherine Mansfield,* edited by Rhoda B. Nathan, pp. 140-50. New York: G. K. Hall & Company, 1993.

[*In the following essay, McFall interprets the different meanings of "bliss" in Mansfield's story of that name, claiming that while on the "mimetic" level the work traces the reversal of its protagonist's joy and expectation into disillusionment, on the narrative level "bliss" represents the power of language and personal vision to compensate for human failure.*]

> Oh, to be a *writer,* a real writer given up to it and to it alone! . . . There are moments when Dickens is possessed by this power of writing: he is carried away. That is bliss.
>
> Katherine Mansfield, 1920
>
> (*Journal,* 203)

"**Bliss**" exemplifies Mansfield's mature fiction shaped by her lyric impulse and her mastery of poetic tradition squaring with the circumstances of her life. Here, her concision, mobilization of imagery and rhythm, irony, ambiguity, and submerged lyric voice require that we read the story with the kind of close attention generally reserved for poems. In doing so, we can see in what respect Mansfield's fiction is poetic. We can also see how, under the pressure of Mansfield's illness and exile, it emerges as a site of revisionary performance, compensating for reality.

When Mansfield wrote "**Bliss**," she was in Bandol, recuperating from a recently diagnosed "spot" on the lung. Aside from Ida Baker, whose arrival in France on 12 February 1918 irritated her, Mansfield had only the 1900 *Oxford Book of English Verse* for companionship.[1] Her steady attention to it resulted, as she told Murry, in its being "full [of] notes" by early March (***Collected Letters***, 2:107). Among the poems there, she fell under the spell of Shelley's "The Question," which she quoted twice in her letters to Murry that month and which she alluded to in her journal. On 18 February she wrote him:

> On my table are wild daffodils . . . They are so lovely that each time I look up I give them to you again. We shall go expeditions in the spring and write down all the *signs* & take a bastick and a small trowel & bring back treasure. Isn't that lovely where Shelley speaks of the "moonlight coloured may" . . .
>
> Its still (I think) very cold & I am in my wadded jacket with the pink 'un round my legs.
>
> (***Collected Letters***, 2:78)

On 19 February Mansfield had her first hemorrhage of the lung. Her anxious thoughts turned immediately to Murry, for she was frightened, and to her work, which she feared would be left incomplete:

> . . . of course I'm frightened . . . I don't want to be ill . . . away from Jack . . . I don't want to find this is real consumption . . . and I shan't have my work written. *That's what matters.* How unbearable it would be to die—leave "scraps," . . . [Mansfield's ellipsis] nothing real finished . . . *Jack and my work*—they are all I think of (mixed with curious visionary longings for gardens in full flower).[2]

Her parenthetical words point to Shelley's poem in the *Oxford Book* ("Methought that of these visionary flowers / I made a nosegay" [715]), and suggest the poem's connection to "**Bliss**," with Bertha's vision of the full, flowering pear tree.[3] Her reference shows how rapidly she had appropriated the poem, how both her experience and Shelley's words were converging even as she worked on "**Bliss**," started seven days before.[4]

In a letter to Murry of 20 and 21 February, she invoked Shelley's poem again:

> Do you remember, or have I mentioned lately that poem of Shelley's *The Question*. It begins: "I dreamed that, as I wandered by the way / Bare Winter suddenly was changed to Spring" . . . [Mansfield's ellipsis] I have learned it by heart since I am here; it is very exquisite, I think. Shelley and Keats I get more and more *attached* to. Nay, to all poetry.
>
> (***Collected Letters***, 2:83)

She quoted these same lines by Shelley in a letter to Ottoline Morrell on 22 February (***Collected Letters***, 2:86). Why "The Question" particularly should have captured Mansfield's imagination is not hard to divine. In the poem, a dreamer gathers an elaborate bouquet of "visionary flowers," only to realize he has no one to give it to. The poem ends:

> I hastened to the spot where I had come,
> That I might there present it—O! to whom?[5]

The dreamer's lush landscape, constituted by language in a detailed listing of flowers, creates a presence in the poem, while the closing question falls on thwarted desire and a recognition of human absence. Mansfield appreciated the poem's movement from longing to deprivation, for it matched her emotional experience with those closest to her, her brother Leslie, whom she had lost in 1915, as well as Murry, whose absence she felt keenly on the heels of his 1916 attraction to Ottoline and the onset of her illness. Her letters record that during this separation, Mansfield dreamed of Murry, only to find him not there upon waking (***Collected Letters***, 2:20). She wrote him: "I have such a longing for you. . . . The absence from you eats at my heart" (***Collected Letters***, 2:81). Although she projected a brave exterior about her illness in her letters to Murry, her hemorrhage understandably accentuated her need of him and her desires for an immediate, happy future together.

Mansfield sketched a movement from longing to deprivation in "**Bliss**." Shelley's lines, which she quoted to Murry and Ottoline, are recapitulated in the second sentence, where Mansfield's dreamer, Bertha, is caught up in a "sudden" transformation: "What can you do if you are thirty and, turning the corner of your own street, you are overcome, suddenly by a feeling of bliss—absolute bliss!"[6]

Shelley's sudden seasonal change (from "Bare Winter" to "Spring") echoes in Bertha's emotional swing. Later in the story, Bertha ascribes her feeling to the season: "She felt quite dizzy, quite drunk. It must have been the spring" (308). Living apart from Murry in a sunny, but chilly France, Mansfield's emotional life was virtually "bare winter." There was every reason why she would have dreamed, like Shelley's dreamer and like Bertha in "**Bliss**," of a sudden spring. In fact, she wrote Murry: "This will all pass & I shall get better, our spring will come—& it will be warm & you will write to me & we shall be together again" (***Collected Letters***, 2:11).

Coupled with Murry's absence was the repressed, yet still troubling matter of Leslie's death, which would have been called up by the passing of his birthday on 21 February, and which she mentioned in a letter to Murry on 26 February (*Collected Letters,* 2:93). Although Mansfield had put the worst of her mourning behind her, her continued longing for him is suggested by the reemergence in **"Bliss"** of imagery from a 1915 entry in her *Journal* following his death. There she wrote recollections of herself and Leslie in the Acacia Road garden, noting the "slender" (83) pear tree, and the "round moon [that] shines over the pear tree" (85). In the entry, the "moonlight deepens" (85) as brother and sister say their good-byes: "The shadows on the grass are long and strange; a puff of strange wind whispers in the ivy and the old moon touches them with silver" (85).

The movement of her journal entry from union to farewell corresponds obliquely enough with Shelley's poem and, inevitably, with **"Bliss"** to show how "The Question" tapped into Mansfield's continued loss and grief. It touched that dreaming part of her that still wished for her brother (in many ways her expectant, but ruined dreams of their shared life parallel Bertha's disillusionment), and figured in the compensatory writing of **"Bliss,"** where Bertha's vision of the flowering pear tree stands removed from human failure and death: "as lovely as ever and as full of flower and as still" (*Stories,* 315). Here was the emotional ground Shelley's poem was laid upon, and in this "soil," to borrow Woolf's figure which she used in criticizing **"Bliss,"**[7] the story took root.

Mansfield was also reading other poems in the *Oxford Book*. She told Murry: "I *keep* (as you see) wanting to quote poetry today—When I get back I shall be like a sort of little private automatic machine in the home. You wind me up & a poem will come out—Ive learned so many here while I lie awake—" (*Collected Letters,* 2:94).

She singled out Marvell's "Upon Appleton House" for quoting in a letter to Murry of 26 February. The lines appeared in the *Oxford Book* as the last six of "A Garden: Written after the Civil War":

> Unhappy! Shall we never more
> That sweet militia restore,
> When gardens only had their towers,
> And all the garrisons were flowers;
> When roses only arms might bear
> And men did rosy garlands wear?
>
> (*Collected Letters,* 2:94; *Oxford,* 386-87)

In her letters to Murry at this time, Mansfield often expressed her wish to regain their garden, which she associated with domestic happiness (*Collected Letters,* 2:77, 93, 97). It is understandable that Marvell's poem appealed to her in that it would have not only called up the past New Zealand gardens of her youth and the 1915 Acacia Road garden she knew with Leslie, but symbolized a future one she hoped to share with Murry. Suffering a triple exile from the "garden," she conflated possibly Marvell's poem as well as Shelley's in her 19 February admission to "curious visionary longings of gardens in full flower" (*Journal,* 129-30).

In any event, her head was full of poetry when she finished **"Bliss"** on 27 February. On that day, she wrote Murry:

> . . . I am so seized with the wonder of the english tongue—of english poetry—and I am so overcome by the idea that you are a poet and that we are going to live for poetry—for writing—that my heart has begun dancing away as if it will never stop—& I can see our cottage and our garden & you leaning against the door & me walking up the path . . .
>
> (*Collected Letters,* 2:97)

On 28 February, she mailed him the story:

> Ive just finished this new story **"Bliss"** and am sending it to you. But though my God! I *have* enjoyed writing it I am an absolute rag for the rest of the day . . . Oh, tell me what you think about *our* new story . . . Please try and like it and I am now free to start another. One extraordinary thing has happened to me since I came over here! Once I start them they haunt me, pursue me and plague me until they are finished and as good as I can do.
>
> (*Collected Letters,* 2:97-98)

In these letters, almost in the manner of Bertha, Mansfield reveals the bliss-producing role of writing in her life. Her exclamation points, her emphasis on **"Bliss"** as *our* story, her sentences such as "one extraordinary thing has happened" and "I am so seized with the wonder of the english tongue" are echoes of the story she had finished. Her request of Murry ("Please try and like it") sounds like Bertha's plea on behalf of Pearl ("Oh, Harry, don't dislike her" [*Stories,* 313]).

Mansfield's composition of the story gave her a new "vision" of her life with Murry, complete with a garden (Marvell's "sweet militia" restored) and a mutual dedication to art, the only third party to their relationship Mansfield could embrace.[8] The story momentarily filled her sense of absence, reawakened and affirmed the 1915 image of union with her brother, and, if we consider her choice of words, supplanted her illness. It is, she tells Murry, her stories that haunt, pursue, and plague her, not the tuberculosis. In other words, a significant mental and emotional alteration was wrought in Mansfield's writing of **"Bliss."** Language redeemed or compensated for an inadequate world, and this sort of transaction is what concerns us in the story.

On the mimetic level, **"Bliss"** depicts Bertha Young's ironic realization that she and her husband love the same woman, Pearl Fulton. Structurally, the story builds on a reversal of Bertha's expectation and ends in what is taken for disillusionment. We witness Bertha at a private moment when she is disabused of any pretense of having an ideal life. As she catches sight of her husband kissing Pearl, her status as wife and friend is called into question, and the precipitous ending of the story just beyond this point forces the reader to consider what for Bertha must be a crushing blow.

Yet the language of the story works against this conclusion and, indeed, achieves what the plot denies. While the plot is cast as a straightforward quest narrative ending in disappointment, the language indicates a different, opposite objective. Managing a second mode of discourse, the story achieves a reformulation of bliss as it occurs tropologically throughout the *Oxford Book* in the poems of Shakespeare, Milton, Wordsworth, and Browning, among others. It plays off the traditional figure of bliss, that is lust, found for example in Shakespeare's sonnet 19 ("a bliss in proof, and proved, a very woe" [*Oxford,* 199]), against what Mansfield felt bliss to be, namely writing or language. Through the story's competing and arguably subversive mode of discourse, language (or subjective vision) balances and compensates for human failure.

Mansfield's appropriation and reformulation of the trope is evident from the beginning of the story in the elaborate account of Bertha's feeling of "absolute bliss": ". . . as though you'd swallowed a bright piece of that late afternoon sun and it burned in your bosom, sending out a little shower of sparks into every particle, into every finger and toe" (*Stories,* 305). Her description harkens directly to the first line of an anonymous sixteenth-century lyric in the *Oxford Book*:

> My heart is high above, my body is full of bliss.
>
> (80)

Bertha's feeling of bliss, which is evoked in language that suggests lust, appears throughout the story as a recurring motif. After her arrival home, she stands in the dusky dining room: "But in her bosom there was still that bright glowing place—that shower of little sparks coming from it" (*Stories,* 305). Later, she holds her baby in the nursery: "And, indeed, she loved little B so much—her neck as she bent forward, her exquisite toes as they shone transparent in the firelight—that all her feeling of bliss came back again" (307). By the time Bertha encounters Pearl, the shower of sparks in her bosom has become a full blaze: "What was there in the touch of that cool arm that could fan—fan—start blazing—blazing the fire of bliss that Bertha did not know what to do with?" (311). Finally, in her momentary dreamlike inspection of the garden with Pearl, she wonders: "How long did they stand there? Both, as it were, caught in that circle of unearthly light, understanding each other perfectly, creatures of another world, and wondering what they were to do in this one with all this blissful treasure that burned in their bosoms and dropped, in silver flowers, from their hair and hands?" (312-13).

If Mansfield's title were not sign enough, certainly her initial description harboring the older trope, and its recurrences throughout the text should tell the reader that Mansfield is up to more than detailing a love triangle from the viewpoint of the betrayed. Playing on "bliss" as it appears in the *Oxford Book,* she deploys it to place vision (indicated by Bertha's pear tree) above or outside human escapades. There are, after all, two things Bertha sees at the end of **"Bliss."** One is her husband kissing Pearl in the foyer; the other is the flowering pear tree in the garden, whose perfection has been, from the start, a subjective "vision," one of Bertha's own making: "The windows of the drawing-room opened on to a balcony overlooking the garden. At the far end, against the wall, there was a tall, slender pear tree in fullest, richest bloom; it stood perfect, as though becalmed against the jade-green sky. Bertha could not help feeling, even from this distance, that it had not a single bud or a faded petal" (308).

It is this vision that remains intact, though Bertha's interpretation of it as a "symbol of her own life" (308) is cast into doubt. The story appears to say: human relations fail; we scarcely know ourselves and are betrayed, if not by ourselves, by others close to us; however, the final vision of the pear tree, a literary figure and the embodiment of Bertha's longing, endures, and stands removed from the disillusioning events that have transpired. Of course, it is because her longing has been thwarted that it remains perfect as represented in her vision of the tree. There are implications here for the writer's task which, in Mansfield's case as we have seen, involved the subordination of absence and longing to the form of fiction.

Just as Mansfield borrows the figure of bliss from the *Oxford Book,* she also appropriates the blossoming tree, a common enough image. She would have found it in Browning's "Home-thoughts, from Abroad" contained in the anthology:

> Hark, where my blossom'd pear-tree in the hedge
> Leans to the field and scatters on the clover
> Blossoms and dewdrops—at the bent spray's edge—.
>
> (866)

Mansfield's anxiety about her appropriation of the image is suggested in her choosing to have Bertha's tree remain full flowering throughout the story. She resists employing it as an equation for inconsistent human feeling and action, which she was unable to do in her poem **"The Lilac Tree"** from 1908; there a lilac tree corresponds with the fruition and loss of love:

> Soon must the tree stand stripped and bare
> And I shall never find her there
> Oh, lilac tree, oh lilac tree
> Shower down thy leaves and cover me.

In **"Bliss,"** nature (insofar as it is part of Bertha's vision) is not subordinated to human crisis, but aloof in all its contrasting perfection. Mansfield has traveled a great distance from her 1908 poem, but the influence of the poets appears as keen if not more so, evidenced by her need to revise the clearly borrowed trope. She reverses Herrick's tact in "To Blossoms," also contained in the *Oxford Book*:

> But you are lovely leaves, where we
>   May read how soon things have
>   Their end, though ne'er so brave:
> And after they have shown their pride
>   Like you awhile, they glide
>   Into the grave.
>
> (269)

Mansfield's contrasting use of the figure (she might have had at least one petal fall from the tree to underscore Bertha's revelation about Harry's affair if this were the story's central concern) shows her unsentimental insistence on the enduring power of subjective vision as it results from longing, and, implicitly, the formalization of it represented by the text, or art.

The irony of the story, which critics generally locate in Bertha's revelation at the end,[9] resides rather in Bertha's inability to express herself (or read people and situations properly) juxtaposed with the text's achievement of expression. Bertha is constantly frustrated by her inarticulateness ("Oh, is there no way you can express it" [*Stories,* 305] and revises her attempts at expression ("No, that about the fiddle is not quite what I mean" [305]). She speaks in phrases marked by Mansfield's inverted commas, indicating these phrases are not authentic:

> "But while I am making coffee in the drawing-room perhaps she will 'give a sign.'" But what she meant by that she did not know, and what would happen after that she could not imagine.
>
> (312)

Mansfield's intention to have Bertha lack authentic expression is revealed in her comment to Murry that Bertha was an "artist manque enough to realise that those words and expressions were not & couldn't be hers—They were, as it were, *quoted* by her, borrowed . . . she'd none of her own" (**Collected Letters,** 2:121).

Yet Bertha appreciates and longs for performance, which is often couched in artistic terms: "Why be given a body if you have to keep it shut up in a case like a rare, rare fiddle?" (**Stories,** 305). Later she wonders: "Why have a baby if it has to be kept—not in a case like a rare, rare fiddle, but in another woman's arms?" (306). Bertha behaves like an eager director, who has set the stage for her acting dinner guests. Her attention to the arrangement of fruit whose color will "bring the carpet up to the table" (306) and her attire that imitates the pear tree hint at her investment in what is about to happen, in what she has earlier thought would be "divine" (305). When the guests finally assemble, they remind her of "a play by Tchekof" (311).

Mansfield once referred to her writing as "regular performance" (**Journal,** 262). That Bertha is duped, that her actors and actresses rewrite the script throws Mansfield's authorial performance into relief. She achieves what is denied Bertha who, upon contemplating being alone with her husband after dinner, jumps up from her chair and runs to the piano:

> "What a pity someone does not play!" she cried. "What a pity somebody does not play."
>
> (**Stories,** 314)

Her anxieties are subverted into a longing for performance that is not fulfilled. The bundle of inadequacies that constitute Bertha's character and the failings of those around her are contrasted by the text in which they appear. Mansfield's performance suggests, through Bertha's concluding vision, that the figure or the fiction endures, whatever the outcome of human events.

This contradiction in what the plot recounts and language implies is signaled in the way language unravels the plot even as it progresses, and holds two levels of discourse in balance: the mimetic depiction of Bertha's dinner party with its ensuing revelation and the play of tropology centering on bliss and the flowering pear tree. Mansfield's process of fiction conforms to Anne Mellor's definition of romantic irony as a "form or structure that simultaneously creates and de-creates itself."[10] (5). The first sentence of the story illustrates this: "Although Bertha Young was thirty she had moments like this when she wanted to run instead of walk, to take dancing steps on and off the pavement, to bowl a hoop, to throw something up in the air and catch it again, or to stand still and laugh at—nothing—at nothing, simply" (305).

Retraction and contradiction mark the sentence where "simply" cannot be said to apply. Immediately following the first sentence, which aims at a mimetic account, a lyric elaboration of Bertha's "bliss" ensues. These two modes of discourse thread throughout the story and are balanced in the final scene:

> Bertha simply ran over to the long windows. "Oh, what is going to happen now?" she cried. But the pear tree was as lovely as ever and as full of flower and as still.

The question of action is answered with a still-life description, a perfect figure, a remaining vision. In Bertha's cry ("Oh, what is going to happen now?") we hear the echo of Shelley's dreamer ("That I might there present it—O! to whom?"). Although the anguish of thwarted desire is implied by both texts, in Mansfield's story it is checked by the compensating vision itself.

Yet even as we track this compensating function of Bertha's vision in the story, **"Bliss"** resists closure. The ambiguity achieved by the juxtaposition of Bertha's sight of her husband kissing Pearl, and the vision of the perfect tree further places the story in the tradition of Romantic irony:

> English Romantic irony, broadly put, consists in the studied avoidance on the artist's part of determinate meanings, even at such times as he might wish to encourage his readers to *produce* such meanings for himself; it involves the refusal of closure, the incorporation of any potentially available "metacomment" within the primary language of the text, the provision of a linguistic sign which moves towards or verges on a "free" status. . . .[11]

Mansfield's refusal to direct us in how we must read the story (though it *is* a lesson in reading) rivets us to her performance as writer. For Mansfield, the text is analogous to Bertha's subjective vision, and maintains a compensating or balancing function in relation to life. As she tells us in a 1922 journal entry: "There is no feeling to be compared with the joy of having written and finished a story. . . . There it was, *new* and complete" (285). Elsewhere, and ironically, given our knowledge of the strain in their relationship, she insists in a 1921 letter to Ottoline Morrell: "Work is the only thing that never fails."[12]

In **"Bliss,"** we have the fusion of Mansfield's life and reading. We witness an active dialectic whereby texts (in this case, poems from the *Oxford Book*) resonate with her experience to produce a fiction whose romantic tropology, identified with subjective experience (and poetry), vies with a linear, mimetic account expected of prose. The situation of **"Bliss,"** involving a triangular relationship, reversal of expectation, and deception, was not new in Mansfield's work. She employed this configuration of elements as early as 1908 in a short sketch entitled **"The Unexpected Must Happen."**[13] What was distinctive about **"Bliss"** was the incorporation of poetic, noncausal elements to reveal the ambiguity of human relationships, and to suggest the triumph of creative vision over pain and disappointment. "Beauty triumphs over ugliness in Life . . ." she wrote. "And that marvellous triumph is what I long to express" (*Letters*, 2:452-53).

Mansfield's **"Bliss,"** far from the love triangle it recounts, points to lyric bliss discovered in the act of writing. It points to longing, whose perfection involves the production of vision or text. Mansfield's bliss was not the lust of the anonymous sixteenth-century lyric or that of Shakespeare's sonnet. It was not Milton's eternal bliss ("On Time," *Oxford*, 318), or Wordsworth's "bliss of solitude" ("Daffodils," *Oxford*, 605), or Browning's "bliss to die with" ("The Last Ride Together," *Oxford*, 865). Mansfield's was the bliss of language that could balance or compensate for an inadequate world.

Notes

1. On 6 February 1918, shortly before Mansfield started "Bliss," she wrote Murry: "Four years ago today Goodyear gave me the Oxford Book of English Verse. I discovered that by chance this morning" (*The Collected Letters of Katherine Mansfield*, ed. Vincent O'Sullivan and Margaret Scott [Oxford: Clarendon Press, 1984-], 2:78; hereafter cited in the text.

2. *Journal of Katherine Mansfield*, ed. John Middleton Murry (London: Constable Books, 1927; New York: Knopf, 1927; Definitive Edition, 1954; London: Hutchinson, 1984), 129—130; hereafter cited in the text.

3. Marilyn Zorn supports this view in her article "Visionary Flowers: Another Study of Mansfield's 'Bliss'" (*Studies in Short Fiction* 17:2 [1980]: 141-47): "'Bliss's' theme encompasses exactly the visionary joy and cry against corruption which we associate with the Romantics. One of the unacknowledged sources for the story is Shelley's poem 'The Question'" (143).

4. In a letter dated 12 and 13 February 1918, Mansfield wrote Murry: "I lay down under a pine tree & though I spent some time saying 'the wells and springs are poisoned' they were not really. I began to construct my new story. Until I get back to you & we are safe in each other's arms there is only one thing to do & that is *work work work*" (*Collected Letters*, 2:70).

5. See Arthur Quiller Couch, ed. *The Oxford Book of English Verse 1250-1900* (Oxford: Clarendon Press, 1900), 715; hereafter cited in the text.

6. *The Stories of Katherine Mansfield*, ed. Antony Alpers (Oxford: Oxford University Press, 1984), 305; hereafter cited in the text.

7. After reading "Bliss" in the August 1918 issue of the *English Review*, Woolf wrote in her *Diary*: "I threw down Bliss with the exclamation, 'she's done for!' Indeed I don't see how much faith in her as a woman or writer can survive that sort of story. . . . her mind is a very thin soil, laid an inch or two deep upon very barren rock. . . . the whole conception is poor, cheap, not the vision, however imperfect, of an interesting mind. She

writes badly too" (*The Diary of Virginia Woolf 1912-1922*, ed. Anne Olivier Bell [New York: Harcourt, 1979] 1:179).

8. That their work became a sign of Mansfield and Murry's love is suggested by an exchange of letters. On 5 February 1918, Murry wrote Mansfield: "I feel that in you & me our love & our work are become the same thing, inextricably knit together" (*Letters*, 111). On 10 and 11 February, she replied: "all I write or ever will write will be the fruit of our love" (*Collected Letters,* 2:66).

9. C. A. Hankin, *Katherine Mansfield and Her Confessional Stories* (New York: St. Martin's Press, 1983), 147.

10. Anne K. Mellor, *English Romantic Irony* (Cambridge: Harvard University Press, 1980), 5.

11. David Simpson, *Irony and Authority in Romantic Poetry* (Totowa: Rowman and Littlefield, 1979), 190.

12. *The Letters of Katherine Mansfield*, ed. John Middleton Murry. 2 vols. (London: Constable, 1929; New York: Knopf, 1929), 2:385; hereafter cited in the text.

13. This sketch is deposited at the Alexander Turnbull Library, Wellington, New Zealand.

Abbreviations

CLKM: *The Collected Letters of Katherine Mansfield.* Ed. Vincent O'Sullivan and Margaret Scott. Oxford: Clarendon Press. 1, 1903-17 (1984); 2, 1918-19 (1987); 3, 1919-20 (1993).

IB: Ida Baker. *Katherine Mansfield: The Memories of L. M.* New York: Taplinger Publishing Company, 1972.

JKM 1927: *The Journal of Katherine Mansfield.* Ed. John Middleton Murry. New York: Knopf, 1927.

JKM 1940: *The Scrapbook of Katherine Mansfield.* Ed. John Middleton Murry. New York: Knopf, 1940.

JKM 1954: *Journal of Katherine Mansfield.* Ed. John Middleton Murry. London: Constable, 1954.

JMM-KM: *The Letters of John Middleton Murry to Katherine Mansfield.* Ed. C. A. Hankin. New York: Franklin Watts, 1983.

LKM: *The Letters of Katherine Mansfield.* Ed. John Middleton Murry. New York: Knopf, 1929.

KM-JMM: *Katherine Mansfield's Letters to John Middleton Murry, 1913-22.* New York: Knopf, 1951.

L & J: *The Letters and Journals of Katherine Mansfield: A Selection.* Ed. C. K. Stead. New York: Penguin, 1977.

SS: *The Short Stories of Katherine Mansfield.* Ed. John Middleton Murry. New York: Knopf, 1937.

Kirsty Cochrane (essay date 1993)

SOURCE: Cochrane, Kirsty. "Katherine Mansfield's Images of Art.'" In *Critical Essays on Katherine Mansfield*, edited by Rhoda B. Nathan, pp. 151-57. New York: G. K. Hall & Company, 1993.

[*In the following essay, Cochrane analyzes Mansfield's "Sun and Moon," focusing specifically on the way the story's imagery functions to "symbolize and enact the condition of art: being fact, metaphor, and emblem."*]

Katherine Mansfield's images of art include living things that have the power to transform something else, or that can themselves be transformed. In **"Sun and Moon,"** flowers are the agent of transformation. Elsewhere, this function is performed by lights or lamps, which may be seen to provide the conditions for awareness of human sympathy and its preciousness. With flowers, however, an elaborate scale of imagistic use can be discerned. First of all, flowers are intrinsic to the stories in their fundamental role of fact and image. Beyond this, they often possess the mediating property of disposing characters toward the experience of art. Ultimately they may be found functioning in ways which both symbolize and enact the condition of art: being fact, metaphor, and emblem.

Already in the nine-year-old Katherine Mansfield's first published story, **"Enna Blake,"** there exists an impulse to reshape in fictional form the primary human experience of gathering plants to bring home and reassemble as objects of beauty or offerings of love in another setting.

> 'I should think it would be very nice to get some moss', Enna said; so off they trudged. The girls spent a very happy day, and got a great many nice ferns and some beautiful moss. And that night Enna thought it was the nicest day she had ever spent in the country.[2]

That child's voice, vision, and impulse, are there with the same purity in stories from Katherine Mansfield's maturity. In these, this fundamental imagery from childhood transforms our view of the adult world; for instance, a child may see the plants and flowers and trees of the outdoor world transfigured in indoor settings, or see the familiar daytime house and garden undergo a mysterious metamorphosis through the effects of night.

The story where this quintessential imagery lies at the very heart of meaning is **"Sun and Moon."** On 10 February 1918 Katherine Mansfield wrote to John Middleton Murry from Bandol, in the South of France:

> I *dreamed* a short story last night, even down to its name, which was **"Sun and Moon."** It was very light. I dreamed it all—about children. I got up at 6.30 and wrote a note or two because I knew it would fade. I'll send it some time this week. It's so nice. I didn't dream that I read it. No, I was in it, part of it, and it played round invisible me. But the hero is not more than 5. In my dream I saw a supper-table with the eyes of 5. It was awfully queer—especially a plate of half-melted ice-cream.[3]

It is almost typical of Katherine Mansfield to trivialize the importance of her story like this. Her attitude in this letter provides a cue for Anthony Alpers to remark in his fine edition of Mansfield: "A case of mental reaction to a major work, written down within hours of finishing **"Je ne parle pas""** (*Stories*, 561). Is this indeed simply a very insignificant story? I don't think so; quite the contrary. This is how it begins.

> In the afternoon the chairs came, a whole big cart full of little gold ones with their legs in the air. And then the flowers came. When you stared down from the balcony at the people carrying them the flower pots looked like funny awfully nice hats nodding up the path.
>
> Moon thought they were hats. She said: 'Look. There's a man wearing a palm on his head.' But she never knew the difference between real things and not real ones.
>
> There was nobody to look after Sun and Moon. Nurse was helping Annie alter Mother's dress which was much-too-long-and-tight-under-the-arms and Mother was running all over the house and telephoning Father to be sure not to forget things. She only had time to say: 'Out of my way, children!'
>
> (*Stories*, 300)

From inside they looked like hats, from outside you might see they were trees being brought in.

"Sun and Moon" was written all in one piece very fast on the same day in 1918 that she wrote to John Middleton Murry about her dream of it. It is remarkable, among her stories of childhood because the children in this case are so very young; they are at the threshold of realizing an individual consciousness. At least, Sun is there; Moon has not yet reached it. It achieves the very delicate task of making very young children real without sentimentality. Where sentimentality is found in the story it belongs to adult characters, not to the narrative consciousness. The story uses a vocabulary which is entirely that of the boy, Sun. The two children are so young they are a world in themselves. They scarcely know that they are boy and girl. "There was nobody to look after Sun and Moon." These names are self-concepts. Chummie, Boy, Sonny, Son: the child makes elementary and total sense of his nickname, and names his sister in terms of his perception. The story comes close to the fundamental sources of individual consciousness. As Katherine Mansfield said, "I was in it, part of it, and it played round invisible me." Her role in it seems to have been that of her "hero," Sun. Perhaps she was sensitive to the psychological truth of this transference. Certainly she was not comfortable about exposing the story without the framing of its larger context, her collection *Bliss.*

Sun and Moon are so young that they exist in a universe that has scarcely formulated a notion of individual identity, though it possesses established routines and expectations of behavior: their real names are unknown to us Their world is upstairs in the nursery. Their experience of larger society is scarcely begun; they have not yet fully comprehended the difference between "real things and not-real ones." From their perspective looking down from the balcony above, the real flowers could be not-real, and again looking up from below into the refrigerator the ice-cream house could be real. When they are dressed for the party they seem decorated, like the table downstairs, for the strange new downstairs world, so that they themselves look not-real to the adults: they look "a picture." "What a picture! Oh the ducks! Oh the lambs! Oh the sweets! Oh the pets!" Not children at all. The known dining-table of their downstairs world has been transformed by flowers and water into an outside garden. The stern behavior of the daytime father is transformed into night-time jolliness. At the end of the story the table, like Mother, is in a disarray never known or countenanced in the daytime world. The little pink house was broken. Sun cannot perceive it was only ice-cream; it was a lovely reality. This is a first experience of disillusionment. There was high-pitched excitement, and joy; there is despair. The newly created world has been destroyed.

> But—oh! oh! what had happened? The ribbons and the roses were all pulled untied. The little red table napkins lay on the floor, all the shining plates were dirty and all the winking glasses. The lovely food that the man had trimmed was all thrown about, and there were bones and bits and fruit peels and shells everywhere. There was even a bottle lying down with stuff coming out of it on to the cloth and nobody stood it up again. And the little pink house with the snow roof and the green windows was broken—broken—half melted away in the centre of the table.
>
> "Come on, Sun," said Father, pretending not to notice.
>
> (*Stories*, 304)

The formulaic symbolism that the story uses to express this first experience of disillusionment works very powerfully, but even more remarkable here is the sustained oblique perspective made up of the elongated or foreshortened view which the children's physical relationship to the adults gives them, together with their innocence. Their sightline is part of their innocent vision. In what sense was the child's original perception of reality not "real"? Perspective in this story is something literal, deriving for instance from the children's line of vision upstairs looking down, so that their "point of view" is something actual, as well as being a matter of emotional attitude. This can cause us to ask: what is real? How can we tell? Is truth after all a matter of perspective?

The images that provide Sun with his insights about reality and the transience of beauty are images of art; the little pink house was a work of art, an emblem of security, placed as the emblematic centerpiece on the dining table decorated also with roses brought in from the outside world, a dining-table that is at the heart of the parameters of his known world. The children themselves, even to the rosettes on Moon's shoes, were presented to the guests as their parents' artificial creations. People become artworks; people destroy their own creations. The sympathetic universe of Sun and Moon is broken. There is no certainty in the world.

Images of change, living images of one thing that becomes another, or that has the capability of allowing one thing to become another, are powerful in Katherine Mansfield's stories. Among these, images of light are innate. Such images may seem to act as agents of alteration, to create the condition of art. Such is the effect of the lighted ship at the end of **"The Wind Blows."** Vehicle of passage, agent of alteration, it holds the potentiality for other kinds of being. The lighted ship is a powerful image *for* art, and its context is an experience of emotional sympathy.

> 'Look, Bogey. Look over there.'
>
> A big black steamer with a long loop of smoke streaming, with the port-holes lighted, with lights everywhere, is putting out to sea. The wind does not stop her; she cuts through the waves, making for the open gate between the pointed rocks that leads to. . . . It's the light that makes her look so awfully beautiful and mysterious. . . . *They* are on board leaning over the rail arm in arm.
>
> '. . . Who are they?'
>
> '. . . Brother and sister.'
>
> 'Look, Bogey, there's the town. Doesn't it look small? There's the post office clock chiming for the last time. There's the esplanade where we walked that windy day. Do you remember? I cried at my music lesson that day—how many years ago! Good-bye, little island, good-bye. . . .'
>
> Now the dark stretches a wing over the tumbling water. They can't see those two any more. Good-bye, good-bye. Don't forget. . . . But the ship is gone, now.
>
> The wind—the wind.
>
> (***Stories***, 194)

Together, in a combined leap of imagination, brother and sister have left the shore and are on board the lighted steamer, looking out toward themselves and the little town. They experience the desire to travel in sympathy with each other. They want to go away—the "where" remains unresolved; it's the departure, the journey itself that is longed for. What is before them? Life is before them; and then there is a sudden change of consciousness and focus towards another, future, farewell, in which "that windy day" is no longer present; and that change helps the reader to emerge at the greater distance in space and time, which is the author's present, and then ours. The image of the lighted ship moving out of the dark harbor to an unknown destination is charged with emotion. With the brother and sister we have moved in and out of consciousness. This powerful image precipitates a further change in our awareness. Behind the theatricality of the adolescent "good-byes" is hidden the scarcely bearable knowledge of a future already in the process of arriving at its final enactment.

The lighted ship is a symbol of passage, through space, in time, and for the transmission of wisdom. The lamp is a symbol Katherine Mansfield uses quite consistently. In **"Prelude"** the new house is first seen by the child Kezia in lamplight; as she is lifted down from the buggy in the darkness it seems a living thing.

> The soft white bulk of it lay stretched upon the green garden like a sleeping beast. And now one and now another of the windows leaped into light. Someone was walking through the empty rooms carrying a lamp. From a window downstairs the light of a fire flickered. A strange beautiful excitement seemed to stream from the house in quivering ripples.
>
> "Where are we?" said Lottie, sitting up. Her reefer cap was all on one side and on her cheek there was the print of an anchor button she had pressed against while sleeping. Tenderly the storeman lifted her, set her cap straight, and pulled down her crumpled clothes. She stood blinking on the lowest verandah step watching Kezia who seemed to come flying through the air to her feet.
>
> "Ooh!" cried Kezia, flinging up her arms. The grandmother came out of the dark hall carrying a little lamp. She was smiling.
>
> "You found your way in the dark?" said she.
>
> "Perfectly well."
>
> (***Stories***, 228)

This living house is itself a potent image, but within it the lamp is described as "a bright breathing thing," and the grandmother trusts Kezia to carry it. The child now brings the lamplight into the drawing room. For her, it illuminates the corners of a stable world, and identifies the real. The lamp makes the house safe and true. Its light brings into focus and isolates those it illuminates. Two evenings later it does this for Linda as she sits remote from others in the room, and she is made restless and wanders outside (where she sees the moonlit aloe), and realizes the difference between her mother's apparently contented inner life and her own. But the image of the lamp properly belongs to a serene grandmother and a peaceful house. When at the bay the children are playing in the washhouse and Kezia begins to fear the shadowy corners, she is comforted by the thought that "somewhere, far away, grandma was lighting a lamp" (*Stories,* 462). But in **"The Voyage,"** the child's emotional trauma is such that even in the company of her father and grandmother the lantern on the wharf "seemed afraid to unfurl its timid, quivering light in all that blackness; it burned softly, as if for itself" (*Stories,* 470). "As if for itself": the normal and natural function of a lamp is to burn for others. Kezia's grandmother lived for others; the lamp is her symbol. Kezia accepts it. The motto of Katherine Mansfield's first Wellington high school is, by a nice coincidence, "lumen accipe et imperti" ("receive the light and pass it on"). The illumination of Katherine Mansfield's art brings much out of darkness into the light of consciousness. In **"The Doll's House,"** "the lamp was perfect. It seemed to smile at Kezia, to say 'I live here'. The lamp was real" (*Stories,* 500). The doll's house is itself an artifact, a creative image of reality, with its lamp inside it. When, at the end, one rejected little Kelvey says to another, "I seen the little lamp," we may see that the lamp has transformed their reality, as it has ours.

But it is with Katherine Mansfield's flower imagery that we find her most fundamental images of art. Flowers in her stories can create an effect of the same kind as that which surrounds the lighted ship, or the grandmother's lamp, whereby the observer's perception of reality is somehow transformed. More profoundly than that, however, they can be found working as both agent and emblem of alteration.

In **"Her First Ball,"** pink and white azaleas are in tune with Leila's mood, becoming flags streaming and eventually a flying wheel, while Leila herself, standing up for her first dance, floated away like a flower that is tossed into a pool. **"The Voyage"** takes place in darkness, and moves toward light. When the Picton ferry was docking in the early dawn Fenella thought, "Oh, it had all been so sad lately. Was it going to change?" Later, as she walks up her grandparents' path, we sense the relief of the transition out of darkness into light. Though the morning is still cold there is some promise, and a new sweetness of smell: "Up a little path of round pebbles they went, with drenched sleeping flowers on either side. Grandma's delicate white picotees were so heavy with dew that they were fallen, but their sweet smell was part of the cold morning" (*Stories,* 475). Those daisies are a catalyst. They offer an intimation of change, and a sense of renewed hope. In **"At the Bay"** the falling flowers of the manuka tree cause Linda to meditate on the meaning of life. "Why, then, flower at all?" (*Stories,* 452)—but these daytime flowers have an intrinsic beauty that makes their existence worthwhile; and feeling this, unexpectedly Linda feels something for her child too. Her brother-in-law Jonathan, relaxed in conversation, offers the garden as a resonant image of undirected energy, and unfulfilled life. "The shortness of life! The shortness of life!" he says. "I've only one night or one day, and there's this vast dangerous garden, waiting out there, undiscovered, unexplored" (*Stories,* 464).

The structural importance of flowers in **"Sun and Moon"** was obvious; they were the locus for transformations of reality. Flowers are brought inside to make an artificial lake and garden; manufactured fabrics are made to imitate flowers. The story is a study in red and white. There were the flowers that arrived looking like hats, the roses and rose-petals that transformed the dining table into a garden with a lake, the red table napkins that were made into roses, Sun's shirt with red and white daisies on it, and the final devastation of untied ribbons and roses. The little ice-cream house, with its nut door-handle, standing in its artificial garden made of real flowers, is a complete, created world, emblem of Sun's reality, and agent of his disillusionment.

To the five-year-old child Kezia in **"Prelude"** flowers are part of a world that needs to be made coherent. The new untamed garden is so large and diverse "she did not believe that she would ever not get lost in this garden" (*Stories,* 238). It needs to be brought within her artist's perspective. The richness and profusion of its flowers delighted her; her impulse is to share this delight, to organize this beauty into a pattern, to offer it as a gift. Her grandmother will be the natural recipient. For instance, the child might begin with an empty matchbox. "First she would put a leaf inside with a big violet lying on it, then she would put a very small white picotee, perhaps, on each side of the violet, and then she would sprinkle some lavender on the top, but not to cover their heads."

She often made these surprises for the grandmother, and they were always most successful.

> 'Do you want a match, my granny?'
>
> 'Why, yes, child, I believe a match is just what I'm looking for.'
>
> The grandmother slowly opened the box and came upon the picture inside.
>
> 'Good gracious, child! How you astonished me!'
>
> (*Stories,* 239)

They are collaborators; they both value the work of art. Here the child's impulse is already the artist's, to record and find pattern and meaning in the living world. The matchbox may be a house for the family group of flowers, framed thus outside in the garden. The matchbox picture both is in itself, and presents to the beholder, an image of art. In **"At the Bay,"** nasturtium leaves and other plants at the beginning were bathed in beneficent dew; but inside at breakfast time the red and yellow nasturtium flowers are found in an old salad bowl decorating the table, and Mrs. Fairfield has a smile of contentment. Grandmother and child share an appreciation of the natural world and the desire to re-create, in a new patterning, its beautiful forms inside. The jar of seapinks on the dresser in their bedroom at the bay is a living and very transitory work of art, bound by time, as are the living woman and child whose pattern of life it enhances. We are told that the seapinks are *like* "a velvet pincushion" (*Stories,* 455)—they no longer just haphazardly exist in natural beauty, they have been remade, and have thus become an artifact. That posy is now a miniature work of art, a microcosm for the story, or an emblem that reminds us of the artist's function to make permanent that which is transient, and renew our vision of the world.

Images of transience and transformation, whether of a lighted ship moving on the water, a lamp flickering within a house, or flowers gathered in a posy, provide Katherine Mansfield with images of art. Supremely through these, she succeeds in her artistic intention of recreating the existentialist moment of experienced life.

Notes

1. Developed from papers given at the Katherine Mansfield Centennial Conferences, Newberry Library Chicago, and Victoria University of Wellington, September-October 1988.

2. *The Stories of Katherine Mansfield,* ed. Antony Alpers (Oxford: Oxford University Press, 1984) 2; hereafter cited in the text as *Stories.*

3. *Letters and Journals of Katherine Mansfield,* ed. C. K. Stead, (Harmondsworth: Penguin Books, 1977), 99.

Abbreviations

CLKM: *The Collected Letters of Katherine Mansfield.* Ed. Vincent O'Sullivan and Margaret Scott. Oxford: Clarendon Press. 1, 1903-17 (1984); 2, 1918-19 (1987); 3, 1919-20 (1993).

IB: Ida Baker. *Katherine Mansfield: The Memories of L. M.* New York: Taplinger Publishing Company, 1972.

JKM 1927: *The Journal of Katherine Mansfield.* Ed. John Middleton Murry. New York: Knopf, 1927.

JKM 1940: *The Scrapbook of Katherine Mansfield.* Ed. John Middleton Murry. New York: Knopf, 1940.

JKM 1954: *Journal of Katherine Mansfield.* Ed. John Middleton Murry. London: Constable, 1954.

JMM-KM: *The Letters of John Middleton Murry to Katherine Mansfield.* Ed. C. A. Hankin. New York: Franklin Watts, 1983.

LKM: *The Letters of Katherine Mansfield.* Ed. John Middleton Murry. New York: Knopf, 1929.

KM-JMM: *Katherine Mansfield's Letters to John Middleton Murry, 1913-22.* New York: Knopf, 1951.

L & J: *The Letters and Journals of Katherine Mansfield: A Selection.* Ed. C. K. Stead. New York: Penguin, 1977.

SS: *The Short Stories of Katherine Mansfield.* Ed. John Middleton Murry. New York: Knopf, 1937.

Patricia Moran (essay date 1996)

SOURCE: Moran, Patricia. "Unholy Meanings: (S)mothering and the Production(s) of Katherine Mansfield." In *Word of Mouth: Body Language in Katherine Mansfield and Virginia Woolf,* pp. 87-116. Charlottesville: University Press of Virginia, 1996.

[*In the following excerpt, Moran asserts that Mansfield was preoccupied with her own maternity and the fear that her femininity would devour her creativity as an artist. According to the critic, this preoccupation is demonstrated by the prevalence of mother-daughter relationships and the idea of the "smothering and suffocating maternal presence" in her stories.*]

I

I feel I am all the time rescuing my nephew and niece from their respective mothers, my two sisters: who have jaguars of wrath in their souls, however they purr to their offspring. The phenomenon of motherhood, in these days, is a strange and rather frightening phenomenon.

    D. H. Lawrence, in a letter to Lady Cynthia Asquith

My cat and kitten are fighting and loving on the couch. First the cat devours the kitten & then the kitten eats up the mother. Lawrence would see an Unholy Meaning in them.

    Katherine Mansfield, in a letter to Ottoline Morrell

I am more like Lawrence than anybody. We are unthinkably alike, in fact.

    Katherine Mansfield, ***Journal of Katherine Mansfield***

Katherine Mansfield first met D. H. Lawrence in 1913, but it was not until she and her husband John Middleton Murry attempted to live with the Lawrences in 1916 that she voiced her revulsion against the matriarchal Frieda, a woman Mansfield saw as devouring and engulfing Lawrence: "When he is in a rage with Frieda he says it is she who has done this to him and that she is 'a bug who has fed on my life.' I think that is true," Mansfield told one friend (*CLKM* [*The Collected Letters of Katherine Mansfield.*] 1 263). To another friend, she put it this way: "The 'dear man' in him whom we all loved is hidden away, absorbed, completely lost, like a little gold ring in that immense german christmas pudding which is Frieda. And with all the appetite in the world one cannot eat ones way through Frieda to find him. One simply looks and waits for someone to come with a knife and cut her up into the smallest pieces that L. may see the light and shine again. But he does not want that to happen at all. And that is the really hopeless part" (*CLKM* 1 267). Mansfield represents Frieda as an inchoate, amorphous, unbounded substance that threatens Lawrence's autonomy, an horrific version of the preoedipal mother in symbiotic fusion with her infant. At the same time, Mansfield sees Frieda as monstrously pregnant, having become so by eating Lawrence, swallowing him up, thus becoming the autonomous, all complete preoedipal mother, but one whose penis/baby resides *within* the maternal body, not outside it.[1] Mansfield longs for someone to rescue Lawrence with an act of violence that is a combination of murder, a cesarean section, and slicing Frieda into dessert portions, but she herself refrains from such destructive and hostile actions. A strange taboo protects the maternal body from the anger and aggression of this woman who felt herself "more like Lawrence than anybody" (*L & J* 127): "with all the appetite in the world" Mansfield cannot feast on Frieda, as if the very desire to kill and devour the phallic mother and rob her of her offspring necessitates the renunciation of female appetite itself. And, having renounced her own appetite, Mansfield seems to project it upon Frieda: here the mother feeds on the child and refuses to expel him. Nurturance thus becomes suffocation; the desire to succor only masks the desire to engulf.[2]

It may seem peculiar to begin a discussion of Mansfield's attitude toward maternity, creativity, and orality with a discussion of her affinity to D. H. Lawrence. But although she dissociated herself from Lawrence's "doctrine of mindlessness," Mansfield repeatedly stressed her sense that they were deeply alike, an affinity that seems to have as its central feature a profound fear of the maternal body and maternal power.[3] Whereas Lawrence could depict that body as alien and other, however, Mansfield struggled with her sense that the maternal body, indeed, her own female flesh, could overwhelm and stifle her subjectivity. Mansfield's sense of affinity with Lawrence, then, discloses a deep-rooted ambivalence toward both female flesh and maternity. Further, by likening herself to Lawrence and other male writers, Mansfield could escape (at least imaginatively) from that troubling female flesh.[4]

Mansfield's ambivalence toward female flesh and maternity is an important key to understanding the role of the preoedipal bond and maternal metaphors in her writing. For, like her contemporaries, Mansfield's work took shape in what Gilbert has called "a cultural context that defined motherhood as the ontological fact from which all other facts, fictions, and myths arise."[5] Her later stories, moreover, feature the mother-daughter plot that has been identified as a hallmark of women's writing of the 1920s: a young woman, frequently an artist, must reconcile her ambitions with the powerful emotions evoked by a seductive maternal figure who advocates a more traditional definition of femininity.[6] Within this framework, Mansfield's career reads as a trajectory of growth—from an early repudiation of maternity in her first collection, *In a German Pension* (1911), to a celebration of maternity as an analogue for female artistry in her well-known **"Prelude"** (1918) and **"At the Bay"** (1921).[7] But this approach simplifies the contradictory aspects of her work, and in particular ignores both the discourse of ambivalence throughout Mansfield's portraits of the mother-daughter bond and the implications of that ambivalence for the creative woman. In Mansfield's texts, the daughter's creativity often enacts (and is enabled by) the mother's *rejection* of her maternity: the daughter's attendant self-hatred and rejection of her female body emerge in a Kleinian language of eating, feeding, starving, and reproducing that translates femininity into a diffuse and engulfing force from which she must defend herself. Creativity becomes, then, a search for principles of boundedness that would defend against feminine materiality. . . .

II

In Mansfield's fiction, the preoccupation with a smothering and suffocating maternal presence emerges in several related narrative patterns. In her earliest work, the child's desire for maternal nurture results in an emotional abandonment that Mansfield figures in images of snow, ice, and winter. In the 1904 sketch **"My Pot-plants,"** for example, the artistic narrator's relationship to a surrogate mother disintegrates when the woman turns into the "Queen of the Snow," a terrifyingly remote figure based upon Hans Christian Andersen's fairy tale "The Snow Queen."[8] And like that figure, Mansfield's Queen of the Snow attracts only to destroy; when the story-telling child imagines that "death shall come and hold me close," the embrace of the mother becomes synonymous with death. Similarly, in an untitled story dated variously 1909 and 1914, the tubercular boy Peter longs for his mother to abandon her plans for a singing career and spend time with him. Instead, her singing—not his tuberculosis—suffocates him, a suffocation Mansfield characterizes as a wintry maternal embrace: "He floated into his mother's singing bosom and rose and fell to her breath. . . . She flew with him out of the window to show him the snow. . . . He felt the snow on his chest and creeping up to his throat it formed a little necklace round his neck. It crept up—

but not to my mouth Mother. Mother, not over my eyes."[9] In both stories, the desire to fuse with the mother makes the child vulnerable: when the mother withdraws emotionally, the child dies.

Although artistry—the mother's or the child's—is a source of conflict in both stories, Mansfield subordinates this theme to her exploration of fusion and abandonment. But increasingly Mansfield focuses on the daughter's desire for self-expression and independence, and increasingly the daughter's story describes the mother's rage and anger about her maternity. In **"The Child-Who-Was-Tired,"** Mansfield's 1911 adaptation of a Chekhov story, an overworked and exploited servant girl smothers a crying infant in an act that simultaneously renders her akin to her own mother and to the dead baby, for the servant girl's mother tried to drown her when she was herself an infant.[10] This kind of boundary confusion between mother and daughter also provides the plot of **"The Woman at the Store"** (1911). Mansfield intensifies the claustrophobic closeness of this mother-daughter bond by isolating the pair in the uninhabited bush of New Zealand, an isolation broken only by the visit of three men. (The daughter's Christmas birthday rounds out the connection between the visit of the magi to the virgin mother and divine son and this unholy alliance). A number of verbal echoes establish the mother's merger with the child, whom she describes as the "dead spit" of herself (*SS* [*The Short Stories of Katherine Mansfield*] 128). The mother's inability to produce milk for the child, for example, had caused the girl to sicken "like a cow" (*SS* 128), an image that inverts their positions: the mother is an inadequate cow; her child is the sick calf. Similarly, she tells her visitors that she wanted her husband "lynched for child murder" (*SS* 131), but it remains unclear whether the murdered child refers to the woman's life or her repeated pregnancies and miscarriages. Perhaps most tellingly, the mother reproduces because she has been "shut up. . . . like a broody 'en" (*SS* 132); when she confines her daughter to the counter in the store, that confinement goads the daughter into drawing the picture "she told me she'd shoot me if I did," a picture of the woman shooting her husband and burying him. The paper the daughter draws upon—a page from "Mumma's account book" (*SS* 134)—ties the daughter's art to the mother's anger and underscores the connection between women's biological and economic subordination: for the woman's relation to her womb parallels the store's relation to the counter, the site where money is exchanged for goods. Although the mother violates that logic by murdering her husband, she cannot escape the reproduction of her mothering: the daughter's pictures are "the creations of a lunatic with a lunatic's cleverness," just as the daughter's "diseased mind" and "mad excitement" reveal her to be the clever lunatic creation of her own mad mother (*SS* 132).[11]

Not surprisingly, Mansfield's use of the biological metaphor of textual production—in which the daughter's texts are analogous to the mother's children—reflects this sense of the mother's anger and maternal reluctance. The mother or the maternal body often inhibits the daughter's creativity; so confused are the boundaries between the two that the maternal body contains the daughter's aborted creative attempts. In the unfinished story **"The New Zealander"** (1909), the city of London becomes a mother, but a mother whose body, initially a source of promise and regeneration, only yields death: "There [London] life seems dead to me—buried. Surely after my terrible sorrow, London seems to lose all her reality. I had thought of her as a gigantic mother in whose womb were bred all the great ones of the earth—and then—suddenly—she was barren, sterile . . . with the travail gone. I felt rather like a frightened child lost in a funeral procession—yes, as bad as that—and came home."[12] And in the *German Pension* story **"The Modern Soul,"** the would-be singer Sonia finds that "My tragedy is my mother. Living with her I live with the coffin of my unborn aspirations" (*SS* 70).

In these early stories, Mansfield suggests that the daughter's inability to create is a consequence of inadequate maternal nurture. Food alone, however, is also inadequate. In **"The Advanced Lady,"** for example, the mother's project of writing a book about maternal sacrifice becomes antithetical to the project of actually caring for her small daughter; neglected by her mother and told to sit quietly in the bedroom, the little girl "always goes down to the kitchen" (*SS* 102). Although this passage seemingly links maternal and physical nurture, the narrator implies that if mothers actually cared for their daughters, daughters would not need to eat or seek sustenance in the kitchen: "'I too would like to write a book, on the advisability of caring for daughters, and taking them for airings and keeping them out of kitchens!'" (*SS* 106).

The *German Pension* stories as a whole, in fact, link eating with self-interest at the expense of others. Frequently men are the greedy and insensitive consumers of women, as in Mansfield's portrait of a bride and her groom in **"Frau Brechenmacher Attends a Wedding"**: "At the head of the centre table sat the bride and bridegroom, she in a white dress trimmed with stripes and bows of coloured ribbon, giving her the appearance of an iced cake all ready to be cut and served in neat little pieces to the bridegroom beside her" (*SS* 59). But such figures of predation are more typically ascribed to mothers, and food, the most common image of maternal nurture, becomes the token of a self-serving maternal practice.[13] Women in the *German Pension* stories become mothers not to care for others, but to achieve economic security from men.[14] One woman advises the narrator to have "handfuls of babies": "Then, as the father of a family, he cannot leave you" (*SS* 55). And these mothers explicitly connect eating with the production of children; they associate fertility with the eating of meat, as if eating flesh made it possible to produce flesh. In **"Germans at Meat,"** a story whose title draws attention to this preoccupation, the German matrons associate the narrator's vegetarianism with her childlessness:

"I have not eaten meat for three years."

"Im-possible! Have you any family?"

"No."

"There, now, you see, that's what you're coming to! Who ever heard of having children upon vegetables? It is not possible. But you never have large families in England now; I suppose you are too busy with your suffragetting."

(*SS* 38)

This passage reveals the unstated hostility toward both mothers and eating that recurs throughout **In a German Pension**: mothers encourage daughters to (eat and) become mothers, rather than encourage them to develop alternative definitions of femininity. For these mothers, the suffrage movement (which was associated with vegetarianism) becomes antithetical to maternity.[15]

Eating becomes, then, a peculiarly feminine mode of participating in the patriarchal economy; **"The Advanced Lady"** even suggests that capital production is based upon the originary model of the female body, which eats that it may have children and thus eat and produce more children. As Herr Langen, a philosophy student, says of "mother earth": "Nature has no heart. . . . She creates that she may destroy. She eats that she may spew up and she spews up that she may eat. That is why we, who are forced to eke out an existence at her trampling feet, consider the world mad, and realise the deadly vulgarity of production" (*SS* 104). Frau Kellerman attempts to replace Herr Langen's vision with her own vision of natural production: "'Come back to this bench in ten years' time and repeat those words to me,' said Frau Kellermann . . . 'and bring with you your young wife, Herr Langen, and watch, perhaps, your little child playing with—' She turned towards Karl [her son], who had rooted an old illustrated paper out of the receptacle, and was spelling over an advertisement for the enlargement of Beautiful Breasts" (*SS* 104). Herr Langen's perception of a nature that eats and vomits that it may eat again is paralleled in the text by women who promote marriage that children may be produced and the social structure be reproduced. "The advertisement for the enlargement of Beautiful Breasts" calls attention to the commercialization and objectification of the female body; the phrase focuses that process on female breasts, enlarged as if to suggest the milk-engorged breasts of the mother, but which function to attract men rather than to nurture babies. The advertisement suggests that men are attracted to women who remind them of their mothers; it also suggests that women embody male fantasies in order to achieve economic security. Through the medium of advertising, Mansfield connects the benign maternal doctrine of Frau Kellermann with the explicitly self-serving one of the Advanced Lady, for an "advance man" is someone hired to promote and publicize theatrical and political events.

Critics of Mansfield tend to read the **German Pension** stories as immature work that is superseded by later stories such as **"Prelude"** (1918) and **"At the Bay"** (1922). And it is true that in these later works Mansfield attempts to valorize maternity and domesticity as forms of female artistry enabling the growth of the artist as a young girl: by self-consciously revising dominant literary narratives that trace the growth of the boy and artist, Mansfield suggests alternative, female-centered accounts of childhood and the child's relation to the mother. **"Prelude"** pays conscious tribute to Wordsworth's poem of the same name, but by making her child-artist a girl rather than a boy, Mansfield draws attention to the way Wordsworth objectifies and transcends the feminine, something the child Kezia is unable to do.[16] Similarly, Mansfield acknowledges her early master Walter Pater's "The Child in the House," but whereas his story ends with the boy's move to a new house, Mansfield begins **"Prelude"** with the mother and grandmother driving away from the children Kezia and Lottie to ready the new home, as if to suggest that the daughter's artistic subjectivity begins with her separation and independence from the conventional lives of her foremothers.[17] Finally, by naming Kezia's cousin "Pip" and his trapped and invalid mother "Dora"—a woman who, in an earlier version of **"Prelude,"** fantasizes about the dead Dora in Charles Dickens's *David Copperfield*[18]—Mansfield marginalizes Dickens's dominant narratives of the growth of the young man, and simultaneously draws attention to the deadening roles women play in such narratives.

Mansfield also seems to revise the multilayered historical scheme of the nineteenth-century theorist Johann Jakob Bachofen, whose work and ideas she may have learned from Frieda and D. H. Lawrence.[19] Bachofen posited a matriarchal stage prior to patriarchy, a matriarchy centered around agriculture and the worship of the great mother goddesses, particularly Demeter. This "lunar stage" was succeeded by the solar, or patriarchal stage, a stage of male dominance, monogamous marriage, and the division of sex roles into public and private spheres. Mansfield clearly adopts lunar and solar imagery to characterize the two adult generations of **"Prelude"** and **"At the Bay."** The grandmother, Mrs. Fairfield, whose name underscores her pastoral associations, is Mansfield's mother goddess, a motherly wise woman associated with mythologically feminine emblems such as the moon, the night, and the sea. She works throughout the stories to reconcile her daughters and granddaughters to the natural processes of birth and death, growth and harvest. While her daughter Linda Burnell gazes at the aloe and dreams of escaping from her husband and childbearing, for example, Mrs. Fairfield evaluates the orchard and dreams of seeing "those pantry shelves thoroughly well stocked with our own jam" (*SS* 259).[20] And like Mrs. Ramsay in *To the Lighthouse,* Mrs. Fairfield's knitting exemplifies her ability to weave diversity into community.

Stanley Burnell is as stereotypically masculine as Mrs. Fairfield is feminine. A conventional pater familias, a domestic tyrant, and insensitive, albeit successful, business man, Stanley sees the world in purely materialistic terms: the home in the country is notable not for its natural beauty but because it was had "dirt cheap" (*SS* 230); his daughters exist only to remind him that he hasn't yet sired a son and heir (*SS* 244); and the entire family becomes the possession upon which he can pin a "brass-edged card. . . . 'Mr. Stanley Burnell and family'" (*SS* 242). Both his wife and his sister-in-law embody the negative consequences of his dominance in the home: Linda is alienated by marriage and childbearing and retreats into invalidism, while Beryl complies with Stanley's and her mother's expectations, retreating into a narcissism Mansfield depicts as the inevitable result of women's economic and sexual subordination.

Mansfield indicates that Kezia's maturation will coincide with the inauguration of a new age. Kezia's name comes from the Book of Job: Kezia is the middle of Job's three daughters, just as Kezia is the second daughter in the Burnell family. Job's three daughters survive the slaughter of his sons; the time frame of **"Prelude"** and **"At the Bay"** indicates that the children will come of age during World War I, a war in which many of Mansfield's male contemporaries, including her only brother, were killed. Certainly Linda Burnell's apocalyptic vision, in which she sees the setting sun (son) as an emblem of the angry Jehovah's wrath, adumbrates the carnage of that conflict: "You remember that at His coming the whole earth will shake into one ruined graveyard" (*SS* 293).[21] The sunset in the West is a traditional image of Christ's death; by collapsing Jehovah and Christ, Old and New Testament deities, Mansfield suggests the coming twilight of the solar stage. Other harbingers of change include Mansfield's systematic diminution and marginalization of patriarchy's heirs: the sons of the Jewish patriarch Samuel Joseph are named "Stanley" (like Kezia's father) and "Moses"; the names of Kezia's cousins, "Pip" and "Rags," carry overtones of insignificance and superfluity.[22] In both stories, boys remain peripheral and undeveloped characters.

At the same time, Mansfield stresses the singularity and potential subversiveness of a female language that inheres, not in meaning, but in sound: Linda speaks to her mother "with the special voice that women use at night to each other as though they spoke in their sleep or from some hollow cave" (*SS* 257).[23] In **"At the Bay,"** female voices similarly celebrate Stanley's departure and the resumption of female community: "Their very voices were changed as they called to one another; they sounded warm and loving and as if they shared a secret" (*SS* 270).[24] But if these passages describe a communal voice that erases female boundaries, they also recall Mansfield's vision of a cavern full of submerged and undifferentiated "seaweed gatherers," a vision that provokes both a fear of feminine materiality and the desire for a bounded "masculine" self. And Mansfield's other images for femininity conform to those she draws on in her biographical texts. In **"At the Bay,"** for example, femininity is persistently associated with water, engulfment, and death: the story opens with boundaries "smothered" by mist and dew "as if the sea had beaten up softly in the darkness" (*SS* 263-64); Alice drowns a teapot as if it were a man (*SS* 271); Mrs. Stubbs's husband dies from dropsy, a liquid that overwhelms him from within (*SS* 286); and Kezia imagines death as "a little man fallen over like a tin soldier by the side of a big black hole" (*SS* 282). Significantly, the very name of the seaside community, Crescent Bay, connects water with the motherly Mrs. Fairfield: at her neck she wears a brooch, "a silver crescent moon with five little owls seated on it" (*SS* 236).[25] Familiar patterns of oral imagery characterize Mrs. Fairfield's relationships to her daughter Linda Burnell and her granddaughter Kezia. Linda, for example, fears an engulfment which Mansfield represents as a simultaneous dread of eating and reproduction but which finally translates into a fear of her own dependence and desire for merger with her mother. For despite the fact that she has had three children and is pregnant with her fourth, Linda seems childishly dependent on Mrs. Fairfield:

> Linda leaned her cheek on her fingers and watched her mother. . . . There was something comforting in the sight of her that Linda felt she could never do without. She needed the sweet smell of her flesh, and the soft feel of her cheeks and her arms and shoulders still softer. She loved the way her hair curled, silver at her forehead, lighter at her neck, and bright brown still in the big coil under the muslin cap. Exquisite were her mother's hands, and the two rings she wore seemed to melt into her creamy skin. And she was always so fresh, so delicious.
>
> (*SS* 238)

The extraordinary sensual detail marks the profoundly erotic nature of this mother-daughter bond. Yet the image of the rings melting into Mrs. Fairfield's flesh, an image that attests to her seductive capacity to fuse and merge with her daughter, resonates with Mansfield's description of Lawrence lost in Frieda's flesh "like a little gold ring" (*CLKM*1 267). And as in earlier Mansfield stories, mother and kitchen become synonymous. "'I'm so hungry,' said Linda: 'where can I get something to eat, mother? This is the first time I've been in the kitchen. It says "mother" all over; everything is in pairs'" (*SS* 237). Mrs. Fairfield is the source of food; more ominously, she mandates that everything come in "pairs." In order to receive Mrs. Fairfield's nurture, Linda must acquiesce to a social structure in which women do not exist singly but in one of two dyadic forms, husband and wife or mother and child. Linda's invalidism is a way of avoiding the first dyad and retaining the second: to grow up for women often means renouncing the mother in order to become her.

Like the narrator in the **German Pension** stories, Linda connects eating with reproduction and initially sees men as devourers and consumers; when with her husband, who is always eating, she refuses to eat meat, as if she can thereby reject sexuality and childbearing.[26] But her horror at her fecundity increasingly centers that horror not on heterosexuality and men but on female flesh, which becomes pregnant orally, not vaginally.[27] In the central dream sequence in **"Prelude,"** Linda envisions a phallic swelling that results in female swelling, in pregnancy and entrapment:

> "How loud the birds are," said Linda in her dream. She was walking with her father through a green paddock sprinkled with daisies. Suddenly he bent down and parted the grasses and showed her a tiny ball of fluff just at her feet. "Oh, Papa, the darling." She made a cup of her hands and caught the tiny bird and stroked its head with her finger. It was quite tame. But a funny thing happened. As she stroked it began to swell, it ruffled and pouched, it grew bigger and bigger and its round eyes seemed to smile knowingly at her. Now her arms were hardly wide enough to hold it and she dropped it into her apron. It had become a baby with a big naked head and a gaping bird-mouth, opening and shutting. Her father broke into a loud clattering laugh and she woke to Burnell standing by the window rattling the Venetian blind up to the very top.
>
> (*SS* 231-32)

Linda equates the phallus with the baby, her father with her husband, a seemingly neat Freudian equation that holds men responsible for engendering devouring infants.[28] Mansfield specifically associates the bird that becomes both phallus and baby with Linda's husband Stanley: in the morning, awake and watching her husband dress for work, she comments that Stanley "look[s] like a big fat turkey" when he pulls on his shirt "only to find some idiot had fastened the neck-band and he was caught" (*SS* 232). This image aligns the headless Stanley with the duck whose head Pat chops off in front of the children,[29] and suggests that Linda's reluctance to eat meat functions as a fear of reproduction.

But if, as Freud would have it, decapitation equals castration, the bird-phallus-baby also suggests that Linda's fear of oral impregnation derives from an archaic infantile fantasy that the maternal body incorporates the father's phallus orally. At the same time, a curious pattern of images connects the bird-baby to Mrs. Fairfield, and the fear of eating becomes a fear of being engulfed from within by the mother's food. As Mary Burgan has pointed out, Linda's dream resembles the episode in Lewis Carroll's *Alice in Wonderland* in which Alice holds a baby that turns into a pig.[30] When Mrs. Fairfield retires for the night, she takes "out her teeth and put them in a glass of water," while outside "some tiny owls, perched on the branches of a lace-bark tree, called 'More pork; more pork'" (*SS* 231). The owls which call for the creation of pork recall the five owls perched on the crescent moon of Mrs. Fairfield's brooch (*SS* 236). Both moon and owls are appropriate mythological emblems for Mrs. Fairfield; the moon because its waxing and waning are evocative of women's menstrual cycles and parturition; owls because they are the symbol of female wisdom. But in this context Mrs. Fairfield's owls take on a sinister cast: owls are predators as well as the emblems of Athena, the goddess who affirmed father right. The power of Mrs. Fairfield's teeth passes to the owls, who call for eating and oral reproduction.[31]

Linda's refusal to eat the fried chops that will result in babies seems, then, not only a refusal of her husband's phallus, but a refusal of her mother's food, food which ominously merges with the mother's own body: the duck which becomes dinner, like Mrs. Fairfield, "hasn't any teeth" (*SS* 250). Like Mrs. Fairfield, too, who wears a "jelly mould cap" and worries about making jam (*SS* 236, 259), the "duck wasn't meat at all but a kind of very superior jelly." The duck thus resembles the steamed suet puddings to which Mansfield frequently compared motherly women. Curiously, a kind of narrative anxiety about devouring the mother seems to provoke the observation that the duck "must have been one of those birds whose mother played to it in infancy upon the German flute" (*SS* 255), a statement that figures the mother as at least complicit in the intent to devour. Once again the fantasy of devouring evokes in turn the fear of being devoured.

Linda's dream reveals that her fear of oral impregnation develops from her relationship with her mother, of whose flesh she feels herself a part. In fact, Linda seems to experience a fear of an internalized preoedipal mother, an inchoate, amorphous, unbounded substance that threatens her from within. Musing about the pattern on the wallpaper, Linda fears "the coming alive of things," a fear which is explicitly sexual and oral: "the strangest part of this coming alive of things was what they did. They listened, they seemed to swell out with some mysterious content, and when they were full she felt that they smiled. But it was not for her, only, their sly, secret smile; they were members of a secret society and they smiled among themselves" (*SS* 234). Linda's "secret society" resembles the smiling object in her dream, as well as the women in Mansfield's journal entry, women who "fill and gorge themselves with their men" and smile a "sly, satisfied smile." As other critics have noted, the secret knowing smile in Mansfield's fiction belongs to women who have experienced childbearing.[32] Linda's desire to distance herself from this secret society necessitates the repudiation of her own female flesh: "THEY saw how she turned her head away as she passed the mirror" (*SS* 234). Linda no longer sees a single image in the mirror; instead, the secret society of mothers—herself and her own mother—confronts her with the knowledge that her flesh can multiply, double, and engulf her from within.

Fantasizing escape from maternity, Linda dreams of finding refuge in the aloe plant that has the qualities of boundedness she herself lacks: its "long sharp thorns" will keep people away; its leaves like a ship will enable her to sail away from the engulfing demands of femininity. When Linda despairs of escape—"What am I guarding myself for so preciously? I shall go on having children and Stanley will go on making money and the children and the gardens will grow bigger and bigger, with whole fleets of aloes in them for me to choose from" (*SS* 258)—she reveals her despair about the meaninglessness of her own life and Stanley's; the repetitive activities of production and reproduction are linked to show how little Linda resembles the solitary aloe, which blooms only once in a hundred years and thus represents an impossible ideal of self unity and autonomy (and presumably the aloe is significant only because it is unique; "whole fleets of aloes" envisions the loss of unitary meaning in multiplication and the dispersal of meaning).[33] That Linda experiences repeated childbearing as self-fragmentation is shown again in **"At the Bay,"** when she compares her life to the flowering of the manuka tree:

> Pretty—yes, if you held one of those flowers on the palm of your hand and looked at it closely, it was an exquisite small thing. Each pale yellow petal shone as if each was the careful work of a loving hand. The tiny tongue in the centre gave it the shape of a bell. And when you turned it over the outside was a deep bronze colour. But as soon as they flowered, they fell and were scattered. You brushed them off your frock as you talked; the horrid little things got caught in one's hair. Why, then, flower at all? Who takes the trouble—or the joy—to make all these things that are wasted, wasted.
>
> (*SS* 277-78)

Like the aloe, a single manuka flower has beauty and significance. But mass production destroys any meaning one flower might have, just as Linda's bleak vision of "whole fleets of aloes" destroys her sense of the solitary aloe's uniqueness. A striking contrast with the aloe that rarely blooms and then only once, the manuka flowers become an image of female fragmentation and waste, at once evoking female genitalia, small children, and coins, all potentially beautiful but now degraded through the appropriation and subordination of female reproduction to the economic and sexual demands of patriarchy. And Linda's sense of childbearing as self-fragmentation subverts any connection between procreation and female artistry, for while the manuka flowers look "as if" they might be "the careful work of a loving hand," they are not—they are mindlessly produced and experienced as a nuisance.[34]

While examining the manuka flowers and again considering the possibility of fleeing her marriage and childbearing, Linda's thoughts turn to her father, who had once promised her that "'As soon as you and I are old enough, Linny, we'll cut off somewhere, we'll escape. Two boys together. I have a fancy I'd like to sail up a river in China'" (*SS* 115). In both stories, fantasies of flight entail escape by boat: the explicit connection between father and boat yokes the desire for a bounded, defended self represented by the aloe with the desire to be male rather than female. Ironically, Linda's turn from her mother does not permit her to escape from engulfing maternity; instead, as her dream suggests, the turn to the father precludes heterosexuality and the swelling phallus that becomes a devouring infant. The escape from the mother ends in becoming her.

* * *

In a sense, **"Prelude"** does define maternity as an analogue for female artistry, for Mansfield develops as a counterpoint to Linda an autobiographical figure of herself as a small girl in the character of Linda's daughter Kezia. Although most analyses of **"Prelude"** see Mrs. Fairfield as a model for Kezia's artistic aspirations, I believe the story suggests that Linda is that model, and that Linda's refusal to assume or accept a maternal role permits her daughter both to consider alternative modes of female activity and to separate from the seductive figure of Mrs. Fairfield.

Kezia echoes her mother's sensual desire for Mrs. Fairfield by begging the old woman to "'Come to bed soon and be my Indian brave'" (*SS* 228). Not yet heterosexually acculturated, Kezia reveals the erotic element of the daughter's desire for merger with the mother's flesh. And Kezia's emulation of Mrs. Fairfield's domestic artistry results in a transformation of nature into culture that reenacts the old woman's transformation of the fruit into jam: "She began to lay the cloth on a pink garden seat. In front of each person she put two geranium leaf plates, a pine needle fork and a twig knife. There were three daisy heads on a laurel leaf for poached eggs, some slices of fuschia petal cold beef, some lovely little rissoles made of earth and water and dandelion seeds, and the chocolate custard which she had decided to serve in the pawa shell she had cooked it in" (*SS* 246). Ominously, Kezia's transformation of nature into culture takes place in relation to food: in

"Prelude," she makes a piece of bread "a dear little sort of gate" by eating a bite of it; in **"At the Bay"** she changes porridge into a landscape: "She had only dug a river down the middle of her porridge, filled it, and was eating the banks away" (*SS* 222, 269). Kezia's productions resemble, then, those of both grandmother and mother: she creates domestic art, but her productions, like those of her mother, focus on food; like her mother, Kezia incorporates in order to produce. Even when Kezia plans on making a present for her grandmother—a matchbox with a "leaf inside with a big violet lying on it, then . . . a very small white picotee, perhaps, on each side of the violet, and then she would sprinkle some lavender on the top, but not to cover their heads" (*SS* 239-40)—her present is a claustrophobic image of creativity that conflates the prolific womb with the funeral coffin.[35]

Kezia's emulation of Mrs. Fairfield thus raises doubt about the efficacy of the magna mater as artistic model, for, as the representative and priestess of nature, Mrs. Fairfield is not a model of the speaking subject or writer.[36] Moreover, Mrs. Fairfield's seductive domesticity is undercut by the presence of the daughter who did, in fact, become what the mother wanted, that is, by Linda Burnell. Although most readers see Mrs. Fairfield as the primary positive model for Kezia, Linda Burnell reveals the cost of compliance with normative middle-class standards of femininity. Rather than creating the single flower of the aloe, women become like the flowers of the manuka: scattered, fragmented, diffuse. Mrs. Fairfield's adherence to "natural" processes is belied by the debilitation Linda embodies and the revulsion she exhibits for those same natural processes. Kezia's "bad" mother, then, turns out to be the necessary wedge between herself and the "good" mother, whose continued nurturance comes at the expense of the daughter's independence.

Kezia's affinities with her mother derive from their shared fear of heterosexuality and its consequences.[37] Linda, for example, calls Stanley her "Newfoundland dog" and wishes "he wouldn't jump at her so, and bark so loudly, and watch her with such eager, loving eyes. He was too strong for her; she had always hated things that rush at her from, from a child" (*SS* 258). Kezia similarly fears "'rushing animals like dogs and parrots. I often dream that animals rush at me—even camels—and while they are rushing their heads swell e-enormous'" (*SS* 225). And just as her mother fears a mysterious "THEY," so Kezia fears a mysterious "IT" that follows her when she's alone: "Kezia was suddenly quite, quite still, with wide open eyes and knees pressed together. She was frightened. She wanted to call Lottie and to go on calling all the while she ran downstairs and out of the house. But IT was just behind her, waiting at the door, at the head of the stairs, at the bottom of the stairs, hiding in the passage, ready to dart out at the back door" (*SS* 223). Although she resembles her mother, whose response to the frightening "THEM" is to lie still and listen with "wide open watchful eyes" (*SS* 235), Kezia has not yet experienced the doubling and splitting of pregnancy that has so devastated her mother's sense of self. Kezia's one exchange with her mother has the aloe as its focal point: her mother tells her the plant's name and its tendency to bloom only once in a hundred years, information she tenders with a dreamy, sleepy smile. What Kezia gains from her mother, then, is an impression that the bounded and defended single self is preferable to maternal (pro)creativity: maternal incompetence and indifference promote the artistic daughter's necessary autonomy and independence.

III

> "Matrophobia" . . . is the fear not of one's mother or of motherhood but of *becoming one's mother* . . . where a mother is hated to the point of matrophobia there may also be a deep underlying pull toward her, a dread that if one relaxes one's guard one will identify with her completely.
>
> Adrienne Rich, *Of Woman Born*

> I am become—Mother. I don't care a *rap* for people.
>
> Katherine Mansfield, **Journal**

In **"Prelude,"** Mansfield attributes female creativity to the desire for bounded, autonomous productions that remain distinct from the female body. But in discussing her own aesthetic, she often invokes the familiar terms of merger and engulfment: "*I am writing* [. . .] until this story is finished I am engulfed. . . . It seizes me—swallows me completely. I am Jonah in the whale and only you could charm that old whale to disgorge me. . . . I'm lost—gone—possessed" (**KM-JMM** [***Katherine Mansfield's Letters to John Middleton Murry, 1913-22***] 583-84). From a writer whose style has frequently been described as a form of impersonation and whose use of oral imagery borders on the obsessive, this apparently conventional description of literary inspiration exemplifies Mansfield's sense of writing as a loss of rigid boundaries and a loss of self: "when I am writing of 'another' I want so to lose myself in the soul of the other that I am not" (*LKM* 365).[38] Although Mansfield envisions this model of impersonality as sexual—"Unless one is free to offer oneself up wholly and solely . . . one receives nothing. Its promiscuous love instead of a living relationship" (IB [Ida Baker, *Katherine Mansfield: The Memories of L. M.*] 158)[39]—when she elaborates upon this process, she represents literary birth as the outcome of an impregnation that differs considerably from that developed in the customary reproductive trope:

> When I pass an apple stall I cannot help stopping and staring until I feel that I, myself, am changing into an apple, too, and that at any moment I may produce an

apple, miraculously—out of my own being, like the conjuror produces the egg. . . . When I write about ducks I swear that I am a white duck. . . . In fact the whole process of becoming the duck (what Lawrence would perhaps call this consummation with the duck or apple) is so thrilling that I can hardly breathe, only to think about it. For although that is as far as most people can get, it is really only the "prelude." There follows the moment when you are *more* duck, *more* apple [. . .] than any of these objects could ever possibly be, and so you *create* them anew.

(***CLKM*** 1 330)⁴⁰

Although she compares her method to Lawrence's model of "consummation," Mansfield describes a kind of parthenogenesis in which the writer merges with and then engulfs her subject before (re)producing it, a model that not only eliminates paternity and insemination but elides the biological mother as well: the conjuror (but not the duck?) who produces an egg does so by sleight of hand and not through conception, labor, and delivery.⁴¹ Mansfield's choice of subjects—egg, apple, duck—connects this process of merger and engulfment to the orally incorporative generativity manifested throughout her work, a connection strengthened by the oblique references to the duck in **"Prelude."**⁴²

Mansfield's aesthetic has been attributed to her belief that the vulnerable fragmented identity required the protection and coherence of the mask.⁴³ Hence her emphasis on the "social self" that so many of her female characters develop as a response to the constraints imposed on women. Yet paradoxically, masking itself constitutes a form of fragmentation that Mansfield finally found untenable. She abandoned her writing in the last year of her life in order to "lose all that is superficial and acquired" and to develop a more "conscious and direct" narrative voice (***L & J*** 278).⁴⁴ This voice, it seems to me, is consistent with Mansfield's desire to combat an engulfing femininity with a bounded singular "phallic" self. For Mansfield's sense of affinity with male writers developed from an apprehension that women—and femininity—represented a threat to her autonomy while men did not: men simply seemed more human to her. Unfortunately, Mansfield never resolved her conflict with the preoedipal mother within. She was never able to integrate her desire to find the "special language" women speak to their mothers "as though they spoke in their sleep or from some hollow cave" with her desire to find in herself a sense of boundedness that resonates with her description of the aloe in **"Prelude"**: a phallic self resembling a "green spear," "untouched by all we acquire and all we shed," "our own particular self . . . free, disentangled, single." The blooming of that plant, she wrote, "is after all the moment we live for—the moment of direct feeling when we are most ourselves and least personal."⁴⁵

Tuberculosis, however, made it impossible for Mansfield to live a life that was "free, disentangled, single."

Increasingly dependent upon women, especially Ida Baker, Mansfield raged, not at her disease, but at the "indecency" of women's willingness to nurture her: "These last days are hideous. It is not being ill that matters; it is the abuse of one's privacy—one's independence—it is having to let people serve you and fighting *every moment* against their desire to 'share.' Why are human beings so indecent?" (***CLKM*** 2 354). Mansfield was honest enough to know that this anger at women was unfair: "I must not forget the long talk L. M. and I had the other evening about *hate*. What is hate? Who has ever described it? Why do I feel it for her?" (***JKM*** 1927, 232-33). She could not analyze what her imagery demonstrates: that the fantasy that turns the nurturing female into the suet pudding one would like to destroy is responsible for the subsequent fantasy that the suet pudding will destroy one in turn. Mansfield's tirades against her caretakers grew increasingly virulent: they are *all* like Ida Baker, vampires, harpies, and ghouls who have made her ill so that they can care for her.⁴⁶ And this anger and rage made her believe that her disease was psychological, not physical. She finally rejected all medical treatment and all caretaking, as well as the diet for tuberculosis, the milk, butter, cream, and eggs she called "female food," thereby hastening her death at the age of thirty-four.⁴⁷ Although she once wrote that "see[ing] into love [. . .] does not rule out hate [. . .] doesn't rule out anger" (***CLKM*** 3 232), Mansfield could not reconcile her dependence upon and need for Ida Baker with her anger and rage against her. Calling herself a "sham" until she "made straight her relations with L. M.," Mansfield concluded, "One of the K. M.'s is so sorry. But of course she is. She has to die. *Don't feed her*" (JKM 1927, 229, 248). She was dead three months later.

Notes

1. Mansfield was not alone in perceiving the Lawrence's relationship in oral terms. In *D. H. Lawrence and the Devouring Mother*, [(Durham: Duke Univ. Press, 1984), Judith] Ruderman cites the following letter by Mansfield's friend S. S. Koteliansky: "If [Frieda] disappeared, Lawrence would be saved, because she is devouring him bit by bit, gradually, permanently. We had a few more quarrels and she shed profuse tears, but, I think, she weeps only to benefit her digestion, after which she eats with an increased appetite and gusto" (16).

2. Mansfield's description of Frieda strongly resembles Melanie Klein's descriptions of infantile fantasies of the maternal body. See Klein, *The Psychoanalysis of Children* (New York: Grove, 1960), esp. 60 and 184-85. A new selection of Klein's important work is *The Selected Melanie Klein*, ed. Juliet Mitchell (New York: Macmillan, 1986), esp. 9-32, 48-51, and 69-83.

Mansfield frequently compares motherly women to a specific kind of steamed suet pudding that more closely resembles an American fruitcake than a custard concoction. Such puddings are relatively popular in England, and contain suet, bread crumbs, and some combination of citrus peels, almonds, walnuts, carrots, dates, figs, plums, cherries, raisins, and currants. At Christmas time it is customary to stir a sixpence into the batter. The pudding is then mounded into a towel or cloth, placed in a basin, and steamed for up to six hours. English steamed puddings tend to be dark, dense, and moist and have the consistency of wet bread. The round shape and dense texture of these puddings uncannily evoke the infantile fantasy that the maternal body (the breast in particular) contains part objects such as milk, babies, and the father's incorporated penis—all of which the infant envies and wishes to devour and destroy.

In light of Mansfield's almost obsessive preoccupation with puddings, it is interesting (and amusing) that Frieda Lawrence invented a pudding and named it after Mansfield. See *Frieda Lawrence: The Memoirs and Correspondence*, ed. E. W. Tedlock Jr. (New York: Knopf, 1964), 426.

3. See Mansfield's December 1920 letter to John Middleton Murry: "Lawrence denies his humanity. . . . His hero and heroine are non-human. They are animals on the prowl. They do not feel: they scarcely speak. . . . They submit to the physical response and for the rest go veiled—blind—*faceless*—mindless. This is the doctrine of mindlessness. . . . I feel privately as though Lawrence had possessed an animal and fallen under a curse" (*KM-JMM* 620-61, emphasis in the original). Mansfield's negative reaction to the explicit sexuality in Lawrence's *The Lost Girl* is tempered by her admiration for his descriptions of the physical world. Although Mansfield shared this love, she typically likens herself to him when she is reacting against maternal engulfment. For a sensitive account of Mansfield's friendship with Lawrence, see chapter 11 of [Claire] Tomalin, *Katherine Mansfield*: [*A Secret Life* (New York: Knopf, 1988))] 145-63. For descriptions of Lawrence's fear of engulfing and devouring mothers, see, in addition to Ruderman (*D. H. Lawrence and the Devouring Mother*), [Sandra M.] Gilbert, "Potent Griselda: ['The LadyBird' and the Great Mother," in *D. H. Lawrence: A Centenary Consideration*, ed. Peter Balbert and Phillip J. Marcus (Ithaca: Cornell Univ. Press, 1985),] 130-61.

4. Sydney Janet Kaplan argues in "Katherine Mansfield's 'Passion for Technique," in *Women's Language and Style*, ed. Douglas Buttruff and Edmund L. Epstein. Studies in Contemporary Language, no. 1 (Akron, Ohio: University of Akron, 1978), that Mansfield's style developed from her desire to distance herself from the feminine: "it speaks to a rejection . . . of the female body—so damp and so fertile, and considered so dangerous by those male artists longing to escape from what they imagined as its powers to entrap them" (122). Kaplan associates this desire for distance with a desire for critical acceptance by men; she explicitly rejects a psychoanalytic explanation that centers on the figure of the mother (121). Kaplan's assessment of Mansfield's style is persuasive; her elision of the figure of the mother is more troubling.

5. Gilbert, "Potent Griselda," 132. For other accounts of the shift from paternal to maternal myths of origins in modernism, see [Susan] Gubar, "The Birth of the Artist as Heroine: [(Re)production, the *Künstlerroman* Tradition, and the Fiction of Katherine Mansfield," in *The Representation of Women in Fiction*, ed. Carolyn G. Heilbrun and Margaret R. Higgonet (Baltimore: Johns Hopkins Univ. Press, 1983),] esp. 19-26; and [Michael] Rogin, "The Great Mother Domesticated: [Sexual Difference and Sexual Indifference in D. W. Griffith's *Intolerance*," *Critical Inquiry* 15 (spring 1989):] 510-55.

6. Moers outlines the shift from the romance plot to a preoccupation with the mother-daughter bond in *Literary Women*: [*The Great Writers* (Garden City: Doubleday, 1977)] 352-68. See also Elizabeth Abel, "Narrative Structure(s) and Female Development: The Case of *Mrs. Dalloway*," in *The Voyage In*: [*Fictions of Female Development*,] ed. [Elizabeth] Abel, [Marianne Hirsch and Elizabeth Langland (Hanover, N.H.: Univ. Press of New England, 1983),] 161-65; [Louise] Bernikow, *Among Women*, [(New York: Harper, 1980)] 160-75; [Rachel Blau] DuPlessis, *Writing Beyond the Ending*: [*Narrative Strategies of Twentieth-Century Women Writers* (Bloomington: Indiana Univ. Press, 1985)] 91-98; [Marianne] Hirsch, *The Mother/Daughter Plot*: [*Narrative, Psychoanalysis, Feminism* (Bloomington: Indiana Univ. Press, 1989)] 91-121; [Jane] Lilienfeld, "Reentering Paradise: [Colette, Woolf, and Their Mothers," in *The Lost Tradition: Mothers and Daughters in Literature*, ed. Cathy N. Davidson and E. M. Broner (New York: Frederick Ungar, 1980)] 160-75.

7. See Mary Burgan, "Childbirth Trauma in Katherine Mansfield's Early Stories," *Modern Fiction Studies* 24, no. 3 (autumn 1978): 395-412; Gubar, "The Birth of the Artist as Heroine"; and Hirsch, *The Mother/Daughter Plot*, 97. It is a commonplace of Mansfield criticism that her style and

material changed around 1915 when she wrote the first draft of what would later be "Prelude"; a number of critics attribute that change to the death of her brother in World War I and her subsequent desire to memorialize him. For explanations of this shift, see, in addition to Burgan, Gubar, and Hirsch, Sylvia Berkman, *Katherine Mansfield: A Critical Study* (London: Oxford Univ. Press, 1951); [Saralyn] Daly, *Katherine Mansfield*, [(New York: Twayne Publisher, 1965)] 62-73; [Kate] Fullbrook, *Katherine Mansfield* [(Bloomington: Indiana Univ. Press, 1986)] 63-7; [Sydney Janet] Kaplan, *Katherine Mansfield and the Origins of Modernism* [(Ithaca: Cornell Univ. Press, 1991)] 127; and [Marvin] Magalaner, *The Fiction of Katherine Mansfield* [(Carbondale: Southern Illinois Univ. Press, 1971)] 1971), 26-27. For relevant biographical information, see [Antony] Alpers, *The Life of Katherine Mansfield* [(New York: Penguin, 1982)]; Gillian Boddy, *Katherine Mansfield: The Woman and the Writer* (New York: Penguin, 1988); [Jeffrey] Meyers, *Katherine Mansfield: [A Biography* (New York: New Directions, 1978)]; and Tomalin, *Katherine Mansfield*. As I argue here, however, patterns of imagery that expose a fear of the maternal body characterize both the early and later fiction. Furthermore, the belief that an acceptance of maternity is concomitant with maturation has lead to what I believe are significant misreadings of women's relationships in "Prelude" and "At the Bay": both Linda Burnell and her mother Mrs. Fairfield are evaluated by their relationship to maternity, and the text itself is widely cited as evidence that Mansfield saw writing as a substitute for childbearing. As I show later in this chapter, a shift in emphasis reveals that Linda's attitude to childbearing is inextricable from the preoedipal concerns with fusion and separation that mark her relationship with her mother.

8. "My Potplants," cited by Cherry Hankin in "Fantasy and the Sense of an Ending in the Work of Katherine Mansfield," *Modern Fiction Studies* 24, no. 3 (autumn 1978): 469. See also *Dulac's "The Snow Queen" and Other Stories from Hans Andersen* (Garden City: Doubleday, 1976). In an early autobiographical story Mansfield mentions "[t]he fairytales that [Juliet] devoured voraciously." See "The Unpublished Manuscripts of Katherine Mansfield," part 1, "Juliet," ed. Margaret Scott, in *The Turnbull Library Record* 3, no. 1 (March 1970): 25.

9. "The Unpublished Manuscripts of Katherine Mansfield," part 4, "Elena and Peter," ed. Margaret Scott, in *The Turnbull Library Record* 5, no. 1 (May 1972): 21-22.

10. Fullbrook, *Katherine Mansfield*, calls "mirroring and doubling . . . the most important meanings of the tale" (39). Although she does not explore this mirroring as a function of mother-daughter fusion, she notes that "the story drives toward the moment . . . when the tormented individual refuses or deforms the role assigned to her by others, but bases her revolt on a revision of forms she already knows" (40). In exploring their mother's murderous impulses, Mansfield's artistic daughters do just that.

11. For a perceptive reading of this story, see Gubar, "The Birth of the Artist as Heroine," 27-92. Gubar notes that "the daughter's 'mad excitement' while drawing is a repetition of the mother's violence" and argues that Mansfield's first girl artist "expresses [Mansfield's] sense of vulnerability and her rage" (28). Note, however, that the daughter's art also articulates the mother's anger at her maternity.

12. This passage is part of an unfinished story published in Ruth Elvish Mantz and John Middleton Murry, *The Life of Katherine Mansfield* (London: Constable, 1933), 320-21. The story clearly derives from Mansfield's disastrous first pregnancy. For a comparable although different reading of this material, see Sydney Janet Kaplan, "'A Gigantic Mother': Katherine Mansfield's London," in *Women Writer and the City: Essays in Feminist Literary Criticism,* ed. Susan Merrill Squier (Knoxville: Univ. of Tennessee Press, 1984), 171.

13. [Mary] Burgan, "Childbirth Trauma in Katherine Mansfield's Early Stories," [in *Illness, Gender and Writing: The Case of Katherine Mansfield* (Baltimore: Johns Hopkins Univ. Press, 1994)] interprets the food imagery in the *German Pension* stories as "common in the folklore and experience of pregnancy" (398-99).

14. Mansfield makes this point repeatedly. The narrator of the *German Pension* stories states that she considers "childbearing the most ignominious of all professions" (55). Another woman expresses her anxiety about the safe delivery of a pregnant daughter, and then adds, "But it is bound to be quite satisfactory. . . . The dear married a banker—the desire of her life" (42). Here the daughter literally swells (with) her husband's capital investment.

15. For the connection between feminism, vegetarianism, and the suffrage movement, see Elaine Showalter, *The Female Malady: Women, Madness, and English Culture, 1830-1980* (New York: Pantheon, 1985), 129.

16. For an account of how women writers define themselves against the Romantic tradition, see Margaret Homans, *Women Writers and Poetic*

16. *Identity* (Princeton: Princeton Univ. Press, 1980), esp. 12-40. For other commentary on Mansfield's debt to Wordsworth, see Berkman, *Katherine Mansfield*, 13; Fullbrook, *Katherine Mansfield*, 68; and Gubar, "The Birth of the Artist as Heroine," 38-39.

17. In his introduction to *The Aloe* (New Zealand: Virago Press, 1985), Vincent O'Sullivan remarks that Pater's story provides a model of how "feeling might be associated with place" (xii). Fullbrook, *Katherine Mansfield*, notes how the move to a new home becomes "an occasion of defamiliarisation and estrangement that prompts a series of moments of self-awareness for the characters" (68). I find both of these readings compatible with the one I offer here.

18. See *The Aloe*, 61-62.

19. See J. J. Bachofen, *Myth, Religion, and Mother-Right: Selected Writings of J. J. Bachofen*, trans. Ralph Manheim (1861; Princeton: Princeton Univ. Press, 1967); Gilbert, "Potent Griselda," esp. 132-40; and Martin Green, *The Von Richthofen Sisters: The Triumphant and the Tragic Modes of Love* (New York: Basic Books, 1974). Gilbert (following Green) points out that Lawrence need not have read Bachofen since Frieda enacted the matriarchal idea (142). The same could be said of Mansfield.

20. Gubar reads this scene as a joint redefinition of the aloe by Linda and her mother ("The Birth of the Artist as Heroine," 37), whereas Burgan finds in it Linda's limited acceptance of natural processes, which are exemplified by her mother's plans ("Childbirth Trauma in Katherine Mansfield's Early Stories," 406). I believe, however, the scene underscores the disjunction between them; I return to Linda's response later in this chapter.

21. In the journal passage widely cited as evidence of the shift in Mansfield's style, Mansfield speaks of her desire to write about her childhood as a means of memorializing her brother; her phrasing anticipates this passage in "At the Bay": "all must be told with a sense of mystery, a radiance, an afterglow, because you, my little sun of it, are set. You have dropped over the dazzling brim of the world. Now I must play my part" (L & J 65-66). In a comparable, although different reading, Gubar also connects this journal passage with the shift from paternal to maternal myths of origins exemplified by "Prelude" and "At the Bay" ("The Birth of the Artist as Heroine," 34).

22. Fullbrook reads the repetition of the name "Stanley" differently; see Fullbrook, *Katherine Mansfield*, 69-70.

23. According to Jane Marcus, Mansfield gave impersonations at a lesbian cabaret called the Cave of Harmony. See Marcus, "Sapphistry: Narration as Lesbian Seduction," in *Virginia Woolf and the Languages of Patriarchy*, [(Bloomington: Indiana Univ. Press, 1987)] 167-69. Marcus's source seems to be Vera Brittain's *Radcliffe Hall: A Case of Obscenity* [(South Brunswick: A. S. Barnes, 1969)]; Brittain says Mansfield appeared there in 1916. Mansfield's biographers give the name as the "Cave of the Golden Calf" and place the date of Mansfield's appearance/appearances there as 1913. See Meyers, *Katherine Mansfield*, 37-38 and Tomalin, *Katherine Mansfield*, 60. It is certainly possible that Mansfield's image of a mother-daughter language that echoes inside a cave derives from the name of this cabaret; an allusion to lesbianism would be compatible with the sensuality and eroticism Mansfield assigns to the mother-daughter bond.

24. Gubar argues that the game in "At the Bay," where the children choose a totem animal and act out its sound, represents a free linguistic play associated with the feminine (42-43). In this connection, Kezia's choice of the bee (in defiance of the rule that she must choose an animal) may indicate her loyalty to the mother goddess, who is often represented by a hive. See, for example, D. H. Lawrence's foreword to *Sons and Lovers*: "we are bees that go between, from the flower home to the hive and the Queen; for she lies at the centre of the hive [and] in her all things are born, both words and bees." Lily Briscoe also imagines Mrs. Ramsay as a hive in Woolf's *To the Lighthouse*, 79-80.

25. Gubar and Fullbrook both interpret the brooch as a positive image of maternal power. Fullbrook finds it indicative of Mrs. Fairfield's "witch-like powers of imposing order on the world" (*Katherine Mansfield*, 72). Gubar notes its resonance with Crescent Bay, which she reads as a positive evocation of the blurred boundaries between the women ("The Birth of the Artist as Heroine," 44-45).

26. Fullbrook notes "the general impulse to devour one another prevalent in the family as a whole" (*Katherine Mansfield*, 72; see also 70). She does not trace preoedipal issues in this impulse.

27. Magalaner identifies swelling as a theme throughout "Prelude" and connects it with sexuality and pregnancy (*The Fiction of Katherine Mansfield*, 29-30). He sees the grandmother's memory of an ant sting that caused Beryl's leg to swell as "apparently unrelated"; I would argue that the swollen leg underscores the connection between pregnancy and other venomous, unwelcome invasions.

28. See, for example, [Sigmund] Freud, "Femininity," [(1931) in *Women and Analysis: Psychoanalytic Dialogues on Femininity*, ed. Jean Strouse (New York: Grossman Publishers, 1974)] 86-87. For a reading that stresses this interpretation, see Burgan, "Childbirth Trauma in Katherine Mansfield's Early Stories," 404.

29. Gubar also makes the connection between the duck and the headless Stanley: "Stanley unwittingly presides at a eucharistic celebration . . . when the ritualistic eating of the bird-phallus is celebrated by the female community which is not only eating the baby to be born to Linda but becoming pregnant with him as well" ("The Birth of the Artist as Heroine," 38). Mansfield suggests, however, that only Isabel and Beryl share Stanley's appetite for meat; they are, significantly, the only characters who unquestioningly accept the patriarchal structure of the family. See "Prelude," *SS* 227, 254-55.

30. Burgan, "Childbirth Trauma in Katherine Mansfield's Early Stories," 404.

31. Fullbrook connects the owls to the devouring impulse characteristic of the family; she does not connect them to Mrs. Fairfield. Mrs. Fairfield's lack of teeth, in Fullbrook's reading, exempt her from this familial impulse (*Katherine Mansfield*, 72).

    Mansfield's use of moonlight in the story strengthens the negative connotations of Mrs. Fairfield's crescent moon, for the moon always symbolizes a manipulative and sexual femininity in Mansfield's work. In "Bliss," for example, the deceitful Pearl Fulton is persistently associated with the moon. Significantly, Linda shivers in the moonlight and retreats to her husband's side (*SS* 244), while Beryl fantasizes about a sexual encounter (*SS* 229). It is also significant that Mrs. Fairfield wears the emblems of Athena, the goddess born from man's mind and not woman's body.

32. Burgan, "Childbirth Trauma in Katherine Mansfield's Early Stories," 400-401; see also Celeste Turner Wright, "Katherine Mansfield and the 'Secret Smile,'" *Literature and Psychology* 5 (August 1955): 44-48.

33. For very different readings of this scene, see Burgan ("Childbirth Trauma in Katherine Mansfield's Early Stories," 406) and Gubar ("The Birth of the Artist as Heroine," 36-37). Burgan argues that Linda's vision of growth and multiplicity represents her "grudging admission of her maternal role in the biological cycle," an admission that makes her link the inevitability of childbirth with "the process of nature which the aloe symbolizes" (406). Gubar sees in this scene a mutual redefinition of the aloe by Linda and her mother, from a phallic threat to a symbol of female resistance, followed by Linda's vision of multiplicity and Mrs. Fairfield's vision of jam, which she sees as evidence of their mutual commitment "to preserving the life of the family" (37). I believe, however, that Mansfield emphasizes a disjunction here: while Linda does indeed speak to her mother with "the special voice that women use to one another," her mother's vision of fruit and jam undercuts Linda's sense that they share a similar vision of rebellion. Resistance and rebellion belong to Linda alone; her vision of multiplicity seems a despairing resignation to female fragmentation. Fullbrook's reading is closer to the one I outline here, but she sees Linda as a character acting perversely and in bad faith (*Katherine Mansfield*, 80-84).

34. Linda's question—"Why, then, flower at all?"—resonates with the murderous mother's question in "The Woman at the Store": "Over and over I tells 'im—you've broken my spirit and spoiled my looks, and wot for. . . . I 'ear them two words knockin' inside me all the time—'Wot for!'" (*SS* 131). In "Frau Brechenmacher Attends a Wedding," the Frau similarly questions women's sexual subordination and reproduction: "what is it all for?" she asks (*SS* 61).

    Burgan interprets Linda's despair as a prelude to her joyful response to her baby boy. But there is no reciprocity of feeling in this scene: the baby gets distracted and rolls over (and away). Mansfield stresses the failure of connection and communication. For readings that emphasizes Linda's change of heart, see Burgan, "Childbirth Trauma in Katherine Mansfield's Early Stories," 407-8; and Gubar, "The Birth of the Artist as Heroine," 42.

35. For a different reading of these passages, see Gubar, "The Birth of the Artist as Heroine," 36.

36. As [Margaret] Homans points out, "Mother Nature is not a helpful model for women aspiring to be poets. She is prolific biologically, not linguistically, and she is as destructive as she is creative. . . . Writing poetry would seem to require of the writer everything that Mother Nature is not, and the first project of any poet who is also a daughter must be to keep herself from becoming her mother" (*Women Writers and Poetic Identity*: [*Dorothy Wordsworth, Emily Brontë, and Emily Dickinson* (Princeton, N.J.: Princeton Univ. Press, 1980)] 13).

37. Kezia's resemblance to her mother is a commonplace of Mansfield criticism. See Burgan, *Illness, Gender, and Writing*, 110; Daly, *Katherine Mans-*

field, 67-68; Fullbrook, *Katherine Mansfield,* 75-77, 82; Gubar, "The Birth of the Artist as Heroine," 36; Kaplan, *Katherine Mansfield and the Origins of Modernism,* 128; and Magalaner, *The Fiction of Katherine Mansfield,* 32-33, for representative readings.

38. Mansfield shares a desire for impersonality with many of her contemporaries. For a study of modernist impersonality, see esp. Daniel Albright, *Personality and Impersonality: Lawrence, Woolf, and Mann* (Chicago: Univ. of Chicago Press, 1978).

39. Mansfield speaks here of a pansy, but this choice of object is not as innocuous as it seems. Mansfield frequently speaks of "offering herself up" to various natural objects, but when it comes to pansies her comments acquire a startling dimension. Not only does she repeatedly compare her feelings for flowers to the way other women feel about babies (see *LKM* 504), she also describes pansies as "nourished on the flesh of dead babies" (*CLKM*3 228).

40. In "Katherine Mansfield's 'Passion for Technique,'" Kaplan reads this passage as demonstrating Mansfield's desire to "defeat the personal": "To *become* the thing is to take the direction away from self. Katherine Mansfield is really speaking of a merging of self and object, distancing without losing the intensity of the original identification with the emotion" (125).

41. In *Virginia Woolf and the Fictions of Psychoanalysis,* [Chicago: Univ. of Chicago Press, 1989] Abel identifies parthenogenesis as a trope of women's writing in the twenties (89, 158 n.14).

42. Gubar makes a comparable connection between this letter and "Prelude" ("The Birth of the Artist as Heroine," 38).

43. See Fullbrook, 16-20; and Kaplan. Fullbrook argues that Mansfield's concept of the mask derives from the symbolists; Kaplan believes Mansfield's "passion for technique" grew out of a need to escape from "the contradictions and the pain of active confrontation with the problems of women's self-identity" (121). Both of these interpretations seem compatible with my assessment that Mansfield's sense of a diffuse inchoate self derives from a fear of preoedipal fusion and merger. Yet it is clear that Mansfield's familiarity with psychoanalysis also inflects her concept of identity. See her journal entry of 1920: "True to oneself! which self? Which of my many—well, really, that's what it looks like coming to—hundreds of selves? For what with complexes and repressions and reactions and vibrations and reflections, there are moments when I feel I am nothing but the small clerk of some hotel without a proprietor, who has all his work cut out to enter the names and hand the keys to the wilful guests" (*L & J* 173). Mansfield immediately contrasts this concept of self to a unified self resembling the aloe in "Prelude." Nonetheless, her vocabulary attests to at least a passing knowledge of psychoanalysis. Mansfield condemned writers for adopting psychoanalytic concepts too facilely—"it's turning Life into a *case*" (*KM-JMM* 560)—but she does not seem to extend her condemnation to psychoanalysis itself.

In light of Mansfield's belief that a mask held the fragmented self together, it is interesting that her only recorded dream of death was a dream of her body breaking up into shards: "It broke up with a violent shock—an earthquake—and it broke like glass. A long terrible shiver, you understand—and the spinal cord and the bones and every bit and particle was a sense of flashing greenish brilliance, like broken glass. When I woke up I thought there had been a violent earthquake. . . . It slowly dawned upon me—the conviction that in that dream I died" (*L & J* 161). Here the coherent self is as fragile as a sheet of glass, an image that conflates the mask with the fragments.

44. Mansfield had several conversations with friends about her plans for developing a new narrative voice and style. See especially A. R. Orage, "Talks with Katherine Mansfield," *Century Magazine,* 87 (November 1924), 36-40. For speculation on these plans, see Alpers, *The Life of Katherine Mansfield,* 380-81; and Tomalin, *Katherine Mansfield,* 235-36.

45. Linda wishes to speak to her mother with a special language in "Prelude," 257. The famous passage about the phallic spear occurs in a journal entry for April 1920 (*L & J* 173).

46. See *CLKM*2 113.

47. I coin the phrase "female food" from the following: "I must get the ancient sisters to simplify their ideas of picnics . . . Today they brought M[urry] boiled beef and trimmings in a saucepan. It's awful to open such a vessel under the very Eye of our Maker. I like eggs, butter-bread and milk at picnics. But M. disagrees. He regards such tastes as female flippancy" (*LKM* 474). Mansfield also repeatedly commented that one could not be cured like a cow if one was not a cow. See JKM 1927, 240, 249, 252. Milk was, of course, part of the prescribed treatment for her tuberculosis.

Abbreviations

CLKM: *The Collected Letters of Katherine Mansfield.* Ed. Vincent O'Sullivan and Margaret Scott. Oxford: Clarendon Press. 1, 1903-17 (1984); 2, 1918-19 (1987); 3, 1919-20 (1993).

IB: Ida Baker. *Katherine Mansfield: The Memories of L. M.* New York: Taplinger Publishing Company, 1972.

JKM 1927: *The Journal of Katherine Mansfield.* Ed. John Middleton Murry. New York: Knopf, 1927.

KM-JMM: *Katherine Mansfield's Letters to John Middleton Murry, 1913-22.* New York: Knopf, 1951.

LKM: *The Letters of Katherine Mansfield.* Ed. John Middleton Murry. New York: Knopf, 1929.

L & J: *The Letters and Journals of Katherine Mansfield: A Selection.* Ed. C. K. Stead. New York: Penguin, 1977.

SS: *The Short Stories of Katherine Mansfield.* Ed. John Middleton Murry. New York: Knopf, 1937.

Pamela Dunbar (essay date 1997)

SOURCE: Dunbar, Pamela. "The Self." In *Radical Mansfield: Double Discourse in Katherine Mansfield's Short Stories,* pp. 73-87. New York: St. Martin's Press, Inc., 1997.

[*In the following essay, Dunbar interprets "Je ne parle pas français" and "A Married Man's Story" as "confessional tales" that evolve into "case studies of their narrators." Also, according to Dunbar, both works question the integrity of the human self while simultaneously deconstructing "traditional and Romantic beliefs regarding the artist."*]

Late in 1917, when on her way to spend the weekend with the 'Bloomsberries' in Lady Ottoline Morrell's country retreat at Garsington near Oxford, Mansfield caught a chill. Her health took a dramatic turn for the worse. A doctor was called, and finding a spot on her lung—the first clear evidence that she was suffering from tuberculosis—ordered her to spend the rest of the winter abroad.

So early in the New Year she set off alone for Bandol in southern France, where two years earlier she and Murry had passed several settled—and highly productive—months. This time Mansfield was less settled. But she did manage to complete two of her most original stories, **'Je Ne Parle Pas Français'** and **'Bliss'**. The first was unlike anything she had produced before—a lengthy monologue delivered apparently *extempore* by its Parisian narrator, a writer and sexual procurer. Then, on her return to England a few months later she began what she described as 'another member of the *Je ne Parle pas* family'.[1] This may have been **'A Married Man's Story'**.[2] Work was resumed—or perhaps begun—on **'A Married Man'** in 1921, only eighteen months or so before her death; but it was never finished.

'Je Ne Parle Pas Français' and **'A Married Man's Story'** are strikingly similar. Both present as confessional tales, then turn into case-studies of their narrators—writers who have suffered childhood trauma. And both investigate the nature of these traumas and the way they have governed the formation of their subjects' personalities.

Both works also interrogate long-held humanist notions of the integrity and stability of the human self. The narrator of **'Je Ne Parle Pas Français'** in particular confounds the traditional view: he is morally dubious, his nature elusive, his sexual preferences confused. But as well as re-visioning the self the portraits deconstruct traditional and Romantic beliefs regarding the artist—his creative autonomy, high endeavour, lack of partisan prejudice; the universality of his work; the heroic nature of his life and personality. These artists have crippling personal problems; their work is represented as a form of predation; and the process of writing itself, though a possible 'way back' to the subject's repressed experience, is offered as a journey which has significance for that artist alone.

'Je Ne Parle Pas' and **'A Married Man's Story'** also investigate the relationship between gender (or gendering) and creativity. As they are the only Mansfield stories to focus on writers it is note-worthy that both are male—this from a woman writer who was deeply concerned with the way her own artistic vision was at times hindered by her domestic, female, role;[3] another indication of her intention to subvert Romantic assumptions regarding the (male) artist's high endeavour.

The Married Man's 'dark secrets' are linked to events which took place within his own first family. So his tale is inevitably concerned with the subject of familial disharmony and its effect upon the child. **'Je Ne Parle Pas Français'** also has this concern, though here the secrets remain largely undisclosed. And both stories deal as well with the effect of those events on the subjects' later ability to form satisfactory relationships.

Though they are themselves engaged with the way trauma is repressed, the tales deal overtly enough with the taboo subjects of child-abuse and child sexuality, Oedipal attachment, the abuse of sexual power, prostitution and procuration in the case of **'Je Ne Parle Pas Français'**; murder, wife-battering, and child sexuality in **'A Married Man's Story'**—making them unquestionably the most daring of all Mansfield's works.

This view is borne out by the reactions of her first readers: Middleton Murry compared **'Je Ne Parle Pas Français'** to Dostoevsky;[4] and Harold Beauchamp, to whom his daughter had sent a copy, carried out his own form of censorship by 'chuck[ing] the thing behind the fireplace'.[5] Mansfield herself commented that it made her feel '*grown up* as a writer'.[6]

The work also met with difficulties from Constable, its mainstream publisher. The first, limited, edition of **'Je Ne Parle Pas Français'** (dated 1919; appeared early 1920) was privately printed by Murry's brother Richard at Mansfield and Murry's own Heron Press, and issued unexpurgated. Where this was noticed by critics it was acclaimed: J. N. Sullivan said in *The Athenaeum*[7] that it 'possesses genius', and Edward Wagenknecht wrote in the *English Journal*[8] that Mansfield had handled her theme 'subtly and delicately'.

But before including the story in the volume **Bliss** (1920) Constable's editor, Michael Sadlier, insisted on cuts. Almost all of these deal with the narrator's childhood seduction and with the subsequent corruption of his vision. Though brief, the censored passages do play a critical role in explaining the narrator's attitude and in building up the story's ironical and slightly seedy tone.[9]

Initially Mansfield rejected Sadleir's stipulation, demanding, 'Shall I pick the eyes out of a story for £40?' (Forty pounds was then a considerable sum of money, equal to almost one-fifth of her annual allowance from her father.) She went on to explain what she considered would be the artistic effect of making the cuts: 'The *outline* would be all blurred. It must have those sharp lines.'[10] But the next day she capitulated, and the story was finally published by Constable in its censored form.

The limited edition was not reprinted, nor the suppressed sections restored to the text, until Antony Alpers's hardback edition of *The Stories of Katherine Mansfield* appeared in 1984. But the Constable/Penguin edition, the one by which the vast majority of Mansfield's readers know her, has turned out the expurgated version to this day.

'Je Ne Parle Pas Français' is set in Paris. It opens with its narrator, Raoul Duquette, musing upon his own personality and past. He goes on to recall his friendship with a young Englishman, Dick Harmon, and the sense of desertion and humiliation he felt when Dick left him to return to England. In fact Dick returned a few months later: though when he did so he was accompanied by his lover, a young woman known only as Mouse. Shortly afterwards Dick abandoned her in order—or so we are told—to return to his mother. Raoul, who admits to feeling a perverse elation at the couple's suffering, also made a point of letting Mouse down. His confessions end with an idle and rather tasteless pronouncement on the allure of the café's proprietress.

Raoul Duquette attempts early on to establish his own identity. This he does by trying out the nineteenth-century realist's thumb-nail portrait. However, the old convention will not hold: his own, more problematic Modernist personality cannot be pinned down in this way. It eludes him, disappearing into the darkness of his repressions:

> My name is Raoul Duquette. I am twenty-six years old and a Parisian, a true Parisian. About my family—it really doesn't matter. I have no family; I don't want any. I never think about my childhood. I've forgotten it.
>
> (p. 66)

A little later he tries again, this time building repression—and irony—into his description:

> I date myself from the moment that I became tenant of a small bachelor flat on the fifth floor of a tall, not too shabby house, in a street that might or might not be discreet. Very useful, that. . . . There I emerged, came out into the light and put out my two horns with a study and a bedroom and a kitchen on my back.
>
> (p. 67)

But between these obfuscatory attempts to define his identity Raoul lets slip a reference to an episode from his childhood that *was* crucial to the formation of his personality—his seduction by the family's laundress:

> When I was about ten our laundress was an African woman, very big, very dark, with . . . frizzy hair. . . . She took me into a little outhouse . . . , caught me up in her arms and began kissing me. Ah, those kisses! Especially those kisses inside my ears that nearly deafened me.
>
> *And then with a soft growl she tore open her bodice and put me to her.* When she set me down she took from her pocket a little round fried cake covered with sugar and I reeled along the passage back to our door.[11]

(Italics mine: the italicised passage is one of those that were omitted from the Constable version.) The transgressive nature of the episode is underlined in the racial identity of the African woman—the incarnation for the white male, European narrator, of the Other.

Raoul's story makes it clear that it is this encounter, repeated once a week throughout his childhood, which has led to the warping of his personality—by, amongst other things, causing him to associate sexual adventure with reward, and confusing for him woman's roles as lover and as mother. The relationship is, it is implied, responsible for his later self-regard, his shiftiness, his activities as gigolo and sexual procurer, his disposition to humiliate women. The tale has him cast frequent glances at the mirror—a reflection, so to speak, of his narcissistic fascination with himself. And, appropriately for such a bankrupt and deceiving personality, neither of his mirrors is paid for.

His attitude towards women is highlighted from the beginning, in his references to life as 'an old hag', an 'old bitch' he might take 'by the throat', and a 'rag-picker on the American cinema shuffling along wrapped in a filthy shawl with her old claws crooked over a stick' (p. 62). And it becomes the focus of the closing episode of the story, when he contributes to an abandoned woman's distress by offering help . . . then calculatedly letting her down.

The closest literary model for Mansfield's hero is the narrator of Dostoevsky's *Notes from Underground,* another first-person confessional tale.[12] Mansfield no doubt got to know the work while Murry was preparing his book on Dostoevsky. This he did during the time they spent together in Bandol, when Mansfield herself was working on an early version of **'Prelude'**. Both Dostoevsky's hero and Mansfield's are socially isolated, and acutely introspective. Both are intended to represent 'modern' urban humanity. Both seem fixated on the psychology of humiliation and revenge, and some of the more perverse aspects of sexual power. And both challenge as just another vanity the kind of self-congratulatory 'truth-telling' which Rousseau makes so much of in the *Confessions*—itself an early attempt to expose Romantic notions regarding the veracity of the first-person subject.

Most strikingly perhaps, Mansfield has taken over Dostoevsky's metaphor of the 'under-ground' and applied it to her own hero's social situation and psychical formation. But in so doing she gives it the explicit referent of psychological repression—something it did not have in the original. The clue to the steal is planted in a passage in which Raoul makes a point of distinguishing himself from the prickly, intense, and pretentiously philosophical Underground Man—and at the same time aligning his preoccupations with those of Freud—by determining to make a name for himself 'as a writer about the *submerged world.* [My italics.] But not as others have done before [him]. Oh, no! Very naïvely, with a sort of tender humour and from the inside, as though it were all quite simple, quite natural' (p. 67).

So Raoul distances himself from the old, high Romantic conception of the self. But although for him personality seems defined according to what was to become the classic Modernist model—fluid and experiential—the cut-and-dried imagery he uses undercuts the Modernist vision. People, he asserts, are 'like portmanteaux—packed with certain things' (p. 60); and the waiter at his favourite café is 'a sort of cross between a coffee-pot and a wine-bottle' (p. 61).

He also declares against any Christian-dualist conception of the mind:

> I don't believe in the human soul. I never have. I believe that people are like portmanteaux—packed with certain things, started going, thrown about, tossed away, dumped down, lost and found, half emptied suddenly, or squeezed fatter than ever, until finally the Ultimate Porter swings them on to the Ultimate Train and away they rattle. . . .
>
> Not but what these portmanteaux can be very fascinating. Oh, but very! I see myself standing in front of them, don't you know, like a Customs official.
>
> 'Have you anything to declare? Any wines, spirits, cigars, perfumes, silks?'
>
> And the moment of hesitation as to whether I am going to be fooled just before I chalk that squiggle, and then the other moment of hesitation just after, as to whether I have been, are perhaps the two most thrilling instants in life.
>
> (pp. 60-1)

This anti-dualist declaration is again undercut in Raoul's preoccupation with 'contents' and 'packaging'. And it is tellingly at odds with the picture he paints of himself in his tale as a whole, as a maimed and fractured personality; and in other distinctions he sets up between the 'submerged' and 'daylit' aspects of the self, and between the self that acts and lives and the self that observes. It is also challenged in the several references he makes to photographs, which play off photography's necessarily two-dimensional revelations against hints of some more elusive, and more complex, notion of identity. And it directly opposes the dualism that is hinted at in his surname 'Du-quette' (my hyphen). (The name also has overtones of 'coquette' and *quéquette*, a French slang term for the penis.) His mirror-glances are relevant here too—particularly as for Mansfield the look in the mirror is consistently associated with a desire, or simulated desire, for self-knowledge.

Raoul's morbid self-absorption, his position on the margins of society, his voyeurism and predatory exploitation of others, his preoccupation with intense feelings, his *maladif* tendency to look too close, all mark him out as a parody of the artist. And the titles of his works confirm his third-rateness—*Wrong Doors, False Coins,* and *Left Umbrellas* (standing presumably for botched opportunities, lack of principle, and psychic residues). As well as his treatment of Mouse, his 'night jobs' of pimp and gigolo reflect the baser aspects of his artistic role. It is also ironically appropriate that he should employ another baldly dualistic metaphor to encapsulate—or to eliminate—the complexities of the artistic process:

> All the while I wrote that last page my other self has been chasing up and down out in the dark there. It left me just when I began to analyse my grand moment, dashed off distracted, like a lost dog who thinks at last, at last, he hears the familiar step again.
>
> (p. 65)

Raoul experienced this 'grand moment' when whiling away the time in his favourite café: 'There! it had come—the moment—the *geste!* And although I was so ready, it caught me, it tumbled me over; I was simply overwhelmed' (p. 64). The 'moment'—brief, intense, overpowering—belongs to the Romantic tradition of revelatory instants. And the self-doubt which precedes it, as well as the way it is triggered by a trivial and contingent circumstance—a 'stupid, stale little phrase: *Je ne parle pas français*' (p. 64) jotted down on a writing-pad—also give it the thumbprint of the revelatory instant.

Yet this tradition too is subverted. Raoul's experience leaves him with a sense of agony rather than any feeling of inspiration, and has been set off moreover by a phrase which is associated for him with the young Englishwoman, whose catchphrase it has become. And she—alone in a foreign capital and deserted by her boyfriend in humiliating circumstances—is also let down later by Raoul himself. So the phrase which triggers Raoul's epiphany becomes linked with Mouse's vulnerability: the narrator has got his 'buzz' from a perverted sense of gratification at the way he has humiliated an apparently helpless woman. Mansfield's delineation may well owe something to the classic Modernist version of the visionary 'moment', Stephen Dedalus' strandside epiphany from Chapter 4 of Joyce's *Portrait of the Artist as a Young Man*, which more subtly undermines its hero's experience.

Raoul's partial repression of his childhood memories has led to the creation of his own 'submerged' psychical world. In logic this would seem to refer back beyond his experiences with his 'sugar-mother', the laundress, to his real mother. But the text remains dark on all aspects of his relationship with his family.

We have already seen how Mansfield uses Raoul to destabilise old certitudes regarding the fixed, and unitary, nature of the self. She also does this by lining up pairs of characters whose individual identities blur or overlap in a fashion reminiscent of Dostoevsky's in his great novels.

Much of **'Je Ne Parle Pas Français'** revolves around signifiers of 'Frenchness' and 'Englishness'. At first glance these seem to be clearly differentiated—and opposed. Raoul, for example, makes frequent allusions both to his own Frenchness and to the Englishness of Dick and Mouse. And Frenchness—the Self as regards the angle of narration in the story but in moral terms the Other—is associated with corruption; Englishness with innocence. The connection is reinforced by a cutting indictment of the French and their sexual mores, inscribed by Mansfield at the head of the notebook containing the first part of the draft of **'Je Ne Parle Pas Français'**:

> But Lord! Lord! how I do hate the French. With them it is always rutting time. See them come dancing and sniffing round a woman's skirt.

> Mademoiselle complains that she has the *pieds glacés*.
>
> 'Then why do you wear such pretty stockings and shoes, Mademoiselle?' leers Monsieur.
>
> 'Eh—oh là—c'est la mode!'
>
> And the fool grins well content with the idiot answer.

However, the text's national associations—especially those which relate to Raoul and Dick—do in fact blur or overlap; a sly indication incidentally of the falseness of the narrator's wholly 'experiential' conception of the self. Raoul has an English writing-table and an English overcoat, and Dick's letter to Mouse is couched in a French that is perhaps 'a shade too French' (p. 74). They are also proficient in each other's languages, and each has a mutual interest in the literature of the other. And seeing Dick for the first time at a literary party Raoul makes enquiries about who he is. He then describes himself in a kind of echo of the response—as if the two of them were indeed *alter egos*:

> 'Who is he?'
>
> 'An Englishman. From London. A writer. And he is making a special study of modern French literature.'
>
> That was enough for me. My little book, *False Coins*, had just been published. I was a young, serious writer who was making a special study of modern English literature.
>
> (p. 71)

The overlap in identities does not end here. Dick's own hapless devotion to his mother is paralleled in the way Raoul's personality has been warped by his own relations with his 'sugar-mother' the laundress. Mouse's declaration 'Je ne parle pas français', which gives both title and *leitmotif* to the story, consists of the first words she speaks to Raoul. As has already been mentioned, it is on account of them that he experiences his ironically named 'grand moment'—itself a semantically exact but imprecise translation of the (inauthentic) French '*le grand moment*': something which itself illustrates the perils of literary interchange. They also turn out to be her final words to Raoul, made after Dick's desertion of her. However, the claim of ignorance in the tag-phrase—which is itself a kind of self-contradiction anyway—is denied by her lover:

> she said, wringing my hand (I'm sure she didn't know it was mine), *je ne parle pas Français*.
>
> 'But I'm sure you do,' I answered, so tender, so reassuring, I might have been a dentist about to draw her first little milk tooth.
>
> 'Of course she does,' Dick swerved back to us.
>
> (p. 78)

And there must be at least a presumption that when Mouse speaks to the *garçon* at the hotel she does so in French.

So the phrase which at first seems to encapsulate Mouse's vulnerability may in fact be evidence of her wary shrewdness—and of her wish to dissociate herself from those attitudes which are signified in the story by 'Frenchness'. Certainly there is little objective evidence for her helplessness: here as elsewhere it is Raoul's assumptions which govern the reader's view.

Just as there is a blending and blurring of Raoul's *national* identity with that of his friend Dick, so there is a corresponding overlap of his sexual and gender characteristics with those of Mouse.[13] His description of himself is laced with indications of femininity:

> I am little and light with an olive skin, black eyes with long lashes, black silky hair cut short, tiny square teeth that show when I smile. My hands are small and supple. A woman in a bread shop once said to me: 'You have the hands for making fine pastries.' I confess, without my clothes I am rather charming. Plump, almost like a girl, with smooth shoulders, and I wear a thin gold bracelet above my left elbow.
>
> (p. 68)

He identifies on occasion with the way he assumes a woman might feel (see e.g. page 73). And he shows a marked sexual attraction towards Dick. Conversely Mouse is associated with boyishness (pp. 78, 90). The link between the two characters is suggested in the image of the butterfly which Raoul connects, first with himself—in a context which invokes notions of role-play and dragdressing, and which therefore points again to the notion of gender as a social artificial construct—and then with Mouse. The image suggests innocence and vulnerability, but also a transformation of identity that is akin to metamorphosis—at one and the same time more natural, and more mysterious, than any Raoul himself could have conceived of:

> I wore a blue kimono embroidered with white birds and my hair was still wet; it lay on my forehead, wet and gleaming.
>
> 'Portrait of Madame Butterfly,' said I, 'on hearing of the arrival of *ce cher Pinkerton.*'
>
> (p. 74)
>
> Mouse . . . came upon you with the same kind of shock that you feel when you have been drinking out of a thin innocent cup and suddenly, at the bottom, you see a tiny creature, half butterfly, half woman. . . .
>
> (p. 80)

This overlapping of identities serves to emphasise Raoul's complex role in the story: like Mouse he is (or fancies himself to have been) deserted, and hence humiliated, by Dick. Here rests one of the burdens of the Madame Butterfly image. And like Dick too, Raoul humiliates Mouse—or at least imagines himself to have humiliated her. So he becomes an *alter ego* of both the other key participants in the drama.

This blurring of identities serves the story's concern to render the modern condition as one of exile: to this end, the literal exile of Mouse and Dick blends with the metaphoric exiles of Raoul (the artist's and the city-dweller's alienation, and the individual's traumatic severance from his own first family) to suggest the multiple estrangements of the modern self.

The tale itself must, however, remain suspect because of doubts over Raoul's veracity . . . as well of course as his judgement. And even its medium remains uncertain: are we to regard this as English, the language both of its author and of the apparently innocent Mouse, or the corrupting French of the narrator Raoul? We have already seen that there are doubts regarding Mouse's own protestations of linguistic incompetence: even she may not be as innocent as she appears.

One further doubt resides, disconcertingly, in the possibility that Raoul himself may be neither as corrupted nor as dangerous as he wishes to believe. There is even evidence both at the beginning of the story and in a lyrical fantasy-passage towards the end, where he finally does perhaps speak candidly, that he himself hankers over Mouse . . . despite (or possibly because of) his own spurning of her. Teasingly the story also entertains the possibility that his deception of Mouse occupied a far larger place in his own unconfident mind than it did in the undisclosed thoughts and preoccupations of Mouse herself; indeed that she is less vulnerable than Raoul believes. Though distressed at Dick's flight, for example, she remains reasonably composed in the face of it. And Raoul is also very far from being able to pin her down as a character: in this respect as well she remains undefeated.

'A Married Man's Story', begun shortly after **'Je Ne Parle Pas Français',** reads like a re-visioning of the earlier work but one which attempts to go beyond the barrier of the central character's repressions. It too offers a portrait of a man whose personality has been warped by a childhood trauma he has undergone, and its subsequent repression. In this case the trauma is a youthful memory—or just possibly an imagined memory, or dream—of the Married Man's mother telling him just before she died that his father had poisoned her. This has affected the man's own family life to the extent that he has become unable to relate to his own wife and child.

But there is a signal difference between the two tales. Where Raoul Duquette attempted to 'bury' his childhood (p. 67) the Married Man, confessing to a fondness for 'débris' (p. 426), burrows resolutely back into his past in the hope of discovering his own buried self—in particular the reason for his present behaviour towards his wife and son:

> But really to explain what happened then I should have to go back and back—I should have to dwindle until

my two hands clutched the banisters, the stair-rail was higher than my head, and I peered through to watch my father padding softly up and down.

(p. 430)

In keeping with Mansfield's developing conception of character as consciousness, the story privileges memory and its contents: as the narrator himself asks, 'Who am I, in fact, as I sit here at this table, but my own past?' (p. 434). The task for him of course is to reach that aspect of his past which has been repressed, and in so doing to get at the truth about himself and his psychological complexities—the implication presumably being that these may then be able to be healed. The tale shows him dedicating himself to this task: where Raoul repeatedly faces us with the darkness of his own repressions the Married Man is resolute in his determination to uncover his past. And as Mansfield is in these tales affirming a relationship between the moral integrity of a writer and the quality of his (or her) work it is entirely appropriate that the Married Man with his dedication should not be subject to the same imputation of third-rateness as Raoul.

Outwardly at least the Married Man also belongs to a more orthodox set-up than his predecessor. In place of Raoul's roving street-life and undisclosed family background we now have someone whose family is 'known', who is a 'family man' himself, and who in the opening scene of his story is placed within a setting of apparently idyllic familial contentment.

Yet, as so often in Mansfield, this appearance of normality is an illusion. The hero, younger at the time of his trauma than Raoul and therefore perhaps more deeply affected by it, is soon shown to be someone apparently without the capacity for feeling; critically unable to relate either to his wife or to their child—of whom he admits, '"I've never accepted him as ours"' (p. 422). Images of dehumanisation and imprisonment thread through his story, contributing to the portrait of him as an emotionally embattled figure. In a haunting image of personal alienation, he compares himself for instance to the 'children who are suckled by wolves and accepted by the tribe, and [who afterwards] move freely among their fleet, grey brothers' (p. 428). Images of imprisonment also figure prominently: he dreams that his family 'were living inside one of [his] father's big coloured bottles' (p. 430) (his father was a chemist), and he confesses to feeling that he himself spent most of his childhood 'like a plant in a cupboard' (p. 432). A fourth image combines hints of dehumanisation and entrapment with an indication that he occupies the victim-position. When he finds a dead bird that his schoolmates have planted in his pocket he identifies it with himself: 'I looked at the dead bird again. . . . And that is the first time that I remember singing—rather . . . listening to a silent voice inside a little cage that was

me' (p. 433). (As I noted in my comments on **'The Canary'**, a story written shortly afterwards, Mansfield frequently applies the 'caged bird' image to herself.)

At school the narrator is nicknamed Gregory Powder. This is a reference to a popular contemporary remedy for constipation—hence of course to the narrator's own emotional blockage. And at his mother's funeral he himself sees his father as a bottle of poison:

'That tall hat so gleaming black and round was like a cork covered with black sealing-wax, and the rest of my father was awfully like a bottle, with his face for the label—*Deadly Poison*. It flashed into my mind as I stood opposite him in the hall. And Deadly Poison, or old D.P., was my private name for him from that day.'

(p. 435)

G. P. is of course son of D. P.—a further, ominous indication that in the absence of self-understanding the son is doomed to follow in his father's footsteps.

When his story opens the Narrator is settled at his writing-table—strategically placed so as to enable him to look out over 'his' domain of the sitting-room. Soon, however, sense-impressions trigger his writer's imagination: it is raining outside, and the sound of the rain leads him out-of-doors as it were and through a series of imagined romantic landscapes. His description of this journey, with its eightfold repetition of the Cartesian 'I am' ('I am here, I am there', 'I am arriving', 'I am conscious of' [p. 423, etc.]) is a Modernist attempt to represent the consciousness, not as some Cartesian prison but as a creative interaction between the mind and the external world. At the same time the Man's efforts to guess at the feelings of his wife and son illustrate a belief in the basically self-enclosed, and self-regarding, nature of the human consciousness. He himself, however—like Mansfield in a famous *Journal* passage envisaging the self as a dual entity composed of multiple superficial sense-impressions and a unified spiritual aspect[14]—soon disregards his own sense-impressions in favour of more inward, and more inspiriting, evidence of his creative powers:

Aren't those just the signs, the traces of my feeling? The bright green streaks made by someone who walks over the dewy grass? Not the feeling itself. And as I think that a mournful, glorious voice begins to sing in my bosom. Yes, perhaps that is nearer what I mean. What a voice! What power! What velvety softness! Marvellous!

(p. 424)

Locked inside the narrator's mind is another formative childhood memory—that of a night-time embrace from one of his father's 'fancy women'. Her sensuous charm triggers a later dream—figured as the bringing to the surface of buried psychical material—in which she is both a focus for his desire and the censurer of it:

> I dreamed she came again—again she drew me to her, something soft, scented, warm and merry hung over me like a cloud. But when I tried to see, her eyes only mocked me, her red lips opened and she hissed, 'Little sneak! Little sneak!' But not as if she were angry,—as if she understood, and her smile somehow was like a rat—hateful!
>
> (p. 436)

Even more disturbingly this dream, which is related in the text to the circumstances of the narrator's mother's death, appears to trigger in him a kind of spiritual rejuvenation—pointed up by suggestions of germination and of renewed vision:

> the shrivelled case of the bud split and fell, the plant in the cupboard came into flower. 'Who am I?' I thought. 'What is all this?' And I looked at my room, at the broken bust of the man called Hahnemann on top of the cupboard, at my little bed with the pillow like an envelope. I saw it all, but not as I had seen before. . . . Everything lived, everything.
>
> (p. 437)

Hahnemann was the founder of homoeopathic medicine, and therefore an appropriate figure to find commemorated (or rejected) in the house of a chemist. But it may also be relevant that a literal translation of the name 'Hahnemann' is 'Cocksman'[15]—something which recalls the Duquette—*quéquette* association made in '**Je Ne Parle Pas Français**,' and which appears to imply that the narrator's earlier feelings of sexual inadequacy are at issue here as well.

The text as we have it ends, however, not with any visionary insight but with a reference—enigmatic but unmistakably ominous—to the narrator turning towards his 'silent brothers' (p. 437). His final return to the human community appears to remain in doubt. The implication in the story as we have it must be that he will himself follow in his father's footsteps. The structure of his own family (father, mother, small son) replicates the one in which he grew up. He himself contributed by his taxing birth to his mother's death. He even confesses to having wished he were his father; to having copied his father's sneer and having lain in the foetal position staring at his father until his image 'remained solid in [his] memory' (p. 431). (It should be noted that the father is to the son's gaze habitually bisected by the shop-counter—another ironic hint at the duality of consciousness.) Even more incriminating, in view of the fact that the death was caused by poisoning, the narrator confesses to knowing the 'mixture'. And it is perhaps prophetic that his wife's and son's present existence should be invaded by an image of instability: he watches from his table as 'her shadow—an immense *Mother and Child*—is here and gone again upon the wall . . .' (p. 423). But as the story was never finished we do not know for sure whether the Married Man's interrogation of himself would have enabled him to break with the destiny which appears to be his.

What is certain is that '**Je Ne Parle Pas Français**' and '**A Married Man's Story**'—experimental in form; radical, even dangerous, in content—marked a new and exciting departure in Mansfield's writing. Yet she wrote nothing else like them, going on instead to cultivate a double discourse which would allow her to cloak the taboo, or repressed, aspects of human character beneath an impeccable surface lyricism. However, the experience she gained in moving from the repressions of a figure like the semi-fictionalised *German Pension* Narrator to those of her key characters—which she was able to confront directly—undoubtedly contributed to the skill and sympathetic understanding with which she worked the subtexts of her later family stories.

Notes

1. Letter to J. M. Murry, 23 and 24 May 1918 [*The Collected Letters of Katherine Mansfield*, ed. Vincent O'Sullivan and Margaret Scott, Oxford, 1984-1993]; ibid., II, p. 188.

2. In his edition of the *Stories*, [*The Stories of Katherine Mansfield*, ed. Antony Alpers, Oxford, 1984], pp. 571-2, Alpers suggests—contrary to an earlier view—that 'A Married Man's Story' was 'wholly written . . . in late August 1921': see also the *Life*, [*The Life of Katherine Mansfield*. New York, 1980], p. 340n.

3. See e.g. her letter to Murry, *Collected Letters*, op. cit., I, pp. 125-6, ?May-June 1913.

4. [John Middleton Murry], *Between Two Worlds*, London, 1935, p. 464.

5. Mansfield recorded in a *Journal* entry for 1921, 'March 9 "I chucked the thing behind the fireplace. It wasn't even clever." Mr. Harold Beauchamp on *Je ne parle pas français*' ([*Journal of Katherine Mansfield*, ed. John Middleton Murry, London, 1954], p. 240).

6. Letter to Murry, 10 February 1918; *Collected Letters*, op. cit., II, p. 66.

7. April 1920.

8. 'Katherine Mansfield'; 1920, p. 274.

9. The story was printed unexpurgated in *The Stories of Katherine Mansfield*, ed. Antony Alpers, op. cit., Auckland and London, 1984. The most significant of the restored passages are to be found on pp. 281 (sentence beginning, 'And then with a soft growl . . .') and 299 (last four lines).

10. Letter to Murry, 6 April 1920; *Collected Letters*, op. cit., III, p. 273.

11. Antony Alpers ed., *The Stories of Katherine Mansfield*, op. cit., p. 281.

12. Middleton Murry was the first to compare 'Je Ne Parle Pas Français' with *Notes from Underground*: 'my sensation is like that which I had when I read

Dostoyevsky's *Letters from the Underworld*. . . . It's utterly unlike any sensation I have ever yet had from any writing of yours, or any writing at all except Dostoyevsky's.' (*Between Two Worlds,* op. cit., p. 464). Saralyn R. Daly, *Katherine Mansfield,* New York, 1965, pp. 73-4, highlights the similarities in characterisation and structure between the two works.

13. See C. A. Hankin, *Katherine Mansfield and Her Confessional Stories,* [New York, 1983], pp. 160-1, for a discussion of the literary relations between Raoul Duquette and Mouse.

14. See *Journal of Katherine Mansfield,* op. cit., p. 205.

15. See Alex Calder, 'My Katherine Mansfield'; *Landfall,* 172 (December 1989), p. 494; article reprinted in *In from the Margin,* ed. Roger Robinson, Louisiana, 1994, pp. 119-36. The figure of Hahnemann was first identified by Antony Alpers in his *Stories of Katherine Mansfield,* op. cit., p. 572.

Jayne Marek (essay date 1998)

SOURCE: Marek, Jayne. "Anxious Narrations: Katherine Mansfield's *In a German Pension.*" *LIT: Literature Interpretation Theory* 8 nos. 3-4 (1998): 279-93.

[*In the following essay, Marek puts forth a feminist narratological reading of* In a German Pension, *noting how Mansfield's "satiric rhetoric" and disruptions in the texts create tension and "a persistent tone of anxiety" in the stories.*]

As intersections between narrative sequence, gender, sexuality, and readerly or spectatorial "desire" have in recent decades altered the trajectory of critical discussion about narrative structures, such intersections might well have included anxiety, for "desire" is another way of naming the anxious energies caused by disruption of the human organism's homeostasis, according to classical psychoanalysis. Freudian theory presumes that the ego necessarily develops in reaction to the pain of reality: the ego appears as an effect of the mind's vacillation between stasis and stimulation (Fischer 12). Taken cumulatively, the channelling of redirected energies caused by human anxieties is responsible for the creation of culture (Fischer 19). Satire, used as a rhetorical and structural device, is an obvious choice for expressing anxiety in literature; highlighting "the way things are" with a pointed humor that suggests "the way things could be" enacts a compromise between drives and sanctions that defends the individual as well as expresses her or his discomfort. When satire explicitly foregrounds issues of sexuality, gender, and social class—such as in the case of Katherine Mansfield's first book of stories, *In a German Pension* (1911)—feminist narratological analysis can help identify the textual disruptions that link the anxieties of an implied author with her or his chosen modalities of discourse.

The elements of local color in ***In a German Pension*** were drawn from Mansfield's trip to Germany late in 1909. She had recently returned to England after an eighteen-month stay in her native New Zealand, but her return did not accord her the freedom to write as she had hoped. Her poverty and an unhappy affair produced a crisis—pregnancy—which Mansfield tried to solve by marrying another man. The solution failed; she left him the next day.[1] Her mother came to England to investigate, insisted that her daughter go abroad to conceal the pregnancy, and attempted to break up Mansfield's "unhealthy" friendship with a school friend, Ida Baker; upon returning home, Mansfield's mother cut her daughter out of her will (Tomalin 67-68). Therefore, along with the anxieties surrounding her pregnancy and the subsequent miscarriage, Mansfield was faced with the emotional pain of losing friendships and family ties, and of having her sexuality—including her relationships with women—held up as a reason for shame.

During her stay in Germany, Mansfield began writing the stories which, in their contents and style, reflect her turmoil as well as the cynicism which was her defense against adversity.[2] Upon her return to London, she took a packet of stories to *The New Age* which printed **"The Child-Who-Was-Tired"** in February 1910, launching Mansfield's career.[3] *New Age* editor A. R. Orage asked for more; the resulting succession of stories were gathered together and published in 1911, when Mansfield was 23. The narrative techniques Mansfield employs show a strong current of anxiety that goes farther than the traditional satiric aim of pointing out social features in need of change. The fact that almost no other evidence remains of those years of Mansfield's life makes the emotional and artistic dynamics of these stories much more intriguing.[4]

This book makes its satiric agenda clear through its premise: in most of the stories, a young Englishwoman staying at a resort in Bavaria engages in critical observations of the people around her, highlighting the disparities between superficial social roles and their underlying delusions. Mansfield manipulates the narrator's ironic distance through a combination of direct speech, indirect discourse, and interior monologue. While the first stories generally develop via humorous direct speech countered by the narrator's mocking internal comments, the tone darkens by the fifth story, related in indirect discourse, which shows a village woman's unhappy home life. The young female narrator appears irregularly thereafter as the book alternates between the comic vignettes she relates, which parody human self-deception, and the more serious stories, which present domestic and sexual oppression. Moving between serious and satiric statements, between first-person and third-person narration, Mansfield destabilizes readers' expectations through an ironic narrative oscillation linked to depictions of women trapped by restricted gender roles or by female biology, creating tension and a persistent tone of anxiety that points to the significance of Mansfield's discourse strategies.

Feminist narratology has identified the *context* of storytelling as crucial to critical discussion of writing by women—that is, "how stories are told, by whom, and for whom" are aspects of narrative positionality strongly affected by gender issues (Mezei 1). Feminist narratology, "the study of narrative structures and strategies in the context of cultural constructions of gender" (Warhol 21), can include analysis of the effects of psychological factors both within the text (as part of the "story" structures) and upon the author (as suggested by "discourse" strategies). Mansfield's satiric rhetoric in *In a German Pension* contrasts various kinds of private commentaries with "polite" public discourses, a contrast that suggests both the psychological interactions of desire, anxiety, and repression and the dynamics between expression and ellipsis that often mark women's fiction.

Even as the interplay of discourses provides much of the humor of the book—expressing some themes while suppressing or disguising others—this interplay also problematizes the narrator's position by calling attention to what Denise Delorey terms a "strategic focus on the parenthetical as a feminist narrative principle" (94). The narrator's use of interior commentary symbolically enacts interruption and independence by reclaiming her presumably devalued personal space, even as her deliberate pretense of misunderstanding her interlocutors is one of her chief defenses, enacting a kind of containment over her situation. This use of parenthetical space, or "aperture" as Delorey terms it, undermines the other characters' social discourse structures and signals a stratum of authorial anxiety via the use of omissions and deflections.

Kathy Mezei notes that "feminist narratology locates and deconstructs sites of ambiguity, indeterminacy, and transgression in aspects of narrative and in the sexuality and gender of author, narrator, character, and reader" (2). One of these aspects of ambiguity concerns the interplay between recognition and critique of societal role expectations, a tension which becomes particularly clear when narrative structures betray anxiety at several levels of discourse and resolution cannot be achieved. At levels that are not specifically verbal—for instance, the use of "the gaze" or "looking"—and at levels that evade social niceties—for instance, parenthetical responses—Mansfield's prose enacts a confrontation with and evasion of particular kinds of dominating discourse as well as of readers' expectations. At times Mansfield's text also demonstrates a tactic used by Virginia Woolf, that of setting material apart from the regular narrative by brackets or by other punctuation, in order to convey crucial information (Delorey 106).

The narrator herself is an outsider, an ironic reinforcement of a major characteristic of the narrative progression: when she challenges the status quo, she is usually misunderstood or ignored; her interlocutors go right on with what they were saying, allowing her disruptive assertions to stand as legitimate responses despite their subversive intent. These stories carry repressed or subverted stories within them which sometimes reinforce and sometimes evade the obvious purposes of Mansfield's satire. The characters' tendency to gossip, a specific aspect of the setting of these tales, is depicted through Mansfield's ironic appropriation of the codes of polite discourse, including "agentless" expressions, "honorifics, thanks, face-saving requests, compliments," and "modalities" like "naturally" and "of course" which point to an established social order (Giltrow 216). As well, the "gendered subjectivity" constructed in Mansfield's stories is problematized by a shifting focalization, at times empathetic to, at times critical of, the figures of young women. This sort of destabilization is echoed in the language of narration, whether embodied by the young female narrator or the indirect discourse of the agentless stories—e.g., those lacking an involved character as narrator (Prince 4). Privately qualifying what is said, amplifying and contradicting, and parrying suggestive verbal thrusts are all characteristic of the speech acts found here. These illusions of communication and violations of complete sentences signal that parenthetical remarks may also violate "a fixed, prefigured, and textual structure and, by extension, an overdetermined social structure," an observation that is often helpful when reading women's writing and that is especially useful when considering Mansfield's sharp-edged take on social conventions (Delorey 105).

In these ways, Mansfield's story structures demonstrate resistant subtexts that arise against the iterations of patriarchal ideology. This style of "simultaneous refusal of, yet submission to, femininity as it is constructed under patriarchy, [in effect depicting] woman's enactment of herself as a lesser male," which some critics find characteristic of women's writings, leads Ruth Parkin-Gounelas to conclude that the stories of *In a German Pension* "represent, on one level, a major attempt to conform to rigorous masculine standards" (45). However, the oscillations of Mansfield's narration, in what Parkin-Gounelas herself calls "a series of evasions of a stable subject position" (44), enact the play of signification not only as an important aspect of the satire but as a marker of anxiety in the implied author, whatever her aspirations may be in terms of accepted literary standards. Such stylistic ruptures are a clear narratological indicator of the most important themes in the book.

Throughout this collection, the unifying thread is spun of three anxiety-producing topics: being friendless among strangers, being a woman in a militantly patriarchal society, and being in danger of motherhood. These themes link to Mansfield's ongoing explorations of "experiences of consciousness within a woman's body: pregnancy and labor, fears of rape, disgust with female submission" (Kaplan 137). Although the Englishwoman does not narrate all of the stories, the anxieties her discourse reveals underlie every major conflict in the book. Some of the rhetoric that points to these anxieties is obvious: for example, the spa owner's remark that "We are such a happy family since my dear man died" (26) and the narrator's mockery of the language of love poetry, in which kissing "close pressed" to her suggests "wardrobes" (23). Mansfield's pattern of narrative markers, however, also complicates and problematizes issues of point-of-view, both in terms of "looking" and of interpretation, which are significant because of the thematic emphasis on self-delusion and undercurrents of sexual anxiety.

These themes unite at once in the first story, **"Germans at Meat,"** which introduces the narrative persona, a young, supposedly married Englishwoman "taking the cure" in Germany alone. She is criticized, as representative of the English, by the German guests, although psychologically she parries them and asserts herself through sarcastic asides about their indelicate habits and foolish aspirations, and what one might call "family values":

> "[You] never have large families in England now; I suppose you are too busy with your suffragetting. Now I have had nine children, and they are all alive, thank God. Fine, healthy babies—though after the first one was born I had to—"
>
> "How *wonderful!*" I cried.
>
> "Wonderful," said the Widow contemptuously . . . "Not at all! A friend of mine had four at the same time. Her husband was so pleased he gave a supper-party and had them placed on the table. Of course she was very proud."
>
> "Germany," boomed the Traveller, biting round a potato which he had speared with his knife, "is the home of the Family."
>
> Followed an appreciative silence.
>
> (16-17)

Besides the link Mansfield draws between the babies and the meal, shocking the reader with the hint of cannibalism, there is a persistent undertone concerning women's "proper" roles, both sexually and politically. In fact, when Herr Rat makes a joke about the British eating the teapot, he looks at the narrator "with an expression which suggested a thousand premeditated invasions"—and since he is known for sexual boasting, one can read Mansfield's rhetoric as carrying more than just military connotations.

Mansfield's satire mingles "amusement and contempt" (Highet 21-22) in a brisk, realistic style, creating what Joanne Trautmann Banks calls a set of "impersonations—quick, vivid, enacted presences":

> The Widow plucks a hairpin from her head and, before returning it, casually uses it to pick her teeth, all the while intoning axioms on the relation of vegetarianism, the English suffragettes, and fecundity. Herr Rat, blowing on his soup, alludes just as casually to his sexual experience, en masse, as it were . . . [The narrator's] stance of mild sarcasm and complete self-possession keeps the gluttons merely funny and in their place.
>
> (64)

In a milieu in which expected proprieties are being violated, the narrator's "self-possessed" observations—her evaluative acts of "looking"—become, as Robyn Warhol characterizes looking in Jane Austen's novels, "an alternative language, a means of communication without recourse to words" (23) which elicits visceral reactions on the narrator's part. Her body, in fact, "comes into the narrative foreground not just as the vehicle of looking . . . but also as the object of the gaze of other characters" (Warhol 23), a structure of reciprocity by which Mansfield's diegesis enacts the narrator's internal resistance to the activity around her. While the narrator's "look" becomes a token of alternative discourse, the reader's "look," on the other hand, perceives this displaced discourse as a signal pointing to certain elements of the story as anxiety-producing or anxiety-containing.

A persistent characteristic of the narrator is her deliberate squelching of the other guests' talk of unappetizing physical functions. The narrator interrupts to avoid hearing about the Traveller's gastric problems with sauerkraut and interrupts again to shut out descriptions of childbirth, both maneuvers which are repeated throughout the book under similar circumstances. By usurping control through censorship, the narrator judges the others from a position that is puritanical and, considering the implied author, hypocritical (Prince 42-43). The narrator's under- or unstated resistance combined with the grotesque humor of the other guests' actions betrays not only Mansfield's satiric intentions but also her concern with issues of sexuality, childbirth, family duties, "propriety," and women's strategies of silence.

In addition to her willingness to judge those around her while revealing very little about herself, the narrator refuses (despite an appearance of frankness) to take the reader entirely into her confidence. Banks points out that the narrator is "smug . . . telling us about herself . . . so that we can thoroughly believe in her . . . She is also protecting herself, of course" (65). Such control is less a sign of power than of anxiety; the narrator's situation is ambiguous, her internalized mockery a defense. Even from the first story, then, it is clear that the apparent self-assurance of this young female narrator is problematic. Her equivocal appropriation of narrative power is ironically clarified by later stories in which she does not appear and which demonstrate unrelievedly negative positions for women, although they also indicate the extremes to which women will go to try to achieve self-determination.

The fifth story, **"Frau Brechenmacher Attends a Wedding,"** is a stunning departure in both approach and tone from the previous four tales. This instance is the first in which there is no first-person narrator, and that change adds to the story's impact for there is no sardonic commentator to relieve the reader's perception of the main character's misery. The Frau herself seems only imperfectly to understand her situation; her internal comments, offset by her and her friends' remarks about the young bride's likely difficulties with her new husband, betray a simultaneous affirmation and denial that demonstrates Frau Brechenmacher's inability to see beyond traditional women's roles. As she walks home from the wedding, she recalls her own wedding night, but cannot specifically acknowledge the pain of her sexual initiation:

> [Suddenly] she remembered how they had come together the first night. Now they had five babies and twice as much money; *but—*
>
> "Na, what is it all for?" she muttered, and not until she had reached home and prepared a little supper of meat and bread for her man did she stop asking herself that silly question.
>
> (39)

Her husband, a conceited oaf, teases her with his own very different recollection—"Remember the night that we came home? You were an innocent one, you were"— while the wife parries with her only defense, verbal denials that Mansfield at once undercuts through indirect narration: "'Get along! Such a time ago I forget.' *Well she remembered*" (40, emphasis added). Despite the accumulation of indignities at her husband's hands which the story outlines—being forced to dress in the dark, to walk behind him, to give up her supper in order to take care of him—it is only when confronted with sex that Frau Brechenmacher briefly overcomes her customary self-sacrificing deference and asserts her anger, albeit briefly and ineffectually.

> But the little Frau seized the candle and went into the next room. The children were all soundly sleeping. She stripped the mattress off the baby's bed to see if he was still dry, then began unfastening her blouse and skirt.
>
> "Always the same," she said—"all over the world the same; but, God in heaven—but *stupid.*"
>
> Then even the memory of the wedding faded quite. She lay down on the bed and put her arm across her face like a child who expected to be hurt as Herr Brechenmacher lurched in.
>
> (40)

The structural conjunction of children, sex, and pain is underlined by the rupture in Frau Brechenmacher's private remarks; compelled to act out her role, she cannot quite articulate her anger and fear, her pity for herself as well as for the new bride, and her resentment of what seems to be the divine plan of making women's situations "all over the world the same." Mansfield's brilliant compression of these themes in the last sentence leaves an aperture in which sex is the unstated but overwhelming source of anxiety for women, linked in this instance less to childbirth than to masculine self-centeredness that segues directly into the brutality of rape.

Immediately following this grim portrayal comes **"The Modern Soul,"** in which the young female narrator returns, bringing some humorous relief after the unrelenting language of **"Frau Brechenmacher."** Mansfield continues to problematize women's attempts to free themselves from imposed roles by adding a twist to the narrator's interactions with another young female guest, an actress visiting with her mother. The actress, Sonia Godowska, claims to reject social restrictions and thus sounds at first interesting to the narrator; however, in her deliberately flamboyant pretensions, Sonia proves to be as silly as the other spa guests. Her unconventional expression of sexuality, though, adds a distinctive spin to this tale, allowing Mansfield to destabilize the narrator's self-assurance by forcing her into hypocritical appeals to the ideology of traditional women's roles as a way of ignoring the actress' expression of sexual autonomy. By upsetting the reader's expectations about the narrator, this destabilization points to another significant locus of anxiety in the implied author.

In this case, Mansfield's narrative strategy presents and then avoids the implications of Sonia's lesbianism, while the narrator hides her true opinions behind ambiguous speculations about the match she suggested between Sonia and another guest, the Herr Professor. The figure of Sonia is described with a marked lack of sympathy. At this point in her life, Mansfield herself had been worrying about her lesbian feelings (Tomalin 67); it is telling that in this story the narrator coldly refuses to recognize Sonia's advances, thus dismissing an opportunity for understanding, or at least kindness. The narrator's refusal to acknowledge a complex personality behind a social exterior indicates that, despite the high-handedness of her internal comments, she is unable to be honest with herself as well as with others. This aspect of the narrator's personality is another clear signal of anxiety indicated by omission and indirection surrounding the overt discourse.

The story begins with a conversation between the narrator and the Herr Professor. Sexual anxiety is initialized by the Professor's condescending, suggestive remarks about finding good cherries to eat. When the narrator refuses his offer of a cherry, he comments:

> "Psychologically I understand your refusal. It is your innate feminine delicacy in preferring etherealised sensations . . . Or perhaps you do not care to eat the worms. All cherries contain worms . . . [It] amounts to this: if one wishes to satisfy the desires of nature one must be strong enough to ignore the facts of nature . . . The conversation is not out of your depth?"
>
> (69)

Of course, his crudity is apparent to her; the narrator sarcastically remarks to herself that she is "grateful" for the Professor's attentions, "without showing undue excitement."

When the mother and daughter Godowska make their entrance, the Professor describes them to the narrator in patronizing terms: "The mother has an internal complaint and the daughter is an actress. Fraulein Sonia is a very modern soul . . . I have once described her in her autograph album as [a] tigress with a flower in the hair" (71-72). Sonia's own self-dramatization plays along with the role in which she has been cast; when she invites the narrator along on an evening walk, her confession of "Sapphism" is couched in language which makes it seem merely another pose and which allows the narrator to dismiss Sonia as easily as she has dismissed other people in what Sydney Janet Kaplan characterizes as "a symptomatic denial on Mansfield's part of her own lesbian experiences" (138):

> "What a night!" she said. "Do you know that poem of Sappho about her hands in the stars . . . I am furiously sapphic. And this is so remarkable—not only am I sapphic, I find in all the works of all the greatest writers, especially in the unedited letters, some touch, some sign of myself—some resemblance, some part of myself, like a thousand reflections of my own hands in a dark mirror."
>
> "But what a bother," said I.
>
> (82)

The narrator brushes off Sonia's advance in the same way that she has refused to listen to other examples of female sexual experience—the same way that she, in a later story, cuts off a young woman's enthusiasm for being engaged, expressed breathlessly as a desire "to give to everybody, to share everything," by remarking "How extremely dangerous" (94). Sonia's additional claim that living with her mother means living "with the coffin of my unborn aspirations" (49) draws no sympathy from the narrator, although Mansfield clearly intends it as an indication of the psychological need to dissociate from one's mother, a detail with a particular sting for Mansfield. When Sonia deliberately faints in response to these rebuffs, the narrator fetches Herr Professor rather than help Sonia "loosen her stays," as the narrator suggestively phrases it. The narrator's refusal to acknowledge Sonia's sexual communication, although she clearly received it, points to female sexual identity as a significant locus of anxiety: both lesbian and heterosexual advances are resisted by the narrator. Delorey's reminder that chastity is a means of maintaining female identity (102-03) is useful, considering Mansfield's portrayals of women who deny, distance themselves from, or misunderstand their sexuality. The point of the story is far more than just Fraulein Sonia's frustration that might lead her to "sell herself into the protection of a bourgeois marriage" (Kaplan 138); it rests on the rhetorical disparity between sexual outspokenness and the seemingly automatic repression and denial figured in the narrator's response.

Mansfield's mockery of so-called "modern women" is articulated against the female characters' repeated failures to recognize their own complicity in their oppression. The most striking section of the book, centered on the two stories **"A Birthday"** and **"The Child-Who-Was-Tired,"** reiterates the linkages of male self-aggrandizement, sexual exploitation, and the physical and psychological problems caused by women's designated roles. The former tale, the only one in which indirect narration takes a male's point of view, depicts villager Andreas Binzer as he talks himself into a frenzy at his own "suffering" while his wife is giving birth upstairs; his self-centeredness serves as an ironic complement to such stories as **Frau Brechenmacher Attends a Wedding."** Binzer's delusions of his own importance are satirized in the specific context of his participation in men's society—an "old boy's club" he plans to perpetuate through his son—and are satirized not only through his self-serving rhetoric but also through the indirect discourse that reveals both Binzer's and his friend Doctor Erb's critical thoughts about each other.

The latter story follows a day's tasks in the person of an abused and abandoned young girl forced into a life of hard labor as a servant. Her escape from the drudgery of work is a daydream she repeats to herself of "a little white road with tall black trees on either side, a little road that led to nowhere" (77). As the abuse escalates and her weariness increases, the Child, told once too often to silence the crying baby and knowing that another baby is on the way, suddenly has "a beautiful, marvellous idea" (85) and enacts it via a description that counterpoints her expected, compliant response with a combination of helplessness and violence:

> "One moment—he is almost asleep," she cried.

> And then gently, smiling, on tiptoe, she brought the pink bolster from the Frau's bed and covered the baby's face with it, pressed with all her might as he struggled, "like a duck with its head off, wriggling," she thought.
>
> She heaved a long sigh, then fell back on the floor, and was walking along a little white road with tall black trees on either side, a little road that led to nowhere, and where nobody walked at all—nobody at all.
>
> (86)

Even the fact that the Child-Who-Was-Tired has no given name suggests her anonymity, the ubiquity of her situation, and her unarticulated rage that erupts in the only available direction. Having acted out her experience of abuse onto a weaker person, the Child returns for comfort to her fairy-tale-like fantasy of a sterile, deathlike landscape, the childish language serving as euphemism for the stark emptiness of lower-class female life, the Child's unspeakable crime, and her inability to understand both what she has done and what was done to her. As the climactic point of the book, this tale—however much it may be traced to Chekhov—provides a center of anxiety toward which all the other stories' narrative strategies point.

Immediately following "The Child-Who-Was-Tired," Mansfield provides some release of tension by bringing back the sarcastic young narrator in "The Advanced Lady," which offers another caricature of a supposedly free-thinking woman whose polemic is no more than a rehash of the self-sacrificing "Angel in the House." Mansfield's irony is especially pointed given that readers have just seen how the Child-Who-Was-Tired tried to break free of the stranglehold of women's work. In this story, Mansfield lampoons "advanced" ideas of spiritual connections between humans, suggesting skepticism of both Freudian and Jungian theories of psychological development and motivation. Proffered by Mansfield's characters as "polite" conversation that also serves the purpose of social and sexual testing, the discourse of psychological speculation in "The Advanced Lady"—as in "Frau Fischer" and "The Modern Soul" earlier—demonstrates a complacent ability to delude oneself that the young woman narrator simultaneously mocks and perpetuates. This lack of self-understanding is reiterated in the final two tales, "A Swing of the Pendulum" and "A Blaze," in which the female leads are carefully described so that the reader, like the characters themselves, can never be sure how self-aware or self-deluded these characters are about the extent to which they exploit their sexuality while denying its power. Throughout the book, a prime feature of Mansfield's satire rests on her ironic manipulation of narrative discourses which reveal the characters' inability to free themselves from their roles or to articulate the true nature of the anxieties driving them.

The alternating viewpoints of these stories create, in effect, an intertextual commentary within the book that foregrounds the subtexts of the satiric tales told by the first-person narrator through comparison to the more serious misapprehensions and self-delusions in the other tales. This oscillation in point-of-view affords Mansfield space for textual play that clarifies the reasons for the young narrator's discomfort with gross physicality—particularly the entrapments of reproduction and female gender roles—enacting a psychodynamic of anxiety that, in the most powerful of these stories, demonstrates "a self-devouring anger that runs to bitterness," as Banks puts it (65). There is a recurrent refusal or inability to become intimately involved with other persons: the men seek to justify their own convenience and protect their pride, while the women and girls exercise far more pervasive self-deception in an attempt to cope with their sexual and economic exploitation. The humorous critique of the class system found in the stories **"The Baron"** and **"The Sister of the Baroness"** is given much darker significance by such stories as **"Frau Brechenmacher Attends a Wedding"** and **"A Birthday,"** which demonstrate the selfishness informing social custom and the folly of suppressing human reality for the sake of convenience.

In all these stories, Mansfield relentlessly condemns human self-delusion, even in her narrator, through narrative choices that seem to reflect the author's personal preoccupations with role-playing and self-dramatization (Parkin-Gounelas 44). Ruth Mantz believes that Mansfield, in writing these stories, presented herself as a "cynical realist" as "part of her plan for protective armour that she should achieve a reputation as one who, having seen through everything, was incapable of further disillusionment" (327). Mansfield's fictionalization of Germans in these stories shows the narrator's sense of inferiority draped in a presumption of superiority, coupled with coarse, condescending ridicule of specific social actions, as is common in the tradition of satire identified by Gilbert Highet (18-21, 233, 238, 240-41). As a New Zealand native looked down on as a "colonial" by "proper" English society, Mansfield, in satirizing her "foreign" characters, demonstrates the folly of approved social discourses and usurps the privilege of censure while symbolically evading it herself.

In a German Pension offers no real solutions to the dilemmas the characters face; the anxieties indicated by Mansfield's narrative strategies are not alleviated either by the characters' attempts at self-analysis or by the young woman narrator's sarcastic distancing. Mansfield's private anxieties about being judged for her sexuality, elliptically suggested in these writings, seem only to issue in cynicism or retreat; her narrative strategies, by the last story, have stopped developing. It should not be surprising that, despite the skill and humor of these early stories, Mansfield was reluctant to reprint this book because it represented, in effect, her response to a period of her life when the voices of self-assertion and of sanction were in clamorous conflict.[5] The disruptive discourses in these stories encode the limitations of social discourses, signifying the clash between individuals and oppressive systems of control, both of which are unable to alleviate—because they are unable to elucidate—their internal contradictions. As a signifier of anxiety in an implied author, Mansfield's narrative technique here clearly indicates a nexus of sexual and social issues that were of consuming importance in her life at the time.

By late 1911, Mansfield was moving away from the sharp tone of the **Pension** stories, beginning to work instead on the first of her New Zealand stories which attempted to restructure—not reject—her colonial heritage and sexual background. Having gained acceptance in English literary circles, Mansfield was ready to move into more finely conceived examinations of her personal and social themes. Feminist narratological analysis reveals the extent of Mansfield's youthful skill as a writer—and her influence as an early modernist—in confronting and "querying subject positions, cultural formation, the laws of genre, and the universality and stability of narrative forms" (Mezei 5). The early satiric exercises of *In a German Pension* prepared Mansfield's skills for the delicacies of narrative irony in her later work, now recognized as one of the great *oeuvres* of short stories in English literature.

Notes

1. "Her inward turmoil was extreme. She found that the experience for which she hungered was shattering. It did not, as she believed it would, issue in self-expression. She was discovering that she could not have life on terms of her own, even when those terms were by no means prudential. Dimly, at the back of her mind, was the purpose of sacrificing herself to life to enrich her art. She would have the experience to express. But Life cannot be managed in that way." Ruth Elvish Mantz and J. Middleton Murry, *The Life of Katherine Mansfield* (London: Constable, 1933) 318. See also Claire Tomalin's explanation of this sequence of events, in *Katherine Mansfield: A Secret Life* (New York: Knopf, 1988) 62-65.

2. Mantz 322, 325. Despite the months of uncertainty, poverty, and fear which Mansfield had endured, Claire Tomalin claims that Mansfield was not particularly upset at being sent to stay in Germany, viewing it as a chance for new experience (69).

3. This story has been shown to be, if not plagiarized, then "remembered" from Chekhov, whom Mansfield had been reading; see Tomalin 79-80.

4. "Introduction," *The Collected Letters of Katherine Mansfield, Vol. 1: 1903-1917*, ed. Vincent O'Sullivan and Margaret Scott (Oxford: Clarendon, 1984) xiii.

5. Mansfield refused to allow the reprinting of *In a German Pension* during the First World War, and although Murry claimed in his introduction to the 1926 Knopf reprint that her refusal represented both a repudiation of the artistic immaturity of that work and a distaste for benefitting personally from English hatred for Germany, such a claim exemplifies Murry's whitewashing of Mansfield's character after her death; the more likely reasons include her fear that the plagiarized story would be discovered and her desire to move beyond the anxieties of her personal life that these stories represent; "Introductory Note," *In a German Pension* 8. Banks also comments that, to Mansfield, the German stories came to represent "clever but trivial juvenilia" (66).

Works Cited

Banks, Joanne Trautmann. "Virginia Woolf and Katherine Mansfield." *The English Short Story 1880-1945: A Critical History*. Ed. Joseph M. Flora. Boston: Twayne, 1985.

Delorey, Denise. "Parsing the Female Sentence: The Paradox of Containment in Virginia Woolf's Narratives." Mezei 93-108.

Fischer, William F. *Theories of Anxiety*. New York: Harper and Row, 1970.

Giltrow, Janet. "Ironies of Politeness in Anita Brookner's *Hotel du Lac*." Mezei 215-37.

Highet, Gilbert. *The Anatomy of Satire*. Princeton: Princeton UP, 1962.

Kaplan, Sydney Janet. *Katherine Mansfield and the Origins of Modernist Fiction*. Ithaca: Cornell UP, 1991.

Mansfield, Katherine. *In a German Pension*. 1911. Harmondsworth: Penguin, 1983.

———. *The Collected Letters of Katherine Mansfield, Vol. 1: 1903-1917*. Ed. Vincent O'Sullivan and Margaret Scott. Oxford: Clarendon, 1984.

Mantz, Ruth Elvish, and J. Middleton Murry. *The Life of Katherine Mansfield*. London: Constable, 1933.

Mezei, Kathy. "Introduction: Contextualizing Feminist Narratology." *Ambiguous Discourse: Feminist Narratology and British Women Writers*. Ed. Kathy Mezei. Chapel Hill: U of North Carolina P, 1996. 1-20.

———. "Who Is Speaking Here? Free Indirect Discourse, Gender, and Authority in *Emma*." Mezei 66-92.

Parkin-Gounelas, Ruth. "Katherine Mansfield Reading Other Women: The Personality of the Text." *Katherine Mansfield: In from the Margin*. Ed. Roger Robinson. Baton Rouge: Louisiana State UP, 1994. 36-52.

Prince, Gerald. *A Dictionary of Narratology.* Lincoln: U of Nebraska P, 1987.

Tomalin, Claire. *Katherine Mansfield: A Secret Life.* New York: Knopf, 1988.

Warhol, Robyn. "The Look, the Body, and the Heroine of *Persuasion*: A Feminist-Narratological View of Jane Austen." Mezei 21-39.

Katherine Murphy Dickson (essay date 1998)

SOURCE: Dickson, Katherine Murphy. "Reality: A Unity." In *Katherine Mansfield's New Zealand Stories*, pp. 49-66. Lanham, Md.: University Press of America, Inc., 1998.

[*In the following essay, Dickson explicates the theme of death and destruction and the numerous instances of death imagery in Mansfield's stories "The Stranger," "Sun and Moon," and "At the Bay."*]

THE REALITY OF DARKNESS

In **"The Stranger," "Sun and Moon,"** and **"At the Bay,"** destruction, from which the characters try to escape, is reality. Each character builds up his defenses against it and the more desperately he does so, the more triumphantly death overwhelms him. The fortifications against death and corruption are torn away; the character is left naked in the face of reality and able only to utter his cry against it. In **"At the Bay,"** Stanley's early morning swim is ruined by Jonathan's presence (p. 103). Then Stanley's breakfast is spoiled because Beryl forgot the sugar for his tea (p. 104); not being able to find his hat and walking stick, he begins a day which is pure Hell (p. 132). He tortures himself all day for not saying goodbye to Linda, and when he discovers that she has been unaware of his intention to punish her or even of his neglect to say goodbye in the morning, he is hurt again. His homecoming, at which he had hoped to find forgiveness, is spoiled. Just as Stanley's swim in the morning has been spoiled, so was Jonathan's—he'd stayed in the water too long (p. 104). Not leaving the water sooner is the beginning of Jonathan's day, during which he is always late. He is late coming to pick up his two children (p. 128). He stays to talk with Linda who thinks he has come to borrow something because the Trouts are always running out of things and coming to borrow from the Burnells at the "last" moment. What Jonathan talks about is his sense of time running out and the fact that he has to spend the best years of his life sitting on a stool in the office from nine to five. Jonathan wants to escape time and destruction: "The shortness of life! The shortness of life! I've only one night or one day and there's this vast dangerous garden, waiting out there, undiscovered, unexplored." ("At the Bay," p. 130.) Linda asked Jonathan if it were not too late, even now, to escape, but he cried that he was too old. For the first time Linda saw Jonathan as weak and touched with age and she wonders:

> What was the matter with Jonathan? He had no ambition; she supposed that was it. And yet one felt he was gifted, exceptional. He was passionately fond of music; every spare penny he had went on books. He was always full of new ideas, schemes, plans. But nothing came of it all. The new fire blazed in Jonathan; you almost heard it roaring softly as he explained, described, and dilated on the new thing; but a moment later it had fallen in and there was nothing but ashes, and Jonathan went about with a look like hunger in his black eyes.
>
> ("At the Bay," p. 129)

Jonathan, regretfully facing middle age, from which he cannot escape, wants desperately to "live," but instead, he is reminded by his graying hair that he must go on living the life of a prisoner or an insect banging its head against the wall in an attempt to escape. As Linda listens to Jonathan's cry against time and death, the sun sets and she thinks:

> Sometimes when those beams of light show in the sky they are very awful. They remind you that up there sits Jehovah, the jealous God, the Almighty, whose eye is upon you, ever watchful, never weary. You remember that at his coming the whole earth will shake into one ruined graveyard; the cold bright angels will drive you this way and that, and there will be no time to explain what could be explained so simply. . . .
>
> ("At the Bay," p. 131)

Death pervades this episode between Jonathan and Linda. The day dies, Jonathan stands on the darkening grass, his voice is shadowy and seems to Linda to boom from beneath the ground as though he were already dead like the new fire in him which "had turned" to ashes. He thinks of himself as a victim under circumstances to which he can never become accustomed.

The women, too, are faced with destruction. After Stanley had left for work in the morning, they think they have the whole perfect day to themselves. A symbolic murder is committed by Alice, the servant girl, who is washing the breakfast dishes:

> "Oh, these men!" said she, and she plunged the teapot into the bowl and held it under the water even after it had stopped bubbling, as if it too was a man and drowning was too good for them.
>
> ("At the Bay," p. 107)

But this is not the only time Alice encounters death on this day. At Mrs. Stubbs', where she has gone for tea on her free afternoon, Alice listens to Mrs. Stubbs talk about her husband's death. After Alice looks at photographs of the dead man and discovers that he died of dropsy and had to be drained of liquid, the very thought of which makes her jump, she wishes she were back in her own kitchen instead of listening to Mrs. Stubbs' deathly discussion (p. 124). Alice carries a sunshade which she calls her "PERISHALL" (p. 121).

Each successive encounter with death or destruction grows in intensity. This is not only because each encounter itself is with a more horrifying form of death, but also because each reference is intensified by the preceding references. The children look for "buried" treasure cast off from wrecks (p. 109). In the middle of the day Kezia and her grandmother discuss death, and later in the wash-house the children are terrified by the dark. Their game of animals has been spoiled. They see a face looking at them through a window and they shriek out in horror before they realize it is only Uncle Jonathan (p. 128).

Beryl is attracted by Mrs. Kember but at the same time this deathly woman fills Beryl with an evil feeling (p. 113). Beryl feels poisoned and imagines Mrs. Kember murdered by her husband (p. 112). Late at night when Beryl is in her room and dreaming about the lover who will take her away and save her from her present life, she sees Harry Kember approaching the house (p. 135). She has been looking out at the beautiful garden from her window. Even the stars seem to conspire with her in sharing the exciting night. When Harry Kember asks her to go for a walk with him she is very much tempted to do so and steps out into the garden. But as soon as she does so, the garden is completely changed and she thinks of the pit of darkness beneath the fuschia bush to which Harry Kember suggests they go (p. 136). This pit of darkness with a showering fuschia bush above is an image similar to several previous ones in the story. The pit is like the grave-like black hole beside which lies the stiff, dead body of Uncle William (p. 119). The shower is an image similar to Alice's holding the teapot/drowning man under the water (p. 107), as well as similar to the stream of water which Pip pours over the squashed boot he finds as buried treasure (p. 109). Lottie, sitting at the edge of the water, is frightened by a "whiskery" wave which threatens to shower her (p. 111). At the horrible parties which the Samuel Josephs give, the Burnell children usually end up getting something poured down their backs (p. 108). Any reference to a shower over anything is distasteful. Mr. Stubbs became a kind of tank which had to be drained before he died of dropsy (p. 123). Although the characters in **"At the Bay"** enjoy swimming, they all want to go in at their rate, and any premature showering is unpleasant and has a death-by-water connotation. When Beryl thinks of the pit of darkness under the bush in the garden which had looked so beautiful from the window of her room, the garden now looks very different to Beryl. "The moonlight stared and glittered; the shadows were like bars of iron" (p. 136). The garden prison image here is the same image Jonathan has of his life. Beryl is momentarily Harry Kember's victim.

Linda, like the other characters, is overwhelmed by death. Sitting in the garden and looking at the flowers on the manuka tree, she asks: "Who takes the trouble—or the joy—to make all these things that are wasted. . . . It was uncanny" (**"At the Bay,"** p. 114). Time is the enemy which prevents her from examining the flowers and knowing nature.

Death, destruction, or corruption interferes in the life of each character and completely overwhelms him. Death is also the frightening power of the unknown. Each character in **"At the Bay"** not only builds up defenses against death but also struggles not to give himself away to the hidden darkness of the unknown. Although Jonathan dreams of discovering the vast, unexplored garden, he does not anticipate hidden dangers in the garden. Neither does Beryl until she is confronted by Harry Kember. Not anticipating danger in the unknown has terrible consequences, as Beryl discovers. Linda thinks of the "eye" of the Jehovah who is always watchful and knows something she does not know. She imagines the day of judgment as a time and situation in which she is unable to communicate, unable to explain or give an account of herself. The all-knowing eye is like the eye Alice imagines watching her as she leaves the house and walks to Mrs. Stubbs' (p. 121). Beryl is watching her, but Alice does not know this. She does not turn around and look but turns her back for fear of being discovered. She is afraid of giving herself up to her fear of the unknown. Beryl turns her back to Mrs. Kember's eyes as she undresses for swimming. She never undresses in front of anyone and feels that because Mrs. Kember is watching her that Mrs. Kember is discovering her and has some power over her. Beryl feels inexperienced in front of Mrs. Kember and feels that Mrs. Kember knows something about her which she doesn't know herself (pp. 111-113). Mrs. Kember is a sphinx-like character who knows about Beryl but is herself completely mysterious to Beryl. She advises Beryl to "enjoy life" and tells Beryl that it is a sin for her to wear clothes, since she has such a lovely figure. Beryl imagines that she would like to "enjoy life" and that it would be fascinating to have the kind of power over other people that Mrs. Kember has over her. Discovering that the unknown is not altogether pleasant, in spite of its tempting appearance, is what Beryl learns when she steps into the garden with Harry Kember. She had dreams of being discovered by a lover who would "save" her, but instead it is Harry Kember, out for a stroll, who discovers her.

Each character feels watched. The children playing in the wash-house are terrified by a watching face:

> Suddenly Lottie gave such a piercing scream that all of them jumped off the forms, all of them screamed too. "A face—a face looking!" shrieked Lottie.
>
> It was true, it was real. Pressed against the window was a pale face, black eyes, a black beard.
>
> ("At the Bay," pp. 127-128)

Of course it turns out to be only Uncle Jonathan. But each character has the experience of being watched and discovered by a powerful eye. Each character fights against giving himself away and being discovered but is unsuccessful in the attempt. For each character the day is spoiled by death, the reality which each one tries to escape. In **"The Stranger,"** John Hammond is completely overcome by death, and the thought that his wife has held a dying man in her arms makes him think that he and his wife will never be alone again. Death has come between them. The stranger here is both death and the unknown. The experience his wife has had is something which John will never share with her. **"Sun and Moon"** likewise ends with the destruction of Sun's vision of the ice house. The child's reality does not allow for change and he expects the party decorations to look the same after the party as they did before it.

ACCEPTING REALITY

"At the Bay" was written in September 1921 and although the former story was conceived as a continuation of **"Prelude"** (1917) and was supposed to be the second part of a projected novel, it is far more closely related to **"The Garden Party."** Anthologies of Katherine Mansfield's short stories follow a chronological order except for having **"At the Bay"** immediately following **"Prelude."** A consideration of **"At the Bay"** in relation to **"The Garden Party"** shows that something is lost in this arrangement. **"The Garden Party"** seems to me to be a resolution of the conflicts in **"At the Bay,"** and therefore printing **"At the Bay"** immediately before **"The Garden Party"** would enhance this relationship. Both **"Prelude"** and **"At the Bay"** are about the same characters, the Burnells, but all of the New Zealand stories have the same or only slightly different characters reappearing in all the stories.[1] The relationship between **"At the Bay"** and **"The Garden Party"** is in the treatment of Death. Reality in **"The Garden Party"** is distinctly different from reality in **"At the Bay."**

Whereas in **"At the Bay"** (and in the stories preceding **"At the Bay"**) death is rejected by each character; in **"The Garden Party"** it is accepted. Death in the former story is something to be feared and escaped but in the latter story it is not only accepted but beautiful. What the characters in **"At the Bay"** fail to come to terms with, Laura in **"The Garden Party"** succeeds in facing. Laura not only succeeds in accepting death, but she escapes the fear of death which haunts the characters in **"At the Bay."** Because she acknowledges the reality of death she is able to transcend the fear of it. This she does by transfiguring death into something beautiful—a marvel. The values of reality in the two stories are reversed, in **"At the Bay"** the very thought of death destroys life for each character who is made unhappy by it. Life is ruined by the thought of death, change, time and destruction. But in **"The Garden Party"** life is enhanced by death. Death not only enhances life but it makes life seem less beautiful than death. It is precisely the absence of death in Mrs. Sheridan's world which makes it so artificial. In **"At the Bay"** death is the enemy which destroys each character's dream, but in **"The Garden Party"** death is so beautiful that it makes life look lacking. As has been pointed out in Chapter III, Mrs. Sheridan's world is sterile and the emotional poverty there makes life less desirable than death. Here life destroys death, but in **"At the Bay"** death destroys life; darkness triumphs. In **"At the Bay"** each character looks upon death as an illusion and tries to build a dream world which excludes death. In **"The Garden Party"** death is a reality which is totally accepted and transmuted into beauty. Death spoils the natural world for the characters in **"At the Bay"** but in **"The Garden Party"** Laura finds beauty in the inevitability of death.[2]

Mrs. Sheridan's world of false light, which is the world of conventional reality, is false because it deletes death. It is a heartless world in which nature is withheld from all except Laura. The story opens with a description of the garden before the party. It is a perfect day in which nature aids and is at the disposal of the Sheridans. A halo of gold envelops the scene. The blue sky "was veiled with a haze of light gold" (p. 285). The opening is casual, conversational, and familiar but at the same time the scene is in some way special, as though the heavenly host were in the background. Even the bushes are bowed down in humility and reverence before the splendor of the natural world. The unique scene is where a garden party is about to take place. The contrast between the beauty offered by the natural world and the failure of the guests to see this beauty is immediately made. Significantly, we are told that the guests only "know" roses, and therefore no other flowers would "impress" them. The loveliness of the garden is withheld from the guests who come to be impressed rather than to see. Everything must be conspicuous or the guests will miss it. The workmen who come to put up the marquee are aware of the blatant pretentions of this world even more than Laura is. When Laura suggests that the marquee be put up on the lily lawn, one of them says, "You want to put it somewhere where it'll give you a bang slap in the eye, if you follow me" (p. 286). The workman suggests that a sufficiently conspicuous place would be against the karaka trees, but Laura thinks:

> Against the karakas, then the karaka trees would be hidden. And they were so lovely, with their broad,

gleaming leaves, and their clusters of yellow fruit. They were like trees you imagined growing on a desert island, proud, solitary, lifting their leaves and fruits to the sun in a kind of silent splendour. Must they be hidden by a marquee? They must.

("The Garden Party," p. 287)

When Laura sees the workman bend down and pinch a sprig of lavender to get to the smell of it, she thinks that the workman, caring for things like the smell of lavender, is very different different from her own friends who do not care for things like this (p. 287). For them the beauties of the natural world do not exist. Laura credits this situation to absurd class distinctions and conventions which she despises.

This world is not only unable to see the beauties of the natural world, but it perpetrates a sinister heartlessness which is repeatedly built up to the point where Mrs. Sheridan refuses to consider the death of the carter as real. During the preparations for the party, Laura's sister Jose, who loved to give orders to the servants as though she were acting a part in a drama, plays the piano unfeelingly: "And although the piano sounded more desperate than ever, her face broke into a brilliant, dreadfully unsympathetic smile." (**"The Garden Party,"** p. 290.) Jose is less interested in the thing she is doing than in her own sense of superiority in doing it. Contrasted with Laura's shocked reaction at the news of the accident, Jose's reaction is completely cruel. When Laura pleads that they stop the party because of the accident, Jose says in amazement:

> Stop the garden party? My dear Laura, don't be absurd. Of course we can't do anything of the kind. Nobody expects us to. Don't be so extravagant.

("The Garden Party," p. 293)

Mrs. Sheridan's reaction to the accident is similar to Jose's. She, too, persists in eliminating death from her world. Mrs. Sheridan succeeds in deleting death but at a price which makes her world deathly in its artificiality. Her world kills all feeling. That someone had the impertinence to die on the day of her party is a social error which polite society will do its best to overlook. Like Jose who lives as though she were acting a part in a play, Mrs. Sheridan lives a life in which her responses are nothing more than an acquired pose. What passes for feeling in her case is nothing more than the learned niceties of social behavior. When Mr. Sheridan mentions the accident after the party, Mrs. Sheridan thinks this is very tactless of her husband (p. 297). Death simply does not belong there.

But Laura, the heroine of the story, is different from the other members of the family. She is the "artistic" one who is sent out to give directions to the men putting up the marquee (p. 236). She is the only one who is affected by the accident, and when her mother suggests taking the leftovers to the party, the suggestion affects her differently than it does the rest of the family. Laura is set apart and unique in her capacity to feel:

> Again, how curious, she seemed to be different from them all. To take scraps from their party. Would the poor woman really like that?

("The Garden Party," p. 297)

Laura questions her mother's attitude and wonders whether her mother is right or wrong. But what makes Laura extraordinarily different from her family and her family's friends is her capacity to accept everything. She not only accepts the death of the carter and reacts to it, but she also accepts her mother's distorted world. Laura is receptive to the beauties of the natural world in a way which the other characters are not. Every gesture Laura makes during the story is one of affirmation. Her sense of the injustice of class distinctions does not prevent her from seeing that the workman, who cares about the smell of the spring of lavender, has the capacity to care which her family lacks. Because he cares, he is more alive than her family and in the end has more of a sense of the earth than they do. Class distinction does not deprive him of very much. The Sheridan's by contrast have nothing—life eludes them because it is life without death. In the midst of plenty they are starving and do not realize it.

The first part of **"The Garden Party,"** the scene of the Sheridan's home and the party itself, contains the beauty of the natural world. The image for the natural world on this afternoon is the flower. "And the perfect afternoon slowly ripened, slowly faded, slowly its petals closed" (p. 296). Within this beauty there is the Sheridan's world which, because of its sterility, only gives the illusion of life. It is the blight within the flower—it is a kind of death which prevents the characters from seeing life or beauty. The false light in which they live is of their own creation, their own determined efforts to delete death.

In the second part of **"The Garden Party,"** the world of the alley and the dead man, the natural world is completely dark, but natural death is beautiful. Both scenes in the story have the parallels of death and beauty but the parallels are reversed. In the first part the natural world is beautiful in comparison to which life is deathly, but in the second part the natural world is dark and ugly while actual death is magnificent. Curiously, the people, except Laura, in both parts are more dead than alive. They live either in the extreme of total light or total darkness both of which extremes have the same consequences for the people. They are all dead. Just as Mrs. Sheridan is unaware of the world beyond her garden gate, the people in the alley are unaware of any world other than their own. In fact, like Mrs. Sheridan who is unaware of the beauty of her own garden, these people in the alley are unaware not only of the Sheridan world, but also of the beauty of death before them. They have something which Mrs. Sheridan doesn't have, but like Mrs. Sheridan they too are unaware of what they *do* have.

Just as Laura accepts her mother's world, she also accepts the dark world of the Scotts and natural death. Once she closes her gate she steps into a dark world where she is the only light:

> Now the broad road was crossed. The lane began, smoky and dark. Women in shawls and men's tweed caps hurried by. Men hung over the palings; the children played in the doorways. A low hum came from the mean little cottages. In some of them there was a flicker of light, and a shadow, crab-like, moved across the window. Laura bent her head and hurried on. She wished now that she had put on a coat. How her frock shone! And the big hat with the velvet streamer—if only it was another hat! Were the people looking at her? They must be. It was a mistake to have come; she knew all along it was a mistake. Should she go back even now?
>
> **("The Garden Party,"** p. 298)

Laura is frightened by the dark squalor, and having come from such brightness, she can hardly find her way in the dark. She feels she is losing her way and venturing farther than she would like to go. "Oh, to be away from this! She actually said, 'Help me, God'" (p. 299). But the point is that she does go on and does not run away. She makes her way as best she can and although the people smile queerly at her, she stops and asks directions. Laura's sense of being out of place and in the unknown is as terrifying to her as the squalor and darkness. She feels that all eyes along the road are on her, and although the figures of the people are indistinct to her, she knows that she is seen plainly. To be discovered by what she cannot understand is horrible. "To be away from those staring eyes, to be covered up in anything, one of those women's shawls even" (p. 200). This situation is similar to one in which each character in **"At the Bay"** feels that an eye is upon him. The characters feel helpless before the all-seeking mysterious eye which catches them frightened. They feel naked and given away in their fright and left without an avenue of escape. But the difference between the characters in **"At the Bay"** and Laura is that Laura does not cry out in horror, she just keeps going: "I'll just leave the basket and go, she decided. I shan't even wait for it to be emptied" (p. 299). The characters in **"At the Bay"** do not escape a final sense of being trapped but Laura, who feels momentarily trapped in several instances, accepts the trap, and because she does she escapes it finally. Mrs. Sheridan traps Laura by the hat and diverts her attention from the death.[3] At first Laura cannot look at herself in the mirror but finally she does (p. 295). If Laura had her own way the party would be postponed but she gives way temporarily to her mother's wishes. Then when Laura arrives at the Scotts', she wants to leave the basket and not go in but she gets trapped in the passageway by Mrs. Scott's sister to whom Laura is unable to communicate. In the kitchen, "Laura only wanted to get out, to get away" (p. 300). The woman manages to get Laura into the bedroom where the dead man lies, and Laura passively follows her to the corpse. Laura doesn't want to look, but just as she finally looked in the mirror which her mother had held before her, she finally looks at death. Laura is the explorer who must see everything and go everywhere no matter how painful or sordid the place or thing may be.

Transcending Darkness

But what Laura finds in death is not desolation but fulfillment:

> There lay a young man, fast asleep—sleeping so soundly, so deeply, that he was far, far away from them both. Oh, so remote, so peaceful. He was dreaming. Never wake him up again. His head was sunk in the pillow, his eyes were closed; they were blind under the closed lids. He was given up to his dream. What did garden parties and baskets and lace frocks matter to him? He was far from all those things. He was wonderful, beautiful. While they were laughing and while the band was playing, this marvel had come to the lane. Happy . . . happy. . . . All is well, said the sleeping face. This is just as it should be. I am content.
>
> **("The Garden Party,"** p. 300)

Laura painfully accepts death and transmutes it into something beautiful.[4] She does this not with resignation but with a sense of death being right—"just as it should be." It is precisely the necessary shadow of death in all things which is the beauty and mystery of life.

Because she accepts death, she does not fear its power over her. The eyes of death are closed, and unlike the staring eyes of the people in the street, these eyes do not discover her and make her desperately want to hide. In **"At the Bay,"** the characters feel helpless in the presence of an eye which discovers them and gives them away. The watching eyes in **"At the Bay"** have the terrifying power of the unknown over the characters. It is not the physical corpse which is beautiful to Laura as much as it is the wonderful mystery of the thing. Laura tells her brother, "It was simply marvellous" (p. 301). But the story does not end on death. Laura returns from her descent into darkness and comes through to her brother and Life. After seeing death, her exit from the dark world is made easily and without the difficulties of the journey to death. On the way back, having seen ultimate darkness, Laura knows her way and is not afraid of getting lost: "And this time she didn't wait for Em's sister. She found her way out the door, down the path, past all those dark people." (**"The Garden Party,"** p. 300.) Out of the shadow steps her brother, the one member of her family with whom she can communicate (when he is not distracted by Laura's hat—the symbol of their mother's artificial world) and with whom as a consequence she shares those explorations where "one must go everywhere; one must see everything" (p. 294), and not be overwhelmed by what one sees. Their conversation immediately turns to life—to which Laura has been reborn:

> "But Laurie—," she stopped, she looked at her brother. "Isn't life," she stammered, "isn't life." But what life was she couldn't explain. No matter. He quite understood. "Isn't it, darling?" said Laurie.
>
> (**"The Garden Party,"** p. 301)

Reality is light and life in both **"The Garden Party"** and **"The Doll's House."** But in both stories it is a reality in which light finally triumphs over darkness precisely because it depends on darkness being there and being accepted. In **"The Doll's House,"** Else, the washerwoman's daughter whose only words in the whole story are the final ones: "I seen the little lamp," (p. 326) is similar to Laura in the way in which they both transcend darkness and apprehend beauty and light. The reality of both heroines includes darkness and light, and is a unity synthesized out of this diversity. Both heroines' vision penetrates through darkness or appearance and finally apprehends light, truth, or reality.[5]

"The Doll's House" is written in such a way that Else's words "I seen the little lamp" symbolizes some universality or truth similar to Laura's unstated vision of reality which compels her to ask: "isn't life?". What this lamp represents is not only indirectly suggested, but it is also difficult to apprehend and hidden to all but the pure in heart. After a series of unveilings are stripped away, the reader, like the Burnell children, finally sees the lamp. The doll's house, which is so heavy that two men must carry it, is kept in the courtyard and not taken into the house because Aunt Beryl objects to the smell of paint. "But the perfect, perfect little house! Who could possibly mind the smell? It was part of the joy, part of the newness." (**"The Doll's House,"** p. 318.) The outside of the house is seen by the children, then the inside in all its detail; and finally Kezia sees the lamp—" an exquisite little amber lamp with a white globe" (p. 319). To Kezia the lamp was the best part of the house. The lamp was "real" and like lamps the children "burn" to tell their friends about the house (p. 319). It is Kezia who reminds her sister, Isabel, to tell their school friends about it (p. 322). Just as the doll's house is banished to the courtyard because of the smell, the Kelvey children are banished from the Burnell world because they are social outcasts—the children of a washerwoman and a gaolbird and not fit company for other people's children (p. 321). They smell, too. Like the lamp behind the housefront, Else Kelvey is seen behind her sister. Both the lamp and Else could easily be overlooked and are overlooked by Aunt Beryl. Else scarcely talks and accepts the abuse of the other children without defending herself. Else has "big, imploring eyes: (p. 324), and in her dumbness she is like the sorrowful bush which says to Beryl in **"At the Bay,"** "We are dumb trees, reaching up in the night, imploring we know not what" (p. 134). And like the imploring bush, Else wants to see the doll's house when the opportunity arises (p. 324). She reaches up out of the dark outsider's world, and in spite of Beryl's success in dispelling them from the garden, Beryl cannot prevent Else's seeing the light. With every disadvantage Else overcomes darkness and sees the light.

The unfinished story, **"Six Years After,"** is Katherine Mansfield's final expression of Reality. The wife continues to seek with the realization that she may never find. Knowing that there may be nothing more to life than final death, she goes on with the hope that there may be something else. Like Else and Laura, this woman has the capacity to see through darkness. But, as with Else and Laura, facing darkness is painful. At first she doesn't dare turn and look back at the lonely gulls, the sea, and the rain because after the steamer passes by there is nothing. She decides she won't look because it is too depressing:

> But immediately, she opened her eyes and looked again. Lonely birds, water lifting, white pale sky—how were they changed?
>
> And it seemed to her there was a presence far out there, between the sky and the water. Someone very desolate and longing watched them pass and cried as if to stop them—but cried to her alone.
>
> (**"Six Years After,"** p. 346)

The presence crying out is the memory of her soldier-son who has been dead six years. But he does not stop her—she goes on and takes his memory with her just as years ago she had taken the child's nightmare back with her from the bedroom into the living room and into the circle of lamplight, where "it had taken its place there like a ghost" (p. 347). The mother's anguish over death is not defeat but persistence in the belief that one can go on although life may be only an illusion, a drama at the end of which there is nothing:

> But softly without a sound the dark curtain has rolled down. There is no more to come. That is the end of the play. But it's cold, it's still. There is nothing to be gained by waiting.
>
> "I can't bear it!" She sits up breathing the words and tosses the dark rug away. It is colder than ever, and now dusk is falling like an ash on the pallid water.
>
> And the little steamer growing determined, throbbed on, pressed on, as if at the end of the journey there waited. . . .
>
> (**"Six Years After,"** pp. 347-348)

The changing function of the boat image parallels the change in Reality from death, destruction, and darkness to life, beauty, and light.[6] In the New Zealand short stories preceding and including **"At the Bay,"** the boat image functions as a symbol of escape, whereas in the stories written after **"At the Bay,"** the boat image functions as a symbol of triumph over the fear of death in the journey through life. In **"Prelude,"** Linda sees the aloe as a ship of escape from life and time (pp. 92-93). In **"At the Bay,"** Linda sits in a "steamer" chair and dreams of the river boats in China in which she escapes time with her father (p. 115). In the same story, Jonathan Trout wants to escape. "I could cut off to sea . . ." (p. 130). But he knows he cannot escape because he is a ship without an "anchor" (p. 131). In **"The Stranger,"** the ship bringing Janey home is stopped by death—the thing which makes escape impossible. By contrast, the ship in **"Six Years After,"** is not stopped by the presence of death but rather grows determined and throbs on in the face of death (p. 348). In **"The Voyage,"** the little girl, Fenella Crane, and her grandmother make the journey in the Picton boat, through the darkness of night after Fenella's mother has died, and safely return home. Although this story was completed August 14, 1921, and therefore predates **"At the Bay"** by one month, the boat image is a symbol of triumph over darkness and death because it is associated with the little girl and grandmother, the two characters who are favored with the ability to accept death. The character of the mother is dispensed with in this story:

> We resist, we are terribly frightened, the little boat enters the dark fearful gulf and our only cry is to escape—"put me on land again." But it's useless. Nobody listens. The shadowy figure rows on. One ought to sit still and uncover one's eyes.[7]

Notes

1. See note 3, Chapter I.
2. The difference between the reality in "At the Bay" and in "The Garden Party" parallels a change in Katherine Mansfield's attitude toward death, corruption, and suffering. The problem of how the ugliness and intolerable corruption of life could be borne (see Notes to Chapter III, n. 3) was resolved finally by her belief that it must be accepted. In her *Journal* for December 19, 1920 ([*Journal of Katherine Mansfield*, ed. John Middleton Murry (London: Constable, 1954)], p. 228), she wrote:

   > There is no limit to human suffering. When one thinks: Now I have touched the bottom of the sea—now I can go no deeper, one goes deeper. And so it is for ever. I thought last year in Italy: Any shadow more would be death. But this year has been so much more terrible that I think with affection of the Casetta! Suffering is boundless, it is eternity. One pang is eternal torment. Physical suffering is child's play. To have one's breast crushed by a great stone—one could laugh!
   >
   > I don't want to die without leaving a record of my belief that suffering can be overcome. For I do believe it. What must one do? There is no question of what Jack (her husband, John Middleton Murry) calls "passing beyond it". This is false.
   >
   > One must *submit*. Do not resist. Take it. Be overwhelmed. Accept it fully. Make it *part of life*.
   >
   > Everything in life that we really accept undergoes a change. So suffering must become Love. This is the mystery. This is what I must do.

3. The hat as a symbol of Mrs. Sheridan's world which is blind to the reality of death is discussed in Chapter III.

4. Not only must corruption be accepted, but it must be transmuted into Beauty.

   > But do you really feel (she wrote to the Honorable Dorothy Brett, March 9, 1922) all beauty is marred by ugliness and the lovely woman has bad teeth? I don't feel quite that. For it seems to me if Beauty were Absolute it would no longer be the kind of Beauty it is. Beauty triumphs over ugliness in Life. That's what I feel. And that marvellous triumph is what I long to express. The poor man lives and the tears glitter in his beard and that is so beautiful one could bow down. Why? Nobody can say. I sit in a waiting-room where all is ugly, where it's dirty, dull, dreadful, where sick people waiting with me to see the doctor are all marked by suffering and sorrow. And a very poor workman comes in, takes off his cap humbly, beautifully, walks in tiptoe, has a look as though he were in Church, has a look as though he believed that behind that doctor's door there shone the miracle of *healing*. And all is changed, all is marvellous. It's only then that one sees for the first time what is happening. No, I don't believe in your frowsty housemaids, really. Life is, all at one and the same time, far more mysterious and far simpler than we know. It's like religion in that. If we want to have faith, and without faith we die, we must *learn to accept*.
   >
   > (*Letters* [*The Letters of Katherine Mansfield*], pp. 452-453)

   About what she wanted to convey in "The Garden Party" Katherine Mansfield wrote to William Gerhardi, March 13, 1922:

   > The diversity of life and how we try to fit in everything, Death included. That is bewildering for a person of Laura's age. She feels things ought to happen differently. First one and then another. But life isn't like that. We haven't the ordering of it. Laura says, "But all these things must not happen at once." And Life answers, "Why not? How are they divided from each other?" And they do all happen, it is inevitable. And it seems to me there is beauty in that inevitability.
   >
   > (*Letters*, p. 454)

5. In Katherine Mansfield's estimation, accepting darkness and light together was the most profound human experience. Praising Dostoevsky for this in a letter to John Middleton Murry, dated November 4, 1917, she described him as "a being who Loved, in spite of everything adored LIFE even while he knew the dark, dark places" (*Letters*, p. 244).

6. Celeste T. Wright, "Katherine Mansfield's Boat Image," *Twentieth Century Literature*, I, 128-132 (October, 1955). Mrs. Wright is particularly interested in the relationship between Katherine Mansfield's life and her work, and she traces parallel use of the boat image in the short stories as well as in all of Katherine Mansfield's writings.

7. *Letters*, Oct. 1920, p. 334.

W. H. New (essay date 1999)

SOURCE: New, W. H. "Reiteration: Stories of Static Action." In *Reading Mansfield and Metaphors of Form*, pp. 103-20. Montreal: McGill-Queen's University Press, 1999.

[*In the following essay, New discusses the thematic importance of reiteration in a number of Mansfield's stories, claiming that the device can be "lexical," "phonological," or "organizational" and that, far from being merely repetitive on the author's part, "reiteration is a deliberate technical strategy," functioning to shed light on the lack of development in Mansfield's characters.*]

The paradox in this chapter title has to do with the nature of reiteration itself, whereby the action of repeating something does little to forward any activity. Such reiteration *reinscribes* instead, perhaps intending to emphasize an observation or idea, perhaps to reaffirm it, perhaps with some other reason in mind. Clearly, the act of reiteration can have an effect, especially on an interlocutor or observer within a story and on the perceptions that a reader (the observer-interlocutor outside it) brings to interpretation. But the act itself is oddly static; it draws attention not to movement or enterprise or vitality but to a lack of progress, a failure of alteration, an inability to embrace change, a resistance to time.[1]

That so many of Mansfield's stories concern themselves with such issues is itself revealing, perhaps suggesting a personal preoccupation with death and thwarted sexuality, a dissatisfaction with degrees of artistic accomplishment, the debilitating pressures of a persistent illness, or an impatience with self-satisfaction, wherever it is to be found. These subjects, indeed, constitute the overt themes of **"A Birthday"** (1911), **"Mr Reginald Peacock's Day"** (1917), **"A Married Man's Story"** (1921), and numerous other stories, and have regularly surfaced as motivating sensibilities in accounts of Mansfield's life. Particular events and phrases within these stories—the scenes of morning exercises, for example—further reinforce a sense that Mansfield's later stories often echoed her earlier ones: the Stanley Burnell of **"At the Bay"** (1921) is in many ways a textual variant of the character-type earlier constructed as Reginald Peacock and (in **"A Birthday"**) Andreas Binzer. But the fascination with the actively immobile should not be construed as evidence for mere repetitiveness on Mansfield's part. Far from it. As these stories reveal—along with two others that can instructively be discussed with them, **"The Wind Blows"** (1915) and **"The Voyage"** (1921)—reiteration is a deliberate technical strategy, functioning to elucidate the attractions of the ostensibly changeless as well as to critique the limitations of a life that does not adequately embrace change. The technique shows up in the way sets of words and phrases are repeated within individual stories for deliberate effects, and in the choice and arrangement of particular verbs.

Something of a circular process operates here, for the deliberateness of these effects is apparent from the pattern of recurrence, though of course not all recurrences involve reiteration. As the following chapters reveal, alternative paradigms of recurrence involve such techniques as reversal, inversion, and fragmentation, and these have their own impact upon interpretive strategies. But the general point is that *reading for form* requires close attention to whatever constitutes the recurrent element in a particular passage of prose, for such an element functions as a kind of formal directive. Such rent elements can be lexical (diction, for example, or specific items of vocabulary, or associated clusters of imagery) or phonological (sound patterns) or organizational (dealing with structure, whether at a micro or macro level: prepositional phrases, formulaic phrases, interrogations, juxtapositions, words in series, negations, syntactic choices, sentence patterning, and the like). To focus on verb choice and form and on specific instances of repetition—in order to clarify how reiteration works as a story-telling strategy—is to examine more closely the effect of the relation between *stasis* and *statement*.

"The Wind Blows" and **"Mr Reginald Peacock's Day"** furnish ready examples of specific kinds of repetition. For instance, the repetition of the single word "wind" in **"The Wind Blows"** (five times compounded as "The wind—the wind," 191, 192, 193, 194) functions not only to reinforce, as though physiologically, the reader's sense of the intensity and persistence of a Wellington windstorm but also as a sort of mantra for the central character, a formulaic verbal utterance that here at once invokes change and mediates against it, producing tension. Reginald Peacock's recurrent phrase, by contrast, is sentence length: "Dear lady, I should be so charmed!" (with two or three variants: 262, 264, 265, 266). For Peacock, a singing teacher, this phrase has become the formula through which he egocentrically ingratiates himself with his wealthy female clients. It is oily and empty, but produces the effect he seems to want. The problem is that it becomes habitual; substituting for both thought and feeling, it begins to impede any real communication, especially between him and his wife. Automatic utterance replaces language, that is, the verbal formula in this instance getting in the way of the medium that would permit him to express his capacity for growth. In consequence, language itself—the field in which the narrative action takes place—is also the narrative *ground* here; it becomes as much of a subject in these stories as are such themes as ego, sacrifice, childhood, childishness, and loss, and because of the deliberateness of Mansfield's technique, it is formally integrated with them.

The opening sentences of **"A Married Man's Story"** demonstrate further how the character of reiteration both conveys and constructs a mode of engagement with (or, in this case, disengagement from) the world. As the story opens, the reader abruptly, but without direction, has access to a screed—a diary?—that the married man of the title, the first-person narrator, is writing. The reader is reading over his shoulder, as it were, and at the same time overhearing his internal meditations on his mother's death (did his father poison her?), his failing marriage (is he planning to murder his wife, or leave her?), and his ideas about freedom (are they solipsistic reveries, mere fancies, or mad, perhaps schizophrenic notions about loss of humanity and death?). This is what the reader first reads:

> It is evening. Supper is over. We have left the small, cold dining room; we have come back to the sitting room where there is a fire. All is as usual. I am sitting at my writing table which is placed across a corner so that I am behind it, as it were, and facing the room. The lamp with the green shade is alight; I have before me two large books of reference, both open, a pile of papers . . . All the paraphernalia, in fact, of an extremely occupied man. My wife, with our little boy on her lap, is in a low chair before the fire. She is about to put him to bed before she clears away the dishes and piles them up in the kitchen for the servant girl tomorrow morning. But the warmth, the quiet, and the sleepy baby, have made her dreamy. One of his red woollen boots is off; one is on. She sits, bent forward, clasping the little bare foot, staring into the glow, and as the fire quickens, falls, flares again, her shadow—an immense *Mother and Child*—is here and gone again upon the wall.
>
> (476-7)

The deliberateness of the technique operating here will shortly become evident, but on first reading, the diary entries seem like disjointed reflections and self-justifications—perhaps even pretentious ones, however artfully scripted on the page. Some time later, after dipping back and forth into the external world and the past ("While I am here, I am there," 477), the story closes in ellipsis, which has led several commentators to treat the whole thing as an unfinished fragment. Certainly the story does not invoke a conventional formal closure; when it comes to its end, this is what the married man finally writes: "I did not consciously turn away from the world of human beings; I had never known it; but I from that night did beyond words consciously turn towards my silent brothers . . ." (486-7).

The text earlier makes clear that the "silent brothers" are, at least metaphorically, creatures of the wild (480), and that the entire narrative is meant to explain why, since "last autumn" (482), the married man has come to see his wife and child as objects of analysis rather than as a family with whom he enjoys a fulfilling and subjective relationship. But the field of relationship through which as an adult he has had access to others has always been verbal, not emotional, and if he is "beyond words" at the end, the ellipses announce a kind of withdrawal from human discourse—mad? solipsistic?—that is a frighteningly effective closure of a different kind. Words have, that is, for the most part provided him some promise of connection. For while, along the way, he has taken a kind of refuge in "reference books" (they sustain his work, yet are also part of the barrier between himself and the room he ostensibly shares with his family) and observation, he has also found some degree of satisfaction in words—he is a writer of some sort, after all—or at least in the look and *taste* of them. But at one point he starts to feel separate even from words: "To live like this . . . I write those words, very carefully, very beautifully. For some reason I feel inclined to sign them" (478). As words in this way become objects, and as he consciously comes to realize this fact, so they, too—like mother and child (the parodic Pietà reference is not accidental)—become correlatives of death instead of life, of stasis instead of renewal or rebirth. Hence the verbal paradigms of the opening sentences do more than simply set the scene. Embodied in them is a pattern of reiteration that spells out the threat that life presents to this married man, and perhaps the threat that he presents to life.

For almost no action occurs in the first paragraph; the predominant verb is *is,* reiterated (in independent and auxiliary forms together) thirteen times, a pattern echoed in the paragraphs that follow. Any activity is assigned primarily to the fire, which *quickens, falls, flares*—the active piling and clearing of dishes is cast into the future; it has not yet happened. The most the man and his wife can do, in this setting of scene, is *to sit* and *to have*—neither of which breaks the sense of immobility that the paragraph designs (or the paragraph-writer, the narrator, as Mansfield designs him). But to recognize that the married man, narrating this paragraph, has to be *writing* the paragraph adds to the complexity of how the syntax behaves. If the man is writing, this fact affirms an action that the paragraph does not directly record; self-reflexively, moreover, the suppression of the one action that is actually shaping this particular narrative scene proclaims a distance between what the married man writes and what his writing reveals. The man's recurrent word is *is*. Ostensibly the lexicon of record, the verb *to be* could in other circumstances affirm simple existence, even celebrate it, or assert factuality, perhaps laying claim to some version of neutrality in the process. Here, however, the illusion of an objective—in fact, *objectifying*—distance seems carefully crafted not to celebrate the way things are (existence, factuality, life) but for the man to justify to himself his nagging, self-pitying disaffection from it. He shapes stasis *in order* to rail against it; no neutrality governs his observations. The lack of activity stems from him: stasis, death, is of his own creation. It is reiterated into existence in words, until his own words become the agents of undoing, of ruin and dissolution, a parable of the loss of creative power.

"A Married Man's Story" is the most dour of the five stories under consideration here, yet its picture of male ego and insensitivity reiterates a characteristic Mansfield motif. The portraits of Binzer and Peacock are related to it, recording earlier instances of men whose shallow command of words reveals a limited capacity for empathy—or perhaps this capacity has been socially limited or stunted, the culture of masculinity being a force that thwarts their capacity to express whatever sensitivity they might once have been able to nurture. The focus in **"The Wind Blows"** and **"The Voyage"** falls on young girls, by contrast, a motif that throws the portraits of men into some relief, for in these stories sensitivity governs the entire waking life of the central characters, the senses being acutely alive to surroundings, feeding, intensifying the imagination.

The word "waking" is important. In all five of the stories expressions of ego and sensitivity are tied with images of the borderland between waking and sleep. Fenella, in **"The Voyage,"** awakes towards the end of her story, after a long dark night of travelling between islands, following the death of her mother and her move to a new home with her caring grandparents. The married man, however, is cursed with wakefulness; neither sleep nor a sleepless state renews him, and his closing identification with the "silent brothers" of the wild merely intensifies the sense that his is a world of suspended animation. The other three stories all open with scenes of characters waking up:

"A Birthday"

Andreas Binzer woke slowly. He turned over on the narrow bed and stretched himself—yawned—opening his mouth as widely as possible and bringing his teeth together afterwards with a sharp "click." The sound of that click fascinated him; he repeated it quickly several times, with a snapping movement of the jaws. What teeth! he thought. Sound as a bell, every man jack of them. Never had one out, never had one stopped . . . He looked up at the sky; it shone, strangely white, unflecked with cloud; he looked down at the row of garden strips and backyards. The fence of these gardens was built along the edge of a gully, spanned by an iron suspension bridge, and the people had a wretched habit of throwing their empty tins over the fence into the gully. Just like them, of course! Andreas started counting the tins, and decided, viciously, to write a letter to the papers about it and sign it—sign it in full.

(58-9)

"The Wind Blows"

Suddenly—dreadfully—she wakes up. What has happened? Something dreadful has happened. No—nothing has happened. It is only the wind shaking the house, rattling the windows, banging a piece of iron on the roof and making her bed tremble. Leaves flutter past the window, up and away; down in the avenue a whole newspaper wags in the air like a lost kite and falls, spiked on a pine tree. It is cold. Summer is over—it is autumn—everything is ugly . . . It is all over! What is? Oh, everything! And she begins to plait her hair with shaking fingers, not daring to look in the glass. Mother is talking to grandmother in the hall.

"A perfect idiot! Imagine leaving anything out on the line in weather like this . . ."

(191)

"Mr Reginald Peacock's Day"

If there was one thing that he hated more than another it was the way she had of waking him in the morning. She did it on purpose, of course. It was her way of establishing her grievance for the day, and he was not going to let her know how successful it was. But really, really, to wake a sensitive person like that was positively dangerous! It took him hours to get over it—simply hours. She came into the room buttoned up in an overall, with a handkerchief over her head—thereby proving that she had been up herself and slaving since dawn—and called in a low, warning voice: "Reginald!"

"Eh! What! What's that? What's the matter?"

"It's time to get up; it's half-past eight." And out she went, shutting the door quietly after her, to gloat over her triumph, he supposed.

He rolled over in the big bed, his heart still beating in quick, dull throbs, and with every throb he felt his energy escaping him, his—his inspiration for the day stifling under those thudding blows.

(259)

These passages are by no means uniform. Binzer is in a narrow bed, Peacock in a big one; Peacock is wakened by his wife, while Binzer and Matilda (in **"The Wind Blows"**) awake on their own; Peacock and Binzer are preoccupied with themselves, whereas Matilda fractionally distances self-preoccupation by resisting looking in the mirror. Yet all three examples insist that the waking state (the verbs in all three passages are predominantly active, emphasizing motion) is punctuated by flashes of ego. Peacock blames his wife for his own inactivity; Matilda's mother blames a servant for doing the wash; Binzer wants to sign his name—in full—to complain about what "the people" do to his property. Ego, however, resists change—it is a psychological expression of emotional stasis—in part because it is the outward expression of a satisfaction taken in ownership, an identification between security and a position in the social hierarchy. It is not only men who express this satisfaction; Matilda's mother occupies a position ratified by her husband's property, and she uses her social authority to dictate order to the world about her. But Mansfield's male characters are the chief exemplars of this state of mind. Binzer and Peacock are both envious and insecure, afraid of being seen through by others, and they use their claims on property and artistic talent, icons of self-definition, as claims upon social recognition. Those who are close to them oddly constitute in their own minds a threat to this self-image; their wives know the reality—the sleeping person, as it were—an identity to which their wakened ego will not admit. At least directly. Binzer's preoccupation with the habits of the people on the suspension bridge can clearly be read as a projection of his own insecurities; Peacock's observation that his wife wears a buttoned overall likewise says something about his own need to remain covered, or (as his habitual, reiterated phrase has it) "charmed." For them, change threatens; the way things are—the static status quo—offers a kind of protection and (in their minds at least) a kind of power. In such circumstances growth (which at least is accessible to Matilda and Fenella) is a difficult proposition, and perhaps impossible to attain.

The relation between ego and power, a motif that surfaces in a range of other Mansfield stories from **"The Doll's House"** to **"The Garden Party"** and **"The Fly,"** provides further direction to the reader of these stories. Towards the end of **"Mr Reginald Peacock's Day"** Peacock attends a champagne party given by Lord Timbuck, where, at one point, he is called "Peacock . . .— not Mr Peacock—but Peacock, as if he were one of them" (265). Immediately, however fatuously, Peacock turns the "as if" into a declaration of reality, failing to read it as a code-word for imitation. When the story closes with him thinking that he *could* confide in his wife *if only* she were not his enemy, *if* she were his friend, *if* he felt she were "here to come back to" (266), then artifice has taken hold; ego has supplanted person. He has turned from "Reginald" into "Peacock," from king into strutter, mistaking projected image for the authority to rule. As empty of functional words as the "married man," Peacock, whose singing lessons exude *performed* emotion, proves himself finally to be incapable of actively expressing the emotional connections that would give his *ordinary* life meaning.

Binzer, too, who ends up saying "'Well, by God! Nobody can accuse *me* of not knowing what suffering is'" (65), returns the focus from others to himself when he is finally told that Anna, his wife, has given birth to a son. (Doctor Erb's actual phrase is "hooked a boy," 65, which is oddly piscatorial for this context.) Binzer does worry about his wife, but he projects this concern in a variety of directions that do little to aid her. He claims himself to be ill; he frets over neighbours' behaviour, government inaction, and old times; and he aspires to eat as well as the doctor does. He seems incapable, that is, not only of accepting that he is not the centre of the universe, especially on this birthing day, but also of giving up his private competition for power and precedence among the other men in his community. Doctor Erb offers the chief rivalry (the German prefix *erb* has to do with inheritance, and the word *Binse* means "rush": *in die Binsen gehen,* an informal phrase, means "to be a wash-out"). Erb represents a style of life that Binzer envies, a life of late hours, plenty of food, numerous possessions, vapid aphorisms ("Good weather is as necessary to a confinement as it is to a washing day," 64), and apparent imperturbability (Erb "thrust his hands into his pockets, and began balancing himself on toe and heel," 64). So insistent is Binzer's jockeying for power in this milieu that he can scarcely see the degree to which this ambition isolates and stultifies him. When he walks from home to fetch the doctor, all the shutters on the street are closed (61); when he is convinced that his wife will die in childbirth, he shuts the drawing-room door behind himself, mopes over a picture of Anna "holding a sheaf of artificial poppies and corn" (65), and regrets the degree to which time has altered how she looks. Erb and the servants take little notice of him, except to judge him "flabby as butter" (65). But there is a paradox here. Infatuated with artifice, Binzer nevertheless admires the fact that Anna at one time had "more 'go' and 'spirit' in her" (64); and he is bothered by stillness—when the wind drops, he is convinced his wife has died: "the whole house was still, terribly still" (65). Conceptualizing this character (the parallel with Stanley Burnell is sustained yet again), Mansfield seems, for all his limitations, to have initially granted him some promise. Yet when Erb announces to him that all is well, Mansfield's phrase for describing Binzer's reaction is curiously, revealingly flat: "He was exultant" (65). *Was.* Tactically, the phrasing emphasizes the state of being rather than the act of doing, as though Binzer aspired *to be seen to be* something, to have others grant him station and authority ("Nobody can accuse *me*"), rather than actually to exercise himself to action: to be seen to be a father of sons rather than actually to spend time raising children, to be exultant rather than to exult.

Investing his faith in the appearance of being powerful (the adjective), he surrenders his claim to live as a person who can actually empower (the verb).

"The Voyage" and **"The Wind Blows"** provide an interesting counterpoint to these stories of male gridlock. For **"The Voyage"** *begins* in disempowerment. Fenella's mother has died; her father cannot keep her; her grandmother comes to take her away; and the words that initially evince her condition reiterate stasis and death. Despite the setting (a boat dock), they imply no immediate possibility of change:

> The Picton boat was due to leave at half-past eleven. It was a beautiful night, mild, starry, only when they got out of the cab and started to walk down the Old Wharf that jutted out into the harbour, a faint wind blowing off the water ruffled under Fenella's hat, and she put up her hand to keep it on. It was dark on the Old Wharf, very dark; the wool sheds, the cattle trucks, the cranes standing up so high, the little squat railway engine, all seemed carved out of solid darkness. Here and there on a rounded wood-pile, that was like the stalk of a huge black mushroom, there hung a lantern, but it seemed afraid to unfurl its timid, quivering light in all that blackness; it burned softly, as if for itself.
>
> (470)

Four repetitions of the verb "was," the intensifying repetition of the word "dark," the *seeming* conversion of the sites of wharf activity to immobile "carvings," the overshadowing immensity of the fungal mushroom, the attachment to the hat, the personified timidity of the light, the closing adverb (as if) with its hint of uncertain hypothesis: all these technical strategies together suggest the bleakness of Fenella's circumstances and the power they exert over her. Against them, the active verbs and present participles exert only a quiet claim on an alternative possibility: started, jutted, blowing, ruffled, standing, unfurl, quivering, burned. But alternatives are precisely what the story opens up. On board, and just before sleep, Fenella sees her grandmother with her head "uncovered," her stays "loosened," breathing "a sigh of relief" as she "slowly and carefully pulled off her elastic-sidedboots and stood them side by side" (473). It is an example of possibility. All will be well, the story promises, or at least an improvement on what has been. But this is no naïve blinding transformation. Mansfield's story works to a different and more sophisticated kind of revelation, one that requires the sense of bleakness to recur and permits the counterpowers of action and life to deal again and yet again with it, before stasis slowly loosens its hold on Fenella's future.

This textual voyage (as distinct from the thematic and psychological voyages that constitute the substance of the overt narrative) records an ongoing exchange, adumbrated in the first paragraph, between verbs of state and verbs of motion.[2] Hence, when the Picton boat draws near its destination, before dawn, the verbs reiterate the opening motif: the apparent immobility of death and mourning. Fenella puts on "her black clothes again"—except that this time they don't quite cover: "a button sprang off one of her gloves and rolled to where she couldn't reach it" (475). Already the containment loosens, although (the antiphonal dialogue continuing) the static verbs return: "But if it had been cold in the cabin, on deck it was like ice. The sun was not up yet, but the stars were dim, and the cold pale sky was the same colour as the cold pale sea" (475). *Had been, was, was not, were, was*: not a dynamic moment. Yet the word "but," signalling a change in syntactic direction, also occurs twice, twice signalling further changes in psychological sensibility as well. Then active verbs re-enter the discourse, though the adjectives and nouns they carry at first do little to combat the sense of a pervasive morbidity in the landscape: "On the land a white mist rose and fell. Now they could see quite plainly dark bush. Even the shapes of the umbrella ferns showed, and those strange silvery withered trees that are like skeletons . . . Now they could see the landing-stage and some little houses, pale too . . . And now the landing-stage came out to meet them" (475). While the other passengers "looked gloomy," Fenella's grandmother "sounded pleased" (475), the difference between passivity in the one instance and animation in the other echoing the slow shift from an inanimate landscape to one inhabited, then peopled, then actively engaging, encouraging connection. But it is not enough that the grandmother should know her landscape; Fenella, so far, remains a stranger, and once they reach shore, the landscape turns still once more, the text reiterating the cyclical phrase that describes the mist: "Not a soul was to be seen; there was not even a feather of smoke. The mist rose and fell, and the sea sounded asleep as slowly it turned on the beach" (475). Almost at once, however, Mr Penreddy, the cart driver, speaks of other people in the community, and of their active concern to help each other. Treated already as though she were one of the local townspeople, Fenella quickly reaches her grandmother's home.

Yet twice more Fenella has to face immobility before the story closes, once for each time she stands on the threshold of a new (and each time smaller, more contained) territory: island, then port-town, then house, then room. At her new home the flowers "were fallen" in front of the "shell-like" house; the blinds "were drawn"; and bluchers and watering-can seem fixed in place on either side of the front door (475). Fenella waits. It is her grandmother who "turned the handle" and who calls out for her husband. And then (the vocabulary of death and timidity reiterated from the beginning here, but this time altering in resonance) the "white cat, that had been folded up like a camel, rose, stretched itself, yawned, and then sprang on to the tips of its toes. Fenella buried one cold little hand in the white, warm fur and smiled timidly while she stroked and listened" (476). When she then goes in to greet her grandfather, who is still lying in bed this early in the morning, and when she sees that above him, on the wall, "there was a big text in a deep-black frame" that speaks of a lost golden hour that *Is Gone For Ever* (476), it seems as though death (or dying) wins out after all. But then the story closes, *in speech*—language in use as a medium of communication between generations, between sexes, between people: "'Yer grandma painted that,' said grandpa. And he ruffled his white tuft and looked at Fenella so merrily she almost thought he winked at her" (476). Six active verbs in a row. They turn away from stasis at the end, and celebrate connection, affirm life, instead.

To turn in more detail to Matilda's story, **"The Wind Blows,"** is to see how another version of Mansfield's reiterative strategy elucidates the contrary appeals of a different personality and a different moment in life: to trace not a story of ego and desiccation, nor one of recuperative rebirth, but one shaped by the tensions of impending adolescence. On the edge of puberty, Matilda is impatient with the way things are and contrarily wants things to stay the same; she desires change and fears change, all at the same time, a state of affairs for which the incessant Wellington wind, moving and yet somehow not changing, is a strikingly apt metaphor. (Jacqueline Bardolph points to several occasions in Mansfield's fiction where the wind appears as a contrary image, associated paradoxically with both liberation and death [161]—that is, with both change and stasis.) Several further motifs here also clearly link **"The Wind Blows"** with other Mansfield stories: hats, for example, and music lessons. Hats, repeatedly, are signs of deference to convention, as when Fenella wears one for propriety's sake, or Laura Sheridan (in **"The Garden Party"**) puts one on at her mother's behest; in **"The Wind Blows"** Matilda (rebelling against her mother) deliberately wears an *old* hat to her music lesson and shouts "'Go to hell'" (192) at her mother as she runs down the road, an imprecation that likely dissipates in the wind. In another parallel, Mr Bullen, the oozingly charming music master to whom Matilda runs, combines features of Reginald Peacock and the pedophiliac old man of **"The Little Governess."** (Still later "music" stories include **"The Singing Lesson"** and, less directly, **"Miss Brill,"** and once again these stories obliquely deal with sexuality.)

Matilda's brother Bogey, like Laura Sheridan's brother Laurie, is the seeming counterfoil who, by his presence, combats the sense (stated, but not actually believed) that "Life is so dreadful" (193) and who can walk out with her into the wind and share her fantasies on the seashore esplanade. Most commentary on this story (though few critics pay it any attention at all) indeed concentrates on Bogey, using the story to romanticize Mansfield's relationship with her brother Leslie (for example, Hankin, 106; Daly, 62), and Saralyn Daly's version of it as a sketch with many tonal changes is a total misreading, arguing as it does that the story ends with a shift in perspective to "many years later" (60), when the narrator is leaving her island home with her brother and asks him to remember their childhood. No one leaves the island, and there is no shift in time. Place alters, in part in the imagination, but the entire action takes place within a single (turbulent, reverberating) day. Only Sydney Janet Kaplan acknowledges that, symbolically, it is "a story about awakening sexuality" (110). Returning the focus to Matilda, and to the story's form, reinforces this interpretation.

Basically the story divides into two sections, the first recording Matilda's waking up to a stormy day and heading off almost immediately to Mr Bullen's, where she is the second of three young girls to take piano lessons. In the second section Matilda and Bogey go for a walk on the esplanade to watch the storm, and when they see a ship leaving harbour, Matilda imagines them both aboard it, leaving behind the world-that-is for a world-that-might-be. In both sections flowers and mirrors repeat as images; in both sections particular phrases are repeated (as when Bullen, anticipating Peacock's "charming" phrase, greets each new student with "Sit . . . in the sofa corner, little lady," 192, 193). The question to ask is what effect the reiteration serves.

The opening paradox—"Something dreadful has happened. No—nothing has happened. It is only the wind" (191)—spells out the tension between change and changelessness that characterizes Matilda's age; at the same time the hint of the "dreadful," coupled with the apparent difficulty in recognizing what constitutes real threat, suggests how a gothic desire for adult adventure goes along, in this instance, with an apparent susceptibility to manipulation. The overriding effect of the first section, which takes Matilda away from her childhood home, is to get the reader to infer how corrupt the outside world is and how much safer Matilda would be if she didn't grow up and away; one effect of the second section is to reminisce on how innocent her (and Bogey's) childhood once was, and how inevitable and positive is the fact of growing up and away. The tension of "static action" with which the story opens, that is, repeats itself in the structural dialogue between the two halves of the story, two halves of a single glimpse of adolescent (and possibly artistic) desire.

The flower references contribute to this tension. Early on, Matilda's neighbour Marie Swainson "runs into the garden . . . to pick the 'chrysanths' before they are ruined" (191). "Ruin" might refer only to the storm's simple physical effect on flowers were it not for the fact that chrysanthemums are conventionally associated with death, and were it not also for the social and sexual innuendo of the succeeding sentence: "Her skirt flies up above her waist; she tries to beat it down, to tuck it between her legs while she stoops, but it is no use—up it flies" (191). Outside, the dust comes "in waves" (192) as Matilda runs to her lesson (sea and land overlapping in the windstorm), but Bullen's "cave"-like drawing-room seems "peaceful" (192) in contrast. What kind of peace can this be? Despite Matilda's fancies about her own maturity and musical sensitivity (she is dismissive of the "girl-before-her," who blushes when Bullen "puts his arms over her shoulders and plays the passage for her," 192), the "passage" she herself is undergoing is far more threatening and demanding than she realizes. The room "smells of art serge and stale smoke and chrysanthemums" (192). Matilda thinks she likes the smell, and likes the images that punctuate the room: the black piano, the pale photograph of Rubenstein on the mantelpiece, the picture of "'Solitude,' a dark, tragic woman" that hangs on the wall. These images, however, describe a room not of life but of seductive death. When Bullen leans over her shoulder ostensibly to play Beethoven and says "'Let's have a little of the old master'" (192), it is hard to ignore the double entendre. When Matilda's fingers "tremble" (and therefore cannot untie the "knot" in her satchel: "It's the wind . . . And her heart beats so hard she feels it must lift her blouse up and down," 192), when she asks if she should "take the repeat," and when Bullen goes on to say "something about 'waiting' and 'marking time' and 'that rare thing, a woman'" (193), the musical vocabulary overlaps with that of seduction. In this artificial indoor room Matilda thinks she can be "comfortable . . . for ever" (193), a moment broken suddenly when Marie Swainson, the student-after-her, arrives early, causing Bullen to stand up quickly and pull away from Matilda. When he reiterates his now-formulaic charge to the next girl, "Sit in the sofa corner, little lady," the first half of the story abruptly stops.

The second half just as abruptly begins "The wind, the wind" (193), with Matilda alone in her own room, where the "bed, the mirror, the white jug and basin gleam like the sky outside," where a pile of stockings lies "knotted up on the quilt like a coil of snakes," and where "It's the bed that is frightening" (193). With the interpenetration of storm and room, the implicitly sexual vocabulary takes a different turn. For if the covertly sexual escapade with Bullen implied stillness and death, the impending adventure with Bogey will at least initially seem active. Together the brother and sister will walk out into the storm, dismissing Shelley ("'I bring fresh flowers to the leaves and showers.' . . . What nonsense," 193[3]) and observing instead that the wind has "bent to the ground" the "pahutukawas" (the New Zealand Christmas flame tree, Mansfield's misspelling, 194). Dressed in identically hooked ulsters—that word "hooked" again (193)—they join arms ("'Hook on,' says Bogey," 194) and "cannot walk fast enough. Their heads bent, their legs just touching, they stride like one eager person through the town, down . . . [to] where the fennel grows wild" (194). At the breakwater "They pull off their hats" (194). Outside and inside coalesce once more: "They are covered with drops; the inside of her mouth tastes wet and cold" (194). And then there follows a passage that not only emphasizes Bogey as Matilda's age-mate but also links their relationship with the sexuality that had been broached in Bullen's music-room:

> Bogey's voice is breaking. When he speaks he rushes up and down the scale. It's funny—it makes you laugh—and yet it just suits the day. The wind carries their voices—away fly the sentences like the narrow ribbons.
>
> "Quicker! Quicker!"
>
> It is getting very dark.
>
> (194)

When they then see a "big black steamer . . . putting out to sea," and characterize *her* (the text emphasizes the female pronoun) as a force that the wind cannot stop, and when the text imagines them on board "arm in arm," the naïve musical morning is made to seem as though it took place "many years ago" (194). The brother and sister together "on board" have transformed the day, in what might be taken as little more than wish-fulfilment, or might be read as a more active sexual experiment.

But what, fundamentally, is it that Matilda wants? Another set of textual repetitions comes into play. First thing that morning she had been reluctant to look in the mirror at all; when she and Bogey leave for their walk, they look together into a glass and "know those two" (193), the familiar faces of their nearly gone childhood ("they have the same excited eyes and hot lips," 193); in the dark at the end of the day "They can't see those two" any more (194). Is it the two that they have imagined, those who are sailing away on board the disappearing ship? or the two in the glass, from earlier? The question remains unanswered; "The wind—the wind" (194) persists at the end, closing the story with the only fixed truth the narrative will admit to—that of change.

But the question does beg for an answer, and however a reader unpacks it reflects back on the whole story. If the sketch is just a narrative of childish dreaming, then it is possible to accept that the couple standing on the shore at the end can just no longer see their mirror-selves at sea, and say so; they have lost their glimpse, in other words, of the adult versions of themselves that they have hypothesized as sophisticated world travellers. This hypothesis raises still further questions, however, and even if it were the only possible interpretation, it would seem a tenuous and unsatisfactory reading. What, for example, does one make of the adult couple? Siblings, they stand arm in arm at the ship's rail like lovers, their innocence extended sexlessly from their early adolescent selves into the indeterminate future. It is only by such a configuration that "The Wind Blows" can be read simply as Mansfield's fond tribute to her real-life brother, but such a reading patently ignores the sexuality of the language of the rest of the story. What, then, if the story has nothing necessarily specific to do with Leslie Beauchamp at all? What if the brother in the story serves a fictional function? What if the story proposes an incestuous relationship rather than merely a strolling friendship? Such a reading would make more sense of the mirror imagery, the "excited eyes and hot lips," and the textual rhythms of music and seduction. Even the idea of "active stasis" (different but the same) gathers a new resonance in this context. This interpretation becomes more tenable, too, to the degree that it also makes sense of the hatless couple in the dark who can no longer see (recognize? catch a glimpse of? look at the world through the eyes of?) their childish selves but who, whatever they have come to realize, are still subject to the wind. It would, however, be a mistake simply to accept a tangentially worded narrative of incest at face value, as though Mansfield were necessarily confessing an autobiographical secret or trumpeting her freedom from a literary taboo. In fact, if she herself was ever the victim of parental or fraternal incest, evidence is indirect at best, and largely absent; if incest was ever a *literary* taboo, by contrast, scores of earlier writers had already transgressed the interdiction, and it is this context that extends even further the implications of **"The Wind Blows."**

Mary Burgan, in *Illness, Gender and Writing,* quotes entries from Mansfield's 1916 journal, after Leslie Beauchamp had died, to suggest that the "brother/sister incest taboo had always shadowed Mansfield's feeling about her little brother; now the longing for some ultimate intimacy with the loved usurper became a passionate identification with him. In imagining her brother as a twin who takes over her body" (102), Burgan argues, Mansfield is not necessarily recalling a physical fact but simply demonstrating a pattern of behaviour—a "displacement" of identity—characteristic among some adolescents, those who have fixed on a sibling as a "twin" and are at once enraged and paralysed when the artificial identification breaks down. Faced with the break from her real brother, Burgan says, Mansfield called "into play an ethic of work, . . . her ideological commitment to writing" (102), to counter her feelings of anger, paralysis, longing for death, and childish vulnerability. It was this sensibility, continues Burgan, that led to the great stories of "childbirth and its possible power of reconciliation," especially **"Prelude"** and **"At the Bay"** (104). **"The Wind Blows,"** of course—in its first incarnation called **"Autumn II"**[4]—appeared in the journal *Signature* on 4 October 1915, three days before Leslie's death in France (Alpers, 555), and Burgan does not mention the story in connection with her argument. But the psychological paradigm she outlines, one that involves writing as therapy, relates interestingly to a line of literary uses of the theme of incest that extends at least from Milton to Byron, Mary Shelley, George Eliot, and beyond.

Surveying women's writing of the nineteenth century in *The Madwoman in the Attic,* Sandra Gilbert and Susan Gubar provide some relevant comments. Arguing that the complicated relation between women writers and Byronic heroes "derived in part from Milton's portrayal of the Sin-Satan relationship" (which produced the child Death), they argue that "admiring, even adoring, Satan's Byronic rebelliousness, his scorn of conventional virtues, his raging energy, the woman writer may have secretly fantasized that she *was* Satan—or Cain, or Manfred, or Prometheus. But at the same time her feelings of female powerlessness manifested themselves in her conviction that the closest she could really get to being Satan was to be his creature" (207). Quoting from Adrienne Rich's "Natural Resources"—to the effect that Will Ladislaw, Dorothea's lover in George Eliot's *Middlemarch,* is a prototype of the kind of man who tries to understand women and who is figured as brother, as twin (530)—they further characterize the incest motif by alluding to Mary Shelley's *Frankenstein*: "For Milton, and therefore for Mary Shelley, who was trying to understand Milton, incest was an inescapable metaphor for the solipsistic fever of self-awareness that Matthew Arnold [in his preface to his *Poems,* 1853] was later to call 'the dialogue of the mind with itself'" (229). The relation between metaphors of sexuality and metaphors of language consequently emphasizes at once the dangers, the isolation, and the ecstasy of creativity:

> To the extent that the desire to violate the incest taboo is a desire to be self-sufficient—self-begetting—it is a divinely interdicted wish to be "as Gods," like the desire for the forbidden fruit of the tree of knowledge, whose taste also meant death. For the woman writer, moreover, even the reflection that the Byronic hero is as much a creature of her mind—an incarnation of her "private, brooding, female resentments"—as she is an invention of his, offers little solace. For if in loving her he [the Byronic hero, Satan, "artist of death, the paradigmatic master of all those perverse aesthetic techniques that pleasure the body rather than the soul, and serve the world rather than God"] loves himself, in loving him she loves herself, and is therefore similarly condemned to the death of the soul that punishes solipsism . . . [D]efining herself as the "creature" of one or the other of these irreligious artists, the woman writer would be confirmed . . . in her fear that she was herself a false creator, . . . for whom the arts of language . . . are . . . only . . . parodies of the language of the angels and the music of the spheres . . . [D]windling by degrees into an infertile drone, she might well conclude that this image of Satan and Eve as the false art-

ists of creation was finally the most demeaning and discouraging avatar of Milton's bogey.

(209-10)

"The Wind Blows," however, does not express discouragement, nor any overt or passive acceptance of a Miltonic world order, though perhaps there is more than the usual rebellious resonance in the fact that Matilda's first, *shouted* words in the story are "Go to hell" (192). It may be difficult to turn either Bullen or Bogey into a Byronic giant, but not hard at all to see Bogey as Matilda's "twin" and therefore an extension of herself with whom she is in some sort of close, impassioned (if finally unproductive) dialogue, nor is it hard to read Bullen as a father-figure agent of creative death. Reading **"The Wind Blows"** as a sketch involving an incest motif does not require a specific Satanic paradigm; it does, nevertheless, return the critical focus to the issue of language and creativity, and to the formal dialogues between stasis and change that structure a number of Mansfield's fictions.

For the paradigms of reiteration have repeatedly concerned themselves with the power to use language creatively. The married man cannot do so, nor can Peacock, or Binzer, or Bullen, yet all make claims on sexual power and on the power that accrues from precedence and social convention. Mansfield's accomplishment in these portraits is in part to demonstrate the emptiness of the social and artistic prototypes that—however much they were granted authority—merely repeat the past. The challenge lay in finding an alternative mode of discourse within which to express a sensibility beyond insecurity. Insecurity, in these stories, produces automatic utterance, formula, coercive texts that inhibit growth and understanding; it expresses itself as mental inactivity because it employs language as a barrier, a "static agent" against the world rather than a means of engaging with the processes of living. If, in consequence, language is a barrier, it functions more like silence than speech, more like death than life, and Mansfield's female characters in particular, often silenced by convention, are textually required to reread their silence and find new ways to express their identities and their claims upon the future. As **"The Voyage"** and **"The Wind Blows"** elucidate this process, the passage into creative language is not smooth, nor is it guaranteed of success. Reiteration can sometimes imply creative failure. But by linking the creativity of language with the creativity of female sexuality, Mansfield emphasized that a dialogue with death and an engagement with the twinned, divided self could also lead alike to social renewal and psycholinguistic rebirth.

Notes

1. In *Fiction and Repetition* J. Hillis Miller draws attention to two kinds of repetition, which, he argues, interrelate, and help to shape the character of the realistic novel. Although his analyses of repetition as subversion, irony, and revelation of the "uncanny" in nineteenth century and Modernist novels is tangential to commentary on Mansfield, his distinction is relevant here: between a "Platonic" model and a "Nietzschean" one (6)—i.e., between one that, through mimesis, acquires its validity by the fact of repeating an original model and one that, however strong the sense of similarity it draws on, can only, in the action of repeating, emphasize its difference from that which preceded it.

2. For a structuralist analysis of "The Voyage," see Bonheim ("Metaphor Boxes"); see also Lojkine-Morelec ("Les Objets comme repères"); and cf Harmat's structuralist analysis of "Miss Brill" ("Essai d'analyse").

3. Shelley's "The Cloud" of course opens "I bring fresh showers for the thirsting flowers"; Mansfield's deliberate misquotation here not only suggests Matilda's limited memory for poetry but also converts the phrase into one that functions more pointedly within the imagery of "The Wind Blows" itself. Clearly, what Matilda's storm of adolescent aspiration is not associated with, in a context of dead chrysanthemums and bent pohutakawas, is "fresh flowers"; the sexual longing that the story obliquely expresses is far less domestic and far more dramatic than that.

4. "Autumn I" also appeared in *Signature* and was subsequently collected, as "The Apple-Tree," in Murry's "Definitive Edition" of Mansfield's *Journal*. While Alpers calls the story "a trivial piece" (*Stories*, 555), and does not collect it in the so-called "Definitive Edition" of Mansfield's *Stories*, the imagery of "Autumn I" is relevant to a reading of "Autumn II." In the earlier sketch an unnamed narrator recalls two orchards from her youth, one a "wild" one (*Stories*, 86) that she and her brother Bogey do not go near, the other one that they do visit, "hidden from the house," where the grass grew "so thick and coarse that it tangled and knotted in your shoes" (86). This latter orchard has a "Forbidden Tree" (87), named so by their father, who anticipates (because an Englishman has told him so) that it will bear special fruit; when they bite into the apples it produces in the autumn, however—even though they lie to their father that the apples are "perfect"—the fruit tastes "floury" and "bitter" and "horrible" and "dry" (89). "Autumn," perhaps coincidentally, is also the season that dates the moment of crisis in the life of the narrator of "The Married Man's Story."

Works Cited

Burgan, Mary. *Illness, Gender and Writing: The Case of Katherine Mansfield*. Baltimore & London: Johns Hopkins University Press 1994.

Daly, Saralyn. *Katherine Mansfield*. New York: Twayne 1965.

Gilbert, Sandra M., and Susan Gubar. *The Madwoman in the Attic: The Woman Writer and the Nineteenth-Century Literary Imagination*. New Haven and London: Yale University Press 1979.

Hankin, C. A. *Katherine Mansfield and Her Confessional Stories*. London: Macmillan 1983.

Kaplan, Sydney Janet. "Katherine Mansfield's 'Passion for Technique.'" In *Women's Language and Style*, ed. Douglas Butturff and Edmund L. Epstein. Akron: University of Akron Press 1978. 119-31.

———. *Katherine Mansfield and the Origins of Modernist Fiction*. Ithaca and London: Cornell University Press 1991.

Mansfield, Katherine. *The Aloe with Prelude*. Ed. Vincent O'Sullivan. Wellington: Port Nicholson Press 1982.

———. *The Collected Letters of Katherine Mansfield*. Ed. Vincent O'Sullivan and Margaret Scott. Vol. 1: *1903-1917*; 2: *1918-1919*; 3: *1919-1920*; 4: *1920-1921*. Oxford: Clarendon 1984, 1987, 1993, 1996.

———. *The Critical Writings of Katherine Mansfield*. Ed. Clare Hanson. London: Macmillan 1987.

———. *Dramatic Sketches*. Intro. David Dowling, Wilhelmina Drummond, and David Drummond. Palmerston North: Nagare Press 1988.

———. *Journal of Katherine Mansfield*. Ed. J. Middleton Murry. Definitive Edition. London: Constable 1962.

———. *Katherine Mansfield: Manuscripts in the Alexander Turnbull Library*. Wellington: Alexander Turnbull Library 1988.

———. *Katherine Mansfield: Publications in Australia, 1907-09*. Ed. Jean E. Stone. Sydney: Wentworth 1977.

———. *The Letters and Journals of Katherine Mansfield*. Ed. C. K. Stead. Harmondsworth: Penguin 1977.

———. Letters and Papers of Katherine Mansfield, 1907-1922. Newberry Library, Chicago. MS Group 44.

———. "[London]." Ed. Margaret Scott. *Turnbull Library Record* 3.3 (Nov. 1970): 129-36.

———. *Poems of Katherine Mansfield*. Ed. Vincent O'Sullivan. Auckland: Oxford 1988.

———. *The Scrapbook of Katherine Mansfield*. Ed. J. Middleton Murry. London: Constable 1939.

———. *The Stories of Katherine Mansfield*. Ed. Antony Alpers. Auckland: Oxford University Press 1984.

———. "Study: The Death of a Rose." *Triad* (Dunedin), 1908, 35.

———. *The Urewera Notebook*. Ed. Ian Gordon. London: Oxford 1978.

R. A. York (essay date 1999)

SOURCE: York, R. A. "Katherine Mansfield: Stories." In *The Rules of Time: Time and Rhythm in the Twentieth-Century Novel*, pp. 82-93. London: Associated University Presses, 1999.

[*In the following essay, York analyzes how Mansfield comically juxtaposes John Hammond's impatience and need for control in "The Stranger," and the slow pace of events forced upon the character. York goes on to describe how Mansfield achieves a level of self-knowledge in the pompous Hammond, who evolves from "complacent ignorance of other people to a sudden confrontation with death and with the variety of people's attachments."*]

Katherine Mansfield's story **"The Stranger"** is about impatience. It concerns John Hammond, a middle-aged man whose wife, Janey, has been away from home (which is presumably in New Zealand) for ten months visiting their daughter in Europe, and it recounts the short time from his waiting for her boat to dock at the harbor to their arrival at a hotel and their first private contact. During this time, John talks with other people waiting for the boat, meets his wife, and observes her farewells to her fellow travelers. They take a short cab drive, settle in at the hotel as her luggage is delivered, and finally have a brief conversation. The story is some 5,000 words long and perhaps narrates some one hour of experience; in other words, a slow reading would take nearly as long as the events recounted. Here is a first paradox; the story is about impatience, but the style of narration is rather leisurely. This might be read, in principle, in one of two ways: either the narration is a demonstration of thorough, sound, systematic storytelling with proper attention to pace and decorum—in which case the implication might be that the haste of the central character is inappropriate—or the narrator is deliberately teasing the readers by withholding the climax that they, like Mr. Hammond, can quite legitimately expect. The reunion of married people after a long break is surely an occasion for eagerness, to say the least; if Mrs. Hammond had returned to find her husband calm and resigned to the delay in her arrival, she might naturally have been upset by his indifference. The situation, we shall see, is actually quite subtle.

The first point to note is the quite heavy emphasis on Hammond's impatience. The opening words of the story are: "It seemed to the little crowd on the wharf that she was never going to move again." The exaggeration is a normal conversational one and certainly not surprising when we learn that the crowd has been waiting for two hours. Still, it may shock a little, especially given the sudden plunge of the reader into the situation, with that initially obscure "she" and "again" (Who is she? When did she last move?). The feeling of a possibly excessive pressure is reinforced by the very heavy stress on the rapidity or brusqueness of Hammond's manner: he has a "quick, eager glance," his eyes "searched anxiously, quickly, the motionless liner," he obsessively consults his watch, he paces quickly up and down—all this within a couple of pages, and persistently counterpointed with the obstinate slowness of everything else: the "old chaps lounging against the gangways" (who, Hammond manages to persuade himself, are not simply idlers but "fine, solid old chaps," "solid" no doubt meaning "slow"), the dusk, which "at least might have the decency to keep off for a bit" but which "came slowly, spreading like a slow stain over the water," the Captain "hanging about in the stream."

This is getting comic, as Hammond's irritability struggles desperately and repeatedly with his sense of respectability and his good nature; it is a comedy born of repetition and disproportion. In other words, it is a comedy depending essentially on a sense of time, on the difference between the pace that is natural to the central character and the pace that is imposed upon him by circumstances and on his inability to cope moderately with this difference. The comedy continues discreetly, throughout the story: rushing onto the liner, the first of the waiting crowd and immediately behind the harbor master, he is greeted by his wife saying coolly, "Well, darling! Have you been waiting long?" She then insists on saying good-bye to all sorts of people ("It was plain as a pikestaff," Hammond consoles himself, "that she was by far the most popular woman on board"), tips the stewardess, and at the very last moment insists on going off to see the ship's doctor, though denying that she has been ill ("That was rather queer of Janey, wasn't it?"). Arriving at the hotel, they seem to be coming closer to the culminating moment of intimacy. Hammond hastily avoids his acquaintances in the public rooms in his longing to be alone with his wife, only to be interrupted ("Would you believe it!") by a porter with the luggage, and at this moment Janey starts showing a quite uncalled-for interest in letters from their children, their father heartlessly insisting that "later on will do." All this is approaching farce, suggesting the Feydeau series of contretemps and obstacles, even though in Feydeau it is not usually marital love that is thus impeded. And this comic perspective throws an important light on the sense of the story: Hammond's impatience is not just natural and respectable; it is also essentially a manifestation of power and possessiveness. Decent, responsible, outgoing, and efficient as he may be, he is also a butt for amusement because of his failure to apprehend what other people are like, his failure to see that other people have other priorities: "They knew, every man-jack of them, that Mrs. Hammond was on that boat, and he was so tremendously excited that it never entered his head not to believe that this marvellous fact meant something to them too." At this point, Hammond's excitement may be quite endearing; so, perhaps, is his first vision of her "between two great clumsy idiots." But we gradually realize that his affection is always of a patronizing and restricted kind, so that his reflection, "How little she looked to have come all that long way and back by herself!" is in fact a way of subordinating her, of denying her independence and responsibility, and is quite consistent with his rejoicing that she is "not a day changed. Just as he'd always known her" and his satisfaction at seeing her luggage labeled with her married name as "Mrs. John Hammond." In short, Hammond is, at bottom, the pompous and self-regarding buffoon who is the mainstay of many comedies—though presented with Katherine Mansfield's usual restraint and discretion.

The rhythm of the story up to now has been a largely comic one; it comprises a number of brief and partially successful attempts by Hammond to gain control of Janey. But the climax of the story changes the pattern as well as the tone of the whole. As Hammond at last embraces her, he feels weariness, his thoughts turn self-pityingly to his own excitements during the day rather than to her ten months away: "There we were, hanging about. What kept you so long?" And the answer, given slowly, hesitantly, thoughtfully, is that she has been held back by death; she has nursed a young man who has died in her arms of some heart trouble, and the delay was caused by medical formalities.

This news retrospectively makes a new kind of sense out of the story; the delay is no longer a simple annoyance, one of many, but is rationally intelligible (the two hours' waiting, we should remember, follows on the departure of "the doctor's launch," Janey has been eager to see the doctor, and even though he is usually unobservant about clothes, Hammond has noted that she is wearing black). The story is a cohesive one, and what gives it its cohesion is the ultimate challenge to the self-assertive pride that typifies Hammond: death and the demands death makes on those who have contact with it. Janey's preoccupation with death arouses immediate jealousy in her husband, of a quite clearly sexual kind: he is particularly aware that the young man has died in her arms and that this physical contact comes obviously by her own will, whereas he implies that her behavior towards him has been generally passive and cool. And this concern of hers for another person has, in his eyes, made a radical difference between them; in a final sentence that elegantly inverts the first, he reflects that "they would never be alone together again." The phrase, moreover, echoes a thoughtless but revealing hyperbolic expression Hammond used at the beginning of their conversation: "I feel I'll never have you to myself again." At the end, that vague discontent has become a profound anxiety. And no doubt he is right, at least in the sense he gives to the words: no doubt he will never again be the only object in her thoughts. The story has attained a new level of decisiveness; from trivial delay it has slipped to significant change, as Hammond has passed from complacent ignorance of other people to a sudden confrontation with death and with the variety of people's attachments.

How is this discovery handled by the processes of narration? Mansfield apparently totally suppresses the personality of the narrator, which gives the impression that the text is nothing but a record of the consciousness of the characters, or of a single character, in this case Hammond. Undoubtedly she achieves an extraordinary success, equaled by very few other authors, in this elimination of narratorial comment or interpretation, leaving an impression of impersonality, objectivity, even inscrutability, in which the reader has to decide for himself or herself on the value and significance of the events portrayed. But this absence of the narrator can only be apparent; the narrator actually survives in the occasional references to things Hammond doesn't see (such as his wife's expression of concern when he queries her health), in the occasional explanations that seem not to be in Hammond's consciousness ("The blow was so sudden that Hammond thought he would faint"), in certain patterns of imagery that the reader finds difficult to associate with his unsophisticated and immediate frame of mind (the grip of the chair he feels as he is shocked by Janey's news of the death [362] recalls the grip of anxiety as he waits [357]), in certain visions that appear to be that of the author rather than that of the character ("the great blind bed, with his coat flung across it like some headless man saying his prayers" [363]). Above all, the act of narration appears in patterns of pace and rhythm. Someone other than Hammond has decided what to narrate in detail, what to summarize, what to omit.

Given the general orientation of the text to the consciousness of the central character, it is inevitable that detailed, apparently unedited narrative should predominate. But this itself has a particular effect. Since readers are accustomed to narratives that (like any other form of communication) are governed by the principle of relevance and do not contain material that does not advance the point of the story, they will be conscious of the various factors of slowness: repetition, recounting of trivia, searching for exact formulations. So, we have, for instance, dialogue that repeats information given as unspoken thought:

> There wasn't a pair of glasses between the whole lot of them.

> "Curious thing, Mr. Scott, that none of us thought of glasses."
>
> (350)

We have dialogue that is completely uninformative, as far as the relationship of the Hammonds is concerned:

> "All well?"
>
> "All well."
>
> "How's mother?"
>
> "Much better."
>
> "Hullo, Jean!"
>
> "Hillo, Aun' Emily!"
>
> (354)

We have an attempt to analyze the impressions given by a rather unsatisfactory kiss:

> It seemed to him there was a tiny pause—but long enough for him to suffer torture—before her lips touched his, firmly, lightly—kissing them as she always kissed him, as though the kiss—how could he describe it?—confirmed what they were saying, signed the contract.
>
> (361)

All this comes from Hammond's consciousness, and it makes his consciousness seem somewhat strange to us. The first example is, of course, an instance of his making conversation while waiting; the activity is normal enough, even if it does drive people into remarks as pointless as this, but the narrative technique underlines the pointlessness and lets us see it as a reflection of Hammond's wish to dominate, to be the center of attention. The chain of greetings is perhaps a little too analytically treated; according to the narrator, the voices "flew to greet each other," but this hardly reads like flying—it looks like a rather obsessive interest in the circumstances of waiting, as opposed to the purpose of it. And the puzzled analysis of the much awaited kiss is very strange: Hammond seeks to describe his sensations to himself, becomes a spectacle for himself; the heightened self-awareness brought about by delay seems to have excluded the intended climax. In short, the chosen method of moment-by-moment narration is one that is essentially alien to the central character's apparent concern for rapid assertion of will and possession; it shows how far life is a matter of dependency and distance, of waiting for other people and of seeking to discover oneself.

The technique of immediate and exhaustive depiction is, in any case, not quite fully maintained. In the earlier parts, at least, of the story, there is some display of economy. There is, for instance, the turning of the ship to come in:

At last! She was slowly, slowly turning round. A bell sounded far over the water and a great spout of steam gushed into the air. The gulls rose; they fluttered away like bits of white paper. And whether that deep throbbing was her engines or his heart Mr. Hammond couldn't say.

This is certainly not rapid narration, but it is a condensation, insofar as it takes much less time to read these fifty words than it does to watch a ship turning. The word "slowly" does much of the work here; that and the throbbing put the emphasis on the recognition of change, on the effect rather than the process, and so imply that moments are being selected by the narrator in view of their importance. The point is even clearer in the one obvious omission that appears in the text: a row of dots covers the time from Hammond's sending for someone to collect the luggage from the ship to the couple's arrival on the wharf. The time cannot be estimated exactly; they have to wait for someone to ensure that the luggage will in fact be collected, walk to the gangway and down it (possibly amidst the general impediments of other disembarking passengers), and find their direction on the wharf. This is no doubt a matter of some minutes. That these minutes are not narrated is a sort of courtesy to the reader, since they can easily be reconstituted, as we have just seen. But there is more to it than that. First, the gap appears to promise a sudden shift in the narrator's attitude; the waiting, we might feel, is over, and we shall now come to the real business of marital communion. This is partly true; we are indeed approaching a sort of climax. But it is not the sort of climax we might be expecting, and we are not approaching as fast as we might think; the narrator is almost teasing us by taking us, fairly slowly, to what may seem to be an anticlimax, to an imperfect and understated contact between the couple. And that teasing is part of the point of the story; we have to learn not to share Hammond's impatience and to reprove ourselves—with humor, no doubt, but not without gravity—if we have been seduced by his eagerness, if we have shared his irritation with waiting crowds and the stewardess needing to be tipped. And second, the omission is not just a courtesy, not just a passing-over of redundant material; it also conceals a difficult transition. Just before this point, Mr. Hammond has been anxious: "And again, as always, he had the feeling he was holding something that never was quite his—his." "As always": the narrator is intruding here, generalizing beyond the moment. And the generalization is one that might apply to quite a lot of Mansfield's characters, including many less dynamic than the present one: it concerns the sense of separation from the desired object. This focuses forcefully what is perhaps the central theme of the story. Hammond reacts with brutal energy: "For God's sake let's get off to the hotel so that we can be by ourselves!," and, momentarily, the narrator appears to share his brusqueness, suddenly—magically, so to speak—placing him on dry land and in a more positive frame of mind: "She took his arm. He had her on his arm again. . . . No more going without his tea or pouring out his own. She was back." The stability achieved here is not going to last, of course, but the brief feint of satisfaction, of delay overcome, of a problem solved, at least writes into the story—obvious as the irony may be—a not quite unsympathetic sense of the desired orderliness of life.

This is the rhythm of what Hammond wants, not of what he has to put up with. The effect is a double one: the moment strengthens such element of sympathy for him as has existed throughout the story so far and so prevents it from becoming too facile a satire on male possessiveness; but it also prepares for his final defeat by making the revelation of Janey's separate concerns come as a surprise, as a sudden blow disproportionate to her mildness of speech and gentleness of manner; it stresses the unpredictability of other people, it shows that their difference from us is incalculable.

It goes, in short, towards allowing the story to be read as an account of a revelation, of a moment in which the familiar is seen afresh (freshness here implying suddenness), and it allows the reader to experience both the unenlightened feeling of a wish for conclusiveness and comfort and also the moment of enlightenment, the discovery of otherness. Certain aspects of narrative proportion in the story as a whole arise from this same structure. The period of waiting accounts for some ten pages and contains various subdivisions (waiting for the boat, boarding, moving to the hotel, receiving the luggage); the final, revealing talk occupies some two and a half pages and is essentially a continuous whole. It appears to be essential that an enlightenment be set against a norm, and it appears that the character of a norm is to be protracted and repetitious; it is therefore essential that the part of the story enacting the norm be fairly long and the part enacting the revelation—by contrast—be fairly brief. But it would also seem to be essential that the account of the moment of enlightenment not be too brief, though the reason is not quite as clear-cut. The reason for length in the presentation of the norm is one of mimesis; life is long-drawn-out and repetitious, and the story should imitate these characteristics. It is not clear that the length of the climax is governed by considerations of imitation. On the one hand, it might be argued that an important discovery (such as that of the profound difference between oneself and one's spouse) is bound to arouse many rapid thoughts and that these ought to be depicted by the writer of fiction; on the other, it might be argued that an important discovery about the nature of human life should not be rushed, that on grounds of dignity and respect for the bases of human life a decorous slowness should be observed. If either of these arguments is correct, there has been a change of attitude to the whole business of storytelling; the bulk of the story is governed by a wish to depict the actual, the climax by a wish to do justice to it. (This is especially clear if we take the second view, that of dignity and profundity; even if we take the first, we are considering how much psychological activity *ought* to be presented). There is a shift from the actual to the normative; rhythm in this way enacts the significance of the story.

Many of Katherine Mansfield's stories follow a similar pattern of expectation and reversal. Fullbrook (1986) sees such reversals, very pertinently, as "moments of truly existential wonder and terror" and rightly stresses their discontinuity with the normal course of (male-dominated) life (32). An earlier critic (Hormasji 1967) notes that Mansfield's subject matter "is the prosaic and the ordinary, the life of the everyday." But he is too simple in saying that "the events which happen in the lives of her characters are not memorable or of any major import" (85). This is true enough, as far as public import is concerned. For the characters themselves, the events are revelations that may utterly disrupt the ordinariness of their lives. The very fine story **"The Garden-Party,"** for instance, again produces an encounter with death as its climax but sets this in a somewhat more complex context: the central character, Laura, wishes to cancel her family's garden party when she hears that a neighboring workman has died, but she is overruled by the rest of the family. At the end of the day, she is sent to deliver a parcel of leftover food to the house of the dead man and is moved at seeing the body, which she finds both impressively serene and somewhat embarrassing. The pattern of contrasts between context and climax is complex: life against death, bustle against repose, middle-class decorum and complacency against working-class unrestraint, enjoyment against gravity, dissipation of emotion against concentration. And the structure is somewhat more complex than in **"The Stranger"** because of the many moments of fine visual observation that make small climaxes in the preparatory part of the story (but that eventually have to be reinterpreted as mere incidents of hedonistic life) and still more because of the moments of tension in the preparatory section as first Laura and then—less radically—her father worry about the propriety of life continuing in the presence of death. The preparatory section is thus not a case of simple waiting but rather of the uncertainties of adolescent impulsiveness or adolescent decency and so acquires an interest in itself and not simply as preparation for a conclusion.

But other Mansfield stories give a more worrying problem to anyone seeking to find patterns in fiction. These are stories in which, one is rather tempted to say, nothing happens; stories in which there seems to be no climax, which might as well, as it seems, have finished a page earlier or gone on a page longer; stories that are nevertheless not demonstrations of literary incompetence but impressive stories that a sensitive reader can read with full absorption and a sense of an enriched life. If this sort of description is accurate, it would seem that, for some fiction at least, climaxes don't matter and that rhythm doesn't therefore matter; all that matters is the delicacy, subtlety, convincingness, humor, or pathos of the writing; it is the quality of the reading experience that matters rather than its shape. And undoubtedly there is much truth in this, and it is a truth that applies to many writers of the period we are considering (as well as to previous writers, such as Chekhov, obviously one of Katherine Mansfield's major influences). Many modern writers do not obviously seek climax; one might even say that their works are a struggle to produce fiction without climaxes, or at the very least to mute such climaxes as may be inevitable.

An example of such writing is **"The Voyage."** This recounts a night boat journey (between the two islands of New Zealand?) in which Fenella, a young girl whose mother has just died, is taken from her father's home by her grandmother to stay with her and her grandfather. Grandmother and granddaughter get on the boat, say farewell to the father, consider buying sandwiches but find them too expensive, go to bed, are visited by the stewardess, arrive on shore, and go to the grandparents' house, where they find the grandfather in bed. During all this time, Fenella has been given charge of her grandmother's swan-necked umbrella, which she has carefully preserved and which she hooks onto the grandfather's bed-rail as they arrive. And that is the story. A hasty reader could certainly say that "nothing has happened," or at least nothing major; the important event in Fenella's life is the death of her mother, and the important change—a fairly normal, even routine one in the circumstances—is that she goes to live with new people. But the death takes place before the story, and the life with the grandparents takes place after it; it seems perverse to focus on a transition, which in itself contains no events beyond the banal: grandmother's prayers, her loosening of her stays, Fenella's not eating a banana.

But there is an event, an event so miraculous as to be almost imperceptible. It is one that depends in large part again on the degree of sympathy or intimacy with the central character that the story allows. The narration essentially follows Fenella's observations, but (unlike the treatment of John Hammond) it does not reproduce her consciousness continuously, and it says little about her response to the things she sees. But the response is not totally absent: she is awkward at the beginning, clutching her hat to keep it on and giving "an undignified little skip" to keep up with her hurrying elders; she seems to be pecked by the umbrella "as if it too wanted her to hurry"; she sees that her father looks tired and sad; she finds the farewell of grandmother and father "awful" and turns away; she asks anxiously how long she is to stay and gets no answer—except a present of a shilling that persuades her that she is going away forever; she notes that her grandmother is praying and later is afraid that she is going to do it again; she overhears the stewardess sentimentally commenting on her as a "poor motherless mite." And as they reach land, the text for once reproduces her thought very explicitly: "Oh, it had all been so sad lately. Was it going to change?" And as they reach the new home, it does change: there is a white cat "folded up like a camel," and a white-bearded grandfather, and it is the grandfather's good humor that ends the story: "And he ruffled his white tuft and looked at Fenella so merrily she almost thought he winked at her." So, there is here, as in **"The Stranger,"** a discovery: whereas Hammond in the midst of his excessive pride and security finds death, Fenella in the midst of her anxiety finds life and welcome. The distinctive thing about **"The Voyage"** is not that there is no climax; it is that the climax is an event that can be seen as climactic only in the given context—it might elsewhere be dull or trivial. And the story does much to mask the climax, which is not surprising, since a meeting with a grandfather is a predictable result of a journey to the home of grandparents, and indeed he has been briefly mentioned (and it is certainly not surprising that a grandfather should smile and have a white beard); it is not conclusive, since we have no guarantee that this welcome is going to continue; it is very brief (a half page out of ten), and the indication of both sides of the contrast, Fenella's anxiety and the grandfather's good humor, is extremely understated and might be overlooked on a cursory reading (the pathos of Fenella's voyage being appreciably undercut by the narrator's humor and by her own sensitivity and curiosity in observation). This, one might say, is a kind of minimalist narration, in which the procedures of expectation and contrasting fulfillment are deployed as discreetly as possible; but they are deployed nevertheless and make for much of the satisfaction the story gives us.

"The Voyage" is the story of a kind of grace, of the gift of happiness as a compensation for hardship, and of the ordeal of an ill-prepared waiting for such grace. It is a story because it implies that the sequence of events in time makes sense and affects the quality of our experience, that waiting affects the way we receive the thing we have waited for. It presents, subtly and imaginatively, an attunement to the future. The short story tends to be a study of waiting, expectation, and apprehension. Our study shows the same to be true of many novels; Katherine Mansfield brings these things to the forefront of the reader's attention. Her work is fascinating, it demands the reader's most delicate sympathy because experiences of the sort depicted might not seem to the uninvolved observer to constitute an event at all because it does not constitute an obvious anecdote with an obvious finality. The correspondence of expectancy and culmination is tenuous; it depends, for one thing, on the author's control of atmosphere through image, recurrent phrasing, point of view, and pace, and for another on the reader's sense of the incompleteness of some kinds of experience and the fullness of others, the conclusiveness of death and love. Two structures are superimposed: a structure of fictional culmination and a structure of discovering ultimate values, and they work together to create a sense of the elusive satisfactoriness of life.

Bibliography

Critical Works are cited throughout by year and page number, the author's name being evident from the text.

Fullbrook, K. *Katherine Mansfield*. Brighton: Harvester, 1986.

Hormasji, N. *Katherine Mansfield, An Appraisal*. London: Collins, 1967.

Diane McGee (essay date 2001)

SOURCE: McGee, Diane. "'Hungry Roaming': Dinners and Non-Dinners in the Stories of Katherine Mansfield." In *Writing the Meal: Dinner in the Fiction of Early Twentieth-Century Women Writers*, pp. 81-107. Toronto: University of Toronto Press, 2001.

[*In the following essay, McGee argues that two key ideas become apparent in Mansfield's treatment of meals in her stories: one, meals paradoxically indicate the absence of "communality, commensality, intimacy, and warmth which the rituals of sharing food are supposed to create"; and two, Mansfield's representation of meals reflects the tensions in women's lives—their acute sense of being trapped between a desire for woman's traditional role and their new-found freedom.*]

Homelessness and Hunger

In her depiction of old New York, Edith Wharton points the way to changes in consciousness that are typical of the modernist period and that affect women and are expressed in the writing of women in very particular ways. The social change traced by her work is well established in the fiction of Katherine Mansfield. If, in Wharton, society is defined in large part by customs of dining and sociability, in Mansfield's short stories, dining and attitudes to food in general are linked to the modern predicaments and modernist themes of homelessness, rootlessness, alienation, and isolation. In sum, Mansfield's meals elucidate the contradictions surrounding changing roles for women in the context of the larger social changes which marked the first part of the century.

Because meals are so central to notions of the home, their literary treatment is a key index to modern experiences of homelessness or a sense of homelessness, and, in Mansfield, reflects a profound ambivalence about that state of being or state of mind. From childhood, as noted in chapter 1, food plays a crucial role in people's lives, not only in forming our habits and tastes, but in defining our feelings of warmth and security. Food figures strongly in our memories of home, usually evoking positive associations: a nostalgia for 'mom's home cooking' is expected, a cliché. In adult life, meals are a crucial element in creating a home—usually the job of a woman. For various reasons, homes are problematic in both *The House of Mirth* and *The Custom of the Country*; however, they are particularly so in Mansfield's work. If circumstances in some of her stories seem to make it impossible for characters to create a home, it may also be a character's choice not to do so, an attempt, perhaps, to liberate herself from the constraints a home might impose. Mostly, the lines are blurred between longing for and rebellion against home, and the two apparently contradictory positions of desire for liberation and anxiety about isolation may fade into each other.

Mansfield's people can be viewed as caught between the limitations of two eras. Consciously rebelling against lingering and tenacious Victorian ideals about the proper role of women, her female characters may be trapped by another constraint: that sense of estrangement—itself, in part, a consequence of the reaction against Victorianism—which is intrinsic to modernity. In other words, the very forms of rebellion contain this sense of alienation; what looks like freedom may, in fact, be oppressive in another way. This peculiarly twentieth-century dilemma is reflected in the structure of a number of stories, which seems to trap the characters, at the same time as the content of the stories explores or at least hints at new ways of living. For instance, although Mansfield's characters present an impression of being in motion, actual mobility is minimal; many of the stories are very contained in both time and space. Indeed, even though the characters may have broken away from the traditional home and family setting, some of the stories seem scarcely to give them breathing room.

Rita Felski writes that '[t]he so-called private sphere, often portrayed as a domain where natural and timeless emotions hold sway, is shown to be radically implicated in patterns of modernization and processes of social change' (*Gender of Modernity* 3).[1] Modernist expressions of alienation and homelessness are indeed congruent with actual historical changes in gender roles and family structure. Although the food reformers succeeded in establishing food science in school and university curricula, they did not, in so doing, cure social ills or solidify the family unit as they had originally hoped to do. The First World War pushed women into new situations which forced them to see themselves differently. In addition, the cultural disillusionment arising from its battlefield horrors had a huge impact on social structures. But even before the cataclysm of the war, there had been changes in the family. Despite the focus of early advertising on the family, referred to in a previous chapter, one can trace a breakdown in family structure beginning in the nineteenth century. Ernest Groves and William Fielding Ogburn's *American Marriage and Family Relationships,* published in 1928, cites the statistic that in the United States, 'Divorce between 1870 and the mid-1920s had risen 35 percent for each ten year period' (Ewen 120).

Certainly, the most cursory look at early twentieth-century fiction reveals a concern with fragmented families. If Ellen Olenska's possible divorce in *The Age of Innocence* is a matter for some discussion among members of the New York aristocracy, divorce is relatively common in *The House of Mirth* and nearly unremarkable in *The Custom of the Country.* As well, many early twentieth-century novels portray orphaned children and parents who do not fulfil a traditional role. As already noted, etiquette manuals were so popular partly because parental guidance was no longer sufficient for the upwardly mobile; thus children of newly wealthy but old-fashioned families like the Spraggs might take charge of the family themselves.[2]

Some early twentieth-century works of fiction portray families in the process of disintegrating completely. One or both parents may be entirely absent, and guardians—like Mrs Peniston in *The House of Mirth*—not completely committed to their responsibilities. Given the destruction of black family structure by slavery, it is perhaps not surprising that in Zora Neale Hurston's *Their Eyes Were Watching God,* Janie is raised by her grandmother. In Nella Larsen's *Quicksand* and *Passing,* the parents of Helga Crane and Clare Kendry are dead, and in both cases, the biracial family situation made the parent-child relationship a complicated and painful one in the first place. However, white families are also portrayed as fragmented. In Kate Chopin's *The Awakening,* Edna's mother has died young, and her father is not a reliable source of paternal guidance; moreover, she leaves her own two young sons motherless. By the end of *The Custom of the Country,* Paul Marvell, having had two fathers rather violently taken away from him, is a lonely and neglected little boy.

The differences in meaning, referred to earlier, between nineteenth- and twentieth-century fictional portrayals of dinner signal a change in the portrayal of families as well. The history of the novel is full of orphans like Pip or Jane Eyre, making their way in the world. In this tradition, however, the family itself is not questioned. What we see in the early twentieth century, on the other hand, is not the unfortunate and unpredictable loss of the family, but the rejection of the family. In the literature of the early modernist era, when characters leave home and set out on their own, it may be because they have to, but, more likely, also because they consider the beliefs and values of their parents and their home to be hopelessly old-fashioned. Thus F. Scott Fitzgerald's Jay Gatsby not only leaves the Midwest but tries to eradicate his origins completely. Carrie in Theodore Dreiser's *Sister Carrie* and Ellen in John Dos Passos's *Manhattan Transfer* are women making their own way in the world more out of desire than because of dire financial necessity.

Geographical mobility, then, also contributes significantly to the sense of homelessness in this period: indeed, it is well known that many of the writers discussed in this study themselves lived in a self-imposed exile, an exile which they found necessary for intellectual, artistic, or psychological survival, even though they may have written longingly and frequently or—as Joyce did—even exclusively about their home country.[3] Edith Wharton's experience is presumably mirrored in that of Ellen Olenska, who, despite her short-lived attempt to integrate back into New York, ultimately does better alone in Paris. It is groundbreaking for a woman to be on her own, creating, by herself, her own home and, thereby, her own stance in relation to society. The conventional marriage plot with the conventional role for women is upended in *The Age of Innocence*.

As Marshall Berman argues, there may be economic reasons for the modernist emphasis on the solitary individual struggling with both loneliness and—apparently inconsistently—the desire for distance from home or roots: the notion of striving and the feeling of mobility are, Berman says, inherent in modern capitalism. Because expansion is necessary, change is necessary as well.[4] On the one hand, in both Marxist and standard capitalist terms, this philosophy is profoundly optimistic; in another sense, it is both frightening and profoundly isolating, as notions of family, community, and even selfhood become fluid. Thus we see a desperate need for intimacy at the same time as traditional group relationships can no longer be assumed, and as it becomes increasingly difficult to be certain of one's own identity (Berman 110).[5] As indicated by the rising interest in psychoanalysis during the early twentieth century, the notion of the self becomes more important at the same time as its very existence becomes questionable. Djuna Barnes's dreamlike *Nightwood* is a striking example of a piece of modernist fiction in which the characters—and indeed the entire narrative—evince a sense of distance and dissociation from self and from what is generally constituted as reality. In Mansfield's fiction, the shifting quality of personal and social identity is frequently associated with a change in the relationship to the home. In particular, the treatment of dining and of food itself expresses both this loss of tradition and the search for a new way of being, especially for women. Loss or rejection of food habits, customs, and rituals may signal various other losses as well.[6]

Much recent criticism of Mansfield includes a strong biographical element. While such criticism may be valuable—interesting and insightful—I am wary of interpreting works of fiction in the light of excerpts from journals and letters.[7] Nevertheless, even as a historical example of women's relationship with food, it is worth noting a 'preoccupation with eating' (Moran, 'Unholy Meanings' 108) in Mansfield's personal writing as well as in her fiction. Like Virginia Woolf, who could not eat during her several breakdowns (Poole ch. 8), Mansfield may have suffered from food-related anxiety and health problems. As a child, she was sensitive about being plump, and her weight remained a source of some tension, especially in her relationship with her mother, until tuberculosis finally cured that problem with a more serious one.

It has been suggested that eating disorders are more common in times of social change, that the disruption, dislocation, and instability inherent in such periods may be indicators for anorexia, and specifically, that the condition 'afflicts many women during periods of change in female roles' (Perlick and Silverstein 81). Thus anorexia has been seen by some as a disease peculiar to the twentieth century. Indeed, there is an anorexic quality to the experience of many of Mansfield's women characters, a rejection of meals which is not based in the popular understanding of anorexia as an obsession with weight dictated by cultural norms of beauty, but which nevertheless involves self-rejection. The potentially liberating movement away from the roles that usually tie women to the provision of meals and the creation of a home seems, in much of Mansfield's fiction, to entail an alienation from the physical self and a lack of interest in the nourishment—both literal and metaphorical—required to sustain that self. In other words, the roles of server and consumer of meals may be conflated: the rejection of the former may involve the rejection of the latter as well. Male modernist characters may generally have been able to assume that, in the end, dinner would somehow be cooked. And, with notable exceptions such as Joyce's Bloom cooking breakfast, they did not need to pay too much attention to how. But Mansfield's women who divorce themselves from such details of mundane existence may sometimes seem to be at risk of starvation. At the very least, they seem to have no pleasure in eating; moreover, the magical, transformatory quality of meals may be lost, forgotten or even deliberately avoided.

In Mansfield's work, then, women who view themselves or are viewed by the author as resisting the mould of Victorianism have a particularly complex and difficult relationship with dinner. Mansfield writes about women alone, in couples, and within the family; in each of these circumstances, characters may evince an attempt to find meaning in food and the rituals of dining, and yet, at the same time, an alienation from eating that reflects a larger sense of social and personal alienation, even despair: what Thomas Hardy, in a very different context, calls 'the ache of modernism' (180). Moreover, as chapter 1 pointed out, food is inextricably tied up with language, and Mansfield's sense of the relationship of food with the forms of discourse that structure people's lives is quite acute. If the dinner table fails in these stories, this failure is frequently linked with a failure of communication as well.

'Ghosts of Saucepans & Primus Stoveses'

> Yes, I hate hate HATE doing these things that you accept just as all men accept of their women. I can only play the servant with very bad grace indeed. Its all very well for females who have nothing else to do . . . & then you say I am a tyrant & wonder because I get tired at night! The trouble with women like me is—they cant keep their nerves out of the job in hand—& . . . I walk about with a mind full of ghosts of saucepans & primus stoveses & 'will there be enough to go round' . . . & you calling . . . isn't there going to be tea. Its five o'clock.[8]
>
> Katherine Mansfield to John Middleton Murray

If Lily Bart is on the cusp of modernity, most of Katherine Mansfield's women lead a definitely 'modern' life. Many of her stories are about independent, mobile people, often young, and looking to reject the past. On the surface, at least, class may be unimportant to them. Sometimes they are intellectuals or artists, people who could be classified as bohemian; often they are single and may have had many lovers, or, if married, have a consciously different view of marriage from their parents. They are the mould for the kind of characters found in the popular short stories of writers like Dorothy Parker, Jean Rhys, and Kay Boyle in the 1920s and 1930s. Unlike Lily, who only begins to recognize the degree of her alienation from society and to discover the depth of her loneliness late in *The House of Mirth,* many of Mansfield's characters do not need to discover their own solitude and anomie: it is rather the milieu in which they move, the air that they breathe. In some of the stories, alienation is so much an accepted state of being that people would be as hard pressed to live otherwise as Lily is to survive outside the Trenors' circle.

In Mansfield, this alienation is frequently expressed in terms of food. The emphasis on eating is a striking characteristic of Mansfield's work: most of her short stories include at least a reference to some kind of meal, tea, or snack. Lily Bart's failure to nourish herself, although in a very different context, has become the norm in many of the stories, where the serving and consuming of dinner and other meals represent major sites of conflict and conceal a tangle of anxiety and unease. Some stories present an arguably neurotic obsession with eating; in many, a meal or a lack of meals is foregrounded as an integral part of the dissociated, solitary, or fragmented lives that the story follows. A character's state of spiritual or psychological well-being, on the one hand, or malaise, on the other, is reflected and made concrete in her relationship with the dinner table. The strong emphasis on food suggests a pervasive hunger that cannot be assuaged, a constant question about survival—physical, emotional, and financial—and the means of survival.[9] However, the importance of the issues raised by meals goes beyond the problems of individual characters; as descriptors of a particular view of the modern and modernist world, issues of food are an integral part of the narrative consciousness and, as such, are woven into the context of the story as a whole.

Overall, two major emphases emerge in Mansfield's treatment of food. First, in many stories, the social event of the meal is reduced to the merely biological level. Thus the presence of food in the story has an almost ironic effect, if not intent: meals underline the absence of that very communality, commensality, intimacy, and warmth which the rituals of sharing food are supposed to create or enhance within families, among friends, and between lovers. Even when such positive associations with food seem about to appear, they are either shown to be false or undercut in some way. In some stories, love, friendship, or family is directly parodied. Although Mansfield usually focuses on the loss of mealtime ritual from a woman's perspective, its effect on men is also demonstrated in a number of stories. Second, the treatment of meals, as part of the larger framework of domesticity in general, particularly reflects and reveals the tensions in women's lives; that is, for women, the modern sense of alienation expresses itself in the context of their traditional roles—especially that of organizing meals—and through each individual woman's position within or against these roles.

In much of Mansfield's work, then, if eating is at all associated with pleasure, sociability, and intimacy, it is solely as an expression of a lack of pleasure, of the absence of sociability or intimacy, of a general sense of unfulfilled desire. The meals in Mansfield's stories often occur within an atmosphere of loneliness, repression, even moral corruption—as in **'Je ne parle pas français'**—and suggest the failure of intimacy, the dashing of hopes. Many of the meals in Mansfield's stories are eaten alone, largely because 'her people are ceaselessly on the move, traveling, wandering, often in foreign or threatening situations . . . Mansfield wrote almost compulsively of outcasts, exiles, minorities, and fringe dwellers' (Robinson 4). In some of Mansfield's stories, then, eating is done on the fly; meals are consumed in nameless restaurants or are replaced by snacks. When eating in restaurants because they are away on holiday, vacationers may seem more like exiles. Sometimes people simply do not get to eat: in **'Poison,'** for instance, the table is set for lunch, but lunch is not eaten; in **'Marriage à la Mode,'** the fruit that the husband brings home for the children somehow just disappears into the chaos of fashionable guests, sardines eaten out of the box for supper, and vanished leftover salmon. In these last two examples, it is largely the man's alienation within the couple that is explored. In both cases, the men seem to be looking for the traditional marriage that their partners reject. Although spurning the traditional couple, the women in these two stories are still in control of meals, and exercise their power by leaving the men hungry, if not physically, then emotionally.

Such an unstructured, if possibly frustrating, manner of eating does, of course, suggest a possible release—for both men and women—not only from the entrenched rituals of the Victorian dinner table, but from the social structures implied and reinforced by such rituals: those, for instance, described in Wharton's *The Age of Innocence*. Most important, perhaps, is the potential liberation from gender roles, even if such does not always actually materialize. However, modern changes to meal structures can also imply a loosening of class distinctions. Eating in restaurants is one expression of the partially illusory democracy inherent in the anonymity of the modern crowd, the twentieth-century street scene which figures prominently in the work of many modernists.[10] Like these street scenes, the fictional restaurant setting conveys the impression of equality. As Joanne Finkelstein says, '[b]y following the formulated modes of sociality accepted in the restaurant one can appear as one desires without the risks of actually crossing social barriers or attempting to realize these imagined postures' (15). In Nella Larsen's *Passing,* Irene Redfield and Clare Kendry drink tea in the roof-top restaurant of a whites-only hotel; with the appropriate clothes and class demeanour, a light-skinned woman can 'pass' in such a situation. When Miss Kilman has tea with Elizabeth Dalloway in the restaurant of a department store—itself a leveller of classes—the anonymity of the tea-room momentarily erases class. However, when Elizabeth has to leave to get ready for her mother's party, the differences of class—and the material and social advantages of class—reappear between her and Miss Kilman. The older woman is left wallowing in self-pity: '"I never go to parties," said Miss Kilman, just to keep Elizabeth from going. "People don't ask me to parties . . . Why should they ask me? . . . I'm plain, I'm unhappy"' (200).

Public dining, then, creates only a superficial equality—defined strictly by one's ability to pay the bill. Moreover, Finkelstein argues that, although it is public, the restaurant meal may not be truly social, even when it is shared. Highly 'stylized' (Finkelstein 13), such meals may in fact preclude rather than encourage interaction. Certainly, the restaurant setting does not inspire the profound resonance of meaning associated with the historic rituals of a culture. Despite its liberating aspects, then, this new world of dining out is not without its price; it may in fact entail a loss of ritual and sociability, which creates or reinforces a sense of loneliness or rootlessness. The above example from *Mrs. Dalloway* suggests not only that Doris Kilman's craving for sweets emerges from her feeling of deprivation, but, moreover, that the tea-room brings out this feeling:

> Elizabeth rather wondered whether Miss Kilman could be hungry. It was her way of eating, eating with intensity, then looking, again and again, at a plate of sugared cakes on the table next them; then, when a lady and a child sat down and the child took the cake, could Miss Kilman really mind it? Yes, Miss Kilman did mind it. She had wanted that cake—the pink one. The pleasure of eating was almost the only pure pleasure left her, and then to be baffled even in that!
>
> (197)

Miss Kilman's desperate loneliness, envy, and unhappiness are especially evident in this tea-room setting, which seems to suggest just the opposite: camaraderie, intimacy, festivity, pleasure.

For women in general, the restaurant meal certainly represents freedom from domestic fetters and liberation from such potentially onerous tasks as organizing, cooking, and serving meals. Yet Mansfield's stories emphasize that dining on the run, especially alone, is both rooted in and symbolic of other things that are missing in a character's life. Obviously, many of the people in the stories eat alone because they are literally alone in the world; others may feel alone or experience themselves as profoundly divided from society or within themselves. Mansfield's heroines may demonstrate at any age a profound alienation from both meals and the world around them. Their sometimes very minimal diet is in keeping with their minimal pleasure and minimal expectations. Moreover, the fact that very small details about food or changes in diet are so terribly important in their lives and carry such subtle nuances of meaning for them shows the tenuousness of their accommodation with life, the fine line between joy and despair.

If left with only the physical necessity of eating, the person feels spiritually bereft. Yet, at the same time, food habits can create meaning even for those who are alone or alienated from social life. **'Miss Brill,'** reminiscent of some of Joyce's stories, describes the simple rituals of the lonely and suggests the importance of these rituals for survival. An English teacher living in France, Miss Brill makes a habit of a weekly Sunday afternoon outing to a park where a band plays. The stop on the way home to buy herself a Sunday piece of honey-cake is a high point of the week, and central to her life: 'Sometimes there was an almond in her slice, sometimes not. It made a great difference. If there was an almond it was like carrying home a tiny present—a surprise—something that might very well not have been there. She hurried on the almond Sundays and struck the match for the kettle in quite a dashing way' (335). Miss Brill's weekly treat of cake, like Miss Kilman's desperate consumption of pink cakes and éclairs, seems laughable, pathetic. But buying the cake reflects more than greed, self-pity, or sublimated desire; it is a ritual, and as such, not only fills a need for Miss Brill, but creates meaning in her life. The secret possibility of a nut hidden in the cake represents a chance prize or gift, a hoped-for yet unexpected bonus or reward, and thus the possibility of optimism. No meal is portrayed in this story; still, even on this very limited scale, food can transform reality. For Miss Brill, finding an almond in her slice of cake creates feelings of gaiety, frivolity, excitement and transforms her afternoon, so that she even lights the gas 'in quite a dashing way.'

The almond in the cake is also related to her sense of a hidden part of herself: sexual, perhaps, or in any case unknown and unappreciated by anyone else. Like buying the cake, wearing her rather moth-eaten old fur piece, a special possession that she treats almost as a pet, is part of the weekly ritual; it represents that weekend self which is hidden from others, a part of her which would surely surprise her pupils and 'the old invalid gentleman to whom she read the newspaper four afternoons a week while he slept in the garden' (334). Although her words are surely wasted on the sleeping man and perhaps on her students as well, Miss Brill is a person who deals in language. She has created for herself a highly significant personal script to describe her Sundays. Wearing her Sunday fur, she is part of the crowd in the park, someone with a place in the world and a knowledge of character and of life, an accomplished actress with a role in a play, a woman who is curious, interested, almost beautiful. Thus, she is devastated when two young lovers sharing her park bench make fun of her fur. The fact that she does not buy her slice of cake that day, depriving herself of that little pleasure and the meaning inherent even in the possibility of finding an almond, indicates the degree of her humiliation. She returns directly home to 'her room like a cupboard' (335) after hearing the couple laugh at her: 'The box that the fur came out of was on the bed. She unclasped the necklet quickly; quickly, without looking, laid it inside. But when she put the lid on she thought she heard something crying' (336). Denying herself her ritual of cake expresses her despair; indeed, it is a kind of suicide of the spirit.

In Mansfield's early story **'The Tiredness of Rosabel,'** the main character is young, and not only lonely, but poor; the fact that she has had little to eat for tea opens the story and sets its context. For a young woman on a limited budget, a shop-girl who understands the world of exchange, dinner must be weighed against other needs. Thus flowers replace the meal.[11] Rosabel has bought 'a bunch of violets, and that was practically the reason why she had so little tea—for a scone and a boiled egg and a cup of cocoa at Lyons are not ample sufficiency after a hard day's work in a millinery establishment . . . [S]he would have sacrificed her soul for a good dinner—roast duck and green peas, chestnut stuffing, pudding with brandy sauce—something very hot and strong' (513). Although written in the third person, this passage represents Rosabel's own text of her life. In fact, despite the cliché of the last sentence, it is obvious that Rosabel would *not* sacrifice her soul: the flowers she buys are 'soul food,' and are at least part of the reason for her eating a minimal dinner.

But Rosabel has also written a second, more romantic script for herself. Fantasizing about the wealthy young couple who came into the shop that day, she imagines the life she would lead if she were in the other woman's place: the food and drink, the invitations to social events, the house, the clothes, and especially the man. She sees herself sharing an elaborate dinner with him—'the soup, and oysters, and pigeons, and creamed potatoes, and champagne, of course, and afterwards coffee and cigarettes'—and later tea: '"Sugar? Milk? Cream?" The little homely questions seemed to suggest a joyous intimacy' (517). Eating together is part of Rosabel's fantasy of sexual desire and fulfilment. As in many of Mansfield's stories, however, food is minimal and desire repressed. For the independent, solitary woman, both social conventions and economic pressures make the expression of sexuality problematic except in fantasy. In fact, Rosabel's fantasy reflects economic realities: delicious meals are linked with both financial security and emotional intimacy. For the self-supporting woman who lives outside the traditional family structure, both may be lacking. Rosabel is not alone in this situation: as she daydreams on the bus, the woman next to her reads a romance novel, the text of which quite probably parallels Rosabel's own rewriting of her life. If nineteenth-century bourgeois dining rituals are disappearing in the early twentieth century, a version of them may still exist in fantasy for the working class.

Even when parts of Rosabel's dream come true for other women—women, that is, who have some money and are not alone—intimacy itself often stays at the level of fantasy. A number of Mansfield's stories depict meals shared by a man and a woman, meals which might automatically suggest intimacy, as the waiting lunch table does for the male narrator in **'Poison'**: 'As always, the sight of the table laid for two—for two people only—and yet so finished, so perfect, there was no possible room for a third, gave me a queer, quick thrill as though

I'd been struck by that silver lightning that quivered over the white cloth, the brilliant glasses, the shadow bowl of freesias' (674). Although such meals *à deux* occur in various situations in Mansfield, any sense of intimacy they suggest always remains potential, if not false. 'Sexually, one devours or is devoured,' Fullbrook (88) says of Mansfield's stories. However, the recurring link between food and sex is more varied and usually more subtle than Fullbrook suggests, and is always part of the all-encompassing context of alienation. To one extent or another, frustration permeates many of the stories, and superficial trappings of intimacy may make the situation all the more painful. If a meal brings the potential for closeness, the failure of this potential is demonstrated sometimes in the inadequate menu, sometimes in the lack of joy or pleasure in eating, and usually in the halting, stunted conversation. As talk sputters and falters, the dinner table fails as the setting for intimacy or even conviviality, as well as for any profound degree of communication.

'**The Honeymoon,**' for instance, is about a newly married couple, but as they drink tea and eat éclairs in the south of France, the story delves beneath the surface of love and the novelty of marriage. The sexual attraction between them is apparent, but the reader is aware of their differences, the woman's attempts to overlook flaws, the beginnings of questions which remain suppressed—perhaps the seeds of the failure of their marriage, as they negotiate the gaps between everyday life and their idealized notions of love. George, practical, insensitive, somewhat boorish, is incapable of understanding his wife's desire for intimacy, a desire that she can scarcely express, even awkwardly: 'So often people, even when they love each other, don't seem to—to— it's so hard to say—know each other perfectly. They don't seem to want to. And I think that's awful. They misunderstand each other about the most important things of all' (396). Even as the couple hold hands across the table, the distance between them cannot really be breached. In the few minutes described in the story, their relationship appears insubstantial, superficial, although sweet and delicious, like the pastries they are eating. Their marriage is, so far, a sweet snack, their vacation a month of honey; whether it will ever really become nourishing remains open to question, but, the story suggests, is unlikely.

A different version of this faltering tea-table discourse appears in '**Psychology,**' where another meal of cake and tea reflects a different kind of limited relationship. A man and a woman—each a writer and an intellectual—are having tea at the woman's home, and seem to be on the verge of becoming lovers. In this story there is a lot of talk, much of it about books and writing, but it is almost compulsive, ultimately boring even for the talkers, covering their fear of being together in silence and of considering another level to their conversation and their relationship. Each is afraid of broaching the subject of the attraction between them. However, the woman tempts the man with her cake: '"Do realise how good it is," she implored. "Eat it imaginatively. Roll your eyes if you can and taste it on the breath. It's not a sandwich from the hatter's bag—it's the kind of cake that might have been mentioned in the Book of Genesis . . ."' (113; ellipsis in original). The man observes that their eating together is significant, but can only speak about it in a halting way: 'It's a queer thing but I always do notice what I eat here and never anywhere else. I suppose it comes of living alone so long and always reading while I feed . . . my habit of looking upon food as just food . . . something that's there, at certain times . . . to be devoured . . . to be . . . not there' (113; ellipses in original). Although the man associates the enjoyment of food with the presence of his companion, and sees that, in her company, food is transformed from a mere physical necessity, to be ignored in so far as possible, into something pleasurable, he seems unable to go any further with this thought, and his resistance to intimacy remains. Both are quick to break a silence or to change the subject to intellectual banalities. In this story, it is not a lack of facility with language that precludes closeness, but the limitations and barriers reinforced by their language itself.

A dinner table or tea table, then, can set the framework of both a relationship and a story. In the humorously titled '**A Dill Pickle,**' a restaurant is the setting for a chance meeting of ex-lovers for the first time in six years. Even though the story is about a man and a woman in a restaurant, it does not describe a meal, a relationship, or even a date, but is almost a parody of all of the above: food is not shared, and the two characters remain separate. A very limited description—'He was seated at one of those little bamboo tables decorated with a Japanese vase of paper daffodils' (167)—suggests a stylish but anonymous décor. Other diners do not seem to exist; the interior reality of memory, imagination, and emotion dominates the external surroundings. Yet years of personal history are evoked at the restaurant table, and food plays a part in their shared but different memories—his, perhaps, romanticized; hers more negative—and defines both their closeness and their distance from each other. Past intimacy is suggested in the fact that the man's eating habits are still recognizable to Vera: 'There was a tall plate of fruit in front of him, and very carefully, in a way she recognised immediately as his "special" way, he was peeling an orange' (167). She, however, declines fruit and takes only coffee, her refusal to eat emphasizing their separateness. There is also a sense of austerity about this choice: Vera takes her coffee black, a detail noted only because, after her departure, the man insists that he not be charged for the unused cream. Both seem to be worried about money. Yet the man presents himself as well off and vaguely successful; Vera, on the other hand, has presumably had to choose food over art and pleasure, for she mentions 'with a little grimace' (170) that she has sold her piano.

The man's story of eating a dill pickle during his trip to Russia, a trip that they once spoke of taking together, sparks Vera's imagination, and she feels that she is 'sitting on the grass beside the mysteriously Black Sea' (171). She even seems able to taste the pickle: 'She sucked in her cheeks; the dill pickle was terribly sour . . .' (171; ellipsis in original). The pickle is more real than what is actually on the table, and the past seems more tangible than the present. The congruence between the pickle and the soured love affair is too comically obvious, yet, indeed, the relationship returns almost as palpably as the taste of the pickle. Across the table, their old dynamic is picked up again: a fleeting illusion of intimacy, as well as competition, ambivalence, pain both felt and inflicted. The vividness with which Vera imagines the pickle also suggests the hunger that characterizes her life—and perhaps her ex-lover's as well. Indeed, both are still alone.

Playing with an even harsher vision of physical vulnerability implicit in sharing a meal, Mansfield takes to the limit her pessimism about the possibility of communion at a shared table. As Margaret Visser observes, during dinner, people have always had to relax their guard and put their weapons aside, even though they are surrounded at the table by tearing teeth and sharp instruments. Moreover, unless we have cooked the meal ourselves, we are ingesting unknown substances. The fear of poisoning is a terrible one, suggesting an absolute failure of trust; if sharing food is a bond, poisoning is the most insidious betrayal, occurring, as it does, from inside the site of communal intimacy. Some of Mansfield's stories draw an analogy between this kind of culinary betrayal and that occurring in love: for example, a husband's poisoning his wife figures in the unfinished **'A Married Man's Story.'** In **'Poison,'** the physical danger of meals is linked with the emotional danger of relationships. Like **'The Honeymoon,'** this story takes place in the south of France, but the couple are sophisticated, even world-weary, and the story is far more cynical, although rather flippant and glossy. The man is trying to convince himself that he is finally sure of his aptly named lover Beatrice: this, despite the fact that her impatience for the postman to appear strongly suggests to the reader that she expects a letter from another man. As noted earlier, the sight of the table set for two people implies a happy intimacy to the man, but not to Beatrice: 'She took my arm. "Let's go on to the terrace—" and I felt her shiver. "Ça sent," she said faintly, "de la cuisine . . ."' (675; ellipsis in original). Her aversion to the smell of cooking suggests a disgust with the physical, the sexual, and her avoidance of the table a rejection of love and intimacy. No lunch is eaten during the story; instead the man is served up an intense and rather dramatic discourse on poisoning. Beatrice becomes 'pale with excitement' at the subject: '"It's the exception to find married people who don't poison each other—married people and lovers"' (679). The 'gleam of the pearl' on her ring begins to look ominous: a poison ring, perhaps? Finally, Beatrice's words transform the taste of his drink into something unpleasant and frightening: 'Good God! Was it fancy? No, it wasn't fancy. [His apéritif] tasted chill, bitter, *queer*' (680; emphasis in original).

If loneliness, unhappiness, a failure to communicate, and even cruelty seem to be endemic and even inevitable at the tables described in these stories, the option of traditional family life, which some characters have either missed or rejected and others still hope for, is not without its drawbacks in Mansfield's fiction. While the treatment of meals in **'The Daughters of the Late Colonel'** is, on one level, quite funny, it also points to the oppression and repression of the family. The very title of the story indicates the family relationship which has destroyed its main characters: Constantia and Josephine ('Jug') have, indeed, been defined as daughters for their entire lives; that they do not know how to be adult women is demonstrated in their relationship to both cooking and eating.

A preoccupation with food runs throughout the story. Tea, meals, and discussions about food occur during the actual time frame of the story, a week after their father's death, and also form a significant part of the sisters' recent memories. Their own role as consumers of food has apparently always been secondary to their father's; now, having lived within the oppressive limits of their father's house for so long, the two women do not know what they want to eat, if they want to eat, or even what it is possible to eat, a state of indecision which causes friction with their servant, Kate:

> 'I think it might be nice to have it fried,' said Constantia. 'On the other hand, of course, boiled fish is very nice. I think I prefer both equally well . . . Unless you . . . In that case—'
>
> 'I shall fry it,' said Kate, and she bounced back, leaving the door open and slamming the door of her kitchen.
>
> (279; ellipses in original)

If they fire the servant, of whom they are terrified, they are not sure what they can manage to cook, or indeed what kind of food there is to buy; nevertheless, the prospect seems childishly exciting:

> 'What it comes to is, if we did'—and this [Jug] barely breathed, glancing at the door—'give Kate notice'—she raised her voice again—'we could manage our own food.'
>
> 'Why not?' cried Constantia. She couldn't help smiling. The idea was so exciting. She clasped her hands. 'What should we live on, Jug?'

'Oh, eggs in various forms!' said Jug, lofty again. 'And, besides, there are all the cooked foods.'

(280)

The lack of regular meals seems to them to be liberating, and they are annoyed that when they rather naïvely invite the voracious Nurse Andrews to stay an extra week, it means having to hold 'regular sit-down meals at the proper times, whereas if they'd been alone they could just have asked Kate if she wouldn't have minded bringing them a tray wherever they were' (265). However, the anticipated informality of their mealtimes is double-edged: if it is liberating, it is also symptomatic of their repression and self-denial. Meals are for other people, perhaps mostly for men; with their father dead, they may not need the cook.

The daughters can, however, organize a tea and serve others. They invite their nephew Cyril from time to time: 'one of their rare treats' (275), if not one of his. Although the form of the family meal is here, there is no content to it. The sisters look to the tea party to transform their everyday reality, to draw their nephew into their world and to create the family they do not have. But Cyril is a disappointing guest; he merely tolerates the tea table, remains detached and leaves as quickly as possible for the real world of friends and business connections. At the last awkward tea before the colonel's death, Cyril—mindful, perhaps, of Persephone's fate—does not want to eat the extravagant cake and meringues which they press upon him: 'Josephine cut recklessly into the rich dark cake that stood for her winter gloves or the soling and heeling of Constantia's only respectable shoes. But Cyril was most unmanlike in appetite' (275). Since there is really nothing to say, food becomes the only subject of conversation at tea, and a banal and meaningless one at that. The discussion of whether or not Cyril's father likes meringues continues from the table into the absurd and finally pathetic scene in the colonel's sickroom where the young man, at his aunts' insistence, tries to tell his grandfather about his father's taste for meringues. The old man has difficulty hearing the young man's words, and then comprehending why they are being spoken; it is a ridiculous exchange across the generations that neither Cyril nor the old man wants.

The sisters, however, do not see the absurdity; for them, speaking is as divorced from meaning as eating is. Both are also potentially terrifying: either making a choice about what to eat or stating something in real words could, perhaps, lead to the frightening prospect of admitting desire, articulating hopes, maybe even seeking fulfilment. At the end of the story, both Constantia and Josephine want to speak about their fragile and tentative desires for the future, but each backs away, claiming to forget what she intended to say. If food is, literally, the text of Cyril's trivial communication about his father, the text of their lives has comprised domestic duties of the most trivial and meaningless sort. Since they have only been servers in their father's home, they have found in domesticity neither content, nor meaning, nor nourishment—only a marking of time.

A preoccupation with the physical and symbolic value of food itself is most evident in Mansfield's first published collection, **In a German Pension**.[12] The stories, most of which are set at a German spa, are both a parody and a critique of bourgeois family life: the ersatz family of guests viewed through the eyes of a young Englishwoman. Diet is presumably one component of the cure, but, more than this, food is the constant obsession of the 'Kurgäste,' who, under the narrator's ironic gaze, appear comical, pathetic, neurotic, even revolting. The opening story, somewhat crudely called **'Germans at Meat,'** begins with the following passage, a dinner-table discussion about food:

> Bread soup was placed upon the table. 'Ah,' said the Herr Rat, leaning upon the table as he peered into the tureen, 'that is what I need. My "magen" has not been in order for several days. Bread soup, and just the right consistency. I am a good cook myself . . . Now at nine o'clock I make myself an English breakfast, but not much. Four slices of bread, two eggs, two slices of cold ham, one plate of soup, two cups of tea—that is nothing to you.'
>
> He asserted the fact so vehemently that I had not the courage to refute it.
>
> All eyes were suddenly turned upon me. I felt I was bearing the burden of the nation's preposterous breakfast—I who drank a cup of coffee while buttoning my blouse in the morning.
>
> (683)

This is more an accusation than an interchange, and is typical of much of the dialogue in the stories. Food is discussed aggressively and eaten aggressively at the large, family-style meals. The 'Kurgäste' talk about the benefits of a good diet throughout **'Germans at Meat,'** at the same time enjoying a multi-course dinner, and finally applying themselves without restraint to cherry cake with whipped cream. Characters in other stories may demonstrate a more dogmatic approach to their choice of food. For instance, a woman in **'The Luft Bad'** attests to 'living entirely on raw vegetables and nuts, and each day I feel my spirit is stronger and purer. After, all, what can you expect? The majority of us are walking about with pig corpuscles and oxen fragments in our brain. The wonder is the world is as good as it is' (731). In either case, food is at the centre of their universe: an explanation and a cure for the ills of individuals and of the world, the subject of talk and testimonials.

In contrast to the other guests, the narrator, like the heroine of **'A Dill Pickle,'** is unmistakably the sort to eat and run. While she dines with the other guests and participates in some other group activities, 'she sets herself in squeamish, often derisory opposition to what is depicted as the gross physicality of those around her—particularly the men—in relation to food, sex and health' (Parkin-Gounelas, 'KM's Piece of Pink Wool' 501). Thus, as a critical observer of the self-righteous, somehow perverse gluttony of most of the characters—women as well as men, contrary to Parkin-Gounelas's point—the narrator seems ascetic, almost ethereal; she never describes herself eating.[13] The narrator also remains an aloof observer of the spa flirtations, in **'Frau Fischer'** concocting a story about a sea-captain husband away on a 'long and perilous voyage' (702). Given the description of the other spa guests, the narrator's detachment seems eminently sensible and may also enhance her powers of observation as a storyteller. But, conversely, her role isolates her, and she herself expresses an ambivalence about being an outsider, admitting to feeling 'a little crushed . . . at the tone—placing me outside the pale—branding me as a foreigner' (692). Her lonely position calls to mind Mansfield's statement of her own internal division: '"I am a writer first and a woman second"' (Parkin-Gounelas, *Fictions of the Female Self* 22).

Swirling around the focal point of food, then, is an exploration of what it means to be a woman, and, beneath that, of the tension between the woman and the artist. Moran argues, from the journals, that 'Mansfield connects eating, impregnation, and engulfment; more ominously, she perceives these "female" functions as inhibiting analysis and self-examination' ('Unholy Meanings' 112). Again, in the ***Pension*** stories, eating is, in itself, not especially gendered; yet, the stories link women's reproductive capacities with their ingestion of—and general connection with—food. In **'Germans at Meat,'** a widow who has nine children advises the narrator that she is childless because she is a vegetarian, and goes on to recount, 'A friend of mine had four at the same time. Her husband was so pleased he gave a supper-party and had them placed on the table. Of course she was very proud' (685). Here, both dinner and children seem to have been produced by the woman to enhance her man's status. In **'Frau Fischer,'** the English woman is thus advised to produce 'handfuls of babies, that is what you are really in need of . . . Then, as the father of a family he cannot leave you' (703). Clearly, the true womanliness of the English narrator is suspect. Frau Fischer refuses to accept seriously her provocative comment, 'I consider child-bearing the most ignominious of all professions' (703), and speculates that the young woman must have suffered greatly to have such views, impossible for a real woman. In **'Germans at Meat,'** the whole table reacts with horror that she does not know her husband's favourite meat: 'A pause. They all looked at me, shaking their heads, their mouths full of cherry stones' (687). And in **'Frau Fischer'** it is considered highly unusual that she is travelling alone, and admits to enjoying sleeping without her husband at her side. Yet widows generally seem glad that their husbands are gone, although they speak of them in a formalized mournful way: for instance, 'Frau Hartmann, in an ashamed, apologetic voice: "We are such a happy family since my dear man died"' (697). For the speaker, there seems to be no inconsistency in this odd statement.

Although always associated with food, which is certainly attacked with vigour, and, generally, pleasure, by both women and men, sexuality, in some ***German Pension*** stories—particularly those characterized by an omniscient narrative voice and set outside of the spa—is presented as frightening and harsh, or at best, confusing for women. In **'At Lehmann's'** and **'Frau Brechenmacher Attends a Wedding,'** images of candy or cake describe fantasies of love, marriage, and motherhood. In the former story, Sabina, a young servant and waitress in a café, 'loved to stand behind the counter, cutting up slices of Anna's marvellous chocolate-spotted confections, or doing up packets of sugar almonds in pink and blue striped bags' (722-3), an image of baby colours underlining the girl's feeling that perhaps 'it would be very sweet to have a little baby to dress and jump up and down' (724). Hitherto apparently ignorant about all matters sexual, and frightened and disgusted by her mistress's pregnancy, she is seduced in the cloakroom by a young man who appears in the café with photographs of naked women. At the end of the story, Sabina, her mistress, and the latter's newborn infant are linked by their intermingling cries of pain, passion, fear, and birth.[14] In **'Frau Brechenmacher Attends a Wedding,'** the bride herself is described as a piece of cake: she wears 'a white dress trimmed with stripes and bows of coloured ribbon, giving her the appearance of an iced cake all ready to be cut and served in neat little pieces to the bridegroom beside her' (706). Just as an intimate meal may be a prelude to seduction, the eating, drinking, and other wedding festivities are a prelude to sexual consummation. But married love is portrayed as an unpleasant, even cruel experience that women must endure, a reality contrary to the sugary, pink confectionery image. Most of the older women express a kind of glee that the bride will soon share their burdens. Frau Brechenmacher's drunken husband recalls their own wedding night: 'Such a clout on the ear as you gave me. . . . But I soon taught you' (ellipsis in original). And things do not seem to have changed between them since. Back at home after the wedding, Frau Brechenmacher 'lay down on the bed and put her arm across her face like a child who expected to be hurt as Herr Brechenmacher lurched in' (711).

As Moran and other recent critics have pointed out, the literal and symbolic connection of food with women's lives and with sexuality in ***In a German Pension*** sets the stage for Mansfield's later New Zealand stories. The themes of homelessness, loneliness, and alienation found in her other stories continue here, although in a rather more subtle and complex way. The stories centring around the Burnells are about an apparently stable family, not lonely, single people, a young woman in exile, or uneasy couples wandering around Europe. Yet an underlying sense of dislocation is implied by the fact that in neither **'Prelude'** nor **'At the Bay'** is the family at home: in the former they are in the process of moving house, as Roger Robinson also points out (4), and in the latter on vacation. In addition to the sense of disruption, there is also a pervasive feeling of isolation experienced by at least some of the family members, and reflected in the context of the stories as a whole. In **'Prelude,'** the family has moved away from town; in **'At the Bay,'** the reader feels the 'sense of isolation of the little summer colony, the sense of there being no "others" in the background' (Alpers, *The Life of KM* 346).[15] In other words, despite the fact that these two stories are about a family, they take place within an uneasy or temporary space rather than an established family setting. Nevertheless, most of the characters are actively working to create a home: Stanley Burnell's role as wage-earner and provider of the home is emphasized, and much of the women's time—especially that of Mrs Fairfield—is spent on domestic chores. As well, Beryl Fairfield dreams of marrying and establishing her own household.

The fact that meals are somehow askew is a major factor contributing to the sense of uneasiness. The first meal in **'Prelude'** introduces, right at the beginning of the story, a sense of being homeless, of bitter satisfactions in exile. The meal is not eaten at the Burnells' home, but at the Josephs,' neighbours with whom Kezia and her sister Lottie have been left behind because there is not enough room in the wagon taking their mother, grandmother, and sister Isabel to their new house: '"We shall simply have to leave them. That is all. We shall simply have to cast them off," said Linda Burnell. A strange little laugh flew from her lips; she leaned back against the buttoned leather cushions and shut her eyes, her lips trembling with laughter' (11). Abandoned, at least temporarily, in favour of what their mother calls 'absolute necessities that I will not let out of my sight for one instant' (11), the girls have tea with a surrogate family, whose dinner-table behaviour is pointedly unfamiliar, as are their customs of discourse. They are outsiders at the family table, excluded from the habits and rituals of a group of initiates. Thus, Kezia does not understand that one of the menu choices is a joke. Offered 'strawberries and cream or bread and dripping' (13) for tea, she naturally chooses the former, much to the delight of the whole table. Everyone laughs at her, and 'beat[s] the table with their teaspoons' (13) because only the latter is in fact available. 'Even Mrs Samuel Josephs, pouring out the milk and water, could not help smiling' (13), an echo of the girls' own mother's laughter at leaving them behind. The fact that the boy who teases her is named Stanley, like her father, sets up another parallel to her own family. In fact, in the first pages of the story, the 'storeman' who drives them to their new house that evening is more friendly than members of either the Burnell or Josephs family.

Fullbrook defines Kezia's licking her tears away at the table rather than allowing the Josephs to see her cry as 'a gesture of emotional self-consumption that . . . sends ripples of meaning through the story' (70). Indeed, her tears become food, while Kezia tries to control her feelings by transforming the actual food into another kind of object: 'Kezia bit a big piece out of her bread and dripping, and then stood the piece up on her plate. With the bite out it made a dear little sort of a gate. Pooh! She didn't care!' (13). A gate is a potent symbol of transitions and limits: an entry, an exit, a potential point of access in a barrier. Mansfield tells us that the two girls stand 'just inside the gate' (11)—a place that was within the family circle but now is on the wrong side—as the cart leaves for the new house. The fundamental loneliness of family life is suggested by Kezia's returning, after the meal, to her family's former house, now empty; indeed, the sentence 'After tea Kezia wandered back to their own house' immediately follows her whisking her tears away. She enters the house through the scullery and the kitchen, and, wandering through the dining-room, drawing-room, and the bedrooms of her parents, her grandmother, and the servant girl, looks for treasures in the detritus of family life.

Throughout **'Prelude,'** there exists an uncomfortable relationship with food. Left outside the Josephs' inner circle, Kezia finds this first meal confusing and painful; however, her mother seems to have put herself permanently in a similar position, outside the normal pattern of eating and away from the table. Thus, when the children arrive at the new house, Stanley and Linda's sister Beryl are having dinner, but Linda sits apart: 'Linda Burnell, in a long cane chair, with her feet on a hassock and a plaid over her knees, lay before a crackling fire. Burnell and Beryl sat at the table in the middle of the room eating a dish of fried chops and drinking tea out of a brown china teapot' (19). Later in the story Stanley says to Beryl, 'You and I are the only ones in this house with a real feeling for food' (50). Only once is Linda portrayed eating, and the occasion is a snack, not a meal. On the first morning in the new house, she comes into the kitchen and says, 'I'm so hungry . . . where can I get something to eat, mother?' (30). Yet she takes only a piece of ginger-bread, and offers Beryl half of it.

Patricia Moran sees as particularly significant Linda's refusal to eat meat: 'Like the narrator in the ***German Pension*** stories, Linda connects eating with reproduction and initially sees men as devourers and consumers; when with her husband, who is always eating, she refuses to eat meat, as if she can thereby reject sexuality and childbearing' ('Unholy Meanings' 118).[16] It is difficult, however, to argue that an appetite for meat is an integral part of gender identification in this story, since other female characters do eat meat: the story pointedly shows Beryl and Isabel eating chops. In fact, Isabel, who has arrived at the new house without her sisters, boasts that she has had meat for supper as if it is symbolic of entry into the adult world. Still, if the consumption of meat is not necessarily linked with men, the technical skills involved in preparing meat are indeed presented as the purview of men in the division of domestic labour:

> Burnell ran his eye along the edge of the carving knife. He prided himself very much upon his carving, upon making a first-class job of it. He hated seeing a woman carve; they were always too slow and they never seemed to care what the meat looked like afterwards. Now he did; he took a real pride in cutting delicate shaves of cold beef, little wads of mutton, just the right thickness, and in dividing a chicken or a duck with nice precision . . .
>
> (50; ellipsis in original)

The source of meat is also emphasized, and specifically the fact that the animal was killed by a man. The duck eaten at dinner in section XI may taste like 'a kind of very superior jelly' (50), but the children have seen the animal beheaded by Pat, the handyman, whose gender is emphasized in Kezia's surprise at a man wearing earrings: 'She put up her hands and touched his ears. She felt something. Slowly she raised her quivering face and looked. Pat wore little round gold ear-rings. She never knew that men wore ear-rings. She was very much surprised' (47).[17]

In any case, it is not just meat that Linda avoids. She shows little interest in her breakfast gingerbread and she also puts aside the gifts of a pineapple, oysters, and cherries that Stanley brings her, calling them 'silly things,' and giving the excuse—a rather lame one, given her general lack of interest in meals—'You don't mind if I save them. They'd spoil my appetite for dinner' (37). The couple treat the fruit in a 'silly' way—Stanley has placed some of the cherries in his buttonhole and she hangs them over his ear. 'Don't do that, darling. They are for you' (37), he says. Her playfulness masks both her reluctance to eat and her rejection of his gift.

Linda's attitude toward food seems to be the opposite of that of the Germans in the **Pension** stories; however, her *not* eating indicates an obsession with food as much as their gluttony does. In her very interesting work on the Middle Ages, Caroline Bynum argues that it was in the area of food that medieval women felt they could make some choices and exert some control: 'Women's food behavior—fasting and feeding—was an effective way of manipulating the environment in a world in which food was woman's primary resource' (30).[18] Fasting was one way for women to assert themselves against their parents and the church; it could be, for instance, an effective way to avoid marriage. Bynum's argument may also have relevance in more recent times. Certainly, in the early twentieth century, a period when the number of cases of eating disorders may have increased,[19] food was still largely women's domain. In **'Prelude,'** it is too late, of course, for Linda to avoid marriage, and, indeed, her husband seems to pay little attention to her eating habits. Still, her avoidance of food makes a statement about her life, at least to herself, and expresses an attitude toward the physical in general: her children, her husband, her body, sexuality—in short, the fecundity, the mortality, and the daily routine of adulthood. In addition, Linda often appears to be somewhat sickly, a reaction, perhaps, to her apparent pregnancy, but also a withdrawal from her identity and responsibilities as a wife and a mother.

While I do not find it helpful to an understanding of **'Prelude'** to debate whether or not Linda suffers from clinical anorexia, to some extent, Linda's case does fit the view of anorexia as an expression of confusion about or a rejection of the sufferer's femininity.[20] Certainly, Linda does not take on the usual roles for a married woman, either in cooking and serving meals or in other aspects of domestic management. Moreover, her attitude toward the children seems at best uninterested. Not only do her belongings have priority over Lottie and Kezia at the start of the story, but, when the two girls reach the new house that evening, her response to their arrival is minimal: '"Are those the children?" But Linda did not really care; she did not even open her eyes to see' (19). She refers to her daughters as 'three great lumps of children' (54), as if still experiencing their bulk in her body before birth. However, it is hard to tell whether Linda is fundamentally questioning gender roles or acquiescing in them. Her response to having finally given birth to a boy in **'At the Bay'** is a standard one, seeming to resolve some of her predicament by ending the necessity of child-bearing, but also affirming her success as a woman in finally giving her husband a male heir and filling the empty place that Stanley sees at the nursery table (38). Moreover, her own preference for boys becomes clear as, looking at the sleeping infant, Linda for the first time feels drawn to one of her babies.[21] The child also reminds Linda of her own youthful fantasies of *being* a boy, of her father promising that the two of them would sail up a river in China: '[W]e'll escape. Two boys together' (221).

Moran insists on Linda's behaviour as a neurotic response to her own mothering. This approach follows Showalter's sources in proposing another definition of anorexia: 'in the rigid control of her eating, the anorexic both expressed her fear of adult sexual desire and enacted an exaggerated form of the deadening life of the dutiful daughter' (*The Female Malady* 129).[22] But it is too simple to cast Mrs Fairfield as the villain of the piece, as Moran sometimes seems to do. It is likely that Mansfield is indeed critical of—or at least ambivalent about—the characteristic expressions of mothering in the culture at large; however, if Mrs Fairfield's effect on her daughter can be read as destructive, her presence also allows Linda the space to protest against and to refuse certain cultural demands and definitions of womanhood. If Linda will not or cannot take on a woman's role, she is able to take this stand—to some extent, perhaps, remaining a child herself—because her mother is still there to run the Burnell family for her. Given the limited possibilities of her world, by refusing to act as a mother, she necessarily remains emotionally a daughter, both supported and repressed by the continuing presence of her own mother.[23] By the standards of her culture, like the standards of the women in the **Pension** stories, Linda must, of course, be considered neurotic or she would be a better mother. However, especially in the context of Mansfield's corpus, Linda's questioning of femininity—inconsistent, to be sure, and expressed in a passively 'feminine' way—cannot be seen as an individual failure, but rather as an indictment of social roles. 'Prelude' calls into question the culture's standards, even if the existence of any other role for Linda is scarcely imaginable within the story.

Women who more actively seek non-traditional roles in other Mansfield stories also rarely find fulfilment; most of Mansfield's people are split, anguished, searching. In **'Prelude,'** and **'At the Bay,'** this fragmentation is made real, as women are divided in two: on the one hand Mrs Fairfield, the nurturing, motherly cook; on the other, the imaginative, but detached, hungry, and unhappy Linda. It is a challenge for the fragmented individual to live in the modern world: stereotyped roles are at the very least unsatisfying, and an identity outside of these roles both dangerous and hard to find. Thus, throughout Mansfield's corpus, the options of the dependent spinster, the independent bachelor girl, the traditional wife and mother, the 'liberated' married woman are all oppressive, each in its own way.

In the wake of Victorianism and, with it, the questioning of traditional social values, roles, and conventions described by meals, many of Mansfield's stories depict a void in people's relationship to the table. For women especially, the collapse of mealtime roles and rituals leaves a hungry vacuum. In portraying the failure of the communality of the table, Mansfield's work examines other failures as well, asserting the difficulties not merely of being human in the twentieth century, but particularly of functioning fully as a female human being. New ideologies may be in the process of replacing the old, but, although Mansfield's fictional worlds at first seem far more open and full of possibilities than, for example, Lily Bart's world in *The House of Mirth*, ultimately there may be a similar lack of room to manoeuvre.

The fact that food is constantly present in Mansfield's stories, then, does not necessarily indicate either physical or spiritual nourishment, but rather a pervasive anxiety about home, security, and loneliness. As I have argued, meals are linked to language on a profound level: not only allowing an opportunity for conversation, but also reflecting its success or failure. Failed, insufficient or non-existent meals mean that meaningful communication suffers as well. The dinner itself—or the non-dinner—is an expressive vehicle for communicating the loss. In Mansfield's work, it is only in the New Zealand stories that there is the beginning of a resolution to this situation. The following chapters will propose other perspectives on these stories which suggest the potential of a more positive relationship to meals.

Notes

1. Felski bases her argument on Gail Finney's 1989 study, *Women in Modern Drama: Freud, Feminism, and European Theater at the Turn of the Century.*

2. On the other hand, children in some novels of the 1920s seem to have no reality; children in *The Great Gatsby,* for instance, and in Carl Van Vechten's *Parties* are treated as dolls by both their parents and the writer.

3. Although she never returned to New Zealand, Katherine Mansfield never felt fully accepted in England either. Quoting from her journals, Gardner McFall reports that 'Mansfield considered herself the "little Colonial walking in the London garden patch—allowed to look perhaps, but not to linger"' (54).

4. Felski sees Berman's definition of modernity as specifically male; however, the 'creative destruction and constant transformation unleashed by the logic of capitalist development' (Felski, *Gender of Modernity* 2) surely had an impact on women as well, and certainly applies to modernist depictions of women and their relationship to the home.

5. The modernist emphasis on questions of identity is reflected, for instance, in Mansfield's interest in the motif of masks and the notion of multiple selves.

6. Patricia Waugh argues that '[i]n modernist fiction the struggle for personal autonomy can be continued only through *opposition* to existing social institutions and conventions. This struggle necessarily involves individual alienation and often ends

with mental dissolution' (10). Waugh's argument is perhaps oversimplified. 'Personal autonomy' is not the clearly definable state she seems to imply. Also, while 'mental dissolution' may seem imminent in *Nightwood,* this is not a very common situation in modernist fiction. Generally, 'individual alienation' is both far more mundane and more subtly pervasive.

7. Mary Burgan's *Illness, Gender, and Writing: The Case of Katherine Mansfield* and Patricia Moran's 'Unholy Meanings: Maternity, Creativity, and Orality in Katherine Mansfield' are examples of recent influential criticism almost completely based in Mansfield's life. Ruth Parkin-Gounelas quite rightly sees problems in the fact that 'all female writing has traditionally been decoded as autobiographical' (*Fictions of the Female Self* 5) and notes in particular 'the unwillingness of readers to separate the popular myths of [Mansfield's biography] from the characters in [her] fiction' (24). In Mansfield's case, this critical approach has sometimes reduced her work to a question of neurosis, leading to her 'being read as a "case" rather than as a writer' (Fullbrook 4).

8. Excerpt from a 1913 letter from Katherine Mansfield to John Middleton Murry (O'Sullivan and Scott 1:125-6; misspellings and first and third ellipsis in original).

9. This question certainly poses itself for the characters within the story, but may also pertain to the writer's relationship with her own work. In an interesting essay on Mary Wilkins Freeman, Virginia Blum suggests that the pervasive poverty faced by Freeman's characters, and their resulting obsession with money, is reflected in an anxiety about food. Like Freeman, Mansfield wrote many of her stories because of an immediate need for money, a fact that Blum sees as significant both in Freeman's work and in her attitudes toward literary value.

10. This relaxation of class demarcations can also be seen in depictions of public transport, another site where classes mix. Except for those in the highest stratum of society, everyone takes the bus, from Mansfield's Rosabel, a hat-shop clerk, to Woolf's Elizabeth Dalloway. But beneath the semblance of equality, class distinctions remain. In *Mrs. Dalloway,* the upper-class Clarissa mingles with the Bond Street crowds; yet her shopping errands remain firmly rooted in her class, their purpose to prepare for the party that she will be hosting as the wife of a member of Parliament. Mrs Dalloway's attention, like that of the other shoppers and strollers, is seized by a passing limousine; but, for readers of the novel, she is distinguished from the crowd by the fact that the prime minister—quite possibly the passenger in the car—will be a guest at her party.

11. Flowers appear frequently in Mansfield's stories, and are often associated with food as well as with femaleness. Unfortunately, a full discussion of their importance is beyond the scope of this study.

12. Mansfield later disavowed this early collection, and resisted having it reprinted. Certainly, the stories are immature, somewhat clumsy, and dwell rather heavily on pre-First World War stereotypes of Germans. Still, as a number of recent critics—Patricia Moran, C. A. Hankin, and others—have pointed out, the collection is quite important in the context of her whole work, and is particularly linked to her New Zealand stories.

13. Mansfield herself spent time at a spa in 1909. While there, she suffered a miscarriage. Presumably her pregnancy was the reason for her being there in the first place.

14. Fullbrook argues that 'At Lehmann's' joins 'images of male assault, female desire, pain, bewilderment and violence as the important aspects of a typical sexual initiation for women' (58).

15. Alpers believes that V. S. Pritchett was responding to this characteristic of Mansfield's work when 'he declared that the sense of a country, the sense of the "unseen character," was . . . weak in her writing' (*The Life of KM* 346).

16. Moran follows the line of thought traced by Elaine Showalter in *The Female Malady*: 'Disgust with meat was a common phenomenon among Victorian girls; a carnivorous diet was associated with sexual precocity' (129).

17. The earrings distract Kezia from the duck's death, but also raise for her the issue of gender, and particularly the relationship between biological gender and its usual surface symbols. Here, as elsewhere in the story, essential gender differences are, at the same time, both alluded to and questioned.

18. Bynum explores the symbolic value of food for medieval women: 'Like body, food must be broken and spilled forth in order to give life. Macerated by teeth before it can be assimilated to give life, food mirrors and recapitulates both sacrifice and service . . . Women's bodies, in the acts of lactation and of giving birth, were analogous both to ordinary food and to the body of Christ, as it died on the cross and gave birth to salvation' (30).

19. Obviously, there are many factors involved in tracking statistics on eating disorders, not least of which is the reliability of diagnosis and reporting of the syndrome. Perlick and Silverstein report,

'At the beginning of the 20th century, disordered eating among females did not appear to be common; however, it increased dramatically, reaching possible epidemic proportions in the 1920s, as evidenced in an emergency meeting of the American Medical Association' (80).

20. '[T]he key to the development of [anorexia] is feeling ambivalent about one's own gender' (Perlick and Silverstein 89).

21. Linda's dual response to gender might fit what Parkin-Gounelas refers to in terms of the woman writer as 'the discourse of the hysteric': in other words, 'a simultaneous refusal of, yet submission to, femininity as it is constructed under patriarchy' ('KM Reading Other Women' 45). Parkin-Gounelas credits Julia Kristeva as the originator of this notion.

22. Bynum also refers to 'the mother-daughter relationship' as key in the treatment of anorectics (202).

23. Linda's dilemma can be seen as an inheritance of the nineteenth-century fictional tradition, in which '"the only choices available to a female protagonist are frequently revealed as negative ones: a stifling and repressive marriage or a form of withdrawal into inwardness which frequently concludes in self-destruction"' (Felski, *Beyond Feminist Aesthetics* 124; quoted in Kaplan, *KM and the Origins* 87).

Works Cited

Alpers, Antony. *The Life of Katherine Mansfield*. New York: Viking Press, 1980.

Berman, Marshall. *All That Is Solid Melts into Air: The Experience of Modernity*. New York: Simon and Schuster, 1982.

Blum, Virginia L. 'Mary Wilkins Freeman and the Taste of Necessity.' *American Literature* 65.1 (1993): 69-94.

Burgan, Mary. *Illness, Gender, and Writing: The Case of Katherine Mansfield*. Baltimore and London: Johns Hopkins University Press, 1994.

Bynum, Caroline Walker. *Holy Feast and Holy Fast: The Religious Significance of Food to Medieval Women*. Berkeley and Los Angeles: University of California Press, 1987.

Chopin, Kate. *The Awakening and Selected Short Stories*. 1899. Toronto, New York, London: Bantam, 1981.

Ewen, Stuart. *Captains of Consciousness*. New York: McGraw-Hill, 1976.

Felski, Rita. *Beyond Feminist Aesthetics*. United Kingdom: Hutchinson Radius, 1989.

———. *The Gender of Modernity*. Cambridge: Harvard University Press, 1995.

Finkelstein, Joanne. *Dining Out: A Sociology of Modern Manners*. Cambridge: Polity Press, 1989.

Fullbrook, Kate. *Katherine Mansfield*. Bloomington and Indianapolis: Indiana University Press, 1986.

Hardy, Thomas. *Tess of the d'Urbervilles*. 1891. Harmondsworth: Penguin Books, 1985.

Hurston, Zora Neale. *Their Eyes Were Watching God*. 1937. Urbana and Chicago: University of Illinois Press, 1978.

Kaplan, Sydney Janet. *Katherine Mansfield and the Origins of Modernist Fiction*. Ithaca and London: Cornell University Press, 1991.

Larsen, Nella. *An Intimation of Things Distant: The Collected Fiction of Nella Larsen*. New York: Doubleday, 1992.

Mansfield, Katherine. *The Collected Stories of Katherine Mansfield*. Constable, 1945. London: Penguin Books, 1981.

McFall, Gardner. 'Katherine Mansfield and the Honourable Dorothy Brett: A Correspondence of Artists.' Robinson 53-69.

Moran, Patricia. 'Unholy Meanings: Maternity, Creativity, and Orality in Katherine Mansfield.' *Feminist Studies* 17.1 (Spring 1991): 105-25.

O'Sullivan, Vincent, and Margaret Scott, eds. *The Collected Letters of Katherine Mansfield*. Oxford: Clarendon Press, 1984.

Parkin-Gounelas, Ruth. *Fictions of the Female Self: Charlotte Brontë, Olive Schreiner, Katherine Mansfield*. New York: St Martin's Press, 1991.

———. 'Katherine Mansfield Reading Other Women: The Personality of the Text.' Robinson 36-52.

———. 'Katherine Mansfield's Piece of Pink Wool: Feminine Signification in "The Luftbad."' *Studies in Short Fiction* 27.4 (Fall 1990): 495-507.

Perlick, Deborah, and Brett Silverstein. 'Faces of Female Discontent: Depression, Disordered Eating, and Changing Gender Roles.' *Feminist Perspectives on Eating Disorders*. Ed. Patricia Fallon, Melanie A. Katzman, and Susan C. Wooley. New York and London: Guilford Press, 1994. 77-93.

Poole, Roger. *The Unknown Virginia Woolf*. 4th ed. Cambridge and New York: Cambridge University Press, 1995.

Robinson, Roger, ed. *Katherine Mansfield: In from the Margin*. Baton Rouge and London: Louisiana State University Press, 1994.

Showalter, Elaine. *The Female Malady: Women, Madness, and English Culture, 1830-1980.* New York: Pantheon Books, 1985.

Waugh, Patricia. *Metafiction: The Theory and Practice of Self-Conscious Fiction.* London and New York: Methuen, 1984.

Wharton, Edith. *The Age of Innocence.* 1920. New York: Collier Books, 1993.

———. *The Custom of the Country.* 1913. London: Constable, 1941.

———. *The House of Mirth.* 1905. New York: Collier Books, 1987.

Woolf, Virginia. *Mrs. Dalloway.* 1925. New York: Harcourt, Brace and World, 1953.

Suzanne Ferguson (essay date 2003)

SOURCE: Ferguson, Suzanne. "Genre and the Work of Reading in Mansfield's 'Prelude' and 'At the Bay.'" In *Postmodern Approaches to the Short Story,* edited by Farhat Iftekharrudin, Joseph Boyden, Joseph Longo, and Mary Rohrberger, pp. 25-38. Westport, Conn.: Praeger Publishers, 2003.

[*In the following essay, Ferguson examines Mansfield's intentional blurring of issues of literary genres in the novel* The Aloe, *its revision as the story "Prelude," and the companion piece "At the Bay," which features the same characters. She maintains that these works challenge the reader to find meaning in and connections between the individual narratives within the larger works.*]

From its beginnings the short story has lent itself to sequencing, by both authors and readers alike: The Hebrew Bible, we now realize, is a cobbled-together short story sequence, as are most epics, romances, and picaresque novels. Put into sequence—chronologically, genealogically, geographically—they "become" a different genre, to be read in parts, perhaps, but understood as a whole. When, in the later nineteenth century, the short story rose to prominence as an artistic genre, sequences (and cycles) grew up side by side with the single story, making possible, for example, the publication and sale of related stories in separate volumes, as in *The Adventures of Sherlock Holmes* or P. G. Wodehouse's many volumes about Bertie and Jeeves. Such volumes we do not think of as "sequences" because, except for the final story in *Tales of Sherlock Holmes,* where Conan Doyle tried to kill off his charismatic hero, they have no governing formal development and denouement. Perhaps Doyle's public so fervently demanded the return of Sherlock Holmes precisely because there was no sequence leading to his "death."

The modernist/impressionist story, however, grew up with "sequences" such as George Moore's *The Untilled Field,* with its themes of Irish emigration and alienation, followed by Joyce's *Dubliners* and Anderson's *Winesburg, Ohio.* The critical enterprise confronting these works must study the meanings of the sequence as a whole as much as of the individual stories. Recently, I have become interested in related stories from this period and after that resist readers' efforts to cast them into sequence: Mansfield's New Zealand stories of the Fairfield/Burnell family from the years 1910-1919; Grace Paley's "Faith Darwin" stories from the 50s through the 80s, Sherman Alexie's "Victor" stories of the early 1990s. These groups have in common that they are autobiographical and were written by authors self-identified as "on the margins" of the mainstream of their society, while they appeal to the mainstream audience and depend for some of their impact on its resistance to their formal challenge: to remain outside the rules of "sequence." Each story tacitly, and sometimes openly (Paley) acknowledges the existence of the others, but doesn't yield to the seduction of plot development, as if denying the authenticity of plot and "sequence."

In their resistance to being read as unified sequences they suggest a curious blurring or overlap of what, just a few years ago, would have seemed fixed: the border between modernist and postmodernist fiction. Rather than a "rage for order" that would respond to New Critical methods of interpretation, these stories confront and accept discontinuity and disorder. They tempt the reader to form sequences, only to leave great gaps and dislocations.

What difference does it make for us as readers whether we read these stories as sequenced or not? One implication of the work of critics Ian Reid, Suzanne Hunter Brown, and others investigating the cognitive side of short-story research is that works whose genre characteristics are mixed or uncertain are more difficult to read (i.e., establish a "reading" of or interpret) and their emotional impact will vary much more from reader to reader than works whose genres are readily identified. Sometimes the mixing of genre characteristics is deliberate: the authors apparently mean to mystify and complicate the reader's task and response, as in Shakespeare's romances or works of postmodern fiction and drama. But sometimes, as when the author is herself trying something new that doesn't seem to fit the conventions of her contemporary mainstream, works emerge that are interesting hybrids, calling on the reader for extra investment of reading effort and perhaps rewarding that readerly work with special pleasures and illuminations.

In writing, the author has available the full arsenal of intentionality, arrangement of episodes, perspectives, diction, imagery, allusion. The reader confronting the printed text has generic expectations internalized and organized from childhood forward. In readers' encounters with generically unusual fictional texts, the work of reading often involves a process of negotiation among conflicting generic expectations. In a short work, full understanding of how to read may develop concurrently with the entire reading experience: only in retrospect, that is, may we be able to "complete" the integration of textual elements into a sense of the work "as a whole." When the reader's sense of the "whole" is a group of "parts" left discrete and separated by the author, the occasion arises for critical interrogation of the formal and social elements that pull the reader toward a sequencing that the author neglected or refused to provide.

On March 25, 1915, Katherine Mansfield wrote to John Middleton Murry that she had begun work on her first *novel*. "I had a great day yesterday. The Muses descended in a ring, like the angels on the Botticelli Nativity roof . . . and I fell into the open arms of my first novel. I have finished a large chunk (***Letters*** I,167-68). She calls the work a "book" in a letter to S. S. Koteliansky of May 4th; to Murry, May 8th and 12th (***Letters*** I, 174, 180, 186); and on the 14th of May she declares, "My work is finished my freedom gained. . . . I have only to polish my work now; its [sic] all really accompli" (188).[1] Nevertheless, in responding to an October 11th, 1917, query from her friend, the painter Dorothy Brett, as to its form, she replied that it was "so difficult to say. As far as I know its [sic] more or less my own invention" (***Letters*** I, 331).[2] This assessment comes after her cuts and revisions to the work gave it the form in which it was to be published, under the title **"Prelude,"** by Leonard and Virginia Woolf at the Hogarth Press in July of 1918 (O'Sullivan, ***The Aloe***, 16). Vincent O'Sullivan claims that in this work Mansfield "is discovering a new way to tell a story" which is "not so much a narrative about events shared by several people, as one where several temperaments unfold in the slantings of perspective, in the tilting gradations of time. . . . The story itself has become how it is being told" (9), and Mansfield herself later referred to "the **'Prelude'** method—it just unfolds and opens" (qtd. in Kaplan, 103).

This long story/novella, with its canonical name **"Prelude,"** was also published in 1930 by Murry in its "original" 1915 form, about a third again as long, under its first title ***The Aloe***. Mansfield's countryman, Vincent O'Sullivan, who has made so many important contributions to Mansfield scholarship in recent decades, made the two versions co-readable in his excellent facing-page edition of 1983, which preserves even passages struck through in the manuscript. The existence of the two versions, in the context of the letters identifying it as a "novel," along with a second work (**"At the Bay,"** 1921) featuring the same characters and a similar form—short sections focusing on different family members unified by an event or a short time period and touching upon a cluster of family themes—and with some additional short stories of more conventionally plotted forms that could nonetheless be seen as related to **"Prelude"** and **"At the Bay,"** provide a tempting case study for considering generic issues in readers' responses to these works. As Perry Meisel has noted: "In reading **'Prelude,'** the issue is not so much creating a subtext or supplement [as it is for other Mansfield stories] as creating a matrix to 'hold' the various strands in a meaningful, coherent whole" (117).

The story, along with its companion piece **"At the Bay,"** has received much critical attention to its form and meaning, notably by such critics as Mary Rohrberger, Saralyn Daly, Sidney Janet Kaplan, Mary Burgan, Vincent O'Sullivan, W. H. New, and Ian Gordon, in his chronological ordering of these stories with other stories of the Fairfield/Burnell and Sheridan families (Mansfield's other autobiographically reminiscent New Zealand family, most notably in **"The Garden Party"**) in ***Undiscovered Country*** (1974), demonstrates the critical impulse to see them as a sequence. In what follows I will try to focus specifically on elements of the story that point to generic frames by which we determine how to read the story, rather than seeking or espousing a particular interpretation. In the text included in ***Bliss and Other Stories*** (1920), **"Prelude"** is about 28,000 words long, divided into twelve irregular sections: something already arguably in the "novella" range, already posing problems of generic framing. Are we to abandon ourselves to "experiencing" the fictional world, as in a novel, or are we to grasp all the aesthetic and ideational parts as a whole, as in reading the short story? We begin in medias res (no help from that!) with the scene of a moving day: everything has been loaded up, and all the family have boarded the van except two little girls. We hear their mother, in the free indirect style that immediately puts us on guard as to how to judge what she is saying, announcing that these two will have to be left behind, as the contents already loaded are "absolute necessities." My most recent students, reading this, began to wonder aloud what was wrong with this mother, an appropriate reaction as it turns out, and a question that is unanswered until sections V and XI. No one in the scene, including the children, however, seems to take her seriously, and after the first moment it seems that she has been joking, with the hysterical exhaustion of a moving day. A provisional topos has been set in motion, however, that of the bad mother and of lost or abandoned children—"Hansel and Gretel" in "modern" dress, a tale with moral and psychological resonances for the reader.

This opening scene appears to have set up not just the teasing of one of the girls by a family of children who are, though more worldly wise, of a lower class (the neighboring "Samuel Josephs" who entertain Kezia and

Lottie while they wait for the store-man who is to bring them along to the new house), but the girl herself, her farewell to the old house, and her unfamiliar framing of it through colored glass that gives odd (and self-consciously artistic) perspectives on what is soon to be the past.

> Kezia bent down to have one more look at a blue lawn with blue arum lilies growing at the gate, and then at a yellow lawn with yellow lilies and a yellow fence. As she looked a little Chinese Lottie came out onto the lawn. . . . Was that really Lottie? Kezia was not quite sure until she had looked through the ordinary window.
>
> (34)

Thus by following Kezia out of the first scene, the reader frames the "story" to be "about" her reaction to the move. This focus on Kezia continues for more than a quarter of the story, but then, in an elegant "turn" in the scene in which the children are reunited with both their parents and grandmother in the new house, it shifts, playing briefly among several of the adults at the end of section III. The reader's first attempt at a story paradigm is overturned, and s/he must cast about for some other way to establish the unity "story" demands.

Here is the first hint that perhaps we are reading a "novel" after all: we are now following the consciousness of four additional characters—the mother, the father, the grandmother, and the children's Aunt Beryl—and will pick up that of the household maid, Alice, as well, in section X. Certainly one interesting act of reading many have performed with the story and its successor, **"At the Bay,"** is to follow the "stories" of the individual characters: Beryl's "story" of her place in the household as the unmarried aunt and her writing of this to her friend Nan; Linda's story of wishing to sail away from her children and especially her husband, Stanley; Stanley's opposing, dissonant story of his success in marriage and family life; Kezia's story of confronting death and ambiguity in the episode in which the handyman Pat demonstrates beheading a duck, only to have it "pad back to the stream" already headless, distressing Kezia until she is distracted by Pat's little gold earrings. For Alice, the housemaid's "story" is not fleshed out until **"At the Bay,"** in which Beryl has a vivid new strand in her story portraying her relationship with the odious Mr. and Mrs. Harry Kember; there, Linda also has a new episode in which she "falls in love" with her new, male child; and a new character, Linda's brother-in-law Jonathan Trout, appears to juxtapose Stanley's story with a contrasting one of male self-consciousness and regret. In the later story, Kezia is relegated to a minor role as one of a group of children participating in what is, in generic terms, clearly an episode rather than a "story," and extends her own story only in the brief scene in which, teasing with her at naptime, she tries to make her grandmother promise never to die.

Whether we project the "strings" as independent horizontal strands layered as in musical polyphony, or as in the plot and subplot of novels, we are seeing the family as a multileveled system, in which the members interact with and affect one another, even as the whole system evolves. By the time the reader has made it to the middle of **"Prelude"** the sense of where the story may be leading, in terms of action or change, is almost completely in abeyance. One reads on to see what (if anything) will happen to bring the strands into a pattern. And indeed, nothing does "happen" to any of the protagonists, nor do they do anything to change their status or resolve their problems. Although by the end Kezia has had an experience of confronting death, Linda has admitted to herself her fear of death through sex and childbirth, and Beryl has admitted her false persona, these "discoveries" seem in themselves quite disparate and tenuous as compared to the dramatic conclusions of such Mansfield stories as **"Bliss"** or **"Marriage à la Mode,"** for example, which deal at least partly with similar themes.

Certainly nothing is concluded in **"Prelude"** for Kezia. After the episode of the duck, she does not return until the very end of the story, where she appears holding a kitten to call her aunt down to meet "a man Stanley had brought from work," neatly concluding Beryl's "plot" with the notion that she will continue to try to find a husband from among a class of men that in her heart she despises. Kezia's "plot," however, ends with the miraculous *not*-breaking of a face-cream jar lid she has put on the kitten to see it aesthetically arranged and anthropomorphized in Beryl's mirror. Some readers have taken this ending to suggest that Kezia will follow Beryl as a poseur and avoider of responsibility; others that the "mystery" of why things happen embodied in the fantasy of the fearful "them" and "it"—unseen forces in and under our world that both Kezia and Linda Burnell experience—is confirmed in this chance happening of "good" that will spare Kezia from her aunt's wrath.

Although the first scene of **"Prelude"** could begin either a novel or a story, the last could not conclude a novel of the kind that has been suggested in the various scenes and plot threads. The "to-be-continued" sense is very strong in the suggestion that Linda Burnell will have the male child Stanley foresees in the empty chair of the nursery and she anticipates in section XI: "What am I guarding myself for so preciously? I shall go on having children and Stanley will go on making money and the children and the gardens will grow bigger and bigger, with whole fleets of aloes in them" (142).[3]

In several ways, **"At the Bay"** does function as a next installment. Beryl's fantasies get her into trouble; Linda has had "the boy" and becomes intrigued with him, suggesting that she will develop into an indulgent and attached mother for the first time with this male child;

Stanley continues to be self-centered and self-indulgent; and Jonathan Trout is introduced as a counter to Stanley. The children continue their childhood games and confront the terror that imagination can bring, and Kezia tries to stop the flow toward death by demanding that her grandmother promise not to die, in what could well be a fore-shadowing of the grandmother's death in an episode never to be written. The housemaid Alice takes a more prominent role in her visit to her assertive widow-friend Mrs. Stubbs, which results in her revulsion against sex and marriage and longing for the safety of her "kitching." There, the only threat is Beryl, whom, as we saw in **"Prelude"** (section X), Alice can "vanquish" by imagined repartée, much as troublesome Stanley can be "drowned" vicariously with the teapot in the dishwater.

"At the Bay" uses the same formal method as **"Prelude,"** but instead of the unifying device of "moving house," it has the cycle of dawn to darkness as its spatiotemporal frame. The long set piece with which it opens, establishing the place as special and magical, and the figures of the shepherd and his dog challenged by Florrie the vacationing cat ("silly young female" in the dog's view [4]), seems to most of my student readers very novelistic, and, for a short story, "excessive." Nothing is "done" with the sheep, the shepherd, or the dog later in the story, so they have to carry their full symbolism from connections established within this first scene, and in juxtaposition to the absurdity of the second scene, in which Stanley's morning "constitutional" vacation swim is spoiled by his talkative, ironic, "failed" brother-in-law, who does not have to go back to work for several days, and who doesn't want to, ever. Although one can read **"At the Bay"** as a separate story, and it has its champions, it seems to depend for resonance on **"Prelude"** and at the same time to be more contrived in its use of the day cycle to display the differences in the worlds of women and men, the stereotypes and anti-types Mansfield manipulates in the story.

Thus neither work fully conforms to the readerly frame of "novel fragment" or "short story." As "novellae," both are still odd "beasts" requiring much work from the reader to give them aesthetic completeness. Mansfield seems to have recognized that *The Aloe* would not do in the state it was when the Woolfs asked her for something to publish at Hogarth Press. She streamlined it, simplifying its plot lines, characters, and themes as she prepared it for printing.[4] One striking difference that marks an important change of "frame" is that of the title from *The Aloe* to **"Prelude,"** reputedly suggested by Murry (O'Sullivan, 14).

The reader, upon encountering **"Prelude,"** quickly surmises that the moving to a new house is itself "prelude"—something before the *ludus*, the play—to other things that will happen to these characters in their "lives." The "completeness" of the prelude can be evaluated on the basis of how subtly and clearly it does predict what will come "after" the events recounted. A "prelude" is also a free-form musical composition that stands on its own, especially in piano music of the romantic period, successor to the "chorale prelude" of baroque organists—embellishments on a well-known tune or theme, developed freely within established conventions of improvisation. The suggestion of communication through oblique hints rather than direct statement also comes from romantic and impressionist musical "preludes," as does the notion of something small and intimate rather than grand and completely "plotted," like a sonata or a symphony.[5]

The title *The Aloe*, on the other hand, was also manifestly wrong for a family novel, but could have worked for a short story, like Lawrence's "Odour of Chrysanthemums" (1911) or Chekhov's "Gooseberries" (1893), both of which use the eponymous plants as focal points for characters' moments of revelation about the meaning of their lives. The aloe plant[6] does work in the story as a many-attributed symbol bringing together Kezia and Linda, and Linda and Mrs. Fairfield, in two memorable scenes. The plant seems to have no direct relation to Stanley or Beryl, though Mansfield's planned cutting-down of the aloe stem while Linda lies ill after giving birth to "the boy" could have brought the other characters into the picture.[7] Nevertheless, like such titles as "Noon Wine," "The Aspern Papers," "The Fox," or "Death in Venice," the titles of *The Aloe*, **"Prelude,"** and **"At the Bay"** suggest central tropes that can easily frame a short fiction—novella or short story—rather than a novel.

With such titles and brevity influencing us on the one hand, and multiple story threads weaving in and out on the other, how do readers decide the appropriate strategies to make sense of and achieve the illusion of wholeness (Poe's "unity of effect") from stories such as **"Prelude"** and **"At the Bay,"** now widely regarded as trailblazers in modernist short-story form? First, we must accept, and hold in suspension, the sometimes rapid shifts in the objects of our attention. Once the focus has shifted from Kezia, in section IV of **"Prelude,"** it moves first to Beryl, readying herself for bed, imagining "in the garden a young man, dark and slender, with mocking eyes," and thinking "how frightfully unreasonable" her brother-in-law can be; within a few paragraphs, the "eye" of the story, movie-like, shifts to Stanley, talking to Linda, then pauses for a moment on Pat the handyman before shifting back to Kezia and her grandmother (56), and finally out into the night itself, where owls call "more pork; more pork," and a bird—the New Zealand equivalent of a kukuburra, apparently—laughs "far away in the bush" (58) to end the section.

Section V begins with the world's coming back to consciousness in light and sound, with Linda Burnell as the center, for the first time, in the midst of a dream that reveals some of the tensions in her character and marriage. In the dream her father (dead at the time of the story) is walking with her and shows her a tiny chick which, attractive at first, grows large and demanding under her touch (58). The dream is broken by Stanley's pulling up the venetian blind with a clatter. This scene was followed by the largest single cut Mansfield made from *The Aloe,* nearly eight full printed pages, about 3500 words, which give more detail on the grandmother, on Linda before her marriage to Stanley, on her father, and on the courtship of Linda by Stanley. These pages filled in background in a conventional novelistic fashion, fleshing out the characters and their interrelationships.

Lacking this background, the **"Prelude"** reader stays with Linda in her bed, tracing flowers on the wallpaper and feeling haunted by an imaginary "them" reminiscent of the fearful "it" that earlier terrified Kezia in the empty town house. Forced to put these feelings of disease together, both by the fact that Kezia and her mother have similar feelings when left alone and that Linda is now only the second character in the story with whose consciousness we are allowed to have extended contact, we begin to narrow down to a finer sense just who is important and of whose situation we will be asked to judge.

Now at midpoint in the story, with the beginning of section VI, the focalization retreats to a general overview of unpacking activity in the kitchen, where Linda arrives some pages later, and from which she walks out into the garden. Kezia, meanwhile, has also begun to explore the garden, and for two pages (over 700 words) Mansfield describes its flowers, then how Kezia likes to surprise her grandmother with tiny artistic creations put together from flowers and leaves (90, 92). At the end of this section, Kezia and Linda meet in contemplation of the giant aloe, and have their sole conversational exchange in the story (94).

There could be no doubt, whether in a story or a novel, that the aloe is set up as some sort of symbol, because of the extensive description and the convergence of the two most prominent characters in its shadow. Yet it is not until the following evening—in section XI—that its meaning for Linda becomes clear. Like Mrs. Ramsay's lighthouse in Woolf, created nearly ten years later,[8] the aloe "is" Linda's symbol: remote, full of spikes and thorns, able to bloom only once "in a hundred years," and embodying both the aggressiveness of her longing to be free and her fear of Stanley's sexual domination. Thus its projected destruction would symbolize her spiritual "death" as the resisting woman. In section XI of **"Prelude"** she sees the plant in the moonlight as a great ship powered by sail and oars that can row her "far away over the top of the garden trees, the paddocks and the dark bush beyond" (138).

In the sections of the story between the two "glimpses" of the aloe, Stanley's satisfaction with the move, his plans for his family, the trivial conflict between Beryl and Alice, and Beryl's flirting with Stanley are described, and there is a substantial section (seven-plus pages, over 2500 words) dealing with the children, including the two male cousins and their long-suffering dog Snooker; and the cutting off of the duck's head which so horrifies Kezia but is soon forgotten in the gender puzzle of Pat's earrings. In *The Aloe,* another four pages contained a scene with Beryl and Linda's married sister (Jonathan's wife) and additional material on Alice, again appropriate for novelistic development, but unnecessary to the themes of **"Prelude,"** which have begun to emerge more clearly around the motif of how the move brings out tensions and reflections that may have remained hidden in the old environment: Linda's fear of sex and childbirth and her longing to escape (even though she recognizes that she has no real will to do so); Beryl's fear of being an old maid, exacerbated by her new isolation in the country (though she is really only attracted to the men of her dreams, and not the men available in her social group). In *The Aloe* as later in **"At the Bay,"** Beryl is uncomfortably aware of her appeal to women (*The Aloe,* 153; "At the Bay," 20-23). A section of the latter also foregrounds Kezia's attraction to and timidity before the spectacle of life and death that unfolds before her.

While the cuts from *The Aloe* seem unexceptionable when one considers the refining and focusing necessary for a short story, all the material would have "fit" perfectly well into a novel, had Mansfield ever chosen to or been able to finish it. She did go on working with the Fairfield/Burnell family after the publication of **"Prelude,"** as she refers in a letter to Murry of December 1917 to a **"Bud of the Aloe"** which was lost in the mail but later, according to Murry, turned up and formed the opening of **"At the Bay"** (*Letters* I, 349). Still later, in 1922, she was working on another "installment," and wrote to her sister Charlotte Perkins: "I am going to write a kind of serial novel for *The Sphere* this summer" that would incorporate both earlier pieces (quoted in Boddy, 186). Although **"The Doll's House"** (published in February 1922) has a more straightforward short-story plot, with its own exposition of the local social structure, it could also easily have become part of the "novel," extending the characters of the children and Beryl.

That it all might have become a novel, had Mansfield lived and been well enough to pursue it, seems plausible enough, though it would have had to be resolved thematically similarly to Woolf's solution in *To the*

Lighthouse (1927). Since the characters were based on her family members, Mansfield might, perhaps, have simply continued to "tell" their lives to some convenient point—Kezia's leaving home, the grandmother's death, some resolution between Linda and Stanley. Beryl's marriage or disgrace or decamping seems only appropriate to a subplot. More interesting than such speculation, however, is how the two long stories became so admired, how they came to seem a new "form" of the short story. The many substantial readings of the stories in recent as well as earlier criticism testify not only to Mansfield's craftiness in interspersing the various episodes dealing with different characters and her success in creating a form similar to the themes and developments of musical preludes, but also in readers' persistence in seeking unities from these pluralities.

Given the basic trope of "moving house" in **"Prelude"** the reader remains open to each new episode as a revelation of what happens to each part of the family as a result. Kate Fulbrook writes: "Moving house is itself used as a metaphor for the possibility of change as the characters are temporarily dislodged from their habits and set roles," a setting which "prompts a series of moments of self-awareness for the characters" (67-68). Thus Kezia's deliberate defamiliarization of the yard and her sister Lottie (by looking through colored panes of glass) at the old house is extrapolated through the night journey to the new house, the explorations around the new environment, and the discovery of the symbolic aloe. The movement from being "packed up" in the first section to being "at home" in the final three sections, provides a framework within which the reader can examine the dramatic tensions within the family and speculate upon "woman's life" as represented in the different generations and social situations of the women of the story.[9]

In the many ingenious readings of the symbolism and structural echoes of **"Prelude"** by such insightful critics as Sylvia Berkman, Mary Rohrberger, Sidney Janet Kaplan, Mary Burgan, Saralynn Daly, Robert Robinson, Kate Fulbrook, Patrick Morrow, and W. H. New, we can see the insistent "rage for order" readers bring to bear upon a work they perceive as a short story. The many internal and corroborative clues to the novelistic origin (and planned destination) of the work are set aside or bracketed as each reader seeks to find the unifying elements. Mansfield's arbitrary foregrounding of the aloe as a central symbol and the "natural" unity provided by the instigation and completion of "moving house" actually do seem to satisfy the reader's desire for coherence even if, with Morrow, we concede that **"Prelude'** is noticeably incomplete" (51).

Having achieved an improvised formal success in **"Prelude,"** Mansfield was able to use the method as the basis for another installment of her family "novel" in **"At the Bay."** Having learned to read the former, the reader is prepared for the latter, though this story is even more thematically fragmented than **"Prelude,"** and indeed stands less well on its own. Having used "moving" as the primary structural trope for **"Prelude,"** Mansfield turned more conventionally in **"At the Bay"** to the time span of the day: a workday (for Stanley) during vacation time, in which the children and the women, along with Jonathan Trout, the unmasculine (because he dislikes work and is thoughtful and sensitive) brother-in-law, engage in their holiday routines of leisure, closer to the elemental rhythms of sea and sun and moon.[10]

The social space of being "on holiday" is a more interesting topos, however, given the tensions between work and leisure, and bondage and freedom that are explored. In this different spatiotemporal setting, a number of the themes raised in **"Prelude"** are revisited: Linda's distance from Stanley and her children, reframed when she is "seduced" by her boy baby; and Beryl's more dangerous flirting which nearly brings her to grief with Harry Kember. The drawn-out scene of the children's game at the center of the work makes sense only in the context of the characters in **"Prelude,"** however charming it may be. Similarly, Alice's tea with Mrs. Stubbs really draws upon her character as established in the earlier story, and though in itself not lacking for appeal, does not "work" very effectively with the other episodes, even though it opens up a window into a social stratum that mimics the tensions and conventions of the Burnells and their neighbors. The reader does put the pieces of this story together, but it lacks the freshness and intensity of **"Prelude,"** many of whose themes and insights seem repeated with less compelling examples. As further episodes from the "unwritten novel," however, it is enjoyable and meaningful, as well as beautiful.

> In some larger sense, it is impossible not to wish that "the novel" had been written, yet the very fact of its being somehow "behind" the two stories gives them a resonance beyond that of the more conventionally plotted stories. That Mansfield discovered the form of "layering" or "collaging"[11] experiences of several characters to show a range of women's experience within a single "work" essentially by accident—having to give the "woolves" a story to publish at a time when she was desirous of making public her tribute to her dead brother—does not detract from its achievement. As Kaplan writes, "What began as a 'novel' eventually became something new: a mixed genre, a multileveled, spatially ordered narrative."
>
> (103)

Though praised as influential, its influence on the short story is difficult, in fact, to follow except in its general principle of presenting episodes that can be read as the traces of a larger theme and plot. The careful neutrality of the omniscient narrator who bridges the episodes and narrates the "dramatic" scenes in which no character's consciousness is observed (and often mediates the characters' consciousness with a dazzling "indirect free style") can also be seen as influential, but as much for novelists (in addition to Woolf, Elizabeth Bowen comes immediately to mind) as later story writers.[12]

Paradoxically, then, it is the fact of **"Prelude"** and **"At the Bay"** having histories as drafts toward novels, trimmed for focus but retaining their multiple strands of plot, that creates the reading task of "framing" short stories, or perhaps more properly, novellas, out of them: that is, using their brevity as a rubric to indicate that a thematic and configural unity must be the aim of the reader. That readers have largely been able to find a thematic unity and process the complexity through conflating both "novel" and "short story" reading techniques suggests both how adaptable readers are and how Mansfield managed to make a virtue of necessity with her **"Gift of the Muses."** By configuration and sequencing of her various plot strands, she calls upon the reader to construct the interrelationship of the family's inner dynamic. Resisting the novel convention of working everything out over time but exploiting its tendency to portray community, she presents a set of examples the reader accepts as a microcosm from which the macrocosm of the family and of the society are projected.

It remains to consider why, then, since the stories did not become parts of a novel, we should also resist "sequencing" them or calling them, even casually, a "sequence" or "cycle." To summarize: like the stories with shared characters by other writers I have listed in the introduction to this paper, Mansfield's fictions about the Sheridans are connected only through the characters and settings. Although they share some themes, the development of the themes is disorganized, and the stories do not form a "whole" with an articulable conclusion. The repeated characters, in Paley's term, are "employed" by the writers to establish a familiarity that can be drawn upon while new themes and emphases are explored by the writer as well as the reader. Although the temptation to forge them into sequences may be irresistible to readers, we should not allow that kind of reading to blind us to the oddities and deliberate strangeness of these stories, nor should we neglect to register the dis-ease that lies behind their refusal to be normalized into sequences. Their very existence resists the pull of plot, the reader's urge to make the crooked straight and the rough places plain: they say to us, "See these lives? See how difficult they are, how marginalized, how fragmented?" As their characters stand outside the mainstream of their social milieux, questioning and challenging their assumptions, so should the reader step aside from the desire to see the tidy fictional package, the reasonable conclusion. Mansfield was right when she wrote to Dorothy Brett that the form of **"Prelude"** and **"At the Bay"** was her own invention. So, too, I would argue, is the "form" that resists formulation, the anti-sequence of the Fairfield/Burnell stories.

Notes

1. Sidney Janet Kaplan notes that in her journal, Mansfield said she was "planning a novel, *Karori*" (216).

2. Mansfield continues with a figure of an island (New Zealand, Atlantis) rising out of the mists of the sea, seen in glimpses and descending again, an image more precisely descriptive of "At the Bay," published three years later.

3. Mansfield also noted her plan to have her brother's birth the conclusion of *The Aloe* in a journal entry.

4. In addition to O'Sullivan, Sidney Janet Kaplan and others have traced and analyzed the excisions.

5. Saralyn Daly likens the appearances and recurrences of symbols as "musical motifs" (91). Compare also T. S. Eliot's "Preludes" as impressionist "glimpses." For a different take on the title, see New, 147-57.

6. The described plant sounds more like the related succulent, the agave, commonly known as "century plant," which blossoms once upon maturing (after thirty years or so), after which the plant itself dies. However new, smaller plants are already growing adjacent to it, in a cluster.

7. Cf. Chekhov's "The Cherry Orchard," or Forster's "Other Kingdom" (ca. 1910) where a Stanley Burnell-like man insists on fencing off a parcel of his forest against his fiancé's will, only to have her disappear, Daphne-like, among the trees.

8. Correspondences between the aloe and the lighthouse, and the possible influence of Mansfield on Woolf here, are explored at length by Angela Smith in her recent *Katherine Mansfield and Virginia Woolf*, 95-105.

9. Thus the third sister can be dispensed with in the short-story version—she merely reiterates aspects of the other women's situation. See also Burgan, 116.

10. Mary Burgan sees in the moon the "female influence. . . . As a final comment on the anxieties of sex and birth, Mansfield thus provides a vision of eternally recurrent nature which both troubles and consoles" (116). See also Ruth Parkin-Gounelas, 51.

11. Both O'Sullivan and Sara Sandley liken the techniques to those of film (in Robinson, ed., 15, 74-77).

12. Some critics, notably Sidney Janet Kaplan, have argued that what Mansfield created was a peculiarly feminine form of narrative: "What makes

'Prelude' so revolutionary as a narrative is its implicit statement that the construction of gender should be the motivating center of the text. . . . It is . . . a rejection of male modes, and this strategy is apparent in its all-over structure: its multiplicity, its fluidity, its lack of a central climax, and its many moments of encoded sexual pleasure" (114).

Works Cited

Berkman, Sylvia. *Katherine Mansfield: A Critical Study*. New Haven, Conn: Yale University Press, 1951.

Boddy, Gillian. "'Finding the Treasure,' Coming Home: Katherine Mansfield in 1921-22." In Robinson, 173-88.

Burgan, Mary. *Illness, Gender, and Writing, The Case of Katherine Mansfield*. Baltimore & London: Johns Hopkins University Press, 1994.

Daly, Saralyn. *Katherine Mansfield*. Revised edition. New York: Twayne, 1994.

Fulbrook, Kate. *Katherine Mansfield*. Bloomington and Indianapolis: Indiana University Press, 1986.

Gordon, Ian, ed. *Undiscovered Country: The New Zealand Stories of Katherine Mansfield*. London: Longman, 1974.

Hunter Brown, Suzanne. "Discourse Analysis and the Short Story." *Short Story Theory at a Crossroads*. Ed. Susan Lohafer and Jo Ellyn Clarey. Baton Rouge: Louisiana State University Press, 1989, 217-48.

Kaplan, Sidney Janet. *Katherine Mansfield and the Origins of Modernist Fiction*. Ithaca: Cornell University Press, 1991.

Mansfield, Katherine. *The Garden Party and other Stories*. New York: Alfred A. Knopf, 1923.

———. *The Collected Letters of Katherine Mansfield*. Edited by Vincent O'Sullivan and Margaret Scott. Vols. 1 and 4. Oxford: Clarendon Press, 1984, 1996.

Meisel, Perry. "What the Reader Knows; or, The French One." In Robinson, 112-18.

Morrow, Patrick D. *Katherine Mansfield's Fiction*. Bowling Green, OH: Bowling Green State University Popular Press, 1993.

New, W. H. *Reading Mansfield and Metaphors of Form*. Montreal & Kingston: McGill-Queen's University Press, 1998.

O'Sullivan, Vincent, ed. *"The Aloe" with "Prelude" by Katherine Mansfield*. Manchester, England: Carcanet New Press Limited, 1983.

———. "'Finding the Pattern, Solving the Problem': Katherine Mansfield, the New Zealand European." In Robinson, 9-24.

Parkin-Gounelas, Ruth. "Katherine Mansfield Reading Other Women: The Personality of the Text." In Robinson, 36-52.

Reid, Ian. "Destabilizing Frames for Story." *Short Story Theory at a Crossroads*. Baton Rouge: Louisiana State University Press, 1989, 299-310.

Robinson, Roger, ed. *Katherine Mansfield, In From the Margin*. Baton Rouge & London: Louisiana University Press 1994.

Rohrberger, Mary. *The Art of Katherine Mansfield*. Ann Arbor, Mich.: University Microfilms, 1977.

Sandley, Sarah. "The Middle of the Note: Katherine Mansfield's 'Glimpses.'" In Robinson, 70-89.

Smith, Angela. *Katherine Mansfield and Virginia Woolf: A Public of Two*. Oxford: Clarendon Press, 1999.

Andrew Bennett (essay date 2004)

SOURCE: Bennett, Andrew. "Katherine Mansfield's 'Vagrant Self.'" In *Katherine Mansfield*, pp. 32-43. Horndon, United Kingdom: Northcote House Publishers Ltd., 2004.

[*In the following essay, Bennett analyzes the theme of displacement and the depiction of exiles and migrants in three of Mansfield's early New Zealand stories: "The Woman at the Store," "Ole Underwood," and "Millie."*]

Katherine Mansfield's identities are bound up with her sense of place and her sense of belonging, national, geographical, cultural, linguistic. But after leaving New Zealand in 1908 Mansfield rarely felt settled and she wrote as a displaced, even, in a certain sense, a homeless person, from a migrant perspective. Hers was what she herself referred to in a letter as a 'vagrant self' (*CLKM* [*The Collected Letters of Katherine Mansfield*] ii. 188). In this chapter we will examine this sense of displacement in Mansfield's writing before going on to discuss the significance of her first home, New Zealand, in and for her writing.

After leaving home and travelling to England for the first time at the age of 14, Mansfield rarely lived in one place for more than a few months at a time, and, despite her efforts to establish a home in England with Murry, for much of her adult life she lived in temporary lodgings, hotels and hostels, guest houses and pensions. Antony Alpers suggests, for example, that at a 'conservative count' Mansfield 'amassed a total of twenty-nine postal addresses' between her arrival in London in 1908 and April 1916 (*L*. [Antony Alpers, *The Life of Katherine Mansfield*] 201). The difficulties involved in finding a place to live were no doubt multiple and included the difficulties in her relationship with Murry, her terminal illness, and a chronic lack of money. But the problem also seems to have been to do with a fundamental sense of unease concerning the question of 'home', which we might link with Mansfield's complex and indeed multiple national and cultural identities. From November 1915 until her death, Mansfield repeatedly travelled to the Continent, moving from one temporary residence to another on the French or Italian Riviera, in Paris or Switzerland, in search of a climate that would help to cure her tuberculosis, usually returning to London for the summer. Her condition during these years—the years of her major work—was that of the exile, the migrant, the nomad. Her condition was characterized by the loss of place, by ungrounding or displacement—cultural, geographical, linguistic, national. But from early on in her life Mansfield herself recognized that this loss of place, of permanence, was also a gain in that it allowed for a fluidity or mobility of identity. In a letter to her cousin Sylvia Payne from London in April 1906, Mansfield comments on how much she is enjoying what she calls 'this Hotel life': 'There is a kind of feeling of irresponsibility about it', she says, 'that is fascinating'. And she links this irresponsible life with writing: 'Would you not like to try *all* sorts of lives', she asks her cousin, 'but that is the satisfaction of writing—one can impersonate so many people' (**CLKM** i. 19).

As Roger Robinson has commented, Mansfield's characters are 'ceaselessly on the move, travelling, wandering, often in foreign or threatening situations', and, as he also comments, her stories are filled with 'outcasts, exiles, minorities, and fringe dwellers'.[1] Often in transit, on the move, then, Mansfield's people are often hotel guests or lodgers, people with no fixed abode, on the way to somewhere else. **'The Woman at the Store'** focuses on a group of travellers in the unwelcoming, uncanny New Zealand backbush; **'Prelude'** concerns the Burnell family's move to a new house in the country; **'Pictures'** centres around Ada Moss's attempt to earn enough money to avoid being evicted for non-payment of rent; the characters in **'The Man without a Temperament'** live uneasily in a hotel on the Italian Riviera; **'The Little Governess'** is concerned with a young woman's difficult, even dangerous journey to Germany; **'Life of Ma Parker'** concludes with Ma Parker's distress over the fact that she has no place to be alone to mourn her life; in **'Marriage à la Mode'** William is made to feel a stranger in his own house by his wife and her fashionably bohemian friends; **'The Voyage'** concerns Fenella's journey by sea to stay with her grandparents after her mother's death; **'The Stranger'** revolves around a husband's anxious wait for his wife's ship to dock after her long absence abroad; **'Epilogue I: Pension Seguin'** revolves around the narrator's attempt to find lodgings in a strange city.

This concern with what is the often disturbing and even threatening nature of travel and with the uncertainties of hotel life is no doubt linked to Mansfield's sense of the insecurities and fragilities of personal identity. But it is also surely impelled, in the first place, by her 'colonial' status, by her move from New Zealand to Europe. As the New Zealand writer and critic C. K. Stead has commented, the cost of Mansfield's 'transplantation' from New Zealand to Europe was 'enormous' and became an important element in her writing, not least in her return to New Zealand as a subject in some of her major stories.[2] But Stead also raises the question of whether Mansfield should be described as a 'New Zealand writer' at all, suggesting that what he calls her 'New Zealandness' is 'hard to pin down' since it has been 'laid over, concealed—deliberately'.[3]

In fact, Mansfield's often somewhat nostalgic desire after her departure in 1908 to return to the place and time of her New Zealand childhood through her writing—'New Zealand is in my very bones,' she writes in one letter; 'what wouldn't I give to have a look at it' (***LKM*** [***The Letters of Katherine Mansfield***] ii. 199)—was no doubt reinforced by the fact that her status in England was that of what she herself called a 'colonial'.[4] Indeed, her notebooks and letters give a powerful sense of the condition of the life of a colonial exile in the metropolitan centre, the condition of being, as Angela Carter puts it, a 'prodigal daughter' in a world 'of which she was subtly never a part'.[5] In one notebook entry, for example, Mansfield remembers—without apparent bitterness—an incident from her time at Queen's College when the Principal referred to her in class as 'a little savage from New Zealand' (***KMN*** [***The Katherine Mansfield Notebooks***] ii. 31). In another notebook entry Mansfield writes a surreal fantasy of being shouted at by the 'red geraniums' who have bought the garden 'over my head':

> But why should they make me feel a stranger? Why should they ask me every time I go near: 'And what are *you* doing in a London garden?' They burn with arrogance & pride. And I am the little colonial walking in the London garden patch—allowed to look, perhaps, but not to linger. If I lie on the grass they positively shout at me. Look at her lying on *our* grass, pretending she lives here, pretending this is her garden & that tall back of the house with the windows open & the coloured curtains lifting is her house. She is a stranger—an alien. She is nothing but a little girl sitting on the Tinakori hills & dreaming: I went to London and married an englishman & we lived in a tall grave house with red geraniums & white daisies in the garden at the back. *Im*-pudence!
>
> (***KMN*** ii. 166)

Mansfield's sense of being a 'stranger', an 'alien', is exacerbated by the unwritten rules that govern one's claim to a place, to a home. Her life in England is only a 'pretence', a dream, even. Mansfield's reaction to such rejection was often extreme. In a notebook, for example, she describes being 'possessed' all day by 'my hate of England', a hatred that is (together with her brief love affair with Francis Carco) her 'one passion—a loathing for England' (**KMN** ii. 5). 'How I have hated England!' she declares later in a letter dated 25 July 1921 from Switzerland: 'Never, never will I live there. It's a kind of negation to me and there is always a kind of silky web or net of complications spread to catch one' (**CLKM** iv. 255). In another notebook, Mansfield's feelings towards her 'typical english husband' are complicated by his 'English' lack of warmth, by the fact that he is not 'ardent, eager, full of quick response, careless, spendthrift of himself, vividly alive, *high spirited*': it is this that she hates in England, a country she never wants to see again: 'No, I don't want England. England is of no use to me' (**KMN** ii. 167).

Mansfield's experience of growing up in New Zealand provided her with a store of memories and, more importantly perhaps, a desire to write herself back to her past and back to her homeland. Her past becomes, indeed, another country. 'Now—now I want to write recollections of my own country', she remarks in a notebook some time after the death of her brother in the First World War, 'not only because it is a "sacred debt" that I pay to my country because my brother & I were born there, but also because in my thoughts I range with him over all the remembered places. I am never far away from them. I long to renew them in writing.' Writing is figured here as a practice that renews the writer's memory, allowing her to re-experience what is lost. As her thoughts on the subject of writing New Zealand develop, she imagines the details of her birthplace:

> And the people, the people we loved there. Of them too I want to write—another 'debt of love'. Oh, I want for one moment to make our undiscovered country leap into the eyes of the old world. It must be mysterious, as though floating—it must take the breath [. . .] I shall tell everything, even of how the laundry basket squeaked at '75'—but all must be told with a sense of mystery, a radiance, an after glow because you, my little sun of it, are set . . .
>
> (**KMN** ii. 32)

Out of this desire to tell of how the laundry basket squeaked at "75"', Mansfield made some of her most accomplished fictions—**'Prelude', 'At the Bay', 'The Garden Party', 'The Doll's House',** and others. But as well as being important 'New Zealand' stories, the ethnic, national, and cultural identifications of many of these narratives are complicated by the way that the class and cultural assumptions of characters' thoughts and actions are overlaid by an 'English' sensibility. As Stead remarks, Mansfield 'neutraliz[es] the background' in many of these stories.[6] In other words, the Burnell and the Sheridan stories may themselves be read as articulations of the placelessness, or perhaps more accurately the multiple placings, the multiple cultural, ethnic, and national identifications of Mansfield's identity.

In a number of earlier stories, however—**'The Woman at the Store', 'Ole Underwood',** and **'Millie'**—Mansfield evokes a colonial cultural identity that is peculiarly un-English, an identity, indeed, constituted by its difference from the English. Although the stories have had a somewhat marginal place in the Mansfield canon, Stead has stressed their importance in a number of essays written since the 1970s and two of them have found a place in Angela Smith's new edition of the Oxford World's Classics **Selected Stories.** In these three stories, Mansfield develops themes and a style that, according to Stead 'indicate a whole line of development she denied herself by becoming a European writer' (*CR* [Jan Pilditch, ed., *The Critical Response to Katherine Mansfield*] 158)—a line of development that is particularly influential in the work of other New Zealand writers of the 1930s-1950s.[7] The three stories may be read both as important literary 'roads not taken' in Mansfield's career and as in themselves interesting and not unproblematic considerations of cultural and national identity. As I will suggest, the stories demonstrate that Mansfield's cultural and national identity as a 'New Zealander' is itself no less complicated than her sense of cultural identity as a 'colonial' in England and Europe.

First published by Murry in *Rhythm* and *The Blue Review* in 1912 and 1913, **'The Woman at the Store', 'Ole Underwood',** and **'Millie'** were begun not long after Mansfield left New Zealand but written in what Antony Alpers characterizes as a state of 'cultural isolation that was total': 'no one who read them in London', comments Alpers, 'could have known what in fact they achieved' (*L*. 155). It is intriguing to contemplate Alpers's sense that Mansfield is not only a displaced person but a displaced author, an author at this point, and in these stories at least, without an audience, living what she termed, in her early fantasy of such a life, a 'dual existence' (**KMN** i. 111). Alpers suggests that Mansfield's cultural and geographical displacement means that her audience—the literary and avant-garde community of London in particular—is, in a certain sense, culturally illiterate with regard to the locations and language of her writing, that her stories have no proper, no properly educated readers. Indeed, Angela Smith remarks that **'The Woman at the Store'** is 'disorientating' for the reader, 'inverting' as it does the 'conventions of European writing' (larks are cacophonous, sunset is sudden and 'grotesque', and so on): 'Nothing is what is seems,' Smith comments, and suggests that the reader feels that she is being 'sneered at'.[8] Mansfield is, of course, well aware of the problem of the possible alienation of her readers from her New Zealand stories. Writing to Murry about the contents of **Bliss and Other Sto-**

ries in February 1920, she says that she couldn't have **'The Woman at the Store'** reprinted in the volume (***CLKM*** iii. 210). And she hints at a reason for this refusal in a review of her compatriot, Jane Mander's, novel *The Story of a New Zealand River* in July of the same year. Her comments seem to confirm Alpers's sense that New Zealand writing is, at some level, unreadable for an English audience. 'In spite of the fact that there is frequent allusion to the magnificent scenery,' she remarks of Mander's novel, 'it profiteth us nothing', since references to indigenous New Zealand plants with alien, Maori names—the 'laurel-like puriris', the 'lacy rimu', the 'hard blackish kahikateas', and the 'oak-like ti-tokis'—can mean little to the English reader. 'What picture can that possibly convey to an English reader?', she asks, 'What emotion can it produce?''

All three of Mansfield's early New Zealand stories centre around violence and lawlessness—indeed, all three centre on an act of murder: **'The Woman at the Store'** concerns a woman living in the isolation of the New Zealand backblocks who, her daughter indicates, has murdered her husband; **'Ole Underwood'** centres on the eponymous protagonist's murder of his unfaithful wife and ends in the suggestion that he will kill again; **'Millie'** tells of the murder of Mr Williamson by his English apprentice farmhand and the blood-lust of those that are hunting him down in order to take their own revenge. These bleak, violent narratives are played out against a raw and unforgiving landscape. Although Mansfield wrote about murder and violence in other stories—indeed, violence is, I will suggest, an ever-present dimension in many of her fictions—in her later work violence is often qualified by (if not constituted as) the decorum of English and European society. In **'The Woman at the Store'**, **'Ole Underwood'**, and **'Millie'**, however, Mansfield seems to suggest that New Zealand society is constituted precisely in its absence, an absence of cultural and social conventions that allows undisguised physical violence—usually unpunished or at least not punished by official legal process and in that sense too outside the law—to predominate.

'The Woman at the Store' is told by one of three travellers in the New Zealand backblocks. The three come near to an isolated store that one of them, Hin, has previously visited. Hin tells his fellow travellers that the store is owned by a man who will 'give yer a bottle of whisky before 'e shakes hands with yer' and his wife who will 'promise you something else before she shakes hands with you' (***SS*** [*Selected Stories*] 10-11). As they arrive at the store, they find the woman alone with her daughter. The woman tells the travellers that her husband is 'away shearin'' (***SS*** 12). She is a disappointment to the travellers, though, for, despite Hin's boast that she is famous for knowing one hundred and twenty-five different ways of kissing (***SS*** 14), she is decidedly unattractive: 'you felt there was nothing but sticks and wires under that pinafore—her front teeth were knocked out, she had red pulpy hands, and she wore on her feet a pair of dirty "Bluchers"' (***SS*** 12). Jo, however, is philosophical, telling Hin that 'she'll look better by night light' and that, anyway, 'she's female flesh!' (***SS*** 14). The woman tells the travellers that she has had four miscarriages since her marriage six years ago and that if they were 'back at the Coast' she would have had her husband 'lynched for child murder': 'Over and over I tells 'im—you've broken my spirit and spoiled my looks', she says (***SS*** 16). 'Trouble with me is', she goes on, 'he left me too much alone' (***SS*** 16), perhaps confirming Hin and the narrator's suspicion that the isolation has made her 'mad' (***SS*** 13). After a night in which the woman's daughter—a 'mean, undersized brat, with whitish hair, and weak eyes' (***SS*** 15)—draws a picture of 'the woman shooting at a man with a rook rifle and then digging a hole to bury him in' (***SS*** 19), Hin and the narrator leave, while Jo, who has apparently tried out some of the woman's 'one hundred and twenty-five ways' of kissing over night, calls ominously to tell them that he'll catch up with them later. Ole Underwood, in the story of the same name, is also, apparently 'cracked' (***SKM*** [*The Stories of Katherine Mansfield*] 132). Tormented by a thudding noise, the noise of something beating in his breast 'like a hammer' (***SKM*** 131), Ole Underwood makes his way into a town (based on Wellington, although it remains unnamed) and into a pub where he is studiously avoided. One of the customers tells another Ole Underwood's story: 'When he was a young fellow, thirty years ago, a man 'ere done in 'is woman, an' 'e foun' out an' killed 'er'—for which he was given twenty years in jail and ended up 'cracked'. The storyteller does not know who 'did in' Underwood's wife: 'Dunno', he says, '"E don' no, nor nobody' (***SKM*** 132). Overhearing the story, Ole Underwood crushes some 'red pinks' that stand in a jar on the counter and is hounded from the bar. Hounded again even from another group of outsiders—a group of Chinese men playing cards—he eventually makes his way to the wharf, which, as an ex-sailor, he remembers well, and into the cabin of a ship. In the cabin a sailor is asleep on a bunk and, to Underwood's crazed imagination, there is a picture of his dead wife above the sailor, 'her picture—his woman's picture—smiling and smiling at the big sleeping man' (***SKM*** 133). The story ends here, but with the suggestion that Underwood will, despite the bar customer's assurance that '"E's 'armless enough'(***SKM*** 132), murder the sleeping—and presumably innocent—man. **'Millie'** is told from the perspective of Millie Evans, who is alone on a farm while her husband, Sid, helps hunt for Harrison, a 'young English "johnny"' who has disappeared after the shooting of Mr Williamson. 'My word! When they caught that young man!' Millie thinks: 'As Sid said, if he wasn't strung up where would they all be?' (***SS*** 24). But when Millie comes across a young man hiding near the house and recognizes Harrison, instead of revealing him, she feeds him and helps him hide. 'Nothing but a kid', she thinks, 'An' all them fellows after 'im. 'E don't stand any more of a chance than a kid would [. . .] They won't ketch 'im. Not if I can 'elp it. Men is all beasts. I don't care wot 'e's done, or wot 'e 'asn't done. See 'im through, Millie Evans,' she tells herself (*SS* 27). The scene changes to the night with Sid and his mates back on the farm. As Harrison tries to escape under cover of darkness, he is discovered and the men run after him. Despite her sense that the 'justice' that the men have been talking about is 'all [. . .] rot', and that you don't 'know what anythink's like till yer do know' (*SS* 27-8), as the men chase after Harrison, Millie's mood changes. She feels 'a strange mad joy' that 'smother[s] everything else' and she laughs, shrieks, and dances, shouting for the men to catch Harrison, to 'Shoot 'im down. Shoot 'im!' (*SS* 28).

The three early stories, then, are uncompromisingly 'colonial' in their New Zealand setting and language, and impelled by relatively straightforward narrative trajectories: each is plotted around a killing that takes place either outside the law, outside society, or within the context of a crude and crudely reasoned logic of retributive justice. And yet the stories are, perhaps, more complicated in their analysis of ethnic and national identity than this sense of a desocialized New Zealand naturalism might suggest, just as the 'naturalism' of Mansfield's prose is itself complicated by devices of parallelism, indirection, and symbolism. While New Zealand is presented as a place of lawlessness and outlawry, a place of the outsider, the stories complicate this sense of a New Zealand 'identity' by suggesting its involvement in a context of British imperialism. While many of Mansfield's later New Zealand stories—**'The Garden Party', 'The Dolls House', 'How Pearl Button was Kidnapped',** and others—suggest that a powerful dimension of New Zealand society is as a simulacrum of England, in **'The Woman at the Store', 'Ole Underwood',** and **'Millie',** the imperial power is represented as an uncanny presence within the otherness of New Zealand settler culture. The three stories are unflinchingly and uncompromisingly brutal in their representation of settler life, but in two of the three stories Mansfield also focuses briefly on the connections and discontinuities of the brutal, working-class New Zealand culture to that of the British colonial power, to an alienated Englishness. In both cases, England becomes the anachronistic and dislocated background—indeed, literally the faded wallpaper—for New Zealand life. In **'The Woman at the Store'** the unnamed woman of the title lives in a house that is an incongruous mix of backblock poverty—almost destitution—and the faded remnants of English gentility:

> It was a large room, the walls plastered with old pages of English periodicals. Queen Victoria's Jubilee appeared to be the most recent number—a table with an ironing board and wash-tub on it—some wooden forms—a black horsehair sofa, and some broken cane chairs pushed against the walls. The mantlepiece above the stove was draped in pink paper, further ornamented with dried grasses and ferns and a coloured print of Richard Seddon.
>
> (*SS* 12)

The symbolism of colonial power, represented not least in its head of state, has been cannibalized and transformed into wallpaper—England *is*, in a sense, the forgotten wallpaper in this scene, overlaid by an alternative governance in the picture of Richard Seddon, the prime minister of New Zealand until 1906. The contrasting savagery of New Zealand is explicitly evoked in the next paragraph: 'There is no twilight to our New Zealand days, but a curious half-hour when everything appears grotesque—it frightens—as though the savage spirit of the country walked abroad and sneered at what it saw' (*SS* 13). While New Zealand—New Zealandness—is, on the one hand, brutal, grotesque, terrifying, this seems to suggest, it is, on the other hand, constituted by an incongruous and anachronistic royalism—one that, however, has been cannibalized and distorted in its transportation to the New Zealand backblocks.

A similar evocation of cultural dislocation is also apparent in **'Millie'**, which once again marks such a difference by the incongruity of the furnishings and fittings of the New Zealand domestic interior:

> She flopped down on the side of the bed and stared at the coloured print on the wall opposite, 'Garden Party at Windsor Castle'. In the foreground emerald lawns planted with immense oak trees, and in their grateful shade, a muddle of ladies and gentlemen and parasols and little tables. The background was filled with the towers of Windsor Castle, flying three Union Jacks, and in the middle of the picture the old Queen, like a tea cosy with a head on top of it. 'I wonder if it really looked like that.' Millie stared at the flowery ladies, who simpered back at her. 'I wouldn't care for that sort of thing. Too much side. What with the Queen an' one thing an' another'.
>
> (*SS* 25)

The Englishness of the print is marked as both overbearing and anachronistic by the image of the three Union Jacks and by the presence of Queen Victoria. And it is contrasted immediately with Millie's contemplation of another scene, specifically of New Zealand but equally fabricated and artificial: she turns from the coloured print to look at a photograph of her wedding, where she and her husband pose in front of 'some fern trees, and a waterfall, and Mount Cook in the distance, covered with snow' (*SS* 25). But the image of colonial power is deeply ironized and its potency as ideology compromised by the very rhetoric of the description. By contrast with the Windsor Castle scene—with its sophistication (including the alienating 'side'), its symbolic complexity (or in Millie's terms 'muddle'), and its aristocratic context (suggested by the 'emerald' lawn, by the gentlemen and ladies, and even by the parasols)—Millie's language is direct and even crude: her language is syntactically repetitive ('and . . . and . . . and . . . and') and she perhaps unwittingly undermines the head of state's dignity by her crass figuration of the Queen as a tea cosy with a head on top. Millie's doubt over whether the tea party at Windsor castle 'really looked like that' is, indeed, a central question in a story involving the murder of a New Zealander by an Englishman. The transplantation of English culture into a New Zealand context leads to the question of what that culture 'really' looks like. In other words, Mansfield suggests that the representational *power* of imperial Britain—the power, that is, to represent—is compromised in its migration to a different hemisphere. The transplantation or transportation of 'English' representational conventions to those of New Zealand settler culture leads not only to a distortion of its pictures of itself, but also to an undermining of the very representational conventions by which empire constitutes itself.

These New Zealand stories, then, with their tales of violence, their setting of economic and cultural deprivation, their raw, colloquial speech patterns, and their harsh, unsentimental idioms, articulate a raw energy of national and cultural origin rarely found elsewhere in Mansfield's work. But the intrusion of Britishness into the cultural background in two of the stories evinces a heightened awareness of the complexity of a New Zealand cultural identity. One of the identities that Mansfield takes on or performs is that of the 'colonial', of the 'little savage from New Zealand'. In other stories this identification is submerged within a different kind of class allegiance and a different kind of cosmopolitanism. But New Zealand—as identity and identification—is a place that defines Mansfield, above all, as displaced, as placeless. Cultural and national identity, we might surmise, was, for Mansfield, another aspect of the complex representation of personal identity and impersonality that we are calling 'impersonation'.

Notes

1. Roger Robinson, 'Introduction: In from the Margin', in Robinson (ed.), *In from the Margin* (Baton Rouge, La.: Louisiana State University Press, 1994), 4.

2. C. K. Stead, 'Katherine Mansfield and T. S. Eliot: A Double Centenary', in Stead, *Answering to the Language: Essays on Modern Writers* (Auckland: Auckland University Press, 1989), 160.

3. C. K. Stead, 'Katherine Mansfield's Life', in ibid. 166.

4. See *Katherine Mansfield: Selected Letters,* ed. Vincent O'Sullivan (Oxford: Oxford University Press, 1989), 257.

5. Quoted in Angela Smith, *Katherine Mansfield: A Literary Life* (Basingstoke: Palgrave, 2000), 1.

6. Stead, 'Life', 167.

7. C. K. Stead, 'Katherine Mansfield as Colonial Realist', in Stead, *The Writer at Work* (Dunedin: University of Otago Press, 2000), 38.

8. Angela Smith, *Katherine Mansfield and Virginia Woolf: A Public of Two* (Oxford: Clarendon Press, 1999), 119. See also Smith, *Literary Life,* 88-94; and see p. 13, on 'The Woman at the Store' as Mansfield's 'most overtly disorientating story'.

9. *The Critical Writings of Katherine Mansfield,* ed. Clare Hanson (Basingstoke: Macmillan, 1987), 102.

Select Bibliography

WORKS BY KATHERINE MANSFIELD

SEPARATE STORY COLLECTIONS

In a German Pension (London: Stephen Swift, 1911).

Bliss and Other Stories (London: Constable, 1920).

The Garden Party and Other Stories (London: Constable, 1922).

The Doves' Nest and Other Stories, ed. John Middleton Murry (London: Constable, 1923).

Something Childish and Other Stories, ed. John Middleton Murry (London: Constable, 1924); and in the USA as *The Little Girl and Other Stories* (New York: Knopf, 1924).

STORIES PUBLISHED SEPARATELY

Prelude (Richmond: Hogarth Press, 1918).

Je ne parle pas français (Hampstead: Heron Press, 1920).

The Aloe, ed. John Middleton Murry (London: Constable, 1930).

The Aloe, with Prelude, ed. Vincent O'Sullivan (Manchester: Carcanet New Press, 1983).

COLLECTED AND SELECTED EDITIONS OF THE SHORT STORIES

Collected Stories of Katherine Mansfield (London: Constable, 1945); republished in paperback (London: Penguin, 1981).

The Stories of Katherine Mansfield, ed. Antony Alpers (Auckland: Oxford University Press, 1984).

Selected Stories, ed. Angela Smith (Oxford University Press, 2002).

Other Works

The Letters of Katherine Mansfield, ed. John Middleton Murry, 2 vols. (London: Constable, 1928). Now superseded by O'Sullivan and Scott's Clarendon Press edition, except for the letters from 1922 in the second volume.

The Letters and Journals of Katherine Mansfield: A Selection, ed. C. K. Stead (London: Allen Lane, 1977).

The Collected Letters of Katherine Mansfield, ed. Vincent O'Sullivan and Margaret Scott, 4 vols. to date (Oxford: Clarendon Press, 1984-96). The definitive edition of the letters, which needs to be supplemented, until the publication of vol. v, by Murry's edition of the letters, vol. ii.

The Critical Writings of Katherine Mansfield, ed. Clare Hanson (Basingstoke: Macmillan, 1987).

The Katherine Mansfield Notebooks, ed. Margaret Scott, 2 vols. (Canterbury, NZ: Lincoln University Press 1997). An accurate scholarly edition of the notebooks.

Bibliography

Kirkpatrick, B. J., *A Bibliography of Katherine Mansfield* (Oxford: Clarendon Press, 1989). The most complete bibliography of Mansfield's work and secondary materials.

Biography

Alpers, Antony, *The Life of Katherine Mansfield* (London; Jonathan Cape, 1980). The fullest, and generally acknowledged to be the standard biography.

Smith, Angela, *Katherine Mansfield: A Literary Life* (Basingstoke: Palgrave, 2000). A useful short life focusing in particular on Mansfield's New Zealand origins and on the influence of post-Impressionism and Fauvism on her work.

Criticism

Pilditch, Jan (ed.), *The Critical Response to Katherine Mansfield* (Westport, Conn.: Greenwood, 1996). A useful collection of essays, ranging from the first reviews to essays published to mark the centenary of Mansfield's birth. Includes influential contributions by V. S. Pritchett, David Daiches, Elizabeth Bowen, Ian A. Gordon, Margaret Scott, Vincent O'Sullivan, C. K. Stead, and others.

Robinson, Roger (ed.), *Katherine Mansfield: In from the Margin* (Baton Rouge, La.: Louisiana State University Press, 1994). An important collection of essays from two centennial conferences held in 1988.

Smith, Angela, *Katherine Mansfield and Virginia Woolf: A Public of Two* (Oxford: Clarendon Press, 1999). An impressive revaluation of the relationship of the two writers, with a Kristevan analysis of abjection and liminality in Mansfield's work.

Abbreviations

CLKM: *The Collected Letters of Katherine Mansfield,* ed. Vincent O'Sullivan and Margaret Scott, 4 vols. to date (Oxford: Clarendon Press, 1984-96).

CR: Jan Pilditch (ed.), *The Critical Response to Katherine Mansfield* (Westport, Conn.: Greenwood Press, 1996).

KMN: *The Katherine Mansfield Notebooks,* ed. Margaret Scott, 2 vols. (Canterbury, NZ: Lincoln University Press, 1997).

L.: Antony Alpers, *The Life of Katherine Mansfield* (London: Jonathan Cape, 1980).

LKM: *The Letters of Katherine Mansfield,* ed. John Middleton Murry, 2 vols. (London: Constable, 1928).

SKM: *The Stories of Katherine Mansfield,* ed. Antony Alpers (Auckland: Oxford University Press, 1984).

SL: Claire Tomalin, *Katherine Mansfield: A Secret Life* (London: Penguin, 1988).

SS: *Selected Stories,* ed. Angela Smith (Oxford: Oxford University Press, 2002).

FURTHER READING

Bibliography

Kirkpatrick, B. J. *A Bibliography of Katherine Mansfield.* Oxford: Clarendon Press, 1989, 396 p.

> Considered the most comprehensive bibliography of the writings of Mansfield and adaptations of her work.

Biographies

Alpers, Antony. *Katherine Mansfield: A Biography.* New York: Alfred A. Knopf, 1953, 376 p.

> Considered the definitive biography of Mansfield, drawn from first-hand accounts of family members, personal acquaintances, and Mansfield's husband, John Middleton Murry.

Baker, Ida. *Katherine Mansfield: The Memories of LM.* London: Michael Joseph, 1971, 240 p.

> Biography of Mansfield written by her companion and personal assistant, Ida Baker, who lived with the author during the last five years of her life.

Moore, James. "Katherine Mansfield." In *Gurdjieff and Mansfield,* pp. 7-18. London: Routledge & Kegan Paul, 1980.

Includes a brief biography of Mansfield, focusing specifically on her relationship with George Ivanovitch Gurdjieff late in her life and her decision to seek treatment at Gurdjieff's Institute for the Harmonious Development of Man, where Mansfield died in January 1923.

Tomalin, Claire. *Katherine Mansfield: A Secret Life.* London: Viking, 1987, 292 p.

Book-length biography of Mansfield that addresses Mansfield's first foray into sexual freedom in 1908 and the impact of her physical and emotional illnesses on important issues in her life.

Criticism

Bennett, Andrew. "Hating Katherine Mansfield." *Angelaki: Journal of the Theoretical Humanities* 7, no. 3 (December 2002): 3-16

Discusses the complex and competitive friendship between Mansfield and fellow author Virginia Woolf, noting especially Woolf's jealousy over Mansfield's success as a writer.

Burgan, Mary. *Illness, Gender, and Writing: The Case of Katherine Mansfield.* Baltimore: Johns Hopkins University Press, 1994, 217 p.

Explores Mansfield's writing in the context of her recurrent emotional and physical illnesses, claiming that the author serves as a model of the woman-artist who attempts to overcome mortality through the power of her narrative.

Cornut-Gentille D'Arcy, Chantal. "Katherine Mansfield's 'Bliss': 'The Rare Fiddle' as Emblem of the Political and Sexual Alienation of Woman." *Papers on Language & Literature* 35, no. 3 (summer 1999): 244-69.

Demonstrates how the delicacy and "elusiveness" of Mansfield's story "Bliss" conceal more subversive themes and convictions of the author, such as the political and sexual alienation of women at the beginning of the twentieth century.

Darrohn, Christine. "'Blown to Bits!': Katherine Mansfield's 'The Garden Party' and the Great War." *Modern Fiction Studies* 44, no. 3 (fall 1998): 513-39.

Interprets "The Garden Party" as a work of war literature, focusing especially on how the carter's death in the story sheds light on the way in which Mansfield and her contemporaries tried to recover from the physical horrors of war.

Dilworth, Thomas. "Monkey Business: Darwin, Displacement, and Literary Form in Katherine Mansfield's 'Bliss.'" *Studies in Short Fiction* 35, no. 2 (spring 1998): 141-52.

Argues that "Bliss" is "a rich and protean work of art," in which the form, structure, and language unite with and symbolize the story's central theme of evolution.

Fullbrook, Kate. *Katherine Mansfield.* Sussex: The Harvester Press, 1986, 146 p.

Applies a new form of feminist critique of Mansfield's literature, attempting to replace the mirror-image dualism of prevailing feminist studies with a methodology that focuses on how women have constructed their own unique versions of meaning in art and life.

Gong, Shifen, ed. *A Fine Pen: The Chinese View of Katherine Mansfield.* Dunedin, New Zealand: University of Otago Press, 2001, 174 p.

Collection of essays on Mansfield and her works, written by Chinese critics from 1923 to 1991.

Gubar, Susan. "The Birth of the Artist as Heroine: (Re)production, the *Künstlerroman* Tradition, and the Fiction of Katherine Mansfield." In *The Representation of Women in Fiction: Selected Papers from the English Institute, 1981,* edited by Carolyn G. Heilbrun and Margaret R. Higonnet, pp. 19-59. Baltimore: Johns Hopkins University Press, 1983.

Draws parallels between the changing social views of pregnancy, maternity, and reproduction at the beginning of the twentieth century with the growing celebration of the female artist and her creations, claiming that Mansfield serves as a model of the woman-artist who redefines women's unique creativity in the space that separates life and art.

Gunsteren, Julia van. *Katherine Mansfield and Literary Impressionism.* Amsterdam: Rodopi B.V., 1990, 271 p.

Traces the impact of Impressionism in the visual arts on Mansfield's aesthetics and fiction.

Hankin, C. A. *Katherine Mansfield and Her Confessional Stories.* London: Macmillan Press Ltd., 1983, 271 p.

Centers the ongoing appeal and interest in Mansfield's work on the confessional nature of her writing, arguing that the author probed her own personality conflicts, in the guise of fiction, in order to achieve a deeper psychological understanding.

Hanson, Clare and Andrew Gurr. *Katherine Mansfield.* London: Macmillan Press Ltd., 1981, 146 p.

Analyze a number of Mansfield's stories, focusing on the central symbolic nature of her work and the evolution of her narrative and technical skills as a writer of short fiction.

Jensen, Margaret M. "Mother/Muse, Psychic Sister?: The Personal and Intertextual Connections between Virginia Woolf and Katherine Mansfield." In *The Open Book: Creative Misreading in the Works of Selected Modern Writers,* pp. 91-130. New York: Palgrave Macmillan, 2002.

Examines the circumstances surrounding Mansfield's friendship with Virginia Woolf and assesses the impact of that relationship on the work of each writer.

Moran, Patricia. "Unholy Meanings: Maternity, Creativity, and Orality in Katherine Mansfield." *Feminist Studies* 17, no. 1 (spring 1991): 105-25.

>Psychoanalytic study that discerns in Mansfield's writings a metaphorical obsession with anorexia—an obsessive revulsion against food and against the devouring power of maternity.

Morrow, Patrick D. *Katherine Mansfield's Fiction.* Bowling Green, Ohio: Bowling Green State University Popular Press, 1993, 158 p.

>Offers interpretations of many of Mansfield's stories, including those often overlooked by critics and scholars as weak and inferior to her best work.

Mortimer, Armine Kotin. "Fortifications of Desire: Reading the Second Story in Katherine Mansfield's 'Bliss.'" *Narrative* 2, no. 1 (January 1994): 41-52.

>Focuses on the subtext, or "second story," present in Mansfield's "Bliss," claiming that the story offers a good example of how events in the work "mirror the way language drives the narrative."

Parkin-Gounelas, Ruth. "Katherine Mansfield's Piece of Pink Wool: Feminine Signification in 'The Luftbad.'" *Studies in Short Fiction* 27, no. 4 (fall 1990): 495-507.

>Compares Mansfield's story "The Luftbad" to her more feminine, sentimental, and "childish" stories, emphasizing the way in which the author ironically deflates the cool, masculine discourse that ridicules women in the story.

Pilditch, Jan, ed. *The Critical Response to Katherine Mansfield.* Westport, Conn.: Greenwood Press, 1996, 249 p.

>Collects nearly one hundred years of criticism and commentary on Mansfield and her work. Also provides useful primary and secondary bibliographies.

Reid, Ian. "Always a Sacrifice: Executing Unities in Two Stories by Katherine Mansfield." *Journal of the Short Story in English* 4 (spring 1985): 77-94.

>Semiotic interpretation of "Prelude" and "At the Bay" that posits that the transformation of rhetorical figures, or metaphors, in the two stories is more important than events or plot in producing connection and unity.

Robinson, Roger, ed. *Katherine Mansfield: In from the Margin.* Baton Rouge: Louisiana State University Press, 1994, 224 p.

>Collection of twelve critical essays on Mansfield and her work taken from two Mansfield centenary conferences that took place in 1981: the Katherine Mansfield Centenary Symposium in Chicago and the Katherine Mansfield Centennial Conference in New Zealand.

Smith, Angela. "Shifts in 'Prelude' and *To the Lighthouse*." In *Katherine Mansfield and Virginia Woolf: A Public of Two*, pp. 91-110. Oxford: Clarendon Press, 1999.

>Compares Mansfield's "Prelude" and Virginia Woolf's *To the Lighthouse*, noting the manner in which each work uses shifts in perspective, ellipses, and disjointed construction to transform the symbolic order of the external world from within the characters and their own experiences.

Tytler, Graeme. "Mansfield's 'The Voyage.'" *The Explicator* 50, no. 1 (fall 1991): 42-5.

>Discusses how contrasting symbols, such as darkness and light, in Mansfield's "The Voyage" support the central theme of love in the story.

Additional coverage of Mansfield's life and career is contained in the following sources published by Thomson Gale: *Beacham's Encyclopedia of Popular Fiction: Biography & Resources*, Vol. 2; *British Writers*, Vol. 7; *Contemporary Authors*, Vols. 104, 134; *Dictionary of Literary Biography*, Vol. 162; *DISCovering Authors*; *DISCovering Authors: British Edition*; *DISCovering Authors: Canadian Edition*; *DISCovering Authors Modules: Most-studied Authors*; *DISCovering Authors 3.0*; *Encyclopedia of World Literature in the 20th Century*, Ed. 3; *Exploring Short Stories*; *Feminist Writers*; *Gay & Lesbian Literature*, Ed. 1; *Literature Resource Center*; *Major 20th-Century Writers*, Ed. 2; *Reference Guide to English Literature*, Ed. 2; *Reference Guide to Short Fiction*, Ed. 2; *Short Stories for Students*, Vols. 2, 8, 10, 11; *Short Story Criticism*, Vols. 9, 23, 38, 81; *Twayne's English Authors*; *Twentieth-Century Literary Criticism*, Vols. 2, 8, 39; *World Literature Criticism*; **and** *World Writers in English*, **Vol. 1.**

How to Use This Index

The main references

> Calvino, Italo
> 1923-1985 .... CLC 5, 8, 11, 22, 33, 39,
> 73; SSC 3, 48

list all author entries in the following Gale Literary Criticism series:

AAL = Asian American Literature
BG = The Beat Generation: A Gale Critical Companion
BLC = Black Literature Criticism
BLCS = Black Literature Criticism Supplement
CLC = Contemporary Literary Criticism
CLR = Children's Literature Review
CMLC = Classical and Medieval Literature Criticism
DC = Drama Criticism
HLC = Hispanic Literature Criticism
HLCS = Hispanic Literature Criticism Supplement
HR = Harlem Renaissance: A Gale Critical Companion
LC = Literature Criticism from 1400 to 1800
NCLC = Nineteenth-Century Literature Criticism
NNAL = Native North American Literature
PC = Poetry Criticism
SSC = Short Story Criticism
TCLC = Twentieth-Century Literary Criticism
WLC = World Literature Criticism, 1500 to the Present
WLCS = World Literature Criticism Supplement

The cross-references

> See also CA 85-88, 116; CANR 23, 61;
> DAM NOV; DLB 196; EW 13; MTCW 1, 2;
> RGSF 2; RGWL 2; SFW 4; SSFS 12

list all author entries in the following Gale biographical and literary sources:

AAYA = Authors & Artists for Young Adults
AFAW = African American Writers
AFW = African Writers
AITN = Authors in the News
AMW = American Writers
AMWR = American Writers Retrospective Supplement
AMWS = American Writers Supplement
ANW = American Nature Writers
AW = Ancient Writers
BEST = Bestsellers
BPFB = Beacham's Encyclopedia of Popular Fiction: Biography and Resources
BRW = British Writers
BRWS = British Writers Supplement
BW = Black Writers
BYA = Beacham's Guide to Literature for Young Adults
CA = Contemporary Authors
CAAS = Contemporary Authors Autobiography Series
CABS = Contemporary Authors Bibliographical Series
CAD = Contemporary American Dramatists
CANR = Contemporary Authors New Revision Series
CAP = Contemporary Authors Permanent Series
CBD = Contemporary British Dramatists
CCA = Contemporary Canadian Authors
CD = Contemporary Dramatists
CDALB = Concise Dictionary of American Literary Biography
CDALBS = Concise Dictionary of American Literary Biography Supplement
CDBLB = Concise Dictionary of British Literary Biography

CMW = *St. James Guide to Crime & Mystery Writers*
CN = *Contemporary Novelists*
CP = *Contemporary Poets*
CPW = *Contemporary Popular Writers*
CSW = *Contemporary Southern Writers*
CWD = *Contemporary Women Dramatists*
CWP = *Contemporary Women Poets*
CWRI = *St. James Guide to Children's Writers*
CWW = *Contemporary World Writers*
DA = *DISCovering Authors*
DA3 = *DISCovering Authors 3.0*
DAB = *DISCovering Authors: British Edition*
DAC = *DISCovering Authors: Canadian Edition*
DAM = *DISCovering Authors: Modules*
   DRAM: *Dramatists Module;* **MST:** *Most-studied Authors Module;*
   MULT: *Multicultural Authors Module;* **NOV:** *Novelists Module;*
   POET: *Poets Module;* **POP:** *Popular Fiction and Genre Authors Module*
DFS = *Drama for Students*
DLB = *Dictionary of Literary Biography*
DLBD = *Dictionary of Literary Biography Documentary Series*
DLBY = *Dictionary of Literary Biography Yearbook*
DNFS = *Literature of Developing Nations for Students*
EFS = *Epics for Students*
EXPN = *Exploring Novels*
EXPP = *Exploring Poetry*
EXPS = *Exploring Short Stories*
EW = *European Writers*
FANT = *St. James Guide to Fantasy Writers*
FW = *Feminist Writers*
GFL = *Guide to French Literature,* Beginnings to 1789, 1798 to the Present
GLL = *Gay and Lesbian Literature*
HGG = *St. James Guide to Horror, Ghost & Gothic Writers*
HW = *Hispanic Writers*
IDFW = *International Dictionary of Films and Filmmakers: Writers and Production Artists*
IDTP = *International Dictionary of Theatre: Playwrights*
LAIT = *Literature and Its Times*
LAW = *Latin American Writers*
JRDA = *Junior DISCovering Authors*
MAICYA = *Major Authors and Illustrators for Children and Young Adults*
MAICYAS = *Major Authors and Illustrators for Children and Young Adults Supplement*
MAWW = *Modern American Women Writers*
MJW = *Modern Japanese Writers*
MTCW = *Major 20th-Century Writers*
NCFS = *Nonfiction Classics for Students*
NFS = *Novels for Students*
PAB = *Poets: American and British*
PFS = *Poetry for Students*
RGAL = *Reference Guide to American Literature*
RGEL = *Reference Guide to English Literature*
RGSF = *Reference Guide to Short Fiction*
RGWL = *Reference Guide to World Literature*
RHW = *Twentieth-Century Romance and Historical Writers*
SAAS = *Something about the Author Autobiography Series*
SATA = *Something about the Author*
SFW = *St. James Guide to Science Fiction Writers*
SSFS = *Short Stories for Students*
TCWW = *Twentieth-Century Western Writers*
WLIT = *World Literature and Its Times*
WP = *World Poets*
YABC = *Yesterday's Authors of Books for Children*
YAW = *St. James Guide to Young Adult Writers*

Literary Criticism Series Cumulative Author Index

20/1631
See Upward, Allen
A/C Cross
See Lawrence, T(homas) E(dward)
Abasiyanik, Sait Faik 1906-1954
See Sait Faik
See also CA 123
Abbey, Edward 1927-1989 .... **CLC 36, 59; TCLC 160**
See also AMWS 13; ANW; CA 45-48; 128; CANR 2, 41, 131; DA3; DLB 256, 275; LATS 1:2; MTCW 2; TCWW 2
Abbott, Edwin A. 1838-1926 .... **TCLC 139**
See also DLB 178
Abbott, Lee K(ittredge) 1947- .... **CLC 48**
See also CA 124; CANR 51, 101; DLB 130
Abe, Kobo 1924-1993 ...... **CLC 8, 22, 53, 81; SSC 61; TCLC 131**
See also CA 65-68; 140; CANR 24, 60; DAM NOV; DFS 14; DLB 182; EWL 3; MJW; MTCW 1, 2; RGWL 3; SFW 4
Abe Kobo
See Abe, Kobo
Abelard, Peter c. 1079-c. 1142 ...... **CMLC 11**
See also DLB 115, 208
Abell, Kjeld 1901-1961 .... **CLC 15**
See also CA 191; 111; DLB 214; EWL 3
Abercrombie, Lascelles
1881-1938 .... **TCLC 141**
See also CA 112; DLB 19; RGEL 2
Abish, Walter 1931- .... **CLC 22; SSC 44**
See also CA 101; CANR 37, 114; CN 7; DLB 130, 227
Abrahams, Peter (Henry) 1919- .... **CLC 4**
See also AFW; BW 1; CA 57-60; CANR 26, 125; CDWLB 3; CN 7; DLB 117, 225; EWL 3; MTCW 1, 2; RGEL 2; WLIT 2
Abrams, M(eyer) H(oward) 1912- ... **CLC 24**
See also CA 57-60; CANR 13, 33; DLB 67
Abse, Dannie 1923- .... **CLC 7, 29; PC 41**
See also CA 53-56; CAAS 1; CANR 4, 46, 74, 124; CBD; CP 7; DAB; DAM POET; DLB 27, 245; MTCW 1
Abutsu 1222(?)-1283 .... **CMLC 46**
See Abutsu-ni
Abutsu-ni
See Abutsu
See also DLB 203
Achebe, (Albert) Chinua(lumogu)
1930- ..... **BLC 1; CLC 1, 3, 5, 7, 11, 26, 51, 75, 127, 152; WLC**
See also AAYA 15; AFW; BPFB 1; BRWC 2; BW 2, 3; CA 1-4R; CANR 6, 26, 47, 124; CDWLB 3; CLR 20; CN 7; CP 7; CWRI 5; DA; DA3; DAB; DAC; DAM MST, MULT, NOV; DLB 117; DNFS 1; EWL 3; EXPN; EXPS; LAIT 2; LATS 1:2; MAICYA 1, 2; MTCW 1, 2; NFS 2; RGEL 2; RGSF 2; SATA 38, 40; SATA-Brief 38; SSFS 3, 13; TWA; WLIT 2; WWE 1

Acker, Kathy 1948-1997 .... **CLC 45, 111**
See also AMWS 12; CA 117; 122; 162; CANR 55; CN 7
Ackroyd, Peter 1949- .... **CLC 34, 52, 140**
See also BRWS 6; CA 123; 127; CANR 51, 74, 99, 132; CN 7; DLB 155, 231; HGG; INT CA-127; MTCW 1; RHW; SATA 153; SUFW 2
Acorn, Milton 1923-1986 .... **CLC 15**
See also CA 103; CCA 1; DAC; DLB 53; INT CA-103
Adamov, Arthur 1908-1970 .... **CLC 4, 25**
See also CA 17-18; 25-28R; CAP 2; DAM DRAM; EWL 3; GFL 1789 to the Present; MTCW 1; RGWL 2, 3
Adams, Alice (Boyd) 1926-1999 .. **CLC 6, 13, 46; SSC 24**
See also CA 81-84; 179; CANR 26, 53, 75, 88; CN 7; CSW; DLB 234; DLBY 1986; INT CANR-26; MTCW 1, 2; SSFS 14
Adams, Andy 1859-1935 .... **TCLC 56**
See also TCWW 2; YABC 1
Adams, (Henry) Brooks
1848-1927 .... **TCLC 80**
See also CA 123; 193; DLB 47
Adams, Douglas (Noel) 1952-2001 .. **CLC 27, 60**
See also AAYA 4, 33; BEST 89:3; BYA 14; CA 106; 197; CANR 34, 64, 124; CPW; DA3; DAM POP; DLB 261; DLBY 1983; JRDA; MTCW 1; NFS 7; SATA 116; SATA-Obit 128; SFW 4
Adams, Francis 1862-1893 .... **NCLC 33**
Adams, Henry (Brooks)
1838-1918 .... **TCLC 4, 52**
See also AMW; CA 104; 133; CANR 77; DA; DAB; DAC; DAM MST; DLB 12, 47, 189, 284; EWL 3; MTCW 1; NCFS 1; RGAL 4; TUS
Adams, John 1735-1826 .... **NCLC 106**
See also DLB 31, 183
Adams, Richard (George) 1920- ... **CLC 4, 5, 18**
See also AAYA 16; AITN 1, 2; BPFB 1; BYA 5; CA 49-52; CANR 3, 35, 128; CLR 20; CN 7; DAM NOV; DLB 261; FANT; JRDA; LAIT 5; MAICYA 1, 2; MTCW 1, 2; NFS 11; SATA 7, 69; YAW
Adamson, Joy(-Friederike Victoria)
1910-1980 .... **CLC 17**
See also CA 69-72; 93-96; CANR 22; MTCW 1; SATA 11; SATA-Obit 22
Adcock, Fleur 1934- .... **CLC 41**
See also CA 25-28R, 182; CAAE 182; CAAS 23; CANR 11, 34, 69, 101; CP 7; CWP; DLB 40; FW; WWE 1

Addams, Charles (Samuel)
1912-1988 .... **CLC 30**
See also CA 61-64; 126; CANR 12, 79
Addams, (Laura) Jane 1860-1935 . **TCLC 76**
See also AMWS 1; CA 194; DLB 303; FW
Addison, Joseph 1672-1719 .... **LC 18**
See also BRW 3; CDBLB 1660-1789; DLB 101; RGEL 2; WLIT 3
Adler, Alfred (F.) 1870-1937 .... **TCLC 61**
See also CA 119; 159
Adler, C(arole) S(chwerdtfeger)
1932- .... **CLC 35**
See also AAYA 4, 41; CA 89-92; CANR 19, 40, 101; CLR 78; JRDA; MAICYA 1, 2; SAAS 15; SATA 26, 63, 102, 126; YAW
Adler, Renata 1938- .... **CLC 8, 31**
See also CA 49-52; CANR 95; CN 7; MTCW 1
Adorno, Theodor W(iesengrund)
1903-1969 .... **TCLC 111**
See also CA 89-92; 25-28R; CANR 89; DLB 242; EWL 3
Ady, Endre 1877-1919 .... **TCLC 11**
See also CA 107; CDWLB 4; DLB 215; EW 9; EWL 3
A.E. .... **TCLC 3, 10**
See Russell, George William
See also DLB 19
Aelfric c. 955-c. 1010 .... **CMLC 46**
See also DLB 146
Aeschines c. 390B.C.-c. 320B.C. .... **CMLC 47**
See also DLB 176
Aeschylus 525(?)B.C.-456(?)B.C. .. **CMLC 11, 51; DC 8; WLCS**
See also AW 1; CDWLB 1; DA; DAB; DAC; DAM DRAM, MST; DFS 5, 10; DLB 176; LMFS 1; RGWL 2, 3; TWA
Aesop 620(?)B.C.-560(?)B.C. .... **CMLC 24**
See also CLR 14; MAICYA 1, 2; SATA 64
Affable Hawk
See MacCarthy, Sir (Charles Otto) Desmond
Africa, Ben
See Bosman, Herman Charles
Afton, Effie
See Harper, Frances Ellen Watkins
Agapida, Fray Antonio
See Irving, Washington
Agee, James (Rufus) 1909-1955 ...... **TCLC 1, 19**
See also AAYA 44; AITN 1; AMW; CA 108; 148; CANR 131; CDALB 1941-1968; DAM NOV; DLB 2, 26, 152; DLBY 1989; EWL 3; LAIT 3; LATS 1:2; MTCW 1; RGAL 4; TUS
Aghill, Gordon
See Silverberg, Robert

349

Agnon, S(hmuel) Y(osef Halevi)
1888-1970 .... **CLC 4, 8, 14; SSC 30; TCLC 151**
See also CA 17-18; 25-28R; CANR 60, 102; CAP 2; EWL 3; MTCW 1, 2; RGSF 2; RGWL 2, 3

Agrippa von Nettesheim, Henry Cornelius
1486-1535 .... **LC 27**

Aguilera Malta, Demetrio
1909-1981 .... **HLCS 1**
See also CA 111; 124; CANR 87; DAM MULT, NOV; DLB 145; EWL 3; HW 1; RGWL 3

Agustini, Delmira 1886-1914 .... **HLCS 1**
See also CA 166; DLB 290; HW 1, 2; LAW

Aherne, Owen
See Cassill, R(onald) V(erlin)

Ai 1947- .... **CLC 4, 14, 69**
See also CA 85-88; CAAS 13; CANR 70; DLB 120; PFS 16

Aickman, Robert (Fordyce)
1914-1981 .... **CLC 57**
See also CA 5-8R; CANR 3, 72, 100; DLB 261; HGG; SUFW 1, 2

Aidoo, (Christina) Ama Ata
1942- .... **BLCS; CLC 177**
See also AFW; BW 1; CA 101; CANR 62; CD 5; CDWLB 3; CN 7; CWD; CWP; DLB 117; DNFS 1, 2; EWL 3; FW; WLIT 2

Aiken, Conrad (Potter) 1889-1973 .... **CLC 1, 3, 5, 10, 52; PC 26; SSC 9**
See also AMW; CA 5-8R; 45-48; CANR 4, 60; CDALB 1929-1941; DAM NOV, POET; DLB 9, 45, 102; EWL 3; EXPS; HGG; MTCW 1, 2; RGAL 4; RGSF 2; SATA 3, 30; SSFS 8; TUS

Aiken, Joan (Delano) 1924-2004 ...... **CLC 35**
See also AAYA 1, 25; CA 9-12R; 182; 223; CAAE 182; CANR 4, 23, 34, 64, 121; CLR 1, 19, 90; DLB 161; FANT; HGG; JRDA; MAICYA 1, 2; MTCW 1; RHW; SAAS 1; SATA 2, 30, 73; SATA-Essay 109; SATA-Obit 152; SUFW 2; WYA; YAW

Ainsworth, William Harrison
1805-1882 .... **NCLC 13**
See also DLB 21; HGG; RGEL 2; SATA 24; SUFW 1

Aitmatov, Chingiz (Torekulovich)
1928- .... **CLC 71**
See Aytmatov, Chingiz
See also CA 103; CANR 38; CWW 2; DLB 302; MTCW 1; RGSF 2; SATA 56

Akers, Floyd
See Baum, L(yman) Frank

Akhmadulina, Bella Akhatovna
1937- .... **CLC 53; PC 43**
See also CA 65-68; CWP; CWW 2; DAM POET; EWL 3

Akhmatova, Anna 1888-1966 ..... **CLC 11, 25, 64, 126; PC 2, 55**
See also CA 19-20; 25-28R; CANR 35; CAP 1; DA3; DAM POET; DLB 295; EW 10; EWL 3; MTCW 1, 2; PFS 18; RGWL 2, 3

Aksakov, Sergei Timofeyvich
1791-1859 .... **NCLC 2**
See also DLB 198

Aksenov, Vasilii (Pavlovich)
See Aksyonov, Vassily (Pavlovich)
See also CWW 2

Aksenov, Vassily
See Aksyonov, Vassily (Pavlovich)

Akst, Daniel 1956- .... **CLC 109**
See also CA 161; CANR 110

Aksyonov, Vassily (Pavlovich)
1932- .... **CLC 22, 37, 101**
See Aksenov, Vasilii (Pavlovich)
See also CA 53-56; CANR 12, 48, 77; DLB 302; EWL 3

Akutagawa Ryunosuke 1892-1927 ... **SSC 44; TCLC 16**
See also CA 117; 154; DLB 180; EWL 3; MJW; RGSF 2; RGWL 2, 3

Alabaster, William 1568-1640 .... **LC 90**
See also DLB 132; RGEL 2

Alain 1868-1951 .... **TCLC 41**
See also CA 163; EWL 3; GFL 1789 to the Present

Alain de Lille c. 1116-c. 1203 .... **CMLC 53**
See also DLB 208

Alain-Fournier .... **TCLC 6**
See Fournier, Henri-Alban
See also DLB 65; EWL 3; GFL 1789 to the Present; RGWL 2, 3

Al-Amin, Jamil Abdullah 1943- .... **BLC 1**
See also BW 1, 3; CA 112; 125; CANR 82; DAM MULT

Alanus de Insluis
See Alain de Lille

Alarcon, Pedro Antonio de
1833-1891 .... **NCLC 1; SSC 64**

Alas (y Urena), Leopoldo (Enrique Garcia)
1852-1901 .... **TCLC 29**
See also CA 113; 131; HW 1; RGSF 2

Albee, Edward (Franklin) (III)
1928- .. **CLC 1, 2, 3, 5, 9, 11, 13, 25, 53, 86, 113; DC 11; WLC**
See also AAYA 51; AITN 1; AMW; CA 5-8R; CABS 3; CAD; CANR 8, 54, 74, 124; CD 5; CDALB 1941-1968; DA; DA3; DAB; DAC; DAM DRAM, MST; DFS 2, 3, 8, 10, 13, 14; DLB 7, 266; EWL 3; INT CANR-8; LAIT 4; LMFS 2; MTCW 1, 2; RGAL 4; TUS

Alberti (Merello), Rafael
See Alberti, Rafael
See also CWW 2

Alberti, Rafael 1902-1999 .... **CLC 7**
See Alberti (Merello), Rafael
See also CA 85-88; 185; CANR 81; DLB 108; EWL 3; HW 2; RGWL 2, 3

Albert the Great 1193(?)-1280 ...... **CMLC 16**
See also DLB 115

Alcaeus c. 620B.C.- .... **CMLC 65**
See also DLB 176

Alcala-Galiano, Juan Valera y
See Valera y Alcala-Galiano, Juan

Alcayaga, Lucila Godoy
See Godoy Alcayaga, Lucila

Alcott, Amos Bronson 1799-1888 .... **NCLC 1**
See also DLB 1, 223

Alcott, Louisa May 1832-1888 . **NCLC 6, 58, 83; SSC 27; WLC**
See also AAYA 20; AMWS 1; BPFB 1; BYA 2; CDALB 1865-1917; CLR 1, 38; DA; DA3; DAB; DAC; DAM MST, NOV; DLB 1, 42, 79, 223, 239, 242; DLBD 14; FW; JRDA; LAIT 2; MAICYA 1, 2; NFS 12; RGAL 4; SATA 100; TUS; WCH; WYA; YABC 1; YAW

Alcuin c. 730-804 .... **CMLC 69**
See also DLB 148

Aldanov, M. A.
See Aldanov, Mark (Alexandrovich)

Aldanov, Mark (Alexandrovich)
1886(?)-1957 .... **TCLC 23**
See also CA 118; 181

Aldington, Richard 1892-1962 .... **CLC 49**
See also CA 85-88; CANR 45; DLB 20, 36, 100, 149; LMFS 2; RGEL 2

Aldiss, Brian W(ilson) 1925- . **CLC 5, 14, 40; SSC 36**
See also AAYA 42; CA 5-8R; 190; CAAE 190; CAAS 2; CANR 5, 28, 64, 121; CN 7; DAM NOV; DLB 14, 261, 271; MTCW 1, 2; SATA 34; SFW 4

Aldrich, Bess Streeter
1881-1954 .... **TCLC 125**
See also CLR 70

Alegria, Claribel
See Alegria, Claribel (Joy)
See also CWW 2; DLB 145, 283

Alegria, Claribel (Joy) 1924- .... **CLC 75; HLCS 1; PC 26**
See Alegria, Claribel
See also CA 131; CAAS 15; CANR 66, 94, 134; DAM MULT; EWL 3; HW 1; MTCW 1; PFS 21

Alegria, Fernando 1918- .... **CLC 57**
See also CA 9-12R; CANR 5, 32, 72; EWL 3; HW 1, 2

Aleichem, Sholom .... **SSC 33; TCLC 1, 35**
See Rabinovitch, Sholem
See also TWA

Aleixandre, Vicente 1898-1984 .... **HLCS 1; TCLC 113**
See also CANR 81; DLB 108; EWL 3; HW 2; RGWL 2, 3

Aleman, Mateo 1547-1615(?) .... **LC 81**

Alencon, Marguerite d'
See de Navarre, Marguerite

Alepoudelis, Odysseus
See Elytis, Odysseus
See also CWW 2

Aleshkovsky, Joseph 1929-
See Aleshkovsky, Yuz
See also CA 121; 128

Aleshkovsky, Yuz .... **CLC 44**
See Aleshkovsky, Joseph

Alexander, Lloyd (Chudley) 1924- ... **CLC 35**
See also AAYA 1, 27; BPFB 1; BYA 5, 6, 7, 9, 10, 11; CA 1-4R; CANR 1, 24, 38, 55, 113; CLR 1, 5, 48; CWRI 5; DLB 52; FANT; JRDA; MAICYA 1, 2; MAICYAS 1; MTCW 1; SAAS 19; SATA 3, 49, 81, 129, 135; SUFW; TUS; WYA; YAW

Alexander, Meena 1951- .... **CLC 121**
See also CA 115; CANR 38, 70; CP 7; CWP; FW

Alexander, Samuel 1859-1938 .... **TCLC 77**

Alexie, Sherman (Joseph, Jr.)
1966- .... **CLC 96, 154; NNAL; PC 53**
See also AAYA 28; BYA 15; CA 138; CANR 65, 95, 133; DA3; DAM MULT; DLB 175, 206, 278; LATS 1:2; MTCW 1; NFS 17; SSFS 18

al-Farabi 870(?)-950 .... **CMLC 58**
See also DLB 115

Alfau, Felipe 1902-1999 .... **CLC 66**
See also CA 137

Alfieri, Vittorio 1749-1803 .... **NCLC 101**
See also EW 4; RGWL 2, 3

Alfred, Jean Gaston
See Ponge, Francis

Alger, Horatio, Jr. 1832-1899 .... **NCLC 8, 83**
See also CLR 87; DLB 42; LAIT 2; RGAL 4; SATA 16; TUS

Al-Ghazali, Muhammad ibn Muhammad
1058-1111 .... **CMLC 50**
See also DLB 115

Algren, Nelson 1909-1981 ..... **CLC 4, 10, 33; SSC 33**
See also AMWS 9; BPFB 1; CA 13-16R; 103; CANR 20, 61; CDALB 1941-1968; DLB 9; DLBY 1981, 1982, 2000; EWL 3; MTCW 1, 2; RGAL 4; RGSF 2

al-Hariri, al-Qasim ibn 'Ali Abu Muhammad al-Basri 1054-1122 .... **CMLC 63**
See also RGWL 3

Ali, Ahmed 1908-1998 .... **CLC 69**
See also CA 25-28R; CANR 15, 34; EWL 3

Ali, Tariq 1943- .... **CLC 173**
See also CA 25-28R; CANR 10, 99

Alighieri, Dante
See Dante

Allan, John B.
See Westlake, Donald E(dwin)

Allan, Sidney
See Hartmann, Sadakichi

Allan, Sydney
See Hartmann, Sadakichi

Allard, Janet .... **CLC 59**

Allen, Edward 1948- .... **CLC 59**

Allen, Fred 1894-1956 .... **TCLC 87**

Allen, Paula Gunn 1939- .... **CLC 84, 202; NNAL**
See also AMWS 4; CA 112; 143; CANR 63, 130; CWP; DA3; DAM MULT; DLB 175; FW; MTCW 1; RGAL 4

Allen, Roland
See Ayckbourn, Alan

Allen, Sarah A.
See Hopkins, Pauline Elizabeth

Allen, Sidney H.
See Hartmann, Sadakichi

Allen, Woody 1935- .... **CLC 16, 52, 195**
See also AAYA 10, 51; CA 33-36R; CANR 27, 38, 63, 128; DAM POP; DLB 44; MTCW 1

Allende, Isabel 1942- ... **CLC 39, 57, 97, 170; HLC 1; SSC 65; WLCS**
See also AAYA 18; CA 125; 130; CANR 51, 74, 129; CDWLB 3; CLR 99; CWW 2; DA3; DAM MULT, NOV; DLB 145; DNFS 1; EWL 3; FW; HW 1, 2; INT CA-130; LAIT 5; LAWS 1; LMFS 2; MTCW 1, 2; NCFS 1; NFS 6, 18; RGSF 2; RGWL 3; SSFS 11, 16; WLIT 1

Alleyn, Ellen
See Rossetti, Christina (Georgina)

Alleyne, Carla D. .... **CLC 65**

Allingham, Margery (Louise) 1904-1966 .... **CLC 19**
See also CA 5-8R; 25-28R; CANR 4, 58; CMW 4; DLB 77; MSW; MTCW 1, 2

Allingham, William 1824-1889 ...... **NCLC 25**
See also DLB 35; RGEL 2

Allison, Dorothy E. 1949- .... **CLC 78, 153**
See also AAYA 53; CA 140; CANR 66, 107; CSW; DA3; FW; MTCW 1; NFS 11; RGAL 4

Alloula, Malek .... **CLC 65**

Allston, Washington 1779-1843 .... **NCLC 2**
See also DLB 1, 235

Almedingen, E. M. .... **CLC 12**
See Almedingen, Martha Edith von
See also SATA 3

Almedingen, Martha Edith von 1898-1971
See Almedingen, E. M.
See also CA 1-4R; CANR 1

Almodovar, Pedro 1949(?)- .... **CLC 114; HLCS 1**
See also CA 133; CANR 72; HW 2

Almqvist, Carl Jonas Love 1793-1866 .... **NCLC 42**

al-Mutanabbi, Ahmad ibn al-Husayn Abu al-Tayyib al-Jufi al-Kindi 915-965 .... **CMLC 66**
See also RGWL 3

Alonso, Damaso 1898-1990 .... **CLC 14**
See also CA 110; 131; 130; CANR 72; DLB 108; EWL 3; HW 1, 2

Alov
See Gogol, Nikolai (Vasilyevich)

al'Sadaawi, Nawal
See El Saadawi, Nawal
See also FW

Al Siddik
See Rolfe, Frederick (William Serafino Austin Lewis Mary)
See also GLL 1; RGEL 2

Alta 1942- .... **CLC 19**
See also CA 57-60

Alter, Robert B(ernard) 1935- .... **CLC 34**
See also CA 49-52; CANR 1, 47, 100

Alther, Lisa 1944- .... **CLC 7, 41**
See also BPFB 1; CA 65-68; CAAS 30; CANR 12, 30, 51; CN 7; CSW; GLL 2; MTCW 1

Althusser, L.
See Althusser, Louis

Althusser, Louis 1918-1990 .... **CLC 106**
See also CA 131; 132; CANR 102; DLB 242

Altman, Robert 1925- .... **CLC 16, 116**
See also CA 73-76; CANR 43

Alurista .... **HLCS 1**
See Urista (Heredia), Alberto (Baltazar)
See also DLB 82; LLW 1

Alvarez, A(lfred) 1929- .... **CLC 5, 13**
See also CA 1-4R; CANR 3, 33, 63, 101, 134; CN 7; CP 7; DLB 14, 40

Alvarez, Alejandro Rodriguez 1903-1965
See Casona, Alejandro
See also CA 131; 93-96; HW 1

Alvarez, Julia 1950- .... **CLC 93; HLCS 1**
See also AAYA 25; AMWS 7; CA 147; CANR 69, 101, 133; DA3; DLB 282; LATS 1:2; LLW 1; MTCW 1; NFS 5, 9; SATA 129; WLIT 1

Alvaro, Corrado 1896-1956 .... **TCLC 60**
See also CA 163; DLB 264; EWL 3

Amado, Jorge 1912-2001 ... **CLC 13, 40, 106; HLC 1**
See also CA 77-80; 201; CANR 35, 74; CWW 2; DAM MULT, NOV; DLB 113, 307; EWL 3; HW 2; LAW; LAWS 1; MTCW 1, 2; RGWL 2, 3; TWA; WLIT 1

Ambler, Eric 1909-1998 .... **CLC 4, 6, 9**
See also BRWS 4; CA 9-12R; 171; CANR 7, 38, 74; CMW 4; CN 7; DLB 77; MSW; MTCW 1, 2; TEA

Ambrose, Stephen E(dward) 1936-2002 .... **CLC 145**
See also AAYA 44; CA 1-4R; 209; CANR 3, 43, 57, 83, 105; NCFS 2; SATA 40, 138

Amichai, Yehuda 1924-2000 .. **CLC 9, 22, 57, 116; PC 38**
See also CA 85-88; 189; CANR 46, 60, 99, 132; CWW 2; EWL 3; MTCW 1

Amichai, Yehudah
See Amichai, Yehuda

Amiel, Henri Frederic 1821-1881 .... **NCLC 4**
See also DLB 217

Amis, Kingsley (William) 1922-1995 ...... **CLC 1, 2, 3, 5, 8, 13, 40, 44, 129**
See also AITN 2; BPFB 1; BRWS 2; CA 9-12R; 150; CANR 8, 28, 54; CDBLB 1945-1960; CN 7; CP 7; DA; DA3; DAB; DAC; DAM MST, NOV; DLB 15, 27, 100, 139; DLBY 1996; EWL 3; HGG; INT CANR-8; MTCW 1, 2; RGEL 2; RGSF 2; SFW 4

Amis, Martin (Louis) 1949- .... **CLC 4, 9, 38, 62, 101**
See also BEST 90:3; BRWS 4; CA 65-68; CANR 8, 27, 54, 73, 95, 132; CN 7; DA3; DLB 14, 194; EWL 3; INT CANR-27; MTCW 1

Ammianus Marcellinus c. 330-c. 395 .... **CMLC 60**
See also AW 2; DLB 211

Ammons, A(rchie) R(andolph) 1926-2001 ...... **CLC 2, 3, 5, 8, 9, 25, 57, 108; PC 16**
See also AITN 1; AMWS 7; CA 9-12R; 193; CANR 6, 36, 51, 73, 107; CP 7; CSW; DAM POET; DLB 5, 165; EWL 3; MTCW 1, 2; PFS 19; RGAL 4

Amo, Tauraatua i
See Adams, Henry (Brooks)

Amory, Thomas 1691(?)-1788 .... **LC 48**
See also DLB 39

Anand, Mulk Raj 1905-2004 ...... **CLC 23, 93**
See also CA 65-68; CANR 32, 64; CN 7; DAM NOV; EWL 3; MTCW 1, 2; RGSF 2

Anatol
See Schnitzler, Arthur

Anaximander c. 611B.C.-c. 546B.C. .... **CMLC 22**

Anaya, Rudolfo A(lfonso) 1937- ...... **CLC 23, 148; HLC 1**
See also AAYA 20; BYA 13; CA 45-48; CAAS 4; CANR 1, 32, 51, 124; CN 7; DAM MULT, NOV; DLB 82, 206, 278; HW 1; LAIT 4; LLW 1; MTCW 1, 2; NFS 12; RGAL 4; RGSF 2; WLIT 1

Andersen, Hans Christian 1805-1875 .... **NCLC 7, 79; SSC 6, 56; WLC**
See also AAYA 57; CLR 6; DA; DA3; DAB; DAC; DAM MST, POP; EW 6; MAICYA 1, 2; RGSF 2; RGWL 2, 3; SATA 100; TWA; WCH; YABC 1

Anderson, C. Farley
See Mencken, H(enry) L(ouis); Nathan, George Jean

Anderson, Jessica (Margaret) Queale 1916- .... **CLC 37**
See also CA 9-12R; CANR 4, 62; CN 7

Anderson, Jon (Victor) 1940- .... **CLC 9**
See also CA 25-28R; CANR 20; DAM POET

Anderson, Lindsay (Gordon) 1923-1994 .... **CLC 20**
See also CA 125; 128; 146; CANR 77

Anderson, Maxwell 1888-1959 .... **TCLC 2, 144**
See also CA 105; 152; DAM DRAM; DFS 16, 20; DLB 7, 228; MTCW 2; RGAL 4

Anderson, Poul (William) 1926-2001 .... **CLC 15**
See also AAYA 5, 34; BPFB 1; BYA 6, 8, 9; CA 1-4R, 181; 199; CAAE 181; CAAS 2; CANR 2, 15, 34, 64, 110; CLR 58; DLB 8; FANT; INT CANR-15; MTCW 1, 2; SATA 90; SATA-Brief 39; SATA-Essay 106; SCFW 2; SFW 4; SUFW 1, 2

Anderson, Robert (Woodruff) 1917- .... **CLC 23**
See also AITN 1; CA 21-24R; CANR 32; DAM DRAM; DLB 7; LAIT 5

Anderson, Roberta Joan
See Mitchell, Joni

Anderson, Sherwood 1876-1941 .. **SSC 1, 46; TCLC 1, 10, 24, 123; WLC**
See also AAYA 30; AMW; AMWS 2; BPFB 1; CA 104; 121; CANR 61; CDALB 1917-1929; DA; DA3; DAB; DAC; DAM MST, NOV; DLB 4, 9, 86; DLBD 1; EWL 3; EXPS; GLL 2; MTCW 1, 2; NFS 4; RGAL 4; RGSF 2; SSFS 4, 10, 11; TUS

Andier, Pierre
See Desnos, Robert

Andouard
See Giraudoux, Jean(-Hippolyte)

Andrade, Carlos Drummond de ..... CLC 18
See Drummond de Andrade, Carlos
See also EWL 3; RGWL 2, 3

Andrade, Mario de .... TCLC 43
See de Andrade, Mario
See also DLB 307; EWL 3; LAW; RGWL 2, 3; WLIT 1

Andreae, Johann V(alentin)
1586-1654 .... LC 32
See also DLB 164

Andreas Capellanus fl. c. 1185- ... CMLC 45
See also DLB 208

Andreas-Salome, Lou 1861-1937 ... TCLC 56
See also CA 178; DLB 66

Andreev, Leonid
See Andreyev, Leonid (Nikolaevich)
See also DLB 295; EWL 3

Andress, Lesley
See Sanders, Lawrence

Andrewes, Lancelot 1555-1626 .... LC 5
See also DLB 151, 172

Andrews, Cicily Fairfield
See West, Rebecca

Andrews, Elton V.
See Pohl, Frederik

Andreyev, Leonid (Nikolaevich)
1871-1919 .... TCLC 3
See Andreev, Leonid
See also CA 104; 185

Andric, Ivo 1892-1975 .... CLC 8; SSC 36; TCLC 135
See also CA 81-84; 57-60; CANR 43, 60; CDWLB 4; DLB 147; EW 11; EWL 3; MTCW 1; RGSF 2; RGWL 2, 3

Androvar
See Prado (Calvo), Pedro

Angelique, Pierre
See Bataille, Georges

Angell, Roger 1920- .... CLC 26
See also CA 57-60; CANR 13, 44, 70; DLB 171, 185

Angelou, Maya 1928- ... BLC 1; CLC 12, 35, 64, 77, 155; PC 32; WLCS
See also AAYA 7, 20; AMWS 4; BPFB 1; BW 2, 3; BYA 2; CA 65-68; CANR 19, 42, 65, 111, 133; CDALBS; CLR 53; CP 7; CSW; CWP; DA; DA3; DAB; DAC; DAM MST, MULT, POET, POP; DLB 38; EWL 3; EXPN; EXPP; LAIT 4; MAICYA 2; MAICYAS 1; MAWW; MTCW 1, 2; NCFS 2; NFS 2; PFS 2, 3; RGAL 4; SATA 49, 136; WYA; YAW

Angouleme, Marguerite d'
See de Navarre, Marguerite

Anna Comnena 1083-1153 .... CMLC 25

Annensky, Innokentii Fedorovich
See Annensky, Innokenty (Fyodorovich)
See also DLB 295

Annensky, Innokenty (Fyodorovich)
1856-1909 .... TCLC 14
See also CA 110; 155; EWL 3

Annunzio, Gabriele d'
See D'Annunzio, Gabriele

Anodos
See Coleridge, Mary E(lizabeth)

Anon, Charles Robert
See Pessoa, Fernando (Antonio Nogueira)

Anouilh, Jean (Marie Lucien Pierre)
1910-1987 . CLC 1, 3, 8, 13, 40, 50; DC 8, 21
See also CA 17-20R; 123; CANR 32; DAM DRAM; DFS 9, 10, 19; EW 13; EWL 3; GFL 1789 to the Present; MTCW 1, 2; RGWL 2, 3; TWA

Anselm of Canterbury
1033(?)-1109 .... CMLC 67
See also DLB 115

Anthony, Florence
See Ai

Anthony, John
See Ciardi, John (Anthony)

Anthony, Peter
See Shaffer, Anthony (Joshua); Shaffer, Peter (Levin)

Anthony, Piers 1934- .... CLC 35
See also AAYA 11, 48; BYA 7; CA 200; CAAE 200; CANR 28, 56, 73, 102, 133; CPW; DAM POP; DLB 8; FANT; MAICYA 2; MAICYAS 1; MTCW 1, 2; SAAS 22; SATA 84, 129; SATA-Essay 129; SFW 4; SUFW 1, 2; YAW

Anthony, Susan B(rownell)
1820-1906 .... TCLC 84
See also CA 211; FW

Antiphon c. 480B.C.-c. 411B.C. .... CMLC 55

Antoine, Marc
See Proust, (Valentin-Louis-George-Eugene) Marcel

Antoninus, Brother
See Everson, William (Oliver)

Antonioni, Michelangelo 1912- .... CLC 20, 144
See also CA 73-76; CANR 45, 77

Antschel, Paul 1920-1970
See Celan, Paul
See also CA 85-88; CANR 33, 61; MTCW 1; PFS 21

Anwar, Chairil 1922-1949 .... TCLC 22
See Chairil Anwar
See also CA 121; 219; RGWL 3

Anzaldua, Gloria (Evanjelina)
1942-2004 .... CLC 200, HLCS 1
See also CA 175; 227; CSW; CWP; DLB 122; FW; LLW 1; RGAL 4; SATA-Obit 154

Apess, William 1798-1839(?) .... NCLC 73; NNAL
See also DAM MULT; DLB 175, 243

Apollinaire, Guillaume 1880-1918 .... PC 7; TCLC 3, 8, 51
See Kostrowitzki, Wilhelm Apollinaris de
See also CA 152; DAM POET; DLB 258; EW 9; EWL 3; GFL 1789 to the Present; MTCW 1; RGWL 2, 3; TWA; WP

Apollonius of Rhodes
See Apollonius Rhodius
See also AW 1; RGWL 2, 3

Apollonius Rhodius c. 300B.C.-c. 220B.C. .... CMLC 28
See Apollonius of Rhodes
See also DLB 176

Appelfeld, Aharon 1932- ... CLC 23, 47; SSC 42
See also CA 112; 133; CANR 86; CWW 2; DLB 299; EWL 3; RGSF 2

Apple, Max (Isaac) 1941- .... CLC 9, 33; SSC 50
See also CA 81-84; CANR 19, 54; DLB 130

Appleman, Philip (Dean) 1926- .... CLC 51
See also CA 13-16R; CAAS 18; CANR 6, 29, 56

Appleton, Lawrence
See Lovecraft, H(oward) P(hillips)

Apteryx
See Eliot, T(homas) S(tearns)

Apuleius, (Lucius Madaurensis)
125(?)-175(?) .... CMLC 1
See also AW 2; CDWLB 1; DLB 211; RGWL 2, 3; SUFW

Aquin, Hubert 1929-1977 .... CLC 15
See also CA 105; DLB 53; EWL 3

Aquinas, Thomas 1224(?)-1274 ..... CMLC 33
See also DLB 115; EW 1; TWA

Aragon, Louis 1897-1982 .... CLC 3, 22; TCLC 123
See also CA 69-72; 108; CANR 28, 71; DAM NOV, POET; DLB 72, 258; EW 11; EWL 3; GFL 1789 to the Present; GLL 2; LMFS 2; MTCW 1, 2; RGWL 2, 3

Arany, Janos 1817-1882 .... NCLC 34

Aranyos, Kakay 1847-1910
See Mikszath, Kalman

Aratus of Soli c. 315B.C.-c. 240B.C. .... CMLC 64
See also DLB 176

Arbuthnot, John 1667-1735 .... LC 1
See also DLB 101

Archer, Herbert Winslow
See Mencken, H(enry) L(ouis)

Archer, Jeffrey (Howard) 1940- .... CLC 28
See also AAYA 16; BEST 89:3; BPFB 1; CA 77-80; CANR 22, 52, 95; CPW; DA3; DAM POP; INT CANR-22

Archer, Jules 1915- .... CLC 12
See also CA 9-12R; CANR 6, 69; SAAS 5; SATA 4, 85

Archer, Lee
See Ellison, Harlan (Jay)

Archilochus c. 7th cent. B.C.- .... CMLC 44
See also DLB 176

Arden, John 1930- .... CLC 6, 13, 15
See also BRWS 2; CA 13-16R; CAAS 4; CANR 31, 65, 67, 124; CBD; CD 5; DAM DRAM; DFS 9; DLB 13, 245; EWL 3; MTCW 1

Arenas, Reinaldo 1943-1990 .. CLC 41; HLC 1
See also CA 124; 128; 133; CANR 73, 106; DAM MULT; DLB 145; EWL 3; GLL 2; HW 1; LAW; LAWS 1; MTCW 1; RGSF 2; RGWL 3; WLIT 1

Arendt, Hannah 1906-1975 .... CLC 66, 98
See also CA 17-20R; 61-64; CANR 26, 60; DLB 242; MTCW 1, 2

Aretino, Pietro 1492-1556 .... LC 12
See also RGWL 2, 3

Arghezi, Tudor .... CLC 80
See Theodorescu, Ion N.
See also CA 167; CDWLB 4; DLB 220; EWL 3

Arguedas, Jose Maria 1911-1969 .... CLC 10, 18; HLCS 1; TCLC 147
See also CA 89-92; CANR 73; DLB 113; EWL 3; HW 1; LAW; RGWL 2, 3; WLIT 1

Argueta, Manlio 1936- .... CLC 31
See also CA 131; CANR 73; CWW 2; DLB 145; EWL 3; HW 1; RGWL 3

Arias, Ron(ald Francis) 1941- .... HLC 1
See also CA 131; CANR 81; DAM MULT; DLB 82; HW 1, 2; MTCW 2

Ariosto, Ludovico 1474-1533 ... LC 6, 87; PC 42
See also EW 2; RGWL 2, 3

Aristides
See Epstein, Joseph

Aristophanes 450B.C.-385B.C. .... CMLC 4, 51; DC 2; WLCS
See also AW 1; CDWLB 1; DA; DA3; DAB; DAC; DAM DRAM, MST; DFS 10; DLB 176; LMFS 1; RGWL 2, 3; TWA

Aristotle 384B.C.-322B.C. .... CMLC 31; WLCS
See also AW 1; CDWLB 1; DA; DA3; DAB; DAC; DAM MST; DLB 176; RGWL 2, 3; TWA

Arlt, Roberto (Godofredo Christophersen)
1900-1942 .... HLC 1; TCLC 29
See also CA 123; 131; CANR 67; DAM MULT; DLB 305; EWL 3; HW 1, 2; LAW

Armah, Ayi Kwei 1939- . **BLC 1; CLC 5, 33, 136**
See also AFW; BRWS 10; BW 1; CA 61-64; CANR 21, 64; CDWLB 3; CN 7; DAM MULT, POET; DLB 117; EWL 3; MTCW 1; WLIT 2

Armatrading, Joan 1950- .... **CLC 17**
See also CA 114; 186

Armitage, Frank
See Carpenter, John (Howard)

Armstrong, Jeannette (C.) 1948- .... **NNAL**
See also CA 149; CCA 1; CN 7; DAC; SATA 102

Arnette, Robert
See Silverberg, Robert

Arnim, Achim von (Ludwig Joachim von Arnim) 1781-1831 ..... **NCLC 5; SSC 29**
See also DLB 90

Arnim, Bettina von 1785-1859 ...... **NCLC 38, 123**
See also DLB 90; RGWL 2, 3

Arnold, Matthew 1822-1888 ..... **NCLC 6, 29, 89, 126; PC 5; WLC**
See also BRW 5; CDBLB 1832-1890; DA; DAB; DAC; DAM MST, POET; DLB 32, 57; EXPP; PAB; PFS 2; TEA; WP

Arnold, Thomas 1795-1842 .... **NCLC 18**
See also DLB 55

Arnow, Harriette (Louisa) Simpson 1908-1986 .... **CLC 2, 7, 18**
See also BPFB 1; CA 9-12R; 118; CANR 14; DLB 6; FW; MTCW 1, 2; RHW; SATA 42; SATA-Obit 47

Arouet, Francois-Marie
See Voltaire

Arp, Hans
See Arp, Jean

Arp, Jean 1887-1966 .... **CLC 5; TCLC 115**
See also CA 81-84; 25-28R; CANR 42, 77; EW 10

Arrabal
See Arrabal, Fernando

Arrabal, Fernando 1932- ... **CLC 2, 9, 18, 58**
See Arrabal (Teran), Fernando
See also CA 9-12R; CANR 15; EWL 3; LMFS 2

Arrabal (Teran), Fernando 1932-
See Arrabal, Fernando
See also CWW 2

Arreola, Juan Jose 1918-2001 .... **CLC 147; HLC 1; SSC 38**
See also CA 113; 131; 200; CANR 81; CWW 2; DAM MULT; DLB 113; DNFS 2; EWL 3; HW 1, 2; LAW; RGSF 2

Arrian c. 89(?)-c. 155(?) .... **CMLC 43**
See also DLB 176

Arrick, Fran .... **CLC 30**
See Gaberman, Judie Angell
See also BYA 6

Arrley, Richmond
See Delany, Samuel R(ay), Jr.

Artaud, Antonin (Marie Joseph) 1896-1948 .... **DC 14; TCLC 3, 36**
See also CA 104; 149; DA3; DAM DRAM; DLB 258; EW 11; EWL 3; GFL 1789 to the Present; MTCW 1; RGWL 2, 3

Arthur, Ruth M(abel) 1905-1979 ..... **CLC 12**
See also CA 9-12R; 85-88; CANR 4; CWRI 5; SATA 7, 26

Artsybashev, Mikhail (Petrovich) 1878-1927 .... **TCLC 31**
See also CA 170; DLB 295

Arundel, Honor (Morfydd) 1919-1973 .... **CLC 17**
See also CA 21-22; 41-44R; CAP 2; CLR 35; CWRI 5; SATA 4; SATA-Obit 24

Arzner, Dorothy 1900-1979 .... **CLC 98**

Asch, Sholem 1880-1957 .... **TCLC 3**
See also CA 105; EWL 3; GLL 2

Ascham, Roger 1516(?)-1568 .... **LC 101**
See also DLB 236

Ash, Shalom
See Asch, Sholem

Ashbery, John (Lawrence) 1927- .. **CLC 2, 3, 4, 6, 9, 13, 15, 25, 41, 77, 125; PC 26**
See Berry, Jonas
See also AMWS 3; CA 5-8R; CANR 9, 37, 66, 102, 132; CP 7; DA3; DAM POET; DLB 5, 165; DLBY 1981; EWL 3; INT CANR-9; MTCW 1, 2; PAB; PFS 11; RGAL 4; WP

Ashdown, Clifford
See Freeman, R(ichard) Austin

Ashe, Gordon
See Creasey, John

Ashton-Warner, Sylvia (Constance) 1908-1984 .... **CLC 19**
See also CA 69-72; 112; CANR 29; MTCW 1, 2

Asimov, Isaac 1920-1992 ..... **CLC 1, 3, 9, 19, 26, 76, 92**
See also AAYA 13; BEST 90:2; BPFB 1; BYA 4, 6, 7, 9; CA 1-4R; 137; CANR 2, 19, 36, 60, 125; CLR 12, 79; CMW 4; CPW; DA3; DAM POP; DLB 8; DLBY 1992; INT CANR-19; JRDA; LAIT 5; LMFS 2; MAICYA 1, 2; MTCW 1, 2; RGAL 4; SATA 1, 26, 74; SCFW 2; SFW 4; SSFS 17; TUS; YAW

Askew, Anne 1521(?)-1546 .... **LC 81**
See also DLB 136

Assis, Joaquim Maria Machado de
See Machado de Assis, Joaquim Maria

Astell, Mary 1666-1731 .... **LC 68**
See also DLB 252; FW

Astley, Thea (Beatrice May) 1925-2004 .... **CLC 41**
See also CA 65-68; 229; CANR 11, 43, 78; CN 7; DLB 289; EWL 3

Astley, William 1855-1911
See Warung, Price

Aston, James
See White, T(erence) H(anbury)

Asturias, Miguel Angel 1899-1974 .... **CLC 3, 8, 13; HLC 1**
See also CA 25-28; 49-52; CANR 32; CAP 2; CDWLB 3; DA3; DAM MULT, NOV; DLB 113, 290; EWL 3; HW 1; LAW; LMFS 2; MTCW 1, 2; RGWL 2, 3; WLIT 1

Atares, Carlos Saura
See Saura (Atares), Carlos

Athanasius c. 295-c. 373 .... **CMLC 48**

Atheling, William
See Pound, Ezra (Weston Loomis)

Atheling, William, Jr.
See Blish, James (Benjamin)

Atherton, Gertrude (Franklin Horn) 1857-1948 .... **TCLC 2**
See also CA 104; 155; DLB 9, 78, 186; HGG; RGAL 4; SUFW 1; TCWW 2

Atherton, Lucius
See Masters, Edgar Lee

Atkins, Jack
See Harris, Mark

Atkinson, Kate 1951- .... **CLC 99**
See also CA 166; CANR 101; DLB 267

Attaway, William (Alexander) 1911-1986 .... **BLC 1; CLC 92**
See also BW 2, 3; CA 143; CANR 82; DAM MULT; DLB 76

Atticus
See Fleming, Ian (Lancaster); Wilson, (Thomas) Woodrow

Atwood, Margaret (Eleanor) 1939- ... **CLC 2, 3, 4, 8, 13, 15, 25, 44, 84, 135; PC 8; SSC 2, 46; WLC**
See also AAYA 12, 47; AMWS 13; BEST 89:2; BPFB 1; CA 49-52; CANR 3, 24, 33, 59, 95, 133; CN 7; CP 7; CPW; CWP; DA; DA3; DAB; DAC; DAM MST, NOV, POET; DLB 53, 251; EWL 3; EXPN; FW; INT CANR-24; LAIT 5; MTCW 1, 2; NFS 4, 12, 13, 14, 19; PFS 7; RGSF 2; SATA 50; SSFS 3, 13; TWA; WWE 1; YAW

Aubigny, Pierre d'
See Mencken, H(enry) L(ouis)

Aubin, Penelope 1685-1731(?) .... **LC 9**
See also DLB 39

Auchincloss, Louis (Stanton) 1917- .. **CLC 4, 6, 9, 18, 45; SSC 22**
See also AMWS 4; CA 1-4R; CANR 6, 29, 55, 87, 130; CN 7; DAM NOV; DLB 2, 244; DLBY 1980; EWL 3; INT CANR-29; MTCW 1; RGAL 4

Auden, W(ystan) H(ugh) 1907-1973 . **CLC 1, 2, 3, 4, 6, 9, 11, 14, 43, 123; PC 1; WLC**
See also AAYA 18; AMWS 2; BRW 7; BRWR 1; CA 9-12R; 45-48; CANR 5, 61, 105; CDBLB 1914-1945; DA; DA3; DAB; DAC; DAM DRAM, MST, POET; DLB 10, 20; EWL 3; EXPP; MTCW 1, 2; PAB; PFS 1, 3, 4, 10; TUS; WP

Audiberti, Jacques 1899-1965 .... **CLC 38**
See also CA 25-28R; DAM DRAM; EWL 3

Audubon, John James 1785-1851 . **NCLC 47**
See also ANW; DLB 248

Auel, Jean M(arie) 1936- .... **CLC 31, 107**
See also AAYA 7, 51; BEST 90:4; BPFB 1; CA 103; CANR 21, 64, 115; CPW; DA3; DAM POP; INT CANR-21; NFS 11; RHW; SATA 91

Auerbach, Erich 1892-1957 .... **TCLC 43**
See also CA 118; 155; EWL 3

Augier, Emile 1820-1889 .... **NCLC 31**
See also DLB 192; GFL 1789 to the Present

August, John
See De Voto, Bernard (Augustine)

Augustine, St. 354-430 .... **CMLC 6; WLCS**
See also DA; DA3; DAB; DAC; DAM MST; DLB 115; EW 1; RGWL 2, 3

Aunt Belinda
See Braddon, Mary Elizabeth

Aunt Weedy
See Alcott, Louisa May

Aurelius
See Bourne, Randolph S(illiman)

Aurelius, Marcus 121-180 .... **CMLC 45**
See Marcus Aurelius
See also RGWL 2, 3

Aurobindo, Sri
See Ghose, Aurabinda

Aurobindo Ghose
See Ghose, Aurabinda

Austen, Jane 1775-1817 .... **NCLC 1, 13, 19, 33, 51, 81, 95, 119, 150; WLC**
See also AAYA 19; BRW 4; BRWC 1; BRWR 2; BYA 3; CDBLB 1789-1832; DA; DA3; DAB; DAC; DAM MST, NOV; DLB 116; EXPN; LAIT 2; LATS 1:1; LMFS 1; NFS 1, 14, 18, 20; TEA; WLIT 3; WYAS 1

Auster, Paul 1947- .... **CLC 47, 131**
See also AMWS 12; CA 69-72; CANR 23, 52, 75, 129; CMW 4; CN 7; DA3; DLB 227; MTCW 1; SUFW 2

Austin, Frank
See Faust, Frederick (Schiller)
See also TCWW 2

Austin, Mary (Hunter) 1868-1934 . **TCLC 25**
See Stairs, Gordon
See also ANW; CA 109; 178; DLB 9, 78, 206, 221, 275; FW; TCWW 2

Averroes 1126-1198 .... **CMLC 7**
See also DLB 115

Avicenna 980-1037 .... **CMLC 16**
See also DLB 115

Avison, Margaret (Kirkland) 1918- .. **CLC 2, 4, 97**
See also CA 17-20R; CANR 134; CP 7; DAC; DAM POET; DLB 53; MTCW 1

Axton, David
See Koontz, Dean R(ay)

Ayckbourn, Alan 1939- ...... **CLC 5, 8, 18, 33, 74; DC 13**
See also BRWS 5; CA 21-24R; CANR 31, 59, 118; CBD; CD 5; DAB; DAM DRAM; DFS 7; DLB 13, 245; EWL 3; MTCW 1, 2

Aydy, Catherine
See Tennant, Emma (Christina)

Ayme, Marcel (Andre) 1902-1967 ... **CLC 11; SSC 41**
See also CA 89-92; CANR 67; CLR 25; DLB 72; EW 12; EWL 3; GFL 1789 to the Present; RGSF 2; RGWL 2, 3; SATA 91

Ayrton, Michael 1921-1975 .... **CLC 7**
See also CA 5-8R; 61-64; CANR 9, 21

Aytmatov, Chingiz
See Aitmatov, Chingiz (Torekulovich)
See also EWL 3

Azorin .... **CLC 11**
See Martinez Ruiz, Jose
See also EW 9; EWL 3

Azuela, Mariano 1873-1952 .. **HLC 1; TCLC 3, 145**
See also CA 104; 131; CANR 81; DAM MULT; EWL 3; HW 1, 2; LAW; MTCW 1, 2

Ba, Mariama 1929-1981 .... **BLCS**
See also AFW; BW 2; CA 141; CANR 87; DNFS 2; WLIT 2

Baastad, Babbis Friis
See Friis-Baastad, Babbis Ellinor

Bab
See Gilbert, W(illiam) S(chwenck)

Babbis, Eleanor
See Friis-Baastad, Babbis Ellinor

Babel, Isaac
See Babel, Isaak (Emmanuilovich)
See also EW 11; SSFS 10

Babel, Isaak (Emmanuilovich) 1894-1941(?) .. **SSC 16, 78; TCLC 2, 13**
See Babel, Isaac
See also CA 104; 155; CANR 113; DLB 272; EWL 3; MTCW 1; RGSF 2; RGWL 2, 3; TWA

Babits, Mihaly 1883-1941 .... **TCLC 14**
See also CA 114; CDWLB 4; DLB 215; EWL 3

Babur 1483-1530 .... **LC 18**

Babylas 1898-1962
See Ghelderode, Michel de

Baca, Jimmy Santiago 1952- . **HLC 1; PC 41**
See also CA 131; CANR 81, 90; CP 7; DAM MULT; DLB 122; HW 1, 2; LLW 1

Baca, Jose Santiago
See Baca, Jimmy Santiago

Bacchelli, Riccardo 1891-1985 .... **CLC 19**
See also CA 29-32R; 117; DLB 264; EWL 3

Bach, Richard (David) 1936- .... **CLC 14**
See also AITN 1; BEST 89:2; BPFB 1; BYA 5; CA 9-12R; CANR 18, 93; CPW; DAM NOV, POP; FANT; MTCW 1; SATA 13

Bache, Benjamin Franklin 1769-1798 .... **LC 74**
See also DLB 43

Bachelard, Gaston 1884-1962 ...... **TCLC 128**
See also CA 97-100; 89-92; DLB 296; GFL 1789 to the Present

Bachman, Richard
See King, Stephen (Edwin)

Bachmann, Ingeborg 1926-1973 .... **CLC 69**
See also CA 93-96; 45-48; CANR 69; DLB 85; EWL 3; RGWL 2, 3

Bacon, Francis 1561-1626 .... **LC 18, 32**
See also BRW 1; CDBLB Before 1660; DLB 151, 236, 252; RGEL 2; TEA

Bacon, Roger 1214(?)-1294 .... **CMLC 14**
See also DLB 115

Bacovia, George 1881-1957 .... **TCLC 24**
See Vasiliu, Gheorghe
See also CDWLB 4; DLB 220; EWL 3

Badanes, Jerome 1937-1995 .... **CLC 59**

Bagehot, Walter 1826-1877 .... **NCLC 10**
See also DLB 55

Bagnold, Enid 1889-1981 .... **CLC 25**
See also BYA 2; CA 5-8R; 103; CANR 5, 40; CBD; CWD; CWRI 5; DAM DRAM; DLB 13, 160, 191, 245; FW; MAICYA 1, 2; RGEL 2; SATA 1, 25

Bagritsky, Eduard .... **TCLC 60**
See Dzyubin, Eduard Georgievich

Bagrjana, Elisaveta
See Belcheva, Elisaveta Lyubomirova

Bagryana, Elisaveta .... **CLC 10**
See Belcheva, Elisaveta Lyubomirova
See also CA 178; CDWLB 4; DLB 147; EWL 3

Bailey, Paul 1937- .... **CLC 45**
See also CA 21-24R; CANR 16, 62, 124; CN 7; DLB 14, 271; GLL 2

Baillie, Joanna 1762-1851 .... **NCLC 71, 151**
See also DLB 93; RGEL 2

Bainbridge, Beryl (Margaret) 1934- . **CLC 4, 5, 8, 10, 14, 18, 22, 62, 130**
See also BRWS 6; CA 21-24R; CANR 24, 55, 75, 88, 128; CN 7; DAM NOV; DLB 14, 231; EWL 3; MTCW 1, 2

Baker, Carlos (Heard) 1909-1987 .... **TCLC 119**
See also CA 5-8R; 122; CANR 3, 63; DLB 103

Baker, Elliott 1922- .... **CLC 8**
See also CA 45-48; CANR 2, 63; CN 7

Baker, Jean H. .... **TCLC 3, 10**
See Russell, George William

Baker, Nicholson 1957- .... **CLC 61, 165**
See also AMWS 13; CA 135; CANR 63, 120; CN 7; CPW; DA3; DAM POP; DLB 227

Baker, Ray Stannard 1870-1946 .... **TCLC 47**
See also CA 118

Baker, Russell (Wayne) 1925- .... **CLC 31**
See also BEST 89:4; CA 57-60; CANR 11, 41, 59; MTCW 1, 2

Bakhtin, M.
See Bakhtin, Mikhail Mikhailovich

Bakhtin, M. M.
See Bakhtin, Mikhail Mikhailovich

Bakhtin, Mikhail
See Bakhtin, Mikhail Mikhailovich

Bakhtin, Mikhail Mikhailovich 1895-1975 .... **CLC 83; TCLC 160**
See also CA 128; 113; DLB 242; EWL 3

Bakshi, Ralph 1938(?)- .... **CLC 26**
See also CA 112; 138; IDFW 3

Bakunin, Mikhail (Alexandrovich) 1814-1876 .... **NCLC 25, 58**
See also DLB 277

Baldwin, James (Arthur) 1924-1987. **BLC 1; CLC 1, 2, 3, 4, 5, 8, 13, 15, 17, 42, 50, 67, 90, 127; DC 1; SSC 10, 33; WLC**
See also AAYA 4, 34; AFAW 1, 2; AMWR 2; AMWS 1; BPFB 1; BW 1; CA 1-4R; 124; CABS 1; CAD; CANR 3, 24; CDALB 1941-1968; CPW; DA; DA3; DAB; DAC; DAM MST, MULT, NOV, POP; DFS 11, 15; DLB 2, 7, 33, 249, 278; DLBY 1987; EWL 3; EXPS; LAIT 5; MTCW 1, 2; NCFS 4; NFS 4; RGAL 4; RGSF 2; SATA 9; SATA-Obit 54; SSFS 2, 18; TUS

Baldwin, William c. 1515-c. 1563 ...... **LC 113**
See also DLB 132

Bale, John 1495-1563 .... **LC 62**
See also DLB 132; RGEL 2; TEA

Ball, Hugo 1886-1927 .... **TCLC 104**

Ballard, J(ames) G(raham) 1930- . **CLC 3, 6, 14, 36, 137; SSC 1, 53**
See also AAYA 3, 52; BRWS 5; CA 5-8R; CANR 15, 39, 65, 107, 133; CN 7; DA3; DAM NOV, POP; DLB 14, 207, 261; EWL 3; HGG; MTCW 1, 2; NFS 8; RGEL 2; RGSF 2; SATA 93; SFW 4

Balmont, Konstantin (Dmitriyevich) 1867-1943 .... **TCLC 11**
See also CA 109; 155; DLB 295; EWL 3

Baltausis, Vincas 1847-1910
See Mikszath, Kalman

Balzac, Honore de 1799-1850 ... **NCLC 5, 35, 53, 153; SSC 5, 59; WLC**
See also DA; DA3; DAB; DAC; DAM MST, NOV; DLB 119; EW 5; GFL 1789 to the Present; LMFS 1; RGSF 2; RGWL 2, 3; SSFS 10; SUFW; TWA

Bambara, Toni Cade 1939-1995 .... **BLC 1; CLC 19, 88; SSC 35; TCLC 116; WLCS**
See also AAYA 5, 49; AFAW 2; AMWS 11; BW 2, 3; BYA 12, 14; CA 29-32R; 150; CANR 24, 49, 81; CDALBS; DA; DA3; DAC; DAM MST, MULT; DLB 38, 218; EXPS; MTCW 1, 2; RGAL 4; RGSF 2; SATA 112; SSFS 4, 7, 12

Bamdad, A.
See Shamlu, Ahmad

Bamdad, Alef
See Shamlu, Ahmad

Banat, D. R.
See Bradbury, Ray (Douglas)

Bancroft, Laura
See Baum, L(yman) Frank

Banim, John 1798-1842 .... **NCLC 13**
See also DLB 116, 158, 159; RGEL 2

Banim, Michael 1796-1874 .... **NCLC 13**
See also DLB 158, 159

Banjo, The
See Paterson, A(ndrew) B(arton)

Banks, Iain
See Banks, Iain M(enzies)

Banks, Iain M(enzies) 1954- .... **CLC 34**
See also CA 123; 128; CANR 61, 106; DLB 194, 261; EWL 3; HGG; INT CA-128; SFW 4

Banks, Lynne Reid .... **CLC 23**
See Reid Banks, Lynne
See also AAYA 6; BYA 7; CLR 86

Banks, Russell (Earl) 1940- .... **CLC 37, 72, 187; SSC 42**
See also AAYA 45; AMWS 5; CA 65-68; CAAS 15; CANR 19, 52, 73, 118; CN 7; DLB 130, 278; EWL 3; NFS 13

Banville, John 1945- .... **CLC 46, 118**
See also CA 117; 128; CANR 104; CN 7; DLB 14, 271; INT CA-128

Banville, Theodore (Faullain) de 1832-1891 .... **NCLC 9**
See also DLB 217; GFL 1789 to the Present

Baraka, Amiri 1934- .... BLC 1; CLC 1, 2, 3, 5, 10, 14, 33, 115; DC 6; PC 4; WLCS
See Jones, LeRoi
See also AFAW 1, 2; AMWS 2; BW 2, 3; CA 21-24R; CABS 3; CAD; CANR 27, 38, 61, 133; CD 5; CDALB 1941-1968; CP 7; CPW; DA; DA3; DAC; DAM MST, MULT, POET, POP; DFS 3, 11, 16; DLB 5, 7, 16, 38; DLBD 8; EWL 3; LMFS 2; MTCW 1, 2; PFS 9; RGAL 4; TUS; WP

Baratynsky, Evgenii Abramovich 1800-1844 .... NCLC 103
See also DLB 205

Barbauld, Anna Laetitia 1743-1825 .... NCLC 50
See also DLB 107, 109, 142, 158; RGEL 2

Barbellion, W. N. P. .... TCLC 24
See Cummings, Bruce F(rederick)

Barber, Benjamin R. 1939- .... CLC 141
See also CA 29-32R; CANR 12, 32, 64, 119

Barbera, Jack (Vincent) 1945- .... CLC 44
See also CA 110; CANR 45

Barbey d'Aurevilly, Jules-Amedee 1808-1889 .... NCLC 1; SSC 17
See also DLB 119; GFL 1789 to the Present

Barbour, John c. 1316-1395 .... CMLC 33
See also DLB 146

Barbusse, Henri 1873-1935 .... TCLC 5
See also CA 105; 154; DLB 65; EWL 3; RGWL 2, 3

Barclay, Alexander c. 1475-1552 .... LC 109
See also DLB 132

Barclay, Bill
See Moorcock, Michael (John)

Barclay, William Ewert
See Moorcock, Michael (John)

Barea, Arturo 1897-1957 .... TCLC 14
See also CA 111; 201

Barfoot, Joan 1946- .... CLC 18
See also CA 105

Barham, Richard Harris 1788-1845 .... NCLC 77
See also DLB 159

Baring, Maurice 1874-1945 .... TCLC 8
See also CA 105; 168; DLB 34; HGG

Baring-Gould, Sabine 1834-1924 ... TCLC 88
See also DLB 156, 190

Barker, Clive 1952- .... CLC 52, 205; SSC 53
See also AAYA 10, 54; BEST 90:3; BPFB 1; CA 121; 129; CANR 71, 111, 133; CPW; DA3; DAM POP; DLB 261; HGG; INT CA-129; MTCW 1, 2; SUFW 2

Barker, George Granville 1913-1991 .... CLC 8, 48
See also CA 9-12R; 135; CANR 7, 38; DAM POET; DLB 20; EWL 3; MTCW 1

Barker, Harley Granville
See Granville-Barker, Harley
See also DLB 10

Barker, Howard 1946- .... CLC 37
See also CA 102; CBD; CD 5; DLB 13, 233

Barker, Jane 1652-1732 .... LC 42, 82
See also DLB 39, 131

Barker, Pat(ricia) 1943- ...... CLC 32, 94, 146
See also BRWS 4; CA 117; 122; CANR 50, 101; CN 7; DLB 271; INT CA-122

Barlach, Ernst (Heinrich) 1870-1938 .... TCLC 84
See also CA 178; DLB 56, 118; EWL 3

Barlow, Joel 1754-1812 .... NCLC 23
See also AMWS 2; DLB 37; RGAL 4

Barnard, Mary (Ethel) 1909- .... CLC 48
See also CA 21-22; CAP 2

Barnes, Djuna 1892-1982 .... CLC 3, 4, 8, 11, 29, 127; SSC 3
See Steptoe, Lydia
See also AMWS 3; CA 9-12R; 107; CAD; CANR 16, 55; CWD; DLB 4, 9, 45; EWL 3; GLL 1; MTCW 1, 2; RGAL 4; TUS

Barnes, Jim 1933- .... NNAL
See also CA 108, 175; CAAE 175; CAAS 28; DLB 175

Barnes, Julian (Patrick) 1946- . CLC 42, 141
See also BRWS 4; CA 102; CANR 19, 54, 115; CN 7; DAB; DLB 194; DLBY 1993; EWL 3; MTCW 1

Barnes, Peter 1931-2004 .... CLC 5, 56
See also CA 65-68; CAAS 12; CANR 33, 34, 64, 113; CBD; CD 5; DFS 6; DLB 13, 233; MTCW 1

Barnes, William 1801-1886 .... NCLC 75
See also DLB 32

Baroja (y Nessi), Pio 1872-1956 .... HLC 1; TCLC 8
See also CA 104; EW 9

Baron, David
See Pinter, Harold

Baron Corvo
See Rolfe, Frederick (William Serafino Austin Lewis Mary)

Barondess, Sue K(aufman) 1926-1977 .... CLC 8
See Kaufman, Sue
See also CA 1-4R; 69-72; CANR 1

Baron de Teive
See Pessoa, Fernando (Antonio Nogueira)

Baroness Von S.
See Zangwill, Israel

Barres, (Auguste-)Maurice 1862-1923 .... TCLC 47
See also CA 164; DLB 123; GFL 1789 to the Present

Barreto, Afonso Henrique de Lima
See Lima Barreto, Afonso Henrique de

Barrett, Andrea 1954- .... CLC 150
See also CA 156; CANR 92

Barrett, Michele .... CLC 65

Barrett, (Roger) Syd 1946- .... CLC 35

Barrett, William (Christopher) 1913-1992 .... CLC 27
See also CA 13-16R; 139; CANR 11, 67; INT CANR-11

Barrett Browning, Elizabeth 1806-1861 ... NCLC 1, 16, 61, 66; PC 6, 62; WLC
See also BRW 4; CDBLB 1832-1890; DA; DA3; DAB; DAC; DAM MST, POET; DLB 32, 199; EXPP; PAB; PFS 2, 16; TEA; WLIT 4; WP

Barrie, J(ames) M(atthew) 1860-1937 .... TCLC 2, 164
See also BRWS 3; BYA 4, 5; CA 104; 136; CANR 77; CDBLB 1890-1914; CLR 16; CWRI 5; DA3; DAB; DAM DRAM; DFS 7; DLB 10, 141, 156; EWL 3; FANT; MAICYA 1, 2; MTCW 1; SATA 100; SUFW; WCH; WLIT 4; YABC 1

Barrington, Michael
See Moorcock, Michael (John)

Barrol, Grady
See Bograd, Larry

Barry, Mike
See Malzberg, Barry N(athaniel)

Barry, Philip 1896-1949 .... TCLC 11
See also CA 109; 199; DFS 9; DLB 7, 228; RGAL 4

Bart, Andre Schwarz
See Schwarz-Bart, Andre

Barth, John (Simmons) 1930- ... CLC 1, 2, 3, 5, 7, 9, 10, 14, 27, 51, 89; SSC 10
See also AITN 1, 2; AMW; BPFB 1; CA 1-4R; CABS 1; CANR 5, 23, 49, 64, 113; CN 7; DAM NOV; DLB 2, 227; EWL 3; FANT; MTCW 1; RGAL 4; RGSF 2; RHW; SSFS 6; TUS

Barthelme, Donald 1931-1989 ... CLC 1, 2, 3, 5, 6, 8, 13, 23, 46, 59, 115; SSC 2, 55
See also AMWS 4; BPFB 1; CA 21-24R; 129; CANR 20, 58; DA3; DAM NOV; DLB 2, 234; DLBY 1980, 1989; EWL 3; FANT; LMFS 2; MTCW 1, 2; RGAL 4; RGSF 2; SATA 7; SATA-Obit 62; SSFS 17

Barthelme, Frederick 1943- ...... CLC 36, 117
See also AMWS 11; CA 114; 122; CANR 77; CN 7; CSW; DLB 244; DLBY 1985; EWL 3; INT CA-122

Barthes, Roland (Gerard) 1915-1980 .... CLC 24, 83; TCLC 135
See also CA 130; 97-100; CANR 66; DLB 296; EW 13; EWL 3; GFL 1789 to the Present; MTCW 1, 2; TWA

Bartram, William 1739-1823 .... NCLC 145
See also ANW; DLB 37

Barzun, Jacques (Martin) 1907- ..... CLC 51, 145
See also CA 61-64; CANR 22, 95

Bashevis, Isaac
See Singer, Isaac Bashevis

Bashkirtseff, Marie 1859-1884 .... NCLC 27

Basho, Matsuo
See Matsuo Basho
See also PFS 18; RGWL 2, 3; WP

Basil of Caesaria c. 330-379 .... CMLC 35

Basket, Raney
See Edgerton, Clyde (Carlyle)

Bass, Kingsley B., Jr.
See Bullins, Ed

Bass, Rick 1958- .... CLC 79, 143; SSC 60
See also ANW; CA 126; CANR 53, 93; CSW; DLB 212, 275

Bassani, Giorgio 1916-2000 .... CLC 9
See also CA 65-68; 190; CANR 33; CWW 2; DLB 128, 177, 299; EWL 3; MTCW 1; RGWL 2, 3

Bastian, Ann .... CLC 70

Bastos, Augusto (Antonio) Roa
See Roa Bastos, Augusto (Antonio)

Bataille, Georges 1897-1962 .... CLC 29; TCLC 155
See also CA 101; 89-92; EWL 3

Bates, H(erbert) E(rnest) 1905-1974 .... CLC 46; SSC 10
See also CA 93-96; 45-48; CANR 34; DA3; DAB; DAM POP; DLB 162, 191; EWL 3; EXPS; MTCW 1, 2; RGSF 2; SSFS 7

Bauchart
See Camus, Albert

Baudelaire, Charles 1821-1867 . NCLC 6, 29, 55; PC 1; SSC 18; WLC
See also DA; DA3; DAB; DAC; DAM MST, POET; DLB 217; EW 7; GFL 1789 to the Present; LMFS 2; PFS 21; RGWL 2, 3; TWA

Baudouin, Marcel
See Peguy, Charles (Pierre)

Baudouin, Pierre
See Peguy, Charles (Pierre)

Baudrillard, Jean 1929- .... CLC 60
See also DLB 296

Baum, L(yman) Frank 1856-1919 .. TCLC 7, 132
See also AAYA 46; BYA 16; CA 108; 133; CLR 15; CWRI 5; DLB 22; FANT; JRDA; MAICYA 1, 2; MTCW 1, 2; NFS 13; RGAL 4; SATA 18, 100; WCH

Baum, Louis F.
See Baum, L(yman) Frank

Baumbach, Jonathan 1933- .... **CLC 6, 23**
See also CA 13-16R; CAAS 5; CANR 12, 66; CN 7; DLBY 1980; INT CANR-12; MTCW 1

Bausch, Richard (Carl) 1945- .... **CLC 51**
See also AMWS 7; CA 101; CAAS 14; CANR 43, 61, 87; CSW; DLB 130

Baxter, Charles (Morley) 1947- . **CLC 45, 78**
See also CA 57-60; CANR 40, 64, 104, 133; CPW; DAM POP; DLB 130; MTCW 2

Baxter, George Owen
See Faust, Frederick (Schiller)

Baxter, James K(eir) 1926-1972 .... **CLC 14**
See also CA 77-80; EWL 3

Baxter, John
See Hunt, E(verette) Howard, (Jr.)

Bayer, Sylvia
See Glassco, John

Baynton, Barbara 1857-1929 .... **TCLC 57**
See also DLB 230; RGSF 2

Beagle, Peter S(oyer) 1939- .... **CLC 7, 104**
See also AAYA 47; BPFB 1; BYA 9, 10, 16; CA 9-12R; CANR 4, 51, 73, 110; DA3; DLBY 1980; FANT; INT CANR-4; MTCW 1; SATA 60, 130; SUFW 1, 2; YAW

Bean, Normal
See Burroughs, Edgar Rice

Beard, Charles A(ustin)
1874-1948 .... **TCLC 15**
See also CA 115; 189; DLB 17; SATA 18

Beardsley, Aubrey 1872-1898 .... **NCLC 6**

Beattie, Ann 1947- ..... **CLC 8, 13, 18, 40, 63, 146; SSC 11**
See also AMWS 5; BEST 90:2; BPFB 1; CA 81-84; CANR 53, 73, 128; CN 7; CPW; DA3; DAM NOV, POP; DLB 218, 278; DLBY 1982; EWL 3; MTCW 1, 2; RGAL 4; RGSF 2; SSFS 9; TUS

Beattie, James 1735-1803 .... **NCLC 25**
See also DLB 109

Beauchamp, Kathleen Mansfield 1888-1923
See Mansfield, Katherine
See also CA 104; 134; DA; DA3; DAC; DAM MST; MTCW 2; TEA

Beaumarchais, Pierre-Augustin Caron de
1732-1799 .... **DC 4; LC 61**
See also DAM DRAM; DFS 14, 16; EW 4; GFL Beginnings to 1789; RGWL 2, 3

Beaumont, Francis 1584(?)-1616 .. **DC 6; LC 33**
See also BRW 2; CDBLB Before 1660; DLB 58; TEA

Beauvoir, Simone (Lucie Ernestine Marie Bertrand) de 1908-1986 .... **CLC 1, 2, 4, 8, 14, 31, 44, 50, 71, 124; SSC 35; WLC**
See also BPFB 1; CA 9-12R; 118; CANR 28, 61; DA; DA3; DAB; DAC; DAM MST, NOV; DLB 72; DLBY 1986; EW 12; EWL 3; FW; GFL 1789 to the Present; LMFS 2; MTCW 1, 2; RGSF 2; RGWL 2, 3; TWA

Becker, Carl (Lotus) 1873-1945 ..... **TCLC 63**
See also CA 157; DLB 17

Becker, Jurek 1937-1997 .... **CLC 7, 19**
See also CA 85-88; 157; CANR 60, 117; CWW 2; DLB 75, 299; EWL 3

Becker, Walter 1950- .... **CLC 26**

Beckett, Samuel (Barclay)
1906-1989 .. **CLC 1, 2, 3, 4, 6, 9, 10, 11, 14, 18, 29, 57, 59, 83; DC 22; SSC 16, 74; TCLC 145; WLC**
See also BRWC 2; BRWR 1; BRWS 1; CA 5-8R; 130; CANR 33, 61; CBD; CDBLB 1945-1960; DA; DA3; DAB; DAC; DAM DRAM, MST, NOV; DFS 2, 7, 18; DLB 13, 15, 233; DLBY 1990; EWL 3; GFL 1789 to the Present; LATS 1:2; LMFS 2; MTCW 1, 2; RGSF 2; RGWL 2, 3; SSFS 15; TEA; WLIT 4

Beckford, William 1760-1844 .... **NCLC 16**
See also BRW 3; DLB 39, 213; HGG; LMFS 1; SUFW

Beckham, Barry (Earl) 1944- .... **BLC 1**
See also BW 1; CA 29-32R; CANR 26, 62; CN 7; DAM MULT; DLB 33

Beckman, Gunnel 1910- .... **CLC 26**
See also CA 33-36R; CANR 15, 114; CLR 25; MAICYA 1, 2; SAAS 9; SATA 6

Becque, Henri 1837-1899 .... **DC 21; NCLC 3**
See also DLB 192; GFL 1789 to the Present

Becquer, Gustavo Adolfo
1836-1870 .... **HLCS 1; NCLC 106**
See also DAM MULT

Beddoes, Thomas Lovell 1803-1849 .. **DC 15; NCLC 3, 154**
See also DLB 96

Bede c. 673-735 .... **CMLC 20**
See also DLB 146; TEA

Bedford, Denton R. 1907-(?) .... **NNAL**

Bedford, Donald F.
See Fearing, Kenneth (Flexner)

Beecher, Catharine Esther
1800-1878 .... **NCLC 30**
See also DLB 1, 243

Beecher, John 1904-1980 .... **CLC 6**
See also AITN 1; CA 5-8R; 105; CANR 8

Beer, Johann 1655-1700 .... **LC 5**
See also DLB 168

Beer, Patricia 1924- .... **CLC 58**
See also CA 61-64; 183; CANR 13, 46; CP 7; CWP; DLB 40; FW

Beerbohm, Max
See Beerbohm, (Henry) Max(imilian)

Beerbohm, (Henry) Max(imilian)
1872-1956 .... **TCLC 1, 24**
See also BRWS 2; CA 104; 154; CANR 79; DLB 34, 100; FANT

Beer-Hofmann, Richard
1866-1945 .... **TCLC 60**
See also CA 160; DLB 81

Beg, Shemus
See Stephens, James

Begiebing, Robert J(ohn) 1946- .... **CLC 70**
See also CA 122; CANR 40, 88

Begley, Louis 1933- .... **CLC 197**
See also CA 140; CANR 98; DLB 299

Behan, Brendan (Francis)
1923-1964 .... **CLC 1, 8, 11, 15, 79**
See also BRWS 2; CA 73-76; CANR 33, 121; CBD; CDBLB 1945-1960; DAM DRAM; DFS 7; DLB 13, 233; EWL 3; MTCW 1, 2

Behn, Aphra 1640(?)-1689 .. **DC 4; LC 1, 30, 42; PC 13; WLC**
See also BRWS 3; DA; DA3; DAB; DAC; DAM DRAM, MST, NOV, POET; DFS 16; DLB 39, 80, 131; FW; TEA; WLIT 3

Behrman, S(amuel) N(athaniel)
1893-1973 .... **CLC 40**
See also CA 13-16; 45-48; CAD; CAP 1; DLB 7, 44; IDFW 3; RGAL 4

Belasco, David 1853-1931 .... **TCLC 3**
See also CA 104; 168; DLB 7; RGAL 4

Belcheva, Elisaveta Lyubomirova
1893-1991 .... **CLC 10**
See Bagryana, Elisaveta

Beldone, Phil "Cheech"
See Ellison, Harlan (Jay)

Beleno
See Azuela, Mariano

Belinski, Vissarion Grigoryevich
1811-1848 .... **NCLC 5**
See also DLB 198

Belitt, Ben 1911- .... **CLC 22**
See also CA 13-16R; CAAS 4; CANR 7, 77; CP 7; DLB 5

Belknap, Jeremy 1744-1798 .... **LC 115**
See also DLB 30, 37

Bell, Gertrude (Margaret Lowthian)
1868-1926 .... **TCLC 67**
See also CA 167; CANR 110; DLB 174

Bell, J. Freeman
See Zangwill, Israel

Bell, James Madison 1826-1902 .... **BLC 1; TCLC 43**
See also BW 1; CA 122; 124; DAM MULT; DLB 50

Bell, Madison Smartt 1957- ...... **CLC 41, 102**
See also AMWS 10; BPFB 1; CA 111, 183; CAAE 183; CANR 28, 54, 73, 134; CN 7; CSW; DLB 218, 278; MTCW 1

Bell, Marvin (Hartley) 1937- .... **CLC 8, 31**
See also CA 21-24R; CAAS 14; CANR 59, 102; CP 7; DAM POET; DLB 5; MTCW 1

Bell, W. L. D.
See Mencken, H(enry) L(ouis)

Bellamy, Atwood C.
See Mencken, H(enry) L(ouis)

Bellamy, Edward 1850-1898 ..... **NCLC 4, 86, 147**
See also DLB 12; NFS 15; RGAL 4; SFW 4

Belli, Gioconda 1948- .... **HLCS 1**
See also CA 152; CWW 2; DLB 290; EWL 3; RGWL 3

Bellin, Edward J.
See Kuttner, Henry

Bello, Andres 1781-1865 .... **NCLC 131**
See also LAW

Belloc, (Joseph) Hilaire (Pierre Sebastien Rene Swanton) 1870-1953 .... **PC 24; TCLC 7, 18**
See also CA 106; 152; CLR 102; CWRI 5; DAM POET; DLB 19, 100, 141, 174; EWL 3; MTCW 1; SATA 112; WCH; YABC 1

Belloc, Joseph Peter Rene Hilaire
See Belloc, (Joseph) Hilaire (Pierre Sebastien Rene Swanton)

Belloc, Joseph Pierre Hilaire
See Belloc, (Joseph) Hilaire (Pierre Sebastien Rene Swanton)

Belloc, M. A.
See Lowndes, Marie Adelaide (Belloc)

Belloc-Lowndes, Mrs.
See Lowndes, Marie Adelaide (Belloc)

Bellow, Saul 1915- . **CLC 1, 2, 3, 6, 8, 10, 13, 15, 25, 33, 34, 63, 79, 190, 200; SSC 14; WLC**
See also AITN 2; AMW; AMWC 2; AMWR 2; BEST 89:3; BPFB 1; CA 5-8R; CABS 1; CANR 29, 53, 95, 132; CDALB 1941-1968; CN 7; DA; DA3; DAB; DAC; DAM MST, NOV, POP; DLB 2, 28, 299; DLBD 3; DLBY 1982; EWL 3; MTCW 1, 2; NFS 4, 14; RGAL 4; RGSF 2; SSFS 12; TUS

Belser, Reimond Karel Maria de 1929-
See Ruyslinck, Ward
See also CA 152

Bely, Andrey .... **PC 11; TCLC 7**
See Bugayev, Boris Nikolayevich
See also DLB 295; EW 9; EWL 3; MTCW 1

Belyi, Andrei
See Bugayev, Boris Nikolayevich
See also RGWL 2, 3

Bembo, Pietro 1470-1547 .... **LC 79**
See also RGWL 2, 3

Benary, Margot
See Benary-Isbert, Margot

Benary-Isbert, Margot 1889-1979 .... **CLC 12**
See also CA 5-8R; 89-92; CANR 4, 72; CLR 12; MAICYA 1, 2; SATA 2; SATA-Obit 21

Benavente (y Martinez), Jacinto 1866-1954 .... **HLCS 1; TCLC 3**
See also CA 106; 131; CANR 81; DAM DRAM, MULT; EWL 3; GLL 2; HW 1, 2; MTCW 1, 2

Benchley, Peter (Bradford) 1940- .. **CLC 4, 8**
See also AAYA 14; AITN 2; BPFB 1; CA 17-20R; CANR 12, 35, 66, 115; CPW; DAM NOV, POP; HGG; MTCW 1, 2; SATA 3, 89

Benchley, Robert (Charles) 1889-1945 .... **TCLC 1, 55**
See also CA 105; 153; DLB 11; RGAL 4

Benda, Julien 1867-1956 .... **TCLC 60**
See also CA 120; 154; GFL 1789 to the Present

Benedict, Ruth (Fulton) 1887-1948 .... **TCLC 60**
See also CA 158; DLB 246

Benedikt, Michael 1935- .... **CLC 4, 14**
See also CA 13-16R; CANR 7; CP 7; DLB 5

Benet, Juan 1927-1993 .... **CLC 28**
See also CA 143; EWL 3

Benet, Stephen Vincent 1898-1943 ..... **PC 64; SSC 10; TCLC 7**
See also AMWS 11; CA 104; 152; DA3; DAM POET; DLB 4, 48, 102, 249, 284; DLBY 1997; EWL 3; HGG; MTCW 1; RGAL 4; RGSF 2; SUFW; WP; YABC 1

Benet, William Rose 1886-1950 ..... **TCLC 28**
See also CA 118; 152; DAM POET; DLB 45; RGAL 4

Benford, Gregory (Albert) 1941- ...... **CLC 52**
See also BPFB 1; CA 69-72, 175; CAAE 175; CAAS 27; CANR 12, 24, 49, 95, 134; CSW; DLBY 1982; SCFW 2; SFW 4

Bengtsson, Frans (Gunnar) 1894-1954 .... **TCLC 48**
See also CA 170; EWL 3

Benjamin, David
See Slavitt, David R(ytman)

Benjamin, Lois
See Gould, Lois

Benjamin, Walter 1892-1940 .... **TCLC 39**
See also CA 164; DLB 242; EW 11; EWL 3

Ben Jelloun, Tahar 1944-
See Jelloun, Tahar ben
See also CA 135; CWW 2; EWL 3; RGWL 3; WLIT 2

Benn, Gottfried 1886-1956 .. **PC 35; TCLC 3**
See also CA 106; 153; DLB 56; EWL 3; RGWL 2, 3

Bennett, Alan 1934- .... **CLC 45, 77**
See also BRWS 8; CA 103; CANR 35, 55, 106; CBD; CD 5; DAB; DAM MST; MTCW 1, 2

Bennett, (Enoch) Arnold 1867-1931 .... **TCLC 5, 20**
See also BRW 6; CA 106; 155; CDBLB 1890-1914; DLB 10, 34, 98, 135; EWL 3; MTCW 2

Bennett, Elizabeth
See Mitchell, Margaret (Munnerlyn)

Bennett, George Harold 1930-
See Bennett, Hal
See also BW 1; CA 97-100; CANR 87

Bennett, Gwendolyn B. 1902-1981 .... **HR 2**
See also BW 1; CA 125; DLB 51; WP

Bennett, Hal .... **CLC 5**
See Bennett, George Harold
See also DLB 33

Bennett, Jay 1912- .... **CLC 35**
See also AAYA 10; CA 69-72; CANR 11, 42, 79; JRDA; SAAS 4; SATA 41, 87; SATA-Brief 27; WYA; YAW

Bennett, Louise (Simone) 1919- .... **BLC 1; CLC 28**
See also BW 2, 3; CA 151; CDWLB 3; CP 7; DAM MULT; DLB 117; EWL 3

Benson, A. C. 1862-1925 .... **TCLC 123**
See also DLB 98

Benson, E(dward) F(rederic) 1867-1940 .... **TCLC 27**
See also CA 114; 157; DLB 135, 153; HGG; SUFW 1

Benson, Jackson J. 1930- .... **CLC 34**
See also CA 25-28R; DLB 111

Benson, Sally 1900-1972 .... **CLC 17**
See also CA 19-20; 37-40R; CAP 1; SATA 1, 35; SATA-Obit 27

Benson, Stella 1892-1933 .... **TCLC 17**
See also CA 117; 154, 155; DLB 36, 162; FANT; TEA

Bentham, Jeremy 1748-1832 .... **NCLC 38**
See also DLB 107, 158, 252

Bentley, E(dmund) C(lerihew) 1875-1956 .... **TCLC 12**
See also CA 108; DLB 70; MSW

Bentley, Eric (Russell) 1916- .... **CLC 24**
See also CA 5-8R; CAD; CANR 6, 67; CBD; CD 5; INT CANR-6

ben Uzair, Salem
See Horne, Richard Henry Hengist

Beranger, Pierre Jean de 1780-1857 .... **NCLC 34**

Berdyaev, Nicolas
See Berdyaev, Nikolai (Aleksandrovich)

Berdyaev, Nikolai (Aleksandrovich) 1874-1948 .... **TCLC 67**
See also CA 120; 157

Berdyayev, Nikolai (Aleksandrovich)
See Berdyaev, Nikolai (Aleksandrovich)

Berendt, John (Lawrence) 1939- ...... **CLC 86**
See also CA 146; CANR 75, 93; DA3; MTCW 1

Beresford, J(ohn) D(avys) 1873-1947 .... **TCLC 81**
See also CA 112; 155; DLB 162, 178, 197; SFW 4; SUFW 1

Bergelson, David (Rafailovich) 1884-1952 .... **TCLC 81**
See Bergelson, Dovid
See also CA 220

Bergelson, Dovid
See Bergelson, David (Rafailovich)
See also EWL 3

Berger, Colonel
See Malraux, (Georges-)Andre

Berger, John (Peter) 1926- .... **CLC 2, 19**
See also BRWS 4; CA 81-84; CANR 51, 78, 117; CN 7; DLB 14, 207

Berger, Melvin H. 1927- .... **CLC 12**
See also CA 5-8R; CANR 4; CLR 32; SAAS 2; SATA 5, 88; SATA-Essay 124

Berger, Thomas (Louis) 1924- .. **CLC 3, 5, 8, 11, 18, 38**
See also BPFB 1; CA 1-4R; CANR 5, 28, 51, 128; CN 7; DAM NOV; DLB 2; DLBY 1980; EWL 3; FANT; INT CANR-28; MTCW 1, 2; RHW; TCWW 2

Bergman, (Ernst) Ingmar 1918- ...... **CLC 16, 72**
See also CA 81-84; CANR 33, 70; CWW 2; DLB 257; MTCW 2

Bergson, Henri(-Louis) 1859-1941 . **TCLC 32**
See also CA 164; EW 8; EWL 3; GFL 1789 to the Present

Bergstein, Eleanor 1938- .... **CLC 4**
See also CA 53-56; CANR 5

Berkeley, George 1685-1753 .... **LC 65**
See also DLB 31, 101, 252

Berkoff, Steven 1937- .... **CLC 56**
See also CA 104; CANR 72; CBD; CD 5

Berlin, Isaiah 1909-1997 .... **TCLC 105**
See also CA 85-88; 162

Bermant, Chaim (Icyk) 1929-1998 ... **CLC 40**
See also CA 57-60; CANR 6, 31, 57, 105; CN 7

Bern, Victoria
See Fisher, M(ary) F(rances) K(ennedy)

Bernanos, (Paul Louis) Georges 1888-1948 .... **TCLC 3**
See also CA 104; 130; CANR 94; DLB 72; EWL 3; GFL 1789 to the Present; RGWL 2, 3

Bernard, April 1956- .... **CLC 59**
See also CA 131

Bernard of Clairvaux 1090-1153 .. **CMLC 71**
See also DLB 208

Berne, Victoria
See Fisher, M(ary) F(rances) K(ennedy)

Bernhard, Thomas 1931-1989 ..... **CLC 3, 32, 61; DC 14**
See also CA 85-88; 127; CANR 32, 57; CDWLB 2; DLB 85, 124; EWL 3; MTCW 1; RGWL 2, 3

Bernhardt, Sarah (Henriette Rosine) 1844-1923 .... **TCLC 75**
See also CA 157

Bernstein, Charles 1950- .... **CLC 142,**
See also CA 129; CAAS 24; CANR 90; CP 7; DLB 169

Bernstein, Ingrid
See Kirsch, Sarah

Beroul fl. c. 1150- .... **CMLC 75**

Berriault, Gina 1926-1999 .... **CLC 54, 109; SSC 30**
See also CA 116; 129; 185; CANR 66; DLB 130; SSFS 7,11

Berrigan, Daniel 1921- .... **CLC 4**
See also CA 33-36R; CAAE 187; CAAS 1; CANR 11, 43, 78; CP 7; DLB 5

Berrigan, Edmund Joseph Michael, Jr. 1934-1983
See Berrigan, Ted
See also CA 61-64; 110; CANR 14, 102

Berrigan, Ted .... **CLC 37**
See Berrigan, Edmund Joseph Michael, Jr.
See also DLB 5, 169; WP

Berry, Charles Edward Anderson 1931-
See Berry, Chuck
See also CA 115

Berry, Chuck .... **CLC 17**
See Berry, Charles Edward Anderson

Berry, Jonas
See Ashbery, John (Lawrence)
See also GLL 1

Berry, Wendell (Erdman) 1934- ... **CLC 4, 6, 8, 27, 46; PC 28**
See also AITN 1; AMWS 10; ANW; CA 73-76; CANR 50, 73, 101, 132; CP 7; CSW; DAM POET; DLB 5, 6, 234, 275; MTCW 1

Berryman, John 1914-1972 ... **CLC 1, 2, 3, 4, 6, 8, 10, 13, 25, 62; PC 64**
See also AMW; CA 13-16; 33-36R; CABS 2; CANR 35; CAP 1; CDALB 1941-1968; DAM POET; DLB 48; EWL 3; MTCW 1, 2; PAB; RGAL 4; WP

Bertolucci, Bernardo 1940- ...... **CLC 16, 157**
See also CA 106; CANR 125

Berton, Pierre (Francis Demarigny) 1920-2004 .... **CLC 104**
See also CA 1-4R; CANR 2, 56; CPW; DLB 68; SATA 99

Bertrand, Aloysius 1807-1841 .... **NCLC 31**
See Bertrand, Louis oAloysiusc

Bertrand, Louis oAloysiusc
See Bertrand, Aloysius
See also DLB 217

Bertran de Born c. 1140-1215 .... **CMLC 5**

Besant, Annie (Wood) 1847-1933 ..... **TCLC 9**
See also CA 105; 185

Bessie, Alvah 1904-1985 .... **CLC 23**
See also CA 5-8R; 116; CANR 2, 80; DLB 26

Bestuzhev, Aleksandr Aleksandrovich
1797-1837 .... **NCLC 131**
See also DLB 198

Bethlen, T. D.
See Silverberg, Robert

Beti, Mongo .... **BLC 1; CLC 27**
See Biyidi, Alexandre
See also AFW; CANR 79; DAM MULT; EWL 3; WLIT 2

Betjeman, John 1906-1984 ...... **CLC 2, 6, 10, 34, 43**
See also BRW 7; CA 9-12R; 112; CANR 33, 56; CDBLB 1945-1960; DA3; DAB; DAM MST, POET; DLB 20; DLBY 1984; EWL 3; MTCW 1, 2

Bettelheim, Bruno 1903-1990 .... **CLC 79; TCLC 143**
See also CA 81-84; 131; CANR 23, 61; DA3; MTCW 1, 2

Betti, Ugo 1892-1953 .... **TCLC 5**
See also CA 104; 155; EWL 3; RGWL 2, 3

Betts, Doris (Waugh) 1932- ..... **CLC 3, 6, 28; SSC 45**
See also CA 13-16R; CANR 9, 66, 77; CN 7; CSW; DLB 218; DLBY 1982; INT CANR-9; RGAL 4

Bevan, Alistair
See Roberts, Keith (John Kingston)

Bey, Pilaff
See Douglas, (George) Norman

Bialik, Chaim Nachman
1873-1934 .... **TCLC 25**
See also CA 170; EWL 3

Bickerstaff, Isaac
See Swift, Jonathan

Bidart, Frank 1939- .... **CLC 33**
See also CA 140; CANR 106; CP 7

Bienek, Horst 1930- .... **CLC 7, 11**
See also CA 73-76; DLB 75

Bierce, Ambrose (Gwinett)
1842-1914(?) ...... **SSC 9, 72; TCLC 1, 7, 44; WLC**
See also AAYA 55; AMW; BYA 11; CA 104; 139; CANR 78; CDALB 1865-1917; DA; DA3; DAC; DAM MST; DLB 11, 12, 23, 71, 74, 186; EWL 3; EXPS; HGG; LAIT 2; RGAL 4; RGSF 2; SSFS 9; SUFW 1

Biggers, Earl Derr 1884-1933 .... **TCLC 65**
See also CA 108; 153; DLB 306

Billiken, Bud
See Motley, Willard (Francis)

Billings, Josh
See Shaw, Henry Wheeler

Billington, (Lady) Rachel (Mary)
1942- .... **CLC 43**
See also AITN 2; CA 33-36R; CANR 44; CN 7

Binchy, Maeve 1940- .... **CLC 153**
See also BEST 90:1; BPFB 1; CA 127; 134; CANR 50, 96, 134; CN 7; CPW; DA3; DAM POP; INT CA-134; MTCW 1; RHW

Binyon, T(imothy) J(ohn) 1936- .... **CLC 34**
See also CA 111; CANR 28

Bion 335B.C.-245B.C. .... **CMLC 39**

Bioy Casares, Adolfo 1914-1999 ... **CLC 4, 8, 13, 88; HLC 1; SSC 17**
See Casares, Adolfo Bioy; Miranda, Javier; Sacastru, Martin
See also CA 29-32R; 177; CANR 19, 43, 66; CWW 2; DAM MULT; DLB 113; EWL 3; HW 1, 2; LAW; MTCW 1, 2

Birch, Allison .... **CLC 65**

Bird, Cordwainer
See Ellison, Harlan (Jay)

Bird, Robert Montgomery
1806-1854 .... **NCLC 1**
See also DLB 202; RGAL 4

Birkerts, Sven 1951- .... **CLC 116**
See also CA 128; 133, 176; CAAE 176; CAAS 29; INT CA-133

Birney, (Alfred) Earle 1904-1995 .. **CLC 1, 4, 6, 11; PC 52**
See also CA 1-4R; CANR 5, 20; CP 7; DAC; DAM MST, POET; DLB 88; MTCW 1; PFS 8; RGEL 2

Biruni, al 973-1048(?) .... **CMLC 28**

Bishop, Elizabeth 1911-1979 ... **CLC 1, 4, 9, 13, 15, 32; PC 3, 34; TCLC 121**
See also AMWR 2; AMWS 1; CA 5-8R; 89-92; CABS 2; CANR 26, 61, 108; CDALB 1968-1988; DA; DA3; DAC; DAM MST, POET; DLB 5, 169; EWL 3; GLL 2; MAWW; MTCW 1, 2; PAB; PFS 6, 12; RGAL 4; SATA-Obit 24; TUS; WP

Bishop, John 1935- .... **CLC 10**
See also CA 105

Bishop, John Peale 1892-1944 ..... **TCLC 103**
See also CA 107; 155; DLB 4, 9, 45; RGAL 4

Bissett, Bill 1939- .... **CLC 18; PC 14**
See also CA 69-72; CAAS 19; CANR 15; CCA 1; CP 7; DLB 53; MTCW 1

Bissoondath, Neil (Devindra)
1955- .... **CLC 120**
See also CA 136; CANR 123; CN 7; DAC

Bitov, Andrei (Georgievich) 1937- ... **CLC 57**
See also CA 142; DLB 302

Biyidi, Alexandre 1932-
See Beti, Mongo
See also BW 1, 3; CA 114; 124; CANR 81; DA3; MTCW 1, 2

Bjarme, Brynjolf
See Ibsen, Henrik (Johan)

Bjoernson, Bjoernstjerne (Martinius)
1832-1910 .... **TCLC 7, 37**
See also CA 104

Black, Robert
See Holdstock, Robert P.

Blackburn, Paul 1926-1971 .... **CLC 9, 43**
See also BG 2; CA 81-84; 33-36R; CANR 34; DLB 16; DLBY 1981

Black Elk 1863-1950 .... **NNAL; TCLC 33**
See also CA 144; DAM MULT; MTCW 1; WP

Black Hawk 1767-1838 .... **NNAL**

Black Hobart
See Sanders, (James) Ed(ward)

Blacklin, Malcolm
See Chambers, Aidan

Blackmore, R(ichard) D(oddridge)
1825-1900 .... **TCLC 27**
See also CA 120; DLB 18; RGEL 2

Blackmur, R(ichard) P(almer)
1904-1965 .... **CLC 2, 24**
See also AMWS 2; CA 11-12; 25-28R; CANR 71; CAP 1; DLB 63; EWL 3

Black Tarantula
See Acker, Kathy

Blackwood, Algernon (Henry)
1869-1951 .... **TCLC 5**
See also CA 105; 150; DLB 153, 156, 178; HGG; SUFW 1

Blackwood, Caroline 1931-1996 .... **CLC 6, 9, 100**
See also BRWS 9; CA 85-88; 151; CANR 32, 61, 65; CN 7; DLB 14, 207; HGG; MTCW 1

Blade, Alexander
See Hamilton, Edmond; Silverberg, Robert

Blaga, Lucian 1895-1961 .... **CLC 75**
See also CA 157; DLB 220; EWL 3

Blair, Eric (Arthur) 1903-1950 .... **TCLC 123**
See Orwell, George
See also CA 104; 132; DA; DA3; DAB; DAC; DAM MST, NOV; MTCW 1, 2; SATA 29

Blair, Hugh 1718-1800 .... **NCLC 75**

Blais, Marie-Claire 1939- .... **CLC 2, 4, 6, 13, 22**
See also CA 21-24R; CAAS 4; CANR 38, 75, 93; CWW 2; DAC; DAM MST; DLB 53; EWL 3; FW; MTCW 1, 2; TWA

Blaise, Clark 1940- .... **CLC 29**
See also AITN 2; CA 53-56; CAAS 3; CANR 5, 66, 106; CN 7; DLB 53; RGSF 2

Blake, Fairley
See De Voto, Bernard (Augustine)

Blake, Nicholas
See Day Lewis, C(ecil)
See also DLB 77; MSW

Blake, Sterling
See Benford, Gregory (Albert)

Blake, William 1757-1827 . **NCLC 13, 37, 57, 127; PC 12, 63; WLC**
See also AAYA 47; BRW 3; BRWR 1; CDBLB 1789-1832; CLR 52; DA; DA3; DAB; DAC; DAM MST, POET; DLB 93, 163; EXPP; LATS 1:1; LMFS 1; MAI-CYA 1, 2; PAB; PFS 2, 12; SATA 30; TEA; WCH; WLIT 3; WP

Blanchot, Maurice 1907-2003 .... **CLC 135**
See also CA 117; 144; 213; DLB 72, 296; EWL 3

Blasco Ibanez, Vicente 1867-1928 . **TCLC 12**
See also BPFB 1; CA 110; 131; CANR 81; DA3; DAM NOV; EW 8; EWL 3; HW 1, 2; MTCW 1

Blatty, William Peter 1928- .... **CLC 2**
See also CA 5-8R; CANR 9, 124; DAM POP; HGG

Bleeck, Oliver
See Thomas, Ross (Elmore)

Blessing, Lee 1949- .... **CLC 54**
See also CAD; CD 5

Blight, Rose
See Greer, Germaine

Blish, James (Benjamin) 1921-1975 . **CLC 14**
See also BPFB 1; CA 1-4R; 57-60; CANR 3; DLB 8; MTCW 1; SATA 66; SCFW 2; SFW 4

Bliss, Frederick
See Card, Orson Scott

Bliss, Reginald
See Wells, H(erbert) G(eorge)

Blixen, Karen (Christentze Dinesen)
1885-1962
See Dinesen, Isak
See also CA 25-28; CANR 22, 50; CAP 2; DA3; DLB 214; LMFS 1; MTCW 1, 2; SATA 44; SSFS 20

Bloch, Robert (Albert) 1917-1994 .... **CLC 33**
See also AAYA 29; CA 5-8R, 179; 146; CAAE 179; CAAS 20; CANR 5, 78; DA3; DLB 44; HGG; INT CANR-5; MTCW 1; SATA 12; SATA-Obit 82; SFW 4; SUFW 1, 2

Blok, Alexander (Alexandrovich)
1880-1921 .... **PC 21; TCLC 5**
See also CA 104; 183; DLB 295; EW 9; EWL 3; LMFS 2; RGWL 2, 3

Blom, Jan
See Breytenbach, Breyten
Bloom, Harold 1930- .... **CLC 24, 103**
See also CA 13-16R; CANR 39, 75, 92, 133; DLB 67; EWL 3; MTCW 1; RGAL 4
Bloomfield, Aurelius
See Bourne, Randolph S(illiman)
Bloomfield, Robert 1766-1823 ..... **NCLC 145**
See also DLB 93
Blount, Roy (Alton), Jr. 1941- .... **CLC 38**
See also CA 53-56; CANR 10, 28, 61, 125; CSW; INT CANR-28; MTCW 1, 2
Blowsnake, Sam 1875-(?) .... **NNAL**
Bloy, Leon 1846-1917 .... **TCLC 22**
See also CA 121; 183; DLB 123; GFL 1789 to the Present
Blue Cloud, Peter (Aroniawenrate)
1933- .... **NNAL**
See also CA 117; CANR 40; DAM MULT
Bluggage, Oranthy
See Alcott, Louisa May
Blume, Judy (Sussman) 1938- .... **CLC 12, 30**
See also AAYA 3, 26; BYA 1, 8, 12; CA 29-32R; CANR 13, 37, 66, 124; CLR 2, 15, 69; CPW; DA3; DAM NOV, POP; DLB 52; JRDA; MAICYA 1, 2; MAICYAS 1; MTCW 1, 2; SATA 2, 31, 79, 142; WYA; YAW
Blunden, Edmund (Charles)
1896-1974 .... **CLC 2, 56**
See also BRW 6; CA 17-18; 45-48; CANR 54; CAP 2; DLB 20, 100, 155; MTCW 1; PAB
Bly, Robert (Elwood) 1926- .... **CLC 1, 2, 5, 10, 15, 38, 128; PC 39**
See also AMWS 4; CA 5-8R; CANR 41, 73, 125; CP 7; DA3; DAM POET; DLB 5; EWL 3; MTCW 1, 2; PFS 6, 17; RGAL 4
Boas, Franz 1858-1942 .... **TCLC 56**
See also CA 115; 181
Bobette
See Simenon, Georges (Jacques Christian)
Boccaccio, Giovanni 1313-1375 ... **CMLC 13, 57; SSC 10**
See also EW 2; RGSF 2; RGWL 2, 3; TWA
Bochco, Steven 1943- .... **CLC 35**
See also AAYA 11; CA 124; 138
Bode, Sigmund
See O'Doherty, Brian
Bodel, Jean 1167(?)-1210 .... **CMLC 28**
Bodenheim, Maxwell 1892-1954 .... **TCLC 44**
See also CA 110; 187; DLB 9, 45; RGAL 4
Bodenheimer, Maxwell
See Bodenheim, Maxwell
Bodker, Cecil 1927-
See Bodker, Cecil
Bodker, Cecil 1927- .... **CLC 21**
See also CA 73-76; CANR 13, 44, 111; CLR 23; MAICYA 1, 2; SATA 14, 133
Boell, Heinrich (Theodor)
1917-1985 ..... **CLC 2, 3, 6, 9, 11, 15, 27, 32, 72; SSC 23; WLC**
See Boll, Heinrich
See also CA 21-24R; 116; CANR 24; DA; DA3; DAB; DAC; DAM MST, NOV; DLB 69; DLBY 1985; MTCW 1, 2; SSFS 20; TWA
Boerne, Alfred
See Doeblin, Alfred
Boethius c. 480-c. 524 .... **CMLC 15**
See also DLB 115; RGWL 2, 3
Boff, Leonardo (Genezio Darci)
1938- .... **CLC 70; HLC 1**
See also CA 150; DAM MULT; HW 2

Bogan, Louise 1897-1970 .... **CLC 4, 39, 46, 93; PC 12**
See also AMWS 3; CA 73-76; 25-28R; CANR 33, 82; DAM POET; DLB 45, 169; EWL 3; MAWW; MTCW 1, 2; PFS 21; RGAL 4
Bogarde, Dirk
See Van Den Bogarde, Derek Jules Gaspard Ulric Niven
See also DLB 14
Bogosian, Eric 1953- .... **CLC 45, 141**
See also CA 138; CAD; CANR 102; CD 5
Bograd, Larry 1953- .... **CLC 35**
See also CA 93-96; CANR 57; SAAS 21; SATA 33, 89; WYA
Boiardo, Matteo Maria 1441-1494 .... **LC 6**
Boileau-Despreaux, Nicolas 1636-1711 . **LC 3**
See also DLB 268; EW 3; GFL Beginnings to 1789; RGWL 2, 3
Boissard, Maurice
See Leautaud, Paul
Bojer, Johan 1872-1959 .... **TCLC 64**
See also CA 189; EWL 3
Bok, Edward W(illiam)
1863-1930 .... **TCLC 101**
See also CA 217; DLB 91; DLBD 16
Boker, George Henry 1823-1890 . **NCLC 125**
See also RGAL 4
Boland, Eavan (Aisling) 1944- .. **CLC 40, 67, 113; PC 58**
See also BRWS 5; CA 143, 207; CAAE 207; CANR 61; CP 7; CWP; DAM POET; DLB 40; FW; MTCW 2; PFS 12
Boll, Heinrich
See Boell, Heinrich (Theodor)
See also BPFB 1; CDWLB 2; EW 13; EWL 3; RGSF 2; RGWL 2, 3
Bolt, Lee
See Faust, Frederick (Schiller)
Bolt, Robert (Oxton) 1924-1995 .... **CLC 14**
See also CA 17-20R; 147; CANR 35, 67; CBD; DAM DRAM; DFS 2; DLB 13, 233; EWL 3; LAIT 1; MTCW 1
Bombal, Maria Luisa 1910-1980 .... **HLCS 1; SSC 37**
See also CA 127; CANR 72; EWL 3; HW 1; LAW; RGSF 2
Bombet, Louis-Alexandre-Cesar
See Stendhal
Bomkauf
See Kaufman, Bob (Garnell)
Bonaventura .... **NCLC 35**
See also DLB 90
Bond, Edward 1934- .... **CLC 4, 6, 13, 23**
See also AAYA 50; BRWS 1; CA 25-28R; CANR 38, 67, 106; CBD; CD 5; DAM DRAM; DFS 3, 8; DLB 13; EWL 3; MTCW 1
Bonham, Frank 1914-1989 .... **CLC 12**
See also AAYA 1; BYA 1, 3; CA 9-12R; CANR 4, 36; JRDA; MAICYA 1, 2; SAAS 3; SATA 1, 49; SATA-Obit 62; TCWW 2; YAW
Bonnefoy, Yves 1923- . **CLC 9, 15, 58; PC 58**
See also CA 85-88; CANR 33, 75, 97; CWW 2; DAM MST, POET; DLB 258; EWL 3; GFL 1789 to the Present; MTCW 1, 2
Bonner, Marita .... **HR 2**
See Occomy, Marita (Odette) Bonner
Bonnin, Gertrude 1876-1938 .... **NNAL**
See Zitkala-Sa
See also CA 150; DAM MULT
Bontemps, Arna(ud Wendell)
1902-1973 ..... **BLC 1; CLC 1, 18; HR 2**
See also BW 1; CA 1-4R; 41-44R; CANR 4, 35; CLR 6; CWRI 5; DA3; DAM MULT, NOV, POET; DLB 48, 51; JRDA; MAICYA 1, 2; MTCW 1, 2; SATA 2, 44; SATA-Obit 24; WCH; WP

Boot, William
See Stoppard, Tom
Booth, Martin 1944-2004 .... **CLC 13**
See also CA 93-96, 188; 223; CAAE 188; CAAS 2; CANR 92
Booth, Philip 1925- .... **CLC 23**
See also CA 5-8R; CANR 5, 88; CP 7; DLBY 1982
Booth, Wayne C(layson) 1921- .... **CLC 24**
See also CA 1-4R; CAAS 5; CANR 3, 43, 117; DLB 67
Borchert, Wolfgang 1921-1947 .... **TCLC 5**
See also CA 104; 188; DLB 69, 124; EWL 3
Borel, Petrus 1809-1859 .... **NCLC 41**
See also DLB 119; GFL 1789 to the Present
Borges, Jorge Luis 1899-1986 ... **CLC 1, 2, 3, 4, 6, 8, 9, 10, 13, 19, 44, 48, 83; HLC 1; PC 22, 32; SSC 4, 41; TCLC 109; WLC**
See also AAYA 26; BPFB 1; CA 21-24R; CANR 19, 33, 75, 105, 133; CDWLB 3; DA; DA3; DAB; DAC; DAM MST, MULT; DLB 113, 283; DLBY 1986; DNFS 1, 2; EWL 3; HW 1, 2; LAW; LMFS 2; MSW; MTCW 1, 2; RGSF 2; RGWL 2, 3; SFW 4; SSFS 17; TWA; WLIT 1
Borowski, Tadeusz 1922-1951 .... **SSC 48; TCLC 9**
See also CA 106; 154; CDWLB 4; DLB 215; EWL 3; RGSF 2; RGWL 3; SSFS 13
Borrow, George (Henry)
1803-1881 .... **NCLC 9**
See also DLB 21, 55, 166
Bosch (Gavino), Juan 1909-2001 ..... **HLCS 1**
See also CA 151; 204; DAM MST, MULT; DLB 145; HW 1, 2
Bosman, Herman Charles
1905-1951 .... **TCLC 49**
See Malan, Herman
See also CA 160; DLB 225; RGSF 2
Bosschere, Jean de 1878(?)-1953 ... **TCLC 19**
See also CA 115; 186
Boswell, James 1740-1795 ... **LC 4, 50; WLC**
See also BRW 3; CDBLB 1660-1789; DA; DAB; DAC; DAM MST; DLB 104, 142; TEA; WLIT 3
Bottomley, Gordon 1874-1948 ..... **TCLC 107**
See also CA 120; 192; DLB 10
Bottoms, David 1949- .... **CLC 53**
See also CA 105; CANR 22; CSW; DLB 120; DLBY 1983
Boucicault, Dion 1820-1890 .... **NCLC 41**
Boucolon, Maryse
See Conde, Maryse
Bourdieu, Pierre 1930-2002 .... **CLC 198**
See also CA 130; 204
Bourget, Paul (Charles Joseph)
1852-1935 .... **TCLC 12**
See also CA 107; 196; DLB 123; GFL 1789 to the Present
Bourjaily, Vance (Nye) 1922- .... **CLC 8, 62**
See also CA 1-4R; CAAS 1; CANR 2, 72; CN 7; DLB 2, 143
Bourne, Randolph S(illiman)
1886-1918 .... **TCLC 16**
See also AMW; CA 117; 155; DLB 63
Bova, Ben(jamin William) 1932- ...... **CLC 45**
See also AAYA 16; CA 5-8R; CAAS 18; CANR 11, 56, 94, 111; CLR 3, 96; DLBY 1981; INT CANR-11; MAICYA 1, 2; MTCW 1; SATA 6, 68, 133; SFW 4
Bowen, Elizabeth (Dorothea Cole)
1899-1973 . **CLC 1, 3, 6, 11, 15, 22, 118; SSC 3, 28, 66; TCLC 148**
See also BRWS 2; CA 17-18; 41-44R; CANR 35, 105; CAP 2; CDBLB 1945-

1960; DA3; DAM NOV; DLB 15, 162; EWL 3; EXPS; FW; HGG; MTCW 1, 2; NFS 13; RGSF 2; SSFS 5; SUFW 1; TEA; WLIT 4

Bowering, George 1935- .... **CLC 15, 47**
See also CA 21-24R; CAAS 16; CANR 10; CP 7; DLB 53

Bowering, Marilyn R(uthe) 1949- .... **CLC 32**
See also CA 101; CANR 49; CP 7; CWP

Bowers, Edgar 1924-2000 .... **CLC 9**
See also CA 5-8R; 188; CANR 24; CP 7; CSW; DLB 5

Bowers, Mrs. J. Milton 1842-1914
See Bierce, Ambrose (Gwinett)

Bowie, David .... **CLC 17**
See Jones, David Robert

Bowles, Jane (Sydney) 1917-1973 ..... **CLC 3, 68**
See Bowles, Jane Auer
See also CA 19-20; 41-44R; CAP 2

Bowles, Jane Auer
See Bowles, Jane (Sydney)
See also EWL 3

Bowles, Paul (Frederick) 1910-1999 . **CLC 1, 2, 19, 53; SSC 3**
See also AMWS 4; CA 1-4R; 186; CAAS 1; CANR 1, 19, 50, 75; CN 7; DA3; DLB 5, 6, 218; EWL 3; MTCW 1, 2; RGAL 4; SSFS 17

Bowles, William Lisle 1762-1850 . **NCLC 103**
See also DLB 93

Box, Edgar
See Vidal, (Eugene Luther) Gore
See also GLL 1

Boyd, James 1888-1944 .... **TCLC 115**
See also CA 186; DLB 9; DLBD 16; RGAL 4; RHW

Boyd, Nancy
See Millay, Edna St. Vincent
See also GLL 1

Boyd, Thomas (Alexander)
1898-1935 .... **TCLC 111**
See also CA 111; 183; DLB 9; DLBD 16

Boyd, William 1952- .... **CLC 28, 53, 70**
See also CA 114; 120; CANR 51, 71, 131; CN 7; DLB 231

Boyesen, Hjalmar Hjorth
1848-1895 .... **NCLC 135**
See also DLB 12, 71; DLBD 13; RGAL 4

Boyle, Kay 1902-1992 .... **CLC 1, 5, 19, 58, 121; SSC 5**
See also CA 13-16R; 140; CAAS 1; CANR 29, 61, 110; DLB 4, 9, 48, 86; DLBY 1993; EWL 3; MTCW 1, 2; RGAL 4; RGSF 2; SSFS 10, 13, 14

Boyle, Mark
See Kienzle, William X(avier)

Boyle, Patrick 1905-1982 .... **CLC 19**
See also CA 127

Boyle, T. C.
See Boyle, T(homas) Coraghessan
See also AMWS 8

Boyle, T(homas) Coraghessan
1948- .... **CLC 36, 55, 90; SSC 16**
See Boyle, T. C.
See also AAYA 47; BEST 90:4; BPFB 1; CA 120; CANR 44, 76, 89, 132; CN 7; CPW; DA3; DAM POP; DLB 218, 278; DLBY 1986; EWL 3; MTCW 2; SSFS 13, 19

Boz
See Dickens, Charles (John Huffam)

Brackenridge, Hugh Henry
1748-1816 .... **NCLC 7**
See also DLB 11, 37; RGAL 4

Bradbury, Edward P.
See Moorcock, Michael (John)
See also MTCW 2

Bradbury, Malcolm (Stanley)
1932-2000 .... **CLC 32, 61**
See also CA 1-4R; CANR 1, 33, 91, 98; CN 7; DA3; DAM NOV; DLB 14, 207; EWL 3; MTCW 1, 2

Bradbury, Ray (Douglas) 1920- .... **CLC 1, 3, 10, 15, 42, 98; SSC 29, 53; WLC**
See also AAYA 15; AITN 1, 2; AMWS 4; BPFB 1; BYA 4, 5, 11; CA 1-4R; CANR 2, 30, 75, 125; CDALB 1968-1988; CN 7; CPW; DA; DA3; DAB; DAC; DAM MST, NOV, POP; DLB 2, 8; EXPN; EXPS; HGG; LAIT 3, 5; LATS 1:2; LMFS 2; MTCW 1, 2; NFS 1; RGAL 4; RGSF 2; SATA 11, 64, 123; SCFW 2; SFW 4; SSFS 1, 20; SUFW 1, 2; TUS; YAW

Braddon, Mary Elizabeth
1837-1915 .... **TCLC 111**
See also BRWS 8; CA 108; 179; CMW 4; DLB 18, 70, 156; HGG

Bradfield, Scott (Michael) 1955- .... **SSC 65**
See also CA 147; CANR 90; HGG; SUFW 2

Bradford, Gamaliel 1863-1932 .... **TCLC 36**
See also CA 160; DLB 17

Bradford, William 1590-1657 .... **LC 64**
See also DLB 24, 30; RGAL 4

Bradley, David (Henry), Jr. 1950- .... **BLC 1; CLC 23, 118**
See also BW 1, 3; CA 104; CANR 26, 81; CN 7; DAM MULT; DLB 33

Bradley, John Ed(mund, Jr.) 1958- . **CLC 55**
See also CA 139; CANR 99; CN 7; CSW

Bradley, Marion Zimmer
1930-1999 .... **CLC 30**
See Chapman, Lee; Dexter, John; Gardner, Miriam; Ives, Morgan; Rivers, Elfrida
See also AAYA 40; BPFB 1; CA 57-60; 185; CAAS 10; CANR 7, 31, 51, 75, 107; CPW; DA3; DAM POP; DLB 8; FANT; FW; MTCW 1, 2; SATA 90, 139; SATA-Obit 116; SFW 4; SUFW 2; YAW

Bradshaw, John 1933- .... **CLC 70**
See also CA 138; CANR 61

Bradstreet, Anne 1612(?)-1672 .... **LC 4, 30; PC 10**
See also AMWS 1; CDALB 1640-1865; DA; DA3; DAC; DAM MST, POET; DLB 24; EXPP; FW; PFS 6; RGAL 4; TUS; WP

Brady, Joan 1939- .... **CLC 86**
See also CA 141

Bragg, Melvyn 1939- .... **CLC 10**
See also BEST 89:3; CA 57-60; CANR 10, 48, 89; CN 7; DLB 14, 271; RHW

Brahe, Tycho 1546-1601 .... **LC 45**
See also DLB 300

Braine, John (Gerard) 1922-1986 . **CLC 1, 3, 41**
See also CA 1-4R; 120; CANR 1, 33; CD-BLB 1945-1960; DLB 15; DLBY 1986; EWL 3; MTCW 1

Braithwaite, William Stanley (Beaumont)
1878-1962 .... **BLC 1; HR 2; PC 52**
See also BW 1; CA 125; DAM MULT; DLB 50, 54

Bramah, Ernest 1868-1942 .... **TCLC 72**
See also CA 156; CMW 4; DLB 70; FANT

Brammer, William 1930(?)-1978 ...... **CLC 31**
See also CA 77-80

Brancati, Vitaliano 1907-1954 .... **TCLC 12**
See also CA 109; DLB 264; EWL 3

Brancato, Robin F(idler) 1936- .... **CLC 35**
See also AAYA 9; BYA 6; CA 69-72; CANR 11, 45; CLR 32; JRDA; MAICYA 2; MAICYAS 1; SAAS 9; SATA 97; WYA; YAW

Brand, Dionne 1953- .... **CLC 192**
See also BW 2; CA 143; CWP

Brand, Max
See Faust, Frederick (Schiller)
See also BPFB 1; TCWW 2

Brand, Millen 1906-1980 .... **CLC 7**
See also CA 21-24R; 97-100; CANR 72

Branden, Barbara .... **CLC 44**
See also CA 148

Brandes, Georg (Morris Cohen)
1842-1927 .... **TCLC 10**
See also CA 105; 189; DLB 300

Brandys, Kazimierz 1916-2000 .... **CLC 62**
See also EWL 3

Branley, Franklyn M(ansfield)
1915-2002 .... **CLC 21**
See also CA 33-36R; 207; CANR 14, 39; CLR 13; MAICYA 1, 2; SAAS 16; SATA 4, 68, 136

Brant, Beth (E.) 1941- .... **NNAL**
See also CA 144; FW

Brant, Sebastian 1457-1521 .... **LC 112**
See also DLB 179; RGWL 2, 3

Brathwaite, Edward Kamau
1930- .... **BLCS; CLC 11; PC 56**
See also BW 2, 3; CA 25-28R; CANR 11, 26, 47, 107; CDWLB 3; CP 7; DAM POET; DLB 125; EWL 3

Brathwaite, Kamau
See Brathwaite, Edward Kamau

Brautigan, Richard (Gary)
1935-1984 .... **CLC 1, 3, 5, 9, 12, 34, 42; TCLC 133**
See also BPFB 1; CA 53-56; 113; CANR 34; DA3; DAM NOV; DLB 2, 5, 206; DLBY 1980, 1984; FANT; MTCW 1; RGAL 4; SATA 56

Brave Bird, Mary .... **NNAL**
See Crow Dog, Mary (Ellen)

Braverman, Kate 1950- .... **CLC 67**
See also CA 89-92

Brecht, (Eugen) Bertolt (Friedrich)
1898-1956 ..... **DC 3; TCLC 1, 6, 13, 35; WLC**
See also CA 104; 133; CANR 62; CDWLB 2; DA; DA3; DAB; DAC; DAM DRAM, MST; DFS 4, 5, 9; DLB 56, 124; EW 11; EWL 3; IDTP; MTCW 1, 2; RGWL 2, 3; TWA

Brecht, Eugen Berthold Friedrich
See Brecht, (Eugen) Bertolt (Friedrich)

Bremer, Fredrika 1801-1865 .... **NCLC 11**
See also DLB 254

Brennan, Christopher John
1870-1932 .... **TCLC 17**
See also CA 117; 188; DLB 230; EWL 3

Brennan, Maeve 1917-1993 ... **CLC 5; TCLC 124**
See also CA 81-84; CANR 72, 100

Brent, Linda
See Jacobs, Harriet A(nn)

Brentano, Clemens (Maria)
1778-1842 .... **NCLC 1**
See also DLB 90; RGWL 2, 3

Brent of Bin Bin
See Franklin, (Stella Maria Sarah) Miles (Lampe)

Brenton, Howard 1942- .... **CLC 31**
See also CA 69-72; CANR 33, 67; CBD; CD 5; DLB 13; MTCW 1

Breslin, James 1930-
See Breslin, Jimmy
See also CA 73-76; CANR 31, 75; DAM NOV; MTCW 1, 2

Breslin, Jimmy .... **CLC 4, 43**
See Breslin, James
See also AITN 1; DLB 185; MTCW 2

Bresson, Robert 1901(?)-1999 .... **CLC 16**
See also CA 110; 187; CANR 49

Breton, Andre 1896-1966 .. **CLC 2, 9, 15, 54; PC 15**
See also CA 19-20; 25-28R; CANR 40, 60; CAP 2; DLB 65, 258; EW 11; EWL 3; GFL 1789 to the Present; LMFS 2; MTCW 1, 2; RGWL 2, 3; TWA; WP

Breytenbach, Breyten 1939(?)- .. **CLC 23, 37, 126**
See also CA 113; 129; CANR 61, 122; CWW 2; DAM POET; DLB 225; EWL 3

Bridgers, Sue Ellen 1942- .... **CLC 26**
See also AAYA 8, 49; BYA 7, 8; CA 65-68; CANR 11, 36; CLR 18; DLB 52; JRDA; MAICYA 1, 2; SAAS 1; SATA 22, 90; SATA-Essay 109; WYA; YAW

Bridges, Robert (Seymour) 1844-1930 .... **PC 28; TCLC 1**
See also BRW 6; CA 104; 152; CDBLB 1890-1914; DAM POET; DLB 19, 98

Bridie, James .... **TCLC 3**
See Mavor, Osborne Henry
See also DLB 10; EWL 3

Brin, David 1950- .... **CLC 34**
See also AAYA 21; CA 102; CANR 24, 70, 125, 127; INT CANR-24; SATA 65; SCFW 2; SFW 4

Brink, Andre (Philippus) 1935- . **CLC 18, 36, 106**
See also AFW; BRWS 6; CA 104; CANR 39, 62, 109, 133; CN 7; DLB 225; EWL 3; INT CA-103; LATS 1:2; MTCW 1, 2; WLIT 2

Brinsmead, H. F(ay)
See Brinsmead, H(esba) F(ay)

Brinsmead, H. F.
See Brinsmead, H(esba) F(ay)

Brinsmead, H(esba) F(ay) 1922- ...... **CLC 21**
See also CA 21-24R; CANR 10; CLR 47; CWRI 5; MAICYA 1, 2; SAAS 5; SATA 18, 78

Brittain, Vera (Mary) 1893(?)-1970 . **CLC 23**
See also BRWS 10; CA 13-16; 25-28R; CANR 58; CAP 1; DLB 191; FW; MTCW 1, 2

Broch, Hermann 1886-1951 .... **TCLC 20**
See also CA 117; 211; CDWLB 2; DLB 85, 124; EW 10; EWL 3; RGWL 2, 3

Brock, Rose
See Hansen, Joseph
See also GLL 1

Brod, Max 1884-1968 .... **TCLC 115**
See also CA 5-8R; 25-28R; CANR 7; DLB 81; EWL 3

Brodkey, Harold (Roy) 1930-1996 .. **CLC 56; TCLC 123**
See also CA 111; 151; CANR 71; CN 7; DLB 130

Brodsky, Iosif Alexandrovich 1940-1996
See Brodsky, Joseph
See also AITN 1; CA 41-44R; 151; CANR 37, 106; DA3; DAM POET; MTCW 1, 2; RGWL 2, 3

Brodsky, Joseph . **CLC 4, 6, 13, 36, 100; PC 9**
See Brodsky, Iosif Alexandrovich
See also AMWS 8; CWW 2; DLB 285; EWL 3; MTCW 1

Brodsky, Michael (Mark) 1948- .... **CLC 19**
See also CA 102; CANR 18, 41, 58; DLB 244

Brodzki, Bella ed. .... **CLC 65**

Brome, Richard 1590(?)-1652 .... **LC 61**
See also BRWS 10; DLB 58

Bromell, Henry 1947- .... **CLC 5**
See also CA 53-56; CANR 9, 115, 116

Bromfield, Louis (Brucker) 1896-1956 .... **TCLC 11**
See also CA 107; 155; DLB 4, 9, 86; RGAL 4; RHW

Broner, E(sther) M(asserman) 1930- .... **CLC 19**
See also CA 17-20R; CANR 8, 25, 72; CN 7; DLB 28

Bronk, William (M.) 1918-1999 .... **CLC 10**
See also CA 89-92; 177; CANR 23; CP 7; DLB 165

Bronstein, Lev Davidovich
See Trotsky, Leon

Bronte, Anne 1820-1849 ..... **NCLC 4, 71, 102**
See also BRW 5; BRWR 1; DA3; DLB 21, 199; TEA

Bronte, (Patrick) Branwell 1817-1848 .... **NCLC 109**

Bronte, Charlotte 1816-1855 ...... **NCLC 3, 8, 33, 58, 105; WLC**
See also AAYA 17; BRW 5; BRWC 2; BRWR 1; BYA 2; CDBLB 1832-1890; DA; DA3; DAB; DAC; DAM MST, NOV, DLB 21, 159, 199; EXPN; LAIT 2; NFS 4; TEA; WLIT 4

Bronte, Emily (Jane) 1818-1848 ... **NCLC 16, 35; PC 8; WLC**
See also AAYA 17; BPFB 1; BRW 5; BRWC 1; BRWR 1; BYA 3; CDBLB 1832-1890; DA; DA3; DAB; DAC; DAM MST, NOV, POET; DLB 21, 32, 199; EXPN; LAIT 1; TEA; WLIT 3

Brontes
See Bronte, Anne; Bronte, Charlotte; Bronte, Emily (Jane)

Brooke, Frances 1724-1789 .... **LC 6, 48**
See also DLB 39, 99

Brooke, Henry 1703(?)-1783 .... **LC 1**
See also DLB 39

Brooke, Rupert (Chawner) 1887-1915 ..... **PC 24; TCLC 2, 7; WLC**
See also BRWS 3; CA 104; 132; CANR 61; CDBLB 1914-1945; DA; DAB; DAC; DAM MST, POET; DLB 19, 216; EXPP; GLL 2; MTCW 1, 2; PFS 7; TEA

Brooke-Haven, P.
See Wodehouse, P(elham) G(renville)

Brooke-Rose, Christine 1926(?)- ...... **CLC 40, 184**
See also BRWS 4; CA 13-16R; CANR 58, 118; CN 7; DLB 14, 231; EWL 3; SFW 4

Brookner, Anita 1928- .. **CLC 32, 34, 51, 136**
See also BRWS 4; CA 114; 120; CANR 37, 56, 87, 130; CN 7; CPW; DA3; DAB; DAM POP; DLB 194; DLBY 1987; EWL 3; MTCW 1, 2; TEA

Brooks, Cleanth 1906-1994 . **CLC 24, 86, 110**
See also AMWS 14; CA 17-20R; 145; CANR 33, 35; CSW; DLB 63; DLBY 1994; EWL 3; INT CANR-35; MTCW 1, 2

Brooks, George
See Baum, L(yman) Frank

Brooks, Gwendolyn (Elizabeth) 1917-2000 ... **BLC 1; CLC 1, 2, 4, 5, 15, 49, 125; PC 7; WLC**
See also AAYA 20; AFAW 1, 2; AITN 1; AMWS 3; BW 2, 3; CA 1-4R; 190; CANR 1, 27, 52, 75, 132; CDALB 1941-1968; CLR 27; CP 7; CWP; DA; DA3; DAC; DAM MST, MULT, POET; DLB 5, 76, 165; EWL 3; EXPP; MAWW; MTCW 1, 2; PFS 1, 2, 4, 6; RGAL 4; SATA 6; SATA-Obit 123; TUS; WP

Brooks, Mel .... **CLC 12**
See Kaminsky, Melvin
See also AAYA 13, 48; DLB 26

Brooks, Peter (Preston) 1938- .... **CLC 34**
See also CA 45-48; CANR 1, 107

Brooks, Van Wyck 1886-1963 .... **CLC 29**
See also AMW; CA 1-4R; CANR 6; DLB 45, 63, 103; TUS

Brophy, Brigid (Antonia) 1929-1995 .... **CLC 6, 11, 29, 105**
See also CA 5-8R; 149; CAAS 4; CANR 25, 53; CBD; CN 7; CWD; DA3; DLB 14, 271; EWL 3; MTCW 1, 2

Brosman, Catharine Savage 1934- ..... **CLC 9**
See also CA 61-64; CANR 21, 46

Brossard, Nicole 1943- .... **CLC 115, 169**
See also CA 122; CAAS 16; CCA 1; CWP; CWW 2; DLB 53; EWL 3; FW; GLL 2; RGWL 3

Brother Antoninus
See Everson, William (Oliver)

The Brothers Quay
See Quay, Stephen; Quay, Timothy

Broughton, T(homas) Alan 1936- ..... **CLC 19**
See also CA 45-48; CANR 2, 23, 48, 111

Broumas, Olga 1949- .... **CLC 10, 73**
See also CA 85-88; CANR 20, 69, 110; CP 7; CWP; GLL 2

Broun, Heywood 1888-1939 .... **TCLC 104**
See also DLB 29, 171

Brown, Alan 1950- .... **CLC 99**
See also CA 156

Brown, Charles Brockden 1771-1810 .... **NCLC 22, 74, 122**
See also AMWS 1; CDALB 1640-1865; DLB 37, 59, 73; FW; HGG; LMFS 1; RGAL 4; TUS

Brown, Christy 1932-1981 .... **CLC 63**
See also BYA 13; CA 105; 104; CANR 72; DLB 14

Brown, Claude 1937-2002 ... **BLC 1; CLC 30**
See also AAYA 7; BW 1, 3; CA 73-76; 205; CANR 81; DAM MULT

Brown, Dee (Alexander) 1908-2002 .... **CLC 18, 47**
See also AAYA 30; CA 13-16R; 212; CAAS 6; CANR 11, 45, 60; CPW; CSW; DA3; DAM POP; DLBY 1980; LAIT 2; MTCW 1, 2; NCFS 5; SATA 5, 110; SATA-Obit 141; TCWW 2

Brown, George
See Wertmueller, Lina

Brown, George Douglas 1869-1902 .... **TCLC 28**
See Douglas, George
See also CA 162

Brown, George Mackay 1921-1996 ... **CLC 5, 48, 100**
See also BRWS 6; CA 21-24R; 151; CAAS 6; CANR 12, 37, 67; CN 7; CP 7; DLB 14, 27, 139, 271; MTCW 1; RGSF 2; SATA 35

Brown, (William) Larry 1951-2004 . **CLC 73**
See also CA 130; 134; CANR 117; CSW; DLB 234; INT CA-134

Brown, Moses
See Barrett, William (Christopher)

Brown, Rita Mae 1944- .... **CLC 18, 43, 79**
See also BPFB 1; CA 45-48; CANR 2, 11, 35, 62, 95; CN 7; CPW; CSW; DA3; DAM NOV, POP; FW; INT CANR-11; MTCW 1, 2; NFS 9; RGAL 4; TUS

Brown, Roderick (Langmere) Haig-
See Haig-Brown, Roderick (Langmere)

Brown, Rosellen 1939- .... **CLC 32, 170**
See also CA 77-80; CAAS 10; CANR 14, 44, 98; CN 7

Brown, Sterling Allen 1901-1989 .... **BLC 1; CLC 1, 23, 59; HR 2; PC 55**
See also AFAW 1, 2; BW 1, 3; CA 85-88; 127; CANR 26; DA3; DAM MULT, POET; DLB 48, 51, 63; MTCW 1, 2; RGAL 4; WP

Brown, Will
See Ainsworth, William Harrison

Brown, William Hill 1765-1793 .... **LC 93**
See also DLB 37

Brown, William Wells 1815-1884 ...... **BLC 1; DC 1; NCLC 2, 89**
See also DAM MULT; DLB 3, 50, 183, 248; RGAL 4

Browne, (Clyde) Jackson 1948(?)- ... **CLC 21**
See also CA 120

Browne, Thomas 1605-1682 .... **LC 111**
See also BW 2; DLB 151

Browning, Robert 1812-1889 . **NCLC 19, 79; PC 2, 61; WLCS**
See also BRW 4; BRWC 2; BRWR 2; CD-BLB 1832-1890; CLR 97; DA; DA3; DAB; DAC; DAM MST, POET; DLB 32, 163; EXPP; LATS 1:1; PAB; PFS 1, 15; RGEL 2; TEA; WLIT 4; WP; YABC 1

Browning, Tod 1882-1962 .... **CLC 16**
See also CA 141; 117

Brownmiller, Susan 1935- .... **CLC 159**
See also CA 103; CANR 35, 75; DAM NOV; FW; MTCW 1, 2

Brownson, Orestes Augustus 1803-1876 .... **NCLC 50**
See also DLB 1, 59, 73, 243

Bruccoli, Matthew J(oseph) 1931- ... **CLC 34**
See also CA 9-12R; CANR 7, 87; DLB 103

Bruce, Lenny .... **CLC 21**
See Schneider, Leonard Alfred

Bruchac, Joseph III 1942- .... **NNAL**
See also AAYA 19; CA 33-36R; CANR 13, 47, 75, 94; CLR 46; CWRI 5; DAM MULT; JRDA; MAICYA 2; MAICYAS 1; MTCW 1; SATA 42, 89, 131

Bruin, John
See Brutus, Dennis

Brulard, Henri
See Stendhal

Brulls, Christian
See Simenon, Georges (Jacques Christian)

Brunetto Latini c. 1220-1294 .... **CMLC 73**

Brunner, John (Kilian Houston) 1934-1995 .... **CLC 8, 10**
See also CA 1-4R; 149; CAAS 8; CANR 2, 37; CPW; DAM POP; DLB 261; MTCW 1, 2; SCFW 2; SFW 4

Bruno, Giordano 1548-1600 .... **LC 27**
See also RGWL 2, 3

Brutus, Dennis 1924- ... **BLC 1; CLC 43; PC 24**
See also AFW; BW 2, 3; CA 49-52; CAAS 14; CANR 2, 27, 42, 81; CDWLB 3; CP 7; DAM MULT, POET; DLB 117, 225; EWL 3

Bryan, C(ourtlandt) D(ixon) B(arnes) 1936- .... **CLC 29**
See also CA 73-76; CANR 13, 68; DLB 185; INT CANR-13

Bryan, Michael
See Moore, Brian
See also CCA 1

Bryan, William Jennings 1860-1925 .... **TCLC 99**
See also DLB 303

Bryant, William Cullen 1794-1878 . **NCLC 6, 46; PC 20**
See also AMWS 1; CDALB 1640-1865; DA; DAB; DAC; DAM MST, POET; DLB 3, 43, 59, 189, 250; EXPP; PAB; RGAL 4; TUS

Bryusov, Valery Yakovlevich 1873-1924 .... **TCLC 10**
See also CA 107; 155; EWL 3; SFW 4

Buchan, John 1875-1940 .... **TCLC 41**
See also CA 108; 145; CMW 4; DAB; DAM POP; DLB 34, 70, 156; HGG; MSW; MTCW 1; RGEL 2; RHW; YABC 2

Buchanan, George 1506-1582 .... **LC 4**
See also DLB 132

Buchanan, Robert 1841-1901 .... **TCLC 107**
See also CA 179; DLB 18, 35

Buchheim, Lothar-Guenther 1918- .... **CLC 6**
See also CA 85-88

Buchner, (Karl) Georg 1813-1837 .... **NCLC 26, 146**
See also CDWLB 2; DLB 133; EW 6; RGSF 2; RGWL 2, 3; TWA

Buchwald, Art(hur) 1925- .... **CLC 33**
See also AITN 1; CA 5-8R; CANR 21, 67, 107; MTCW 1, 2; SATA 10

Buck, Pearl S(ydenstricker) 1892-1973 .... **CLC 7, 11, 18, 127**
See also AAYA 42; AITN 1; AMWS 2; BPFB 1; CA 1-4R; 41-44R; CANR 1, 34; CDALBS; DA; DA3; DAB; DAC; DAM MST, NOV; DLB 9, 102; EWL 3; LAIT 3; MTCW 1, 2; RGAL 4; RHW; SATA 1, 25; TUS

Buckler, Ernest 1908-1984 .... **CLC 13**
See also CA 11-12; 114; CAP 1; CCA 1; DAC; DAM MST; DLB 68; SATA 47

Buckley, Christopher (Taylor) 1952- .... **CLC 165**
See also CA 139; CANR 119

Buckley, Vincent (Thomas) 1925-1988 .... **CLC 57**
See also CA 101; DLB 289

Buckley, William F(rank), Jr. 1925- . **CLC 7, 18, 37**
See also AITN 1; BPFB 1; CA 1-4R; CANR 1, 24, 53, 93, 133; CMW 4; CPW; DA3; DAM POP; DLB 137; DLBY 1980; INT CANR-24; MTCW 1, 2; TUS

Buechner, (Carl) Frederick 1926- . **CLC 2, 4, 6, 9**
See also AMWS 12; BPFB 1; CA 13-16R; CANR 11, 39, 64, 114; CN 7; DAM NOV; DLBY 1980; INT CANR-11; MTCW 1, 2

Buell, John (Edward) 1927- .... **CLC 10**
See also CA 1-4R; CANR 71; DLB 53

Buero Vallejo, Antonio 1916-2000 ... **CLC 15, 46, 139; DC 18**
See also CA 106; 189; CANR 24, 49, 75; CWW 2; DFS 11; EWL 3; HW 1; MTCW 1, 2

Bufalino, Gesualdo 1920-1996 .... **CLC 74**
See also CA 209; CWW 2; DLB 196

Bugayev, Boris Nikolayevich 1880-1934 .... **PC 11; TCLC 7**
See Bely, Andrey; Belyi, Andrei
See also CA 104; 165; MTCW 1

Bukowski, Charles 1920-1994 ... **CLC 2, 5, 9, 41, 82, 108; PC 18; SSC 45**
See also CA 17-20R; 144; CANR 40, 62, 105; CPW; DA3; DAM NOV, POET; DLB 5, 130, 169; EWL 3; MTCW 1, 2

Bulgakov, Mikhail (Afanas'evich) 1891-1940 ..... **SSC 18; TCLC 2, 16, 159**
See also BPFB 1; CA 105; 152; DAM DRAM, NOV; DLB 272; EWL 3; NFS 8; RGSF 2; RGWL 2, 3; SFW 4; TWA

Bulgya, Alexander Alexandrovich 1901-1956 .... **TCLC 53**
See Fadeev, Aleksandr Aleksandrovich; Fadeev, Alexandr Alexandrovich; Fadeyev, Alexander
See also CA 117; 181

Bullins, Ed 1935- ... **BLC 1; CLC 1, 5, 7; DC 6**
See also BW 2, 3; CA 49-52; CAAS 16; CAD; CANR 24, 46, 73, 134; CD 5; DAM DRAM, MULT; DLB 7, 38, 249; EWL 3; MTCW 1, 2; RGAL 4

Bulosan, Carlos 1911-1956 .... **AAL**
See also CA 216; RGAL 4

Bulwer-Lytton, Edward (George Earle Lytton) 1803-1873 .... **NCLC 1, 45**
See also DLB 21; RGEL 2; SFW 4; SUFW 1; TEA

Bunin, Ivan Alexeyevich 1870-1953 ... **SSC 5; TCLC 6**
See also CA 104; EWL 3; RGSF 2; RGWL 2, 3; TWA

Bunting, Basil 1900-1985 ...... **CLC 10, 39, 47**
See also BRWS 7; CA 53-56; 115; CANR 7; DAM POET; DLB 20; EWL 3; RGEL 2

Bunuel, Luis 1900-1983 ... **CLC 16, 80; HLC 1**
See also CA 101; 110; CANR 32, 77; DAM MULT; HW 1

Bunyan, John 1628-1688 ..... **LC 4, 69; WLC**
See also BRW 2; BYA 5; CDBLB 1660-1789; DA; DAB; DAC; DAM MST; DLB 39; RGEL 2; TEA; WCH; WLIT 3

Buravsky, Alexandr .... **CLC 59**

Burckhardt, Jacob (Christoph) 1818-1897 .... **NCLC 49**
See also EW 6

Burford, Eleanor
See Hibbert, Eleanor Alice Burford

Burgess, Anthony . **CLC 1, 2, 4, 5, 8, 10, 13, 15, 22, 40, 62, 81, 94**
See Wilson, John (Anthony) Burgess
See also AAYA 25; AITN 1; BRWS 1; CD-BLB 1960 to Present; DAB; DLB 14, 194, 261; DLBY 1998; EWL 3; MTCW 1; RGEL 2; RHW; SFW 4; YAW

Burke, Edmund 1729(?)-1797 .... **LC 7, 36; WLC**
See also BRW 3; DA; DA3; DAB; DAC; DAM MST; DLB 104, 252; RGEL 2; TEA

Burke, Kenneth (Duva) 1897-1993 ... **CLC 2, 24**
See also AMW; CA 5-8R; 143; CANR 39, 74; DLB 45, 63; EWL 3; MTCW 1, 2; RGAL 4

Burke, Leda
See Garnett, David

Burke, Ralph
See Silverberg, Robert

Burke, Thomas 1886-1945 .... **TCLC 63**
See also CA 113; 155; CMW 4; DLB 197

Burney, Fanny 1752-1840 .... **NCLC 12, 54, 107**
See also BRWS 3; DLB 39; NFS 16; RGEL 2; TEA

Burney, Frances
See Burney, Fanny

Burns, Robert 1759-1796 ..... **LC 3, 29, 40; PC 6; WLC**
See also AAYA 51; BRW 3; CDBLB 1789-1832; DA; DA3; DAB; DAC; DAM MST, POET; DLB 109; EXPP; PAB; RGEL 2; TEA; WP

Burns, Tex
See L'Amour, Louis (Dearborn)
See also TCWW 2

Burnshaw, Stanley 1906- .... **CLC 3, 13, 44**
See also CA 9-12R; CP 7; DLB 48; DLBY 1997

Burr, Anne 1937- .... **CLC 6**
See also CA 25-28R

Burroughs, Edgar Rice 1875-1950 . **TCLC 2, 32**
See also AAYA 11; BPFB 1; BYA 4, 9; CA 104; 132; CANR 131; DA3; DAM NOV; DLB 8; FANT; MTCW 1, 2; RGAL 4; SATA 41; SCFW 2; SFW 4; TUS; YAW

Burroughs, William S(eward) 1914-1997 .. **CLC 1, 2, 5, 15, 22, 42, 75, 109; TCLC 121; WLC**
See Lee, William; Lee, Willy
See also AAYA 60; AITN 2; AMWS 3; BG 2; BPFB 1; CA 9-12R; 160; CANR 20, 52, 104; CN 7; CPW; DA; DA3; DAB;

DAC; DAM MST, NOV, POP; DLB 2, 8, 16, 152, 237; DLBY 1981, 1997; EWL 3; HGG; LMFS 2; MTCW 1, 2; RGAL 4; SFW 4

Burton, Sir Richard F(rancis)
1821-1890 .... **NCLC 42**
See also DLB 55, 166, 184

Burton, Robert 1577-1640 .... **LC 74**
See also DLB 151; RGEL 2

Buruma, Ian 1951- .... **CLC 163**
See also CA 128; CANR 65

Busch, Frederick 1941- ... **CLC 7, 10, 18, 47, 166**
See also CA 33-36R; CAAS 1; CANR 45, 73, 92; CN 7; DLB 6, 218

Bush, Barney (Furman) 1946- .... **NNAL**
See also CA 145

Bush, Ronald 1946- .... **CLC 34**
See also CA 136

Bustos, F(rancisco)
See Borges, Jorge Luis

Bustos Domecq, H(onorio)
See Bioy Casares, Adolfo; Borges, Jorge Luis

Butler, Octavia E(stelle) 1947- .. **BLCS; CLC 38, 121**
See also AAYA 18, 48; AFAW 2; AMWS 13; BPFB 1; BW 2, 3; CA 73-76; CANR 12, 24, 38, 73; CLR 65; CPW; DA3; DAM MULT, POP; DLB 33; LATS 1:2; MTCW 1, 2; NFS 8; SATA 84; SCFW 2; SFW 4; SSFS 6; YAW

Butler, Robert Olen, (Jr.) 1945- ...... **CLC 81, 162**
See also AMWS 12; BPFB 1; CA 112; CANR 66; CSW; DAM POP; DLB 173; INT CA-112; MTCW 1; SSFS 11

Butler, Samuel 1612-1680 .... **LC 16, 43**
See also DLB 101, 126; RGEL 2

Butler, Samuel 1835-1902 .... **TCLC 1, 33; WLC**
See also BRWS 2; CA 143; CDBLB 1890-1914; DA; DA3; DAB; DAC; DAM MST, NOV; DLB 18, 57, 174; RGEL 2; SFW 4; TEA

Butler, Walter C.
See Faust, Frederick (Schiller)

Butor, Michel (Marie Francois)
1926- .... **CLC 1, 3, 8, 11, 15, 161**
See also CA 9-12R; CANR 33, 66; CWW 2; DLB 83; EW 13; EWL 3; GFL 1789 to the Present; MTCW 1, 2

Butts, Mary 1890(?)-1937 .... **TCLC 77**
See also CA 148; DLB 240

Buxton, Ralph
See Silverstein, Alvin; Silverstein, Virginia B(arbara Opshelor)

Buzo, Alex
See Buzo, Alexander (John)
See also DLB 289

Buzo, Alexander (John) 1944- .... **CLC 61**
See also CA 97-100; CANR 17, 39, 69; CD 5

Buzzati, Dino 1906-1972 .... **CLC 36**
See also CA 160; 33-36R; DLB 177; RGWL 2, 3; SFW 4

Byars, Betsy (Cromer) 1928- .... **CLC 35**
See also AAYA 19; BYA 3; CA 33-36R, 183; CAAE 183; CANR 18, 36, 57, 102; CLR 1, 16, 72; DLB 52; INT CANR-18; JRDA; MAICYA 1, 2; MAICYAS 1; MTCW 1; SAAS 1; SATA 4, 46, 80; SATA-Essay 108; WYA; YAW

Byatt, A(ntonia) S(usan Drabble)
1936- .... **CLC 19, 65, 136**
See also BPFB 1; BRWC 2; BRWS 4; CA 13-16R; CANR 13, 33, 50, 75, 96, 133; DA3; DAM NOV, POP; DLB 14, 194; EWL 3; MTCW 1, 2; RGSF 2; RHW; TEA

Byrd, Willam II 1674-1744 .... **LC 112**
See also DLB 24, 140; RGAL 4

Byrne, David 1952- .... **CLC 26**
See also CA 127

Byrne, John Keyes 1926-
See Leonard, Hugh
See also CA 102; CANR 78; INT CA-102

Byron, George Gordon (Noel)
1788-1824 ..... **DC 24; NCLC 2, 12, 109, 149; PC 16; WLC**
See also BRW 4; BRWC 2; CDBLB 1789-1832; DA; DA3; DAB; DAC; DAM MST, POET; DLB 96, 110; EXPP; LMFS 1; PAB; PFS 1, 14; RGEL 2; TEA; WLIT 3; WP

Byron, Robert 1905-1941 .... **TCLC 67**
See also CA 160; DLB 195

C. 3. 3.
See Wilde, Oscar (Fingal O'Flahertie Wills)

Caballero, Fernan 1796-1877 .... **NCLC 10**

Cabell, Branch
See Cabell, James Branch

Cabell, James Branch 1879-1958 .... **TCLC 6**
See also CA 105; 152; DLB 9, 78; FANT; MTCW 1; RGAL 4; SUFW 1

Cabeza de Vaca, Alvar Nunez
1490-1557(?) .... **LC 61**

Cable, George Washington
1844-1925 .... **SSC 4; TCLC 4**
See also CA 104; 155; DLB 12, 74; DLBD 13; RGAL 4; TUS

Cabral de Melo Neto, Joao
1920-1999 .... **CLC 76**
See Melo Neto, Joao Cabral de
See also CA 151; DAM MULT; DLB 307; LAW; LAWS 1

Cabrera Infante, G(uillermo) 1929- . **CLC 5, 25, 45, 120; HLC 1; SSC 39**
See also CA 85-88; CANR 29, 65, 110; CDWLB 3; CWW 2; DA3; DAM MULT; DLB 113; EWL 3; HW 1, 2; LAW; LAWS 1; MTCW 1, 2; RGSF 2; WLIT 1

Cade, Toni
See Bambara, Toni Cade

Cadmus and Harmonia
See Buchan, John

Caedmon fl. 658-680 .... **CMLC 7**
See also DLB 146

Caeiro, Alberto
See Pessoa, Fernando (Antonio Nogueira)

Caesar, Julius .... **CMLC 47**
See Julius Caesar
See also AW 1; RGWL 2, 3

Cage, John (Milton, Jr.)
1912-1992 .... **CLC 41; PC 58**
See also CA 13-16R; 169; CANR 9, 78; DLB 193; INT CANR-9

Cahan, Abraham 1860-1951 .... **TCLC 71**
See also CA 108; 154; DLB 9, 25, 28; RGAL 4

Cain, G.
See Cabrera Infante, G(uillermo)

Cain, Guillermo
See Cabrera Infante, G(uillermo)

Cain, James M(allahan) 1892-1977 .. **CLC 3, 11, 28**
See also AITN 1; BPFB 1; CA 17-20R; 73-76; CANR 8, 34, 61; CMW 4; DLB 226; EWL 3; MSW; MTCW 1; RGAL 4

Caine, Hall 1853-1931 .... **TCLC 97**
See also RHW

Caine, Mark
See Raphael, Frederic (Michael)

Calasso, Roberto 1941- .... **CLC 81**
See also CA 143; CANR 89

Calderon de la Barca, Pedro
1600-1681 .... **DC 3; HLCS 1; LC 23**
See also EW 2; RGWL 2, 3; TWA

Caldwell, Erskine (Preston)
1903-1987 .... **CLC 1, 8, 14, 50, 60; SSC 19; TCLC 117**
See also AITN 1; AMW; BPFB 1; CA 1-4R; 121; CAAS 1; CANR 2, 33; DA3; DAM NOV; DLB 9, 86; EWL 3; MTCW 1, 2; RGAL 4; RGSF 2; TUS

Caldwell, (Janet Miriam) Taylor (Holland)
1900-1985 .... **CLC 2, 28, 39**
See also BPFB 1; CA 5-8R; 116; CANR 5; DA3; DAM NOV, POP; DLBD 17; RHW

Calhoun, John Caldwell
1782-1850 .... **NCLC 15**
See also DLB 3, 248

Calisher, Hortense 1911- ..... **CLC 2, 4, 8, 38, 134; SSC 15**
See also CA 1-4R; CANR 1, 22, 117; CN 7; DA3; DAM NOV; DLB 2, 218; INT CANR-22; MTCW 1, 2; RGAL 4; RGSF 2

Callaghan, Morley Edward
1903-1990 ..... **CLC 3, 14, 41, 65; TCLC 145**
See also CA 9-12R; 132; CANR 33, 73; DAC; DAM MST; DLB 68; EWL 3; MTCW 1, 2; RGEL 2; RGSF 2; SSFS 19

Callimachus c. 305B.C.-c.
240B.C. .... **CMLC 18**
See also AW 1; DLB 176; RGWL 2, 3

Calvin, Jean
See Calvin, John
See also GFL Beginnings to 1789

Calvin, John 1509-1564 .... **LC 37**
See Calvin, Jean

Calvino, Italo 1923-1985 .... **CLC 5, 8, 11, 22, 33, 39, 73; SSC 3, 48**
See also AAYA 58; CA 85-88; 116; CANR 23, 61, 132; DAM NOV; DLB 196; EW 13; EWL 3; MTCW 1, 2; RGSF 2; RGWL 2, 3; SFW 4; SSFS 12

Camara Laye
See Laye, Camara
See also EWL 3

Camden, William 1551-1623 .... **LC 77**
See also DLB 172

Cameron, Carey 1952- .... **CLC 59**
See also CA 135

Cameron, Peter 1959- .... **CLC 44**
See also AMWS 12; CA 125; CANR 50, 117; DLB 234; GLL 2

Camoens, Luis Vaz de 1524(?)-1580
See Camoes, Luis de
See also EW 2

Camoes, Luis de 1524(?)-1580 . **HLCS 1; LC 62; PC 31**
See Camoens, Luis Vaz de
See also DLB 287; RGWL 2, 3

Campana, Dino 1885-1932 .... **TCLC 20**
See also CA 117; DLB 114; EWL 3

Campanella, Tommaso 1568-1639 .... **LC 32**
See also RGWL 2, 3

Campbell, John W(ood, Jr.)
1910-1971 .... **CLC 32**
See also CA 21-22; 29-32R; CANR 34; CAP 2; DLB 8; MTCW 1; SCFW; SFW 4

Campbell, Joseph 1904-1987 .... **CLC 69; TCLC 140**
See also AAYA 3; BEST 89:2; CA 1-4R; 124; CANR 3, 28, 61, 107; DA3; MTCW 1, 2

Campbell, Maria 1940- .... **CLC 85; NNAL**
See also CA 102; CANR 54; CCA 1; DAC

Campbell, (John) Ramsey 1946- ..... **CLC 42; SSC 19**
See also AAYA 51; CA 57-60, 228; CAAE 228; CANR 7, 102; DLB 261; HGG; INT CANR-7; SUFW 1, 2

Campbell, (Ignatius) Roy (Dunnachie)
1901-1957 .... **TCLC 5**
See also AFW; CA 104; 155; DLB 20, 225; EWL 3; MTCW 2; RGEL 2

Campbell, Thomas 1777-1844 .... **NCLC 19**
See also DLB 93, 144; RGEL 2

Campbell, Wilfred .... **TCLC 9**
See Campbell, William

Campbell, William 1858(?)-1918
See Campbell, Wilfred
See also CA 106; DLB 92

Campion, Jane 1954- .... **CLC 95**
See also AAYA 33; CA 138; CANR 87

Campion, Thomas 1567-1620 .... **LC 78**
See also CDBLB Before 1660; DAM POET; DLB 58, 172; RGEL 2

Camus, Albert 1913-1960 ...... **CLC 1, 2, 4, 9, 11, 14, 32, 63, 69, 124; DC 2; SSC 9, 76; WLC**
See also AAYA 36; AFW; BPFB 1; CA 89-92; CANR 131; DA; DA3; DAB; DAC; DAM DRAM, MST, NOV; DLB 72; EW 13; EWL 3; EXPN; EXPS; GFL 1789 to the Present; LATS 1:2; LMFS 2; MTCW 1, 2; NFS 6, 16; RGSF 2; RGWL 2, 3; SSFS 4; TWA

Canby, Vincent 1924-2000 .... **CLC 13**
See also CA 81-84; 191

Cancale
See Desnos, Robert

Canetti, Elias 1905-1994 .. **CLC 3, 14, 25, 75, 86; TCLC 157**
See also CA 21-24R; 146; CANR 23, 61, 79; CDWLB 2; CWW 2; DA3; DLB 85, 124; EW 12; EWL 3; MTCW 1, 2; RGWL 2, 3; TWA

Canfield, Dorothea F.
See Fisher, Dorothy (Frances) Canfield

Canfield, Dorothea Frances
See Fisher, Dorothy (Frances) Canfield

Canfield, Dorothy
See Fisher, Dorothy (Frances) Canfield

Canin, Ethan 1960- .... **CLC 55; SSC 70**
See also CA 131; 135

Cankar, Ivan 1876-1918 .... **TCLC 105**
See also CDWLB 4; DLB 147; EWL 3

Cannon, Curt
See Hunter, Evan

Cao, Lan 1961- .... **CLC 109**
See also CA 165

Cape, Judith
See Page, P(atricia) K(athleen)
See also CCA 1

Capek, Karel 1890-1938 .... **DC 1; SSC 36; TCLC 6, 37; WLC**
See also CA 104; 140; CDWLB 4; DA; DA3; DAB; DAC; DAM DRAM, MST, NOV; DFS 7, 11; DLB 215; EW 10; EWL 3; MTCW 1; RGSF 2; RGWL 2, 3; SCFW 2; SFW 4

Capote, Truman 1924-1984 . **CLC 1, 3, 8, 13, 19, 34, 38, 58; SSC 2, 47; TCLC 164; WLC**
See also AMWS 3; BPFB 1; CA 5-8R; 113; CANR 18, 62; CDALB 1941-1968; CPW; DA; DA3; DAB; DAC; DAM MST, NOV, POP; DLB 2, 185, 227; DLBY 1980, 1984; EWL 3; EXPS; GLL 1; LAIT 3; MTCW 1, 2; NCFS 2; RGAL 4; RGSF 2; SATA 91; SSFS 2; TUS

Capra, Frank 1897-1991 .... **CLC 16**
See also AAYA 52; CA 61-64; 135

Caputo, Philip 1941- .... **CLC 32**
See also AAYA 60; CA 73-76; CANR 40, 135; YAW

Caragiale, Ion Luca 1852-1912 ...... **TCLC 76**
See also CA 157

Card, Orson Scott 1951- .... **CLC 44, 47, 50**
See also AAYA 11, 42; BPFB 1; BYA 5, 8; CA 102; CANR 27, 47, 73, 102, 106, 133; CPW; DA3; DAM POP; FANT; INT CANR-27; MTCW 1, 2; NFS 5; SATA 83, 127; SCFW 2; SFW 4; SUFW 2; YAW

Cardenal, Ernesto 1925- .... **CLC 31, 161; HLC 1; PC 22**
See also CA 49-52; CANR 2, 32, 66; CWW 2; DAM MULT, POET; DLB 290; EWL 3; HW 1, 2; LAWS 1; MTCW 1, 2; RGWL 2, 3

Cardinal, Marie 1929-2001 .... **CLC 189**
See also CA 177; CWW 2; DLB 83; FW

Cardozo, Benjamin N(athan)
1870-1938 .... **TCLC 65**
See also CA 117; 164

Carducci, Giosue (Alessandro Giuseppe)
1835-1907 .... **PC 46; TCLC 32**
See also CA 163; EW 7; RGWL 2, 3

Carew, Thomas 1595(?)-1640 . **LC 13; PC 29**
See also BRW 2; DLB 126; PAB; RGEL 2

Carey, Ernestine Gilbreth 1908- .... **CLC 17**
See also CA 5-8R; CANR 71; SATA 2

Carey, Peter 1943- .... **CLC 40, 55, 96, 183**
See also CA 123; 127; CANR 53, 76, 117; CN 7; DLB 289; EWL 3; INT CA-127; MTCW 1, 2; RGSF 2; SATA 94

Carleton, William 1794-1869 .... **NCLC 3**
See also DLB 159; RGEL 2; RGSF 2

Carlisle, Henry (Coffin) 1926- .... **CLC 33**
See also CA 13-16R; CANR 15, 85

Carlsen, Chris
See Holdstock, Robert P.

Carlson, Ron(ald F.) 1947- .... **CLC 54**
See also CA 105, 189; CAAE 189; CANR 27; DLB 244

Carlyle, Thomas 1795-1881 ..... **NCLC 22, 70**
See also BRW 4; CDBLB 1789-1832; DA; DAB; DAC; DAM MST; DLB 55, 144, 254; RGEL 2; TEA

Carman, (William) Bliss 1861-1929 ... **PC 34; TCLC 7**
See also CA 104; 152; DAC; DLB 92; RGEL 2

Carnegie, Dale 1888-1955 .... **TCLC 53**
See also CA 218

Carossa, Hans 1878-1956 .... **TCLC 48**
See also CA 170; DLB 66; EWL 3

Carpenter, Don(ald Richard)
1931-1995 .... **CLC 41**
See also CA 45-48; 149; CANR 1, 71

Carpenter, Edward 1844-1929 .... **TCLC 88**
See also CA 163; GLL 1

Carpenter, John (Howard) 1948- ... **CLC 161**
See also AAYA 2; CA 134; SATA 58

Carpenter, Johnny
See Carpenter, John (Howard)

Carpentier (y Valmont), Alejo
1904-1980 . **CLC 8, 11, 38, 110; HLC 1; SSC 35**
See also CA 65-68; 97-100; CANR 11, 70; CDWLB 3; DAM MULT; DLB 113; EWL 3; HW 1, 2; LAW; LMFS 2; RGSF 2; RGWL 2, 3; WLIT 1

Carr, Caleb 1955- .... **CLC 86**
See also CA 147; CANR 73, 134; DA3

Carr, Emily 1871-1945 .... **TCLC 32**
See also CA 159; DLB 68; FW; GLL 2

Carr, John Dickson 1906-1977 .... **CLC 3**
See Fairbairn, Roger
See also CA 49-52; 69-72; CANR 3, 33, 60; CMW 4; DLB 306; MSW; MTCW 1, 2

Carr, Philippa
See Hibbert, Eleanor Alice Burford

Carr, Virginia Spencer 1929- .... **CLC 34**
See also CA 61-64; DLB 111

Carrere, Emmanuel 1957- .... **CLC 89**
See also CA 200

Carrier, Roch 1937- .... **CLC 13, 78**
See also CA 130; CANR 61; CCA 1; DAC; DAM MST; DLB 53; SATA 105

Carroll, James Dennis
See Carroll, Jim

Carroll, James P. 1943(?)- .... **CLC 38**
See also CA 81-84; CANR 73; MTCW 1

Carroll, Jim 1951- .... **CLC 35, 143**
See also AAYA 17; CA 45-48; CANR 42, 115; NCFS 5

Carroll, Lewis ..... **NCLC 2, 53, 139; PC 18; WLC**
See Dodgson, Charles L(utwidge)
See also AAYA 39; BRW 5; BYA 5, 13; CDBLB 1832-1890; CLR 2, 18; DLB 18, 163, 178; DLBY 1998; EXPN; EXPP; FANT; JRDA; LAIT 1; NFS 7; PFS 11; RGEL 2; SUFW 1; TEA; WCH

Carroll, Paul Vincent 1900-1968 ...... **CLC 10**
See also CA 9-12R; 25-28R; DLB 10; EWL 3; RGEL 2

Carruth, Hayden 1921- ..... **CLC 4, 7, 10, 18, 84; PC 10**
See also CA 9-12R; CANR 4, 38, 59, 110; CP 7; DLB 5, 165; INT CANR-4; MTCW 1, 2; SATA 47

Carson, Anne 1950- .... **CLC 185; PC 64**
See also AMWS 12; CA 203; DLB 193; PFS 18

Carson, Ciaran 1948- .... **CLC 201**
See also CA 153; CA-Brief 112; CANR 113; CP 7

Carson, Rachel
See Carson, Rachel Louise
See also AAYA 49; DLB 275

Carson, Rachel Louise 1907-1964 .... **CLC 71**
See Carson, Rachel
See also AMWS 9; ANW; CA 77-80; CANR 35; DA3; DAM POP; FW; LAIT 4; MTCW 1, 2; NCFS 1; SATA 23

Carter, Angela (Olive) 1940-1992 ...... **CLC 5, 41, 76; SSC 13; TCLC 139**
See also BRWS 3; CA 53-56; 136; CANR 12, 36, 61, 106; DA3; DLB 14, 207, 261; EXPS; FANT; FW; MTCW 1, 2; RGSF 2; SATA 66; SATA-Obit 70; SFW 4; SSFS 4, 12; SUFW 2; WLIT 4

Carter, Nick
See Smith, Martin Cruz

Carver, Raymond 1938-1988 ...... **CLC 22, 36, 53, 55, 126; PC 54; SSC 8, 51**
See also AAYA 44; AMWS 3; BPFB 1; CA 33-36R; 126; CANR 17, 34, 61, 103; CPW; DA3; DAM NOV; DLB 130; DLBY 1984, 1988; EWL 3; MTCW 1, 2; PFS 17; RGAL 4; RGSF 2; SSFS 3, 6, 12, 13; TCWW 2; TUS

Cary, Elizabeth, Lady Falkland
1585-1639 .... **LC 30**

Cary, (Arthur) Joyce (Lunel)
1888-1957 .... **TCLC 1, 29**
See also BRW 7; CA 104; 164; CDBLB 1914-1945; DLB 15, 100; EWL 3; MTCW 2; RGEL 2; TEA

Casal, Julian del 1863-1893 .... **NCLC 131**
See also DLB 283; LAW

Casanova de Seingalt, Giovanni Jacopo
1725-1798 .... **LC 13**

Casares, Adolfo Bioy
See Bioy Casares, Adolfo
See also RGSF 2

Casas, Bartolome de las 1474-1566
See Las Casas, Bartolome de
See also WLIT 1

Casely-Hayford, J(oseph) E(phraim)
1866-1903 .... **BLC 1; TCLC 24**
See also BW 2; CA 123; 152; DAM MULT

Casey, John (Dudley) 1939- .... **CLC 59**
See also BEST 90:2; CA 69-72; CANR 23, 100
Casey, Michael 1947- .... **CLC 2**
See also CA 65-68; CANR 109; DLB 5
Casey, Patrick
See Thurman, Wallace (Henry)
Casey, Warren (Peter) 1935-1988 .... **CLC 12**
See also CA 101; 127; INT CA-101
Casona, Alejandro .... **CLC 49**
See Alvarez, Alejandro Rodriguez
See also EWL 3
Cassavetes, John 1929-1989 .... **CLC 20**
See also CA 85-88; 127; CANR 82
Cassian, Nina 1924- .... **PC 17**
See also CWP; CWW 2
Cassill, R(onald) V(erlin) 1919-2002 .... **CLC 4, 23**
See also CA 9-12R; 208; CAAS 1; CANR 7, 45; CN 7; DLB 6, 218; DLBY 2002
Cassiodorus, Flavius Magnus c. 490(?)-c. 583(?) .... **CMLC 43**
Cassirer, Ernst 1874-1945 .... **TCLC 61**
See also CA 157
Cassity, (Allen) Turner 1929- .... **CLC 6, 42**
See also CA 17-20R, 223; CAAE 223; CAAS 8; CANR 11; CSW; DLB 105
Castaneda, Carlos (Cesar Aranha) 1931(?)-1998 .... **CLC 12, 119**
See also CA 25-28R; CANR 32, 66, 105; DNFS 1; HW 1; MTCW 1
Castedo, Elena 1937- .... **CLC 65**
See also CA 132
Castedo-Ellerman, Elena
See Castedo, Elena
Castellanos, Rosario 1925-1974 .... **CLC 66; HLC 1; SSC 39, 68**
See also CA 131; 53-56; CANR 58; CDWLB 3; DAM MULT; DLB 113, 290; EWL 3; FW; HW 1; LAW; MTCW 1; RGSF 2; RGWL 2, 3
Castelvetro, Lodovico 1505-1571 .... **LC 12**
Castiglione, Baldassare 1478-1529 ...... **LC 12**
See Castiglione, Baldesar
See also LMFS 1; RGWL 2, 3
Castiglione, Baldesar
See Castiglione, Baldassare
See also EW 2
Castillo, Ana (Hernandez Del) 1953- .... **CLC 151**
See also AAYA 42; CA 131; CANR 51, 86, 128; CWP; DLB 122, 227; DNFS 2; FW; HW 1; LLW 1; PFS 21
Castle, Robert
See Hamilton, Edmond
Castro (Ruz), Fidel 1926(?)- .... **HLC 1**
See also CA 110; 129; CANR 81; DAM MULT; HW 2
Castro, Guillen de 1569-1631 .... **LC 19**
Castro, Rosalia de 1837-1885 ... **NCLC 3, 78; PC 41**
See also DAM MULT
Cather, Willa (Sibert) 1873-1947 . **SSC 2, 50; TCLC 1, 11, 31, 99, 132, 152; WLC**
See also AAYA 24; AMW; AMWC 1; AMWR 1; BPFB 1; CA 104; 128; CDALB 1865-1917; CLR 98; DA; DA3; DAB; DAC; DAM MST, NOV; DLB 9, 54, 78, 256; DLBD 1; EWL 3; EXPN; EXPS; LAIT 3; LATS 1:1; MAWW; MTCW 1, 2; NFS 19; RGAL 4; RGSF 2; RHW; SATA 30; SSFS 2, 7, 16; TCWW 2; TUS
Catherine II
See Catherine the Great
See also DLB 150
Catherine the Great 1729-1796 .... **LC 69**
See Catherine II

Cato, Marcus Porcius 234B.C.-149B.C. .... **CMLC 21**
See Cato the Elder
Cato, Marcus Porcius, the Elder
See Cato, Marcus Porcius
Cato the Elder
See Cato, Marcus Porcius
See also DLB 211
Catton, (Charles) Bruce 1899-1978 . **CLC 35**
See also AITN 1; CA 5-8R; 81-84; CANR 7, 74; DLB 17; SATA 2; SATA-Obit 24
Catullus c. 84B.C.-54B.C. .... **CMLC 18**
See also AW 2; CDWLB 1; DLB 211; RGWL 2, 3
Cauldwell, Frank
See King, Francis (Henry)
Caunitz, William J. 1933-1996 .... **CLC 34**
See also BEST 89:3; CA 125; 130; 152; CANR 73; INT CA-130
Causley, Charles (Stanley) 1917-2003 .... **CLC 7**
See also CA 9-12R; 223; CANR 5, 35, 94; CLR 30; CWRI 5; DLB 27; MTCW 1; SATA 3, 66; SATA-Obit 149
Caute, (John) David 1936- .... **CLC 29**
See also CA 1-4R; CAAS 4; CANR 1, 33, 64, 120; CBD; CD 5; CN 7; DAM NOV; DLB 14, 231
Cavafy, C(onstantine) P(eter) .... **PC 36; TCLC 2, 7**
See Kavafis, Konstantinos Petrou
See also CA 148; DA3; DAM POET; EW 8; EWL 3; MTCW 1; PFS 19; RGWL 2, 3; WP
Cavalcanti, Guido c. 1250-c. 1300 .... **CMLC 54**
See also RGWL 2, 3
Cavallo, Evelyn
See Spark, Muriel (Sarah)
Cavanna, Betty .... **CLC 12**
See Harrison, Elizabeth (Allen) Cavanna
See also JRDA; MAICYA 1; SAAS 4; SATA 1, 30
Cavendish, Margaret Lucas 1623-1673 .... **LC 30**
See also DLB 131, 252, 281; RGEL 2
Caxton, William 1421(?)-1491(?) .... **LC 17**
See also DLB 170
Cayer, D. M.
See Duffy, Maureen
Cayrol, Jean 1911- .... **CLC 11**
See also CA 89-92; DLB 83; EWL 3
Cela (y Trulock), Camilo Jose
See Cela, Camilo Jose
See also CWW 2
Cela, Camilo Jose 1916-2002 .... **CLC 4, 13, 59, 122; HLC 1; SSC 71**
See Cela (y Trulock), Camilo Jose
See also BEST 90:2; CA 21-24R; 206; CAAS 10; CANR 21, 32, 76; DAM MULT; DLBY 1989; EW 13; EWL 3; HW 1; MTCW 1, 2; RGSF 2; RGWL 2, 3
Celan, Paul .... **CLC 10, 19, 53, 82; PC 10**
See Antschel, Paul
See also CDWLB 2; DLB 69; EWL 3; RGWL 2, 3
Celine, Louis-Ferdinand .. **CLC 1, 3, 4, 7, 9, 15, 47, 124**
See Destouches, Louis-Ferdinand
See also DLB 72; EW 11; EWL 3; GFL 1789 to the Present; RGWL 2, 3
Cellini, Benvenuto 1500-1571 .... **LC 7**
Cendrars, Blaise .... **CLC 18, 106**
See Sauser-Hall, Frederic
See also DLB 258; EWL 3; GFL 1789 to the Present; RGWL 2, 3; WP
Centlivre, Susanna 1669(?)-1723 .... **DC 25; LC 65**
See also DLB 84; RGEL 2

Cernuda (y Bidon), Luis 1902-1963 .... **CLC 54; PC 62**
See also CA 131; 89-92; DAM POET; DLB 134; EWL 3; GLL 1; HW 1; RGWL 2, 3
Cervantes, Lorna Dee 1954- ..... **HLCS 1; PC 35**
See also CA 131; CANR 80; CWP; DLB 82; EXPP; HW 1; LLW 1
Cervantes (Saavedra), Miguel de 1547-1616 .... **HLCS 1; LC 6, 23, 93; SSC 12; WLC**
See also AAYA 56; BYA 1, 14; DA; DAB; DAC; DAM MST, NOV; EW 2; LAIT 1; LATS 1:1; LMFS 1; NFS 8; RGSF 2; RGWL 2, 3; TWA
Cesaire, Aime (Fernand) 1913- .... **BLC 1; CLC 19, 32, 112; DC 22; PC 25**
See also BW 2, 3; CA 65-68; CANR 24, 43, 81; CWW 2; DA3; DAM MULT, POET; EWL 3; GFL 1789 to the Present; MTCW 1, 2; WP
Chabon, Michael 1963- ... **CLC 55, 149; SSC 59**
See also AAYA 45; AMWS 11; CA 139; CANR 57, 96, 127; DLB 278; SATA 145
Chabrol, Claude 1930- .... **CLC 16**
See also CA 110
Chairil Anwar
See Anwar, Chairil
See also EWL 3
Challans, Mary 1905-1983
See Renault, Mary
See also CA 81-84; 111; CANR 74; DA3; MTCW 2; SATA 23; SATA-Obit 36; TEA
Challis, George
See Faust, Frederick (Schiller)
See also TCWW 2
Chambers, Aidan 1934- .... **CLC 35**
See also AAYA 27; CA 25-28R; CANR 12, 31, 58, 116; JRDA; MAICYA 1, 2; SAAS 12; SATA 1, 69, 108; WYA; YAW
Chambers, James 1948-
See Cliff, Jimmy
See also CA 124
Chambers, Jessie
See Lawrence, D(avid) H(erbert Richards)
See also GLL 1
Chambers, Robert W(illiam) 1865-1933 .... **TCLC 41**
See also CA 165; DLB 202; HGG; SATA 107; SUFW 1
Chambers, (David) Whittaker 1901-1961 .... **TCLC 129**
See also CA 89-92; DLB 303
Chamisso, Adelbert von 1781-1838 .... **NCLC 82**
See also DLB 90; RGWL 2, 3; SUFW 1
Chance, James T.
See Carpenter, John (Howard)
Chance, John T.
See Carpenter, John (Howard)
Chandler, Raymond (Thornton) 1888-1959 .... **SSC 23; TCLC 1, 7**
See also AAYA 25; AMWC 2; AMWS 4; BPFB 1; CA 104; 129; CANR 60, 107; CDALB 1929-1941; CMW 4; DA3; DLB 226, 253; DLBD 6; EWL 3; MSW; MTCW 1, 2; NFS 17; RGAL 4; TUS
Chang, Diana 1934- .... **AAL**
See also CA 228; CWP; EXPP
Chang, Eileen 1921-1995 .... **AAL; SSC 28**
See Chang Ai-Ling; Zhang Ailing
See also CA 166
Chang, Jung 1952- .... **CLC 71**
See also CA 142
Chang Ai-Ling
See Chang, Eileen
See also EWL 3

Channing, William Ellery
1780-1842 .... **NCLC 17**
See also DLB 1, 59, 235; RGAL 4

Chao, Patricia 1955- .... **CLC 119**
See also CA 163

Chaplin, Charles Spencer
1889-1977 .... **CLC 16**
See Chaplin, Charlie
See also CA 81-84; 73-76

Chaplin, Charlie
See Chaplin, Charles Spencer
See also DLB 44

Chapman, George 1559(?)-1634 . **DC 19; LC 22**
See also BRW 1; DAM DRAM; DLB 62, 121; LMFS 1; RGEL 2

Chapman, Graham 1941-1989 .... **CLC 21**
See Monty Python
See also CA 116; 129; CANR 35, 95

Chapman, John Jay 1862-1933 .... **TCLC 7**
See also AMWS 14; CA 104; 191

Chapman, Lee
See Bradley, Marion Zimmer
See also GLL 1

Chapman, Walker
See Silverberg, Robert

Chappell, Fred (Davis) 1936- .... **CLC 40, 78, 162**
See also CA 5-8R, 198; CAAE 198; CAAS 4; CANR 8, 33, 67, 110; CN 7; CP 7; CSW; DLB 6, 105; HGG

Char, Rene(-Emile) 1907-1988 .... **CLC 9, 11, 14, 55; PC 56**
See also CA 13-16R; 124; CANR 32; DAM POET; DLB 258; EWL 3; GFL 1789 to the Present; MTCW 1, 2; RGWL 2, 3

Charby, Jay
See Ellison, Harlan (Jay)

Chardin, Pierre Teilhard de
See Teilhard de Chardin, (Marie Joseph) Pierre

Chariton fl. 1st cent. (?)- .... **CMLC 49**

Charlemagne 742-814 .... **CMLC 37**

Charles I 1600-1649 .... **LC 13**

Charriere, Isabelle de 1740-1805 .. **NCLC 66**

Chartier, Alain c. 1392-1430 .... **LC 94**
See also DLB 208

Chartier, Emile-Auguste
See Alain

Charyn, Jerome 1937- .... **CLC 5, 8, 18**
See also CA 5-8R; CAAS 1; CANR 7, 61, 101; CMW 4; CN 7; DLBY 1983; MTCW 1

Chase, Adam
See Marlowe, Stephen

Chase, Mary (Coyle) 1907-1981 .... **DC 1**
See also CA 77-80; 105; CAD; CWD; DFS 11; DLB 228; SATA 17; SATA-Obit 29

Chase, Mary Ellen 1887-1973 .... **CLC 2; TCLC 124**
See also CA 13-16; 41-44R; CAP 1; SATA 10

Chase, Nicholas
See Hyde, Anthony
See also CCA 1

Chateaubriand, Francois Rene de
1768-1848 .... **NCLC 3, 134**
See also DLB 119; EW 5; GFL 1789 to the Present; RGWL 2, 3; TWA

Chatterje, Sarat Chandra 1876-1936(?)
See Chatterji, Saratchandra
See also CA 109

Chatterji, Bankim Chandra
1838-1894 .... **NCLC 19**

Chatterji, Saratchandra .... **TCLC 13**
See Chatterje, Sarat Chandra
See also CA 186; EWL 3

Chatterton, Thomas 1752-1770 ...... **LC 3, 54**
See also DAM POET; DLB 109; RGEL 2

Chatwin, (Charles) Bruce
1940-1989 .... **CLC 28, 57, 59**
See also AAYA 4; BEST 90:1; BRWS 4; CA 85-88; 127; CPW; DAM POP; DLB 194, 204; EWL 3

Chaucer, Daniel
See Ford, Ford Madox
See also RHW

Chaucer, Geoffrey 1340(?)-1400 .. **LC 17, 56; PC 19, 58; WLCS**
See also BRW 1; BRWC 1; BRWR 2; CD-BLB Before 1660; DA; DA3; DAB; DAC; DAM MST, POET; DLB 146; LAIT 1; PAB; PFS 14; RGEL 2; TEA; WLIT 3; WP

Chavez, Denise (Elia) 1948- .... **HLC 1**
See also CA 131; CANR 56, 81; DAM MULT; DLB 122; FW; HW 1, 2; LLW 1; MTCW 2

Chaviaras, Strates 1935-
See Haviaras, Stratis
See also CA 105

Chayefsky, Paddy .... **CLC 23**
See Chayefsky, Sidney
See also CAD; DLB 7, 44; DLBY 1981; RGAL 4

Chayefsky, Sidney 1923-1981
See Chayefsky, Paddy
See also CA 9-12R; 104; CANR 18; DAM DRAM

Chedid, Andree 1920- .... **CLC 47**
See also CA 145; CANR 95; EWL 3

Cheever, John 1912-1982 ..... **CLC 3, 7, 8, 11, 15, 25, 64; SSC 1, 38, 57; WLC**
See also AMWS 1; BPFB 1; CA 5-8R; 106; CABS 1; CANR 5, 27, 76; CDALB 1941-1968; CPW; DA; DA3; DAB; DAC; DAM MST, NOV, POP; DLB 2, 102, 227; DLBY 1980, 1982; EWL 3; EXPS; INT CANR-5; MTCW 1, 2; RGAL 4; RGSF 2; SSFS 2, 14; TUS

Cheever, Susan 1943- .... **CLC 18, 48**
See also CA 103; CANR 27, 51, 92; DLBY 1982; INT CANR-27

Chekhonte, Antosha
See Chekhov, Anton (Pavlovich)

Chekhov, Anton (Pavlovich)
1860-1904 ...... **DC 9; SSC 2, 28, 41, 51; TCLC 3, 10, 31, 55, 96, 163; WLC**
See also BYA 14; CA 104; 124; DA; DA3; DAB; DAC; DAM DRAM, MST; DFS 1, 5, 10, 12; DLB 277; EW 7; EWL 3; EXPS; LAIT 3; LATS 1:1; RGSF 2; RGWL 2, 3; SATA 90; SSFS 5, 13, 14; TWA

Cheney, Lynne V. 1941- .... **CLC 70**
See also CA 89-92; CANR 58, 117; SATA 152

Chernyshevsky, Nikolai Gavrilovich
See Chernyshevsky, Nikolay Gavrilovich
See also DLB 238

Chernyshevsky, Nikolay Gavrilovich
1828-1889 .... **NCLC 1**
See Chernyshevsky, Nikolai Gavrilovich

Cherry, Carolyn Janice 1942-
See Cherryh, C. J.
See also CA 65-68; CANR 10

Cherryh, C. J. .... **CLC 35**
See Cherry, Carolyn Janice
See also AAYA 24; BPFB 1; DLBY 1980; FANT; SATA 93; SCFW 2; SFW 4; YAW

Chesnutt, Charles W(addell)
1858-1932 .... **BLC 1; SSC 7, 54; TCLC 5, 39**
See also AFAW 1, 2; AMWS 14; BW 1, 3; CA 106; 125; CANR 76; DAM MULT; DLB 12, 50, 78; EWL 3; MTCW 1, 2; RGAL 4; RGSF 2; SSFS 11

Chester, Alfred 1929(?)-1971 .... **CLC 49**
See also CA 196; 33-36R; DLB 130

Chesterton, G(ilbert) K(eith)
1874-1936 . **PC 28; SSC 1, 46; TCLC 1, 6, 64**
See also AAYA 57; BRW 6; CA 104; 132; CANR 73, 131; CDBLB 1914-1945; CMW 4; DAM NOV, POET; DLB 10, 19, 34, 70, 98, 149, 178; EWL 3; FANT; MSW; MTCW 1, 2; RGEL 2; RGSF 2; SATA 27; SUFW 1

Chettle, Henry c. 1564-c. 1606 .... **LC 112**
See also DLB 136; RGEL 2

Chiang, Pin-chin 1904-1986
See Ding Ling
See also CA 118

Chief Joseph 1840-1904 .... **NNAL**
See also CA 152; DA3; DAM MULT

Chief Seattle 1786(?)-1866 .... **NNAL**
See also DA3; DAM MULT

Ch'ien, Chung-shu 1910-1998 .... **CLC 22**
See Qian Zhongshu
See also CA 130; CANR 73; MTCW 1, 2

Chikamatsu Monzaemon 1653-1724 ... **LC 66**
See also RGWL 2, 3

Child, L. Maria
See Child, Lydia Maria

Child, Lydia Maria 1802-1880 .. **NCLC 6, 73**
See also DLB 1, 74, 243; RGAL 4; SATA 67

Child, Mrs.
See Child, Lydia Maria

Child, Philip 1898-1978 .... **CLC 19, 68**
See also CA 13-14; CAP 1; DLB 68; RHW; SATA 47

Childers, (Robert) Erskine
1870-1922 .... **TCLC 65**
See also CA 113; 153; DLB 70

Childress, Alice 1920-1994 . **BLC 1; CLC 12, 15, 86, 96; DC 4; TCLC 116**
See also AAYA 8; BW 2, 3; BYA 2; CA 45-48; 146; CAD; CANR 3, 27, 50, 74; CLR 14; CWD; DA3; DAM DRAM, MULT, NOV; DFS 2, 8, 14; DLB 7, 38, 249; JRDA; LAIT 5; MAICYA 1, 2; MAIC-YAS 1; MTCW 1, 2; RGAL 4; SATA 7, 48, 81; TUS; WYA; YAW

Chin, Frank (Chew, Jr.) 1940- .... **CLC 135; DC 7**
See also CA 33-36R; CANR 71; CD 5; DAM MULT; DLB 206; LAIT 5; RGAL 4

Chin, Marilyn (Mei Ling) 1955- .... **PC 40**
See also CA 129; CANR 70, 113; CWP

Chislett, (Margaret) Anne 1943- ...... **CLC 34**
See also CA 151

Chitty, Thomas Willes 1926- .... **CLC 11**
See Hinde, Thomas
See also CA 5-8R; CN 7

Chivers, Thomas Holley
1809-1858 .... **NCLC 49**
See also DLB 3, 248; RGAL 4

Choi, Susan 1969- .... **CLC 119**
See also CA 223

Chomette, Rene Lucien 1898-1981
See Clair, Rene
See also CA 103

Chomsky, (Avram) Noam 1928- ..... **CLC 132**
See also CA 17-20R; CANR 28, 62, 110, 132; DA3; DLB 246; MTCW 1, 2

Chona, Maria 1845(?)-1936 .... **NNAL**
See also CA 144

Chopin, Kate .... **SSC 8, 68; TCLC 127; WLCS**
See Chopin, Katherine
See also AAYA 33; AMWR 2; AMWS 1; BYA 11, 15; CDALB 1865-1917; DA; DAB; DLB 12, 78; EXPN; EXPS; FW; LAIT 3; MAWW; NFS 3; RGAL 4; RGSF 2; SSFS 17; TUS

Chopin, Katherine 1851-1904
See Chopin, Kate
See also CA 104; 122; DA3; DAC; DAM MST, NOV

Chretien de Troyes c. 12th cent. -. **CMLC 10**
See also DLB 208; EW 1; RGWL 2, 3; TWA

Christie
See Ichikawa, Kon

Christie, Agatha (Mary Clarissa) 1890-1976 .. **CLC 1, 6, 8, 12, 39, 48, 110**
See also AAYA 9; AITN 1, 2; BPFB 1; BRWS 2; CA 17-20R; 61-64; CANR 10, 37, 108; CBD; CDBLB 1914-1945; CMW 4; CPW; CWD; DA3; DAB; DAC; DAM NOV; DFS 2; DLB 13, 77, 245; MSW; MTCW 1, 2; NFS 8; RGEL 2; RHW; SATA 36; TEA; YAW

Christie, Philippa .... **CLC 21**
See Pearce, Philippa
See also BYA 5; CANR 109; CLR 9; DLB 161; MAICYA 1; SATA 1, 67, 129

Christine de Pizan 1365(?)-1431(?) .... **LC 9**
See also DLB 208; RGWL 2, 3

Chuang Tzu c. 369B.C.-c. 286B.C. .... **CMLC 57**

Chubb, Elmer
See Masters, Edgar Lee

Chulkov, Mikhail Dmitrievich 1743-1792 .... **LC 2**
See also DLB 150

Churchill, Caryl 1938- .... **CLC 31, 55, 157; DC 5**
See Churchill, Chick
See also BRWS 4; CA 102; CANR 22, 46, 108; CBD; CWD; DFS 12, 16; DLB 13; EWL 3; FW; MTCW 1; RGEL 2

Churchill, Charles 1731-1764 .... **LC 3**
See also DLB 109; RGEL 2

Churchill, Chick
See Churchill, Caryl
See also CD 5

Churchill, Sir Winston (Leonard Spencer) 1874-1965 .... **TCLC 113**
See also BRW 6; CA 97-100; CDBLB 1890-1914; DA3; DLB 100; DLBD 16; LAIT 4; MTCW 1, 2

Chute, Carolyn 1947- .... **CLC 39**
See also CA 123; CANR 135

Ciardi, John (Anthony) 1916-1986 . **CLC 10, 40, 44, 129**
See also CA 5-8R; 118; CAAS 2; CANR 5, 33; CLR 19; CWRI 5; DAM POET; DLB 5; DLBY 1986; INT CANR-5; MAICYA 1, 2; MTCW 1, 2; RGAL 4; SAAS 26; SATA 1, 65; SATA-Obit 46

Cibber, Colley 1671-1757 .... **LC 66**
See also DLB 84; RGEL 2

Cicero, Marcus Tullius 106B.C.-43B.C. .... **CMLC 3**
See also AW 1; CDWLB 1; DLB 211; RGWL 2, 3

Cimino, Michael 1943- .... **CLC 16**
See also CA 105

Cioran, E(mil) M. 1911-1995 .... **CLC 64**
See also CA 25-28R; 149; CANR 91; DLB 220; EWL 3

Cisneros, Sandra 1954- .... **CLC 69, 118, 193; HLC 1; PC 64; SSC 32, 72**
See also AAYA 9, 53; AMWS 7; CA 131; CANR 64, 118; CWP; DA3; DAM MULT; DLB 122, 152; EWL 3; EXPN; FW; HW 1, 2; LAIT 5; LATS 1:2; LLW 1; MAICYA 1, 2; MTCW 2; NFS 2; PFS 19; RGAL 4; RGSF 2; SSFS 3, 13; WLIT 1; YAW

Cixous, Helene 1937- .... **CLC 92**
See also CA 126; CANR 55, 123; CWW 2; DLB 83, 242; EWL 3; FW; GLL 2; MTCW 1, 2; TWA

Clair, Rene .... **CLC 20**
See Chomette, Rene Lucien

Clampitt, Amy 1920-1994 .... **CLC 32; PC 19**
See also AMWS 9; CA 110; 146; CANR 29, 79; DLB 105

Clancy, Thomas L., Jr. 1947-
See Clancy, Tom
See also CA 125; 131; CANR 62, 105; DA3; INT CA-131; MTCW 1, 2

Clancy, Tom .... **CLC 45, 112**
See Clancy, Thomas L., Jr.
See also AAYA 9, 51; BEST 89:1, 90:1; BPFB 1; BYA 10, 11; CANR 132; CMW 4; CPW; DAM NOV, POP; DLB 227

Clare, John 1793-1864 .. **NCLC 9, 86; PC 23**
See also DAB; DAM POET; DLB 55, 96; RGEL 2

Clarin
See Alas (y Urena), Leopoldo (Enrique Garcia)

Clark, Al C.
See Goines, Donald

Clark, (Robert) Brian 1932- .... **CLC 29**
See also CA 41-44R; CANR 67; CBD; CD 5

Clark, Curt
See Westlake, Donald E(dwin)

Clark, Eleanor 1913-1996 .... **CLC 5, 19**
See also CA 9-12R; 151; CANR 41; CN 7; DLB 6

Clark, J. P.
See Clark Bekederemo, J(ohnson) P(epper)
See also CDWLB 3; DLB 117

Clark, John Pepper
See Clark Bekederemo, J(ohnson) P(epper)
See also AFW; CD 5; CP 7; RGEL 2

Clark, Kenneth (Mackenzie) 1903-1983 .... **TCLC 147**
See also CA 93-96; 109; CANR 36; MTCW 1, 2

Clark, M. R.
See Clark, Mavis Thorpe

Clark, Mavis Thorpe 1909-1999 .... **CLC 12**
See also CA 57-60; CANR 8, 37, 107; CLR 30; CWRI 5; MAICYA 1, 2; SAAS 5; SATA 8, 74

Clark, Walter Van Tilburg 1909-1971 .... **CLC 28**
See also CA 9-12R; 33-36R; CANR 63, 113; DLB 9, 206; LAIT 2; RGAL 4; SATA 8

Clark Bekederemo, J(ohnson) P(epper) 1935- .... **BLC 1; CLC 38; DC 5**
See Clark, J. P.; Clark, John Pepper
See also BW 1; CA 65-68; CANR 16, 72; DAM DRAM, MULT; DFS 13; EWL 3; MTCW 1

Clarke, Arthur C(harles) 1917- .... **CLC 1, 4, 13, 18, 35, 136; SSC 3**
See also AAYA 4, 33; BPFB 1; BYA 13; CA 1-4R; CANR 2, 28, 55, 74, 130; CN 7; CPW; DA3; DAM POP; DLB 261; JRDA; LAIT 5; MAICYA 1, 2; MTCW 1, 2; SATA 13, 70, 115; SCFW; SFW 4; SSFS 4, 18; YAW

Clarke, Austin 1896-1974 .... **CLC 6, 9**
See also CA 29-32; 49-52; CAP 2; DAM POET; DLB 10, 20; EWL 3; RGEL 2

Clarke, Austin C(hesterfield) 1934- .. **BLC 1; CLC 8, 53; SSC 45**
See also BW 1; CA 25-28R; CAAS 16; CANR 14, 32, 68; CN 7; DAC; DAM MULT; DLB 53, 125; DNFS 2; RGSF 2

Clarke, Gillian 1937- .... **CLC 61**
See also CA 106; CP 7; CWP; DLB 40

Clarke, Marcus (Andrew Hislop) 1846-1881 .... **NCLC 19**
See also DLB 230; RGEL 2; RGSF 2

Clarke, Shirley 1925-1997 .... **CLC 16**
See also CA 189

Clash, The
See Headon, (Nicky) Topper; Jones, Mick; Simonon, Paul; Strummer, Joe

Claudel, Paul (Louis Charles Marie) 1868-1955 .... **TCLC 2, 10**
See also CA 104; 165; DLB 192, 258; EW 8; EWL 3; GFL 1789 to the Present; RGWL 2, 3; TWA

Claudian 370(?)-404(?) .... **CMLC 46**
See also RGWL 2, 3

Claudius, Matthias 1740-1815 .... **NCLC 75**
See also DLB 97

Clavell, James (duMaresq) 1925-1994 .... **CLC 6, 25, 87**
See also BPFB 1; CA 25-28R; 146; CANR 26, 48; CPW; DA3; DAM NOV, POP; MTCW 1, 2; NFS 10; RHW

Clayman, Gregory .... **CLC 65**

Cleaver, (Leroy) Eldridge 1935-1998 .... **BLC 1; CLC 30, 119**
See also BW 1, 3; CA 21-24R; 167; CANR 16, 75; DA3; DAM MULT; MTCW 2; YAW

Cleese, John (Marwood) 1939- .... **CLC 21**
See Monty Python
See also CA 112; 116; CANR 35; MTCW 1

Cleishbotham, Jebediah
See Scott, Sir Walter

Cleland, John 1710-1789 .... **LC 2, 48**
See also DLB 39; RGEL 2

Clemens, Samuel Langhorne 1835-1910
See Twain, Mark
See also CA 104; 135; CDALB 1865-1917; DA; DA3; DAB; DAC; DAM MST, NOV; DLB 12, 23, 64, 74, 186, 189; JRDA; LMFS 1; MAICYA 1, 2; NCFS 4; NFS 20; SATA 100; SSFS 16; YABC 2

Clement of Alexandria 150(?)-215(?) .... **CMLC 41**

Cleophil
See Congreve, William

Clerihew, E.
See Bentley, E(dmund) C(lerihew)

Clerk, N. W.
See Lewis, C(live) S(taples)

Cleveland, John 1613-1658 .... **LC 106**
See also DLB 126; RGEL 2

Cliff, Jimmy .... **CLC 21**
See Chambers, James
See also CA 193

Cliff, Michelle 1946- .... **BLCS; CLC 120**
See also BW 2; CA 116; CANR 39, 72; CDWLB 3; DLB 157; FW; GLL 2

Clifford, Lady Anne 1590-1676 .... **LC 76**
See also DLB 151

Clifton, (Thelma) Lucille 1936- .... **BLC 1; CLC 19, 66, 162; PC 17**
See also AFAW 2; BW 2, 3; CA 49-52; CANR 2, 24, 42, 76, 97; CLR 5; CP 7; CSW; CWP; CWRI 5; DA3; DAM MULT, POET; DLB 5, 41; EXPP; MAICYA 1, 2; MTCW 1, 2; PFS 1, 14; SATA 20, 69, 128; WP

Clinton, Dirk
See Silverberg, Robert

Clough, Arthur Hugh 1819-1861 ... **NCLC 27**
See also BRW 5; DLB 32; RGEL 2

Clutha, Janet Paterson Frame 1924-2004
See Frame, Janet
See also CA 1-4R; 224; CANR 2, 36, 76, 135; MTCW 1, 2; SATA 119

Clyne, Terence
See Blatty, William Peter

Cobalt, Martin
See Mayne, William (James Carter)

Cobb, Irvin S(hrewsbury)
1876-1944 .... **TCLC 77**
See also CA 175; DLB 11, 25, 86

Cobbett, William 1763-1835 .... **NCLC 49**
See also DLB 43, 107, 158; RGEL 2

Coburn, D(onald) L(ee) 1938- .... **CLC 10**
See also CA 89-92

Cocteau, Jean (Maurice Eugene Clement)
1889-1963 ...... **CLC 1, 8, 15, 16, 43; DC 17; TCLC 119; WLC**
See also CA 25-28; CANR 40; CAP 2; DA; DA3; DAB; DAC; DAM DRAM, MST, NOV; DLB 65, 258; EW 10; EWL 3; GFL 1789 to the Present; MTCW 1, 2; RGWL 2, 3; TWA

Codrescu, Andrei 1946- .... **CLC 46, 121**
See also CA 33-36R; CAAS 19; CANR 13, 34, 53, 76, 125; DA3; DAM POET; MTCW 2

Coe, Max
See Bourne, Randolph S(illiman)

Coe, Tucker
See Westlake, Donald E(dwin)

Coen, Ethan 1958- .... **CLC 108**
See also AAYA 54; CA 126; CANR 85

Coen, Joel 1955- .... **CLC 108**
See also AAYA 54; CA 126; CANR 119

The Coen Brothers
See Coen, Ethan; Coen, Joel

Coetzee, J(ohn) M(axwell) 1940- ..... **CLC 23, 33, 66, 117, 161, 162**
See also AAYA 37; AFW; BRWS 6; CA 77-80; CANR 41, 54, 74, 114, 133; CN 7; DA3; DAM NOV; DLB 225; EWL 3; LMFS 2; MTCW 1, 2; WLIT 2; WWE 1

Coffey, Brian
See Koontz, Dean R(ay)

Coffin, Robert P(eter) Tristram
1892-1955 .... **TCLC 95**
See also CA 123; 169; DLB 45

Cohan, George M(ichael)
1878-1942 .... **TCLC 60**
See also CA 157; DLB 249; RGAL 4

Cohen, Arthur A(llen) 1928-1986 ...... **CLC 7, 31**
See also CA 1-4R; 120; CANR 1, 17, 42; DLB 28

Cohen, Leonard (Norman) 1934- ...... **CLC 3, 38**
See also CA 21-24R; CANR 14, 69; CN 7; CP 7; DAC; DAM MST; DLB 53; EWL 3; MTCW 1

Cohen, Matt(hew) 1942-1999 .... **CLC 19**
See also CA 61-64; 187; CAAS 18; CANR 40; CN 7; DAC; DLB 53

Cohen-Solal, Annie 19(?)- .... **CLC 50**

Colegate, Isabel 1931- .... **CLC 36**
See also CA 17-20R; CANR 8, 22, 74; CN 7; DLB 14, 231; INT CANR-22; MTCW 1

Coleman, Emmett
See Reed, Ishmael

Coleridge, Hartley 1796-1849 .... **NCLC 90**
See also DLB 96

Coleridge, M. E.
See Coleridge, Mary E(lizabeth)

Coleridge, Mary E(lizabeth)
1861-1907 .... **TCLC 73**
See also CA 116; 166; DLB 19, 98

Coleridge, Samuel Taylor
1772-1834 ...... **NCLC 9, 54, 99, 111; PC 11, 39; WLC**
See also BRW 4; BRWR 2; BYA 4; CDBLB 1789-1832; DA; DA3; DAB; DAC; DAM MST, POET; DLB 93, 107; EXPP; LATS 1:1; LMFS 1; PAB; PFS 4, 5; RGEL 2; TEA; WLIT 3; WP

Coleridge, Sara 1802-1852 .... **NCLC 31**
See also DLB 199

Coles, Don 1928- .... **CLC 46**
See also CA 115; CANR 38; CP 7

Coles, Robert (Martin) 1929- .... **CLC 108**
See also CA 45-48; CANR 3, 32, 66, 70, 135; INT CANR-32; SATA 23

Colette, (Sidonie-Gabrielle)
1873-1954 .... **SSC 10; TCLC 1, 5, 16**
See Willy, Colette
See also CA 104; 131; DA3; DAM NOV; DLB 65; EW 9; EWL 3; GFL 1789 to the Present; MTCW 1, 2; RGWL 2, 3; TWA

Collett, (Jacobine) Camilla (Wergeland)
1813-1895 .... **NCLC 22**

Collier, Christopher 1930- .... **CLC 30**
See also AAYA 13; BYA 2; CA 33-36R; CANR 13, 33, 102; JRDA; MAICYA 1, 2; SATA 16, 70; WYA; YAW 1

Collier, James Lincoln 1928- .... **CLC 30**
See also AAYA 13; BYA 2; CA 9-12R; CANR 4, 33, 60, 102; CLR 3; DAM POP; JRDA; MAICYA 1, 2; SAAS 21; SATA 8, 70; WYA; YAW 1

Collier, Jeremy 1650-1726 .... **LC 6**

Collier, John 1901-1980 . **SSC 19; TCLC 127**
See also CA 65-68; 97-100; CANR 10; DLB 77, 255; FANT; SUFW 1

Collier, Mary 1690-1762 .... **LC 86**
See also DLB 95

Collingwood, R(obin) G(eorge)
1889(?)-1943 .... **TCLC 67**
See also CA 117; 155; DLB 262

Collins, Hunt
See Hunter, Evan

Collins, Linda 1931- .... **CLC 44**
See also CA 125

Collins, Tom
See Furphy, Joseph
See also RGEL 2

Collins, (William) Wilkie
1824-1889 .... **NCLC 1, 18, 93**
See also BRWS 6; CDBLB 1832-1890; CMW 4; DLB 18, 70, 159; MSW; RGEL 2; RGSF 2; SUFW 1; WLIT 4

Collins, William 1721-1759 .... **LC 4, 40**
See also BRW 3; DAM POET; DLB 109; RGEL 2

Collodi, Carlo .... **NCLC 54**
See Lorenzini, Carlo
See also CLR 5; WCH

Colman, George
See Glassco, John

Colman, George, the Elder
1732-1794 .... **LC 98**
See also RGEL 2

Colonna, Vittoria 1492-1547 .... **LC 71**
See also RGWL 2, 3

Colt, Winchester Remington
See Hubbard, L(afayette) Ron(ald)

Colter, Cyrus J. 1910-2002 .... **CLC 58**
See also BW 1; CA 65-68; 205; CANR 10, 66; CN 7; DLB 33

Colton, James
See Hansen, Joseph
See also GLL 1

Colum, Padraic 1881-1972 .... **CLC 28**
See also BYA 4; CA 73-76; 33-36R; CANR 35; CLR 36; CWRI 5; DLB 19; MAICYA 1, 2; MTCW 1; RGEL 2; SATA 15; WCH

Colvin, James
See Moorcock, Michael (John)

Colwin, Laurie (E.) 1944-1992 .... **CLC 5, 13, 23, 84**
See also CA 89-92; 139; CANR 20, 46; DLB 218; DLBY 1980; MTCW 1

Comfort, Alex(ander) 1920-2000 .... **CLC 7**
See also CA 1-4R; 190; CANR 1, 45; CP 7; DAM POP; MTCW 1

Comfort, Montgomery
See Campbell, (John) Ramsey

Compton-Burnett, I(vy)
1892(?)-1969 .... **CLC 1, 3, 10, 15, 34**
See also BRW 7; CA 1-4R; 25-28R; CANR 4; DAM NOV; DLB 36; EWL 3; MTCW 1; RGEL 2

Comstock, Anthony 1844-1915 ...... **TCLC 13**
See also CA 110; 169

Comte, Auguste 1798-1857 .... **NCLC 54**

Conan Doyle, Arthur
See Doyle, Sir Arthur Conan
See also BPFB 1; BYA 4, 5, 11

Conde (Abellan), Carmen
1901-1996 .... **HLCS 1**
See also CA 177; CWW 2; DLB 108; EWL 3; HW 2

Conde, Maryse 1937- ...... **BLCS; CLC 52, 92**
See also BW 2, 3; CA 110, 190; CAAE 190; CANR 30, 53, 76; CWW 2; DAM MULT; EWL 3; MTCW 1

Condillac, Etienne Bonnot de
1714-1780 .... **LC 26**

Condon, Richard (Thomas)
1915-1996 .... **CLC 4, 6, 8, 10, 45, 100**
See also BEST 90:3; BPFB 1; CA 1-4R; 151; CAAS 1, 2, 23; CMW 4; CN 7; DAM NOV; INT CANR-23; MTCW 1, 2

Condorcet 1743-1794 .... **LC 104**
See also GFL Beginnings to 1789

Confucius 551B.C.-479B.C. ..... **CMLC 19, 65; WLCS**
See also DA; DA3; DAB; DAC; DAM MST

Congreve, William 1670-1729 ... **DC 2; LC 5, 21; WLC**
See also BRW 2; CDBLB 1660-1789; DA; DAB; DAC; DAM DRAM, MST, POET; DFS 15; DLB 39, 84; RGEL 2; WLIT 3

Conley, Robert J(ackson) 1940- .... **NNAL**
See also CA 41-44R; CANR 15, 34, 45, 96; DAM MULT

Connell, Evan S(helby), Jr. 1924- . **CLC 4, 6, 45**
See also AAYA 7; AMWS 14; CA 1-4R; CAAS 2; CANR 2, 39, 76, 97; CN 7; DAM NOV; DLB 2; DLBY 1981; MTCW 1, 2

Connelly, Marc(us Cook) 1890-1980 . **CLC 7**
See also CA 85-88; 102; CANR 30; DFS 12; DLB 7; DLBY 1980; RGAL 4; SATA-Obit 25

Connor, Ralph .... **TCLC 31**
See Gordon, Charles William
See also DLB 92; TCWW 2

Conrad, Joseph 1857-1924 ..... **SSC 9, 67, 69, 71; TCLC 1, 6, 13, 25, 43, 57; WLC**
See also AAYA 26; BPFB 1; BRW 6; BRWC 1; BRWR 2; BYA 2; CA 104; 131; CANR 60; CDBLB 1890-1914; DA; DA3; DAB; DAC; DAM MST, NOV; DLB 10, 34, 98, 156; EWL 3; EXPN; EXPS; LAIT 2; LATS 1:1; LMFS 1; MTCW 1, 2; NFS 2, 16; RGEL 2; RGSF 2; SATA 27; SSFS 1, 12; TEA; WLIT 4

Conrad, Robert Arnold
See Hart, Moss

Conroy, (Donald) Pat(rick) 1945- ... **CLC 30, 74**
See also AAYA 8, 52; AITN 1; BPFB 1; CA 85-88; CANR 24, 53, 129; CPW; CSW; DA3; DAM NOV, POP; DLB 6; LAIT 5; MTCW 1, 2

Constant (de Rebecque), (Henri) Benjamin
1767-1830 .... **NCLC 6**
See also DLB 119; EW 4; GFL 1789 to the Present

Conway, Jill K(er) 1934- .... **CLC 152**
See also CA 130; CANR 94

Conybeare, Charles Augustus
See Eliot, T(homas) S(tearns)

Cook, Michael 1933-1994 .... **CLC 58**
See also CA 93-96; CANR 68; DLB 53

Cook, Robin 1940- .... **CLC 14**
See also AAYA 32; BEST 90:2; BPFB 1; CA 108; 111; CANR 41, 90, 109; CPW; DA3; DAM POP; HGG; INT CA-111

Cook, Roy
See Silverberg, Robert

Cooke, Elizabeth 1948- .... **CLC 55**
See also CA 129

Cooke, John Esten 1830-1886 .... **NCLC 5**
See also DLB 3, 248; RGAL 4

Cooke, John Estes
See Baum, L(yman) Frank

Cooke, M. E.
See Creasey, John

Cooke, Margaret
See Creasey, John

Cooke, Rose Terry 1827-1892 ...... **NCLC 110**
See also DLB 12, 74

Cook-Lynn, Elizabeth 1930- .... **CLC 93; NNAL**
See also CA 133; DAM MULT; DLB 175

Cooney, Ray .... **CLC 62**
See also CBD

Cooper, Anthony Ashley 1671-1713 .. **LC 107**
See also DLB 101

Cooper, Dennis 1953- .... **CLC 203**
See also CA 133; CANR 72, 86; GLL 1; St. James Guide to Horror, Ghost, and Gothic Writers.

Cooper, Douglas 1960- .... **CLC 86**

Cooper, Henry St. John
See Creasey, John

Cooper, J(oan) California (?)- .... **CLC 56**
See also AAYA 12; BW 1; CA 125; CANR 55; DAM MULT; DLB 212

Cooper, James Fenimore
1789-1851 .... **NCLC 1, 27, 54**
See also AAYA 22; AMW; BPFB 1; CDALB 1640-1865; DA3; DLB 3, 183, 250, 254; LAIT 1; NFS 9; RGAL 4; SATA 19; TUS; WCH

Cooper, Susan Fenimore
1813-1894 .... **NCLC 129**
See also ANW; DLB 239, 254

Coover, Robert (Lowell) 1932- .... **CLC 3, 7, 15, 32, 46, 87, 161; SSC 15**
See also AMWS 5; BPFB 1; CA 45-48; CANR 3, 37, 58, 115; CN 7; DAM NOV; DLB 2, 227; DLBY 1981; EWL 3; MTCW 1, 2; RGAL 4; RGSF 2

Copeland, Stewart (Armstrong)
1952- .... **CLC 26**

Copernicus, Nicolaus 1473-1543 .... **LC 45**

Coppard, A(lfred) E(dgar)
1878-1957 .... **SSC 21; TCLC 5**
See also BRWS 8; CA 114; 167; DLB 162; EWL 3; HGG; RGEL 2; RGSF 2; SUFW 1; YABC 1

Coppee, Francois 1842-1908 .... **TCLC 25**
See also CA 170; DLB 217

Coppola, Francis Ford 1939- ... **CLC 16, 126**
See also AAYA 39; CA 77-80; CANR 40, 78; DLB 44

Copway, George 1818-1869 .... **NNAL**
See also DAM MULT; DLB 175, 183

Corbiere, Tristan 1845-1875 .... **NCLC 43**
See also DLB 217; GFL 1789 to the Present

Corcoran, Barbara (Asenath)
1911- .... **CLC 17**
See also AAYA 14; CA 21-24R; 191; CAAE 191; CAAS 2; CANR 11, 28, 48; CLR 50; DLB 52; JRDA; MAICYA 2; MAIC-YAS 1; RHW; SAAS 20; SATA 3, 77; SATA-Essay 125

Cordelier, Maurice
See Giraudoux, Jean(-Hippolyte)

Corelli, Marie .... **TCLC 51**
See Mackay, Mary
See also DLB 34, 156; RGEL 2; SUFW 1

Corinna c. 225B.C.-c. 305B.C. .... **CMLC 72**

Corman, Cid .... **CLC 9**
See Corman, Sidney
See also CAAS 2; DLB 5, 193

Corman, Sidney 1924-2004
See Corman, Cid
See also CA 85-88; 225; CANR 44; CP 7; DAM POET

Cormier, Robert (Edmund)
1925-2000 .... **CLC 12, 30**
See also AAYA 3, 19; BYA 1, 2, 6, 8, 9; CA 1-4R; CANR 5, 23, 76, 93; CDALB 1968-1988; CLR 12, 55; DA; DAB; DAC; DAM MST, NOV; DLB 52; EXPN; INT CANR-23; JRDA; LAIT 5; MAICYA 1, 2; MTCW 1, 2; NFS 2, 18; SATA 10, 45, 83; SATA-Obit 122; WYA; YAW

Corn, Alfred (DeWitt III) 1943- .... **CLC 33**
See also CA 179; CAAE 179; CAAS 25; CANR 44; CP 7; CSW; DLB 120, 282; DLBY 1980

Corneille, Pierre 1606-1684 ... **DC 21; LC 28**
See also DAB; DAM MST; DLB 268; EW 3; GFL Beginnings to 1789; RGWL 2, 3; TWA

Cornwell, David (John Moore)
1931- .... **CLC 9, 15**
See le Carre, John
See also CA 5-8R; CANR 13, 33, 59, 107, 132; DA3; DAM POP; MTCW 1, 2

Cornwell, Patricia (Daniels) 1956- . **CLC 155**
See also AAYA 16, 56; BPFB 1; CA 134; CANR 53, 131; CMW 4; CPW; CSW; DAM POP; DLB 306; MSW; MTCW 1

Corso, (Nunzio) Gregory 1930-2001 . **CLC 1, 11; PC 33**
See also AMWS 12; BG 2; CA 5-8R; 193; CANR 41, 76, 132; CP 7; DA3; DLB 5, 16, 237; LMFS 2; MTCW 1, 2; WP

Cortazar, Julio 1914-1984 ... **CLC 2, 3, 5, 10, 13, 15, 33, 34, 92; HLC 1; SSC 7, 76**
See also BPFB 1; CA 21-24R; CANR 12, 32, 81; CDWLB 3; DA3; DAM MULT, NOV; DLB 113; EWL 3; EXPS; HW 1, 2; LAW; MTCW 1, 2; RGSF 2; RGWL 2, 3; SSFS 3, 20; TWA; WLIT 1

Cortes, Hernan 1485-1547 .... **LC 31**

Corvinus, Jakob
See Raabe, Wilhelm (Karl)

Corwin, Cecil
See Kornbluth, C(yril) M.

Cosic, Dobrica 1921- .... **CLC 14**
See also CA 122; 138; CDWLB 4; CWW 2; DLB 181; EWL 3

Costain, Thomas B(ertram)
1885-1965 .... **CLC 30**
See also BYA 3; CA 5-8R; 25-28R; DLB 9; RHW

Costantini, Humberto 1924(?)-1987 . **CLC 49**
See also CA 131; 122; EWL 3; HW 1

Costello, Elvis 1954- .... **CLC 21**
See also CA 204

Costenoble, Philostene
See Ghelderode, Michel de

Cotes, Cecil V.
See Duncan, Sara Jeannette

Cotter, Joseph Seamon Sr.
1861-1949 .... **BLC 1; TCLC 28**
See also BW 1; CA 124; DAM MULT; DLB 50

Couch, Arthur Thomas Quiller
See Quiller-Couch, Sir Arthur (Thomas)

Coulton, James
See Hansen, Joseph

Couperus, Louis (Marie Anne)
1863-1923 .... **TCLC 15**
See also CA 115; EWL 3; RGWL 2, 3

Coupland, Douglas 1961- .... **CLC 85, 133**
See also AAYA 34; CA 142; CANR 57, 90, 130; CCA 1; CPW; DAC; DAM POP

Court, Wesli
See Turco, Lewis (Putnam)

Courtenay, Bryce 1933- .... **CLC 59**
See also CA 138; CPW

Courtney, Robert
See Ellison, Harlan (Jay)

Cousteau, Jacques-Yves 1910-1997 .. **CLC 30**
See also CA 65-68; 159; CANR 15, 67; MTCW 1; SATA 38, 98

Coventry, Francis 1725-1754 .... **LC 46**

Coverdale, Miles c. 1487-1569 .... **LC 77**
See also DLB 167

Cowan, Peter (Walkinshaw)
1914-2002 .... **SSC 28**
See also CA 21-24R; CANR 9, 25, 50, 83; CN 7; DLB 260; RGSF 2

Coward, Noel (Peirce) 1899-1973 . **CLC 1, 9, 29, 51**
See also AITN 1; BRWS 2; CA 17-18; 41-44R; CANR 35, 132; CAP 2; CDBLB 1914-1945; DA3; DAM DRAM; DFS 3, 6; DLB 10, 245; EWL 3; IDFW 3, 4; MTCW 1, 2; RGEL 2; TEA

Cowley, Abraham 1618-1667 .... **LC 43**
See also BRW 2; DLB 131, 151; PAB; RGEL 2

Cowley, Malcolm 1898-1989 .... **CLC 39**
See also AMWS 2; CA 5-8R; 128; CANR 3, 55; DLB 4, 48; DLBY 1981, 1989; EWL 3; MTCW 1, 2

Cowper, William 1731-1800 ..... **NCLC 8, 94; PC 40**
See also BRW 3; DA3; DAM POET; DLB 104, 109; RGEL 2

Cox, William Trevor 1928-
See Trevor, William
See also CA 9-12R; CANR 4, 37, 55, 76, 102; DAM NOV; INT CANR-37; MTCW 1, 2; TEA

Coyne, P. J.
See Masters, Hilary

Cozzens, James Gould 1903-1978 . **CLC 1, 4, 11, 92**
See also AMW; BPFB 1; CA 9-12R; 81-84; CANR 19; CDALB 1941-1968; DLB 9, 294; DLBD 2; DLBY 1984, 1997; EWL 3; MTCW 1, 2; RGAL 4

Crabbe, George 1754-1832 ..... **NCLC 26, 121**
See also BRW 3; DLB 93; RGEL 2

Crace, Jim 1946- .... **CLC 157; SSC 61**
See also CA 128; 135; CANR 55, 70, 123; CN 7; DLB 231; INT CA-135

Craddock, Charles Egbert
See Murfree, Mary Noailles

Craig, A. A.
See Anderson, Poul (William)

Craik, Mrs.
See Craik, Dinah Maria (Mulock)
See also RGEL 2

Craik, Dinah Maria (Mulock)
1826-1887 .... **NCLC 38**
See Craik, Mrs.; Mulock, Dinah Maria
See also DLB 35, 163; MAICYA 1, 2; SATA 34

Cram, Ralph Adams 1863-1942 ..... **TCLC 45**
See also CA 160

Cranch, Christopher Pearse
1813-1892 .... **NCLC 115**
See also DLB 1, 42, 243

Crane, (Harold) Hart 1899-1932 .... **PC** 3; **TCLC** 2, 5, 80; **WLC**
See also AMW; AMWR 2; CA 104; 127; CDALB 1917-1929; DA; DA3; DAB; DAC; DAM MST, POET; DLB 4, 48; EWL 3; MTCW 1, 2; RGAL 4; TUS

Crane, R(onald) S(almon) 1886-1967 .... **CLC** 27
See also CA 85-88; DLB 63

Crane, Stephen (Townley) 1871-1900 ...... **SSC** 7, 56, 70; **TCLC** 11, 17, 32; **WLC**
See also AAYA 21; AMW; AMWC 1; BPFB 1; BYA 3; CA 109; 140; CANR 84; CDALB 1865-1917; DA; DA3; DAB; DAC; DAM MST, NOV, POET; DLB 12, 54, 78; EXPN; EXPS; LAIT 2; LMFS 2; NFS 4, 20; PFS 9; RGAL 4; RGSF 2; SSFS 4; TUS; WYA; YABC 2

Cranmer, Thomas 1489-1556 .... **LC** 95
See also DLB 132, 213

Cranshaw, Stanley
See Fisher, Dorothy (Frances) Canfield

Crase, Douglas 1944- .... **CLC** 58
See also CA 106

Crashaw, Richard 1612(?)-1649 .... **LC** 24
See also BRW 2; DLB 126; PAB; RGEL 2

Cratinus c. 519B.C.-c. 422B.C. ..... **CMLC** 54
See also LMFS 1

Craven, Margaret 1901-1980 .... **CLC** 17
See also BYA 2; CA 103; CCA 1; DAC; LAIT 5

Crawford, F(rancis) Marion 1854-1909 .... **TCLC** 10
See also CA 107; 168; DLB 71; HGG; RGAL 4; SUFW 1

Crawford, Isabella Valancy 1850-1887 .... **NCLC** 12, 127
See also DLB 92; RGEL 2

Crayon, Geoffrey
See Irving, Washington

Creasey, John 1908-1973 .... **CLC** 11
See Marric, J. J.
See also CA 5-8R; 41-44R; CANR 8, 59; CMW 4; DLB 77; MTCW 1

Crebillon, Claude Prosper Jolyot de (fils) 1707-1777 .... **LC** 1, 28
See also GFL Beginnings to 1789

Credo
See Creasey, John

Credo, Alvaro J. de
See Prado (Calvo), Pedro

Creeley, Robert (White) 1926- .. **CLC** 1, 2, 4, 8, 11, 15, 36, 78
See also AMWS 4; CA 1-4R; CAAS 10; CANR 23, 43, 89; CP 7; DA3; DAM POET; DLB 5, 16, 169; DLBD 17; EWL 3; MTCW 1, 2; PFS 21; RGAL 4; WP

de Crenne, Hélisenne c. 1510-c. 1560 .... **LC** 113

Crevecoeur, Hector St. John de
See Crevecoeur, Michel Guillaume Jean de
See also ANW

Crevecoeur, Michel Guillaume Jean de 1735-1813 .... **NCLC** 105
See Crevecoeur, Hector St. John de
See also AMWS 1; DLB 37

Crevel, Rene 1900-1935 .... **TCLC** 112
See also GLL 2

Crews, Harry (Eugene) 1935- ..... **CLC** 6, 23, 49
See also AITN 1; AMWS 11; BPFB 1; CA 25-28R; CANR 20, 57; CN 7; CSW; DA3; DLB 6, 143, 185; MTCW 1, 2; RGAL 4

Crichton, (John) Michael 1942- .... **CLC** 2, 6, 54, 90
See also AAYA 10, 49; AITN 2; BPFB 1; CA 25-28R; CANR 13, 40, 54, 76, 127; CMW 4; CN 7; CPW; DA3; DAM NOV, POP; DLB 292; DLBY 1981; INT CANR-13; JRDA; MTCW 1, 2; SATA 9, 88; SFW 4; YAW

Crispin, Edmund .... **CLC** 22
See Montgomery, (Robert) Bruce
See also DLB 87; MSW

Cristofer, Michael 1945(?)- .... **CLC** 28
See also CA 110; 152; CAD; CD 5; DAM DRAM; DFS 15; DLB 7

Criton
See Alain

Croce, Benedetto 1866-1952 .... **TCLC** 37
See also CA 120; 155; EW 8; EWL 3

Crockett, David 1786-1836 .... **NCLC** 8
See also DLB 3, 11, 183, 248

Crockett, Davy
See Crockett, David

Crofts, Freeman Wills 1879-1957 .. **TCLC** 55
See also CA 115; 195; CMW 4; DLB 77; MSW

Croker, John Wilson 1780-1857 .... **NCLC** 10
See also DLB 110

Crommelynck, Fernand 1885-1970 .. **CLC** 75
See also CA 189; 89-92; EWL 3

Cromwell, Oliver 1599-1658 .... **LC** 43

Cronenberg, David 1943- .... **CLC** 143
See also CA 138; CCA 1

Cronin, A(rchibald) J(oseph) 1896-1981 .... **CLC** 32
See also BPFB 1; CA 1-4R; 102; CANR 5; DLB 191; SATA 47; SATA-Obit 25

Cross, Amanda
See Heilbrun, Carolyn G(old)
See also BPFB 1; CMW; CPW; DLB 306; MSW

Crothers, Rachel 1878-1958 .... **TCLC** 19
See also CA 113; 194; CAD; CWD; DLB 7, 266; RGAL 4

Croves, Hal
See Traven, B.

Crow Dog, Mary (Ellen) (?)- .... **CLC** 93
See Brave Bird, Mary
See also CA 154

Crowfield, Christopher
See Stowe, Harriet (Elizabeth) Beecher

Crowley, Aleister .... **TCLC** 7
See Crowley, Edward Alexander
See also GLL 1

Crowley, Edward Alexander 1875-1947
See Crowley, Aleister
See also CA 104; HGG

Crowley, John 1942- .... **CLC** 57
See also AAYA 57; BPFB 1; CA 61-64; CANR 43, 98; DLBY 1982; FANT; SATA 65, 140; SFW 4; SUFW 2

Crowne, John 1641-1712 .... **LC** 104
See also DLB 80; RGEL 2

Crud
See Crumb, R(obert)

Crumarums
See Crumb, R(obert)

Crumb, R(obert) 1943- .... **CLC** 17
See also CA 106; CANR 107

Crumbum
See Crumb, R(obert)

Crumski
See Crumb, R(obert)

Crum the Bum
See Crumb, R(obert)

Crunk
See Crumb, R(obert)

Crustt
See Crumb, R(obert)

Crutchfield, Les
See Trumbo, Dalton

Cruz, Victor Hernandez 1949- ... **HLC** 1; **PC** 37
See also BW 2; CA 65-68; CAAS 17; CANR 14, 32, 74, 132; CP 7; DAM MULT, POET; DLB 41; DNFS 1; EXPP; HW 1, 2; LLW 1; MTCW 1; PFS 16; WP

Cryer, Gretchen (Kiger) 1935- .... **CLC** 21
See also CA 114; 123

Csath, Geza 1887-1919 .... **TCLC** 13
See also CA 111

Cudlip, David R(ockwell) 1933- .... **CLC** 34
See also CA 177

Cullen, Countee 1903-1946 .... **BLC** 1; **HR** 2; **PC** 20; **TCLC** 4, 37; **WLCS**
See also AFAW 2; AMWS 4; BW 1; CA 108; 124; CDALB 1917-1929; DA; DA3; DAC; DAM MST, MULT, POET; DLB 4, 48, 51; EWL 3; EXPP; LMFS 2; MTCW 1, 2; PFS 3; RGAL 4; SATA 18; WP

Culleton, Beatrice 1949- .... **NNAL**
See also CA 120; CANR 83; DAC

Cum, R.
See Crumb, R(obert)

Cummings, Bruce F(rederick) 1889-1919
See Barbellion, W. N. P.
See also CA 123

Cummings, E(dward) E(stlin) 1894-1962 ... **CLC** 1, 3, 8, 12, 15, 68; **PC** 5; **TCLC** 137; **WLC**
See also AAYA 41; AMW; CA 73-76; CANR 31; CDALB 1929-1941; DA; DA3; DAB; DAC; DAM MST, POET; DLB 4, 48; EWL 3; EXPP; MTCW 1, 2; PAB; PFS 1, 3, 12, 13, 19; RGAL 4; TUS; WP

Cummins, Maria Susanna 1827-1866 .... **NCLC** 139
See also DLB 42; YABC 1

Cunha, Euclides (Rodrigues Pimenta) da 1866-1909 .... **TCLC** 24
See also CA 123; 219; DLB 307; LAW; WLIT 1

Cunningham, E. V.
See Fast, Howard (Melvin)

Cunningham, J(ames) V(incent) 1911-1985 .... **CLC** 3, 31
See also CA 1-4R; 115; CANR 1, 72; DLB 5

Cunningham, Julia (Woolfolk) 1916- .... **CLC** 12
See also CA 9-12R; CANR 4, 19, 36; CWRI 5; JRDA; MAICYA 1, 2; SAAS 2; SATA 1, 26, 132

Cunningham, Michael 1952- .... **CLC** 34
See also CA 136; CANR 96; DLB 292; GLL 2

Cunninghame Graham, R. B.
See Cunninghame Graham, Robert (Gallnigad) Bontine

Cunninghame Graham, Robert (Gallnigad) Bontine 1852-1936 .... **TCLC** 19
See Graham, R(obert) B(ontine) Cunninghame
See also CA 119; 184

Curnow, (Thomas) Allen (Monro) 1911-2001 .... **PC** 48
See also CA 69-72; 202; CANR 48, 99; CP 7; EWL 3; RGEL 2

Currie, Ellen 19(?)- .... **CLC** 44

Curtin, Philip
See Lowndes, Marie Adelaide (Belloc)

Curtin, Phillip
See Lowndes, Marie Adelaide (Belloc)

Curtis, Price
See Ellison, Harlan (Jay)

Cusanus, Nicolaus 1401-1464 .... **LC** 80
See Nicholas of Cusa

Cutrate, Joe
See Spiegelman, Art

Cynewulf c. 770- .... **CMLC 23**
See also DLB 146; RGEL 2
Cyrano de Bergerac, Savinien de
1619-1655 .... **LC 65**
See also DLB 268; GFL Beginnings to 1789; RGWL 2, 3
Cyril of Alexandria c. 375-c. 430 . **CMLC 59**
Czaczkes, Shmuel Yosef Halevi
See Agnon, S(hmuel) Y(osef Halevi)
Dabrowska, Maria (Szumska)
1889-1965 .... **CLC 15**
See also CA 106; CDWLB 4; DLB 215; EWL 3
Dabydeen, David 1955- .... **CLC 34**
See also BW 1; CA 125; CANR 56, 92; CN 7; CP 7
Dacey, Philip 1939- .... **CLC 51**
See also CA 37-40R; CAAS 17; CANR 14, 32, 64; CP 7; DLB 105
Dacre, Charlotte c. 1772-1825? ... **NCLC 151**
Dafydd ap Gwilym c. 1320-c. 1380 ..... **PC 56**
Dagerman, Stig (Halvard)
1923-1954 .... **TCLC 17**
See also CA 117; 155; DLB 259; EWL 3
D'Aguiar, Fred 1960- .... **CLC 145**
See also CA 148; CANR 83, 101; CP 7; DLB 157; EWL 3
Dahl, Roald 1916-1990 .... **CLC 1, 6, 18, 79**
See also AAYA 15; BPFB 1; BRWS 4; BYA 5; CA 1-4R; 133; CANR 6, 32, 37, 62; CLR 1, 7, 41; CPW; DA3; DAB; DAC; DAM MST, NOV, POP; DLB 139, 255; HGG; JRDA; MAICYA 1, 2; MTCW 1, 2; RGSF 2; SATA 1, 26, 73; SATA-Obit 65; SSFS 4; TEA; YAW
Dahlberg, Edward 1900-1977 .. **CLC 1, 7, 14**
See also CA 9-12R; 69-72; CANR 31, 62; DLB 48; MTCW 1; RGAL 4
Daitch, Susan 1954- .... **CLC 103**
See also CA 161
Dale, Colin .... **TCLC 18**
See Lawrence, T(homas) E(dward)
Dale, George E.
See Asimov, Isaac
Dalton, Roque 1935-1975(?) ..... **HLCS 1; PC 36**
See also CA 176; DLB 283; HW 2
Daly, Elizabeth 1878-1967 .... **CLC 52**
See also CA 23-24; 25-28R; CANR 60; CAP 2; CMW 4
Daly, Mary 1928- .... **CLC 173**
See also CA 25-28R; CANR 30, 62; FW; GLL 1; MTCW 1
Daly, Maureen 1921- .... **CLC 17**
See also AAYA 5, 58; BYA 6; CANR 37, 83, 108; CLR 96; JRDA; MAICYA 1, 2; SAAS 1; SATA 2, 129; WYA; YAW
Damas, Leon-Gontran 1912-1978 .... **CLC 84**
See also BW 1; CA 125; 73-76; EWL 3
Dana, Richard Henry Sr.
1787-1879 .... **NCLC 53**
Daniel, Samuel 1562(?)-1619 .... **LC 24**
See also DLB 62; RGEL 2
Daniels, Brett
See Adler, Renata
Dannay, Frederic 1905-1982 .... **CLC 11**
See Queen, Ellery
See also CA 1-4R; 107; CANR 1, 39; CMW 4; DAM POP; DLB 137; MTCW 1
D'Annunzio, Gabriele 1863-1938 ... **TCLC 6, 40**
See also CA 104; 155; EW 8; EWL 3; RGWL 2, 3; TWA
Danois, N. le
See Gourmont, Remy(-Marie-Charles) de

Dante 1265-1321 .... **CMLC 3, 18, 39, 70; PC 21; WLCS**
See also DA; DA3; DAB; DAC; DAM MST, POET; EFS 1; EW 1; LAIT 1; RGWL 2, 3; TWA; WP
d'Antibes, Germain
See Simenon, Georges (Jacques Christian)
Danticat, Edwidge 1969- .... **CLC 94, 139**
See also AAYA 29; CA 152, 192; CAAE 192; CANR 73, 129; DNFS 1; EXPS; LATS 1:2; MTCW 1; SSFS 1; YAW
Danvers, Dennis 1947- .... **CLC 70**
Danziger, Paula 1944-2004 .... **CLC 21**
See also AAYA 4, 36; BYA 6, 7, 14; CA 112; 115; 229; CANR 37, 132; CLR 20; JRDA; MAICYA 1, 2; SATA 36, 63, 102, 149; SATA-Brief 30; WYA; YAW
Da Ponte, Lorenzo 1749-1838 .... **NCLC 50**
Dario, Ruben 1867-1916 .... **HLC 1; PC 15; TCLC 4**
See also CA 131; CANR 81; DAM MULT; DLB 290; EWL 3; HW 1, 2; LAW; MTCW 1, 2; RGWL 2, 3
Darley, George 1795-1846 .... **NCLC 2**
See also DLB 96; RGEL 2
Darrow, Clarence (Seward)
1857-1938 .... **TCLC 81**
See also CA 164; DLB 303
Darwin, Charles 1809-1882 .... **NCLC 57**
See also BRWS 7; DLB 57, 166; LATS 1:1; RGEL 2; TEA; WLIT 4
Darwin, Erasmus 1731-1802 .... **NCLC 106**
See also DLB 93; RGEL 2
Daryush, Elizabeth 1887-1977 ...... **CLC 6, 19**
See also CA 49-52; CANR 3, 81; DLB 20
Das, Kamala 1934- .... **CLC 191; PC 43**
See also CA 101; CANR 27, 59; CP 7; CWP; FW
Dasgupta, Surendranath
1887-1952 .... **TCLC 81**
See also CA 157
Dashwood, Edmee Elizabeth Monica de la Pasture 1890-1943
See Delafield, E. M.
See also CA 119; 154
da Silva, Antonio Jose
1705-1739 .... **NCLC 114**
Daudet, (Louis Marie) Alphonse
1840-1897 .... **NCLC 1**
See also DLB 123; GFL 1789 to the Present; RGSF 2
d'Aulnoy, Marie-Catherine c.
1650-1705 .... **LC 100**
Daumal, Rene 1908-1944 .... **TCLC 14**
See also CA 114; EWL 3
Davenant, William 1606-1668 .... **LC 13**
See also DLB 58, 126; RGEL 2
Davenport, Guy (Mattison, Jr.)
1927-2005 .... **CLC 6, 14, 38; SSC 16**
See also CA 33-36R; CANR 23, 73; CN 7; CSW; DLB 130
David, Robert
See Nezval, Vitezslav
Davidson, Avram (James) 1923-1993
See Queen, Ellery
See also CA 101; 171; CANR 26; DLB 8; FANT; SFW 4; SUFW 1, 2
Davidson, Donald (Grady)
1893-1968 .... **CLC 2, 13, 19**
See also CA 5-8R; 25-28R; CANR 4, 84; DLB 45
Davidson, Hugh
See Hamilton, Edmond
Davidson, John 1857-1909 .... **TCLC 24**
See also CA 118; 217; DLB 19; RGEL 2
Davidson, Sara 1943- .... **CLC 9**
See also CA 81-84; CANR 44, 68; DLB 185

Davie, Donald (Alfred) 1922-1995 .... **CLC 5, 8, 10, 31; PC 29**
See also BRWS 6; CA 1-4R; 149; CAAS 3; CANR 1, 44; CP 7; DLB 27; MTCW 1; RGEL 2
Davie, Elspeth 1919-1995 .... **SSC 52**
See also CA 120; 126; 150; DLB 139
Davies, Ray(mond Douglas) 1944- ... **CLC 21**
See also CA 116; 146; CANR 92
Davies, Rhys 1901-1978 .... **CLC 23**
See also CA 9-12R; 81-84; CANR 4; DLB 139, 191
Davies, (William) Robertson
1913-1995 .... **CLC 2, 7, 13, 25, 42, 75, 91; WLC**
See Marchbanks, Samuel
See also BEST 89:2; BPFB 1; CA 33-36R; 150; CANR 17, 42, 103; CN 7; CPW; DA; DA3; DAB; DAC; DAM MST, NOV, POP; DLB 68; EWL 3; HGG; INT CANR-17; MTCW 1, 2; RGEL 2; TWA
Davies, Sir John 1569-1626 .... **LC 85**
See also DLB 172
Davies, Walter C.
See Kornbluth, C(yril) M.
Davies, William Henry 1871-1940 ... **TCLC 5**
See also CA 104; 179; DLB 19, 174; EWL 3; RGEL 2
Da Vinci, Leonardo 1452-1519 ..... **LC 12, 57, 60**
See also AAYA 40
Davis, Angela (Yvonne) 1944- .... **CLC 77**
See also BW 2, 3; CA 57-60; CANR 10, 81; CSW; DA3; DAM MULT; FW
Davis, B. Lynch
See Bioy Casares, Adolfo; Borges, Jorge Luis
Davis, Frank Marshall 1905-1987 ...... **BLC 1**
See also BW 2, 3; CA 125; 123; CANR 42, 80; DAM MULT; DLB 51
Davis, Gordon
See Hunt, E(verette) Howard, (Jr.)
Davis, H(arold) L(enoir) 1896-1960 . **CLC 49**
See also ANW; CA 178; 89-92; DLB 9, 206; SATA 114
Davis, Natalie Z(emon) 1928- .... **CLC 204**
See also CA 53-56; CANR 58, 100
Davis, Rebecca (Blaine) Harding
1831-1910 .... **SSC 38; TCLC 6**
See also CA 104; 179; DLB 74, 239; FW; NFS 14; RGAL 4; TUS
Davis, Richard Harding
1864-1916 .... **TCLC 24**
See also CA 114; 179; DLB 12, 23, 78, 79, 189; DLBD 13; RGAL 4
Davison, Frank Dalby 1893-1970 ..... **CLC 15**
See also CA 217; 116; DLB 260
Davison, Lawrence H.
See Lawrence, D(avid) H(erbert Richards)
Davison, Peter (Hubert) 1928- .... **CLC 28**
See also CA 9-12R; CAAS 4; CANR 3, 43, 84; CP 7; DLB 5
Davys, Mary 1674-1732 .... **LC 1, 46**
See also DLB 39
Dawson, (Guy) Fielding (Lewis)
1930-2002 .... **CLC 6**
See also CA 85-88; 202; CANR 108; DLB 130; DLBY 2002
Dawson, Peter
See Faust, Frederick (Schiller)
See also TCWW 2, 2
Day, Clarence (Shepard, Jr.)
1874-1935 .... **TCLC 25**
See also CA 108; 199; DLB 11
Day, John 1574(?)-1640(?) .... **LC 70**
See also DLB 62, 170; RGEL 2
Day, Thomas 1748-1789 .... **LC 1**
See also DLB 39; YABC 1

Day Lewis, C(ecil) 1904-1972 . **CLC 1, 6, 10; PC 11**
See Blake, Nicholas
See also BRWS 3; CA 13-16; 33-36R; CANR 34; CAP 1; CWRI 5; DAM POET; DLB 15, 20; EWL 3; MTCW 1, 2; RGEL 2

Dazai Osamu .... **SSC 41; TCLC 11**
See Tsushima, Shuji
See also CA 164; DLB 182; EWL 3; MJW; RGSF 2; RGWL 2, 3; TWA

de Andrade, Carlos Drummond
See Drummond de Andrade, Carlos

de Andrade, Mario 1892(?)-1945
See Andrade, Mario de
See also CA 178; HW 2

Deane, Norman
See Creasey, John

Deane, Seamus (Francis) 1940- ...... **CLC 122**
See also CA 118; CANR 42

de Beauvoir, Simone (Lucie Ernestine Marie Bertrand)
See Beauvoir, Simone (Lucie Ernestine Marie Bertrand) de

de Beer, P.
See Bosman, Herman Charles

de Botton, Alain 1969- .... **CLC 203**
See also CA 159; CANR 96

de Brissac, Malcolm
See Dickinson, Peter (Malcolm de Brissac)

de Campos, Alvaro
See Pessoa, Fernando (Antonio Nogueira)

de Chardin, Pierre Teilhard
See Teilhard de Chardin, (Marie Joseph) Pierre

de Crenne, Hélisenne c. 1510-c. 1560 .... **LC 113**

Dee, John 1527-1608 .... **LC 20**
See also DLB 136, 213

Deer, Sandra 1940- .... **CLC 45**
See also CA 186

De Ferrari, Gabriella 1941- .... **CLC 65**
See also CA 146

de Filippo, Eduardo 1900-1984 ... **TCLC 127**
See also CA 132; 114; EWL 3; MTCW 1; RGWL 2, 3

Defoe, Daniel 1660(?)-1731 .... **LC 1, 42, 108; WLC**
See also AAYA 27; BRW 3; BRWR 1; BYA 4; CDBLB 1660-1789; CLR 61; DA; DA3; DAB; DAC; DAM MST, NOV; DLB 39, 95, 101; JRDA; LAIT 1; LMFS 1; MAICYA 1, 2; NFS 9, 13; RGEL 2; SATA 22; TEA; WCH; WLIT 3

de Gourmont, Remy(-Marie-Charles)
See Gourmont, Remy(-Marie-Charles) de

de Gournay, Marie le Jars 1566-1645 .... **LC 98**
See also FW

de Hartog, Jan 1914-2002 .... **CLC 19**
See also CA 1-4R; 210; CANR 1; DFS 12

de Hostos, E. M.
See Hostos (y Bonilla), Eugenio Maria de

de Hostos, Eugenio M.
See Hostos (y Bonilla), Eugenio Maria de

Deighton, Len .... **CLC 4, 7, 22, 46**
See Deighton, Leonard Cyril
See also AAYA 6; BEST 89:2; BPFB 1; CDBLB 1960 to Present; CMW 4; CN 7; CPW; DLB 87

Deighton, Leonard Cyril 1929-
See Deighton, Len
See also AAYA 57; CA 9-12R; CANR 19, 33, 68; DA3; DAM NOV, POP; MTCW 1, 2

Dekker, Thomas 1572(?)-1632 ..... **DC 12; LC 22**
See also CDBLB Before 1660; DAM DRAM; DLB 62, 172; LMFS 1; RGEL 2

de Laclos, Pierre Ambroise Franois
See Laclos, Pierre Ambroise Francois

Delacroix, (Ferdinand-Victor-)Eugene 1798-1863 .... **NCLC 133**
See also EW 5

Delafield, E. M. .... **TCLC 61**
See Dashwood, Edmee Elizabeth Monica de la Pasture
See also DLB 34; RHW

de la Mare, Walter (John) 1873-1956 . **SSC 14; TCLC 4, 53; WLC**
See also CA 163; CDBLB 1914-1945; CLR 23; CWRI 5; DA3; DAB; DAC; DAM MST, POET; DLB 19, 153, 162, 255, 284; EWL 3; EXPP; HGG; MAICYA 1, 2; MTCW 1; RGEL 2; RGSF 2; SATA 16; SUFW 1; TEA; WCH

de Lamartine, Alphonse (Marie Louis Prat)
See Lamartine, Alphonse (Marie Louis Prat) de

Delaney, Franey
See O'Hara, John (Henry)

Delaney, Shelagh 1939- .... **CLC 29**
See also CA 17-20R; CANR 30, 67; CBD; CD 5; CDBLB 1960 to Present; CWD; DAM DRAM; DFS 7; DLB 13; MTCW 1

Delany, Martin Robison 1812-1885 .... **NCLC 93**
See also DLB 50; RGAL 4

Delany, Mary (Granville Pendarves) 1700-1788 .... **LC 12**

Delany, Samuel R(ay), Jr. 1942- .... **BLC 1; CLC 8, 14, 38, 141**
See also AAYA 24; AFAW 2; BPFB 1; BW 2, 3; CA 81-84; CANR 27, 43, 115, 116; CN 7; DAM MULT; DLB 8, 33; FANT; MTCW 1, 2; RGAL 4; SATA 92; SCFW; SFW 4; SUFW 2

De la Ramee, Marie Louise (Ouida) 1839-1908
See Ouida
See also CA 204; SATA 20

de la Roche, Mazo 1879-1961 .... **CLC 14**
See also CA 85-88; CANR 30; DLB 68; RGEL 2; RHW; SATA 64

De La Salle, Innocent
See Hartmann, Sadakichi

de Laureamont, Comte
See Lautreamont

Delbanco, Nicholas (Franklin) 1942- .... **CLC 6, 13, 167**
See also CA 17-20R, 189; CAAE 189; CAAS 2; CANR 29, 55, 116; DLB 6, 234

del Castillo, Michel 1933- .... **CLC 38**
See also CA 109; CANR 77

Deledda, Grazia (Cosima) 1875(?)-1936 .... **TCLC 23**
See also CA 123; 205; DLB 264; EWL 3; RGWL 2, 3

Deleuze, Gilles 1925-1995 .... **TCLC 116**
See also DLB 296

Delgado, Abelardo (Lalo) B(arrientos) 1930-2004 .... **HLC 1**
See also CA 131; CAAS 15; CANR 90; DAM MST, MULT; DLB 82; HW 1, 2

Delibes, Miguel .... **CLC 8, 18**
See Delibes Setien, Miguel
See also EWL 3

Delibes Setien, Miguel 1920-
See Delibes, Miguel
See also CA 45-48; CANR 1, 32; CWW 2; HW 1; MTCW 1

DeLillo, Don 1936- ..... **CLC 8, 10, 13, 27, 39, 54, 76, 143**
See also AMWC 2; AMWS 6; BEST 89:1; BPFB 1; CA 81-84; CANR 21, 76, 92, 133; CN 7; CPW; DA3; DAM NOV, POP; DLB 6, 173; EWL 3; MTCW 1, 2; RGAL 4; TUS

de Lisser, H. G.
See De Lisser, H(erbert) G(eorge)
See also DLB 117

De Lisser, H(erbert) G(eorge) 1878-1944 .... **TCLC 12**
See de Lisser, H. G.
See also BW 2; CA 109; 152

Deloire, Pierre
See Peguy, Charles (Pierre)

Deloney, Thomas 1543(?)-1600 .... **LC 41**
See also DLB 167; RGEL 2

Deloria, Ella (Cara) 1889-1971(?) ..... **NNAL**
See also CA 152; DAM MULT; DLB 175

Deloria, Vine (Victor), Jr. 1933- ...... **CLC 21, 122; NNAL**
See also CA 53-56; CANR 5, 20, 48, 98; DAM MULT; DLB 175; MTCW 1; SATA 21

del Valle-Inclan, Ramon (Maria)
See Valle-Inclan, Ramon (Maria) del

Del Vecchio, John M(ichael) 1947- .. **CLC 29**
See also CA 110; DLBD 9

de Man, Paul (Adolph Michel) 1919-1983 .... **CLC 55**
See also CA 128; 111; CANR 61; DLB 67; MTCW 1, 2

DeMarinis, Rick 1934- .... **CLC 54**
See also CA 57-60, 184; CAAE 184; CAAS 24; CANR 9, 25, 50; DLB 218

de Maupassant, (Henri Rene Albert) Guy
See Maupassant, (Henri Rene Albert) Guy de

Dembry, R. Emmet
See Murfree, Mary Noailles

Demby, William 1922- .... **BLC 1; CLC 53**
See also BW 1, 3; CA 81-84; CANR 81; DAM MULT; DLB 33

de Menton, Francisco
See Chin, Frank (Chew, Jr.)

Demetrius of Phalerum c. 307B.C.- .... **CMLC 34**

Demijohn, Thom
See Disch, Thomas M(ichael)

De Mille, James 1833-1880 .... **NCLC 123**
See also DLB 99, 251

Deming, Richard 1915-1983
See Queen, Ellery
See also CA 9-12R; CANR 3, 94; SATA 24

Democritus c. 460B.C.-c. 370B.C. . **CMLC 47**

de Montaigne, Michel (Eyquem)
See Montaigne, Michel (Eyquem) de

de Montherlant, Henry (Milon)
See Montherlant, Henry (Milon) de

Demosthenes 384B.C.-322B.C. .... **CMLC 13**
See also AW 1; DLB 176; RGWL 2, 3

de Musset, (Louis Charles) Alfred
See Musset, (Louis Charles) Alfred de

de Natale, Francine
See Malzberg, Barry N(athaniel)

de Navarre, Marguerite 1492-1549 ..... **LC 61**
See Marguerite d'Angouleme; Marguerite de Navarre

Denby, Edwin (Orr) 1903-1983 .... **CLC 48**
See also CA 138; 110

de Nerval, Gerard
See Nerval, Gerard de

Denham, John 1615-1669 .... **LC 73**
See also DLB 58, 126; RGEL 2

Denis, Julio
See Cortazar, Julio

Denmark, Harrison
See Zelazny, Roger (Joseph)

Dennis, John 1658-1734 .... **LC 11**
See also DLB 101; RGEL 2

Dennis, Nigel (Forbes) 1912-1989 .... **CLC 8**
See also CA 25-28R; 129; DLB 13, 15, 233; EWL 3; MTCW 1

Dent, Lester 1904-1959 .... **TCLC 72**
See also CA 112; 161; CMW 4; DLB 306; SFW 4

De Palma, Brian (Russell) 1940- ...... **CLC 20**
See also CA 109

De Quincey, Thomas 1785-1859 ..... **NCLC 4, 87**
See also BRW 4; CDBLB 1789-1832; DLB 110, 144; RGEL 2

Deren, Eleanora 1908(?)-1961
See Deren, Maya
See also CA 192; 111

Deren, Maya .... **CLC 16, 102**
See Deren, Eleanora

Derleth, August (William) 1909-1971 .... **CLC 31**
See also BPFB 1; BYA 9, 10; CA 1-4R; 29-32R; CANR 4; CMW 4; DLB 9; DLBD 17; HGG; SATA 5; SUFW 1

Der Nister 1884-1950 .... **TCLC 56**
See Nister, Der

Der Stricker c. 1190-c. 1250 .... **CMLC 75**

de Routisie, Albert
See Aragon, Louis

Derrida, Jacques 1930-2004 .... **CLC 24, 87**
See also CA 124; 127; CANR 76, 98, 133; DLB 242; EWL 3; LMFS 2; MTCW 1; TWA

Derry Down Derry
See Lear, Edward

Dersonnes, Jacques
See Simenon, Georges (Jacques Christian)

Desai, Anita 1937- .... **CLC 19, 37, 97, 175**
See also BRWS 5; CA 81-84; CANR 33, 53, 95, 133; CN 7; CWRI 5; DA3; DAB; DAM NOV; DLB 271; DNFS 2; EWL 3; FW; MTCW 1, 2; SATA 63, 126

Desai, Kiran 1971- .... **CLC 119**
See also BYA 16; CA 171; CANR 127

de Saint-Luc, Jean
See Glassco, John

de Saint Roman, Arnaud
See Aragon, Louis

Desbordes-Valmore, Marceline 1786-1859 .... **NCLC 97**
See also DLB 217

Descartes, Rene 1596-1650 .... **LC 20, 35**
See also DLB 268; EW 3; GFL Beginnings to 1789

Deschamps, Eustache 1340(?)-1404 .. **LC 103**
See also DLB 208

De Sica, Vittorio 1901(?)-1974 .... **CLC 20**
See also CA 117

Desnos, Robert 1900-1945 .... **TCLC 22**
See also CA 121; 151; CANR 107; DLB 258; EWL 3; LMFS 2

Destouches, Louis-Ferdinand 1894-1961 .... **CLC 9, 15**
See Celine, Louis-Ferdinand
See also CA 85-88; CANR 28; MTCW 1

de Tolignac, Gaston
See Griffith, D(avid Lewelyn) W(ark)

Deutsch, Babette 1895-1982 .... **CLC 18**
See also BYA 3; CA 1-4R; 108; CANR 4, 79; DLB 45; SATA 1; SATA-Obit 33

Devenant, William 1606-1649 .... **LC 13**

Devkota, Laxmiprasad 1909-1959 . **TCLC 23**
See also CA 123

De Voto, Bernard (Augustine) 1897-1955 .... **TCLC 29**
See also CA 113; 160; DLB 256

De Vries, Peter 1910-1993 ..... **CLC 1, 2, 3, 7, 10, 28, 46**
See also CA 17-20R; 142; CANR 41; DAM NOV; DLB 6; DLBY 1982; MTCW 1, 2

Dewey, John 1859-1952 .... **TCLC 95**
See also CA 114; 170; DLB 246, 270; RGAL 4

Dexter, John
See Bradley, Marion Zimmer
See also GLL 1

Dexter, Martin
See Faust, Frederick (Schiller)
See also TCWW 2

Dexter, Pete 1943- .... **CLC 34, 55**
See also BEST 89:2; CA 127; 131; CANR 129; CPW; DAM POP; INT CA-131; MTCW 1

Diamano, Silmang
See Senghor, Leopold Sedar

Diamond, Neil 1941- .... **CLC 30**
See also CA 108

Diaz del Castillo, Bernal 1496-1584 .... **HLCS 1; LC 31**
See also LAW

di Bassetto, Corno
See Shaw, George Bernard

Dick, Philip K(indred) 1928-1982 ... **CLC 10, 30, 72; SSC 57**
See also AAYA 24; BPFB 1; BYA 11; CA 49-52; 106; CANR 2, 16, 132; CPW; DA3; DAM NOV, POP; DLB 8; MTCW 1, 2; NFS 5; SCFW; SFW 4

Dickens, Charles (John Huffam) 1812-1870 .... **NCLC 3, 8, 18, 26, 37, 50, 86, 105, 113; SSC 17, 49; WLC**
See also AAYA 23; BRW 5; BRWC 1, 2; BYA 1, 2, 3, 13, 14; CDBLB 1832-1890; CLR 95; CMW 4; DA; DA3; DAB; DAC; DAM MST, NOV; DLB 21, 55, 70, 159, 166; EXPN; HGG; JRDA; LAIT 1, 2; LATS 1:1; LMFS 1; MAICYA 1, 2; NFS 4, 5, 10, 14, 20; RGEL 2; RGSF 2; SATA 15; SUFW 1; TEA; WCH; WLIT 4; WYA

Dickey, James (Lafayette) 1923-1997 ..... **CLC 1, 2, 4, 7, 10, 15, 47, 109; PC 40; TCLC 151**
See also AAYA 50; AITN 1, 2; AMWS 4; BPFB 1; CA 9-12R; 156; CABS 2; CANR 10, 48, 61, 105; CDALB 1968-1988; CP 7; CPW; CSW; DA3; DAM NOV, POET, POP; DLB 5, 193; DLBD 7; DLBY 1982, 1993, 1996, 1997, 1998; EWL 3; INT CANR-10; MTCW 1, 2; NFS 9; PFS 6, 11; RGAL 4; TUS

Dickey, William 1928-1994 .... **CLC 3, 28**
See also CA 9-12R; 145; CANR 24, 79; DLB 5

Dickinson, Charles 1951- .... **CLC 49**
See also CA 128

Dickinson, Emily (Elizabeth) 1830-1886 ... **NCLC 21, 77; PC 1; WLC**
See also AAYA 22; AMW; AMWR 1; CDALB 1865-1917; DA; DA3; DAB; DAC; DAM MST, POET; DLB 1, 243; EXPP; MAWW; PAB; PFS 1, 2, 3, 4, 5, 6, 8, 10, 11, 13, 16; RGAL 4; SATA 29; TUS; WP; WYA

Dickinson, Mrs. Herbert Ward
See Phelps, Elizabeth Stuart

Dickinson, Peter (Malcolm de Brissac) 1927- .... **CLC 12, 35**
See also AAYA 9, 49; BYA 5; CA 41-44R; CANR 31, 58, 88, 134; CLR 29; CMW 4; DLB 87, 161, 276; JRDA; MAICYA 1, 2; SATA 5, 62, 95, 150; SFW 4; WYA; YAW

Dickson, Carr
See Carr, John Dickson

Dickson, Carter
See Carr, John Dickson

Diderot, Denis 1713-1784 .... **LC 26**
See also EW 4; GFL Beginnings to 1789; LMFS 1; RGWL 2, 3

Didion, Joan 1934- . **CLC 1, 3, 8, 14, 32, 129**
See also AITN 1; AMWS 4; CA 5-8R; CANR 14, 52, 76, 125; CDALB 1968-1988; CN 7; DA3; DAM NOV; DLB 2, 173, 185; DLBY 1981, 1986; EWL 3; MAWW; MTCW 1, 2; NFS 3; RGAL 4; TCWW 2; TUS

di Donato, Pietro 1911-1992 .... **TCLC 159**
See also CA 101; 136; DLB 9

Dietrich, Robert
See Hunt, E(verette) Howard, (Jr.)

Difusa, Pati
See Almodovar, Pedro

Dillard, Annie 1945- .... **CLC 9, 60, 115**
See also AAYA 6, 43; AMWS 6; ANW; CA 49-52; CANR 3, 43, 62, 90, 125; DA3; DAM NOV; DLB 275, 278; DLBY 1980; LAIT 4, 5; MTCW 1, 2; NCFS 1; RGAL 4; SATA 10, 140; TUS

Dillard, R(ichard) H(enry) W(ilde) 1937- .... **CLC 5**
See also CA 21-24R; CAAS 7; CANR 10; CP 7; CSW; DLB 5, 244

Dillon, Eilis 1920-1994 .... **CLC 17**
See also CA 9-12R, 182; 147; CAAE 182; CAAS 3; CANR 4, 38, 78; CLR 26; MAICYA 1, 2; MAICYAS 1; SATA 2, 74; SATA-Essay 105; SATA-Obit 83; YAW

Dimont, Penelope
See Mortimer, Penelope (Ruth)

Dinesen, Isak ..... **CLC 10, 29, 95; SSC 7, 75**
See Blixen, Karen (Christentze Dinesen)
See also EW 10; EWL 3; EXPS; FW; HGG; LAIT 3; MTCW 1; NCFS 2; NFS 9; RGSF 2; RGWL 2, 3; SSFS 3, 6, 13; WLIT 2

Ding Ling .... **CLC 68**
See Chiang, Pin-chin
See also RGWL 3

Diphusa, Patty
See Almodovar, Pedro

Disch, Thomas M(ichael) 1940- ... **CLC 7, 36**
See Disch, Tom
See also AAYA 17; BPFB 1; CA 21-24R; CAAS 2; CANR 17, 36, 54, 89; CLR 18; CP 7; DA3; DLB 8; HGG; MAICYA 1, 2; MTCW 1, 2; SAAS 15; SATA 92; SCFW; SFW 4; SUFW 2

Disch, Tom
See Disch, Thomas M(ichael)
See also DLB 282

d'Isly, Georges
See Simenon, Georges (Jacques Christian)

Disraeli, Benjamin 1804-1881 ... **NCLC 2, 39, 79**
See also BRW 4; DLB 21, 55; RGEL 2

Ditcum, Steve
See Crumb, R(obert)

Dixon, Paige
See Corcoran, Barbara (Asenath)

Dixon, Stephen 1936- .... **CLC 52; SSC 16**
See also AMWS 12; CA 89-92; CANR 17, 40, 54, 91; CN 7; DLB 130

Dixon, Thomas 1864-1946 .... **TCLC 163**
See also RHW

Djebar, Assia 1936- .... **CLC 182**
See also CA 188; EWL 3; RGWL 3; WLIT 2

Doak, Annie
See Dillard, Annie

Dobell, Sydney Thompson 1824-1874 .... **NCLC 43**
See also DLB 32; RGEL 2

Doblin, Alfred .... **TCLC 13**
See Doeblin, Alfred
See also CDWLB 2; EWL 3; RGWL 2, 3

Dobroliubov, Nikolai Aleksandrovich
See Dobrolyubov, Nikolai Alexandrovich
See also DLB 277

Dobrolyubov, Nikolai Alexandrovich 1836-1861 .... **NCLC 5**
See Dobroliubov, Nikolai Aleksandrovich

Dobson, Austin 1840-1921 .... **TCLC 79**
See also DLB 35, 144

Dobyns, Stephen 1941- .... **CLC 37**
See also AMWS 13; CA 45-48; CANR 2, 18, 99; CMW 4; CP 7

Doctorow, E(dgar) L(aurence)
1931- .... **CLC 6, 11, 15, 18, 37, 44, 65, 113**
See also AAYA 22; AITN 2; AMWS 4; BEST 89:3; BPFB 1; CA 45-48; CANR 2, 33, 51, 76, 97, 133; CDALB 1968-1988; CN 7; CPW; DA3; DAM NOV, POP; DLB 2, 28, 173; DLBY 1980; EWL 3; LAIT 3; MTCW 1, 2; NFS 6; RGAL 4; RHW; TUS

Dodgson, Charles L(utwidge) 1832-1898
See Carroll, Lewis
See also CLR 2; DA; DA3; DAB; DAC; DAM MST, NOV, POET; MAICYA 1, 2; SATA 100; YABC 2

Dodsley, Robert 1703-1764 .... **LC 97**
See also DLB 95; RGEL 2

Dodson, Owen (Vincent) 1914-1983 .. **BLC 1; CLC 79**
See also BW 1; CA 65-68; 110; CANR 24; DAM MULT; DLB 76

Doeblin, Alfred 1878-1957 .... **TCLC 13**
See Doblin, Alfred
See also CA 110; 141; DLB 66

Doerr, Harriet 1910-2002 .... **CLC 34**
See also CA 117; 122; 213; CANR 47; INT CA-122; LATS 1:2

Domecq, H(onorio Bustos)
See Bioy Casares, Adolfo

Domecq, H(onorio) Bustos
See Bioy Casares, Adolfo; Borges, Jorge Luis

Domini, Rey
See Lorde, Audre (Geraldine)
See also GLL 1

Dominique
See Proust, (Valentin-Louis-George-Eugene) Marcel

Don, A
See Stephen, Sir Leslie

Donaldson, Stephen R(eeder)
1947- .... **CLC 46, 138**
See also AAYA 36; BPFB 1; CA 89-92; CANR 13, 55, 99; CPW; DAM POP; FANT; INT CANR-13; SATA 121; SFW 4; SUFW 1, 2

Donleavy, J(ames) P(atrick) 1926- .... **CLC 1, 4, 6, 10, 45**
See also AITN 2; BPFB 1; CA 9-12R; CANR 24, 49, 62, 80, 124; CBD; CD 5; CN 7; DLB 6, 173; INT CANR-24; MTCW 1, 2; RGAL 4

Donnadieu, Marguerite
See Duras, Marguerite

Donne, John 1572-1631 ... **LC 10, 24, 91; PC 1, 43; WLC**
See also BRW 1; BRWC 1; BRWR 2; CDBLB Before 1660; DA; DAB; DAC; DAM MST, POET; DLB 121, 151; EXPP; PAB; PFS 2, 11; RGEL 3; TEA; WLIT 3; WP

Donnell, David 1939(?)- .... **CLC 34**
See also CA 197

Donoghue, P. S.
See Hunt, E(verette) Howard, (Jr.)

Donoso (Yanez), Jose 1924-1996 ... **CLC 4, 8, 11, 32, 99; HLC 1; SSC 34; TCLC 133**
See also CA 81-84; 155; CANR 32, 73; CDWLB 3; CWW 2; DAM MULT; DLB 113; EWL 3; HW 1, 2; LAW; LAWS 1; MTCW 1, 2; RGSF 2; WLIT 1

Donovan, John 1928-1992 .... **CLC 35**
See also AAYA 20; CA 97-100; 137; CLR 3; MAICYA 1, 2; SATA 72; SATA-Brief 29; YAW

Don Roberto
See Cunninghame Graham, Robert (Gallnigad) Bontine

Doolittle, Hilda 1886-1961 . **CLC 3, 8, 14, 31, 34, 73; PC 5; WLC**
See H. D.
See also AMWS 1; CA 97-100; CANR 35, 131; DA; DAC; DAM MST, POET; DLB 4, 45; EWL 3; FW; GLL 1; LMFS 2; MAWW; MTCW 1, 2; PFS 6; RGAL 4

Doppo, Kunikida .... **TCLC 99**
See Kunikida Doppo

Dorfman, Ariel 1942- .... **CLC 48, 77, 189; HLC 1**
See also CA 124; 130; CANR 67, 70, 135; CWW 2; DAM MULT; DFS 4; EWL 3; HW 1, 2; INT CA-130; WLIT 1

Dorn, Edward (Merton)
1929-1999 .... **CLC 10, 18**
See also CA 93-96; 187; CANR 42, 79; CP 7; DLB 5; INT CA-93-96; WP

Dor-Ner, Zvi .... **CLC 70**

Dorris, Michael (Anthony)
1945-1997 .... **CLC 109; NNAL**
See also AAYA 20; BEST 90:1; BYA 12; CA 102; 157; CANR 19, 46, 75; CLR 58; DA3; DAM MULT, NOV; DLB 175; LAIT 5; MTCW 2; NFS 3; RGAL 4; SATA 75; SATA-Obit 94; TCWW 2; YAW

Dorris, Michael A.
See Dorris, Michael (Anthony)

Dorsan, Luc
See Simenon, Georges (Jacques Christian)

Dorsange, Jean
See Simenon, Georges (Jacques Christian)

Dorset
See Sackville, Thomas

Dos Passos, John (Roderigo)
1896-1970 ... **CLC 1, 4, 8, 11, 15, 25, 34, 82; WLC**
See also AMW; BPFB 1; CA 1-4R; 29-32R; CANR 3; CDALB 1929-1941; DA; DA3; DAB; DAC; DAM MST, NOV; DLB 4, 9, 274; DLBD 1, 15; DLBY 1996; EWL 3; MTCW 1, 2; NFS 14; RGAL 4; TUS

Dossage, Jean
See Simenon, Georges (Jacques Christian)

Dostoevsky, Fedor Mikhailovich
1821-1881 .. **NCLC 2, 7, 21, 33, 43, 119; SSC 2, 33, 44; WLC**
See Dostoevsky, Fyodor
See also AAYA 40; DA; DA3; DAB; DAC; DAM MST, NOV; EW 7; EXPN; NFS 3, 8; RGSF 2; RGWL 2, 3; SSFS 8; TWA

Dostoevsky, Fyodor
See Dostoevsky, Fedor Mikhailovich
See also DLB 238; LATS 1:1; LMFS 1, 2

Doty, M. R.
See Doty, Mark (Alan)

Doty, Mark
See Doty, Mark (Alan)

Doty, Mark (Alan) 1953(?)- .... **CLC 176; PC 53**
See also AMWS 11; CA 161, 183; CAAE 183; CANR 110

Doty, Mark A.
See Doty, Mark (Alan)

Doughty, Charles M(ontagu)
1843-1926 .... **TCLC 27**
See also CA 115; 178; DLB 19, 57, 174

Douglas, Ellen .... **CLC 73**
See Haxton, Josephine Ayres; Williamson, Ellen Douglas
See also CN 7; CSW; DLB 292

Douglas, Gavin 1475(?)-1522 .... **LC 20**
See also DLB 132; RGEL 2

Douglas, George
See Brown, George Douglas
See also RGEL 2

Douglas, Keith (Castellain)
1920-1944 .... **TCLC 40**
See also BRW 7; CA 160; DLB 27; EWL 3; PAB; RGEL 2

Douglas, Leonard
See Bradbury, Ray (Douglas)

Douglas, Michael
See Crichton, (John) Michael

Douglas, (George) Norman
1868-1952 .... **TCLC 68**
See also BRW 6; CA 119; 157; DLB 34, 195; RGEL 2

Douglas, William
See Brown, George Douglas

Douglass, Frederick 1817(?)-1895 ..... **BLC 1; NCLC 7, 55, 141; WLC**
See also AAYA 48; AFAW 1, 2; AMWC 1; AMWS 3; CDALB 1640-1865; DA; DA3; DAC; DAM MST, MULT; DLB 1, 43, 50, 79, 243; FW; LAIT 2; NCFS 2; RGAL 4; SATA 29

Dourado, (Waldomiro Freitas) Autran
1926- .... **CLC 23, 60**
See also CA 25-28R, 179; CANR 34, 81; DLB 145, 307; HW 2

Dourado, Waldomiro Freitas Autran
See Dourado, (Waldomiro Freitas) Autran

Dove, Rita (Frances) 1952- . **BLCS; CLC 50, 81; PC 6**
See also AAYA 46; AMWS 4; BW 2; CA 109; CAAS 19; CANR 27, 42, 68, 76, 97, 132; CDALBS; CP 7; CSW; CWP; DA3; DAM MULT, POET; DLB 120; EWL 3; EXPP; MTCW 1; PFS 1, 15; RGAL 4

Doveglion
See Villa, Jose Garcia

Dowell, Coleman 1925-1985 .... **CLC 60**
See also CA 25-28R; 117; CANR 10; DLB 130; GLL 2

Dowson, Ernest (Christopher)
1867-1900 .... **TCLC 4**
See also CA 105; 150; DLB 19, 135; RGEL 2

Doyle, A. Conan
See Doyle, Sir Arthur Conan

Doyle, Sir Arthur Conan
1859-1930 .... **SSC 12; TCLC 7; WLC**
See Conan Doyle, Arthur
See also AAYA 14; BRWS 2; CA 104; 122; CANR 131; CDBLB 1890-1914; CMW 4; DA; DA3; DAB; DAC; DAM MST, NOV; DLB 18, 70, 156, 178; EXPS; HGG; LAIT 2; MSW; MTCW 1, 2; RGEL 2; RGSF 2; RHW; SATA 24; SCFW 2; SFW 4; SSFS 2; TEA; WCH; WLIT 4; WYA; YAW

Doyle, Conan
See Doyle, Sir Arthur Conan

Doyle, John
See Graves, Robert (von Ranke)

Doyle, Roddy 1958(?)- .... **CLC 81, 178**
See also AAYA 14; BRWS 5; CA 143; CANR 73, 128; CN 7; DA3; DLB 194

Doyle, Sir A. Conan
See Doyle, Sir Arthur Conan

Dr. A
See Asimov, Isaac; Silverstein, Alvin; Silverstein, Virginia B(arbara Opshelor)

Drabble, Margaret 1939- ...... **CLC 2, 3, 5, 8, 10, 22, 53, 129**
See also BRWS 4; CA 13-16R; CANR 18, 35, 63, 112, 131; CDBLB 1960 to Present; CN 7; CPW; DA3; DAB; DAC; DAM MST, NOV, POP; DLB 14, 155, 231; EWL 3; FW; MTCW 1, 2; RGEL 2; SATA 48; TEA

Drakulic, Slavenka 1949- .... **CLC 173**
See also CA 144; CANR 92

Drakulic-Ilic, Slavenka
See Drakulic, Slavenka
Drapier, M. B.
See Swift, Jonathan
Drayham, James
See Mencken, H(enry) L(ouis)
Drayton, Michael 1563-1631 .... **LC 8**
See also DAM POET; DLB 121; RGEL 2
Dreadstone, Carl
See Campbell, (John) Ramsey
Dreiser, Theodore (Herman Albert)
1871-1945 .... **SSC 30; TCLC 10, 18, 35, 83; WLC**
See also AMW; AMWC 2; AMWR 2; BYA 15, 16; CA 106; 132; CDALB 1865-1917; DA; DA3; DAC; DAM MST, NOV; DLB 9, 12, 102, 137; DLBD 1; EWL 3; LAIT 2; LMFS 2; MTCW 1, 2; NFS 8, 17; RGAL 4; TUS
Drexler, Rosalyn 1926- .... **CLC 2, 6**
See also CA 81-84; CAD; CANR 68, 124; CD 5; CWD
Dreyer, Carl Theodor 1889-1968 ...... **CLC 16**
See also CA 116
Drieu la Rochelle, Pierre(-Eugene)
1893-1945 .... **TCLC 21**
See also CA 117; DLB 72; EWL 3; GFL 1789 to the Present
Drinkwater, John 1882-1937 .... **TCLC 57**
See also CA 109; 149; DLB 10, 19, 149; RGEL 2
Drop Shot
See Cable, George Washington
Droste-Hulshoff, Annette Freiin von
1797-1848 .... **NCLC 3, 133**
See also CDWLB 2; DLB 133; RGSF 2; RGWL 2, 3
Drummond, Walter
See Silverberg, Robert
Drummond, William Henry
1854-1907 .... **TCLC 25**
See also CA 160; DLB 92
Drummond de Andrade, Carlos
1902-1987 .... **CLC 18; TCLC 139**
See Andrade, Carlos Drummond de
See also CA 132; 123; DLB 307; LAW
Drummond of Hawthornden, William
1585-1649 .... **LC 83**
See also DLB 121, 213; RGEL 2
Drury, Allen (Stuart) 1918-1998 .... **CLC 37**
See also CA 57-60; 170; CANR 18, 52; CN 7; INT CANR-18
Druse, Eleanor
See King, Stephen (Edwin)
Dryden, John 1631-1700 ..... **DC 3; LC 3, 21, 115; PC 25; WLC**
See also BRW 2; CDBLB 1660-1789; DA; DAB; DAC; DAM DRAM, MST, POET; DLB 80, 101, 131; EXPP; IDTP; LMFS 1; RGEL 2; TEA; WLIT 3
du Bellay, Joachim 1524-1560 .... **LC 92**
See also GFL Beginnings to 1789; RGWL 2, 3
Duberman, Martin (Bauml) 1930- ..... **CLC 8**
See also CA 1-4R; CAD; CANR 2, 63; CD 5
Dubie, Norman (Evans) 1945- .... **CLC 36**
See also CA 69-72; CANR 12, 115; CP 7; DLB 120; PFS 12
Du Bois, W(illiam) E(dward) B(urghardt)
1868-1963 ..... **BLC 1; CLC 1, 2, 13, 64, 96; HR 2; WLC**
See also AAYA 40; AFAW 1, 2; AMWC 1; AMWS 2; BW 1, 3; CA 85-88; CANR 34, 82, 132; CDALB 1865-1917; DA; DA3; DAC; DAM MST, MULT, NOV; DLB 47, 50, 91, 246, 284; EWL 3; EXPP; LAIT 2; LMFS 2; MTCW 1, 2; NCFS 1; PFS 13; RGAL 4; SATA 42

Dubus, Andre 1936-1999 ..... **CLC 13, 36, 97; SSC 15**
See also AMWS 7; CA 21-24R; 177; CANR 17; CN 7; CSW; DLB 130; INT CANR-17; RGAL 4; SSFS 10
Duca Minimo
See D'Annunzio, Gabriele
Ducharme, Rejean 1941- .... **CLC 74**
See also CA 165; DLB 60
du Chatelet, Emilie 1706-1749 .... **LC 96**
Duchen, Claire .... **CLC 65**
Duclos, Charles Pinot- 1704-1772 .... **LC 1**
See also GFL Beginnings to 1789
Dudek, Louis 1918-2001 .... **CLC 11, 19**
See also CA 45-48; 215; CAAS 14; CANR 1; CP 7; DLB 88
Duerrenmatt, Friedrich 1921-1990 ... **CLC 1, 4, 8, 11, 15, 43, 102**
See Durrenmatt, Friedrich
See also CA 17-20R; CANR 33; CMW 4; DAM DRAM; DLB 69, 124; MTCW 1, 2
Duffy, Bruce 1953(?)- .... **CLC 50**
See also CA 172
Duffy, Maureen 1933- .... **CLC 37**
See also CA 25-28R; CANR 33, 68; CBD; CN 7; CP 7; CWD; CWP; DFS 15; DLB 14; FW; MTCW 1
Du Fu
See Tu Fu
See also RGWL 2, 3
Dugan, Alan 1923-2003 .... **CLC 2, 6**
See also CA 81-84; 220; CANR 119; CP 7; DLB 5; PFS 10
du Gard, Roger Martin
See Martin du Gard, Roger
Duhamel, Georges 1884-1966 .... **CLC 8**
See also CA 81-84; 25-28R; CANR 35; DLB 65; EWL 3; GFL 1789 to the Present; MTCW 1
Dujardin, Edouard (Emile Louis)
1861-1949 .... **TCLC 13**
See also CA 109; DLB 123
Duke, Raoul
See Thompson, Hunter S(tockton)
Dulles, John Foster 1888-1959 .... **TCLC 72**
See also CA 115; 149
Dumas, Alexandre (pere)
1802-1870 .... **NCLC 11, 71; WLC**
See also AAYA 22; BYA 3; DA; DA3; DAB; DAC; DAM MST, NOV; DLB 119, 192; EW 6; GFL 1789 to the Present; LAIT 1, 2; NFS 14, 19; RGWL 2, 3; SATA 18; TWA; WCH
Dumas, Alexandre (fils) 1824-1895 ...... **DC 1; NCLC 9**
See also DLB 192; GFL 1789 to the Present; RGWL 2, 3
Dumas, Claudine
See Malzberg, Barry N(athaniel)
Dumas, Henry L. 1934-1968 .... **CLC 6, 62**
See also BW 1; CA 85-88; DLB 41; RGAL 4
du Maurier, Daphne 1907-1989 .. **CLC 6, 11, 59; SSC 18**
See also AAYA 37; BPFB 1; BRWS 3; CA 5-8R; 128; CANR 6, 55; CMW 4; CPW; DA3; DAB; DAC; DAM MST, POP; DLB 191; HGG; LAIT 3; MSW; MTCW 1, 2; NFS 12; RGEL 2; RGSF 2; RHW; SATA 27; SATA-Obit 60; SSFS 14, 16; TEA
Du Maurier, George 1834-1896 .... **NCLC 86**
See also DLB 153, 178; RGEL 2
Dunbar, Paul Laurence 1872-1906 ... **BLC 1; PC 5; SSC 8; TCLC 2, 12; WLC**
See also AFAW 1, 2; AMWS 2; BW 1, 3; CA 104; 124; CANR 79; CDALB 1865-1917; DA; DA3; DAC; DAM MST, MULT, POET; DLB 50, 54, 78; EXPP; RGAL 4; SATA 34

Dunbar, William 1460(?)-1520(?) .... **LC 20**
See also BRWS 8; DLB 132, 146; RGEL 2
Dunbar-Nelson, Alice .... **HR 2**
See Nelson, Alice Ruth Moore Dunbar
Duncan, Dora Angela
See Duncan, Isadora
Duncan, Isadora 1877(?)-1927 .... **TCLC 68**
See also CA 118; 149
Duncan, Lois 1934- .... **CLC 26**
See also AAYA 4, 34; BYA 6, 8; CA 1-4R; CANR 2, 23, 36, 111; CLR 29; JRDA; MAICYA 1, 2; MAICYAS 1; SAAS 2; SATA 1, 36, 75, 133, 141; SATA-Essay 141; WYA; YAW
Duncan, Robert (Edward)
1919-1988 .... **CLC 1, 2, 4, 7, 15, 41, 55; PC 2**
See also BG 2; CA 9-12R; 124; CANR 28, 62; DAM POET; DLB 5, 16, 193; EWL 3; MTCW 1, 2; PFS 13; RGAL 4; WP
Duncan, Sara Jeannette
1861-1922 .... **TCLC 60**
See also CA 157; DLB 92
Dunlap, William 1766-1839 .... **NCLC 2**
See also DLB 30, 37, 59; RGAL 4
Dunn, Douglas (Eaglesham) 1942- .... **CLC 6, 40**
See also BRWS 10; CA 45-48; CANR 2, 33, 126; CP 7; DLB 40; MTCW 1
Dunn, Katherine (Karen) 1945- .... **CLC 71**
See also CA 33-36R; CANR 72; HGG; MTCW 1
Dunn, Stephen (Elliott) 1939- .... **CLC 36**
See also AMWS 11; CA 33-36R; CANR 12, 48, 53, 105; CP 7; DLB 105; PFS 21
Dunne, Finley Peter 1867-1936 ...... **TCLC 28**
See also CA 108; 178; DLB 11, 23; RGAL 4
Dunne, John Gregory 1932-2003 ..... **CLC 28**
See also CA 25-28R; 222; CANR 14, 50; CN 7; DLBY 1980
Dunsany, Lord .... **TCLC 2, 59**
See Dunsany, Edward John Moreton Drax Plunkett
See also DLB 77, 153, 156, 255; FANT; IDTP; RGEL 2; SFW 4; SUFW 1
Dunsany, Edward John Moreton Drax
Plunkett 1878-1957
See Dunsany, Lord
See also CA 104; 148; DLB 10; MTCW 1
Duns Scotus, John 1266(?)-1308 ... **CMLC 59**
See also DLB 115
du Perry, Jean
See Simenon, Georges (Jacques Christian)
Durang, Christopher (Ferdinand)
1949- .... **CLC 27, 38**
See also CA 105; CAD; CANR 50, 76, 130; CD 5; MTCW 1
Duras, Claire de 1777-1828 .... **NCLC 154**
Duras, Marguerite 1914-1996 . **CLC 3, 6, 11, 20, 34, 40, 68, 100; SSC 40**
See also BPFB 1; CA 25-28R; 151; CANR 50; CWW 2; DLB 83; EWL 3; GFL 1789 to the Present; IDFW 4; MTCW 1, 2; RGWL 2, 3; TWA
Durban, (Rosa) Pam 1947- .... **CLC 39**
See also CA 123; CANR 98; CSW
Durcan, Paul 1944- .... **CLC 43, 70**
See also CA 134; CANR 123; CP 7; DAM POET; EWL 3
Durfey, Thomas 1653-1723 .... **LC 94**
See also DLB 80; RGEL 2
Durkheim, Emile 1858-1917 .... **TCLC 55**
Durrell, Lawrence (George)
1912-1990 ..... **CLC 1, 4, 6, 8, 13, 27, 41**
See also BPFB 1; BRWS 1; CA 9-12R; 132; CANR 40, 77; CDBLB 1945-1960; DAM NOV; DLB 15, 27, 204; DLBY 1990; EWL 3; MTCW 1, 2; RGEL 2; SFW 4; TEA

Durrenmatt, Friedrich
See Duerrenmatt, Friedrich
See also CDWLB 2; EW 13; EWL 3; RGWL 2, 3

Dutt, Michael Madhusudan
1824-1873 .... NCLC 118

Dutt, Toru 1856-1877 .... NCLC 29
See also DLB 240

Dwight, Timothy 1752-1817 .... NCLC 13
See also DLB 37; RGAL 4

Dworkin, Andrea 1946- .... CLC 43, 123
See also CA 77-80; CAAS 21; CANR 16, 39, 76, 96; FW; GLL 1; INT CANR-16; MTCW 1, 2

Dwyer, Deanna
See Koontz, Dean R(ay)

Dwyer, K. R.
See Koontz, Dean R(ay)

Dybek, Stuart 1942- .... CLC 114; SSC 55
See also CA 97-100; CANR 39; DLB 130

Dye, Richard
See De Voto, Bernard (Augustine)

Dyer, Geoff 1958- .... CLC 149
See also CA 125; CANR 88

Dyer, George 1755-1841 .... NCLC 129
See also DLB 93

Dylan, Bob 1941- .... CLC 3, 4, 6, 12, 77; PC 37
See also CA 41-44R; CANR 108; CP 7; DLB 16

Dyson, John 1943- .... CLC 70
See also CA 144

Dzyubin, Eduard Georgievich 1895-1934
See Bagritsky, Eduard
See also CA 170

E. V. L.
See Lucas, E(dward) V(errall)

Eagleton, Terence (Francis) 1943- .. CLC 63, 132
See also CA 57-60; CANR 7, 23, 68, 115; DLB 242; LMFS 2; MTCW 1, 2

Eagleton, Terry
See Eagleton, Terence (Francis)

Early, Jack
See Scoppettone, Sandra
See also GLL 1

East, Michael
See West, Morris L(anglo)

Eastaway, Edward
See Thomas, (Philip) Edward

Eastlake, William (Derry)
1917-1997 .... CLC 8
See also CA 5-8R; 158; CAAS 1; CANR 5, 63; CN 7; DLB 6, 206; INT CANR-5; TCWW 2

Eastman, Charles A(lexander)
1858-1939 .... NNAL; TCLC 55
See also CA 179; CANR 91; DAM MULT; DLB 175; YABC 1

Eaton, Edith Maude 1865-1914 .... AAL
See Far, Sui Sin
See also CA 154; DLB 221; FW

Eaton, (Lillie) Winnifred 1875-1954 .... AAL
See also CA 217; DLB 221; RGAL 4

Eberhart, Richard (Ghormley)
1904- .... CLC 3, 11, 19, 56
See also AMW; CA 1-4R; CANR 2, 125; CDALB 1941-1968; CP 7; DAM POET; DLB 48; MTCW 1; RGAL 4

Eberstadt, Fernanda 1960- .... CLC 39
See also CA 136; CANR 69, 128

Echegaray (y Eizaguirre), Jose (Maria Waldo) 1832-1916 .... HLCS 1; TCLC 4
See also CA 104; CANR 32; EWL 3; HW 1; MTCW 1

Echeverria, (Jose) Esteban (Antonino)
1805-1851 .... NCLC 18
See also LAW

Echo
See Proust, (Valentin-Louis-George-Eugene) Marcel

Eckert, Allan W. 1931- .... CLC 17
See also AAYA 18; BYA 2; CA 13-16R; CANR 14, 45; INT CANR-14; MAICYA 2; MAICYAS 1; SAAS 21; SATA 29, 91; SATA-Brief 27

Eckhart, Meister 1260(?)-1327(?) ... CMLC 9
See also DLB 115; LMFS 1

Eckmar, F. R.
See de Hartog, Jan

Eco, Umberto 1932- .... CLC 28, 60, 142
See also BEST 90:1; BPFB 1; CA 77-80; CANR 12, 33, 55, 110, 131; CPW; CWW 2; DA3; DAM NOV, POP; DLB 196, 242; EWL 3; MSW; MTCW 1, 2; RGWL 3

Eddison, E(ric) R(ucker)
1882-1945 .... TCLC 15
See also CA 109; 156; DLB 255; FANT; SFW 4; SUFW 1

Eddy, Mary (Ann Morse) Baker
1821-1910 .... TCLC 71
See also CA 113; 174

Edel, (Joseph) Leon 1907-1997 .. CLC 29, 34
See also CA 1-4R; 161; CANR 1, 22, 112; DLB 103; INT CANR-22

Eden, Emily 1797-1869 .... NCLC 10

Edgar, David 1948- .... CLC 42
See also CA 57-60; CANR 12, 61, 112; CBD; CD 5; DAM DRAM; DFS 15; DLB 13, 233; MTCW 1

Edgerton, Clyde (Carlyle) 1944- .... CLC 39
See also AAYA 17; CA 118; 134; CANR 64, 125; CSW; DLB 278; INT CA-134; YAW

Edgeworth, Maria 1768-1849 .... NCLC 1, 51
See also BRWS 3; DLB 116, 159, 163; FW; RGEL 2; SATA 21; TEA; WLIT 3

Edmonds, Paul
See Kuttner, Henry

Edmonds, Walter D(umaux)
1903-1998 .... CLC 35
See also BYA 2; CA 5-8R; CANR 2; CWRI 5; DLB 9; LAIT 1; MAICYA 1, 2; RHW; SAAS 4; SATA 1, 27; SATA-Obit 99

Edmondson, Wallace
See Ellison, Harlan (Jay)

Edson, Margaret 1961- ...... CLC 199; DC 24
See also CA 190; DFS 13; DLB 266

Edson, Russell 1935- .... CLC 13
See also CA 33-36R; CANR 115; DLB 244; WP

Edwards, Bronwen Elizabeth
See Rose, Wendy

Edwards, G(erald) B(asil)
1899-1976 .... CLC 25
See also CA 201; 110

Edwards, Gus 1939- .... CLC 43
See also CA 108; INT CA-108

Edwards, Jonathan 1703-1758 .... LC 7, 54
See also AMW; DA; DAC; DAM MST; DLB 24, 270; RGAL 4; TUS

Edwards, Sarah Pierpont 1710-1758 .. LC 87
See also DLB 200

Efron, Marina Ivanovna Tsvetaeva
See Tsvetaeva (Efron), Marina (Ivanovna)

Egeria fl. 4th cent. - .... CMLC 70

Egoyan, Atom 1960- .... CLC 151
See also CA 157

Ehle, John (Marsden, Jr.) 1925- .... CLC 27
See also CA 9-12R; CSW

Ehrenbourg, Ilya (Grigoryevich)
See Ehrenburg, Ilya (Grigoryevich)

Ehrenburg, Ilya (Grigoryevich)
1891-1967 .... CLC 18, 34, 62
See Erenburg, Il'ia Grigor'evich
See also CA 102; 25-28R; EWL 3

Ehrenburg, Ilyo (Grigoryevich)
See Ehrenburg, Ilya (Grigoryevich)

Ehrenreich, Barbara 1941- .... CLC 110
See also BEST 90:4; CA 73-76; CANR 16, 37, 62, 117; DLB 246; FW; MTCW 1, 2

Eich, Gunter
See Eich, Gunter
See also RGWL 2, 3

Eich, Gunter 1907-1972 .... CLC 15
See Eich, Gunter
See also CA 111; 93-96; DLB 69, 124; EWL 3

Eichendorff, Joseph 1788-1857 .... NCLC 8
See also DLB 90; RGWL 2, 3

Eigner, Larry .... CLC 9
See Eigner, Laurence (Joel)
See also CAAS 23; DLB 5; WP

Eigner, Laurence (Joel) 1927-1996
See Eigner, Larry
See also CA 9-12R; 151; CANR 6, 84; CP 7; DLB 193

Eilhart von Oberge c. 1140-c. 1195 .... CMLC 67
See also DLB 148

Einhard c. 770-840 .... CMLC 50
See also DLB 148

Einstein, Albert 1879-1955 .... TCLC 65
See also CA 121; 133; MTCW 1, 2

Eiseley, Loren
See Eiseley, Loren Corey
See also DLB 275

Eiseley, Loren Corey 1907-1977 .... CLC 7
See Eiseley, Loren
See also AAYA 5; ANW; CA 1-4R; 73-76; CANR 6; DLBD 17

Eisenstadt, Jill 1963- .... CLC 50
See also CA 140

Eisenstein, Sergei (Mikhailovich)
1898-1948 .... TCLC 57
See also CA 114; 149

Eisner, Simon
See Kornbluth, C(yril) M.

Ekeloef, (Bengt) Gunnar
1907-1968 .... CLC 27; PC 23
See Ekelof, (Bengt) Gunnar
See also CA 123; 25-28R; DAM POET

Ekelof, (Bengt) Gunnar 1907-1968
See Ekeloef, (Bengt) Gunnar
See also DLB 259; EW 12; EWL 3

Ekelund, Vilhelm 1880-1949 .... TCLC 75
See also CA 189; EWL 3

Ekwensi, C. O. D.
See Ekwensi, Cyprian (Odiatu Duaka)

Ekwensi, Cyprian (Odiatu Duaka)
1921- .... BLC 1; CLC 4
See also AFW; BW 2, 3; CA 29-32R; CANR 18, 42, 74, 125; CDWLB 3; CN 7; CWRI 5; DAM MULT; DLB 117; EWL 3; MTCW 1, 2; RGEL 2; SATA 66; WLIT 2

Elaine .... TCLC 18
See Leverson, Ada Esther

El Crummo
See Crumb, R(obert)

Elder, Lonne III 1931-1996 ..... BLC 1; DC 8
See also BW 1, 3; CA 81-84; 152; CAD; CANR 25; DAM MULT; DLB 7, 38, 44

Eleanor of Aquitaine 1122-1204 ... CMLC 39

Elia
See Lamb, Charles

Eliade, Mircea 1907-1986 .... CLC 19
See also CA 65-68; 119; CANR 30, 62; CDWLB 4; DLB 220; EWL 3; MTCW 1; RGWL 3; SFW 4

Eliot, A. D.
See Jewett, (Theodora) Sarah Orne

Eliot, Alice
See Jewett, (Theodora) Sarah Orne

Eliot, Dan
See Silverberg, Robert

Eliot, George 1819-1880 ...... **NCLC 4, 13, 23, 41, 49, 89, 118; PC 20; SSC 72; WLC**
See Evans, Mary Ann
See also BRW 5; BRWC 1, 2; BRWR 2; CDBLB 1832-1890; CN 7; CPW; DA; DA3; DAB; DAC; DAM MST, NOV; DLB 21, 35, 55; LATS 1:1; LMFS 1; NFS 17; RGEL 2; RGSF 2; SSFS 8; TEA; WLIT 3

Eliot, John 1604-1690 .... **LC 5**
See also DLB 24

Eliot, T(homas) S(tearns)
1888-1965 ...... **CLC 1, 2, 3, 6, 9, 10, 13, 15, 24, 34, 41, 55, 57, 113; PC 5, 31; WLC**
See also AAYA 28; AMW; AMWC 1; AMWR 1; BRW 7; BRWR 2; CA 5-8R; 25-28R; CANR 41; CDALB 1929-1941; DA; DA3; DAB; DAC; DAM DRAM, MST, POET; DFS 4, 13; DLB 7, 10, 45, 63, 245; DLBY 1988; EWL 3; EXPP; LAIT 3; LATS 1:1; LMFS 2; MTCW 1, 2; NCFS 5; PAB; PFS 1, 7, 20; RGAL 4; RGEL 2; TUS; WLIT 4; WP

Elizabeth 1866-1941 .... **TCLC 41**

Elkin, Stanley L(awrence)
1930-1995 .. **CLC 4, 6, 9, 14, 27, 51, 91; SSC 12**
See also AMWS 6; BPFB 1; CA 9-12R; 148; CANR 8, 46; CN 7; CPW; DAM NOV, POP; DLB 2, 28, 218, 278; DLBY 1980; EWL 3; INT CANR-8; MTCW 1, 2; RGAL 4

Elledge, Scott .... **CLC 34**

Elliott, Don
See Silverberg, Robert

Elliott, George P(aul) 1918-1980 .... **CLC 2**
See also CA 1-4R; 97-100; CANR 2; DLB 244

Elliott, Janice 1931-1995 .... **CLC 47**
See also CA 13-16R; CANR 8, 29, 84; CN 7; DLB 14; SATA 119

Elliott, Sumner Locke 1917-1991 ..... **CLC 38**
See also CA 5-8R; 134; CANR 2, 21; DLB 289

Elliott, William
See Bradbury, Ray (Douglas)

Ellis, A. E. .... **CLC 7**

Ellis, Alice Thomas .... **CLC 40**
See Haycraft, Anna (Margaret)
See also DLB 194; MTCW 1

Ellis, Bret Easton 1964- ...... **CLC 39, 71, 117**
See also AAYA 2, 43; CA 118; 123; CANR 51, 74, 126; CN 7; CPW; DA3; DAM POP; DLB 292; HGG; INT CA-123; MTCW 1; NFS 11

Ellis, (Henry) Havelock
1859-1939 .... **TCLC 14**
See also CA 109; 169; DLB 190

Ellis, Landon
See Ellison, Harlan (Jay)

Ellis, Trey 1962- .... **CLC 55**
See also CA 146; CANR 92

Ellison, Harlan (Jay) 1934- ... **CLC 1, 13, 42, 139; SSC 14**
See also AAYA 29; BPFB 1; BYA 14; CA 5-8R; CANR 5, 46, 115; CPW; DAM POP; DLB 8; HGG; INT CANR-5; MTCW 1, 2; SCFW 2; SFW 4; SSFS 13, 14, 15; SUFW 1, 2

Ellison, Ralph (Waldo) 1914-1994 .... **BLC 1; CLC 1, 3, 11, 54, 86, 114; SSC 26, 79; WLC**
See also AAYA 19; AFAW 1, 2; AMWC 2; AMWR 2; AMWS 2; BPFB 1; BW 1, 3; BYA 2; CA 9-12R; 145; CANR 24, 53; CDALB 1941-1968; CSW; DA; DA3; DAB; DAC; DAM MST, MULT, NOV;

DLB 2, 76, 227; DLBY 1994; EWL 3; EXPN; EXPS; LAIT 4; MTCW 1, 2; NCFS 3; NFS 2; RGAL 4; RGSF 2; SSFS 1, 11; YAW

Ellmann, Lucy (Elizabeth) 1956- ..... **CLC 61**
See also CA 128

Ellmann, Richard (David)
1918-1987 .... **CLC 50**
See also BEST 89:2; CA 1-4R; 122; CANR 2, 28, 61; DLB 103; DLBY 1987; MTCW 1, 2

Elman, Richard (Martin)
1934-1997 .... **CLC 19**
See also CA 17-20R; 163; CAAS 3; CANR 47

Elron
See Hubbard, L(afayette) Ron(ald)

El Saadawi, Nawal 1931- .... **CLC 196**
See al'Sadaawi, Nawal; Sa'adawi, al-Nawal; Saadawi, Nawal El; Sa'dawi, Nawal al-
See also CA 118; CAAS 11; CANR 44, 92

Eluard, Paul .... **PC 38; TCLC 7, 41**
See Grindel, Eugene
See also EWL 3; GFL 1789 to the Present; RGWL 2, 3

Elyot, Thomas 1490(?)-1546 .... **LC 11**
See also DLB 136; RGEL 2

Elytis, Odysseus 1911-1996 .... **CLC 15, 49, 100; PC 21**
See Alepoudelis, Odysseus
See also CA 102; 151; CANR 94; CWW 2; DAM POET; EW 13; EWL 3; MTCW 1, 2; RGWL 2, 3

Emecheta, (Florence Onye) Buchi
1944- .... **BLC 2; CLC 14, 48, 128**
See also AFW; BW 2, 3; CA 81-84; CANR 27, 81, 126; CDWLB 3; CN 7; CWRI 5; DA3; DAM MULT; DLB 117; EWL 3; FW; MTCW 1, 2; NFS 12, 14; SATA 66; WLIT 2

Emerson, Mary Moody
1774-1863 .... **NCLC 66**

Emerson, Ralph Waldo 1803-1882 . **NCLC 1, 38, 98; PC 18; WLC**
See also AAYA 60; AMW; ANW; CDALB 1640-1865; DA; DA3; DAB; DAC; DAM MST, POET; DLB 1, 59, 73, 183, 223, 270; EXPP; LAIT 2; LMFS 1; NCFS 3; PFS 4, 17; RGAL 4; TUS; WP

Eminescu, Mihail 1850-1889 .. **NCLC 33, 131**

Empedocles 5th cent. B.C.- .... **CMLC 50**
See also DLB 176

Empson, William 1906-1984 ... **CLC 3, 8, 19, 33, 34**
See also BRWS 2; CA 17-20R; 112; CANR 31, 61; DLB 20; EWL 3; MTCW 1, 2; RGEL 2

Enchi, Fumiko (Ueda) 1905-1986 ..... **CLC 31**
See Enchi Fumiko
See also CA 129; 121; FW; MJW

Enchi Fumiko
See Enchi, Fumiko (Ueda)
See also DLB 182; EWL 3

Ende, Michael (Andreas Helmuth)
1929-1995 .... **CLC 31**
See also BYA 5; CA 118; 124; 149; CANR 36, 110; CLR 14; DLB 75; MAICYA 1, 2; MAICYAS 1; SATA 61, 130; SATA-Brief 42; SATA-Obit 86

Endo, Shusaku 1923-1996 ...... **CLC 7, 14, 19, 54, 99; SSC 48; TCLC 152**
See Endo Shusaku
See also CA 29-32R; 153; CANR 21, 54, 131; DA3; DAM NOV; MTCW 1, 2; RGSF 2; RGWL 2, 3

Endo Shusaku
See Endo, Shusaku
See also CWW 2; DLB 182; EWL 3

Engel, Marian 1933-1985 .... **CLC 36; TCLC 137**
See also CA 25-28R; CANR 12; DLB 53; FW; INT CANR-12

Engelhardt, Frederick
See Hubbard, L(afayette) Ron(ald)

Engels, Friedrich 1820-1895 .. **NCLC 85, 114**
See also DLB 129; LATS 1:1

Enright, D(ennis) J(oseph)
1920-2002 .... **CLC 4, 8, 31**
See also CA 1-4R; 211; CANR 1, 42, 83; CP 7; DLB 27; EWL 3; SATA 25; SATA-Obit 140

Enzensberger, Hans Magnus
1929- .... **CLC 43; PC 28**
See also CA 116; 119; CANR 103; CWW 2; EWL 3

Ephron, Nora 1941- .... **CLC 17, 31**
See also AAYA 35; AITN 2; CA 65-68; CANR 12, 39, 83

Epicurus 341B.C.-270B.C. .... **CMLC 21**
See also DLB 176

Epsilon
See Betjeman, John

Epstein, Daniel Mark 1948- .... **CLC 7**
See also CA 49-52; CANR 2, 53, 90

Epstein, Jacob 1956- .... **CLC 19**
See also CA 114

Epstein, Jean 1897-1953 .... **TCLC 92**

Epstein, Joseph 1937- .... **CLC 39, 204**
See also AMWS 14; CA 112; 119; CANR 50, 65, 117

Epstein, Leslie 1938- .... **CLC 27**
See also AMWS 12; CA 73-76, 215; CAAE 215; CAAS 12; CANR 23, 69; DLB 299

Equiano, Olaudah 1745(?)-1797 . **BLC 2; LC 16**
See also AFAW 1, 2; CDWLB 3; DAM MULT; DLB 37, 50; WLIT 2

Erasmus, Desiderius 1469(?)-1536 ..... **LC 16, 93**
See also DLB 136; EW 2; LMFS 1; RGWL 2, 3; TWA

Erdman, Paul E(mil) 1932- .... **CLC 25**
See also AITN 1; CA 61-64; CANR 13, 43, 84

Erdrich, Louise 1954- .... **CLC 39, 54, 120, 176; NNAL; PC 52**
See also AAYA 10, 47; AMWS 4; BEST 89:1; BPFB 1; CA 114; CANR 41, 62, 118; CDALBS; CN 7; CP 7; CPW; CWP; DA3; DAM MULT, NOV, POP; DLB 152, 175, 206; EWL 3; EXPP; LAIT 5; LATS 1:2; MTCW 1; NFS 5; PFS 14; RGAL 4; SATA 94, 141; SSFS 14; TCWW 2

Erenburg, Ilya (Grigoryevich)
See Ehrenburg, Ilya (Grigoryevich)

Erickson, Stephen Michael 1950-
See Erickson, Steve
See also CA 129; SFW 4

Erickson, Steve .... **CLC 64**
See Erickson, Stephen Michael
See also CANR 60, 68; SUFW 2

Erickson, Walter
See Fast, Howard (Melvin)

Ericson, Walter
See Fast, Howard (Melvin)

Eriksson, Buntel
See Bergman, (Ernst) Ingmar

Eriugena, John Scottus c.
810-877 .... **CMLC 65**
See also DLB 115

Ernaux, Annie 1940- .... **CLC 88, 184**
See also CA 147; CANR 93; NCFS 3, 5

Erskine, John 1879-1951 .... **TCLC 84**
See also CA 112; 159; DLB 9, 102; FANT

Eschenbach, Wolfram von
See Wolfram von Eschenbach
See also RGWL 3

Eseki, Bruno
See Mphahlele, Ezekiel
Esenin, Sergei (Alexandrovich)
1895-1925 .... **TCLC 4**
See Yesenin, Sergey
See also CA 104; RGWL 2, 3
Eshleman, Clayton 1935- .... **CLC 7**
See also CA 33-36R, 212; CAAE 212; CAAS 6; CANR 93; CP 7; DLB 5
Espriella, Don Manuel Alvarez
See Southey, Robert
Espriu, Salvador 1913-1985 .... **CLC 9**
See also CA 154; 115; DLB 134; EWL 3
Espronceda, Jose de 1808-1842 ..... **NCLC 39**
Esquivel, Laura 1951(?)- ... **CLC 141; HLCS 1**
See also AAYA 29; CA 143; CANR 68, 113; DA3; DNFS 2; LAIT 3; LMFS 2; MTCW 1; NFS 5; WLIT 1
Esse, James
See Stephens, James
Esterbrook, Tom
See Hubbard, L(afayette) Ron(ald)
Estleman, Loren D. 1952- .... **CLC 48**
See also AAYA 27; CA 85-88; CANR 27, 74; CMW 4; CPW; DA3; DAM NOV, POP; DLB 226; INT CANR-27; MTCW 1, 2
Etherege, Sir George 1636-1692 . **DC 23; LC 78**
See also BRW 2; DAM DRAM; DLB 80; PAB; RGEL 2
Euclid 306B.C.-283B.C. .... **CMLC 25**
Eugenides, Jeffrey 1960(?)- .... **CLC 81**
See also AAYA 51; CA 144; CANR 120
Euripides c. 484B.C.-406B.C. .... **CMLC 23, 51; DC 4; WLCS**
See also AW 1; CDWLB 1; DA; DA3; DAB; DAC; DAM DRAM, MST; DFS 1, 4, 6; DLB 176; LAIT 1; LMFS 1; RGWL 2, 3
Evan, Evin
See Faust, Frederick (Schiller)
Evans, Caradoc 1878-1945 ... **SSC 43; TCLC 85**
See also DLB 162
Evans, Evan
See Faust, Frederick (Schiller)
See also TCWW 2
Evans, Marian
See Eliot, George
Evans, Mary Ann
See Eliot, George
See also NFS 20
Evarts, Esther
See Benson, Sally
Everett, Percival
See Everett, Percival L.
See also CSW
Everett, Percival L. 1956- .... **CLC 57**
See Everett, Percival
See also BW 2; CA 129; CANR 94, 134
Everson, R(onald) G(ilmour)
1903-1992 .... **CLC 27**
See also CA 17-20R; DLB 88
Everson, William (Oliver)
1912-1994 .... **CLC 1, 5, 14**
See also BG 2; CA 9-12R; 145; CANR 20; DLB 5, 16, 212; MTCW 1
Evtushenko, Evgenii Aleksandrovich
See Yevtushenko, Yevgeny (Alexandrovich)
See also CWW 2; RGWL 2, 3
Ewart, Gavin (Buchanan)
1916-1995 .... **CLC 13, 46**
See also BRWS 7; CA 89-92; 150; CANR 17, 46; CP 7; DLB 40; MTCW 1
Ewers, Hanns Heinz 1871-1943 ..... **TCLC 12**
See also CA 109; 149

Ewing, Frederick R.
See Sturgeon, Theodore (Hamilton)
Exley, Frederick (Earl) 1929-1992 .... **CLC 6, 11**
See also AITN 2; BPFB 1; CA 81-84; 138; CANR 117; DLB 143; DLBY 1981
Eynhardt, Guillermo
See Quiroga, Horacio (Sylvestre)
Ezekiel, Nissim (Moses) 1924-2004 .. **CLC 61**
See also CA 61-64; 223; CP 7; EWL 3
Ezekiel, Tish O'Dowd 1943- .... **CLC 34**
See also CA 129
Fadeev, Aleksandr Aleksandrovich
See Bulgya, Alexander Alexandrovich
See also DLB 272
Fadeev, Alexandr Alexandrovich
See Bulgya, Alexander Alexandrovich
See also EWL 3
Fadeyev, A.
See Bulgya, Alexander Alexandrovich
Fadeyev, Alexander .... **TCLC 53**
See Bulgya, Alexander Alexandrovich
Fagen, Donald 1948- .... **CLC 26**
Fainzilberg, Ilya Arnoldovich 1897-1937
See Ilf, Ilya
See also CA 120; 165
Fair, Ronald L. 1932- .... **CLC 18**
See also BW 1; CA 69-72; CANR 25; DLB 33
Fairbairn, Roger
See Carr, John Dickson
Fairbairns, Zoe (Ann) 1948- .... **CLC 32**
See also CA 103; CANR 21, 85; CN 7
Fairfield, Flora
See Alcott, Louisa May
Fairman, Paul W. 1916-1977
See Queen, Ellery
See also CA 114; SFW 4
Falco, Gian
See Papini, Giovanni
Falconer, James
See Kirkup, James
Falconer, Kenneth
See Kornbluth, C(yril) M.
Falkland, Samuel
See Heijermans, Herman
Fallaci, Oriana 1930- .... **CLC 11, 110**
See also CA 77-80; CANR 15, 58, 134; FW; MTCW 1
Faludi, Susan 1959- .... **CLC 140**
See also CA 138; CANR 126; FW; MTCW 1; NCFS 3
Faludy, George 1913- .... **CLC 42**
See also CA 21-24R
Faludy, Gyoergy
See Faludy, George
Fanon, Frantz 1925-1961 .... **BLC 2; CLC 74**
See also BW 1; CA 116; 89-92; DAM MULT; DLB 296; LMFS 2; WLIT 2
Fanshawe, Ann 1625-1680 .... **LC 11**
Fante, John (Thomas) 1911-1983 .... **CLC 60; SSC 65**
See also AMWS 11; CA 69-72; 109; CANR 23, 104; DLB 130; DLBY 1983
Far, Sui Sin .... **SSC 62**
See Eaton, Edith Maude
See also SSFS 4
Farah, Nuruddin 1945- .... **BLC 2; CLC 53, 137**
See also AFW; BW 2, 3; CA 106; CANR 81; CDWLB 3; CN 7; DAM MULT; DLB 125; EWL 3; WLIT 2
Fargue, Leon-Paul 1876(?)-1947 .... **TCLC 11**
See also CA 109; CANR 107; DLB 258; EWL 3
Farigoule, Louis
See Romains, Jules

Farina, Richard 1936(?)-1966 .... **CLC 9**
See also CA 81-84; 25-28R
Farley, Walter (Lorimer)
1915-1989 .... **CLC 17**
See also AAYA 58; BYA 14; CA 17-20R; CANR 8, 29, 84; DLB 22; JRDA; MAICYA 1, 2; SATA 2, 43, 132; YAW
Farmer, Philip Jose 1918- .... **CLC 1, 19**
See also AAYA 28; BPFB 1; CA 1-4R; CANR 4, 35, 111; DLB 8; MTCW 1; SATA 93; SCFW 2; SFW 4
Farquhar, George 1677-1707 .... **LC 21**
See also BRW 2; DAM DRAM; DLB 84; RGEL 2
Farrell, J(ames) G(ordon)
1935-1979 .... **CLC 6**
See also CA 73-76; 89-92; CANR 36; DLB 14, 271; MTCW 1; RGEL 2; RHW; WLIT 4
Farrell, James T(homas) 1904-1979 . **CLC 1, 4, 8, 11, 66; SSC 28**
See also AMW; BPFB 1; CA 5-8R; 89-92; CANR 9, 61; DLB 4, 9, 86; DLBD 2; EWL 3; MTCW 1, 2; RGAL 4
Farrell, Warren (Thomas) 1943- ...... **CLC 70**
See also CA 146; CANR 120
Farren, Richard J.
See Betjeman, John
Farren, Richard M.
See Betjeman, John
Fassbinder, Rainer Werner
1946-1982 .... **CLC 20**
See also CA 93-96; 106; CANR 31
Fast, Howard (Melvin) 1914-2003 .. **CLC 23, 131**
See also AAYA 16; BPFB 1; CA 1-4R, 181; 214; CAAE 181; CAAS 18; CANR 1, 33, 54, 75, 98; CMW 4; CN 7; CPW; DAM NOV; DLB 9; INT CANR-33; LATS 1:1; MTCW 1; RHW; SATA 7; SATA-Essay 107; TCWW 2; YAW
Faulcon, Robert
See Holdstock, Robert P.
Faulkner, William (Cuthbert)
1897-1962 .... **CLC 1, 3, 6, 8, 9, 11, 14, 18, 28, 52, 68; SSC 1, 35, 42; TCLC 141; WLC**
See also AAYA 7; AMW; AMWR 1; BPFB 1; BYA 5, 15; CA 81-84; CANR 33; CDALB 1929-1941; DA; DA3; DAB; DAC; DAM MST, NOV; DLB 9, 11, 44, 102; DLBD 2; DLBY 1986, 1997; EWL 3; EXPN; EXPS; LAIT 2; LATS 1:1; LMFS 2; MTCW 1, 2; NFS 4, 8, 13; RGAL 4; RGSF 2; SSFS 2, 5, 6, 12; TUS
Fauset, Jessie Redmon
1882(?)-1961 .. **BLC 2; CLC 19, 54; HR 2**
See also AFAW 2; BW 1; CA 109; CANR 83; DAM MULT; DLB 51; FW; LMFS 2; MAWW
Faust, Frederick (Schiller)
1892-1944(?) .... **TCLC 49**
See Austin, Frank; Brand, Max; Challis, George; Dawson, Peter; Dexter, Martin; Evans, Evan; Frederick, John; Frost, Frederick; Manning, David; Silver, Nicholas
See also CA 108; 152; DAM POP; DLB 256; TUS
Faust, Irvin 1924- .... **CLC 8**
See also CA 33-36R; CANR 28, 67; CN 7; DLB 2, 28, 218, 278; DLBY 1980
Faustino, Domingo 1811-1888 ...... **NCLC 123**
Fawkes, Guy
See Benchley, Robert (Charles)
Fearing, Kenneth (Flexner)
1902-1961 .... **CLC 51**
See also CA 93-96; CANR 59; CMW 4; DLB 9; RGAL 4

Fecamps, Elise
See Creasey, John

Federman, Raymond 1928- .... **CLC 6, 47**
See also CA 17-20R, 208; CAAE 208; CAAS 8; CANR 10, 43, 83, 108; CN 7; DLBY 1980

Federspiel, J(uerg) F. 1931- .... **CLC 42**
See also CA 146

Feiffer, Jules (Ralph) 1929- ...... **CLC 2, 8, 64**
See also AAYA 3; CA 17-20R; CAD; CANR 30, 59, 129; CD 5; DAM DRAM; DLB 7, 44; INT CANR-30; MTCW 1; SATA 8, 61, 111

Feige, Hermann Albert Otto Maximilian
See Traven, B.

Feinberg, David B. 1956-1994 .... **CLC 59**
See also CA 135; 147

Feinstein, Elaine 1930- .... **CLC 36**
See also CA 69-72; CAAS 1; CANR 31, 68, 121; CN 7; CP 7; CWP; DLB 14, 40; MTCW 1

Feke, Gilbert David .... **CLC 65**

Feldman, Irving (Mordecai) 1928- ..... **CLC 7**
See also CA 1-4R; CANR 1; CP 7; DLB 169

Felix-Tchicaya, Gerald
See Tchicaya, Gerald Felix

Fellini, Federico 1920-1993 .... **CLC 16, 85**
See also CA 65-68; 143; CANR 33

Felltham, Owen 1602(?)-1668 .... **LC 92**
See also DLB 126, 151

Felsen, Henry Gregor 1916-1995 ..... **CLC 17**
See also CA 1-4R; 180; CANR 1; SAAS 2; SATA 1

Felski, Rita .... **CLC 65**

Fenno, Jack
See Calisher, Hortense

Fenollosa, Ernest (Francisco) 1853-1908 .... **TCLC 91**

Fenton, James Martin 1949- .... **CLC 32**
See also CA 102; CANR 108; CP 7; DLB 40; PFS 11

Ferber, Edna 1887-1968 .... **CLC 18, 93**
See also AITN 1; CA 5-8R; 25-28R; CANR 68, 105; DLB 9, 28, 86, 266; MTCW 1, 2; RGAL 4; RHW; SATA 7; TCWW 2

Ferdowsi, Abu'l Qasem 940-1020 . **CMLC 43**
See also RGWL 2, 3

Ferguson, Helen
See Kavan, Anna

Ferguson, Niall 1964- .... **CLC 134**
See also CA 190

Ferguson, Samuel 1810-1886 .... **NCLC 33**
See also DLB 32; RGEL 2

Fergusson, Robert 1750-1774 .... **LC 29**
See also DLB 109; RGEL 2

Ferling, Lawrence
See Ferlinghetti, Lawrence (Monsanto)

Ferlinghetti, Lawrence (Monsanto) 1919(?)- ..... **CLC 2, 6, 10, 27, 111; PC 1**
See also CA 5-8R; CANR 3, 41, 73, 125; CDALB 1941-1968; CP 7; DA3; DAM POET; DLB 5, 16; MTCW 1, 2; RGAL 4; WP

Fern, Fanny
See Parton, Sara Payson Willis

Fernandez, Vicente Garcia Huidobro
See Huidobro Fernandez, Vicente Garcia

Fernandez-Armesto, Felipe .... **CLC 70**

Fernandez de Lizardi, Jose Joaquin
See Lizardi, Jose Joaquin Fernandez de

Ferre, Rosario 1938- ...... **CLC 139; HLCS 1; SSC 36**
See also CA 131; CANR 55, 81, 134; CWW 2; DLB 145; EWL 3; HW 1, 2; LAWS 1; MTCW 1; WLIT 1

Ferrer, Gabriel (Francisco Victor) Miro
See Miro (Ferrer), Gabriel (Francisco Victor)

Ferrier, Susan (Edmonstone) 1782-1854 .... **NCLC 8**
See also DLB 116; RGEL 2

Ferrigno, Robert 1948(?)- .... **CLC 65**
See also CA 140; CANR 125

Ferron, Jacques 1921-1985 .... **CLC 94**
See also CA 117; 129; CCA 1; DAC; DLB 60; EWL 3

Feuchtwanger, Lion 1884-1958 .... **TCLC 3**
See also CA 104; 187; DLB 66; EWL 3

Feuerbach, Ludwig 1804-1872 ..... **NCLC 139**
See also DLB 133

Feuillet, Octave 1821-1890 .... **NCLC 45**
See also DLB 192

Feydeau, Georges (Leon Jules Marie) 1862-1921 .... **TCLC 22**
See also CA 113; 152; CANR 84; DAM DRAM; DLB 192; EWL 3; GFL 1789 to the Present; RGWL 2, 3

Fichte, Johann Gottlieb 1762-1814 .... **NCLC 62**
See also DLB 90

Ficino, Marsilio 1433-1499 .... **LC 12**
See also LMFS 1

Fiedeler, Hans
See Doeblin, Alfred

Fiedler, Leslie A(aron) 1917-2003 ..... **CLC 4, 13, 24**
See also AMWS 13; CA 9-12R; 212; CANR 7, 63; CN 7; DLB 28, 67; EWL 3; MTCW 1, 2; RGAL 4; TUS

Field, Andrew 1938- .... **CLC 44**
See also CA 97-100; CANR 25

Field, Eugene 1850-1895 .... **NCLC 3**
See also DLB 23, 42, 140; DLBD 13; MAICYA 1, 2; RGAL 4; SATA 16

Field, Gans T.
See Wellman, Manly Wade

Field, Michael 1915-1971 .... **TCLC 43**
See also CA 29-32R

Field, Peter
See Hobson, Laura Z(ametkin)
See also TCWW 2

Fielding, Helen 1958- .... **CLC 146**
See also CA 172; CANR 127; DLB 231

Fielding, Henry 1707-1754 .... **LC 1, 46, 85; WLC**
See also BRW 3; BRWR 1; CDBLB 1660-1789; DA; DA3; DAB; DAC; DAM DRAM, MST, NOV; DLB 39, 84, 101; NFS 18; RGEL 2; TEA; WLIT 3

Fielding, Sarah 1710-1768 .... **LC 1, 44**
See also DLB 39; RGEL 2; TEA

Fields, W. C. 1880-1946 .... **TCLC 80**
See also DLB 44

Fierstein, Harvey (Forbes) 1954- ..... **CLC 33**
See also CA 123; 129; CAD; CD 5; CPW; DA3; DAM DRAM, POP; DFS 6; DLB 266; GLL

Figes, Eva 1932- .... **CLC 31**
See also CA 53-56; CANR 4, 44, 83; CN 7; DLB 14, 271; FW

Filippo, Eduardo de
See de Filippo, Eduardo

Finch, Anne 1661-1720 .... **LC 3; PC 21**
See also BRWS 9; DLB 95

Finch, Robert (Duer Claydon) 1900-1995 .... **CLC 18**
See also CA 57-60; CANR 9, 24, 49; CP 7; DLB 88

Findley, Timothy (Irving Frederick) 1930-2002 .... **CLC 27, 102**
See also CA 25-28R; 206; CANR 12, 42, 69, 109; CCA 1; CN 7; DAC; DAM MST; DLB 53; FANT; RHW

Fink, William
See Mencken, H(enry) L(ouis)

Firbank, Louis 1942-
See Reed, Lou
See also CA 117

Firbank, (Arthur Annesley) Ronald 1886-1926 .... **TCLC 1**
See also BRWS 2; CA 104; 177; DLB 36; EWL 3; RGEL 2

Fish, Stanley
See Fish, Stanley Eugene

Fish, Stanley E.
See Fish, Stanley Eugene

Fish, Stanley Eugene 1938- .... **CLC 142**
See also CA 112; 132; CANR 90; DLB 67

Fisher, Dorothy (Frances) Canfield 1879-1958 .... **TCLC 87**
See also CA 114; 136; CANR 80; CLR 71,; CWRI 5; DLB 9, 102, 284; MAICYA 1, 2; YABC 1

Fisher, M(ary) F(rances) K(ennedy) 1908-1992 .... **CLC 76, 87**
See also CA 77-80; 138; CANR 44; MTCW 1

Fisher, Roy 1930- .... **CLC 25**
See also CA 81-84; CAAS 10; CANR 16; CP 7; DLB 40

Fisher, Rudolph 1897-1934 .... **BLC 2; HR 2; SSC 25; TCLC 11**
See also BW 1, 3; CA 107; 124; CANR 80; DAM MULT; DLB 51, 102

Fisher, Vardis (Alvero) 1895-1968 .... **CLC 7; TCLC 140**
See also CA 5-8R; 25-28R; CANR 68; DLB 9, 206; RGAL 4; TCWW 2

Fiske, Tarleton
See Bloch, Robert (Albert)

Fitch, Clarke
See Sinclair, Upton (Beall)

Fitch, John IV
See Cormier, Robert (Edmund)

Fitzgerald, Captain Hugh
See Baum, L(yman) Frank

FitzGerald, Edward 1809-1883 .... **NCLC 9, 153**
See also BRW 4; DLB 32; RGEL 2

Fitzgerald, F(rancis) Scott (Key) 1896-1940 ... **SSC 6, 31, 75; TCLC 1, 6, 14, 28, 55, 157; WLC**
See also AAYA 24; AITN 1; AMW; AMWC 2; AMWR 1; BPFB 1; CA 110; 123; CDALB 1917-1929; DA; DA3; DAB; DAC; DAM MST, NOV; DLB 4, 9, 86, 219, 273; DLBD 1, 15, 16; DLBY 1981, 1996; EWL 3; EXPN; EXPS; LAIT 3; MTCW 1, 2; NFS 2, 19, 20; RGAL 4; RGSF 2; SSFS 4, 15; TUS

Fitzgerald, Penelope 1916-2000 . **CLC 19, 51, 61, 143**
See also BRWS 5; CA 85-88; 190; CAAS 10; CANR 56, 86, 131; CN 7; DLB 14, 194; EWL 3; MTCW 2

Fitzgerald, Robert (Stuart) 1910-1985 .... **CLC 39**
See also CA 1-4R; 114; CANR 1; DLBY 1980

FitzGerald, Robert D(avid) 1902-1987 .... **CLC 19**
See also CA 17-20R; DLB 260; RGEL 2

Fitzgerald, Zelda (Sayre) 1900-1948 .... **TCLC 52**
See also AMWS 9; CA 117; 126; DLBY 1984

Flanagan, Thomas (James Bonner) 1923-2002 .... **CLC 25, 52**
See also CA 108; 206; CANR 55; CN 7; DLBY 1980; INT CA-108; MTCW 1; RHW

Flaubert, Gustave 1821-1880 .... **NCLC 2, 10, 19, 62, 66, 135; SSC 11, 60; WLC**
See also DA; DA3; DAB; DAC; DAM MST, NOV; DLB 119, 301; EW 7; EXPS; GFL 1789 to the Present; LAIT 2; LMFS 1; NFS 14; RGSF 2; RGWL 2, 3; SSFS 6; TWA

Flavius Josephus
See Josephus, Flavius

Flecker, Herman Elroy
See Flecker, (Herman) James Elroy

Flecker, (Herman) James Elroy 1884-1915 .... **TCLC 43**
See also CA 109; 150; DLB 10, 19; RGEL 2

Fleming, Ian (Lancaster) 1908-1964 . **CLC 3, 30**
See also AAYA 26; BPFB 1; CA 5-8R; CANR 59; CDBLB 1945-1960; CMW 4; CPW; DA3; DAM POP; DLB 87, 201; MSW; MTCW 1, 2; RGEL 2; SATA 9; TEA; YAW

Fleming, Thomas (James) 1927- ...... **CLC 37**
See also CA 5-8R; CANR 10, 102; INT CANR-10; SATA 8

Fletcher, John 1579-1625 .... **DC 6; LC 33**
See also BRW 2; CDBLB Before 1660; DLB 58; RGEL 2; TEA

Fletcher, John Gould 1886-1950 .... **TCLC 35**
See also CA 107; 167; DLB 4, 45; LMFS 2; RGAL 4

Fleur, Paul
See Pohl, Frederik

Flieg, Helmut
See Heym, Stefan

Flooglebuckle, Al
See Spiegelman, Art

Flora, Fletcher 1914-1969
See Queen, Ellery
See also CA 1-4R; CANR 3, 85

Flying Officer X
See Bates, H(erbert) E(rnest)

Fo, Dario 1926- .... **CLC 32, 109; DC 10**
See also CA 116; 128; CANR 68, 114, 134; CWW 2; DA3; DAM DRAM; DLBY 1997; EWL 3; MTCW 1, 2

Fogarty, Jonathan Titulescu Esq.
See Farrell, James T(homas)

Follett, Ken(neth Martin) 1949- .... **CLC 18**
See also AAYA 6, 50; BEST 89:4; BPFB 1; CA 81-84; CANR 13, 33, 54, 102; CMW 4; CPW; DA3; DAM NOV, POP; DLB 87; DLBY 1981; INT CANR-33; MTCW 1

Fondane, Benjamin 1898-1944 ..... **TCLC 159**

Fontane, Theodor 1819-1898 .... **NCLC 26**
See also CDWLB 2; DLB 129; EW 6; RGWL 2, 3; TWA

Fontenot, Chester .... **CLC 65**

Fonvizin, Denis Ivanovich 1744(?)-1792 .... **LC 81**
See also DLB 150; RGWL 2, 3

Foote, Horton 1916- .... **CLC 51, 91**
See also CA 73-76; CAD; CANR 34, 51, 110; CD 5; CSW; DA3; DAM DRAM; DFS 20; DLB 26, 266; EWL 3; INT CANR-34

Foote, Mary Hallock 1847-1938 .. **TCLC 108**
See also DLB 186, 188, 202, 221

Foote, Samuel 1721-1777 .... **LC 106**
See also DLB 89; RGEL 2

Foote, Shelby 1916- .... **CLC 75**
See also AAYA 40; CA 5-8R; CANR 3, 45, 74, 131; CN 7; CPW; CSW; DA3; DAM NOV, POP; DLB 2, 17; MTCW 2; RHW

Forbes, Cosmo
See Lewton, Val

Forbes, Esther 1891-1967 .... **CLC 12**
See also AAYA 17; BYA 2; CA 13-14; 25-28R; CAP 1; CLR 27; DLB 22; JRDA; MAICYA 1, 2; RHW; SATA 2, 100; YAW

Forche, Carolyn (Louise) 1950- .... **CLC 25, 83, 86; PC 10**
See also CA 109; 117; CANR 50, 74; CP 7; CWP; DA3; DAM POET; DLB 5, 193; INT CA-117; MTCW 1; PFS 18; RGAL 4

Ford, Elbur
See Hibbert, Eleanor Alice Burford

Ford, Ford Madox 1873-1939 ... **TCLC 1, 15, 39, 57**
See Chaucer, Daniel
See also BRW 6; CA 104; 132; CANR 74; CDBLB 1914-1945; DA3; DAM NOV; DLB 34, 98, 162; EWL 3; MTCW 1, 2; RGEL 2; TEA

Ford, Henry 1863-1947 .... **TCLC 73**
See also CA 115; 148

Ford, Jack
See Ford, John

Ford, John 1586-1639 .... **DC 8; LC 68**
See also BRW 2; CDBLB Before 1660; DA3; DAM DRAM; DFS 7; DLB 58; IDTP; RGEL 2

Ford, John 1895-1973 .... **CLC 16**
See also CA 187; 45-48

Ford, Richard 1944- .... **CLC 46, 99, 205**
See also AMWS 5; CA 69-72; CANR 11, 47, 86, 128; CN 7; CSW; DLB 227; EWL 3; MTCW 1; RGAL 4; RGSF 2

Ford, Webster
See Masters, Edgar Lee

Foreman, Richard 1937- .... **CLC 50**
See also CA 65-68; CAD; CANR 32, 63; CD 5

Forester, C(ecil) S(cott) 1899-1966 . **CLC 35; TCLC 152**
See also CA 73-76; 25-28R; CANR 83; DLB 191; RGEL 2; RHW; SATA 13

Forez
See Mauriac, Francois (Charles)

Forman, James
See Forman, James D(ouglas)

Forman, James D(ouglas) 1932- .... **CLC 21**
See also AAYA 17; CA 9-12R; CANR 4, 19, 42; JRDA; MAICYA 1, 2; SATA 8, 70; YAW

Forman, Milos 1932- .... **CLC 164**
See also CA 109

Fornes, Maria Irene 1930- .... **CLC 39, 61, 187; DC 10; HLCS 1**
See also CA 25-28R; CAD; CANR 28, 81; CD 5; CWD; DLB 7; HW 1, 2; INT CANR-28; LLW 1; MTCW 1; RGAL 4

Forrest, Leon (Richard) 1937-1997 .... **BLCS; CLC 4**
See also AFAW 2; BW 2; CA 89-92; 162; CAAS 7; CANR 25, 52, 87; CN 7; DLB 33

Forster, E(dward) M(organ) 1879-1970 ...... **CLC 1, 2, 3, 4, 9, 10, 13, 15, 22, 45, 77; SSC 27; TCLC 125; WLC**
See also AAYA 2, 37; BRW 6; BRWR 2; BYA 12; CA 13-14; 25-28R; CANR 45; CAP 1; CDBLB 1914-1945; DA; DA3; DAB; DAC; DAM MST, NOV; DLB 34, 98, 162, 178, 195; DLBD 10; EWL 3; EXPN; LAIT 3; LMFS 1; MTCW 1, 2; NCFS 1; NFS 3, 10, 11; RGEL 2; RGSF 2; SATA 57; SUFW 1; TEA; WLIT 4

Forster, John 1812-1876 .... **NCLC 11**
See also DLB 144, 184

Forster, Margaret 1938- .... **CLC 149**
See also CA 133; CANR 62, 115; CN 7; DLB 155, 271

Forsyth, Frederick 1938- .... **CLC 2, 5, 36**
See also BEST 89:4; CA 85-88; CANR 38, 62, 115; CMW 4; CN 7; CPW; DAM NOV, POP; DLB 87; MTCW 1, 2

Forten, Charlotte L. 1837-1914 .... **BLC 2; TCLC 16**
See Grimke, Charlotte L(ottie) Forten
See also DLB 50, 239

Fortinbras
See Grieg, (Johan) Nordahl (Brun)

Foscolo, Ugo 1778-1827 .... **NCLC 8, 97**
See also EW 5

Fosse, Bob .... **CLC 20**
See Fosse, Robert Louis

Fosse, Robert Louis 1927-1987
See Fosse, Bob
See also CA 110; 123

Foster, Hannah Webster 1758-1840 .... **NCLC 99**
See also DLB 37, 200; RGAL 4

Foster, Stephen Collins 1826-1864 .... **NCLC 26**
See also RGAL 4

Foucault, Michel 1926-1984 . **CLC 31, 34, 69**
See also CA 105; 113; CANR 34; DLB 242; EW 13; EWL 3; GFL 1789 to the Present; GLL 1; LMFS 2; MTCW 1, 2; TWA

Fouque, Friedrich (Heinrich Karl) de la Motte 1777-1843 .... **NCLC 2**
See also DLB 90; RGWL 2, 3; SUFW 1

Fourier, Charles 1772-1837 .... **NCLC 51**

Fournier, Henri-Alban 1886-1914
See Alain-Fournier
See also CA 104; 179

Fournier, Pierre 1916- .... **CLC 11**
See Gascar, Pierre
See also CA 89-92; CANR 16, 40

Fowles, John (Robert) 1926- . **CLC 1, 2, 3, 4, 6, 9, 10, 15, 33, 87; SSC 33**
See also BPFB 1; BRWS 1; CA 5-8R; CANR 25, 71, 103; CDBLB 1960 to Present; CN 7; DA3; DAB; DAC; DAM MST; DLB 14, 139, 207; EWL 3; HGG; MTCW 1, 2; RGEL 2; RHW; SATA 22; TEA; WLIT 4

Fox, Paula 1923- .... **CLC 2, 8, 121**
See also AAYA 3, 37; BYA 3, 8; CA 73-76; CANR 20, 36, 62, 105; CLR 1, 44, 96; DLB 52; JRDA; MAICYA 1, 2; MTCW 1; NFS 12; SATA 17, 60, 120; WYA; YAW

Fox, William Price (Jr.) 1926- .... **CLC 22**
See also CA 17-20R; CAAS 19; CANR 11; CSW; DLB 2; DLBY 1981

Foxe, John 1517(?)-1587 .... **LC 14**
See also DLB 132

Frame, Janet .. **CLC 2, 3, 6, 22, 66, 96; SSC 29**
See Clutha, Janet Paterson Frame
See also CN 7; CWP; EWL 3; RGEL 2; RGSF 2; TWA

France, Anatole .... **TCLC 9**
See Thibault, Jacques Anatole Francois
See also DLB 123; EWL 3; GFL 1789 to the Present; MTCW 1; RGWL 2, 3; SUFW 1

Francis, Claude .... **CLC 50**
See also CA 192

Francis, Richard Stanley 1920- ... **CLC 2, 22, 42, 102**
See also AAYA 5, 21; BEST 89:3; BPFB 1; CA 5-8R; CANR 9, 42, 68, 100; CDBLB 1960 to Present; CMW 4; CN 7; DA3; DAM POP; DLB 87; INT CANR-9; MSW; MTCW 1, 2

Francis, Robert (Churchill) 1901-1987 .... **CLC 15; PC 34**
See also AMWS 9; CA 1-4R; 123; CANR 1; EXPP; PFS 12

Francis, Lord Jeffrey
See Jeffrey, Francis
See also DLB 107

Frank, Anne(lies Marie)
1929-1945 .... **TCLC 17; WLC**
See also AAYA 12; BYA 1; CA 113; 133; CANR 68; CLR 101; DA; DA3; DAB; DAC; DAM MST; LAIT 4; MAICYA 2; MAICYAS 1; MTCW 1, 2; NCFS 2; SATA 87; SATA-Brief 42; WYA; YAW

Frank, Bruno 1887-1945 .... **TCLC 81**
See also CA 189; DLB 118; EWL 3

Frank, Elizabeth 1945- .... **CLC 39**
See also CA 121; 126; CANR 78; INT CA-126

Frankl, Viktor E(mil) 1905-1997 ...... **CLC 93**
See also CA 65-68; 161

Franklin, Benjamin
See Hasek, Jaroslav (Matej Frantisek)

Franklin, Benjamin 1706-1790 .... **LC 25; WLCS**
See also AMW; CDALB 1640-1865; DA; DA3; DAB; DAC; DAM MST; DLB 24, 43, 73, 183; LAIT 1; RGAL 4; TUS

Franklin, (Stella Maria Sarah) Miles (Lampe) 1879-1954 .... **TCLC 7**
See also CA 104; 164; DLB 230; FW; MTCW 2; RGEL 2; TWA

Franzen, Jonathan 1959- .... **CLC 202**
See also CA 129; CANR 105

Fraser, Antonia (Pakenham) 1932- . **CLC 32, 107**
See also AAYA 57; CA 85-88; CANR 44, 65, 119; CMW; DLB 276; MTCW 1, 2; SATA-Brief 32

Fraser, George MacDonald 1925- ...... **CLC 7**
See also CA 45-48; CA 45-48, 180; CAAE 180; CANR 2, 48, 74; MTCW 1; RHW

Fraser, Sylvia 1935- .... **CLC 64**
See also CA 45-48; CANR 1, 16, 60; CCA 1

Frayn, Michael 1933- . **CLC 3, 7, 31, 47, 176**
See also BRWC 2; BRWS 7; CA 5-8R; CANR 30, 69, 114, 133; CBD; CD 5; CN 7; DAM DRAM, NOV; DLB 13, 14, 194, 245; FANT; MTCW 1, 2; SFW 4

Fraze, Candida (Merrill) 1945- .... **CLC 50**
See also CA 126

Frazer, Andrew
See Marlowe, Stephen

Frazer, J(ames) G(eorge)
1854-1941 .... **TCLC 32**
See also BRWS 3; CA 118; NCFS 5

Frazer, Robert Caine
See Creasey, John

Frazer, Sir James George
See Frazer, J(ames) G(eorge)

Frazier, Charles 1950- .... **CLC 109**
See also AAYA 34; CA 161; CANR 126; CSW; DLB 292

Frazier, Ian 1951- .... **CLC 46**
See also CA 130; CANR 54, 93

Frederic, Harold 1856-1898 .... **NCLC 10**
See also AMW; DLB 12, 23; DLBD 13; RGAL 4

Frederick, John
See Faust, Frederick (Schiller)
See also TCWW 2

Frederick the Great 1712-1786 .... **LC 14**

Fredro, Aleksander 1793-1876 .... **NCLC 8**

Freeling, Nicolas 1927-2003 .... **CLC 38**
See also CA 49-52; 218; CAAS 12; CANR 1, 17, 50, 84; CMW 4; CN 7; DLB 87

Freeman, Douglas Southall
1886-1953 .... **TCLC 11**
See also CA 109; 195; DLB 17; DLBD 17

Freeman, Judith 1946- .... **CLC 55**
See also CA 148; CANR 120; DLB 256

Freeman, Mary E(leanor) Wilkins
1852-1930 .... **SSC 1, 47; TCLC 9**
See also CA 106; 177; DLB 12, 78, 221; EXPS; FW; HGG; MAWW; RGAL 4; RGSF 2; SSFS 4, 8; SUFW 1; TUS

Freeman, R(ichard) Austin
1862-1943 .... **TCLC 21**
See also CA 113; CANR 84; CMW 4; DLB 70

French, Albert 1943- .... **CLC 86**
See also BW 3; CA 167

French, Antonia
See Kureishi, Hanif

French, Marilyn 1929- .. **CLC 10, 18, 60, 177**
See also BPFB 1; CA 69-72; CANR 3, 31, 134; CN 7; CPW; DAM DRAM, NOV, POP; FW; INT CANR-31; MTCW 1, 2

French, Paul
See Asimov, Isaac

Freneau, Philip Morin 1752-1832 .. **NCLC 1, 111**
See also AMWS 2; DLB 37, 43; RGAL 4

Freud, Sigmund 1856-1939 .... **TCLC 52**
See also CA 115; 133; CANR 69; DLB 296; EW 8; EWL 3; LATS 1:1; MTCW 1, 2; NCFS 3; TWA

Freytag, Gustav 1816-1895 .... **NCLC 109**
See also DLB 129

Friedan, Betty (Naomi) 1921- .... **CLC 74**
See also CA 65-68; CANR 18, 45, 74; DLB 246; FW; MTCW 1, 2; NCFS 5

Friedlander, Saul 1932- .... **CLC 90**
See also CA 117; 130; CANR 72

Friedman, B(ernard) H(arper)
1926- .... **CLC 7**
See also CA 1-4R; CANR 3, 48

Friedman, Bruce Jay 1930- ...... **CLC 3, 5, 56**
See also CA 9-12R; CAD; CANR 25, 52, 101; CD 5; CN 7; DLB 2, 28, 244; INT CANR-25; SSFS 18

Friel, Brian 1929- .... **CLC 5, 42, 59, 115; DC 8; SSC 76**
See also BRWS 5; CA 21-24R; CANR 33, 69, 130; DAM DRAM; CD 5; DFS 11; DLB 13; EWL 3; MTCW 1; RGEL 2; TEA

Friis-Baastad, Babbis Ellinor
1921-1970 .... **CLC 12**
See also CA 17-20R; 134; SATA 7

Frisch, Max (Rudolf) 1911-1991 ... **CLC 3, 9, 14, 18, 32, 44; TCLC 121**
See also CA 85-88; 134; CANR 32, 74; CD-WLB 2; DAM DRAM, NOV; DLB 69, 124; EW 13; EWL 3; MTCW 1, 2; RGWL 2, 3

Fromentin, Eugene (Samuel Auguste)
1820-1876 .... **NCLC 10, 125**
See also DLB 123; GFL 1789 to the Present

Frost, Frederick
See Faust, Frederick (Schiller)
See also TCWW 2

Frost, Robert (Lee) 1874-1963 .. **CLC 1, 3, 4, 9, 10, 13, 15, 26, 34, 44; PC 1, 39; WLC**
See also AAYA 21; AMW; AMWR 1; CA 89-92; CANR 33; CDALB 1917-1929; CLR 67; DA; DA3; DAB; DAC; DAM MST, POET; DLB 54, 284; DLBD 7; EWL 3; EXPP; MTCW 1, 2; PAB; PFS 1, 2, 3, 4, 5, 6, 7, 10, 13; RGAL 4; SATA 14; TUS; WP; WYA

Froude, James Anthony
1818-1894 .... **NCLC 43**
See also DLB 18, 57, 144

Froy, Herald
See Waterhouse, Keith (Spencer)

Fry, Christopher 1907- .... **CLC 2, 10, 14**
See also BRWS 3; CA 17-20R; CAAS 23; CANR 9, 30, 74, 132; CBD; CD 5; CP 7; DAM DRAM; DLB 13; EWL 3; MTCW 1, 2; RGEL 2; SATA 66; TEA

Frye, (Herman) Northrop
1912-1991 .... **CLC 24, 70**
See also CA 5-8R; 133; CANR 8, 37; DLB 67, 68, 246; EWL 3; MTCW 1, 2; RGAL 4; TWA

Fuchs, Daniel 1909-1993 .... **CLC 8, 22**
See also CA 81-84; 142; CAAS 5; CANR 40; DLB 9, 26, 28; DLBY 1993

Fuchs, Daniel 1934- .... **CLC 34**
See also CA 37-40R; CANR 14, 48

Fuentes, Carlos 1928- .. **CLC 3, 8, 10, 13, 22, 41, 60, 113; HLC 1; SSC 24; WLC**
See also AAYA 4, 45; AITN 2; BPFB 1; CA 69-72; CANR 10, 32, 68, 104; CD-WLB 3; CWW 2; DA; DA3; DAB; DAC; DAM MST, MULT, NOV; DLB 113; DNFS 2; EWL 3; HW 1, 2; LAIT 3; LATS 1:2; LAW; LAWS 1; LMFS 2; MTCW 1, 2; NFS 8; RGSF 2; RGWL 2, 3; TWA; WLIT 1

Fuentes, Gregorio Lopez y
See Lopez y Fuentes, Gregorio

Fuertes, Gloria 1918-1998 .... **PC 27**
See also CA 178; 180; DLB 108; HW 2; SATA 115

Fugard, (Harold) Athol 1932- . **CLC 5, 9, 14, 25, 40, 80; DC 3**
See also AAYA 17; AFW; CA 85-88; CANR 32, 54, 118; CD 5; DAM DRAM; DFS 3, 6, 10; DLB 225; EWL 3; LATS 1:2; MTCW 1; RGEL 2; WLIT 2

Fugard, Sheila 1932- .... **CLC 48**
See also CA 125

Fukuyama, Francis 1952- .... **CLC 131**
See also CA 140; CANR 72, 125

Fuller, Charles (H.), (Jr.) 1939- .... **BLC 2; CLC 25; DC 1**
See also BW 2; CA 108; 112; CAD; CANR 87; CD 5; DAM DRAM, MULT; DFS 8; DLB 38, 266; EWL 3; INT CA-112; MTCW 1

Fuller, Henry Blake 1857-1929 .... **TCLC 103**
See also CA 108; 177; DLB 12; RGAL 4

Fuller, John (Leopold) 1937- .... **CLC 62**
See also CA 21-24R; CANR 9, 44; CP 7; DLB 40

Fuller, Margaret
See Ossoli, Sarah Margaret (Fuller)
See also AMWS 2; DLB 183, 223, 239

Fuller, Roy (Broadbent) 1912-1991 ... **CLC 4, 28**
See also BRWS 7; CA 5-8R; 135; CAAS 10; CANR 53, 83; CWRI 5; DLB 15, 20; EWL 3; RGEL 2; SATA 87

Fuller, Sarah Margaret
See Ossoli, Sarah Margaret (Fuller)

Fuller, Sarah Margaret
See Ossoli, Sarah Margaret (Fuller)
See also DLB 1, 59, 73

Fuller, Thomas 1608-1661 .... **LC 111**
See also DLB 151

Fulton, Alice 1952- .... **CLC 52**
See also CA 116; CANR 57, 88; CP 7; CWP; DLB 193

Furphy, Joseph 1843-1912 .... **TCLC 25**
See Collins, Tom
See also CA 163; DLB 230; EWL 3; RGEL 2

Fuson, Robert H(enderson) 1927- .... **CLC 70**
See also CA 89-92; CANR 103

Fussell, Paul 1924- .... **CLC 74**
See also BEST 90:1; CA 17-20R; CANR 8, 21, 35, 69, 135; INT CANR-21; MTCW 1, 2

Futabatei, Shimei 1864-1909 .... **TCLC 44**
See Futabatei Shimei
See also CA 162; MJW

Futabatei Shimei
See Futabatei, Shimei
See also DLB 180; EWL 3

Futrelle, Jacques 1875-1912 .... **TCLC 19**
See also CA 113; 155; CMW 4

Gaboriau, Emile 1835-1873 .... **NCLC 14**
See also CMW 4; MSW

Gadda, Carlo Emilio 1893-1973 ...... **CLC 11; TCLC 144**
See also CA 89-92; DLB 177; EWL 3

Gaddis, William 1922-1998 ... **CLC 1, 3, 6, 8, 10, 19, 43, 86**
See also AMWS 4; BPFB 1; CA 17-20R; 172; CANR 21, 48; CN 7; DLB 2, 278; EWL 3; MTCW 1, 2; RGAL 4

Gaelique, Moruen le
See Jacob, (Cyprien-)Max

Gage, Walter
See Inge, William (Motter)

Gaiman, Neil (Richard) 1960- .... **CLC 195**
See also AAYA 19, 42; CA 133; CANR 81, 129; DLB 261; HGG; SATA 85, 146; SFW 4; SUFW 2

Gaines, Ernest J(ames) 1933- .. **BLC 2; CLC 3, 11, 18, 86, 181; SSC 68**
See also AAYA 18; AFAW 1, 2; AITN 1; BPFB 2; BW 2, 3; BYA 6; CA 9-12R; CANR 6, 24, 42, 75, 126; CDALB 1968-1988; CLR 62; CN 7; CSW; DA3; DAM MULT; DLB 2, 33, 152; DLBY 1980; EWL 3; EXPN; LAIT 5; LATS 1:2; MTCW 1, 2; NFS 5, 7, 16; RGAL 4; RGSF 2; RHW; SATA 86; SSFS 5; YAW

Gaitskill, Mary (Lawrence) 1954- ..... **CLC 69**
See also CA 128; CANR 61; DLB 244

Gaius Suetonius Tranquillus
See Suetonius

Galdos, Benito Perez
See Perez Galdos, Benito
See also EW 7

Gale, Zona 1874-1938 .... **TCLC 7**
See also CA 105; 153; CANR 84; DAM DRAM; DFS 17; DLB 9, 78, 228; RGAL 4

Galeano, Eduardo (Hughes) 1940- . **CLC 72; HLCS 1**
See also CA 29-32R; CANR 13, 32, 100; HW 1

Galiano, Juan Valera y Alcala
See Valera y Alcala-Galiano, Juan

Galilei, Galileo 1564-1642 .... **LC 45**

Gallagher, Tess 1943- .... **CLC 18, 63; PC 9**
See also CA 106; CP 7; CWP; DAM POET; DLB 120, 212, 244; PFS 16

Gallant, Mavis 1922- ..... **CLC 7, 18, 38, 172; SSC 5, 78**
See also CA 69-72; CANR 29, 69, 117; CCA 1; CN 7; DAC; DAM MST; DLB 53; EWL 3; MTCW 1, 2; RGEL 2; RGSF 2

Gallant, Roy A(rthur) 1924- .... **CLC 17**
See also CA 5-8R; CANR 4, 29, 54, 117; CLR 30; MAICYA 1, 2; SATA 4, 68, 110

Gallico, Paul (William) 1897-1976 ..... **CLC 2**
See also AITN 1; CA 5-8R; 69-72; CANR 23; DLB 9, 171; FANT; MAICYA 1, 2; SATA 13

Gallo, Max Louis 1932- .... **CLC 95**
See also CA 85-88

Gallois, Lucien
See Desnos, Robert

Gallup, Ralph
See Whitemore, Hugh (John)

Galsworthy, John 1867-1933 .... **SSC 22; TCLC 1, 45; WLC**
See also BRW 6; CA 104; 141; CANR 75; CDBLB 1890-1914; DA; DA3; DAB; DAC; DAM DRAM, MST, NOV; DLB 10, 34, 98, 162; DLBD 16; EWL 3; MTCW 1; RGEL 2; SSFS 3; TEA

Galt, John 1779-1839 .... **NCLC 1, 110**
See also DLB 99, 116, 159; RGEL 2; RGSF 2

Galvin, James 1951- .... **CLC 38**
See also CA 108; CANR 26

Gamboa, Federico 1864-1939 .... **TCLC 36**
See also CA 167; HW 2; LAW

Gandhi, M. K.
See Gandhi, Mohandas Karamchand

Gandhi, Mahatma
See Gandhi, Mohandas Karamchand

Gandhi, Mohandas Karamchand 1869-1948 .... **TCLC 59**
See also CA 121; 132; DA3; DAM MULT; MTCW 1, 2

Gann, Ernest Kellogg 1910-1991 ..... **CLC 23**
See also AITN 1; BPFB 2; CA 1-4R; 136; CANR 1, 83; RHW

Gao Xingjian 1940- .... **CLC 167**
See Xingjian, Gao

Garber, Eric 1943(?)-
See Holleran, Andrew
See also CANR 89

Garcia, Cristina 1958- .... **CLC 76**
See also AMWS 11; CA 141; CANR 73, 130; DLB 292; DNFS 1; EWL 3; HW 2; LLW 1

Garcia Lorca, Federico 1898-1936 .... **DC 2; HLC 2; PC 3; TCLC 1, 7, 49; WLC**
See Lorca, Federico Garcia
See also AAYA 46; CA 104; 131; CANR 81; DA; DA3; DAB; DAC; DAM DRAM, MST, MULT, POET; DFS 4, 10; DLB 108; EWL 3; HW 1, 2; LATS 1:2; MTCW 1, 2; TWA

Garcia Marquez, Gabriel (Jose) 1928- .... **CLC 2, 3, 8, 10, 15, 27, 47, 55, 68, 170; HLC 1; SSC 8; WLC**
See also AAYA 3, 33; BEST 89:1, 90:4; BPFB 2; BYA 12, 16; CA 33-36R; CANR 10, 28, 50, 75, 82, 128; CDWLB 3; CPW; CWW 2; DA; DA3; DAB; DAC; DAM MST, MULT, NOV, POP; DLB 113; DNFS 1, 2; EWL 3; EXPN; EXPS; HW 1, 2; LAIT 2; LATS 1:2; LAW; LAWS 1; LMFS 2; MTCW 1, 2; NCFS 1; NFS 1, 5, 10; RGSF 2; RGWL 2, 3; SSFS 1, 6, 16; TWA; WLIT 1

Garcilaso de la Vega, El Inca 1503-1536 .... **HLCS 1**
See also LAW

Gard, Janice
See Latham, Jean Lee

Gard, Roger Martin du
See Martin du Gard, Roger

Gardam, Jane (Mary) 1928- .... **CLC 43**
See also CA 49-52; CANR 2, 18, 33, 54, 106; CLR 12; DLB 14, 161, 231; MAICYA 1, 2; MTCW 1; SAAS 9; SATA 39, 76, 130; SATA-Brief 28; YAW

Gardner, Herb(ert George) 1934-2003 .... **CLC 44**
See also CA 149; 220; CAD; CANR 119; CD 5; DFS 18, 20

Gardner, John (Champlin), Jr. 1933-1982 ...... **CLC 2, 3, 5, 7, 8, 10, 18, 28, 34; SSC 7**
See also AAYA 45; AITN 1; AMWS 6; BPFB 2; CA 65-68; 107; CANR 33, 73; CDALBS; CPW; DA3; DAM NOV, POP; DLB 2; DLBY 1982; EWL 3; FANT; LATS 1:2; MTCW 1; NFS 3; RGAL 4; RGSF 2; SATA 40; SATA-Obit 31; SSFS 8

Gardner, John (Edmund) 1926- .... **CLC 30**
See also CA 103; CANR 15, 69, 127; CMW 4; CPW; DAM POP; MTCW 1

Gardner, Miriam
See Bradley, Marion Zimmer
See also GLL 1

Gardner, Noel
See Kuttner, Henry

Gardons, S. S.
See Snodgrass, W(illiam) D(e Witt)

Garfield, Leon 1921-1996 .... **CLC 12**
See also AAYA 8; BYA 1, 3; CA 17-20R; 152; CANR 38, 41, 78; CLR 21; DLB 161; JRDA; MAICYA 1, 2; MAICYAS 1; SATA 1, 32, 76; SATA-Obit 90; TEA; WYA; YAW

Garland, (Hannibal) Hamlin 1860-1940 .... **SSC 18; TCLC 3**
See also CA 104; DLB 12, 71, 78, 186; RGAL 4; RGSF 2; TCWW 2

Garneau, (Hector de) Saint-Denys 1912-1943 .... **TCLC 13**
See also CA 111; DLB 88

Garner, Alan 1934- .... **CLC 17**
See also AAYA 18; BYA 3, 5; CA 73-76; 178; CAAE 178; CANR 15, 64, 134; CLR 20; CPW; DAB; DAM POP; DLB 161, 261; FANT; MAICYA 1, 2; MTCW 1, 2; SATA 18, 69; SATA-Essay 108; SUFW 1, 2; YAW

Garner, Hugh 1913-1979 .... **CLC 13**
See Warwick, Jarvis
See also CA 69-72; CANR 31; CCA 1; DLB 68

Garnett, David 1892-1981 .... **CLC 3**
See also CA 5-8R; 103; CANR 17, 79; DLB 34; FANT; MTCW 2; RGEL 2; SFW 4; SUFW 1

Garos, Stephanie
See Katz, Steve

Garrett, George (Palmer) 1929- .. **CLC 3, 11, 51; SSC 30**
See also AMWS 7; BPFB 2; CA 1-4R; 202; CAAE 202; CAAS 5; CANR 1, 42, 67, 109; CN 7; CP 7; CSW; DLB 2, 5, 130, 152; DLBY 1983

Garrick, David 1717-1779 .... **LC 15**
See also DAM DRAM; DLB 84, 213; RGEL 2

Garrigue, Jean 1914-1972 .... **CLC 2, 8**
See also CA 5-8R; 37-40R; CANR 20

Garrison, Frederick
See Sinclair, Upton (Beall)

Garrison, William Lloyd 1805-1879 .... **NCLC 149**
See also CDALB 1640-1865; DLB 1, 43, 235

Garro, Elena 1920(?)-1998 .. **HLCS 1; TCLC 153**
See also CA 131; 169; CWW 2; DLB 145; EWL 3; HW 1; LAWS 1; WLIT 1

Garth, Will
See Hamilton, Edmond; Kuttner, Henry

Garvey, Marcus (Moziah, Jr.) 1887-1940 .... **BLC 2; HR 2; TCLC 41**
See also BW 1; CA 120; 124; CANR 79; DAM MULT

Gary, Romain .... **CLC 25**
See Kacew, Romain
See also DLB 83, 299

Gascar, Pierre .... **CLC 11**
See Fournier, Pierre
See also EWL 3

Gascoigne, George 1539-1577 .... **LC 108**
See also DLB 136; RGEL 2

Gascoyne, David (Emery)
1916-2001 .... **CLC 45**
See also CA 65-68; 200; CANR 10, 28, 54; CP 7; DLB 20; MTCW 1; RGEL 2

Gaskell, Elizabeth Cleghorn
1810-1865 .... **NCLC 5, 70, 97, 137; SSC 25**
See also BRW 5; CDBLB 1832-1890; DAB; DAM MST; DLB 21, 144, 159; RGEL 2; RGSF 2; TEA

Gass, William H(oward) 1924- . **CLC 1, 2, 8, 11, 15, 39, 132; SSC 12**
See also AMWS 6; CA 17-20R; CANR 30, 71, 100; CN 7; DLB 2, 227; EWL 3; MTCW 1, 2; RGAL 4

Gassendi, Pierre 1592-1655 .... **LC 54**
See also GFL Beginnings to 1789

Gasset, Jose Ortega y
See Ortega y Gasset, Jose

Gates, Henry Louis, Jr. 1950- ... **BLCS; CLC 65**
See also BW 2, 3; CA 109; CANR 25, 53, 75, 125; CSW; DA3; DAM MULT; DLB 67; EWL 3; MTCW 1; RGAL 4

Gautier, Theophile 1811-1872 .. **NCLC 1, 59; PC 18; SSC 20**
See also DAM POET; DLB 119; EW 6; GFL 1789 to the Present; RGWL 2, 3; SUFW; TWA

Gawsworth, John
See Bates, H(erbert) E(rnest)

Gay, John 1685-1732 .... **LC 49**
See also BRW 3; DAM DRAM; DLB 84, 95; RGEL 2; WLIT 3

Gay, Oliver
See Gogarty, Oliver St. John

Gay, Peter (Jack) 1923- .... **CLC 158**
See also CA 13-16R; CANR 18, 41, 77; INT CANR-18

Gaye, Marvin (Pentz, Jr.)
1939-1984 .... **CLC 26**
See also CA 195; 112

Gebler, Carlo (Ernest) 1954- .... **CLC 39**
See also CA 119; 133; CANR 96; DLB 271

Gee, Maggie (Mary) 1948- .... **CLC 57**
See also CA 130; CANR 125; CN 7; DLB 207

Gee, Maurice (Gough) 1931- .... **CLC 29**
See also AAYA 42; CA 97-100; CANR 67, 123; CLR 56; CN 7; CWRI 5; EWL 3; MAICYA 2; RGSF 2; SATA 46, 101

Geiogamah, Hanay 1945- .... **NNAL**
See also CA 153; DAM MULT; DLB 175

Gelbart, Larry (Simon) 1928- .... **CLC 21, 61**
See Gelbart, Larry
See also CA 73-76; CANR 45, 94

Gelbart, Larry 1928-
See Gelbart, Larry (Simon)
See also CAD; CD 5

Gelber, Jack 1932-2003 ...... **CLC 1, 6, 14, 79**
See also CA 1-4R; 216; CAD; CANR 2; DLB 7, 228

Gellhorn, Martha (Ellis)
1908-1998 .... **CLC 14, 60**
See also CA 77-80; 164; CANR 44; CN 7; DLBY 1982, 1998

Genet, Jean 1910-1986 . **DC 25; CLC 1, 2, 5, 10, 14, 44, 46; TCLC 128**
See also CA 13-16R; CANR 18; DA3; DAM DRAM; DFS 10; DLB 72; DLBY 1986; EW 13; EWL 3; GFL 1789 to the Present; GLL 1; LMFS 2; MTCW 1, 2; RGWL 2, 3; TWA

Gent, Peter 1942- .... **CLC 29**
See also AITN 1; CA 89-92; DLBY 1982

Gentile, Giovanni 1875-1944 .... **TCLC 96**
See also CA 119

Gentlewoman in New England, A
See Bradstreet, Anne

Gentlewoman in Those Parts, A
See Bradstreet, Anne

Geoffrey of Monmouth c.
1100-1155 .... **CMLC 44**
See also DLB 146; TEA

George, Jean
See George, Jean Craighead

George, Jean Craighead 1919- .... **CLC 35**
See also AAYA 8; BYA 2, 4; CA 5-8R; CANR 25; CLR 1; 80; DLB 52; JRDA; MAICYA 1, 2; SATA 2, 68, 124; WYA; YAW

George, Stefan (Anton) 1868-1933 . **TCLC 2, 14**
See also CA 104; 193; EW 8; EWL 3

Georges, Georges Martin
See Simenon, Georges (Jacques Christian)

Gerald of Wales c. 1146-c. 1223 ... **CMLC 60**

Gerhardi, William Alexander
See Gerhardie, William Alexander

Gerhardie, William Alexander
1895-1977 .... **CLC 5**
See also CA 25-28R; 73-76; CANR 18; DLB 36; RGEL 2

Gerson, Jean 1363-1429 .... **LC 77**
See also DLB 208

Gersonides 1288-1344 .... **CMLC 49**
See also DLB 115

Gerstler, Amy 1956- .... **CLC 70**
See also CA 146; CANR 99

Gertler, T. .... **CLC 34**
See also CA 116; 121

Gertsen, Aleksandr Ivanovich
See Herzen, Aleksandr Ivanovich

Ghalib .... **NCLC 39, 78**
See Ghalib, Asadullah Khan

Ghalib, Asadullah Khan 1797-1869
See Ghalib
See also DAM POET; RGWL 2, 3

Ghelderode, Michel de 1898-1962 ..... **CLC 6, 11; DC 15**
See also CA 85-88; CANR 40, 77; DAM DRAM; EW 11; EWL 3; TWA

Ghiselin, Brewster 1903-2001 .... **CLC 23**
See also CA 13-16R; CAAS 10; CANR 13; CP 7

Ghose, Aurabinda 1872-1950 .... **TCLC 63**
See Ghose, Aurobindo
See also CA 163

Ghose, Aurobindo
See Ghose, Aurabinda
See also EWL 3

Ghose, Zulfikar 1935- .... **CLC 42, 200**
See also CA 65-68; CANR 67; CN 7; CP 7; EWL 3

Ghosh, Amitav 1956- .... **CLC 44, 153**
See also CA 147; CANR 80; CN 7; WWE 1

Giacosa, Giuseppe 1847-1906 .... **TCLC 7**
See also CA 104

Gibb, Lee
See Waterhouse, Keith (Spencer)

Gibbon, Edward 1737-1794 .... **LC 97**
See also BRW 3; DLB 104; RGEL 2

Gibbon, Lewis Grassic .... **TCLC 4**
See Mitchell, James Leslie
See also RGEL 2

Gibbons, Kaye 1960- .... **CLC 50, 88, 145**
See also AAYA 34; AMWS 10; CA 151; CANR 75, 127; CSW; DA3; DAM POP; DLB 292; MTCW 1; NFS 3; RGAL 4; SATA 117

Gibran, Kahlil 1883-1931 . **PC 9; TCLC 1, 9**
See also CA 104; 150; DA3; DAM POET, POP; EWL 3; MTCW 2

Gibran, Khalil
See Gibran, Kahlil

Gibson, William 1914- .... **CLC 23**
See also CA 9-12R; CAD 2; CANR 9, 42, 75, 125; CD 5; DA; DAB; DAC; DAM DRAM, MST; DFS 2; DLB 7; LAIT 2; MTCW 2; SATA 66; YAW

Gibson, William (Ford) 1948- ... **CLC 39, 63, 186, 192; SSC 52**
See also AAYA 12, 59; BPFB 2; CA 126; 133; CANR 52, 90, 106; CN 7; CPW; DA3; DAM POP; DLB 251; MTCW 2; SCFW 2; SFW 4

Gide, Andre (Paul Guillaume)
1869-1951 ..... **SSC 13; TCLC 5, 12, 36; WLC**
See also CA 104; 124; DA; DA3; DAB; DAC; DAM MST, NOV; DLB 65; EW 8; EWL 3; GFL 1789 to the Present; MTCW 1, 2; RGSF 2; RGWL 2, 3; TWA

Gifford, Barry (Colby) 1946- .... **CLC 34**
See also CA 65-68; CANR 9, 30, 40, 90

Gilbert, Frank
See De Voto, Bernard (Augustine)

Gilbert, W(illiam) S(chwenck)
1836-1911 .... **TCLC 3**
See also CA 104; 173; DAM DRAM, POET; RGEL 2; SATA 36

Gilbreth, Frank B(unker), Jr.
1911-2001 .... **CLC 17**
See also CA 9-12R; SATA 2

Gilchrist, Ellen (Louise) 1935- .. **CLC 34, 48, 143; SSC 14, 63**
See also BPFB 2; CA 113; 116; CANR 41, 61, 104; CN 7; CPW; CSW; DAM POP; DLB 130; EWL 3; EXPS; MTCW 1, 2; RGAL 4; RGSF 2; SSFS 9

Giles, Molly 1942- .... **CLC 39**
See also CA 126; CANR 98

Gill, Eric 1882-1940 .... **TCLC 85**
See Gill, (Arthur) Eric (Rowton Peter Joseph)

Gill, (Arthur) Eric (Rowton Peter Joseph)
1882-1940
See Gill, Eric
See also CA 120; DLB 98

Gill, Patrick
See Creasey, John

Gillette, Douglas .... **CLC 70**

Gilliam, Terry (Vance) 1940- .... **CLC 21, 141**
See Monty Python
See also AAYA 19, 59; CA 108; 113; CANR 35; INT CA-113

Gillian, Jerry
See Gilliam, Terry (Vance)

Gilliatt, Penelope (Ann Douglass)
1932-1993 .... **CLC 2, 10, 13, 53**
See also AITN 2; CA 13-16R; 141; CANR 49; DLB 14

Gilman, Charlotte (Anna) Perkins (Stetson)
1860-1935 ...... **SSC 13, 62; TCLC 9, 37, 117**
See also AMWS 11; BYA 11; CA 106; 150; DLB 221; EXPS; FW; HGG; LAIT 2; MAWW; MTCW 1; RGAL 4; RGSF 2; SFW 4; SSFS 1, 18

Gilmour, David 1946- .... **CLC 35**

Gilpin, William 1724-1804 .... **NCLC 30**

Gilray, J. D.
See Mencken, H(enry) L(ouis)

Gilroy, Frank D(aniel) 1925- .... **CLC 2**
See also CA 81-84; CAD; CANR 32, 64, 86; CD 5; DFS 17; DLB 7

Gilstrap, John 1957(?)- .... **CLC 99**
See also CA 160; CANR 101

Ginsberg, Allen 1926-1997 .... **CLC 1, 2, 3, 4, 6, 13, 36, 69, 109; PC 4, 47; TCLC 120; WLC**
See also AAYA 33; AITN 1; AMWC 1; AMWS 2; BG 2; CA 1-4R; 157; CANR 2, 41, 63, 95; CDALB 1941-1968; CP 7;

DA; DA3; DAB; DAC; DAM MST, POET; DLB 5, 16, 169, 237; EWL 3; GLL 1; LMFS 2; MTCW 1, 2; PAB; PFS 5; RGAL 4; TUS; WP

Ginzburg, Eugenia .... **CLC 59**
See Ginzburg, Evgeniia

Ginzburg, Evgeniia 1904-1977
See Ginzburg, Eugenia
See also DLB 302

Ginzburg, Natalia 1916-1991 .... **CLC 5, 11, 54, 70; SSC 65; TCLC 156**
See also CA 85-88; 135; CANR 33; DFS 14; DLB 177; EW 13; EWL 3; MTCW 1, 2; RGWL 2, 3

Giono, Jean 1895-1970 .... **CLC 4, 11; TCLC 124**
See also CA 45-48; 29-32R; CANR 2, 35; DLB 72; EWL 3; GFL 1789 to the Present; MTCW 1; RGWL 2, 3

Giovanni, Nikki 1943- ...... **BLC 2; CLC 2, 4, 19, 64, 117; PC 19; WLCS**
See also AAYA 22; AITN 1; BW 2, 3; CA 29-32R; CAAS 6; CANR 18, 41, 60, 91, 130; CDALBS; CLR 6, 73; CP 7; CSW; CWP; CWRI 5; DA; DA3; DAB; DAC; DAM MST, MULT, POET; DLB 5, 41; EWL 3; EXPP; INT CANR-18; MAICYA 1, 2; MTCW 1, 2; PFS 17; RGAL 4; SATA 24, 107; TUS; YAW

Giovene, Andrea 1904-1998 .... **CLC 7**
See also CA 85-88

Gippius, Zinaida (Nikolaevna) 1869-1945
See Hippius, Zinaida (Nikolaevna)
See also CA 106; 212

Giraudoux, Jean(-Hippolyte) 1882-1944 .... **TCLC 2, 7**
See also CA 104; 196; DAM DRAM; DLB 65; EW 9; EWL 3; GFL 1789 to the Present; RGWL 2, 3; TWA

Gironella, Jose Maria (Pous) 1917-2003 .... **CLC 11**
See also CA 101; 212; EWL 3; RGWL 2, 3

Gissing, George (Robert) 1857-1903 .... **SSC 37; TCLC 3, 24, 47**
See also BRW 5; CA 105; 167; DLB 18, 135, 184; RGEL 2; TEA

Gitlin, Todd 1943- .... **CLC 201**
See also CA 29-32R; CANR 25, 50, 88

Giurlani, Aldo
See Palazzeschi, Aldo

Gladkov, Fedor Vasil'evich
See Gladkov, Fyodor (Vasilyevich)
See also DLB 272

Gladkov, Fyodor (Vasilyevich) 1883-1958 .... **TCLC 27**
See Gladkov, Fedor Vasil'evich
See also CA 170; EWL 3

Glancy, Diane 1941- .... **NNAL**
See also CA 136, 225; CAAE 225; CAAS 24; CANR 87; DLB 175

Glanville, Brian (Lester) 1931- .... **CLC 6**
See also CA 5-8R; CAAS 9; CANR 3, 70; CN 7; DLB 15, 139; SATA 42

Glasgow, Ellen (Anderson Gholson) 1873-1945 .... **SSC 34; TCLC 2, 7**
See also AMW; CA 104; 164; DLB 9, 12; MAWW; MTCW 2; RGAL 4; RHW; SSFS 9; TUS

Glaspell, Susan 1882(?)-1948 ..... **DC 10; SSC 41; TCLC 55**
See also AMWS 3; CA 110; 154; DFS 8, 18; DLB 7, 9, 78, 228; MAWW; RGAL 4; SSFS 3; TCWW 2; TUS; YABC 2

Glassco, John 1909-1981 .... **CLC 9**
See also CA 13-16R; 102; CANR 15; DLB 68

Glasscock, Amnesia
See Steinbeck, John (Ernst)

Glasser, Ronald J. 1940(?)- .... **CLC 37**
See also CA 209

Glassman, Joyce
See Johnson, Joyce

Gleick, James (W.) 1954- .... **CLC 147**
See also CA 131; 137; CANR 97; INT CA-137

Glendinning, Victoria 1937- .... **CLC 50**
See also CA 120; 127; CANR 59, 89; DLB 155

Glissant, Edouard (Mathieu) 1928- .... **CLC 10, 68**
See also CA 153; CANR 111; CWW 2; DAM MULT; EWL 3; RGWL 3

Gloag, Julian 1930- .... **CLC 40**
See also AITN 1; CA 65-68; CANR 10, 70; CN 7

Glowacki, Aleksander
See Prus, Boleslaw

Gluck, Louise (Elisabeth) 1943- .. **CLC 7, 22, 44, 81, 160; PC 16**
See also AMWS 5; CA 33-36R; CANR 40, 69, 108, 133; CP 7; CWP; DA3; DAM POET; DLB 5; MTCW 2; PFS 5, 15; RGAL 4

Glyn, Elinor 1864-1943 .... **TCLC 72**
See also DLB 153; RHW

Gobineau, Joseph-Arthur 1816-1882 .... **NCLC 17**
See also DLB 123; GFL 1789 to the Present

Godard, Jean-Luc 1930- .... **CLC 20**
See also CA 93-96

Godden, (Margaret) Rumer 1907-1998 .... **CLC 53**
See also AAYA 6; BPFB 2; BYA 2, 5; CA 5-8R; 172; CANR 4, 27, 36, 55, 80; CLR 20; CN 7; CWRI 5; DLB 161; MAICYA 1, 2; RHW; SAAS 12; SATA 3, 36; SATA-Obit 109; TEA

Godoy Alcayaga, Lucila 1899-1957 .. **HLC 2; PC 32; TCLC 2**
See Mistral, Gabriela
See also BW 2; CA 104; 131; CANR 81; DAM MULT; DNFS; HW 1, 2; MTCW 1, 2

Godwin, Gail (Kathleen) 1937- ..... **CLC 5, 8, 22, 31, 69, 125**
See also BPFB 2; CA 29-32R; CANR 15, 43, 69, 132; CN 7; CPW; CSW; DA3; DAM POP; DLB 6, 234; INT CANR-15; MTCW 1, 2

Godwin, William 1756-1836 .. **NCLC 14, 130**
See also CDBLB 1789-1832; CMW 4; DLB 39, 104, 142, 158, 163, 262; HGG; RGEL 2

Goebbels, Josef
See Goebbels, (Paul) Joseph

Goebbels, (Paul) Joseph 1897-1945 .... **TCLC 68**
See also CA 115; 148

Goebbels, Joseph Paul
See Goebbels, (Paul) Joseph

Goethe, Johann Wolfgang von 1749-1832 . **DC 20; NCLC 4, 22, 34, 90, 154; PC 5; SSC 38; WLC**
See also CDWLB 2; DA; DA3; DAB; DAC; DAM DRAM, MST, POET; DLB 94; EW 5; LATS 1; LMFS 1:1; RGWL 2, 3; TWA

Gogarty, Oliver St. John 1878-1957 .... **TCLC 15**
See also CA 109; 150; DLB 15, 19; RGEL 2

Gogol, Nikolai (Vasilyevich) 1809-1852 .... **DC 1; NCLC 5, 15, 31; SSC 4, 29, 52; WLC**
See also DA; DAB; DAC; DAM DRAM, MST; DFS 12; DLB 198; EW 6; EXPS; RGSF 2; RGWL 2, 3; SSFS 7; TWA

Goines, Donald 1937(?)-1974 ... **BLC 2; CLC 80**
See also AITN 1; BW 1, 3; CA 124; 114; CANR 82; CMW 4; DA3; DAM MULT, POP; DLB 33

Gold, Herbert 1924- ... **CLC 4, 7, 14, 42, 152**
See also CA 9-12R; CANR 17, 45, 125; CN 7; DLB 2; DLBY 1981

Goldbarth, Albert 1948- .... **CLC 5, 38**
See also AMWS 12; CA 53-56; CANR 6, 40; CP 7; DLB 120

Goldberg, Anatol 1910-1982 .... **CLC 34**
See also CA 131; 117

Goldemberg, Isaac 1945- .... **CLC 52**
See also CA 69-72; CAAS 12; CANR 11, 32; EWL 3; HW 1; WLIT 1

Golding, Arthur 1536-1606 .... **LC 101**
See also DLB 136

Golding, William (Gerald) 1911-1993 ...... **CLC 1, 2, 3, 8, 10, 17, 27, 58, 81; WLC**
See also AAYA 5, 44; BPFB 2; BRWR 1; BRWS 1; BYA 2; CA 5-8R; 141; CANR 13, 33, 54; CDBLB 1945-1960; CLR 94; DA; DA3; DAB; DAC; DAM MST, NOV; DLB 15, 100, 255; EWL 3; EXPN; HGG; LAIT 4; MTCW 1, 2; NFS 2; RGEL 2; RHW; SFW 4; TEA; WLIT 4; YAW

Goldman, Emma 1869-1940 .... **TCLC 13**
See also CA 110; 150; DLB 221; FW; RGAL 4; TUS

Goldman, Francisco 1954- .... **CLC 76**
See also CA 162

Goldman, William (W.) 1931- ...... **CLC 1, 48**
See also BPFB 2; CA 9-12R; CANR 29, 69, 106; CN 7; DLB 44; FANT; IDFW 3, 4

Goldmann, Lucien 1913-1970 .... **CLC 24**
See also CA 25-28; CAP 2

Goldoni, Carlo 1707-1793 .... **LC 4**
See also DAM DRAM; EW 4; RGWL 2, 3

Goldsberry, Steven 1949- .... **CLC 34**
See also CA 131

Goldsmith, Oliver 1730-1774 .... **DC 8; LC 2, 48; WLC**
See also BRW 3; CDBLB 1660-1789; DA; DAB; DAC; DAM DRAM, MST, NOV, POET; DFS 1; DLB 39, 89, 104, 109, 142; IDTP; RGEL 2; SATA 26; TEA; WLIT 3

Goldsmith, Peter
See Priestley, J(ohn) B(oynton)

Gombrowicz, Witold 1904-1969 .... **CLC 4, 7, 11, 49**
See also CA 19-20; 25-28R; CANR 105; CAP 2; CDWLB 4; DAM DRAM; DLB 215; EW 12; EWL 3; RGWL 2, 3; TWA

Gomez de Avellaneda, Gertrudis 1814-1873 .... **NCLC 111**
See also LAW

Gomez de la Serna, Ramon 1888-1963 .... **CLC 9**
See also CA 153; 116; CANR 79; EWL 3; HW 1, 2

Goncharov, Ivan Alexandrovich 1812-1891 .... **NCLC 1, 63**
See also DLB 238; EW 6; RGWL 2, 3

Goncourt, Edmond (Louis Antoine Huot) de 1822-1896 .... **NCLC 7**
See also DLB 123; EW 7; GFL 1789 to the Present; RGWL 2, 3

Goncourt, Jules (Alfred Huot) de 1830-1870 .... **NCLC 7**
See also DLB 123; EW 7; GFL 1789 to the Present; RGWL 2, 3

Gongora (y Argote), Luis de 1561-1627 .... **LC 72**
See also RGWL 2, 3

Gontier, Fernande 19(?)- .... **CLC 50**

Gonzalez Martinez, Enrique
See Gonzalez Martinez, Enrique
See also DLB 290

Gonzalez Martinez, Enrique
1871-1952 .... **TCLC 72**
See Gonzalez Martinez, Enrique
See also CA 166; CANR 81; EWL 3; HW 1, 2

Goodison, Lorna 1947- .... **PC 36**
See also CA 142; CANR 88; CP 7; CWP; DLB 157; EWL 3

Goodman, Paul 1911-1972 ..... **CLC 1, 2, 4, 7**
See also CA 19-20; 37-40R; CAD; CANR 34; CAP 2; DLB 130, 246; MTCW 1; RGAL 4

GoodWeather, Harley
See King, Thomas

Googe, Barnabe 1540-1594 .... **LC 94**
See also DLB 132; RGEL 2

Gordimer, Nadine 1923- ...... **CLC 3, 5, 7, 10, 18, 33, 51, 70, 123, 160, 161; SSC 17, 80; WLCS**
See also AAYA 39; AFW; BRWS 2; CA 5-8R; CANR 3, 28, 56, 88, 131; CN 7; DA; DA3; DAB; DAC; DAM MST, NOV; DLB 225; EWL 3; EXPS; INT CANR-28; LATS 1:2; MTCW 1, 2; NFS 4; RGEL 2; RGSF 2; SSFS 2, 14, 19; TWA; WLIT 2; YAW

Gordon, Adam Lindsay
1833-1870 .... **NCLC 21**
See also DLB 230

Gordon, Caroline 1895-1981 . **CLC 6, 13, 29, 83; SSC 15**
See also AMW; CA 11-12; 103; CANR 36; CAP 1; DLB 4, 9, 102; DLBD 17; DLBY 1981; EWL 3; MTCW 1, 2; RGAL 4; RGSF 2

Gordon, Charles William 1860-1937
See Connor, Ralph
See also CA 109

Gordon, Mary (Catherine) 1949- .... **CLC 13, 22, 128; SSC 59**
See also AMWS 4; BPFB 2; CA 102; CANR 44, 92; CN 7; DLB 6; DLBY 1981; FW; INT CA-102; MTCW 1

Gordon, N. J.
See Bosman, Herman Charles

Gordon, Sol 1923- .... **CLC 26**
See also CA 53-56; CANR 4; SATA 11

Gordone, Charles 1925-1995 .. **CLC 1, 4; DC 8**
See also BW 1, 3; CA 93-96, 180; 150; CAAE 180; CAD; CANR 55; DAM DRAM; DLB 7; INT CA-93-96; MTCW 1

Gore, Catherine 1800-1861 .... **NCLC 65**
See also DLB 116; RGEL 2

Gorenko, Anna Andreevna
See Akhmatova, Anna

Gorky, Maxim .... **SSC 28; TCLC 8; WLC**
See Peshkov, Alexei Maximovich
See also DAB; DFS 9; DLB 295; EW 8; EWL 3; MTCW 2; TWA

Goryan, Sirak
See Saroyan, William

Gosse, Edmund (William)
1849-1928 .... **TCLC 28**
See also CA 117; DLB 57, 144, 184; RGEL 2

Gotlieb, Phyllis (Fay Bloom) 1926- .. **CLC 18**
See also CA 13-16R; CANR 7, 135; DLB 88, 251; SFW 4

Gottesman, S. D.
See Kornbluth, C(yril) M.; Pohl, Frederik

Gottfried von Strassburg fl. c. 1170-1215 .... **CMLC 10**
See also CDWLB 2; DLB 138; EW 1; RGWL 2, 3

Gotthelf, Jeremias 1797-1854 .... **NCLC 117**
See also DLB 133; RGWL 2, 3

Gottschalk, Laura Riding
See Jackson, Laura (Riding)

Gould, Lois 1932(?)-2002 .... **CLC 4, 10**
See also CA 77-80; 208; CANR 29; MTCW 1

Gould, Stephen Jay 1941-2002 .... **CLC 163**
See also AAYA 26; BEST 90:2; CA 77-80; 205; CANR 10, 27, 56, 75, 125; CPW; INT CANR-27; MTCW 1, 2

Gourmont, Remy(-Marie-Charles) de
1858-1915 .... **TCLC 17**
See also CA 109; 150; GFL 1789 to the Present; MTCW 2

Gournay, Marie le Jars de
See de Gournay, Marie le Jars

Govier, Katherine 1948- .... **CLC 51**
See also CA 101; CANR 18, 40, 128; CCA 1

Gower, John c. 1330-1408 .... **LC 76; PC 59**
See also BRW 1; DLB 146; RGEL 2

Goyen, (Charles) William
1915-1983 .... **CLC 5, 8, 14, 40**
See also AITN 2; CA 5-8R; 110; CANR 6, 71; DLB 2, 218; DLBY 1983; EWL 3; INT CANR-6

Goytisolo, Juan 1931- .... **CLC 5, 10, 23, 133; HLC 1**
See also CA 85-88; CANR 32, 61, 131; CWW 2; DAM MULT; EWL 3; GLL 2; HW 1, 2; MTCW 1, 2

Gozzano, Guido 1883-1916 .... **PC 10**
See also CA 154; DLB 114; EWL 3

Gozzi, (Conte) Carlo 1720-1806 .... **NCLC 23**

Grabbe, Christian Dietrich
1801-1836 .... **NCLC 2**
See also DLB 133; RGWL 2, 3

Grace, Patricia Frances 1937- .... **CLC 56**
See also CA 176; CANR 118; CN 7; EWL 3; RGSF 2

Gracian y Morales, Baltasar
1601-1658 .... **LC 15**

Gracq, Julien .... **CLC 11, 48**
See Poirier, Louis
See also CWW 2; DLB 83; GFL 1789 to the Present

Grade, Chaim 1910-1982 .... **CLC 10**
See also CA 93-96; 107; EWL 3

Graduate of Oxford, A
See Ruskin, John

Grafton, Garth
See Duncan, Sara Jeannette

Grafton, Sue 1940- .... **CLC 163**
See also AAYA 11, 49; BEST 90:3; CA 108; CANR 31, 55, 111, 134; CMW 4; CPW; CSW; DA3; DAM POP; DLB 226; FW; MSW

Graham, John
See Phillips, David Graham

Graham, Jorie 1951- .... **CLC 48, 118; PC 59**
See also CA 111; CANR 63, 118; CP 7; CWP; DLB 120; EWL 3; PFS 10, 17

Graham, R(obert) B(ontine) Cunninghame
See Cunninghame Graham, Robert (Gallnigad) Bontine
See also DLB 98, 135, 174; RGEL 2; RGSF 2

Graham, Robert
See Haldeman, Joe (William)

Graham, Tom
See Lewis, (Harry) Sinclair

Graham, W(illiam) S(idney)
1918-1986 .... **CLC 29**
See also BRWS 7; CA 73-76; 118; DLB 20; RGEL 2

Graham, Winston (Mawdsley)
1910-2003 .... **CLC 23**
See also CA 49-52; 218; CANR 2, 22, 45, 66; CMW 4; CN 7; DLB 77; RHW

Grahame, Kenneth 1859-1932 ...... **TCLC 64, 136**
See also BYA 5; CA 108; 136; CANR 80; CLR 5; CWRI 5; DA3; DAB; DLB 34, 141, 178; FANT; MAICYA 1, 2; MTCW 2; NFS 20; RGEL 2; SATA 100; TEA; WCH; YABC 1

Granger, Darius John
See Marlowe, Stephen

Granin, Daniil 1918- .... **CLC 59**
See also DLB 302

Granovsky, Timofei Nikolaevich
1813-1855 .... **NCLC 75**
See also DLB 198

Grant, Skeeter
See Spiegelman, Art

Granville-Barker, Harley
1877-1946 .... **TCLC 2**
See Barker, Harley Granville
See also CA 104; 204; DAM DRAM; RGEL 2

Granzotto, Gianni
See Granzotto, Giovanni Battista

Granzotto, Giovanni Battista
1914-1985 .... **CLC 70**
See also CA 166

Grass, Guenter (Wilhelm) 1927- ... **CLC 1, 2, 4, 6, 11, 15, 22, 32, 49, 88; WLC**
See Grass, Gunter (Wilhelm)
See also BPFB 2; CA 13-16R; CANR 20, 75, 93, 133; CDWLB 2; DA; DA3; DAB; DAC; DAM MST, NOV; DLB 75, 124; EW 13; EWL 3; MTCW 1, 2; RGWL 2, 3; TWA

Grass, Gunter (Wilhelm)
See Grass, Guenter (Wilhelm)
See also CWW 2

Gratton, Thomas
See Hulme, T(homas) E(rnest)

Grau, Shirley Ann 1929- .... **CLC 4, 9, 146; SSC 15**
See also CA 89-92; CANR 22, 69; CN 7; CSW; DLB 2, 218; INT CA-89-92, CANR-22; MTCW 1

Gravel, Fern
See Hall, James Norman

Graver, Elizabeth 1964- .... **CLC 70**
See also CA 135; CANR 71, 129

Graves, Richard Perceval
1895-1985 .... **CLC 44**
See also CA 65-68; CANR 9, 26, 51

Graves, Robert (von Ranke)
1895-1985 .. **CLC 1, 2, 6, 11, 39, 44, 45; PC 6**
See also BPFB 2; BRW 7; BYA 4; CA 5-8R; 117; CANR 5, 36; CDBLB 1914-1945; DA3; DAB; DAC; DAM MST, POET; DLB 20, 100, 191; DLBD 18; DLBY 1985; EWL 3; LATS 1:1; MTCW 1, 2; NCFS 2; RGEL 2; RHW; SATA 45; TEA

Graves, Valerie
See Bradley, Marion Zimmer

Gray, Alasdair (James) 1934- .... **CLC 41**
See also BRWS 9; CA 126; CANR 47, 69, 106; CN 7; DLB 194, 261; HGG; INT CA-126; MTCW 1, 2; RGSF 2; SUFW 2

Gray, Amlin 1946- .... **CLC 29**
See also CA 138**

Gray, Francine du Plessix 1930- ..... **CLC 22, 153**
See also BEST 90:3; CA 61-64; CAAS 2; CANR 11, 33, 75, 81; DAM NOV; INT CANR-11; MTCW 1, 2

Gray, John (Henry) 1866-1934 ...... **TCLC 19**
See also CA 119; 162; RGEL 2

Gray, Simon (James Holliday) 1936- .... **CLC 9, 14, 36**
See also AITN 1; CA 21-24R; CAAS 3; CANR 32, 69; CD 5; DLB 13; EWL 3; MTCW 1; RGEL 2

Gray, Spalding 1941-2004 .... **CLC 49, 112; DC 7**
See also CA 128; 225; CAD; CANR 74; CD 5; CPW; DAM POP; MTCW 2

Gray, Thomas 1716-1771 .... **LC 4, 40; PC 2; WLC**
See also BRW 3; CDBLB 1660-1789; DA; DA3; DAB; DAC; DAM MST; DLB 109; EXPP; PAB; PFS 9; RGEL 2; TEA; WP

Grayson, David
See Baker, Ray Stannard

Grayson, Richard (A.) 1951- .... **CLC 38**
See also CA 85-88, 210; CAAE 210; CANR 14, 31, 57; DLB 234

Greeley, Andrew M(oran) 1928- ...... **CLC 28**
See also BPFB 2; CA 5-8R; CAAS 7; CANR 7, 43, 69, 104; CMW 4; CPW; DA3; DAM POP; MTCW 1, 2

Green, Anna Katharine 1846-1935 .... **TCLC 63**
See also CA 112; 159; CMW 4; DLB 202, 221; MSW

Green, Brian
See Card, Orson Scott

Green, Hannah
See Greenberg, Joanne (Goldenberg)

Green, Hannah 1927(?)-1996 .... **CLC 3**
See also CA 73-76; CANR 59, 93; NFS 10

Green, Henry .... **CLC 2, 13, 97**
See Yorke, Henry Vincent
See also BRWS 2; CA 175; DLB 15; EWL 3; RGEL 2

Green, Julien (Hartridge) 1900-1998
See Green, Julian
See also CA 21-24R; 169; CANR 33, 87; CWW 2; DLB 4, 72; MTCW 1

Green, Julian .... **CLC 3, 11, 77**
See Green, Julien (Hartridge)
See also EWL 3; GFL 1789 to the Present; MTCW 2

Green, Paul (Eliot) 1894-1981 .... **CLC 25**
See also AITN 1; CA 5-8R; 103; CANR 3; DAM DRAM; DLB 7, 9, 249; DLBY 1981; RGAL 4

Greenaway, Peter 1942- .... **CLC 159**
See also CA 127

Greenberg, Ivan 1908-1973
See Rahv, Philip
See also CA 85-88

Greenberg, Joanne (Goldenberg) 1932- .... **CLC 7, 30**
See also AAYA 12; CA 5-8R; CANR 14, 32, 69; CN 7; SATA 25; YAW

Greenberg, Richard 1959(?)- .... **CLC 57**
See also CA 138; CAD; CD 5

Greenblatt, Stephen J(ay) 1943- ...... **CLC 70**
See also CA 49-52; CANR 115

Greene, Bette 1934- .... **CLC 30**
See also AAYA 7; BYA 3; CA 53-56; CANR 4; CLR 2; CWRI 5; JRDA; LAIT 4; MAICYA 1, 2; NFS 10; SAAS 16; SATA 8, 102; WYA; YAW

Greene, Gael .... **CLC 8**
See also CA 13-16R; CANR 10

Greene, Graham (Henry) 1904-1991 .... **CLC 1, 3, 6, 9, 14, 18, 27, 37, 70, 72, 125; SSC 29; WLC**
See also AITN 2; BPFB 2; BRWR 2; BRWS 1; BYA 3; CA 13-16R; 133; CANR 35, 61, 131; CBD; CDBLB 1945-1960; CMW 4; DA; DA3; DAB; DAC; DAM MST, NOV; DLB 13, 15, 77, 100, 162, 201, 204; DLBY 1991; EWL 3; MSW; MTCW 1, 2; NFS 16; RGEL 2; SATA 20; SSFS 14; TEA; WLIT 4

Greene, Robert 1558-1592 .... **LC 41**
See also BRWS 8; DLB 62, 167; IDTP; RGEL 2; TEA

Greer, Germaine 1939- .... **CLC 131**
See also AITN 1; CA 81-84; CANR 33, 70, 115, 133; FW; MTCW 1, 2

Greer, Richard
See Silverberg, Robert

Gregor, Arthur 1923- .... **CLC 9**
See also CA 25-28R; CAAS 10; CANR 11; CP 7; SATA 36

Gregor, Lee
See Pohl, Frederik

Gregory, Lady Isabella Augusta (Persse) 1852-1932 .... **TCLC 1**
See also BRW 6; CA 104; 184; DLB 10; IDTP; RGEL 2

Gregory, J. Dennis
See Williams, John A(lfred)

Grekova, I. .... **CLC 59**
See Ventsel, Elena Sergeevna
See also CWW 2

Grendon, Stephen
See Derleth, August (William)

Grenville, Kate 1950- .... **CLC 61**
See also CA 118; CANR 53, 93

Grenville, Pelham
See Wodehouse, P(elham) G(renville)

Greve, Felix Paul (Berthold Friedrich) 1879-1948
See Grove, Frederick Philip
See also CA 104; 141, 175; CANR 79; DAC; DAM MST

Greville, Fulke 1554-1628 .... **LC 79**
See also DLB 62, 172; RGEL 2

Grey, Lady Jane 1537-1554 .... **LC 93**
See also DLB 132

Grey, Zane 1872-1939 .... **TCLC 6**
See also BPFB 2; CA 104; 132; DA3; DAM POP; DLB 9, 212; MTCW 1, 2; RGAL 4; TCWW 2; TUS

Griboedov, Aleksandr Sergeevich 1795(?)-1829 .... **NCLC 129**
See also DLB 205; RGWL 2, 3

Grieg, (Johan) Nordahl (Brun) 1902-1943 .... **TCLC 10**
See also CA 107; 189; EWL 3

Grieve, C(hristopher) M(urray) 1892-1978 .... **CLC 11, 19**
See MacDiarmid, Hugh; Pteleon
See also CA 5-8R; 85-88; CANR 33, 107; DAM POET; MTCW 1; RGEL 2

Griffin, Gerald 1803-1840 .... **NCLC 7**
See also DLB 159; RGEL 2

Griffin, John Howard 1920-1980 ..... **CLC 68**
See also AITN 1; CA 1-4R; 101; CANR 2

Griffin, Peter 1942- .... **CLC 39**
See also CA 136

Griffith, D(avid Lewelyn) W(ark) 1875(?)-1948 .... **TCLC 68**
See also CA 119; 150; CANR 80

Griffith, Lawrence
See Griffith, D(avid Lewelyn) W(ark)

Griffiths, Trevor 1935- .... **CLC 13, 52**
See also CA 97-100; CANR 45; CBD; CD 5; DLB 13, 245

Griggs, Sutton (Elbert) 1872-1930 .... **TCLC 77**
See also CA 123; 186; DLB 50

Grigson, Geoffrey (Edward Harvey) 1905-1985 .... **CLC 7, 39**
See also CA 25-28R; 118; CANR 20, 33; DLB 27; MTCW 1, 2

Grile, Dod
See Bierce, Ambrose (Gwinett)

Grillparzer, Franz 1791-1872 .... **DC 14; NCLC 1, 102; SSC 37**
See also CDWLB 2; DLB 133; EW 5; RGWL 2, 3; TWA

Grimble, Reverend Charles James
See Eliot, T(homas) S(tearns)

Grimke, Angelina (Emily) Weld 1880-1958 .... **HR 2**
See Weld, Angelina (Emily) Grimke
See also BW 1; CA 124; DAM POET; DLB 50, 54

Grimke, Charlotte L(ottie) Forten 1837(?)-1914
See Forten, Charlotte L.
See also BW 1; CA 117; 124; DAM MULT, POET

Grimm, Jacob Ludwig Karl 1785-1863 .... **NCLC 3, 77; SSC 36**
See also DLB 90; MAICYA 1, 2; RGSF 2; RGWL 2, 3; SATA 22; WCH

Grimm, Wilhelm Karl 1786-1859 .. **NCLC 3, 77; SSC 36**
See also CDWLB 2; DLB 90; MAICYA 1, 2; RGSF 2; RGWL 2, 3; SATA 22; WCH

Grimmelshausen, Hans Jakob Christoffel von
See Grimmelshausen, Johann Jakob Christoffel von
See also RGWL 2, 3

Grimmelshausen, Johann Jakob Christoffel von 1621-1676 .... **LC 6**
See Grimmelshausen, Hans Jakob Christoffel von
See also CDWLB 2; DLB 168

Grindel, Eugene 1895-1952
See Eluard, Paul
See also CA 104; 193; LMFS 2

Grisham, John 1955- .... **CLC 84**
See also AAYA 14, 47; BPFB 2; CA 138; CANR 47, 69, 114, 133; CMW 4; CN 7; CPW; CSW; DA3; DAM POP; MSW; MTCW 2

Grosseteste, Robert 1175(?)-1253 . **CMLC 62**
See also DLB 115

Grossman, David 1954- .... **CLC 67**
See also CA 138; CANR 114; CWW 2; DLB 299; EWL 3

Grossman, Vasilii Semenovich
See Grossman, Vasily (Semenovich)
See also DLB 272

Grossman, Vasily (Semenovich) 1905-1964 .... **CLC 41**
See Grossman, Vasilii Semenovich
See also CA 124; 130; MTCW 1

Grove, Frederick Philip .... **TCLC 4**
See Greve, Felix Paul (Berthold Friedrich)
See also DLB 92; RGEL 2

Grubb
See Crumb, R(obert)

Grumbach, Doris (Isaac) 1918- . **CLC 13, 22, 64**
See also CA 5-8R; CAAS 2; CANR 9, 42, 70, 127; CN 7; INT CANR-9; MTCW 2

Grundtvig, Nicolai Frederik Severin 1783-1872 .... **NCLC 1**
See also DLB 300

Grunge
See Crumb, R(obert)

Grunwald, Lisa 1959- .... **CLC 44**
See also CA 120

Gryphius, Andreas 1616-1664 .... **LC 89**
See also CDWLB 2; DLB 164; RGWL 2, 3
Guare, John 1938- .... **CLC 8, 14, 29, 67; DC 20**
See also CA 73-76; CAD; CANR 21, 69, 118; CD 5; DAM DRAM; DFS 8, 13; DLB 7, 249; EWL 3; MTCW 1, 2; RGAL 4
Guarini, Battista 1537-1612 .... **LC 102**
Gubar, Susan (David) 1944- .... **CLC 145**
See also CA 108; CANR 45, 70; FW; MTCW 1; RGAL 4
Gudjonsson, Halldor Kiljan 1902-1998
See Halldor Laxness
See also CA 103; 164
Guenter, Erich
See Eich, Gunter
Guest, Barbara 1920- .... **CLC 34; PC 55**
See also BG 2; CA 25-28R; CANR 11, 44, 84; CP 7; CWP; DLB 5, 193
Guest, Edgar A(lbert) 1881-1959 ... **TCLC 95**
See also CA 112; 168
Guest, Judith (Ann) 1936- .... **CLC 8, 30**
See also AAYA 7; CA 77-80; CANR 15, 75; DA3; DAM NOV, POP; EXPN; INT CANR-15; LAIT 5; MTCW 1, 2; NFS 1
Guevara, Che .... **CLC 87; HLC 1**
See Guevara (Serna), Ernesto
Guevara (Serna), Ernesto 1928-1967 .... **CLC 87; HLC 1**
See Guevara, Che
See also CA 127; 111; CANR 56; DAM MULT; HW 1
Guicciardini, Francesco 1483-1540 ..... **LC 49**
Guild, Nicholas M. 1944- .... **CLC 33**
See also CA 93-96
Guillemin, Jacques
See Sartre, Jean-Paul
Guillen, Jorge 1893-1984 . **CLC 11; HLCS 1; PC 35**
See also CA 89-92; 112; DAM MULT, POET; DLB 108; EWL 3; HW 1; RGWL 2, 3
Guillen, Nicolas (Cristobal) 1902-1989 .... **BLC 2; CLC 48, 79; HLC 1; PC 23**
See also BW 2; CA 116; 125; 129; CANR 84; DAM MST, MULT, POET; DLB 283; EWL 3; HW 1; LAW; RGWL 2, 3; WP
Guillen y Alvarez, Jorge
See Guillen, Jorge
Guillevic, (Eugene) 1907-1997 .... **CLC 33**
See also CA 93-96; CWW 2
Guillois
See Desnos, Robert
Guillois, Valentin
See Desnos, Robert
Guimaraes Rosa, Joao 1908-1967 .... **HLCS 2**
See Rosa, Joao Guimaraes
See also CA 175; LAW; RGSF 2; RGWL 2, 3
Guiney, Louise Imogen 1861-1920 .... **TCLC 41**
See also CA 160; DLB 54; RGAL 4
Guinizelli, Guido c. 1230-1276 ...... **CMLC 49**
Guiraldes, Ricardo (Guillermo) 1886-1927 .... **TCLC 39**
See also CA 131; EWL 3; HW 1; LAW; MTCW 1
Gumilev, Nikolai (Stepanovich) 1886-1921 .... **TCLC 60**
See Gumilyov, Nikolay Stepanovich
See also CA 165; DLB 295
Gumilyov, Nikolay Stepanovich
See Gumilev, Nikolai (Stepanovich)
See also EWL 3
Gump, P. Q.
See Card, Orson Scott

Gunesekera, Romesh 1954- .... **CLC 91**
See also BRWS 10; CA 159; CN 7; DLB 267
Gunn, Bill .... **CLC 5**
See Gunn, William Harrison
See also DLB 38
Gunn, Thom(son William) 1929-2004 . **CLC 3, 6, 18, 32, 81; PC 26**
See also BRWS 4; CA 17-20R; 227; CANR 9, 33, 116; CDBLB 1960 to Present; CP 7; DAM POET; DLB 27; INT CANR-33; MTCW 1; PFS 9; RGEL 2
Gunn, William Harrison 1934(?)-1989
See Gunn, Bill
See also AITN 1; BW 1, 3; CA 13-16R; 128; CANR 12, 25, 76
Gunn Allen, Paula
See Allen, Paula Gunn
Gunnars, Kristjana 1948- .... **CLC 69**
See also CA 113; CCA 1; CP 7; CWP; DLB 60
Gunter, Erich
See Eich, Gunter
Gurdjieff, G(eorgei) I(vanovich) 1877(?)-1949 .... **TCLC 71**
See also CA 157
Gurganus, Allan 1947- .... **CLC 70**
See also BEST 90:1; CA 135; CANR 114; CN 7; CPW; CSW; DAM POP; GLL 1
Gurney, A. R.
See Gurney, A(lbert) R(amsdell), Jr.
See also DLB 266
Gurney, A(lbert) R(amsdell), Jr. 1930- .... **CLC 32, 50, 54**
See Gurney, A. R.
See also AMWS 5; CA 77-80; CAD; CANR 32, 64, 121; CD 5; DAM DRAM; EWL 3
Gurney, Ivor (Bertie) 1890-1937 ... **TCLC 33**
See also BRW 6; CA 167; DLBY 2002; PAB; RGEL 2
Gurney, Peter
See Gurney, A(lbert) R(amsdell), Jr.
Guro, Elena (Genrikhovna) 1877-1913 .... **TCLC 56**
See also DLB 295
Gustafson, James M(oody) 1925- ... **CLC 100**
See also CA 25-28R; CANR 37
Gustafson, Ralph (Barker) 1909-1995 .... **CLC 36**
See also CA 21-24R; CANR 8, 45, 84; CP 7; DLB 88; RGEL 2
Gut, Gom
See Simenon, Georges (Jacques Christian)
Guterson, David 1956- .... **CLC 91**
See also CA 132; CANR 73, 126; DLB 292; MTCW 2; NFS 13
Guthrie, A(lfred) B(ertram), Jr. 1901-1991 .... **CLC 23**
See also CA 57-60; 134; CANR 24; DLB 6, 212; SATA 62; SATA-Obit 67
Guthrie, Isobel
See Grieve, C(hristopher) M(urray)
Guthrie, Woodrow Wilson 1912-1967
See Guthrie, Woody
See also CA 113; 93-96
Guthrie, Woody .... **CLC 35**
See Guthrie, Woodrow Wilson
See also DLB 303; LAIT 3
Gutierrez Najera, Manuel 1859-1895 .... **HLCS 2; NCLC 133**
See also DLB 290; LAW
Guy, Rosa (Cuthbert) 1925- .... **CLC 26**
See also AAYA 4, 37; BW 2; CA 17-20R; CANR 14, 34, 83; CLR 13; DLB 33; DNFS 1; JRDA; MAICYA 1, 2; SATA 14, 62, 122; YAW
Gwendolyn
See Bennett, (Enoch) Arnold

H. D. .... **CLC 3, 8, 14, 31, 34, 73; PC 5**
See Doolittle, Hilda
H. de V.
See Buchan, John
Haavikko, Paavo Juhani 1931- .. **CLC 18, 34**
See also CA 106; CWW 2; EWL 3
Habbema, Koos
See Heijermans, Herman
Habermas, Juergen 1929- .... **CLC 104**
See also CA 109; CANR 85; DLB 242
Habermas, Jurgen
See Habermas, Juergen
Hacker, Marilyn 1942- ...... **CLC 5, 9, 23, 72, 91; PC 47**
See also CA 77-80; CANR 68, 129; CP 7; CWP; DAM POET; DLB 120, 282; FW; GLL 2; PFS 19
Hadewijch of Antwerp fl. 1250- ... **CMLC 61**
See also RGWL 3
Hadrian 76-138 .... **CMLC 52**
Haeckel, Ernst Heinrich (Philipp August) 1834-1919 .... **TCLC 83**
See also CA 157
Hafiz c. 1326-1389(?) .... **CMLC 34**
See also RGWL 2, 3
Hagedorn, Jessica T(arahata) 1949- .... **CLC 185**
See also CA 139; CANR 69; CWP; RGAL 4
Haggard, H(enry) Rider 1856-1925 .... **TCLC 11**
See also BRWS 3; BYA 4, 5; CA 108; 148; CANR 112; DLB 70, 156, 174, 178; FANT; LMFS 1; MTCW 2; RGEL 2; RHW; SATA 16; SCFW; SFW 4; SUFW 1; WLIT 4
Hagiosy, L.
See Larbaud, Valery (Nicolas)
Hagiwara, Sakutaro 1886-1942 .... **PC 18; TCLC 60**
See Hagiwara Sakutaro
See also CA 154; RGWL 3
Hagiwara Sakutaro
See Hagiwara, Sakutaro
See also EWL 3
Haig, Fenil
See Ford, Ford Madox
Haig-Brown, Roderick (Langmere) 1908-1976 .... **CLC 21**
See also CA 5-8R; 69-72; CANR 4, 38, 83; CLR 31; CWRI 5; DLB 88; MAICYA 1, 2; SATA 12
Haight, Rip
See Carpenter, John (Howard)
Hailey, Arthur 1920- .... **CLC 5**
See also AITN 2; BEST 90:3; BPFB 2; CA 1-4R; CANR 2, 36, 75; CCA 1; CN 7; CPW; DAM NOV, POP; DLB 88; DLBY 1982; MTCW 1, 2
Hailey, Elizabeth Forsythe 1938- ...... **CLC 40**
See also CA 93-96; 188; CAAE 188; CAAS 1; CANR 15, 48; INT CANR-15
Haines, John (Meade) 1924- .... **CLC 58**
See also AMWS 12; CA 17-20R; CANR 13, 34; CSW; DLB 5, 212
Hakluyt, Richard 1552-1616 .... **LC 31**
See also DLB 136; RGEL 2
Haldeman, Joe (William) 1943- .... **CLC 61**
See Graham, Robert
See also AAYA 38; CA 53-56; 179; CAAE 179; CAAS 25; CANR 6, 70, 72, 130; DLB 8; INT CANR-6; SCFW 2; SFW 4
Hale, Janet Campbell 1947- .... **NNAL**
See also CA 49-52; CANR 45, 75; DAM MULT; DLB 175; MTCW 2
Hale, Sarah Josepha (Buell) 1788-1879 .... **NCLC 75**
See also DLB 1, 42, 73, 243

Halevy, Elie 1870-1937 .... **TCLC 104**
Haley, Alex(ander Murray Palmer)
    1921-1992 .... **BLC 2; CLC 8, 12, 76;
    TCLC 147**
    See also AAYA 26; BPFB 2; BW 2, 3; CA
    77-80; 136; CANR 61; CDALBS; CPW;
    CSW; DA; DA3; DAB; DAC; DAM MST,
    MULT, POP; DLB 38; LAIT 5; MTCW
    1, 2; NFS 9
Haliburton, Thomas Chandler
    1796-1865 .... **NCLC 15, 149**
    See also DLB 11, 99; RGEL 2; RGSF 2
Hall, Donald (Andrew, Jr.) 1928- ...... **CLC 1,
    13, 37, 59, 151**
    See also CA 5-8R; CAAS 7; CANR 2, 44,
    64, 106, 133; CP 7; DAM POET; DLB 5;
    MTCW 1; RGAL 4; SATA 23, 97
Hall, Frederic Sauser
    See Sauser-Hall, Frederic
Hall, James
    See Kuttner, Henry
Hall, James Norman 1887-1951 ..... **TCLC 23**
    See also CA 123; 173; LAIT 1; RHW 1;
    SATA 21
Hall, Joseph 1574-1656 .... **LC 91**
    See also DLB 121, 151; RGEL 2
Hall, (Marguerite) Radclyffe
    1880-1943 .... **TCLC 12**
    See also BRWS 6; CA 110; 150; CANR 83;
    DLB 191; MTCW 2; RGEL 2; RHW
Hall, Rodney 1935- .... **CLC 51**
    See also CA 109; CANR 69; CN 7; CP 7;
    DLB 289
Hallam, Arthur Henry
    1811-1833 .... **NCLC 110**
    See also DLB 32
Halldor Laxness .... **CLC 25**
    See Gudjonsson, Halldor Kiljan
    See also DLB 293; EW 12; EWL 3; RGWL
    2, 3
Halleck, Fitz-Greene 1790-1867 .... **NCLC 47**
    See also DLB 3, 250; RGAL 4
Halliday, Michael
    See Creasey, John
Halpern, Daniel 1945- .... **CLC 14**
    See also CA 33-36R; CANR 93; CP 7
Hamburger, Michael (Peter Leopold)
    1924- .... **CLC 5, 14**
    See also CA 5-8R, 196; CAAE 196; CAAS
    4; CANR 2, 47; CP 7; DLB 27
Hamill, Pete 1935- .... **CLC 10**
    See also CA 25-28R; CANR 18, 71, 127
Hamilton, Alexander
    1755(?)-1804 .... **NCLC 49**
    See also DLB 37
Hamilton, Clive
    See Lewis, C(live) S(taples)
Hamilton, Edmond 1904-1977 .... **CLC 1**
    See also CA 1-4R; CANR 3, 84; DLB 8;
    SATA 118; SFW 4
Hamilton, Elizabeth 1758-1816 ... **NCLC 153**
    See also DLB 116, 158
Hamilton, Eugene (Jacob) Lee
    See Lee-Hamilton, Eugene (Jacob)
Hamilton, Franklin
    See Silverberg, Robert
Hamilton, Gail
    See Corcoran, Barbara (Asenath)
Hamilton, (Robert) Ian 1938-2001 . **CLC 191**
    See also CA 106; 203; CANR 41, 67; CP 7;
    DLB 40, 155
Hamilton, Jane 1957- .... **CLC 179**
    See also CA 147; CANR 85, 128
Hamilton, Mollie
    See Kaye, M(ary) M(argaret)
Hamilton, (Anthony Walter) Patrick
    1904-1962 .... **CLC 51**
    See also CA 176; 113; DLB 10, 191

Hamilton, Virginia (Esther)
    1936-2002 .... **CLC 26**
    See also AAYA 2, 21; BW 2, 3; BYA 1, 2,
    8; CA 25-28R; 206; CANR 20, 37, 73,
    126; CLR 1, 11, 40; DAM MULT; DLB
    33, 52; DLBY 01; INT CANR-20; JRDA;
    LAIT 5; MAICYA 1, 2; MAICYAS 1;
    MTCW 1, 2; SATA 4, 56, 79, 123; SATA-
    Obit 132; WYA; YAW
Hammett, (Samuel) Dashiell
    1894-1961 .... **CLC 3, 5, 10, 19, 47; SSC
    17**
    See also AAYA 59; AITN 1; AMWS 4;
    BPFB 2; CA 81-84; CANR 42; CDALB
    1929-1941; CMW 4; DA3; DLB 226, 280;
    DLBD 6; DLBY 1996; EWL 3; LAIT 3;
    MSW; MTCW 1, 2; RGAL 4; RGSF 2;
    TUS
Hammon, Jupiter 1720(?)-1800(?) .... **BLC 2;
    NCLC 5; PC 16**
    See also DAM MULT, POET; DLB 31, 50
Hammond, Keith
    See Kuttner, Henry
Hamner, Earl (Henry), Jr. 1923- ...... **CLC 12**
    See also AITN 2; CA 73-76; DLB 6
Hampton, Christopher (James)
    1946- .... **CLC 4**
    See also CA 25-28R; CD 5; DLB 13;
    MTCW 1
Hamsun, Knut .... **TCLC 2, 14, 49, 151**
    See Pedersen, Knut
    See also DLB 297; EW 8; EWL 3; RGWL
    2, 3
Handke, Peter 1942- .... **CLC 5, 8, 10, 15, 38,
    134; DC 17**
    See also CA 77-80; CANR 33, 75, 104, 133;
    CWW 2; DAM DRAM, NOV; DLB 85,
    124; EWL 3; MTCW 1, 2; TWA
Handy, W(illiam) C(hristopher)
    1873-1958 .... **TCLC 97**
    See also BW 3; CA 121; 167
Hanley, James 1901-1985 ..... **CLC 3, 5, 8, 13**
    See also CA 73-76; 117; CANR 36; CBD;
    DLB 191; EWL 3; MTCW 1; RGEL 2
Hannah, Barry 1942- .... **CLC 23, 38, 90**
    See also BPFB 2; CA 108; 110; CANR 43,
    68, 113; CN 7; CSW; DLB 6, 234; INT
    CA-110; MTCW 1; RGSF 2
Hannon, Ezra
    See Hunter, Evan
Hansberry, Lorraine (Vivian)
    1930-1965 ... **BLC 2; CLC 17, 62; DC 2**
    See also AAYA 25; AFAW 1, 2; AMWS 4;
    BW 1, 3; CA 109; 25-28R; CABS 3;
    CAD; CANR 58; CDALB 1941-1968;
    CWD; DA; DA3; DAB; DAC; DAM
    DRAM, MST, MULT; DFS 2; DLB 7, 38;
    EWL 3; FW; LAIT 4; MTCW 1, 2; RGAL
    4; TUS
Hansen, Joseph 1923- .... **CLC 38**
    See Brock, Rose; Colton, James
    See also BPFB 2; CA 29-32R; CAAS 17;
    CANR 16, 44, 66, 125; CMW 4; DLB
    226; GLL 1; INT CANR-16
Hansen, Martin A(lfred)
    1909-1955 .... **TCLC 32**
    See also CA 167; DLB 214; EWL 3
Hansen and Philipson eds. .... **CLC 65**
Hanson, Kenneth O(stlin) 1922- ...... **CLC 13**
    See also CA 53-56; CANR 7
Hardwick, Elizabeth (Bruce) 1916- . **CLC 13**
    See also AMWS 3; CA 5-8R; CANR 3, 32,
    70, 100; CN 7; CSW; DA3; DAM NOV;
    DLB 6; MAWW; MTCW 1, 2
Hardy, Thomas 1840-1928 .... **PC 8; SSC 2,
    60; TCLC 4, 10, 18, 32, 48, 53, 72, 143,
    153; WLC**
    See also BRW 6; BRWC 1, 2; BRWR 1;
    CA 104; 123; CDBLB 1890-1914; DA;
    DA3; DAB; DAC; DAM MST, NOV,
    POET; DLB 18, 19, 135, 284; EWL 3;
    EXPN; EXPP; LAIT 2; MTCW 1, 2; NFS
    3, 11, 15, 19; PFS 3, 4, 18; RGEL 2;
    RGSF 2; TEA; WLIT 4
Hare, David 1947- .... **CLC 29, 58, 136**
    See also BRWS 4; CA 97-100; CANR 39,
    91; CBD; CD 5; DFS 4, 7, 16; DLB 13;
    MTCW 1; TEA
Harewood, John
    See Van Druten, John (William)
Harford, Henry
    See Hudson, W(illiam) H(enry)
Hargrave, Leonie
    See Disch, Thomas M(ichael)
**Hariri, Al- al-Qasim ibn 'Ali Abu
    Muhammad al-Basri**
    See al-Hariri, al-Qasim ibn 'Ali Abu Mu-
    hammad al-Basri
Harjo, Joy 1951- ..... **CLC 83; NNAL; PC 27**
    See also AMWS 12; CA 114; CANR 35,
    67, 91, 129; CP 7; CWP; DAM MULT;
    DLB 120, 175; EWL 3; MTCW 2; PFS
    15; RGAL 4
Harlan, Louis R(udolph) 1922- .... **CLC 34**
    See also CA 21-24R; CANR 25, 55, 80
Harling, Robert 1951(?)- .... **CLC 53**
    See also CA 147
Harmon, William (Ruth) 1938- .... **CLC 38**
    See also CA 33-36R; CANR 14, 32, 35;
    SATA 65
Harper, F. E. W.
    See Harper, Frances Ellen Watkins
Harper, Frances E. W.
    See Harper, Frances Ellen Watkins
Harper, Frances E. Watkins
    See Harper, Frances Ellen Watkins
Harper, Frances Ellen
    See Harper, Frances Ellen Watkins
Harper, Frances Ellen Watkins
    1825-1911 ..... **BLC 2; PC 21; TCLC 14**
    See also AFAW 1, 2; BW 1, 3; CA 111; 125;
    CANR 79; DAM MULT, POET; DLB 50,
    221; MAWW; RGAL 4
Harper, Michael S(teven) 1938- ... **CLC 7, 22**
    See also AFAW 2; BW 1; CA 33-36R; 224;
    CAAE 224; CANR 24, 108; CP 7; DLB
    41; RGAL 4
Harper, Mrs. F. E. W.
    See Harper, Frances Ellen Watkins
Harpur, Charles 1813-1868 .... **NCLC 114**
    See also DLB 230; RGEL 2
Harris, Christie
    See Harris, Christie (Lucy) Irwin
Harris, Christie (Lucy) Irwin
    1907-2002 .... **CLC 12**
    See also CA 5-8R; CANR 6, 83; CLR 47;
    DLB 88; JRDA; MAICYA 1, 2; SAAS 10;
    SATA 6, 74; SATA-Essay 116
Harris, Frank 1856-1931 .... **TCLC 24**
    See also CA 109; 150; CANR 80; DLB 156,
    197; RGEL 2
Harris, George Washington
    1814-1869 .... **NCLC 23**
    See also DLB 3, 11, 248; RGAL 4
Harris, Joel Chandler 1848-1908 ..... **SSC 19;
    TCLC 2**
    See also CA 104; 137; CANR 80; CLR 49;
    DLB 11, 23, 42, 78, 91; LAIT 2; MAI-
    CYA 1, 2; RGSF 2; SATA 100; WCH;
    YABC 1
**Harris, John (Wyndham Parkes Lucas)
    Beynon** 1903-1969
    See Wyndham, John
    See also CA 102; 89-92; CANR 84; SATA
    118; SFW 4
Harris, MacDonald .... **CLC 9**
    See Heiney, Donald (William)

Harris, Mark 1922- .... **CLC 19**
See also CA 5-8R; CAAS 3; CANR 2, 55, 83; CN 7; DLB 2; DLBY 1980

Harris, Norman .... **CLC 65**

Harris, (Theodore) Wilson 1921- .... **CLC 25, 159**
See also BRWS 5; BW 2, 3; CA 65-68; CAAS 16; CANR 11, 27, 69, 114; CDWLB 3; CN 7; CP 7; DLB 117; EWL 3; MTCW 1; RGEL 2

Harrison, Barbara Grizzuti
1934-2002 .... **CLC 144**
See also CA 77-80; 205; CANR 15, 48; INT CANR-15

Harrison, Elizabeth (Allen) Cavanna
1909-2001
See Cavanna, Betty
See also CA 9-12R; 200; CANR 6, 27, 85, 104, 121; MAICYA 2; SATA 142; YAW

Harrison, Harry (Max) 1925- .... **CLC 42**
See also CA 1-4R; CANR 5, 21, 84; DLB 8; SATA 4; SCFW 2; SFW 4

Harrison, James (Thomas) 1937- ...... **CLC 6, 14, 33, 66, 143; SSC 19**
See Harrison, Jim
See also CA 13-16R; CANR 8, 51, 79; CN 7; CP 7; DLBY 1982; INT CANR-8

Harrison, Jim
See Harrison, James (Thomas)
See also AMWS 8; RGAL 4; TCWW 2; TUS

Harrison, Kathryn 1961- .... **CLC 70, 151**
See also CA 144; CANR 68, 122

Harrison, Tony 1937- .... **CLC 43, 129**
See also BRWS 5; CA 65-68; CANR 44, 98; CBD; CD 5; CP 7; DLB 40, 245; MTCW 1; RGEL 2

Harriss, Will(ard Irvin) 1922- .... **CLC 34**
See also CA 111

Hart, Ellis
See Ellison, Harlan (Jay)

Hart, Josephine 1942(?)- .... **CLC 70**
See also CA 138; CANR 70; CPW; DAM POP

Hart, Moss 1904-1961 .... **CLC 66**
See also CA 109; 89-92; CANR 84; DAM DRAM; DFS 1; DLB 7, 266; RGAL 4

Harte, (Francis) Bret(t)
1836(?)-1902 ... **SSC 8, 59; TCLC 1, 25; WLC**
See also AMWS 2; CA 104; 140; CANR 80; CDALB 1865-1917; DA; DA3; DAC; DAM MST; DLB 12, 64, 74, 79, 186; EXPS; LAIT 2; RGAL 4; RGSF 2; SATA 26; SSFS 3; TUS

Hartley, L(eslie) P(oles) 1895-1972 ... **CLC 2, 22**
See also BRWS 7; CA 45-48; 37-40R; CANR 33; DLB 15, 139; EWL 3; HGG; MTCW 1, 2; RGEL 2; RGSF 2; SUFW 1

Hartman, Geoffrey H. 1929- .... **CLC 27**
See also CA 117; 125; CANR 79; DLB 67

Hartmann, Sadakichi 1869-1944 ... **TCLC 73**
See also CA 157; DLB 54

Hartmann von Aue c. 1170-c. 1210 .... **CMLC 15**
See also CDWLB 2; DLB 138; RGWL 2, 3

Hartog, Jan de
See de Hartog, Jan

Haruf, Kent 1943- .... **CLC 34**
See also AAYA 44; CA 149; CANR 91, 131

Harvey, Caroline
See Trollope, Joanna

Harvey, Gabriel 1550(?)-1631 .... **LC 88**
See also DLB 167, 213, 281

Harwood, Ronald 1934- .... **CLC 32**
See also CA 1-4R; CANR 4, 55; CBD; CD 5; DAM DRAM, MST; DLB 13

Hasegawa Tatsunosuke
See Futabatei, Shimei

Hasek, Jaroslav (Matej Frantisek)
1883-1923 .... **SSC 69; TCLC 4**
See also CA 104; 129; CDWLB 4; DLB 215; EW 9; EWL 3; MTCW 1, 2; RGSF 2; RGWL 2, 3

Hass, Robert 1941- ... **CLC 18, 39, 99; PC 16**
See also AMWS 6; CA 111; CANR 30, 50, 71; CP 7; DLB 105, 206; EWL 3; RGAL 4; SATA 94

Hastings, Hudson
See Kuttner, Henry

Hastings, Selina .... **CLC 44**

Hathorne, John 1641-1717 .... **LC 38**

Hatteras, Amelia
See Mencken, H(enry) L(ouis)

Hatteras, Owen .... **TCLC 18**
See Mencken, H(enry) L(ouis); Nathan, George Jean

Hauptmann, Gerhart (Johann Robert)
1862-1946 .... **SSC 37; TCLC 4**
See also CA 104; 153; CDWLB 2; DAM DRAM; DLB 66, 118; EW 8; EWL 3; RGSF 2; RGWL 2, 3; TWA

Havel, Vaclav 1936- ..... **CLC 25, 58, 65, 123; DC 6**
See also CA 104; CANR 36, 63, 124; CDWLB 4; CWW 2; DA3; DAM DRAM; DFS 10; DLB 232; EWL 3; LMFS 2; MTCW 1, 2; RGWL 3

Haviaras, Stratis .... **CLC 33**
See Chaviaras, Strates

Hawes, Stephen 1475(?)-1529(?) .... **LC 17**
See also DLB 132; RGEL 2

Hawkes, John (Clendennin Burne, Jr.)
1925-1998 .. **CLC 1, 2, 3, 4, 7, 9, 14, 15, 27, 49**
See also BPFB 2; CA 1-4R; 167; CANR 2, 47, 64; CN 7; DLB 2, 7, 227; DLBY 1980, 1998; EWL 3; MTCW 1, 2; RGAL 4

Hawking, S. W.
See Hawking, Stephen W(illiam)

Hawking, Stephen W(illiam) 1942- . **CLC 63, 105**
See also AAYA 13; BEST 89:1; CA 126; 129; CANR 48, 115; CPW; DA3; MTCW 2

Hawkins, Anthony Hope
See Hope, Anthony

Hawthorne, Julian 1846-1934 .... **TCLC 25**
See also CA 165; HGG

Hawthorne, Nathaniel 1804-1864 ... **NCLC 2, 10, 17, 23, 39, 79, 95; SSC 3, 29, 39; WLC**
See also AAYA 18; AMW; AMWC 1; AMWR 1; BPFB 2; BYA 3; CDALB 1640-1865; DA; DA3; DAB; DAC; DAM MST, NOV; DLB 1, 74, 183, 223, 269; EXPN; EXPS; HGG; LAIT 1; NFS 1, 20; RGAL 4; RGSF 2; SSFS 1, 7, 11, 15; SUFW 1; TUS; WCH; YABC 2

Hawthorne, Sophia Peabody
1809-1871 .... **NCLC 150**
See also DLB 183, 239

Haxton, Josephine Ayres 1921-
See Douglas, Ellen
See also CA 115; CANR 41, 83

Hayaseca y Eizaguirre, Jorge
See Echegaray (y Eizaguirre), Jose (Maria Waldo)

Hayashi, Fumiko 1904-1951 .... **TCLC 27**
See Hayashi Fumiko
See also CA 161

Hayashi Fumiko
See Hayashi, Fumiko
See also DLB 180; EWL 3

Haycraft, Anna (Margaret) 1932-
See Ellis, Alice Thomas
See also CA 122; CANR 85, 90; MTCW 2

Hayden, Robert E(arl) 1913-1980 ..... **BLC 2; CLC 5, 9, 14, 37; PC 6**
See also AFAW 1, 2; AMWS 2; BW 1, 3; CA 69-72; 97-100; CABS 2; CANR 24, 75, 82; CDALB 1941-1968; DA; DAC; DAM MST, MULT, POET; DLB 5, 76; EWL 3; EXPP; MTCW 1, 2; PFS 1; RGAL 4; SATA 19; SATA-Obit 26; WP

Haydon, Benjamin Robert
1786-1846 .... **NCLC 146**
See also DLB 110

Hayek, F(riedrich) A(ugust von)
1899-1992 .... **TCLC 109**
See also CA 93-96; 137; CANR 20; MTCW 1, 2

Hayford, J(oseph) E(phraim) Casely
See Casely-Hayford, J(oseph) E(phraim)

Hayman, Ronald 1932- .... **CLC 44**
See also CA 25-28R; CANR 18, 50, 88; CD 5; DLB 155

Hayne, Paul Hamilton 1830-1886 . **NCLC 94**
See also DLB 3, 64, 79, 248; RGAL 4

Hays, Mary 1760-1843 .... **NCLC 114**
See also DLB 142, 158; RGEL 2

Haywood, Eliza (Fowler)
1693(?)-1756 .... **LC 1, 44**
See also DLB 39; RGEL 2

Hazlitt, William 1778-1830 ...... **NCLC 29, 82**
See also BRW 4; DLB 110, 158; RGEL 2; TEA

Hazzard, Shirley 1931- .... **CLC 18**
See also CA 9-12R; CANR 4, 70, 127; CN 7; DLB 289; DLBY 1982; MTCW 1

Head, Bessie 1937-1986 .... **BLC 2; CLC 25, 67; SSC 52**
See also AFW; BW 2, 3; CA 29-32R; 119; CANR 25, 82; CDWLB 3; DA3; DAM MULT; DLB 117, 225; EWL 3; EXPS; FW; MTCW 1, 2; RGSF 2; SSFS 5, 13; WLIT 2; WWE 1

Headon, (Nicky) Topper 1956(?)- ...... **CLC 30**

Heaney, Seamus (Justin) 1939- ...... **CLC 5, 7, 14, 25, 37, 74, 91, 171; PC 18; WLCS**
See also BRWR 1; BRWS 2; CA 85-88; CANR 25, 48, 75, 91, 128; CDBLB 1960 to Present; CP 7; DA3; DAB; DAM POET; DLB 40; DLBY 1995; EWL 3; EXPP; MTCW 1, 2; PAB; PFS 2, 5, 8, 17; RGEL 2; TEA; WLIT 4

Hearn, (Patricio) Lafcadio (Tessima Carlos)
1850-1904 .... **TCLC 9**
See also CA 105; 166; DLB 12, 78, 189; HGG; RGAL 4

Hearne, Samuel 1745-1792 .... **LC 95**
See also DLB 99

Hearne, Vicki 1946-2001 .... **CLC 56**
See also CA 139; 201

Hearon, Shelby 1931- .... **CLC 63**
See also AITN 2; AMWS 8; CA 25-28R; CANR 18, 48, 103; CSW

Heat-Moon, William Least .... **CLC 29**
See Trogdon, William (Lewis)
See also AAYA 9

Hebbel, Friedrich 1813-1863 . **DC 21; NCLC 43**
See also CDWLB 2; DAM DRAM; DLB 129; EW 6; RGWL 2, 3

Hebert, Anne 1916-2000 .... **CLC 4, 13, 29**
See also CA 85-88; 187; CANR 69, 126; CCA 1; CWP; CWW 2; DA3; DAC; DAM MST, POET; DLB 68; EWL 3; GFL 1789 to the Present; MTCW 1, 2; PFS 20

Hecht, Anthony (Evan) 1923-2004 .... CLC 8, 13, 19
See also AMWS 10; CA 9-12R; CANR 6, 108; CP 7; DAM POET; DLB 5, 169; EWL 3; PFS 6; WP

Hecht, Ben 1894-1964 ..... CLC 8; TCLC 101
See also CA 85-88; DFS 9; DLB 7, 9, 25, 26, 28, 86; FANT; IDFW 3, 4; RGAL 4

Hedayat, Sadeq 1903-1951 .... TCLC 21
See also CA 120; EWL 3; RGSF 2

Hegel, Georg Wilhelm Friedrich 1770-1831 .... NCLC 46, 151
See also DLB 90; TWA

Heidegger, Martin 1889-1976 .... CLC 24
See also CA 81-84; 65-68; CANR 34; DLB 296; MTCW 1, 2

Heidenstam, (Carl Gustaf) Verner von 1859-1940 .... TCLC 5
See also CA 104

Heidi Louise
See Erdrich, Louise

Heifner, Jack 1946- .... CLC 11
See also CA 105; CANR 47

Heijermans, Herman 1864-1924 .... TCLC 24
See also CA 123; EWL 3

Heilbrun, Carolyn G(old) 1926-2003 .... CLC 25, 173
See Cross, Amanda
See also CA 45-48; 220; CANR 1, 28, 58, 94; FW

Hein, Christoph 1944- .... CLC 154
See also CA 158; CANR 108; CDWLB 2; CWW 2; DLB 124

Heine, Heinrich 1797-1856 .... NCLC 4, 54, 147; PC 25
See also CDWLB 2; DLB 90; EW 5; RGWL 2, 3; TWA

Heinemann, Larry (Curtiss) 1944- .... CLC 50
See also CA 110; CAAS 21; CANR 31, 81; DLBD 9; INT CANR-31

Heiney, Donald (William) 1921-1993
See Harris, MacDonald
See also CA 1-4R; 142; CANR 3, 58; FANT

Heinlein, Robert A(nson) 1907-1988 . CLC 1, 3, 8, 14, 26, 55; SSC 55
See also AAYA 17; BPFB 2; BYA 4, 13; CA 1-4R; 125; CANR 1, 20, 53; CLR 75; CPW; DA3; DAM POP; DLB 8; EXPS; JRDA; LAIT 5; LMFS 2; MAICYA 1, 2; MTCW 1, 2; RGAL 4; SATA 9, 69; SATA-Obit 56; SCFW; SFW 4; SSFS 7; YAW

Helforth, John
See Doolittle, Hilda

Heliodorus fl. 3rd cent. - .... CMLC 52

Hellenhofferu, Vojtech Kapristian z
See Hasek, Jaroslav (Matej Frantisek)

Heller, Joseph 1923-1999 . CLC 1, 3, 5, 8, 11, 36, 63; TCLC 131, 151; WLC
See also AAYA 24; AITN 1; AMWS 4; BPFB 2; BYA 1; CA 5-8R; 187; CABS 1; CANR 8, 42, 66, 126; CN 7; CPW; DA; DA3; DAB; DAC; DAM MST, NOV, POP; DLB 2, 28, 227; DLBY 1980, 2002; EWL 3; EXPN; INT CANR-8; LAIT 4; MTCW 1, 2; NFS 1; RGAL 4; TUS; YAW

Hellman, Lillian (Florence) 1906-1984 .. CLC 2, 4, 8, 14, 18, 34, 44, 52; DC 1; TCLC 119
See also AAYA 47; AITN 1, 2; AMWS 1; CA 13-16R; 112; CAD; CANR 33; CWD; DA3; DAM DRAM; DFS 1, 3, 14; DLB 7, 228; DLBY 1984; EWL 3; FW; LAIT 3; MAWW; MTCW 1, 2; RGAL 4; TUS

Helprin, Mark 1947- .... CLC 7, 10, 22, 32
See also CA 81-84; CANR 47, 64, 124; CDALBS; CPW; DA3; DAM NOV, POP; DLBY 1985; FANT; MTCW 1, 2; SUFW 2

Helvetius, Claude-Adrien 1715-1771 .. LC 26

Helyar, Jane Penelope Josephine 1933-
See Poole, Josephine
See also CA 21-24R; CANR 10, 26; CWRI 5; SATA 82, 138; SATA-Essay 138

Hemans, Felicia 1793-1835 ...... NCLC 29, 71
See also DLB 96; RGEL 2

Hemingway, Ernest (Miller) 1899-1961 ... CLC 1, 3, 6, 8, 10, 13, 19, 30, 34, 39, 41, 44, 50, 61, 80; SSC 1, 25, 36, 40, 63; TCLC 115; WLC
See also AAYA 19; AMW; AMWC 1; AMWR 1; BPFB 2, 3, 13, 15; CA 77-80; CANR 34; CDALB 1917-1929; DA; DA3; DAB; DAC; DAM MST, NOV; DLB 4, 9, 102, 210, 308; DLBD 1, 15, 16; DLBY 1981, 1987, 1996, 1998; EWL 3; EXPN; EXPS; LAIT 3, 4; LATS 1:1; MTCW 1, 2; NFS 1, 5, 6, 14; RGAL 4; RGSF 2; SSFS 17; TUS; WYA

Hempel, Amy 1951- .... CLC 39
See also CA 118; 137; CANR 70; DA3; DLB 218; EXPS; MTCW 2; SSFS 2

Henderson, F. C.
See Mencken, H(enry) L(ouis)

Henderson, Sylvia
See Ashton-Warner, Sylvia (Constance)

Henderson, Zenna (Chlarson) 1917-1983 .... SSC 29
See also CA 1-4R; 133; CANR 1, 84; DLB 8; SATA 5; SFW 4

Henkin, Joshua .... CLC 119
See also CA 161

Henley, Beth .... CLC 23; DC 6, 14
See Henley, Elizabeth Becker
See also CABS 3; CAD; CD 5; CSW; CWD; DFS 2; DLBY 1986; FW

Henley, Elizabeth Becker 1952-
See Henley, Beth
See also CA 107; CANR 32, 73; DA3; DAM DRAM, MST; MTCW 1, 2

Henley, William Ernest 1849-1903 .. TCLC 8
See also CA 105; DLB 19; RGEL 2

Hennissart, Martha 1929-
See Lathen, Emma
See also CA 85-88; CANR 64

Henry VIII 1491-1547 .... LC 10
See also DLB 132

Henry, O. ..... SSC 5, 49; TCLC 1, 19; WLC
See Porter, William Sydney
See also AAYA 41; AMWS 2; EXPS; RGAL 4; RGSF 2; SSFS 2, 18

Henry, Patrick 1736-1799 .... LC 25
See also LAIT 1

Henryson, Robert 1430(?)-1506(?) ..... LC 20, 110
See also BRWS 7; DLB 146; RGEL 2

Henschke, Alfred
See Klabund

Henson, Lance 1944- .... NNAL
See also CA 146; DLB 175

Hentoff, Nat(han Irving) 1925- .... CLC 26
See also AAYA 4, 42; BYA 6; CA 1-4R; CAAS 6; CANR 5, 25, 77, 114; CLR 1, 52; INT CANR-25; JRDA; MAICYA 1, 2; SATA 42, 69, 133; SATA-Brief 27; WYA; YAW

Heppenstall, (John) Rayner 1911-1981 .... CLC 10
See also CA 1-4R; 103; CANR 29; EWL 3

Heraclitus c. 540B.C.-c. 450B.C. ... CMLC 22
See also DLB 176

Herbert, Frank (Patrick) 1920-1986 .... CLC 12, 23, 35, 44, 85
See also AAYA 21; BPFB 2; BYA 4, 14; CA 53-56; 118; CANR 5, 43; CDALBS; CPW; DAM POP; DLB 8; INT CANR-5; LAIT 5; MTCW 1, 2; NFS 17; SATA 9, 37; SATA-Obit 47; SCFW 2; SFW 4; YAW

Herbert, George 1593-1633 ...... LC 24; PC 4
See also BRW 2; BRWR 2; CDBLB Before 1660; DAB; DAM POET; DLB 126; EXPP; RGEL 2; TEA; WP

Herbert, Zbigniew 1924-1998 ..... CLC 9, 43; PC 50
See also CA 89-92; 169; CANR 36, 74; CDWLB 4; CWW 2; DAM POET; DLB 232; EWL 3; MTCW 1

Herbst, Josephine (Frey) 1897-1969 .... CLC 34
See also CA 5-8R; 25-28R; DLB 9

Herder, Johann Gottfried von 1744-1803 .... NCLC 8
See also DLB 97; EW 4; TWA

Heredia, Jose Maria 1803-1839 .... HLCS 2
See also LAW

Hergesheimer, Joseph 1880-1954 ... TCLC 11
See also CA 109; 194; DLB 102, 9; RGAL 4

Herlihy, James Leo 1927-1993 .... CLC 6
See also CA 1-4R; 143; CAD; CANR 2

Herman, William
See Bierce, Ambrose (Gwinett)

Hermogenes fl. c. 175- .... CMLC 6

Hernandez, Jose 1834-1886 .... NCLC 17
See also LAW; RGWL 2, 3; WLIT 1

Herodotus c. 484B.C.-c. 420B.C. .. CMLC 17
See also AW 1; CDWLB 1; DLB 176; RGWL 2, 3; TWA

Herrick, Robert 1591-1674 .... LC 13; PC 9
See also BRW 2; BRWC 2; DA; DAB; DAC; DAM MST, POP; DLB 126; EXPP; PFS 13; RGAL 4; RGEL 2; TEA; WP

Herring, Guilles
See Somerville, Edith Oenone

Herriot, James 1916-1995 .... CLC 12
See Wight, James Alfred
See also AAYA 1, 54; BPFB 2; CA 148; CANR 40; CLR 80; CPW; DAM POP; LAIT 3; MAICYA 2; MAICYAS 1; MTCW 2; SATA 86, 135; TEA; YAW

Herris, Violet
See Hunt, Violet

Herrmann, Dorothy 1941- .... CLC 44
See also CA 107

Herrmann, Taffy
See Herrmann, Dorothy

Hersey, John (Richard) 1914-1993 .... CLC 1, 2, 7, 9, 40, 81, 97
See also AAYA 29; BPFB 2; CA 17-20R; 140; CANR 33; CDALBS; CPW; DAM POP; DLB 6, 185, 278, 299; MTCW 1, 2; SATA 25; SATA-Obit 76; TUS

Herzen, Aleksandr Ivanovich 1812-1870 .... NCLC 10, 61
See Herzen, Alexander

Herzen, Alexander
See Herzen, Aleksandr Ivanovich
See also DLB 277

Herzl, Theodor 1860-1904 .... TCLC 36
See also CA 168

Herzog, Werner 1942- .... CLC 16
See also CA 89-92

Hesiod c. 8th cent. B.C.- .... CMLC 5
See also AW 1; DLB 176; RGWL 2, 3

Hesse, Hermann 1877-1962 ... CLC 1, 2, 3, 6, 11, 17, 25, 69; SSC 9, 49; TCLC 148; WLC
See also AAYA 43; BPFB 2; CA 17-18; CAP 2; CDWLB 2; DA; DA3; DAB; DAC; DAM MST, NOV; DLB 66; EW 9; EWL 3; EXPN; LAIT 1; MTCW 1, 2; NFS 6, 15; RGWL 2, 3; SATA 50; TWA

Hewes, Cady
See De Voto, Bernard (Augustine)

Heyen, William 1940- .... CLC 13, 18
See also CA 33-36R; 220; CAAE 220; CAAS 9; CANR 98; CP 7; DLB 5

Heyerdahl, Thor 1914-2002 .... **CLC 26**
See also CA 5-8R; 207; CANR 5, 22, 66, 73; LAIT 4; MTCW 1, 2; SATA 2, 52

Heym, Georg (Theodor Franz Arthur)
1887-1912 .... **TCLC 9**
See also CA 106; 181

Heym, Stefan 1913-2001 .... **CLC 41**
See also CA 9-12R; 203; CANR 4; CWW 2; DLB 69; EWL 3

Heyse, Paul (Johann Ludwig von)
1830-1914 .... **TCLC 8**
See also CA 104; 209; DLB 129

Heyward, (Edwin) DuBose
1885-1940 .... **HR 2; TCLC 59**
See also CA 108; 157; DLB 7, 9, 45, 249; SATA 21

Heywood, John 1497(?)-1580(?) .... **LC 65**
See also DLB 136; RGEL 2

Heywood, Thomas 1573(?)-1641 .... **LC 111**
See also DLB 62; DAM DRAM; LMFS 1; RGEL 2; TWA

Hibbert, Eleanor Alice Burford
1906-1993 .... **CLC 7**
See Holt, Victoria
See also BEST 90:4; CA 17-20R; 140; CANR 9, 28, 59; CMW 4; CPW; DAM POP; MTCW 2; RHW; SATA 2; SATA-Obit 74

Hichens, Robert (Smythe)
1864-1950 .... **TCLC 64**
See also CA 162; DLB 153; HGG; RHW; SUFW

Higgins, Aidan 1927- .... **SSC 68**
See also CA 9-12R; CANR 70, 115; CN 7; DLB 14

Higgins, George V(incent)
1939-1999 .... **CLC 4, 7, 10, 18**
See also BPFB 2; CA 77-80; 186; CAAS 5; CANR 17, 51, 89, 96; CMW 4; CN 7; DLB 2; DLBY 1981, 1998; INT CANR-17; MSW; MTCW 1

Higginson, Thomas Wentworth
1823-1911 .... **TCLC 36**
See also CA 162; DLB 1, 64, 243

Higgonet, Margaret ed. .... **CLC 65**

Highet, Helen
See MacInnes, Helen (Clark)

Highsmith, (Mary) Patricia
1921-1995 .... **CLC 2, 4, 14, 42, 102**
See Morgan, Claire
See also AAYA 48; BRWS 5; CA 1-4R; 147; CANR 1, 20, 48, 62, 108; CMW 4; CPW; DA3; DAM NOV, POP; DLB 306; MSW; MTCW 1, 2

Highwater, Jamake (Mamake)
1942(?)-2001 .... **CLC 12**
See also AAYA 7; BPFB 2; BYA 4; CA 65-68; 199; CAAS 7; CANR 10, 34, 84; CLR 17; CWRI 5; DLB 52; DLBY 1985; JRDA; MAICYA 1, 2; SATA 32, 69; SATA-Brief 30

Highway, Tomson 1951- ...... **CLC 92; NNAL**
See also CA 151; CANR 75; CCA 1; CD 5; DAC; DAM MULT; DFS 2; MTCW 2

Hijuelos, Oscar 1951- .... **CLC 65; HLC 1**
See also AAYA 25; AMWS 8; BEST 90:1; CA 123; CANR 50, 75, 125; CPW; DA3; DAM MULT, POP; DLB 145; HW 1, 2; LLW 1; MTCW 2; NFS 17; RGAL 4; WLIT 1

Hikmet, Nazim 1902(?)-1963 .... **CLC 40**
See also CA 141; 93-96; EWL 3

Hildegard von Bingen 1098-1179 . **CMLC 20**
See also DLB 148

Hildesheimer, Wolfgang 1916-1991 .. **CLC 49**
See also CA 101; 135; DLB 69, 124; EWL 3

Hill, Geoffrey (William) 1932- ...... **CLC 5, 8, 18, 45**
See also BRWS 5; CA 81-84; CANR 21, 89; CDBLB 1960 to Present; CP 7; DAM POET; DLB 40; EWL 3; MTCW 1; RGEL 2

Hill, George Roy 1921-2002 .... **CLC 26**
See also CA 110; 122; 213

Hill, John
See Koontz, Dean R(ay)

Hill, Susan (Elizabeth) 1942- ...... **CLC 4, 113**
See also CA 33-36R; CANR 29, 69, 129; CN 7; DAB; DAM MST, NOV; DLB 14, 139; HGG; MTCW 1; RHW

Hillard, Asa G. III .... **CLC 70**

Hillerman, Tony 1925- .... **CLC 62, 170**
See also AAYA 40; BEST 89:1; BPFB 2; CA 29-32R; CANR 21, 42, 65, 97, 134; CMW 4; CPW; DA3; DAM POP; DLB 206, 306; MSW; RGAL 4; SATA 6; TCWW 2; YAW

Hillesum, Etty 1914-1943 .... **TCLC 49**
See also CA 137

Hilliard, Noel (Harvey) 1929-1996 ... **CLC 15**
See also CA 9-12R; CANR 7, 69; CN 7

Hillis, Rick 1956- .... **CLC 66**
See also CA 134

Hilton, James 1900-1954 .... **TCLC 21**
See also CA 108; 169; DLB 34, 77; FANT; SATA 34

Hilton, Walter (?)-1396 .... **CMLC 58**
See also DLB 146; RGEL 2

Himes, Chester (Bomar) 1909-1984 .. **BLC 2; CLC 2, 4, 7, 18, 58, 108; TCLC 139**
See also AFAW 2; BPFB 2; BW 2; CA 25-28R; 114; CANR 22, 89; CMW 4; DAM MULT; DLB 2, 76, 143, 226; EWL 3; MSW; MTCW 1, 2; RGAL 4

Himmelfarb, Gertrude 1922- .... **CLC 202**
See also CA 49-52; CANR 28, 66, 102;

Hinde, Thomas .... **CLC 6, 11**
See Chitty, Thomas Willes
See also EWL 3

Hine, (William) Daryl 1936- .... **CLC 15**
See also CA 1-4R; CAAS 15; CANR 1, 20; CP 7; DLB 60

Hinkson, Katharine Tynan
See Tynan, Katharine

Hinojosa(-Smith), Rolando (R.)
1929- .... **HLC 1**
See Hinojosa-Smith, Rolando
See also CA 131; CAAS 16; CANR 62; DAM MULT; DLB 82; HW 1, 2; LLW 1; MTCW 2; RGAL 4

Hinton, S(usan) E(loise) 1950- .. **CLC 30, 111**
See also AAYA 2, 33; BPFB 2; BYA 2, 3; CA 81-84; CANR 32, 62, 92, 133; CDALBS; CLR 3, 23; CPW; DA; DA3; DAB; DAC; DAM MST, NOV; JRDA; LAIT 5; MAICYA 1, 2; MTCW 1, 2; NFS 5, 9, 15, 16; SATA 19, 58, 115; WYA; YAW

Hippius, Zinaida (Nikolaevna) .... **TCLC 9**
See Gippius, Zinaida (Nikolaevna)
See also DLB 295; EWL 3

Hiraoka, Kimitake 1925-1970
See Mishima, Yukio
See also CA 97-100; 29-32R; DA3; DAM DRAM; GLL 1; MTCW 1, 2

Hirsch, E(ric) D(onald), Jr. 1928- .... **CLC 79**
See also CA 25-28R; CANR 27, 51; DLB 67; INT CANR-27; MTCW 1

Hirsch, Edward 1950- .... **CLC 31, 50**
See also CA 104; CANR 20, 42, 102; CP 7; DLB 120

Hitchcock, Alfred (Joseph)
1899-1980 .... **CLC 16**
See also AAYA 22; CA 159; 97-100; SATA 27; SATA-Obit 24

Hitchens, Christopher (Eric)
1949- .... **CLC 157**
See also CA 152; CANR 89

Hitler, Adolf 1889-1945 .... **TCLC 53**
See also CA 117; 147

Hoagland, Edward 1932- .... **CLC 28**
See also ANW; CA 1-4R; CANR 2, 31, 57, 107; CN 7; DLB 6; SATA 51; TCWW 2

Hoban, Russell (Conwell) 1925- ... **CLC 7, 25**
See also BPFB 2; CA 5-8R; CANR 23, 37, 66, 114; CLR 3, 69; CN 7; CWRI 5; DAM NOV; DLB 52; FANT; MAICYA 1, 2; MTCW 1, 2; SATA 1, 40, 78, 136; SFW 4; SUFW 2

Hobbes, Thomas 1588-1679 .... **LC 36**
See also DLB 151, 252, 281; RGEL 2

Hobbs, Perry
See Blackmur, R(ichard) P(almer)

Hobson, Laura Z(ametkin)
1900-1986 .... **CLC 7, 25**
See Field, Peter
See also BPFB 2; CA 17-20R; 118; CANR 55; DLB 28; SATA 52

Hoccleve, Thomas c. 1368-c. 1437 ...... **LC 75**
See also DLB 146; RGEL 2

Hoch, Edward D(entinger) 1930-
See Queen, Ellery
See also CA 29-32R; CANR 11, 27, 51, 97; CMW 4; DLB 306; SFW 4

Hochhuth, Rolf 1931- .... **CLC 4, 11, 18**
See also CA 5-8R; CANR 33, 75; CWW 2; DAM DRAM; DLB 124; EWL 3; MTCW 1, 2

Hochman, Sandra 1936- .... **CLC 3, 8**
See also CA 5-8R; DLB 5

Hochwaelder, Fritz 1911-1986 .... **CLC 36**
See Hochwalder, Fritz
See also CA 29-32R; 120; CANR 42; DAM DRAM; MTCW 1; RGWL 3

Hochwalder, Fritz
See Hochwaelder, Fritz
See also EWL 3; RGWL 2

Hocking, Mary (Eunice) 1921- .... **CLC 13**
See also CA 101; CANR 18, 40

Hodgins, Jack 1938- .... **CLC 23**
See also CA 93-96; CN 7; DLB 60

Hodgson, William Hope
1877(?)-1918 .... **TCLC 13**
See also CA 111; 164; CMW 4; DLB 70, 153, 156, 178; HGG; MTCW 2; SFW 4; SUFW 1

Hoeg, Peter 1957- .... **CLC 95, 156**
See also CA 151; CANR 75; CMW 4; DA3; DLB 214; EWL 3; MTCW 2; NFS 17; RGWL 3; SSFS 18

Hoffman, Alice 1952- .... **CLC 51**
See also AAYA 37; AMWS 10; CA 77-80; CANR 34, 66, 100; CN 7; CPW; DAM NOV; DLB 292; MTCW 1, 2

Hoffman, Daniel (Gerard) 1923- . **CLC 6, 13, 23**
See also CA 1-4R; CANR 4; CP 7; DLB 5

Hoffman, Eva 1945- .... **CLC 182**
See also CA 132

Hoffman, Stanley 1944- .... **CLC 5**
See also CA 77-80

Hoffman, William 1925- .... **CLC 141**
See also CA 21-24R; CANR 9, 103; CSW; DLB 234

Hoffman, William M(oses) 1939- ..... **CLC 40**
See Hoffman, William M.
See also CA 57-60; CANR 11, 71

Hoffmann, E(rnst) T(heodor) A(madeus)
1776-1822 .... **NCLC 2; SSC 13**
See also CDWLB 2; DLB 90; EW 5; RGSF 2; RGWL 2, 3; SATA 27; SUFW 1; WCH

Hofmann, Gert 1931- .... **CLC 54**
See also CA 128; EWL 3

Hofmannsthal, Hugo von 1874-1929 ... **DC 4; TCLC 11**
See also CA 106; 153; CDWLB 2; DAM DRAM; DFS 17; DLB 81, 118; EW 9; EWL 3; RGWL 2, 3

Hogan, Linda 1947- ..... **CLC 73; NNAL; PC 35**
See also AMWS 4; ANW; BYA 12; CA 120, 226; CAAE 226; CANR 45, 73, 129; CWP; DAM MULT; DLB 175; SATA 132; TCWW 2

Hogarth, Charles
See Creasey, John

Hogarth, Emmett
See Polonsky, Abraham (Lincoln)

Hogarth, William 1697-1764 .... **LC 112**
See also AAYA 56

Hogg, James 1770-1835 .... **NCLC 4, 109**
See also BRWS 10; DLB 93, 116, 159; HGG; RGEL 2; SUFW 1

Holbach, Paul Henri Thiry Baron 1723-1789 .... **LC 14**

Holberg, Ludvig 1684-1754 .... **LC 6**
See also DLB 300; RGWL 2, 3

Holcroft, Thomas 1745-1809 .... **NCLC 85**
See also DLB 39, 89, 158; RGEL 2

Holden, Ursula 1921- .... **CLC 18**
See also CA 101; CAAS 8; CANR 22

Holderlin, (Johann Christian) Friedrich 1770-1843 .... **NCLC 16; PC 4**
See also CDWLB 2; DLB 90; EW 5; RGWL 2, 3

Holdstock, Robert
See Holdstock, Robert P.

Holdstock, Robert P. 1948- .... **CLC 39**
See also CA 131; CANR 81; DLB 261; FANT; HGG; SFW 4; SUFW 2

Holinshed, Raphael fl. 1580- .... **LC 69**
See also DLB 167; RGEL 2

Holland, Isabelle (Christian) 1920-2002 .... **CLC 21**
See also AAYA 11; CA 21-24R; 205; CAAE 181; CANR 10, 25, 47; CLR 57; CWRI 5; JRDA; LAIT 4; MAICYA 1, 2; SATA 8, 70; SATA-Essay 103; SATA-Obit 132; WYA

Holland, Marcus
See Caldwell, (Janet Miriam) Taylor (Holland)

Hollander, John 1929- .... **CLC 2, 5, 8, 14**
See also CA 1-4R; CANR 1, 52; CP 7; DLB 5; SATA 13

Hollander, Paul
See Silverberg, Robert

Holleran, Andrew 1943(?)- .... **CLC 38**
See Garber, Eric
See also CA 144; GLL 1

Holley, Marietta 1836(?)-1926 .... **TCLC 99**
See also CA 118; DLB 11

Hollinghurst, Alan 1954- .... **CLC 55, 91**
See also BRWS 10; CA 114; CN 7; DLB 207; GLL 1

Hollis, Jim
See Summers, Hollis (Spurgeon, Jr.)

Holly, Buddy 1936-1959 .... **TCLC 65**
See also CA 213

Holmes, Gordon
See Shiel, M(atthew) P(hipps)

Holmes, John
See Souster, (Holmes) Raymond

Holmes, John Clellon 1926-1988 ...... **CLC 56**
See also BG 2; CA 9-12R; 125; CANR 4; DLB 16, 237

Holmes, Oliver Wendell, Jr. 1841-1935 .... **TCLC 77**
See also CA 114; 186

Holmes, Oliver Wendell 1809-1894 .... **NCLC 14, 81**
See also AMWS 1; CDALB 1640-1865; DLB 1, 189, 235; EXPP; RGAL 4; SATA 34

Holmes, Raymond
See Souster, (Holmes) Raymond

Holt, Victoria
See Hibbert, Eleanor Alice Burford
See also BPFB 2

Holub, Miroslav 1923-1998 .... **CLC 4**
See also CA 21-24R; 169; CANR 10; CDWLB 4; CWW 2; DLB 232; EWL 3; RGWL 3

Holz, Detlev
See Benjamin, Walter

Homer c. 8th cent. B.C.- .... **CMLC 1, 16, 61; PC 23; WLCS**
See also AW 1; CDWLB 1; DA; DA3; DAB; DAC; DAM MST, POET; DLB 176; EFS 1; LAIT 1; LMFS 1; RGWL 2, 3; TWA; WP

Hongo, Garrett Kaoru 1951- .... **PC 23**
See also CA 133; CAAS 22; CP 7; DLB 120; EWL 3; EXPP; RGAL 4

Honig, Edwin 1919- .... **CLC 33**
See also CA 5-8R; CAAS 8; CANR 4, 45; CP 7; DLB 5

Hood, Hugh (John Blagdon) 1928- . **CLC 15, 28; SSC 42**
See also CA 49-52; CAAS 17; CANR 1, 33, 87; CN 7; DLB 53; RGSF 2

Hood, Thomas 1799-1845 .... **NCLC 16**
See also BRW 4; DLB 96; RGEL 2

Hooker, (Peter) Jeremy 1941- .... **CLC 43**
See also CA 77-80; CANR 22; CP 7; DLB 40

Hooker, Richard 1554-1600 .... **LC 95**
See also BRW 1; DLB 132; RGEL 2

hooks, bell
See Watkins, Gloria Jean

Hope, A(lec) D(erwent) 1907-2000 .... **CLC 3, 51; PC 56**
See also BRWS 7; CA 21-24R; 188; CANR 33, 74; DLB 289; EWL 3; MTCW 1, 2; PFS 8; RGEL 2

Hope, Anthony 1863-1933 .... **TCLC 83**
See also CA 157; DLB 153, 156; RGEL 2; RHW

Hope, Brian
See Creasey, John

Hope, Christopher (David Tully) 1944- .... **CLC 52**
See also AFW; CA 106; CANR 47, 101; CN 7; DLB 225; SATA 62

Hopkins, Gerard Manley 1844-1889 .... **NCLC 17; PC 15; WLC**
See also BRW 5; BRWR 2; CDBLB 1890-1914; DA; DA3; DAB; DAC; DAM MST, POET; DLB 35, 57; EXPP; PAB; RGEL 2; TEA; WP

Hopkins, John (Richard) 1931-1998 .. **CLC 4**
See also CA 85-88; 169; CBD; CD 5

Hopkins, Pauline Elizabeth 1859-1930 .... **BLC 2; TCLC 28**
See also AFAW 2; BW 2, 3; CA 141; CANR 82; DAM MULT; DLB 50

Hopkinson, Francis 1737-1791 .... **LC 25**
See also DLB 31; RGAL 4

Hopley-Woolrich, Cornell George 1903-1968
See Woolrich, Cornell
See also CA 13-14; CANR 58; CAP 1; CMW 4; DLB 226; MTCW 2

Horace 65B.C.-8B.C. .... **CMLC 39; PC 46**
See also AW 2; CDWLB 1; DLB 211; RGWL 2, 3

Horatio
See Proust, (Valentin-Louis-George-Eugene) Marcel

Horgan, Paul (George Vincent O'Shaughnessy) 1903-1995 .. **CLC 9, 53**
See also BPFB 2; CA 13-16R; 147; CANR 9, 35; DAM NOV; DLB 102, 212; DLBY 1985; INT CANR-9; MTCW 1, 2; SATA 13; SATA-Obit 84; TCWW 2

Horkheimer, Max 1895-1973 .... **TCLC 132**
See also CA 216; 41-44R; DLB 296

Horn, Peter
See Kuttner, Henry

Horne, Frank (Smith) 1899-1974 .... **HR 2**
See also BW 1; CA 125; 53-56; DLB 51; WP

Horne, Richard Henry Hengist 1802(?)-1884 .... **NCLC 127**
See also DLB 32; SATA 29

Hornem, Horace Esq.
See Byron, George Gordon (Noel)

Horney, Karen (Clementine Theodore Danielsen) 1885-1952 .... **TCLC 71**
See also CA 114; 165; DLB 246; FW

Hornung, E(rnest) W(illiam) 1866-1921 .... **TCLC 59**
See also CA 108; 160; CMW 4; DLB 70

Horovitz, Israel (Arthur) 1939- .... **CLC 56**
See also CA 33-36R; CAD; CANR 46, 59; CD 5; DAM DRAM; DLB 7

Horton, George Moses 1797(?)-1883(?) .... **NCLC 87**
See also DLB 50

Horvath, odon von 1901-1938
See von Horvath, Odon
See also EWL 3

Horvath, Oedoen von -1938
See von Horvath, Odon

Horwitz, Julius 1920-1986 .... **CLC 14**
See also CA 9-12R; 119; CANR 12

Hospital, Janette Turner 1942- .... **CLC 42, 145**
See also CA 108; CANR 48; CN 7; DLBY 2002; RGSF 2

Hostos, E. M. de
See Hostos (y Bonilla), Eugenio Maria de

Hostos, Eugenio M. de
See Hostos (y Bonilla), Eugenio Maria de

Hostos, Eugenio Maria
See Hostos (y Bonilla), Eugenio Maria de

Hostos (y Bonilla), Eugenio Maria de 1839-1903 .... **TCLC 24**
See also CA 123; 131; HW 1

Houdini
See Lovecraft, H(oward) P(hillips)

Houellebecq, Michel 1958- .... **CLC 179**
See also CA 185

Hougan, Carolyn 1943- .... **CLC 34**
See also CA 139

Household, Geoffrey (Edward West) 1900-1988 .... **CLC 11**
See also CA 77-80; 126; CANR 58; CMW 4; DLB 87; SATA 14; SATA-Obit 59

Housman, A(lfred) E(dward) 1859-1936 .... **PC 2, 43; TCLC 1, 10; WLCS**
See also BRW 6; CA 104; 125; DA; DA3; DAB; DAC; DAM MST, POET; DLB 19, 284; EWL 3; EXPP; MTCW 1, 2; PAB; PFS 4, 7; RGEL 2; TEA; WP

Housman, Laurence 1865-1959 .... **TCLC 7**
See also CA 106; 155; DLB 10; FANT; RGEL 2; SATA 25

Houston, Jeanne (Toyo) Wakatsuki 1934- .... **AAL**
See also AAYA 49; CA 103; CAAS 16; CANR 29, 123; LAIT 4; SATA 78

Howard, Elizabeth Jane 1923- ..... **CLC 7, 29**
See also CA 5-8R; CANR 8, 62; CN 7

Howard, Maureen 1930- .... **CLC 5, 14, 46, 151**
See also CA 53-56; CANR 31, 75; CN 7; DLBY 1983; INT CANR-31; MTCW 1, 2

Howard, Richard 1929- .... **CLC 7, 10, 47**
See also AITN 1; CA 85-88; CANR 25, 80; CP 7; DLB 5; INT CANR-25

Howard, Robert E(rvin) 1906-1936 .... **TCLC 8**
See also BPFB 2; BYA 5; CA 105; 157; FANT; SUFW 1

Howard, Warren F.
See Pohl, Frederik

Howe, Fanny (Quincy) 1940- .... **CLC 47**
See also CA 117, 187; CAAE 187; CAAS 27; CANR 70, 116; CP 7; CWP; SATA-Brief 52

Howe, Irving 1920-1993 .... **CLC 85**
See also AMWS 6; CA 9-12R; 141; CANR 21, 50; DLB 67; EWL 3; MTCW 1, 2

Howe, Julia Ward 1819-1910 .... **TCLC 21**
See also CA 117; 191; DLB 1, 189, 235; FW

Howe, Susan 1937- .... **CLC 72, 152; PC 54**
See also AMWS 4; CA 160; CP 7; CWP; DLB 120; FW; RGAL 4

Howe, Tina 1937- .... **CLC 48**
See also CA 109; CAD; CANR 125; CD 5; CWD

Howell, James 1594(?)-1666 .... **LC 13**
See also DLB 151

Howells, W. D.
See Howells, William Dean

Howells, William D.
See Howells, William Dean

Howells, William Dean 1837-1920 ... **SSC 36; TCLC 7, 17, 41**
See also AMW; CA 104; 134; CDALB 1865-1917; DLB 12, 64, 74, 79, 189; LMFS 1; MTCW 2; RGAL 4; TUS

Howes, Barbara 1914-1996 .... **CLC 15**
See also CA 9-12R; 151; CAAS 3; CANR 53; CP 7; SATA 5

Hrabal, Bohumil 1914-1997 ...... **CLC 13, 67; TCLC 155**
See also CA 106; 156; CAAS 12; CANR 57; CWW 2; DLB 232; EWL 3; RGSF 2

Hrotsvit of Gandersheim c. 935-c. 1000 .... **CMLC 29**
See also DLB 148

Hsi, Chu 1130-1200 .... **CMLC 42**

Hsun, Lu
See Lu Hsun

Hubbard, L(afayette) Ron(ald) 1911-1986 .... **CLC 43**
See also CA 77-80; 118; CANR 52; CPW; DA3; DAM POP; FANT; MTCW 2; SFW 4

Huch, Ricarda (Octavia) 1864-1947 .... **TCLC 13**
See also CA 111; 189; DLB 66; EWL 3

Huddle, David 1942- .... **CLC 49**
See also CA 57-60; CAAS 20; CANR 89; DLB 130

Hudson, Jeffrey
See Crichton, (John) Michael

Hudson, W(illiam) H(enry) 1841-1922 .... **TCLC 29**
See also CA 115; 190; DLB 98, 153, 174; RGEL 2; SATA 35

Hueffer, Ford Madox
See Ford, Ford Madox

Hughart, Barry 1934- .... **CLC 39**
See also CA 137; FANT; SFW 4; SUFW 2

Hughes, Colin
See Creasey, John

Hughes, David (John) 1930- .... **CLC 48**
See also CA 116; 129; CN 7; DLB 14

Hughes, Edward James
See Hughes, Ted
See also DA3; DAM MST, POET

Hughes, (James Mercer) Langston 1902-1967 ..... **BLC 2; CLC 1, 5, 10, 15, 35, 44, 108; DC 3; HR 2; PC 1, 53; SSC 6; WLC**
See also AAYA 12; AFAW 1, 2; AMWR 1; AMWS 1; BW 1, 3; CA 1-4R; 25-28R; CANR 1, 34, 82; CDALB 1929-1941; CLR 17; DA; DA3; DAB; DAC; DAM DRAM, MST, MULT, POET; DFS 6, 18; DLB 4, 7, 48, 51, 86, 228; EWL 3; EXPP; EXPS; JRDA; LAIT 3; LMFS 2; MAICYA 1, 2; MTCW 1, 2; PAB; PFS 1, 3, 6, 10, 15; RGAL 4; RGSF 2; SATA 4, 33; SSFS 4, 7; TUS; WCH; WP; YAW

Hughes, Richard (Arthur Warren) 1900-1976 .... **CLC 1, 11**
See also CA 5-8R; 65-68; CANR 4; DAM NOV; DLB 15, 161; EWL 3; MTCW 1; RGEL 2; SATA 8; SATA-Obit 25

Hughes, Ted 1930-1998 . **CLC 2, 4, 9, 14, 37, 119; PC 7**
See Hughes, Edward James
See also BRWC 2; BRWR 2; BRWS 1; CA 1-4R; 171; CANR 1, 33, 66, 108; CLR 3; CP 7; DAB; DAC; DLB 40, 161; EWL 3; EXPP; MAICYA 1, 2; MTCW 1, 2; PAB; PFS 4, 19; RGEL 2; SATA 49; SATA-Brief 27; SATA-Obit 107; TEA; YAW

Hugo, Richard
See Huch, Ricarda (Octavia)

Hugo, Richard F(ranklin) 1923-1982 .... **CLC 6, 18, 32**
See also AMWS 6; CA 49-52; 108; CANR 3; DAM POET; DLB 5, 206; EWL 3; PFS 17; RGAL 4

Hugo, Victor (Marie) 1802-1885 .... **NCLC 3, 10, 21; PC 17; WLC**
See also AAYA 28; DA; DA3; DAB; DAC; DAM DRAM, MST, NOV, POET; DLB 119, 192, 217; EFS 2; EW 6; EXPN; GFL 1789 to the Present; LAIT 1, 2; NFS 5, 20; RGWL 2, 3; SATA 47; TWA

Huidobro, Vicente
See Huidobro Fernandez, Vicente Garcia
See also DLB 283; EWL 3; LAW

Huidobro Fernandez, Vicente Garcia 1893-1948 .... **TCLC 31**
See Huidobro, Vicente
See also CA 131; HW 1

Hulme, Keri 1947- .... **CLC 39, 130**
See also CA 125; CANR 69; CN 7; CP 7; CWP; EWL 3; FW; INT CA-125

Hulme, T(homas) E(rnest) 1883-1917 .... **TCLC 21**
See also BRWS 6; CA 117; 203; DLB 19

Humboldt, Wilhelm von 1767-1835 .... **NCLC 134**
See also DLB 90

Hume, David 1711-1776 .... **LC 7, 56**
See also BRWS 3; DLB 104, 252; LMFS 1; TEA

Humphrey, William 1924-1997 .... **CLC 45**
See also AMWS 9; CA 77-80; 160; CANR 68; CN 7; CSW; DLB 6, 212, 234, 278; TCWW 2

Humphreys, Emyr Owen 1919- .... **CLC 47**
See also CA 5-8R; CANR 3, 24; CN 7; DLB 15

Humphreys, Josephine 1945- ..... **CLC 34, 57**
See also CA 121; 127; CANR 97; CSW; DLB 292; INT CA-127

Huneker, James Gibbons 1860-1921 .... **TCLC 65**
See also CA 193; DLB 71; RGAL 4

Hungerford, Hesba Fay
See Brinsmead, H(esba) F(ay)

Hungerford, Pixie
See Brinsmead, H(esba) F(ay)

Hunt, E(verette) Howard, (Jr.) 1918- .... **CLC 3**
See also AITN 1; CA 45-48; CANR 2, 47, 103; CMW 4

Hunt, Francesca
See Holland, Isabelle (Christian)

Hunt, Howard
See Hunt, E(verette) Howard, (Jr.)

Hunt, Kyle
See Creasey, John

Hunt, (James Henry) Leigh 1784-1859 .... **NCLC 1, 70**
See also DAM POET; DLB 96, 110, 144; RGEL 2; TEA

Hunt, Marsha 1946- .... **CLC 70**
See also BW 2, 3; CA 143; CANR 79

Hunt, Violet 1866(?)-1942 .... **TCLC 53**
See also CA 184; DLB 162, 197

Hunter, E. Waldo
See Sturgeon, Theodore (Hamilton)

Hunter, Evan 1926- .... **CLC 11, 31**
See McBain, Ed
See also AAYA 39; BPFB 2; CA 5-8R; CANR 5, 38, 62, 97; CMW 4; CN 7; CPW; DAM POP; DLB 306; DLBY 1982; INT CANR-5; MSW; MTCW 1; SATA 25; SFW 4

Hunter, Kristin
See Lattany, Kristin (Elaine Eggleston) Hunter

Hunter, Mary
See Austin, Mary (Hunter)

Hunter, Mollie 1922- .... **CLC 21**
See McIlwraith, Maureen Mollie Hunter
See also AAYA 13; BYA 6; CANR 37, 78; CLR 25; DLB 161; JRDA; MAICYA 1, 2; SAAS 7; SATA 54, 106, 139; SATA-Essay 139; WYA; YAW

Hunter, Robert (?)-1734 .... **LC 7**

Hurston, Zora Neale 1891-1960 .... **BLC 2; CLC 7, 30, 61; DC 12; HR 2; SSC 4, 80; TCLC 121, 131; WLCS**
See also AAYA 15; AFAW 1, 2; AMWS 6; BW 1, 3; BYA 12; CA 85-88; CANR 61; CDALBS; DA; DA3; DAC; DAM MST, MULT, NOV; DFS 6; DLB 51, 86; EWL 3; EXPN; EXPS; FW; LAIT 3; LATS 1:1; LMFS 2; MAWW; MTCW 1, 2; NFS 3; RGAL 4; RGSF 2; SSFS 1, 6, 11, 19; TUS; YAW

Husserl, E. G.
See Husserl, Edmund (Gustav Albrecht)

Husserl, Edmund (Gustav Albrecht) 1859-1938 .... **TCLC 100**
See also CA 116; 133; DLB 296

Huston, John (Marcellus) 1906-1987 .... **CLC 20**
See also CA 73-76; 123; CANR 34; DLB 26

Hustvedt, Siri 1955- .... **CLC 76**
See also CA 137

Hutten, Ulrich von 1488-1523 .... **LC 16**
See also DLB 179

Huxley, Aldous (Leonard) 1894-1963 .... **CLC 1, 3, 4, 5, 8, 11, 18, 35, 79; SSC 39; WLC**
See also AAYA 11; BPFB 2; BRW 7; CA 85-88; CANR 44, 99; CDBLB 1914-1945; DA; DA3; DAB; DAC; DAM MST, NOV; DLB 36, 100, 162, 195, 255; EWL 3; EXPN; LAIT 5; LMFS 2; MTCW 1, 2; NFS 6; RGEL 2; SATA 63; SCFW 2; SFW 4; TEA; YAW

Huxley, T(homas) H(enry) 1825-1895 .... **NCLC 67**
See also DLB 57; TEA

Huygens, Constantijn 1596-1687 .... **LC 114**
See also

Huysmans, Joris-Karl 1848-1907 ... **TCLC 7, 69**
See also CA 104; 165; DLB 123; EW 7; GFL 1789 to the Present; LMFS 2; RGWL 2, 3

Hwang, David Henry 1957- .... **CLC 55, 196; DC 4, 23**
See also CA 127; 132; CAD; CANR 76, 124; CD 5; DA3; DAM DRAM; DFS 11, 18; DLB 212, 228; INT CA-132; MTCW 2; RGAL 4

Hyde, Anthony 1946- .... **CLC 42**
See Chase, Nicholas
See also CA 136; CCA 1

Hyde, Margaret O(ldroyd) 1917- ...... **CLC 21**
See also CA 1-4R; CANR 1, 36; CLR 23; JRDA; MAICYA 1, 2; SAAS 8; SATA 1, 42, 76, 139

Hynes, James 1956(?)- .... **CLC 65**
See also CA 164; CANR 105

Hypatia c. 370-415 .... **CMLC 35**

Ian, Janis 1951- .... **CLC 21**
See also CA 105; 187

Ibanez, Vicente Blasco
See Blasco Ibanez, Vicente

Ibarbourou, Juana de
1895(?)-1979 .... **HLCS 2**
See also DLB 290; HW 1; LAW

Ibarguengoitia, Jorge 1928-1983 ..... **CLC 37; TCLC 148**
See also CA 124; 113; EWL 3; HW 1

Ibn Battuta, Abu Abdalla
1304-1368(?) .... **CMLC 57**
See also WLIT 2

Ibn Hazm 994-1064 .... **CMLC 64**

Ibsen, Henrik (Johan) 1828-1906 .... **DC 2; TCLC 2, 8, 16, 37, 52; WLC**
See also AAYA 46; CA 104; 141; DA; DA3; DAB; DAC; DAM DRAM, MST; DFS 1, 6, 8, 10, 11, 15, 16; EW 7; LAIT 2; LATS 1:1; RGWL 2, 3

Ibuse, Masuji 1898-1993 .... **CLC 22**
See Ibuse Masuji
See also CA 127; 141; MJW; RGWL 3

Ibuse Masuji
See Ibuse, Masuji
See also CWW 2; DLB 180; EWL 3

Ichikawa, Kon 1915- .... **CLC 20**
See also CA 121

Ichiyo, Higuchi 1872-1896 .... **NCLC 49**
See also MJW

Idle, Eric 1943- .... **CLC 21**
See Monty Python
See also CA 116; CANR 35, 91

Idris, Yusuf 1927-1991 .... **SSC 74**
See also AFW; EWL 3; RGSF 2, 3; RGWL 3; WLIT 2

Ignatow, David 1914-1997 .... **CLC 4, 7, 14, 40; PC 34**
See also CA 9-12R; 162; CAAS 3; CANR 31, 57, 96; CP 7; DLB 5; EWL 3

Ignotus
See Strachey, (Giles) Lytton

Ihimaera, Witi (Tame) 1944- .... **CLC 46**
See also CA 77-80; CANR 130; CN 7; RGSF 2; SATA 148

Ilf, Ilya .... **TCLC 21**
See Fainzilberg, Ilya Arnoldovich
See also EWL 3

Illyes, Gyula 1902-1983 .... **PC 16**
See also CA 114; 109; CDWLB 4; DLB 215; EWL 3; RGWL 2, 3

Imalayen, Fatima-Zohra
See Djebar, Assia

Immermann, Karl (Lebrecht)
1796-1840 .... **NCLC 4, 49**
See also DLB 133

Ince, Thomas H. 1882-1924 .... **TCLC 89**
See also IDFW 3, 4

Inchbald, Elizabeth 1753-1821 ...... **NCLC 62**
See also DLB 39, 89; RGEL 2

Inclan, Ramon (Maria) del Valle
See Valle-Inclan, Ramon (Maria) del

Infante, G(uillermo) Cabrera
See Cabrera Infante, G(uillermo)

Ingalls, Rachel (Holmes) 1940- .... **CLC 42**
See also CA 123; 127

Ingamells, Reginald Charles
See Ingamells, Rex

Ingamells, Rex 1913-1955 .... **TCLC 35**
See also CA 167; DLB 260

Inge, William (Motter) 1913-1973 ..... **CLC 1, 8, 19**
See also CA 9-12R; CDALB 1941-1968; DA3; DAM DRAM; DFS 1, 3, 5, 8; DLB 7, 249; EWL 3; MTCW 1, 2; RGAL 4; TUS

Ingelow, Jean 1820-1897 .... **NCLC 39, 107**
See also DLB 35, 163; FANT; SATA 33

Ingram, Willis J.
See Harris, Mark

Innaurato, Albert (F.) 1948(?)- ... **CLC 21, 60**
See also CA 115; 122; CAD; CANR 78; CD 5; INT CA-122

Innes, Michael
See Stewart, J(ohn) I(nnes) M(ackintosh)
See also DLB 276; MSW

Innis, Harold Adams 1894-1952 .... **TCLC 77**
See also CA 181; DLB 88

Insluis, Alanus de
See Alain de Lille

Iola
See Wells-Barnett, Ida B(ell)

Ionesco, Eugene 1912-1994 ... **CLC 1, 4, 6, 9, 11, 15, 41, 86; DC 12; WLC**
See also CA 9-12R; 144; CANR 55, 132; CWW 2; DA; DA3; DAB; DAC; DAM DRAM, MST; DFS 4, 9; EW 13; EWL 3; GFL 1789 to the Present; LMFS 2; MTCW 1, 2; RGWL 2, 3; SATA 7; SATA-Obit 79; TWA

Iqbal, Muhammad 1877-1938 .... **TCLC 28**
See also CA 215; EWL 3

Ireland, Patrick
See O'Doherty, Brian

Irenaeus St. 130- .... **CMLC 42**

Irigaray, Luce 1930- .... **CLC 164**
See also CA 154; CANR 121; FW

Iron, Ralph
See Schreiner, Olive (Emilie Albertina)

Irving, John (Winslow) 1942- ... **CLC 13, 23, 38, 112, 175**
See also AAYA 8; AMWS 6; BEST 89:3; BPFB 2; CA 25-28R; CANR 28, 73, 112, 133; CN 7; CPW; DA3; DAM NOV, POP; DLB 6, 278; DLBY 1982; EWL 3; MTCW 1, 2; NFS 12, 14; RGAL 4; TUS

Irving, Washington 1783-1859 . **NCLC 2, 19, 95; SSC 2, 37; WLC**
See also AAYA 56; AMW; CDALB 1640-1865; CLR 97; DA; DA3; DAB; DAC; DAM MST; DLB 3, 11, 30, 59, 73, 74, 183, 186, 250, 254; EXPS; LAIT 1; RGAL 4; RGSF 2; SSFS 1, 8, 16; SUFW 1; TUS; WCH; YABC 2

Irwin, P. K.
See Page, P(atricia) K(athleen)

Isaacs, Jorge Ricardo 1837-1895 ... **NCLC 70**
See also LAW

Isaacs, Susan 1943- .... **CLC 32**
See also BEST 89:1; BPFB 2; CA 89-92; CANR 20, 41, 65, 112, 134; CPW; DA3; DAM POP; INT CANR-20; MTCW 1, 2

Isherwood, Christopher (William Bradshaw) 1904-1986 .... **CLC 1, 9, 11, 14, 44; SSC 56**
See also AMWS 14; BRW 7; CA 13-16R; 117; CANR 35, 97, 133; DA3; DAM DRAM, NOV; DLB 15, 195; DLBY 1986; EWL 3; IDTP; MTCW 1, 2; RGAL 4; RGEL 2; TUS; WLIT 4

Ishiguro, Kazuo 1954- .. **CLC 27, 56, 59, 110**
See also AAYA 58; BEST 90:2; BPFB 2; BRWS 4; CA 120; CANR 49, 95, 133; CN 7; DA3; DAM NOV; DLB 194; EWL 3; MTCW 1, 2; NFS 13; WLIT 4; WWE 1

Ishikawa, Hakuhin
See Ishikawa, Takuboku

Ishikawa, Takuboku 1886(?)-1912 ...... **PC 10; TCLC 15**
See Ishikawa Takuboku
See also CA 113; 153; DAM POET

Iskander, Fazil (Abdulovich) 1929- .. **CLC 47**
See Iskander, Fazil' Abdulevich
See also CA 102; EWL 3

Iskander, Fazil' Abdulevich
See Iskander, Fazil (Abdulovich)
See also DLB 302

Isler, Alan (David) 1934- .... **CLC 91**
See also CA 156; CANR 105

Ivan IV 1530-1584 .... **LC 17**

Ivanov, Vyacheslav Ivanovich
1866-1949 .... **TCLC 33**
See also CA 122; EWL 3

Ivask, Ivar Vidrik 1927-1992 .... **CLC 14**
See also CA 37-40R; 139; CANR 24

Ives, Morgan
See Bradley, Marion Zimmer
See also GLL 1

Izumi Shikibu c. 973-c. 1034 .... **CMLC 33**

J. R. S.
See Gogarty, Oliver St. John

Jabran, Kahlil
See Gibran, Kahlil

Jabran, Khalil
See Gibran, Kahlil

Jackson, Daniel
See Wingrove, David (John)

Jackson, Helen Hunt 1830-1885 .... **NCLC 90**
See also DLB 42, 47, 186, 189; RGAL 4

Jackson, Jesse 1908-1983 .... **CLC 12**
See also BW 1; CA 25-28R; 109; CANR 27; CLR 28; CWRI 5; MAICYA 1, 2; SATA 2, 29; SATA-Obit 48

Jackson, Laura (Riding) 1901-1991 .... **PC 44**
See Riding, Laura
See also CA 65-68; 135; CANR 28, 89; DLB 48

Jackson, Sam
See Trumbo, Dalton

Jackson, Sara
See Wingrove, David (John)

Jackson, Shirley 1919-1965 . **CLC 11, 60, 87; SSC 9, 39; WLC**
See also AAYA 9; AMWS 9; BPFB 2; CA 1-4R; 25-28R; CANR 4, 52; CDALB 1941-1968; DA; DA3; DAC; DAM MST; DLB 6, 234; EXPS; HGG; LAIT 4; MTCW 2; RGAL 4; RGSF 2; SATA 2; SSFS 1; SUFW 1, 2

Jacob, (Cyprien-)Max 1876-1944 .... **TCLC 6**
See also CA 104; 193; DLB 258; EWL 3; GFL 1789 to the Present; GLL 2; RGWL 2, 3

Jacobs, Harriet A(nn)
1813(?)-1897 .... **NCLC 67**
See also AFAW 1, 2; DLB 239; FW; LAIT 2; RGAL 4

Jacobs, Jim 1942- .... **CLC 12**
See also CA 97-100; INT CA-97-100

Jacobs, W(illiam) W(ymark)
1863-1943 .... **SSC 73; TCLC 22**
See also CA 121; 167; DLB 135; EXPS; HGG; RGEL 2; RGSF 2; SSFS 2; SUFW 1

Jacobsen, Jens Peter 1847-1885 .... **NCLC 34**

Jacobsen, Josephine (Winder)
1908-2003 .... **CLC 48, 102; PC 62**
See also CA 33-36R; 218; CAAS 18; CANR 23, 48; CCA 1; CP 7; DLB 244

Jacobson, Dan 1929- .... **CLC 4, 14**
See also AFW; CA 1-4R; CANR 2, 25, 66; CN 7; DLB 14, 207, 225; EWL 3; MTCW 1; RGSF 2

Jacqueline
See Carpentier (y Valmont), Alejo

Jacques de Vitry c. 1160-1240 ...... **CMLC 63**
See also DLB 208

Jagger, Mick 1944- .... **CLC 17**

Jahiz, al- c. 780-c. 869 .... **CMLC 25**

Jakes, John (William) 1932- .... **CLC 29**
See also AAYA 32; BEST 89:4; BPFB 2; CA 57-60, 214; CAAE 214; CANR 10, 43, 66, 111; CPW; CSW; DA3; DAM NOV, POP; DLB 278; DLBY 1983; FANT; INT CANR-10; MTCW 1, 2; RHW; SATA 62; SFW 4; TCWW 2

James I 1394-1437 .... **LC 20**
See also RGEL 2

James, Andrew
See Kirkup, James

James, C(yril) L(ionel) R(obert)
1901-1989 .... **BLCS; CLC 33**
See also BW 2; CA 117; 125; 128; CANR 62; DLB 125; MTCW 1

James, Daniel (Lewis) 1911-1988
See Santiago, Danny
See also CA 174; 125

James, Dynely
See Mayne, William (James Carter)

James, Henry Sr. 1811-1882 .... **NCLC 53**

James, Henry 1843-1916 .... **SSC 8, 32, 47; TCLC 2, 11, 24, 40, 47, 64; WLC**
See also AMW; AMWC 1; AMWR 1; BPFB 2; BRW 6; CA 104; 132; CDALB 1865-1917; DA; DA3; DAB; DAC; DAM MST, NOV; DLB 12, 71, 74, 189; DLBD 13; EWL 3; EXPS; HGG; LAIT 2; MTCW 1, 2; NFS 12, 16, 19; RGAL 4; RGEL 2; RGSF 2; SSFS 9; SUFW 1; TUS

James, M. R.
See James, Montague (Rhodes)
See also DLB 156, 201

James, Montague (Rhodes)
1862-1936 .... **SSC 16; TCLC 6**
See James, M. R.
See also CA 104; 203; HGG; RGEL 2; RGSF 2; SUFW 1

James, P. D. .... **CLC 18, 46, 122**
See White, Phyllis Dorothy James
See also BEST 90:2; BPFB 2; BRWS 4; CDBLB 1960 to Present; DLB 87, 276; DLBD 17; MSW

James, Philip
See Moorcock, Michael (John)

James, Samuel
See Stephens, James

James, Seumas
See Stephens, James

James, Stephen
See Stephens, James

James, William 1842-1910 .... **TCLC 15, 32**
See also AMW; CA 109; 193; DLB 270, 284; NCFS 5; RGAL 4

Jameson, Anna 1794-1860 .... **NCLC 43**
See also DLB 99, 166

Jameson, Fredric (R.) 1934- .... **CLC 142**
See also CA 196; DLB 67; LMFS 2

James VI of Scotland 1566-1625 .... **LC 109**
See also DLB 151, 172

Jami, Nur al-Din 'Abd al-Rahman
1414-1492 .... **LC 9**

Jammes, Francis 1868-1938 .... **TCLC 75**
See also CA 198; EWL 3; GFL 1789 to the Present

Jandl, Ernst 1925-2000 .... **CLC 34**
See also CA 200; EWL 3

Janowitz, Tama 1957- .... **CLC 43, 145**
See also CA 106; CANR 52, 89, 129; CN 7; CPW; DAM POP; DLB 292

Japrisot, Sebastien 1931- .... **CLC 90**
See Rossi, Jean-Baptiste
See also CMW 4; NFS 18

Jarrell, Randall 1914-1965 .... **CLC 1, 2, 6, 9, 13, 49; PC 41**
See also AMW; BYA 5; CA 5-8R; 25-28R; CABS 2; CANR 6, 34; CDALB 1941-1968; CLR 6; CWRI 5; DAM POET; DLB 48, 52; EWL 3; EXPP; MAICYA 1, 2; MTCW 1, 2; PAB; PFS 2; RGAL 4; SATA 7

Jarry, Alfred 1873-1907 .... **SSC 20; TCLC 2, 14, 147**
See also CA 104; 153; DA3; DAM DRAM; DFS 8; DLB 192, 258; EW 9; EWL 3; GFL 1789 to the Present; RGWL 2, 3; TWA

Jarvis, E. K.
See Ellison, Harlan (Jay)

Jawien, Andrzej
See John Paul II, Pope

Jaynes, Roderick
See Coen, Ethan

Jeake, Samuel, Jr.
See Aiken, Conrad (Potter)

Jean Paul 1763-1825 .... **NCLC 7**

Jefferies, (John) Richard
1848-1887 .... **NCLC 47**
See also DLB 98, 141; RGEL 2; SATA 16; SFW 4

Jeffers, (John) Robinson 1887-1962 .. **CLC 2, 3, 11, 15, 54; PC 17; WLC**
See also AMWS 2; CA 85-88; CANR 35; CDALB 1917-1929; DA; DAC; DAM MST, POET; DLB 45, 212; EWL 3; MTCW 1, 2; PAB; PFS 3, 4; RGAL 4

Jefferson, Janet
See Mencken, H(enry) L(ouis)

Jefferson, Thomas 1743-1826 . **NCLC 11, 103**
See also AAYA 54; ANW; CDALB 1640-1865; DA3; DLB 31, 183; LAIT 1; RGAL 4

Jeffrey, Francis 1773-1850 .... **NCLC 33**
See Francis, Lord Jeffrey

Jelakowitch, Ivan
See Heijermans, Herman

Jelinek, Elfriede 1946- .... **CLC 169**
See also CA 154; DLB 85; FW

Jellicoe, (Patricia) Ann 1927- .... **CLC 27**
See also CA 85-88; CBD; CD 5; CWD; CWRI 5; DLB 13, 233; FW

Jelloun, Tahar ben 1944- .... **CLC 180**
See Ben Jelloun, Tahar
See also CA 162; CANR 100

Jemyma
See Holley, Marietta

Jen, Gish .... **AAL; CLC 70, 198**
See Jen, Lillian
See also AMWC 2

Jen, Lillian 1956(?)-
See Jen, Gish
See also CA 135; CANR 89, 130

Jenkins, (John) Robin 1912- .... **CLC 52**
See also CA 1-4R; CANR 1, 135; CN 7; DLB 14, 271

Jennings, Elizabeth (Joan)
1926-2001 .... **CLC 5, 14, 131**
See also BRWS 5; CA 61-64; 200; CAAS 5; CANR 8, 39, 66, 127; CP 7; CWP; DLB 27; EWL 3; MTCW 1; SATA 66

Jennings, Waylon 1937- .... **CLC 21**

Jensen, Johannes V(ilhelm)
1873-1950 .... **TCLC 41**
See also CA 170; DLB 214; EWL 3; RGWL 3

Jensen, Laura (Linnea) 1948- .... **CLC 37**
See also CA 103

Jerome, Saint 345-420 .... **CMLC 30**
See also RGWL 3

Jerome, Jerome K(lapka)
1859-1927 .... **TCLC 23**
See also CA 119; 177; DLB 10, 34, 135; RGEL 2

Jerrold, Douglas William
1803-1857 .... **NCLC 2**
See also DLB 158, 159; RGEL 2

Jewett, (Theodora) Sarah Orne
1849-1909 .... **SSC 6, 44; TCLC 1, 22**
See also AMW; AMWC 2; AMWR 2; CA 108; 127; CANR 71; DLB 12, 74, 221; EXPS; FW; MAWW; NFS 15; RGAL 4; RGSF 2; SATA 15; SSFS 4

Jewsbury, Geraldine (Endsor)
1812-1880 .... **NCLC 22**
See also DLB 21

Jhabvala, Ruth Prawer 1927- . **CLC 4, 8, 29, 94, 138**
See also BRWS 5; CA 1-4R; CANR 2, 29, 51, 74, 91, 128; CN 7; DAB; DAM NOV; DLB 139, 194; EWL 3; IDFW 3, 4; INT CANR-29; MTCW 1, 2; RGSF 2; RGWL 2; RHW; TEA

Jibran, Kahlil
See Gibran, Kahlil

Jibran, Khalil
See Gibran, Kahlil

Jiles, Paulette 1943- .... **CLC 13, 58**
See also CA 101; CANR 70, 124; CWP

Jimenez (Mantecon), Juan Ramon
1881-1958 .... **HLC 1; PC 7; TCLC 4**
See also CA 104; 131; CANR 74; DAM MULT, POET; DLB 134; EW 9; EWL 3; HW 1; MTCW 1, 2; RGWL 2, 3

Jimenez, Ramon
See Jimenez (Mantecon), Juan Ramon

Jimenez Mantecon, Juan
See Jimenez (Mantecon), Juan Ramon

Jin, Ha .... **CLC 109**
See Jin, Xuefei
See also CA 152; DLB 244, 292; SSFS 17

Jin, Xuefei 1956-
See Jin, Ha
See also CANR 91, 130; SSFS 17

Joel, Billy .... **CLC 26**
See Joel, William Martin

Joel, William Martin 1949-
See Joel, Billy
See also CA 108

John, Saint 10(?)-100 .... **CMLC 27, 63**

John of Salisbury c. 1115-1180 ..... **CMLC 63**

John of the Cross, St. 1542-1591 .... **LC 18**
See also RGWL 2, 3

John Paul II, Pope 1920- .... **CLC 128**
See also CA 106; 133

Johnson, B(ryan) S(tanley William)
1933-1973 .... **CLC 6, 9**
See also CA 9-12R; 53-56; CANR 9; DLB 14, 40; EWL 3; RGEL 2

Johnson, Benjamin F., of Boone
See Riley, James Whitcomb

Johnson, Charles (Richard) 1948- .... **BLC 2; CLC 7, 51, 65, 163**
See also AFAW 2; AMWS 6; BW 2, 3; CA 116; CAAS 18; CANR 42, 66, 82, 129; CN 7; DAM MULT; DLB 33, 278; MTCW 2; RGAL 4; SSFS 16

Johnson, Charles S(purgeon) 1893-1956 .... **HR 3**
See also BW 1, 3; CA 125; CANR 82; DLB 51, 91

Johnson, Denis 1949- . **CLC 52, 160; SSC 56**
See also CA 117; 121; CANR 71, 99; CN 7; DLB 120

Johnson, Diane 1934- .... **CLC 5, 13, 48**
See also BPFB 2; CA 41-44R; CANR 17, 40, 62, 95; CN 7; DLBY 1980; INT CANR-17; MTCW 1

Johnson, E. Pauline 1861-1913 .... **NNAL**
See also CA 150; DAC; DAM MULT; DLB 92, 175

Johnson, Eyvind (Olof Verner) 1900-1976 .... **CLC 14**
See also CA 73-76; 69-72; CANR 34, 101; DLB 259; EW 12; EWL 3

Johnson, Fenton 1888-1958 .... **BLC 2**
See also BW 1; CA 118; 124; DAM MULT; DLB 45, 50

Johnson, Georgia Douglas (Camp) 1880-1966 .... **HR 3**
See also BW 1; CA 125; DLB 51, 249; WP

Johnson, Helene 1907-1995 .... **HR 3**
See also CA 181; DLB 51; WP

Johnson, J. R.
See James, C(yril) L(ionel) R(obert)

Johnson, James Weldon 1871-1938 .. **BLC 2; HR 3; PC 24; TCLC 3, 19**
See also AFAW 1, 2; BW 1, 3; CA 104; 125; CANR 82; CDALB 1917-1929; CLR 32; DA3; DAM MULT, POET; DLB 51; EWL 3; EXPP; LMFS 2; MTCW 1, 2; PFS 1; RGAL 4; SATA 31; TUS

Johnson, Joyce 1935- .... **CLC 58**
See also BG 3; CA 125; 129; CANR 102

Johnson, Judith (Emlyn) 1936- .... **CLC 7, 15**
See Sherwin, Judith Johnson
See also CA 25-28R; 153; CANR 34

Johnson, Lionel (Pigot) 1867-1902 .... **TCLC 19**
See also CA 117; 209; DLB 19; RGEL 2

Johnson, Marguerite Annie
See Angelou, Maya

Johnson, Mel
See Malzberg, Barry N(athaniel)

Johnson, Pamela Hansford 1912-1981 .... **CLC 1, 7, 27**
See also CA 1-4R; 104; CANR 2, 28; DLB 15; MTCW 1, 2; RGEL 2

Johnson, Paul (Bede) 1928- .... **CLC 147**
See also BEST 89:4; CA 17-20R; CANR 34, 62, 100

Johnson, Robert .... **CLC 70**

Johnson, Robert 1911(?)-1938 .... **TCLC 69**
See also BW 3; CA 174

Johnson, Samuel 1709-1784 .... **LC 15, 52; WLC**
See also BRW 3; BRWR 1; CDBLB 1660-1789; DA; DAB; DAC; DAM MST; DLB 39, 95, 104, 142, 213; LMFS 1; RGEL 2; TEA

Johnson, Uwe 1934-1984 .. **CLC 5, 10, 15, 40**
See also CA 1-4R; 112; CANR 1, 39; CDWLB 3; DLB 75; EWL 3; MTCW 1; RGWL 2, 3

Johnston, Basil H. 1929- .... **NNAL**
See also CA 69-72; CANR 11, 28, 66; DAC; DAM MULT; DLB 60

Johnston, George (Benson) 1913- .... **CLC 51**
See also CA 1-4R; CANR 5, 20; CP 7; DLB 88

Johnston, Jennifer (Prudence) 1930- .... **CLC 7, 150**
See also CA 85-88; CANR 92; CN 7; DLB 14

Joinville, Jean de 1224(?)-1317 ..... **CMLC 38**

Jolley, (Monica) Elizabeth 1923- ...... **CLC 46; SSC 19**
See also CA 127; CAAS 13; CANR 59; CN 7; EWL 3; RGSF 2

Jones, Arthur Llewellyn 1863-1947
See Machen, Arthur
See also CA 104; 179; HGG

Jones, D(ouglas) G(ordon) 1929- ...... **CLC 10**
See also CA 29-32R; CANR 13, 90; CP 7; DLB 53

Jones, David (Michael) 1895-1974 .... **CLC 2, 4, 7, 13, 42**
See also BRW 6; BRWS 7; CA 9-12R; 53-56; CANR 28; CDBLB 1945-1960; DLB 20, 100; EWL 3; MTCW 1; PAB; RGEL 2

Jones, David Robert 1947-
See Bowie, David
See also CA 103; CANR 104

Jones, Diana Wynne 1934- .... **CLC 26**
See also AAYA 12; BYA 6, 7, 9, 11, 13, 16; CA 49-52; CANR 4, 26, 56, 120; CLR 23; DLB 161; FANT; JRDA; MAICYA 1, 2; SAAS 7; SATA 9, 70, 108; SFW 4; SUFW 2; YAW

Jones, Edward P. 1950- .... **CLC 76**
See also BW 2, 3; CA 142; CANR 79, 134; CSW

Jones, Gayl 1949- ...... **BLC 2; CLC 6, 9, 131**
See also AFAW 1, 2; BW 2, 3; CA 77-80; CANR 27, 66, 122; CN 7; CSW; DA3; DAM MULT; DLB 33, 278; MTCW 1, 2; RGAL 4

Jones, James 1921-1977 ...... **CLC 1, 3, 10, 39**
See also AITN 1, 2; AMWS 11; BPFB 2; CA 1-4R; 69-72; CANR 6; DLB 2, 143; DLBD 17; DLBY 1998; EWL 3; MTCW 1; RGAL 4

Jones, John J.
See Lovecraft, H(oward) P(hillips)

Jones, LeRoi .... **CLC 1, 2, 3, 5, 10, 14**
See Baraka, Amiri
See also MTCW 2

Jones, Louis B. 1953- .... **CLC 65**
See also CA 141; CANR 73

Jones, Madison (Percy, Jr.) 1925- ...... **CLC 4**
See also CA 13-16R; CAAS 11; CANR 7, 54, 83; CN 7; CSW; DLB 152

Jones, Mervyn 1922- .... **CLC 10, 52**
See also CA 45-48; CAAS 5; CANR 1, 91; CN 7; MTCW 1

Jones, Mick 1956(?)- .... **CLC 30**

Jones, Nettie (Pearl) 1941- .... **CLC 34**
See also BW 2; CA 137; CAAS 20; CANR 88

Jones, Peter 1802-1856 .... **NNAL**

Jones, Preston 1936-1979 .... **CLC 10**
See also CA 73-76; 89-92; DLB 7

Jones, Robert F(rancis) 1934-2003 .... **CLC 7**
See also CA 49-52; CANR 2, 61, 118

Jones, Rod 1953- .... **CLC 50**
See also CA 128

Jones, Terence Graham Parry 1942- .... **CLC 21**
See Jones, Terry; Monty Python
See also CA 112; 116; CANR 35, 93; INT CA-116; SATA 127

Jones, Terry
See Jones, Terence Graham Parry
See also SATA 67; SATA-Brief 51

Jones, Thom (Douglas) 1945(?)- ...... **CLC 81; SSC 56**
See also CA 157; CANR 88; DLB 244

Jong, Erica 1942- .... **CLC 4, 6, 8, 18, 83**
See also AITN 1; AMWS 5; BEST 90:2; BPFB 2; CA 73-76; CANR 26, 52, 75, 132; CN 7; CP 7; CPW; DA3; DAM NOV, POP; DLB 2, 5, 28, 152; FW; INT CANR-26; MTCW 1, 2

Jonson, Ben(jamin) 1572(?)-1637 . **DC 4; LC 6, 33, 110; PC 17; WLC**
See also BRW 1; BRWC 1; BRWR 1; CDBLB Before 1660; DA; DAB; DAC; DAM DRAM, MST, POET; DFS 4, 10; DLB 62, 121; LMFS 1; RGEL 2; TEA; WLIT 3

Jordan, June (Meyer) 1936-2002 .. **BLCS; CLC 5, 11, 23, 114; PC 38**
See also AAYA 2; AFAW 1, 2; BW 2, 3; CA 33-36R; 206; CANR 25, 70, 114; CLR 10; CP 7; CWP; DAM MULT, POET; DLB 38; GLL 2; LAIT 5; MAICYA 1, 2; MTCW 1; SATA 4, 136; YAW

Jordan, Neil (Patrick) 1950- .... **CLC 110**
See also CA 124; 130; CANR 54; CN 7; GLL 2; INT CA-130

Jordan, Pat(rick M.) 1941- .... **CLC 37**
See also CA 33-36R; CANR 121

Jorgensen, Ivar
See Ellison, Harlan (Jay)

Jorgenson, Ivar
See Silverberg, Robert

Joseph, George Ghevarughese .... **CLC 70**

Josephson, Mary
See O'Doherty, Brian

Josephus, Flavius c. 37-100 .... **CMLC 13**
See also AW 2; DLB 176

Josiah Allen's Wife
See Holley, Marietta

Josipovici, Gabriel (David) 1940- ...... **CLC 6, 43, 153**
See also CA 37-40R; 224; CAAE 224; CAAS 8; CANR 47, 84; CN 7; DLB 14

Joubert, Joseph 1754-1824 .... **NCLC 9**

Jouve, Pierre Jean 1887-1976 .... **CLC 47**
See also CA 65-68; DLB 258; EWL 3

Jovine, Francesco 1902-1950 .... **TCLC 79**
See also DLB 264; EWL 3

Joyce, James (Augustine Aloysius) 1882-1941 .... **DC 16; PC 22; SSC 3, 26, 44, 64; TCLC 3, 8, 16, 35, 52, 159; WLC**
See also AAYA 42; BRW 7; BRWC 1; BRWR 1; BYA 11, 13; CA 104; 126; CDBLB 1914-1945; DA; DA3; DAB; DAC; DAM MST, NOV, POET; DLB 10, 19, 36, 162, 247; EWL 3; EXPN; EXPS; LAIT 3; LMFS 1, 2; MTCW 1, 2; NFS 7; RGSF 2; SSFS 1, 19; TEA; WLIT 4

Jozsef, Attila 1905-1937 .... **TCLC 22**
See also CA 116; CDWLB 4; DLB 215; EWL 3

Juana Ines de la Cruz, Sor 1651(?)-1695 ...... **HLCS 1; LC 5; PC 24**
See also DLB 305; FW; LAW; RGWL 2, 3; WLIT 1

Juana Inez de La Cruz, Sor
See Juana Ines de la Cruz, Sor

Judd, Cyril
See Kornbluth, C(yril) M.; Pohl, Frederik

Juenger, Ernst 1895-1998 .... **CLC 125**
See Junger, Ernst
See also CA 101; 167; CANR 21, 47, 106; DLB 56

Julian of Norwich 1342(?)-1416(?) . **LC 6, 52**
See also DLB 146; LMFS 1

Julius Caesar 100B.C.-44B.C.
See Caesar, Julius
See also CDWLB 1; DLB 211

Junger, Ernst
See Juenger, Ernst
See also CDWLB 2; EWL 3; RGWL 2, 3

Junger, Sebastian 1962- .... **CLC 109**
See also AAYA 28; CA 165; CANR 130

Juniper, Alex
See Hospital, Janette Turner

Junius
See Luxemburg, Rosa

Just, Ward (Swift) 1935- .... **CLC 4, 27**
See also CA 25-28R; CANR 32, 87; CN 7; INT CANR-32

Justice, Donald (Rodney)
1925-2004 .... **CLC 6, 19, 102; PC 64**
See also AMWS 7; CA 5-8R; CANR 26, 54, 74, 121, 122; CP 7; CSW; DAM POET; DLBY 1983; EWL 3; INT CANR-26; MTCW 2; PFS 14

Juvenal c. 60-c. 130 .... **CMLC 8**
See also AW 2; CDWLB 1; DLB 211; RGWL 2, 3

Juvenis
See Bourne, Randolph S(illiman)

K., Alice
See Knapp, Caroline

Kabakov, Sasha .... **CLC 59**

Kabir 1398(?)-1448(?) .... **LC 109; PC 56**
See also RGWL 2, 3

Kacew, Romain 1914-1980
See Gary, Romain
See also CA 108; 102

Kadare, Ismail 1936- .... **CLC 52, 190**
See also CA 161; EWL 3; RGWL 3

Kadohata, Cynthia 1956(?)- ...... **CLC 59, 122**
See also CA 140; CANR 124

Kafka, Franz 1883-1924 ... **SSC 5, 29, 35, 60; TCLC 2, 6, 13, 29, 47, 53, 112; WLC**
See also AAYA 31; BPFB 2; CA 105; 126; CDWLB 2; DA; DA3; DAB; DAC; DAM MST, NOV; DLB 81; EW 3; EWL 3; EXPS; LATS 1:1; LMFS 2; MTCW 1, 2; NFS 7; RGSF 2; RGWL 2, 3; SFW 4; SSFS 3, 7, 12; TWA

Kahanovitsch, Pinkhes
See Der Nister

Kahn, Roger 1927- .... **CLC 30**
See also CA 25-28R; CANR 44, 69; DLB 171; SATA 37

Kain, Saul
See Sassoon, Siegfried (Lorraine)

Kaiser, Georg 1878-1945 .... **TCLC 9**
See also CA 106; 190; CDWLB 2; DLB 124; EWL 3; LMFS 2; RGWL 2, 3

Kaledin, Sergei .... **CLC 59**

Kaletski, Alexander 1946- .... **CLC 39**
See also CA 118; 143

Kalidasa fl. c. 400-455 .... **CMLC 9; PC 22**
See also RGWL 2, 3

Kallman, Chester (Simon)
1921-1975 .... **CLC 2**
See also CA 45-48; 53-56; CANR 3

Kaminsky, Melvin 1926-
See Brooks, Mel
See also CA 65-68; CANR 16

Kaminsky, Stuart M(elvin) 1934- ...... **CLC 59**
See also CA 73-76; CANR 29, 53, 89; CMW 4

Kamo no Chomei 1153(?)-1216 .... **CMLC 66**
See also DLB 203

Kamo no Nagaakira
See Kamo no Chomei

Kandinsky, Wassily 1866-1944 .... **TCLC 92**
See also CA 118; 155

Kane, Francis
See Robbins, Harold

Kane, Henry 1918-
See Queen, Ellery
See also CA 156; CMW 4

Kane, Paul
See Simon, Paul (Frederick)

Kanin, Garson 1912-1999 .... **CLC 22**
See also AITN 1; CA 5-8R; 177; CAD; CANR 7, 78; DLB 7; IDFW 3, 4

Kaniuk, Yoram 1930- .... **CLC 19**
See also CA 134; DLB 299

Kant, Immanuel 1724-1804 ..... **NCLC 27, 67**
See also DLB 94

Kantor, MacKinlay 1904-1977 .... **CLC 7**
See also CA 61-64; 73-76; CANR 60, 63; DLB 9, 102; MTCW 2; RHW; TCWW 2

Kanze Motokiyo
See Zeami

Kaplan, David Michael 1946- .... **CLC 50**
See also CA 187

Kaplan, James 1951- .... **CLC 59**
See also CA 135; CANR 121

Karadzic, Vuk Stefanovic
1787-1864 .... **NCLC 115**
See also CDWLB 4; DLB 147

Karageorge, Michael
See Anderson, Poul (William)

Karamzin, Nikolai Mikhailovich
1766-1826 .... **NCLC 3**
See also DLB 150; RGSF 2

Karapanou, Margarita 1946- .... **CLC 13**
See also CA 101

Karinthy, Frigyes 1887-1938 .... **TCLC 47**
See also CA 170; DLB 215; EWL 3

Karl, Frederick R(obert)
1927-2004 .... **CLC 34**
See also CA 5-8R; 226; CANR 3, 44

Karr, Mary 1955- .... **CLC 188**
See also AMWS 11; CA 151; CANR 100; NCFS 5

Kastel, Warren
See Silverberg, Robert

Kataev, Evgeny Petrovich 1903-1942
See Petrov, Evgeny
See also CA 120

Kataphusin
See Ruskin, John

Katz, Steve 1935- .... **CLC 47**
See also CA 25-28R; CAAS 14, 64; CANR 12; CN 7; DLBY 1983

Kauffman, Janet 1945- .... **CLC 42**
See also CA 117; CANR 43, 84; DLB 218; DLBY 1986

Kaufman, Bob (Garnell) 1925-1986 . **CLC 49**
See also BG 3; BW 1; CA 41-44R; 118; CANR 22; DLB 16, 41

Kaufman, George S. 1889-1961 .... **CLC 38; DC 17**
See also CA 108; 93-96; DAM DRAM; DFS 1, 10; DLB 7; INT CA-108; MTCW 2; RGAL 4; TUS

Kaufman, Sue .... **CLC 3, 8**
See Barondess, Sue K(aufman)

Kavafis, Konstantinos Petrou 1863-1933
See Cavafy, C(onstantine) P(eter)
See also CA 104

Kavan, Anna 1901-1968 .... **CLC 5, 13, 82**
See also BRWS 7; CA 5-8R; CANR 6, 57; DLB 255; MTCW 1; RGEL 2; SFW 4

Kavanagh, Dan
See Barnes, Julian (Patrick)

Kavanagh, Julie 1952- .... **CLC 119**
See also CA 163

Kavanagh, Patrick (Joseph)
1904-1967 .... **CLC 22; PC 33**
See also BRWS 7; CA 123; 25-28R; DLB 15, 20; EWL 3; MTCW 1; RGEL 2

Kawabata, Yasunari 1899-1972 ..... **CLC 2, 5, 9, 18, 107; SSC 17**
See Kawabata Yasunari
See also CA 93-96; 33-36R; CANR 88; DAM MULT; MJW; MTCW 2; RGSF 2; RGWL 2, 3

Kawabata Yasunari
See Kawabata, Yasunari
See also DLB 180; EWL 3

Kaye, M(ary) M(argaret)
1908-2004 .... **CLC 28**
See also CA 89-92; 223; CANR 24, 60, 102; MTCW 1, 2; RHW; SATA 62; SATA-Obit 152

Kaye, Mollie
See Kaye, M(ary) M(argaret)

Kaye-Smith, Sheila 1887-1956 .... **TCLC 20**
See also CA 118; 203; DLB 36

Kaymor, Patrice Maguilene
See Senghor, Leopold Sedar

Kazakov, Iurii Pavlovich
See Kazakov, Yuri Pavlovich
See also DLB 302

Kazakov, Yuri Pavlovich 1927-1982 . **SSC 43**
See Kazakov, Iurii Pavlovich; Kazakov, Yury
See also CA 5-8R; CANR 36; MTCW 1; RGSF 2

Kazakov, Yury
See Kazakov, Yuri Pavlovich
See also EWL 3

Kazan, Elia 1909-2003 .... **CLC 6, 16, 63**
See also CA 21-24R; 220; CANR 32, 78

Kazantzakis, Nikos 1883(?)-1957 .... **TCLC 2, 5, 33**
See also BPFB 2; CA 105; 132; DA3; EW 9; EWL 3; MTCW 1, 2; RGWL 2, 3

Kazin, Alfred 1915-1998 ..... **CLC 34, 38, 119**
See also AMWS 8; CA 1-4R; CAAS 7; CANR 1, 45, 79; DLB 67; EWL 3

Keane, Mary Nesta (Skrine) 1904-1996
See Keane, Molly
See also CA 108; 114; 151; CN 7; RHW

Keane, Molly .... **CLC 31**
See Keane, Mary Nesta (Skrine)
See also INT CA-114

Keates, Jonathan 1946(?)- .... **CLC 34**
See also CA 163; CANR 126

Keaton, Buster 1895-1966 .... **CLC 20**
See also CA 194

Keats, John 1795-1821 ...... **NCLC 8, 73, 121; PC 1; WLC**
See also AAYA 58; BRW 4; BRWR 1; CDBLB 1789-1832; DA; DA3; DAB; DAC; DAM MST, POET; DLB 96, 110; EXPP; LMFS 1; PAB; PFS 1, 2, 3, 9, 17; RGEL 2; TEA; WLIT 3; WP

Keble, John 1792-1866 .... **NCLC 87**
See also DLB 32, 55; RGEL 2

Keene, Donald 1922- .... **CLC 34**
See also CA 1-4R; CANR 5, 119

Keillor, Garrison .... **CLC 40, 115**
See Keillor, Gary (Edward)
See also AAYA 2; BEST 89:3; BPFB 2; DLBY 1987; EWL 3; SATA 58; TUS

Keillor, Gary (Edward) 1942-
See Keillor, Garrison
See also CA 111; 117; CANR 36, 59, 124; CPW; DA3; DAM POP; MTCW 1, 2

Keith, Carlos
See Lewton, Val

Keith, Michael
See Hubbard, L(afayette) Ron(ald)

Keller, Gottfried 1819-1890 .... **NCLC 2; SSC 26**
See also CDWLB 2; DLB 129; EW; RGSF 2; RGWL 2, 3

Keller, Nora Okja 1965- .... **CLC 109**
See also CA 187

Kellerman, Jonathan 1949- .... **CLC 44**
See also AAYA 35; BEST 90:1; CA 106; CANR 29, 51; CMW 4; CPW; DA3; DAM POP; INT CANR-29

Kelley, William Melvin 1937- .... **CLC 22**
See also BW 1; CA 77-80; CANR 27, 83; CN 7; DLB 33; EWL 3

Kellogg, Marjorie 1922- .... **CLC 2**
See also CA 81-84

Kellow, Kathleen
See Hibbert, Eleanor Alice Burford

Kelly, M(ilton) T(errence) 1947- .... **CLC 55**
See also CA 97-100; CAAS 22; CANR 19, 43, 84; CN 7

Kelly, Robert 1935- .... **SSC 50**
See also CA 17-20R; CAAS 19; CANR 47; CP 7; DLB 5, 130, 165

Kelman, James 1946- .... **CLC 58, 86**
See also BRWS 5; CA 148; CANR 85, 130; CN 7; DLB 194; RGSF 2; WLIT 4

Kemal, Yasar
See Kemal, Yashar
See also CWW 2; EWL 3

Kemal, Yashar 1923(?)- .... **CLC 14, 29**
See also CA 89-92; CANR 44

Kemble, Fanny 1809-1893 .... **NCLC 18**
See also DLB 32

Kemelman, Harry 1908-1996 .... **CLC 2**
See also AITN 1; BPFB 2; CA 9-12R; 155; CANR 6, 71; CMW 4; DLB 28

Kempe, Margery 1373(?)-1440(?) ... **LC 6, 56**
See also DLB 146; RGEL 2

Kempis, Thomas a 1380-1471 .... **LC 11**

Kendall, Henry 1839-1882 .... **NCLC 12**
See also DLB 230

Keneally, Thomas (Michael) 1935- ... **CLC 5, 8, 10, 14, 19, 27, 43, 117**
See also BRWS 4; CA 85-88; CANR 10, 50, 74, 130; CN 7; CPW; DA3; DAM NOV; DLB 289, 299; EWL 3; MTCW 1, 2; NFS 17; RGEL 2; RHW

Kennedy, A(lison) L(ouise) 1965- ... **CLC 188**
See also CA 168, 213; CAAE 213; CANR 108; CD 5; CN 7; DLB 271; RGSF 2

Kennedy, Adrienne (Lita) 1931- .... **BLC 2; CLC 66; DC 5**
See also AFAW 2; BW 2, 3; CA 103; CAAS 20; CABS 3; CANR 26, 53, 82; CD 5; DAM MULT; DFS 9; DLB 38; FW

Kennedy, John Pendleton
1795-1870 .... **NCLC 2**
See also DLB 3, 248, 254; RGAL 4

Kennedy, Joseph Charles 1929-
See Kennedy, X. J.
See also CA 1-4R, 201; CAAE 201; CANR 4, 30, 40; CP 7; CWRI 5; MAICYA 2; MAICYAS 1; SATA 14, 86, 130; SATA-Essay 130

Kennedy, William 1928- ... **CLC 6, 28, 34, 53**
See also AAYA 1; AMWS 7; BPFB 2; CA 85-88; CANR 14, 31, 76, 134; CN 7; DA3; DAM NOV; DLB 143; DLBY 1985; EWL 3; INT CANR-31; MTCW 1, 2; SATA 57

Kennedy, X. J. .... **CLC 8, 42**
See Kennedy, Joseph Charles
See also CAAS 9; CLR 27; DLB 5; SAAS 22

Kenny, Maurice (Francis) 1929- ..... **CLC 87; NNAL**
See also CA 144; CAAS 22; DAM MULT; DLB 175

Kent, Kelvin
See Kuttner, Henry

Kenton, Maxwell
See Southern, Terry

Kenyon, Jane 1947-1995 .... **PC 57**
See also AMWS 7; CA 118; 148; CANR 44, 69; CP 7; CWP; DLB 120; PFS 9, 17; RGAL 4

Kenyon, Robert O.
See Kuttner, Henry

Kepler, Johannes 1571-1630 .... **LC 45**

Ker, Jill
See Conway, Jill K(er)

Kerkow, H. C.
See Lewton, Val

Kerouac, Jack 1922-1969 ...... **CLC 1, 2, 3, 5, 14, 29, 61; TCLC 117; WLC**
See Kerouac, Jean-Louis Lebris de
See also AAYA 25; AMWC 1; AMWS 3; BG 3; BPFB 2; CDALB 1941-1968; CPW; DLB 2, 16, 237; DLBD 3; DLBY 1995; EWL 3; GLL 1; LAIT 1:2; LMFS 2; MTCW 2; NFS 8; RGAL 4; TUS; WP

Kerouac, Jean-Louis Lebris de 1922-1969
See Kerouac, Jack
See also AITN 1; CA 5-8R; 25-28R; CANR 26, 54, 95; DA; DA3; DAB; DAC; DAM MST, NOV, POET, POP; MTCW 1, 2

Kerr, (Bridget) Jean (Collins)
1923(?)-2003 .... **CLC 22**
See also CA 5-8R; 212; CANR 7; INT CANR-7

Kerr, M. E. .... **CLC 12, 35**
See Meaker, Marijane (Agnes)
See also AAYA 2, 23; BYA 1, 7, 8; CLR 29; SAAS 1; WYA

Kerr, Robert .... **CLC 55**

Kerrigan, (Thomas) Anthony 1918- .. **CLC 4, 6**
See also CA 49-52; CAAS 11; CANR 4

Kerry, Lois
See Duncan, Lois

Kesey, Ken (Elton) 1935-2001 ... **CLC 1, 3, 6, 11, 46, 64, 184; WLC**
See also AAYA 25; BG 3; BPFB 2; CA 1-4R; 204; CANR 22, 38, 66, 124; CDALB 1968-1988; CN 7; CPW; DA; DA3; DAB; DAC; DAM MST, NOV, POP; DLB 2, 16, 206; EWL 3; EXPN; LAIT 4; MTCW 1, 2; NFS 2; RGAL 4; SATA 66; SATA-Obit 131; TUS; YAW

Kesselring, Joseph (Otto)
1902-1967 .... **CLC 45**
See also CA 150; DAM DRAM, MST; DFS 20

Kessler, Jascha (Frederick) 1929- ...... **CLC 4**
See also CA 17-20R; CANR 8, 48, 111

Kettelkamp, Larry (Dale) 1933- .... **CLC 12**
See also CA 29-32R; CANR 16; SAAS 3; SATA 2

Key, Ellen (Karolina Sofia)
1849-1926 .... **TCLC 65**
See also DLB 259

Keyber, Conny
See Fielding, Henry

Keyes, Daniel 1927- .... **CLC 80**
See also AAYA 23; BYA 11; CA 17-20R, 181; CAAE 181; CANR 10, 26, 54, 74; DA; DA3; DAC; DAM MST, NOV; EXPN; LAIT 4; MTCW 2; NFS 2; SATA 37; SFW 4

Keynes, John Maynard
1883-1946 .... **TCLC 64**
See also CA 114; 162, 163; DLBD 10; MTCW 2

Khanshendel, Chiron
See Rose, Wendy

Khayyam, Omar 1048-1131 ... **CMLC 11; PC 8**
See Omar Khayyam
See also DA3; DAM POET

Kherdian, David 1931- .... **CLC 6, 9**
See also AAYA 42; CA 21-24R, 192; CAAE 192; CAAS 2; CANR 39, 78; CLR 24; JRDA; LAIT 3; MAICYA 1, 2; SATA 16, 74; SATA-Essay 125

Khlebnikov, Velimir .... **TCLC 20**
See Khlebnikov, Viktor Vladimirovich
See also DLB 295; EW 10; EWL 3; RGWL 2, 3

Khlebnikov, Viktor Vladimirovich 1885-1922
See Khlebnikov, Velimir
See also CA 117; 217

Khodasevich, Vladislav (Felitsianovich)
1886-1939 .... **TCLC 15**
See also CA 115; EWL 3

Kielland, Alexander Lange
1849-1906 .... **TCLC 5**
See also CA 104

Kiely, Benedict 1919- ... **CLC 23, 43; SSC 58**
See also CA 1-4R; CANR 2, 84; CN 7; DLB 15

Kienzle, William X(avier)
1928-2001 .... **CLC 25**
See also CA 93-96; 203; CAAS 1; CANR 9, 31, 59, 111; CMW 4; DA3; DAM POP; INT CANR-31; MSW; MTCW 1, 2

Kierkegaard, Soren 1813-1855 ..... **NCLC 34, 78, 125**
See also DLB 300; EW 6; LMFS 2; RGWL 3; TWA

Kieslowski, Krzysztof 1941-1996 .... **CLC 120**
See also CA 147; 151

Killens, John Oliver 1916-1987 .... **CLC 10**
See also BW 2; CA 77-80; 123; CAAS 2; CANR 26; DLB 33; EWL 3

Killigrew, Anne 1660-1685 .... **LC 4, 73**
See also DLB 131

Killigrew, Thomas 1612-1683 .... **LC 57**
See also DLB 58; RGEL 2

Kim
See Simenon, Georges (Jacques Christian)

Kincaid, Jamaica 1949- ...... **BLC 2; CLC 43, 68, 137; SSC 72**
See also AAYA 13, 56; AFAW 2; AMWS 7; BRWS 7; BW 2, 3; CA 125; CANR 47, 59, 95, 133; CDALBS; CDWLB 3; CLR 63; CN 7; DA3; DAM MULT, NOV; DLB 157, 227; DNFS 1; EWL 3; EXPS; FW; LATS 1:2; LMFS 2; MTCW 2; NCFS 1; NFS 3; SSFS 5, 7; TUS; WWE 1; YAW

King, Francis (Henry) 1923- .... **CLC 8, 53, 145**
See also CA 1-4R; CANR 1, 33, 86; CN 7; DAM NOV; DLB 15, 139; MTCW 1

King, Kennedy
See Brown, George Douglas

King, Martin Luther, Jr. 1929-1968 . **BLC 2; CLC 83; WLCS**
See also BW 2, 3; CA 25-28; CANR 27, 44; CAP 2; DA; DA3; DAB; DAC; DAM MST, MULT; LAIT 5; LATS 1:2; MTCW 1, 2; SATA 14

King, Stephen (Edwin) 1947- .... **CLC 12, 26, 37, 61, 113; SSC 17, 55**
See also AAYA 1, 17; AMWS 5; BEST 90:1; BPFB 2; CA 61-64; CANR 1, 30, 52, 76, 119, 134; CPW; DA3; DAM NOV, POP; DLB 143; DLBY 1980; HGG; JRDA; LAIT 5; MTCW 1, 2; RGAL 4; SATA 9, 55; SUFW 1, 2; WYAS 1; YAW

King, Steve
See King, Stephen (Edwin)

King, Thomas 1943- .... **CLC 89, 171; NNAL**
See also CA 144; CANR 95; CCA 1; CN 7; DAC; DAM MULT; DLB 175; SATA 96

Kingman, Lee .... **CLC 17**
See Natti, (Mary) Lee
See also CWRI 5; SAAS 3; SATA 1, 67

Kingsley, Charles 1819-1875 .... **NCLC 35**
See also CLR 77; DLB 21, 32, 163, 178, 190; FANT; MAICYA 2; MAICYAS 1; RGEL 2; WCH; YABC 2

Kingsley, Henry 1830-1876 .... **NCLC 107**
See also DLB 21, 230; RGEL 2

Kingsley, Sidney 1906-1995 .... **CLC 44**
See also CA 85-88; 147; CAD; DFS 14, 19; DLB 7; RGAL 4

Kingsolver, Barbara 1955- . **CLC 55, 81, 130**
See also AAYA 15; AMWS 7; CA 129; 134; CANR 60, 96, 133; CDALBS; CPW; CSW; DA3; DAM POP; DLB 206; INT CA-134; LAIT 5; MTCW 2; NFS 5, 10, 12; RGAL 4

Kingston, Maxine (Ting Ting) Hong 1940- .... **AAL; CLC 12, 19, 58, 121; WLCS**
See also AAYA 8, 55; AMWS 5; BPFB 2; CA 69-72; CANR 13, 38, 74, 87, 128; CDALBS; CN 7; DA3; DAM MULT, NOV; DLB 173, 212; DLBY 1980; EWL 3; FW; INT CANR-13; LAIT 5; MAWW; MTCW 1, 2; NFS 6; RGAL 4; SATA 53; SSFS 3

Kinnell, Galway 1927- ..... **CLC 1, 2, 3, 5, 13, 29, 129; PC 26**
See also AMWS 3; CA 9-12R; CANR 10, 34, 66, 116; CP 7; DLB 5; DLBY 1987; EWL 3; INT CANR-34; MTCW 1, 2; PAB; PFS 9; RGAL 4; WP

Kinsella, Thomas 1928- .... **CLC 4, 19, 138**
See also BRWS 5; CA 17-20R; CANR 15, 122; CP 7; DLB 27; EWL 3; MTCW 1, 2; RGEL 2; TEA

Kinsella, W(illiam) P(atrick) 1935- . **CLC 27, 43, 166**
See also AAYA 7, 60; BPFB 2; CA 97-100, 222; CAAE 222; CAAS 7; CANR 21, 35, 66, 75, 129; CN 7; CPW; DAC; DAM NOV, POP; FANT; INT CANR-21; LAIT 5; MTCW 1, 2; NFS 15; RGSF 2

Kinsey, Alfred C(harles) 1894-1956 .... **TCLC 91**
See also CA 115; 170; MTCW 2

Kipling, (Joseph) Rudyard 1865-1936 . **PC 3; SSC 5, 54; TCLC 8, 17; WLC**
See also AAYA 32; BRW 6; BRWC 1, 2; BYA 4; CA 105; 120; CANR 33; CDBLB 1890-1914; CLR 39, 65; CWRI 5; DA; DA3; DAB; DAC; DAM MST, POET; DLB 19, 34, 141, 156; EWL 3; EXPS; FANT; LAIT 3; LMFS 1; MAICYA 1, 2; MTCW 1, 2; RGEL 2; RGSF 2; SATA 100; SFW 4; SSFS 8; SUFW 1; TEA; WCH; WLIT 4; YABC 2

Kirk, Russell (Amos) 1918-1994 .. **TCLC 119**
See also AITN 1; CA 1-4R; 145; CAAS 9; CANR 1, 20, 60; HGG; INT CANR-20; MTCW 1, 2

Kirkham, Dinah
See Card, Orson Scott

Kirkland, Caroline M. 1801-1864 . **NCLC 85**
See also DLB 3, 73, 74, 250, 254; DLBD 13

Kirkup, James 1918- .... **CLC 1**
See also CA 1-4R; CAAS 4; CANR 2; CP 7; DLB 27; SATA 12

Kirkwood, James 1930(?)-1989 .... **CLC 9**
See also AITN 2; CA 1-4R; 128; CANR 6, 40; GLL 2

Kirsch, Sarah 1935- .... **CLC 176**
See also CA 178; CWW 2; DLB 75; EWL 3

Kirshner, Sidney
See Kingsley, Sidney

Kis, Danilo 1935-1989 .... **CLC 57**
See also CA 109; 118; 129; CANR 61; CDWLB 4; DLB 181; EWL 3; MTCW 1; RGSF 2; RGWL 2, 3

Kissinger, Henry A(lfred) 1923- ..... **CLC 137**
See also CA 1-4R; CANR 2, 33, 66, 109; MTCW 1

Kivi, Aleksis 1834-1872 .... **NCLC 30**

Kizer, Carolyn (Ashley) 1925- ... **CLC 15, 39, 80**
See also CA 65-68; CAAS 5; CANR 24, 70, 134; CP 7; CWP; DAM POET; DLB 5, 169; EWL 3; MTCW 2; PFS 18

Klabund 1890-1928 .... **TCLC 44**
See also CA 162; DLB 66

Klappert, Peter 1942- .... **CLC 57**
See also CA 33-36R; CSW; DLB 5

Klein, A(braham) M(oses) 1909-1972 .... **CLC 19**
See also CA 101; 37-40R; DAB; DAC; DAM MST; DLB 68; EWL 3; RGEL 2

Klein, Joe
See Klein, Joseph

Klein, Joseph 1946- .... **CLC 154**
See also CA 85-88; CANR 55

Klein, Norma 1938-1989 .... **CLC 30**
See also AAYA 2, 35; BPFB 2; BYA 6, 7, 8; CA 41-44R; 128; CANR 15, 37; CLR 2, 19; INT CANR-15; JRDA; MAICYA 1, 2; SAAS 1; SATA 7, 57; WYA; YAW

Klein, T(heodore) E(ibon) D(onald) 1947- .... **CLC 34**
See also CA 119; CANR 44, 75; HGG

Kleist, Heinrich von 1777-1811 ...... **NCLC 2, 37; SSC 22**
See also CDWLB 2; DAM DRAM; DLB 90; EW 5; RGSF 2; RGWL 2, 3

Klima, Ivan 1931- .... **CLC 56, 172**
See also CA 25-28R; CANR 17, 50, 91; CDWLB 4; CWW 2; DAM NOV; DLB 232; EWL 3; RGWL 3

Klimentev, Andrei Platonovich
See Klimentov, Andrei Platonovich

Klimentov, Andrei Platonovich 1899-1951 .... **SSC 42; TCLC 14**
See Platonov, Andrei Platonovich; Platonov, Andrey Platonovich
See also CA 108

Klinger, Friedrich Maximilian von 1752-1831 .... **NCLC 1**
See also DLB 94

Klingsor the Magician
See Hartmann, Sadakichi

Klopstock, Friedrich Gottlieb 1724-1803 .... **NCLC 11**
See also DLB 97; EW 4; RGWL 2, 3

Kluge, Alexander 1932- .... **SSC 61**
See also CA 81-84; DLB 75

Knapp, Caroline 1959-2002 .... **CLC 99**
See also CA 154; 207

Knebel, Fletcher 1911-1993 .... **CLC 14**
See also AITN 1; CA 1-4R; 140; CAAS 3; CANR 1, 36; SATA 36; SATA-Obit 75

Knickerbocker, Diedrich
See Irving, Washington

Knight, Etheridge 1931-1991 ... **BLC 2; CLC 40; PC 14**
See also BW 1, 3; CA 21-24R; 133; CANR 23, 82; DAM POET; DLB 41; MTCW 2; RGAL 4

Knight, Sarah Kemble 1666-1727 .... **LC 7**
See also DLB 24, 200

Knister, Raymond 1899-1932 .... **TCLC 56**
See also CA 186; DLB 68; RGEL 2

Knowles, John 1926-2001 ... **CLC 1, 4, 10, 26**
See also AAYA 10; AMWS 12; BPFB 2; BYA 3; CA 17-20R; 203; CANR 40, 74, 76, 132; CDALB 1968-1988; CLR 98; CN 7; DA; DAC; DAM MST, NOV; DLB 6; EXPN; MTCW 1, 2; NFS 2; RGAL 4; SATA 8, 89; SATA-Obit 134; YAW

Knox, Calvin M.
See Silverberg, Robert

Knox, John c. 1505-1572 .... **LC 37**
See also DLB 132

Knye, Cassandra
See Disch, Thomas M(ichael)

Koch, C(hristopher) J(ohn) 1932- .... **CLC 42**
See also CA 127; CANR 84; CN 7; DLB 289

Koch, Christopher
See Koch, C(hristopher) J(ohn)

Koch, Kenneth (Jay) 1925-2002 .... **CLC 5, 8, 44**
See also CA 1-4R; 207; CAD; CANR 6, 36, 57, 97, 131; CD 5; CP 7; DAM POET; DLB 5; INT CANR-36; MTCW 2; PFS 20; SATA 65; WP

Kochanowski, Jan 1530-1584 .... **LC 10**
See also RGWL 2, 3

Kock, Charles Paul de 1794-1871 . **NCLC 16**

Koda Rohan
See Koda Shigeyuki

Koda Rohan
See Koda Shigeyuki
See also DLB 180

Koda Shigeyuki 1867-1947 .... **TCLC 22**
See Koda Rohan
See also CA 121; 183

Koestler, Arthur 1905-1983 ... **CLC 1, 3, 6, 8, 15, 33**
See also BRWS 1; CA 1-4R; 109; CANR 1, 33; CDBLB 1945-1960; DLBY 1983; EWL 3; MTCW 1, 2; NFS 19; RGEL 2

Kogawa, Joy Nozomi 1935- .... **CLC 78, 129**
See also AAYA 47; CA 101; CANR 19, 62, 126; CN 7; CWP; DAC; DAM MST, MULT; FW; MTCW 2; NFS 3; SATA 99

Kohout, Pavel 1928- .... **CLC 13**
See also CA 45-48; CANR 3

Koizumi, Yakumo
See Hearn, (Patricio) Lafcadio (Tessima Carlos)

Kolmar, Gertrud 1894-1943 .... **TCLC 40**
See also CA 167; EWL 3

Komunyakaa, Yusef 1947- .. **BLCS; CLC 86, 94; PC 51**
See also AFAW 2; AMWS 13; CA 147; CANR 83; CP 7; CSW; DLB 120; EWL 3; PFS 5, 20; RGAL 4

Konrad, George
See Konrad, Gyorgy

Konrad, Gyorgy 1933- .... **CLC 4, 10, 73**
See also CA 85-88; CANR 97; CDWLB 4; CWW 2; DLB 232; EWL 3

Konwicki, Tadeusz 1926- .... **CLC 8, 28, 54, 117**
See also CA 101; CAAS 9; CANR 39, 59; CWW 2; DLB 232; EWL 3; IDFW 3; MTCW 1

Koontz, Dean R(ay) 1945- .... **CLC 78**
See also AAYA 9, 31; BEST 89:3, 90:2; CA 108; CANR 19, 36, 52, 95; CMW 4; CPW; DA3; DAM NOV, POP; DLB 292; HGG; MTCW 1; SATA 92; SFW 4; SUFW 2; YAW

Kopernik, Mikolaj
See Copernicus, Nicolaus

Kopit, Arthur (Lee) 1937- .... **CLC 1, 18, 33**
See also AITN 1; CA 81-84; CABS 3; CD 5; DAM DRAM; DFS 7, 14; DLB 7; MTCW 1; RGAL 4

Kopitar, Jernej (Bartholomaus) 1780-1844 .... **NCLC 117**

Kops, Bernard 1926- .... **CLC 4**
See also CA 5-8R; CANR 84; CBD; CN 7; CP 7; DLB 13

Kornbluth, C(yril) M. 1923-1958 .... **TCLC 8**
See also CA 105; 160; DLB 8; SFW 4

Korolenko, V. G.
See Korolenko, Vladimir Galaktionovich

Korolenko, Vladimir
See Korolenko, Vladimir Galaktionovich

Korolenko, Vladimir G.
See Korolenko, Vladimir Galaktionovich
Korolenko, Vladimir Galaktionovich
1853-1921 .... **TCLC 22**
See also CA 121; DLB 277
Korzybski, Alfred (Habdank Skarbek)
1879-1950 .... **TCLC 61**
See also CA 123; 160
Kosinski, Jerzy (Nikodem)
1933-1991 .... **CLC 1, 2, 3, 6, 10, 15, 53, 70**
See also AMWS 7; BPFB 2; CA 17-20R; 134; CANR 9, 46; DA3; DAM NOV; DLB 2, 299; DLBY 1982; EWL 3; HGG; MTCW 1, 2; NFS 12; RGAL 4; TUS
Kostelanetz, Richard (Cory) 1940- .. **CLC 28**
See also CA 13-16R; CAAS 8; CANR 38, 77; CN 7; CP 7
Kostrowitzki, Wilhelm Apollinaris de
1880-1918
See Apollinaire, Guillaume
See also CA 104
Kotlowitz, Robert 1924- .... **CLC 4**
See also CA 33-36R; CANR 36
Kotzebue, August (Friedrich Ferdinand) von
1761-1819 .... **NCLC 25**
See also DLB 94
Kotzwinkle, William 1938- ..... **CLC 5, 14, 35**
See also BPFB 2; CA 45-48; CANR 3, 44, 84, 129; CLR 6; DLB 173; FANT; MAICYA 1, 2; SATA 24, 70, 146; SFW 4; SUFW 2; YAW
Kowna, Stancy
See Szymborska, Wislawa
Kozol, Jonathan 1936- .... **CLC 17**
See also AAYA 46; CA 61-64; CANR 16, 45, 96
Kozoll, Michael 1940(?)- .... **CLC 35**
Kramer, Kathryn 19(?)- .... **CLC 34**
Kramer, Larry 1935- .... **CLC 42; DC 8**
See also CA 124; 126; CANR 60, 132; DAM POP; DLB 249; GLL 1
Krasicki, Ignacy 1735-1801 .... **NCLC 8**
Krasinski, Zygmunt 1812-1859 .... **NCLC 4**
See also RGWL 2, 3
Kraus, Karl 1874-1936 .... **TCLC 5**
See also CA 104; 216; DLB 118; EWL 3
Kreve (Mickevicius), Vincas
1882-1954 .... **TCLC 27**
See also CA 170; DLB 220; EWL 3
Kristeva, Julia 1941- .... **CLC 77, 140**
See also CA 154; CANR 99; DLB 242; EWL 3; FW; LMFS 2
Kristofferson, Kris 1936- .... **CLC 26**
See also CA 104
Krizanc, John 1956- .... **CLC 57**
See also CA 187
Krleza, Miroslav 1893-1981 .... **CLC 8, 114**
See also CA 97-100; 105; CANR 50; CDWLB 4; DLB 147; EW 11; RGWL 2, 3
Kroetsch, Robert 1927- .. **CLC 5, 23, 57, 132**
See also CA 17-20R; CANR 8, 38; CCA 1; CN 7; CP 7; DAC; DAM POET; DLB 53; MTCW 1
Kroetz, Franz
See Kroetz, Franz Xaver
Kroetz, Franz Xaver 1946- .... **CLC 41**
See also CA 130; CWW 2; EWL 3
Kroker, Arthur (W.) 1945- .... **CLC 77**
See also CA 161
Kropotkin, Peter (Aleksieevich)
1842-1921 .... **TCLC 36**
See Kropotkin, Petr Alekseevich
See also CA 119; 219
Kropotkin, Petr Alekseevich
See Kropotkin, Peter (Aleksieevich)
See also DLB 277
Krotkov, Yuri 1917-1981 .... **CLC 19**
See also CA 102

Krumb
See Crumb, R(obert)
Krumgold, Joseph (Quincy)
1908-1980 .... **CLC 12**
See also BYA 1, 2; CA 9-12R; 101; CANR 7; MAICYA 1, 2; SATA 1, 48; SATA-Obit 23; YAW
Krumwitz
See Crumb, R(obert)
Krutch, Joseph Wood 1893-1970 ..... **CLC 24**
See also ANW; CA 1-4R; 25-28R; CANR 4; DLB 63, 206, 275
Krutzch, Gus
See Eliot, T(homas) S(tearns)
Krylov, Ivan Andreevich
1768(?)-1844 .... **NCLC 1**
See also DLB 150
Kubin, Alfred (Leopold Isidor)
1877-1959 .... **TCLC 23**
See also CA 112; 149; CANR 104; DLB 81
Kubrick, Stanley 1928-1999 .... **CLC 16; TCLC 112**
See also AAYA 30; CA 81-84; 177; CANR 33; DLB 26
Kumin, Maxine (Winokur) 1925- ..... **CLC 5, 13, 28, 164; PC 15**
See also AITN 2; AMWS 4; ANW; CA 1-4R; CAAS 8; CANR 1, 21, 69, 115; CP 7; CWP; DA3; DAM POET; DLB 5; EWL 3; EXPP; MTCW 1, 2; PAB; PFS 18; SATA 12
Kundera, Milan 1929- . **CLC 4, 9, 19, 32, 68, 115, 135; SSC 24**
See also AAYA 2; BPFB 2; CA 85-88; CANR 19, 52, 74; CDWLB 4; CWW 2; DA3; DAM NOV; DLB 232; EW 13; EWL 3; MTCW 1, 2; NFS 18; RGSF 2; RGWL 3; SSFS 10
Kunene, Mazisi (Raymond) 1930- ... **CLC 85**
See also BW 1, 3; CA 125; CANR 81; CP 7; DLB 117
Kung, Hans .... **CLC 130**
See Kung, Hans
Kung, Hans 1928-
See Kung, Hans
See also CA 53-56; CANR 66, 134; MTCW 1, 2
Kunikida Doppo 1869(?)-1908
See Doppo, Kunikida
See also DLB 180; EWL 3
Kunitz, Stanley (Jasspon) 1905- .. **CLC 6, 11, 14, 148; PC 19**
See also AMWS 3; CA 41-44R; CANR 26, 57, 98; CP 7; DA3; DLB 48; INT CANR-26; MTCW 1, 2; PFS 11; RGAL 4
Kunze, Reiner 1933- .... **CLC 10**
See also CA 93-96; CWW 2; DLB 75; EWL 3
Kuprin, Aleksander Ivanovich
1870-1938 .... **TCLC 5**
See Kuprin, Aleksandr Ivanovich; Kuprin, Alexandr Ivanovich
See also CA 104; 182
Kuprin, Aleksandr Ivanovich
See Kuprin, Aleksander Ivanovich
See also DLB 295
Kuprin, Alexandr Ivanovich
See Kuprin, Aleksander Ivanovich
See also EWL 3
Kureishi, Hanif 1954(?)- .... **CLC 64, 135**
See also CA 139; CANR 113; CBD; CD 5; CN 7; DLB 194, 245; GLL 2; IDFW 4; WLIT 4; WWE 1
Kurosawa, Akira 1910-1998 ..... **CLC 16, 119**
See also AAYA 11; CA 101; 170; CANR 46; DAM MULT

Kushner, Tony 1956(?)- ..... **CLC 81, 203; DC 10**
See also AMWS 9; CA 144; CAD; CANR 74, 130; CD 5; DA3; DAM DRAM; DFS 5; DLB 228; EWL 3; GLL 1; LAIT 5; MTCW 2; RGAL 4
Kuttner, Henry 1915-1958 .... **TCLC 10**
See also CA 107; 157; DLB 8; FANT; SCFW 2; SFW 4
Kutty, Madhavi
See Das, Kamala
Kuzma, Greg 1944- .... **CLC 7**
See also CA 33-36R; CANR 70
Kuzmin, Mikhail (Alekseevich)
1872(?)-1936 .... **TCLC 40**
See also CA 170; DLB 295; EWL 3
Kyd, Thomas 1558-1594 .... **DC 3; LC 22**
See also BRW 1; DAM DRAM; DLB 62; IDTP; LMFS 1; RGEL 2; TEA; WLIT 3
Kyprianos, Iossif
See Samarakis, Antonis
L. S.
See Stephen, Sir Leslie
Laȝamon
See Layamon
See also DLB 146
Labrunie, Gerard
See Nerval, Gerard de
La Bruyere, Jean de 1645-1696 .... **LC 17**
See also DLB 268; EW 3; GFL Beginnings to 1789
Lacan, Jacques (Marie Emile)
1901-1981 .... **CLC 75**
See also CA 121; 104; DLB 296; EWL 3; TWA
Laclos, Pierre Ambroise Francois
1741-1803 .... **NCLC 4, 87**
See also EW 4; GFL Beginnings to 1789; RGWL 2, 3
Lacolere, Francois
See Aragon, Louis
La Colere, Francois
See Aragon, Louis
La Deshabilleuse
See Simenon, Georges (Jacques Christian)
Lady Gregory
See Gregory, Lady Isabella Augusta (Persse)
Lady of Quality, A
See Bagnold, Enid
La Fayette, Marie-(Madelaine Pioche de la Vergne) 1634-1693 .... **LC 2**
See Lafayette, Marie-Madeleine
See also GFL Beginnings to 1789; RGWL 2, 3
Lafayette, Marie-Madeleine
See La Fayette, Marie-(Madelaine Pioche de la Vergne)
See also DLB 268
Lafayette, Rene
See Hubbard, L(afayette) Ron(ald)
La Flesche, Francis 1857(?)-1932 ...... **NNAL**
See also CA 144; CANR 83; DLB 175
La Fontaine, Jean de 1621-1695 .... **LC 50**
See also DLB 268; EW 3; GFL Beginnings to 1789; MAICYA 1, 2; RGWL 2, 3; SATA 18
Laforgue, Jules 1860-1887 . **NCLC 5, 53; PC 14; SSC 20**
See also DLB 217; EW 7; GFL 1789 to the Present; RGWL 2, 3
Lagerkvist, Paer (Fabian)
1891-1974 ..... **CLC 7, 10, 13, 54; TCLC 144**
See Lagerkvist, Par
See also CA 85-88; 49-52; DA3; DAM DRAM, NOV; MTCW 1, 2; TWA

Lagerkvist, Par .... **SSC 12**
See Lagerkvist, Paer (Fabian)
See also DLB 259; EW 10; EWL 3; MTCW 2; RGSF 2; RGWL 2, 3

Lagerloef, Selma (Ottiliana Lovisa)
1858-1940 .... **TCLC 4, 36**
See Lagerlof, Selma (Ottiliana Lovisa)
See also CA 108; MTCW 2; SATA 15

Lagerlof, Selma (Ottiliana Lovisa)
See Lagerloef, Selma (Ottiliana Lovisa)
See also CLR 7; SATA 15

La Guma, (Justin) Alex(ander)
1925-1985 . **BLCS; CLC 19; TCLC 140**
See also AFW; BW 1, 3; CA 49-52; 118; CANR 25, 81; CDWLB 3; DAM NOV; DLB 117, 225; EWL 3; MTCW 1, 2; WLIT 2; WWE 1

Laidlaw, A. K.
See Grieve, C(hristopher) M(urray)

Lainez, Manuel Mujica
See Mujica Lainez, Manuel
See also HW 1

Laing, R(onald) D(avid) 1927-1989 . **CLC 95**
See also CA 107; 129; CANR 34; MTCW 1

Laishley, Alex
See Booth, Martin

Lamartine, Alphonse (Marie Louis Prat) de
1790-1869 .... **NCLC 11; PC 16**
See also DAM POET; DLB 217; GFL 1789 to the Present; RGWL 2, 3

Lamb, Charles 1775-1834 ..... **NCLC 10, 113; WLC**
See also BRW 4; CDBLB 1789-1832; DA; DAB; DAC; DAM MST; DLB 93, 107, 163; RGEL 2; SATA 17; TEA

Lamb, Lady Caroline 1785-1828 ... **NCLC 38**
See also DLB 116

Lamb, Mary Ann 1764-1847 .... **NCLC 125**
See also DLB 163; SATA 17

Lame Deer 1903(?)-1976 .... **NNAL**
See also CA 69-72

Lamming, George (William) 1927- ... **BLC 2; CLC 2, 4, 66, 144**
See also BW 2, 3; CA 85-88; CANR 26, 76; CDWLB 3; CN 7; DAM MULT; DLB 125; EWL 3; MTCW 1, 2; NFS 15; RGEL 2

L'Amour, Louis (Dearborn)
1908-1988 .... **CLC 25, 55**
See Burns, Tex; Mayo, Jim
See also AAYA 16; AITN 2; BEST 89:2; BPFB 2; CA 1-4R; 125; CANR 3, 25, 40; CPW; DA3; DAM NOV, POP; DLB 206; DLBY 1980; MTCW 1, 2; RGAL 4

Lampedusa, Giuseppe (Tomasi) di
.... **TCLC 13**
See Tomasi di Lampedusa, Giuseppe
See also CA 164; EW 11; MTCW 2; RGWL 2, 3

Lampman, Archibald 1861-1899 ... **NCLC 25**
See also DLB 92; RGEL 2; TWA

Lancaster, Bruce 1896-1963 .... **CLC 36**
See also CA 9-10; CANR 70; CAP 1; SATA 9

Lanchester, John 1962- .... **CLC 99**
See also CA 194; DLB 267

Landau, Mark Alexandrovich
See Aldanov, Mark (Alexandrovich)

Landau-Aldanov, Mark Alexandrovich
See Aldanov, Mark (Alexandrovich)

Landis, Jerry
See Simon, Paul (Frederick)

Landis, John 1950- .... **CLC 26**
See also CA 112; 122; CANR 128

Landolfi, Tommaso 1908-1979 .... **CLC 11, 49**
See also CA 127; 117; DLB 177; EWL 3

Landon, Letitia Elizabeth
1802-1838 .... **NCLC 15**
See also DLB 96

Landor, Walter Savage
1775-1864 .... **NCLC 14**
See also BRW 4; DLB 93, 107; RGEL 2

Landwirth, Heinz 1927-
See Lind, Jakov
See also CA 9-12R; CANR 7

Lane, Patrick 1939- .... **CLC 25**
See also CA 97-100; CANR 54; CP 7; DAM POET; DLB 53; INT CA-97-100

Lang, Andrew 1844-1912 .... **TCLC 16**
See also CA 114; 137; CANR 85; CLR 101; DLB 98, 141, 184; FANT; MAICYA 1, 2; RGEL 2; SATA 16; WCH

Lang, Fritz 1890-1976 .... **CLC 20, 103**
See also CA 77-80; 69-72; CANR 30

Lange, John
See Crichton, (John) Michael

Langer, Elinor 1939- .... **CLC 34**
See also CA 121

Langland, William 1332(?)-1400(?) ..... **LC 19**
See also BRW 1; DA; DAB; DAC; DAM MST, POET; DLB 146; RGEL 2; TEA; WLIT 3

Langstaff, Launcelot
See Irving, Washington

Lanier, Sidney 1842-1881 . **NCLC 6, 118; PC 50**
See also AMWS 1; DAM POET; DLB 64; DLBD 13; EXPP; MAICYA 1; PFS 14; RGAL 4; SATA 18

Lanyer, Aemilia 1569-1645 .... **LC 10, 30, 83; PC 60**
See also DLB 121

Lao-Tzu
See Lao Tzu

Lao Tzu c. 6th cent. B.C.-3rd cent.
B.C. .... **CMLC 7**

Lapine, James (Elliot) 1949- .... **CLC 39**
See also CA 123; 130; CANR 54, 128; INT CA-130

Larbaud, Valery (Nicolas)
1881-1957 .... **TCLC 9**
See also CA 106; 152; EWL 3; GFL 1789 to the Present

Lardner, Ring
See Lardner, Ring(gold) W(ilmer)
See also BPFB 2; CDALB 1917-1929; DLB 11, 25, 86, 171; DLBD 16; RGAL 4; RGSF 2

Lardner, Ring W., Jr.
See Lardner, Ring(gold) W(ilmer)

Lardner, Ring(gold) W(ilmer)
1885-1933 .... **SSC 32; TCLC 2, 14**
See Lardner, Ring
See also AMW; CA 104; 131; MTCW 1, 2; TUS

Laredo, Betty
See Codrescu, Andrei

Larkin, Maia
See Wojciechowska, Maia (Teresa)

Larkin, Philip (Arthur) 1922-1985 ... **CLC 3, 5, 8, 9, 13, 18, 33, 39, 64; PC 21**
See also BRWS 1; CA 5-8R; 117; CANR 24, 62; CDBLB 1960 to Present; DA3; DAB; DAM MST, POET; DLB 27; EWL 3; MTCW 1, 2; PFS 3, 4, 12; RGEL 2

La Roche, Sophie von
1730-1807 .... **NCLC 121**
See also DLB 94

La Rochefoucauld, Francois
1613-1680 .... **LC 108**

Larra (y Sanchez de Castro), Mariano Jose de 1809-1837 .... **NCLC 17, 130**

Larsen, Eric 1941- .... **CLC 55**
See also CA 132

Larsen, Nella 1893(?)-1963 .... **BLC 2; CLC 37; HR 3**
See also AFAW 1, 2; BW 1; CA 125; CANR 83; DAM MULT; DLB 51; FW; LATS 1:1; LMFS 2

Larson, Charles R(aymond) 1938- ... **CLC 31**
See also CA 53-56; CANR 4, 121

Larson, Jonathan 1961-1996 .... **CLC 99**
See also AAYA 28; CA 156

La Sale, Antoine de c. 1386-1460(?) . **LC 104**
See also DLB 208

Las Casas, Bartolome de
1474-1566 .... **HLCS; LC 31**
See Casas, Bartolome de las
See also LAW

Lasch, Christopher 1932-1994 .... **CLC 102**
See also CA 73-76; 144; CANR 25, 118; DLB 246; MTCW 1, 2

Lasker-Schueler, Else 1869-1945 ... **TCLC 57**
See Lasker-Schuler, Else
See also CA 183; DLB 66, 124

Lasker-Schuler, Else
See Lasker-Schueler, Else
See also EWL 3

Laski, Harold J(oseph) 1893-1950 . **TCLC 79**
See also CA 188

Latham, Jean Lee 1902-1995 .... **CLC 12**
See also AITN 1; BYA 1; CA 5-8R; CANR 7, 84; CLR 50; MAICYA 1, 2; SATA 2, 68; YAW

Latham, Mavis
See Clark, Mavis Thorpe

Lathen, Emma .... **CLC 2**
See Hennissart, Martha; Latsis, Mary J(ane)
See also BPFB 2; CMW 4; DLB 306

Lathrop, Francis
See Leiber, Fritz (Reuter, Jr.)

Latsis, Mary J(ane) 1927-1997
See Lathen, Emma
See also CA 85-88; 162; CMW 4

Lattany, Kristin
See Lattany, Kristin (Elaine Eggleston) Hunter

Lattany, Kristin (Elaine Eggleston) Hunter
1931- .... **CLC 35**
See also AITN 1; BW 1; BYA 3; CA 13-16R; CANR 13, 108; CLR 3; CN 7; DLB 33; INT CANR-13; MAICYA 1, 2; SAAS 10; SATA 12, 132; YAW

Lattimore, Richmond (Alexander)
1906-1984 .... **CLC 3**
See also CA 1-4R; 112; CANR 1

Laughlin, James 1914-1997 .... **CLC 49**
See also CA 21-24R; 162; CAAS 22; CANR 9, 47; CP 7; DLB 48; DLBY 1996, 1997

Laurence, (Jean) Margaret (Wemyss)
1926-1987 . **CLC 3, 6, 13, 50, 62; SSC 7**
See also BYA 13; CA 5-8R; 121; CANR 33; DAC; DAM MST; DLB 53; EWL 3; FW; MTCW 1, 2; NFS 11; RGEL 2; RGSF 2; SATA-Obit 50; TCWW 2

Laurent, Antoine 1952- .... **CLC 50**

Lauscher, Hermann
See Hesse, Hermann

Lautreamont 1846-1870 .. **NCLC 12; SSC 14**
See Lautreamont, Isidore Lucien Ducasse
See also GFL 1789 to the Present; RGWL 2, 3

Lautreamont, Isidore Lucien Ducasse
See Lautreamont
See also DLB 217

Lavater, Johann Kaspar
1741-1801 .... **NCLC 142**
See also DLB 97

Laverty, Donald
See Blish, James (Benjamin)

Lavin, Mary 1912-1996 . **CLC 4, 18, 99; SSC 4, 67**
See also CA 9-12R; 151; CANR 33; CN 7; DLB 15; FW; MTCW 1; RGEL 2; RGSF 2

Lavond, Paul Dennis
See Kornbluth, C(yril) M.; Pohl, Frederik

Lawes Henry 1596-1662 .... **LC 113**
See also DLB 126

Lawler, Ray
See Lawler, Raymond Evenor
See also DLB 289

Lawler, Raymond Evenor 1922- .... **CLC 58**
See Lawler, Ray
See also CA 103; CD 5; RGEL 2

Lawrence, D(avid) H(erbert Richards)
1885-1930 .... **PC 54; SSC 4, 19, 73; TCLC 2, 9, 16, 33, 48, 61, 93; WLC**
See Chambers, Jessie
See also BPFB 2; BRW 7; BRWR 2; CA 104; 121; CANR 131; CDBLB 1914-1945; DA; DA3; DAB; DAC; DAM MST, NOV, POET; DLB 10, 19, 36, 98, 162, 195; EWL 3; EXPP; EXPS; LAIT 2, 3; MTCW 1, 2; NFS 18; PFS 6; RGEL 2; RGSF 2; SSFS 2, 6; TEA; WLIT 4; WP

Lawrence, T(homas) E(dward)
1888-1935 .... **TCLC 18**
See Dale, Colin
See also BRWS 2; CA 115; 167; DLB 195

Lawrence of Arabia
See Lawrence, T(homas) E(dward)

Lawson, Henry (Archibald Hertzberg)
1867-1922 .... **SSC 18; TCLC 27**
See also CA 120; 181; DLB 230; RGEL 2; RGSF 2

Lawton, Dennis
See Faust, Frederick (Schiller)

Layamon fl. c. 1200- .... **CMLC 10**
See Laʒamon
See also DLB 146; RGEL 2

Laye, Camara 1928-1980 ..... **BLC 2; CLC 4, 38**
See Camara Laye
See also AFW; BW 1; CA 85-88; 97-100; CANR 25; DAM MULT; MTCW 1, 2; WLIT 2

Layton, Irving (Peter) 1912- .... **CLC 2, 15, 164**
See also CA 1-4R; CANR 2, 33, 43, 66, 129; CP 7; DAC; DAM MST, POET; DLB 88; EWL 3; MTCW 1, 2; PFS 12; RGEL 2

Lazarus, Emma 1849-1887 ...... **NCLC 8, 109**

Lazarus, Felix
See Cable, George Washington

Lazarus, Henry
See Slavitt, David R(ytman)

Lea, Joan
See Neufeld, John (Arthur)

Leacock, Stephen (Butler)
1869-1944 .... **SSC 39; TCLC 2**
See also CA 104; 141; CANR 80; DAC; DAM MST; DLB 92; EWL 3; MTCW 2; RGEL 2; RGSF 2

Lead, Jane Ward 1623-1704 .... **LC 72**
See also DLB 131

Leapor, Mary 1722-1746 .... **LC 80**
See also DLB 109

Lear, Edward 1812-1888 .... **NCLC 3**
See also AAYA 48; BRW 5; CLR 1, 75; DLB 32, 163, 166; MAICYA 1, 2; RGEL 2; SATA 18, 100; WCH; WP

Lear, Norman (Milton) 1922- .... **CLC 12**
See also CA 73-76

Leautaud, Paul 1872-1956 .... **TCLC 83**
See also CA 203; DLB 65; GFL 1789 to the Present

Leavis, F(rank) R(aymond)
1895-1978 .... **CLC 24**
See also BRW 7; CA 21-24R; 77-80; CANR 44; DLB 242; EWL 3; MTCW 1, 2; RGEL 2

Leavitt, David 1961- .... **CLC 34**
See also CA 116; 122; CANR 50, 62, 101, 134; CPW; DA3; DAM POP; DLB 130; GLL 1; INT CA-122; MTCW 2

Leblanc, Maurice (Marie Emile)
1864-1941 .... **TCLC 49**
See also CA 110; CMW 4

Lebowitz, Fran(ces Ann) 1951(?)- ... **CLC 11, 36**
See also CA 81-84; CANR 14, 60, 70; INT CANR-14; MTCW 1

Lebrecht, Peter
See Tieck, (Johann) Ludwig

le Carre, John .... **CLC 3, 5, 9, 15, 28**
See Cornwell, David (John Moore)
See also AAYA 42; BEST 89:4; BPFB 2; BRWS 2; CDBLB 1960 to Present; CMW 4; CN 7; CPW; DLB 87; EWL 3; MSW; MTCW 2; RGEL 2; TEA

Le Clezio, J(ean) M(arie) G(ustave)
1940- .... **CLC 31, 155**
See also CA 116; 128; CWW 2; DLB 83; EWL 3; GFL 1789 to the Present; RGSF 2

Leconte de Lisle, Charles-Marie-Rene
1818-1894 .... **NCLC 29**
See also DLB 217; EW 6; GFL 1789 to the Present

Le Coq, Monsieur
See Simenon, Georges (Jacques Christian)

Leduc, Violette 1907-1972 .... **CLC 22**
See also CA 13-14; 33-36R; CANR 69; CAP 1; EWL 3; GFL 1789 to the Present; GLL 1

Ledwidge, Francis 1887(?)-1917 .... **TCLC 23**
See also CA 123; 203; DLB 20

Lee, Andrea 1953- .... **BLC 2; CLC 36**
See also BW 1, 3; CA 125; CANR 82; DAM MULT

Lee, Andrew
See Auchincloss, Louis (Stanton)

Lee, Chang-rae 1965- .... **CLC 91**
See also CA 148; CANR 89; LATS 1:2

Lee, Don L. .... **CLC 2**
See Madhubuti, Haki R.

Lee, George W(ashington)
1894-1976 .... **BLC 2; CLC 52**
See also BW 1; CA 125; CANR 83; DAM MULT; DLB 51

Lee, (Nelle) Harper 1926- . **CLC 12, 60, 194; WLC**
See also AAYA 13; AMWS 8; BPFB 2; BYA 3; CA 13-16R; CANR 51, 128; CDALB 1941-1968; CSW; DA; DA3; DAB; DAC; DAM MST, NOV; DLB 6; EXPN; LAIT 3; MTCW 1, 2; NFS 2; SATA 11; WYA; YAW

Lee, Helen Elaine 1959(?)- .... **CLC 86**
See also CA 148

Lee, John .... **CLC 70**

Lee, Julian
See Latham, Jean Lee

Lee, Larry
See Lee, Lawrence

Lee, Laurie 1914-1997 .... **CLC 90**
See also CA 77-80; 158; CANR 33, 73; CP 7; CPW; DAB; DAM POP; DLB 27; MTCW 1; RGEL 2

Lee, Lawrence 1941-1990 .... **CLC 34**
See also CA 131; CANR 43

Lee, Li-Young 1957- .... **CLC 164; PC 24**
See also CA 153; CANR 118; CP 7; DLB 165; LMFS 2; PFS 11, 15, 17

Lee, Manfred B(ennington)
1905-1971 .... **CLC 11**
See Queen, Ellery
See also CA 1-4R; 29-32R; CANR 2; CMW 4; DLB 137

Lee, Nathaniel 1645(?)-1692 .... **LC 103**
See also DLB 80; RGEL 2

Lee, Shelton Jackson 1957(?)- .. **BLCS; CLC 105**
See Lee, Spike
See also BW 2, 3; CA 125; CANR 42; DAM MULT

Lee, Spike
See Lee, Shelton Jackson
See also AAYA 4, 29

Lee, Stan 1922- .... **CLC 17**
See also AAYA 5, 49; CA 108; 111; CANR 129; INT CA-111

Lee, Tanith 1947- .... **CLC 46**
See also AAYA 15; CA 37-40R; CANR 53, 102; DLB 261; FANT; SATA 8, 88, 134; SFW 4; SUFW 1, 2; YAW

Lee, Vernon .... **SSC 33; TCLC 5**
See Paget, Violet
See also DLB 57, 153, 156, 174, 178; GLL 1; SUFW 1

Lee, William
See Burroughs, William S(eward)
See also GLL 1

Lee, Willy
See Burroughs, William S(eward)
See also GLL 1

Lee-Hamilton, Eugene (Jacob)
1845-1907 .... **TCLC 22**
See also CA 117

Leet, Judith 1935- .... **CLC 11**
See also CA 187

Le Fanu, Joseph Sheridan
1814-1873 .... **NCLC 9, 58; SSC 14**
See also CMW 4; DA3; DAM POP; DLB 21, 70, 159, 178; HGG; RGEL 2; RGSF 2; SUFW 1

Leffland, Ella 1931- .... **CLC 19**
See also CA 29-32R; CANR 35, 78, 82; DLBY 1984; INT CANR-35; SATA 65

Leger, Alexis
See Leger, (Marie-Rene Auguste) Alexis Saint-Leger

Leger, (Marie-Rene Auguste) Alexis
Saint-Leger 1887-1975 .. **CLC 4, 11, 46; PC 23**
See Perse, Saint-John; Saint-John Perse
See also CA 13-16R; 61-64; CANR 43; DAM POET; MTCW 1

Leger, Saintleger
See Leger, (Marie-Rene Auguste) Alexis Saint-Leger

Le Guin, Ursula K(roeber) 1929- ...... **CLC 8, 13, 22, 45, 71, 136; SSC 12, 69**
See also AAYA 9, 27; AITN 1; BPFB 2; BYA 5, 8, 11, 14; CA 21-24R; CANR 9, 32, 52, 74, 132; CDALB 1968-1988; CLR 3, 28, 91; CN 7; CPW; DA3; DAB; DAC; DAM MST, POP; DLB 8, 52, 256, 275; EXPS; FANT; FW; INT CANR-32; JRDA; LAIT 5; MAICYA 1, 2; MTCW 1, 2; NFS 6, 9; SATA 4, 52, 99, 149; SCFW; SFW 4; SSFS 2; SUFW 1, 2; WYA; YAW

Lehmann, Rosamond (Nina)
1901-1990 .... **CLC 5**
See also CA 77-80; 131; CANR 8, 73; DLB 15; MTCW 2; RGEL 2; RHW

Leiber, Fritz (Reuter, Jr.)
1910-1992 .... **CLC 25**
See also BPFB 2; CA 45-48; 139; CANR 2, 40, 86; DLB 8; FANT; HGG; MTCW 1, 2; SATA 45; SATA-Obit 73; SCFW 2; SFW 4; SUFW 1, 2

Leibniz, Gottfried Wilhelm von
1646-1716 .... **LC 35**
See also DLB 168

Leimbach, Martha 1963-
See Leimbach, Marti
See also CA 130

Leimbach, Marti .... **CLC 65**
See Leimbach, Martha

Leino, Eino .... **TCLC 24**
See Lonnbohm, Armas Eino Leopold
See also EWL 3

Leiris, Michel (Julien) 1901-1990 ..... **CLC 61**
See also CA 119; 128; 132; EWL 3; GFL 1789 to the Present

Leithauser, Brad 1953- .... **CLC 27**
See also CA 107; CANR 27, 81; CP 7; DLB 120, 282

le Jars de Gournay, Marie
See de Gournay, Marie le Jars

Lelchuk, Alan 1938- .... **CLC 5**
See also CA 45-48; CAAS 20; CANR 1, 70; CN 7

Lem, Stanislaw 1921- ...... **CLC 8, 15, 40, 149**
See also CA 105; CAAS 1; CANR 32; CWW 2; MTCW 1; SCFW 2; SFW 4

Lemann, Nancy (Elise) 1956- .... **CLC 39**
See also CA 118; 136; CANR 121

Lemonnier, (Antoine Louis) Camille
1844-1913 .... **TCLC 22**
See also CA 121

Lenau, Nikolaus 1802-1850 .... **NCLC 16**

L'Engle, Madeleine (Camp Franklin)
1918- .... **CLC 12**
See also AAYA 28; AITN 2; BPFB 2; BYA 2, 4, 5, 7; CA 1-4R; CANR 3, 21, 39, 66, 107; CLR 1, 14, 57; CPW; CWRI 5; DA3; DAM POP; DLB 52; JRDA; MAICYA 1, 2; MTCW 1, 2; SAAS 15; SATA 1, 27, 75, 128; SFW 4; WYA; YAW

Lengyel, Jozsef 1896-1975 .... **CLC 7**
See also CA 85-88; 57-60; CANR 71; RGSF 2

Lenin 1870-1924
See Lenin, V. I.
See also CA 121; 168

Lenin, V. I. .... **TCLC 67**
See Lenin

Lennon, John (Ono) 1940-1980 .. **CLC 12, 35**
See also CA 102; SATA 114

Lennox, Charlotte Ramsay
1729(?)-1804 .... **NCLC 23, 134**
See also DLB 39; RGEL 2

Lentricchia, Frank, (Jr.) 1940- .... **CLC 34**
See also CA 25-28R; CANR 19, 106; DLB 246

Lenz, Gunter .... **CLC 65**

Lenz, Jakob Michael Reinhold
1751-1792 .... **LC 100**
See also DLB 94; RGWL 2, 3

Lenz, Siegfried 1926- .... **CLC 27; SSC 33**
See also CA 89-92; CANR 80; CWW 2; DLB 75; EWL 3; RGSF 2; RGWL 2, 3

Leon, David
See Jacob, (Cyprien-)Max

Leonard, Elmore (John, Jr.) 1925- . **CLC 28, 34, 71, 120**
See also AAYA 22, 59; AITN 1; BEST 89:1, 90:4; BPFB 2; CA 81-84; CANR 12, 28, 53, 76, 96, 133; CMW 4; CN 7; CPW; DA3; DAM POP; DLB 173, 226; INT CANR-28; MSW; MTCW 1, 2; RGAL 4; TCWW 2

Leonard, Hugh .... **CLC 19**
See Byrne, John Keyes
See also CBD; CD 5; DFS 13; DLB 13

Leonov, Leonid (Maximovich)
1899-1994 .... **CLC 92**
See Leonov, Leonid Maksimovich
See also CA 129; CANR 74, 76; DAM NOV; EWL 3; MTCW 1, 2

Leonov, Leonid Maksimovich
See Leonov, Leonid (Maximovich)
See also DLB 272

Leopardi, (Conte) Giacomo
1798-1837 .... **NCLC 22, 129; PC 37**
See also EW 5; RGWL 2, 3; WP

Le Reveler
See Artaud, Antonin (Marie Joseph)

Lerman, Eleanor 1952- .... **CLC 9**
See also CA 85-88; CANR 69, 124

Lerman, Rhoda 1936- .... **CLC 56**
See also CA 49-52; CANR 70

Lermontov, Mikhail Iur'evich
See Lermontov, Mikhail Yuryevich
See also DLB 205

Lermontov, Mikhail Yuryevich
1814-1841 .... **NCLC 5, 47, 126; PC 18**
See Lermontov, Mikhail Iur'evich
See also EW 6; RGWL 2, 3; TWA

Leroux, Gaston 1868-1927 .... **TCLC 25**
See also CA 108; 136; CANR 69; CMW 4; NFS 20; SATA 65

Lesage, Alain-Rene 1668-1747 .... **LC 2, 28**
See also EW 3; GFL Beginnings to 1789; RGWL 2, 3

Leskov, N(ikolai) S(emenovich) 1831-1895
See Leskov, Nikolai (Semyonovich)

Leskov, Nikolai (Semyonovich)
1831-1895 .... **NCLC 25; SSC 34**
See Leskov, Nikolai Semenovich

Leskov, Nikolai Semenovich
See Leskov, Nikolai (Semyonovich)
See also DLB 238

Lesser, Milton
See Marlowe, Stephen

Lessing, Doris (May) 1919- ... **CLC 1, 2, 3, 6, 10, 15, 22, 40, 94, 170; SSC 6, 61; WLCS**
See also AAYA 57; AFW; BRWS 1; CA 9-12R; CAAS 14; CANR 33, 54, 76, 122; CD 5; CDBLB 1960 to Present; CN 7; DA; DA3; DAB; DAC; DAM MST, NOV; DFS 20; DLB 15, 139; DLBY 1985; EWL 3; EXPS; FW; LAIT 4; MTCW 1, 2; RGEL 2; RGSF 2; SFW 4; SSFS 1, 12, 20; TEA; WLIT 2, 4

Lessing, Gotthold Ephraim 1729-1781 . **LC 8**
See also CDWLB 2; DLB 97; EW 4; RGWL 2, 3

Lester, Richard 1932- .... **CLC 20**

Levenson, Jay .... **CLC 70**

Lever, Charles (James)
1806-1872 .... **NCLC 23**
See also DLB 21; RGEL 2

Leverson, Ada Esther
1862(?)-1933(?) .... **TCLC 18**
See Elaine
See also CA 117; 202; DLB 153; RGEL 2

Levertov, Denise 1923-1997 .. **CLC 1, 2, 3, 5, 8, 15, 28, 66; PC 11**
See also AMWS 3; CA 1-4R, 178; 163; CAAE 178; CAAS 19; CANR 3, 29, 50, 108; CDALBS; CP 7; CWP; DAM POET; DLB 5, 165; EWL 3; EXPP; FW; INT CANR-29; MTCW 1, 2; PAB; PFS 7, 17; RGAL 4; TUS; WP

Levi, Carlo 1902-1975 .... **TCLC 125**
See also CA 65-68; 53-56; CANR 10; EWL 3; RGWL 2, 3

Levi, Jonathan .... **CLC 76**
See also CA 197

Levi, Peter (Chad Tigar)
1931-2000 .... **CLC 41**
See also CA 5-8R; 187; CANR 34, 80; CP 7; DLB 40

Levi, Primo 1919-1987 ...... **CLC 37, 50; SSC 12; TCLC 109**
See also CA 13-16R; 122; CANR 12, 33, 61, 70, 132; DLB 177, 299; EWL 3; MTCW 1, 2; RGWL 2, 3

Levin, Ira 1929- .... **CLC 3, 6**
See also CA 21-24R; CANR 17, 44, 74; CMW 4; CN 7; CPW; DA3; DAM POP; HGG; MTCW 1, 2; SATA 66; SFW 4

Levin, Meyer 1905-1981 .... **CLC 7**
See also AITN 1; CA 9-12R; 104; CANR 15; DAM POP; DLB 9, 28; DLBY 1981; SATA 21; SATA-Obit 27

Levine, Norman 1924- .... **CLC 54**
See also CA 73-76; CAAS 23; CANR 14, 70; DLB 88

Levine, Philip 1928- .. **CLC 2, 4, 5, 9, 14, 33, 118; PC 22**
See also AMWS 5; CA 9-12R; CANR 9, 37, 52, 116; CP 7; DAM POET; DLB 5; EWL 3; PFS 8

Levinson, Deirdre 1931- .... **CLC 49**
See also CA 73-76; CANR 70

Levi-Strauss, Claude 1908- .... **CLC 38**
See also CA 1-4R; CANR 6, 32, 57; DLB 242; EWL 3; GFL 1789 to the Present; MTCW 1, 2; TWA

Levitin, Sonia (Wolff) 1934- .... **CLC 17**
See also AAYA 13, 48; CA 29-32R; CANR 14, 32, 79; CLR 53; JRDA; MAICYA 1, 2; SAAS 2; SATA 4, 68, 119, 131; SATA-Essay 131; YAW

Levon, O. U.
See Kesey, Ken (Elton)

Levy, Amy 1861-1889 .... **NCLC 59**
See also DLB 156, 240

Lewes, George Henry 1817-1878 ... **NCLC 25**
See also DLB 55, 144

Lewis, Alun 1915-1944 .... **SSC 40; TCLC 3**
See also BRW 7; CA 104; 188; DLB 20, 162; PAB; RGEL 2

Lewis, C. Day
See Day Lewis, C(ecil)

Lewis, C(live) S(taples) 1898-1963 .... **CLC 1, 3, 6, 14, 27, 124; WLC**
See also AAYA 3, 39; BPFB 2; BRWS 3; BYA 15, 16; CA 81-84; CANR 33, 71, 132; CDBLB 1945-1960; CLR 3, 27; CWRI 5; DA; DA3; DAB; DAC; DAM MST, NOV, POP; DLB 15, 100, 160, 255; EWL 3; FANT; JRDA; LMFS 2; MAICYA 1, 2; MTCW 1, 2; RGEL 2; SATA 13, 100; SCFW; SFW 4; SUFW 1; TEA; WCH; WYA; YAW

Lewis, Cecil Day
See Day Lewis, C(ecil)

Lewis, Janet 1899-1998 .... **CLC 41**
See Winters, Janet Lewis
See also CA 9-12R; 172; CANR 29, 63; CAP 1; CN 7; DLBY 1987; RHW; TCWW 2

Lewis, Matthew Gregory
1775-1818 .... **NCLC 11, 62**
See also DLB 39, 158, 178; HGG; LMFS 1; RGEL 2; SUFW

Lewis, (Harry) Sinclair 1885-1951 . **TCLC 4, 13, 23, 39; WLC**
See also AMW; AMWC 1; BPFB 2; CA 104; 133; CANR 132; CDALB 1917-1929; DA; DA3; DAB; DAC; DAM MST, NOV; DLB 9, 102, 284; DLBD 1; EWL 3; LAIT 3; MTCW 1, 2; NFS 15, 19; RGAL 4; TUS

Lewis, (Percy) Wyndham
1884(?)-1957 .. **SSC 34; TCLC 2, 9, 104**
See also BRW 7; CA 104; 157; DLB 15;
EWL 3; FANT; MTCW 2; RGEL 2

Lewisohn, Ludwig 1883-1955 .... **TCLC 19**
See also CA 107; 203; DLB 4, 9, 28, 102

Lewton, Val 1904-1951 .... **TCLC 76**
See also CA 199; IDFW 3, 4

Leyner, Mark 1956- .... **CLC 92**
See also CA 110; CANR 28, 53; DA3; DLB
292; MTCW 2

Lezama Lima, Jose 1910-1976 .... **CLC 4, 10, 101; HLCS 2**
See also CA 77-80; CANR 71; DAM
MULT; DLB 113, 283; EWL 3; HW 1, 2;
LAW; RGWL 2, 3

L'Heureux, John (Clarke) 1934- ...... **CLC 52**
See also CA 13-16R; CANR 23, 45, 88;
DLB 244

Li Ch'ing-chao 1081(?)-1141(?) .... **CMLC 71**

Liddell, C. H.
See Kuttner, Henry

Lie, Jonas (Lauritz Idemil)
1833-1908(?) .... **TCLC 5**
See also CA 115

Lieber, Joel 1937-1971 .... **CLC 6**
See also CA 73-76; 29-32R

Lieber, Stanley Martin
See Lee, Stan

Lieberman, Laurence (James)
1935- .... **CLC 4, 36**
See also CA 17-20R; CANR 8, 36, 89; CP
7

Lieh Tzu fl. 7th cent. B.C.-5th cent.
B.C. .... **CMLC 27**

Lieksman, Anders
See Haavikko, Paavo Juhani

Li Fei-kan 1904-
See Pa Chin
See also CA 105; TWA

Lifton, Robert Jay 1926- .... **CLC 67**
See also CA 17-20R; CANR 27, 78; INT
CANR-27; SATA 66

Lightfoot, Gordon 1938- .... **CLC 26**
See also CA 109

Lightman, Alan P(aige) 1948- .... **CLC 81**
See also CA 141; CANR 63, 105

Ligotti, Thomas (Robert) 1953- ...... **CLC 44; SSC 16**
See also CA 123; CANR 49, 135; HGG;
SUFW 2

Li Ho 791-817 .... **PC 13**

Li Ju-chen c. 1763-c. 1830 .... **NCLC 137**

Lilar, Francoise
See Mallet-Joris, Francoise

**Liliencron, (Friedrich Adolf Axel) Detlev
von** 1844-1909 .... **TCLC 18**
See also CA 117

Lille, Alain de
See Alain de Lille

Lilly, William 1602-1681 .... **LC 27**

Lima, Jose Lezama
See Lezama Lima, Jose

Lima Barreto, Afonso Henrique de
1881-1922 .... **TCLC 23**
See Lima Barreto, Afonso Henriques de
See also CA 117; 181; LAW

Lima Barreto, Afonso Henriques de
See Lima Barreto, Afonso Henrique de
See also DLB 307

Limonov, Edward 1944- .... **CLC 67**
See also CA 137

Lin, Frank
See Atherton, Gertrude (Franklin Horn)

Lin, Yutang 1895-1976 .... **TCLC 149**
See also CA 45-48; 65-68; CANR 2; RGAL
4

Lincoln, Abraham 1809-1865 .... **NCLC 18**
See also LAIT 2

Lind, Jakov .... **CLC 1, 2, 4, 27, 82**
See Landwirth, Heinz
See also CAAS 4; DLB 299; EWL 3

Lindbergh, Anne (Spencer) Morrow
1906-2001 .... **CLC 82**
See also BPFB 2; CA 17-20R; 193; CANR
16, 73; DAM NOV; MTCW 1, 2; SATA
33; SATA-Obit 125; TUS

Lindsay, David 1878(?)-1945 .... **TCLC 15**
See also CA 113; 187; DLB 255; FANT;
SFW 4; SUFW 1

Lindsay, (Nicholas) Vachel
1879-1931 .... **PC 23; TCLC 17; WLC**
See also AMWS 1; CA 114; 135; CANR
79; CDALB 1865-1917; DA; DA3; DAC;
DAM MST, POET; DLB 54; EWL 3;
EXPP; RGAL 4; SATA 40; WP

Linke-Poot
See Doeblin, Alfred

Linney, Romulus 1930- .... **CLC 51**
See also CA 1-4R; CAD; CANR 40, 44,
79; CD 5; CSW; RGAL 4

Linton, Eliza Lynn 1822-1898 .... **NCLC 41**
See also DLB 18

Li Po 701-763 .... **CMLC 2; PC 29**
See also PFS 20; WP

Lipsius, Justus 1547-1606 .... **LC 16**

Lipsyte, Robert (Michael) 1938- ...... **CLC 21**
See also AAYA 7, 45; CA 17-20R; CANR
8, 57; CLR 23, 76; DA; DA3; DAC;
DAM MST, NOV; JRDA; LAIT 5; MAICYA 1,
2; SATA 5, 68, 113; WYA; YAW

Lish, Gordon (Jay) 1934- ... **CLC 45; SSC 18**
See also CA 113; 117; CANR 79; DLB 130;
INT CA-117

Lispector, Clarice 1925(?)-1977 .... **CLC 43; HLCS 2; SSC 34**
See also CA 139; 116; CANR 71; CDWLB
3; DLB 113, 307; DNFS 1; EWL 3; FW;
HW 2; LAW; RGSF 2; RGWL 2, 3; WLIT
1

Littell, Robert 1935(?)- .... **CLC 42**
See also CA 109; 112; CANR 64, 115;
CMW 4

Little, Malcolm 1925-1965
See Malcolm X
See also BW 1, 3; CA 125; 111; CANR 82;
DA; DA3; DAB; DAC; DAM MST,
MULT; MTCW 1, 2

Littlewit, Humphrey Gent.
See Lovecraft, H(oward) P(hillips)

Litwos
See Sienkiewicz, Henryk (Adam Alexander
Pius)

Liu, E. 1857-1909 .... **TCLC 15**
See also CA 115; 190

Lively, Penelope (Margaret) 1933- .. **CLC 32, 50**
See also BPFB 2; CA 41-44R; CANR 29,
67, 79, 131; CLR 7; CN 7; CWRI 5;
DAM NOV; DLB 14, 161, 207; FANT;
JRDA; MAICYA 1, 2; MTCW 1, 2; SATA
7, 60, 101; TEA

Livesay, Dorothy (Kathleen)
1909-1996 .... **CLC 4, 15, 79**
See also AITN 2; CA 25-28R; CAAS 8;
CANR 36, 67; DAC; DAM MST, POET;
DLB 68; FW; MTCW 1; RGEL 2; TWA

Livy c. 59B.C.-c. 12 .... **CMLC 11**
See also AW 2; CDWLB 1; DLB 211;
RGWL 2, 3

Lizardi, Jose Joaquin Fernandez de
1776-1827 .... **NCLC 30**
See also LAW

Llewellyn, Richard
See Llewellyn Lloyd, Richard Dafydd Vivian
See also DLB 15

Llewellyn Lloyd, Richard Dafydd Vivian
1906-1983 .... **CLC 7, 80**
See Llewellyn, Richard
See also CA 53-56; 111; CANR 7, 71;
SATA 11; SATA-Obit 37

Llosa, (Jorge) Mario (Pedro) Vargas
See Vargas Llosa, (Jorge) Mario (Pedro)
See also RGWL 3

Llosa, Mario Vargas
See Vargas Llosa, (Jorge) Mario (Pedro)

Lloyd, Manda
See Mander, (Mary) Jane

Lloyd Webber, Andrew 1948-
See Webber, Andrew Lloyd
See also AAYA 1, 38; CA 116; 149; DAM
DRAM; SATA 56

Llull, Ramon c. 1235-c. 1316 .... **CMLC 12**

Lobb, Ebenezer
See Upward, Allen

Locke, Alain (Le Roy)
1886-1954 .... **BLCS; HR 3; TCLC 43**
See also AMWS 14; BW 1, 3; CA 106; 124;
CANR 79; DLB 51; LMFS 2; RGAL 4

Locke, John 1632-1704 .... **LC 7, 35**
See also DLB 31, 101, 213, 252; RGEL 2;
WLIT 3

Locke-Elliott, Sumner
See Elliott, Sumner Locke

Lockhart, John Gibson 1794-1854 .. **NCLC 6**
See also DLB 110, 116, 144

Lockridge, Ross (Franklin), Jr.
1914-1948 .... **TCLC 111**
See also CA 108; 145; CANR 79; DLB 143;
DLBY 1980; RGAL 4; RHW

Lockwood, Robert
See Johnson, Robert

Lodge, David (John) 1935- .... **CLC 36, 141**
See also BEST 90:1; BRWS 4; CA 17-20R;
CANR 19, 53, 92; CN 7; CPW; DAM
POP; DLB 14, 194; EWL 3; INT CANR-
19; MTCW 1, 2

Lodge, Thomas 1558-1625 .... **LC 41**
See also DLB 172; RGEL 2

Loewinsohn, Ron(ald William)
1937- .... **CLC 52**
See also CA 25-28R; CANR 71

Logan, Jake
See Smith, Martin Cruz

Logan, John (Burton) 1923-1987 .... **CLC 5**
See also CA 77-80; 124; CANR 45; DLB 5

Lo Kuan-chung 1330(?)-1400(?) .... **LC 12**

Lombard, Nap
See Johnson, Pamela Hansford

Lombard, Peter 1100(?)-1160(?) ... **CMLC 72**

London, Jack 1876-1916 .. **SSC 4, 49; TCLC 9, 15, 39; WLC**
See London, John Griffith
See also AAYA 13; AITN 2; AMW; BPFB
2; BYA 4, 13; CDALB 1865-1917; DLB
8, 12, 78, 212; EWL 3; EXPS; LAIT 3;
NFS 8; RGAL 4; RGSF 2; SATA 18; SFW
4; SSFS 7; TCWW 2; TUS; WYA; YAW

London, John Griffith 1876-1916
See London, Jack
See also CA 110; 119; CANR 73; DA; DA3;
DAB; DAC; DAM MST, NOV; JRDA;
MAICYA 1, 2; MTCW 1, 2; NFS 19

Long, Emmett
See Leonard, Elmore (John, Jr.)

Longbaugh, Harry
See Goldman, William (W.)

Longfellow, Henry Wadsworth
1807-1882 .... **NCLC 2, 45, 101, 103; PC 30; WLCS**
See also AMW; AMWR 2; CDALB 1640-1865; CLR 99; DA; DA3; DAB; DAC; DAM MST, POET; DLB 1, 59, 235; EXPP; PAB; PFS 2, 7, 17; RGAL 4; SATA 19; TUS; WP

Longinus c. 1st cent. - .... **CMLC 27**
See also AW 2; DLB 176

Longley, Michael 1939- .... **CLC 29**
See also BRWS 8; CA 102; CP 7; DLB 40

Longus fl. c. 2nd cent. - .... **CMLC 7**

Longway, A. Hugh
See Lang, Andrew

Lonnbohm, Armas Eino Leopold 1878-1926
See Leino, Eino
See also CA 123

Lonnrot, Elias 1802-1884 .... **NCLC 53**
See also EFS 1

Lonsdale, Roger ed. .... **CLC 65**

Lopate, Phillip 1943- .... **CLC 29**
See also CA 97-100; CANR 88; DLBY 1980; INT CA-97-100

Lopez, Barry (Holstun) 1945- .... **CLC 70**
See also AAYA 9; ANW; CA 65-68; CANR 7, 23, 47, 68, 92; DLB 256, 275; INT CANR-7, -23; MTCW 1; RGAL 4; SATA 67

Lopez Portillo (y Pacheco), Jose
1920-2004 .... **CLC 46**
See also CA 129; 224; HW 1

Lopez y Fuentes, Gregorio
1897(?)-1966 .... **CLC 32**
See also CA 131; EWL 3; HW 1

Lorca, Federico Garcia
See Garcia Lorca, Federico
See also DFS 4; EW 11; PFS 20; RGWL 2, 3; WP

Lord, Audre
See Lorde, Audre (Geraldine)
See also EWL 3

Lord, Bette Bao 1938- .... **AAL; CLC 23**
See also BEST 90:3; BPFB 2; CA 107; CANR 41, 79; INT CA-107; SATA 58

Lord Auch
See Bataille, Georges

Lord Brooke
See Greville, Fulke

Lord Byron
See Byron, George Gordon (Noel)

Lorde, Audre (Geraldine)
1934-1992 .. **BLC 2; CLC 18, 71; PC 12**
See Domini, Rey; Lord, Audre
See also AFAW 1, 2; BW 1, 3; CA 25-28R; 142; CANR 16, 26, 46, 82; DA3; DAM MULT, POET; DLB 41; FW; MTCW 1, 2; PFS 16; RGAL 4

Lord Houghton
See Milnes, Richard Monckton

Lord Jeffrey
See Jeffrey, Francis

Loreaux, Nichol .... **CLC 65**

Lorenzini, Carlo 1826-1890
See Collodi, Carlo
See also MAICYA 1, 2; SATA 29, 100

Lorenzo, Heberto Padilla
See Padilla (Lorenzo), Heberto

Loris
See Hofmannsthal, Hugo von

Loti, Pierre .... **TCLC 11**
See Viaud, (Louis Marie) Julien
See also DLB 123; GFL 1789 to the Present

Lou, Henri
See Andreas-Salome, Lou

Louie, David Wong 1954- .... **CLC 70**
See also CA 139; CANR 120

Louis, Adrian C. .... **NNAL**
See also CA 223

Louis, Father M.
See Merton, Thomas (James)

Louise, Heidi
See Erdrich, Louise

Lovecraft, H(oward) P(hillips)
1890-1937 .... **SSC 3, 52; TCLC 4, 22**
See also AAYA 14; BPFB 2; CA 104; 133; CANR 106; DA3; DAM POP; HGG; MTCW 1, 2; RGAL 4; SCFW; SFW 4; SUFW

Lovelace, Earl 1935- .... **CLC 51**
See also BW 2; CA 77-80; CANR 41, 72, 114; CD 5; CDWLB 3; CN 7; DLB 125; EWL 3; MTCW 1

Lovelace, Richard 1618-1657 .... **LC 24**
See also BRW 2; DLB 131; EXPP; PAB; RGEL 2

Lowe, Pardee 1904- .... **AAL**

Lowell, Amy 1874-1925 ... **PC 13; TCLC 1, 8**
See also AAYA 57; AMW; CA 104; 151; DAM POET; DLB 54, 140; EWL 3; EXPP; LMFS 2; MAWW; MTCW 2; RGAL 4; TUS

Lowell, James Russell 1819-1891 ... **NCLC 2, 90**
See also AMWS 1; CDALB 1640-1865; DLB 1, 11, 64, 79, 189, 235; RGAL 4

Lowell, Robert (Traill Spence, Jr.)
1917-1977 .... **CLC 1, 2, 3, 4, 5, 8, 9, 11, 15, 37, 124; PC 3; WLC**
See also AMW; AMWC 2; AMWR 2; CA 9-12R; 73-76; CABS 2; CANR 26, 60; CDALBS; DA; DA3; DAB; DAC; DAM MST, NOV; DLB 5, 169; EWL 3; MTCW 1, 2; PAB; PFS 6, 7; RGAL 4; WP

Lowenthal, Michael (Francis)
1969- .... **CLC 119**
See also CA 150; CANR 115

Lowndes, Marie Adelaide (Belloc)
1868-1947 .... **TCLC 12**
See also CA 107; CMW 4; DLB 70; RHW

Lowry, (Clarence) Malcolm
1909-1957 .... **SSC 31; TCLC 6, 40**
See also BPFB 2; BRWS 3; CA 105; 131; CANR 62, 105; CDBLB 1945-1960; DLB 15; EWL 3; MTCW 1, 2; RGEL 2

Lowry, Mina Gertrude 1882-1966
See Loy, Mina
See also CA 113

Loxsmith, John
See Brunner, John (Kilian Houston)

Loy, Mina .... **CLC 28; PC 16**
See Lowry, Mina Gertrude
See also DAM POET; DLB 4, 54; PFS 20

Loyson-Bridet
See Schwob, Marcel (Mayer Andre)

Lucan 39-65 .... **CMLC 33**
See also AW 2; DLB 211; EFS 2; RGWL 2, 3

Lucas, Craig 1951- .... **CLC 64**
See also CA 137; CAD; CANR 71, 109; CD 5; GLL 2

Lucas, E(dward) V(errall)
1868-1938 .... **TCLC 73**
See also CA 176; DLB 98, 149, 153; SATA 20

Lucas, George 1944- .... **CLC 16**
See also AAYA 1, 23; CA 77-80; CANR 30; SATA 56

Lucas, Hans
See Godard, Jean-Luc

Lucas, Victoria
See Plath, Sylvia

Lucian c. 125-c. 180 .... **CMLC 32**
See also AW 2; DLB 176; RGWL 2, 3

Lucretius c. 94B.C.-c. 49B.C. .... **CMLC 48**
See also AW 2; CDWLB 1; DLB 211; EFS 2; RGWL 2, 3

Ludlam, Charles 1943-1987 .... **CLC 46, 50**
See also CA 85-88; 122; CAD; CANR 72, 86; DLB 266

Ludlum, Robert 1927-2001 .... **CLC 22, 43**
See also AAYA 10, 59; BEST 89:1, 90:3; BPFB 2; CA 33-36R; 195; CANR 25, 41, 68, 105, 131; CMW 4; CPW; DA3; DAM NOV, POP; DLBY 1982; MSW; MTCW 1, 2

Ludwig, Ken .... **CLC 60**
See also CA 195; CAD

Ludwig, Otto 1813-1865 .... **NCLC 4**
See also DLB 129

Lugones, Leopoldo 1874-1938 .... **HLCS 2; TCLC 15**
See also CA 116; 131; CANR 104; DLB 283; EWL 3; HW 1; LAW

Lu Hsun .... **SSC 20; TCLC 3**
See Shu-Jen, Chou
See also EWL 3

Lukacs, George .... **CLC 24**
See Lukacs, Gyorgy (Szegeny von)

Lukacs, Gyorgy (Szegeny von) 1885-1971
See Lukacs, George
See also CA 101; 29-32R; CANR 62; CDWLB 4; DLB 215, 242; EW 10; EWL 3; MTCW 2

Luke, Peter (Ambrose Cyprian)
1919-1995 .... **CLC 38**
See also CA 81-84; 147; CANR 72; CBD; CD 5; DLB 13

Lunar, Dennis
See Mungo, Raymond

Lurie, Alison 1926- ..... **CLC 4, 5, 18, 39, 175**
See also BPFB 2; CA 1-4R; CANR 2, 17, 50, 88; CN 7; DLB 2; MTCW 1; SATA 46, 112

Lustig, Arnost 1926- .... **CLC 56**
See also AAYA 3; CA 69-72; CANR 47, 102; CWW 2; DLB 232, 299; EWL 3; SATA 56

Luther, Martin 1483-1546 .... **LC 9, 37**
See also CDWLB 2; DLB 179; EW 2; RGWL 2, 3

Luxemburg, Rosa 1870(?)-1919 ..... **TCLC 63**
See also CA 118

Luzi, Mario 1914- .... **CLC 13**
See also CA 61-64; CANR 9, 70; CWW 2; DLB 128; EWL 3

L'vov, Arkady .... **CLC 59**

Lydgate, John c. 1370-1450(?) .... **LC 81**
See also BRW 1; DLB 146; RGEL 2

Lyly, John 1554(?)-1606 .... **DC 7; LC 41**
See also BRW 1; DAM DRAM; DLB 62, 167; RGEL 2

L'Ymagier
See Gourmont, Remy(-Marie-Charles) de

Lynch, B. Suarez
See Borges, Jorge Luis

Lynch, David (Keith) 1946- ...... **CLC 66, 162**
See also AAYA 55; CA 124; 129; CANR 111

Lynch, James
See Andreyev, Leonid (Nikolaevich)

Lyndsay, Sir David 1485-1555 .... **LC 20**
See also RGEL 2

Lynn, Kenneth S(chuyler)
1923-2001 .... **CLC 50**
See also CA 1-4R; 196; CANR 3, 27, 65

Lynx
See West, Rebecca

Lyons, Marcus
See Blish, James (Benjamin)

Lyotard, Jean-Francois
1924-1998 .... **TCLC 103**
See also DLB 242; EWL 3

Lyre, Pinchbeck
See Sassoon, Siegfried (Lorraine)

Lytle, Andrew (Nelson) 1902-1995 ... **CLC 22**
See also CA 9-12R; 150; CANR 70; CN 7; CSW; DLB 6; DLBY 1995; RGAL 4; RHW

Lyttelton, George 1709-1773 .... **LC 10**
See also RGEL 2

Lytton of Knebworth, Baron
See Bulwer-Lytton, Edward (George Earle Lytton)

Maas, Peter 1929-2001 .... **CLC 29**
See also CA 93-96; 201; INT CA-93-96; MTCW 2

Macaulay, Catherine 1731-1791 .... **LC 64**
See also DLB 104

Macaulay, (Emilie) Rose
1881(?)-1958 .... **TCLC 7, 44**
See also CA 104; DLB 36; EWL 3; RGEL 2; RHW

Macaulay, Thomas Babington
1800-1859 .... **NCLC 42**
See also BRW 4; CDBLB 1832-1890; DLB 32, 55; RGEL 2

MacBeth, George (Mann)
1932-1992 .... **CLC 2, 5, 9**
See also CA 25-28R; 136; CANR 61, 66; DLB 40; MTCW 1; PFS 8; SATA 4; SATA-Obit 70

MacCaig, Norman (Alexander)
1910-1996 .... **CLC 36**
See also BRWS 6; CA 9-12R; CANR 3, 34; CP 7; DAB; DAM POET; DLB 27; EWL 3; RGEL 2

MacCarthy, Sir (Charles Otto) Desmond
1877-1952 .... **TCLC 36**
See also CA 167

MacDiarmid, Hugh .... **CLC 2, 4, 11, 19, 63; PC 9**
See Grieve, C(hristopher) M(urray)
See also CDBLB 1945-1960; DLB 20; EWL 3; RGEL 2

MacDonald, Anson
See Heinlein, Robert A(nson)

Macdonald, Cynthia 1928- .... **CLC 13, 19**
See also CA 49-52; CANR 4, 44; DLB 105

MacDonald, George 1824-1905 .... **TCLC 9, 113**
See also AAYA 57; BYA 5; CA 106; 137; CANR 80; CLR 67; DLB 18, 163, 178; FANT; MAICYA 1, 2; RGEL 2; SATA 33, 100; SFW 4; SUFW; WCH

Macdonald, John
See Millar, Kenneth

MacDonald, John D(ann)
1916-1986 .... **CLC 3, 27, 44**
See also BPFB 2; CA 1-4R; CANR 1, 19, 60; CMW 4; CPW; DAM NOV, POP; DLB 8, 306; DLBY 1986; MSW; MTCW 1, 2; SFW 4

Macdonald, John Ross
See Millar, Kenneth

Macdonald, Ross ..... **CLC 1, 2, 3, 14, 34, 41**
See Millar, Kenneth
See also AMWS 4; BPFB 2; DLBD 6; MSW; RGAL 4

MacDougal, John
See Blish, James (Benjamin)

MacDougal, John
See Blish, James (Benjamin)

MacDowell, John
See Parks, Tim(othy Harold)

MacEwen, Gwendolyn (Margaret)
1941-1987 .... **CLC 13, 55**
See also CA 9-12R; 124; CANR 7, 22; DLB 53, 251; SATA 50; SATA-Obit 55

Macha, Karel Hynek 1810-1846 .... **NCLC 46**

Machado (y Ruiz), Antonio
1875-1939 .... **TCLC 3**
See also CA 104; 174; DLB 108; EW 9; EWL 3; HW 2; RGWL 2, 3

Machado de Assis, Joaquim Maria
1839-1908 .... **BLC 2; HLCS 2; SSC 24; TCLC 10**
See also CA 107; 153; CANR 91; DLB 307; LAW; RGSF 2; RGWL 2, 3; TWA; WLIT 1

Machaut, Guillaume de c.
1300-1377 .... **CMLC 64**
See also DLB 208

Machen, Arthur .... **SSC 20; TCLC 4**
See Jones, Arthur Llewellyn
See also CA 179; DLB 156, 178; RGEL 2; SUFW 1

Machiavelli, Niccolo 1469-1527 ... **DC 16; LC 8, 36; WLCS**
See also AAYA 58; DA; DAB; DAC; DAM MST; EW 2; LAIT 1; LMFS 1; NFS 9; RGWL 2, 3; TWA

MacInnes, Colin 1914-1976 .... **CLC 4, 23**
See also CA 69-72; 65-68; CANR 21; DLB 14; MTCW 1, 2; RGEL 2; RHW

MacInnes, Helen (Clark)
1907-1985 .... **CLC 27, 39**
See also BPFB 2; CA 1-4R; 117; CANR 1, 28, 58; CMW 4; CPW; DAM POP; DLB 87; MSW; MTCW 1, 2; SATA 22; SATA-Obit 44

Mackay, Mary 1855-1924
See Corelli, Marie
See also CA 118; 177; FANT; RHW

Mackay, Shena 1944- .... **CLC 195**
See also CA 104; CANR 88; DLB 231

Mackenzie, Compton (Edward Montague)
1883-1972 .... **CLC 18; TCLC 116**
See also CA 21-22; 37-40R; CAP 2; DLB 34, 100; RGEL 2

Mackenzie, Henry 1745-1831 .... **NCLC 41**
See also DLB 39; RGEL 2

Mackey, Nathaniel (Ernest) 1947- .... **PC 49**
See also CA 153; CANR 114; CP 7; DLB 169

MacKinnon, Catharine A. 1946- .... **CLC 181**
See also CA 128; 132; CANR 73; FW; MTCW 2

Mackintosh, Elizabeth 1896(?)-1952
See Tey, Josephine
See also CA 110; CMW 4

MacLaren, James
See Grieve, C(hristopher) M(urray)

Mac Laverty, Bernard 1942- .... **CLC 31**
See also CA 116; 118; CANR 43, 88; CN 7; DLB 267; INT CA-118; RGSF 2

MacLean, Alistair (Stuart)
1922(?)-1987 .... **CLC 3, 13, 50, 63**
See also CA 57-60; 121; CANR 28, 61; CMW 4; CPW; DAM POP; DLB 276; MTCW 1; SATA 23; SATA-Obit 50; TCWW 2

Maclean, Norman (Fitzroy)
1902-1990 .... **CLC 78; SSC 13**
See also AMWS 14; CA 102; 132; CANR 49; CPW; DAM POP; DLB 206; TCWW 2

MacLeish, Archibald 1892-1982 ... **CLC 3, 8, 14, 68; PC 47**
See also AMW; CA 9-12R; 106; CAD; CANR 33, 63; CDALBS; DAM POET; DFS 15; DLB 4, 7, 45; DLBY 1982; EWL 3; EXPP; MTCW 1, 2; PAB; PFS 5; RGAL 4; TUS

MacLennan, (John) Hugh
1907-1990 .... **CLC 2, 14, 92**
See also CA 5-8R; 142; CANR 33; DAC; DAM MST; DLB 68; EWL 3; MTCW 1, 2; RGEL 2; TWA

MacLeod, Alistair 1936- .... **CLC 56, 165**
See also CA 123; CCA 1; DAC; DAM MST; DLB 60; MTCW 2; RGSF 2

Macleod, Fiona
See Sharp, William
See also RGEL 2; SUFW

MacNeice, (Frederick) Louis
1907-1963 .... **CLC 1, 4, 10, 53; PC 61**
See also BRW 7; CA 85-88; CANR 61; DAB; DAM POET; DLB 10, 20; EWL 3; MTCW 1, 2; RGEL 2

MacNeill, Dand
See Fraser, George MacDonald

Macpherson, James 1736-1796 .... **LC 29**
See Ossian
See also BRWS 8; DLB 109; RGEL 2

Macpherson, (Jean) Jay 1931- .... **CLC 14**
See also CA 5-8R; CANR 90; CP 7; CWP; DLB 53

Macrobius fl. 430- .... **CMLC 48**

MacShane, Frank 1927-1999 .... **CLC 39**
See also CA 9-12R; 186; CANR 3, 33; DLB 111

Macumber, Mari
See Sandoz, Mari(e Susette)

Madach, Imre 1823-1864 .... **NCLC 19**

Madden, (Jerry) David 1933- .... **CLC 5, 15**
See also CA 1-4R; CAAS 3; CANR 4, 45; CN 7; CSW; DLB 6; MTCW 1

Maddern, Al(an)
See Ellison, Harlan (Jay)

Madhubuti, Haki R. 1942- ... **BLC 2; CLC 6, 73; PC 5**
See Lee, Don L.
See also BW 2, 3; CA 73-76; CANR 24, 51, 73; CP 7; CSW; DAM MULT, POET; DLB 5, 41; DLBD 8; EWL 3; MTCW 2; RGAL 4

Madison, James 1751-1836 .... **NCLC 126**
See also DLB 37

Maepenn, Hugh
See Kuttner, Henry

Maepenn, K. H.
See Kuttner, Henry

Maeterlinck, Maurice 1862-1949 ..... **TCLC 3**
See also CA 104; 136; DAM DRAM; DLB 192; EW 8; EWL 3; GFL 1789 to the Present; LMFS 2; RGWL 2, 3; SATA 66; TWA

Maginn, William 1794-1842 .... **NCLC 8**
See also DLB 110, 159

Mahapatra, Jayanta 1928- .... **CLC 33**
See also CA 73-76; CAAS 9; CANR 15, 33, 66, 87; CP 7; DAM MULT

Mahfouz, Naguib (Abdel Aziz Al-Sabilgi)
1911(?)- .... **CLC 153; SSC 66**
See Mahfuz, Najib (Abdel Aziz al-Sabilgi)
See also AAYA 49; BEST 89:2; CA 128; CANR 55, 101; DA3; DAM NOV; MTCW 1, 2; RGWL 2, 3; SSFS 9

Mahfuz, Najib (Abdel Aziz al-Sabilgi)
.... **CLC 52, 55**
See Mahfouz, Naguib (Abdel Aziz Al-Sabilgi)
See also AFW; CWW 2; DLBY 1988; EWL 3; RGSF 2; WLIT 2

Mahon, Derek 1941- .... **CLC 27; PC 60**
See also BRWS 6; CA 113; 128; CANR 88; CP 7; DLB 40; EWL 3

Maiakovskii, Vladimir
See Mayakovski, Vladimir (Vladimirovich)
See also IDTP; RGWL 2, 3

Mailer, Norman (Kingsley) 1923- . **CLC 1, 2, 3, 4, 5, 8, 11, 14, 28, 39, 74, 111**
See also AAYA 31; AITN 2; AMW; AMWC 2; AMWR 2; BPFB 2; CA 9-12R; CABS 1; CANR 28, 74, 77, 130; CDALB 1968-1988; CN 7; CPW; DA; DA3; DAB; DAC; DAM MST, NOV, POP; DLB 2, 16, 28, 185, 278; DLBD 3; DLBY 1980, 1983; EWL 3; MTCW 1, 2; NFS 10; RGAL 4; TUS

Maillet, Antonine 1929- .... **CLC 54, 118**
See also CA 115; 120; CANR 46, 74, 77, 134; CCA 1; CWW 2; DAC; DLB 60; INT CA-120; MTCW 2

Mais, Roger 1905-1955 .... **TCLC 8**
See also BW 1, 3; CA 105; 124; CANR 82; CDWLB 3; DLB 125; EWL 3; MTCW 1; RGEL 2

Maistre, Joseph 1753-1821 .... **NCLC 37**
See also GFL 1789 to the Present

Maitland, Frederic William 1850-1906 .... **TCLC 65**

Maitland, Sara (Louise) 1950- .... **CLC 49**
See also CA 69-72; CANR 13, 59; DLB 271; FW

Major, Clarence 1936- ... **BLC 2; CLC 3, 19, 48**
See also AFAW 2; BW 2, 3; CA 21-24R; CAAS 6; CANR 13, 25, 53, 82; CN 7; CP 7; CSW; DAM MULT; DLB 33; EWL 3; MSW

Major, Kevin (Gerald) 1949- .... **CLC 26**
See also AAYA 16; CA 97-100; CANR 21, 38, 112; CLR 11; DAC; DLB 60; INT CANR-21; JRDA; MAICYA 1, 2; MAICYAS 1; SATA 32, 82, 134; WYA; YAW

Maki, James
See Ozu, Yasujiro

Makine, Andrei 1957- .... **CLC 198**
See also CA 176; CANR 103

Malabaila, Damiano
See Levi, Primo

Malamud, Bernard 1914-1986 .. **CLC 1, 2, 3, 5, 8, 9, 11, 18, 27, 44, 78, 85; SSC 15; TCLC 129; WLC**
See also AAYA 16; AMWS 1; BPFB 2; BYA 15; CA 5-8R; 118; CABS 1; CANR 28, 62, 114; CDALB 1941-1968; CPW; DA; DA3; DAB; DAC; DAM MST, NOV, POP; DLB 2, 28, 152; DLBY 1980, 1986; EWL 3; EXPS; LAIT 4; LATS 1:1; MTCW 1, 2; NFS 4, 9; RGAL 4; RGSF 2; SSFS 8, 13, 16; TUS

Malan, Herman
See Bosman, Herman Charles; Bosman, Herman Charles

Malaparte, Curzio 1898-1957 .... **TCLC 52**
See also DLB 264

Malcolm, Dan
See Silverberg, Robert

Malcolm, Janet 1934- .... **CLC 201**
See also CA 123; CANR 89; NCFS 1

Malcolm X .... **BLC 2; CLC 82, 117; WLCS**
See Little, Malcolm
See also LAIT 5; NCFS 3

Malherbe, Francois de 1555-1628 .... **LC 5**
See also GFL Beginnings to 1789

Mallarme, Stephane 1842-1898 ...... **NCLC 4, 41; PC 4**
See also DAM POET; DLB 217; EW 7; GFL 1789 to the Present; LMFS 2; RGWL 2, 3; TWA

Mallet-Joris, Francoise 1930- .... **CLC 11**
See also CA 65-68; CANR 17; CWW 2; DLB 83; EWL 3; GFL 1789 to the Present

Malley, Ern
See McAuley, James Phillip

Mallon, Thomas 1951- .... **CLC 172**
See also CA 110; CANR 29, 57, 92

Mallowan, Agatha Christie
See Christie, Agatha (Mary Clarissa)

Maloff, Saul 1922- .... **CLC 5**
See also CA 33-36R

Malone, Louis
See MacNeice, (Frederick) Louis

Malone, Michael (Christopher) 1942- .... **CLC 43**
See also CA 77-80; CANR 14, 32, 57, 114

Malory, Sir Thomas 1410(?)-1471(?) . **LC 11, 88; WLCS**
See also BRW 1; BRWR 2; CDBLB Before 1660; DA; DAB; DAC; DAM MST; DLB 146; EFS 2; RGEL 2; SATA 59; SATA-Brief 33; TEA; WLIT 3

Malouf, (George Joseph) David 1934- .... **CLC 28, 86**
See also CA 124; CANR 50, 76; CN 7; CP 7; DLB 289; EWL 3; MTCW 2

Malraux, (Georges-)Andre 1901-1976 .... **CLC 1, 4, 9, 13, 15, 57**
See also BPFB 2; CA 21-22; 69-72; CANR 34, 58; CAP 2; DA3; DAM NOV; DLB 72; EW 12; EWL 3; GFL 1789 to the Present; MTCW 1, 2; RGWL 2, 3; TWA

Malthus, Thomas Robert 1766-1834 .... **NCLC 145**
See also DLB 107, 158; RGEL 2

Malzberg, Barry N(athaniel) 1939- ... **CLC 7**
See also CA 61-64; CAAS 4; CANR 16; CMW 4; DLB 8; SFW 4

Mamet, David (Alan) 1947- .. **CLC 9, 15, 34, 46, 91, 166; DC 4, 24**
See also AAYA 3, 60; AMWS 14; CA 81-84; CABS 3; CANR 15, 41, 67, 72, 129; CD 5; DA3; DAM DRAM; DFS 2, 3, 6, 12, 15; DLB 7; EWL 3; IDFW 4; MTCW 1, 2; RGAL 4

Mamoulian, Rouben (Zachary) 1897-1987 .... **CLC 16**
See also CA 25-28R; 124; CANR 85

Mandelshtam, Osip
See Mandelstam, Osip (Emilievich)
See also EW 10; EWL 3; RGWL 2, 3

Mandelstam, Osip (Emilievich) 1891(?)-1943(?) .... **PC 14; TCLC 2, 6**
See Mandelshtam, Osip
See also CA 104; 150; MTCW 2; TWA

Mander, (Mary) Jane 1877-1949 ... **TCLC 31**
See also CA 162; RGEL 2

Mandeville, Bernard 1670-1733 .... **LC 82**
See also DLB 101

Mandeville, Sir John fl. 1350- ...... **CMLC 19**
See also DLB 146

Mandiargues, Andre Pieyre de .... **CLC 41**
See Pieyre de Mandiargues, Andre
See also DLB 83

Mandrake, Ethel Belle
See Thurman, Wallace (Henry)

Mangan, James Clarence 1803-1849 .... **NCLC 27**
See also RGEL 2

Maniere, J.-E.
See Giraudoux, Jean(-Hippolyte)

Mankiewicz, Herman (Jacob) 1897-1953 .... **TCLC 85**
See also CA 120; 169; DLB 26; IDFW 3, 4

Manley, (Mary) Delariviere 1672(?)-1724 .... **LC 1, 42**
See also DLB 39, 80; RGEL 2

Mann, Abel
See Creasey, John

Mann, Emily 1952- .... **DC 7**
See also CA 130; CAD; CANR 55; CD 5; CWD; DLB 266

Mann, (Luiz) Heinrich 1871-1950 ... **TCLC 9**
See also CA 106; 164; 181; DLB 66, 118; EW 8; EWL 3; RGWL 2, 3

Mann, (Paul) Thomas 1875-1955 .... **SSC 5, 80; TCLC 2, 8, 14, 21, 35, 44, 60; WLC**
See also BPFB 2; CA 104; 128; CANR 133; CDWLB 2; DA; DA3; DAB; DAC; DAM MST, NOV; DLB 66; EW 9; EWL 3; GLL 1; LATS 1:1; LMFS 1; MTCW 1, 2; NFS 17; RGSF 2; RGWL 2, 3; SSFS 4, 9; TWA

Mannheim, Karl 1893-1947 .... **TCLC 65**
See also CA 204

Manning, David
See Faust, Frederick (Schiller)
See also TCWW 2

Manning, Frederic 1882-1935 .... **TCLC 25**
See also CA 124; 216; DLB 260

Manning, Olivia 1915-1980 .... **CLC 5, 19**
See also CA 5-8R; 101; CANR 29; EWL 3; FW; MTCW 1; RGEL 2

Mano, D. Keith 1942- .... **CLC 2, 10**
See also CA 25-28R; CAAS 6; CANR 26, 57; DLB 6

Mansfield, Katherine .... **SSC 9, 23, 38, 81; TCLC 2, 8, 39, 164; WLC**
See Beauchamp, Kathleen Mansfield
See also BPFB 2; BRW 7; DAB; DLB 162; EWL 3; EXPS; FW; GLL 1; RGEL 2; RGSF 2; SSFS 2, 8, 10, 11; WWE 1

Manso, Peter 1940- .... **CLC 39**
See also CA 29-32R; CANR 44

Mantecon, Juan Jimenez
See Jimenez (Mantecon), Juan Ramon

Mantel, Hilary (Mary) 1952- .... **CLC 144**
See also CA 125; CANR 54, 101; CN 7; DLB 271; RHW

Manton, Peter
See Creasey, John

Man Without a Spleen, A
See Chekhov, Anton (Pavlovich)

Manzoni, Alessandro 1785-1873 ... **NCLC 29, 98**
See also EW 5; RGWL 2, 3; TWA

Map, Walter 1140-1209 .... **CMLC 32**

Mapu, Abraham (ben Jekutiel) 1808-1867 .... **NCLC 18**

Mara, Sally
See Queneau, Raymond

Maracle, Lee 1950- .... **NNAL**
See also CA 149

Marat, Jean Paul 1743-1793 .... **LC 10**

Marcel, Gabriel Honore 1889-1973 . **CLC 15**
See also CA 102; 45-48; EWL 3; MTCW 1, 2

March, William 1893-1954 .... **TCLC 96**
See also CA 216

Marchbanks, Samuel
See Davies, (William) Robertson
See also CCA 1

Marchi, Giacomo
See Bassani, Giorgio

Marcus Aurelius
See Aurelius, Marcus
See also AW 2

Marguerite
See de Navarre, Marguerite

Marguerite d'Angouleme
See de Navarre, Marguerite
See also GFL Beginnings to 1789

Marguerite de Navarre
See de Navarre, Marguerite
See also RGWL 2, 3

Margulies, Donald 1954- .... **CLC 76**
See also AAYA 57; CA 200; DFS 13; DLB 228

Marie de France c. 12th cent. - ...... **CMLC 8; PC 22**
See also DLB 208; FW; RGWL 2, 3

Marie de l'Incarnation 1599-1672 ...... **LC 10**

Marier, Captain Victor
See Griffith, D(avid Lewelyn) W(ark)

Mariner, Scott
See Pohl, Frederik

Marinetti, Filippo Tommaso 1876-1944 .... **TCLC 10**
See also CA 107; DLB 114, 264; EW 9; EWL 3

Marivaux, Pierre Carlet de Chamblain de 1688-1763 .... **DC 7; LC 4**
See also GFL Beginnings to 1789; RGWL 2, 3; TWA

Markandaya, Kamala .... **CLC 8, 38**
See Taylor, Kamala (Purnaiya)
See also BYA 13; CN 7; EWL 3

Markfield, Wallace 1926-2002 .... **CLC 8**
See also CA 69-72; 208; CAAS 3; CN 7; DLB 2, 28; DLBY 2002

Markham, Edwin 1852-1940 .... **TCLC 47**
See also CA 160; DLB 54, 186; RGAL 4

Markham, Robert
See Amis, Kingsley (William)

Markoosie .... **NNAL**
See Patsauq, Markoosie
See also CLR 23; DAM MULT

Marks, J.
See Highwater, Jamake (Mamake)

Marks, J
See Highwater, Jamake (Mamake)

Marks-Highwater, J
See Highwater, Jamake (Mamake)

Marks-Highwater, J.
See Highwater, Jamake (Mamake)

Markson, David M(errill) 1927- .... **CLC 67**
See also CA 49-52; CANR 1, 91; CN 7

Marlatt, Daphne (Buckle) 1942- ..... **CLC 168**
See also CA 25-28R; CANR 17, 39; CN 7; CP 7; CWP; DLB 60; FW

Marley, Bob .... **CLC 17**
See Marley, Robert Nesta

Marley, Robert Nesta 1945-1981
See Marley, Bob
See also CA 107; 103

Marlowe, Christopher 1564-1593 . **DC 1; LC 22, 47; PC 57; WLC**
See also BRW 1; BRWR 1; CDBLB Before 1660; DA; DA3; DAB; DAC; DAM DRAM, MST; DFS 1, 5, 13; DLB 62; EXPP; LMFS 1; RGEL 2; TEA; WLIT 3

Marlowe, Stephen 1928- .... **CLC 70**
See Queen, Ellery
See also CA 13-16R; CANR 6, 55; CMW 4; SFW 4

Marmion, Shakerley 1603-1639 .... **LC 89**
See also DLB 58; RGEL 2

Marmontel, Jean-Francois 1723-1799 .. **LC 2**

Maron, Monika 1941- .... **CLC 165**
See also CA 201

Marquand, John P(hillips) 1893-1960 .... **CLC 2, 10**
See also AMW; BPFB 2; CA 85-88; CANR 73; CMW 4; DLB 9, 102; EWL 3; MTCW 2; RGAL 4

Marques, Rene 1919-1979 .. **CLC 96; HLC 2**
See also CA 97-100; 85-88; CANR 78; DAM MULT; DLB 305; EWL 3; HW 1, 2; LAW; RGSF 2

Marquez, Gabriel (Jose) Garcia
See Garcia Marquez, Gabriel (Jose)

Marquis, Don(ald Robert Perry) 1878-1937 .... **TCLC 7**
See also CA 104; 166; DLB 11, 25; RGAL 4

Marquis de Sade
See Sade, Donatien Alphonse Francois

Marric, J. J.
See Creasey, John
See also MSW

Marryat, Frederick 1792-1848 .... **NCLC 3**
See also DLB 21, 163; RGEL 2; WCH

Marsden, James
See Creasey, John

Marsh, Edward 1872-1953 .... **TCLC 99**

Marsh, (Edith) Ngaio 1895-1982 .. **CLC 7, 53**
See also CA 9-12R; CANR 6, 58; CMW 4; CPW; DAM POP; DLB 77; MSW; MTCW 1, 2; RGEL 2; TEA

Marshall, Garry 1934- .... **CLC 17**
See also AAYA 3; CA 111; SATA 60

Marshall, Paule 1929- .. **BLC 3; CLC 27, 72; SSC 3**
See also AFAW 1, 2; AMWS 11; BPFB 2; BW 2, 3; CA 77-80; CANR 25, 73, 129; CN 7; DA3; DAM MULT; DLB 33, 157, 227; EWL 3; LATS 1:2; MTCW 1, 2; RGAL 4; SSFS 15

Marshallik
See Zangwill, Israel

Marsten, Richard
See Hunter, Evan

Marston, John 1576-1634 .... **LC 33**
See also BRW 2; DAM DRAM; DLB 58, 172; RGEL 2

Martel, Yann 1963- .... **CLC 192**
See also CA 146; CANR 114

Martha, Henry
See Harris, Mark

Marti, Jose
See Marti (y Perez), Jose (Julian)
See also DLB 290

Marti (y Perez), Jose (Julian) 1853-1895 .... **HLC 2; NCLC 63**
See Marti, Jose
See also DAM MULT; HW 2; LAW; RGWL 2, 3; WLIT 1

Martial c. 40-c. 104 .... **CMLC 35; PC 10**
See also AW 2; CDWLB 1; DLB 211; RGWL 2, 3

Martin, Ken
See Hubbard, L(afayette) Ron(ald)

Martin, Richard
See Creasey, John

Martin, Steve 1945- .... **CLC 30**
See also AAYA 53; CA 97-100; CANR 30, 100; DFS 19; MTCW 1

Martin, Valerie 1948- .... **CLC 89**
See also BEST 90:2; CA 85-88; CANR 49, 89

Martin, Violet Florence 1862-1915 .. **SSC 56; TCLC 51**

Martin, Webber
See Silverberg, Robert

Martindale, Patrick Victor
See White, Patrick (Victor Martindale)

Martin du Gard, Roger 1881-1958 .... **TCLC 24**
See also CA 118; CANR 94; DLB 65; EWL 3; GFL 1789 to the Present; RGWL 2, 3

Martineau, Harriet 1802-1876 ...... **NCLC 26, 137**
See also DLB 21, 55, 159, 163, 166, 190; FW; RGEL 2; YABC 2

Martines, Julia
See O'Faolain, Julia

Martinez, Enrique Gonzalez
See Gonzalez Martinez, Enrique

Martinez, Jacinto Benavente y
See Benavente (y Martinez), Jacinto

Martinez de la Rosa, Francisco de Paula 1787-1862 .... **NCLC 102**
See also TWA

Martinez Ruiz, Jose 1873-1967
See Azorin; Ruiz, Jose Martinez
See also CA 93-96; HW 1

Martinez Sierra, Gregorio 1881-1947 .... **TCLC 6**
See also CA 115; EWL 3

Martinez Sierra, Maria (de la O'LeJarraga) 1874-1974 .... **TCLC 6**
See also CA 115; EWL 3

Martinsen, Martin
See Follett, Ken(neth Martin)

Martinson, Harry (Edmund) 1904-1978 .... **CLC 14**
See also CA 77-80; CANR 34, 130; DLB 259; EWL 3

Martyn, Edward 1859-1923 .... **TCLC 131**
See also CA 179; DLB 10; RGEL 2

Marut, Ret
See Traven, B.

Marut, Robert
See Traven, B.

Marvell, Andrew 1621-1678 .... **LC 4, 43; PC 10; WLC**
See also BRW 2; BRWR 2; CDBLB 1660-1789; DA; DAB; DAC; DAM MST, POET; DLB 131; EXPP; PFS 5; RGEL 2; TEA; WP

Marx, Karl (Heinrich) 1818-1883 .... **NCLC 17, 114**
See also DLB 129; LATS 1:1; TWA

Masaoka, Shiki -1902 .... **TCLC 18**
See Masaoka, Tsunenori
See also RGWL 3

Masaoka, Tsunenori 1867-1902
See Masaoka, Shiki
See also CA 117; 191; TWA

Masefield, John (Edward) 1878-1967 .... **CLC 11, 47**
See also CA 19-20; 25-28R; CANR 33; CAP 2; CDBLB 1890-1914; DAM POET; DLB 10, 19, 153, 160; EWL 3; EXPP; FANT; MTCW 1, 2; PFS 5; RGEL 2; SATA 19

Maso, Carole 19(?)- .... **CLC 44**
See also CA 170; GLL 2; RGAL 4

Mason, Bobbie Ann 1940- ... **CLC 28, 43, 82, 154; SSC 4**
See also AAYA 5, 42; AMWS 8; BPFB 2; CA 53-56; CANR 11, 31, 58, 83, 125; CDALBS; CN 7; CSW; DA3; DLB 173; DLBY 1987; EWL 3; EXPS; INT CANR-31; MTCW 1, 2; NFS 4; RGAL 4; RGSF 2; SSFS 3, 8, 20; YAW

Mason, Ernst
See Pohl, Frederik

Mason, Hunni B.
See Sternheim, (William Adolf) Carl

Mason, Lee W.
See Malzberg, Barry N(athaniel)

Mason, Nick 1945- .... **CLC 35**

Mason, Tally
See Derleth, August (William)

Mass, Anna .... **CLC 59**

Mass, William
See Gibson, William

Massinger, Philip 1583-1640 .... **LC 70**
See also DLB 58; RGEL 2

Master Lao
See Lao Tzu

Masters, Edgar Lee 1868-1950 .... **PC 1, 36; TCLC 2, 25; WLCS**
See also AMWS 1; CA 104; 133; CDALB 1865-1917; DA; DAC; DAM MST, POET; DLB 54; EWL 3; EXPP; MTCW 1, 2; RGAL 4; TUS; WP

Masters, Hilary 1928- .... **CLC 48**
See also CA 25-28R; 217; CAAE 217; CANR 13, 47, 97; CN 7; DLB 244

Mastrosimone, William 19(?)- .... **CLC 36**
See also CA 186; CAD; CD 5

Mathe, Albert
See Camus, Albert

Mather, Cotton 1663-1728 .... **LC 38**
See also AMWS 2; CDALB 1640-1865; DLB 24, 30, 140; RGAL 4; TUS

Mather, Increase 1639-1723 .... **LC 38**
See also DLB 24

Matheson, Richard (Burton) 1926- .. **CLC 37**
See also AAYA 31; CA 97-100; CANR 88, 99; DLB 8, 44; HGG; INT CA-97-100; SCFW 2; SFW 4; SUFW 2

Mathews, Harry 1930- .... **CLC 6, 52**
See also CA 21-24R; CAAS 6; CANR 18, 40, 98; CN 7

Mathews, John Joseph 1894-1979 .. **CLC 84; NNAL**
See also CA 19-20; 142; CANR 45; CAP 2; DAM MULT; DLB 175

Mathias, Roland (Glyn) 1915- .... **CLC 45**
See also CA 97-100; CANR 19, 41; CP 7; DLB 27

Matsuo Basho 1644-1694 .... **LC 62; PC 3**
See Basho, Matsuo
See also DAM POET; PFS 2, 7

Matheson, Rodney
See Creasey, John

Matthews, (James) Brander 1852-1929 .... **TCLC 95**
See also DLB 71, 78; DLBD 13

Matthews, (James) Brander 1852-1929 .... **TCLC 95**
See also CA 181; DLB 71, 78; DLBD 13

Matthews, Greg 1949- .... **CLC 45**
See also CA 135

Matthews, William (Procter III) 1942-1997 .... **CLC 40**
See also AMWS 9; CA 29-32R; 162; CAAS 18; CANR 12, 57; CP 7; DLB 5

Matthias, John (Edward) 1941- .... **CLC 9**
See also CA 33-36R; CANR 56; CP 7

Matthiessen, F(rancis) O(tto) 1902-1950 .... **TCLC 100**
See also CA 185; DLB 63

Matthiessen, Peter 1927- ... **CLC 5, 7, 11, 32, 64**
See also AAYA 6, 40; AMWS 5; ANW; BEST 90:4; BPFB 2; CA 9-12R; CANR 21, 50, 73, 100; CN 7; DA3; DAM NOV; DLB 6, 173, 275; MTCW 1, 2; SATA 27

Maturin, Charles Robert 1780(?)-1824 .... **NCLC 6**
See also BRWS 8; DLB 178; HGG; LMFS 1; RGEL 2; SUFW

Matute (Ausejo), Ana Maria 1925- .. **CLC 11**
See also CA 89-92; CANR 129; CWW 2; EWL 3; MTCW 1; RGSF 2

Maugham, W. S.
See Maugham, W(illiam) Somerset

Maugham, W(illiam) Somerset 1874-1965 .. **CLC 1, 11, 15, 67, 93; SSC 8; WLC**
See also AAYA 55; BPFB 2; BRW 6; CA 5-8R; 25-28R; CANR 40, 127; CDBLB 1914-1945; CMW 4; DA; DA3; DAB; DAC; DAM DRAM, MST, NOV; DLB 10, 36, 77, 100, 162, 195; EWL 3; LAIT 3; MTCW 1, 2; RGEL 2; RGSF 2; SATA 54; SSFS 17

Maugham, William Somerset
See Maugham, W(illiam) Somerset

Maupassant, (Henri Rene Albert) Guy de 1850-1893 . **NCLC 1, 42, 83; SSC 1, 64; WLC**
See also BYA 14; DA; DA3; DAB; DAC; DAM MST; DLB 123; EW 7; EXPS; GFL 1789 to the Present; LAIT 2; LMFS 1; RGSF 2; RGWL 2, 3; SSFS 4; SUFW; TWA

Maupin, Armistead (Jones, Jr.) 1944- .... **CLC 95**
See also CA 125; 130; CANR 58, 101; CPW; DA3; DAM POP; DLB 278; GLL 1; INT CA-130; MTCW 2

Maurhut, Richard
See Traven, B.

Mauriac, Claude 1914-1996 .... **CLC 9**
See also CA 89-92; 152; CWW 2; DLB 83; EWL 3; GFL 1789 to the Present

Mauriac, Francois (Charles) 1885-1970 .... **CLC 4, 9, 56; SSC 24**
See also CA 25-28; CAP 2; DLB 65; EW 10; EWL 3; GFL 1789 to the Present; MTCW 1, 2; RGWL 2, 3; TWA

Mavor, Osborne Henry 1888-1951
See Bridie, James
See also CA 104

Maxwell, William (Keepers, Jr.) 1908-2000 .... **CLC 19**
See also AMWS 8; CA 93-96; 189; CANR 54, 95; CN 7; DLB 218, 278; DLBY 1980; INT CA-93-96; SATA-Obit 128

May, Elaine 1932- .... **CLC 16**
See also CA 124; 142; CAD; CWD; DLB 44

Mayakovski, Vladimir (Vladimirovich) 1893-1930 .... **TCLC 4, 18**
See Maiakovskii, Vladimir; Mayakovsky, Vladimir
See also CA 104; 158; EWL 3; MTCW 2; SFW 4; TWA

Mayakovsky, Vladimir
See Mayakovski, Vladimir (Vladimirovich)
See also EW 11; WP

Mayhew, Henry 1812-1887 .... **NCLC 31**
See also DLB 18, 55, 190

Mayle, Peter 1939(?)- .... **CLC 89**
See also CA 139; CANR 64, 109

Maynard, Joyce 1953- .... **CLC 23**
See also CA 111; 129; CANR 64

Mayne, William (James Carter) 1928- .... **CLC 12**
See also AAYA 20; CA 9-12R; CANR 37, 80, 100; CLR 25; FANT; JRDA; MAICYA 1, 2; MAICYAS 1; SAAS 11; SATA 6, 68, 122; SUFW 2; YAW

Mayo, Jim
See L'Amour, Louis (Dearborn)
See also TCWW 2

Maysles, Albert 1926- .... **CLC 16**
See also CA 29-32R

Maysles, David 1932-1987 .... **CLC 16**
See also CA 191

Mazer, Norma Fox 1931- .... **CLC 26**
See also AAYA 5, 36; BYA 1, 8; CA 69-72; CANR 12, 32, 66, 129; CLR 23; JRDA; MAICYA 1, 2; SAAS 1; SATA 24, 67, 105; WYA; YAW

Mazzini, Guiseppe 1805-1872 .... **NCLC 34**

McAlmon, Robert (Menzies) 1895-1956 .... **TCLC 97**
See also CA 107; 168; DLB 4, 45; DLBD 15; GLL 1

McAuley, James Phillip 1917-1976 .. **CLC 45**
See also CA 97-100; DLB 260; RGEL 2

McBain, Ed
See Hunter, Evan
See also MSW

McBrien, William (Augustine) 1930- .... **CLC 44**
See also CA 107; CANR 90

McCabe, Patrick 1955- .... **CLC 133**
See also BRWS 9; CA 130; CANR 50, 90; CN 7; DLB 194

McCaffrey, Anne (Inez) 1926- .... **CLC 17**
See also AAYA 6, 34; AITN 2; BEST 89:2; BPFB 2; BYA 5; CA 25-28R; 227; CAAE 227; CANR 15, 35, 55, 96; CLR 49; CPW; DA3; DAM NOV, POP; DLB 8; JRDA; MAICYA 1, 2; MTCW 1, 2; SAAS 11; SATA 8, 70, 116, 152; SATA-Essay 152; SFW 4; SUFW 2; WYA; YAW

McCall, Nathan 1955(?)- .... **CLC 86**
See also AAYA 59; BW 3; CA 146; CANR 88

McCann, Arthur
See Campbell, John W(ood, Jr.)

McCann, Edson
See Pohl, Frederik

McCarthy, Charles, Jr. 1933-
See McCarthy, Cormac
See also CANR 42, 69, 101; CN 7; CPW; CSW; DA3; DAM POP; MTCW 2

McCarthy, Cormac ...... **CLC 4, 57, 101, 204**
See McCarthy, Charles, Jr.
See also AAYA 41; AMWS 8; BPFB 2; CA 13-16R; CANR 10; DLB 6, 143, 256; EWL 3; LATS 1:2; TCWW 2

McCarthy, Mary (Therese) 1912-1989 .. **CLC 1, 3, 5, 14, 24, 39, 59; SSC 24**
See also AMW; BPFB 2; CA 5-8R; 129; CANR 16, 50, 64; DA3; DLB 2; DLBY 1981; EWL 3; FW; INT CANR-16; MAWW; MTCW 1, 2; RGAL 4; TUS

McCartney, (James) Paul 1942- . **CLC 12, 35**
See also CA 146; CANR 111

McCauley, Stephen (D.) 1955- .... **CLC 50**
See also CA 141

McClaren, Peter .... **CLC 70**

McClure, Michael (Thomas) 1932- ... **CLC 6, 10**
See also BG 3; CA 21-24R; CAD; CANR 17, 46, 77, 131; CD 5; CP 7; DLB 16; WP

McCorkle, Jill (Collins) 1958- .... **CLC 51**
See also CA 121; CANR 113; CSW; DLB 234; DLBY 1987

McCourt, Frank 1930- .... **CLC 109**
See also AMWS 12; CA 157; CANR 97; NCFS 1

McCourt, James 1941- .... **CLC 5**
See also CA 57-60; CANR 98

McCourt, Malachy 1931- .... **CLC 119**
See also SATA 126

McCoy, Horace (Stanley) 1897-1955 .... **TCLC 28**
See also AMWS 13; CA 108; 155; CMW 4; DLB 9

McCrae, John 1872-1918 .... **TCLC 12**
See also CA 109; DLB 92; PFS 5

McCreigh, James
See Pohl, Frederik

McCullers, (Lula) Carson (Smith) 1917-1967 .... **CLC 1, 4, 10, 12, 48, 100; SSC 9, 24; TCLC 155; WLC**
See also AAYA 21; AMW; AMWC 2; BPFB 2; CA 5-8R; 25-28R; CABS 1, 3; CANR 18, 132; CDALB 1941-1968; DA; DA3; DAB; DAC; DAM MST, NOV; DFS 5, 18; DLB 2, 7, 173, 228; EWL 3; EXPS; FW; GLL 1; LAIT 3, 4; MAWW; MTCW 1, 2; NFS 6, 13; RGAL 4; RGSF 2; SATA 27; SSFS 5; TUS; YAW

McCulloch, John Tyler
See Burroughs, Edgar Rice

McCullough, Colleen 1938(?)- .. **CLC 27, 107**
See also AAYA 36; BPFB 2; CA 81-84; CANR 17, 46, 67, 98; CPW; DA3; DAM NOV, POP; MTCW 1, 2; RHW

McCunn, Ruthanne Lum 1946- .... **AAL**
See also CA 119; CANR 43, 96; LAIT 2; SATA 63

McDermott, Alice 1953- .... **CLC 90**
See also CA 109; CANR 40, 90, 126; DLB 292

McElroy, Joseph 1930- .... **CLC 5, 47**
See also CA 17-20R; CN 7

McEwan, Ian (Russell) 1948- .... **CLC 13, 66, 169**
See also BEST 90:4; BRWS 4; CA 61-64; CANR 14, 41, 69, 87, 132; CN 7; DAM NOV; DLB 14, 194; HGG; MTCW 1, 2; RGSF 2; SUFW 2; TEA

McFadden, David 1940- .... **CLC 48**
See also CA 104; CP 7; DLB 60; INT CA-104

McFarland, Dennis 1950- .... **CLC 65**
See also CA 165; CANR 110

McGahern, John 1934- ... **CLC 5, 9, 48, 156; SSC 17**
See also CA 17-20R; CANR 29, 68, 113; CN 7; DLB 14, 231; MTCW 1

McGinley, Patrick (Anthony) 1937- . **CLC 41**
See also CA 120; 127; CANR 56; INT CA-127

McGinley, Phyllis 1905-1978 .... **CLC 14**
See also CA 9-12R; 77-80; CANR 19; CWRI 5; DLB 11, 48; PFS 9, 13; SATA 2, 44; SATA-Obit 24

McGinniss, Joe 1942- .... **CLC 32**
See also AITN 2; BEST 89:2; CA 25-28R; CANR 26, 70; CPW; DLB 185; INT CANR-26

McGivern, Maureen Daly
See Daly, Maureen

McGrath, Patrick 1950- .... **CLC 55**
See also CA 136; CANR 65; CN 7; DLB 231; HGG; SUFW 2

McGrath, Thomas (Matthew)
1916-1990 .... **CLC 28, 59**
See also AMWS 10; CA 9-12R; 132; CANR 6, 33, 95; DAM POET; MTCW 1; SATA 41; SATA-Obit 66

McGuane, Thomas (Francis III)
1939- .... **CLC 3, 7, 18, 45, 127**
See also AITN 2; BPFB 2; CA 49-52; CANR 5, 24, 49, 94; CN 7; DLB 2, 212; DLBY 1980; EWL 3; INT CANR-24; MTCW 1; TCWW 2

McGuckian, Medbh 1950- .... **CLC 48, 174; PC 27**
See also BRWS 5; CA 143; CP 7; CWP; DAM POET; DLB 40

McHale, Tom 1942(?)-1982 .... **CLC 3, 5**
See also AITN 1; CA 77-80; 106

McHugh, Heather 1948- .... **PC 61**
See also CA 69-72; CANR 11, 28, 55, 92; CP 7; CWP

McIlvanney, William 1936- .... **CLC 42**
See also CA 25-28R; CANR 61; CMW 4; DLB 14, 207

McIlwraith, Maureen Mollie Hunter
See Hunter, Mollie
See also SATA 2

McInerney, Jay 1955- .... **CLC 34, 112**
See also AAYA 18; BPFB 2; CA 116; 123; CANR 45, 68, 116; CN 7; CPW; DA3; DAM POP; DLB 292; INT CA-123; MTCW 2

McIntyre, Vonda N(eel) 1948- .... **CLC 18**
See also CA 81-84; CANR 17, 34, 69; MTCW 1; SFW 4; YAW

McKay, Claude .... **BLC 3; HR 3; PC 2; TCLC 7, 41; WLC**
See McKay, Festus Claudius
See also AFAW 1, 2; AMWS 10; DAB; DLB 4, 45, 51, 117; EWL 3; EXPP; GLL 2; LAIT 3; LMFS 2; PAB; PFS 4; RGAL 4; WP

McKay, Festus Claudius 1889-1948
See McKay, Claude
See also BW 1, 3; CA 104; 124; CANR 73; DA; DAC; DAM MST, MULT, NOV, POET; MTCW 1, 2; TUS

McKuen, Rod 1933- .... **CLC 1, 3**
See also AITN 1; CA 41-44R; CANR 40

McLoughlin, R. B.
See Mencken, H(enry) L(ouis)

McLuhan, (Herbert) Marshall
1911-1980 .... **CLC 37, 83**
See also CA 9-12R; 102; CANR 12, 34, 61; DLB 88; INT CANR-12; MTCW 1, 2

McManus, Declan Patrick Aloysius
See Costello, Elvis

McMillan, Terry (L.) 1951- . **BLCS; CLC 50, 61, 112**
See also AAYA 21; AMWS 13; BPFB 2; BW 2, 3; CA 140; CANR 60, 104, 131; CPW; DA3; DAM MULT, NOV, POP; MTCW 2; RGAL 4; YAW

McMurtry, Larry (Jeff) 1936- .. **CLC 2, 3, 7, 11, 27, 44, 127**
See also AAYA 15; AITN 2; AMWS 5; BEST 89:2; BPFB 2; CA 5-8R; CANR 19, 43, 64, 103; CDALB 1968-1988; CN 7; CPW; CSW; DA3; DAM NOV, POP; DLB 2, 143, 256; DLBY 1980, 1987; EWL 3; MTCW 1, 2; RGAL 4; TCWW 2

McNally, T. M. 1961- .... **CLC 82**

McNally, Terrence 1939- .... **CLC 4, 7, 41, 91**
See also AMWS 13; CA 45-48; CAD; CANR 2, 56, 116; CD 5; DA3; DAM DRAM; DFS 16, 19; DLB 7, 249; EWL 3; GLL 1; MTCW 2

McNamer, Deirdre 1950- .... **CLC 70**

McNeal, Tom .... **CLC 119**

McNeile, Herman Cyril 1888-1937
See Sapper
See also CA 184; CMW 4; DLB 77

McNickle, (William) D'Arcy
1904-1977 .... **CLC 89; NNAL**
See also CA 9-12R; 85-88; CANR 5, 45; DAM MULT; DLB 175, 212; RGAL 4; SATA-Obit 22

McPhee, John (Angus) 1931- .... **CLC 36**
See also AMWS 3; ANW; BEST 90:1; CA 65-68; CANR 20, 46, 64, 69, 121; CPW; DLB 185, 275; MTCW 1, 2; TUS

McPherson, James Alan 1943- . **BLCS; CLC 19, 77**
See also BW 1, 3; CA 25-28R; CAAS 17; CANR 24, 74; CN 7; CSW; DLB 38, 244; EWL 3; MTCW 1, 2; RGAL 4; RGSF 2

McPherson, William (Alexander)
1933- .... **CLC 34**
See also CA 69-72; CANR 28; INT CANR-28

McTaggart, J. McT. Ellis
See McTaggart, John McTaggart Ellis

McTaggart, John McTaggart Ellis
1866-1925 .... **TCLC 105**
See also CA 120; DLB 262

Mead, George Herbert 1863-1931 . **TCLC 89**
See also CA 212; DLB 270

Mead, Margaret 1901-1978 .... **CLC 37**
See also AITN 1; CA 1-4R; 81-84; CANR 4; DA3; FW; MTCW 1, 2; SATA-Obit 20

Meaker, Marijane (Agnes) 1927-
See Kerr, M. E.
See also CA 107; CANR 37, 63; INT CA-107; JRDA; MAICYA 1, 2; MAICYAS 1; MTCW 1; SATA 20, 61, 99; SATA-Essay 111; YAW

Medoff, Mark (Howard) 1940- .... **CLC 6, 23**
See also AITN 1; CA 53-56; CAD; CANR 5; CD 5; DAM DRAM; DFS 4; DLB 7; INT CANR-5

Medvedev, P. N.
See Bakhtin, Mikhail Mikhailovich

Meged, Aharon
See Megged, Aharon

Meged, Aron
See Megged, Aharon

Megged, Aharon 1920- .... **CLC 9**
See also CA 49-52; CAAS 13; CANR 1; EWL 3

Mehta, Gita 1943- .... **CLC 179**
See also CA 225; DNFS 2

Mehta, Ved (Parkash) 1934- .... **CLC 37**
See also CA 1-4R; 212; CAAE 212; CANR 2, 23, 69; MTCW 1

Melanchthon, Philipp 1497-1560 .... **LC 90**
See also DLB 179

Melanter
See Blackmore, R(ichard) D(oddridge)

Meleager c. 140B.C.-c. 70B.C. ...... **CMLC 53**

Melies, Georges 1861-1938 .... **TCLC 81**

Melikow, Loris
See Hofmannsthal, Hugo von

Melmoth, Sebastian
See Wilde, Oscar (Fingal O'Flahertie Wills)

Melo Neto, Joao Cabral de
See Cabral de Melo Neto, Joao
See also CWW 2; EWL 3

Meltzer, Milton 1915- .... **CLC 26**
See also AAYA 8, 45; BYA 2, 6; CA 13-16R; CANR 38, 92, 107; CLR 13; DLB 61; JRDA; MAICYA 1, 2; SAAS 1; SATA 1, 50, 80, 128; SATA-Essay 124; WYA; YAW

Melville, Herman 1819-1891 ..... **NCLC 3, 12, 29, 45, 49, 91, 93, 123; SSC 1, 17, 46; WLC**
See also AAYA 25; AMW; AMWR 1; CDALB 1640-1865; DA; DA3; DAB; DAC; DAM MST, NOV; DLB 3, 74, 250, 254; EXPN; EXPS; LAIT 1, 2; NFS 7, 9; RGAL 4; RGSF 2; SATA 59; SSFS 3; TUS

Members, Mark
See Powell, Anthony (Dymoke)

Membreno, Alejandro .... **CLC 59**

Menander c. 342B.C.-c. 293B.C. .... **CMLC 9, 51; DC 3**
See also AW 1; CDWLB 1; DAM DRAM; DLB 176; LMFS 1; RGWL 2, 3

Menchu, Rigoberta 1959- .. **CLC 160; HLCS 2**
See also CA 175; DNFS 1; WLIT 1

Mencken, H(enry) L(ouis)
1880-1956 .... **TCLC 13**
See also AMW; CA 105; 125; CDALB 1917-1929; DLB 11, 29, 63, 137, 222; EWL 3; MTCW 1, 2; NCFS 4; RGAL 4; TUS

Mendelsohn, Jane 1965- .... **CLC 99**
See also CA 154; CANR 94

Menton, Francisco de
See Chin, Frank (Chew, Jr.)

Mercer, David 1928-1980 .... **CLC 5**
See also CA 9-12R; 102; CANR 23; CBD; DAM DRAM; DLB 13; MTCW 1; RGEL 2

Merchant, Paul
See Ellison, Harlan (Jay)

Meredith, George 1828-1909 .. **PC 60; TCLC 17, 43**
See also CA 117; 153; CANR 80; CDBLB 1832-1890; DAM POET; DLB 18, 35, 57, 159; RGEL 2; TEA

Meredith, William (Morris) 1919- .... **CLC 4, 13, 22, 55; PC 28**
See also CA 9-12R; CAAS 14; CANR 6, 40, 129; CP 7; DAM POET; DLB 5

Merezhkovsky, Dmitrii Sergeevich
See Merezhkovsky, Dmitry Sergeyevich
See also DLB 295

Merezhkovsky, Dmitry Sergeyevich
See Merezhkovsky, Dmitry Sergeyevich
See also EWL 3

Merezhkovsky, Dmitry Sergeyevich
1865-1941 .... **TCLC 29**
See Merezhkovsky, Dmitrii Sergeevich; Merezhkovsky, Dmitry Sergeevich
See also CA 169

Merimee, Prosper 1803-1870 ... **NCLC 6, 65; SSC 7, 77**
See also DLB 119, 192; EW 6; EXPS; GFL 1789 to the Present; RGSF 2; RGWL 2, 3; SSFS 8; SUFW

Merkin, Daphne 1954- .... **CLC 44**
See also CA 123

Merleau-Ponty, Maurice
1908-1961 .... **TCLC 156**
See also CA 114; 89-92; DLB 296; GFL 1789 to the Present

Merlin, Arthur
See Blish, James (Benjamin)

Mernissi, Fatima 1940- .... **CLC 171**
See also CA 152; FW

Merrill, James (Ingram) 1926-1995 .. **CLC 2, 3, 6, 8, 13, 18, 34, 91; PC 28**
See also AMWS 3; CA 13-16R; 147; CANR 10, 49, 63, 108; DA3; DAM POET; DLB 5, 165; DLBY 1985; EWL 3; INT CANR-10; MTCW 1, 2; PAB; RGAL 4

Merriman, Alex
See Silverberg, Robert

Merriman, Brian 1747-1805 .... **NCLC 70**

Merritt, E. B.
See Waddington, Miriam

Merton, Thomas (James)
1915-1968 . **CLC 1, 3, 11, 34, 83; PC 10**
See also AMWS 8; CA 5-8R; 25-28R; CANR 22, 53, 111, 131; DA3; DLB 48; DLBY 1981; MTCW 1, 2

Merwin, W(illiam) S(tanley) 1927- ... **CLC 1, 2, 3, 5, 8, 13, 18, 45, 88; PC 45**
See also AMWS 3; CA 13-16R; CANR 15, 51, 112; CP 7; DA3; DAM POET; DLB 5, 169; EWL 3; INT CANR-15; MTCW 1, 2; PAB; PFS 5, 15; RGAL 4

Metastasio, Pietro 1698-1782 .... **LC 115**
See also RGWL 2, 3

Metcalf, John 1938- .... **CLC 37; SSC 43**
See also CA 113; CN 7; DLB 60; RGSF 2; TWA

Metcalf, Suzanne
See Baum, L(yman) Frank

Mew, Charlotte (Mary) 1870-1928 .. **TCLC 8**
See also CA 105; 189; DLB 19, 135; RGEL 2

Mewshaw, Michael 1943- .... **CLC 9**
See also CA 53-56; CANR 7, 47; DLBY 1980

Meyer, Conrad Ferdinand
1825-1898 .... **NCLC 81; SSC 30**
See also DLB 129; EW; RGWL 2, 3

Meyer, Gustav 1868-1932
See Meyrink, Gustav
See also CA 117; 190

Meyer, June
See Jordan, June (Meyer)

Meyer, Lynn
See Slavitt, David R(ytman)

Meyers, Jeffrey 1939- .... **CLC 39**
See also CA 73-76, 186; CAAE 186; CANR 54, 102; DLB 111

Meynell, Alice (Christina Gertrude Thompson) 1847-1922 .... **TCLC 6**
See also CA 104; 177; DLB 19, 98; RGEL 2

Meyrink, Gustav .... **TCLC 21**
See Meyer, Gustav
See also DLB 81; EWL 3

Michaels, Leonard 1933-2003 ..... **CLC 6, 25; SSC 16**
See also CA 61-64; 216; CANR 21, 62, 119; CN 7; DLB 130; MTCW 1

Michaux, Henri 1899-1984 .... **CLC 8, 19**
See also CA 85-88; 114; DLB 258; EWL 3; GFL 1789 to the Present; RGWL 2, 3

Micheaux, Oscar (Devereaux)
1884-1951 .... **TCLC 76**
See also BW 3; CA 174; DLB 50; TCWW 2

Michelangelo 1475-1564 .... **LC 12**
See also AAYA 43

Michelet, Jules 1798-1874 .... **NCLC 31**
See also EW 5; GFL 1789 to the Present

Michels, Robert 1876-1936 .... **TCLC 88**
See also CA 212

Michener, James A(lbert)
1907(?)-1997 .. **CLC 1, 5, 11, 29, 60, 109**
See also AAYA 27; AITN 1; BEST 90:1; BPFB 2; CA 5-8R; 161; CANR 21, 45, 68; CN 7; CPW; DA3; DAM NOV, POP; DLB 6; MTCW 1, 2; RHW

Mickiewicz, Adam 1798-1855 . **NCLC 3, 101; PC 38**
See also EW 5; RGWL 2, 3

Middleton, (John) Christopher
1926- .... **CLC 13**
See also CA 13-16R; CANR 29, 54, 117; CP 7; DLB 40

Middleton, Richard (Barham)
1882-1911 .... **TCLC 56**
See also CA 187; DLB 156; HGG

Middleton, Stanley 1919- .... **CLC 7, 38**
See also CA 25-28R; CAAS 23; CANR 21, 46, 81; CN 7; DLB 14

Middleton, Thomas 1580-1627 ...... **DC 5; LC 33**
See also BRW 2; DAM DRAM, MST; DFS 18; DLB 58; RGEL 2

Migueis, Jose Rodrigues 1901-1980 . **CLC 10**
See also DLB 287

Mikszath, Kalman 1847-1910 .... **TCLC 31**
See also CA 170

Miles, Jack .... **CLC 100**
See also CA 200

Miles, John Russiano
See Miles, Jack

Miles, Josephine (Louise)
1911-1985 .... **CLC 1, 2, 14, 34, 39**
See also CA 1-4R; 116; CANR 2, 55; DAM POET; DLB 48

Militant
See Sandburg, Carl (August)

Mill, Harriet (Hardy) Taylor
1807-1858 .... **NCLC 102**
See also FW

Mill, John Stuart 1806-1873 .... **NCLC 11, 58**
See also CDBLB 1832-1890; DLB 55, 190, 262; FW 1; RGEL 2; TEA

Millar, Kenneth 1915-1983 .... **CLC 14**
See Macdonald, Ross
See also CA 9-12R; 110; CANR 16, 63, 107; CMW 4; CPW; DA3; DAM POP; DLB 2, 226; DLBD 6; DLBY 1983; MTCW 1, 2

Millay, E. Vincent
See Millay, Edna St. Vincent

Millay, Edna St. Vincent 1892-1950 ..... **PC 6, 61; TCLC 4, 49; WLCS**
See Boyd, Nancy
See also AMW; CA 104; 130; CDALB 1917-1929; DA; DA3; DAB; DAC; DAM MST, POET; DLB 45, 249; EWL 3; EXPP; MAWW; MTCW 1, 2; PAB; PFS 3, 17; RGAL 4; TUS; WP

Miller, Arthur 1915- ...... **CLC 1, 2, 6, 10, 15, 26, 47, 78, 179; DC 1; WLC**
See also AAYA 15; AITN 1; AMW; AMWC 1; CA 1-4R; CABS 3; CAD; CANR 2, 30, 54, 76, 132; CD 5; CDALB 1941-1968; DA; DA3; DAB; DAC; DAM DRAM, MST; DFS 1, 3, 8; DLB 7, 266; EWL 3; LAIT 1, 4; LATS 1:2; MTCW 1, 2; RGAL 4; TUS; WYAS 1

Miller, Henry (Valentine)
1891-1980 .... **CLC 1, 2, 4, 9, 14, 43, 84; WLC**
See also AMW; BPFB 2; CA 9-12R; 97-100; CANR 33, 64; CDALB 1929-1941; DA; DA3; DAB; DAC; DAM MST, NOV; DLB 4, 9; DLBY 1980; EWL 3; MTCW 1, 2; RGAL 4; TUS

Miller, Hugh 1802-1856 .... **NCLC 143**
See also DLB 190

Miller, Jason 1939(?)-2001 .... **CLC 2**
See also AITN 1; CA 73-76; 197; CAD; CANR 130; DFS 12; DLB 7

Miller, Sue 1943- .... **CLC 44**
See also AMWS 12; BEST 90:3; CA 139; CANR 59, 91, 128; DA3; DAM POP; DLB 143

Miller, Walter M(ichael, Jr.)
1923-1996 .... **CLC 4, 30**
See also BPFB 2; CA 85-88; CANR 108; DLB 8; SCFW 1; SFW 4

Millett, Kate 1934- .... **CLC 67**
See also AITN 1; CA 73-76; CANR 32, 53, 76, 110; DA3; DLB 246; FW; GLL 1; MTCW 1, 2

Millhauser, Steven (Lewis) 1943- .... **CLC 21, 54, 109; SSC 57**
See also CA 110; 111; CANR 63, 114, 133; CN 7; DA3; DLB 2; FANT; INT CA-111; MTCW 2

Millin, Sarah Gertrude 1889-1968 ... **CLC 49**
See also CA 102; 93-96; DLB 225; EWL 3

Milne, A(lan) A(lexander)
1882-1956 .... **TCLC 6, 88**
See also BRWS 5; CA 104; 133; CLR 1, 26; CMW 4; CWRI 5; DA3; DAB; DAC; DAM MST; DLB 10, 77, 100, 160; FANT; MAICYA 1, 2; MTCW 1, 2; RGEL 2; SATA 100; WCH; YABC 1

Milner, Ron(ald) 1938-2004 ..... **BLC 3; CLC 56**
See also AITN 1; BW 1; CA 73-76; CAD; CANR 24, 81; CD 5; DAM MULT; DLB 38; MTCW 1

Milnes, Richard Monckton
1809-1885 .... **NCLC 61**
See also DLB 32, 184

Milosz, Czeslaw 1911- .... **CLC 5, 11, 22, 31, 56, 82; PC 8; WLCS**
See also CA 81-84; CANR 23, 51, 91, 126; CDWLB 4; CWW 2; DA3; DAM MST, POET; DLB 215; EW 13; EWL 3; MTCW 1, 2; PFS 16; RGWL 2, 3

Milton, John 1608-1674 ..... **LC 9, 43, 92; PC 19, 29; WLC**
See also BRW 2; BRWR 2; CDBLB 1660-1789; DA; DA3; DAB; DAC; DAM MST, POET; DLB 131, 151, 281; EFS 1; EXPP; LAIT 1; PAB; PFS 3, 17; RGEL 2; TEA; WLIT 3; WP

Min, Anchee 1957- .... **CLC 86**
See also CA 146; CANR 94

Minehaha, Cornelius
See Wedekind, (Benjamin) Frank(lin)

Miner, Valerie 1947- .... **CLC 40**
See also CA 97-100; CANR 59; FW; GLL 2

Minimo, Duca
See D'Annunzio, Gabriele

Minot, Susan 1956- .... **CLC 44, 159**
See also AMWS 6; CA 134; CANR 118; CN 7

Minus, Ed 1938- .... **CLC 39**
See also CA 185

Mirabai 1498(?)-1550(?) .... **PC 48**

Miranda, Javier
See Bioy Casares, Adolfo
See also CWW 2

Mirbeau, Octave 1848-1917 .... **TCLC 55**
See also CA 216; DLB 123, 192; GFL 1789 to the Present

Mirikitani, Janice 1942- .... **AAL**
See also CA 211; RGAL 4

Mirk, John (?)-c. 1414 .... **LC 105**
See also DLB 146

Miro (Ferrer), Gabriel (Francisco Victor)
1879-1930 .... **TCLC 5**
See also CA 104; 185; EWL 3

Misharin, Alexandr .... **CLC 59**
Mishima, Yukio ... **CLC 2, 4, 6, 9, 27; DC 1; SSC 4, TCLC 161**
See Hiraoka, Kimitake
See also AAYA 50; BPFB 2; GLL 1; MJW; MTCW 2; RGSF 2; RGWL 2, 3; SSFS 5, 12
Mistral, Frederic 1830-1914 .... **TCLC 51**
See also CA 122; 213; GFL 1789 to the Present
Mistral, Gabriela
See Godoy Alcayaga, Lucila
See also DLB 283; DNFS 1; EWL 3; LAW; RGWL 2, 3; WP
Mistry, Rohinton 1952- ... **CLC 71, 196; SSC 73**
See also BRWS 10; CA 141; CANR 86, 114; CCA 1; CN 7; DAC; SSFS 6
Mitchell, Clyde
See Ellison, Harlan (Jay)
Mitchell, Emerson Blackhorse Barney 1945- .... **NNAL**
See also CA 45-48
Mitchell, James Leslie 1901-1935
See Gibbon, Lewis Grassic
See also CA 104; 188; DLB 15
Mitchell, Joni 1943- .... **CLC 12**
See also CA 112; CCA 1
Mitchell, Joseph (Quincy) 1908-1996 .... **CLC 98**
See also CA 77-80; 152; CANR 69; CN 7; CSW; DLB 185; DLBY 1996
Mitchell, Margaret (Munnerlyn) 1900-1949 .... **TCLC 11**
See also AAYA 23; BPFB 2; BYA 1; CA 109; 125; CANR 55, 94; CDALBS; DA3; DAM NOV, POP; DLB 9; LAIT 2; MTCW 1, 2; NFS 9; RGAL 4; RHW; TUS; WYAS 1; YAW
Mitchell, Peggy
See Mitchell, Margaret (Munnerlyn)
Mitchell, S(ilas) Weir 1829-1914 .... **TCLC 36**
See also CA 165; DLB 202; RGAL 4
Mitchell, W(illiam) O(rmond) 1914-1998 .... **CLC 25**
See also CA 77-80; 165; CANR 15, 43; CN 7; DAC; DAM MST; DLB 88
Mitchell, William (Lendrum) 1879-1936 .... **TCLC 81**
See also CA 213
Mitford, Mary Russell 1787-1855 ... **NCLC 4**
See also DLB 110, 116; RGEL 2
Mitford, Nancy 1904-1973 .... **CLC 44**
See also BRWS 10; CA 9-12R; DLB 191; RGEL 2
Miyamoto, (Chujo) Yuriko 1899-1951 .... **TCLC 37**
See Miyamoto Yuriko
See also CA 170, 174
Miyamoto Yuriko
See Miyamoto, (Chujo) Yuriko
See also DLB 180
Miyazawa, Kenji 1896-1933 .... **TCLC 76**
See Miyazawa Kenji
See also CA 157; RGWL 3
Miyazawa Kenji
See Miyazawa, Kenji
See also EWL 3
Mizoguchi, Kenji 1898-1956 .... **TCLC 72**
See also CA 167
Mo, Timothy (Peter) 1950(?)- ... **CLC 46, 134**
See also CA 117; CANR 128; CN 7; DLB 194; MTCW 1; WLIT 4; WWE 1
Modarressi, Taghi (M.) 1931-1997 ... **CLC 44**
See also CA 121; 134; INT CA-134
Modiano, Patrick (Jean) 1945- .... **CLC 18**
See also CA 85-88; CANR 17, 40, 115; CWW 2; DLB 83, 299; EWL 3

Mofolo, Thomas (Mokopu) 1875(?)-1948 .... **BLC 3; TCLC 22**
See also AFW; CA 121; 153; CANR 83; DAM MULT; DLB 225; EWL 3; MTCW 2; WLIT 2
Mohr, Nicholasa 1938- .... **CLC 12; HLC 2**
See also AAYA 8, 46; CA 49-52; CANR 1, 32, 64; CLR 22; DAM MULT; DLB 145; HW 1, 2; JRDA; LAIT 5; LLW 1; MAICYA 2; MAICYAS 1; RGAL 4; SAAS 8; SATA 8, 97; SATA-Essay 113; WYA; YAW
Moi, Toril 1953- .... **CLC 172**
See also CA 154; CANR 102; FW
Mojtabai, A(nn) G(race) 1938- ..... **CLC 5, 9, 15, 29**
See also CA 85-88; CANR 88
Moliere 1622-1673 ..... **DC 13; LC 10, 28, 64; WLC**
See also DA; DA3; DAB; DAC; DAM DRAM, MST; DFS 13, 18, 20; DLB 268; EW 3; GFL Beginnings to 1789; LATS 1:1; RGWL 2, 3; TWA
Molin, Charles
See Mayne, William (James Carter)
Molnar, Ferenc 1878-1952 .... **TCLC 20**
See also CA 109; 153; CANR 83; CDWLB 4; DAM DRAM; DLB 215; EWL 3; RGWL 2, 3
Momaday, N(avarre) Scott 1934- ...... **CLC 2, 19, 85, 95, 160; NNAL; PC 25; WLCS**
See also AAYA 11; AMWS 4; ANW; BPFB 2; BYA 12; CA 25-28R; CANR 14, 34, 68, 134; CDALBS; CN 7; CPW; DA; DA3; DAB; DAC; DAM MST, MULT, NOV, POP; DLB 143, 175, 256; EWL 3; EXPP; INT CANR-14; LAIT 4; LATS 1:2; MTCW 1, 2; NFS 10; PFS 2, 11; RGAL 4; SATA 48; SATA-Brief 30; WP; YAW
Monette, Paul 1945-1995 .... **CLC 82**
See also AMWS 10; CA 139; 147; CN 7; GLL 1
Monroe, Harriet 1860-1936 .... **TCLC 12**
See also CA 109; 204; DLB 54, 91
Monroe, Lyle
See Heinlein, Robert A(nson)
Montagu, Elizabeth 1720-1800 .... **NCLC 7, 117**
See also FW
Montagu, Mary (Pierrepont) Wortley 1689-1762 .... **LC 9, 57; PC 16**
See also DLB 95, 101; RGEL 2
Montagu, W. H.
See Coleridge, Samuel Taylor
Montague, John (Patrick) 1929- ..... **CLC 13, 46**
See also CA 9-12R; CANR 9, 69, 121; CP 7; DLB 40; EWL 3; MTCW 1; PFS 12; RGEL 2
Montaigne, Michel (Eyquem) de 1533-1592 .... **LC 8, 105; WLC**
See also DA; DAB; DAC; DAM MST; EW 2; GFL Beginnings to 1789; LMFS 1; RGWL 2, 3; TWA
Montale, Eugenio 1896-1981 ... **CLC 7, 9, 18; PC 13**
See also CA 17-20R; 104; CANR 30; DLB 114; EW 11; EWL 3; MTCW 1; RGWL 2, 3; TWA
Montesquieu, Charles-Louis de Secondat 1689-1755 .... **LC 7, 69**
See also EW 3; GFL Beginnings to 1789; TWA
Montessori, Maria 1870-1952 .... **TCLC 103**
See also CA 115; 147
Montgomery, (Robert) Bruce 1921(?)-1978
See Crispin, Edmund
See also CA 179; 104; CMW 4

Montgomery, L(ucy) M(aud) 1874-1942 .... **TCLC 51, 140**
See also AAYA 12; BYA 1; CA 108; 137; CLR 8, 91; DA3; DAC; DAM MST; DLB 92; DLBD 14; JRDA; MAICYA 1, 2; MTCW 2; RGEL 2; SATA 100; TWA; WCH; WYA; YABC 1
Montgomery, Marion H., Jr. 1925- .... **CLC 7**
See also AITN 1; CA 1-4R; CANR 3, 48; CSW; DLB 6
Montgomery, Max
See Davenport, Guy (Mattison, Jr.)
Montherlant, Henry (Milon) de 1896-1972 .... **CLC 8, 19**
See also CA 85-88; 37-40R; DAM DRAM; DLB 72; EW 11; EWL 3; GFL 1789 to the Present; MTCW 1
Monty Python
See Chapman, Graham; Cleese, John (Marwood); Gilliam, Terry (Vance); Idle, Eric; Jones, Terence Graham Parry; Palin, Michael (Edward)
See also AAYA 7
Moodie, Susanna (Strickland) 1803-1885 .... **NCLC 14, 113**
See also DLB 99
Moody, Hiram (F. III) 1961-
See Moody, Rick
See also CA 138; CANR 64, 112
Moody, Minerva
See Alcott, Louisa May
Moody, Rick .... **CLC 147**
See Moody, Hiram (F. III)
Moody, William Vaughan 1869-1910 .... **TCLC 105**
See also CA 110; 178; DLB 7, 54; RGAL 4
Mooney, Edward 1951-
See Mooney, Ted
See also CA 130
Mooney, Ted .... **CLC 25**
See Mooney, Edward
Moorcock, Michael (John) 1939- ...... **CLC 5, 27, 58**
See Bradbury, Edward P.
See also AAYA 26; CA 45-48; CAAS 5; CANR 2, 17, 38, 64, 122; CN 7; DLB 14, 231, 261; FANT; MTCW 1, 2; SATA 93; SCFW 2; SFW 4; SUFW 1, 2
Moore, Brian 1921-1999 ... **CLC 1, 3, 5, 7, 8, 19, 32, 90**
See Bryan, Michael
See also BRWS 9; CA 1-4R; 174; CANR 1, 25, 42, 63; CCA 1; CN 7; DAB; DAC; DAM MST; DLB 251; EWL 3; FANT; MTCW 1, 2; RGEL 2
Moore, Edward
See Muir, Edwin
See also RGEL 2
Moore, G. E. 1873-1958 .... **TCLC 89**
See also DLB 262
Moore, George Augustus 1852-1933 .... **SSC 19; TCLC 7**
See also BRW 6; CA 104; 177; DLB 10, 18, 57, 135; EWL 3; RGEL 2; RGSF 2
Moore, Lorrie .... **CLC 39, 45, 68**
See Moore, Marie Lorena
See also AMWS 10; DLB 234; SSFS 19
Moore, Marianne (Craig) 1887-1972 .... **CLC 1, 2, 4, 8, 10, 13, 19, 47; PC 4, 49; WLCS**
See also AMW; CA 1-4R; 33-36R; CANR 3, 61; CDALB 1929-1941; DA; DA3; DAB; DAC; DAM MST, POET; DLB 45; DLBD 7; EWL 3; EXPP; MAWW; MTCW 1, 2; PAB; PFS 14, 17; RGAL 4; SATA 20; TUS; WP
Moore, Marie Lorena 1957- .... **CLC 165**
See Moore, Lorrie
See also CA 116; CANR 39, 83; CN 7; DLB 234

Moore, Thomas 1779-1852 .... **NCLC 6, 110**
See also DLB 96, 144; RGEL 2

Moorhouse, Frank 1938- .... **SSC 40**
See also CA 118; CANR 92; CN 7; DLB 289; RGSF 2

Mora, Pat(ricia) 1942- .... **HLC 2**
See also AMWS 13; CA 129; CANR 57, 81, 112; CLR 58; DAM MULT; DLB 209; HW 1, 2; LLW 1; MAICYA 2; SATA 92, 134

Moraga, Cherrie 1952- ...... **CLC 126; DC 22**
See also CA 131; CANR 66; DAM MULT; DLB 82, 249; FW; GLL 1; HW 1, 2; LLW 1

Morand, Paul 1888-1976 .... **CLC 41; SSC 22**
See also CA 184; 69-72; DLB 65; EWL 3

Morante, Elsa 1918-1985 .... **CLC 8, 47**
See also CA 85-88; 117; CANR 35; DLB 177; EWL 3; MTCW 1, 2; RGWL 2, 3

Moravia, Alberto .... **CLC 2, 7, 11, 27, 46; SSC 26**
See Pincherle, Alberto
See also DLB 177; EW 12; EWL 3; MTCW 2; RGSF 2; RGWL 2, 3

More, Hannah 1745-1833 ...... **NCLC 27, 141**
See also DLB 107, 109, 116, 158; RGEL 2

More, Henry 1614-1687 .... **LC 9**
See also DLB 126, 252

More, Sir Thomas 1478(?)-1535 .... **LC 10, 32**
See also BRWC 1; BRWS 7; DLB 136, 281; LMFS 1; RGEL 2; TEA

Moreas, Jean .... **TCLC 18**
See Papadiamantopoulos, Johannes
See also GFL 1789 to the Present

Moreton, Andrew Esq.
See Defoe, Daniel

Morgan, Berry 1919-2002 .... **CLC 6**
See also CA 49-52; 208; DLB 6

Morgan, Claire
See Highsmith, (Mary) Patricia
See also GLL 1

Morgan, Edwin (George) 1920- .... **CLC 31**
See also BRWS 9; CA 5-8R; CANR 3, 43, 90; CP 7; DLB 27

Morgan, (George) Frederick 1922-2004 .... **CLC 23**
See also CA 17-20R; 224; CANR 21; CP 7

Morgan, Harriet
See Mencken, H(enry) L(ouis)

Morgan, Jane
See Cooper, James Fenimore

Morgan, Janet 1945- .... **CLC 39**
See also CA 65-68

Morgan, Lady 1776(?)-1859 .... **NCLC 29**
See also DLB 116, 158; RGEL 2

Morgan, Robin (Evonne) 1941- .... **CLC 2**
See also CA 69-72; CANR 29, 68; FW; GLL 2; MTCW 1; SATA 80

Morgan, Scott
See Kuttner, Henry

Morgan, Seth 1949(?)-1990 .... **CLC 65**
See also CA 185; 132

Morgenstern, Christian (Otto Josef Wolfgang) 1871-1914 .... **TCLC 8**
See also CA 105; 191; EWL 3

Morgenstern, S.
See Goldman, William (W.)

Mori, Rintaro
See Mori Ogai
See also CA 110

Moricz, Zsigmond 1879-1942 .... **TCLC 33**
See also CA 165; DLB 215; EWL 3

Morike, Eduard (Friedrich) 1804-1875 .... **NCLC 10**
See also DLB 133; RGWL 2, 3

Mori Ogai 1862-1922 .... **TCLC 14**
See Ogai
See also CA 164; DLB 180; EWL 3; RGWL 3; TWA

Moritz, Karl Philipp 1756-1793 .... **LC 2**
See also DLB 94

Morland, Peter Henry
See Faust, Frederick (Schiller)

Morley, Christopher (Darlington) 1890-1957 .... **TCLC 87**
See also CA 112; 213; DLB 9; RGAL 4

Morren, Theophil
See Hofmannsthal, Hugo von

Morris, Bill 1952- .... **CLC 76**
See also CA 225

Morris, Julian
See West, Morris L(anglo)

Morris, Steveland Judkins 1950(?)-
See Wonder, Stevie
See also CA 111

Morris, William 1834-1896 . **NCLC 4; PC 55**
See also BRW 5; CDBLB 1832-1890; DLB 18, 35, 57, 156, 178, 184; FANT; RGEL 2; SFW 4; SUFW

Morris, Wright 1910-1998 .. **CLC 1, 3, 7, 18, 37; TCLC 107**
See also AMW; CA 9-12R; 167; CANR 21, 81; CN 7; DLB 2, 206, 218; DLBY 1981; EWL 3; MTCW 1, 2; RGAL 4; TCWW 2

Morrison, Arthur 1863-1945 .... **SSC 40; TCLC 72**
See also CA 120; 157; CMW 4; DLB 70, 135, 197; RGEL 2

Morrison, Chloe Anthony Wofford
See Morrison, Toni

Morrison, James Douglas 1943-1971
See Morrison, Jim
See also CA 73-76; CANR 40

Morrison, Jim .... **CLC 17**
See Morrison, James Douglas

Morrison, Toni 1931- ...... **BLC 3; CLC 4, 10, 22, 55, 81, 87, 173, 194**
See also AAYA 1, 22; AFAW 1, 2; AMWC 1; AMWS 3; BPFB 2; BW 2, 3; CA 29-32R; CANR 27, 42, 67, 113, 124; CDALB 1968-1988; CLR 99; CN 7; CPW; DA; DA3; DAB; DAC; DAM MST, MULT, NOV, POP; DLB 6, 33, 143; DLBY 1981; EWL 3; EXPN; FW; LAIT 2, 4; LATS 1:2; LMFS 2; MAWW; MTCW 1, 2; NFS 1, 6, 8, 14; RGAL 4; RHW; SATA 57, 144; SSFS 5; TUS; YAW

Morrison, Van 1945- .... **CLC 21**
See also CA 116; 168

Morrissy, Mary 1957- .... **CLC 99**
See also CA 205; DLB 267

Mortimer, John (Clifford) 1923- ..... **CLC 28, 43**
See also CA 13-16R; CANR 21, 69, 109; CD 5; CDBLB 1960 to Present; CMW 4; CN 7; CPW; DA3; DAM DRAM, POP; DLB 13, 245, 271; INT CANR-21; MSW; MTCW 1, 2; RGEL 2

Mortimer, Penelope (Ruth) 1918-1999 .... **CLC 5**
See also CA 57-60; 187; CANR 45, 88; CN 7

Mortimer, Sir John
See Mortimer, John (Clifford)

Morton, Anthony
See Creasey, John

Morton, Thomas 1579(?)-1647(?) .... **LC 72**
See also DLB 24; RGEL 2

Mosca, Gaetano 1858-1941 .... **TCLC 75**

Moses, Daniel David 1952- .... **NNAL**
See also CA 186

Mosher, Howard Frank 1943- .... **CLC 62**
See also CA 139; CANR 65, 115

Mosley, Nicholas 1923- .... **CLC 43, 70**
See also CA 69-72; CANR 41, 60, 108; CN 7; DLB 14, 207

Mosley, Walter 1952- .... **BLCS; CLC 97, 184**
See also AAYA 57; AMWS 13; BPFB 2; BW 2; CA 142; CANR 57, 92; CMW 4; CPW; DA3; DAM MULT, POP; DLB 306; MSW; MTCW 2

Moss, Howard 1922-1987 . **CLC 7, 14, 45, 50**
See also CA 1-4R; 123; CANR 1, 44; DAM POET; DLB 5

Mossgiel, Rab
See Burns, Robert

Motion, Andrew (Peter) 1952- .... **CLC 47**
See also BRWS 7; CA 146; CANR 90; CP 7; DLB 40

Motley, Willard (Francis) 1909-1965 .... **CLC 18**
See also BW 1; CA 117; 106; CANR 88; DLB 76, 143

Motoori, Norinaga 1730-1801 .... **NCLC 45**

Mott, Michael (Charles Alston) 1930- .... **CLC 15, 34**
See also CA 5-8R; CAAS 7; CANR 7, 29

Mountain Wolf Woman 1884-1960 . **CLC 92; NNAL**
See also CA 144; CANR 90

Moure, Erin 1955- .... **CLC 88**
See also CA 113; CP 7; CWP; DLB 60

Mourning Dove 1885(?)-1936 .... **NNAL**
See also CA 144; CANR 90; DAM MULT; DLB 175, 221

Mowat, Farley (McGill) 1921- .... **CLC 26**
See also AAYA 1, 50; BYA 2; CA 1-4R; CANR 4, 24, 42, 68, 108; CLR 20; CPW; DAC; DAM MST; DLB 68; INT CANR-24; JRDA; MAICYA 1, 2; MTCW 1, 2; SATA 3, 55; YAW

Mowatt, Anna Cora 1819-1870 ..... **NCLC 74**
See also RGAL 4

Moyers, Bill 1934- .... **CLC 74**
See also AITN 2; CA 61-64; CANR 31, 52

Mphahlele, Es'kia
See Mphahlele, Ezekiel
See also AFW; CDWLB 3; DLB 125, 225; RGSF 2; SSFS 11

Mphahlele, Ezekiel 1919- ... **BLC 3; CLC 25, 133**
See Mphahlele, Es'kia
See also BW 2, 3; CA 81-84; CANR 26, 76; CN 7; DA3; DAM MULT; EWL 3; MTCW 2; SATA 119

Mqhayi, S(amuel) E(dward) K(rune Loliwe) 1875-1945 .... **BLC 3; TCLC 25**
See also CA 153; CANR 87; DAM MULT

Mrozek, Slawomir 1930- .... **CLC 3, 13**
See also CA 13-16R; CAAS 10; CANR 29; CDWLB 4; CWW 2; DLB 232; EWL 3; MTCW 1

Mrs. Belloc-Lowndes
See Lowndes, Marie Adelaide (Belloc)

Mrs. Fairstar
See Horne, Richard Henry Hengist

M'Taggart, John M'Taggart Ellis
See McTaggart, John McTaggart Ellis

Mtwa, Percy (?)- .... **CLC 47**

Mueller, Lisel 1924- .... **CLC 13, 51; PC 33**
See also CA 93-96; CP 7; DLB 105; PFS 9, 13

Muggeridge, Malcolm (Thomas) 1903-1990 .... **TCLC 120**
See also AITN 1; CA 101; CANR 33, 63; MTCW 1, 2

Muhammad 570-632 .... **WLCS**
See also DA; DAB; DAC; DAM MST

Muir, Edwin 1887-1959 . **PC 49; TCLC 2, 87**
See Moore, Edward
See also BRWS 6; CA 104; 193; DLB 20, 100, 191; EWL 3; RGEL 2

Muir, John 1838-1914 .... **TCLC 28**
See also AMWS 9; ANW; CA 165; DLB 186, 275

Mujica Lainez, Manuel 1910-1984 ... **CLC 31**
See Lainez, Manuel Mujica
See also CA 81-84; 112; CANR 32; EWL 3; HW 1

Mukherjee, Bharati 1940- ..... **AAL; CLC 53, 115; SSC 38**
See also AAYA 46; BEST 89:2; CA 107; CANR 45, 72, 128; CN 7; DAM NOV; DLB 60, 218; DNFS 1, 2; EWL 3; FW; MTCW 1, 2; RGAL 4; RGSF 2; SSFS 7; TUS; WWE 1

Muldoon, Paul 1951- .... **CLC 32, 72, 166**
See also BRWS 4; CA 113; 129; CANR 52, 91; CP 7; DAM POET; DLB 40; INT CA-129; PFS 7

Mulisch, Harry (Kurt Victor) 1927- .... **CLC 42**
See also CA 9-12R; CANR 6, 26, 56, 110; CWW 2; DLB 299; EWL 3

Mull, Martin 1943- .... **CLC 17**
See also CA 105

Muller, Wilhelm .... **NCLC 73**

Mulock, Dinah Maria
See Craik, Dinah Maria (Mulock)
See also RGEL 2

Munday, Anthony 1560-1633 .... **LC 87**
See also DLB 62, 172; RGEL 2

Munford, Robert 1737(?)-1783 .... **LC 5**
See also DLB 31

Mungo, Raymond 1946- .... **CLC 72**
See also CA 49-52; CANR 2

Munro, Alice 1931- .... **CLC 6, 10, 19, 50, 95; SSC 3; WLCS**
See also AITN 2; BPFB 2; CA 33-36R; CANR 33, 53, 75, 114; CCA 1; CN 7; DA3; DAC; DAM MST, NOV; DLB 53; EWL 3; MTCW 1, 2; RGEL 2; RGSF 2; SATA 29; SSFS 5, 13, 19; WWE 1

Munro, H(ector) H(ugh) 1870-1916 .... **WLC**
See Saki
See also AAYA 56; CA 104; 130; CANR 104; CDBLB 1890-1914; DA; DA3; DAB; DAC; DAM MST, NOV; DLB 34, 162; EXPS; MTCW 1, 2; RGEL 2; SSFS 15

Murakami, Haruki 1949- .... **CLC 150**
See Murakami Haruki
See also CA 165; CANR 102; MJW; RGWL 3; SFW 4

Murakami Haruki
See Murakami, Haruki
See also CWW 2; DLB 182; EWL 3

Murasaki, Lady
See Murasaki Shikibu

Murasaki Shikibu 978(?)-1026(?) ... **CMLC 1**
See also EFS 2; LATS 1:1; RGWL 2, 3

Murdoch, (Jean) Iris 1919-1999 ... **CLC 1, 2, 3, 4, 6, 8, 11, 15, 22, 31, 51**
See also BRWS 1; CA 13-16R; 179; CANR 8, 43, 68, 103; CDBLB 1960 to Present; CN 7; CWD; DA3; DAB; DAC; DAM MST, NOV; DLB 14, 194, 233; EWL 3; INT CANR-8; MTCW 1, 2; NFS 18; RGEL 2; TEA; WLIT 4

Murfree, Mary Noailles 1850-1922 .. **SSC 22; TCLC 135**
See also CA 122; 176; DLB 12, 74; RGAL 4

Murnau, Friedrich Wilhelm
See Plumpe, Friedrich Wilhelm

Murphy, Richard 1927- .... **CLC 41**
See also BRWS 5; CA 29-32R; CP 7; DLB 40; EWL 3

Murphy, Sylvia 1937- .... **CLC 34**
See also CA 121

Murphy, Thomas (Bernard) 1935- ... **CLC 51**
See also CA 101

Murray, Albert L. 1916- .... **CLC 73**
See also BW 2; CA 49-52; CANR 26, 52, 78; CSW; DLB 38

Murray, James Augustus Henry 1837-1915 .... **TCLC 117**

Murray, Judith Sargent 1751-1820 .... **NCLC 63**
See also DLB 37, 200

Murray, Les(lie Allan) 1938- .... **CLC 40**
See also BRWS 7; CA 21-24R; CANR 11, 27, 56, 103; CP 7; DAM POET; DLB 289; DLBY 2001; EWL 3; RGEL 2

Murry, J. Middleton
See Murry, John Middleton

Murry, John Middleton 1889-1957 .... **TCLC 16**
See also CA 118; 217; DLB 149

Musgrave, Susan 1951- .... **CLC 13, 54**
See also CA 69-72; CANR 45, 84; CCA 1; CP 7; CWP

Musil, Robert (Edler von) 1880-1942 .... **SSC 18; TCLC 12, 68**
See also CA 109; CANR 55, 84; CDWLB 2; DLB 81, 124; EW 9; EWL 3; MTCW 2; RGSF 2; RGWL 2, 3

Muske, Carol .... **CLC 90**
See Muske-Dukes, Carol (Anne)

Muske-Dukes, Carol (Anne) 1945-
See Muske, Carol
See also CA 65-68, 203; CAAE 203; CANR 32, 70; CWP

Musset, (Louis Charles) Alfred de 1810-1857 .... **NCLC 7, 150**
See also DLB 192, 217; EW 6; GFL 1789 to the Present; RGWL 2, 3; TWA

Mussolini, Benito (Amilcare Andrea) 1883-1945 .... **TCLC 96**
See also CA 116

Mutanabbi, Al-
See al-Mutanabbi, Ahmad ibn al-Husayn Abu al-Tayyib al-Jufi al-Kindi

My Brother's Brother
See Chekhov, Anton (Pavlovich)

Myers, L(eopold) H(amilton) 1881-1944 .... **TCLC 59**
See also CA 157; DLB 15; EWL 3; RGEL 2

Myers, Walter Dean 1937- .. **BLC 3; CLC 35**
See also AAYA 4, 23; BW 2; BYA 6, 8, 11; CA 33-36R; CANR 20, 42, 67, 108; CLR 4, 16, 35; DAM MULT, NOV; DLB 33; INT CANR-20; JRDA; LAIT 5; MAICYA 1, 2; MAICYAS 1; MTCW 2; SAAS 2; SATA 41, 71, 109; SATA-Brief 27; WYA; YAW

Myers, Walter M.
See Myers, Walter Dean

Myles, Symon
See Follett, Ken(neth Martin)

Nabokov, Vladimir (Vladimirovich) 1899-1977 .... **CLC 1, 2, 3, 6, 8, 11, 15, 23, 44, 46, 64; SSC 11; TCLC 108; WLC**
See also AAYA 45; AMW; AMWC 1; AMWR 1; BPFB 2; CA 5-8R; 69-72; CANR 20, 102; CDALB 1941-1968; DA; DA3; DAB; DAC; DAM MST, NOV; DLB 2, 244, 278; DLBD 3; DLBY 1980, 1991; EWL 3; EXPS; LATS 1:2; MTCW 1, 2; NCFS 4; NFS 9; RGAL 4; RGSF 2; SSFS 6, 15; TUS

Naevius c. 265B.C.-201B.C. .... **CMLC 37**
See also DLB 211

Nagai, Kafu .... **TCLC 51**
See Nagai, Sokichi
See also DLB 180

Nagai, Sokichi 1879-1959
See Nagai, Kafu
See also CA 117

Nagy, Laszlo 1925-1978 .... **CLC 7**
See also CA 129; 112

Naidu, Sarojini 1879-1949 .... **TCLC 80**
See also EWL 3; RGEL 2

Naipaul, Shiva(dhar Srinivasa) 1945-1985 .... **CLC 32, 39; TCLC 153**
See also CA 110; 112; 116; CANR 33; DA3; DAM NOV; DLB 157; DLBY 1985; EWL 3; MTCW 1, 2

Naipaul, V(idiadhar) S(urajprasad) 1932- .... **CLC 4, 7, 9, 13, 18, 37, 105, 199; SSC 38**
See also BPFB 2; BRWS 1; CA 1-4R; CANR 1, 33, 51, 91, 126; CDBLB 1960 to Present; CDWLB 3; CN 7; DA3; DAB; DAC; DAM MST, NOV; DLB 125, 204, 207; DLBY 1985, 2001; EWL 3; LATS 1:2; MTCW 1, 2; RGEL 2; RGSF 2; TWA; WLIT 4; WWE 1

Nakos, Lilika 1903(?)-1989 .... **CLC 29**

Napoleon
See Yamamoto, Hisaye

Narayan, R(asipuram) K(rishnaswami) 1906-2001 . **CLC 7, 28, 47, 121; SSC 25**
See also BPFB 2; CA 81-84; 196; CANR 33, 61, 112; CN 7; DA3; DAM NOV; DNFS 1; EWL 3; MTCW 1, 2; RGEL 2; RGSF 2; SATA 62; SSFS 5; WWE 1

Nash, (Frediric) Ogden 1902-1971 . **CLC 23; PC 21; TCLC 109**
See also CA 13-14; 29-32R; CANR 34, 61; CAP 1; DAM POET; DLB 11; MAICYA 1, 2; MTCW 1, 2; RGAL 4; SATA 2, 46; WP

Nashe, Thomas 1567-1601(?) .... **LC 41, 89**
See also DLB 167; RGEL 2

Nathan, Daniel
See Dannay, Frederic

Nathan, George Jean 1882-1958 .... **TCLC 18**
See Hatteras, Owen
See also CA 114; 169; DLB 137

Natsume, Kinnosuke
See Natsume, Soseki

Natsume, Soseki 1867-1916 .... **TCLC 2, 10**
See Natsume Soseki; Soseki
See also CA 104; 195; RGWL 2, 3; TWA

Natsume Soseki
See Natsume, Soseki
See also DLB 180; EWL 3

Natti, (Mary) Lee 1919-
See Kingman, Lee
See also CA 5-8R; CANR 2

Navarre, Marguerite de
See de Navarre, Marguerite

Naylor, Gloria 1950- ..... **BLC 3; CLC 28, 52, 156; WLCS**
See also AAYA 6, 39; AFAW 1, 2; AMWS 8; BW 2, 3; CA 107; CANR 27, 51, 74, 130; CN 7; CPW; DA; DA3; DAC; DAM MST, MULT, NOV, POP; DLB 173; EWL 3; FW; MTCW 1, 2; NFS 4, 7; RGAL 4; TUS

Neff, Debra .... **CLC 59**

Neihardt, John Gneisenau 1881-1973 .... **CLC 32**
See also CA 13-14; CANR 65; CAP 1; DLB 9, 54, 256; LAIT 2

Nekrasov, Nikolai Alekseevich 1821-1878 .... **NCLC 11**
See also DLB 277

Nelligan, Emile 1879-1941 .... **TCLC 14**
See also CA 114; 204; DLB 92; EWL 3

Nelson, Willie 1933- .... **CLC 17**
See also CA 107; CANR 114

Nemerov, Howard (Stanley) 1920-1991 .... **CLC 2, 6, 9, 36; PC 24; TCLC 124**
See also AMW; CA 1-4R; 134; CABS 2; CANR 1, 27, 53; DAM POET; DLB 5, 6; DLBY 1983; EWL 3; INT CANR-27; MTCW 1, 2; PFS 10, 14; RGAL 4

Neruda, Pablo 1904-1973 .. **CLC 1, 2, 5, 7, 9, 28, 62; HLC 2; PC 4, 64; WLC**
See also CA 19-20; 45-48; CANR 131; CAP 2; DA; DA3; DAB; DAC; DAM MST, MULT, POET; DLB 283; DNFS 2; EWL 3; HW 1; LAW; MTCW 1, 2; PFS 11; RGWL 2, 3; TWA; WLIT 1; WP

Nerval, Gerard de 1808-1855 ... **NCLC 1, 67; PC 13; SSC 18**
See also DLB 217; EW 6; GFL 1789 to the Present; RGSF 2; RGWL 2, 3

Nervo, (Jose) Amado (Ruiz de) 1870-1919 .... **HLCS 2; TCLC 11**
See also CA 109; 131; DLB 290; EWL 3; HW 1; LAW

Nesbit, Malcolm
See Chester, Alfred

Nessi, Pio Baroja y
See Baroja (y Nessi), Pio

Nestroy, Johann 1801-1862 .... **NCLC 42**
See also DLB 133; RGWL 2, 3

Netterville, Luke
See O'Grady, Standish (James)

Neufeld, John (Arthur) 1938- .... **CLC 17**
See also AAYA 11; CA 25-28R; CANR 11, 37, 56; CLR 52; MAICYA 1, 2; SAAS 3; SATA 6, 81, 131; SATA-Essay 131; YAW

Neumann, Alfred 1895-1952 .... **TCLC 100**
See also CA 183; DLB 56

Neumann, Ferenc
See Molnar, Ferenc

Neville, Emily Cheney 1919- .... **CLC 12**
See also BYA 2; CA 5-8R; CANR 3, 37, 85; JRDA; MAICYA 1, 2; SAAS 2; SATA 1; YAW

Newbound, Bernard Slade 1930-
See Slade, Bernard
See also CA 81-84; CANR 49; CD 5; DAM DRAM

Newby, P(ercy) H(oward) 1918-1997 .... **CLC 2, 13**
See also CA 5-8R; 161; CANR 32, 67; CN 7; DAM NOV; DLB 15; MTCW 1; RGEL 2

Newcastle
See Cavendish, Margaret Lucas

Newlove, Donald 1928- .... **CLC 6**
See also CA 29-32R; CANR 25

Newlove, John (Herbert) 1938- .... **CLC 14**
See also CA 21-24R; CANR 9, 25; CP 7

Newman, Charles 1938- .... **CLC 2, 8**
See also CA 21-24R; CANR 84; CN 7

Newman, Edwin (Harold) 1919- ...... **CLC 14**
See also AITN 1; CA 69-72; CANR 5

Newman, John Henry 1801-1890 . **NCLC 38, 99**
See also BRWS 7; DLB 18, 32, 55; RGEL 2

Newton, (Sir) Isaac 1642-1727 ...... **LC 35, 53**
See also DLB 252

Newton, Suzanne 1936- .... **CLC 35**
See also BYA 7; CA 41-44R; CANR 14; JRDA; SATA 5, 77

New York Dept. of Ed. .... **CLC 70**

Nexo, Martin Andersen 1869-1954 .... **TCLC 43**
See also CA 202; DLB 214; EWL 3

Nezval, Vitezslav 1900-1958 .... **TCLC 44**
See also CA 123; CDWLB 4; DLB 215; EWL 3

Ng, Fae Myenne 1957(?)- .... **CLC 81**
See also BYA 11; CA 146

Ngema, Mbongeni 1955- .... **CLC 57**
See also BW 2; CA 143; CANR 84; CD 5

Ngugi, James T(hiong'o) . **CLC 3, 7, 13, 182**
See Ngugi wa Thiong'o

Ngugi wa Thiong'o
See Ngugi wa Thiong'o
See also DLB 125; EWL 3

Ngugi wa Thiong'o 1938- ... **BLC 3; CLC 36, 182**
See Ngugi, James T(hiong'o); Ngugi wa Thiong'o
See also AFW; BRWS 8; BW 2; CA 81-84; CANR 27, 58; CDWLB 3; DAM MULT, NOV; DNFS 2; MTCW 1, 2; RGEL 2; WWE 1

Niatum, Duane 1938- .... **NNAL**
See also CA 41-44R; CANR 21, 45, 83; DLB 175

Nichol, B(arrie) P(hillip) 1944-1988 . **CLC 18**
See also CA 53-56; DLB 53; SATA 66

Nicholas of Cusa 1401-1464 .... **LC 80**
See also DLB 115

Nichols, John (Treadwell) 1940- .... **CLC 38**
See also AMWS 13; CA 9-12R, 190; CAAE 190; CAAS 2; CANR 6, 70, 121; DLBY 1982; LATS 1:2; TCWW 2

Nichols, Leigh
See Koontz, Dean R(ay)

Nichols, Peter (Richard) 1927- .... **CLC 5, 36, 65**
See also CA 104; CANR 33, 86; CBD; CD 5; DLB 13, 245; MTCW 1

Nicholson, Linda ed. .... **CLC 65**

Ni Chuilleanain, Eilean 1942- .... **PC 34**
See also CA 126; CANR 53, 83; CP 7; CWP; DLB 40

Nicolas, F. R. E.
See Freeling, Nicolas

Niedecker, Lorine 1903-1970 ..... **CLC 10, 42; PC 42**
See also CA 25-28; CAP 2; DAM POET; DLB 48

Nietzsche, Friedrich (Wilhelm) 1844-1900 .... **TCLC 10, 18, 55**
See also CA 107; 121; CDWLB 2; DLB 129; EW 7; RGWL 2, 3; TWA

Nievo, Ippolito 1831-1861 .... **NCLC 22**

Nightingale, Anne Redmon 1943-
See Redmon, Anne
See also CA 103

Nightingale, Florence 1820-1910 ... **TCLC 85**
See also CA 188; DLB 166

Nijo Yoshimoto 1320-1388 .... **CMLC 49**
See also DLB 203

Nik. T. O.
See Annensky, Innokenty (Fyodorovich)

Nin, Anais 1903-1977 ..... **CLC 1, 4, 8, 11, 14, 60, 127; SSC 10**
See also AITN 2; AMWS 10; BPFB 2; CA 13-16R; 69-72; CANR 22, 53; DAM NOV, POP; DLB 2, 4, 152; EWL 3; GLL 2; MAWW; MTCW 1, 2; RGAL 4; RGSF 2

Nisbet, Robert A(lexander) 1913-1996 .... **TCLC 117**
See also CA 25-28R; 153; CANR 17; INT CANR-17

Nishida, Kitaro 1870-1945 .... **TCLC 83**

Nishiwaki, Junzaburo
See Nishiwaki, Junzaburo
See also CA 194

Nishiwaki, Junzaburo 1894-1982 .... **PC 15**
See Nishiwaki, Junzaburo; Nishiwaki Junzaburo
See also CA 194; 107; MJW; RGWL 3

Nishiwaki Junzaburo
See Nishiwaki, Junzaburo
See also EWL 3

Nissenson, Hugh 1933- .... **CLC 4, 9**
See also CA 17-20R; CANR 27, 108; CN 7; DLB 28

Nister, Der
See Der Nister

Niven, Larry .... **CLC 8**
See Niven, Laurence Van Cott
See also AAYA 27; BPFB 2; BYA 10; DLB 8; SCFW 2

Niven, Laurence Van Cott 1938-
See Niven, Larry
See also CA 21-24R, 207; CAAE 207; CAAS 12; CANR 14, 44, 66, 113; CPW; DAM POP; MTCW 1, 2; SATA 95; SFW 4

Nixon, Agnes Eckhardt 1927- .... **CLC 21**
See also CA 110

Nizan, Paul 1905-1940 .... **TCLC 40**
See also CA 161; DLB 72; EWL 3; GFL 1789 to the Present

Nkosi, Lewis 1936- .... **BLC 3; CLC 45**
See also BW 1, 3; CA 65-68; CANR 27, 81; CBD; CD 5; DAM MULT; DLB 157, 225; WWE 1

Nodier, (Jean) Charles (Emmanuel) 1780-1844 .... **NCLC 19**
See also DLB 119; GFL 1789 to the Present

Noguchi, Yone 1875-1947 .... **TCLC 80**

Nolan, Christopher 1965- .... **CLC 58**
See also CA 111; CANR 88

Noon, Jeff 1957- .... **CLC 91**
See also CA 148; CANR 83; DLB 267; SFW 4

Norden, Charles
See Durrell, Lawrence (George)

Nordhoff, Charles Bernard 1887-1947 .... **TCLC 23**
See also CA 108; 211; DLB 9; LAIT 1; RHW 1; SATA 23

Norfolk, Lawrence 1963- .... **CLC 76**
See also CA 144; CANR 85; CN 7; DLB 267

Norman, Marsha 1947- . **CLC 28, 186; DC 8**
See also CA 105; CABS 3; CAD; CANR 41, 131; CD 5; CSW; CWD; DAM DRAM; DFS 2; DLB 266; DLBY 1984; FW

Normyx
See Douglas, (George) Norman

Norris, (Benjamin) Frank(lin, Jr.) 1870-1902 .... **SSC 28; TCLC 24, 155**
See also AAYA 57; AMW; AMWC 2; BPFB 2; CA 110; 160; CDALB 1865-1917; DLB 12, 71, 186; LMFS 2; NFS 12; RGAL 4; TCWW 2; TUS

Norris, Leslie 1921- .... **CLC 14**
See also CA 11-12; CANR 14, 117; CAP 1; CP 7; DLB 27, 256

North, Andrew
See Norton, Andre

North, Anthony
See Koontz, Dean R(ay)

North, Captain George
See Stevenson, Robert Louis (Balfour)

North, Captain George
See Stevenson, Robert Louis (Balfour)

North, Milou
See Erdrich, Louise

Northrup, B. A.
See Hubbard, L(afayette) Ron(ald)

North Staffs
See Hulme, T(homas) E(rnest)

Northup, Solomon 1808-1863 .... **NCLC 105**

Norton, Alice Mary
See Norton, Andre
See also MAICYA 1; SATA 1, 43

Norton, Andre 1912- .... **CLC 12**
See Norton, Alice Mary
See also AAYA 14; BPFB 2; BYA 4, 10, 12; CA 1-4R; CANR 68; CLR 50; DLB 8, 52; JRDA; MAICYA 2; MTCW 1; SATA 91; SUFW 1, 2; YAW

Norton, Caroline 1808-1877 .... **NCLC 47**
See also DLB 21, 159, 199

Norway, Nevil Shute 1899-1960
See Shute, Nevil
See also CA 102; 93-96; CANR 85; MTCW 2

Norwid, Cyprian Kamil
1821-1883 .... **NCLC 17**
See also RGWL 3

Nosille, Nabrah
See Ellison, Harlan (Jay)

Nossack, Hans Erich 1901-1978 .... **CLC 6**
See also CA 93-96; 85-88; DLB 69; EWL 3

Nostradamus 1503-1566 .... **LC 27**

Nosu, Chuji
See Ozu, Yasujiro

Notenburg, Eleanora (Genrikhovna) von
See Guro, Elena (Genrikhovna)

Nova, Craig 1945- .... **CLC 7, 31**
See also CA 45-48; CANR 2, 53, 127

Novak, Joseph
See Kosinski, Jerzy (Nikodem)

Novalis 1772-1801 .... **NCLC 13**
See also CDWLB 2; DLB 90; EW 5; RGWL 2, 3

Novick, Peter 1934- .... **CLC 164**
See also CA 188

Novis, Emile
See Weil, Simone (Adolphine)

Nowlan, Alden (Albert) 1933-1983 ... **CLC 15**
See also CA 9-12R; CANR 5; DAC; DAM MST; DLB 53; PFS 12

Noyes, Alfred 1880-1958 .... **PC 27; TCLC 7**
See also CA 104; 188; DLB 20; EXPP; FANT; PFS 4; RGEL 2

Nugent, Richard Bruce 1906(?)-1987 ... **HR 3**
See also BW 1; CA 125; DLB 51; GLL 2

Nunn, Kem .... **CLC 34**
See also CA 159

Nussbaum, Martha 1947- .... **CLC 203**
See also CA 134; CANR 102

Nwapa, Flora (Nwanzuruaha)
1931-1993 .... **BLCS; CLC 133**
See also BW 2; CA 143; CANR 83; CDWLB 3; CWRI 5; DLB 125; EWL 3; WLIT 2

Nye, Robert 1939- .... **CLC 13, 42**
See also BRWS 10; CA 33-36R; CANR 29, 67, 107; CN 7; CP 7; CWRI 5; DAM NOV; DLB 14, 271; FANT; HGG; MTCW 1; RHW; SATA 6

Nyro, Laura 1947-1997 .... **CLC 17**
See also CA 194

Oates, Joyce Carol 1938- .. **CLC 1, 2, 3, 6, 9, 11, 15, 19, 33, 52, 108, 134; SSC 6, 70; WLC**
See also AAYA 15, 52; AITN 1; AMWS 2; BEST 89:2; BPFB 3; BYA 11; CA 5-8R; CANR 25, 45, 74, 113, 129; CDALB 1968-1988; CN 7; CP 7; CPW; DA; DA3; DAB; DAC; DAM MST, NOV, POP; DLB 2, 5, 130; DLBY 1981; EWL 3; EXPS; FW; HGG; INT CANR-25; LAIT 4; MAWW; MTCW 1, 2; NFS 8; RGAL 4; RGSF 2; SSFS 17; SUFW 2; TUS

O'Brian, E. G.
See Clarke, Arthur C(harles)

O'Brian, Patrick 1914-2000 .... **CLC 152**
See also AAYA 55; CA 144; 187; CANR 74; CPW; MTCW 2; RHW

O'Brien, Darcy 1939-1998 .... **CLC 11**
See also CA 21-24R; 167; CANR 8, 59

O'Brien, Edna 1932- ...... **CLC 3, 5, 8, 13, 36, 65, 116; SSC 10, 77**
See also BRWS 5; CA 1-4R; CANR 6, 41, 65, 102; CDBLB 1960 to Present; CN 7; DA3; DAM NOV; DLB 14, 231; EWL 3; FW; MTCW 1, 2; RGSF 2; WLIT 4

O'Brien, Fitz-James 1828-1862 ..... **NCLC 21**
See also DLB 74; RGAL 4; SUFW

O'Brien, Flann .... **CLC 1, 4, 5, 7, 10, 47**
See O Nuallain, Brian
See also BRWS 2; DLB 231; EWL 3; RGEL 2

O'Brien, Richard 1942- .... **CLC 17**
See also CA 124

O'Brien, (William) Tim(othy) 1946- . **CLC 7, 19, 40, 103; SSC 74**
See also AAYA 16; AMWS 5; CA 85-88; CANR 40, 58, 133; CDALBS; CN 7; CPW; DA3; DAM POP; DLB 152; DLBD 9; DLBY 1980; LATS 1:2; MTCW 2; RGAL 4; SSFS 5, 15

Obstfelder, Sigbjoern 1866-1900 .... **TCLC 23**
See also CA 123

O'Casey, Sean 1880-1964 .... **CLC 1, 5, 9, 11, 15, 88; DC 12; WLCS**
See also BRW 7; CA 89-92; CANR 62; CBD; CDBLB 1914-1945; DA3; DAB; DAC; DAM DRAM, MST; DFS 19; DLB 10; EWL 3; MTCW 1, 2; RGEL 2; TEA; WLIT 4

O'Cathasaigh, Sean
See O'Casey, Sean

Occom, Samson 1723-1792 .... **LC 60; NNAL**
See also DLB 175

Ochs, Phil(ip David) 1940-1976 .... **CLC 17**
See also CA 185; 65-68

O'Connor, Edwin (Greene)
1918-1968 .... **CLC 14**
See also CA 93-96; 25-28R

O'Connor, (Mary) Flannery
1925-1964 .... **CLC 1, 2, 3, 6, 10, 13, 15, 21, 66, 104; SSC 1, 23, 61; TCLC 132; WLC**
See also AAYA 7; AMW; AMWR 2; BPFB 3; BYA 16; CA 1-4R; CANR 3, 41; CDALB 1941-1968; DA; DA3; DAB; DAC; DAM MST, NOV; DLB 2, 152; DLBD 12; DLBY 1980; EWL 3; EXPS; LAIT 5; MAWW; MTCW 1, 2; NFS 3; RGAL 4; RGSF 2; SSFS 2, 7, 10, 19; TUS

O'Connor, Frank .... **CLC 23; SSC 5**
See O'Donovan, Michael Francis
See also DLB 162; EWL 3; RGSF 2; SSFS 5

O'Dell, Scott 1898-1989 .... **CLC 30**
See also AAYA 3, 44; BPFB 3; BYA 1, 2, 3, 5; CA 61-64; 129; CANR 12, 30, 112; CLR 1, 16; DLB 52; JRDA; MAICYA 1, 2; SATA 12, 60, 134; WYA; YAW

Odets, Clifford 1906-1963 ..... **CLC 2, 28, 98; DC 6**
See also AMWS 2; CA 85-88; CAD; CANR 62; DAM DRAM; DFS 3, 17, 20; DLB 7, 26; EWL 3; MTCW 1, 2; RGAL 4; TUS

O'Doherty, Brian 1928- .... **CLC 76**
See also CA 105; CANR 108

O'Donnell, K. M.
See Malzberg, Barry N(athaniel)

O'Donnell, Lawrence
See Kuttner, Henry

O'Donovan, Michael Francis
1903-1966 .... **CLC 14**
See O'Connor, Frank
See also CA 93-96; CANR 84

Oe, Kenzaburo 1935- .. **CLC 10, 36, 86, 187; SSC 20**
See Oe Kenzaburo
See also CA 97-100; CANR 36, 50, 74, 126; DA3; DAM NOV; DLB 182; DLBY 1994; LATS 1:2; MJW; MTCW 1, 2; RGSF 2; RGWL 2, 3

Oe Kenzaburo
See Oe, Kenzaburo
See also CWW 2; EWL 3

O'Faolain, Julia 1932- .... **CLC 6, 19, 47, 108**
See also CA 81-84; CAAS 2; CANR 12, 61; CN 7; DLB 14, 231; FW; MTCW 1; RHW

O'Faolain, Sean 1900-1991 ...... **CLC 1, 7, 14, 32, 70; SSC 13; TCLC 143**
See also CA 61-64; 134; CANR 12, 66; DLB 15, 162; MTCW 1, 2; RGEL 2; RGSF 2

O'Flaherty, Liam 1896-1984 .... **CLC 5, 34; SSC 6**
See also CA 101; 113; CANR 35; DLB 36, 162; DLBY 1984; MTCW 1, 2; RGEL 2; RGSF 2; SSFS 5, 20

Ogai
See Mori Ogai
See also MJW

Ogilvy, Gavin
See Barrie, J(ames) M(atthew)

O'Grady, Standish (James)
1846-1928 .... **TCLC 5**
See also CA 104; 157

O'Grady, Timothy 1951- .... **CLC 59**
See also CA 138

O'Hara, Frank 1926-1966 .... **CLC 2, 5, 13, 78; PC 45**
See also CA 9-12R; 25-28R; CANR 33; DA3; DAM POET; DLB 5, 16, 193; EWL 3; MTCW 1, 2; PFS 8; 12; RGAL 4; WP

O'Hara, John (Henry) 1905-1970 . **CLC 1, 2, 3, 6, 11, 42; SSC 15**
See also AMW; BPFB 3; CA 5-8R; 25-28R; CANR 31, 60; CDALB 1929-1941; DAM NOV; DLB 9, 86; DLBD 2; EWL 3; MTCW 1, 2; NFS 11; RGAL 4; RGSF 2

O Hehir, Diana 1922- .... **CLC 41**
See also CA 93-96

Ohiyesa
See Eastman, Charles A(lexander)

Okada, John 1923-1971 .... **AAL**
See also BYA 14; CA 212

Okigbo, Christopher (Ifenayichukwu)
1932-1967 .... **BLC 3; CLC 25, 84; PC 7**
See also AFW; BW 1, 3; CA 77-80; CANR 74; CDWLB 3; DAM MULT, POET; DLB 125; EWL 3; MTCW 1, 2; RGEL 2

Okri, Ben 1959- .... **CLC 87**
See also AFW; BRWS 5; BW 2, 3; CA 130; 138; CANR 65, 128; CN 7; DLB 157, 231; EWL 3; INT CA-138; MTCW 2; RGSF 2; SSFS 20; WLIT 2; WWE 1

Olds, Sharon 1942- .. **CLC 32, 39, 85; PC 22**
See also AMWS 10; CA 101; CANR 18, 41, 66, 98, 135; CP 7; CPW; DAM POET; DLB 120; MTCW 2; PFS 17

Oldstyle, Jonathan
See Irving, Washington

Olesha, Iurii
See Olesha, Yuri (Karlovich)
See also RGWL 2

Olesha, Iurii Karlovich
See Olesha, Yuri (Karlovich)
See also DLB 272

Olesha, Yuri (Karlovich) 1899-1960 . **CLC 8; SSC 69; TCLC 136**
See Olesha, Iurii; Olesha, Iurii Karlovich; Olesha, Yury Karlovich
See also CA 85-88; EW 11; RGWL 3

Olesha, Yury Karlovich
See Olesha, Yuri (Karlovich)
See also EWL 3

Oliphant, Mrs.
See Oliphant, Margaret (Oliphant Wilson)
See also SUFW

Oliphant, Laurence 1829(?)-1888 .. **NCLC 47**
See also DLB 18, 166

Oliphant, Margaret (Oliphant Wilson)
1828-1897 .... **NCLC 11, 61; SSC 25**
See Oliphant, Mrs.
See also BRWS 10; DLB 18, 159, 190; HGG; RGEL 2; RGSF 2

Oliver, Mary 1935- .... **CLC 19, 34, 98**
See also AMWS 7; CA 21-24R; CANR 9, 43, 84, 92; CP 7; CWP; DLB 5, 193; EWL 3; PFS 15

Olivier, Laurence (Kerr) 1907-1989 . **CLC 20**
See also CA 111; 150; 129

Olsen, Tillie 1912- ... **CLC 4, 13, 114; SSC 11**
See also AAYA 51; AMWS 13; BYA 11; CA 1-4R; CANR 1, 43, 74, 132; CDALBS; CN 7; DA; DA3; DAB; DAC; DAM MST; DLB 28, 206; DLBY 1980; EWL 3; EXPS; FW; MTCW 1, 2; RGAL 4; RGSF 1; SSFS 1; TUS

Olson, Charles (John) 1910-1970 .. **CLC 1, 2, 5, 6, 9, 11, 29; PC 19**
See also AMWS 2; CA 13-16; 25-28R; CABS 2; CANR 35, 61; CAP 1; DAM POET; DLB 5, 193; EWL 3; MTCW 1, 2; RGAL 4; WP

Olson, Toby 1937- .... **CLC 28**
See also CA 65-68; CANR 9, 31, 84; CP 7

Olyesha, Yuri
See Olesha, Yuri (Karlovich)

Olympiodorus of Thebes c. 375-c. 430 .... **CMLC 59**

Omar Khayyam
See Khayyam, Omar
See also RGWL 2, 3

Ondaatje, (Philip) Michael 1943- .... **CLC 14, 29, 51, 76, 180; PC 28**
See also CA 77-80; CANR 42, 74, 109, 133; CN 7; CP 7; DA3; DAB; DAC; DAM MST; DLB 60; EWL 3; LATS 1:2; LMFS 2; MTCW 2; PFS 8, 19; TWA; WWE 1

Oneal, Elizabeth 1934-
See Oneal, Zibby
See also CA 106; CANR 28, 84; MAICYA 1, 2; SATA 30, 82; YAW

Oneal, Zibby .... **CLC 30**
See Oneal, Elizabeth
See also AAYA 5, 41; BYA 13; CLR 13; JRDA; WYA

O'Neill, Eugene (Gladstone)
1888-1953 ... **DC 20; TCLC 1, 6, 27, 49; WLC**
See also AAYA 54; AITN 1; AMW; AMWC 1; CA 110; 132; CAD; CANR 131; CDALB 1929-1941; DA; DA3; DAB; DAC; DAM DRAM, MST; DFS 2, 4, 5, 6, 9, 11, 12, 16, 20; DLB 7; EWL 3; LAIT 3; LMFS 2; MTCW 1, 2; RGAL 4; TUS

Onetti, Juan Carlos 1909-1994 ... **CLC 7, 10; HLCS 2; SSC 23; TCLC 131**
See also CA 85-88; 145; CANR 32, 63; CDWLB 3; CWW 2; DAM MULT, NOV; DLB 113; EWL 3; HW 1, 2; LAW; MTCW 1, 2; RGSF 2

O Nuallain, Brian 1911-1966
See O'Brien, Flann
See also CA 21-22; 25-28R; CAP 2; DLB 231; FANT; TEA

Ophuls, Max 1902-1957 .... **TCLC 79**
See also CA 113

Opie, Amelia 1769-1853 .... **NCLC 65**
See also DLB 116, 159; RGEL 2

Oppen, George 1908-1984 ..... **CLC 7, 13, 34; PC 35; TCLC 107**
See also CA 13-16R; 113; CANR 8, 82; DLB 5, 165

Oppenheim, E(dward) Phillips
1866-1946 .... **TCLC 45**
See also CA 111; 202; CMW 4; DLB 70

Opuls, Max
See Ophuls, Max

Orage, A(lfred) R(ichard)
1873-1934 .... **TCLC 157**
See also CA 122

Origen c. 185-c. 254 .... **CMLC 19**

Orlovitz, Gil 1918-1973 .... **CLC 22**
See also CA 77-80; 45-48; DLB 2, 5

Orris
See Ingelow, Jean

Ortega y Gasset, Jose 1883-1955 ...... **HLC 2; TCLC 9**
See also CA 106; 130; DAM MULT; EW 9; EWL 3; HW 1, 2; MTCW 1, 2

Ortese, Anna Maria 1914-1998 .... **CLC 89**
See also DLB 177; EWL 3

Ortiz, Simon J(oseph) 1941- .... **CLC 45; NNAL; PC 17**
See also AMWS 4; CA 134; CANR 69, 118; CP 7; DAM MULT, POET; DLB 120, 175, 256; EXPP; PFS 4, 16; RGAL 4

Orton, Joe ...... **CLC 4, 13, 43; DC 3; TCLC 157**
See Orton, John Kingsley
See also BRWS 5; CBD; CDBLB 1960 to Present; DFS 3, 6; DLB 13; GLL 1; MTCW 2; RGEL 2; TEA; WLIT 4

Orton, John Kingsley 1933-1967
See Orton, Joe
See also CA 85-88; CANR 35, 66; DAM DRAM; MTCW 1, 2

Orwell, George ...... **SSC 68; TCLC 2, 6, 15, 31, 51, 128, 129; WLC**
See Blair, Eric (Arthur)
See also BPFB 3; BRW 7; BYA 5; CDBLB 1945-1960; CLR 68; DAB; DLB 15, 98, 195, 255; EWL 3; EXPN; LAIT 4, 5; LATS 1:1; NFS 3, 7; RGEL 2; SCFW 2; SFW 4; SSFS 4; TEA; WLIT 4; YAW

Osborne, David
See Silverberg, Robert

Osborne, George
See Silverberg, Robert

Osborne, John (James) 1929-1994 .... **CLC 1, 2, 5, 11, 45; TCLC 153; WLC**
See also BRWS 1; CA 13-16R; 147; CANR 21, 56; CDBLB 1945-1960; DA; DAB; DAC; DAM DRAM, MST; DFS 4, 19; DLB 13; EWL 3; MTCW 1, 2; RGEL 2

Osborne, Lawrence 1958- .... **CLC 50**
See also CA 189

Osbourne, Lloyd 1868-1947 .... **TCLC 93**

Osgood, Frances Sargent
1811-1850 .... **NCLC 141**
See also DLB 250

Oshima, Nagisa 1932- .... **CLC 20**
See also CA 116; 121; CANR 78

Oskison, John Milton
1874-1947 .... **NNAL; TCLC 35**
See also CA 144; CANR 84; DAM MULT; DLB 175

Ossian c. 3rd cent. - .... **CMLC 28**
See Macpherson, James

Ossoli, Sarah Margaret (Fuller)
1810-1850 .... **NCLC 5, 50**
See Fuller, Margaret; Fuller, Sarah Margaret
See also CDALB 1640-1865; FW; LMFS 1; SATA 25

Ostriker, Alicia (Suskin) 1937- .... **CLC 132**
See also CA 25-28R; CAAS 24; CANR 10, 30, 62, 99; CWP; DLB 120; EXPP; PFS 19

Ostrovsky, Aleksandr Nikolaevich
See Ostrovsky, Alexander
See also DLB 277

Ostrovsky, Alexander 1823-1886 .. **NCLC 30, 57**
See Ostrovsky, Aleksandr Nikolaevich

Otero, Blas de 1916-1979 .... **CLC 11**
See also CA 89-92; DLB 134; EWL 3

O'Trigger, Sir Lucius
See Horne, Richard Henry Hengist

Otto, Rudolf 1869-1937 .... **TCLC 85**

Otto, Whitney 1955- .... **CLC 70**
See also CA 140; CANR 120

Otway, Thomas 1652-1685 ... **DC 24; LC 106**
See also DAM DRAM; DLB 80; RGEL 2

Ouida .... **TCLC 43**
See De la Ramee, Marie Louise (Ouida)
See also DLB 18, 156; RGEL 2

Ouologuem, Yambo 1940- .... **CLC 146**
See also CA 111; 176

Ousmane, Sembene 1923- ... **BLC 3; CLC 66**
See Sembene, Ousmane
See also BW 1, 3; CA 117; 125; CANR 81; CWW 2; MTCW 1

Ovid 43B.C.-17 .... **CMLC 7; PC 2**
See also AW 2; CDWLB 1; DA3; DAM POET; DLB 211; RGWL 2, 3; WP

Owen, Hugh
See Faust, Frederick (Schiller)

Owen, Wilfred (Edward Salter)
1893-1918 ... **PC 19; TCLC 5, 27; WLC**
See also BRW 6; CA 104; 141; CDBLB 1914-1945; DA; DAB; DAC; DAM MST, POET; DLB 20; EWL 3; EXPP; MTCW 2; PFS 10; RGEL 2; WLIT 4

Owens, Louis (Dean) 1948-2002 .... **NNAL**
See also CA 137; 179; 207; CAAE 179; CAAS 24; CANR 71

Owens, Rochelle 1936- .... **CLC 8**
See also CA 17-20R; CAAS 2; CAD; CANR 39; CD 5; CP 7; CWD; CWP

Oz, Amos 1939- ...... **CLC 5, 8, 11, 27, 33, 54; SSC 66**
See also CA 53-56; CANR 27, 47, 65, 113; CWW 2; DAM NOV; EWL 3; MTCW 1, 2; RGSF 2; RGWL 3

Ozick, Cynthia 1928- .... **CLC 3, 7, 28, 62, 155; SSC 15, 60**
See also AMWS 5; BEST 90:1; CA 17-20R; CANR 23, 58, 116; CN 7; CPW; DA3; DAM NOV, POP; DLB 28, 152, 299; DLBY 1982; EWL 3; EXPS; INT CANR-23; MTCW 1, 2; RGAL 4; RGSF 2; SSFS 3, 12

Ozu, Yasujiro 1903-1963 .... **CLC 16**
See also CA 112

Pabst, G. W. 1885-1967 .... **TCLC 127**

Pacheco, C.
See Pessoa, Fernando (Antonio Nogueira)

Pacheco, Jose Emilio 1939- .... **HLC 2**
See also CA 111; 131; CANR 65; CWW 2; DAM MULT; DLB 290; EWL 3; HW 1, 2; RGSF 2

Pa Chin .... **CLC 18**
See Li Fei-kan
See also EWL 3

Pack, Robert 1929- .... **CLC 13**
See also CA 1-4R; CANR 3, 44, 82; CP 7; DLB 5; SATA 118

Padgett, Lewis
See Kuttner, Henry

Padilla (Lorenzo), Heberto
1932-2000 .... **CLC 38**
See also AITN 1; CA 123; 131; 189; CWW 2; EWL 3; HW 1

Page, James Patrick 1944-
See Page, Jimmy
See also CA 204

Page, Jimmy 1944- .... **CLC 12**
See Page, James Patrick

Page, Louise 1955- .... **CLC 40**
See also CA 140; CANR 76; CBD; CD 5; CWD; DLB 233

Page, P(atricia) K(athleen) 1916- ...... CLC 7, 18; PC 12
See Cape, Judith
See also CA 53-56; CANR 4, 22, 65; CP 7; DAC; DAM MST; DLB 68; MTCW 1; RGEL 2

Page, Stanton
See Fuller, Henry Blake

Page, Stanton
See Fuller, Henry Blake

Page, Thomas Nelson 1853-1922 .... SSC 23
See also CA 118; 177; DLB 12, 78; DLBD 13; RGAL 4

Pagels, Elaine Hiesey 1943- .... CLC 104
See also CA 45-48; CANR 2, 24, 51; FW; NCFS 4

Paget, Violet 1856-1935
See Lee, Vernon
See also CA 104; 166; GLL 1; HGG

Paget-Lowe, Henry
See Lovecraft, H(oward) P(hillips)

Paglia, Camille (Anna) 1947- .... CLC 68
See also CA 140; CANR 72; CPW; FW; GLL 2; MTCW 2

Paige, Richard
See Koontz, Dean R(ay)

Paine, Thomas 1737-1809 .... NCLC 62
See also AMWS 1; CDALB 1640-1865; DLB 31, 43, 73, 158; LAIT 1; RGAL 4; RGEL 2; TUS

Pakenham, Antonia
See Fraser, Antonia (Pakenham)

Palamas, Costis
See Palamas, Kostes

Palamas, Kostes 1859-1943 .... TCLC 5
See Palamas, Kostis
See also CA 105; 190; RGWL 2, 3

Palamas, Kostis
See Palamas, Kostes
See also EWL 3

Palazzeschi, Aldo 1885-1974 .... CLC 11
See also CA 89-92; 53-56; DLB 114, 264; EWL 3

Pales Matos, Luis 1898-1959 .... HLCS 2
See Pales Matos, Luis
See also DLB 290; HW 1; LAW

Paley, Grace 1922- .. CLC 4, 6, 37, 140; SSC 8
See also AMWS 6; CA 25-28R; CANR 13, 46, 74, 118; CN 7; CPW; DA3; DAM POP; DLB 28, 218; EWL 3; EXPS; FW; INT CANR-13; MAWW; MTCW 1, 2; RGAL 4; RGSF 2; SSFS 3, 20

Palin, Michael (Edward) 1943- .... CLC 21
See Monty Python
See also CA 107; CANR 35, 109; SATA 67

Palliser, Charles 1947- .... CLC 65
See also CA 136; CANR 76; CN 7

Palma, Ricardo 1833-1919 .... TCLC 29
See also CA 168; LAW

Pamuk, Orhan 1952- .... CLC 185
See also CA 142; CANR 75, 127; CWW 2

Pancake, Breece Dexter 1952-1979
See Pancake, Breece D'J
See also CA 123; 109

Pancake, Breece D'J .... CLC 29; SSC 61
See Pancake, Breece Dexter
See also DLB 130

Panchenko, Nikolai .... CLC 59

Pankhurst, Emmeline (Goulden) 1858-1928 .... TCLC 100
See also CA 116; FW

Panko, Rudy
See Gogol, Nikolai (Vasilyevich)

Papadiamantis, Alexandros 1851-1911 .... TCLC 29
See also CA 168; EWL 3

Papadiamantopoulos, Johannes 1856-1910
See Moreas, Jean
See also CA 117

Papini, Giovanni 1881-1956 .... TCLC 22
See also CA 121; 180; DLB 264

Paracelsus 1493-1541 .... LC 14
See also DLB 179

Parasol, Peter
See Stevens, Wallace

Pardo Bazan, Emilia 1851-1921 .... SSC 30
See also EWL 3; FW; RGSF 2; RGWL 2, 3

Pareto, Vilfredo 1848-1923 .... TCLC 69
See also CA 175

Paretsky, Sara 1947- .... CLC 135
See also AAYA 30; BEST 90:3; CA 125; 129; CANR 59, 95; CMW 4; CPW; DA3; DAM POP; DLB 306; INT CA-129; MSW; RGAL 4

Parfenie, Maria
See Codrescu, Andrei

Parini, Jay (Lee) 1948- .... CLC 54, 133
See also CA 97-100, 229; CAAE 229; CAAS 16; CANR 32, 87

Park, Jordan
See Kornbluth, C(yril) M.; Pohl, Frederik

Park, Robert E(zra) 1864-1944 ..... TCLC 73
See also CA 122; 165

Parker, Bert
See Ellison, Harlan (Jay)

Parker, Dorothy (Rothschild) 1893-1967 . CLC 15, 68; PC 28; SSC 2; TCLC 143
See also AMWS 9; CA 19-20; 25-28R; CAP 2; DA3; DAM POET; DLB 11, 45, 86; EXPP; FW; MAWW; MTCW 1, 2; PFS 18; RGAL 4; RGSF 2; TUS

Parker, Robert B(rown) 1932- .... CLC 27
See also AAYA 28; BEST 89:4; BPFB 3; CA 49-52; CANR 1, 26, 52, 89, 128; CMW 4; CPW; DAM NOV, POP; DLB 306; INT CANR-26; MSW; MTCW 1

Parkin, Frank 1940- .... CLC 43
See also CA 147

Parkman, Francis, Jr. 1823-1893 .. NCLC 12
See also AMWS 2; DLB 1, 30, 183, 186, 235; RGAL 4

Parks, Gordon (Alexander Buchanan) 1912- .... BLC 3; CLC 1, 16
See also AAYA 36; AITN 2; BW 2, 3; CA 41-44R; CANR 26, 66; DA3; DAM MULT; DLB 33; MTCW 2; SATA 8, 108

Parks, Suzan-Lori 1964(?)- .... DC 23
See also AAYA 55; CA 201; CAD; CD 5; CWD; RGAL 4

Parks, Tim(othy Harold) 1954- ...... CLC 147
See also CA 126; 131; CANR 77; DLB 231; INT CA-131

Parmenides c. 515B.C.-c. 450B.C. .... CMLC 22
See also DLB 176

Parnell, Thomas 1679-1718 .... LC 3
See also DLB 95; RGEL 2

Parr, Catherine c. 1513(?)-1548 .... LC 86
See also DLB 136

Parra, Nicanor 1914- ... CLC 2, 102; HLC 2; PC 39
See also CA 85-88; CANR 32; CWW 2; DAM MULT; DLB 283; EWL 3; HW 1; LAW; MTCW 1

Parra Sanojo, Ana Teresa de la 1890-1936 .... HLCS 2
See de la Parra, (Ana) Teresa (Sonojo)
See also LAW

Parrish, Mary Frances
See Fisher, M(ary) F(rances) K(ennedy)

Parshchikov, Aleksei 1954- .... CLC 59
See Parshchikov, Aleksei Maksimovich

Parshchikov, Aleksei Maksimovich
See Parshchikov, Aleksei
See also DLB 285

Parson, Professor
See Coleridge, Samuel Taylor

Parson Lot
See Kingsley, Charles

Parton, Sara Payson Willis 1811-1872 .... NCLC 86
See also DLB 43, 74, 239

Partridge, Anthony
See Oppenheim, E(dward) Phillips

Pascal, Blaise 1623-1662 .... LC 35
See also DLB 268; EW 3; GFL Beginnings to 1789; RGWL 2, 3; TWA

Pascoli, Giovanni 1855-1912 .... TCLC 45
See also CA 170; EW 7; EWL 3

Pasolini, Pier Paolo 1922-1975 .. CLC 20, 37, 106; PC 17
See also CA 93-96; 61-64; CANR 63; DLB 128, 177; EWL 3; MTCW 1; RGWL 2, 3

Pasquini
See Silone, Ignazio

Pastan, Linda (Olenik) 1932- .... CLC 27
See also CA 61-64; CANR 18, 40, 61, 113; CP 7; CSW; CWP; DAM POET; DLB 5; PFS 8

Pasternak, Boris (Leonidovich) 1890-1960 ...... CLC 7, 10, 18, 63; PC 6; SSC 31; WLC
See also BPFB 3; CA 127; 116; DA; DA3; DAB; DAC; DAM MST, NOV, POET; DLB 302; EW 10; MTCW 1, 2; RGSF 2; RGWL 2, 3; TWA; WP

Patchen, Kenneth 1911-1972 .... CLC 1, 2, 18
See also BG 3; CA 1-4R; 33-36R; CANR 3, 35; DAM POET; DLB 16, 48; EWL 3; MTCW 1; RGAL 4

Pater, Walter (Horatio) 1839-1894 . NCLC 7, 90
See also BRW 5; CDBLB 1832-1890; DLB 57, 156; RGEL 2; TEA

Paterson, A(ndrew) B(arton) 1864-1941 .... TCLC 32
See also CA 155; DLB 230; RGEL 2; SATA 97

Paterson, Banjo
See Paterson, A(ndrew) B(arton)

Paterson, Katherine (Womeldorf) 1932- .... CLC 12, 30
See also AAYA 1, 31; BYA 1, 2, 7; CA 21-24R; CANR 28, 59, 111; CLR 7, 50; CWRI 5; DLB 52; JRDA; LAIT 4; MAICYA 1, 2; MAICYAS 1; MTCW 1; SATA 13, 53, 92, 133; WYA; YAW

Patmore, Coventry Kersey Dighton 1823-1896 .... NCLC 9; PC 59
See also DLB 35, 98; RGEL 2; TEA

Paton, Alan (Stewart) 1903-1988 .... CLC 4, 10, 25, 55, 106; WLC
See also AAYA 26; AFW; BPFB 3; BRWS 2; BYA 1; CA 13-16; 125; CANR 22; CAP 1; DA; DA3; DAB; DAC; DAM MST, NOV; DLB 225; DLBD 17; EWL 3; EXPN; LAIT 4; MTCW 1, 2; NFS 3, 12; RGEL 2; SATA 11; SATA-Obit 56; TWA; WLIT 2; WWE 1

Paton Walsh, Gillian 1937- .... CLC 35
See Paton Walsh, Jill; Walsh, Jill Paton
See also AAYA 11; CANR 38, 83; CLR 2, 65; DLB 161; JRDA; MAICYA 1, 2; SAAS 3; SATA 4, 72, 109; YAW

Paton Walsh, Jill
See Paton Walsh, Gillian
See also AAYA 47; BYA 1, 8

Patterson, (Horace) Orlando (Lloyd) 1940- .... BLCS
See also BW 1; CA 65-68; CANR 27, 84; CN 7

Patton, George S(mith), Jr.
1885-1945 .... **TCLC 79**
See also CA 189

Paulding, James Kirke 1778-1860 ... **NCLC 2**
See also DLB 3, 59, 74, 250; RGAL 4

Paulin, Thomas Neilson 1949-
See Paulin, Tom
See also CA 123; 128; CANR 98; CP 7

Paulin, Tom .... **CLC 37, 177**
See Paulin, Thomas Neilson
See also DLB 40

Pausanias c. 1st cent. - .... **CMLC 36**

Paustovsky, Konstantin (Georgievich)
1892-1968 .... **CLC 40**
See also CA 93-96; 25-28R; DLB 272;
EWL 3

Pavese, Cesare 1908-1950 .... **PC 13; SSC 19; TCLC 3**
See also CA 104; 169; DLB 128, 177; EW 12; EWL 3; PFS 20; RGSF 2; RGWL 2, 3; TWA

Pavic, Milorad 1929- .... **CLC 60**
See also CA 136; CDWLB 4; CWW 2; DLB 181; EWL 3; RGWL 3

Pavlov, Ivan Petrovich 1849-1936 . **TCLC 91**
See also CA 118; 180

Pavlova, Karolina Karlovna
1807-1893 .... **NCLC 138**
See also DLB 205

Payne, Alan
See Jakes, John (William)

Paz, Gil
See Lugones, Leopoldo

Paz, Octavio 1914-1998 . **CLC 3, 4, 6, 10, 19, 51, 65, 119; HLC 2; PC 1, 48; WLC**
See also AAYA 50; CA 73-76; 165; CANR 32, 65, 104; CWW 2; DA; DA3; DAB; DAC; DAM MST, MULT, POET; DLB 290; DLBY 1990; DNFS 1; EWL 3; HW 1, 2; LAW; LAWS 1; MTCW 1, 2; PFS 18; RGWL 2, 3; SSFS 13; TWA; WLIT 1

p'Bitek, Okot 1931-1982 .... **BLC 3; CLC 96; TCLC 149**
See also AFW; BW 2, 3; CA 124; 107; CANR 82; DAM MULT; DLB 125; EWL 3; MTCW 1, 2; RGEL 2; WLIT 2

Peacock, Molly 1947- .... **CLC 60**
See also CA 103; CAAS 21; CANR 52, 84; CP 7; CWP; DLB 120, 282

Peacock, Thomas Love
1785-1866 .... **NCLC 22**
See also BRW 4; DLB 96, 116; RGEL 2; RGSF 2

Peake, Mervyn 1911-1968 .... **CLC 7, 54**
See also CA 5-8R; 25-28R; CANR 3; DLB 15, 160, 255; FANT; MTCW 1; RGEL 2; SATA 23; SFW 4

Pearce, Philippa
See Christie, Philippa
See also CA 5-8R; CANR 4, 109; CWRI 5; FANT; MAICYA 2

Pearl, Eric
See Elman, Richard (Martin)

Pearson, T(homas) R(eid) 1956- .... **CLC 39**
See also CA 120; 130; CANR 97; CSW; INT CA-130

Peck, Dale 1967- .... **CLC 81**
See also CA 146; CANR 72, 127; GLL 2

Peck, John (Frederick) 1941- .... **CLC 3**
See also CA 49-52; CANR 3, 100; CP 7

Peck, Richard (Wayne) 1934- .... **CLC 21**
See also AAYA 1, 24; BYA 1, 6, 8, 11; CA 85-88; CANR 19, 38, 129; CLR 15; INT CANR-19; JRDA; MAICYA 1, 2; SAAS 2; SATA 18, 55, 97; SATA-Essay 110; WYA; YAW

Peck, Robert Newton 1928- .... **CLC 17**
See also AAYA 3, 43; BYA 1, 6; CA 81-84, 182; CAAE 182; CANR 31, 63, 127; CLR 45; DA; DAC; DAM MST; JRDA; LAIT 3; MAICYA 1, 2; SAAS 1; SATA 21, 62, 111; SATA-Essay 108; WYA; YAW

Peckinpah, (David) Sam(uel)
1925-1984 .... **CLC 20**
See also CA 109; 114; CANR 82

Pedersen, Knut 1859-1952
See Hamsun, Knut
See also CA 104; 119; CANR 63; MTCW 1, 2

Peele, George .... **LC 115**
See also BW 1; DLB 62, 167; RGEL 2

Peeslake, Gaffer
See Durrell, Lawrence (George)

Peguy, Charles (Pierre)
1873-1914 .... **TCLC 10**
See also CA 107; 193; DLB 258; EWL 3; GFL 1789 to the Present

Peirce, Charles Sanders
1839-1914 .... **TCLC 81**
See also CA 194; DLB 270

Pellicer, Carlos 1897(?)-1977 .... **HLCS 2**
See also CA 153; 69-72; DLB 290; EWL 3; HW 1

Pena, Ramon del Valle y
See Valle-Inclan, Ramon (Maria) del

Pendennis, Arthur Esquir
See Thackeray, William Makepeace

Penn, Arthur
See Matthews, (James) Brander

Penn, William 1644-1718 .... **LC 25**
See also DLB 24

PEPECE
See Prado (Calvo), Pedro

Pepys, Samuel 1633-1703 ... **LC 11, 58; WLC**
See also BRW 2; CDBLB 1660-1789; DA; DA3; DAB; DAC; DAM MST; DLB 101, 213; NCFS 4; RGEL 2; TEA; WLIT 3

Percy, Thomas 1729-1811 .... **NCLC 95**
See also DLB 104

Percy, Walker 1916-1990 .... **CLC 2, 3, 6, 8, 14, 18, 47, 65**
See also AMWS 3; BPFB 3; CA 1-4R; 131; CANR 1, 23, 64; CPW; CSW; DA3; DAM NOV, POP; DLB 2; DLBY 1980, 1990; EWL 3; MTCW 1, 2; RGAL 4; TUS

Percy, William Alexander
1885-1942 .... **TCLC 84**
See also CA 163; MTCW 2

Perec, Georges 1936-1982 .... **CLC 56, 116**
See also CA 141; DLB 83, 299; EWL 3; GFL 1789 to the Present; RGWL 3

Pereda (y Sanchez de Porrua), Jose Maria de 1833-1906 .... **TCLC 16**
See also CA 117

Pereda y Porrua, Jose Maria de
See Pereda (y Sanchez de Porrua), Jose Maria de

Peregoy, George Weems
See Mencken, H(enry) L(ouis)

Perelman, S(idney) J(oseph)
1904-1979 .. **CLC 3, 5, 9, 15, 23, 44, 49; SSC 32**
See also AITN 1, 2; BPFB 3; CA 73-76; 89-92; CANR 18; DAM DRAM; DLB 11, 44; MTCW 1, 2; RGAL 4

Peret, Benjamin 1899-1959 .... **PC 33; TCLC 20**
See also CA 117; 186; GFL 1789 to the Present

Peretz, Isaac Leib
See Peretz, Isaac Loeb
See also CA 201

Peretz, Isaac Loeb 1851(?)-1915 ...... **SSC 26; TCLC 16**
See Peretz, Isaac Leib
See also CA 109

Peretz, Yitzkhok Leibush
See Peretz, Isaac Loeb

Perez Galdos, Benito 1843-1920 ..... **HLCS 2; TCLC 27**
See Galdos, Benito Perez
See also CA 125; 153; EWL 3; HW 1; RGWL 2, 3

Peri Rossi, Cristina 1941- .. **CLC 156; HLCS 2**
See also CA 131; CANR 59, 81; CWW 2; DLB 145, 290; EWL 3; HW 1, 2

Perlata
See Peret, Benjamin

Perloff, Marjorie G(abrielle)
1931- .... **CLC 137**
See also CA 57-60; CANR 7, 22, 49, 104

Perrault, Charles 1628-1703 .... **LC 2, 56**
See also BYA 4; CLR 79; DLB 268; GFL Beginnings to 1789; MAICYA 1, 2; RGWL 2, 3; SATA 25; WCH

Perry, Anne 1938- .... **CLC 126**
See also CA 101; CANR 22, 50, 84; CMW 4; CN 7; CPW; DLB 276

Perry, Brighton
See Sherwood, Robert E(mmet)

Perse, St.-John
See Leger, (Marie-Rene Auguste) Alexis Saint-Leger

Perse, Saint-John
See Leger, (Marie-Rene Auguste) Alexis Saint-Leger
See also DLB 258; RGWL 3

Persius 34-62 .... **CMLC 74**
See also AW 2; DLB 211; RGWL 2, 3

Perutz, Leo(pold) 1882-1957 .... **TCLC 60**
See also CA 147; DLB 81

Peseenz, Tulio F.
See Lopez y Fuentes, Gregorio

Pesetsky, Bette 1932- .... **CLC 28**
See also CA 133; DLB 130

Peshkov, Alexei Maximovich 1868-1936
See Gorky, Maxim
See also CA 105; 141; CANR 83; DA; DAC; DAM DRAM, MST, NOV; MTCW 2

Pessoa, Fernando (Antonio Nogueira)
1888-1935 ..... **HLC 2; PC 20; TCLC 27**
See also CA 125; 183; DAM MULT; DLB 287; EW 10; EWL 3; RGWL 2, 3; WP

Peterkin, Julia Mood 1880-1961 ...... **CLC 31**
See also CA 102; DLB 9

Peters, Joan K(aren) 1945- .... **CLC 39**
See also CA 158; CANR 109

Peters, Robert L(ouis) 1924- .... **CLC 7**
See also CA 13-16R; CAAS 8; CP 7; DLB 105

Petofi, Sandor 1823-1849 .... **NCLC 21**
See also RGWL 2, 3

Petrakis, Harry Mark 1923- .... **CLC 3**
See also CA 9-12R; CANR 4, 30, 85; CN 7

Petrarch 1304-1374 .... **CMLC 20; PC 8**
See also DA3; DAM POET; EW 2; LMFS 1; RGWL 2, 3

Petronius c. 20-66 .... **CMLC 34**
See also AW 2; CDWLB 1; DLB 211; RGWL 2, 3

Petrov, Evgeny .... **TCLC 21**
See Kataev, Evgeny Petrovich

Petry, Ann (Lane) 1908-1997 .. **CLC 1, 7, 18; TCLC 112**
See also AFAW 1, 2; BPFB 3; BW 1, 3; BYA 2; CA 5-8R; 157; CAAS 6; CANR 4, 46; CLR 12; CN 7; DLB 76; EWL 3; JRDA; LAIT 1; MAICYA 1, 2; MAICYAS 1; MTCW 1; RGAL 4; SATA 5; SATA-Obit 94; TUS

Petursson, Halligrimur 1614-1674 .... **LC 8**
Peychinovich
   See Vazov, Ivan (Minchov)
Phaedrus c. 15B.C.-c. 50 .... **CMLC 25**
   See also DLB 211
Phelps (Ward), Elizabeth Stuart
   See Phelps, Elizabeth Stuart
   See also FW
Phelps, Elizabeth Stuart
   1844-1911 .... **TCLC 113**
   See Phelps (Ward), Elizabeth Stuart
   See also DLB 74
Philips, Katherine 1632-1664 . **LC 30; PC 40**
   See also DLB 131; RGEL 2
Philipson, Morris H. 1926- .... **CLC 53**
   See also CA 1-4R; CANR 4
Phillips, Caryl 1958- .... **BLCS; CLC 96**
   See also BRWS 5; BW 2; CA 141; CANR
   63, 104; CBD; CD 5; CN 7; DA3; DAM
   MULT; DLB 157; EWL 3; MTCW 2;
   WLIT 4; WWE 1
Phillips, David Graham
   1867-1911 .... **TCLC 44**
   See also CA 108; 176; DLB 9, 12, 303;
   RGAL 4
Phillips, Jack
   See Sandburg, Carl (August)
Phillips, Jayne Anne 1952- .... **CLC 15, 33,
   139; SSC 16**
   See also AAYA 57; BPFB 3; CA 101;
   CANR 24, 50, 96; CN 7; CSW; DLBY
   1980; INT CANR-24; MTCW 1, 2; RGAL
   4; RGSF 2; SSFS 4
Phillips, Richard
   See Dick, Philip K(indred)
Phillips, Robert (Schaeffer) 1938- .... **CLC 28**
   See also CA 17-20R; CAAS 13; CANR 8;
   DLB 105
Phillips, Ward
   See Lovecraft, H(oward) P(hillips)
Philostratus, Flavius c. 179-c.
   244 .... **CMLC 62**
Piccolo, Lucio 1901-1969 .... **CLC 13**
   See also CA 97-100; DLB 114; EWL 3
Pickthall, Marjorie L(owry) C(hristie)
   1883-1922 .... **TCLC 21**
   See also CA 107; DLB 92
Pico della Mirandola, Giovanni
   1463-1494 .... **LC 15**
   See also LMFS 1
Piercy, Marge 1936- .... **CLC 3, 6, 14, 18, 27,
   62, 128; PC 29**
   See also BPFB 3; CA 21-24R, 187; CAAE
   187; CAAS 1; CANR 13, 43, 66, 111; CN
   7; CP 7; CWP; DLB 120, 227; EXPP;
   FW; MTCW 1, 2; PFS 9; SFW 4
Piers, Robert
   See Anthony, Piers
Pieyre de Mandiargues, Andre 1909-1991
   See Mandiargues, Andre Pieyre de
   See also CA 103; 136; CANR 22, 82; EWL
   3; GFL 1789 to the Present
Pilnyak, Boris 1894-1938 . **SSC 48; TCLC 23**
   See Vogau, Boris Andreyevich
   See also EWL 3
Pinchback, Eugene
   See Toomer, Jean
Pincherle, Alberto 1907-1990 ...... **CLC 11, 18**
   See Moravia, Alberto
   See also CA 25-28R; 132; CANR 33, 63;
   DAM NOV; MTCW 1
Pinckney, Darryl 1953- .... **CLC 76**
   See also BW 2, 3; CA 143; CANR 79
Pindar 518(?)B.C.-438(?)B.C. .... **CMLC 12;
   PC 19**
   See also AW 1; CDWLB 1; DLB 176;
   RGWL 2
Pineda, Cecile 1942- .... **CLC 39**
   See also CA 118; DLB 209

Pinero, Arthur Wing 1855-1934 .... **TCLC 32**
   See also CA 110; 153; DAM DRAM; DLB
   10; RGEL 2
Pinero, Miguel (Antonio Gomez)
   1946-1988 .... **CLC 4, 55**
   See also CA 61-64; 125; CAD; CANR 29,
   90; DLB 266; HW 1; LLW 1
Pinget, Robert 1919-1997 .... **CLC 7, 13, 37**
   See also CA 85-88; 160; CWW 2; DLB 83;
   EWL 3; GFL 1789 to the Present
Pink Floyd
   See Barrett, (Roger) Syd; Gilmour, David;
   Mason, Nick; Waters, Roger; Wright, Rick
Pinkney, Edward 1802-1828 .... **NCLC 31**
   See also DLB 248
Pinkwater, Daniel
   See Pinkwater, Daniel Manus
Pinkwater, Daniel Manus 1941- .... **CLC 35**
   See also AAYA 1, 46; BYA 9; CA 29-32R;
   CANR 12, 38, 89; CLR 4; CSW; FANT;
   JRDA; MAICYA 1, 2; SAAS 3; SATA 8,
   46, 76, 114; SFW 4; YAW
Pinkwater, Manus
   See Pinkwater, Daniel Manus
Pinsky, Robert 1940- .... **CLC 9, 19, 38, 94,
   121; PC 27**
   See also AMWS 6; CA 29-32R; CAAS 4;
   CANR 58, 97; CP 7; DA3; DAM POET;
   DLBY 1982, 1998; MTCW 2; PFS 18;
   RGAL 4
Pinta, Harold
   See Pinter, Harold
Pinter, Harold 1930- ... **CLC 1, 3, 6, 9, 11, 15,
   27, 58, 73, 199; DC 15; WLC**
   See also BRWR 1; BRWS 1; CA 5-8R;
   CANR 33, 65, 112; CBD; CD 5; CDBLB
   1960 to Present; DA; DA3; DAB; DAC;
   DAM DRAM, MST; DFS 3, 5, 7, 14;
   DLB 13; EWL 3; IDFW 3, 4; LMFS 2;
   MTCW 1, 2; RGEL 2; TEA
Piozzi, Hester Lynch (Thrale)
   1741-1821 .... **NCLC 57**
   See also DLB 104, 142
Pirandello, Luigi 1867-1936 .. **DC 5; SSC 22;
   TCLC 4, 29; WLC**
   See also CA 104; 153; CANR 103; DA;
   DA3; DAB; DAC; DAM DRAM, MST;
   DFS 4, 9; DLB 264; EW 8; EWL 3;
   MTCW 2; RGSF 2; RGWL 2, 3
Pirsig, Robert M(aynard) 1928- ... **CLC 4, 6,
   73**
   See also CA 53-56; CANR 42, 74; CPW 1;
   DA3; DAM POP; MTCW 1, 2; SATA 39
Pisarev, Dmitrii Ivanovich
   See Pisarev, Dmitry Ivanovich
   See also DLB 277
Pisarev, Dmitry Ivanovich
   1840-1868 .... **NCLC 25**
   See Pisarev, Dmitrii Ivanovich
Pix, Mary (Griffith) 1666-1709 .... **LC 8**
   See also DLB 80
Pixerecourt, (Rene Charles) Guilbert de
   1773-1844 .... **NCLC 39**
   See also DLB 192; GFL 1789 to the Present
Plaatje, Sol(omon) T(shekisho)
   1878-1932 .... **BLCS; TCLC 73**
   See also BW 2, 3; CA 141; CANR 79; DLB
   125, 225
Plaidy, Jean
   See Hibbert, Eleanor Alice Burford
Planche, James Robinson
   1796-1880 .... **NCLC 42**
   See also RGEL 2
Plant, Robert 1948- .... **CLC 12**
Plante, David (Robert) 1940- . **CLC 7, 23, 38**
   See also CA 37-40R; CANR 12, 36, 58, 82;
   CN 7; DAM NOV; DLBY 1983; INT
   CANR-12; MTCW 1

Plath, Sylvia 1932-1963 ..... **CLC 1, 2, 3, 5, 9,
   11, 14, 17, 50, 51, 62, 111; PC 1, 37;
   WLC**
   See also AAYA 13; AMWR 2; AMWS 1;
   BPFB 3; CA 19-20; CANR 34, 101; CAP
   2; CDALB 1941-1968; DA; DA3; DAB;
   DAC; DAM MST, POET; DLB 5, 6, 152;
   EWL 3; EXPN; EXPP; FW; LAIT 4;
   MAWW; MTCW 1, 2; NFS 1; PAB; PFS
   1, 15; RGAL 4; SATA 96; TUS; WP;
   YAW
Plato c. 428B.C.-347B.C. .... **CMLC 8, 75;
   WLCS**
   See also AW 1; CDWLB 1; DA; DA3;
   DAB; DAC; DAM MST; DLB 176; LAIT
   1; LATS 1:1; RGWL 2, 3
Platonov, Andrei
   See Klimentov, Andrei Platonovich
Platonov, Andrei Platonovich
   See Klimentov, Andrei Platonovich
   See also DLB 272
Platonov, Andrey Platonovich
   See Klimentov, Andrei Platonovich
   See also EWL 3
Platt, Kin 1911- .... **CLC 26**
   See also AAYA 11; CA 17-20R; CANR 11;
   JRDA; SAAS 17; SATA 21, 86; WYA
Plautus c. 254B.C.-c. 184B.C. ...... **CMLC 24;
   DC 6**
   See also AW 1; CDWLB 1; DLB 211;
   RGWL 2, 3
Plick et Plock
   See Simenon, Georges (Jacques Christian)
Plieksans, Janis
   See Rainis, Janis
Plimpton, George (Ames)
   1927-2003 .... **CLC 36**
   See also AITN 1; CA 21-24R; 224; CANR
   32, 70, 103, 133; DLB 185, 241; MTCW
   1, 2; SATA 10; SATA-Obit 150
Pliny the Elder c. 23-79 .... **CMLC 23**
   See also DLB 211
Pliny the Younger c. 61-c. 112 .... **CMLC 62**
   See also AW 2; DLB 211
Plomer, William Charles Franklin
   1903-1973 .... **CLC 4, 8**
   See also AFW; CA 21-22; CANR 34; CAP
   2; DLB 20, 162, 191, 225; EWL 3;
   MTCW 1; RGEL 2; RGSF 2; SATA 24
Plotinus 204-270 .... **CMLC 46**
   See also CDWLB 1; DLB 176
Plowman, Piers
   See Kavanagh, Patrick (Joseph)
Plum, J.
   See Wodehouse, P(elham) G(renville)
Plumly, Stanley (Ross) 1939- .... **CLC 33**
   See also CA 108; 110; CANR 97; CP 7;
   DLB 5, 193; INT CA-110
Plumpe, Friedrich Wilhelm
   1888-1931 .... **TCLC 53**
   See also CA 112
Plutarch c. 46-c. 120 .... **CMLC 60**
   See also AW 2; CDWLB 1; DLB 176;
   RGWL 2, 3; TWA
Po Chu-i 772-846 .... **CMLC 24**
Podhoretz, Norman 1930- .... **CLC 189**
   See also AMWS 8; CA 9-12R; CANR 7,
   78, 135
Poe, Edgar Allan 1809-1849 ..... **NCLC 1, 16,
   55, 78, 94, 97, 117; PC 1, 54; SSC 1,
   22, 34, 35, 54; WLC**
   See also AAYA 14; AMW; AMWC 1;
   AMWR 2; BPFB 3; BYA 5, 11; CDALB
   1640-1865; CMW 4; DA; DA3; DAB;
   DAC; DAM MST, POET; DLB 3, 59, 73,
   74, 248, 254; EXPP; EXPS; HGG; LAIT
   2; LATS 1:1; LMFS 1; MSW; PAB; PFS

1, 3, 9; RGAL 4; RGSF 2; SATA 23; SCFW 2; SFW 4; SSFS 2, 4, 7, 8, 16; SUFW; TUS; WP; WYA

Poet of Titchfield Street, The
See Pound, Ezra (Weston Loomis)

Pohl, Frederick 1919- .... **CLC 18; SSC 25**
See also AAYA 24; CA 61-64, 188; CAAE 188; CAAS 1; CANR 11, 37, 81; CN 7; DLB 8; INT CANR-11; MTCW 1, 2; SATA 24; SCFW 2; SFW 4

Poirier, Louis 1910-
See Gracq, Julien
See also CA 122; 126

Poitier, Sidney 1927- .... **CLC 26**
See also AAYA 60; BW 1; CA 117; CANR 94

Pokagon, Simon 1830-1899 .... **NNAL**
See also DAM MULT

Polanski, Roman 1933- .... **CLC 16, 178**
See also CA 77-80

Poliakoff, Stephen 1952- .... **CLC 38**
See also CA 106; CANR 116; CBD; CD 5; DLB 13

Police, The
See Copeland, Stewart (Armstrong); Summers, Andrew James

Polidori, John William 1795-1821 . **NCLC 51**
See also DLB 116; HGG

Pollitt, Katha 1949- .... **CLC 28, 122**
See also CA 120; 122; CANR 66, 108; MTCW 1, 2

Pollock, (Mary) Sharon 1936- .... **CLC 50**
See also CA 141; CANR 132; CD 5; CWD; DAC; DAM DRAM, MST; DFS 3; DLB 60; FW

Pollock, Sharon 1936- .... **DC 20**

Polo, Marco 1254-1324 .... **CMLC 15**

Polonsky, Abraham (Lincoln) 1910-1999 .... **CLC 92**
See also CA 104; 187; DLB 26; INT CA-104

Polybius c. 200B.C.-c. 118B.C. .... **CMLC 17**
See also AW 1; DLB 176; RGWL 2, 3

Pomerance, Bernard 1940- .... **CLC 13**
See also CA 101; CAD; CANR 49, 134; CD 5; DAM DRAM; DFS 9; LAIT 2

Ponge, Francis 1899-1988 .... **CLC 6, 18**
See also CA 85-88; 126; CANR 40, 86; DAM POET; DLBY 2002; EWL 3; GFL 1789 to the Present; RGWL 2, 3

Poniatowska, Elena 1933- . **CLC 140; HLC 2**
See also CA 101; CANR 32, 66, 107; CDWLB 3; CWW 2; DAM MULT; DLB 113; EWL 3; HW 1, 2; LAWS 1; WLIT 1

Pontoppidan, Henrik 1857-1943 .... **TCLC 29**
See also CA 170; DLB 300

Ponty, Maurice Merleau
See Merleau-Ponty, Maurice

Poole, Josephine .... **CLC 17**
See Helyar, Jane Penelope Josephine
See also SAAS 2; SATA 5

Popa, Vasko 1922-1991 .... **CLC 19**
See also CA 112; 148; CDWLB 4; DLB 181; EWL 3; RGWL 2, 3

Pope, Alexander 1688-1744 ...... **LC 3, 58, 60, 64; PC 26; WLC**
See also BRW 3; BRWC 1; BRWR 1; CDBLB 1660-1789; DA; DA3; DAB; DAC; DAM MST, POET; DLB 95, 101, 213; EXPP; PAB; PFS 12; RGEL 2; WLIT 3; WP

Popov, Evgenii Anatol'evich
See Popov, Yevgeny
See also DLB 285

Popov, Yevgeny .... **CLC 59**
See Popov, Evgenii Anatol'evich

Poquelin, Jean-Baptiste
See Moliere

Porete, Marguerite c. 1250-1310 .. **CMLC 73**
See also DLB 208

Porphyry c. 233-c. 305 .... **CMLC 71**

Porter, Connie (Rose) 1959(?)- .... **CLC 70**
See also BW 2, 3; CA 142; CANR 90, 109; SATA 81, 129

Porter, Gene(va Grace) Stratton .. **TCLC 21**
See Stratton-Porter, Gene(va Grace)
See also BPFB 3; CA 112; CWRI 5; RHW

Porter, Katherine Anne 1890-1980 ... **CLC 1, 3, 7, 10, 13, 15, 27, 101; SSC 4, 31, 43**
See also AAYA 42; AITN 2; AMW; BPFB 3; CA 1-4R; 101; CANR 1, 65; CDALBS; DA; DA3; DAB; DAC; DAM MST, NOV; DLB 4, 9, 102; DLBD 12; DLBY 1980; EWL 3; EXPS; LAIT 3; MAWW; MTCW 1, 2; NFS 14; RGAL 4; RGSF 2; SATA 39; SATA-Obit 23; SSFS 1, 8, 11, 16; TUS

Porter, Peter (Neville Frederick) 1929- .... **CLC 5, 13, 33**
See also CA 85-88; CP 7; DLB 40, 289; WWE 1

Porter, William Sydney 1862-1910
See Henry, O.
See also CA 104; 131; CDALB 1865-1917; DA; DA3; DAB; DAC; DAM MST; DLB 12, 78, 79; MTCW 1, 2; TUS; YABC 2

Portillo (y Pacheco), Jose Lopez
See Lopez Portillo (y Pacheco), Jose

Portillo Trambley, Estela 1927-1998 .... **HLC 2; TCLC 163**
See Trambley, Estela Portillo
See also CANR 32; DAM MULT; DLB 209; HW 1

Posey, Alexander (Lawrence) 1873-1908 .... **NNAL**
See also CA 144; CANR 80; DAM MULT; DLB 175

Posse, Abel .... **CLC 70**

Post, Melville Davisson 1869-1930 .... **TCLC 39**
See also CA 110; 202; CMW 4

Potok, Chaim 1929-2002 ... **CLC 2, 7, 14, 26, 112**
See also AAYA 15, 50; AITN 1, 2; BPFB 3; BYA 1; CA 17-20R; 208; CANR 19, 35, 64, 98; CLR 92; CN 7; DA3; DAM NOV; DLB 28, 152; EXPN; INT CANR-19; LAIT 4; MTCW 1, 2; NFS 4; SATA 33, 106; SATA-Obit 134; TUS; YAW

Potok, Herbert Harold -2002
See Potok, Chaim

Potok, Herman Harold
See Potok, Chaim

Potter, Dennis (Christopher George) 1935-1994 .... **CLC 58, 86, 123**
See also BRWS 10; CA 107; 145; CANR 33, 61; CBD; DLB 233; MTCW 1

Pound, Ezra (Weston Loomis) 1885-1972 .. **CLC 1, 2, 3, 4, 5, 7, 10, 13, 18, 34, 48, 50, 112; PC 4; WLC**
See also AAYA 47; AMW; AMWR 1; CA 5-8R; 37-40R; CANR 40; CDALB 1917-1929; DA; DA3; DAB; DAC; DAM MST, POET; DLB 4, 45, 63; DLBD 15; EFS 2; EWL 3; EXPP; LMFS 2; MTCW 1, 2; PAB; PFS 2, 8, 16; RGAL 4; TUS; WP

Povod, Reinaldo 1959-1994 .... **CLC 44**
See also CA 136; 146; CANR 83

Powell, Adam Clayton, Jr. 1908-1972 .... **BLC 3; CLC 89**
See also BW 1, 3; CA 102; 33-36R; CANR 86; DAM MULT

Powell, Anthony (Dymoke) 1905-2000 .... **CLC 1, 3, 7, 9, 10, 31**
See also BRW 7; CA 1-4R; 189; CANR 1, 32, 62, 107; CDBLB 1945-1960; CN 7; DLB 15; EWL 3; MTCW 1, 2; RGEL 2; TEA

Powell, Dawn 1896(?)-1965 .... **CLC 66**
See also CA 5-8R; CANR 121; DLBY 1997

Powell, Padgett 1952- .... **CLC 34**
See also CA 126; CANR 63, 101; CSW; DLB 234; DLBY 01

Powell, (Oval) Talmage 1920-2000
See Queen, Ellery
See also CA 5-8R; CANR 2, 80

Power, Susan 1961- .... **CLC 91**
See also BYA 14; CA 160; CANR 135; NFS 11

Powers, J(ames) F(arl) 1917-1999 ..... **CLC 1, 4, 8, 57; SSC 4**
See also CA 1-4R; 181; CANR 2, 61; CN 7; DLB 130; MTCW 1; RGAL 4; RGSF 2

Powers, John J(ames) 1945-
See Powers, John R.
See also CA 69-72

Powers, John R. .... **CLC 66**
See Powers, John J(ames)

Powers, Richard (S.) 1957- .... **CLC 93**
See also AMWS 9; BPFB 3; CA 148; CANR 80; CN 7

Pownall, David 1938- .... **CLC 10**
See also CA 89-92, 180; CAAS 18; CANR 49, 101; CBD; CD 5; CN 7; DLB 14

Powys, John Cowper 1872-1963 ... **CLC 7, 9, 15, 46, 125**
See also CA 85-88; CANR 106; DLB 15, 255; EWL 3; FANT; MTCW 1, 2; RGEL 2; SUFW

Powys, T(heodore) F(rancis) 1875-1953 .... **TCLC 9**
See also BRWS 8; CA 106; 189; DLB 36, 162; EWL 3; FANT; RGEL 2; SUFW

Prado (Calvo), Pedro 1886-1952 ... **TCLC 75**
See also CA 131; DLB 283; HW 1; LAW

Prager, Emily 1952- .... **CLC 56**
See also CA 204

Pratchett, Terry 1948- .... **CLC 197**
See also AAYA 19, 54; BPFB 3; CA 143; CANR 87, 126; CLR 64; CN 7; CPW; CWRI 5; FANT; SATA 82, 139; SFW 4; SUFW 2

Pratolini, Vasco 1913-1991 .... **TCLC 124**
See also CA 211; DLB 177; EWL 3; RGWL 2, 3

Pratt, E(dwin) J(ohn) 1883(?)-1964 . **CLC 19**
See also CA 141; 93-96; CANR 77; DAC; DAM POET; DLB 92; EWL 3; RGEL 2; TWA

Premchand .... **TCLC 21**
See Srivastava, Dhanpat Rai
See also EWL 3

Preseren, France 1800-1849 .... **NCLC 127**
See also CDWLB 4; DLB 147

Preussler, Otfried 1923- .... **CLC 17**
See also CA 77-80; SATA 24

Prevert, Jacques (Henri Marie) 1900-1977 .... **CLC 15**
See also CA 77-80; 69-72; CANR 29, 61; DLB 258; EWL 3; GFL 1789 to the Present; IDFW 3, 4; MTCW 1; RGWL 2, 3; SATA-Obit 30

Prevost, (Antoine Francois) 1697-1763 .... **LC 1**
See also EW 4; GFL Beginnings to 1789; RGWL 2, 3

Price, (Edward) Reynolds 1933- ... **CLC 3, 6, 13, 43, 50, 63; SSC 22**
See also AMWS 6; CA 1-4R; CANR 1, 37, 57, 87, 128; CN 7; CSW; DAM NOV; DLB 2, 218, 278; EWL 3; INT CANR-37; NFS 18

Price, Richard 1949- .... **CLC 6, 12**
See also CA 49-52; CANR 3; DLBY 1981

Prichard, Katharine Susannah
1883-1969 .... **CLC 46**
See also CA 11-12; CANR 33; CAP 1; DLB 260; MTCW 1; RGEL 2; RGSF 2; SATA 66

Priestley, J(ohn) B(oynton)
1894-1984 .... **CLC 2, 5, 9, 34**
See also BRW 7; CA 9-12R; 113; CANR 33; CDBLB 1914-1945; DA3; DAM DRAM, NOV; DLB 10, 34, 77, 100, 139; DLBY 1984; EWL 3; MTCW 1, 2; RGEL 2; SFW 4

Prince 1958- .... **CLC 35**
See also CA 213

Prince, F(rank) T(empleton)
1912-2003 .... **CLC 22**
See also CA 101; 219; CANR 43, 79; CP 7; DLB 20

Prince Kropotkin
See Kropotkin, Peter (Alekseievich)

Prior, Matthew 1664-1721 .... **LC 4**
See also DLB 95; RGEL 2

Prishvin, Mikhail 1873-1954 .... **TCLC 75**
See Prishvin, Mikhail Mikhailovich

Prishvin, Mikhail Mikhailovich
See Prishvin, Mikhail
See also DLB 272; EWL 3

Pritchard, William H(arrison)
1932- .... **CLC 34**
See also CA 65-68; CANR 23, 95; DLB 111

Pritchett, V(ictor) S(awdon)
1900-1997 ... **CLC 5, 13, 15, 41; SSC 14**
See also BPFB 3; BRWS 3; CA 61-64; 157; CANR 31, 63; CN 7; DA3; DAM NOV; DLB 15, 139; EWL 3; MTCW 1, 2; RGEL 2; RGSF 2; TEA

Private 19022
See Manning, Frederic

Probst, Mark 1925- .... **CLC 59**
See also CA 130

Prokosch, Frederic 1908-1989 ...... **CLC 4, 48**
See also CA 73-76; 128; CANR 82; DLB 48; MTCW 2

Propertius, Sextus c. 50B.C.-c. 16B.C. .... **CMLC 32**
See also AW 2; CDWLB 1; DLB 211; RGWL 2, 3

Prophet, The
See Dreiser, Theodore (Herman Albert)

Prose, Francine 1947- .... **CLC 45**
See also CA 109; 112; CANR 46, 95, 132; DLB 234; SATA 101, 149

Proudhon
See Cunha, Euclides (Rodrigues Pimenta) da

Proulx, Annie
See Proulx, E(dna) Annie

Proulx, E(dna) Annie 1935- ...... **CLC 81, 158**
See also AMWS 7; BPFB 3; CA 145; CANR 65, 110; CN 7; CPW 1; DA3; DAM POP; MTCW 2; SSFS 18

Proust, (Valentin-Louis-George-Eugene) Marcel 1871-1922 ..... **SSC 75; TCLC 7, 13, 33, 161; WLC**
See also AAYA 58; BPFB 3; CA 104; 120; CANR 110; DA; DA3; DAB; DAC; DAM MST, NOV; DLB 65; EW 8; EWL 3; GFL 1789 to the Present; MTCW 1, 2; RGWL 2, 3; TWA

Prowler, Harley
See Masters, Edgar Lee

Prus, Boleslaw 1845-1912 .... **TCLC 48**
See also RGWL 2, 3

Pryor, Richard (Franklin Lenox Thomas)
1940- .... **CLC 26**
See also CA 122; 152

Przybyszewski, Stanislaw
1868-1927 .... **TCLC 36**
See also CA 160; DLB 66; EWL 3

Pteleon
See Grieve, C(hristopher) M(urray)
See also DAM POET

Puckett, Lute
See Masters, Edgar Lee

Puig, Manuel 1932-1990 .... **CLC 3, 5, 10, 28, 65, 133; HLC 2**
See also BPFB 3; CA 45-48; CANR 2, 32, 63; CDWLB 3; DA3; DAM MULT; DLB 113; DNFS 1; EWL 3; GLL 1; HW 1, 2; LAW; MTCW 1, 2; RGWL 2, 3; TWA; WLIT 1

Pulitzer, Joseph 1847-1911 .... **TCLC 76**
See also CA 114; DLB 23

Purchas, Samuel 1577(?)-1626 .... **LC 70**
See also DLB 151

Purdy, A(lfred) W(ellington)
1918-2000 .... **CLC 3, 6, 14, 50**
See also CA 81-84; 189; CAAS 17; CANR 42, 66; CP 7; DAC; DAM MST, POET; DLB 88; PFS 5; RGEL 2

Purdy, James (Amos) 1923- .... **CLC 2, 4, 10, 28, 52**
See also AMWS 7; CA 33-36R; CAAS 1; CANR 19, 51, 132; CN 7; DLB 2, 218; EWL 3; INT CANR-19; MTCW 1; RGAL 4

Pure, Simon
See Swinnerton, Frank Arthur

Pushkin, Aleksandr Sergeevich
See Pushkin, Alexander (Sergeyevich)
See also DLB 205

Pushkin, Alexander (Sergeyevich)
1799-1837 .... **NCLC 3, 27, 83; PC 10; SSC 27, 55; WLC**
See Pushkin, Aleksandr Sergeevich
See also DA; DA3; DAB; DAC; DAM DRAM, MST, POET; EW 5; EXPS; RGSF 2; RGWL 2, 3; SATA 61; SSFS 9; TWA

P'u Sung-ling 1640-1715 .... **LC 49; SSC 31**

Putnam, Arthur Lee
See Alger, Horatio, Jr.

Puzo, Mario 1920-1999 .... **CLC 1, 2, 6, 36, 107**
See also BPFB 3; CA 65-68; 185; CANR 4, 42, 65, 99, 131; CN 7; CPW; DA3; DAM NOV, POP; DLB 6; MTCW 1, 2; NFS 16; RGAL 4

Pygge, Edward
See Barnes, Julian (Patrick)

Pyle, Ernest Taylor 1900-1945
See Pyle, Ernie
See also CA 115; 160

Pyle, Ernie .... **TCLC 75**
See Pyle, Ernest Taylor
See also DLB 29; MTCW 2

Pyle, Howard 1853-1911 .... **TCLC 81**
See also AAYA 57; BYA 2, 4; CA 109; 137; CLR 22; DLB 42, 188; DLBD 13; LAIT 1; MAICYA 1, 2; SATA 16, 100; WCH; YAW

Pym, Barbara (Mary Crampton)
1913-1980 .... **CLC 13, 19, 37, 111**
See also BPFB 3; BRWS 2; CA 13-14; 97-100; CANR 13, 34; CAP 1; DLB 14, 207; DLBY 1987; EWL 3; MTCW 1, 2; RGEL 2; TEA

Pynchon, Thomas (Ruggles, Jr.)
1937- .... **CLC 2, 3, 6, 9, 11, 18, 33, 62, 72, 123, 192; SSC 14; WLC**
See also AMWS 2; BEST 90:2; BPFB 3; CA 17-20R; CANR 22, 46, 73; CN 7; CPW 1; DA; DA3; DAB; DAC; DAM MST, NOV, POP; DLB 2, 173; EWL 3; MTCW 1, 2; RGAL 4; SFW 4; TUS

Pythagoras c. 582B.C.-c. 507B.C. . **CMLC 22**
See also DLB 176

Q
See Quiller-Couch, Sir Arthur (Thomas)

Qian, Chongzhu
See Ch'ien, Chung-shu

Qian, Sima 145B.C.-c. 89B.C. .... **CMLC 72**

Qian Zhongshu
See Ch'ien, Chung-shu
See also CWW 2

Qroll
See Dagerman, Stig (Halvard)

Quarrington, Paul (Lewis) 1953- ...... **CLC 65**
See also CA 129; CANR 62, 95

Quasimodo, Salvatore 1901-1968 .... **CLC 10; PC 47**
See also CA 13-16; 25-28R; CAP 1; DLB 114; EW 12; EWL 3; MTCW 1; RGWL 2, 3

Quatermass, Martin
See Carpenter, John (Howard)

Quay, Stephen 1947- .... **CLC 95**
See also CA 189

Quay, Timothy 1947- .... **CLC 95**
See also CA 189

Queen, Ellery .... **CLC 3, 11**
See Dannay, Frederic; Davidson, Avram (James); Deming, Richard; Fairman, Paul W.; Flora, Fletcher; Hoch, Edward D(entinger); Kane, Henry; Lee, Manfred B(ennington); Marlowe, Stephen; Powell, (Oval) Talmage; Sheldon, Walter J(ames); Sturgeon, Theodore (Hamilton); Tracy, Don(ald Fiske); Vance, John Holbrook
See also BPFB 3; CMW 4; MSW; RGAL 4

Queen, Ellery, Jr.
See Dannay, Frederic; Lee, Manfred B(ennington)

Queneau, Raymond 1903-1976 ..... **CLC 2, 5, 10, 42**
See also CA 77-80; 69-72; CANR 32; DLB 72, 258; EW 12; EWL 3; GFL 1789 to the Present; MTCW 1, 2; RGWL 2, 3

Quevedo, Francisco de 1580-1645 .... **LC 23**

Quiller-Couch, Sir Arthur (Thomas)
1863-1944 .... **TCLC 53**
See also CA 118; 166; DLB 135, 153, 190; HGG; RGEL 2; SUFW 1

Quin, Ann (Marie) 1936-1973 .... **CLC 6**
See also CA 9-12R; 45-48; DLB 14, 231

Quincey, Thomas de
See De Quincey, Thomas

Quindlen, Anna 1953- .... **CLC 191**
See also AAYA 35; CA 138; CANR 73, 126; DA3; DLB 292; MTCW 2

Quinn, Martin
See Smith, Martin Cruz

Quinn, Peter 1947- .... **CLC 91**
See also CA 197

Quinn, Simon
See Smith, Martin Cruz

Quintana, Leroy V. 1944- ...... **HLC 2; PC 36**
See also CA 131; CANR 65; DAM MULT; DLB 82; HW 1, 2

Quiroga, Horacio (Sylvestre)
1878-1937 .... **HLC 2; TCLC 20**
See also CA 117; 131; DAM MULT; EWL 3; HW 1; LAW; MTCW 1; RGSF 2; WLIT 1

Quoirez, Francoise 1935- .... **CLC 9**
See Sagan, Francoise
See also CA 49-52; CANR 6, 39, 73; MTCW 1, 2; TWA

Raabe, Wilhelm (Karl) 1831-1910 . **TCLC 45**
See also CA 167; DLB 129

Rabe, David (William) 1940- .. **CLC 4, 8, 33, 200; DC 16**
See also CA 85-88; CABS 3; CAD; CANR 59, 129; CD 5; DAM DRAM; DFS 3, 8, 13; DLB 7, 228; EWL 3

Rabelais, Francois 1494-1553 .... **LC 5, 60;
WLC**
See also DA; DAB; DAC; DAM MST; EW
2; GFL Beginnings to 1789; LMFS 1;
RGWL 2, 3; TWA
Rabinovitch, Sholem 1859-1916
See Aleichem, Sholom
See also CA 104
Rabinyan, Dorit 1972- .... **CLC 119**
See also CA 170
Rachilde
See Vallette, Marguerite Eymery; Vallette,
Marguerite Eymery
See also EWL 3
Racine, Jean 1639-1699 .... **LC 28, 113**
See also DA3; DAB; DAM MST; DLB 268;
EW 3; GFL Beginnings to 1789; LMFS
1; RGWL 2, 3; TWA
Radcliffe, Ann (Ward) 1764-1823 ... **NCLC 6,
55, 106**
See also DLB 39, 178; HGG; LMFS 1;
RGEL 2; SUFW; WLIT 3
Radclyffe-Hall, Marguerite
See Hall, (Marguerite) Radclyffe
Radiguet, Raymond 1903-1923 ...... **TCLC 29**
See also CA 162; DLB 65; EWL 3; GFL
1789 to the Present; RGWL 2, 3
Radnoti, Miklos 1909-1944 .... **TCLC 16**
See also CA 118; 212; CDWLB 4; DLB
215; EWL 3; RGWL 2, 3
Rado, James 1939- .... **CLC 17**
See also CA 105
Radvanyi, Netty 1900-1983
See Seghers, Anna
See also CA 85-88; 110; CANR 82
Rae, Ben
See Griffiths, Trevor
Raeburn, John (Hay) 1941- .... **CLC 34**
See also CA 57-60
Ragni, Gerome 1942-1991 .... **CLC 17**
See also CA 105; 134
Rahv, Philip .... **CLC 24**
See Greenberg, Ivan
See also DLB 137
Raimund, Ferdinand Jakob
1790-1836 .... **NCLC 69**
See also DLB 90
Raine, Craig (Anthony) 1944- .. **CLC 32, 103**
See also CA 108; CANR 29, 51, 103; CP 7;
DLB 40; PFS 7
Raine, Kathleen (Jessie) 1908-2003 .. **CLC 7,
45**
See also CA 85-88; 218; CANR 46, 109;
CP 7; DLB 20; EWL 3; MTCW 1; RGEL
2
Rainis, Janis 1865-1929 .... **TCLC 29**
See also CA 170; CDWLB 4; DLB 220;
EWL 3
Rakosi, Carl .... **CLC 47**
See Rawley, Callman
See also CA 228; CAAS 5; CP 7; DLB 193
Ralegh, Sir Walter
See Raleigh, Sir Walter
See also BRW 1; RGEL 2; WP
Raleigh, Richard
See Lovecraft, H(oward) P(hillips)
Raleigh, Sir Walter 1554(?)-1618 .... **LC 31,
39; PC 31**
See Ralegh, Sir Walter
See also CDBLB Before 1660; DLB 172;
EXPP; PFS 14; TEA
Rallentando, H. P.
See Sayers, Dorothy L(eigh)
Ramal, Walter
See de la Mare, Walter (John)

Ramana Maharshi 1879-1950 .... **TCLC 84**
Ramoacn y Cajal, Santiago
1852-1934 .... **TCLC 93**
Ramon, Juan
See Jimenez (Mantccon), Juan Ramon
Ramos, Graciliano 1892-1953 .... **TCLC 32**
See also CA 167; DLB 307; EWL 3; HW 2;
LAW; WLIT 1
Rampersad, Arnold 1941- .... **CLC 44**
See also BW 2, 3; CA 127; 133; CANR 81;
DLB 111; INT CA-133
Rampling, Anne
See Rice, Anne
See also GLL 2
Ramsay, Allan 1686(?)-1758 .... **LC 29**
See also DLB 95; RGEL 2
Ramsay, Jay
See Campbell, (John) Ramsey
Ramuz, Charles-Ferdinand
1878-1947 .... **TCLC 33**
See also CA 165; EWL 3
Rand, Ayn 1905-1982 ...... **CLC 3, 30, 44, 79;
WLC**
See also AAYA 10; AMWS 4; BPFB 3;
BYA 12; CA 13-16R; 105; CANR 27, 73;
CDALBS; CPW; DA; DA3; DAC; DAM
MST, NOV, POP; DLB 227, 279; MTCW
1, 2; NFS 10, 16; RGAL 4; SFW 4; TUS;
YAW
Randall, Dudley (Felker) 1914-2000 . **BLC 3;
CLC 1, 135**
See also BW 1, 3; CA 25-28R; 189; CANR
23, 82; DAM MULT; DLB 41; PFS 5
Randall, Robert
See Silverberg, Robert
Ranger, Ken
See Creasey, John
Rank, Otto 1884-1939 .... **TCLC 115**
Ransom, John Crowe 1888-1974 .. **CLC 2, 4,
5, 11, 24; PC 61**
See also AMW; CA 5-8R; 49-52; CANR 6,
34; CDALBS; DA3; DAM POET; DLB
45, 63; EWL 3; EXPP; MTCW 1, 2;
RGAL 4; TUS
Rao, Raja 1909- .... **CLC 25, 56**
See also CA 73-76; CANR 51; CN 7; DAM
NOV; EWL 3; MTCW 1, 2; RGEL 2;
RGSF 2
Raphael, Frederic (Michael) 1931- ... **CLC 2,
14**
See also CA 1-4R; CANR 1, 86; CN 7;
DLB 14
Ratcliffe, James P.
See Mencken, H(enry) L(ouis)
Rathbone, Julian 1935- .... **CLC 41**
See also CA 101; CANR 34, 73
Rattigan, Terence (Mervyn)
1911-1977 .... **CLC 7; DC 18**
See also BRWS 7; CA 85-88; 73-76; CBD;
CDBLB 1945-1960; DAM DRAM; DFS
8; DLB 13; IDFW 3, 4; MTCW 1, 2;
RGEL 2
Ratushinskaya, Irina 1954- .... **CLC 54**
See also CA 129; CANR 68; CWW 2
Raven, Simon (Arthur Noel)
1927-2001 .... **CLC 14**
See also CA 81-84; 197; CANR 86; CN 7;
DLB 271
Ravenna, Michael
See Welty, Eudora (Alice)
Rawley, Callman 1903-2004
See Rakosi, Carl
See also CA 21-24R; CANR 12, 32, 91
Rawlings, Marjorie Kinnan
1896-1953 .... **TCLC 4**
See also AAYA 20; AMWS 10; ANW;
BPFB 3; BYA 3; CA 104; 137; CANR 74;
CLR 63; DLB 9, 22, 102; DLBD 17;
JRDA; MAICYA 1, 2; MTCW 2; RGAL
4; SATA 100; WCH; YABC 1; YAW

Ray, Satyajit 1921-1992 .... **CLC 16, 76**
See also CA 114; 137; DAM MULT
Read, Herbert Edward 1893-1968 ..... **CLC 4**
See also BRW 6; CA 85-88; 25-28R; DLB
20, 149; EWL 3; PAB; RGEL 2
Read, Piers Paul 1941- .... **CLC 4, 10, 25**
See also CA 21-24R; CANR 38, 86; CN 7;
DLB 14; SATA 21
Reade, Charles 1814-1884 .... **NCLC 2, 74**
See also DLB 21; RGEL 2
Reade, Hamish
See Gray, Simon (James Holliday)
Reading, Peter 1946- .... **CLC 47**
See also BRWS 8; CA 103; CANR 46, 96;
CP 7; DLB 40
Reaney, James 1926- .... **CLC 13**
See also CA 41-44R; CAAS 15; CANR 42;
CD 5; CP 7; DAC; DAM MST; DLB 68;
RGEL 2; SATA 43
Rebreanu, Liviu 1885-1944 .... **TCLC 28**
See also CA 165; DLB 220; EWL 3
Rechy, John (Francisco) 1934- ...... **CLC 1, 7,
14, 18, 107; HLC 2**
See also CA 5-8R, 195; CAAE 195; CAAS
4; CANR 6, 32, 64; CN 7; DAM MULT;
DLB 122, 278; DLBY 1982; HW 1, 2;
INT CANR-6; LLW 1; RGAL 4
Redcam, Tom 1870-1933 .... **TCLC 25**
Reddin, Keith .... **CLC 67**
See also CAD
Redgrove, Peter (William)
1932-2003 .... **CLC 6, 41**
See also BRWS 6; CA 1-4R; 217; CANR 3,
39, 77; CP 7; DLB 40
Redmon, Anne .... **CLC 22**
See Nightingale, Anne Redmon
See also DLBY 1986
Reed, Eliot
See Ambler, Eric
Reed, Ishmael 1938- ...... **BLC 3; CLC 2, 3, 5,
6, 13, 32, 60, 174**
See also AFAW 1, 2; AMWS 10; BPFB 3;
BW 2, 3; CA 21-24R; CANR 25, 48, 74,
128; CN 7; CP 7; CSW; DA3; DAM
MULT; DLB 2, 5, 33, 169, 227; DLBD 8;
EWL 3; LMFS 2; MSW; MTCW 1, 2;
PFS 6; RGAL 4; TCWW 2
Reed, John (Silas) 1887-1920 .... **TCLC 9**
See also CA 106; 195; TUS
Reed, Lou .... **CLC 21**
See Firbank, Louis
Reese, Lizette Woodworth 1856-1935 . **PC 29**
See also CA 180; DLB 54
Reeve, Clara 1729-1807 .... **NCLC 19**
See also DLB 39; RGEL 2
Reich, Wilhelm 1897-1957 .... **TCLC 57**
See also CA 199
Reid, Christopher (John) 1949- .... **CLC 33**
See also CA 140; CANR 89; CP 7; DLB
40; EWL 3
Reid, Desmond
See Moorcock, Michael (John)
Reid Banks, Lynne 1929-
See Banks, Lynne Reid
See also AAYA 49; CA 1-4R; CANR 6, 22,
38, 87; CLR 24; CN 7; JRDA; MAICYA
1, 2; SATA 22, 75, 111; YAW
Reilly, William K.
See Creasey, John
Reiner, Max
See Caldwell, (Janet Miriam) Taylor
(Holland)
Reis, Ricardo
See Pessoa, Fernando (Antonio Nogueira)
Reizenstein, Elmer Leopold
See Rice, Elmer (Leopold)
See also EWL 3

Remarque, Erich Maria 1898-1970 . **CLC 21**
See also AAYA 27; BPFB 3; CA 77-80; 29-32R; CDWLB 2; DA; DA3; DAB; DAC; DAM MST, NOV; DLB 56; EWL 3; EXPN; LAIT 3; MTCW 1, 2; NFS 4; RGWL 2, 3

Remington, Frederic 1861-1909 ..... **TCLC 89**
See also CA 108; 169; DLB 12, 186, 188; SATA 41

Remizov, A.
See Remizov, Aleksei (Mikhailovich)

Remizov, A. M.
See Remizov, Aleksei (Mikhailovich)

Remizov, Aleksei (Mikhailovich)
1877-1957 .... **TCLC 27**
See Remizov, Alexey Mikhaylovich
See also CA 125; 133; DLB 295

Remizov, Alexey Mikhaylovich
See Remizov, Aleksei (Mikhailovich)
See also EWL 3

Renan, Joseph Ernest 1823-1892 . **NCLC 26, 145**
See also GFL 1789 to the Present

Renard, Jules(-Pierre) 1864-1910 .. **TCLC 17**
See also CA 117; 202; GFL 1789 to the Present

Renault, Mary .... **CLC 3, 11, 17**
See Challans, Mary
See also BPFB 3; BYA 2; DLBY 1983; EWL 3; GLL 1; LAIT 1; MTCW 2; RGEL 2; RHW

Rendell, Ruth (Barbara) 1930- .. **CLC 28, 48**
See Vine, Barbara
See also BPFB 3; BRWS 9; CA 109; CANR 32, 52, 74, 127; CN 7; CPW; DAM POP; DLB 87, 276; INT CANR-32; MSW; MTCW 1, 2

Renoir, Jean 1894-1979 .... **CLC 20**
See also CA 129; 85-88

Resnais, Alain 1922- .... **CLC 16**

Revard, Carter (Curtis) 1931- .... **NNAL**
See also CA 144; CANR 81; PFS 5

Reverdy, Pierre 1889-1960 .... **CLC 53**
See also CA 97-100; 89-92; DLB 258; EWL 3; GFL 1789 to the Present

Rexroth, Kenneth 1905-1982 .... **CLC 1, 2, 6, 11, 22, 49, 112; PC 20**
See also BG 3; CA 5-8R; 107; CANR 14, 34, 63; CDALB 1941-1968; DAM POET; DLB 16, 48, 165, 212; DLBY 1982; EWL 3; INT CANR-14; MTCW 1, 2; RGAL 4

Reyes, Alfonso 1889-1959 .... **HLCS 2; TCLC 33**
See also CA 131; EWL 3; HW 1; LAW

Reyes y Basoalto, Ricardo Eliecer Neftali
See Neruda, Pablo

Reymont, Wladyslaw (Stanislaw)
1868(?)-1925 .... **TCLC 5**
See also CA 104; EWL 3

Reynolds, John Hamilton
1794-1852 .... **NCLC 146**
See also DLB 96

Reynolds, Jonathan 1942- .... **CLC 6, 38**
See also CA 65-68; CANR 28

Reynolds, Joshua 1723-1792 .... **LC 15**
See also DLB 104

Reynolds, Michael S(hane)
1937-2000 .... **CLC 44**
See also CA 65-68; 189; CANR 9, 89, 97

Reznikoff, Charles 1894-1976 .... **CLC 9**
See also AMWS 14; CA 33-36; 61-64; CAP 2; DLB 28, 45; WP

Rezzori (d'Arezzo), Gregor von
1914-1998 .... **CLC 25**
See also CA 122; 136; 167

Rhine, Richard
See Silverstein, Alvin; Silverstein, Virginia B(arbara Opshelor)

Rhodes, Eugene Manlove
1869-1934 .... **TCLC 53**
See also CA 198; DLB 256

R'hoone, Lord
See Balzac, Honore de

Rhys, Jean 1890-1979 .... **CLC 2, 4, 6, 14, 19, 51, 124; SSC 21, 76**
See also BRWS 2; CA 25-28R; 85-88; CANR 35, 62; CDBLB 1945-1960; CDWLB 3; DA3; DAM NOV; DLB 36, 117, 162; DNFS 2; EWL 3; LATS 1:1; MTCW 1, 2; RGEL 2; RGSF 2; RHW; TEA; WWE 1

Ribeiro, Darcy 1922-1997 .... **CLC 34**
See also CA 33-36R; 156; EWL 3

Ribeiro, Joao Ubaldo (Osorio Pimentel)
1941- .... **CLC 10, 67**
See also CA 81-84; CWW 2; EWL 3

Ribman, Ronald (Burt) 1932- .... **CLC 7**
See also CA 21-24R; CAD; CANR 46, 80; CD 5

Ricci, Nino (Pio) 1959- .... **CLC 70**
See also CA 137; CANR 130; CCA 1

Rice, Anne 1941- .... **CLC 41, 128**
See Rampling, Anne
See also AAYA 9, 53; AMWS 7; BEST 89:2; BPFB 3; CA 65-68; CANR 12, 36, 53, 74, 100, 133; CN 7; CPW; CSW; DA3; DAM POP; DLB 292; GLL 2; HGG; MTCW 2; SUFW 2; YAW

Rice, Elmer (Leopold) 1892-1967 ...... **CLC 7, 49**
See Reizenstein, Elmer Leopold
See also CA 21-22; 25-28R; CAP 2; DAM DRAM; DFS 12; DLB 4, 7; MTCW 1, 2; RGAL 4

Rice, Tim(othy Miles Bindon)
1944- .... **CLC 21**
See also CA 103; CANR 46; DFS 7

Rich, Adrienne (Cecile) 1929- ... **CLC 3, 6, 7, 11, 18, 36, 73, 76, 125; PC 5**
See also AMWR 2; AMWS 1; CA 9-12R; CANR 20, 53, 74, 128; CDALBS; CP 7; CSW; CWP; DA3; DAM POET; DLB 5, 67; EWL 3; EXPP; FW; MAWW; MTCW 1, 2; PAB; PFS 15; RGAL 4; WP

Rich, Barbara
See Graves, Robert (von Ranke)

Rich, Robert
See Trumbo, Dalton

Richard, Keith .... **CLC 17**
See Richards, Keith

Richards, David Adams 1950- .... **CLC 59**
See also CA 93-96; CANR 60, 110; DAC; DLB 53

Richards, I(vor) A(rmstrong)
1893-1979 .... **CLC 14, 24**
See also BRWS 2; CA 41-44R; 89-92; CANR 34, 74; DLB 27; EWL 3; MTCW 2; RGEL 2

Richards, Keith 1943-
See Richard, Keith
See also CA 107; CANR 77

Richardson, Anne
See Roiphe, Anne (Richardson)

Richardson, Dorothy Miller
1873-1957 .... **TCLC 3**
See also CA 104; 192; DLB 36; EWL 3; FW; RGEL 2

Richardson (Robertson), Ethel Florence Lindesay 1870-1946
See Richardson, Henry Handel
See also CA 105; 190; DLB 230; RHW

Richardson, Henry Handel .... **TCLC 4**
See Richardson (Robertson), Ethel Florence Lindesay
See also DLB 197; EWL 3; RGEL 2; RGSF 2

Richardson, John 1796-1852 .... **NCLC 55**
See also CCA 1; DAC; DLB 99

Richardson, Samuel 1689-1761 ...... **LC 1, 44; WLC**
See also BRW 3; CDBLB 1660-1789; DA; DAB; DAC; DAM MST, NOV; DLB 39; RGEL 2; TEA; WLIT 3

Richardson, Willis 1889-1977 .... **HR 3**
See also BW 1; CA 124; DLB 51; SATA 60

Richler, Mordecai 1931-2001 .... **CLC 3, 5, 9, 13, 18, 46, 70, 185**
See also AITN 1; CA 65-68; 201; CANR 31, 62, 111; CCA 1; CLR 17; CWRI 5; DAC; DAM MST, NOV; DLB 53; EWL 3; MAICYA 1, 2; MTCW 1, 2; RGEL 2; SATA 44, 98; SATA-Brief 27; TWA

Richter, Conrad (Michael)
1890-1968 .... **CLC 30**
See also AAYA 21; BYA 2; CA 5-8R; 25-28R; CANR 23; DLB 9, 212; LAIT 1; MTCW 1, 2; RGAL 4; SATA 3; TCWW 2; TUS; YAW

Ricostranza, Tom
See Ellis, Trey

Riddell, Charlotte 1832-1906 .... **TCLC 40**
See Riddell, Mrs. J. H.
See also CA 165; DLB 156

Riddell, Mrs. J. H.
See Riddell, Charlotte
See also HGG; SUFW

Ridge, John Rollin 1827-1867 ...... **NCLC 82; NNAL**
See also CA 144; DAM MULT; DLB 175

Ridgeway, Jason
See Marlowe, Stephen

Ridgway, Keith 1965- .... **CLC 119**
See also CA 172

Riding, Laura .... **CLC 3, 7**
See Jackson, Laura (Riding)
See also RGAL 4

Riefenstahl, Berta Helene Amalia 1902-2003
See Riefenstahl, Leni
See also CA 108; 220

Riefenstahl, Leni .... **CLC 16, 190**
See Riefenstahl, Berta Helene Amalia

Riffe, Ernest
See Bergman, (Ernst) Ingmar

Riggs, (Rolla) Lynn
1899-1954 .... **NNAL; TCLC 56**
See also CA 144; DAM MULT; DLB 175

Riis, Jacob A(ugust) 1849-1914 ..... **TCLC 80**
See also CA 113; 168; DLB 23

Riley, James Whitcomb 1849-1916 .... **PC 48; TCLC 51**
See also CA 118; 137; DAM POET; MAICYA 1, 2; RGAL 4; SATA 17

Riley, Tex
See Creasey, John

Rilke, Rainer Maria 1875-1926 .... **PC 2; TCLC 1, 6, 19**
See also CA 104; 132; CANR 62, 99; CDWLB 2; DA3; DAM POET; DLB 81; EW 9; EWL 3; MTCW 1, 2; PFS 19; RGWL 2, 3; TWA; WP

Rimbaud, (Jean Nicolas) Arthur
1854-1891 ... **NCLC 4, 35, 82; PC 3, 57; WLC**
See also DA; DA3; DAB; DAC; DAM MST, POET; DLB 217; EW 7; GFL 1789 to the Present; LMFS 2; RGWL 2, 3; TWA; WP

Rinehart, Mary Roberts
1876-1958 .... **TCLC 52**
See also BPFB 3; CA 108; 166; RGAL 4; RHW

Ringmaster, The
See Mencken, H(enry) L(ouis)

Ringwood, Gwen(dolyn Margaret) Pharis
1910-1984 .... **CLC 48**
See also CA 148; 112; DLB 88

Rio, Michel 1945(?)- .... **CLC 43**
See also CA 201

Rios, Alberto (Alvaro) 1952- .... **PC 57**
See also AMWS 4; CA 113; CANR 34, 79; CP 7; DLB 122; HW 2; PFS 11

Ritsos, Giannes
See Ritsos, Yannis

Ritsos, Yannis 1909-1990 .... **CLC 6, 13, 31**
See also CA 77-80; 133; CANR 39, 61; EW 12; EWL 3; MTCW 1; RGWL 2, 3

Ritter, Erika 1948(?)- .... **CLC 52**
See also CD 5; CWD

Rivera, Jose Eustasio 1889-1928 ... **TCLC 35**
See also CA 162; EWL 3; HW 1, 2; LAW

Rivera, Tomas 1935-1984 .... **HLCS 2**
See also CA 49-52; CANR 32; DLB 82; HW 1; LLW 1; RGAL 4; SSFS 15; TCWW 2; WLIT 1

Rivers, Conrad Kent 1933-1968 .... **CLC 1**
See also BW 1; CA 85-88; DLB 41

Rivers, Elfrida
See Bradley, Marion Zimmer
See also GLL 1

Riverside, John
See Heinlein, Robert A(nson)

Rizal, Jose 1861-1896 .... **NCLC 27**

Roa Bastos, Augusto (Antonio)
1917- .... **CLC 45; HLC 2**
See also CA 131; CWW 2; DAM MULT; DLB 113; EWL 3; HW 1; LAW; RGSF 2; WLIT 1

Robbe-Grillet, Alain 1922- .... **CLC 1, 2, 4, 6, 8, 10, 14, 43, 128**
See also BPFB 3; CA 9-12R; CANR 33, 65, 115; CWW 2; DLB 83; EW 13; EWL 3; GFL 1789 to the Present; IDFW 3, 4; MTCW 1, 2; RGWL 2, 3; SSFS 15

Robbins, Harold 1916-1997 .... **CLC 5**
See also BPFB 3; CA 73-76; 162; CANR 26, 54, 112; DA3; DAM NOV; MTCW 1, 2

Robbins, Thomas Eugene 1936-
See Robbins, Tom
See also CA 81-84; CANR 29, 59, 95; CN 7; CPW; CSW; DA3; DAM NOV, POP; MTCW 1, 2

Robbins, Tom .... **CLC 9, 32, 64**
See Robbins, Thomas Eugene
See also AAYA 32; AMWS 10; BEST 90:3; BPFB 3; DLBY 1980; MTCW 2

Robbins, Trina 1938- .... **CLC 21**
See also CA 128

Roberts, Charles G(eorge) D(ouglas)
1860-1943 .... **TCLC 8**
See also CA 105; 188; CLR 33; CWRI 5; DLB 92; RGEL 2; RGSF 2; SATA 88; SATA-Brief 29

Roberts, Elizabeth Madox
1886-1941 .... **TCLC 68**
See also CA 111; 166; CLR 100; CWRI 5; DLB 9, 54, 102; RGAL 4; RHW; SATA 33; SATA-Brief 27; WCH

Roberts, Kate 1891-1985 .... **CLC 15**
See also CA 107; 116

Roberts, Keith (John Kingston)
1935-2000 .... **CLC 14**
See also BRWS 10; CA 25-28R; CANR 46; DLB 261; SFW 4

Roberts, Kenneth (Lewis)
1885-1957 .... **TCLC 23**
See also CA 109; 199; DLB 9; RGAL 4; RHW

Roberts, Michele (Brigitte) 1949- .... **CLC 48, 178**
See also CA 115; CANR 58, 120; CN 7; DLB 231; FW

Robertson, Ellis
See Ellison, Harlan (Jay); Silverberg, Robert

Robertson, Thomas William
1829-1871 .... **NCLC 35**
See Robertson, Tom
See also DAM DRAM

Robertson, Tom
See Robertson, Thomas William
See also RGEL 2

Robeson, Kenneth
See Dent, Lester

Robinson, Edwin Arlington
1869-1935 .... **PC 1, 35; TCLC 5, 101**
See also AMW; CA 104; 133; CDALB 1865-1917; DA; DAC; DAM MST, POET; DLB 54; EWL 3; EXPP; MTCW 1, 2; PAB; PFS 4; RGAL 4; WP

Robinson, Henry Crabb
1775-1867 .... **NCLC 15**
See also DLB 107

Robinson, Jill 1936- .... **CLC 10**
See also CA 102; CANR 120; INT CA-102

Robinson, Kim Stanley 1952- .... **CLC 34**
See also AAYA 26; CA 126; CANR 113; CN 7; SATA 109; SCFW 2; SFW 4

Robinson, Lloyd
See Silverberg, Robert

Robinson, Marilynne 1944- ...... **CLC 25, 180**
See also CA 116; CANR 80; CN 7; DLB 206

Robinson, Mary 1758-1800 .... **NCLC 142**
See also DLB 158; FW

Robinson, Smokey .... **CLC 21**
See Robinson, William, Jr.

Robinson, William, Jr. 1940-
See Robinson, Smokey
See also CA 116

Robison, Mary 1949- .... **CLC 42, 98**
See also CA 113; 116; CANR 87; CN 7; DLB 130; INT CA-116; RGSF 2

Rochester
See Wilmot, John
See also RGEL 2

Rod, Edouard 1857-1910 .... **TCLC 52**

Roddenberry, Eugene Wesley 1921-1991
See Roddenberry, Gene
See also CA 110; 135; CANR 37; SATA 45; SATA-Obit 69

Roddenberry, Gene .... **CLC 17**
See Roddenberry, Eugene Wesley
See also AAYA 5; SATA-Obit 69

Rodgers, Mary 1931- .... **CLC 12**
See also BYA 5; CA 49-52; CANR 8, 55, 90; CLR 20; CWRI 5; INT CANR-8; JRDA; MAICYA 1, 2; SATA 8, 130

Rodgers, W(illiam) R(obert)
1909-1969 .... **CLC 7**
See also CA 85-88; DLB 20; RGEL 2

Rodman, Eric
See Silverberg, Robert

Rodman, Howard 1920(?)-1985 .... **CLC 65**
See also CA 118

Rodman, Maia
See Wojciechowska, Maia (Teresa)

Rodo, Jose Enrique 1871(?)-1917 .... **HLCS 2**
See also CA 178; EWL 3; HW 2; LAW

Rodolph, Utto
See Ouologuem, Yambo

Rodriguez, Claudio 1934-1999 .... **CLC 10**
See also CA 188; DLB 134

Rodriguez, Richard 1944- .... **CLC 155; HLC 2**
See also AMWS 14; CA 110; CANR 66, 116; DAM MULT; DLB 82, 256; HW 1, 2; LAIT 5; LLW 1; NCFS 3; WLIT 1

Roelvaag, O(le) E(dvart) 1876-1931
See Rolvaag, O(le) E(dvart)
See also CA 117; 171

Roethke, Theodore (Huebner)
1908-1963 .... **CLC 1, 3, 8, 11, 19, 46, 101; PC 15**
See also AMW; CA 81-84; CABS 2; CDALB 1941-1968; DA3; DAM POET; DLB 5, 206; EWL 3; EXPP; MTCW 1, 2; PAB; PFS 3; RGAL 4; WP

Rogers, Carl R(ansom)
1902-1987 .... **TCLC 125**
See also CA 1-4R; 121; CANR 1, 18; MTCW 1

Rogers, Samuel 1763-1855 .... **NCLC 69**
See also DLB 93; RGEL 2

Rogers, Thomas Hunton 1927- .... **CLC 57**
See also CA 89-92; INT CA-89-92

Rogers, Will(iam Penn Adair)
1879-1935 .... **NNAL; TCLC 8, 71**
See also CA 105; 144; DA3; DAM MULT; DLB 11; MTCW 2

Rogin, Gilbert 1929- .... **CLC 18**
See also CA 65-68; CANR 15

Rohan, Koda
See Koda Shigeyuki

Rohlfs, Anna Katharine Green
See Green, Anna Katharine

Rohmer, Eric .... **CLC 16**
See Scherer, Jean-Marie Maurice

Rohmer, Sax .... **TCLC 28**
See Ward, Arthur Henry Sarsfield
See also DLB 70; MSW; SUFW

Roiphe, Anne (Richardson) 1935- .. **CLC 3, 9**
See also CA 89-92; CANR 45, 73; DLBY 1980; INT CA-89-92

Rojas, Fernando de 1475-1541 ... **HLCS 1, 2; LC 23**
See also DLB 286; RGWL 2, 3

Rojas, Gonzalo 1917- .... **HLCS 2**
See also CA 178; HW 2; LAWS 1

Roland, Marie-Jeanne 1754-1793 .... **LC 98**

Rolfe, Frederick (William Serafino Austin Lewis Mary) 1860-1913 .... **TCLC 12**
See Al Siddik
See also CA 107; 210; DLB 34, 156; RGEL 2

Rolland, Romain 1866-1944 .... **TCLC 23**
See also CA 118; 197; DLB 65, 284; EWL 3; GFL 1789 to the Present; RGWL 2, 3

Rolle, Richard c. 1300-c. 1349 .... **CMLC 21**
See also DLB 146; LMFS 1; RGEL 2

Rolvaag, O(le) E(dvart) .... **TCLC 17**
See Roelvaag, O(le) E(dvart)
See also DLB 9, 212; NFS 5; RGAL 4

Romain Arnaud, Saint
See Aragon, Louis

Romains, Jules 1885-1972 .... **CLC 7**
See also CA 85-88; CANR 34; DLB 65; EWL 3; GFL 1789 to the Present; MTCW 1

Romero, Jose Ruben 1890-1952 .... **TCLC 14**
See also CA 114; 131; EWL 3; HW 1; LAW

Ronsard, Pierre de 1524-1585 . **LC 6, 54; PC 11**
See also EW 2; GFL Beginnings to 1789; RGWL 2, 3; TWA

Rooke, Leon 1934- .... **CLC 25, 34**
See also CA 25-28R; CANR 23, 53; CCA 1; CPW; DAM POP

Roosevelt, Franklin Delano
1882-1945 .... **TCLC 93**
See also CA 116; 173; LAIT 3

Roosevelt, Theodore 1858-1919 ..... **TCLC 69**
See also CA 115; 170; DLB 47, 186, 275

Roper, William 1498-1578 .... **LC 10**

Roquelaure, A. N.
See Rice, Anne

Rosa, Joao Guimaraes 1908-1967 ... **CLC 23; HLCS 1**
See Guimaraes Rosa, Joao
See also CA 89-92; DLB 113, 307; EWL 3; WLIT 1

Rose, Wendy 1948- . **CLC 85; NNAL; PC 13**
See also CA 53-56; CANR 5, 51; CWP; DAM MULT; DLB 175; PFS 13; RGAL 4; SATA 12

Rosen, R. D.
See Rosen, Richard (Dean)

Rosen, Richard (Dean) 1949- .... **CLC 39**
See also CA 77-80; CANR 62, 120; CMW 4; INT CANR-30

Rosenberg, Isaac 1890-1918 .... **TCLC 12**
See also BRW 6; CA 107; 188; DLB 20, 216; EWL 3; PAB; RGEL 2

Rosenblatt, Joe .... **CLC 15**
See Rosenblatt, Joseph

Rosenblatt, Joseph 1933-
See Rosenblatt, Joe
See also CA 89-92; CP 7; INT CA-89-92

Rosenfeld, Samuel
See Tzara, Tristan

Rosenstock, Sami
See Tzara, Tristan

Rosenstock, Samuel
See Tzara, Tristan

Rosenthal, M(acha) L(ouis)
1917-1996 .... **CLC 28**
See also CA 1-4R; 152; CAAS 6; CANR 4, 51; CP 7; DLB 5; SATA 59

Ross, Barnaby
See Dannay, Frederic

Ross, Bernard L.
See Follett, Ken(neth Martin)

Ross, J. H.
See Lawrence, T(homas) E(dward)

Ross, John Hume
See Lawrence, T(homas) E(dward)

Ross, Martin 1862-1915
See Martin, Violet Florence
See also DLB 135; GLL 2; RGEL 2; RGSF 2

Ross, (James) Sinclair 1908-1996 ... **CLC 13; SSC 24**
See also CA 73-76; CANR 81; CN 7; DAC; DAM MST; DLB 88; RGEL 2; RGSF 2; TCWW 2

Rossetti, Christina (Georgina)
1830-1894 .... **NCLC 2, 50, 66; PC 7; WLC**
See also AAYA 51; BRW 5; BYA 4; DA; DA3; DAB; DAC; DAM MST, POET; DLB 35, 163, 240; EXPP; LATS 1:1; MAICYA 1, 2; PFS 10, 14; RGEL 2; SATA 20; TEA; WCH

Rossetti, Dante Gabriel 1828-1882 . **NCLC 4, 77; PC 44; WLC**
See also AAYA 51; BRW 5; CDBLB 1832-1890; DA; DAB; DAC; DAM MST, POET; DLB 35; EXPP; RGEL 2; TEA

Rossi, Cristina Peri
See Peri Rossi, Cristina

Rossi, Jean-Baptiste 1931-2003
See Japrisot, Sebastien
See also CA 201; 215

Rossner, Judith (Perelman) 1935- . **CLC 6, 9, 29**
See also AITN 2; BEST 90:3; BPFB 3; CA 17-20R; CANR 18, 51, 73; CN 7; DLB 6; INT CANR-18; MTCW 1, 2

Rostand, Edmond (Eugene Alexis)
1868-1918 .... **DC 10; TCLC 6, 37**
See also CA 104; 126; DA; DA3; DAB; DAC; DAM DRAM, MST; DFS 1; DLB 192; LAIT 1; MTCW 1; RGWL 2, 3; TWA

Roth, Henry 1906-1995 ..... **CLC 2, 6, 11, 104**
See also AMWS 9; CA 11-12; 149; CANR 38, 63; CAP 1; CN 7; DA3; DLB 28; EWL 3; MTCW 1, 2; RGAL 4

Roth, (Moses) Joseph 1894-1939 ... **TCLC 33**
See also CA 160; DLB 85; EWL 3; RGWL 2, 3

Roth, Philip (Milton) 1933- ... **CLC 1, 2, 3, 4, 6, 9, 15, 22, 31, 47, 66, 86, 119, 201; SSC 26; WLC**
See also AMWR 2; AMWS 3; BEST 90:3; BPFB 3; CA 1-4R; CANR 1, 22, 36, 55, 89, 132; CDALB 1968-1988; CN 7; CPW 1; DA; DA3; DAB; DAC; DAM MST, NOV, POP; DLB 2, 28, 173; DLBY 1982; EWL 3; MTCW 1, 2; RGAL 4; RGSF 2; SSFS 12, 18; TUS

Rothenberg, Jerome 1931- .... **CLC 6, 57**
See also CA 45-48; CANR 1, 106; CP 7; DLB 5, 193

Rotter, Pat ed. .... **CLC 65**

Roumain, Jacques (Jean Baptiste)
1907-1944 .... **BLC 3; TCLC 19**
See also BW 1; CA 117; 125; DAM MULT; EWL 3

Rourke, Constance Mayfield
1885-1941 .... **TCLC 12**
See also CA 107; 200; YABC 1

Rousseau, Jean-Baptiste 1671-1741 ...... **LC 9**

Rousseau, Jean-Jacques 1712-1778 .... **LC 14, 36; WLC**
See also DA; DA3; DAB; DAC; DAM MST; EW 4; GFL Beginnings to 1789; LMFS 1; RGWL 2, 3; TWA

Roussel, Raymond 1877-1933 .... **TCLC 20**
See also CA 117; 201; EWL 3; GFL 1789 to the Present

Rovit, Earl (Herbert) 1927- .... **CLC 7**
See also CA 5-8R; CANR 12

Rowe, Elizabeth Singer 1674-1737 ..... **LC 44**
See also DLB 39, 95

Rowe, Nicholas 1674-1718 .... **LC 8**
See also DLB 84; RGEL 2

Rowlandson, Mary 1637(?)-1678 .... **LC 66**
See also DLB 24, 200; RGAL 4

Rowley, Ames Dorrance
See Lovecraft, H(oward) P(hillips)

Rowley, William 1585(?)-1626 .... **LC 100**
See also DLB 58; RGEL 2

Rowling, J(oanne) K(athleen)
1966- .... **CLC 137**
See also AAYA 34; BYA 11, 13, 14; CA 173; CANR 128; CLR 66, 80; MAICYA 2; SATA 109; SUFW 2

Rowson, Susanna Haswell
1762(?)-1824 .... **NCLC 5, 69**
See also DLB 37, 200; RGAL 4

Roy, Arundhati 1960(?)- .... **CLC 109**
See also CA 163; CANR 90, 126; DLBY 1997; EWL 3; LATS 1:2; WWE 1

Roy, Gabrielle 1909-1983 .... **CLC 10, 14**
See also CA 53-56; 110; CANR 5, 61; CCA 1; DAB; DAC; DAM MST; DLB 68; EWL 3; MTCW 1; RGWL 2, 3; SATA 104

Royko, Mike 1932-1997 .... **CLC 109**
See also CA 89-92; 157; CANR 26, 111; CPW

Rozanov, Vasilii Vasil'evich
See Rozanov, Vassili
See also DLB 295

Rozanov, Vasily Vasilyevich
See Rozanov, Vassili
See also EWL 3

Rozanov, Vassili 1856-1919 .... **TCLC 104**
See Rozanov, Vasilii Vasil'evich; Rozanov, Vasily Vasilyevich

Rozewicz, Tadeusz 1921- ...... **CLC 9, 23, 139**
See also CA 108; CANR 36, 66; CWW 2; DA3; DAM POET; DLB 232; EWL 3; MTCW 1, 2; RGWL 3

Ruark, Gibbons 1941- .... **CLC 3**
See also CA 33-36R; CAAS 23; CANR 14, 31, 57; DLB 120

Rubens, Bernice (Ruth) 1923-2004 . **CLC 19, 31**
See also CA 25-28R; CANR 33, 65, 128; CN 7; DLB 14, 207; MTCW 1

Rubin, Harold
See Robbins, Harold

Rudkin, (James) David 1936- .... **CLC 14**
See also CA 89-92; CBD; CD 5; DLB 13

Rudnik, Raphael 1933- .... **CLC 7**
See also CA 29-32R

Ruffian, M.
See Hasek, Jaroslav (Matej Frantisek)

Ruiz, Jose Martinez .... **CLC 11**
See Martinez Ruiz, Jose

Ruiz, Juan c. 1283-c. 1350 .... **CMLC 66**

Rukeyser, Muriel 1913-1980 . **CLC 6, 10, 15, 27; PC 12**
See also AMWS 6; CA 5-8R; 93-96; CANR 26, 60; DA3; DAM POET; DLB 48; EWL 3; FW; GLL 2; MTCW 1, 2; PFS 10; RGAL 4; SATA-Obit 22

Rule, Jane (Vance) 1931- .... **CLC 27**
See also CA 25-28R; CAAS 18; CANR 12, 87; CN 7; DLB 60; FW

Rulfo, Juan 1918-1986 .. **CLC 8, 80; HLC 2; SSC 25**
See also CA 85-88; 118; CANR 26; CD-WLB 3; DAM MULT; DLB 113; EWL 3; HW 1, 2; LAW; MTCW 1, 2; RGSF 2; RGWL 2, 3; WLIT 1

Rumi, Jalal al-Din 1207-1273 ...... **CMLC 20; PC 45**
See also RGWL 2, 3; WP

Runeberg, Johan 1804-1877 .... **NCLC 41**

Runyon, (Alfred) Damon
1884(?)-1946 .... **TCLC 10**
See also CA 107; 165; DLB 11, 86, 171; MTCW 2; RGAL 4

Rush, Norman 1933- .... **CLC 44**
See also CA 121; 126; CANR 130; INT CA-126

Rushdie, (Ahmed) Salman 1947- .... **CLC 23, 31, 55, 100, 191; WLCS**
See also BEST 89:3; BPFB 3; BRWS 4; CA 108; 111; CANR 33, 56, 108, 133; CN 7; CPW 1; DA3; DAB; DAC; DAM MST, NOV, POP; DLB 194; EWL 3; FANT; INT CA-111; LATS 1:2; LMFS 2; MTCW 1, 2; RGEL 2; RGSF 2; TEA; WLIT 4; WWE 1

Rushforth, Peter (Scott) 1945- .... **CLC 19**
See also CA 101

Ruskin, John 1819-1900 .... **TCLC 63**
See also BRW 5; BYA 5; CA 114; 129; CD-BLB 1832-1890; DLB 55, 163, 190; RGEL 2; SATA 24; TEA; WCH

Russ, Joanna 1937- .... **CLC 15**
See also BPFB 3; CA 5-28R; CANR 11, 31, 65; CN 7; DLB 8; FW; GLL 1; MTCW 1; SCFW 2; SFW 4

Russ, Richard Patrick
See O'Brian, Patrick

Russell, George William 1867-1935
See A.E.; Baker, Jean H.
See also BRWS 8; CA 104; 153; CDBLB 1890-1914; DAM POET; EWL 3; RGEL 2

Russell, Jeffrey Burton 1934- .... **CLC 70**
See also CA 25-28R; CANR 11, 28, 52

Russell, (Henry) Ken(neth Alfred)
1927- .... **CLC 16**
See also CA 105

Russell, William Martin 1947-
See Russell, Willy
See also CA 164; CANR 107
Russell, Willy .... **CLC 60**
See Russell, William Martin
See also CBD; CD 5; DLB 233
Russo, Richard 1949- .... **CLC 181**
See also AMWS 12; CA 127; 133; CANR 87, 114
Rutherford, Mark .... **TCLC 25**
See White, William Hale
See also DLB 18; RGEL 2
Ruyslinck, Ward .... **CLC 14**
See Belser, Reimond Karel Maria de
Ryan, Cornelius (John) 1920-1974 ..... **CLC 7**
See also CA 69-72; 53-56; CANR 38
Ryan, Michael 1946- .... **CLC 65**
See also CA 49-52; CANR 109; DLBY 1982
Ryan, Tim
See Dent, Lester
Rybakov, Anatoli (Naumovich) 1911-1998 .... **CLC 23, 53**
See Rybakov, Anatolii (Naumovich)
See also CA 126; 135; 172; SATA 79; SATA-Obit 108
Rybakov, Anatolii (Naumovich)
See Rybakov, Anatolii (Naumovich)
See also DLB 302
Ryder, Jonathan
See Ludlum, Robert
Ryga, George 1932-1987 .... **CLC 14**
See also CA 101; 124; CANR 43, 90; CCA 1; DAC; DAM MST; DLB 60
S. H.
See Hartmann, Sadakichi
S. S.
See Sassoon, Siegfried (Lorraine)
Sa'adawi, al- Nawal
See El Saadawi, Nawal
See also AFW; EWL 3
Saadawi, Nawal El
See El Saadawi, Nawal
See also WLIT 2
Saba, Umberto 1883-1957 .... **TCLC 33**
See also CA 144; CANR 79; DLB 114; EWL 3; RGWL 2, 3
Sabatini, Rafael 1875-1950 .... **TCLC 47**
See also BPFB 3; CA 162; RHW
Sabato, Ernesto (R.) 1911- .... **CLC 10, 23; HLC 2**
See also CA 97-100; CANR 32, 65; CDWLB 3; CWW 2; DAM MULT; DLB 145; EWL 3; HW 1, 2; LAW; MTCW 1, 2
Sa-Carneiro, Mario de 1890-1916 . **TCLC 83**
See also DLB 287; EWL 3
Sacastru, Martin
See Bioy Casares, Adolfo
See also CWW 2
Sacher-Masoch, Leopold von 1836(?)-1895 .... **NCLC 31**
Sachs, Hans 1494-1576 .... **LC 95**
See also CDWLB 2; DLB 179; RGWL 2, 3
Sachs, Marilyn (Stickle) 1927- .... **CLC 35**
See also AAYA 2; BYA 6; CA 17-20R; CANR 13, 47; CLR 2; JRDA; MAICYA 1, 2; SAAS 2; SATA 3, 68; SATA-Essay 110; WYA; YAW
Sachs, Nelly 1891-1970 .... **CLC 14, 98**
See also CA 17-18; 25-28R; CANR 87; CAP 2; EWL 3; MTCW 2; PFS 20; RGWL 2, 3
Sackler, Howard (Oliver) 1929-1982 .... **CLC 14**
See also CA 61-64; 108; CAD; CANR 30; DFS 15; DLB 7
Sacks, Oliver (Wolf) 1933- .... **CLC 67, 202**
See also CA 53-56; CANR 28, 50, 76; CPW; DA3; INT CANR-28; MTCW 1, 2

Sackville, Thomas 1536-1608 .... **LC 98**
See also DAM DRAM; DLB 62, 132; RGEL 2
Sadakichi
See Hartmann, Sadakichi
Sa'dawi, Nawal al-
See El Saadawi, Nawal
See also CWW 2
Sade, Donatien Alphonse Francois 1740-1814 .... **NCLC 3, 47**
See also EW 4; GFL Beginnings to 1789; RGWL 2, 3
Sade, Marquis de
See Sade, Donatien Alphonse Francois
Sadoff, Ira 1945- .... **CLC 9**
See also CA 53-56; CANR 5, 21, 109; DLB 120
Saetone
See Camus, Albert
Safire, William 1929- .... **CLC 10**
See also CA 17-20R; CANR 31, 54, 91
Sagan, Carl (Edward) 1934-1996 .... **CLC 30, 112**
See also AAYA 2; CA 25-28R; 155; CANR 11, 36, 74; CPW; DA3; MTCW 1, 2; SATA 58; SATA-Obit 94
Sagan, Francoise .... **CLC 3, 6, 9, 17, 36**
See Quoirez, Francoise
See also CWW 2; DLB 83; EWL 3; GFL 1789 to the Present; MTCW 2
Sahgal, Nayantara (Pandit) 1927- .... **CLC 41**
See also CA 9-12R; CANR 11, 88; CN 7
Said, Edward W. 1935-2003 .... **CLC 123**
See also CA 21-24R; 220; CANR 45, 74, 107, 131; DLB 67; MTCW 2
Saint, H(arry) F. 1941- .... **CLC 50**
See also CA 127
St. Aubin de Teran, Lisa 1953-
See Teran, Lisa St. Aubin de
See also CA 118; 126; CN 7; INT CA-126
Saint Birgitta of Sweden c. 1303-1373 .... **CMLC 24**
Sainte-Beuve, Charles Augustin 1804-1869 .... **NCLC 5**
See also DLB 217; EW 6; GFL 1789 to the Present
Saint-Exupery, Antoine (Jean Baptiste Marie Roger) de 1900-1944 .... **TCLC 2, 56; WLC**
See also BPFB 3; BYA 3; CA 108; 132; CLR 10; DA3; DAM NOV; DLB 72; EW 12; EWL 3; GFL 1789 to the Present; LAIT 3; MAICYA 1, 2; MTCW 1, 2; RGWL 2, 3; SATA 20; TWA
St. John, David
See Hunt, E(verette) Howard, (Jr.)
St. John, J. Hector
See Crevecoeur, Michel Guillaume Jean de
Saint-John Perse
See Leger, (Marie-Rene Auguste) Alexis Saint-Leger
See also EW 10; EWL 3; GFL 1789 to the Present; RGWL 2
Saintsbury, George (Edward Bateman) 1845-1933 .... **TCLC 31**
See also CA 160; DLB 57, 149
Sait Faik .... **TCLC 23**
See Abasiyanik, Sait Faik
Saki .... **SSC 12; TCLC 3**
See Munro, H(ector) H(ugh)
See also BRWS 6; BYA 11; LAIT 2; MTCW 2; RGEL 2; SSFS 1; SUFW
Sala, George Augustus 1828-1895 . **NCLC 46**
Saladin 1138-1193 .... **CMLC 38**
Salama, Hannu 1936- .... **CLC 18**
See also EWL 3
Salamanca, J(ack) R(ichard) 1922- .. **CLC 4, 15**
See also CA 25-28R, 193; CAAE 193

Salas, Floyd Francis 1931- .... **HLC 2**
See also CA 119; CAAS 27; CANR 44, 75, 93; DAM MULT; DLB 82; HW 1, 2; MTCW 2
Sale, J. Kirkpatrick
See Sale, Kirkpatrick
Sale, Kirkpatrick 1937- .... **CLC 68**
See also CA 13-16R; CANR 10
Salinas, Luis Omar 1937- ... **CLC 90; HLC 2**
See also AMWS 13; CA 131; CANR 81; DAM MULT; DLB 82; HW 1, 2
Salinas (y Serrano), Pedro 1891(?)-1951 .... **TCLC 17**
See also CA 117; DLB 134; EWL 3
Salinger, J(erome) D(avid) 1919- .. **CLC 1, 3, 8, 12, 55, 56, 138; SSC 2, 28, 65; WLC**
See also AAYA 2, 36; AMW; AMWC 1; BPFB 3; CA 5-8R; CANR 39, 129; CDALB 1941-1968; CLR 18; CN 7; CPW 1; DA; DA3; DAB; DAC; DAM MST, NOV, POP; DLB 2, 102, 173; EWL 3; EXPN; LAIT 4; MAICYA 1, 2; MTCW 1, 2; NFS 1; RGAL 4; RGSF 2; SATA 67; SSFS 17; TUS; WYA; YAW
Salisbury, John
See Caute, (John) David
Sallust c. 86B.C.-35B.C. .... **CMLC 68**
See also AW 2; CDWLB 1; DLB 211; RGWL 2, 3
Salter, James 1925- ... **CLC 7, 52, 59; SSC 58**
See also AMWS 9; CA 73-76; CANR 107; DLB 130
Saltus, Edgar (Everton) 1855-1921 . **TCLC 8**
See also CA 105; DLB 202; RGAL 4
Saltykov, Mikhail Evgrafovich 1826-1889 .... **NCLC 16**
See also DLB 238:
Saltykov-Shchedrin, N.
See Saltykov, Mikhail Evgrafovich
Samarakis, Andonis
See Samarakis, Antonis
See also EWL 3
Samarakis, Antonis 1919-2003 .... **CLC 5**
See Samarakis, Andonis
See also CA 25-28R; 224; CAAS 16; CANR 36
Sanchez, Florencio 1875-1910 .... **TCLC 37**
See also CA 153; DLB 305; EWL 3; HW 1; LAW
Sanchez, Luis Rafael 1936- .... **CLC 23**
See also CA 128; DLB 305; EWL 3; HW 1; WLIT 1
Sanchez, Sonia 1934- .... **BLC 3; CLC 5, 116; PC 9**
See also BW 2, 3; CA 33-36R; CANR 24, 49, 74, 115; CLR 18; CP 7; CSW; CWP; DA3; DAM MULT; DLB 41; DLBD 8; EWL 3; MAICYA 1, 2; MTCW 1, 2; SATA 22, 136; WP
Sancho, Ignatius 1729-1780 .... **LC 84**
Sand, George 1804-1876 ..... **NCLC 2, 42, 57; WLC**
See also DA; DA3; DAB; DAC; DAM MST, NOV; DLB 119, 192; EW 6; FW; GFL 1789 to the Present; RGWL 2, 3; TWA
Sandburg, Carl (August) 1878-1967 . **CLC 1, 4, 10, 15, 35; PC 2, 41; WLC**
See also AAYA 24; AMW; BYA 1, 3; CA 5-8R; 25-28R; CANR 35; CDALB 1865-1917; CLR 67; DA; DA3; DAB; DAC; DAM MST, POET; DLB 17, 54, 284; EWL 3; EXPP; LAIT 2; MAICYA 1, 2; MTCW 1, 2; PAB; PFS 3, 6, 12; RGAL 4; SATA 8; TUS; WCH; WP; WYA
Sandburg, Charles
See Sandburg, Carl (August)
Sandburg, Charles A.
See Sandburg, Carl (August)

Sanders, (James) Ed(ward) 1939- .... **CLC 53**
See Sanders, Edward
See also BG 3; CA 13-16R; CAAS 21; CANR 13, 44, 78; CP 7; DAM POET; DLB 16, 244

Sanders, Edward
See Sanders, (James) Ed(ward)
See also DLB 244

Sanders, Lawrence 1920-1998 .... **CLC 41**
See also BEST 89:4; BPFB 3; CA 81-84; 165; CANR 33, 62; CMW 4; CPW; DA3; DAM POP; MTCW 1

Sanders, Noah
See Blount, Roy (Alton), Jr.

Sanders, Winston P.
See Anderson, Poul (William)

Sandoz, Mari(e Susette) 1900-1966 .. **CLC 28**
See also CA 1-4R; 25-28R; CANR 17, 64; DLB 9, 212; LAIT 2; MTCW 1, 2; SATA 5; TCWW 2

Sandys, George 1578-1644 .... **LC 80**
See also DLB 24, 121

Saner, Reg(inald Anthony) 1931- .... **CLC 9**
See also CA 65-68; CP 7

Sankara 788-820 .... **CMLC 32**

Sannazaro, Jacopo 1456(?)-1530 .... **LC 8**
See also RGWL 2, 3

Sansom, William 1912-1976 . **CLC 2, 6; SSC 21**
See also CA 5-8R; 65-68; CANR 42; DAM NOV; DLB 139; EWL 3; MTCW 1; RGEL 2; RGSF 2

Santayana, George 1863-1952 .... **TCLC 40**
See also AMW; CA 115; 194; DLB 54, 71, 246, 270; DLBD 13; EWL 3; RGAL 4; TUS

Santiago, Danny .... **CLC 33**
See James, Daniel (Lewis)
See also DLB 122

Santillana, Íñigo López de Mendoza, Marqués de 1398-1458 .... **LC 111**
See also DLB 286

Santmyer, Helen Hooven 1895-1986 .... **CLC 33; TCLC 133**
See also CA 1-4R; 118; CANR 15, 33; DLBY 1984; MTCW 1; RHW

Santoka, Taneda 1882-1940 .... **TCLC 72**

Santos, Bienvenido N(uqui) 1911-1996 ... **AAL; CLC 22; TCLC 156**
See also CA 101; 151; CANR 19, 46; DAM MULT; EWL; RGAL 4; SSFS 19

Sapir, Edward 1884-1939 .... **TCLC 108**
See also CA 211; DLB 92

Sapper .... **TCLC 44**
See McNeile, Herman Cyril

Sapphire
See Sapphire, Brenda

Sapphire, Brenda 1950- .... **CLC 99**

Sappho fl. 6th cent. B.C.- ... **CMLC 3, 67; PC 5**
See also CDWLB 1; DA3; DAM POET; DLB 176; PFS 20; RGWL 2, 3; WP

Saramago, Jose 1922- ..... **CLC 119; HLCS 1**
See also CA 153; CANR 96; CWW 2; DLB 287; EWL 3; LATS 1:2

Sarduy, Severo 1937-1993 .... **CLC 6, 97; HLCS 2**
See also CA 89-92; 142; CANR 58, 81; CWW 2; DLB 113; EWL 3; HW 1, 2; LAW

Sargeson, Frank 1903-1982 .... **CLC 31**
See also CA 25-28R; 106; CANR 38, 79; EWL 3; GLL 2; RGEL 2; RGSF 2; SSFS 20

Sarmiento, Domingo Faustino 1811-1888 .... **HLCS 2**
See also LAW; WLIT 1

Sarmiento, Felix Ruben Garcia
See Dario, Ruben

Saro-Wiwa, Ken(ule Beeson) 1941-1995 .... **CLC 114**
See also BW 2; CA 142; 150; CANR 60; DLB 157

Saroyan, William 1908-1981 ... **CLC 1, 8, 10, 29, 34, 56; SSC 21; TCLC 137; WLC**
See also CA 5-8R; 103; CAD; CANR 30; CDALBS; DA; DA3; DAB; DAC; DAM DRAM, MST, NOV; DFS 17; DLB 7, 9, 86; DLBY 1981; EWL 3; LAIT 4; MTCW 1, 2; RGAL 4; RGSF 2; SATA 23; SATA-Obit 24; SSFS 14; TUS

Sarraute, Nathalie 1900-1999 .... **CLC 1, 2, 4, 8, 10, 31, 80; TCLC 145**
See also BPFB 3; CA 9-12R; 187; CANR 23, 66, 134; CWW 2; DLB 83; EW 12; EWL 3; GFL 1789 to the Present; MTCW 1, 2; RGWL 2, 3

Sarton, (Eleanor) May 1912-1995 ..... **CLC 4, 14, 49, 91; PC 39; TCLC 120**
See also AMWS 8; CA 1-4R; 149; CANR 1, 34, 55, 116; CN 7; CP 7; DAM POET; DLB 48; DLBY 1981; EWL 3; FW; INT CANR-34; MTCW 1, 2; RGAL 4; SATA 36; SATA-Obit 86; TUS

Sartre, Jean-Paul 1905-1980 . **CLC 1, 4, 7, 9, 13, 18, 24, 44, 50, 52; DC 3; SSC 32; WLC**
See also CA 9-12R; 97-100; CANR 21; DA; DA3; DAB; DAC; DAM DRAM, MST, NOV; DFS 5; DLB 72, 296; EW 12; EWL 3; GFL 1789 to the Present; LMFS 2; MTCW 1, 2; RGSF 2; RGWL 2, 3; SSFS 9; TWA

Sassoon, Siegfried (Lorraine) 1886-1967 .... **CLC 36, 130; PC 12**
See also BRW 6; CA 104; 25-28R; CANR 36; DAB; DAM MST, NOV, POET; DLB 20, 191; DLBD 18; EWL 3; MTCW 1, 2; PAB; RGEL 2; TEA

Satterfield, Charles
See Pohl, Frederik

Satyremont
See Peret, Benjamin

Saul, John (W. III) 1942- .... **CLC 46**
See also AAYA 10; BEST 90:4; CA 81-84; CANR 16, 40, 81; CPW; DAM NOV, POP; HGG; SATA 98

Saunders, Caleb
See Heinlein, Robert A(nson)

Saura (Atares), Carlos 1932-1998 .... **CLC 20**
See also CA 114; 131; CANR 79; HW 1

Sauser, Frederic Louis
See Sauser-Hall, Frederic

Sauser-Hall, Frederic 1887-1961 ...... **CLC 18**
See Cendrars, Blaise
See also CA 102; 93-96; CANR 36, 62; MTCW 1

Saussure, Ferdinand de 1857-1913 .... **TCLC 49**
See also DLB 242

Savage, Catharine
See Brosman, Catharine Savage

Savage, Richard 1697(?)-1743 .... **LC 96**
See also DLB 95; RGEL 2

Savage, Thomas 1915-2003 .... **CLC 40**
See also CA 126; 132; 218; CAAS 15; CN 7; INT CA-132; SATA-Obit 147; TCWW 2

Savan, Glenn 1953-2003 .... **CLC 50**
See also CA 225

Sax, Robert
See Johnson, Robert

Saxo Grammaticus c. 1150-c. 1222 .... **CMLC 58**

Saxton, Robert
See Johnson, Robert

Sayers, Dorothy L(eigh) 1893-1957 . **SSC 71; TCLC 2, 15**
See also BPFB 3; BRWS 3; CA 104; 119; CANR 60; CDBLB 1914-1945; CMW 4; DAM POP; DLB 10, 36, 77, 100; MSW; MTCW 1, 2; RGEL 2; SSFS 12; TEA

Sayers, Valerie 1952- .... **CLC 50, 122**
See also CA 134; CANR 61; CSW

Sayles, John (Thomas) 1950- .... **CLC 7, 10, 14, 198**
See also CA 57-60; CANR 41, 84; DLB 44

Scammell, Michael 1935- .... **CLC 34**
See also CA 156

Scannell, Vernon 1922- .... **CLC 49**
See also CA 5-8R; CANR 8, 24, 57; CP 7; CWRI 5; DLB 27; SATA 59

Scarlett, Susan
See Streatfeild, (Mary) Noel

Scarron 1847-1910
See Mikszath, Kalman

Schaeffer, Susan Fromberg 1941- ..... **CLC 6, 11, 22**
See also CA 49-52; CANR 18, 65; CN 7; DLB 28, 299; MTCW 1, 2; SATA 22

Schama, Simon (Michael) 1945- ..... **CLC 150**
See also BEST 89:4; CA 105; CANR 39, 91

Schary, Jill
See Robinson, Jill

Scarron 1847-1910
See Mikszath, Kalman

Schell, Jonathan 1943- .... **CLC 35**
See also CA 73-76; CANR 12, 117

Schelling, Friedrich Wilhelm Joseph von 1775-1854 .... **NCLC 30**
See also DLB 90

Scherer, Jean-Marie Maurice 1920-
See Rohmer, Eric
See also CA 110

Schevill, James (Erwin) 1920- .... **CLC 7**
See also CA 5-8R; CAAS 12; CAD; CD 5

Schiller, Friedrich von 1759-1805 ...... **DC 12; NCLC 39, 69**
See also CDWLB 2; DAM DRAM; DLB 94; EW 5; RGWL 2, 3; TWA

Schisgal, Murray (Joseph) 1926- .... **CLC 6**
See also CA 21-24R; CAD; CANR 48, 86; CD 5

Schlee, Ann 1934- .... **CLC 35**
See also CA 101; CANR 29, 88; SATA 44; SATA-Brief 36

Schlegel, August Wilhelm von 1767-1845 .... **NCLC 15, 142**
See also DLB 94; RGWL 2, 3

Schlegel, Friedrich 1772-1829 .... **NCLC 45**
See also DLB 90; EW 5; RGWL 2, 3; TWA

Schlegel, Johann Elias (von) 1719(?)-1749 .... **LC 5**

Schleiermacher, Friedrich 1768-1834 .... **NCLC 107**
See also DLB 90

Schlesinger, Arthur M(eier), Jr. 1917- .... **CLC 84**
See also AITN 1; CA 1-4R; CANR 1, 28, 58, 105; DLB 17; INT CANR-28; MTCW 1, 2; SATA 61

Schlink, Bernhard 1944- .... **CLC 174**
See also CA 163; CANR 116

Schmidt, Arno (Otto) 1914-1979 ...... **CLC 56**
See also CA 128; 109; DLB 69; EWL 3

Schmitz, Aron Hector 1861-1928
See Svevo, Italo
See also CA 104; 122; MTCW 1

Schnackenberg, Gjertrud (Cecelia) 1953- .... **CLC 40; PC 45**
See also CA 116; CANR 100; CP 7; CWP; DLB 120, 282; PFS 13

Schneider, Leonard Alfred 1925-1966
See Bruce, Lenny
See also CA 89-92

Schnitzler, Arthur 1862-1931 ..... **DC 17; SSC 15, 61; TCLC 4**
See also CA 104; CDWLB 2; DLB 81, 118; EW 8; EWL 3; RGSF 2; RGWL 2, 3

Schoenberg, Arnold Franz Walter 1874-1951 .... **TCLC 75**
See also CA 109; 188

Schonberg, Arnold
See Schoenberg, Arnold Franz Walter

Schopenhauer, Arthur 1788-1860 .. **NCLC 51**
See also DLB 90; EW 5

Schor, Sandra (M.) 1932(?)-1990 ..... **CLC 65**
See also CA 132

Schorer, Mark 1908-1977 .... **CLC 9**
See also CA 5-8R; 73-76; CANR 7; DLB 103

Schrader, Paul (Joseph) 1946- .... **CLC 26**
See also CA 37-40R; CANR 41; DLB 44

Schreber, Daniel 1842-1911 .... **TCLC 123**

Schreiner, Olive (Emilie Albertina) 1855-1920 .... **TCLC 9**
See also AFW; BRWS 2; CA 105; 154; DLB 18, 156, 190, 225; EWL 3; FW; RGEL 2; TWA; WLIT 2; WWE 1

Schulberg, Budd (Wilson) 1914- .. **CLC 7, 48**
See also BPFB 3; CA 25-28R; CANR 19, 87; CN 7; DLB 6, 26, 28; DLBY 1981, 2001

Schulman, Arnold
See Trumbo, Dalton

Schulz, Bruno 1892-1942 .. **SSC 13; TCLC 5, 51**
See also CA 115; 123; CANR 86; CDWLB 4; DLB 215; EWL 3; MTCW 2; RGSF 2; RGWL 2, 3

Schulz, Charles M(onroe) 1922-2000 .... **CLC 12**
See also AAYA 39; CA 9-12R; 187; CANR 6, 132; INT CANR-6; SATA 10; SATA-Obit 118

Schumacher, E(rnst) F(riedrich) 1911-1977 .... **CLC 80**
See also CA 81-84; 73-76; CANR 34, 85

Schumann, Robert 1810-1856 ...... **NCLC 143**

Schuyler, George Samuel 1895-1977 .... **HR 3**
See also BW 2; CA 81-84; 73-76; CANR 42; DLB 29, 51

Schuyler, James Marcus 1923-1991 .. **CLC 5, 23**
See also CA 101; 134; DAM POET; DLB 5, 169; EWL 3; INT CA-101; WP

Schwartz, Delmore (David) 1913-1966 ... **CLC 2, 4, 10, 45, 87; PC 8**
See also AMWS 2; CA 17-18; 25-28R; CANR 35; CAP 2; DLB 28, 48; EWL 3; MTCW 1, 2; PAB; RGAL 4; TUS

Schwartz, Ernst
See Ozu, Yasujiro

Schwartz, John Burnham 1965- .... **CLC 59**
See also CA 132; CANR 116

Schwartz, Lynne Sharon 1939- .... **CLC 31**
See also CA 103; CANR 44, 89; DLB 218; MTCW 2

Schwartz, Muriel A.
See Eliot, T(homas) S(tearns)

Schwarz-Bart, Andre 1928- .... **CLC 2, 4**
See also CA 89-92; CANR 109; DLB 299

Schwarz-Bart, Simone 1938- . **BLCS; CLC 7**
See also BW 2; CA 97-100; CANR 117; EWL 3

Schwerner, Armand 1927-1999 .... **PC 42**
See also CA 9-12R; 179; CANR 50, 85; CP 7; DLB 165

Schwitters, Kurt (Hermann Edward Karl Julius) 1887-1948 .... **TCLC 95**
See also CA 158

Schwob, Marcel (Mayer Andre) 1867-1905 .... **TCLC 20**
See also CA 117; 168; DLB 123; GFL 1789 to the Present

Sciascia, Leonardo 1921-1989 .. **CLC 8, 9, 41**
See also CA 85-88; 130; CANR 35; DLB 177; EWL 3; MTCW 1; RGWL 2, 3

Scoppettone, Sandra 1936- .... **CLC 26**
See Early, Jack
See also AAYA 11; BYA 8; CA 5-8R; CANR 41, 73; GLL 1; MAICYA 2; MAICYAS 1; SATA 9, 92; WYA; YAW

Scorsese, Martin 1942- .... **CLC 20, 89**
See also AAYA 38; CA 110; 114; CANR 46, 85

Scotland, Jay
See Jakes, John (William)

Scott, Duncan Campbell 1862-1947 .... **TCLC 6**
See also CA 104; 153; DAC; DLB 92; RGEL 2

Scott, Evelyn 1893-1963 .... **CLC 43**
See also CA 104; 112; CANR 64; DLB 9, 48; RHW

Scott, F(rancis) R(eginald) 1899-1985 .... **CLC 22**
See also CA 101; 114; CANR 87; DLB 88; INT CA-101; RGEL 2

Scott, Frank
See Scott, F(rancis) R(eginald)

Scott, Joan .... **CLC 65**

Scott, Joanna 1960- .... **CLC 50**
See also CA 126; CANR 53, 92

Scott, Paul (Mark) 1920-1978 .... **CLC 9, 60**
See also BRWS 1; CA 81-84; 77-80; CANR 33; DLB 14, 207; EWL 3; MTCW 1; RGEL 2; RHW; WWE 1

Scott, Ridley 1937- .... **CLC 183**
See also AAYA 13, 43

Scott, Sarah 1723-1795 .... **LC 44**
See also DLB 39

Scott, Sir Walter 1771-1832 .... **NCLC 15, 69, 110; PC 13; SSC 32; WLC**
See also AAYA 22; BRW 4; BYA 2; CDBLB 1789-1832; DA; DAB; DAC; DAM MST, NOV, POET; DLB 93, 107, 116, 144, 159; HGG; LAIT 1; RGEL 2; RGSF 2; SSFS 10; SUFW 1; TEA; WLIT 3; YABC 2

Scribe, (Augustin) Eugene 1791-1861 . **DC 5; NCLC 16**
See also DAM DRAM; DLB 192; GFL 1789 to the Present; RGWL 2, 3

Scrum, R.
See Crumb, R(obert)

Scudery, Georges de 1601-1667 .... **LC 75**
See also GFL Beginnings to 1789

Scudery, Madeleine de 1607-1701 .. **LC 2, 58**
See also DLB 268; GFL Beginnings to 1789

Scum
See Crumb, R(obert)

Scumbag, Little Bobby
See Crumb, R(obert)

Seabrook, John
See Hubbard, L(afayette) Ron(ald)

Seacole, Mary Jane Grant 1805-1881 .... **NCLC 147**
See also DLB 166

Sealy, I(rwin) Allan 1951- .... **CLC 55**
See also CA 136; CN 7

Search, Alexander
See Pessoa, Fernando (Antonio Nogueira)

Sebald, W(infried) G(eorg) 1944-2001 .... **CLC 194**
See also BRWS 8; CA 159; 202; CANR 98

Sebastian, Lee
See Silverberg, Robert

Sebastian Owl
See Thompson, Hunter S(tockton)

Sebestyen, Igen
See Sebestyen, Ouida

Sebestyen, Ouida 1924- .... **CLC 30**
See also AAYA 8; BYA 7; CA 107; CANR 40, 114; CLR 17; JRDA; MAICYA 2; SAAS 10; SATA 39, 140; WYA; YAW

Sebold, Alice 1963(?)- .... **CLC 193**
See also AAYA 56; CA 203

Second Duke of Buckingham
See Villiers, George

Secundus, H. Scriblerus
See Fielding, Henry

Sedges, John
See Buck, Pearl S(ydenstricker)

Sedgwick, Catharine Maria 1789-1867 .... **NCLC 19, 98**
See also DLB 1, 74, 183, 239, 243, 254; RGAL 4

Seelye, John (Douglas) 1931- .... **CLC 7**
See also CA 97-100; CANR 70; INT CA-97-100; TCWW 2

Seferiades, Giorgos Stylianou 1900-1971
See Seferis, George
See also CA 5-8R; 33-36R; CANR 5, 36; MTCW 1

Seferis, George .... **CLC 5, 11**
See Seferiades, Giorgos Stylianou
See also EW 12; EWL 3; RGWL 2, 3

Segal, Erich (Wolf) 1937- .... **CLC 3, 10**
See also BEST 89:1; BPFB 3; CA 25-28R; CANR 20, 36, 65, 113; CPW; DAM POP; DLBY 1986; INT CANR-20; MTCW 1

Seger, Bob 1945- .... **CLC 35**

Seghers, Anna .... **CLC 7**
See Radvanyi, Netty
See also CDWLB 2; DLB 69; EWL 3

Seidel, Frederick (Lewis) 1936- .... **CLC 18**
See also CA 13-16R; CANR 8, 99; CP 7; DLBY 1984

Seifert, Jaroslav 1901-1986 . **CLC 34, 44, 93; PC 47**
See also CA 127; CDWLB 4; DLB 215; EWL 3; MTCW 1, 2

Sei Shonagon c. 966-1017(?) .... **CMLC 6**

Sejour, Victor 1817-1874 .... **DC 10**
See also DLB 50

Sejour Marcou et Ferrand, Juan Victor
See Sejour, Victor

Selby, Hubert, Jr. 1928-2004 ..... **CLC 1, 2, 4, 8; SSC 20**
See also CA 13-16R; 226; CANR 33, 85; CN 7; DLB 2, 227

Selzer, Richard 1928- .... **CLC 74**
See also CA 65-68; CANR 14, 106

Sembene, Ousmane
See Ousmane, Sembene
See also AFW; EWL 3; WLIT 2

Senancour, Etienne Pivert de 1770-1846 .... **NCLC 16**
See also DLB 119; GFL 1789 to the Present

Sender, Ramon (Jose) 1902-1982 ...... **CLC 8; HLC 2; TCLC 136**
See also CA 5-8R; 105; CANR 8; DAM MULT; EWL 3; HW 1; MTCW 1; RGWL 2, 3

Seneca, Lucius Annaeus c. 4B.C.-c. 65 .... **CMLC 6; DC 5**
See also AW 2; CDWLB 1; DAM DRAM; DLB 211; RGWL 2, 3; TWA

Senghor, Leopold Sedar 1906-2001 ... **BLC 3; CLC 54, 130; PC 25**
See also AFW; BW 2; CA 116; 125; 203; CANR 47, 74, 134; CWW 2; DAM MULT, POET; DNFS 2; EWL 3; GFL 1789 to the Present; MTCW 1, 2; TWA

Senior, Olive (Marjorie) 1941- .... **SSC 78**
See also BW 3; CA 154; CANR 86, 126; CN 7; CP 7; CWP; DLB 157; EWL 3; RGSF 2

Senna, Danzy 1970- .... **CLC 119**
See also CA 169; CANR 130
Serling, (Edward) Rod(man)
1924-1975 .... **CLC 30**
See also AAYA 14; AITN 1; CA 162; 57-60; DLB 26; SFW 4
Serna, Ramon Gomez de la
See Gomez de la Serna, Ramon
Serpieres
See Guillevic, (Eugene)
Service, Robert
See Service, Robert W(illiam)
See also BYA 4; DAB; DLB 92
Service, Robert W(illiam)
1874(?)-1958 .... **TCLC 15; WLC**
See Service, Robert
See also CA 115; 140; CANR 84; DA; DAC; DAM MST, POET; PFS 10; RGEL 2; SATA 20
Seth, Vikram 1952- .... **CLC 43, 90**
See also BRWS 10; CA 121; 127; CANR 50, 74, 131; CN 7; CP 7; DA3; DAM MULT; DLB 120, 271, 282; EWL 3; INT CA-127; MTCW 2; WWE 1
Seton, Cynthia Propper 1926-1982 .. **CLC 27**
See also CA 5-8R; 108; CANR 7
Seton, Ernest (Evan) Thompson
1860-1946 .... **TCLC 31**
See also ANW; BYA 3; CA 109; 204; CLR 59; DLB 92; DLBD 13; JRDA; SATA 18
Seton-Thompson, Ernest
See Seton, Ernest (Evan) Thompson
Settle, Mary Lee 1918- .... **CLC 19, 61**
See also BPFB 3; CA 89-92; CAAS 1; CANR 44, 87, 126; CAS; CSW; DLB 6; INT CA-89-92
Seuphor, Michel
See Arp, Jean
Sevigne, Marie (de Rabutin-Chantal)
1626-1696 .... **LC 11**
See Sevigne, Marie de Rabutin Chantal
See also GFL Beginnings to 1789; TWA
Sevigne, Marie de Rabutin Chantal
See Sevigne, Marie (de Rabutin-Chantal)
See also DLB 268
Sewall, Samuel 1652-1730 .... **LC 38**
See also DLB 24; RGAL 4
Sexton, Anne (Harvey) 1928-1974 ..... **CLC 2, 4, 6, 8, 10, 15, 53, 123; PC 2; WLC**
See also AMWS 2; CA 1-4R; 53-56; CABS 2; CANR 3, 36; CDALB 1941-1968; DA; DA3; DAB; DAC; DAM MST, POET; DLB 5, 169; EWL 3; EXPP; FW; MAWW; MTCW 1, 2; PAB; PFS 4, 14; RGAL 4; SATA 10; TUS
Shaara, Jeff 1952- .... **CLC 119**
See also CA 163; CANR 109
Shaara, Michael (Joseph, Jr.)
1929-1988 .... **CLC 15**
See also AITN 1; BPFB 3; CA 102; 125; CANR 52, 85; DAM POP; DLBY 1983
Shackleton, C. C.
See Aldiss, Brian W(ilson)
Shacochis, Bob .... **CLC 39**
See Shacochis, Robert G.
Shacochis, Robert G. 1951-
See Shacochis, Bob
See also CA 119; 124; CANR 100; INT CA-124
Shadwell, Thomas 1641?-1692 .... **LC 114**
See also DLB 80; IDTP; RGEL 2
Shaffer, Anthony (Joshua)
1926-2001 .... **CLC 19**
See also CA 110; 116; 200; CBD; CD 5; DAM DRAM; DFS 13; DLB 13

Shaffer, Peter (Levin) 1926- .. **CLC 5, 14, 18, 37, 60; DC 7**
See also BRWS 1; CA 25-28R; CANR 25, 47, 74, 118; CBD; CD 5; CDBLB 1960 to Present; DA3; DAB; DAM DRAM, MST; DFS 5, 13; DLB 13, 233; EWL 3; MTCW 1, 2; RGEL 2; TEA
Shakespeare, William 1564-1616 .... **WLC**
See also AAYA 35; BRW 1; CDBLB Before 1660; DA; DA3; DAB; DAC; DAM DRAM, MST, POET; DFS 20; DLB 62, 172, 263; EXPP; LAIT 1; LATS 1:1; LMFS 1; PAB; PFS 1, 2, 3, 4, 5, 8, 9; RGEL 2; TEA; WLIT 3; WP; WS; WYA
Shakey, Bernard
See Young, Neil
Shalamov, Varlam (Tikhonovich)
1907-1982 .... **CLC 18**
See also CA 129; 105; DLB 302; RGSF 2
Shamloo, Ahmad
See Shamlu, Ahmad
Shamlou, Ahmad
See Shamlu, Ahmad
Shamlu, Ahmad 1925-2000 .... **CLC 10**
See also CA 216; CWW 2
Shammas, Anton 1951- .... **CLC 55**
See also CA 199
Shandling, Arline
See Berriault, Gina
Shange, Ntozake 1948- ... **BLC 3; CLC 8, 25, 38, 74, 126; DC 3**
See also AAYA 9; AFAW 1, 2; BW 2; CA 85-88; CABS 3; CAD; CANR 27, 48, 74, 131; CD 5; CP 7; CWD; CWP; DA3; DAM DRAM, MULT; DFS 2, 11; DLB 38, 249; FW; LAIT 5; MTCW 1, 2; NFS 11; RGAL 4; YAW
Shanley, John Patrick 1950- .... **CLC 75**
See also AMWS 14; CA 128; 133; CAD; CANR 83; CD 5
Shapcott, Thomas W(illiam) 1935- .. **CLC 38**
See also CA 69-72; CANR 49, 83, 103; CP 7; DLB 289
Shapiro, Jane 1942- .... **CLC 76**
See also CA 196
Shapiro, Karl (Jay) 1913-2000 ...... **CLC 4, 8, 15, 53; PC 25**
See also AMWS 2; CA 1-4R; 188; CAAS 6; CANR 1, 36, 66; CP 7; DLB 48; EWL 3; EXPP; MTCW 1, 2; PFS 3; RGAL 4
Sharp, William 1855-1905 .... **TCLC 39**
See Macleod, Fiona
See also CA 160; DLB 156; RGEL 2
Sharpe, Thomas Ridley 1928-
See Sharpe, Tom
See also CA 114; 122; CANR 85; INT CA-122
Sharpe, Tom .... **CLC 36**
See Sharpe, Thomas Ridley
See also CN 7; DLB 14, 231
Shatrov, Mikhail .... **CLC 59**
Shaw, Bernard
See Shaw, George Bernard
See also DLB 190
Shaw, G. Bernard
See Shaw, George Bernard
Shaw, George Bernard 1856-1950 ..... **DC 23; TCLC 3, 9, 21, 45; WLC**
See Shaw, Bernard
See also BRW 6; BRWC 1; BRWR 2; CA 104; 128; CDBLB 1914-1945; DA; DA3; DAB; DAC; DAM DRAM, MST; DFS 1, 3, 6, 11, 19; DLB 10, 57; EWL 3; LAIT 3; LATS 1:1; MTCW 1, 2; RGEL 2; TEA; WLIT 4
Shaw, Henry Wheeler 1818-1885 .. **NCLC 15**
See also DLB 11; RGAL 4

Shaw, Irwin 1913-1984 .... **CLC 7, 23, 34**
See also AITN 1; BPFB 3; CA 13-16R; 112; CANR 21; CDALB 1941-1968; CPW; DAM DRAM, POP; DLB 6, 102; DLBY 1984; MTCW 1, 21
Shaw, Robert 1927-1978 .... **CLC 5**
See also AITN 1; CA 1-4R; 81-84; CANR 4; DLB 13, 14
Shaw, T. E.
See Lawrence, T(homas) E(dward)
Shawn, Wallace 1943- .... **CLC 41**
See also CA 112; CAD; CD 5; DLB 266
Shchedrin, N.
See Saltykov, Mikhail Evgrafovich
Shea, Lisa 1953- .... **CLC 86**
See also CA 147
Sheed, Wilfrid (John Joseph) 1930- . **CLC 2, 4, 10, 53**
See also CA 65-68; CANR 30, 66; CN 7; DLB 6; MTCW 1, 2
Sheehy, Gail 1937- .... **CLC 171**
See also CA 49-52; CANR 1, 33, 55, 92; CPW; MTCW 1
Sheldon, Alice Hastings Bradley
1915(?)-1987
See Tiptree, James, Jr.
See also CA 108; 122; CANR 34; INT CA-108; MTCW 1
Sheldon, John
See Bloch, Robert (Albert)
Sheldon, Walter J(ames) 1917-1996
See Queen, Ellery
See also AITN 1; CA 25-28R; CANR 10
Shelley, Mary Wollstonecraft (Godwin)
1797-1851 ...... **NCLC 14, 59, 103; WLC**
See also AAYA 20; BPFB 3; BRW 3; BRWC 2; BRWS 3; BYA 5; CDBLB 1789-1832; DA; DA3; DAB; DAC; DAM MST, NOV; DLB 110, 116, 159, 178; EXPN; HGG; LAIT 1; LMFS 1, 2; NFS 1; RGEL 2; SATA 29; SCFW; SFW 4; TEA; WLIT 3
Shelley, Percy Bysshe 1792-1822 .. **NCLC 18, 93, 143; PC 14; WLC**
See also BRW 4; BRWR 1; CDBLB 1789-1832; DA; DA3; DAB; DAC; DAM MST, POET; DLB 96, 110, 158; EXPP; LMFS 1; PAB; PFS 2; RGEL 2; TEA; WLIT 3; WP
Shepard, Jim 1956- .... **CLC 36**
See also CA 137; CANR 59, 104; SATA 90
Shepard, Lucius 1947- .... **CLC 34**
See also CA 128; 141; CANR 81, 124; HGG; SCFW 2; SFW 4; SUFW 2
Shepard, Sam 1943- .... **CLC 4, 6, 17, 34, 41, 44, 169; DC 5**
See also AAYA 1, 58; AMWS 3; CA 69-72; CABS 3; CAD; CANR 22, 120; CD 5; DA3; DAM DRAM; DFS 3, 6, 7, 14; DLB 7, 212; EWL 3; IDFW 3, 4; MTCW 1, 2; RGAL 4
Shepherd, Michael
See Ludlum, Robert
Sherburne, Zoa (Lillian Morin)
1912-1995 .... **CLC 30**
See also AAYA 13; CA 1-4R; 176; CANR 3, 37; MAICYA 1, 2; SAAS 18; SATA 3; YAW
Sheridan, Frances 1724-1766 .... **LC 7**
See also DLB 39, 84
Sheridan, Richard Brinsley
1751-1816 ...... **DC 1; NCLC 5, 91; WLC**
See also BRW 3; CDBLB 1660-1789; DA; DAB; DAC; DAM DRAM, MST; DFS 15; DLB 89; WLIT 3
Sherman, Jonathan Marc .... **CLC 55**
Sherman, Martin 1941(?)- .... **CLC 19**
See also CA 116; 123; CAD; CANR 86; CD 5; DFS 20; DLB 228; GLL 1; IDTP

Sherwin, Judith Johnson
See Johnson, Judith (Emlyn)
See also CANR 85; CP 7; CWP

Sherwood, Frances 1940- .... **CLC 81**
See also CA 146, 220; CAAE 220

Sherwood, Robert E(mmet)
1896-1955 .... **TCLC 3**
See also CA 104; 153; CANR 86; DAM DRAM; DFS 11, 15, 17; DLB 7, 26, 249; IDFW 3, 4; RGAL 4

Shestov, Lev 1866-1938 .... **TCLC 56**

Shevchenko, Taras 1814-1861 .... **NCLC 54**

Shiel, M(atthew) P(hipps)
1865-1947 .... **TCLC 8**
See Holmes, Gordon
See also CA 106; 160; DLB 153; HGG; MTCW 2; SFW 4; SUFW

Shields, Carol (Ann) 1935-2003 ...... **CLC 91, 113, 193**
See also AMWS 7; CA 81-84; 218; CANR 51, 74, 98, 133; CCA 1; CN 7; CPW; DA3; DAC; MTCW 2

Shields, David (Jonathan) 1956- ...... **CLC 97**
See also CA 124; CANR 48, 99, 112

Shiga, Naoya 1883-1971 ..... **CLC 33; SSC 23**
See Shiga Naoya
See also CA 101; 33-36R; MJW; RGWL 3

Shiga Naoya
See Shiga, Naoya
See also DLB 180; EWL 3; RGWL 3

Shilts, Randy 1951-1994 .... **CLC 85**
See also AAYA 19; CA 115; 127; 144; CANR 45; DA3; GLL 1; INT CA-127; MTCW 2

Shimazaki, Haruki 1872-1943
See Shimazaki Toson
See also CA 105; 134; CANR 84; RGWL 3

Shimazaki Toson .... **TCLC 5**
See Shimazaki, Haruki
See also DLB 180; EWL 3

Shirley, James 1596-1666 .... **DC 25; LC 96**
See also DLB 58; RGEL 2

Sholokhov, Mikhail (Aleksandrovich)
1905-1984 .... **CLC 7, 15**
See also CA 101; 112; DLB 272; EWL 3; MTCW 1, 2; RGWL 2, 3; SATA-Obit 36

Shone, Patric
See Hanley, James

Showalter, Elaine 1941- .... **CLC 169**
See also CA 57-60; CANR 58, 106; DLB 67; FW; GLL 2

Shreve, Susan
See Shreve, Susan Richards

Shreve, Susan Richards 1939- .... **CLC 23**
See also CA 49-52; CAAS 5; CANR 5, 38, 69, 100; MAICYA 1, 2; SATA 46, 95, 152; SATA-Brief 41

Shue, Larry 1946-1985 .... **CLC 52**
See also CA 145; 117; DAM DRAM; DFS 7

Shu-Jen, Chou 1881-1936
See Lu Hsun
See also CA 104

Shulman, Alix Kates 1932- .... **CLC 2, 10**
See also CA 29-32R; CANR 43; FW; SATA 7

Shuster, Joe 1914-1992 .... **CLC 21**
See also AAYA 50

Shute, Nevil .... **CLC 30**
See Norway, Nevil Shute
See also BPFB 3; DLB 255; NFS 9; RHW; SFW 4

Shuttle, Penelope (Diane) 1947- .... **CLC 7**
See also CA 93-96; CANR 39, 84, 92, 108; CP 7; CWP; DLB 14, 40

Shvarts, Elena 1948- .... **PC 50**
See also CA 147

Sidhwa, Bapsy (N.) 1938- .... **CLC 168**
See also CA 108; CANR 25, 57; CN 7; FW

Sidney, Mary 1561-1621 .... **LC 19, 39**
See Sidney Herbert, Mary

Sidney, Sir Philip 1554-1586 . **LC 19, 39; PC 32**
See also BRW 1; BRWR 2; CDBLB Before 1660; DA; DA3; DAB; DAC; DAM MST, POET; DLB 167; EXPP; PAB; RGEL 2; TEA; WP

Sidney Herbert, Mary
See Sidney, Mary
See also DLB 167

Siegel, Jerome 1914-1996 .... **CLC 21**
See Siegel, Jerry
See also CA 116; 169; 151

Siegel, Jerry
See Siegel, Jerome
See also AAYA 50

Sienkiewicz, Henryk (Adam Alexander Pius)
1846-1916 .... **TCLC 3**
See also CA 104; 134; CANR 84; EWL 3; RGSF 2; RGWL 2, 3

Sierra, Gregorio Martinez
See Martinez Sierra, Gregorio

Sierra, Maria (de la O'LeJarraga) Martinez
See Martinez Sierra, Maria (de la O'LeJarraga)

Sigal, Clancy 1926- .... **CLC 7**
See also CA 1-4R; CANR 85; CN 7

Siger of Brabant 1240(?)-1284(?) . **CMLC 69**
See also DLB 115

Sigourney, Lydia H.
See Sigourney, Lydia Howard (Huntley)
See also DLB 73, 183

Sigourney, Lydia Howard (Huntley)
1791-1865 .... **NCLC 21, 87**
See Sigourney, Lydia H.; Sigourney, Lydia Huntley
See also DLB 1

Sigourney, Lydia Huntley
See Sigourney, Lydia Howard (Huntley)
See also DLB 42, 239, 243

Siguenza y Gongora, Carlos de
1645-1700 .... **HLCS 2; LC 8**
See also LAW

Sigurjonsson, Johann
See Sigurjonsson, Johann

Sigurjonsson, Johann 1880-1919 ... **TCLC 27**
See also CA 170; DLB 293; EWL 3

Sikelianos, Angelos 1884-1951 .... **PC 29; TCLC 39**
See also EWL 3; RGWL 2, 3

Silkin, Jon 1930-1997 .... **CLC 2, 6, 43**
See also CA 5-8R; CAAS 5; CANR 89; CP 7; DLB 27

Silko, Leslie (Marmon) 1948- .... **CLC 23, 74, 114; NNAL; SSC 37, 66; WLCS**
See also AAYA 14; AMWS 4; ANW; BYA 12; CA 115; 122; CANR 45, 65, 118; CN 7; CP 7; CPW 1; CWP; DA; DA3; DAC; DAM MST, MULT, POP; DLB 143, 175, 256, 275; EWL 3; EXPS; LAIT 4; MTCW 2; NFS 4; PFS 9, 16; RGAL 4; RGSF 2; SSFS 4, 8, 10, 11

Sillanpaa, Frans Eemil 1888-1964 ... **CLC 19**
See also CA 129; 93-96; EWL 3; MTCW 1

Sillitoe, Alan 1928- .. **CLC 1, 3, 6, 10, 19, 57, 148**
See also AITN 1; BRWS 5; CA 9-12R, 191; CAAE 191; CAAS 2; CANR 8, 26, 55; CDBLB 1960 to Present; CN 7; DLB 14, 139; EWL 3; MTCW 1, 2; RGEL 2; RGSF 2; SATA 61

Silone, Ignazio 1900-1978 .... **CLC 4**
See also CA 25-28; 81-84; CANR 34; CAP 2; DLB 264; EW 12; EWL 3; MTCW 1; RGSF 2; RGWL 2, 3

Silone, Ignazione
See Silone, Ignazio

Silver, Joan Micklin 1935- .... **CLC 20**
See also CA 114; 121; INT CA-121

Silver, Nicholas
See Faust, Frederick (Schiller)
See also TCWW 2

Silverberg, Robert 1935- .... **CLC 7, 140**
See also AAYA 24; BPFB 3; BYA 7, 9; CA 1-4R, 186; CAAE 186; CAAS 3; CANR 1, 20, 36, 85; CLR 59; CN 7; CPW; DAM POP; DLB 8; INT CANR-20; MAICYA 1, 2; MTCW 1, 2; SATA 13, 91; SATA-Essay 104; SCFW 2; SFW 4; SUFW 2

Silverstein, Alvin 1933- .... **CLC 17**
See also CA 49-52; CANR 2; CLR 25; JRDA; MAICYA 1, 2; SATA 8, 69, 124

Silverstein, Shel(don Allan)
1932-1999 .... **PC 49**
See also AAYA 40; BW 3; CA 107; 179; CANR 47, 74, 81; CLR 5, 96; CWRI 5; JRDA; MAICYA 1, 2; MTCW 2; SATA 33, 92; SATA-Brief 27; SATA-Obit 116

Silverstein, Virginia B(arbara Opshelor)
1937- .... **CLC 17**
See also CA 49-52; CANR 2; CLR 25; JRDA; MAICYA 1, 2; SATA 8, 69, 124

Sim, Georges
See Simenon, Georges (Jacques Christian)

Simak, Clifford D(onald) 1904-1988 . **CLC 1, 55**
See also CA 1-4R; 125; CANR 1, 35; DLB 8; MTCW 1; SATA-Obit 56; SFW 4

Simenon, Georges (Jacques Christian)
1903-1989 .... **CLC 1, 2, 3, 8, 18, 47**
See also BPFB 3; CA 85-88; 129; CANR 35; CMW 4; DA3; DAM POP; DLB 72; DLBY 1989; EW 12; EWL 3; GFL 1789 to the Present; MSW; MTCW 1, 2; RGWL 2, 3

Simic, Charles 1938- .... **CLC 6, 9, 22, 49, 68, 130**
See also AMWS 8; CA 29-32R; CAAS 4; CANR 12, 33, 52, 61, 96; CP 7; DA3; DAM POET; DLB 105; MTCW 2; PFS 7; RGAL 4; WP

Simmel, Georg 1858-1918 .... **TCLC 64**
See also CA 157; DLB 296

Simmons, Charles (Paul) 1924- .... **CLC 57**
See also CA 89-92; INT CA-89-92

Simmons, Dan 1948- .... **CLC 44**
See also AAYA 16, 54; CA 138; CANR 53, 81, 126; CPW; DAM POP; HGG; SUFW 2

Simmons, James (Stewart Alexander)
1933- .... **CLC 43**
See also CA 105; CAAS 21; CP 7; DLB 40

Simms, William Gilmore
1806-1870 .... **NCLC 3**
See also DLB 3, 30, 59, 73, 248, 254; RGAL 4

Simon, Carly 1945- .... **CLC 26**
See also CA 105

Simon, Claude (Eugene Henri)
1913-2005 .... **CLC 4, 9, 15, 39**
See also CA 89-92; CANR 33, 117; CWW 2; DAM NOV; DLB 83; EW 13; EWL 3; GFL 1789 to the Present; MTCW 1

Simon, Myles
See Follett, Ken(neth Martin)

Simon, (Marvin) Neil 1927- ... **CLC 6, 11, 31, 39, 70; DC 14**
See also AAYA 32; AITN 1; AMWS 4; CA 21-24R; CANR 26, 54, 87, 126; CD 5; DA3; DAM DRAM; DFS 2, 6, 12, 18; DLB 7, 266; LAIT 4; MTCW 1, 2; RGAL 4; TUS

Simon, Paul (Frederick) 1941(?)- ...... **CLC 17**
See also CA 116; 153

Simonon, Paul 1956(?)- .... **CLC 30**
Simonson, Rick ed. .... **CLC 70**
Simpson, Harriette
    See Arnow, Harriette (Louisa) Simpson
Simpson, Louis (Aston Marantz)
    1923- .... **CLC 4, 7, 9, 32, 149**
    See also AMWS 9; CA 1-4R; CAAS 4; CANR 1, 61; CP 7; DAM POET; DLB 5; MTCW 1, 2; PFS 7, 11, 14; RGAL 4
Simpson, Mona (Elizabeth) 1957- ... **CLC 44, 146**
    See also CA 122; 135; CANR 68, 103; CN 7; EWL 3
Simpson, N(orman) F(rederick)
    1919- .... **CLC 29**
    See also CA 13-16R; CBD; DLB 13; RGEL 2
Sinclair, Andrew (Annandale) 1935- . **CLC 2, 14**
    See also CA 9-12R; CAAS 5; CANR 14, 38, 91; CN 7; DLB 14; FANT; MTCW 1
Sinclair, Emil
    See Hesse, Hermann
Sinclair, Iain 1943- .... **CLC 76**
    See also CA 132; CANR 81; CP 7; HGG
Sinclair, Iain MacGregor
    See Sinclair, Iain
Sinclair, Irene
    See Griffith, D(avid Lewelyn) W(ark)
Sinclair, Mary Amelia St. Clair 1865(?)-1946
    See Sinclair, May
    See also CA 104; HGG; RHW
Sinclair, May .... **TCLC 3, 11**
    See Sinclair, Mary Amelia St. Clair
    See also CA 166; DLB 36, 135; EWL 3; RGEL 2; SUFW
Sinclair, Roy
    See Griffith, D(avid Lewelyn) W(ark)
Sinclair, Upton (Beall) 1878-1968 ..... **CLC 1, 11, 15, 63; TCLC 160; WLC**
    See also AMWS 5; BPFB 3; BYA 2; CA 5-8R; 25-28R; CANR 7; CDALB 1929-1941; DA; DA3; DAB; DAC; DAM MST, NOV; DLB 9; EWL 3; INT CANR-7; LAIT 3; MTCW 1, 2; NFS 6; RGAL 4; SATA 9; TUS; YAW
Singe, (Edmund) J(ohn) M(illington)
    1871-1909 .... **WLC**
Singer, Isaac
    See Singer, Isaac Bashevis
Singer, Isaac Bashevis 1904-1991 .. **CLC 1, 3, 6, 9, 11, 15, 23, 38, 69, 111; SSC 3, 53, 80; WLC**
    See also AAYA 32; AITN 1, 2; AMW; AMWR 2; BPFB 3; BYA 1, 4; CA 1-4R; 134; CANR 1, 39, 106; CDALB 1941-1968; CLR 1; CWRI 5; DA; DA3; DAB; DAC; DAM MST, NOV; DLB 6, 28, 52, 278; DLBY 1991; EWL 3; EXPS; HGG; JRDA; LAIT 3; MAICYA 1, 2; MTCW 1, 2; RGAL 4; RGSF 2; SATA 3, 27; SATA-Obit 68; SSFS 2, 12, 16; TUS; TWA
Singer, Israel Joshua 1893-1944 .... **TCLC 33**
    See also CA 169; EWL 3
Singh, Khushwant 1915- .... **CLC 11**
    See also CA 9-12R; CAAS 9; CANR 6, 84; CN 7; EWL 3; RGEL 2
Singleton, Ann
    See Benedict, Ruth (Fulton)
Singleton, John 1968(?)- .... **CLC 156**
    See also AAYA 50; BW 2, 3; CA 138; CANR 67, 82; DAM MULT
Siniavskii, Andrei
    See Sinyavsky, Andrei (Donatevich)
    See also CWW 2
Sinjohn, John
    See Galsworthy, John

Sinyavsky, Andrei (Donatevich)
    1925-1997 .... **CLC 8**
    See Siniavskii, Andrei; Sinyavsky, Andrey Donatovich; Tertz, Abram
    See also CA 85-88; 159
Sinyavsky, Andrey Donatovich
    See Sinyavsky, Andrei (Donatevich)
    See also EWL 3
Sirin, V.
    See Nabokov, Vladimir (Vladimirovich)
Sissman, L(ouis) E(dward)
    1928-1976 .... **CLC 9, 18**
    See also CA 21-24R; 65-68; CANR 13; DLB 5
Sisson, C(harles) H(ubert)
    1914-2003 .... **CLC 8**
    See also CA 1-4R; 220; CAAS 3; CANR 3, 48, 84; CP 7; DLB 27
Sitting Bull 1831(?)-1890 .... **NNAL**
    See also DA3; DAM MULT
Sitwell, Dame Edith 1887-1964 ..... **CLC 2, 9, 67; PC 3**
    See also BRW 7; CA 9-12R; CANR 35; CDBLB 1945-1960; DAM POET; DLB 20; EWL 3; MTCW 1, 2; RGEL 2; TEA
Siwaarmill, H. P.
    See Sharp, William
Sjoewall, Maj 1935- .... **CLC 7**
    See Sjowall, Maj
    See also CA 65-68; CANR 73
Sjowall, Maj
    See Sjoewall, Maj
    See also BPFB 3; CMW 4; MSW
Skelton, John 1460(?)-1529 ..... **LC 71; PC 25**
    See also BRW 1; DLB 136; RGEL 2
Skelton, Robin 1925-1997 .... **CLC 13**
    See Zuk, Georges
    See also AITN 2; CA 5-8R; 160; CAAS 5; CANR 28, 89; CCA 1; CP 7; DLB 27, 53
Skolimowski, Jerzy 1938- .... **CLC 20**
    See also CA 128
Skram, Amalie (Bertha)
    1847-1905 .... **TCLC 25**
    See also CA 165
Skvorecky, Josef (Vaclav) 1924- ...... **CLC 15, 39, 69, 152**
    See also CA 61-64; CAAS 1; CANR 10, 34, 63, 108; CDWLB 4; CWW 2; DA3; DAC; DAM NOV; DLB 232; EWL 3; MTCW 1, 2
Slade, Bernard .... **CLC 11, 46**
    See Newbound, Bernard Slade
    See also CAAS 9; CCA 1; DLB 53
Slaughter, Carolyn 1946- .... **CLC 56**
    See also CA 85-88; CANR 85; CN 7
Slaughter, Frank G(ill) 1908-2001 ... **CLC 29**
    See also AITN 2; CA 5-8R; 197; CANR 5, 85; INT CANR-5; RHW
Slavitt, David R(ytman) 1935- ...... **CLC 5, 14**
    See also CA 21-24R; CAAS 3; CANR 41, 83; CP 7; DLB 5, 6
Slesinger, Tess 1905-1945 .... **TCLC 10**
    See also CA 107; 199; DLB 102
Slessor, Kenneth 1901-1971 .... **CLC 14**
    See also CA 102; 89-92; DLB 260; RGEL 2
Slowacki, Juliusz 1809-1849 .... **NCLC 15**
    See also RGWL 3
Smart, Christopher 1722-1771 . **LC 3; PC 13**
    See also DAM POET; DLB 109; RGEL 2
Smart, Elizabeth 1913-1986 .... **CLC 54**
    See also CA 81-84; 118; DLB 88
Smiley, Jane (Graves) 1949- ...... **CLC 53, 76, 144**
    See also AMWS 6; BPFB 3; CA 104; CANR 30, 50, 74, 96; CN 7; CPW 1; DA3; DAM POP; DLB 227, 234; EWL 3; INT CANR-30; SSFS 19

Smith, A(rthur) J(ames) M(arshall)
    1902-1980 .... **CLC 15**
    See also CA 1-4R; 102; CANR 4; DAC; DLB 88; RGEL 2
Smith, Adam 1723(?)-1790 .... **LC 36**
    See also DLB 104, 252; RGEL 2
Smith, Alexander 1829-1867 .... **NCLC 59**
    See also DLB 32, 55
Smith, Anna Deavere 1950- .... **CLC 86**
    See also CA 133; CANR 103; CD 5; DFS 2
Smith, Betty (Wehner) 1904-1972 .... **CLC 19**
    See also BPFB 3; BYA 3; CA 5-8R; 33-36R; DLBY 1982; LAIT 3; RGAL 4; SATA 6
Smith, Charlotte (Turner)
    1749-1806 .... **NCLC 23, 115**
    See also DLB 39, 109; RGEL 2; TEA
Smith, Clark Ashton 1893-1961 .... **CLC 43**
    See also CA 143; CANR 81; FANT; HGG; MTCW 2; SCFW 2; SFW 4; SUFW
Smith, Dave .... **CLC 22, 42**
    See Smith, David (Jeddie)
    See also CAAS 7; DLB 5
Smith, David (Jeddie) 1942-
    See Smith, Dave
    See also CA 49-52; CANR 1, 59, 120; CP 7; CSW; DAM POET
Smith, Florence Margaret 1902-1971
    See Smith, Stevie
    See also CA 17-18; 29-32R; CANR 35; CAP 2; DAM POET; MTCW 1, 2; TEA
Smith, Iain Crichton 1928-1998 .... **CLC 64**
    See also BRWS 9; CA 21-24R; 171; CN 7; CP 7; DLB 40, 139; RGSF 2
Smith, John 1580(?)-1631 .... **LC 9**
    See also DLB 24, 30; TUS
Smith, Johnston
    See Crane, Stephen (Townley)
Smith, Joseph, Jr. 1805-1844 .... **NCLC 53**
Smith, Lee 1944- .... **CLC 25, 73**
    See also CA 114; 119; CANR 46, 118; CSW; DLB 143; DLBY 1983; EWL 3; INT CA-119; RGAL 4
Smith, Martin
    See Smith, Martin Cruz
Smith, Martin Cruz 1942- .. **CLC 25; NNAL**
    See also BEST 89:4; BPFB 3; CA 85-88; CANR 6, 23, 43, 65, 119; CMW 4; CPW; DAM MULT, POP; HGG; INT CANR-23; MTCW 2; RGAL 4
Smith, Patti 1946- .... **CLC 12**
    See also CA 93-96; CANR 63
Smith, Pauline (Urmson)
    1882-1959 .... **TCLC 25**
    See also DLB 225; EWL 3
Smith, Rosamond
    See Oates, Joyce Carol
Smith, Sheila Kaye
    See Kaye-Smith, Sheila
Smith, Stevie .... **CLC 3, 8, 25, 44; PC 12**
    See Smith, Florence Margaret
    See also BRWS 2; DLB 20; EWL 3; MTCW 2; PAB; PFS 3; RGEL 2
Smith, Wilbur (Addison) 1933- .... **CLC 33**
    See also CA 13-16R; CANR 7, 46, 66, 134; CPW; MTCW 1, 2
Smith, William Jay 1918- .... **CLC 6**
    See also AMWS 13; CA 5-8R; CANR 44, 106; CP 7; CSW; CWRI 5; DLB 5; MAICYA 1, 2; SAAS 22; SATA 2, 68, 154; SATA-Essay 154
Smith, Woodrow Wilson
    See Kuttner, Henry
Smith, Zadie 1976- .... **CLC 158**
    See also AAYA 50; CA 193

Smolenskin, Peretz 1842-1885 .... **NCLC 30**

Smollett, Tobias (George) 1721-1771 ... **LC 2, 46**
See also BRW 3; CDBLB 1660-1789; DLB 39, 104; RGEL 2; TEA

Snodgrass, W(illiam) D(e Witt) 1926- .... **CLC 2, 6, 10, 18, 68**
See also AMWS 6; CA 1-4R; CANR 6, 36, 65, 85; CP 7; DAM POET; DLB 5; MTCW 1, 2; RGAL 4

Snorri Sturluson 1179-1241 .... **CMLC 56**
See also RGWL 2, 3

Snow, C(harles) P(ercy) 1905-1980 ... **CLC 1, 4, 6, 9, 13, 19**
See also BRW 7; CA 5-8R; 101; CANR 28; CDBLB 1945-1960; DAM NOV; DLB 15, 77; DLBD 17; EWL 3; MTCW 1, 2; RGEL 2; TEA

Snow, Frances Compton
See Adams, Henry (Brooks)

Snyder, Gary (Sherman) 1930- . **CLC 1, 2, 5, 9, 32, 120; PC 21**
See also AMWS 8; ANW; BG 3; CA 17-20R; CANR 30, 60, 125; CP 7; DA3; DAM POET; DLB 5, 16, 165, 212, 237, 275; EWL 3; MTCW 2; PFS 9, 19; RGAL 4; WP

Snyder, Zilpha Keatley 1927- .... **CLC 17**
See also AAYA 15; BYA 1; CA 9-12R; CANR 38; CLR 31; JRDA; MAICYA 1, 2; SAAS 2; SATA 1, 28, 75, 110; SATA-Essay 112; YAW

Soares, Bernardo
See Pessoa, Fernando (Antonio Nogueira)

Sobh, A.
See Shamlu, Ahmad

Sobh, Alef
See Shamlu, Ahmad

Sobol, Joshua 1939- .... **CLC 60**
See Sobol, Yehoshua
See also CA 200

Sobol, Yehoshua 1939-
See Sobol, Joshua
See also CWW 2

Socrates 470B.C.-399B.C. .... **CMLC 27**

Soderberg, Hjalmar 1869-1941 ...... **TCLC 39**
See also DLB 259; EWL 3; RGSF 2

Soderbergh, Steven 1963- .... **CLC 154**
See also AAYA 43

Sodergran, Edith (Irene) 1892-1923
See Soedergran, Edith (Irene)
See also CA 202; DLB 259; EW 11; EWL 3; RGWL 2, 3

Soedergran, Edith (Irene) 1892-1923 .... **TCLC 31**
See Sodergran, Edith (Irene)

Softly, Edgar
See Lovecraft, H(oward) P(hillips)

Softly, Edward
See Lovecraft, H(oward) P(hillips)

Sokolov, Alexander V(sevolodovich) 1943-
See Sokolov, Sasha
See also CA 73-76

Sokolov, Raymond 1941- .... **CLC 7**
See also CA 85-88

Sokolov, Sasha .... **CLC 59**
See Sokolov, Alexander V(sevolodovich)
See also CWW 2; DLB 285; EWL 3; RGWL 2, 3

Solo, Jay
See Ellison, Harlan (Jay)

Sologub, Fyodor .... **TCLC 9**
See Teternikov, Fyodor Kuzmich
See also EWL 3

Solomons, Ikey Esquir
See Thackeray, William Makepeace

Solomos, Dionysios 1798-1857 .... **NCLC 15**

Solwoska, Mara
See French, Marilyn

Solzhenitsyn, Aleksandr I(sayevich) 1918- .. **CLC 1, 2, 4, 7, 9, 10, 18, 26, 34, 78, 134; SSC 32; WLC**
See Solzhenitsyn, Aleksandr Isaevich
See also AAYA 49; AITN 1; BPFB 3; CA 69-72; CANR 40, 65, 116; DA; DA3; DAB; DAC; DAM MST, NOV; DLB 302; EW 13; EXPS; LAIT 4; MTCW 1, 2; NFS 6; RGSF 2; RGWL 2, 3; SSFS 9; TWA

Solzhenitsyn, Aleksandr Isaevich
See Solzhenitsyn, Aleksandr I(sayevich)
See also CWW 2; EWL 3

Somers, Jane
See Lessing, Doris (May)

Somerville, Edith Oenone 1858-1949 .... **SSC 56; TCLC 51**
See also CA 196; DLB 135; RGEL 2; RGSF 2

Somerville & Ross
See Martin, Violet Florence; Somerville, Edith Oenone

Sommer, Scott 1951- .... **CLC 25**
See also CA 106

Sommers, Christina Hoff 1950- ...... **CLC 197**
See also CA 153; CANR 95

Sondheim, Stephen (Joshua) 1930- . **CLC 30, 39, 147; DC 22**
See also AAYA 11; CA 103; CANR 47, 67, 125; DAM DRAM; LAIT 4

Sone, Monica 1919- .... **AAL**

Song, Cathy 1955- .... **AAL; PC 21**
See also CA 154; CANR 118; CWP; DLB 169; EXPP; FW; PFS 5

Sontag, Susan 1933- .... **CLC 1, 2, 10, 13, 31, 105, 195**
See also AMWS 3; CA 17-20R; CANR 25, 51, 74, 97; CN 7; CPW; DA3; DAM POP; DLB 2, 67; EWL 3; MAWW; MTCW 1, 2; RGAL 4; RHW; SSFS 10

Sophocles 496(?)B.C.-406(?)B.C. .... **CMLC 2, 47, 51; DC 1; WLCS**
See also AW 1; CDWLB 1; DA; DA3; DAB; DAC; DAM DRAM, MST; DFS 1, 4, 8; DLB 176; LAIT 1; LATS 1:1; LMFS 1; RGWL 2, 3; TWA

Sordello 1189-1269 .... **CMLC 15**

Sorel, Georges 1847-1922 .... **TCLC 91**
See also CA 118; 188

Sorel, Julia
See Drexler, Rosalyn

Sorokin, Vladimir .... **CLC 59**
See Sorokin, Vladimir Georgievich

Sorokin, Vladimir Georgievich
See Sorokin, Vladimir
See also DLB 285

Sorrentino, Gilbert 1929- .. **CLC 3, 7, 14, 22, 40**
See also CA 77-80; CANR 14, 33, 115; CN 7; CP 7; DLB 5, 173; DLBY 1980; INT CANR-14

Soseki
See Natsume, Soseki
See also MJW

Soto, Gary 1952- ... **CLC 32, 80; HLC 2; PC 28**
See also AAYA 10, 37; BYA 11; CA 119; 125; CANR 50, 74, 107; CLR 38; CP 7; DAM MULT; DLB 82; EWL 3; EXPP; HW 1, 2; INT CA-125; JRDA; LLW 1; MAICYA 2; MAICYAS 1; MTCW 2; PFS 7; RGAL 4; SATA 80, 120; WYA; YAW

Soupault, Philippe 1897-1990 .... **CLC 68**
See also CA 116; 147; 131; EWL 3; GFL 1789 to the Present; LMFS 2

Souster, (Holmes) Raymond 1921- .... **CLC 5, 14**
See also CA 13-16R; CAAS 14; CANR 13, 29, 53; CP 7; DA3; DAC; DAM POET; DLB 88; RGEL 2; SATA 63

Southern, Terry 1924(?)-1995 .... **CLC 7**
See also AMWS 11; BPFB 3; CA 1-4R; 150; CANR 1, 55, 107; CN 7; DLB 2; IDFW 3, 4

Southerne, Thomas 1660-1746 .... **LC 99**
See also DLB 80; RGEL 2

Southey, Robert 1774-1843 .... **NCLC 8, 97**
See also BRW 4; DLB 93, 107, 142; RGEL 2; SATA 54

Southwell, Robert 1561(?)-1595 .... **LC 108**
See also DLB 167; RGEL 2; TEA

Southworth, Emma Dorothy Eliza Nevitte 1819-1899 .... **NCLC 26**
See also DLB 239

Souza, Ernest
See Scott, Evelyn

Soyinka, Wole 1934- .. **BLC 3; CLC 3, 5, 14, 36, 44, 179; DC 2; WLC**
See also AFW; BW 2, 3; CA 13-16R; CANR 27, 39, 82; CD 5; CDWLB 3; CN 7; CP 7; DA; DA3; DAB; DAC; DAM DRAM, MST, MULT; DFS 10; DLB 125; EWL 3; MTCW 1, 2; RGEL 2; TWA; WLIT 2; WWE 1

Spackman, W(illiam) M(ode) 1905-1990 .... **CLC 46**
See also CA 81-84; 132

Spacks, Barry (Bernard) 1931- .... **CLC 14**
See also CA 154; CANR 33, 109; CP 7; DLB 105

Spanidou, Irini 1946- .... **CLC 44**
See also CA 185

Spark, Muriel (Sarah) 1918- ...... **CLC 2, 3, 5, 8, 13, 18, 40, 94; SSC 10**
See also BRWS 1; CA 5-8R; CANR 12, 36, 76, 89, 131; CDBLB 1945-1960; CN 7; CP 7; DA3; DAB; DAC; DAM MST, NOV; DLB 15, 139; EWL 3; FW; INT CANR-12; LAIT 4; MTCW 1, 2; RGEL 2; TEA; WLIT 4; YAW

Spaulding, Douglas
See Bradbury, Ray (Douglas)

Spaulding, Leonard
See Bradbury, Ray (Douglas)

Speght, Rachel 1597-c. 1630 .... **LC 97**
See also DLB 126

Spelman, Elizabeth .... **CLC 65**

Spence, J. A. D.
See Eliot, T(homas) S(tearns)

Spencer, Anne 1882-1975 .... **HR 3**
See also BW 2; CA 161; DLB 51, 54

Spencer, Elizabeth 1921- .... **CLC 22; SSC 57**
See also CA 13-16R; CANR 32, 65, 87; CN 7; CSW; DLB 6, 218; EWL 3; MTCW 1; RGAL 4; SATA 14

Spencer, Leonard G.
See Silverberg, Robert

Spencer, Scott 1945- .... **CLC 30**
See also CA 113; CANR 51; DLBY 1986

Spender, Stephen (Harold) 1909-1995 .... **CLC 1, 2, 5, 10, 41, 91**
See also BRWS 2; CA 9-12R; 149; CANR 31, 54; CDBLB 1945-1960; CP 7; DA3; DAM POET; DLB 20; EWL 3; MTCW 1, 2; PAB; RGEL 2; TEA

Spengler, Oswald (Arnold Gottfried) 1880-1936 .... **TCLC 25**
See also CA 118; 189

Spenser, Edmund 1552(?)-1599 ..... **LC 5, 39; PC 8, 42; WLC**
See also AAYA 60; BRW 1; CDBLB Before 1660; DA; DA3; DAB; DAC; DAM MST, POET; DLB 167; EFS 2; EXPP; PAB; RGEL 2; TEA; WLIT 3; WP

Spicer, Jack 1925-1965 .... **CLC 8, 18, 72**
See also BG 3; CA 85-88; DAM POET; DLB 5, 16, 193; GLL 1; WP

Spiegelman, Art 1948- .... **CLC 76, 178**
See also AAYA 10, 46; CA 125; CANR 41, 55, 74, 124; DLB 299; MTCW 2; SATA 109; YAW

Spielberg, Peter 1929- .... **CLC 6**
See also CA 5-8R; CANR 4, 48; DLBY 1981

Spielberg, Steven 1947- .... **CLC 20, 188**
See also AAYA 8, 24; CA 77-80; CANR 32; SATA 32

Spillane, Frank Morrison 1918-
See Spillane, Mickey
See also CA 25-28R; CANR 28, 63, 125; DA3; MTCW 1, 2; SATA 66

Spillane, Mickey .... **CLC 3, 13**
See Spillane, Frank Morrison
See also BPFB 3; CMW 4; DLB 226; MSW; MTCW 2

Spinoza, Benedictus de 1632-1677 .. **LC 9, 58**

Spinrad, Norman (Richard) 1940- ... **CLC 46**
See also BPFB 3; CA 37-40R; CAAS 19; CANR 20, 91; DLB 8; INT CANR-20; SFW 4

Spitteler, Carl (Friedrich Georg)
1845-1924 .... **TCLC 12**
See also CA 109; DLB 129; EWL 3

Spivack, Kathleen (Romola Drucker)
1938- .... **CLC 6**
See also CA 49-52

Spoto, Donald 1941- .... **CLC 39**
See also CA 65-68; CANR 11, 57, 93

Springsteen, Bruce (F.) 1949- .... **CLC 17**
See also CA 111

Spurling, (Susan) Hilary 1940- .... **CLC 34**
See also CA 104; CANR 25, 52, 94

Spyker, John Howland
See Elman, Richard (Martin)

Squared, A.
See Abbott, Edwin A.

Squires, (James) Radcliffe
1917-1993 .... **CLC 51**
See also CA 1-4R; 140; CANR 6, 21

Srivastava, Dhanpat Rai 1880(?)-1936
See Premchand
See also CA 118; 197

Stacy, Donald
See Pohl, Frederik

Stael
See Stael-Holstein, Anne Louise Germaine Necker
See also EW 5; RGWL 2, 3

Stael, Germaine de
See Stael-Holstein, Anne Louise Germaine Necker
See also DLB 119, 192; FW; GFL 1789 to the Present; TWA

Stael-Holstein, Anne Louise Germaine
Necker 1766-1817 .... **NCLC 3, 91**
See also Stael; Stael, Germaine de

Stafford, Jean 1915-1979 .. **CLC 4, 7, 19, 68;**
SSC 26
See also CA 1-4R; 85-88; CANR 3, 65; DLB 2, 173; MTCW 1, 2; RGAL 4; RGSF 2; SATA-Obit 22; TCWW 2; TUS

Stafford, William (Edgar)
1914-1993 .... **CLC 4, 7, 29**
See also AMWS 11; CA 5-8R; 142; CAAS 3; CANR 5, 22; DAM POET; DLB 5, 206; EXPP; INT CANR-22; PFS 2, 8, 16; RGAL 4; WP

Stagnelius, Eric Johan 1793-1823 . **NCLC 61**

Staines, Trevor
See Brunner, John (Kilian Houston)

Stairs, Gordon
See Austin, Mary (Hunter)
See also TCWW 2

Stalin, Joseph 1879-1953 .... **TCLC 92**

Stampa, Gaspara c. 1524-1554 .... **PC 43; LC 114**
See also RGWL 2, 3

Stampflinger, K. A.
See Benjamin, Walter

Stancykowna
See Szymborska, Wislawa

Standing Bear, Luther
1868(?)-1939(?) .... **NNAL**
See also CA 113; 144; DAM MULT

Stannard, Martin 1947- .... **CLC 44**
See also CA 142; DLB 155

Stanton, Elizabeth Cady
1815-1902 .... **TCLC 73**
See also CA 171; DLB 79; FW

Stanton, Maura 1946- .... **CLC 9**
See also CA 89-92; CANR 15, 123; DLB 120

Stanton, Schuyler
See Baum, L(yman) Frank

Stapledon, (William) Olaf
1886-1950 .... **TCLC 22**
See also CA 111; 162; DLB 15, 255; SFW 4

Starbuck, George (Edwin)
1931-1996 .... **CLC 53**
See also CA 21-24R; 153; CANR 23; DAM POET

Stark, Richard
See Westlake, Donald E(dwin)

Staunton, Schuyler
See Baum, L(yman) Frank

Stead, Christina (Ellen) 1902-1983 ... **CLC 2, 5, 8, 32, 80**
See also BRWS 4; CA 13-16R; 109; CANR 33, 40; DLB 260; EWL 3; FW; MTCW 1, 2; RGEL 2; RGSF 2; WWE 1

Stead, William Thomas
1849-1912 .... **TCLC 48**
See also CA 167

Stebnitsky, M.
See Leskov, Nikolai (Semyonovich)

Steele, Sir Richard 1672-1729 .... **LC 18**
See also BRW 3; CDBLB 1660-1789; DLB 84, 101; RGEL 2; WLIT 3

Steele, Timothy (Reid) 1948- .... **CLC 45**
See also CA 93-96; CANR 16, 50, 92; CP 7; DLB 120, 282

Steffens, (Joseph) Lincoln
1866-1936 .... **TCLC 20**
See also CA 117; 198; DLB 303

Stegner, Wallace (Earle) 1909-1993 .. **CLC 9, 49, 81; SSC 27**
See also AITN 1; AMWS 4; ANW; BEST 90:3; BPFB 3; CA 1-4R; 141; CAAS 9; CANR 1, 21, 46; DAM NOV; DLB 9, 206, 275; DLBY 1993; EWL 3; MTCW 1, 2; RGAL 4; TCWW 2; TUS

Stein, Gertrude 1874-1946 .... **DC 19; PC 18; SSC 42; TCLC 1, 6, 28, 48; WLC**
See also AMW; AMWC 2; CA 104; 132; CANR 108; CDALB 1917-1929; DA; DA3; DAB; DAC; DAM MST, NOV, POET; DLB 4, 54, 86, 228; DLBD 15; EWL 3; EXPS; GLL 1; MAWW; MTCW 1, 2; NCFS 4; RGAL 4; RGSF 2; SSFS 5; TUS; WP

Steinbeck, John (Ernst) 1902-1968 ... **CLC 1, 5, 9, 13, 21, 34, 45, 75, 124; SSC 11, 37, 77; TCLC 135; WLC**
See also AAYA 12; AMW; BPFB 3; BYA 2, 3, 13; CA 1-4R; 25-28R; CANR 1, 35; CDALB 1929-1941; DA; DA3; DAB; DAC; DAM DRAM, MST, NOV; DLB 7, 9, 212, 275, 309; DLBD 2; EWL 3; EXPS; LAIT 3; MTCW 1, 2; NFS 1, 5, 7, 17, 19; RGAL 4; RGSF 2; RHW; SATA 9; SSFS 3, 6; TCWW 2; TUS; WYA; YAW

Steinem, Gloria 1934- .... **CLC 63**
See also CA 53-56; CANR 28, 51; DLB 246; FW; MTCW 1, 2

Steiner, George 1929- .... **CLC 24**
See also CA 73-76; CANR 31, 67, 108; DAM NOV; DLB 67, 299; EWL 3; MTCW 1, 2; SATA 62

Steiner, K. Leslie
See Delany, Samuel R(ay), Jr.

Steiner, Rudolf 1861-1925 .... **TCLC 13**
See also CA 107

Stendhal 1783-1842 .. **NCLC 23, 46; SSC 27; WLC**
See also DA; DA3; DAB; DAC; DAM MST, NOV; DLB 119; EW 5; GFL 1789 to the Present; RGWL 2, 3; TWA

Stephen, Adeline Virginia
See Woolf, (Adeline) Virginia

Stephen, Sir Leslie 1832-1904 .... **TCLC 23**
See also BRW 5; CA 123; DLB 57, 144, 190

Stephen, Sir Leslie
See Stephen, Sir Leslie

Stephen, Virginia
See Woolf, (Adeline) Virginia

Stephens, James 1882(?)-1950 .... **SSC 50; TCLC 4**
See also CA 104; 192; DLB 19, 153, 162; EWL 3; FANT; RGEL 2; SUFW

Stephens, Reed
See Donaldson, Stephen R(eeder)

Steptoe, Lydia
See Barnes, Djuna
See also GLL 1

Sterchi, Beat 1949- .... **CLC 65**
See also CA 203

Sterling, Brett
See Bradbury, Ray (Douglas); Hamilton, Edmond

Sterling, Bruce 1954- .... **CLC 72**
See also CA 119; CANR 44, 135; SCFW 2; SFW 4

Sterling, George 1869-1926 .... **TCLC 20**
See also CA 117; 165; DLB 54

Stern, Gerald 1925- .... **CLC 40, 100**
See also AMWS 9; CA 81-84; CANR 28, 94; CP 7; DLB 105; RGAL 4

Stern, Richard (Gustave) 1928- ... **CLC 4, 39**
See also CA 1-4R; CANR 1, 25, 52, 120; CN 7; DLB 218; DLBY 1987; INT CANR-25

Sternberg, Josef von 1894-1969 .... **CLC 20**
See also CA 81-84

Sterne, Laurence 1713-1768 .... **LC 2, 48; WLC**
See also BRW 3; BRWC 1; CDBLB 1660-1789; DA; DAB; DAC; DAM MST, NOV; DLB 39; RGEL 2; TEA

Sternheim, (William Adolf) Carl
1878-1942 .... **TCLC 8**
See also CA 105; 193; DLB 56, 118; EWL 3; RGWL 2, 3

Stevens, Mark 1951- .... **CLC 34**
See also CA 122

Stevens, Wallace 1879-1955 . **PC 6; TCLC 3, 12, 45; WLC**
See also AMW; AMWR 1; CA 104; 124; CDALB 1929-1941; DA; DA3; DAB; DAC; DAM MST, POET; DLB 54; EWL 3; EXPP; MTCW 1, 2; PAB; PFS 13, 16; RGAL 4; TUS; WP

Stevenson, Anne (Katharine) 1933- .. **CLC 7, 33**
See also BRWS 6; CA 17-20R; CAAS 9; CANR 9, 33, 123; CP 7; CWP; DLB 40; MTCW 1; RHW

Stevenson, Robert Louis (Balfour) 1850-1894 ...... **NCLC 5, 14, 63; SSC 11, 51; WLC**
See also AAYA 24; BPFB 3; BRW 5; BRWC 1; BRWR 1; BYA 1, 2, 4, 13; CDBLB 1890-1914; CLR 10, 11; DA; DA3; DAB; DAC; DAM MST, NOV; DLB 18, 57, 141, 156, 174; DLBD 13; HGG; JRDA; LAIT 1, 3; MAICYA 1, 2; NFS 11, 20; RGEL 2; RGSF 2; SATA 100; SUFW; TEA; WCH; WLIT 4; WYA; YABC 2; YAW

Stewart, J(ohn) I(nnes) M(ackintosh) 1906-1994 .... **CLC 7, 14, 32**
See Innes, Michael
See also CA 85-88; 147; CAAS 3; CANR 47; CMW 4; MTCW 1, 2

Stewart, Mary (Florence Elinor) 1916- .... **CLC 7, 35, 117**
See also AAYA 29; BPFB 3; CA 1-4R; CANR 1, 59, 130; CMW 4; CPW; DAB; FANT; RHW; SATA 12; YAW

Stewart, Mary Rainbow
See Stewart, Mary (Florence Elinor)

Stifle, June
See Campbell, Maria

Stifter, Adalbert 1805-1868 .. **NCLC 41; SSC 28**
See also CDWLB 2; DLB 133; RGSF 2; RGWL 2, 3

Still, James 1906-2001 .... **CLC 49**
See also CA 65-68; 195; CAAS 17; CANR 10, 26; CSW; DLB 9; DLBY 01; SATA 29; SATA-Obit 127

Sting 1951-
See Sumner, Gordon Matthew
See also CA 167

Stirling, Arthur
See Sinclair, Upton (Beall)

Stitt, Milan 1941- .... **CLC 29**
See also CA 69-72

Stockton, Francis Richard 1834-1902
See Stockton, Frank R.
See also CA 108; 137; MAICYA 1, 2; SATA 44; SFW 4

Stockton, Frank R. .... **TCLC 47**
See Stockton, Francis Richard
See also BYA 4, 13; DLB 42, 74; DLBD 13; EXPS; SATA-Brief 32; SSFS 3; SUFW; WCH

Stoddard, Charles
See Kuttner, Henry

Stoker, Abraham 1847-1912
See Stoker, Bram
See also CA 105; 150; DA; DA3; DAC; DAM MST, NOV; HGG; SATA 29

Stoker, Bram .. **SSC 62; TCLC 8, 144; WLC**
See Stoker, Abraham
See also AAYA 23; BPFB 3; BRWS 3; BYA 5; CDBLB 1890-1914; DAB; DLB 304; LATS 1:1; NFS 18; RGEL 2; SUFW; TEA; WLIT 4

Stolz, Mary (Slattery) 1920- .... **CLC 12**
See also AAYA 8; AITN 1; CA 5-8R; CANR 13, 41, 112; JRDA; MAICYA 1, 2; SAAS 3; SATA 10, 71, 133; YAW

Stone, Irving 1903-1989 .... **CLC 7**
See also AITN 1; BPFB 3; CA 1-4R; 129; CAAS 3; CANR 1, 23; CPW; DA3; DAM POP; INT CANR-23; MTCW 1, 2; RHW; SATA 3; SATA-Obit 64

Stone, Oliver (William) 1946- .... **CLC 73**
See also AAYA 15; CA 110; CANR 55, 125

Stone, Robert (Anthony) 1937- ... **CLC 5, 23, 42, 175**
See also AMWS 5; BPFB 3; CA 85-88; CANR 23, 66, 95; CN 7; DLB 152; EWL 3; INT CANR-23; MTCW 1

Stone, Ruth 1915- .... **PC 53**
See also CA 45-48; CANR 2, 91; CP 7; CSW; DLB 105; PFS 19

Stone, Zachary
See Follett, Ken(neth Martin)

Stoppard, Tom 1937- ... **CLC 1, 3, 4, 5, 8, 15, 29, 34, 63, 91; DC 6; WLC**
See also BRWC 1; BRWR 2; BRWS 1; CA 81-84; CANR 39, 67, 125; CBD; CD 5; CDBLB 1960 to Present; DA; DA3; DAB; DAC; DAM DRAM, MST; DFS 2, 5, 8, 11, 13, 16; DLB 13, 233; DLBY 1985; EWL 3; LATS 1:2; MTCW 1, 2; RGEL 2; TEA; WLIT 4

Storey, David (Malcolm) 1933- . **CLC 2, 4, 5, 8**
See also BRWS 1; CA 81-84; CANR 36; CBD; CD 5; CN 7; DAM DRAM; DLB 13, 14, 207, 245; EWL 3; MTCW 1; RGEL 2

Storm, Hyemeyohsts 1935- ... **CLC 3; NNAL**
See also CA 81-84; CANR 45; DAM MULT

Storm, (Hans) Theodor (Woldsen) 1817-1888 .... **NCLC 1; SSC 27**
See also CDWLB 2; DLB 129; EW; RGSF 2; RGWL 2, 3

Storni, Alfonsina 1892-1938 . **HLC 2; PC 33; TCLC 5**
See also CA 104; 131; DAM MULT; DLB 283; HW 1; LAW

Stoughton, William 1631-1701 .... **LC 38**
See also DLB 24

Stout, Rex (Todhunter) 1886-1975 ..... **CLC 3**
See also AITN 2; BPFB 3; CA 61-64; CANR 71; CMW 4; DLB 306; MSW; RGAL 4

Stow, (Julian) Randolph 1935- ... **CLC 23, 48**
See also CA 13-16R; CANR 33; CN 7; DLB 260; MTCW 1; RGEL 2

Stowe, Harriet (Elizabeth) Beecher 1811-1896 .... **NCLC 3, 50, 133; WLC**
See also AAYA 53; AMWS 1; CDALB 1865-1917; DA; DA3; DAB; DAC; DAM MST, NOV; DLB 1, 12, 42, 74, 189, 239, 243; EXPN; JRDA; LAIT 2; MAICYA 1, 2; NFS 6; RGAL 4; TUS; YABC 1

Strabo c. 64B.C.-c. 25 .... **CMLC 37**
See also DLB 176

Strachey, (Giles) Lytton 1880-1932 .... **TCLC 12**
See also BRWS 2; CA 110; 178; DLB 149; DLBD 10; EWL 3; MTCW 2; NCFS 4

Stramm, August 1874-1915 .... **PC 50**
See also CA 195; EWL 3

Strand, Mark 1934- .. **CLC 6, 18, 41, 71; PC 63**
See also AMWS 4; CA 21-24R; CANR 40, 65, 100; CP 7; DAM POET; DLB 5; EWL 3; PAB; PFS 9, 18; RGAL 4; SATA 41

Stratton-Porter, Gene(va Grace) 1863-1924
See Porter, Gene(va Grace) Stratton
See also ANW; CA 137; CLR 87; DLB 221; DLBD 14; MAICYA 1, 2; SATA 15

Straub, Peter (Francis) 1943- ... **CLC 28, 107**
See also BEST 89:1; BPFB 3; CA 85-88; CANR 28, 65, 109; CPW; DAM POP; DLBY 1984; HGG; MTCW 1, 2; SUFW 2

Strauss, Botho 1944- .... **CLC 22**
See also CA 157; CWW 2; DLB 124

Strauss, Leo 1899-1973 .... **TCLC 141**
See also CA 101; 45-48; CANR 122

Streatfeild, (Mary) Noel 1897(?)-1986 .... **CLC 21**
See also CA 81-84; 120; CANR 31; CLR 17, 83; CWRI 5; DLB 160; MAICYA 1, 2; SATA 20; SATA-Obit 48

Stribling, T(homas) S(igismund) 1881-1965 .... **CLC 23**
See also CA 189; 107; CMW 4; DLB 9; RGAL 4

Strindberg, (Johan) August 1849-1912 ... **DC 18; TCLC 1, 8, 21, 47; WLC**
See also CA 104; 135; DA; DA3; DAB; DAC; DAM DRAM, MST; DFS 4, 9; DLB 259; EW 7; EWL 3; IDTP; LMFS 2; MTCW 2; RGWL 2, 3; TWA

Stringer, Arthur 1874-1950 .... **TCLC 37**
See also CA 161; DLB 92

Stringer, David
See Roberts, Keith (John Kingston)

Stroheim, Erich von 1885-1957 ..... **TCLC 71**

Strugatskii, Arkadii (Natanovich) 1925-1991 .... **CLC 27**
See Strugatsky, Arkadii Natanovich
See also CA 106; 135; SFW 4

Strugatskii, Boris (Natanovich) 1933- .... **CLC 27**
See Strugatsky, Boris (Natanovich)
See also CA 106; SFW 4

Strugatsky, Arkadii Natanovich
See Strugatskii, Arkadii (Natanovich)
See also DLB 302

Strugatsky, Boris (Natanovich)
See Strugatskii, Boris (Natanovich)
See also DLB 302

Strummer, Joe 1953(?)- .... **CLC 30**

Strunk, William, Jr. 1869-1946 ...... **TCLC 92**
See also CA 118; 164; NCFS 5

Stryk, Lucien 1924- .... **PC 27**
See also CA 13-16R; CANR 10, 28, 55, 110; CP 7

Stuart, Don A.
See Campbell, John W(ood, Jr.)

Stuart, Ian
See MacLean, Alistair (Stuart)

Stuart, Jesse (Hilton) 1906-1984 ... **CLC 1, 8, 11, 14, 34; SSC 31**
See also CA 5-8R; 112; CANR 31; DLB 9, 48, 102; DLBY 1984; SATA 2; SATA-Obit 36

Stubblefield, Sally
See Trumbo, Dalton

Sturgeon, Theodore (Hamilton) 1918-1985 .... **CLC 22, 39**
See Queen, Ellery
See also AAYA 51; BPFB 3; BYA 9, 10; CA 81-84; 116; CANR 32, 103; DLB 8; DLBY 1985; HGG; MTCW 1, 2; SCFW; SFW 4; SUFW

Sturges, Preston 1898-1959 .... **TCLC 48**
See also CA 114; 149; DLB 26

Styron, William 1925- .... **CLC 1, 3, 5, 11, 15, 60; SSC 25**
See also AMW; AMWC 2; BEST 90:4; BPFB 3; CA 5-8R; CANR 6, 33, 74, 126; CDALB 1968-1988; CN 7; CPW; CSW; DA3; DAM NOV, POP; DLB 2, 143, 299; DLBY 1980; EWL 3; INT CANR-6; LAIT 2; MTCW 1, 2; NCFS 1; RGAL 4; RHW; TUS

Su, Chien 1884-1918
See Su Man-shu
See also CA 123

Suarez Lynch, B.
See Bioy Casares, Adolfo; Borges, Jorge Luis

Suassuna, Ariano Vilar 1927- .... **HLCS 1**
See also CA 178; DLB 307; HW 2; LAW

Suckert, Kurt Erich
See Malaparte, Curzio
Suckling, Sir John 1609-1642 . **LC 75; PC 30**
See also BRW 2; DAM POET; DLB 58, 126; EXPP; PAB; RGEL 2
Suckow, Ruth 1892-1960 .... **SSC 18**
See also CA 193; 113; DLB 9, 102; RGAL 4; TCWW 2
Sudermann, Hermann 1857-1928 .. **TCLC 15**
See also CA 107; 201; DLB 118
Sue, Eugene 1804-1857 .... **NCLC 1**
See also DLB 119
Sueskind, Patrick 1949- .... **CLC 44, 182**
See also Suskind, Patrick
Suetonius c. 70-c. 130 .... **CMLC 60**
See also AW 2; DLB 211; RGWL 2, 3
Sukenick, Ronald 1932-2004 ..... **CLC 3, 4, 6, 48**
See also CA 25-28R; 209; 229; CAAE 209; CAAS 8; CANR 32, 89; CN 7; DLB 173; DLBY 1981
Suknaski, Andrew 1942- .... **CLC 19**
See also CA 101; CP 7; DLB 53
Sullivan, Vernon
See Vian, Boris
Sully Prudhomme, Rene-Francois-Armand
1839-1907 .... **TCLC 31**
See also GFL 1789 to the Present
Su Man-shu .... **TCLC 24**
See Su, Chien
See also EWL 3
Sumarokov, Aleksandr Petrovich
1717-1777 .... **LC 104**
See also DLB 150
Summerforest, Ivy B.
See Kirkup, James
Summers, Andrew James 1942- .... **CLC 26**
Summers, Andy
See Summers, Andrew James
Summers, Hollis (Spurgeon, Jr.)
1916- .... **CLC 10**
See also CA 5-8R; CANR 3; DLB 6
Summers, (Alphonsus Joseph-Mary Augustus) Montague
1880-1948 .... **TCLC 16**
See also CA 118; 163
Sumner, Gordon Matthew .... **CLC 26**
See Police, The; Sting
Sun Tzu c. 400B.C.-c. 320B.C. ...... **CMLC 56**
Surrey, Henry Howard 1517-1574 ...... **PC 59**
See also BRW 1; RGEL 2
Surtees, Robert Smith 1805-1864 .. **NCLC 14**
See also DLB 21; RGEL 2
Susann, Jacqueline 1921-1974 .... **CLC 3**
See also AITN 1; BPFB 3; CA 65-68; 53-56; MTCW 1, 2
Su Shi
See Su Shih
See also RGWL 2, 3
Su Shih 1036-1101 .... **CMLC 15**
See Su Shi
Suskind, Patrick .... **CLC 182**
See Sueskind, Patrick
See also BPFB 3; CA 145; CWW 2
Sutcliff, Rosemary 1920-1992 .... **CLC 26**
See also AAYA 10; BYA 1, 4; CA 5-8R; 139; CANR 37; CLR 1, 37; CPW; DAB; DAC; DAM MST, POP; JRDA; LATS 1:1; MAICYA 1, 2; MAICYAS 1; RHW; SATA 6, 44, 78; SATA-Obit 73; WYA; YAW
Sutro, Alfred 1863-1933 .... **TCLC 6**
See also CA 105; 185; DLB 10; RGEL 2
Sutton, Henry
See Slavitt, David R(ytman)
Suzuki, D. T.
See Suzuki, Daisetz Teitaro

Suzuki, Daisetz T.
See Suzuki, Daisetz Teitaro
Suzuki, Daisetz Teitaro
1870-1966 .... **TCLC 109**
See also CA 121; 111; MTCW 1, 2
Suzuki, Teitaro
See Suzuki, Daisetz Teitaro
Svevo, Italo .... **SSC 25; TCLC 2, 35**
See Schmitz, Aron Hector
See also DLB 264; EW 8; EWL 3; RGWL 2, 3
Swados, Elizabeth (A.) 1951- .... **CLC 12**
See also CA 97-100; CANR 49; INT CA-97-100
Swados, Harvey 1920-1972 .... **CLC 5**
See also CA 5-8R; 37-40R; CANR 6; DLB 2
Swan, Gladys 1934- .... **CLC 69**
See also CA 101; CANR 17, 39
Swanson, Logan
See Matheson, Richard (Burton)
Swarthout, Glendon (Fred)
1918-1992 .... **CLC 35**
See also AAYA 55; CA 1-4R; 139; CANR 1, 47; LAIT 5; SATA 26; TCWW 2; YAW
Swedenborg, Emanuel 1688-1772 ..... **LC 105**
Sweet, Sarah C.
See Jewett, (Theodora) Sarah Orne
Swenson, May 1919-1989 ...... **CLC 4, 14, 61, 106; PC 14**
See also AMWS 4; CA 5-8R; 130; CANR 36, 61, 131; DA; DAB; DAC; DAM MST, POET; DLB 5; EXPP; GLL 2; MTCW 1, 2; PFS 16; SATA 15; WP
Swift, Augustus
See Lovecraft, H(oward) P(hillips)
Swift, Graham (Colin) 1949- ...... **CLC 41, 88**
See also BRWC 2; BRWS 5; CA 117; 122; CANR 46, 71, 128; CN 7; DLB 194; MTCW 2; NFS 18; RGSF 2
Swift, Jonathan 1667-1745 ..... **LC 1, 42, 101; PC 9; WLC**
See also AAYA 41; BRW 3; BRWC 1; BRWR 1; BYA 5, 14; CDBLB 1660-1789; CLR 53; DA; DA3; DAB; DAC; DAM MST, NOV, POET; DLB 39, 95, 101; EXPN; LAIT 1; NFS 6; RGEL 2; SATA 19; TEA; WCH; WLIT 3
Swinburne, Algernon Charles
1837-1909 ... **PC 24; TCLC 8, 36; WLC**
See also BRW 5; CA 105; 140; CDBLB 1832-1890; DA; DA3; DAB; DAC; DAM MST, POET; DLB 35, 57; PAB; RGEL 2; TEA
Swinfen, Ann .... **CLC 34**
See also CA 202
Swinnerton, Frank Arthur
1884-1982 .... **CLC 31**
See also CA 108; DLB 34
Swithen, John
See King, Stephen (Edwin)
Sylvia
See Ashton-Warner, Sylvia (Constance)
Symmes, Robert Edward
See Duncan, Robert (Edward)
Symonds, John Addington
1840-1893 .... **NCLC 34**
See also DLB 57, 144
Symons, Arthur 1865-1945 .... **TCLC 11**
See also CA 107; 189; DLB 19, 57, 149; RGEL 2
Symons, Julian (Gustave)
1912-1994 .... **CLC 2, 14, 32**
See also CA 49-52; 147; CAAS 3; CANR 3, 33, 59; CMW 4; DLB 87, 155; DLBY 1992; MSW; MTCW 1

Synge, (Edmund) J(ohn) M(illington)
1871-1909 .... **DC 2; TCLC 6, 37**
See also BRW 6; BRWR 1; CA 104; 141; CDBLB 1890-1914; DAM DRAM; DFS 18; DLB 10, 19; EWL 3; RGEL 2; TEA; WLIT 4
Syruc, J.
See Milosz, Czeslaw
Szirtes, George 1948- .... **CLC 46; PC 51**
See also CA 109; CANR 27, 61, 117; CP 7
Szymborska, Wislawa 1923- ... **CLC 99, 190; PC 44**
See also CA 154; CANR 91, 133; CDWLB 4; CWP; CWW 2; DA3; DLB 232; DLBY 1996; EWL 3; MTCW 2; PFS 15; RGWL 3
T. O., Nik
See Annensky, Innokenty (Fyodorovich)
Tabori, George 1914- .... **CLC 19**
See also CA 49-52; CANR 4, 69; CBD; CD 5; DLB 245
Tacitus c. 55-c. 117 .... **CMLC 56**
See also AW 2; CDWLB 1; DLB 211; RGWL 2, 3
Tagore, Rabindranath 1861-1941 .... **PC 8; SSC 48; TCLC 3, 53**
See also CA 104; 120; DA3; DAM DRAM, POET; EWL 3; MTCW 1, 2; PFS 18; RGEL 2; RGSF 2; RGWL 2, 3; TWA
Taine, Hippolyte Adolphe
1828-1893 .... **NCLC 15**
See also EW 7; GFL 1789 to the Present
Talayesva, Don C. 1890-(?) .... **NNAL**
Talese, Gay 1932- .... **CLC 37**
See also AITN 1; CA 1-4R; CANR 9, 58; DLB 185; INT CANR-9; MTCW 1, 2
Tallent, Elizabeth (Ann) 1954- .... **CLC 45**
See also CA 117; CANR 72; DLB 130
Tallmountain, Mary 1918-1997 .... **NNAL**
See also CA 146; 161; DLB 193
Tally, Ted 1952- .... **CLC 42**
See also CA 120; 124; CAD; CANR 125; CD 5; INT CA-124
Talvik, Heiti 1904-1947 .... **TCLC 87**
See also EWL 3
Tamayo y Baus, Manuel
1829-1898 .... **NCLC 1**
Tammsaare, A(nton) H(ansen)
1878-1940 .... **TCLC 27**
See also CA 164; CDWLB 4; DLB 220; EWL 3
Tam'si, Tchicaya U
See Tchicaya, Gerald Felix
Tan, Amy (Ruth) 1952- . **AAL; CLC 59, 120, 151**
See also AAYA 9, 48; AMWS 10; BEST 89:3; BPFB 3; CA 136; CANR 54, 105, 132; CDALBS; CN 7; CPW 1; DA3; DAM MULT, NOV, POP; DLB 173; EXPN; FW; LAIT 3, 5; MTCW 2; NFS 1, 13, 16; RGAL 4; SATA 75; SSFS 9; YAW
Tandem, Felix
See Spitteler, Carl (Friedrich Georg)
Tanizaki, Jun'ichiro 1886-1965 ... **CLC 8, 14, 28; SSC 21**
See Tanizaki Jun'ichiro
See also CA 93-96; 25-28R; MJW; MTCW 2; RGSF 2; RGWL 2
Tanizaki Jun'ichiro
See Tanizaki, Jun'ichiro
See also DLB 180; EWL 3
Tanner, William
See Amis, Kingsley (William)
Tao Lao
See Storni, Alfonsina
Tapahonso, Luci 1953- .... **NNAL**
See also CA 145; CANR 72, 127; DLB 175

Tarantino, Quentin (Jerome)
1963- .... **CLC 125**
See also AAYA 58; CA 171; CANR 125

Tarassoff, Lev
See Troyat, Henri

Tarbell, Ida M(inerva) 1857-1944 . **TCLC 40**
See also CA 122; 181; DLB 47

Tarkington, (Newton) Booth
1869-1946 .... **TCLC 9**
See also BPFB 3; BYA 3; CA 110; 143; CWRI 5; DLB 9, 102; MTCW 2; RGAL 4; SATA 17

Tarkovskii, Andrei Arsen'evich
See Tarkovsky, Andrei (Arsenyevich)

Tarkovsky, Andrei (Arsenyevich)
1932-1986 .... **CLC 75**
See also CA 127

Tartt, Donna 1963- .... **CLC 76**
See also AAYA 56; CA 142

Tasso, Torquato 1544-1595 .... **LC 5, 94**
See also EFS 2; EW 2; RGWL 2, 3

Tate, (John Orley) Allen 1899-1979 .. **CLC 2, 4, 6, 9, 11, 14, 24; PC 50**
See also AMW; CA 5-8R; 85-88; CANR 32, 108; DLB 4, 45, 63; DLBD 17; EWL 3; MTCW 1, 2; RGAL 4; RHW

Tate, Ellalice
See Hibbert, Eleanor Alice Burford

Tate, James (Vincent) 1943- .. **CLC 2, 6, 25**
See also CA 21-24R; CANR 29, 57, 114; CP 7; DLB 5, 169; EWL 3; PFS 10, 15; RGAL 4; WP

Tate, Nahum 1652(?)-1715 .... **LC 109**
See also DLB 80; RGEL 2

Tauler, Johannes c. 1300-1361 ...... **CMLC 37**
See also DLB 179; LMFS 1

Tavel, Ronald 1940- .... **CLC 6**
See also CA 21-24R; CAD; CANR 33; CD 5

Taviani, Paolo 1931- .... **CLC 70**
See also CA 153

Taylor, Bayard 1825-1878 .... **NCLC 89**
See also DLB 3, 189, 250, 254; RGAL 4

Taylor, C(ecil) P(hilip) 1929-1981 .. **CLC 27**
See also CA 25-28R; 105; CANR 47; CBD

Taylor, Edward 1642(?)-1729 . **LC 11; PC 63**
See also AMW; DA; DAB; DAC; DAM MST, POET; DLB 24; EXPP; RGAL 4; TUS

Taylor, Eleanor Ross 1920- .... **CLC 5**
See also CA 81-84; CANR 70

Taylor, Elizabeth 1932-1975 ..... **CLC 2, 4, 29**
See also CA 13-16R; CANR 9, 70; DLB 139; MTCW 1; RGEL 2; SATA 13

Taylor, Frederick Winslow
1856-1915 .... **TCLC 76**
See also CA 188

Taylor, Henry (Splawn) 1942- .... **CLC 44**
See also CA 33-36R; CAAS 7; CANR 31; CP 7; DLB 5; PFS 10

Taylor, Kamala (Purnaiya) 1924-2004
See Markandaya, Kamala
See also CA 77-80; 227; NFS 13

Taylor, Mildred D(elois) 1943- .... **CLC 21**
See also AAYA 10, 47; BW 1; BYA 3, 8; CA 85-88; CANR 25, 115; CLR 9, 59, 90; CSW; DLB 52; JRDA; LAIT 3; MAICYA 1, 2; SAAS 5; SATA 135; WYA; YAW

Taylor, Peter (Hillsman) 1917-1994 .. **CLC 1, 4, 18, 37, 44, 50, 71; SSC 10**
See also AMWS 5; BPFB 3; CA 13-16R; 147; CANR 9, 50; CSW; DLB 218, 278; DLBY 1981, 1994; EWL 3; EXPS; INT CANR-9; MTCW 1, 2; RGSF 2; SSFS 9; TUS

Taylor, Robert Lewis 1912-1998 .... **CLC 14**
See also CA 1-4R; 170; CANR 3, 64; SATA 10

Tchekhov, Anton
See Chekhov, Anton (Pavlovich)

Tchicaya, Gerald Felix 1931-1988 .. **CLC 101**
See Tchicaya U Tam'si
See also CA 129; 125; CANR 81

Tchicaya U Tam'si
See Tchicaya, Gerald Felix
See also EWL 3

Teasdale, Sara 1884-1933 .... **PC 31; TCLC 4**
See also CA 104; 163; DLB 45; GLL 1; PFS 14; RGAL 4; SATA 32; TUS

Tecumseh 1768-1813 .... **NNAL**
See also DAM MULT

Tegner, Esaias 1782-1846 .... **NCLC 2**

Fujiwara no Teika 1162-1241 .... **CMLC 73**
See also DLB 203

Teilhard de Chardin, (Marie Joseph) Pierre
1881-1955 .... **TCLC 9**
See also CA 105; 210; GFL 1789 to the Present

Temple, Ann
See Mortimer, Penelope (Ruth)

Tennant, Emma (Christina) 1937- .. **CLC 13, 52**
See also BRWS 9; CA 65-68; CAAS 9; CANR 10, 38, 59, 88; CN 7; DLB 14; EWL 3; SFW 4

Tenneshaw, S. M.
See Silverberg, Robert

Tenney, Tabitha Gilman
1762-1837 .... **NCLC 122**
See also DLB 37, 200

Tennyson, Alfred 1809-1892 ... **NCLC 30, 65, 115; PC 6; WLC**
See also AAYA 50; BRW 4; CDBLB 1832-1890; DA; DA3; DAB; DAC; DAM MST, POET; DLB 32; EXPP; PAB; PFS 1, 2, 4, 11, 15, 19; RGEL 2; TEA; WLIT 4; WP

Teran, Lisa St. Aubin de .... **CLC 36**
See St. Aubin de Teran, Lisa

Terence c. 184B.C.-c. 159B.C. .... **CMLC 14; DC 7**
See also AW 1; CDWLB 1; DLB 211; RGWL 2, 3; TWA

Teresa de Jesus, St. 1515-1582 .... **LC 18**

Terkel, Louis 1912-
See Terkel, Studs
See also CA 57-60; CANR 18, 45, 67, 132; DA3; MTCW 1, 2

Terkel, Studs .... **CLC 38**
See Terkel, Louis
See also AAYA 32; AITN 1; MTCW 2; TUS

Terry, C. V.
See Slaughter, Frank G(ill)

Terry, Megan 1932- .... **CLC 19; DC 13**
See also CA 77-80; CABS 3; CAD; CANR 43; CD 5; CWD; DFS 18; DLB 7, 249; GLL 2

Tertullian c. 155-c. 245 .... **CMLC 29**

Tertz, Abram
See Sinyavsky, Andrei (Donatevich)
See also RGSF 2

Tesich, Steve 1943(?)-1996 .... **CLC 40, 69**
See also CA 105; 152; CAD; DLBY 1983

Tesla, Nikola 1856-1943 .... **TCLC 88**

Teternikov, Fyodor Kuzmich 1863-1927
See Sologub, Fyodor
See also CA 104

Tevis, Walter 1928-1984 .... **CLC 42**
See also CA 113; SFW 4

Tey, Josephine .... **TCLC 14**
See Mackintosh, Elizabeth
See also DLB 77; MSW

Thackeray, William Makepeace
1811-1863 .... **NCLC 5, 14, 22, 43; WLC**
See also BRW 5; BRWC 2; CDBLB 1832-1890; DA; DA3; DAB; DAC; DAM MST, NOV; DLB 21, 55, 159, 163; NFS 13; RGEL 2; SATA 23; TEA; WLIT 3

Thakura, Ravindranatha
See Tagore, Rabindranath

Thames, C. H.
See Marlowe, Stephen

Tharoor, Shashi 1956- .... **CLC 70**
See also CA 141; CANR 91; CN 7

Thelwell, Michael Miles 1939- .... **CLC 22**
See also BW 2; CA 101

Theobald, Lewis, Jr.
See Lovecraft, H(oward) P(hillips)

Theocritus c. 310B.C.- .... **CMLC 45**
See also AW 1; DLB 176; RGWL 2, 3

Theodorescu, Ion N. 1880-1967
See Arghezi, Tudor
See also CA 116

Theriault, Yves 1915-1983 .... **CLC 79**
See also CA 102; CCA 1; DAC; DAM MST; DLB 88; EWL 3

Theroux, Alexander (Louis) 1939- .... **CLC 2, 25**
See also CA 85-88; CANR 20, 63; CN 7

Theroux, Paul (Edward) 1941- ...... **CLC 5, 8, 11, 15, 28, 46**
See also AAYA 28; AMWS 8; BEST 89:4; BPFB 3; CA 33-36R; CANR 20, 45, 74, 133; CDALBS; CN 7; CPW 1; DA3; DAM POP; DLB 2, 218; EWL 3; HGG; MTCW 1, 2; RGAL 4; SATA 44, 109; TUS

Thesen, Sharon 1946- .... **CLC 56**
See also CA 163; CANR 125; CP 7; CWP

Thespis fl. 6th cent. B.C.- .... **CMLC 51**
See also LMFS 1

Thevenin, Denis
See Duhamel, Georges

Thibault, Jacques Anatole Francois
1844-1924
See France, Anatole
See also CA 106; 127; DA3; DAM NOV; MTCW 1, 2; TWA

Thiele, Colin (Milton) 1920- .... **CLC 17**
See also CA 29-32R; CANR 12, 28, 53, 105; CLR 27; DLB 289; MAICYA 1, 2; SAAS 2; SATA 14, 72, 125; YAW

Thistlethwaite, Bel
See Wetherald, Agnes Ethelwyn

Thomas, Audrey (Callahan) 1935- .... **CLC 7, 13, 37, 107; SSC 20**
See also AITN 2; CA 21-24R; CAAS 19; CANR 36, 58; CN 7; DLB 60; MTCW 1; RGSF 2

Thomas, Augustus 1857-1934 .... **TCLC 97**

Thomas, D(onald) M(ichael) 1935- . **CLC 13, 22, 31, 132**
See also BPFB 3; BRWS 4; CA 61-64; CAAS 11; CANR 17, 45, 75; CDBLB 1960 to Present; CN 7; CP 7; DA3; DLB 40, 207, 299; HGG; INT CANR-17; MTCW 1, 2; SFW 4

Thomas, Dylan (Marlais) 1914-1953 .... **PC 2, 52; SSC 3, 44; TCLC 1, 8, 45, 105; WLC**
See also AAYA 45; BRWS 1; CA 104; 120; CANR 65; CDBLB 1945-1960; DA; DA3; DAB; DAC; DAM DRAM, MST, POET; DLB 13, 20, 139; EWL 3; EXPP; LAIT 3; MTCW 1, 2; PAB; PFS 1, 3, 8; RGEL 2; RGSF 2; SATA 60; TEA; WLIT 4; WP

Thomas, (Philip) Edward 1878-1917 . **PC 53; TCLC 10**
See also BRW 6; BRWS 3; CA 106; 153; DAM POET; DLB 19, 98, 156, 216; EWL 3; PAB; RGEL 2

Thomas, Joyce Carol 1938- .... **CLC 35**
See also AAYA 12, 54; BW 2, 3; CA 113; 116; CANR 48, 114, 135; CLR 19; DLB 33; INT CA-116; JRDA; MAICYA 1, 2; MTCW 1, 2; SAAS 7; SATA 40, 78, 123, 137; SATA-Essay 137; WYA; YAW

Thomas, Lewis 1913-1993 .... **CLC 35**
See also ANW; CA 85-88; 143; CANR 38, 60; DLB 275; MTCW 1, 2
Thomas, M. Carey 1857-1935 .... **TCLC 89**
See also FW
Thomas, Paul
See Mann, (Paul) Thomas
Thomas, Piri 1928- .... **CLC 17; HLCS 2**
See also CA 73-76; HW 1; LLW 1
Thomas, R(onald) S(tuart)
1913-2000 .... **CLC 6, 13, 48**
See also CA 89-92; 189; CAAS 4; CANR 30; CDBLB 1960 to Present; CP 7; DAB; DAM POET; DLB 27; EWL 3; MTCW 1; RGEL 2
Thomas, Ross (Elmore) 1926-1995 .. **CLC 39**
See also CA 33-36R; 150; CANR 22, 63; CMW 4
Thompson, Francis (Joseph)
1859-1907 .... **TCLC 4**
See also BRW 5; CA 104; 189; CDBLB 1890-1914; DLB 19; RGEL 2; TEA
Thompson, Francis Clegg
See Mencken, H(enry) L(ouis)
Thompson, Hunter S(tockton)
1937(?)- .... **CLC 9, 17, 40, 104**
See also AAYA 45; BEST 89:1; BPFB 3; CA 17-20R; CANR 23, 46, 74, 77, 111, 133; CPW; CSW; DA3; DAM POP; DLB 185; MTCW 1, 2; TUS
Thompson, James Myers
See Thompson, Jim (Myers)
Thompson, Jim (Myers)
1906-1977(?) .... **CLC 69**
See also BPFB 3; CA 140; CMW 4; CPW; DLB 226; MSW
Thompson, Judith .... **CLC 39**
See also CWD
Thomson, James 1700-1748 .... **LC 16, 29, 40**
See also BRWS 3; DAM POET; DLB 95; RGEL 2
Thomson, James 1834-1882 .... **NCLC 18**
See also DAM POET; DLB 35; RGEL 2
Thoreau, Henry David 1817-1862 .. **NCLC 7, 21, 61, 138; PC 30; WLC**
See also AAYA 42; AMW; ANW; BYA 3; CDALB 1640-1865; DA; DA3; DAB; DAC; DAM MST; DLB 1, 183, 223, 270, 298; LAIT 2; LMFS 1; NCFS 3; RGAL 4; TUS
Thorndike, E. L.
See Thorndike, Edward L(ee)
Thorndike, Edward L(ee)
1874-1949 .... **TCLC 107**
See also CA 121
Thornton, Hall
See Silverberg, Robert
Thorpe, Adam 1956- .... **CLC 176**
See also CA 129; CANR 92; DLB 231
Thubron, Colin (Gerald Dryden)
1939- .... **CLC 163**
See also CA 25-28R; CANR 12, 29, 59, 95; CN 7; DLB 204, 231
Thucydides c. 455B.C.-c. 395B.C. .. **CMLC 17**
See also AW 1; DLB 176; RGWL 2, 3
Thumboo, Edwin Nadason 1933- .... **PC 30**
See also CA 194
Thurber, James (Grover)
1894-1961 .. **CLC 5, 11, 25, 125; SSC 1, 47**
See also AAYA 56; AMWS 1; BPFB 3; BYA 5; CA 73-76; CANR 17, 39; CDALB 1929-1941; CWRI 5; DA; DA3; DAB; DAC; DAM DRAM, MST, NOV; DLB 4, 11, 22, 102; EWL 3; EXPS; FANT; LAIT 3; MAICYA 1, 2; MTCW 1, 2; RGAL 2; RGSF 2; SATA 13; SSFS 1, 10, 19; SUFW; TUS

Thurman, Wallace (Henry)
1902-1934 .... **BLC 3; HR 3; TCLC 6**
See also BW 1, 3; CA 104; 124; CANR 81; DAM MULT; DLB 51
Tibullus c. 54B.C.-c. 18B.C. .... **CMLC 36**
See also AW 2; DLB 211; RGWL 2, 3
Ticheburn, Cheviot
See Ainsworth, William Harrison
Tieck, (Johann) Ludwig
1773-1853 .... **NCLC 5, 46; SSC 31**
See also CDWLB 2; DLB 90; EW 5; IDTP; RGSF 2; RGWL 2, 3; SUFW
Tiger, Derry
See Ellison, Harlan (Jay)
Tilghman, Christopher 1946- .... **CLC 65**
See also CA 159; CANR 135; CSW; DLB 244
Tillich, Paul (Johannes)
1886-1965 .... **CLC 131**
See also CA 5-8R; 25-28R; CANR 33; MTCW 1, 2
Tillinghast, Richard (Williford)
1940- .... **CLC 29**
See also CA 29-32R; CAAS 23; CANR 26, 51, 96; CP 7; CSW
Timrod, Henry 1828-1867 .... **NCLC 25**
See also DLB 3, 248; RGAL 4
Tindall, Gillian (Elizabeth) 1938- ...... **CLC 7**
See also CA 21-24R; CANR 11, 65, 107; CN 7
Tiptree, James, Jr. .... **CLC 48, 50**
See Sheldon, Alice Hastings Bradley
See also DLB 8; SCFW 2; SFW 4
Tirone Smith, Mary-Ann 1944- .... **CLC 39**
See also CA 118; 136; CANR 113; SATA 143
Tirso de Molina 1580(?)-1648 .... **DC 13; HLCS 2; LC 73**
See also RGWL 2, 3
Titmarsh, Michael Angelo
See Thackeray, William Makepeace
Tocqueville, Alexis (Charles Henri Maurice Clerel Comte) de 1805-1859 .. **NCLC 7, 63**
See also EW 6; GFL 1789 to the Present; TWA
Toer, Pramoedya Ananta 1925- ...... **CLC 186**
See also CA 197; RGWL 3
Toffler, Alvin 1928- .... **CLC 168**
See also CA 13-16R; CANR 15, 46, 67; CPW; DAM POP; MTCW 1, 2
Toibin, Colm
See Toibin, Colm
See also DLB 271
Toibin, Colm 1955- .... **CLC 162**
See Toibin, Colm
See also CA 142; CANR 81
Tolkien, J(ohn) R(onald) R(euel)
1892-1973 .... **CLC 1, 2, 3, 8, 12, 38; TCLC 137; WLC**
See also AAYA 10; AITN 1; BPFB 3; BRWC 2; BRWS 2; CA 17-18; 45-48; CANR 36, 134; CAP 2; CDBLB 1914-1945; CLR 56; CPW 1; CWRI 5; DA; DA3; DAB; DAC; DAM MST, NOV, POP; DLB 15, 160, 255; EFS 2; EWL 3; FANT; JRDA; LAIT 1; LATS 1:2; LMFS 2; MAICYA 1, 2; MTCW 1, 2; NFS 8; RGEL 2; SATA 2, 32, 100; SATA-Obit 24; SFW 4; SUFW; TEA; WCH; WYA; YAW
Toller, Ernst 1893-1939 .... **TCLC 10**
See also CA 107; 186; DLB 124; EWL 3; RGWL 2, 3
Tolson, M. B.
See Tolson, Melvin B(eaunorus)

Tolson, Melvin B(eaunorus)
1898(?)-1966 .... **BLC 3; CLC 36, 105**
See also AFAW 1, 2; BW 1, 3; CA 124; 89-92; CANR 80; DAM MULT, POET; DLB 48, 76; RGAL 4
Tolstoi, Aleksei Nikolaevich
See Tolstoy, Alexey Nikolaevich
Tolstoi, Lev
See Tolstoy, Leo (Nikolaevich)
See also RGSF 2; RGWL 2, 3
Tolstoy, Aleksei Nikolaevich
See Tolstoy, Alexey Nikolaevich
See also DLB 272
Tolstoy, Alexey Nikolaevich
1882-1945 .... **TCLC 18**
See Tolstoi, Aleksei Nikolaevich
See also CA 107; 158; EWL 3; SFW 4
Tolstoy, Leo (Nikolaevich)
1828-1910 . **SSC 9, 30, 45, 54; TCLC 4, 11, 17, 28, 44, 79; WLC**
See Tolstoi, Lev
See also AAYA 56; CA 104; 123; DA; DA3; DAB; DAC; DAM MST, NOV; DLB 238; EFS 2; EW 7; EXPS; IDTP; LAIT 2; LATS 1:1; LMFS 1; NFS 10; SATA 26; SSFS 5; TWA
Tolstoy, Count Leo
See Tolstoy, Leo (Nikolaevich)
Tomalin, Claire 1933- .... **CLC 166**
See also CA 89-92; CANR 52, 88; DLB 155
Tomasi di Lampedusa, Giuseppe 1896-1957
See Lampedusa, Giuseppe (Tomasi) di
See also CA 111; DLB 177; EWL 3
Tomlin, Lily .... **CLC 17**
See Tomlin, Mary Jean
Tomlin, Mary Jean 1939(?)-
See Tomlin, Lily
See also CA 117
Tomline, F. Latour
See Gilbert, W(illiam) S(chwenck)
Tomlinson, (Alfred) Charles 1927- .... **CLC 2, 4, 6, 13, 45; PC 17**
See also CA 5-8R; CANR 33; CP 7; DAM POET; DLB 40
Tomlinson, H(enry) M(ajor)
1873-1958 .... **TCLC 71**
See also CA 118; 161; DLB 36, 100, 195
Tonna, Charlotte Elizabeth
1790-1846 .... **NCLC 135**
See also DLB 163
Tonson, Jacob fl. 1655(?)-1736 .... **LC 86**
See also DLB 170
Toole, John Kennedy 1937-1969 ..... **CLC 19, 64**
See also BPFB 3; CA 104; DLBY 1981; MTCW 2
Toomer, Eugene
See Toomer, Jean
Toomer, Eugene Pinchback
See Toomer, Jean
Toomer, Jean 1894-1967 .. **BLC 3; CLC 1, 4, 13, 22; HR 3; PC 7; SSC 1, 45; WLCS**
See also AFAW 1, 2; AMWS 3, 9; BW 1; CA 85-88; CDALB 1917-1929; DA3; DAM MULT; DLB 45, 51; EWL 3; EXPP; EXPS; LMFS 2; MTCW 1, 2; NFS 11; RGAL 4; RGSF 2; SSFS 5
Toomer, Nathan Jean
See Toomer, Jean
Toomer, Nathan Pinchback
See Toomer, Jean
Torley, Luke
See Blish, James (Benjamin)
Tornimparte, Alessandra
See Ginzburg, Natalia
Torre, Raoul della
See Mencken, H(enry) L(ouis)

Torrence, Ridgely 1874-1950 .... **TCLC 97**
See also DLB 54, 249

Torrey, E(dwin) Fuller 1937- .... **CLC 34**
See also CA 119; CANR 71

Torsvan, Ben Traven
See Traven, B.

Torsvan, Benno Traven
See Traven, B.

Torsvan, Berick Traven
See Traven, B.

Torsvan, Berwick Traven
See Traven, B.

Torsvan, Bruno Traven
See Traven, B.

Torsvan, Traven
See Traven, B.

Tourneur, Cyril 1575(?)-1626 .... **LC 66**
See also BRW 2; DAM DRAM; DLB 58; RGEL 2

Tournier, Michel (Edouard) 1924- .... **CLC 6, 23, 36, 95**
See also CA 49-52; CANR 3, 36, 74; CWW 2; DLB 83; EWL 3; GFL 1789 to the Present; MTCW 1, 2; SATA 23

Tournimparte, Alessandra
See Ginzburg, Natalia

Towers, Ivar
See Kornbluth, C(yril) M.

Towne, Robert (Burton) 1936(?)- ..... **CLC 87**
See also CA 108; DLB 44; IDFW 3, 4

Townsend, Sue .... **CLC 61**
See also Townsend, Susan Lilian
See also AAYA 28; CA 119; 127; CANR 65, 107; CBD; CD 5; CPW; CWD; DAB; DAC; DAM MST; DLB 271; INT CA-127; SATA 55, 93; SATA-Brief 48; YAW

Townsend, Susan Lilian 1946-
See Townsend, Sue

Townshend, Pete
See Townshend, Peter (Dennis Blandford)

Townshend, Peter (Dennis Blandford) 1945- .... **CLC 17, 42**
See also CA 107

Tozzi, Federigo 1883-1920 .... **TCLC 31**
See also CA 160; CANR 110; DLB 264; EWL 3

Tracy, Don(ald Fiske) 1905-1970(?)
See Queen, Ellery
See also CA 1-4R; 176; CANR 2

Trafford, F. G.
See Riddell, Charlotte

Traherne, Thomas 1637(?)-1674 .... **LC 99**
See also BRW 2; DLB 131; PAB; RGEL 2

Traill, Catharine Parr 1802-1899 .. **NCLC 31**
See also DLB 99

Trakl, Georg 1887-1914 .... **PC 20; TCLC 5**
See also CA 104; 165; EW 10; EWL 3; LMFS 2; MTCW 2; RGWL 2, 3

Tranquilli, Secondino
See Silone, Ignazio

Transtroemer, Tomas Gosta
See Transtromer, Tomas (Goesta)

Transtromer, Tomas (Gosta)
See Transtromer, Tomas (Goesta)
See also CWW 2

Transtromer, Tomas (Goesta) 1931- .... **CLC 52, 65**
See Transtromer, Tomas (Gosta)
See also CA 117; 129; CAAS 17; CANR 115; DAM POET; DLB 257; EWL 3; PFS 21

Transtromer, Tomas Gosta
See Transtromer, Tomas (Goesta)

Traven, B. 1882(?)-1969 .... **CLC 8, 11**
See also CA 19-20; 25-28R; CAP 2; DLB 9, 56; EWL 3; MTCW 1; RGAL 4

Trediakovsky, Vasilii Kirillovich 1703-1769 .... **LC 68**
See also DLB 150

Treitel, Jonathan 1959- .... **CLC 70**
See also CA 210; DLB 267

Trelawny, Edward John 1792-1881 .... **NCLC 85**
See also DLB 110, 116, 144

Tremain, Rose 1943- .... **CLC 42**
See also CA 97-100; CANR 44, 95; CN 7; DLB 14, 271; RGSF 2; RHW

Tremblay, Michel 1942- .... **CLC 29, 102**
See also CA 116; 128; CCA 1; CWW 2; DAC; DAM MST; DLB 60; EWL 3; GLL 1; MTCW 1, 2

Trevanian .... **CLC 29**
See Whitaker, Rod(ney)

Trevor, Glen
See Hilton, James

Trevor, William .. **CLC 7, 9, 14, 25, 71, 116; SSC 21, 58**
See Cox, William Trevor
See also BRWS 4; CBD; CD 5; CN 7; DLB 14, 139; EWL 3; LATS 1:2; MTCW 2; RGEL 2; RGSF 2; SSFS 10

Trifonov, Iurii (Valentinovich)
See Trifonov, Yuri (Valentinovich)
See also DLB 302; RGWL 2, 3

Trifonov, Yuri (Valentinovich) 1925-1981 .... **CLC 45**
See Trifonov, Iurii (Valentinovich); Trifonov, Yury Valentinovich
See also CA 126; 103; MTCW 1

Trifonov, Yury Valentinovich
See Trifonov, Yuri (Valentinovich)
See also EWL 3

Trilling, Diana (Rubin) 1905-1996 . **CLC 129**
See also CA 5-8R; 154; CANR 10, 46; INT CANR-10; MTCW 1, 2

Trilling, Lionel 1905-1975 ..... **CLC 9, 11, 24; SSC 75**
See also AMWS 3; CA 9-12R; 61-64; CANR 10, 105; DLB 28, 63; EWL 3; INT CANR-10; MTCW 1, 2; RGAL 4; TUS

Trimball, W. H.
See Mencken, H(enry) L(ouis)

Tristan
See Gomez de la Serna, Ramon

Tristram
See Housman, A(lfred) E(dward)

Trogdon, William (Lewis) 1939-
See Heat-Moon, William Least
See also CA 115; 119; CANR 47, 89; CPW; INT CA-119

Trollope, Anthony 1815-1882 .... **NCLC 6, 33, 101; SSC 28; WLC**
See also BRW 5; CDBLB 1832-1890; DA; DA3; DAB; DAC; DAM MST, NOV; DLB 21, 57, 159; RGEL 2; RGSF 2; SATA 22

Trollope, Frances 1779-1863 .... **NCLC 30**
See also DLB 21, 166

Trollope, Joanna 1943- .... **CLC 186**
See also CA 101; CANR 58, 95; CPW; DLB 207; RHW

Trotsky, Leon 1879-1940 .... **TCLC 22**
See also CA 118; 167

Trotter (Cockburn), Catharine 1679-1749 .... **LC 8**
See also DLB 84, 252

Trotter, Wilfred 1872-1939 .... **TCLC 97**

Trout, Kilgore
See Farmer, Philip Jose

Trow, George W. S. 1943- .... **CLC 52**
See also CA 126; CANR 91

Troyat, Henri 1911- .... **CLC 23**
See also CA 45-48; CANR 2, 33, 67, 117; GFL 1789 to the Present; MTCW 1

Trudeau, G(arretson) B(eekman) 1948-
See Trudeau, Garry B.
See also AAYA 60; CA 81-84; CANR 31; SATA 35

Trudeau, Garry B. .... **CLC 12**
See Trudeau, G(arretson) B(eekman)
See also AAYA 10; AITN 2

Truffaut, Francois 1932-1984 ... **CLC 20, 101**
See also CA 81-84; 113; CANR 34

Trumbo, Dalton 1905-1976 .... **CLC 19**
See also CA 21-24R; 69-72; CANR 10; DLB 26; IDFW 3, 4; YAW

Trumbull, John 1750-1831 .... **NCLC 30**
See also DLB 31; RGAL 4

Trundlett, Helen B.
See Eliot, T(homas) S(tearns)

Truth, Sojourner 1797(?)-1883 .... **NCLC 94**
See also DLB 239; FW; LAIT 2

Tryon, Thomas 1926-1991 .... **CLC 3, 11**
See also AITN 1; BPFB 3; CA 29-32R; 135; CANR 32, 77; CPW; DA3; DAM POP; HGG; MTCW 1

Tryon, Tom
See Tryon, Thomas

Ts'ao Hsueh-ch'in 1715(?)-1763 .... **LC 1**

Tsushima, Shuji 1909-1948
See Dazai Osamu
See also CA 107

Tsvetaeva (Efron), Marina (Ivanovna) 1892-1941 .... **PC 14; TCLC 7, 35**
See also CA 104; 128; CANR 73; DLB 295; EW 11; MTCW 1, 2; RGWL 2, 3

Tuck, Lily 1938- .... **CLC 70**
See also CA 139; CANR 90

Tu Fu 712-770 .... **PC 9**
See Du Fu
See also DAM MULT; TWA; WP

Tunis, John R(oberts) 1889-1975 ..... **CLC 12**
See also BYA 1; CA 61-64; CANR 62; DLB 22, 171; JRDA; MAICYA 1, 2; SATA 37; SATA-Brief 30; YAW

Tuohy, Frank .... **CLC 37**
See Tuohy, John Francis
See also DLB 14, 139

Tuohy, John Francis 1925-
See Tuohy, Frank
See also CA 5-8R; 178; CANR 3, 47; CN 7

Turco, Lewis (Putnam) 1934- ..... **CLC 11, 63**
See also CA 13-16R; CAAS 22; CANR 24, 51; CP 7; DLBY 1984

Turgenev, Ivan (Sergeevich) 1818-1883 ...... **DC 7; NCLC 21, 37, 122; SSC 7, 57; WLC**
See also AAYA 58; DA; DAB; DAC; DAM MST, NOV; DFS 6; DLB 238, 284; EW 6; LATS 1:1; NFS 16; RGSF 2; RGWL 2, 3; TWA

Turgot, Anne-Robert-Jacques 1727-1781 .... **LC 26**

Turner, Frederick 1943- .... **CLC 48**
See also CA 73-76, 227; CAAE 227; CAAS 10; CANR 12, 30, 56; DLB 40, 282

Turton, James
See Crace, Jim

Tutu, Desmond M(pilo) 1931- .. **BLC 3; CLC 80**
See also BW 1, 3; CA 125; CANR 67, 81; DAM MULT

Tutuola, Amos 1920-1997 ..... **BLC 3; CLC 5, 14, 29**
See also AFW; BW 2, 3; CA 9-12R; 159; CANR 27, 66; CDWLB 3; CN 7; DA3; DAM MULT; DLB 125; DNFS 2; EWL 3; MTCW 1, 2; RGEL 2; WLIT 2

Twain, Mark .... SSC 6, 26, 34; TCLC 6, 12, 19, 36, 48, 59, 161; WLC
See Clemens, Samuel Langhorne
See also AAYA 20; AMW; AMWC 1; BPFB 3; BYA 2, 3, 11, 14; CLR 58, 60, 66; DLB 11; EXPN; EXPS; FANT; LAIT 2; NCFS 4; NFS 1, 6; RGAL 4; RGSF 2; SFW 4; SSFS 1, 7; SUFW; TUS; WCH; WYA; YAW

Tyler, Anne 1941- . CLC 7, 11, 18, 28, 44, 59, 103, 205
See also AAYA 18, 60; AMWS 4; BEST 89:1; BPFB 3; BYA 12; CA 9-12R; CANR 11, 33, 53, 109, 132; CDALBS; CN 7; CPW; CSW; DAM NOV, POP; DLB 6, 143; DLBY 1982; EWL 3; EXPN; LATS 1:2; MAWW; MTCW 1, 2; NFS 2, 7, 10; RGAL 4; SATA 7, 90; SSFS 17; TUS; YAW

Tyler, Royall 1757-1826 .... NCLC 3
See also DLB 37; RGAL 4

Tynan, Katharine 1861-1931 .... TCLC 3
See also CA 104; 167; DLB 153, 240; FW

Tyndale, William c. 1484-1536 .... LC 103
See also DLB 132

Tyutchev, Fyodor 1803-1873 .... NCLC 34

Tzara, Tristan 1896-1963 ..... CLC 47; PC 27
See also CA 153; 89-92; DAM POET; EWL 3; MTCW 2

Uchida, Yoshiko 1921-1992 .... AAL
See also AAYA 16; BYA 2, 3; CA 13-16R; 139; CANR 6, 22, 47, 61; CDALBS; CLR 6, 56; CWRI 5; JRDA; MAICYA 1, 2; MTCW 1, 2; SAAS 1; SATA 1, 53; SATA-Obit 72

Udall, Nicholas 1504-1556 .... LC 84
See also DLB 62; RGEL 2

Ueda Akinari 1734-1809 .... NCLC 131

Uhry, Alfred 1936- .... CLC 55
See also CA 127; 133; CAD; CANR 112; CD 5; CSW; DA3; DAM DRAM, POP; DFS 11, 15; INT CA-133

Ulf, Haerved
See Strindberg, (Johan) August

Ulf, Harved
See Strindberg, (Johan) August

Ulibarri, Sabine R(eyes)
1919-2003 .... CLC 83; HLCS 2
See also CA 131; 214; CANR 81; DAM MULT; DLB 82; HW 1, 2; RGSF 2

Unamuno (y Jugo), Miguel de
1864-1936 .. HLC 2; SSC 11, 69; TCLC 2, 9, 148
See also CA 104; 131; CANR 81; DAM MULT, NOV; DLB 108; EW 8; EWL 3; HW 1, 2; MTCW 1, 2; RGSF 2; RGWL 2, 3; SSFS 20; TWA

Uncle Shelby
See Silverstein, Shel(don Allan)

Undercliffe, Errol
See Campbell, (John) Ramsey

Underwood, Miles
See Glassco, John

Undset, Sigrid 1882-1949 ..... TCLC 3; WLC
See also CA 104; 129; DA; DA3; DAB; DAC; DAM MST, NOV; DLB 293; EW 9; EWL 3; FW; MTCW 1, 2; RGWL 2, 3

Ungaretti, Giuseppe 1888-1970 ... CLC 7, 11, 15; PC 57
See also CA 19-20; 25-28R; CAP 2; DLB 114; EW 10; EWL 3; PFS 20; RGWL 2, 3

Unger, Douglas 1952- .... CLC 34
See also CA 130; CANR 94

Unsworth, Barry (Forster) 1930- .... CLC 76, 127
See also BRWS 7; CA 25-28R; CANR 30, 54, 125; CN 7; DLB 194

Updike, John (Hoyer) 1932- . CLC 1, 2, 3, 5, 7, 9, 13, 15, 23, 34, 43, 70, 139; SSC 13, 27; WLC
See also AAYA 36; AMW; AMWC 1; AMWR 1; BPFB 3; BYA 12; CA 1-4R; CABS 1; CANR 4, 33, 51, 94, 133; CDALB 1968-1988; CN 7; CP 7; CPW 1; DA; DA3; DAB; DAC; DAM MST, NOV, POET, POP; DLB 2, 5, 143, 218, 227; DLBD 3; DLBY 1980, 1982, 1997; EWL 3; EXPP; HGG; MTCW 1, 2; NFS 12; RGAL 4; RGSF 2; SSFS 3, 19; TUS

Upshaw, Margaret Mitchell
See Mitchell, Margaret (Munnerlyn)

Upton, Mark
See Sanders, Lawrence

Upward, Allen 1863-1926 .... TCLC 85
See also CA 117; 187; DLB 36

Urdang, Constance (Henriette)
1922-1996 .... CLC 47
See also CA 21-24R; CANR 9, 24; CP 7; CWP

Uriel, Henry
See Faust, Frederick (Schiller)

Uris, Leon (Marcus) 1924-2003 ... CLC 7, 32
See also AITN 1, 2; BEST 89:2; BPFB 3; CA 1-4R; 217; CANR 1, 40, 65, 123; CN 7; CPW 1; DA3; DAM NOV, POP; MTCW 1, 2; SATA 49; SATA-Obit 146

Urista (Heredia), Alberto (Baltazar)
1947- .... HLCS 1; PC 34
See Alurista
See also CA 45-48, 182; CANR 2, 32; HW 1

Urmuz
See Codrescu, Andrei

Urquhart, Guy
See McAlmon, Robert (Menzies)

Urquhart, Jane 1949- .... CLC 90
See also CA 113; CANR 32, 68, 116; CCA 1; DAC

Usigli, Rodolfo 1905-1979 .... HLCS 1
See also CA 131; DLB 305; EWL 3; HW 1; LAW

Ustinov, Peter (Alexander)
1921-2004 .... CLC 1
See also AITN 1; CA 13-16R; 225; CANR 25, 51; CBD; CD 5; DLB 13; MTCW 2

U Tam'si, Gerald Felix Tchicaya
See Tchicaya, Gerald Felix

U Tam'si, Tchicaya
See Tchicaya, Gerald Felix

Vachss, Andrew (Henry) 1942- .... CLC 106
See also CA 118; 214; CAAE 214; CANR 44, 95; CMW 4

Vachss, Andrew H.
See Vachss, Andrew (Henry)

Vaculik, Ludvik 1926- .... CLC 7
See also CA 53-56; CANR 72; CWW 2; DLB 232; EWL 3

Vaihinger, Hans 1852-1933 .... TCLC 71
See also CA 116; 166

Valdez, Luis (Miguel) 1940- ..... CLC 84; DC 10; HLC 2
See also CA 101; CAD; CANR 32, 81; CD 5; DAM MULT; DFS 5; DLB 122; EWL 3; HW 1; LAIT 4; LLW 1

Valenzuela, Luisa 1938- .... CLC 31, 104; HLCS 2; SSC 14
See also CA 101; CANR 32, 65, 123; CD-WLB 3; CWW 2; DAM MULT; DLB 113; EWL 3; FW; HW 1, 2; LAW; RGSF 2; RGWL 3

Valera y Alcala-Galiano, Juan
1824-1905 .... TCLC 10
See also CA 106

Valerius Maximus fl. 20- .... CMLC 64
See also DLB 211

Valery, (Ambroise) Paul (Toussaint Jules)
1871-1945 .... PC 9; TCLC 4, 15
See also CA 104; 122; DA3; DAM POET; DLB 258; EW 8; EWL 3; GFL 1789 to the Present; MTCW 1, 2; RGWL 2, 3; TWA

Valle-Inclan, Ramon (Maria) del
1866-1936 .... HLC 2; TCLC 5
See also CA 106; 153; CANR 80; DAM MULT; DLB 134; EW 8; EWL 3; HW 2; RGSF 2; RGWL 2, 3

Vallejo, Antonio Buero
See Buero Vallejo, Antonio

Vallejo, Cesar (Abraham)
1892-1938 .... HLC 2; TCLC 3, 56
See also CA 105; 153; DAM MULT; DLB 290; EWL 3; HW 1; LAW; RGWL 2, 3

Valles, Jules 1832-1885 .... NCLC 71
See also DLB 123; GFL 1789 to the Present

Vallette, Marguerite Eymery
1860-1953 .... TCLC 67
See Rachilde
See also CA 182; DLB 123, 192

Valle Y Pena, Ramon del
See Valle-Inclan, Ramon (Maria) del

Van Ash, Cay 1918-1994 .... CLC 34
See also CA 220

Vanbrugh, Sir John 1664-1726 .... LC 21
See also BRW 2; DAM DRAM; DLB 80; IDTP; RGEL 2

Van Campen, Karl
See Campbell, John W(ood, Jr.)

Vance, Gerald
See Silverberg, Robert

Vance, Jack .... CLC 35
See Vance, John Holbrook
See also DLB 8; FANT; SCFW 2; SFW 4; SUFW 1, 2

Vance, John Holbrook 1916-
See Queen, Ellery; Vance, Jack
See also CA 29-32R; CANR 17, 65; CMW 4; MTCW 1

Van Den Bogarde, Derek Jules Gaspard Ulric Niven 1921-1999 .... CLC 14
See Bogarde, Dirk
See also CA 77-80; 179

Vandenburgh, Jane .... CLC 59
See also CA 168

Vanderhaeghe, Guy 1951- .... CLC 41
See also BPFB 3; CA 113; CANR 72

van der Post, Laurens (Jan)
1906-1996 .... CLC 5
See also AFW; CA 5-8R; 155; CANR 35; CN 7; DLB 204; RGEL 2

van de Wetering, Janwillem 1931- ... CLC 47
See also CA 49-52; CANR 4, 62, 90; CMW 4

Van Dine, S. S. .... TCLC 23
See Wright, Willard Huntington
See also DLB 306; MSW

Van Doren, Carl (Clinton)
1885-1950 .... TCLC 18
See also CA 111; 168

Van Doren, Mark 1894-1972 .... CLC 6, 10
See also CA 1-4R; 37-40R; CANR 3; DLB 45, 284; MTCW 1, 2; RGAL 4

Van Druten, John (William)
1901-1957 .... TCLC 2
See also CA 104; 161; DLB 10; RGAL 4

Van Duyn, Mona (Jane) 1921- ...... CLC 3, 7, 63, 116
See also CA 9-12R; CANR 7, 38, 60, 116; CP 7; CWP; DAM POET; DLB 5; PFS 20

Van Dyne, Edith
See Baum, L(yman) Frank

van Itallie, Jean-Claude 1936- .... CLC 3
See also CA 45-48; CAAS 2; CAD; CANR 1, 48; CD 5; DLB 7

Van Loot, Cornelius Obenchain
See Roberts, Kenneth (Lewis)

van Ostaijen, Paul 1896-1928 .... **TCLC 33**
See also CA 163

Van Peebles, Melvin 1932- .... **CLC 2, 20**
See also BW 2, 3; CA 85-88; CANR 27, 67, 82; DAM MULT

van Schendel, Arthur(-Francois-Emile) 1874-1946 .... **TCLC 56**
See also EWL 3

Vansittart, Peter 1920- .... **CLC 42**
See also CA 1-4R; CANR 3, 49, 90; CN 7; RHW

Van Vechten, Carl 1880-1964 ... **CLC 33; HR 3**
See also AMWS 2; CA 183; 89-92; DLB 4, 9, 51; RGAL 4

van Vogt, A(lfred) E(lton) 1912-2000 . **CLC 1**
See also BPFB 3; BYA 13, 14; CA 21-24R; 190; CANR 28; DLB 8, 251; SATA 14; SATA-Obit 124; SCFW; SFW 4

Vara, Madeleine
See Jackson, Laura (Riding)

Varda, Agnes 1928- .... **CLC 16**
See also CA 116; 122

Vargas Llosa, (Jorge) Mario (Pedro) 1939- .... **CLC 3, 6, 9, 10, 15, 31, 42, 85, 181; HLC 2**
See Llosa, (Jorge) Mario (Pedro) Vargas
See also BPFB 3; CA 73-76; CANR 18, 32, 42, 67, 116; CDWLB 3; CWW 2; DA; DA3; DAB; DAC; DAM MST, MULT, NOV; DLB 145; DNFS 2; EWL 3; HW 1, 2; LAIT 5; LATS 1:2; LAW; LAWS 1; MTCW 1, 2; RGWL 2; SSFS 14; TWA; WLIT 1

Varnhagen von Ense, Rahel 1771-1833 .... **NCLC 130**
See also DLB 90

Vasari, Giorgio 1511-1574 .... **LC 114**

Vasiliu, George
See Bacovia, George

Vasiliu, Gheorghe
See Bacovia, George
See also CA 123; 189

Vassa, Gustavus
See Equiano, Olaudah

Vassilikos, Vassilis 1933- .... **CLC 4, 8**
See also CA 81-84; CANR 75; EWL 3

Vaughan, Henry 1621-1695 .... **LC 27**
See also BRW 2; DLB 131; PAB; RGEL 2

Vaughn, Stephanie .... **CLC 62**

Vazov, Ivan (Minchov) 1850-1921 . **TCLC 25**
See also CA 121; 167; CDWLB 4; DLB 147

Veblen, Thorstein B(unde) 1857-1929 .... **TCLC 31**
See also AMWS 1; CA 115; 165; DLB 246

Vega, Lope de 1562-1635 .... **HLCS 2; LC 23**
See also EW 2; RGWL 2, 3

Vendler, Helen (Hennessy) 1933- ... **CLC 138**
See also CA 41-44R; CANR 25, 72; MTCW 1, 2

Venison, Alfred
See Pound, Ezra (Weston Loomis)

Ventsel, Elena Sergeevna 1907-2002
See Grekova, I.
See also CA 154

Verdi, Marie de
See Mencken, H(enry) L(ouis)

Verdu, Matilde
See Cela, Camilo Jose

Verga, Giovanni (Carmelo) 1840-1922 .... **SSC 21; TCLC 3**
See also CA 104; 123; CANR 101; EW 7; EWL 3; RGSF 2; RGWL 2, 3

Vergil 70B.C.-19B.C. ... **CMLC 9, 40; PC 12; WLCS**
See Virgil
See also AW 2; DA; DA3; DAB; DAC; DAM MST, POET; EFS 1; LMFS 1

Vergil, Polydore c. 1470-1555 .... **LC 108**
See also DLB 132

Verhaeren, Emile (Adolphe Gustave) 1855-1916 .... **TCLC 12**
See also CA 109; EWL 3; GFL 1789 to the Present

Verlaine, Paul (Marie) 1844-1896 .. **NCLC 2, 51; PC 2, 32**
See also DAM POET; DLB 217; EW 7; GFL 1789 to the Present; LMFS 2; RGWL 2, 3; TWA

Verne, Jules (Gabriel) 1828-1905 ... **TCLC 6, 52**
See also AAYA 16; BYA 4; CA 110; 131; CLR 88; DA3; DLB 123; GFL 1789 to the Present; JRDA; LAIT 2; LMFS 2; MAICYA 1, 2; RGWL 2, 3; SATA 21; SCFW; SFW 4; TWA; WCH

Verus, Marcus Annius
See Aurelius, Marcus

Very, Jones 1813-1880 .... **NCLC 9**
See also DLB 1, 243; RGAL 4

Vesaas, Tarjei 1897-1970 .... **CLC 48**
See also CA 190; 29-32R; DLB 297; EW 11; EWL 3; RGWL 3

Vialis, Gaston
See Simenon, Georges (Jacques Christian)

Vian, Boris 1920-1959(?) .... **TCLC 9**
See also CA 106; 164; CANR 111; DLB 72; EWL 3; GFL 1789 to the Present; MTCW 2; RGWL 2, 3

Viaud, (Louis Marie) Julien 1850-1923
See Loti, Pierre
See also CA 107

Vicar, Henry
See Felsen, Henry Gregor

Vicente, Gil 1465-c. 1536 .... **LC 99**
See also DLB 287; RGWL 2, 3

Vicker, Angus
See Felsen, Henry Gregor

Vidal, (Eugene Luther) Gore 1925- .. **CLC 2, 4, 6, 8, 10, 22, 33, 72, 142**
See Box, Edgar
See also AITN 1; AMWS 4; BEST 90:2; BPFB 3; CA 5-8R; CAD; CANR 13, 45, 65, 100, 132; CD 5; CDALBS; CN 7; CPW; DA3; DAM NOV, POP; DFS 2; DLB 6, 152; EWL 3; INT CANR-13; MTCW 1, 2; RGAL 4; RHW; TUS

Viereck, Peter (Robert Edwin) 1916- .... **CLC 4; PC 27**
See also CA 1-4R; CANR 1, 47; CP 7; DLB 5; PFS 9, 14

Vigny, Alfred (Victor) de 1797-1863 .... **NCLC 7, 102; PC 26**
See also DAM POET; DLB 119, 192, 217; EW 5; GFL 1789 to the Present; RGWL 2, 3

Vilakazi, Benedict Wallet 1906-1947 .... **TCLC 37**
See also CA 168

Villa, Jose Garcia 1914-1997 .... **AAL; PC 22**
See also CA 25-28R; CANR 12, 118; EWL 3; EXPP

Villa, Jose Garcia 1914-1997
See Villa, Jose Garcia

Villa, Jose Garcia 1914-1997 .... **AAL; PC 22**
See also CA 25-28R; CANR 12, 118; EWL 3; EXPP

Villard, Oswald Garrison 1872-1949 .... **TCLC 160**
See also CA 113, 162; DLB 25, 91

Villaurrutia, Xavier 1903-1950 ...... **TCLC 80**
See also CA 192; EWL 3; HW 1; LAW

Villaverde, Cirilo 1812-1894 .... **NCLC 121**
See also LAW

Villehardouin, Geoffroi de 1150(?)-1218(?) .... **CMLC 38**

Villiers, George 1628-1687 .... **LC 107**
See also DLB 80; RGEL 2

Villiers de l'Isle Adam, Jean Marie Mathias Philippe Auguste 1838-1889 ... **NCLC 3; SSC 14**
See also DLB 123, 192; GFL 1789 to the Present; RGSF 2

Villon, Francois 1431-1463(?) . **LC 62; PC 13**
See also DLB 208; EW 2; RGWL 2, 3; TWA

Vine, Barbara .... **CLC 50**
See Rendell, Ruth (Barbara)
See also BEST 90:4

Vinge, Joan (Carol) D(ennison) 1948- .... **CLC 30; SSC 24**
See also AAYA 32; BPFB 3; CA 93-96; CANR 72; SATA 36, 113; SFW 4; YAW

Viola, Herman J(oseph) 1938- .... **CLC 70**
See also CA 61-64; CANR 8, 23, 48, 91; SATA 126

Violis, G.
See Simenon, Georges (Jacques Christian)

Viramontes, Helena Maria 1954- .... **HLCS 2**
See also CA 159; DLB 122; HW 2; LLW 1

Virgil
See Vergil
See also CDWLB 1; DLB 211; LAIT 1; RGWL 2, 3; WP

Visconti, Luchino 1906-1976 .... **CLC 16**
See also CA 81-84; 65-68; CANR 39

Vitry, Jacques de
See Jacques de Vitry

Vittorini, Elio 1908-1966 .... **CLC 6, 9, 14**
See also CA 133; 25-28R; DLB 264; EW 12; EWL 3; RGWL 2, 3

Vivekananda, Swami 1863-1902 .... **TCLC 88**

Vizenor, Gerald Robert 1934- .... **CLC 103; NNAL**
See also CA 13-16R, 205; CAAE 205; CAAS 22; CANR 5, 21, 44, 67; DAM MULT; DLB 175, 227; MTCW 2; TCWW 2

Vizinczey, Stephen 1933- .... **CLC 40**
See also CA 128; CCA 1; INT CA-128

Vliet, R(ussell) G(ordon) 1929-1984 .... **CLC 22**
See also CA 37-40R; 112; CANR 18

Vogau, Boris Andreyevich 1894-1938
See Pilnyak, Boris
See also CA 123; 218

Vogel, Paula A(nne) 1951- ... **CLC 76; DC 19**
See also CA 108; CAD; CANR 119; CD 5; CWD; DFS 14; RGAL 4

Voigt, Cynthia 1942- .... **CLC 30**
See also AAYA 3, 30; BYA 1, 3, 6, 7, 8; CA 106; CANR 18, 37, 40, 94; CLR 13, 48; INT CANR-18; JRDA; LAIT 5; MAICYA 1, 2; MAICYAS 1; SATA 48, 79, 116; SATA-Brief 33; WYA; YAW

Voigt, Ellen Bryant 1943- .... **CLC 54**
See also CA 69-72; CANR 11, 29, 55, 115; CP 7; CSW; CWP; DLB 120

Voinovich, Vladimir (Nikolaevich) 1932- .... **CLC 10, 49, 147**
See also CA 81-84; CAAS 12; CANR 33, 67; CWW 2; DLB 302; MTCW 1

Vollmann, William T. 1959- .... **CLC 89**
See also CA 134; CANR 67, 116; CPW; DA3; DAM NOV, POP; MTCW 2

Voloshinov, V. N.
See Bakhtin, Mikhail Mikhailovich

Voltaire 1694-1778 . **LC 14, 79, 110; SSC 12; WLC**
See also BYA 13; DA; DA3; DAB; DAC; DAM DRAM, MST; EW 4; GFL Beginnings to 1789; LATS 1:1; LMFS 1; NFS 7; RGWL 2, 3; TWA

von Aschendrof, Baron Ignatz
See Ford, Ford Madox

von Chamisso, Adelbert
See Chamisso, Adelbert von

von Daeniken, Erich 1935- .... **CLC 30**
See also AITN 1; CA 37-40R; CANR 17, 44

von Daniken, Erich
See von Daeniken, Erich

von Hartmann, Eduard
1842-1906 .... **TCLC 96**

von Hayek, Friedrich August
See Hayek, F(riedrich) A(ugust von)

von Heidenstam, (Carl Gustaf) Verner
See Heidenstam, (Carl Gustaf) Verner von

von Heyse, Paul (Johann Ludwig)
See Heyse, Paul (Johann Ludwig von)

von Hofmannsthal, Hugo
See Hofmannsthal, Hugo von

von Horvath, Odon
See von Horvath, Odon

von Horvath, Odon
See von Horvath, Odon

von Horvath, Odon 1901-1938 .... **TCLC 45**
See von Horvath, Oedoen
See also CA 118; 194; DLB 85, 124; RGWL 2, 3

von Horvath, Oedoen
See von Horvath, Odon
See also CA 184

von Kleist, Heinrich
See Kleist, Heinrich von

von Liliencron, (Friedrich Adolf Axel) Detlev
See Liliencron, (Friedrich Adolf Axel) Detlev von

Vonnegut, Kurt, Jr. 1922- . **CLC 1, 2, 3, 4, 5, 8, 12, 22, 40, 60, 111; SSC 8; WLC**
See also AAYA 6, 44; AITN 1; AMWS 2; BEST 90:4; BPFB 3; BYA 3, 14; CA 1-4R; CANR 1, 25, 49, 75, 92; CDALB 1968-1988; CN 7; CPW 1; DA; DA3; DAB; DAC; DAM MST, NOV, POP; DLB 2, 8, 152; DLBD 3; DLBY 1980; EWL 3; EXPN; EXPS; LAIT 4; LMFS 2; MTCW 1, 2; NFS 3; RGAL 4; SCFW; SFW 4; SSFS 5; TUS; YAW

Von Rachen, Kurt
See Hubbard, L(afayette) Ron(ald)

von Rezzori (d'Arezzo), Gregor
See Rezzori (d'Arezzo), Gregor von

von Sternberg, Josef
See Sternberg, Josef von

Vorster, Gordon 1924- .... **CLC 34**
See also CA 133

Vosce, Trudie
See Ozick, Cynthia

Voznesensky, Andrei (Andreievich)
1933- .... **CLC 1, 15, 57**
See Voznesensky, Andrey
See also CA 89-92; CANR 37; CWW 2; DAM POET; MTCW 1

Voznesensky, Andrey
See Voznesensky, Andrei (Andreievich)
See also EWL 3

Wace, Robert c. 1100-c. 1175 .... **CMLC 55**
See also DLB 146

Waddington, Miriam 1917-2004 .... **CLC 28**
See also CA 21-24R; 225; CANR 12, 30; CCA 1; CP 7; DLB 68

Wagman, Fredrica 1937- .... **CLC 7**
See also CA 97-100; INT CA-97-100

Wagner, Linda W.
See Wagner-Martin, Linda (C.)

Wagner, Linda Welshimer
See Wagner-Martin, Linda (C.)

Wagner, Richard 1813-1883 ..... **NCLC 9, 119**
See also DLB 129; EW 6

Wagner-Martin, Linda (C.) 1936- .... **CLC 50**
See also CA 159; CANR 135

Wagoner, David (Russell) 1926- .... **CLC 3, 5, 15; PC 33**
See also AMWS 9; CA 1-4R; CAAS 3; CANR 2, 71; CN 7; CP 7; DLB 5, 256; SATA 14; TCWW 2

Wah, Fred(erick James) 1939- .... **CLC 44**
See also CA 107; 141; CP 7; DLB 60

Wahloo, Per 1926-1975 .... **CLC 7**
See also BPFB 3; CA 61-64; CANR 73; CMW 4; MSW

Wahloo, Peter
See Wahloo, Per

Wain, John (Barrington) 1925-1994 . **CLC 2, 11, 15, 46**
See also CA 5-8R; 145; CAAS 4; CANR 23, 54; CDBLB 1960 to Present; DLB 15, 27, 139, 155; EWL 3; MTCW 1, 2

Wajda, Andrzej 1926- .... **CLC 16**
See also CA 102

Wakefield, Dan 1932- .... **CLC 7**
See also CA 21-24R, 211; CAAE 211; CAAS 7; CN 7

Wakefield, Herbert Russell
1888-1965 .... **TCLC 120**
See also CA 5-8R; CANR 77; HGG; SUFW

Wakoski, Diane 1937- ...... **CLC 2, 4, 7, 9, 11, 40; PC 15**
See also CA 13-16R, 216; CAAE 216; CAAS 1; CANR 9, 60, 106; CP 7; CWP; DAM POET; DLB 5; INT CANR-9; MTCW 2

Wakoski-Sherbell, Diane
See Wakoski, Diane

Walcott, Derek (Alton) 1930- ... **BLC 3; CLC 2, 4, 9, 14, 25, 42, 67, 76, 160; DC 7; PC 46**
See also BW 2; CA 89-92; CANR 26, 47, 75, 80, 130; CBD; CD 5; CDWLB 3; CP 7; DA3; DAB; DAC; DAM MST, MULT, POET; DLB 117; DLBY 1981; DNFS 1; EFS 1; EWL 3; LMFS 2; MTCW 1, 2; PFS 6; RGEL 2; TWA; WWE 1

Waldman, Anne (Lesley) 1945- .... **CLC 7**
See also BG 3; CA 37-40R; CAAS 17; CANR 34, 69, 116; CP 7; CWP; DLB 16

Waldo, E. Hunter
See Sturgeon, Theodore (Hamilton)

Waldo, Edward Hamilton
See Sturgeon, Theodore (Hamilton)

Walker, Alice (Malsenior) 1944- .... **BLC 3; CLC 5, 6, 9, 19, 27, 46, 58, 103, 167; PC 30; SSC 5; WLCS**
See also AAYA 3, 33; AFAW 1, 2; AMWS 3; BEST 89:4; BPFB 3; BW 2, 3; CA 37-40R; CANR 9, 27, 49, 66, 82, 131; CDALB 1968-1988; CN 7; CPW; CSW; DA; DA3; DAB; DAC; DAM MST, MULT, NOV, POET, POP; DLB 6, 33, 143; EWL 3; EXPN; EXPS; FW; INT CANR-27; LAIT 3; MAWW; MTCW 1, 2; NFS 5; RGAL 4; RGSF 2; SATA 31; SSFS 2, 11; TUS; YAW

Walker, David Harry 1911-1992 ...... **CLC 14**
See also CA 1-4R; 137; CANR 1; CWRI 5; SATA 8; SATA-Obit 71

Walker, Edward Joseph 1934-2004
See Walker, Ted
See also CA 21-24R; 226; CANR 12, 28, 53; CP 7

Walker, George F. 1947- .... **CLC 44, 61**
See also CA 103; CANR 21, 43, 59; CD 5; DAB; DAC; DAM MST; DLB 60

Walker, Joseph A. 1935- .... **CLC 19**
See also BW 1, 3; CA 89-92; CAD; CANR 26; CD 5; DAM DRAM, MST; DFS 12; DLB 38

Walker, Margaret (Abigail)
1915-1998 .... **BLC; CLC 1, 6; PC 20; TCLC 129**
See also AFAW 1, 2; BW 2, 3; CA 73-76; 172; CANR 26, 54, 76; CN 7; CP 7; CSW; DAM MULT; DLB 76, 152; EXPP; FW; MTCW 1, 2; RGAL 4; RHW

Walker, Ted .... **CLC 13**
See Walker, Edward Joseph
See also DLB 40

Wallace, David Foster 1962- ... **CLC 50, 114; SSC 68**
See also AAYA 50; AMWS 10; CA 132; CANR 59, 133; DA3; MTCW 2

Wallace, Dexter
See Masters, Edgar Lee

Wallace, (Richard Horatio) Edgar
1875-1932 .... **TCLC 57**
See also CA 115; 218; CMW 4; DLB 70; MSW; RGEL 2

Wallace, Irving 1916-1990 .... **CLC 7, 13**
See also AITN 1; BPFB 3; CA 1-4R; 132; CAAS 1; CANR 1, 27; CPW; DAM NOV, POP; INT CANR-27; MTCW 1, 2

Wallant, Edward Lewis 1926-1962 ... **CLC 5, 10**
See also CA 1-4R; CANR 22; DLB 2, 28, 143, 299; EWL 3; MTCW 1, 2; RGAL 4

Wallas, Graham 1858-1932 .... **TCLC 91**

Waller, Edmund 1606-1687 .... **LC 86**
See also BRW 2; DAM POET; DLB 126; PAB; RGEL 2

Walley, Byron
See Card, Orson Scott

Walpole, Horace 1717-1797 .... **LC 2, 49**
See also BRW 3; DLB 39, 104, 213; HGG; LMFS 1; RGEL 2; SUFW 1; TEA

Walpole, Hugh (Seymour)
1884-1941 .... **TCLC 5**
See also CA 104; 165; DLB 34; HGG; MTCW 2; RGEL 2; RHW

Walrond, Eric (Derwent) 1898-1966 ..... **HR 3**
See also BW 1; CA 125; DLB 51

Walser, Martin 1927- .... **CLC 27, 183**
See also CA 57-60; CANR 8, 46; CWW 2; DLB 75, 124; EWL 3

Walser, Robert 1878-1956 ..... **SSC 20; TCLC 18**
See also CA 118; 165; CANR 100; DLB 66; EWL 3

Walsh, Gillian Paton
See Paton Walsh, Gillian

Walsh, Jill Paton .... **CLC 35**
See Paton Walsh, Gillian
See also CLR 2, 65; WYA

Walter, Villiam Christian
See Andersen, Hans Christian

Walters, Anna L(ee) 1946- .... **NNAL**
See also CA 73-76

Walther von der Vogelweide c.
1170-1228 .... **CMLC 56**

Walton, Izaak 1593-1683 .... **LC 72**
See also BRW 2; CDBLB Before 1660; DLB 151, 213; RGEL 2

Wambaugh, Joseph (Aloysius), Jr.
1937- .... **CLC 3, 18**
See also AITN 1; BEST 89:3; BPFB 3; CA 33-36R; CANR 42, 65, 115; CMW 4; CPW 1; DA3; DAM NOV, POP; DLB 6; DLBY 1983; MSW; MTCW 1, 2

Wang Wei 699(?)-761(?) .... **PC 18**
See also TWA

Warburton, William 1698-1779 .... **LC 97**
See also DLB 104

Ward, Arthur Henry Sarsfield 1883-1959
See Rohmer, Sax
See also CA 108; 173; CMW 4; HGG

Ward, Douglas Turner 1930- .... **CLC 19**
See also BW 1; CA 81-84; CAD; CANR 27; CD 5; DLB 7, 38

Ward, E. D.
See Lucas, E(dward) V(errall)

Ward, Mrs. Humphry 1851-1920
See Ward, Mary Augusta
See also RGEL 2

Ward, Mary Augusta 1851-1920 ... **TCLC 55**
See Ward, Mrs. Humphry
See also DLB 18

Ward, Nathaniel 1578(?)-1652 .... **LC 114**
See also DLB 24

Ward, Peter
See Faust, Frederick (Schiller)

Warhol, Andy 1928(?)-1987 .... **CLC 20**
See also AAYA 12; BEST 89:4; CA 89-92; 121; CANR 34

Warner, Francis (Robert le Plastrier)
1937- .... **CLC 14**
See also CA 53-56; CANR 11

Warner, Marina 1946- .... **CLC 59**
See also CA 65-68; CANR 21, 55, 118; CN 7; DLB 194

Warner, Rex (Ernest) 1905-1986 ...... **CLC 45**
See also CA 89-92; 119; DLB 15; RGEL 2; RHW

Warner, Susan (Bogert)
1819-1885 .... **NCLC 31, 146**
See also DLB 3, 42, 239, 250, 254

Warner, Sylvia (Constance) Ashton
See Ashton-Warner, Sylvia (Constance)

Warner, Sylvia Townsend
1893-1978 .. **CLC 7, 19; SSC 23; TCLC 131**
See also BRWS 7; CA 61-64; 77-80; CANR 16, 60, 104; DLB 34, 139; EWL 3; FANT; FW; MTCW 1, 2; RGEL 2; RGSF 2; RHW

Warren, Mercy Otis 1728-1814 ..... **NCLC 13**
See also DLB 31, 200; RGAL 4; TUS

Warren, Robert Penn 1905-1989 .. **CLC 1, 4, 6, 8, 10, 13, 18, 39, 53, 59; PC 37; SSC 4, 58; WLC**
See also AITN 1; AMW; AMWC 2; BPFB 3; BYA 1; CA 13-16R; 129; CANR 10, 47; CDALB 1968-1988; DA; DA3; DAB; DAC; DAM MST, NOV, POET; DLB 2, 48, 152; DLBY 1980, 1989; EWL 3; INT CANR-10; MTCW 1, 2; NFS 13; RGAL 4; RGSF 2; RHW; SATA 46; SATA-Obit 63; SSFS 8; TUS

Warrigal, Jack
See Furphy, Joseph

Warshofsky, Isaac
See Singer, Isaac Bashevis

Warton, Joseph 1722-1800 .... **NCLC 118**
See also DLB 104, 109; RGEL 2

Warton, Thomas 1728-1790 .... **LC 15, 82**
See also DAM POET; DLB 104, 109; RGEL 2

Waruk, Kona
See Harris, (Theodore) Wilson

Warung, Price .... **TCLC 45**
See Astley, William
See also DLB 230; RGEL 2

Warwick, Jarvis
See Garner, Hugh
See also CCA 1

Washington, Alex
See Harris, Mark

Washington, Booker T(aliaferro)
1856-1915 .... **BLC 3; TCLC 10**
See also BW 1; CA 114; 125; DA3; DAM MULT; LAIT 2; RGAL 4; SATA 28

Washington, George 1732-1799 .... **LC 25**
See also DLB 31

Wassermann, (Karl) Jakob
1873-1934 .... **TCLC 6**
See also CA 104; 163; DLB 66; EWL 3

Wasserstein, Wendy 1950- ... **CLC 32, 59, 90, 183; DC 4**
See also CA 121; 129; CABS 3; CAD; CANR 53, 75, 128; CD 5; CWD; DA3; DAM DRAM; DFS 5, 17; DLB 228; EWL 3; FW; INT CA-129; MTCW 2; SATA 94

Waterhouse, Keith (Spencer) 1929- . **CLC 47**
See also CA 5-8R; CANR 38, 67, 109; CBD; CN 7; DLB 13, 15; MTCW 1, 2

Waters, Frank (Joseph) 1902-1995 .. **CLC 88**
See also CA 5-8R; 149; CAAS 13; CANR 3, 18, 63, 121; DLB 212; DLBY 1986; RGAL 4; TCWW 2

Waters, Mary C. .... **CLC 70**

Waters, Roger 1944- .... **CLC 35**

Watkins, Frances Ellen
See Harper, Frances Ellen Watkins

Watkins, Gerrold
See Malzberg, Barry N(athaniel)

Watkins, Gloria Jean 1952(?)- .... **CLC 94**
See also BW 2; CA 143; CANR 87, 126; DLB 246; MTCW 2; SATA 115

Watkins, Paul 1964- .... **CLC 55**
See also CA 132; CANR 62, 98

Watkins, Vernon Phillips
1906-1967 .... **CLC 43**
See also CA 9-10; 25-28R; CAP 1; DLB 20; EWL 3; RGEL 2

Watson, Irving S.
See Mencken, H(enry) L(ouis)

Watson, John H.
See Farmer, Philip Jose

Watson, Richard F.
See Silverberg, Robert

Watts, Ephraim
See Horne, Richard Henry Hengist

Watts, Isaac 1674-1748 .... **LC 98**
See also DLB 95; RGEL 2; SATA 52

Waugh, Auberon (Alexander)
1939-2001 .... **CLC 7**
See also CA 45-48; 192; CANR 6, 22, 92; DLB 14, 194

Waugh, Evelyn (Arthur St. John)
1903-1966 .. **CLC 1, 3, 8, 13, 19, 27, 44, 107; SSC 41; WLC**
See also BPFB 3; BRW 7; CA 85-88; 25-28R; CANR 22; CDBLB 1914-1945; DA; DA3; DAB; DAC; DAM MST, NOV, POP; DLB 15, 162, 195; EWL 3; MTCW 1, 2; NFS 13, 17; RGEL 2; RGSF 2; TEA; WLIT 4

Waugh, Harriet 1944- .... **CLC 6**
See also CA 85-88; CANR 22

Ways, C. R.
See Blount, Roy (Alton), Jr.

Waystaff, Simon
See Swift, Jonathan

Webb, Beatrice (Martha Potter)
1858-1943 .... **TCLC 22**
See also CA 117; 162; DLB 190; FW

Webb, Charles (Richard) 1939- .... **CLC 7**
See also CA 25-28R; CANR 114

Webb, Frank J. .... **NCLC 143**
See also DLB 50

Webb, James H(enry), Jr. 1946- ...... **CLC 22**
See also CA 81-84

Webb, Mary Gladys (Meredith)
1881-1927 .... **TCLC 24**
See also CA 182; 123; DLB 34; FW

Webb, Mrs. Sidney
See Webb, Beatrice (Martha Potter)

Webb, Phyllis 1927- .... **CLC 18**
See also CA 104; CANR 23; CCA 1; CP 7; CWP; DLB 53

Webb, Sidney (James) 1859-1947 .. **TCLC 22**
See also CA 117; 163; DLB 190

Webber, Andrew Lloyd .... **CLC 21**
See Lloyd Webber, Andrew
See also DFS 7

Weber, Lenora Mattingly
1895-1971 .... **CLC 12**
See also CA 19-20; 29-32R; CAP 1; SATA 2; SATA-Obit 26

Weber, Max 1864-1920 .... **TCLC 69**
See also CA 109; 189; DLB 296

Webster, John 1580(?)-1634(?) ...... **DC 2; LC 33, 84; WLC**
See also BRW 2; CDBLB Before 1660; DA; DAB; DAC; DAM DRAM, MST; DFS 17, 19; DLB 58; IDTP; RGEL 2; WLIT 3

Webster, Noah 1758-1843 .... **NCLC 30**
See also DLB 1, 37, 42, 43, 73, 243

Wedekind, (Benjamin) Frank(lin)
1864-1918 .... **TCLC 7**
See also CA 104; 153; CANR 121, 122; CDWLB 2; DAM DRAM; DLB 118; EW 8; EWL 3; LMFS 2; RGWL 2, 3

Wehr, Demaris .... **CLC 65**

Weidman, Jerome 1913-1998 .... **CLC 7**
See also AITN 2; CA 1-4R; 171; CAD; CANR 1; DLB 28

Weil, Simone (Adolphine)
1909-1943 .... **TCLC 23**
See also CA 117; 159; EW 12; EWL 3; FW; GFL 1789 to the Present; MTCW 2

Weininger, Otto 1880-1903 .... **TCLC 84**

Weinstein, Nathan
See West, Nathanael

Weinstein, Nathan von Wallenstein
See West, Nathanael

Weir, Peter (Lindsay) 1944- .... **CLC 20**
See also CA 113; 123

Weiss, Peter (Ulrich) 1916-1982 .. **CLC 3, 15, 51; TCLC 152**
See also CA 45-48; 106; CANR 3; DAM DRAM; DFS 3; DLB 69, 124; EWL 3; RGWL 2, 3

Weiss, Theodore (Russell)
1916-2003 .... **CLC 3, 8, 14**
See also CA 9-12R; 189; 216; CAAE 189; CAAS 2; CANR 46, 94; CP 7; DLB 5

Welch, (Maurice) Denton
1915-1948 .... **TCLC 22**
See also BRWS 8, 9; CA 121; 148; RGEL 2

Welch, James (Phillip) 1940-2003 ..... **CLC 6, 14, 52; NNAL; PC 62**
See also CA 85-88; 219; CANR 42, 66, 107; CN 7; CP 7; CPW; DAM MULT, POP; DLB 175, 256; LATS 1:1; RGAL 4; TCWW 2

Weldon, Fay 1931- . **CLC 6, 9, 11, 19, 36, 59, 122**
See also BRWS 4; CA 21-24R; CANR 16, 46, 63, 97; CDBLB 1960 to Present; CN 7; CPW; DAM POP; DLB 14, 194; EWL 3; FW; HGG; INT CANR-16; MTCW 1, 2; RGEL 2; RGSF 2

Wellek, Rene 1903-1995 .... **CLC 28**
See also CA 5-8R; 150; CAAS 7; CANR 8; DLB 63; EWL 3; INT CANR-8

Weller, Michael 1942- .... **CLC 10, 53**
See also CA 85-88; CAD; CD 5

Weller, Paul 1958- .... **CLC 26**

Wellershoff, Dieter 1925- .... **CLC 46**
See also CA 89-92; CANR 16, 37

Welles, (George) Orson 1915-1985 .. **CLC 20, 80**
See also AAYA 40; CA 93-96; 117

Wellman, John McDowell 1945-
See Wellman, Mac
See also CA 166; CD 5

Wellman, Mac .... **CLC 65**
See Wellman, John McDowell; Wellman, John McDowell
See also CAD; RGAL 4

Wellman, Manly Wade 1903-1986 ... **CLC 49**
See also CA 1-4R; 118; CANR 6, 16, 44; FANT; SATA 6; SATA-Obit 47; SFW 4; SUFW

Wells, Carolyn 1869(?)-1942 .... **TCLC 35**
See also CA 113; 185; CMW 4; DLB 11

Wells, H(erbert) G(eorge) 1866-1946 . **SSC 6, 70; TCLC 6, 12, 19, 133; WLC**
See also AAYA 18; BPFB 3; BRW 6; CA 110; 121; CDBLB 1914-1945; CLR 64; DA; DA3; DAB; DAC; DAM MST, NOV; DLB 34, 70, 156, 178; EWL 3; EXPS; HGG; LAIT 3; LMFS 2; MTCW 1, 2; NFS 17, 20; RGEL 2; RGSF 2; SATA 20; SCFW; SFW 4; SSFS 3; SUFW; TEA; WCH; WLIT 4; YAW

Wells, Rosemary 1943- .... **CLC 12**
See also AAYA 13; BYA 7, 8; CA 85-88; CANR 48, 120; CLR 16, 69; CWRI 5; MAICYA 1, 2; SAAS 1; SATA 18, 69, 114; YAW

Wells-Barnett, Ida B(ell) 1862-1931 .... **TCLC 125**
See also CA 182; DLB 23, 221

Welsh, Irvine 1958- .... **CLC 144**
See also CA 173; DLB 271

Welty, Eudora (Alice) 1909-2001 .. **CLC 1, 2, 5, 14, 22, 33, 105; SSC 1, 27, 51; WLC**
See also AAYA 48; AMW; AMWR 1; BPFB 3; CA 9-12R; 199; CABS 1; CANR 32, 65, 128; CDALB 1941-1968; CN 7; CSW; DA; DA3; DAB; DAC; DAM MST, NOV; DLB 2, 102, 143; DLBD 12; DLBY 1987, 2001; EWL 3; EXPS; HGG; LAIT 3; MAWW; MTCW 1, 2; NFS 13, 15; RGAL 4; RGSF 2; RHW; SSFS 2, 10; TUS

Wen I-to 1899-1946 .... **TCLC 28**
See also EWL 3

Wentworth, Robert
See Hamilton, Edmond

Werfel, Franz (Viktor) 1890-1945 ... **TCLC 8**
See also CA 104; 161; DLB 81, 124; EWL 3; RGWL 2, 3

Wergeland, Henrik Arnold 1808-1845 .... **NCLC 5**

Wersba, Barbara 1932- .... **CLC 30**
See also AAYA 2, 30; BYA 6, 12, 13; CA 29-32R, 182; CAAE 182; CANR 16, 38; CLR 3, 78; DLB 52; JRDA; MAICYA 1, 2; SAAS 2; SATA 1, 58; SATA-Essay 103; WYA; YAW

Wertmueller, Lina 1928- .... **CLC 16**
See also CA 97-100; CANR 39, 78

Wescott, Glenway 1901-1987 .. **CLC 13; SSC 35**
See also CA 13-16R; 121; CANR 23, 70; DLB 4, 9, 102; RGAL 4

Wesker, Arnold 1932- .... **CLC 3, 5, 42**
See also CA 1-4R; CAAS 7; CANR 1, 33; CBD; CD 5; CDBLB 1960 to Present; DAB; DAM DRAM; DLB 13; EWL 3; MTCW 1; RGEL 2; TEA

Wesley, John 1703-1791 .... **LC 88**
See also DLB 104

Wesley, Richard (Errol) 1945- .... **CLC 7**
See also BW 1; CA 57-60; CAD; CANR 27; CD 5; DLB 38

Wessel, Johan Herman 1742-1785 .... **LC 7**
See also DLB 300

West, Anthony (Panther) 1914-1987 .... **CLC 50**
See also CA 45-48; 124; CANR 3, 19; DLB 15

West, C. P.
See Wodehouse, P(elham) G(renville)

West, Cornel (Ronald) 1953- .... **BLCS; CLC 134**
See also CA 144; CANR 91; DLB 246

West, Delno C(loyde), Jr. 1936- .... **CLC 70**
See also CA 57-60

West, Dorothy 1907-1998 .. **HR 3; TCLC 108**
See also BW 2; CA 143; 169; DLB 76

West, (Mary) Jessamyn 1902-1984 ... **CLC 7, 17**
See also CA 9-12R; 112; CANR 27; DLB 6; DLBY 1984; MTCW 1, 2; RGAL 4; RHW; SATA-Obit 37; TCWW 2; TUS; YAW

West, Morris
See West, Morris L(anglo)
See also DLB 289

West, Morris L(anglo) 1916-1999 ..... **CLC 6, 33**
See West, Morris
See also BPFB 3; CA 5-8R; 187; CANR 24, 49, 64; CN 7; CPW; MTCW 1, 2

West, Nathanael 1903-1940 .. **SSC 16; TCLC 1, 14, 44**
See also AMW; AMWR 2; BPFB 3; CA 104; 125; CDALB 1929-1941; DA3; DLB 4, 9, 28; EWL 3; MTCW 1, 2; NFS 16; RGAL 4; TUS

West, Owen
See Koontz, Dean R(ay)

West, Paul 1930- .... **CLC 7, 14, 96**
See also CA 13-16R; CAAS 7; CANR 22, 53, 76, 89; CN 7; DLB 14; INT CANR-22; MTCW 2

West, Rebecca 1892-1983 ... **CLC 7, 9, 31, 50**
See also BPFB 3; BRWS 3; CA 5-8R; 109; CANR 19; DLB 36; DLBY 1983; EWL 3; FW; MTCW 1, 2; NCFS 4; RGEL 2; TEA

Westall, Robert (Atkinson) 1929-1993 .... **CLC 17**
See also AAYA 12; BYA 2, 6, 7, 8, 9, 15; CA 69-72; 141; CANR 18, 68; CLR 13; FANT; JRDA; MAICYA 1, 2; MAICYAS 1; SAAS 2; SATA 23, 69; SATA-Obit 75; WYA; YAW

Westermarck, Edward 1862-1939 . **TCLC 87**

Westlake, Donald E(dwin) 1933- . **CLC 7, 33**
See also BPFB 3; CA 17-20R; CAAS 13; CANR 16, 44, 65, 94; CMW 4; CPW; DAM POP; INT CANR-16; MSW; MTCW 2

Westmacott, Mary
See Christie, Agatha (Mary Clarissa)

Weston, Allen
See Norton, Andre

Wetcheek, J. L.
See Feuchtwanger, Lion

Wetering, Janwillem van de
See van de Wetering, Janwillem

Wetherald, Agnes Ethelwyn 1857-1940 .... **TCLC 81**
See also CA 202; DLB 99

Wetherell, Elizabeth
See Warner, Susan (Bogert)

Whale, James 1889-1957 .... **TCLC 63**

Whalen, Philip (Glenn) 1923-2002 .... **CLC 6, 29**
See also BG 3; CA 9-12R; 209; CANR 5, 39; CP 7; DLB 16; WP

Wharton, Edith (Newbold Jones) 1862-1937 ... **SSC 6; TCLC 3, 9, 27, 53, 129, 149; WLC**
See also AAYA 25; AMW; AMWC 2; AMWR 1; BPFB 3; CA 104; 132; CDALB 1865-1917; DA; DA3; DAB; DAC; DAM MST, NOV; DLB 4, 9, 12, 78, 189; DLBD 13; EWL 3; EXPS; HGG; LAIT 2, 3; LATS 1:1; MAWW; MTCW 1, 2; NFS 5, 11, 15, 20; RGAL 4; RGSF 2; RHW; SSFS 6, 7; SUFW; TUS

Wharton, James
See Mencken, H(enry) L(ouis)

Wharton, William (a pseudonym) . **CLC 18, 37**
See also CA 93-96; DLBY 1980; INT CA-93-96

Wheatley (Peters), Phillis 1753(?)-1784 ... **BLC 3; LC 3, 50; PC 3; WLC**
See also AFAW 1, 2; CDALB 1640-1865; DA; DA3; DAC; DAM MST, MULT, POET; DLB 31, 50; EXPP; PFS 13; RGAL 4

Wheelock, John Hall 1886-1978 .... **CLC 14**
See also CA 13-16R; 77-80; CANR 14; DLB 45

Whim-Wham
See Curnow, (Thomas) Allen (Monro)

White, Babington
See Braddon, Mary Elizabeth

White, E(lwyn) B(rooks) 1899-1985 .... **CLC 10, 34, 39**
See also AITN 2; AMWS 1; CA 13-16R; 116; CANR 16, 37; CDALBS; CLR 1, 21; CPW; DA3; DAM POP; DLB 11, 22; EWL 3; FANT; MAICYA 1, 2; MTCW 1, 2; NCFS 5; RGAL 4; SATA 2, 29, 100; SATA-Obit 44; TUS

White, Edmund (Valentine III) 1940- .... **CLC 27, 110**
See also AAYA 7; CA 45-48; CANR 3, 19, 36, 62, 107, 133; CN 7; DA3; DAM POP; DLB 227; MTCW 1, 2

White, Hayden V. 1928- .... **CLC 148**
See also CA 128; CANR 135; DLB 246

White, Patrick (Victor Martindale) 1912-1990 .... **CLC 3, 4, 5, 7, 9, 18, 65, 69; SSC 39**
See also BRWS 1; CA 81-84; 132; CANR 43; DLB 260; EWL 3; MTCW 1; RGEL 2; RGSF 2; RHW; TWA; WWE 1

White, Phyllis Dorothy James 1920-
See James, P. D.
See also CA 21-24R; CANR 17, 43, 65, 112; CMW 4; CN 7; CPW; DA3; DAM POP; MTCW 1, 2; TEA

White, T(erence) H(anbury) 1906-1964 .... **CLC 30**
See also AAYA 22; BPFB 3; BYA 4, 5; CA 73-76; CANR 37; DLB 160; FANT; JRDA; LAIT 1; MAICYA 1, 2; RGEL 2; SATA 12; SUFW 1; YAW

White, Terence de Vere 1912-1994 ... **CLC 49**
See also CA 49-52; 145; CANR 3

White, Walter
See White, Walter F(rancis)

White, Walter F(rancis) 1893-1955 ... **BLC 3; HR 3; TCLC 15**
See also BW 1; CA 115; 124; DAM MULT; DLB 51

White, William Hale 1831-1913
See Rutherford, Mark
See also CA 121; 189

Whitehead, Alfred North 1861-1947 .... **TCLC 97**
See also CA 117; 165; DLB 100, 262

Whitehead, E(dward) A(nthony) 1933- .... **CLC 5**
See also CA 65-68; CANR 58, 118; CBD; CD 5

Whitehead, Ted
See Whitehead, E(dward) A(nthony)

Whiteman, Roberta J. Hill 1947- ...... **NNAL**
See also CA 146

Whitemore, Hugh (John) 1936- .... **CLC 37**
See also CA 132; CANR 77; CBD; CD 5; INT CA-132

Whitman, Sarah Helen (Power) 1803-1878 .... **NCLC 19**
See also DLB 1, 243

Whitman, Walt(er) 1819-1892 .. **NCLC 4, 31, 81; PC 3; WLC**
See also AAYA 42; AMW; AMWR 1; CDALB 1640-1865; DA; DA3; DAB; DAC; DAM MST, POET; DLB 3, 64, 224, 250; EXPP; LAIT 2; LMFS 1; PAB; PFS 2, 3, 13; RGAL 4; SATA 20; TUS; WP; WYAS 1

Whitney, Phyllis A(yame) 1903- .... **CLC 42**
See also AAYA 36; AITN 2; BEST 90:3; CA 1-4R; CANR 3, 25, 38, 60; CLR 59; CMW 4; CPW; DA3; DAM POP; JRDA; MAICYA 1, 2; MTCW 2; RHW; SATA 1, 30; YAW

Whittemore, (Edward) Reed, Jr. 1919- .... **CLC 4**
See also CA 9-12R, 219; CAAE 219; CAAS 8; CANR 4, 119; CP 7; DLB 5

Whittier, John Greenleaf 1807-1892 .... **NCLC 8, 59**
See also AMWS 1; DLB 1, 243; RGAL 4

Whittlebot, Hernia
See Coward, Noel (Peirce)

Wicker, Thomas Grey 1926-
See Wicker, Tom
See also CA 65-68; CANR 21, 46

Wicker, Tom .... **CLC 7**
See Wicker, Thomas Grey

Wideman, John Edgar 1941- ... **BLC 3; CLC 5, 34, 36, 67, 122; SSC 62**
See also AFAW 1, 2; AMWS 10; BPFB 4; BW 2, 3; CA 85-88; CANR 14, 42, 67, 109; CN 7; DAC; DAM MULT; DLB 33, 143; MTCW 2; RGAL 4; RGSF 2; SSFS 6, 12

Wiebe, Rudy (Henry) 1934- .. **CLC 6, 11, 14, 138**
See also CA 37-40R; CANR 42, 67, 123; CN 7; DAC; DAM MST; DLB 60; RHW

Wieland, Christoph Martin 1733-1813 .... **NCLC 17**
See also DLB 97; EW 4; LMFS 1; RGWL 2, 3

Wiene, Robert 1881-1938 .... **TCLC 56**

Wieners, John 1934- .... **CLC 7**
See also BG 3; CA 13-16R; CP 7; DLB 16; WP

Wiesel, Elie(zer) 1928- .... **CLC 3, 5, 11, 37, 165; WLCS**
See also AAYA 7, 54; AITN 1; CA 5-8R; CAAS 4; CANR 8, 40, 65, 125; CDALBS; CWW 2; DA; DA3; DAB; DAC; DAM MST, NOV; DLB 83, 299; EWL 3; INT CANR-8; LAIT 4; MTCW 1, 2; NCFS 4; NFS 4; RGWL 3; SATA 56; YAW

Wiggins, Marianne 1947- .... **CLC 57**
See also BEST 89:3; CA 130; CANR 60

Wigglesworth, Michael 1631-1705 .... **LC 106**
See also DLB 24; RGAL 4

Wiggs, Susan .... **CLC 70**
See also CA 201

Wight, James Alfred 1916-1995
See Herriot, James
See also CA 77-80; SATA 55; SATA-Brief 44

Wilbur, Richard (Purdy) 1921- ..... **CLC 3, 6, 9, 14, 53, 110; PC 51**
See also AMWS 3; CA 1-4R; CABS 2; CANR 2, 29, 76, 93; CDALBS; CP 7; DA; DAB; DAC; DAM MST, POET; DLB 5, 169; EWL 3; EXPP; INT CANR-29; MTCW 1, 2; PAB; PFS 11, 12, 16; RGAL 4; SATA 9, 108; WP

Wild, Peter 1940- .... **CLC 14**
See also CA 37-40R; CP 7; DLB 5

Wilde, Oscar (Fingal O'Flahertie Wills) 1854(?)-1900 .... **DC 17; SSC 11, 77; TCLC 1, 8, 23, 41; WLC**
See also AAYA 49; BRW 5; BRWC 1, 2; BRWR 2; BYA 15; CA 104; 119; CANR 112; CDBLB 1890-1914; DA; DA3; DAB; DAC; DAM DRAM, MST, NOV; DFS 4, 8, 9; DLB 10, 19, 34, 57, 141, 156, 190; EXPS; FANT; LATS 1:1; NFS 20; RGEL 2; RGSF 2; SATA 24; SSFS 7; SUFW; TEA; WCH; WLIT 4

Wilder, Billy .... **CLC 20**
See Wilder, Samuel
See also DLB 26

Wilder, Samuel 1906-2002
See Wilder, Billy
See also CA 89-92; 205

Wilder, Stephen
See Marlowe, Stephen

Wilder, Thornton (Niven) 1897-1975 .. **CLC 1, 5, 6, 10, 15, 35, 82; DC 1, 24; WLC**
See also AAYA 29; AITN 2; AMW; CA 13-16R; 61-64; CAD; CANR 40, 132; CDALB; DA; DA3; DAB; DAC; DAM DRAM, MST, NOV; DFS 1, 4, 16; DLB 4, 7, 9, 228; DLBY 1997; EWL 3; LAIT 3; MTCW 1, 2; RGAL 4; RHW; WYAS 1

Wilding, Michael 1942- ...... **CLC 73; SSC 50**
See also CA 104; CANR 24, 49, 106; CN 7; RGSF 2

Wiley, Richard 1944- .... **CLC 44**
See also CA 121; 129; CANR 71

Wilhelm, Kate .... **CLC 7**
See Wilhelm, Katie (Gertrude)
See also AAYA 20; BYA 16; CAAS 5; DLB 8; INT CANR-17; SCFW 2

Wilhelm, Katie (Gertrude) 1928-
See Wilhelm, Kate
See also CA 37-40R; CANR 17, 36, 60, 94; MTCW 1; SFW 4

Wilkins, Mary
See Freeman, Mary E(leanor) Wilkins

Willard, Nancy 1936- .... **CLC 7, 37**
See also BYA 5; CA 89-92; CANR 10, 39, 68, 107; CLR 5; CWP; CWRI 5; DLB 5, 52; FANT; MAICYA 1, 2; MTCW 1; SATA 37, 71, 127; SATA-Brief 30; SUFW 2

William of Malmesbury c. 1090B.C.-c. 1140B.C. .... **CMLC 57**

William of Ockham 1290-1349 ..... **CMLC 32**

Williams, Ben Ames 1889-1953 ..... **TCLC 89**
See also CA 183; DLB 102

Williams, C(harles) K(enneth) 1936- .... **CLC 33, 56, 148**
See also CA 37-40R; CAAS 26; CANR 57, 106; CP 7; DAM POET; DLB 5

Williams, Charles
See Collier, James Lincoln

Williams, Charles (Walter Stansby) 1886-1945 .... **TCLC 1, 11**
See also BRWS 9; CA 104; 163; DLB 100, 153, 255; FANT; RGEL 2; SUFW 1

Williams, Ella Gwendolen Rees
See Rhys, Jean

Williams, (George) Emlyn 1905-1987 .... **CLC 15**
See also CA 104; 123; CANR 36; DAM DRAM; DLB 10, 77; IDTP; MTCW 1

Williams, Hank 1923-1953 .... **TCLC 81**
See Williams, Hiram King

Williams, Helen Maria 1761-1827 .... **NCLC 135**
See also DLB 158

Williams, Hiram Hank
See Williams, Hank

Williams, Hiram King
See Williams, Hank
See also CA 188

Williams, Hugo (Mordaunt) 1942- ... **CLC 42**
See also CA 17-20R; CANR 45, 119; CP 7; DLB 40

Williams, J. Walker
See Wodehouse, P(elham) G(renville)

Williams, John A(lfred) 1925- . **BLC 3; CLC 5, 13**
See also AFAW 2; BW 2, 3; CA 53-56, 195; CAAE 195; CAAS 3; CANR 6, 26, 51, 118; CN 7; CSW; DAM MULT; DLB 2, 33; EWL 3; INT CANR-6; RGAL 4; SFW 4

Williams, Jonathan (Chamberlain) 1929- .... **CLC 13**
See also CA 9-12R; CAAS 12; CANR 8, 108; CP 7; DLB 5

Williams, Joy 1944- .... **CLC 31**
See also CA 41-44R; CANR 22, 48, 97

Williams, Norman 1952- .... **CLC 39**
See also CA 118

Williams, Sherley Anne 1944-1999 ... **BLC 3; CLC 89**
See also AFAW 2; BW 2, 3; CA 73-76; 185; CANR 25, 82; DAM MULT, POET; DLB 41; INT CANR-25; SATA 78; SATA-Obit 116

Williams, Shirley
See Williams, Sherley Anne

Williams, Tennessee 1911-1983 . **CLC 1, 2, 5, 7, 8, 11, 15, 19, 30, 39, 45, 71, 111; DC 4; SSC 81; WLC**
See also AAYA 31; AITN 1, 2; AMW; AMWC 1; CA 5-8R; 108; CABS 3; CAD; CANR 31, 132; CDALB 1941-1968; DA; DA3; DAB; DAC; DAM DRAM, MST; DFS 17; DLB 7; DLBD 4; DLBY 1983; EWL 3; GLL 1; LAIT 4; LATS 1:2; MTCW 1, 2; RGAL 4; TUS

Williams, Thomas (Alonzo) 1926-1990 .... **CLC 14**
See also CA 1-4R; 132; CANR 2

Williams, William C.
See Williams, William Carlos

Williams, William Carlos 1883-1963 .... **CLC 1, 2, 5, 9, 13, 22, 42, 67; PC 7; SSC 31**
See also AAYA 46; AMW; AMWR 1; CA 89-92; CANR 34; CDALB 1917-1929; DA; DA3; DAB; DAC; DAM MST, POET; DLB 4, 16, 54, 86; EWL 3; EXPP; MTCW 1, 2; NCFS 4; PAB; PFS 1, 6, 11; RGAL 4; RGSF 2; TUS; WP

Williamson, David (Keith) 1942- ..... **CLC 56**
See also CA 103; CANR 41; CD 5; DLB 289

Williamson, Ellen Douglas 1905-1984
See Douglas, Ellen
See also CA 17-20R; 114; CANR 39

Williamson, Jack .... **CLC 29**
See Williamson, John Stewart
See also CAAS 8; DLB 8; SCFW 2

Williamson, John Stewart 1908-
See Williamson, Jack
See also CA 17-20R; CANR 23, 70; SFW 4

Willie, Frederick
See Lovecraft, H(oward) P(hillips)

Willingham, Calder (Baynard, Jr.)
1922-1995 .... **CLC 5, 51**
See also CA 5-8R; 147; CANR 3; CSW; DLB 2, 44; IDFW 3, 4; MTCW 1

Willis, Charles
See Clarke, Arthur C(harles)

Willy
See Colette, (Sidonie-Gabrielle)

Willy, Colette
See Colette, (Sidonie-Gabrielle)
See also GLL 1

Wilmot, John 1647-1680 .... **LC 75**
See Rochester
See also BRW 2; DLB 131; PAB

Wilson, A(ndrew) N(orman) 1950- .. **CLC 33**
See also BRWS 6; CA 112; 122; CN 7; DLB 14, 155, 194; MTCW 2

Wilson, Angus (Frank Johnstone)
1913-1991 . **CLC 2, 3, 5, 25, 34; SSC 21**
See also BRWS 1; CA 5-8R; 134; CANR 21; DLB 15, 139, 155; EWL 3; MTCW 1, 2; RGEL 2; RGSF 2

Wilson, August 1945- ... **BLC 3; CLC 39, 50, 63, 118; DC 2; WLCS**
See also AAYA 16; AFAW 2; AMWS 8; BW 2, 3; CA 115; 122; CAD; CANR 42, 54, 76, 128; CD 5; DA; DA3; DAB; DAC; DAM DRAM, MST, MULT; DFS 3, 7, 15, 17; DLB 228; EWL 3; LAIT 4; LATS 1:2; MTCW 1, 2; RGAL 4

Wilson, Brian 1942- .... **CLC 12**

Wilson, Colin 1931- .... **CLC 3, 14**
See also CA 1-4R; CAAS 5; CANR 1, 22, 33, 77; CMW 4; CN 7; DLB 14, 194; HGG; MTCW 1; SFW 4

Wilson, Dirk
See Pohl, Frederik

Wilson, Edmund 1895-1972 .. **CLC 1, 2, 3, 8, 24**
See also AMW; CA 1-4R; 37-40R; CANR 1, 46, 110; DLB 63; EWL 3; MTCW 1, 2; RGAL 4; TUS

Wilson, Ethel Davis (Bryant)
1888(?)-1980 .... **CLC 13**
See also CA 102; DAC; DAM POET; DLB 68; MTCW 1; RGEL 2

Wilson, Harriet
See Wilson, Harriet E. Adams
See also DLB 239

Wilson, Harriet E.
See Wilson, Harriet E. Adams
See also DLB 243

Wilson, Harriet E. Adams
1827(?)-1863(?) .... **BLC 3; NCLC 78**
See Wilson, Harriet; Wilson, Harriet E.
See also DAM MULT; DLB 50

Wilson, John 1785-1854 .... **NCLC 5**

Wilson, John (Anthony) Burgess 1917-1993
See Burgess, Anthony
See also CA 1-4R; 143; CANR 2, 46; DA3; DAC; DAM NOV; MTCW 1, 2; NFS 15; TEA

Wilson, Lanford 1937- .. **CLC 7, 14, 36, 197; DC 19**
See also CA 17-20R; CABS 3; CAD; CANR 45, 96; CD 5; DAM DRAM; DFS 4, 9, 12, 16, 20; DLB 7; EWL 3; TUS

Wilson, Robert M. 1941- .... **CLC 7, 9**
See also CA 49-52; CAD; CANR 2, 41; CD 5; MTCW 1

Wilson, Robert McLiam 1964- .... **CLC 59**
See also CA 132; DLB 267

Wilson, Sloan 1920-2003 .... **CLC 32**
See also CA 1-4R; 216; CANR 1, 44; CN 7

Wilson, Snoo 1948- .... **CLC 33**
See also CA 69-72; CBD; CD 5

Wilson, William S(mith) 1932- .... **CLC 49**
See also CA 81-84

Wilson, (Thomas) Woodrow
1856-1924 .... **TCLC 79**
See also CA 166; DLB 47

Wilson and Warnke eds. .... **CLC 65**

Winchilsea, Anne (Kingsmill) Finch
1661-1720
See Finch, Anne
See also RGEL 2

Windham, Basil
See Wodehouse, P(elham) G(renville)

Wingrove, David (John) 1954- .... **CLC 68**
See also CA 133; SFW 4

Winnemucca, Sarah 1844-1891 .... **NCLC 79; NNAL**
See also DAM MULT; DLB 175; RGAL 4

Winstanley, Gerrard 1609-1676 .... **LC 52**

Wintergreen, Jane
See Duncan, Sara Jeannette

Winters, Janet Lewis .... **CLC 41**
See Lewis, Janet
See also DLBY 1987

Winters, (Arthur) Yvor 1900-1968 .... **CLC 4, 8, 32**
See also AMWS 2; CA 11-12; 25-28R; CAP 1; DLB 48; EWL 3; MTCW 1; RGAL 4

Winterson, Jeanette 1959- .... **CLC 64, 158**
See also BRWS 4; CA 136; CANR 58, 116; CN 7; CPW; DA3; DAM POP; DLB 207, 261; FANT; FW; GLL 1; MTCW 2; RHW

Winthrop, John 1588-1649 .... **LC 31, 107**
See also DLB 24, 30

Wirth, Louis 1897-1952 .... **TCLC 92**
See also CA 210

Wiseman, Frederick 1930- .... **CLC 20**
See also CA 159

Wister, Owen 1860-1938 .... **TCLC 21**
See also BPFB 3; CA 108; 162; DLB 9, 78, 186; RGAL 4; SATA 62; TCWW 2

Wither, George 1588-1667 .... **LC 96**
See also DLB 121; RGEL 2

Witkacy
See Witkiewicz, Stanislaw Ignacy

Witkiewicz, Stanislaw Ignacy
1885-1939 .... **TCLC 8**
See also CA 105; 162; CDWLB 4; DLB 215; EW 10; EWL 3; RGWL 2, 3; SFW 4

Wittgenstein, Ludwig (Josef Johann)
1889-1951 .... **TCLC 59**
See also CA 113; 164; DLB 262; MTCW 2

Wittig, Monique 1935(?)-2003 .... **CLC 22**
See also CA 116; 135; 212; CWW 2; DLB 83; EWL 3; FW; GLL 1

Wittlin, Jozef 1896-1976 .... **CLC 25**
See also CA 49-52; 65-68; CANR 3; EWL 3

Wodehouse, P(elham) G(renville)
1881-1975 . **CLC 1, 2, 5, 10, 22; SSC 2; TCLC 108**
See also AITN 2; BRWS 3; CA 45-48; 57-60; CANR 3, 33; CDBLB 1914-1945; CPW 1; DA3; DAB; DAC; DAM NOV; DLB 34, 162; EWL 3; MTCW 1, 2; RGEL 2; RGSF 2; SATA 22; SSFS 10

Woiwode, L.
See Woiwode, Larry (Alfred)

Woiwode, Larry (Alfred) 1941- ... **CLC 6, 10**
See also CA 73-76; CANR 16, 94; CN 7; DLB 6; INT CANR-16

Wojciechowska, Maia (Teresa)
1927-2002 .... **CLC 26**
See also AAYA 8, 46; BYA 3; CA 9-12R, 183; 209; CAAE 183; CANR 4, 41; CLR 1; JRDA; MAICYA 1, 2; SAAS 1; SATA 1, 28, 83; SATA-Essay 104; SATA-Obit 134; YAW

Wojtyla, Karol
See John Paul II, Pope

Wolf, Christa 1929- .... **CLC 14, 29, 58, 150**
See also CA 85-88; CANR 45, 123; CDWLB 2; CWW 2; DLB 75; EWL 3; FW; MTCW 1; RGWL 2, 3; SSFS 14

Wolf, Naomi 1962- .... **CLC 157**
See also CA 141; CANR 110; FW

Wolfe, Gene (Rodman) 1931- .... **CLC 25**
See also AAYA 35; CA 57-60; CAAS 9; CANR 6, 32, 60; CPW; DAM POP; DLB 8; FANT; MTCW 2; SATA 118; SCFW 2; SFW 4; SUFW 2

Wolfe, George C. 1954- .... **BLCS; CLC 49**
See also CA 149; CAD; CD 5

Wolfe, Thomas (Clayton)
1900-1938 ... **SSC 33; TCLC 4, 13, 29, 61; WLC**
See also AMW; BPFB 3; CA 104; 132; CANR 102; CDALB 1929-1941; DA; DA3; DAB; DAC; DAM MST, NOV; DLB 9, 102, 229; DLBD 2, 16; DLBY 1985, 1997; EWL 3; MTCW 1, 2; NFS 18; RGAL 4; TUS

Wolfe, Thomas Kennerly, Jr.
1931- .... **CLC 147**
See Wolfe, Tom
See also CA 13-16R; CANR 9, 33, 70, 104; DA3; DAM POP; DLB 185; EWL 3; INT CANR-9; MTCW 1, 2; SSFS 18; TUS

Wolfe, Tom .... **CLC 1, 2, 9, 15, 35, 51**
See Wolfe, Thomas Kennerly, Jr.
See also AAYA 8; AITN 2; AMWS 3; BEST 89:1; BPFB 3; CN 7; CPW; CSW; DLB 152; LAIT 5; RGAL 4

Wolff, Geoffrey (Ansell) 1937- .... **CLC 41**
See also CA 29-32R; CANR 29, 43, 78

Wolff, Sonia
See Levitin, Sonia (Wolff)

Wolff, Tobias (Jonathan Ansell)
1945- .... **CLC 39, 64, 172; SSC 63**
See also AAYA 16; AMWS 7; BEST 90:2; BYA 12; CA 114; 117; CAAS 22; CANR 54, 76, 96; CN 7; CSW; DA3; DLB 130; EWL 3; INT CA-117; MTCW 2; RGAL 4; RGSF 2; SSFS 4, 11

Wolfram von Eschenbach c. 1170-c. 1220 .... **CMLC 5**
See Eschenbach, Wolfram von
See also CDWLB 2; DLB 138; EW 1; RGWL 2

Wolitzer, Hilma 1930- .... **CLC 17**
See also CA 65-68; CANR 18, 40; INT CANR-18; SATA 31; YAW

Wollstonecraft, Mary 1759-1797 .... **LC 5, 50, 90**
See also BRWS 3; CDBLB 1789-1832; DLB 39, 104, 158, 252; FW; LAIT 1; RGEL 2; TEA; WLIT 3

Wonder, Stevie .... **CLC 12**
See Morris, Steveland Judkins

Wong, Jade Snow 1922- .... **CLC 17**
See also CA 109; CANR 91; SATA 112

Woodberry, George Edward
1855-1930 .... **TCLC 73**
See also CA 165; DLB 71, 103

Woodcott, Keith
See Brunner, John (Kilian Houston)

Woodruff, Robert W.
See Mencken, H(enry) L(ouis)

Woolf, (Adeline) Virginia 1882-1941 .. **SSC 7, 79; TCLC 1, 5, 20, 43, 56, 101, 123, 128; WLC**
See also AAYA 44; BPFB 3; BRW 7; BRWC 2; BRWR 1; CA 104; 130; CANR 64, 132; CDBLB 1914-1945; DA; DA3; DAB; DAC; DAM MST, NOV; DLB 36, 100, 162; DLBD 10; EWL 3; EXPS; FW; LAIT 3; LATS 1:1; LMFS 2; MTCW 1, 2; NCFS 2; NFS 8, 12; RGEL 2; RGSF 2; SSFS 4, 12; TEA; WLIT 4

Woollcott, Alexander (Humphreys)
    1887-1943 .... **TCLC 5**
    See also CA 105; 161; DLB 29
Woolrich, Cornell .... **CLC 77**
    See Hopley-Woolrich, Cornell George
    See also MSW
Woolson, Constance Fenimore
    1840-1894 .... **NCLC 82**
    See also DLB 12, 74, 189, 221; RGAL 4
Wordsworth, Dorothy 1771-1855 . **NCLC 25, 138**
    See also DLB 107
Wordsworth, William 1770-1850 .. **NCLC 12, 38, 111; PC 4; WLC**
    See also BRW 4; BRWC 1; CDBLB 1789-1832; DA; DA3; DAB; DAC; DAM MST, POET; DLB 93, 107; EXPP; LATS 1:1; LMFS 1; PAB; PFS 2; RGEL 2; TEA; WLIT 3; WP
Wotton, Sir Henry 1568-1639 .... **LC 68**
    See also DLB 121; RGEL 2
Wouk, Herman 1915- .... **CLC 1, 9, 38**
    See also BPFB 2, 3; CA 5-8R; CANR 6, 33, 67; CDALBS; CN 7; CPW; DA3; DAM NOV, POP; DLBY 1982; INT CANR-6; LAIT 4; MTCW 1, 2; NFS 7; TUS
Wright, Charles (Penzel, Jr.) 1935- .. **CLC 6, 13, 28, 119, 146**
    See also AMWS 5; CA 29-32R; CAAS 7; CANR 23, 36, 62, 88, 135; CP 7; DLB 165; DLBY 1982; EWL 3; MTCW 1, 2; PFS 10
Wright, Charles Stevenson 1932- ..... **BLC 3; CLC 49**
    See also BW 1; CA 9-12R; CANR 26; CN 7; DAM MULT, POET; DLB 33
Wright, Frances 1795-1852 .... **NCLC 74**
    See also DLB 73
Wright, Frank Lloyd 1867-1959 .... **TCLC 95**
    See also AAYA 33; CA 174
Wright, Jack R.
    See Harris, Mark
Wright, James (Arlington)
    1927-1980 .... **CLC 3, 5, 10, 28; PC 36**
    See also AITN 2; AMWS 3; CA 49-52; 97-100; CANR 4, 34, 64; CDALBS; DAM POET; DLB 5, 169; EWL 3; EXPP; MTCW 1, 2; PFS 7, 8; RGAL 4; TUS; WP
Wright, Judith (Arundell)
    1915-2000 .... **CLC 11, 53; PC 14**
    See also CA 13-16R; 188; CANR 31, 76, 93; CP 7; CWP; DLB 260; EWL 3; MTCW 1, 2; PFS 8; RGEL 2; SATA 14; SATA-Obit 121
Wright, L(aurali) R. 1939- .... **CLC 44**
    See also CA 138; CMW 4
Wright, Richard (Nathaniel)
    1908-1960 ... **BLC 3; CLC 1, 3, 4, 9, 14, 21, 48, 74; SSC 2; TCLC 136; WLC**
    See also AAYA 5, 42; AFAW 2; AMW; BPFB 3; BW 1; BYA 2; CA 108; CANR 64; CDALB 1929-1941; DA; DA3; DAB; DAC; DAM MST, MULT, NOV; DLB 76, 102; DLBD 2; EWL 3; EXPN; LAIT 3, 4; MTCW 1, 2; NCFS 1; NFS 1, 7; RGAL 4; RGSF 2; SSFS 3, 9, 15, 20; TUS; YAW
Wright, Richard B(ruce) 1937- .... **CLC 6**
    See also CA 85-88; CANR 120; DLB 53
Wright, Rick 1945- .... **CLC 35**
Wright, Rowland
    See Wells, Carolyn
Wright, Stephen 1946- .... **CLC 33**
Wright, Willard Huntington 1888-1939
    See Van Dine, S. S.
    See also CA 115; 189; CMW 4; DLBD 16
Wright, William 1930- .... **CLC 44**
    See also CA 53-56; CANR 7, 23

Wroth, Lady Mary 1587-1653(?) .... **LC 30; PC 38**
    See also DLB 121
Wu Ch'eng-en 1500(?)-1582(?) .... **LC 7**
Wu Ching-tzu 1701-1754 .... **LC 2**
Wulfstan c. 10th cent. -1023 .... **CMLC 59**
Wurlitzer, Rudolph 1938(?)- .... **CLC 2, 4, 15**
    See also CA 85-88; CN 7; DLB 173
Wyatt, Sir Thomas c. 1503-1542 . **LC 70; PC 27**
    See also BRW 1; DLB 132; EXPP; RGEL 2; TEA
Wycherley, William 1640-1716 .... **LC 8, 21, 102**
    See also BRW 2; CDBLB 1660-1789; DAM DRAM; DLB 80; RGEL 2
Wyclif, John c. 1330-1384 .... **CMLC 70**
    See also DLB 146
Wylie, Elinor (Morton Hoyt)
    1885-1928 .... **PC 23; TCLC 8**
    See also AMWS 1; CA 105; 162; DLB 9, 45; EXPP; RGAL 4
Wylie, Philip (Gordon) 1902-1971 ... **CLC 43**
    See also CA 21-22; 33-36R; CAP 2; DLB 9; SFW 4
Wyndham, John .... **CLC 19**
    See Harris, John (Wyndham Parkes Lucas) Beynon
    See also DLB 255; SCFW 2
Wyss, Johann David Von
    1743-1818 .... **NCLC 10**
    See also CLR 92; JRDA; MAICYA 1, 2; SATA 29; SATA-Brief 27
Xenophon c. 430B.C.-c. 354B.C. ... **CMLC 17**
    See also AW 1; DLB 176; RGWL 2, 3
Xingjian, Gao 1940-
    See Gao Xingjian
    See also CA 193; RGWL 3
Yakamochi 718-785 .... **CMLC 45; PC 48**
Yakumo Koizumi
    See Hearn, (Patricio) Lafcadio (Tessima Carlos)
Yamada, Mitsuye (May) 1923- .... **PC 44**
    See also CA 77-80
Yamamoto, Hisaye 1921- .... **AAL; SSC 34**
    See also CA 214; DAM MULT; LAIT 4; SSFS 14
Yamauchi, Wakako 1924- .... **AAL**
    See also CA 214
Yanez, Jose Donoso
    See Donoso (Yanez), Jose
Yanovsky, Basile S.
    See Yanovsky, V(assily) S(emenovich)
Yanovsky, V(assily) S(emenovich)
    1906-1989 .... **CLC 2, 18**
    See also CA 97-100; 129
Yates, Richard 1926-1992 .... **CLC 7, 8, 23**
    See also AMWS 11; CA 5-8R; 139; CANR 10, 43; DLB 2, 234; DLBY 1981, 1992; INT CANR-10
Yau, John 1950- .... **PC 61**
    See also CA 154; CANR 89; CP 7; DLB 234
Yeats, W. B.
    See Yeats, William Butler
Yeats, William Butler 1865-1939 . **PC 20, 51; TCLC 1, 11, 18, 31, 93, 116; WLC**
    See also AAYA 48; BRW 6; BRWR 1; CA 104; 127; CANR 45; CDBLB 1890-1914; DA; DA3; DAB; DAC; DAM DRAM, MST, POET; DLB 10, 19, 98, 156; EWL 3; EXPP; MTCW 1, 2; NCFS 3; PAB; PFS 1, 2, 5, 7, 13, 15; RGEL 2; TEA; WLIT 4; WP
Yehoshua, A(braham) B. 1936- .. **CLC 13, 31**
    See also CA 33-36R; CANR 43, 90; CWW 2; EWL 3; RGSF 2; RGWL 3
Yellow Bird
    See Ridge, John Rollin

Yep, Laurence Michael 1948- .... **CLC 35**
    See also AAYA 5, 31; BYA 7; CA 49-52; CANR 1, 46, 92; CLR 3, 17, 54; DLB 52; FANT; JRDA; MAICYA 1, 2; MAICYAS 1; SATA 7, 69, 123; WYA; YAW
Yerby, Frank G(arvin) 1916-1991 ..... **BLC 3; CLC 1, 7, 22**
    See also BPFB 3; BW 1, 3; CA 9-12R; 136; CANR 16, 52; DAM MULT; DLB 76; INT CANR-16; MTCW 1; RGAL 4; RHW
Yesenin, Sergei Alexandrovich
    See Esenin, Sergei (Alexandrovich)
Yesenin, Sergey
    See Esenin, Sergei (Alexandrovich)
    See also EWL 3
Yevtushenko, Yevgeny (Alexandrovich)
    1933- ...... **CLC 1, 3, 13, 26, 51, 126; PC 40**
    See Evtushenko, Evgenii Aleksandrovich
    See also CA 81-84; CANR 33, 54; DAM POET; EWL 3; MTCW 1
Yezierska, Anzia 1885(?)-1970 .... **CLC 46**
    See also CA 126; 89-92; DLB 28, 221; FW; MTCW 1; RGAL 4; SSFS 15
Yglesias, Helen 1915- .... **CLC 7, 22**
    See also CA 37-40R; CAAS 20; CANR 15, 65, 95; CN 7; INT CANR-15; MTCW 1
Yokomitsu, Riichi 1898-1947 .... **TCLC 47**
    See also CA 170; EWL 3
Yonge, Charlotte (Mary)
    1823-1901 .... **TCLC 48**
    See also CA 109; 163; DLB 18, 163; RGEL 2; SATA 17; WCH
York, Jeremy
    See Creasey, John
York, Simon
    See Heinlein, Robert A(nson)
Yorke, Henry Vincent 1905-1974 ..... **CLC 13**
    See Green, Henry
    See also CA 85-88; 49-52
Yosano Akiko 1878-1942 .... **PC 11; TCLC 59**
    See also CA 161; EWL 3; RGWL 3
Yoshimoto, Banana .... **CLC 84**
    See Yoshimoto, Mahoko
    See also AAYA 50; NFS 7
Yoshimoto, Mahoko 1964-
    See Yoshimoto, Banana
    See also CA 144; CANR 98; SSFS 16
Young, Al(bert James) 1939- ... **BLC 3; CLC 19**
    See also BW 2, 3; CA 29-32R; CANR 26, 65, 109; CN 7; CP 7; DAM MULT; DLB 33
Young, Andrew (John) 1885-1971 .... **CLC 5**
    See also CA 5-8R; CANR 7, 29; RGEL 2
Young, Collier
    See Bloch, Robert (Albert)
Young, Edward 1683-1765 .... **LC 3, 40**
    See also DLB 95; RGEL 2
Young, Marguerite (Vivian)
    1909-1995 .... **CLC 82**
    See also CA 13-16; 150; CAP 1; CN 7
Young, Neil 1945- .... **CLC 17**
    See also CA 110; CCA 1
Young Bear, Ray A. 1950- ... **CLC 94; NNAL**
    See also CA 146; DAM MULT; DLB 175
Yourcenar, Marguerite 1903-1987 ... **CLC 19, 38, 50, 87**
    See also BPFB 3; CA 69-72; CANR 23, 60, 93; DAM NOV; DLB 72; DLBY 1988; EW 12; EWL 3; GFL 1789 to the Present; GLL 1; MTCW 1, 2; RGWL 2, 3
Yuan, Chu 340(?)B.C.-278(?)B.C. . **CMLC 36**
Yurick, Sol 1925- .... **CLC 6**
    See also CA 13-16R; CANR 25; CN 7
Zabolotsky, Nikolai Alekseevich
    1903-1958 .... **TCLC 52**
    See Zabolotsky, Nikolay Alekseevich
    See also CA 116; 164

Zabolotsky, Nikolay Alekseevich
See Zabolotsky, Nikolai Alekseevich
See also EWL 3

Zagajewski, Adam 1945- .... **PC 27**
See also CA 186; DLB 232; EWL 3

Zalygin, Sergei -2000 .... **CLC 59**

Zalygin, Sergei (Pavlovich)
1913-2000 .... **CLC 59**
See also DLB 302

Zamiatin, Evgenii
See Zamyatin, Evgeny Ivanovich
See also RGSF 2; RGWL 2, 3

Zamiatin, Evgenii Ivanovich
See Zamyatin, Evgeny Ivanovich
See also DLB 272

Zamiatin, Yevgenii
See Zamyatin, Evgeny Ivanovich

Zamora, Bernice (B. Ortiz) 1938- .. **CLC 89; HLC 2**
See also CA 151; CANR 80; DAM MULT; DLB 82; HW 1, 2

Zamyatin, Evgeny Ivanovich
1884-1937 .... **TCLC 8, 37**
See Zamiatin, Evgenii; Zamiatin, Evgenii Ivanovich; Zamyatin, Yevgeny Ivanovich
See also CA 105; 166; EW 10; SFW 4

Zamyatin, Yevgeny Ivanovich
See Zamyatin, Evgeny Ivanovich
See also EWL 3

Zangwill, Israel 1864-1926 ... **SSC 44; TCLC 16**
See also CA 109; 167; CMW 4; DLB 10, 135, 197; RGEL 2

Zappa, Francis Vincent, Jr. 1940-1993
See Zappa, Frank
See also CA 108; 143; CANR 57

Zappa, Frank .... **CLC 17**
See Zappa, Francis Vincent, Jr.

Zaturenska, Marya 1902-1982 ..... **CLC 6, 11**
See also CA 13-16R; 105; CANR 22

Zayas y Sotomayor, Maria de 1590-c. 1661 .... **LC 102**
See also RGSF 2

Zeami 1363-1443 .... **DC 7; LC 86**
See also DLB 203; RGWL 2, 3

Zelazny, Roger (Joseph) 1937-1995 . **CLC 21**
See also AAYA 7; BPFB 3; CA 21-24R; 148; CANR 26, 60; CN 7; DLB 8; FANT; MTCW 1, 2; SATA 57; SATA-Brief 39; SCFW; SFW 4; SUFW 1, 2

Zhang Ailing
See Chang, Eileen
See also CWW 2; RGSF 2

Zhdanov, Andrei Alexandrovich
1896-1948 .... **TCLC 18**
See also CA 117; 167

Zhukovsky, Vasilii Andreevich
See Zhukovsky, Vasily (Andreevich)
See also DLB 205

Zhukovsky, Vasily (Andreevich)
1783-1852 .... **NCLC 35**
See Zhukovsky, Vasilii Andreevich

Ziegenhagen, Eric .... **CLC 55**

Zimmer, Jill Schary
See Robinson, Jill

Zimmerman, Robert
See Dylan, Bob

Zindel, Paul 1936-2003 ...... **CLC 6, 26; DC 5**
See also AAYA 2, 37; BYA 2, 3, 8, 11, 14; CA 73-76; 213; CAD; CANR 31, 65, 108; CD 5; CDALBS; CLR 3, 45, 85; DA; DA3; DAB; DAC; DAM DRAM, MST, NOV; DFS 12; DLB 7, 52; JRDA; LAIT 5; MAICYA 1, 2; MTCW 1, 2; NFS 14; SATA 16, 58, 102; SATA-Obit 142; WYA; YAW

Zinn, Howard 1922- .... **CLC 199**
See also CA 1-4R; CANR 2, 33, 90

Zinov'Ev, A. A.
See Zinoviev, Alexander (Aleksandrovich)

Zinov'ev, Aleksandr (Aleksandrovich)
See Zinoviev, Alexander (Aleksandrovich)
See also DLB 302

Zinoviev, Alexander (Aleksandrovich)
1922- .... **CLC 19**
See Zinov'ev, Aleksandr (Aleksandrovich)
See also CA 116; 133; CAAS 10

Zizek, Slavoj 1949- .... **CLC 188**
See also CA 201

Zoilus
See Lovecraft, H(oward) P(hillips)

Zola, Emile (Edouard Charles Antoine)
1840-1902 ...... **TCLC 1, 6, 21, 41; WLC**
See also CA 104; 138; DA; DA3; DAB; DAC; DAM MST, NOV; DLB 123; EW 7; GFL 1789 to the Present; IDTP; LMFS 1, 2; RGWL 2; TWA

Zoline, Pamela 1941- .... **CLC 62**
See also CA 161; SFW 4

Zoroaster 628(?)B.C.-551(?)B.C. ... **CMLC 40**

Zorrilla y Moral, Jose 1817-1893 .... **NCLC 6**

Zoshchenko, Mikhail (Mikhailovich)
1895-1958 .... **SSC 15; TCLC 15**
See also CA 115; 160; EWL 3; RGSF 2; RGWL 3

Zuckmayer, Carl 1896-1977 .... **CLC 18**
See also CA 69-72; DLB 56, 124; EWL 3; RGWL 2, 3

Zuk, Georges
See Skelton, Robin
See also CCA 1

Zukofsky, Louis 1904-1978 ... **CLC 1, 2, 4, 7, 11, 18; PC 11**
See also AMWS 3; CA 9-12R; 77-80; CANR 39; DAM POET; DLB 5, 165; EWL 3; MTCW 1; RGAL 4

Zweig, Paul 1935-1984 .... **CLC 34, 42**
See also CA 85-88; 113

Zweig, Stefan 1881-1942 .... **TCLC 17**
See also CA 112; 170; DLB 81, 118; EWL 3

Zwingli, Huldreich 1484-1531 .... **LC 37**
See also DLB 179

Literary Criticism Series Cumulative Topic Index

This index lists all topic entries in Gale's *Children's Literature Review* (CLR), *Classical and Medieval Literature Criticism* (CMLC), *Contemporary Literary Criticism* (CLC), *Drama Criticism* (DC), *Literature Criticism from 1400 to 1800* (LC), *Nineteenth-Century Literature Criticism* (NCLC), *Short Story Criticism* (SSC), and *Twentieth-Century Literary Criticism* (TCLC). The index also lists topic entries in the Gale Critical Companion Collection, which includes the following publications: *The Beat Generation* (BG), and *Harlem Renaissance* (HR).

Abbey Theatre in the Irish Literary Renaissance TCLC 154: 1-114
 origins and development, 2-14
 major figures, 14-30
 plays and controversies, 30-59
 artistic vision and significance, 59-114

Abolitionist Literature of Cuba and Brazil, Nineteenth-Century NCLC 132: 1-94
 overviews, 2-11
 origins and development, 11-23
 sociopolitical concerns, 23-39
 poetry, 39-47
 prose, 47-93

The Aborigine in Nineteenth-Century Australian Literature NCLC 120: 1-88
 overviews, 2-27
 representations of the Aborigine in Australian literature, 27-58
 Aboriginal myth, literature, and oral tradition, 58-88

The Aesopic Fable LC 51: 1-100
 the British Aesopic Fable, 1-54
 the Aesopic tradition in non-English-speaking cultures, 55-66
 political uses of the Aesopic fable, 67-88
 the evolution of the Aesopic fable, 89-99

African-American Folklore and Literature TCLC 126: 1-67
 African-American folk tradition, 1-16
 representative writers, 16-34
 hallmark works, 35-48
 the study of African-American literature and folklore, 48-64

Age of Johnson LC 15: 1-87
 Johnson's London, 3-15
 aesthetics of neoclassicism, 15-36
 "age of prose and reason," 36-45
 clubmen and bluestockings, 45-56
 printing technology, 56-62
 periodicals: "a map of busy life," 62-74
 transition, 74-86

Age of Spenser LC 39: 1-70
 overviews and general studies, 2-21
 literary style, 22-34
 poets and the crown, 34-70

AIDS in Literature CLC 81: 365-416

Alcohol and Literature TCLC 70: 1-58
 overview, 2-8
 fiction, 8-48
 poetry and drama, 48-58

American Abolitionism NCLC 44: 1-73
 overviews and general studies, 2-26
 abolitionist ideals, 26-46
 the literature of abolitionism, 46-72

American Autobiography TCLC 86: 1-115
 overviews and general studies, 3-36
 American authors and autobiography, 36-82
 African-American autobiography, 82-114

American Black Humor Fiction TCLC 54: 1-85
 characteristics of black humor, 2-13
 origins and development, 13-38
 black humor distinguished from related literary trends, 38-60
 black humor and society, 60-75
 black humor reconsidered, 75-83

American Civil War in Literature NCLC 32: 1-109
 overviews and general studies, 2-20
 regional perspectives, 20-54
 fiction popular during the war, 54-79
 the historical novel, 79-108

American Frontier in Literature NCLC 28: 1-103
 definitions, 2-12
 development, 12-17
 nonfiction writing about the frontier, 17-30
 frontier fiction, 30-45
 frontier protagonists, 45-66
 portrayals of Native Americans, 66-86
 feminist readings, 86-98
 twentieth-century reaction against frontier literature, 98-100

American Humor Writing NCLC 52: 1-59
 overviews and general studies, 2-12
 the Old Southwest, 12-42
 broader impacts, 42-5
 women humorists, 45-58

American Naturalism in Short Fiction SSC 77: 1-103
 overviews and general studies, 2-30
 major authors of American literary Naturalism, 30-102
  Ambrose Bierce, 30
  Stephen Crane, 30-53
  Theodore Dreiser, 53-65
  Jack London, 65-80
  Frank Norris, 80-9
  Edith Wharton, 89-102

American Novel of Manners TCLC 130: 1-42
 history of the Novel of Manners in America, 4-10
 representative writers, 10-18
 relevancy of the Novel of Manners, 18-24
 hallmark works in the Novel of Manners, 24-36
 Novel of Manners and other media, 36-40

American Mercury, **The** TCLC 74: 1-80

American Popular Song, Golden Age of TCLC 42: 1-49
 background and major figures, 2-34
 the lyrics of popular songs, 34-47

American Proletarian Literature TCLC 54: 86-175
 overviews and general studies, 87-95
 American proletarian literature and the American Communist Party, 95-111
 ideology and literary merit, 111-17
 novels, 117-36
 Gastonia, 136-48
 drama, 148-54
 journalism, 154-9
 proletarian literature in the United States, 159-74

American Realism NCLC 120: 89-246
 overviews, 91-112
 background and sources, 112-72
 social issues, 172-223
 women and realism, 223-45

American Renaissance SSC 64: 46-193
 overviews and general studies, 47-103
 major authors of short fiction, 103-92

American Romanticism NCLC 44: 74-138
 overviews and general studies, 74-84
 sociopolitical influences, 84-104
 Romanticism and the American frontier, 104-15
 thematic concerns, 115-37

American Western Literature TCLC 46: 1-100

definition and development of American Western literature, 2-7
characteristics of the Western novel, 8-23
Westerns as history and fiction, 23-34
critical reception of American Western literature, 34-41
the Western hero, 41-73
women in Western fiction, 73-91
later Western fiction, 91-9

American Writers in Paris TCLC 98: 1-156
overviews and general studies, 2-155

Anarchism NCLC 84: 1-97
overviews and general studies, 2-23
the French anarchist tradition, 23-56
Anglo-American anarchism, 56-68
anarchism: incidents and issues, 68-97

Animals in Literature TCLC 106: 1-120
overviews and general studies, 2-8
animals in American literature, 8-45
animals in Canadian literature, 45-57
animals in European literature, 57-100
animals in Latin American literature, 100-06
animals in women's literature, 106-20

Antebellum South, Literature of the NCLC 112:1-188
overviews, 4-55
culture of the Old South, 55-68
antebellum fiction: pastoral and heroic romance, 68-120
role of women: a subdued rebellion, 120-59
slavery and the slave narrative, 159-85

Anti-Americanism TCLC 158: 1-98
overviews and general studies, 3-18
literary and intellectual perspectives, 18-36
social and political reactions, 36-98

Anti-Apartheid TCLC 162: 1-121
overviews, 3-45
major authors, 45-74
anti-apartheid literature and the liberal tradition, 74-101
writing under apartheid: historical views, 101-20

The Apocalyptic Movement TCLC 106: 121-69

Aristotle CMLC 31:1-397
philosophy, 3-100
poetics, 101-219
rhetoric, 220-301
science, 302-397

Art and Literature TCLC 54: 176-248
overviews and general studies, 176-93
definitions, 193-219
influence of visual arts on literature, 219-31
spatial form in literature, 231-47

Arthurian Literature CMLC 10: 1-127
historical context and literary beginnings, 2-27
development of the legend through Malory, 27-64
development of the legend from Malory to the Victorian Age, 65-81
themes and motifs, 81-95
principal characters, 95-125

Arthurian Revival NCLC 36: 1-77
overviews and general studies, 2-12
Tennyson and his influence, 12-43
other leading figures, 43-73
the Arthurian legend in the visual arts, 73-6

Australian Cultural Identity in Nineteenth-Century Literature NCLC 124: 1-164
overviews and general studies, 4-22
poetry, 22-67
fiction, 67-135
role of women writers, 135-64

Australian Literature TCLC 50: 1-94
origins and development, 2-21
characteristics of Australian literature, 21-33
historical and critical perspectives, 33-41
poetry, 41-58
fiction, 58-76
drama, 76-82
Aboriginal literature, 82-91

The Beat Generation BG 1:1-562
the Beat Generation: an overview, 1-137
primary sources, 3-32
overviews and general studies, 32-47
Beat Generation as a social phenomenon, 47-65
drugs, inspiration, and the Beat Generation, 65-92
religion and the Beat Generation, 92-124
women of the Beat Generation, 124-36
Beat "scene": East and West, 139-259
primary sources, 141-77
Beat scene in the East, 177-218
Beat scene in the West, 218-59
Beat Generation publishing: periodicals, small presses, and censorship, 261-349
primary sources, 263-74
overview, 274-88
Beat periodicals: "little magazines," 288-311
Beat publishing: small presses, 311-24
Beat battles with censorship, 324-49
performing arts and the Beat Generation, 351-417
primary sources, 353-58
Beats and film, 358-81
Beats and music, 381-415
visual arts and the Beat Generation, 419-91
primary sources, 421-24
critical commentary, 424-90

Beat Generation, Literature of the TCLC 42: 50-102
overviews and general studies, 51-9
the Beat generation as a social phenomenon, 59-62
development, 62-5
Beat literature, 66-96
influence, 97-100

The Bell Curve Controversy CLC 91: 281-330

***Bildungsroman* in Nineteenth-Century Literature** NCLC 20: 92-168
surveys, 93-113
in Germany, 113-40
in England, 140-56
female *Bildungsroman*, 156-67
NCLC 152: 1-129
overview, 3-16
definition and issues, 16-52
female *Bildungsromane*, 52-83
ideology and nationhood, 83-128

Bloomsbury Group TCLC 34: 1-73
history and major figures, 2-13
definitions, 13-7
influences, 17-27
thought, 27-40
prose, 40-52
and literary criticism, 52-4
political ideals, 54-61
response to, 61-71

The Bloomsbury Group TCLC 138: 1-59
representative members of the Bloomsbury Group, 9-24
literary relevance of the Bloomsbury Group, 24-36
Bloomsbury's hallmark works, 36-48
other modernists studied with the Bloomsbury Group, 48-54

The Blues in Literature TCLC 82: 1-71

Bly, Robert, *Iron John: A Book about Men and Men's Work* CLC 70: 414-62

The Book of J CLC 65: 289-311

Brazilian Literature TCLC 134: 1-126
overviews and general studies, 3-33
Brazilian poetry, 33-48
contemporary Brazilian writing, 48-76
culture, politics, and race in Brazilian writing, 76-100
modernism and postmodernism in Brazil, 100-25

British Ephemeral Literature LC 59: 1-70
overviews and general studies, 1-9
broadside ballads, 10-40
chapbooks, jestbooks, pamphlets, and newspapers, 40-69

Buddhism and Literature TCLC 70: 59-164
eastern literature, 60-113
western literature, 113-63

The *Bulletin* and the Rise of Australian Literary Nationalism NCLC 116: 1-121
overviews, 3-32
legend of the nineties, 32-55
Bulletin style, 55-71
Australian literary nationalism, 71-98
myth of the bush, 98-120

Businessman in American Literature TCLC 26: 1-48
portrayal of the businessman, 1-32
themes and techniques in business fiction, 32-47

The Calendar LC 55: 1-92
overviews and general studies, 2-19
measuring time, 19-28
calendars and culture, 28-60
calendar reform, 60-92

Captivity Narratives LC 82: 71-172
overviews, 72-107
captivity narratives and Puritanism, 108-34
captivity narratives and Native Americans, 134-49
influence on American literature, 149-72

Caribbean Literature TCLC 138: 60-135
overviews and general studies, 61-9
ethnic and national identity, 69-107
expatriate Caribbean literature, 107-23
literary histoiography, 123-35

Catholicism in Nineteenth-Century American Literature NCLC 64: 1-58
overviews, 3-14
polemical literature, 14-46
Catholicism in literature, 47-57

Cavalier Poetry and Drama LC 107: 1-71
overviews, 2-36
Cavalier drama, 36-48
major figures, 48-70

Celtic Mythology CMLC 26: 1-111
overviews and general studies, 2-22
Celtic myth as literature and history, 22-48
Celtic religion: Druids and divinities, 48-80
Fionn MacCuhaill and the Fenian cycle, 80-111

Celtic Twilight See Irish Literary Renaissance

Censorship and Contemporary World Literature CLC 194: 1-80
overviews and general studies, 2-19
notorious cases, 19-59
censorship in the global context, 59-79

Censorship in Twentieth-Century Literature TCLC 154: 115-238

overviews and general studies, 117-25
censorship and obscenity trials, 125-61
censorship and sexual politics, 161-81
censorship and war, 181-207
political censorship and the state, 207-28
censorship and the writer, 228-38

The Chartist Movement and Literature NCLC 60: 1-84
overview: nineteenth-century working-class fiction, 2-19
Chartist fiction and poetry, 19-73
the Chartist press, 73-84

The Chicago Renaissance TCLC 154: 239-341
overviews and general studies, 240-60
definitions and growth, 260-82
the language debate, 282-318
major authors, 318-40

Chicano/a Literature, Contemporary CLC 205: 82-181
overviews, 84-124
Chicana studies, 124-40
some representative works, 140-80

Child Labor in Nineteenth-Century Literature NCLC 108: 1-133
overviews, 3-10
climbing boys and chimney sweeps, 10-16
the international traffic in children, 16-45
critics and reformers, 45-82
fictional representations of child laborers, 83-132

Children's Literature, Nineteenth-Century NCLC 52: 60-135
overviews and general studies, 61-72
moral tales, 72-89
fairy tales and fantasy, 90-119
making men/making women, 119-34

Christianity in Twentieth-Century Literature TCLC 110: 1-79
overviews and general studies, 2-31
Christianity in twentieth-century fiction, 31-78

Chronicle Plays LC 89: 1-106
development of the genre, 2-33
historiography and literature, 33-56
genre and performance, 56-88
politics and ideology, 88-106

The City and Literature TCLC 90: 1-124
overviews and general studies, 2-9
the city in American literature, 9-86
the city in European literature, 86-124

Civic Critics, Russian NCLC 20: 402-46
principal figures and background, 402-9
and Russian Nihilism, 410-6
aesthetic and critical views, 416-45

The Cockney School NCLC 68: 1-64
overview, 2-7
Blackwood's Magazine and the contemporary critical response, 7-24
the political and social import of the Cockneys and their critics, 24-63

Colonial America: The Intellectual Background LC 25: 1-98
overviews and general studies, 2-17
philosophy and politics, 17-31
early religious influences in Colonial America, 31-60
consequences of the Revolution, 60-78
religious influences in post-revolutionary America, 78-87
colonial literary genres, 87-97

Colonialism in Victorian English Literature NCLC 56: 1-77
overviews and general studies, 2-34
colonialism and gender, 34-51
monsters and the occult, 51-76

Columbus, Christopher, Books on the Quincentennial of His Arrival in the New World CLC 70: 329-60

Comic Books TCLC 66: 1-139
historical and critical perspectives, 2-48
superheroes, 48-67
underground comix, 67-88
comic books and society, 88-122
adult comics and graphic novels, 122-36

Comedy of Manners LC 92: 1-75
overviews, 2-21
comedy of manners and society, 21-47
comedy of manners and women, 47-74

Commedia dell'Arte LC 83: 1-147
overviews, 2-7
origins and development, 7-23
characters and actors, 23-45
performance, 45-62
texts and authors, 62-100
influence in Europe, 100-46

Conduct Books in Nineteenth-Century Literature NCLC 152: 130-229
women's education, 131-68
feminist revisions, 168-82
American behavioral literature: cultivating national identity, 182-209
English behavioral literature: defining a middle class, 209-27

Connecticut Wits NCLC 48: 1-95
overviews and general studies, 2-40
major works, 40-76
intellectual context, 76-95

Contemporary Black Humor CLC 196: 1-128
overviews and general studies, 2-18
black humor in American fiction, 18-28
development and history, 29-62
major authors, 62-115
technique and narrative, 115-127

Contemporary Feminist Criticism CLC 180: 1-103
overviews and general studies, 2-59
modern French feminist theory, 59-102

Contemporary Gay and Lesbian Literature CLC 171: 1-130
overviews and general studies, 2-43
contemporary gay literature, 44-95
lesbianism in contemporary literature, 95-129

Contemporary Southern Literature CLC 167: 1-132
criticism, 2-131

Crime in Literature TCLC 54: 249-307
evolution of the criminal figure in literature, 250-61
crime and society, 261-77
literary perspectives on crime and punishment, 277-88
writings by criminals, 288-306

Crime-Mystery-Detective Stories SSC 59:89-226
overviews and general studies, 90-140
origins and early masters of the crime-mystery-detective story, 140-73
hard-boiled crime-mystery-detective fiction, 173-209
diversity in the crime-mystery-detective story, 210-25

The Crusades CMLC 38: 1-144
history of the Crusades, 3-60
literature of the Crusades, 60-116
the Crusades and the people: attitudes and influences, 116-44

Cyberpunk TCLC 106: 170-366
overviews and general studies, 171-88
feminism and cyberpunk, 188-230
history and cyberpunk, 230-70
sexuality and cyberpunk, 270-98
social issues and cyberpunk, 299-366

Cyberpunk Short Fiction SSC 60: 44-108
overviews and general studies, 46-78
major writers of cyberpunk fiction, 78-81
sexuality and cyberpunk fiction, 81-97
additional pieces, 97-108

Czechoslovakian Literature of the Twentieth Century TCLC 42:103-96
through World War II, 104-35
de-Stalinization, the Prague Spring, and contemporary literature, 135-72
Slovak literature, 172-85
Czech science fiction, 185-93

Dadaism TCLC 46: 101-71
background and major figures, 102-16
definitions, 116-26
manifestos and commentary by Dadaists, 126-40
theater and film, 140-58
nature and characteristics of Dadaist writing, 158-70

Danish Literature See Twentieth-Century Danish Literature

Darwinism and Literature NCLC 32: 110-206
background, 110-31
direct responses to Darwin, 131-71
collateral effects of Darwinism, 171-205

Death in American Literature NCLC 92: 1-170
overviews and general studies, 2-32
death in the works of Emily Dickinson, 32-72
death in the works of Herman Melville, 72-101
death in the works of Edgar Allan Poe, 101-43
death in the works of Walt Whitman, 143-70

Death in Nineteenth-Century British Literature NCLC 68: 65-142
overviews and general studies, 66-92
responses to death, 92-102
feminist perspectives, 103-17
striving for immortality, 117-41

Death in Literature TCLC 78:1-183
fiction, 2-115
poetry, 115-46
drama, 146-81

Deconstruction TCLC 138: 136-256
overviews and general studies, 137-83
deconstruction and literature, 183-221
deconstruction in philosophy and history, 221-56

de Man, Paul, Wartime Journalism of CLC 55: 382-424

Detective Fiction, Nineteenth-Century NCLC 36: 78-148
origins of the genre, 79-100
history of nineteenth-century detective fiction, 101-33
significance of nineteenth-century detective fiction, 133-46
NCLC 148: 1-161
overviews, 3-26
origins and influences, 26-63
major authors, 63-134
Freud and detective fiction, 134-59

Detective Fiction, Twentieth-Century TCLC 38: 1-96
genesis and history of the detective story, 3-22
defining detective fiction, 22-32
evolution and varieties, 32-77
the appeal of detective fiction, 77-90

Detective Story See Crime-Mystery-Detective Stories

Dime Novels NCLC 84: 98-168
- overviews and general studies, 99-123
- popular characters, 123-39
- major figures and influences, 139-52
- socio-political concerns, 152-167

Disease and Literature TCLC 66: 140-283
- overviews and general studies, 141-65
- disease in nineteenth-century literature, 165-81
- tuberculosis and literature, 181-94
- women and disease in literature, 194-221
- plague literature, 221-53
- AIDS in literature, 253-82

El Dorado, The Legend of See The Legend of El Dorado

The Double in Nineteenth-Century Literature NCLC 40: 1-95
- genesis and development of the theme, 2-15
- the double and Romanticism, 16-27
- sociological views, 27-52
- psychological interpretations, 52-87
- philosophical considerations, 87-95

Dramatic Realism NCLC 44: 139-202
- overviews and general studies, 140-50
- origins and definitions, 150-66
- impact and influence, 166-93
- realist drama and tragedy, 193-201

Drugs and Literature TCLC 78: 184-282
- overviews and general studies, 185-201
- pre-twentieth-century literature, 201-42
- twentieth-century literature, 242-82

Dystopias in Contemporary Literature CLC 168: 1-91
- overviews and general studies, 2-52
- dystopian views in Margaret Atwood's *The Handmaid's Tale* (1985), 52-71
- feminist readings of dystopias, 71-90

Eastern Mythology CMLC 26: 112-92
- heroes and kings, 113-51
- cross-cultural perspective, 151-69
- relations to history and society, 169-92

Ecocriticism and Nineteenth-Century Literature NCLC 140: 1-168
- overviews, 3-20
- American literature: Romantics and Realists, 20-76
- American explorers and naturalists, 76-123
- English literature: Romantics and Victorians, 123-67

Ecofeminism and Nineteenth-Century Literature NCLC 136: 1-110
- overviews, 2-24
- the local landscape, 24-72
- travel writing, 72-109

Eighteenth-Century British Periodicals LC 63: 1-123
- rise of periodicals, 2-31
- impact and influence of periodicals, 31-64
- periodicals and society, 64-122

Eighteenth-Century Travel Narratives LC 77: 252-355
- overviews and general studies, 254-79
- eighteenth-century European travel narratives, 279-334
- non-European eighteenth-century travel narratives, 334-55

Electronic "Books": Hypertext and Hyperfiction CLC 86: 367-404
- books vs. CD-ROMS, 367-76
- hypertext and hyperfiction, 376-95
- implications for publishing, libraries, and the public, 395-403

Eliot, T. S., Centenary of Birth CLC 55: 345-75

Elizabethan Drama LC 22: 140-240
- origins and influences, 142-67
- characteristics and conventions, 167-83
- theatrical production, 184-200
- histories, 200-12
- comedy, 213-20
- tragedy, 220-30

Elizabethan Prose Fiction LC 41: 1-70
- overviews and general studies, 1-15
- origins and influences, 15-43
- style and structure, 43-69

The Emergence of the Short Story in the Nineteenth Century NCLC 140: 169-279
- overviews, 171-74
- the American short story, 174-214
- the short story in Great Britain and Ireland, 214-235
- stories by women in English, 235-45
- the short story in France and Russia, 245-66
- the Latin American short story, 266-77

Enclosure of the English Common NCLC 88: 1-57
- overviews and general studies, 1-12
- early reaction to enclosure, 12-23
- nineteenth-century reaction to enclosure, 23-56

The Encyclopedists LC 26: 172-253
- overviews and general studies, 173-210
- intellectual background, 210-32
- views on esthetics, 232-41
- views on women, 241-52

English Abolitionist Literature of the Nineteenth Century NCLC 136: 111-235
- overview, 112-35
- origins and development, 135-42
- poetry, 142-58
- prose, 158-80
- sociopolitical concerns, 180-95
- English abolitionist literature and feminism, 195-233

English Caroline Literature LC 13: 221-307
- background, 222-41
- evolution and varieties, 241-62
- the Cavalier mode, 262-75
- court and society, 275-91
- politics and religion, 291-306

English Decadent Literature of the 1890s NCLC 28: 104-200
- fin de siècle: the Decadent period, 105-19
- definitions, 120-37
- major figures: "the tragic generation," 137-50
- French literature and English literary Decadence, 150-7
- themes, 157-61
- poetry, 161-82
- periodicals, 182-96

English Essay, Rise of the LC 18: 238-308
- definitions and origins, 236-54
- influence on the essay, 254-69
- historical background, 269-78
- the essay in the seventeenth century, 279-93
- the essay in the eighteenth century, 293-307

English Mystery Cycle Dramas LC 34: 1-88
- overviews and general studies, 1-27
- the nature of dramatic performances, 27-42
- the medieval worldview and the mystery cycles, 43-67
- the doctrine of repentance and the mystery cycles, 67-76
- the fall from grace in the mystery cycles, 76-88

The English Realist Novel, 1740-1771 LC 51: 102-98
- overviews and general studies, 103-22
- from Romanticism to Realism, 123-58
- women and the novel, 159-175
- the novel and other literary forms, 176-197

English Revolution, Literature of the LC 43: 1-58
- overviews and general studies, 2-24
- pamphlets of the English Revolution, 24-38
- political sermons of the English Revolution, 38-48
- poetry of the English Revolution, 48-57

English Romantic Hellenism NCLC 68: 143-250
- overviews and general studies, 144-69
- historical development of English Romantic Hellenism, 169-91
- influence of Greek mythology on the Romantics, 191-229
- influence of Greek literature, art, and culture on the Romantics, 229-50

English Romantic Poetry NCLC 28: 201-327
- overviews and reputation, 202-37
- major subjects and themes, 237-67
- forms of Romantic poetry, 267-78
- politics, society, and Romantic poetry, 278-99
- philosophy, religion, and Romantic poetry, 299-324

The Epistolary Novel LC 59: 71-170
- overviews and general studies, 72-96
- women and the Epistolary novel, 96-138
- principal figures: Britain, 138-53
- principal figures: France, 153-69

Espionage Literature TCLC 50: 95-159
- overviews and general studies, 96-113
- espionage fiction/formula fiction, 113-26
- spies in fact and fiction, 126-38
- the female spy, 138-44
- social and psychological perspectives, 144-58

European Debates on the Conquest of the Americas LC 67: 1-129
- overviews and general studies, 3-56
- major Spanish figures, 56-98
- English perceptions of Native Americans, 98-129

European Romanticism NCLC 36: 149-284
- definitions, 149-77
- origins of the movement, 177-82
- Romantic theory, 182-200
- themes and techniques, 200-23
- Romanticism in Germany, 223-39
- Romanticism in France, 240-61
- Romanticism in Italy, 261-4
- Romanticism in Spain, 264-8
- impact and legacy, 268-82

Exile in Literature TCLC 122: 1-129
- overviews and general studies, 2-33
- exile in fiction, 33-92
- German literature in exile, 92-129

Existentialism and Literature TCLC 42: 197-268
- overviews and definitions, 198-209
- history and influences, 209-19
- Existentialism critiqued and defended, 220-35
- philosophical and religious perspectives, 235-41
- Existentialist fiction and drama, 241-67

Ezra Pound Controversy TCLC 150: 1-132
- politics of Ezra Pound, 3-42
- anti-semitism of Ezra Pound, 42-57
- the Bollingen Award controversy, 57-76
- Pound's later writing, 76-104
- criticism of *The Pisan Cantos*, 104-32

Familiar Essay NCLC 48: 96-211
- definitions and origins, 97-130
- overview of the genre, 130-43
- elements of form and style, 143-59

elements of content, 159-73
the Cockneys: Hazlitt, Lamb, and Hunt, 173-91
status of the genre, 191-210

Fantasy in Contemporary Literature CLC 193: 137-250
overviews and general studies, 139-57
language, form, and theory, 157-91
major writers, 191-230
women writers and fantasy, 230-50

Fashion in Nineteenth-Century Literature NCLC 128: 104-93
overviews and general studies, 105-38
fashion and American literature, 138-46
fashion and English literature, 146-74
fashion and French literature, 174-92

The Faust Legend LC 47: 1-117

Fear in Literature TCLC 74: 81-258
overviews and general studies, 81
pre-twentieth-century literature, 123
twentieth-century literature, 182

Feminism in the 1990s: Commentary on Works by Naomi Wolf, Susan Faludi, and Camille Paglia CLC 76: 377-415

Feminist Criticism See Contemporary Feminist Criticism

Feminist Criticism in 1990 CLC 65: 312-60

Fifteenth-Century English Literature LC 17: 248-334
background, 249-72
poetry, 272-315
drama, 315-23
prose, 323-33

Fifteenth-Century Spanish Poetry LC 100:82-173
overviews and general studies, 83-101
the Cancioneros, 101-57
major figures, 157-72

Film and Literature TCLC 38: 97-226
overviews and general studies, 97-119
film and theater, 119-34
film and the novel, 134-45
the art of the screenplay, 145-66
genre literature/genre film, 167-79
the writer and the film industry, 179-90
authors on film adaptations of their works, 190-200
fiction into film: comparative essays, 200-23

Finance and Money as Represented in Nineteenth-Century Literature NCLC 76: 1-69
historical perspectives, 2-20
the image of money, 20-37
the dangers of money, 37-50
women and money, 50-69

Folklore and Literature TCLC 86: 116-293
overviews and general studies, 118-144
Native American literature, 144-67
African-American literature, 167-238
folklore and the American West, 238-57
modern and postmodern literature, 257-91

Food in Literature TCLC 114: 1-133
food and children's literature, 2-14
food as a literary device, 14-32
rituals invloving food, 33-45
food and social and ethnic identity, 45-90
women's relationship with food, 91-132

Food in Nineteenth-Century Literature NCLC 108: 134-288
overviews, 136-74
food and social class, 174-85
food and gender, 185-219
food and love, 219-31
food and sex, 231-48
eating disorders, 248-70

vegetarians, carnivores, and cannibals, 270-87

French Drama in the Age of Louis XIV LC 28: 94-185
overview, 95-127
tragedy, 127-46
comedy, 146-66
tragicomedy, 166-84

French Enlightenment LC 14: 81-145
the question of definition, 82-9
le siècle des lumières, 89-94
women and the salons, 94-105
censorship, 105-15
the philosophy of reason, 115-31
influence and legacy, 131-44

French New Novel TCLC 98: 158-234
overviews and general studies, 158-92
influences, 192-213
themes, 213-33

French Realism NCLC 52: 136-216
origins and definitions, 137-70
issues and influence, 170-98
realism and representation, 198-215

French Revolution and English Literature NCLC 40: 96-195
history and theory, 96-123
romantic poetry, 123-50
the novel, 150-81
drama, 181-92
children's literature, 192-5

French Symbolist Poetry NCLC 144: 1-107
overviews, 2-14
Symbolist aesthetics, 14-47
the Symbolist lyric, 47-60
history and influence, 60-105

Futurism, Italian TCLC 42: 269-354
principles and formative influences, 271-9
manifestos, 279-88
literature, 288-303
theater, 303-19
art, 320-30
music, 330-6
architecture, 336-9
and politics, 339-46
reputation and significance, 346-51

Gaelic Revival See Irish Literary Renaissance

Gates, Henry Louis, Jr., and African-American Literary Criticism CLC 65: 361-405

Gaucho Literature TCLC 158: 99-195
overviews and general studies, 101-43
major works, 143-95

Gay and Lesbian Literature CLC 76: 416-39

Gay and Lesbian Literature See also Contemporary Gay and Lesbian Literature

Generation of 1898 Short Fiction SSC 75: 182-287
overviews and general studies, 182-210
major short story writers of the Generation of 1898, 210-86
Azorín, 210-16
Emilia Pardo Bazán, 216-34
Vicente Blasco Ibáñez, 234-36
Gabriel Miró, 236-43
Miguel de Unamuno, 243-68
Ramon del Valle-Inclán, 268-86

German Exile Literature TCLC 30: 1-58
the writer and the Nazi state, 1-10
definition of, 10-4
life in exile, 14-32
surveys, 32-50
Austrian literature in exile, 50-2
German publishing in the United States, 52-7

German Expressionism TCLC 34: 74-160
history and major figures, 76-85
aesthetic theories, 85-109
drama, 109-26
poetry, 126-38
film, 138-42
painting, 142-7
music, 147-53
and politics, 153-8

The Ghost Story SSC 58: 1-142
overviews and general studies, 1-21
the ghost story in American literature, 21-49
the ghost story in Asian literature, 49-53
the ghost story in European and English literature, 54-89
major figures, 89-141

The Gilded Age NCLC 84: 169-271
popular themes, 170-90
Realism, 190-208
Aestheticism, 208-26
socio-political concerns, 226-70

***Glasnost* and Contemporary Soviet Literature** CLC 59: 355-97

Gothic Drama NCLC 132: 95-198
overviews, 97-125
sociopolitical contexts, 125-58
Gothic playwrights, 158-97

Gothic Novel NCLC 28: 328-402
development and major works, 328-34
definitions, 334-50
themes and techniques, 350-78
in America, 378-85
in Scotland, 385-91
influence and legacy, 391-400

The Governess in Nineteenth-Century Literature NCLC 104: 1-131
overviews and general studies, 3-28
social roles and economic conditions, 28-86
fictional governesses, 86-131

The Grail Theme in Twentieth-Century Literature TCLC 142: 1-89
overviews and general studies, 2-20
major works, 20-89

Graphic Narratives CLC 86: 405-32
history and overviews, 406-21
the "Classics Illustrated" series, 421-2
reviews of recent works, 422-32

Graphic Novels CLC 177: 163-299
overviews and general studies, 165-198
critical readings of major works, 198-286
reviews of recent graphic novels, 286-299

Graveyard Poets LC 67: 131-212
origins and development, 131-52
major figures, 152-75
major works, 175-212

Greek Historiography CMLC 17: 1-49

Greek Mythology CMLC 26: 193-320
overviews and general studies, 194-209
origins and development of Greek mythology, 209-29
cosmogonies and divinities in Greek mythology, 229-54
heroes and heroines in Greek mythology, 254-80
women in Greek mythology, 280-320

Greek Theater CMLC 51: 1-58
criticism, 2-58

Hard-Boiled Fiction TCLC 118: 1-109
overviews and general studies, 2-39
major authors, 39-76
women and hard-boiled fiction, 76-109

The Harlem Renaissance HR 1: 1-563
overviews and general studies of the Harlem Renaissance, 1-137
primary sources, 3-12

overviews, 12-38
background and sources of the Harlem Renaissance, 38-56
the New Negro aesthetic, 56-91
patrons, promoters, and the New York Public Library, 91-121
women of the Harlem Renaissance, 121-37
social, economic, and political factors that influenced the Harlem Renaissance, 139-240
primary sources, 141-53
overviews, 153-87
social and economic factors, 187-213
Black intellectual and political thought, 213-40
publishing and periodicals during the Harlem Renaissance, 243-339
primary sources, 246-52
overviews, 252-68
African American writers and mainstream publishers, 268-91
anthologies: *The New Negro* and others, 291-309
African American periodicals and the Harlem Renaissance, 309-39
performing arts during the Harlem Renaissance, 341-465
primary sources, 343-48
overviews, 348-64
drama of the Harlem Renaissance, 364-92
influence of music on Harlem Renaissance writing, 437-65
visual arts during the Harlem Renaissance, 467-563
primary sources, 470-71
overviews, 471-517
painters, 517-36
sculptors, 536-58
photographers, 558-63

Harlem Renaissance TCLC 26: 49-125
principal issues and figures, 50-67
the literature and its audience, 67-74
theme and technique in poetry, fiction, and drama, 74-115
and American society, 115-21
achievement and influence, 121-2

Havel, Václav, Playwright and President CLC 65: 406-63

Heroic Drama LC 91: 249-373
definitions and overviews, 251-78
politics and heroic drama, 278-303
early plays: Dryden and Orrery, 303-51
later plays: Lee and Otway, 351-73

Historical Fiction, Nineteenth-Century NCLC 48: 212-307
definitions and characteristics, 213-36
Victorian historical fiction, 236-65
American historical fiction, 265-88
realism in historical fiction, 288-306

Hollywood and Literature TCLC 118: 110-251
overviews and general studies, 111-20
adaptations, 120-65
socio-historical and cultural impact, 165-206
theater and hollywood, 206-51

Holocaust and the Atomic Bomb: Fifty Years Later CLC 91: 331-82
the Holocaust remembered, 333-52
Anne Frank revisited, 352-62
the atomic bomb and American memory, 362-81

Holocaust Denial Literature TCLC 58: 1-110
overviews and general studies, 1-30
Robert Faurisson and Noam Chomsky, 30-52
Holocaust denial literature in America, 52-71
library access to Holocaust denial literature, 72-5
the authenticity of Anne Frank's diary, 76-90
David Irving and the "normalization" of Hitler, 90-109

Holocaust, Literature of the TCLC 42: 355-450
historical overview, 357-61
critical overview, 361-70
diaries and memoirs, 370-95
novels and short stories, 395-425
poetry, 425-41
drama, 441-8

Homosexuality in Nineteenth-Century Literature NCLC 56: 78-182
defining homosexuality, 80-111
Greek love, 111-44
trial and danger, 144-81

Humors Comedy LC 85: 194-324
overviews, 195-251
major figures: Ben Jonson, 251-93
major figures: William Shakespeare, 293-324

Hungarian Literature of the Twentieth Century TCLC 26: 126-88
surveys of, 126-47
Nyugat and early twentieth-century literature, 147-56
mid-century literature, 156-68
and politics, 168-78
since the 1956 revolt, 178-87

Hysteria in Nineteenth-Century Literature NCLC 64: 59-184
the history of hysteria, 60-75
the gender of hysteria, 75-103
hysteria and women's narratives, 103-57
hysteria in nineteenth-century poetry, 157-83

Image of the Noble Savage in Literature LC 79: 136-252
overviews and development, 136-76
the Noble Savage in the New World, 176-221
Rousseau and the French Enlightenment's view of the noble savage, 221-51

Imagism TCLC 74: 259-454
history and development, 260
major figures, 288
sources and influences, 352
Imagism and other movements, 397
influence and legacy, 431

Immigrants in Nineteenth-Century Literature, Representation of NCLC 112: 188-298
overview, 189-99
immigrants in America, 199-223
immigrants and labor, 223-60
immigrants in England, 260-97

Incest in Nineteenth-Century American Literature NCLC 76: 70-141
overview, 71-88
the concern for social order, 88-117
authority and authorship, 117-40

Incest in Victorian Literature NCLC 92: 172-318
overviews and general studies, 173-85
novels, 185-276
plays, 276-84
poetry, 284-318

Indian Literature in English TCLC 54: 308-406
overview, 309-13
origins and major figures, 313-25
the Indo-English novel, 325-55
Indo-English poetry, 355-67
Indo-English drama, 367-72
critical perspectives on Indo-English literature, 372-80
modern Indo-English literature, 380-9
Indo-English authors on their work, 389-404

The Industrial Revolution in Literature NCLC 56: 183-273
historical and cultural perspectives, 184-201
contemporary reactions to the machine, 201-21
themes and symbols in literature, 221-73

The Influence of Ernest Hemingway TCLC 162: 122-259
overviews, 123-43
writers on Hemingway, 143-58
Hemingway's evocation of place, 158-84
gender and identity, 184-229
Hemingway and the quest for meaning, 229-58

The Irish Famine as Represented in Nineteenth-Century Literature NCLC 64: 185-261
overviews and general studies, 187-98
historical background, 198-212
famine novels, 212-34
famine poetry, 234-44
famine letters and eye-witness accounts, 245-61

Irish Literary Renaissance TCLC 46: 172-287
overview, 173-83
development and major figures, 184-202
influence of Irish folklore and mythology, 202-22
Irish poetry, 222-34
Irish drama and the Abbey Theatre, 234-56
Irish fiction, 256-86

Irish Nationalism and Literature NCLC 44: 203-73
the Celtic element in literature, 203-19
anti-Irish sentiment and the Celtic response, 219-34
literary ideals in Ireland, 234-45
literary expressions, 245-73

The Irish Novel NCLC 80: 1-130
overviews and general studies, 3-9
principal figures, 9-22
peasant and middle class Irish novelists, 22-76
aristocratic Irish and Anglo-Irish novelists, 76-129

Israeli Literature TCLC 94: 1-137
overviews and general studies, 2-18
Israeli fiction, 18-33
Israeli poetry, 33-62
Israeli drama, 62-91
women and Israeli literature, 91-112
Arab characters in Israeli literature, 112-36

Italian Futurism See Futurism, Italian

Italian Humanism LC 12: 205-77
origins and early development, 206-18
revival of classical letters, 218-23
humanism and other philosophies, 224-39
humanism and humanists, 239-46
the plastic arts, 246-57
achievement and significance, 258-76

Italian Romanticism NCLC 60: 85-145
origins and overviews, 86-101
Italian Romantic theory, 101-25
the language of Romanticism, 125-45

Jacobean Drama LC 33: 1-37
the Jacobean worldview: an era of transition, 2-14
the moral vision of Jacobean drama, 14-22

Jacobean tragedy, 22-3
the Jacobean masque, 23-36

Jazz and Literature TCLC 102: 3-124

Jewish-American Fiction TCLC 62: 1-181
overviews and general studies, 2-24
major figures, 24-48
Jewish writers and American life, 48-78
Jewish characters in American fiction, 78-108
themes in Jewish-American fiction, 108-43
Jewish-American women writers, 143-59
the Holocaust and Jewish-American fiction, 159-81

Jews in Literature TCLC 118: 252-417
overviews and general studies, 253-97
representing the Jew in literature, 297-351
the Holocaust in literature, 351-416

The Journals of Lewis and Clark NCLC 100: 1-88
overviews and general studies, 4-30
journal-keeping methods, 30-46
Fort Mandan, 46-51
the Clark journal, 51-65
the journals as literary texts, 65-87

Kabuki LC 73: 118-232
overviews and general studies, 120-40
the development of Kabuki, 140-65
major works, 165-95
Kabuki and society, 195-231

The Kit-Kat Club LC 71: 66-112
overviews and general studies, 67-88
major figures, 88-107
attacks on the Kit-Kat Club, 107-12

The Knickerbocker Group NCLC 56: 274-341
overviews and general studies, 276-314
Knickerbocker periodicals, 314-26
writers and artists, 326-40

Künstlerroman TCLC 150: 133-260
overviews and general studies, 135-51
major works, 151-212
feminism in the *Künstlerroman,* 212-49
minority *Künstlerroman,* 249-59

The Lake Poets NCLC 52: 217-304
characteristics of the Lake Poets and their works, 218-27
literary influences and collaborations, 227-66
defining and developing Romantic ideals, 266-84
embracing Conservatism, 284-303

Language Poets TCLC 126: 66-172
overviews and general studies, 67-122
selected major figures in language poetry, 122-72

Larkin, Philip, Controversy CLC 81: 417-64

Latin American Literature, Twentieth-Century TCLC 58: 111-98
historical and critical perspectives, 112-36
the novel, 136-45
the short story, 145-9
drama, 149-60
poetry, 160-7
the writer and society, 167-86
Native Americans in Latin American literature, 186-97

Law and Literature TCLC 126: 173-347
overviews and general studies, 174-253
fiction critiquing the law, 253-88
literary responses to the law, 289-346

The Legend of El Dorado LC 74: 248-350
overviews, 249-308
major explorations for El Dorado, 308-50

The Levellers LC 51: 200-312
overviews and general studies, 201-29
principal figures, 230-86

religion, political philosophy, and pamphleteering, 287-311

Literary Criticism in the Nineteenth Century, American NCLC 128: 1-103
overviews and general studies, 2-44
the trancendentalists, 44-65
"young America," 65-71
James Russell Lowell, 71-9
Edgar Allan Poe, 79-97
Walt Whitman, 97-102

Literary Expressionism TCLC 142: 90-185
overviews and general studies, 91-138
themes in literary expressionism, 138-61
expressionism in Germany, 161-84

The Literary Marketplace Nineteenth-Century NCLC 128: 194-368
overviews and general studies, 197-228
British literary marketplace, 228-66
French literary marketplace, 266-82
American literary marketplace, 282-323
Women in the literary marketplace, 323-67

Literary Prizes TCLC 122: 130-203
overviews and general studies, 131-34
the Nobel Prize in Literature, 135-83
the Pulitzer Prize, 183-203

Literature and Millenial Lists CLC 119: 431-67
The Modern Library list, 433
The Waterstone list, 438-439

Literature in Response to the September 11 Attacks CLC 174: 1-46
Major works about September 11, 2001, 2-22
Critical, artistic, and journalistic responses, 22-45

Literature of the American Cowboy NCLC 96: 1-60
overview, 3-20
cowboy fiction, 20-36
cowboy poetry and songs, 36-59

Literature of the California Gold Rush NCLC 92: 320-85
overviews and general studies, 322-24
early California Gold Rush fiction, 324-44
Gold Rush folklore and legend, 344-51
the rise of Western local color, 351-60
social relations and social change, 360-385

Literature of the Counter-Reformation LC 109: 213-56
overviews and general studies, 214-33
influential figures, 233-56

The Living Theatre DC 16: 154-214

Luddism in Nineteenth-Century Literature NCLC 140: 280-365
overviews, 281-322
the literary response, 322-65

Lynching in Nineteenth-Century Literature NCLC 148: 162-247
lynching in literature and music, 163-92
Ida B. Wells-Barnett and the anti-lynching movement, 192-221
resistance to lynching in society and the press, 221-46

Madness in Nineteenth-Century Literature NCLC 76: 142-284
overview, 143-54
autobiography, 154-68
poetry, 168-215
fiction, 215-83

Madness in Twentieth-Century Literature TCLC 50: 160-225
overviews and general studies, 161-71
madness and the creative process, 171-86
suicide, 186-91
madness in American literature, 191-207

madness in German literature, 207-13
madness and feminist artists, 213-24

Magic Realism TCLC 110: 80-327
overviews and general studies, 81-94
magic realism in African literature, 95-110
magic realism in American literature, 110-32
magic realism in Canadian literature, 132-46
magic realism in European literature, 146-66
magic realism in Asian literature, 166-79
magic realism in Latin-American literature, 179-223
magic realism in Israeli literature and the novels of Salman Rushdie, 223-38
magic realism in literature written by women, 239-326

The Martin Marprelate Tracts LC 101: 165-240
criticism, 166-240

Marxist Criticism TCLC 134: 127-57
overviews and general studies, 128-67
Marxist interpretations, 167-209
cultural and literary Marxist theory, 209-49
Marxism and feminist critical theory, 250-56

The Masque LC 63: 124-265
development of the masque, 125-62
sources and structure, 162-220
race and gender in the masque, 221-64

Medical Writing LC 55: 93-195
colonial America, 94-110
enlightenment, 110-24
medieval writing, 124-40
sexuality, 140-83
vernacular, 185-95

Memoirs of Trauma CLC 109: 419-466
overview, 420
criticism, 429

Metafiction TCLC 130: 43-228
overviews and general studies, 44-85
Spanish metafiction, 85-117
studies of metafictional authors and works, 118-228

Metaphysical Poets LC 24: 356-439
early definitions, 358-67
surveys and overviews, 367-92
cultural and social influences, 392-406
stylistic and thematic variations, 407-38

Missionaries in the Nineteenth-Century, Literature of NCLC 112: 299-392
history and development, 300-16
uses of ethnography, 316-31
sociopolitical concerns, 331-82
David Livingstone, 382-91

The Modern Essay TCLC 58: 199-273
overview, 200-7
the essay in the early twentieth century, 207-19
characteristics of the modern essay, 219-32
modern essayists, 232-45
the essay as a literary genre, 245-73

Modern French Literature TCLC 122: 205-359
overviews and general studies, 207-43
French theater, 243-77
gender issues and French women writers, 277-315
ideology and politics, 315-24
modern French poetry, 324-41
resistance literature, 341-58

Modern Irish Literature TCLC 102: 125-321
overview, 129-44
dramas, 144-70
fiction, 170-247
poetry, 247-321

Modern Japanese Literature TCLC 66: 284-389
- poetry, 285-305
- drama, 305-29
- fiction, 329-61
- western influences, 361-87

Modernism TCLC 70: 165-275
- definitions, 166-84
- Modernism and earlier influences, 184-200
- stylistic and thematic traits, 200-29
- poetry and drama, 229-42
- redefining Modernism, 242-75

Monasticism and Literature CMLC 74: 88-294
- major figures, 89-132
- secular influences, 132-54
- monastic principles and literary practices, 154-232
- women and monasticism, 232-93

Muckraking Movement in American Journalism TCLC 34: 161-242
- development, principles, and major figures, 162-70
- publications, 170-9
- social and political ideas, 179-86
- targets, 186-208
- fiction, 208-19
- decline, 219-29
- impact and accomplishments, 229-40

Multiculturalism CLC 189: 167-254
- overviews and general studies, 168-93
- the effects of multiculturalism on global literature, 193-213
- multicultural themes in specific contemporary works, 213-53

Multiculturalism in Literature and Education CLC 70: 361-413

Music and Modern Literature TCLC 62: 182-329
- overviews and general studies, 182-211
- musical form/literary form, 211-32
- music in literature, 232-50
- the influence of music on literature, 250-73
- literature and popular music, 273-303
- jazz and poetry, 303-28

Mystery Story See Crime-Mystery-Detective Stories

Native American Literature CLC 76: 440-76

Natural School, Russian NCLC 24: 205-40
- history and characteristics, 205-25
- contemporary criticism, 225-40

Naturalism NCLC 36: 285-382
- definitions and theories, 286-305
- critical debates on Naturalism, 305-16
- Naturalism in theater, 316-32
- European Naturalism, 332-61
- American Naturalism, 361-72
- the legacy of Naturalism, 372-81

Negritude TCLC 50: 226-361
- origins and evolution, 227-56
- definitions, 256-91
- Negritude in literature, 291-343
- Negritude reconsidered, 343-58

Negritude TCLC 158: 196-280
- overviews and general studies, 197-208
- major figures, 208-25
- Negritude and humanism, 225-29
- poetry of Negritude, 229-47
- politics of Negritude, 247-68
- the Negritude debate, 268-79

New Criticism TCLC 34: 243-318
- development and ideas, 244-70
- debate and defense, 270-99
- influence and legacy, 299-315

TCLC 146: 1-108
- overviews and general studies, 3-19
- defining New Criticism, 19-28
- place in history, 28-51
- poetry and New Criticism, 51-78
- major authors, 78-108

The New Humanists TCLC 162: 260-341
- overviews, 261-92
- major figures, 292-310
- New Humanism in education and literature, 310-41

New South, Literature of the NCLC 116: 122-240
- overviews, 124-66
- the novel in the New South, 166-209
- myth of the Old South in the New, 209-39

The New World in Renaissance Literature LC 31: 1-51
- overview, 1-18
- utopia vs. terror, 18-31
- explorers and Native Americans, 31-51

New York Intellectuals and *Partisan Review* TCLC 30: 117-98
- development and major figures, 118-28
- influence of Judaism, 128-39
- *Partisan Review,* 139-57
- literary philosophy and practice, 157-75
- political philosophy, 175-87
- achievement and significance, 187-97

The New Yorker TCLC 58: 274-357
- overviews and general studies, 274-95
- major figures, 295-304
- *New Yorker* style, 304-33
- fiction, journalism, and humor at *The New Yorker,* 333-48
- the new *New Yorker,* 348-56

Newgate Novel NCLC 24: 166-204
- development of Newgate literature, 166-73
- *Newgate Calendar,* 173-7
- Newgate fiction, 177-95
- Newgate drama, 195-204

New Zealand Literature TCLC 134: 258-368
- overviews and general studies, 260-300
- Maori literature, 300-22
- New Zealand drama, 322-32
- New Zealand fiction, 332-51
- New Zealand poetry, 351-67

Nigerian Literature of the Twentieth Century TCLC 30: 199-265
- surveys of, 199-227
- English language and African life, 227-45
- politics and the Nigerian writer, 245-54
- Nigerian writers and society, 255-62

Nihilism and Literature TCLC 110: 328-93
- overviews and general studies, 328-44
- European and Russian nihilism, 344-73
- nihilism in the works of Albert Camus, Franz Kafka, and John Barth, 373-92

Nineteenth-Century Captivity Narratives NCLC 80:131-218
- overview, 132-37
- the political significance of captivity narratives, 137-67
- images of gender, 167-96
- moral instruction, 197-217

Nineteenth-Century Euro-American Literary Representations of Native Americans NCLC 104: 132-264
- overviews and general studies, 134-53
- Native American history, 153-72
- the Indians of the Northeast, 172-93
- the Indians of the Southeast, 193-212
- the Indians of the West, 212-27
- Indian-hater fiction, 227-43
- the Indian as exhibit, 243-63

Nineteenth-Century Native American Autobiography NCLC 64: 262-389
- overview, 263-8
- problems of authorship, 268-81
- the evolution of Native American autobiography, 281-304
- political issues, 304-15
- gender and autobiography, 316-62
- autobiographical works during the turn of the century, 362-88

Nineteenth-Century Pornography NCLC 144: 108-202
- nineteenth-century pornographers, 110-64
- pornography and literature, 164-91
- pornography and censorship, 191-201

Noh Drama LC 103: 189-270
- overviews, 190-94
- origins and development, 194-214
- structure, 214-28
- types of plays, 228-45
- masks in Noh drama, 245-57
- Noh drama and the audience, 257-69

Norse Mythology CMLC 26: 321-85
- history and mythological tradition, 322-44
- Eddic poetry, 344-74
- Norse mythology and other traditions, 374-85

Northern Humanism LC 16: 281-356
- background, 282-305
- precursor of the Reformation, 305-14
- the Brethren of the Common Life, the Devotio Moderna, and education, 314-40
- the impact of printing, 340-56

The Novel of Manners NCLC 56: 342-96
- social and political order, 343-53
- domestic order, 353-73
- depictions of gender, 373-83
- the American novel of manners, 383-95

Novels of the Ming and Early Ch'ing Dynasties LC 76: 213-356
- overviews and historical development, 214-45
- major works—overview, 245-85
- genre studies, 285-325
- cultural and social themes, 325-55

Nuclear Literature: Writings and Criticism in the Nuclear Age TCLC 46: 288-390
- overviews and general studies, 290-301
- fiction, 301-35
- poetry, 335-8
- nuclear war in Russo-Japanese literature, 338-55
- nuclear war and women writers, 355-67
- the nuclear referent and literary criticism, 367-88

Occultism in Modern Literature TCLC 50: 362-406
- influence of occultism on literature, 363-72
- occultism, literature, and society, 372-87
- fiction, 387-96
- drama, 396-405

Opium and the Nineteenth-Century Literary Imagination NCLC 20:250-301
- original sources, 250-62
- historical background, 262-71
- and literary society, 271-9
- and literary creativity, 279-300

Orientalism NCLC 96: 149-364
- overviews and general studies, 150-98
- Orientalism and imperialism, 198-229
- Orientalism and gender, 229-59
- Orientalism and the nineteenth-century novel, 259-321
- Orientalism in nineteenth-century poetry, 321-63

The Oxford Movement NCLC 72: 1-197
- overviews and general studies, 2-24
- background, 24-59
- and education, 59-69
- religious responses, 69-128

literary aspects, 128-178
political implications, 178-196

The Parnassian Movement NCLC 72: 198-241
overviews and general studies, 199-231
and epic form, 231-38
and positivism, 238-41

Pastoral Literature of the English Renaissance LC 59: 171-282
overviews and general studies, 172-214
principal figures of the Elizabethan period, 214-33
principal figures of the later Renaissance, 233-50
pastoral drama, 250-81

Periodicals, Nineteenth-Century American NCLC 132: 199-374
overviews, chronology, and development, 200-41
literary periodicals, 241-83
regional periodicals, 283-317
women's magazines and gender issues, 317-47
minority periodicals, 347-72

Periodicals, Nineteenth-Century British NCLC 24: 100-65
overviews and general studies, 100-30
in the Romantic Age, 130-41
in the Victorian era, 142-54
and the reviewer, 154-64

Picaresque Literature of the Sixteenth and Seventeenth Centuries LC 78: 223-355
context and development, 224-71
genre, 271-98
the picaro, 299-326
the picara, 326-53

Plath, Sylvia, and the Nature of Biography CLC 86: 433-62
the nature of biography, 433-52
reviews of *The Silent Woman*, 452-61

Political Theory from the 15th to the 18th Century LC 36: 1-55
overview, 1-26
natural law, 26-42
empiricism, 42-55

Polish Romanticism NCLC 52: 305-71
overviews and general studies, 306-26
major figures, 326-40
Polish Romantic drama, 340-62
influences, 362-71

Politics and Literature TCLC 94: 138-61
overviews and general studies, 139-96
Europe, 196-226
Latin America, 226-48
Africa and the Caribbean, 248-60

Popular Literature TCLC 70: 279-382
overviews and general studies, 280-324
"formula" fiction, 324-336
readers of popular literature, 336-351
evolution of popular literature, 351-382

The Portrayal of Jews in Nineteenth-Century English Literature NCLC 72: 242-368
overviews and general studies, 244-77
Anglo-Jewish novels, 277-303
depictions by non-Jewish writers, 303-44
Hebraism versus Hellenism, 344-67

The Portrayal of Mormonism NCLC 96: 61-148
overview, 63-72
early Mormon literature, 72-100
Mormon periodicals and journals, 100-10
women writers, 110-22
Mormonism and nineteenth-century literature, 122-42
Mormon poetry, 142-47

Post-apartheid Literature CLC 187: 284-382
overviews and general studies, 286-318
the post-apartheid novel, 318-65
post-apartheid drama, 365-81

Postcolonial African Literature TCLC 146: 110-239
overviews and general studies, 111-45
ideology and theory, 145-62
postcolonial testimonial literature, 162-99
major authors, 199-239

Postcolonialism TCLC 114: 134-239
overviews and general studies, 135-153
African postcolonial writing, 153-72
Asian/Pacific literature, 172-78
postcolonial literary theory, 178-213
postcolonial women's writing, 213-38

Postmodernism TCLC 90:125-307
overview, 126-166
criticism, 166-224
fiction, 224-282
poetry, 282-300
drama, 300-307

Pre-Raphaelite Movement NCLC 20: 302-401
overview, 302-4
genesis, 304-12
Germ and *Oxford and Cambridge Magazine*, 312-20
Robert Buchanan and the "Fleshly School of Poetry," 320-31
satires and parodies, 331-4
surveys, 334-51
aesthetics, 351-75
sister arts of poetry and painting, 375-94
influence, 394-9

Pre-romanticism LC 40: 1-56
overviews and general studies, 2-14
defining the period, 14-23
new directions in poetry and prose, 23-45
the focus on the self, 45-56

Pre-Socratic Philosophy CMLC 22: 1-56
overviews and general studies, 3-24
the Ionians and the Pythagoreans, 25-35
Heraclitus, the Eleatics, and the Atomists, 36-47
the Sophists, 47-55

The Prison in Nineteenth-Century Literature NCLC 116: 241-357
overview, 242-60
romantic prison, 260-78
domestic prison, 278-316
America as prison, 316-24
physical prisons and prison authors, 324-56

Protestant Hagiography and Martyrology LC 84: 106-217
overview, 106-37
John Foxe's *Book of Martyrs*, 137-97
martyrology and the feminine perspective, 198-216

Protestant Reformation, Literature of the LC 37: 1-83
overviews and general studies, 1-49
humanism and scholasticism, 49-69
the reformation and literature, 69-82

Psychoanalysis and Literature TCLC 38: 227-338
overviews and general studies, 227-46
Freud on literature, 246-51
psychoanalytic views of the literary process, 251-61
psychoanalytic theories of response to literature, 261-88
psychoanalysis and literary criticism, 288-312
psychoanalysis as literature/literature as psychoanalysis, 313-34

The Quarrel between the Ancients and the Moderns LC 63: 266-381
overviews and general studies, 267-301
Renaissance origins, 301-32
Quarrel between the Ancients and the Moderns in France, 332-58
Battle of the Books in England, 358-80

Racism in Literature TCLC 138: 257-373
overviews and general studies, 257-326
racism and literature by and about African Americans, 292-326
theme of racism in literature, 326-773

Rap Music CLC 76: 477-50

Reader-Response Criticism TCLC 146: 240-357
overviews and general studies, 241-88
critical approaches to reader response, 288-342
reader-response interpretation, 342-57

Realism in Short Fiction SSC 63: 128-57
overviews and general studies, 129-37
realist short fiction in France, 137-62
realist short fiction in Russia, 162-215
realist short fiction in England, 215-31
realist short fiction in the United States, 231-56

Regionalism and Local Color in Short Fiction SSC 65: 160-289
overviews and general studies, 163-205
regionalism/local color fiction of the west, 205-42
regionalism/local color fiction of the midwest, 242-57
regionalism/local color fiction of the south, 257-88

Renaissance Natural Philosophy LC 27: 201-87
cosmology, 201-28
astrology, 228-54
magic, 254-86

Representations of Africa in Nineteenth-Century Literature NCLC 148: 248-351
overview, 251-66
Northeast and Central Africa, 266-76
South Africa, 276-301
West Africa, 301-49

Representations of the Devil in Nineteenth-Century Literature NCLC 100: 89-223
overviews and general studies, 90-115
the Devil in American fiction, 116-43
English Romanticism: the satanic school, 143-89
Luciferian discourse in European literature, 189-222

Restoration Drama LC 21: 184-275
general overviews and general studies, 185-230
Jeremy Collier stage controversy, 230-9
other critical interpretations, 240-75

Revenge Tragedy LC 71: 113-242
overviews and general studies, 113-51
Elizabethan attitudes toward revenge, 151-88
the morality of revenge, 188-216
reminders and remembrance, 217-41

Revising the Literary Canon CLC 81: 465-509

Revising the Literary Canon TCLC 114: 240-84
overviews and general studies, 241-85
canon change in American literature, 285-339
gender and the literary canon, 339-59
minority and third-world literature and the canon, 359-84

Revolutionary Astronomers LC 51: 314-65
overviews and general studies, 316-25

Robin Hood, Legend of LC 19: 205-58
   principal figures, 325-51
   Revolutionary astronomical models, 352-64

Robin Hood, Legend of LC 19: 205-58
   origins and development of the Robin Hood legend, 206-20
   representations of Robin Hood, 220-44
   Robin Hood as hero, 244-56

Romantic Literary Criticism NCLC 144: 203-357
   background and overviews, 205-30
   literary reviews, 230-38
   the German Romantics, 238-81
   Wordsworth and Coleridge, 281-326
   variations on Romantic critical theory, 326-56

Rushdie, Salman, *Satanic Verses* Controversy CLC 55: 214-63; 59:404-56

Russian Nihilism NCLC 28: 403-47
   definitions and overviews, 404-17
   women and Nihilism, 417-27
   literature as reform: the Civic Critics, 427-33
   Nihilism and the Russian novel: Turgenev and Dostoevsky, 433-47

Russian Thaw TCLC 26: 189-247
   literary history of the period, 190-206
   theoretical debate of socialist realism, 206-11
   Novy Mir, 211-7
   Literary Moscow, 217-24
   Pasternak, *Zhivago,* and the Nobel prize, 224-7
   poetry of liberation, 228-31
   Brodsky trial and the end of the Thaw, 231-6
   achievement and influence, 236-46

Salem Witch Trials LC 38: 1-145
   overviews and general studies, 2-30
   historical background, 30-65
   judicial background, 65-78
   the search for causes, 78-115
   the role of women in the trials, 115-44

Salinger, J. D., Controversy Surrounding *In Search of J. D. Salinger* CLC 55: 325-44

Samizdat Literature TCLC 150: 261-342
   overviews and general studies, 262-64
   history and development, 264-309
   politics and Samizdat, 309-22
   voices of Samizdat, 322-42

Sanitation Reform, Nineteenth-Century NCLC 124: 165-257
   overviews and general studies, 166
   primary texts, 186-89
   social context, 189-221
   public health in literature, 221-56

Science and Modern Literature TCLC 90: 308-419
   overviews and general studies, 295-333
   fiction, 333-95
   poetry, 395-405
   drama, 405-19

Science in Nineteenth-Century Literature NCLC 100: 224-366
   overviews and general studies, 225-65
   major figures, 265-336
   sociopolitical concerns, 336-65

Science Fiction, Nineteenth-Century NCLC 24: 241-306
   background, 242-50
   definitions of the genre, 251-56
   representative works and writers, 256-75
   themes and conventions, 276-305

Scottish Chaucerians LC 20: 363-412

Scottish Poetry, Eighteenth-Century LC 29: 95-167
   overviews and general studies, 96-114
   the Scottish Augustans, 114-28
   the Scots Vernacular Revival, 132-63
   Scottish poetry after Burns, 163-66

The Sea in Literature TCLC 82: 72-191
   drama, 73-9
   poetry, 79-119
   fiction, 119-91

The Sea in Nineteenth-Century English and American Literature NCLC 104: 265-362
   overviews and general studies, 267-306
   major figures in American sea fiction—Cooper and Melville, 306-29
   American sea poetry and short stories, 329-45
   English sea literature, 345-61

The Sensation Novel NCLC 80: 219-330
   overviews and general studies, 221-46
   principal figures, 246-62
   nineteenth-century reaction, 262-91
   feminist criticism, 291-329

The Sentimental Novel NCLC 60: 146-245
   overviews and general studies, 147-58
   the politics of domestic fiction, 158-79
   a literature of resistance and repression, 179-212
   the reception of sentimental fiction, 213-44

September 11 Attacks See Literature in Response to the September 11 Attacks

Sex and Literature TCLC 82: 192-434
   overviews and general studies, 193-216
   drama, 216-63
   poetry, 263-87
   fiction, 287-431

Sherlock Holmes Centenary TCLC 26: 248-310
   Doyle's life and the composition of the Holmes stories, 248-59
   life and character of Holmes, 259-78
   method, 278-79
   Holmes and the Victorian world, 279-92
   Sherlockian scholarship, 292-301
   Doyle and the development of the detective story, 301-07
   Holmes's continuing popularity, 307-09

Short Science Fiction, Golden Age of, 1938-1950 SSC 73: 1-145
   overviews and general studies, 3-48
   publishing history of Golden Age Short Science Fiction, 48-65
   major Golden Age Short Science Fiction authors and editors
     Isaac Asimov, 65-77
     Ray Bradbury, 77-92
     John W. Campbell, 92-106
     Arthur C. Clarke, 106-15
     Robert A. Heinlein, 115-29
     Damon Knight, 129-40
     Frederik Pohl, 141-43

Short-Short Fiction SSC 61: 311-36
   overviews and general studies, 312-19
   major short-short fiction writers, 319-35

The Silver Fork Novel NCLC 88: 58-140
   criticism, 59-139

Slave Narratives, American NCLC 20: 1-91
   background, 2-9
   overviews and general studies, 9-24
   contemporary responses, 24-7
   language, theme, and technique, 27-70
   historical authenticity, 70-5
   antecedents, 75-83
   role in development of Black American literature, 83-8

The Slave Trade in British and American Literature LC 59: 283-369
   overviews and general studies, 284-91
   depictions by white writers, 291-331
   depictions by former slaves, 331-67

Social Conduct Literature LC 55: 196-298
   overviews and general studies, 196-223
   prescriptive ideology in other literary forms, 223-38
   role of the press, 238-63
   impact of conduct literature, 263-87
   conduct literature and the perception of women, 287-96
   women writing for women, 296-98

Social Protest Literature Outside England, Nineteenth-Century NCLC 124: 258-350
   overviews and general studies, 259-72
   oppression revealed, 272-306
   literature to incite or prevent reform, 306-50

Socialism NCLC 88: 141-237
   origins, 142-54
   French socialism, 154-83
   Anglo-American socialism, 183-205
   Socialist-Feminism, 205-36

Southern Gothic Literature TCLC 142: 186-270
   overviews and general studies, 187-97
   major authors in southern Gothic literature, 197-230
   structure and technique in southern Gothic literature, 230-50
   themes in southern Gothic literature, 250-70

Southern Literature See Contemporary Southern Literature

Southern Literature of the Reconstruction NCLC 108: 289-369
   overview, 290-91
   reconstruction literature: the consequences of war, 291-321
   old south to new: continuities in southern culture, 321-68

Southwestern Humor SSC 81: 105-248
   overviews, 106-83
   Mark Twain, 183-97
   George Washington Harris, 197-208
   other major figures, 208-46

Spanish Civil War Literature TCLC 26: 311-85
   topics in, 312-33
   British and American literature, 333-59
   French literature, 359-62
   Spanish literature, 362-73
   German literature, 373-75
   political idealism and war literature, 375-83

Spanish Golden Age Literature LC 23: 262-332
   overviews and general studies, 263-81
   verse drama, 281-304
   prose fiction, 304-19
   lyric poetry, 319-31

Sparta in Literature CMLC 70: 145-271
   overviews, 147-61
   Spartan poetry, 161-72
   the Spartan myth, 172-200
   historical background, 200-27
   Spartan society and culture, 227-69

Spasmodic School of Poetry NCLC 24: 307-52
   history and major figures, 307-21
   the Spasmodics on poetry, 321-7
   Firmilian and critical disfavor, 327-39
   theme and technique, 339-47
   influence, 347-51

Sports in Literature TCLC 86: 294-445
   overviews and general studies, 295-324
   major writers and works, 324-402
   sports, literature, and social issues, 402-45

Steinbeck, John, Fiftieth Anniversary of *The Grapes of Wrath* CLC 59: 311-54

Sturm und Drang NCLC 40: 196-276
   definitions, 197-238

poetry and poetics, 238-58
drama, 258-75

Supernatural Fiction in the Nineteenth Century NCLC 32: 207-87
major figures and influences, 208-35
the Victorian ghost story, 236-54
the influence of science and occultism, 254-66
supernatural fiction and society, 266-86

Supernatural Fiction, Modern TCLC 30: 59-116
evolution and varieties, 60-74
"decline" of the ghost story, 74-86
as a literary genre, 86-92
technique, 92-101
nature and appeal, 101-15

Surrealism TCLC 30: 334-406
history and formative influences, 335-43
manifestos, 343-54
philosophic, aesthetic, and political principles, 354-75
poetry, 375-81
novel, 381-6
drama, 386-92
film, 392-8
painting and sculpture, 398-403
achievement, 403-5

Surrealism in Children's Literature CLR 103: 127-200
overviews and general studies, 130-52
critical analysis of surrealist children's authors and works, 152-99

Sylvia Beach and Company TCLC 158: 281-370
overviews and general studies, 282-97
Shakespeare and Company, 297-314
the business of publishing, 315-40
Sylvia Beach and James Joyce, 341-70

Symbolism, Russian TCLC 30: 266-333
doctrines and major figures, 267-92
theories, 293-8
and French Symbolism, 298-310
themes in poetry, 310-4
theater, 314-20
and the fine arts, 320-32

Symbolist Movement, French NCLC 20: 169-249
background and characteristics, 170-86
principles, 186-91
attacked and defended, 191-7
influences and predecessors, 197-211
and Decadence, 211-6
theater, 216-26
prose, 226-33
decline and influence, 233-47

Television and Literature TCLC 78: 283-426
television and literacy, 283-98
reading vs. watching, 298-341
adaptations, 341-62
literary genres and television, 362-90
television genres and literature, 390-410
children's literature/children's television, 410-25

Theater of the Absurd TCLC 38: 339-415
"The Theater of the Absurd," 340-7
major plays and playwrights, 347-58
and the concept of the absurd, 358-86
theatrical techniques, 386-94
predecessors of, 394-402
influence of, 402-13

Tin Pan Alley See American Popular Song, Golden Age of

Tobacco Culture LC 55: 299-366
social and economic attitudes toward tobacco, 299-344

tobacco trade between the old world and the new world, 344-55
tobacco smuggling in Great Britain, 355-66

Transcendentalism, American NCLC 24: 1-99
overviews and general studies, 3-23
contemporary documents, 23-41
theological aspects of, 42-52
and social issues, 52-74
literature of, 74-96

Travel Narratives in Contemporary Literature CLC 204: 260-351
overviews, 261-76
major authors, 276-311
modern travel writing, 311-31
women writers and travel, 331-51

Travel Writing in the Nineteenth Century NCLC 44: 274-392
the European grand tour, 275-303
the Orient, 303-47
North America, 347-91

Travel Writing in the Twentieth Century TCLC 30: 407-56
conventions and traditions, 407-27
and fiction writing, 427-43
comparative essays on travel writers, 443-54

Treatment of Death in Children's Literature CLR 101: 152-201
overviews and general studies, 155-80
analytical and bibliographical reviews of death in children's literature, 180-97
death of animals in children's literature, 197-200

Tristan and Isolde Legend CMLC 42: 311-404

Troubadours CMLC 66: 244-383
overviews, 245-91
politics, economics, history, and the troubadours, 291-344
troubadours and women, 344-82

True-Crime Literature CLC 99: 333-433
history and analysis, 334-407
reviews of true-crime publications, 407-23
writing instruction, 424-29
author profiles, 429-33

Twentieth-Century Danish Literature TCLC 142: 271-344
major works, 272-84
major authors, 284-344

Ulysses **and the Process of Textual Reconstruction** TCLC 26:386-416
evaluations of the new *Ulysses,* 386-94
editorial principles and procedures, 394-401
theoretical issues, 401-16

Unconventional Family in Children's Literature CLR 102: 146-213
overviews and general studies, 149-79
analytical and bibliographical reviews, 179-97
types of unconventional families: foster, adopted, homosexual, 197-212

Utilitarianism NCLC 84: 272-340
J. S. Mill's Utilitarianism: liberty, equality, justice, 273-313
Jeremy Bentham's Utilitarianism: the science of happiness, 313-39

Utopianism NCLC 88: 238-346
overviews: Utopian literature, 239-59
Utopianism in American literature, 259-99
Utopianism in British literature, 299-311
Utopianism and Feminism, 311-45

Utopian Literature, Nineteenth-Century NCLC 24: 353-473
definitions, 354-74
overviews and general studies, 374-88

theory, 388-408
communities, 409-26
fiction, 426-53
women and fiction, 454-71

Utopian Literature, Renaissance LC 32: 1-63
overviews and general studies, 2-25
classical background, 25-33
utopia and the social contract, 33-9
origins in mythology, 39-48
utopia and the Renaissance country house, 48-52
influence of millenarianism, 52-62

Vampire in Literature TCLC 46: 391-454
origins and evolution, 392-412
social and psychological perspectives, 413-44
vampire fiction and science fiction, 445-53

Vernacular Bibles LC 67: 214-388
overviews and general studies, 215-59
the English Bible, 259-355
the German Bible, 355-88

Victorian Autobiography NCLC 40: 277-363
development and major characteristics, 278-88
themes and techniques, 289-313
the autobiographical tendency in Victorian prose and poetry, 313-47
Victorian women's autobiographies, 347-62
NCLC 152: 230-365
overviews and general studies, 232-61
autobiography and the self, 261-93
autobiography and gender, 293-307
autobiography and class, 307-36
autobiography and fiction, 336-64

Victorian Critical Theory NCLC 136: 236-379
overviews and general studies, 237-86
Matthew Arnold, 286-324
Walter Pater and aestheticism, 324-36
other Victorian critics, 336-78

Victorian Fantasy Literature NCLC 60: 246-384
overviews and general studies, 247-91
major figures, 292-366
women in Victorian fantasy literature, 366-83

Victorian Hellenism NCLC 68: 251-376
overviews and general studies, 252-78
the meanings of Hellenism, 278-335
the literary influence, 335-75

Victorian Illustrated Fiction NCLC 120: 247-356
overviews and development, 128-76
technical and material aspects of book illustration, 276-84
Charles Dickens and his illustrators, 284-320
William Makepeace Thackeray, 320-31
George Eliot and Frederic Leighton, 331-51
Lewis Carroll and John Tenniel, 351-56

Victorian Novel NCLC 32: 288-454
development and major characteristics, 290-310
themes and techniques, 310-58
social criticism in the Victorian novel, 359-97
urban and rural life in the Victorian novel, 397-406
women in the Victorian novel, 406-25
Mudie's Circulating Library, 425-34
the late-Victorian novel, 434-51

Vietnamese Literature TCLC 102: 322-386

Vietnam War in Literature and Film CLC 91: 383-437
overview, 384-8
prose, 388-412

film and drama, 412-24
poetry, 424-35

The Vietnam War in Short Fiction SSC 79: 83-177
  overviews and general studies, 84-93
  women authors of Vietnam War short fiction, 93-116
  Robert Olen Butler: *A Good Scent from a Strange Mountain* (1992), 116-31
  Barry Hannah: *Airships* (1978), 131-50
  Tim O'Brien: *The Things They Carried* (1990), 150-65
  Tobias Wolff: *Back in the World* (1985), 165-69
  other authors and works, 169-76

Violence in Literature TCLC 98: 235-358
  overviews and general studies, 236-74
  violence in the works of modern authors, 274-358

Vorticism TCLC 62: 330-426
  Wyndham Lewis and Vorticism, 330-8
  characteristics and principles of Vorticism, 338-65
  Lewis and Pound, 365-82
  Vorticist writing, 382-416
  Vorticist painting, 416-26

The Well-Made Play NCLC 80: 331-370
  overviews and general studies, 332-45
  Scribe's style, 345-56
  the influence of the well-made play, 356-69

Women's Autobiography, Nineteenth Century NCLC 76: 285-368
  overviews and general studies, 287-300
  autobiographies concerned with religious and political issues, 300-15
  autobiographies by women of color, 315-38
  autobiographies by women pioneers, 338-51
  autobiographies by women of letters, 351-68

Women's Diaries, Nineteenth-Century NCLC 48: 308-54
  overview, 308-13
  diary as history, 314-25
  sociology of diaries, 325-34
  diaries as psychological scholarship, 334-43
  diary as autobiography, 343-8
  diary as literature, 348-53

Women in Modern Literature TCLC 94: 262-425
  overviews and general studies, 263-86
  American literature, 286-304
  other national literatures, 304-33
  fiction, 333-94
  poetry, 394-407
  drama, 407-24

Women Writers, Seventeenth-Century LC 30: 2-58
  overview, 2-15
  women and education, 15-9
  women and autobiography, 19-31
  women's diaries, 31-9
  early feminists, 39-58

World War I Literature TCLC 34: 392-486
  overview, 393-403
  English, 403-27
  German, 427-50
  American, 450-66
  French, 466-74
  and modern history, 474-82

World War I Short Fiction SSC 71: 187-347
  overviews and general studies, 187-206
  female short fiction writers of World War I, 206-36
  Central Powers
    Czechoslovakian writers of short fiction, 236-44
    German writers of short fiction, 244-61
  Entente/Allied Alliance
    Australian writers of short fiction, 261-73
    English writers of short fiction, 273-305
    French writers of short fiction, 305-11
  Associated Power: American writers of short fiction, 311-46

Yellow Journalism NCLC 36: 383-456
  overviews and general studies, 384-96
  major figures, 396-413

Yiddish Literature TCLC 130: 229-364
  overviews and general studies, 230-54
  major authors, 254-305
  Yiddish literature in America, 305-34
  Yiddish and Judaism, 334-64

Young Playwrights Festival
  1988 CLC 55: 376-81
  1989 CLC 59: 398-403
  1990 CLC 65: 444-8

TCLC Cumulative Nationality Index

AMERICAN

Abbey, Edward **160**
Adams, Andy **56**
Adams, Brooks **80**
Adams, Henry (Brooks) **4, 52**
Addams, Jane **76**
Agee, James (Rufus) **1, 19**
Aldrich, Bess (Genevra) Streeter **125**
Allen, Fred **87**
Anderson, Maxwell **2, 144**
Anderson, Sherwood **1, 10, 24, 123**
Anthony, Susan B(rownell) **84**
Atherton, Gertrude (Franklin Horn) **2**
Austin, Mary (Hunter) **25**
Baker, Ray Stannard **47**
Baker, Carlos (Heard) **119**
Bambara, Toni Cade **116**
Barry, Philip **11**
Baum, L(yman) Frank **7, 132**
Beard, Charles A(ustin) **15**
Becker, Carl (Lotus) **63**
Belasco, David **3**
Bell, James Madison **43**
Benchley, Robert (Charles) **1, 55**
Benedict, Ruth (Fulton) **60**
Benét, Stephen Vincent **7**
Benét, William Rose **28**
Bettelheim, Bruno **143**
Bierce, Ambrose (Gwinett) **1, 7, 44**
Biggers, Earl Derr **65**
Bishop, Elizabeth **121**
Bishop, John Peale **103**
Black Elk **33**
Boas, Franz **56**
Bodenheim, Maxwell **44**
Bok, Edward W. **101**
Bourne, Randolph S(illiman) **16**
Boyd, James **115**
Boyd, Thomas (Alexander) **111**
Bradford, Gamaliel **36**
Brautigan, Richard **133**
Brennan, Christopher John **17**
Brennan, Maeve **124**
Brodkey, Harold (Roy) **123**
Bromfield, Louis (Brucker) **11**
Broun, Heywood **104**
Bryan, William Jennings **99**
Burroughs, Edgar Rice **2, 32**
Burroughs, William S(eward) **121**
Cabell, James Branch **6**
Cable, George Washington **4**
Cahan, Abraham **71**
Caldwell, Erskine (Preston) **117**
Campbell, Joseph **140**
Capote, Truman **164**
Cardozo, Benjamin N(athan) **65**
Carnegie, Dale **53**
Cather, Willa (Sibert) **1, 11, 31, 99, 132, 152**
Chambers, Robert W(illiam) **41**
Chambers, (David) Whittaker **129**
Chandler, Raymond (Thornton) **1, 7**
Chapman, John Jay **7**
Chase, Mary Ellen **124**
Chesnutt, Charles W(addell) **5, 39**
Childress, Alice **116**
Chopin, Katherine **5, 14, 127**
Cobb, Irvin S(hrewsbury) **77**
Coffin, Robert P(eter) Tristram **95**
Cohan, George M(ichael) **60**
Comstock, Anthony **13**
Cotter, Joseph Seamon Sr. **28**
Cram, Ralph Adams **45**
Crane, (Harold) Hart **2, 5, 80**
Crane, Stephen (Townley) **11, 17, 32**
Crawford, F(rancis) Marion **10**
Crothers, Rachel **19**
Cullen, Countée **4, 37**
Cummings, E. E. **137**
Darrow, Clarence (Seward) **81**
Davis, Rebecca (Blaine) Harding **6**
Davis, Richard Harding **24**
Day, Clarence (Shepard Jr.) **25**
Dent, Lester **72**
De Voto, Bernard (Augustine) **29**
Dewey, John **95**
Dickey, James **151**
Dixon, Thomas, Jr. **163**
di Donato, Pietro **159**
Dreiser, Theodore (Herman Albert) **10, 18, 35, 83**
Dulles, John Foster **72**
Dunbar, Paul Laurence **2, 12**
Duncan, Isadora **68**
Dunne, Finley Peter **28**
Eastman, Charles A(lexander) **55**
Eddy, Mary (Ann Morse) Baker **71**
Einstein, Albert **65**
Erskine, John **84**
Faulkner, William **141**
Faust, Frederick (Schiller) **49**
Fenollosa, Ernest (Francisco) **91**
Fields, W. C. **80**
Fisher, Dorothy (Frances) Canfield **87**
Fisher, Rudolph **11**
Fisher, Vardis **140**
Fitzgerald, F(rancis) Scott (Key) **1, 6, 14, 28, 55, 157**
Fitzgerald, Zelda (Sayre) **52**
Fletcher, John Gould **35**
Foote, Mary Hallock **108**
Ford, Henry **73**
Forten, Charlotte L. **16**
Freeman, Douglas Southall **11**
Freeman, Mary E(leanor) Wilkins **9**
Fuller, Henry Blake **103**
Futrelle, Jacques **19**
Gale, Zona **7**
Garland, (Hannibal) Hamlin **3**
Gilman, Charlotte (Anna) Perkins (Stetson) **9, 37, 117**
Ginsberg, Allen **120**
Glasgow, Ellen (Anderson Gholson) **2, 7**
Glaspell, Susan **55**
Goldman, Emma **13**
Green, Anna Katharine **63**
Grey, Zane **6**
Griffith, D(avid Lewelyn) W(ark) **68**
Griggs, Sutton (Elbert) **77**
Guest, Edgar A(lbert) **95**
Guiney, Louise Imogen **41**
Haley, Alex **147**
Hall, James Norman **23**
Handy, W(illiam) C(hristopher) **97**
Harper, Frances Ellen Watkins **14**
Harris, Joel Chandler **2**
Harte, (Francis) Bret(t) **1, 25**
Hartmann, Sadakichi **73**
Hatteras, Owen **18**
Hawthorne, Julian **25**
Hearn, (Patricio) Lafcadio (Tessima Carlos) **9**
Hecht, Ben **101**
Heller, Joseph **131, 151**
Hellman, Lillian (Florence) **119**
Hemingway, Ernest (Miller) **115**
Henry, O. **1, 19**
Hergesheimer, Joseph **11**
Heyward, (Edwin) DuBose **59**
Higginson, Thomas Wentworth **36**
Himes, Chester **139**
Holley, Marietta **99**
Holly, Buddy **65**
Holmes, Oliver Wendell Jr. **77**
Hopkins, Pauline Elizabeth **28**
Horney, Karen (Clementine Theodore Danielsen) **71**
Howard, Robert E(rvin) **8**
Howe, Julia Ward **21**
Howells, William Dean **7, 17, 41**
Huneker, James Gibbons **65**
Hurston, Zora Neale **121, 131**
Ince, Thomas H. **89**
James, Henry **2, 11, 24, 40, 47, 64**
James, William **15, 32**
Jewett, (Theodora) Sarah Orne **1, 22**
Johnson, James Weldon **3, 19**
Johnson, Robert **69**
Kerouac, Jack **117**
Kinsey, Alfred C(harles) **91**
Kirk, Russell (Amos) **119**
Kornbluth, C(yril) M. **8**
Korzybski, Alfred (Habdank Skarbek) **61**
Kubrick, Stanley **112**
Kuttner, Henry **10**
Lardner, Ring(gold) W(ilmer) **2, 14**
Lewis, (Harry) Sinclair **4, 13, 23, 39**
Lewisohn, Ludwig **19**
Lewton, Val **76**
Lindsay, (Nicholas) Vachel **17**
Locke, Alain (Le Roy) **43**
Lockridge, Ross (Franklin) Jr. **111**
London, Jack **9, 15, 39**
Lovecraft, H(oward) P(hillips) **4, 22**
Lowell, Amy **1, 8**
Malamud, Bernard **129**
Mankiewicz, Herman (Jacob) **85**
March, William **96**
Markham, Edwin **47**
Marquis, Don(ald Robert Perry) **7**

Masters, Edgar Lee **2, 25**
Matthews, (James) Brander **95**
Matthiessen, F(rancis) O(tto) **100**
McAlmon, Robert (Menzies) **97**
McCoy, Horace (Stanley) **28**
McCullers, Carson **155**
Mead, George Herbert **89**
Mencken, H(enry) L(ouis) **13**
Micheaux, Oscar (Devereaux) **76**
Millay, Edna St. Vincent **4, 49**
Mitchell, Margaret (Munnerlyn) **11**
Mitchell, S(ilas) Weir **36**
Mitchell, William **81**
Monroe, Harriet **12**
Moody, William Vaughan **105**
Morley, Christopher (Darlington) **87**
Morris, Wright **107**
Muir, John **28**
Murfree, Mary Noailles **135**
Nash, (Fredric) Ogden **109**
Nathan, George Jean **18**
Nemerov, Howard (Stanley) **124F**
Neumann, Alfred **100**
Nisbet, Robert A(lexander) **117**
Nordhoff, Charles (Bernard) **23**
Norris, (Benjamin) Frank(lin Jr.) **24, 155**
O'Connor, Flannery **132**
O'Neill, Eugene (Gladstone) **1, 6, 27, 49**
Oppen, George **107**
Osbourne, Lloyd **93**
Oskison, John Milton **35**
Park, Robert E(zra) **73**
Parker, Dorothy **143**
Patton, George S(mith) Jr. **79**
Peirce, Charles Sanders **81**
Percy, William Alexander **84**
Petry, Ann (Lane) **112**
Phelps, Elizabeth Stuart **113**
Phillips, David Graham **44**
Portillo Trambley, Estela **163**
Post, Melville Davisson **39**
Pulitzer, Joseph **76**
Pyle, Ernie **75**
Pyle, Howard **81**
Rawlings, Marjorie Kinnan **4**
Reed, John (Silas) **9**
Reich, Wilhelm **57**
Remington, Frederic **89**
Rhodes, Eugene Manlove **53**
Riggs, (Rolla) Lynn **56**
Riis, Jacob A(ugust) **80**
Riley, James Whitcomb **51**
Rinehart, Mary Roberts **52**
Roberts, Elizabeth Madox **68**
Roberts, Kenneth (Lewis) **23**
Robinson, Edwin Arlington **5, 101**
Rogers, Carl **125**
Rogers, Will(iam Penn Adair) **8, 71**
Roosevelt, Franklin Delano **93**
Roosevelt, Theodore **69**
Rourke, Constance (Mayfield) **12**
Runyon, (Alfred) Damon **10**
Saltus, Edgar (Everton) **8**
Santayana, George **40**
Santmyer, Helen Hooven **133**
Santos, Bienvenido N. **156**
Sapir, Edward **108**
Saroyan, William **137**
Schoenberg, Arnold Franz Walter **75**
Sherwood, Robert E(mmet) **3**
Sinclair, Upton **160**
Slesinger, Tess **10**
Stanton, Elizabeth Cady **73**
Steffens, (Joseph) Lincoln **20**
Stein, Gertrude **1, 6, 28, 48**
Steinbeck, John **135**
Sterling, George **20**
Stevens, Wallace **3, 12, 45**
Stockton, Frank R. **47**
Stroheim, Erich von **71**
Strunk, William Jr. **92**
Sturges, Preston **48**
Tarbell, Ida M(inerva) **40**
Tarkington, (Newton) Booth **9**
Taylor, Frederick Winslow **76**
Teasdale, Sara **4**
Tesla, Nikola **88**
Thomas, Augustus **97**
Thomas, M. Carey **89**
Thorndike, Edward L(ee) **107**
Thurman, Wallace (Henry) **6**
Torrence, Ridgely **97**
Twain, Mark **6, 12, 19, 36, 48, 59, 161**
Van Doren, Carl (Clinton) **18**
Veblen, Thorstein B(unde) **31**
Villard, Oswald Garrison **160**
Walker, Margaret **129**
Washington, Booker T(aliaferro) **10**
Wells, Carolyn **35**
Wells-Barnett, Ida B(ell) **125**
West, Dorothy **108**
West, Nathanael **1, 14, 44**
Whale, James **63**
Wharton, Edith (Newbold Jones) **3, 9, 27, 53, 129, 149**
White, Walter F(rancis) **15**
Williams, Ben Ames **89**
Williams, Hank **81**
Wilson, (Thomas) Woodrow **79**
Wirth, Louis **92**
Wister, Owen **21**
Wolfe, Thomas (Clayton) **4, 13, 29, 61**
Woodberry, George Edward **73**
Woollcott, Alexander (Humphreys) **5**
Wright, Frank Lloyd **95**
Wright, Richard **136**
Wylie, Elinor (Morton Hoyt) **8**

ARGENTINIAN

Arlt, Roberto (Godofredo Christophersen) **29**
Borges, Jorge Luis **109**
Güiraldes, Ricardo (Guillermo) **39**
Hudson, W(illiam) H(enry) **29**
Lugones, Leopoldo **15**
Storni, Alfonsina **5**

AUSTRALIAN

Baynton, Barbara **57**
Franklin, (Stella Maria Sarah) Miles (Lampe) **7**
Furphy, Joseph **25**
Ingamells, Rex **35**
Lawson, Henry (Archibald Hertzberg) **27**
Paterson, A(ndrew) B(arton) **32**
Warung, Price **45**

AUSTRIAN

Beer-Hofmann, Richard **60**
Broch, Hermann **20**
Brod, Max **115**
Freud, Sigmund **52**
Hayek, F(riedrich) A(ugust von) **109**
Hofmannsthal, Hugo von **11**
Kafka, Franz **2, 6, 13, 29, 47, 53, 112**
Kraus, Karl **5**
Kubin, Alfred (Leopold Isidor) **23**
Meyrink, Gustav **21**
Musil, Robert (Edler von) **12, 68**
Pabst, G. W. **127**
Perutz, Leo(pold) **60**
Rank, Otto **115**
Roth, (Moses) Joseph **33**
Schnitzler, Arthur **4**
Steiner, Rudolf **13**
Stroheim, Erich von **71**
Trakl, Georg **5**
Weininger, Otto **84**
Werfel, Franz (Viktor) **8**
Zweig, Stefan **17**

BELGIAN

Bosschere, Jean de **19**
Lemonnier, (Antoine Louis) Camille **22**
Maeterlinck, Maurice **3**
Sarton, May (Eleanor) **120**
van Ostaijen, Paul **33**
Verhaeren, Émile (Adolphe Gustave) **12**

BRAZILIAN

Cunha, Euclides (Rodrigues Pimenta) da **24**
Drummond de Andrade, Carlos **139**
Lima Barreto, Afonso Henrique de **23**
Machado de Assis, Joaquim Maria **10**
Ramos, Graciliano **32**

BULGARIAN

Vazov, Ivan (Minchov) **25**

CANADIAN

Campbell, Wilfred **9**
Carman, (William) Bliss **7**
Carr, Emily **32**
Connor, Ralph **31**
Drummond, William Henry **25**
Duncan, Sara Jeannette **60**
Engel, Marian **137**
Garneau, (Hector de) Saint-Denys **13**
Innis, Harold Adams **77**
Knister, Raymond **56**
Leacock, Stephen (Butler) **2**
Lewis, (Percy) Wyndham **2, 9, 104**
McCrae, John **12**
Montgomery, L(ucy) M(aud) **51, 140**
Nelligan, Emile **14**
Pickthall, Marjorie L(owry) C(hristie) **21**
Roberts, Charles G(eorge) D(ouglas) **8**
Scott, Duncan Campbell **6**
Service, Robert W(illiam) **15**
Seton, Ernest (Evan) Thompson **31**
Stringer, Arthur **37**
Wetherald, Agnes Ethelwyn **81**

CHILEAN

Donoso, José **133**
Godoy Alcayaga, Lucila **2**
Huidobro Fernandez, Vicente Garcia **31**
Prado (Calvo), Pedro **75**

CHINESE

Lin, Yutang **149**
Liu, E. **15**
Lu Hsun **3**
Su Man-shu **24**
Wen I-to **28**

COLOMBIAN

Rivera, José Eustasio **35**

CZECH

Brod, Max **115**
Chapek, Karel **6, 37**
Freud, Sigmund **52**
Hasek, Jaroslav (Matej Frantisek) **4**
Hrabal, Bohumil **155**
Kafka, Franz **2, 6, 13, 29, 47, 53, 112**
Nezval, Vitezslav **44**

DANISH

Brandes, Georg (Morris Cohen) **10**
Hansen, Martin A(lfred) **32**
Jensen, Johannes V. **41**
Nexo, Martin Andersen **43**
Pontoppidan, Henrik **29**

DUTCH

Bok, Edward W. **101**
Couperus, Louis (Marie Anne) **15**
Heijermans, Herman **24**

Hillesum, Etty **49**
van Schendel, Arthur(-Francois-Émile) **56**

ENGLISH

Abbott, Edwin **139**
Abercrombie, Lascelles **141**
Alexander, Samuel **77**
Barbellion, W. N. P. **24**
Baring, Maurice **8**
Baring-Gould, Sabine **88**
Beerbohm, (Henry) Max(imilian) **1, 24**
Bell, Gertrude (Margaret Lowthian) **67**
Belloc, (Joseph) Hilaire (Pierre Sebastien Rene Swanton) **7, 18**
Bennett, (Enoch) Arnold **5, 20**
Benson, A.C. **123**
Benson, E(dward) F(rederic) **27**
Benson, Stella **17**
Bentley, E(dmund) C(lerihew) **12**
Beresford, J(ohn) D(avys) **81**
Besant, Annie (Wood) **9**
Blackmore, R(ichard) D(oddridge) **27**
Blackwood, Algernon (Henry) **5**
Bottomley, Gordon **107**
Bowen, Elizabeth **148**
Braddon, Mary Elizabeth **111**
Bramah, Ernest **72**
Bridges, Robert (Seymour) **1**
Brooke, Rupert (Chawner) **2, 7**
Buchanan, Robert **107**
Burke, Thomas **63**
Butler, Samuel **1, 33**
Butts, Mary **77**
Byron, Robert **67**
Caine, Hall **97**
Carpenter, Edward **88**
Carter, Angela **139**
Chesterton, G(ilbert) K(eith) **1, 6, 64**
Childers, (Robert) Erskine **65**
Churchill, Winston (Leonard Spencer) **113**
Clark, Kenneth Mackenzie **147**
Coleridge, Mary E(lizabeth) **73**
Collier, John **127**
Collingwood, R(obin) G(eorge) **67**
Conrad, Joseph **1, 6, 13, 25, 43, 57**
Coppard, A(lfred) E(dgar) **5**
Corelli, Marie **51**
Crofts, Freeman Wills **55**
Crowley, Aleister **7**
Dale, Colin **18**
Davies, William Henry **5**
Delafield, E. M. **61**
de la Mare, Walter (John) **4, 53**
Dobson, Austin **79**
Doughty, Charles M(ontagu) **27**
Douglas, Keith (Castellain) **40**
Dowson, Ernest (Christopher) **4**
Doyle, Arthur Conan **7**
Drinkwater, John **57**
Dunsany **2, 59**
Eddison, E(ric) R(ucker) **15**
Elaine **18**
Elizabeth **41**
Ellis, (Henry) Havelock **14**
Firbank, (Arthur Annesley) Ronald **1**
Flecker, (Herman) James Elroy **43**
Ford, Ford Madox **1, 15, 39, 57**
Forester, C(ecil) S(cott) **152**
Forster, E(dward) M(organ) **125**
Freeman, R(ichard) Austin **21**
Galsworthy, John **1, 45**
Gilbert, W(illiam) S(chwenck) **3**
Gill, Eric **85**
Gissing, George (Robert) **3, 24, 47**
Glyn, Elinor **72**
Gosse, Edmund (William) **28**
Grahame, Kenneth **64, 136**
Granville-Barker, Harley **2**
Gray, John (Henry) **19**
Gurney, Ivor (Bertie) **33**
Haggard, H(enry) Rider **11**
Hall, (Margueritc) Radclyffe **12**

Hardy, Thomas **4, 10, 18, 32, 48, 53, 72, 143, 153**
Henley, William Ernest **8**
Hilton, James **21**
Hodgson, William Hope **13**
Hope, Anthony **83**
Housman, A(lfred) E(dward) **1, 10**
Housman, Laurence **7**
Hudson, W(illiam) H(enry) **29**
Hulme, T(homas) E(rnest) **21**
Hunt, Violet **53**
Jacobs, W(illiam) W(ymark) **22**
James, Montague (Rhodes) **6**
Jerome, Jerome K(lapka) **23**
Johnson, Lionel (Pigot) **19**
Kaye-Smith, Sheila **20**
Keynes, John Maynard **64**
Kipling, (Joseph) Rudyard **8, 17**
Laski, Harold J(oseph) **79**
Lawrence, D(avid) H(erbert Richards) **2, 9, 16, 33, 48, 61, 93**
Lawrence, T(homas) E(dward) **18**
Lee, Vernon **5**
Lee-Hamilton, Eugene (Jacob) **22**
Leverson, Ada **18**
Lindsay, David **15**
Lowndes, Marie Adelaide (Belloc) **12**
Lowry, (Clarence) Malcolm **6, 40**
Lucas, E(dward) V(errall) **73**
Macaulay, (Emilie) Rose **7, 44**
MacCarthy, (Charles Otto) Desmond **36**
Mackenzie, Compton (Edward Montague) **116**
Maitland, Frederic William **65**
Manning, Frederic **25**
Marsh, Edward **99**
McTaggart, John McTaggart Ellis **105**
Meredith, George **17, 43**
Mew, Charlotte (Mary) **8**
Meynell, Alice (Christina Gertrude Thompson) **6**
Middleton, Richard (Barham) **56**
Milne, A(lan) A(lexander) **6, 88**
Moore, G. E. **89**
Morrison, Arthur **72**
Muggeridge, Thomas (Malcom) **120**
Murry, John Middleton **16**
Myers, L(eopold) H(amilton) **59**
Nightingale, Florence **85**
Naipaul, Shiva(dhar) (Srinivasa) **153**
Noyes, Alfred **7**
Oppenheim, E(dward) Phillips **45**
Orage, Alfred Richard **157**
Orton, Joe **157**
Orwell, George **2, 6, 15, 31, 51, 128, 129**
Osborne, John **153**
Owen, Wilfred (Edward Salter) **5, 27**
Pankhurst, Emmeline (Goulden) **100**
Pinero, Arthur Wing **32**
Powys, T(heodore) F(rancis) **9**
Quiller-Couch, Arthur (Thomas) **53**
Richardson, Dorothy Miller **3**
Rolfe, Frederick (William Serafino Austin Lewis Mary) **12**
Rosenberg, Isaac **12**
Ruskin, John **20**
Sabatini, Rafael **47**
Saintsbury, George (Edward Bateman) **31**
Sapper **44**
Sayers, Dorothy L(eigh) **2, 15**
Shiel, M(atthew) P(hipps) **8**
Sinclair, May **3, 11**
Stapledon, (William) Olaf **22**
Stead, William Thomas **48**
Stephen, Leslie **23**
Strachey, (Giles) Lytton **12**
Summers, (Alphonsus Joseph-Mary Augustus) Montague **16**
Sutro, Alfred **6**
Swinburne, Algernon Charles **8, 36**
Symons, Arthur **11**
Thomas, (Philip) Edward **10**

Thompson, Francis (Joseph) **4**
Tolkien, J. R. R. **137**
Tomlinson, H(enry) M(ajor) **71**
Trotter, Wilfred **97**
Upward, Allen **85**
Van Druten, John (William) **2**
Wakefield, Herbert (Russell) **120**
Wallace, (Richard Horatio) Edgar **57**
Wallas, Graham **91**
Walpole, Hugh (Seymour) **5**
Ward, Mary Augusta **55**
Warner, Sylvia Townsend **131**
Warung, Price **45**
Webb, Mary Gladys (Meredith) **24**
Webb, Sidney (James) **22**
Welch, (Maurice) Denton **22**
Wells, H(erbert) G(eorge) **6, 12, 19, 133**
Whitehead, Alfred North **97**
Williams, Charles (Walter Stansby) **1, 11**
Wodehouse, P(elham) G(renville) **108**
Woolf, (Adeline) Virginia **1, 5, 20, 43, 56, 101, 128**
Yonge, Charlotte (Mary) **48**
Zangwill, Israel **16**

ESTONIAN

Talvik, Heiti **87**
Tammsaare, A(nton) H(ansen) **27**

FINNISH

Leino, Eino **24**
Soedergran, Edith (Irene) **31**
Westermarck, Edward **87**

FRENCH

Alain **41**
Apollinaire, Guillaume **3, 8, 51**
Arp, Jean **115**
Artaud, Antonin (Marie Joseph) **3, 36**
Bachelard, Gaston **128**
Barbusse, Henri **5**
Barrès, (Auguste-)Maurice **47**
Barthes, Roland **135**
Bataille, Georges **155**
Benda, Julien **60**
Bergson, Henri(-Louis) **32**
Bernanos, (Paul Louis) Georges **3**
Bernhardt, Sarah (Henriette Rosine) **75**
Bloy, Léon **22**
Bourget, Paul (Charles Joseph) **12**
Claudel, Paul (Louis Charles Marie) **2, 10**
Cocteau, Jean (Maurice Eugene Clement) **119**
Colette, (Sidonie-Gabrielle) **1, 5, 16**
Coppee, Francois **25**
Crevel, Rene **112**
Daumal, Rene **14**
Deleuze, Gilles **116**
Desnos, Robert **22**
Drieu la Rochelle, Pierre(-Eugène) **21**
Dujardin, Edouard (Emile Louis) **13**
Durkheim, Emile **55**
Epstein, Jean **92**
Fargue, Leon-Paul **11**
Feydeau, Georges (Léon Jules Marie) **22**
Fondane, Benjamin **159**
Genet, Jean **128**
Gide, André (Paul Guillaume) **5, 12, 36**
Giono, Jean **124**
Giraudoux, Jean(-Hippolyte) **2, 7**
Gourmont, Remy(-Marie-Charles) de **17**
Halévy, Elie **104**
Huysmans, Joris-Karl **7, 69**
Jacob, (Cyprien-)Max **6**
Jammes, Francis **75**
Jarry, Alfred **2, 14, 147**
Larbaud, Valery (Nicolas) **9**
Léautaud, Paul **83**
Leblanc, Maurice (Marie Emile) **49**
Leroux, Gaston **25**
Lyotard, Jean-François **103**

Martin du Gard, Roger **24**
Melies, Georges **81**
Merlau-Ponty, Maurice **156**
Mirbeau, Octave **55**
Mistral, Frédéric **51**
Nizan, Paul **40**
Péguy, Charles (Pierre) **10**
Péret, Benjamin **20**
Proust, (Valentin-Louis-George-Eugène-)Marcel **7, 13, 33, 161**
Radiguet, Raymond **29**
Renard, Jules **17**
Rolland, Romain **23**
Rostand, Edmond (Eugene Alexis) **6, 37**
Roussel, Raymond **20**
Saint-Exupéry, Antoine (Jean Baptiste Marie Roger) de **2, 56**
Schwob, Marcel (Mayer André) **20**
Sorel, Georges **91**
Sully Prudhomme, René-François-Armand **31**
Teilhard de Chardin, (Marie Joseph) Pierre **9**
Valéry, (Ambroise) Paul (Toussaint Jules) **4, 15**
Vallette, Marguerite Eymery **67**
Verne, Jules (Gabriel) **6, 52**
Vian, Boris **9**
Weil, Simone (Adolphine) **23**
Zola, Émile (Édouard Charles Antoine) **1, 6, 21, 41**

GERMAN

Adorno, Theodor W(iesengrund) **111**
Andreas-Salome, Lou **56**
Arp, Jean **115**
Auerbach, Erich **43**
Ball, Hugo **104**
Barlach, Ernst (Heinrich) **84**
Benjamin, Walter **39**
Benn, Gottfried **3**
Borchert, Wolfgang **5**
Brecht, (Eugen) Bertolt (Friedrich) **1, 6, 13, 35**
Carossa, Hans **48**
Cassirer, Ernst **61**
Doeblin, Alfred **13**
Einstein, Albert **65**
Ewers, Hanns Heinz **12**
Feuchtwanger, Lion **3**
Frank, Bruno **81**
George, Stefan (Anton) **2, 14**
Goebbels, (Paul) Joseph **68**
Haeckel, Ernst Heinrich (Philipp August) **83**
Hauptmann, Gerhart (Johann Robert) **4**
Heym, Georg (Theodor Franz Arthur) **9**
Heyse, Paul (Johann Ludwig von) **8**
Hitler, Adolf **53**
Horkheimer, Max **132**
Horney, Karen (Clementine Theodore Danielsen) **71**
Huch, Ricarda (Octavia) **13**
Husserl, Edmund (Gustav Albrecht) **100**
Kaiser, Georg **9**
Klabund **44**
Kolmar, Gertrud **40**
Lasker-Schueler, Else **57**
Liliencron, (Friedrich Adolf Axel) Detlev von **18**
Luxemburg, Rosa **63**
Mann, (Luiz) Heinrich **9**
Mann, (Paul) Thomas **2, 8, 14, 21, 35, 44, 60**
Mannheim, Karl **65**
Michels, Robert **88**
Morgenstern, Christian (Otto Josef Wolfgang) **8**
Neumann, Alfred **100**
Nietzsche, Friedrich (Wilhelm) **10, 18, 55**
Ophuls, Max **79**
Otto, Rudolf **85**
Plumpe, Friedrich Wilhelm **53**
Raabe, Wilhelm (Karl) **45**
Rilke, Rainer Maria **1, 6, 19**
Schreber, Daniel Paul **123**
Schwitters, Kurt (Hermann Edward Karl Julius) **95**
Simmel, Georg **64**
Spengler, Oswald (Arnold Gottfried) **25**
Sternheim, (William Adolf) Carl **8**
Strauss, Leo **141**
Sudermann, Hermann **15**
Toller, Ernst **10**
Vaihinger, Hans **71**
von Hartmann, Eduard **96**
Wassermann, (Karl) Jakob **6**
Weber, Max **69**
Wedekind, (Benjamin) Frank(lin) **7**
Wiene, Robert **56**

GHANIAN

Casely-Hayford, J(oseph) E(phraim) **24**

GREEK

Cavafy, C(onstantine) P(eter) **2, 7**
Kazantzakis, Nikos **2, 5, 33**
Palamas, Kostes **5**
Papadiamantis, Alexandros **29**
Sikelianos, Angelos **39**

HAITIAN

Roumain, Jacques (Jean Baptiste) **19**

HUNGARIAN

Ady, Endre **11**
Babits, Mihaly **14**
Csath, Geza **13**
Herzl, Theodor **36**
Horváth, Ödön von **45**
Jozsef, Attila **22**
Karinthy, Frigyes **47**
Mikszath, Kalman **31**
Molnár, Ferenc **20**
Moricz, Zsigmond **33**
Radnóti, Miklós **16**

ICELANDIC

Sigurjonsson, Johann **27**

INDIAN

Chatterji, Saratchandra **13**
Dasgupta, Surendranath **81**
Gandhi, Mohandas Karamchand **59**
Ghose, Aurabinda **63**
Iqbal, Muhammad **28**
Naidu, Sarojini **80**
Premchand **21**
Ramana Maharshi **84**
Tagore, Rabindranath **3, 53**
Vivekananda, Swami **88**

INDONESIAN

Anwar, Chairil **22**

IRANIAN

Hedabayat, Sādeq **21**

IRISH

A.E. **3, 10**
Baker, Jean H. **3, 10**
Cary, (Arthur) Joyce (Lunel) **1, 29**
Gogarty, Oliver St. John **15**
Gregory, Isabella Augusta (Persse) **1**
Harris, Frank **24**
Joyce, James (Augustine Aloysius) **3, 8, 16, 35, 52, 159**
Ledwidge, Francis **23**
Martin, Violet Florence **51**
Martyn, Edward **131**
Moore, George Augustus **7**
O'Faolain, Sean **143**
O'Grady, Standish (James) **5**
Shaw, George Bernard **3, 9, 21, 45**
Somerville, Edith Oenone **51**
Stephens, James **4**
Stoker, Bram **8, 144**
Synge, (Edmund) J(ohn) M(illington) **6, 37**
Tynan, Katharine **3**
Wilde, Oscar (Fingal O'Flahertie Wills) **1, 8, 23, 41**
Yeats, William Butler **1, 11, 18, 31, 93, 116**

ISRAELI

Agnon, S(hmuel) Y(osef Halevi) **151**

ITALIAN

Alvaro, Corrado **60**
Betti, Ugo **5**
Brancati, Vitaliano **12**
Campana, Dino **20**
Carducci, Giosuè (Alessandro Giuseppe) **32**
Croce, Benedetto **37**
D'Annunzio, Gabriele **6, 40**
de Filippo, Eduardo **127**
Deledda, Grazia (Cosima) **23**
Gadda, Carlo Emilio **144**
Gentile, Giovanni **96**
Giacosa, Giuseppe **7**
Ginzburg, Natalia **156**
Jovine, Francesco **79**
Levi, Carlo **125**
Levi, Primo **109**
Malaparte, Curzio **52**
Marinetti, Filippo Tommaso **10**
Montessori, Maria **103**
Mosca, Gaetano **75**
Mussolini, Benito (Amilcare Andrea) **96**
Papini, Giovanni **22**
Pareto, Vilfredo **69**
Pascoli, Giovanni **45**
Pavese, Cesare **3**
Pirandello, Luigi **4, 29**
Protolini, Vasco **124**
Saba, Umberto **33**
Tozzi, Federigo **31**
Verga, Giovanni (Carmelo) **3**

JAMAICAN

De Lisser, H(erbert) G(eorge) **12**
Garvey, Marcus (Moziah Jr.) **41**
Mais, Roger **8**
Redcam, Tom **25**

JAPANESE

Abé, Kōbō **131**
Akutagawa Ryunosuke **16**
Dazai Osamu **11**
Endō, Shūsaku **152**
Futabatei, Shimei **44**
Hagiwara, Sakutaro **60**
Hayashi, Fumiko **27**
Ishikawa, Takuboku **15**
Kunikida, Doppo **99**
Masaoka, Shiki **18**
Mishima, Yukio **161**
Miyamoto, (Chujo) Yuriko **37**
Miyazawa, Kenji **76**
Mizoguchi, Kenji **72**
Mori Ogai **14**
Nagai, Kafu **51**
Nishida, Kitaro **83**
Noguchi, Yone **80**
Santoka, Taneda **72**
Shimazaki Toson **5**
Suzuki, Daisetz Teitaro **109**
Yokomitsu, Riichi **47**
Yosano Akiko **59**

LATVIAN

Berlin, Isaiah **105**
Rainis, Jānis **29**

LEBANESE

Gibran, Kahlil **1, 9**

LESOTHAN
Mofolo, Thomas (Mokopu) 22

LITHUANIAN
Kreve (Mickevicius), Vincas 27

MEXICAN
Azuela, Mariano 3
Gamboa, Federico 36
Garro, Elena 153
Gonzalez Martinez, Enrique 72
Ibargüengoitia, Jorge 148
Nervo, (Jose) Amado (Ruiz de) 11
Reyes, Alfonso 33
Romero, José Rubén 14
Villaurrutia, Xavier 80

NEPALI
Devkota, Laxmiprasad 23

NEW ZEALANDER
Mander, (Mary) Jane 31
Mansfield, Katherine 2, 8, 39, 164

NICARAGUAN
Darío, Rubén 4

NORWEGIAN
Bjoernson, Bjoernstjerne (Martinius) 7, 37
Bojer, Johan 64
Grieg, (Johan) Nordahl (Brun) 10
Hamsun, Knut 151
Ibsen, Henrik (Johan) 2, 8, 16, 37, 52
Kielland, Alexander Lange 5
Lie, Jonas (Lauritz Idemil) 5
Obstfelder, Sigbjoern 23
Skram, Amalie (Bertha) 25
Undset, Sigrid 3

PAKISTANI
Iqbal, Muhammad 28

PERUVIAN
Arguedas, José María 147
Palma, Ricardo 29
Vallejo, César (Abraham) 3, 56

POLISH
Asch, Sholem 3
Borowski, Tadeusz 9
Conrad, Joseph 1, 6, 13, 25, 43, 57
Peretz, Isaac Loeb 16
Prus, Boleslaw 48
Przybyszewski, Stanislaw 36
Reymont, Wladyslaw (Stanislaw) 5
Schulz, Bruno 5, 51
Sienkiewicz, Henryk (Adam Alexander Pius) 3
Singer, Israel Joshua 33
Witkiewicz, Stanislaw Ignacy 8

PORTUGUESE
Pessoa, Fernando (António Nogueira) 27
Sa-Carniero, Mario de 83

PUERTO RICAN
Hostos (y Bonilla), Eugenio Maria de 24

ROMANIAN
Bacovia, George 24
Caragiale, Ion Luca 76
Rebreanu, Liviu 28

RUSSIAN
Aldanov, Mark (Alexandrovich) 23
Andreyev, Leonid (Nikolaevich) 3
Annensky, Innokenty (Fyodorovich) 14
Artsybashev, Mikhail (Petrovich) 31
Babel, Isaak (Emmanuilovich) 2, 13
Bagritsky, Eduard 60
Bakhtin, Mikhail 160
Balmont, Konstantin (Dmitriyevich) 11
Bely, Andrey 7
Berdyaev, Nikolai (Aleksandrovich) 67
Bergelson, David 81
Blok, Alexander (Alexandrovich) 5
Bryusov, Valery Yakovlevich 10
Bulgakov, Mikhail (Afanas'evich) 2, 16, 159
Bulgya, Alexander Alexandrovich 53
Bunin, Ivan Alexeyevich 6
Chekhov, Anton (Pavlovich) 3, 10, 31, 55, 96, 163
Der Nister 56
Eisenstein, Sergei (Mikhailovich) 57
Esenin, Sergei (Alexandrovich) 4
Fadeyev, Alexander 53
Gladkov, Fyodor (Vasilyevich) 27
Gumilev, Nikolai (Stepanovich) 60
Gurdjieff, G(eorgei) I(vanovich) 71
Guro, Elena 56
Hippius, Zinaida 9
Ilf, Ilya 21
Ivanov, Vyacheslav Ivanovich 33
Kandinsky, Wassily 92
Khlebnikov, Velimir 20
Khodasevich, Vladislav (Felitsianovich) 15
Klimentov, Andrei Platonovich 14
Korolenko, Vladimir Galaktionovich 22
Kropotkin, Peter (Aleksieevich) 36
Kuprin, Aleksander Ivanovich 5
Kuzmin, Mikhail 40
Lenin, V. I. 67
Mandelstam, Osip (Emilievich) 2, 6
Mayakovski, Vladimir (Vladimirovich) 4, 18
Merezhkovsky, Dmitry Sergeyevich 29
Nabokov, Vladimir (Vladimirovich) 108
Olesha, Yuri 136
Pavlov, Ivan Petrovich 91
Petrov, Evgeny 21
Pilnyak, Boris 23
Prishvin, Mikhail 75
Remizov, Aleksei (Mikhailovich) 27
Rozanov, Vassili 104
Shestov, Lev 56
Sologub, Fyodor 9
Stalin, Joseph 92
Tolstoy, Alexey Nikolaevich 18
Tolstoy, Leo (Nikolaevich) 4, 11, 17, 28, 44, 79
Trotsky, Leon 22
Tsvetaeva (Efron), Marina (Ivanovna) 7, 35
Zabolotsky, Nikolai Alekseevich 52
Zamyatin, Evgeny Ivanovich 8, 37
Zhdanov, Andrei Alexandrovich 18
Zoshchenko, Mikhail (Mikhailovich) 15

SCOTTISH
Barrie, J(ames) M(atthew) 2, 164
Brown, George Douglas 28
Buchan, John 41
Cunninghame Graham, Robert (Gallnigad) Bontine 19
Davidson, John 24
Doyle, Arthur Conan 7
Frazer, J(ames) G(eorge) 32
Lang, Andrew 16
MacDonald, George 9, 113
Muir, Edwin 2, 87
Murray, James Augustus Henry 117
Sharp, William 39
Tey, Josephine 14

SLOVENIAN
Cankar, Ivan 105

SOUTH AFRICAN
Bosman, Herman Charles 49
Campbell, (Ignatius) Roy (Dunnachie) 5
La Guma, Alex 140
Mqhayi, S(amuel) E(dward) K(rune Loliwe) 25
Plaatje, Sol(omon) T(shekisho) 73
Schreiner, Olive (Emilie Albertina) 9
Smith, Pauline (Urmson) 25
Vilakazi, Benedict Wallet 37

SPANISH
Alas (y Urena), Leopoldo (Enrique Garcia) 29
Aleixandre, Vicente 113
Barea, Arturo 14
Baroja (y Nessi), Pio 8
Benavente (y Martinez), Jacinto 3
Blasco Ibáñez, Vicente 12
Echegaray (y Eizaguirre), Jose (Maria Waldo) 4
García Lorca, Federico 1, 7, 49
Jiménez (Mantecón), Juan Ramón 4
Machado (y Ruiz), Antonio 3
Martinez Sierra, Gregorio 6
Martinez Sierra, Maria (de la O'LeJarraga) 6
Miro (Ferrer), Gabriel (Francisco Victor) 5
Onetti, Juan Carlos 131
Ortega y Gasset, José 9
Pereda (y Sanchez de Porrua), Jose Maria de 16
Pérez Galdós, Benito 27
Ramoacn y Cajal, Santiago 93
Salinas (y Serrano), Pedro 17
Sender, Ramón 136
Unamuno (y Jugo), Miguel de 2, 9, 148
Valera y Alcala-Galiano, Juan 10
Valle-Inclán, Ramón (Maria) del 5

SWEDISH
Bengtsson, Frans (Gunnar) 48
Dagerman, Stig (Halvard) 17
Ekelund, Vilhelm 75
Heidenstam, (Carl Gustaf) Verner von 5
Key, Ellen (Karolina Sofia) 65
Lagerkvist, Pär 144
Lagerloef, Selma (Ottiliana Lovisa) 4, 36
Söderberg, Hjalmar 39
Strindberg, (Johan) August 1, 8, 21, 47
Weiss, Peter 152

SWISS
Canetti, Elias 157
Frisch, Max (Rudolf) 121
Hesse, Herman 148
Ramuz, Charles-Ferdinand 33
Rod, Edouard 52
Saussure, Ferdinand de 49
Spitteler, Carl (Friedrich Georg) 12
Walser, Robert 18

SYRIAN
Gibran, Kahlil 1, 9

TURKISH
Sait Faik 23

UKRAINIAN
Aleichem, Sholom 1, 35
Bialik, Chaim Nachman 25

UGANDAN
p'Bitek, Okot 149

URUGUAYAN
Quiroga, Horacio (Sylvestre) 20
Sánchez, Florencio 37

WELSH
Davies, William Henry 5
Evans, Caradoc 85
Lewis, Alun 3
Thomas, Dylan (Marlais) 1, 8, 45, 105

YUGOSLAVIAN
Andrić, Ivo 135

TCLC-164 Title Index

The Admirable Crichton (Barrie) **164**:7, 37, 39, 80
The Adored One (Barrie) **164**:39
"The Advanced Lady" (Mansfield) **164**:269-70, 293
Alice Sit-by-the-Fire (Barrie) **164**:36
The Aloe (Mansfield) **164**:250-54, 332, 334-35
"Among the Paths to Eden" (Capote) **164**:99-100, 104-5
"Angel in the House" (Mansfield) **164**:239
"Answer" (Capote) **164**:171
Answered Prayers (Capote) **164**:123, 134, 151, 170, 199, 204
"At Lehmann's" (Mansfield) **164**:325
"At the Bay" (Mansfield) **164**:241, 248-49, 253, 255, 266-68, 270-71, 273-74, 295-97, 299-302, 309, 326-28, 332-37, 340
Auld Licht Idylls (Barrie) **164**:14-15, 61-62
"Autumn II" (Mansfield) **164**:309
"The Baron" (Mansfield) **164**:293
"A Beautiful Child" (Capote) **164**:200
"A Birthday" (Mansfield) **164**:292-93, 302, 304
"A Blaze" (Mansfield) **164**:293
Bliss and Other Stories (Mansfield) **164**:264, 332, 340-41
"Bliss" (Mansfield) **164**:225, 227-33, 239, 241, 247-49, 258-62, 281, 333
The Boy Castaways (Barrie) **164**:62
The Boy David (Barrie) **164**:8-9, 16-17, 25
Breakfast at Tiffany's (Capote) **164**:100, 102, 111, 115, 129, 155-57, 159-61, 168-69, 208, 218
"Bud of the Aloe" (Mansfield) **164**:335
"The Canary" (Mansfield) **164**:249, 286
"The Child-Who-Was-Tired" (Mansfield) **164**:237, 269, 288, 292-93
"Children on Their Birthdays" (Capote) **164**:100, 110, 112, 114, 155-61
A Christmas Memory (Capote) **164**:112, 157
The Collected Letters of Katherine Mansfield (Mansfield) **164**:258-59, 261, 268, 275, 338-41
Collected Stories (Mansfield) **164**:241
"Conversational Portraits" (Capote) **164**:153, 199
"The Corner" (Capote) **164**:168, 177
"The Daughters of the Late Colonel" (Mansfield) **164**:237-38, 323
"A Day's Work" (Capote) **164**:142, 144
"Dazzle" (Capote) **164**:200
Dear Brutus (Barrie) **164**:8
"Derringdo" (Capote) **164**:200
"A Diamond Guitar" (Capote) **164**:105, 111-12, 115
"A Dill Pickle" (Mansfield) **164**:239, 248, 322, 324
The Dogs Bark (Capote) **164**:137, 139, 142, 153, 199-204
"The Doll's House" (Mansfield) **164**:249, 300, 305, 335, 340, 342
"The Duke in His Domain" (Capote) **164**:137, 142, 150, 199-200
An Edinburgh Eleven (Barrie) **164**:61
"Enna Blake" (Mansfield) **164**:263

"Epilogue I: Pension Seguin" (Mansfield) **164**:339
"The Escape" (Mansfield) **164**:241
Farewell, Miss Julie Logan (Barrie) **164**:8, 14-16, 29, 37
"Feuille d'Album" (Mansfield) **164**:247, 249
"The Fly" (Mansfield) **164**:240, 305
"Frau Brechenmacher Attends a Wedding" (Mansfield) **164**:269, 291-93, 325
"Frau Fischer" (Mansfield) **164**:293, 325
The Garden Party (Mansfield) **164**:244
"The Garden Party" (Mansfield) **164**:239, 247, 297-98, 300, 305, 307, 315, 332, 340, 342
"Germans at Meat" (Mansfield) **164**:270, 290, 324-25
"Gift of the Muses" (Mansfield) **164**:337
The Grass Harp (Capote) **164**:100, 111-12, 115, 146, 155-57, 159, 168, 176
The Greenwood Hat (Barrie) **164**:14
"Haiti" (Capote) **164**:200
Handcarved Coffins (Capote) **164**:122-23, 134, 138, 142, 150-54, 202-4
"The Headless Hawk" (Capote) **164**:99-103, 109-10, 112, 158, 199
"Hello Stranger" (Capote) **164**:138
"Her First Ball" (Mansfield) **164**:247-48, 266266
"Hidden Gardens" (Capote) **164**:142
"The Honeymoon" (Mansfield) **164**:322-23
"Hospitality" (Capote) **164**:200
House of Flowers (Capote) **164**:100, 114
"A House on the Heights" (Capote) **164**:201-2
"How Pearl Button was Kidnapped" (Mansfield) **164**:342
"The Ideal Family" (Mansfield) **164**:240
In a German Pension (Mansfield) **164**:268-70, 288-89, 293-94, 324-27, 272271
In Cold Blood (Capote) **164**:105, 113, 116-18, 122-23, 129-32, 134-35, 137-40, 143, 145-46, 148, 150-53, 162, 165, 167-71, 173, 176-89, 201, 208
"Je ne parle pas français" (Mansfield) **164**:241-44, 264, 281-82, 284-85, 287, 319
The Journal of Katherine Mansfield (Mansfield) **164**:250-51, 253, 257, 259, 261, 267, 275, 286
"A Jug of Silver" (Capote) **164**:100, 109-12, 115, 146
The Katherine Mansfield Notebooks (Mansfield) **164**:339-40
Katherine Mansfield's Letters to John Middleton Murry, 1913-22 (Mansfield) **164**:280
"A Lamp in a Window" (Capote) **164**:200
The Letters and Journals of Katherine Mansfield: A Selection (Mansfield) **164**:268, 275
The Letters of J. M. Barrie (Barrie) **164**:14
The Letters of Katherine Mansfield (Mansfield) **164**:250, 252-53, 262, 274, 332, 339
"The Life of Ma Parker" (Mansfield) **164**:237, 248, 339
"The Lilac Tree" (Mansfield) **164**:261
"The Little Girl" (Mansfield) **164**:251

"The Little Governess" (Mansfield) **164**:252, 307, 339
Little Mary (Barrie) **164**:63, 69
The Little Minister (Barrie) **164**:6, 14
The Little White Bird (Barrie) **164**:6-8, 28, 62, 66, 80
Local Color (Capote) **164**:150, 199, 201
"The Luft Bad" (Mansfield) **164**:324
"Maata" (Mansfield) **164**:250
"The Man without a Temperament" (Mansfield) **164**:339
Margaret Ogilvy (Barrie) **164**:22, 24, 38-39
"Marriage à la Mode" (Mansfield) **164**:248, 320, 333, 339
"A Married Man's Story" (Mansfield) **164**:281, 285, 287, 302-4, 323
Mary Rose (Barrie) **164**:8-9, 16, 18, 22, 26-27, 29-33, 35
"Master Misery" (Capote) **164**:99-100, 103-4, 106, 109, 112, 115, 156, 199
"Millie" (Mansfield) **164**:340-42
"A Mink of One's Own" (Capote) **164**:99-102, 106
"Miriam" (Capote) **164**:99-103, 109-10, 112, 115, 142
"Miss Brill" (Mansfield) **164**:236, 244, 247, 307, 320
"The Modern Soul" (Mansfield) **164**:269, 291, 293
"Mojave" (Capote) **164**:99, 105-6
"Mr. and Mrs. Dove" (Mansfield) **164**:240
"Mr. Reginald Peacock's Day" (Mansfield) **164**:235-36, 302, 304-5
The Muses Are Heard (Capote) **164**:116-17, 130, 142, 144, 150, 201
Music for Chameleons (Capote) **164**:116-17, 123, 134, 138-39, 144-46, 151, 153-54, 199-204
"My Potplants" (Mansfield) **164**:268
"My Side of the Matter" (Capote) **164**:108-10, 112
"New Dresses" (Mansfield) **164**:251
"The New Zealander" (Mansfield) **164**:269
"Nocturnal Turnings" (Capote) **164**:154, 204
"Notes for the Aloe" (Mansfield) **164**:253
Observations (Capote) **164**:199
"Ole Underwood" (Mansfield) **164**:340-42
One Christmas (Capote) **164**:199
Other Voices, Other Rooms (Capote) **164**:100, 105-6, 108, 111-12, 115, 129, 136, 142, 150, 167-68, 190-93, 195-97, 199, 201, 205-14, 216-18
Pantaloon (Barrie) **164**:7, 66
Pension (Mansfield) **164**:239
Peter and Wendy (Barrie) **164**:53, 70, 73
Peter Pan; or, the Boy Who Wouldn't Grow Up (Barrie) **164**:6-8, 11-13, 18-22, 25, 32-33, 36-39, 41, 45, 53-58, 61-65, 67-70, 73, 80, 87-88, 90-94
"Pictures" (Mansfield) **164**:236-37, 239, 339
"Poison" (Mansfield) **164**:320-21, 323
"Preacher's Legend" (Capote) **164**:100, 107-8
"Prelude" (Mansfield) **164**:241, 247-51, 253-55,

265-66, 268, 270-75, 283, 297, 301, 309, 326-28, 332-37, 339-40
"Psychology" (Mansfield) **164**:229, 247-48, 322
Quality Street (Barrie) **164**:7, 63
"Revelations" (Mansfield) **164**:240-41
Richard Savage (Barrie) **164**:16
"A Ride through Spain" (Capote) **164**:137
Selected Stories (Mansfield) **164**:341-42
Sentimental Tommy (Barrie) **164**:5, 67-68, 80, 82
Shall We Join the Ladies? (Barrie) **164**:29
"The Shape of Things" (Capote) **164**:100, 106
The Short Stories of Katherine Mansfield (Mansfield) **164**:225-27, 269, 271, 273-74
"Shut a Final Door" (Capote) **164**:99-100, 102-3, 109, 112, 115
"The Singing Lesson" (Mansfield) **164**:235, 307
"The Sister of the Baroness" (Mansfield) **164**:293
"Six Years After" (Mansfield) **164**:300-301

"Something Childish But Very Natural" (Mansfield) **164**:247-48
The Stories of Katherine Mansfield (Mansfield) **164**:254, 259-61, 264-66, 282, 341
"The Stranger" (Mansfield) **164**:295, 297, 301, 311, 315-16, 339
"Sun and Moon" (Mansfield) **164**:231, 233, 239, 249-50, 263-64, 266, 295, 297
"A Swing of the Pendulum" (Mansfield) **164**:293
"Tangier" (Capote) **164**:200
The Thanksgiving Visitor (Capote) **164**:100, 111-14, 199
"The Tiredness of Rosabel" (Mansfield) **164**:321
Tommy and Grizel (Barrie) **164**:5-6, 66, 82-86
A Tree of Night (Capote) **164**:142, 146, 150
"A Tree of Night" (Capote) **164**:99-101, 106-8, 110, 112, 142, 199
"A Truthful Adventure" (Mansfield) **164**:235

The Twelve-Pound Look (Barrie) **164**:39
Undiscovered Country (Mansfield) **164**:332
"The Unexpected Must Happen" (Mansfield) **164**:262
"A Voice from a Cloud" (Capote) **164**:199
"The Voyage" (Mansfield) **164**:266, 301-2, 304, 306, 310, 315-16, 339
Walker, London (Barrie) **164**:5
"The Walls Are Cold" (Capote) **164**:99-100, 102-3
A Well-Remembered Voice (Barrie) **164**:36-37
What Every Woman Knows (Barrie) **164**:39, 80
The Will (Barrie) **164**:37
"The Wind Blows" (Mansfield) **164**:252-53, 265, 302, 304, 306-7, 309-10
A Window in Thrums (Barrie) **164**:61, 80
"The Woman at the Store" (Mansfield) **164**:269, 339-42
"The Young Girl" (Mansfield) **164**:239

ISBN 0-7876-8918-1